D1195320

ADVERTISING

and Integrated Brand Promotion, 3e

ADVERTISING
and Integrated Brand Promotion, 3e

Thomas C. O'Guinn
Professor
University of Illinois at Urbana-Champaign

Chris T. Allen
Arthur Beerman Professor of Marketing
University of Cincinnati

Richard J. Semenik
Professor of Marketing and Dean
Montana State University
Board of Directors of American Advertising Museum

Australia · Canada · Mexico · Singapore · Spain · United Kingdom · United States

THOMSON
SOUTH-WESTERN

Advertising and Integrated Brand Promotion, Third Edition
Thomas C. O'Guinn, Chris T. Allen, Richard J. Semenik

VP/Editor-in-Chief:
Jack Calhoun

Team Leader:
Melissa Acuña

Acquisitions Editor:
Steve Hazelwood

Developmental Editor:
Leslie Kauffman/LEAP
Mardell Toomey

Marketing Manager:
Marc Callahan

Production Editor:
Tamborah Moore

Manufacturing Coordinator:
Diane Lohman

Compositor:
Lachina Publishing Services, Inc.

Printer:
Quebecor World Versailles

Internal Designer:
Craig Ramsdell

Cover Designer:
Michael H. Stratton

Cover Illustration:
Lou Beach

Printed in the United States of America
2 3 4 5 05 04 03 02

For more information contact South-Western,
5191 Natorp Boulevard,
Mason, Ohio 45040.
Or you can visit our Internet site at: http://www.swcollege.com

Library of Congress Cataloging-in-Publication Data
O'Guinn, Thomas C.
Advertising and integrated brand promotion/Thomas C. O'Guinn, Chris T. Allen, Richard J. Semenik.--3rd ed.
p.cm.
Includes bibliographical references and index
ISBN: 0-324-11380-3
1. Advertising. 2. Advertising media planning. I. Allen, Chris T. II. Semenik, Richard J. III. Title.

HF5821 O34 2002
659.1--dc21 2002019662

ISBN: 0-324-11380-3

To

To Connie Mae Johnson, and her parents, Arthur and June Johnson, for their love and kindness.
Thomas Clayton O'Guinn

To Gillian and Maddy,
My shining stars.
Chris Allen

To Andi,
my favorite creative.
Rich Semenik

PREFACE

Welcome to our third edition! We're glad you're here and we think you will really enjoy it.

We have retained all the content and chapter features that students and instructors alike have enjoyed in our previous editions. Building on the success of those editions, we have also made a few important improvements: First, advertising as a brand-building process receives greater emphasis in the third edition. Also, a wide range of communication tools are now discussed as contributors to the brand-building process; hence, *Advertising and Integrated Brand Promotion* as the new title better reflects the full range of coverage of this well-rounded text. Another important improvement is the even greater number of ads used in the third edition. We tried to always give a concrete visual example of what we discuss. This makes reading and understanding the book easier and more enjoyable. It does the same for teaching.

We were very selective in choosing the chapters that received heavy revision and targeted only a few chapters to avoid detracting from the book's success. These chapters have some new text, and a lot of new ads. But even in these cases, there is still a lot of familiar material. **Chapter 7: (Advertising and Promotion Research)** was significantly revised to reflect new realities in the profession, including attention to account planning. **Chapter 10: (Creativity and Advertising)** is now more practically focused. It still goes into something rarely discussed: the basic nature of creativity and why creative people can be so "difficult"—or, from the creatives' perspective, why account executives and brand managers are such soulless "suits." We deal with the case of the 500-pound gorilla that is present in all account meetings, but who seems to be invisible by consensus. The traditional approach is to think that if you don't notice him, he will go away. Close to a hundred years of industry experience, however, says he won't. So we wrote about this typically ignored aspect of advertising and promotion management. But this time, we spent more time specifically focusing on the suit/creative interface from an organizational/reward management perspective. The result is a thought-provoking and entertaining treatment like no other. In **Chapter 15: Advertising on the Internet,** we observe that the Internet represents so much more to the marketer than an advertising medium. Rather, it is emerging as a distribution system that carries advertising and communications of various sorts. The merging of Web site communication with sales transaction and fulfillment makes this a very different commercial communication environment than originally thought. There is also an extensive new discussion of security and privacy issues and a very substantive discussion of measuring the effectiveness of using the Internet. We believe this is unique to our book. **Chapter 18: Sales Promotion** has two new, extensive sections. The first is sales promotion techniques for the business market (added to the original discussions of the consumer market and the trade market). The second new section "Sales Promotion, the Internet, and New Media," talks about using new distribution and communication techniques for sales promotion.

The use of examples in this edition is very strong. We think that the book is tighter, with each visual example being right on target with the point being made in the text. We worked really hard on this . . . and we think it shows.

We moved a couple of chapters around in an effort to better organize the book for instructors and students, and to accommodate our added attention to promotion and integrated brand communication. Basically, we put all the promotion chapters together (Part 5). We moved the Internet chapter to the media section. Now everything is better bundled and provides a more flexible package for instructors who have different time constraints (modules, quarters, semesters) and different interests. For example, it is now very easy for our communication adopters to simply skip the promotions chapters if they choose, and for our business-school adopters to skip the more detailed creative chapters, if they choose. At the same time, we have done a good job of integrating key concepts throughout the book.

The soul of the book, however, remains the same. When we introduced the first edition of *Advertising,* we summed up our attitudes about our subject in this way:

Advertising is a lot of things. It's democratic pop culture, capitalist tool, oppressor, liberator, art, and theater, all rolled into one. It's free speech, it's creative flow, it's information, and it helps businesses get things sold. Above all, it's fun.

Advertising is fun, and this book reflects it. Advertising is also business, and this edition clearly conveys that message. Like other aspects of business, advertising is the result of hard work and careful planning. Creating good advertising is an enormous challenge . . . and we understand that. We understand advertising and promotion in its business and marketing context.

This book was written by three people with lots of experience in both academic and professional settings. They have collectively been consultants for many firms and their agencies. Thus, this book is grounded in real-world experience. It is, however, a book that seeks not to sell you a show-and-tell coffee-table book about the advertising industry. Advertising and promotion in the name of brands is a topic worthy of academic attention. The story of the 20th century was in no small part the story of the rise of consumer and advertising culture. Many academic disciplines want to understand how it works. We, as academic researchers, are in a unique and enviable position: We get to discuss advertising from the perspective of knowledge gathered in university settings as well as in daily practice. So we wrote a book that is both practically engaging and academically solid.

Much has happened since we released the first edition that has strengthened our resolve to write and deliver the best advertising and promotions book on the market. First, we learned from our adopters (over 300 of you) and from our students that the book's (sometimes brutally) honest discussion of advertising practice was welcomed and applauded. We are not here to be cheerleaders for advertising, or to tell you we possess the magic bullet. We truly love advertising, but we also know that it is not always wonderful: It can be totally frustrating to work with, particularly when you first learn there is no magic bullet. Advertising can have a dark side. We understand that, and try to put advertising in a realistic context. We treat students like adults. When the best answer is "no one knows," we tell you that.

Advertising continues to be buffeted by the turbulent world of ad industry evolution, "new" media expansion, and global competition. We were compelled to re-release this book just to keep current. In this edition, you will find the most current and extensive references to support our discussions of every aspect of advertising and lots and lots of detail.

As much as we respected our academic and practitioner colleagues the first and second times around, we respect them even more now. Research for the third edition turned up phenomenal industry talent, and we share our findings and surprises with you. This book is completely real-world, but the real world is also explained in terms of some really smart scholarship.

This book copies no one, yet pays homage to many. More than anything, this book seeks to be honest, thoughtful, and imaginative. It acknowledges the complexity of human communication and consumer behavior while retaining a point of view. It tells you what the cutting-edge thinking is on various topics and what we're fairly certain about in the way of good advertising practices, but it also quickly admits that, on certain issues, no one really knows the "right way" to do it. We tell it to you straight.

In terms of content and features, this book is loaded, simultaneously attuned to the vanguard and mindful of accepted wisdom. We pay particular attention to "new" media options such as advertising on the World Wide Web. We have guarded against immediate outdating by underlying our discussions of new media with principles and perspectives that will endure well after specific examples are obsolete. We have also tried our best to make life easier for the overworked instructor by offering a wide variety of ancillary materials that will assist in teaching from the book and in fully engaging students on this fascinating topic.

Students will like this book. They have liked the last two editions, and they will like this one even more. We spent considerable time reviewing student and instructor likes and dislikes of other advertising textbooks in addition to examining their reactions to our own book. With this feedback, we devote pages and pictures, ideas and intelligence to creating a place for student and teacher to meet and to discuss one of the most important and intrinsically interesting phenomena of contemporary times: advertising and promotion in the service of brands.

From Chapter 1 to Chapter 20. *Advertising and Integrated Brand Promotion,* 3e is different in that it explicitly acknowledges that advertising and promotion are all about brands. Brands can be goods or services, things or people (for example, political candidates, performers), and advertising and promotion are about projecting brands for marketers into the consciousness of consumers.

The third edition is also about taking a wider view of advertising and promotion. The truth these days is that any boundary between advertising and other forms of promotion is a pretty porous border. We acknowledge that, without making a really big deal of it or moving away from traditional advertising. In fact, we have made it very easy for instructors to cover what they want. This is still, first and foremost, an advertising book. We think that advertising and promotion should be discussed between the covers of the same book, as should their coordinated integration.

Organization. The third edition is divided into five parts. These parts are organized in a slightly different way than in the two previous editions. Due to the book's wide success for two editions, it has been adopted in courses from introductory to MBA level. Some instructors teach the whole book, while others use only selected chapters. So we have made it easier for people with different teaching objectives to use the book.

It seems that almost everyone uses Parts 1 and 2 (Chapters 1 through 9). That's where the book's core resides.

Part 3 (Chapters 10 through 13) is all about creativity: creativity in general, as a managerial issue, art direction, copy writing, and message strategy. Most adopters in advertising and communication use this section, while some business-school adopters (particularly those on 6- and 10-week modules or classes) skip some of the creative chapters in Part 3. Almost everyone uses Chapter 11, "Message Development: Strategies and Methods."

Part 4 (Chapters 14 through 16) is all about media, including the Internet.

Part 5 (Chapters 17 through 20) covers integrated brand promotion. In this edition, we bundled these four chapters together, since they are often used by our business-school adopters. We think they are good for everyone.

Our support package was designed and written for use in all advertising and/or promotion classes taught anywhere: in business and journalism schools as well as in mass communication and advertising departments.

Compelling Fundamentals. We fully expect our book to continue to set the standard for coverage of new media topics. It is loaded with features and insights and commonsense advertising perspectives about the new media. We were at the right place at the right time to build these issues into the first edition of *Advertising*. Now we have built on that competitive advantage and have incorporated new media coverage in *every* chapter.

That said, the real strength of this book is in its treatment of the fundamentals of advertising. One cannot appreciate the role of the new media today without a solid understanding of the fundamentals. If you doubt our commitment to the fundamentals, take a good look at Chapters 2 through 9. Here we present compelling coverage of the key issues involved in preparing a sound advertising plan. Chapter 2 begins this process by providing students with a perspective on the structure of the advertising industry and the economic roots of the process. In Chapters 3 and 4, students will gain further insights by studying the evolution of modern-day advertising along with social, ethical, and regulatory aspects. Chapter 5 provides a comprehensive treatment of how analysis of consumer behavior serves as the basis for sound advertising plans, and Chapter 6 establishes advertising's key role in executing coherent marketing strategies with respect to market segmentation, targeting, and positioning. The role of marketing and advertising research in laying the foundation for the plan is considered in Chapter 7, and the essentials of ad planning are consolidated and spelled out in Chapter 8.

Notice that we don't wait until the end of the book to bring international considerations into students' thinking. Global topics are integrated in every chapter throughout the text, because today's students must possess a global view. We incorporate our international chapter into the heart of the book—Chapter 9. Chapter 9 builds on the discussions in Chapter 8 and gives students a full view of the global advertising planning process.

Chapters 10 through 20 cover the full array of issues that must be attended to in executing an advertising plan, from message development to media planning and evaluation to promotion.

Balanced New Media Coverage. Most chapters contain a boxed insert headed *E-Commerce,* which furnish contemporary examples of how the new media are affecting various aspects of advertising practice. And every chapter contains *e-Sightings,* application activities designed to bring chapter ads into real time, and the concept of new media to life. Every chapter ends with *Using the Internet* exercises that can be pursued via the Internet to help students learn about advertising, generally, and the Internet, specifically. In-depth consideration of new media vehicles is provided in Part 4 of the book, "Placing the Message." Chapter 16 is all about advertising and marketing on the Internet and reviews many technical considerations for working with this now not-so-new, but still challenging and evolving medium.

IBP Coverage. Advertising is about brands. The marketing and advertising worlds have always known this, but have placed intense focus on brands in the last few years. So we make things explicit: This book is about advertising and promotion in the service of brands. Further, it must be an integrated effort. Integrated efforts have come to be the norm.

But the IBP coverage doesn't stop there—not by a long shot. Another unique feature of *Advertising and Integrated Brand Promotion* is the end-of-part case history, "From Principles to Practice: A Comprehensive IBP Case," which we developed in conjunction with Cincinnati Bell and its former agency, Northlich. This five-part case takes students inside a company and an ad agency to learn how IBP campaigns are planned and executed. The result illustrates the full array of considerations involved in implementing advertising and integrated brand promotion. As you will see, Cincinnati Bell provided us with all the planning, strategy, and implementation information from its campaign to introduce Cincinnati Bell Wireless services. We track the evolution of this campaign from its inception through its multimedia execution. This unique and comprehensive case history vividly illustrates what it means to speak to the customer with multiple tools, but *in a single voice,* to build and sustain a client's brand.

Student Engagement and Learning. You will find that this book provides a sophisticated examination of advertising fundamentals in lively, concise language. We don't beat around the bush, and we're not shy about challenging conventions. In addition, the book features an attractive internal design and hundreds of illustrations. Reading this book will be an engaging experience for students of advertising.

The markers of our commitment to student learning are easily identified throughout the book. Every chapter begins with a statement of the *learning objectives* for that chapter. (For a quick appreciation of the coverage provided by this book, take a pass through it and read the learning objectives on the first page of each chapter.) Chapters are organized to deliver content that responds to each learning objective, and the *chapter summaries* are written to reflect what the chapter has offered with respect to each learning objective.

We also believe that students must be challenged to go beyond their reading to think about the issues raised in the book. Thus, you will note that the *Questions* at the end of each chapter demand thoughtful analysis rather than mere regurgitation, and the *Experiential Exercises* will help students put their learning to use in ways that will help them take more away from the course than just textbook learning. Complete use of this text and its ancillary materials will yield a dramatic and engaging learning experience for students of all ages who are studying advertising for the first time.

A Closer Look at Some Third Edition Features.

How the Text Is Organized. *Advertising and Integrated Brand Promotion* is divided into five major parts:

- The Process of Advertising (Part 1)
- The Planning of Advertising (Part 2)
- Preparing the Advertising Message (Part 3)

- Placing the Advertising Message (Part 4)
- Integrated Brand Promotion (Part 5)

Now, let us call your attention to some important chapter highlights:

PART ONE

Part 1: Process: Advertising in Business and Society.

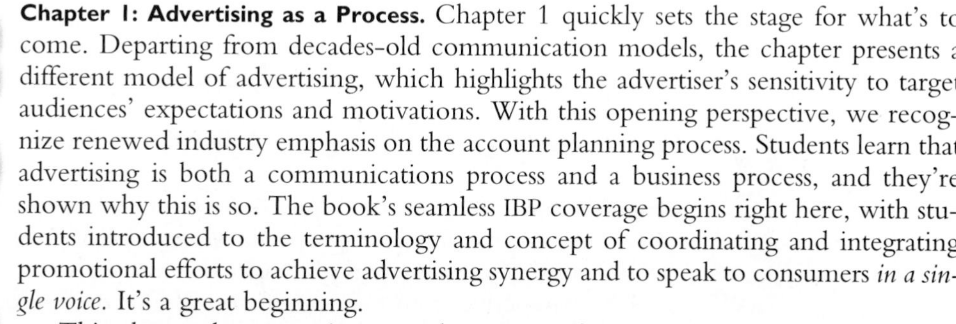

Chapter 1: Advertising as a Process. Chapter 1 quickly sets the stage for what's to come. Departing from decades-old communication models, the chapter presents a different model of advertising, which highlights the advertiser's sensitivity to target audiences' expectations and motivations. With this opening perspective, we recognize renewed industry emphasis on the account planning process. Students learn that advertising is both a communications process and a business process, and they're shown why this is so. The book's seamless IBP coverage begins right here, with students introduced to the terminology and concept of coordinating and integrating promotional efforts to achieve advertising synergy and to speak to consumers *in a single voice*. It's a great beginning.

This chapter has extensive new discussions of the concept of the brand, brand extensions, and brand equity. The concept of advertising and brand management is introduced here as the premise for the integrated brand promotion dimension of the text. IBP is the logical next step in IMC. We are not abandoning integrated marketing communication, but the key achievement of IMC is integrated brand promotion (IBP).

Chapter 2: The Structure of the Advertising Industry: Advertisers, Advertising Agencies, and Support Organizations. In Chapter 2, students read about trends that are transforming the advertising industry today and the seismic changes the industry experienced at the end of the millennium. Students will see who the participants in the ad industry are today and the role each plays in the formulation and execution of ad campaigns.

The main point is that advertisers are rethinking the way they try to communicate with consumers. Fundamentally, there is a greater focus on integrating more tools with the overall advertising effort into brand promotion programs. More than ever, advertisers are looking to the full complement of promotional opportunities in sales promotions, event sponsorships, new media options, and public relations as means to support and enhance the primary advertising effort for brands. There is much more emphasis on the role of the trade in the communications effort.

Chapter 3: The Evolution of Advertising. Chapter 3 puts advertising in a historical context. But before the history lesson begins, students are given the straight scoop about advertising as a product of fundamental economic and social conditions—capitalism, the Industrial Revolution, manufacturers' pursuit of power, and modern mass communication—without which there would be no advertising process. Students then study the history of advertising through 10 eras, seeing how advertising has changed and evolved, and how it is forged out of its social setting This chapter is rich with some of the most interesting ads representing advertising as a faithful documentation of social life in America. Definitely an entertaining and provocative chapter, it also gives students a necessary and important perspective on advertising before launching into advertising planning concepts and issues. Most strategies were created decades ago, and if you can learn how advertisers took advantage of various social conditions and trends yesterday, you can learn a lot about how to do it tomorrow.

Chapter 4: Social, Ethical, and Regulatory Aspects of Advertising. Advertising is dynamic and controversial. In Chapter 4, students will examine a variety of issues concerning advertising's effects on societal well-being. Is advertising intrusive, manipulative, and deceptive? Does it waste resources, promote materialism, and perpetuate stereotypes? Or does it inform, give exposure to important issues, and raise the standard of living? After debating the social merits of advertising, students will explore the ethical considerations that underlie the development of campaigns and learn about the regulatory agencies that set guidelines for advertisers. Lastly, students are introduced to the concept of self-regulation and why advertisers must practice it.

There are a couple of important and extensive changes in the third edition. First, the issue of privacy is discussed extensively as both a social and ethical issue, given new technologies that can track and profile consumers through the communication process. New sections were added on regulatory issues in direct marketing and e-commerce, in sales promotion, and in public relations.

PART TWO

Part 2: Planning: Analyzing the Advertising Environment.

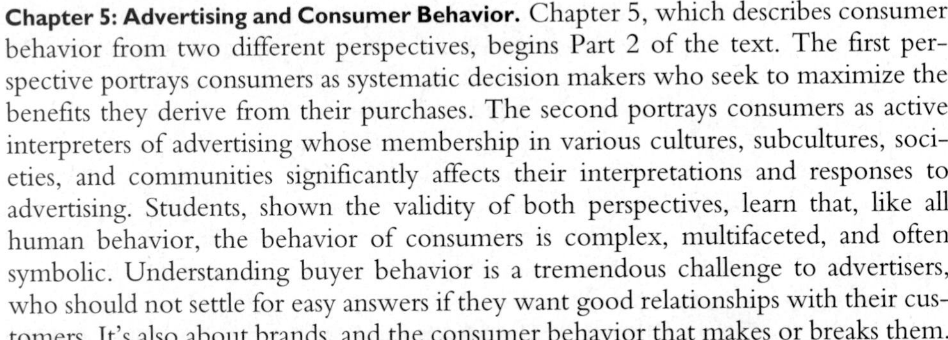

Chapter 5: Advertising and Consumer Behavior. Chapter 5, which describes consumer behavior from two different perspectives, begins Part 2 of the text. The first perspective portrays consumers as systematic decision makers who seek to maximize the benefits they derive from their purchases. The second portrays consumers as active interpreters of advertising whose membership in various cultures, subcultures, societies, and communities significantly affects their interpretations and responses to advertising. Students, shown the validity of both perspectives, learn that, like all human behavior, the behavior of consumers is complex, multifaceted, and often symbolic. Understanding buyer behavior is a tremendous challenge to advertisers, who should not settle for easy answers if they want good relationships with their customers. It's also about brands, and the consumer behavior that makes or breaks them.

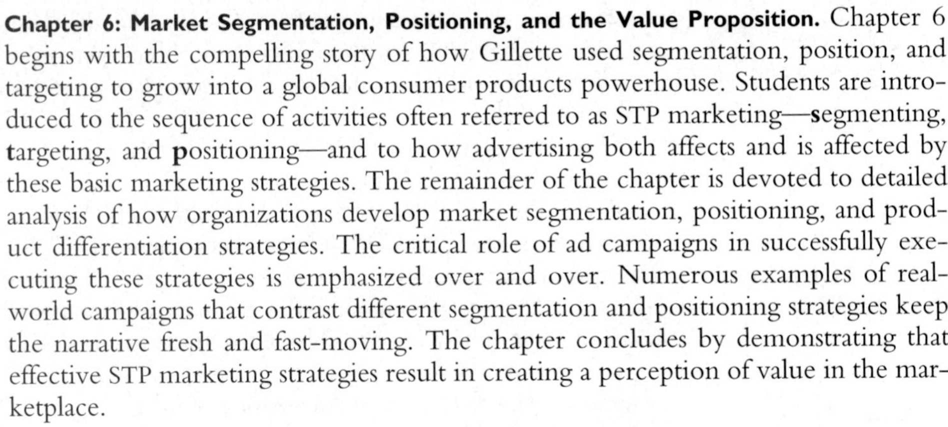

Chapter 6: Market Segmentation, Positioning, and the Value Proposition. Chapter 6 begins with the compelling story of how Gillette used segmentation, position, and targeting to grow into a global consumer products powerhouse. Students are introduced to the sequence of activities often referred to as STP marketing—**s**egmenting, **t**argeting, and **p**ositioning—and to how advertising both affects and is affected by these basic marketing strategies. The remainder of the chapter is devoted to detailed analysis of how organizations develop market segmentation, positioning, and product differentiation strategies. The critical role of ad campaigns in successfully executing these strategies is emphasized over and over. Numerous examples of real-world campaigns that contrast different segmentation and positioning strategies keep the narrative fresh and fast-moving. The chapter concludes by demonstrating that effective STP marketing strategies result in creating a perception of value in the marketplace.

Chapter 7: Advertising Research. Chapter 7, which contains a lot of new content, covers the methods used in developmental research, the procedures used for pretesting messages prior to the launch of a campaign, the methods used to track the effectiveness of ads during and after a launch, and the many sources of secondary data that can aid the ad-planning effort. This chapter also provides coverage of the agency's new emphasis on account planning as a distinct part of the planning process.

Chapter 8: The Advertising Plan. Chapter 8 begins by recounting the sequence of events and strategies behind the launch of Apple's colorful iMac computer. Through this opening vignette, students see the importance of constructing a sound ad plan before launching any campaign. But in addition, this introductory campaign for the iMac is an extraordinary example of IBP at work. After reading this chapter, students will be familiar with the basic components of an ad plan. They will understand two fundamental approaches for setting advertising objectives—the budgeting process and the role of the ad agency in formulating an advertising plan. By the end of the chapter, students will understand the significance of the opening commentary in this chapter: ". . . you don't go out and spend $100 million promoting a new product that is vital to the success of a firm without giving the entire endeavor considerable forethought. Such an endeavor calls for a plan."

Chapter 9: Advertising Planning: An International Perspective. We begin Chapter 9 with some of the many blunders in international advertising that make for some good belly laughs. But aside from the compelling content of this chapter, one of its most noteworthy features is the placement. While many books bury their international chapter at the end, we chose to place this chapter in the heart of the book, where it belongs, as part of the overall advertising planning effort. We think you'll find the chapter impressive in the number of international ads that are included and impressive in the way the fast-moving discussion unfolds: from a discussion of cultural barriers and overcoming them to an examination of the creative, media, and regulatory challenges that international advertising presents. The chapter ends with an insightful discussion of the differences between globalized and localized campaigns.

Part 3: Preparing the Message.

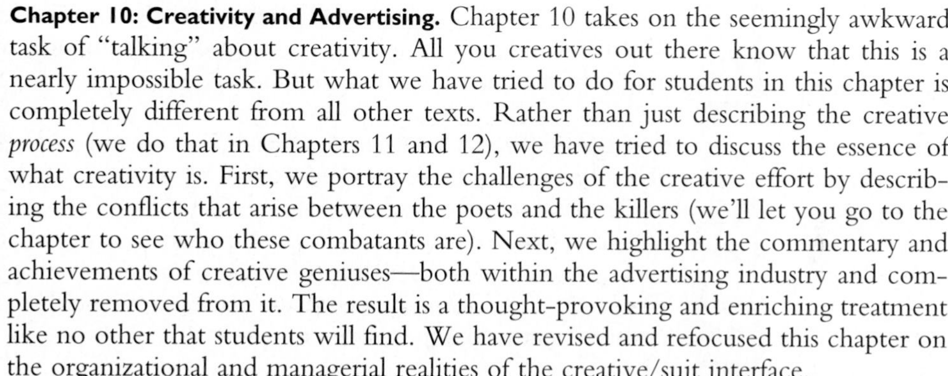

Chapter 10: Creativity and Advertising. Chapter 10 takes on the seemingly awkward task of "talking" about creativity. All you creatives out there know that this is a nearly impossible task. But what we have tried to do for students in this chapter is completely different from all other texts. Rather than just describing the creative *process* (we do that in Chapters 11 and 12), we have tried to discuss the essence of what creativity is. First, we portray the challenges of the creative effort by describing the conflicts that arise between the poets and the killers (we'll let you go to the chapter to see who these combatants are). Next, we highlight the commentary and achievements of creative geniuses—both within the advertising industry and completely removed from it. The result is a thought-provoking and enriching treatment like no other that students will find. We have revised and refocused this chapter on the organizational and managerial realities of the creative/suit interface.

Chapter 11: Message Development: Strategies and Methods. Building on Chapter 10, Chapter 11 explores the role of creativity in message strategy from a refreshingly honest perspective—no one knows exactly how advertising creativity works. Ten message strategy objectives are presented along with the creative methods used to accomplish the objectives, including humor ads, slice-of-life ads, anxiety ads, sexual-appeal ads, slogan ads, and repetition ads. This chapter makes excellent use of visuals to dramatize the concepts presented. Quite a bit of revision went into this signature chapter. Many ads are offered here as concrete examples.

Chapter 12: Copywriting. Chapter 12 flows logically from the chapter on message development. In this chapter students learn about the copywriting process and the importance of good, hard-hitting copy in the development of print, radio, and television advertising. Guidelines for writing headlines, subheads, and body copy for print ads are given, as are guidelines for writing radio and television ad copy. The chapter closes with a discussion of the most common mistakes copywriters make and a discussion of the copy approval process. And, of course, this chapter considers the issues surrounding the copywriting process in the highly constrained creative environment of the Internet.

Chapter 13: Art Direction and Production. The adopters of the first edition of *Advertising* told us that two chapters on art direction and production was overkill. We heeded your plea. Chapter 13 now combines discussion of print and broadcast media. Here, students learn about the strategic and creative impact of illustration, design, and layout, and the production steps required to get to the final ad. Numerous engaging full-color ads are included that illustrate important design, illustration, and layout concepts.

We also introduce students to what is often thought of as the most glamorous side of advertising: television advertising. Students learn about the role of the creative team and the many agency and production company participants involved in the direction and production processes. Students are given six creative guidelines for television ads, with examples of each. Radio is not treated as a second-class citizen in this chapter but is given full treatment, including six guidelines for the production of creative and effective radio ads. This chapter is comprehensive and informative without getting bogged down in production details.

Part 4: Placing the Message.

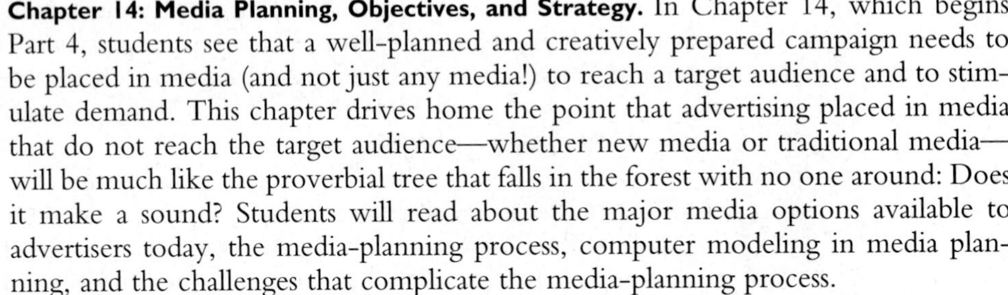

Chapter 14: Media Planning, Objectives, and Strategy. In Chapter 14, which begins Part 4, students see that a well-planned and creatively prepared campaign needs to be placed in media (and not just any media!) to reach a target audience and to stimulate demand. This chapter drives home the point that advertising placed in media that do not reach the target audience—whether new media or traditional media—will be much like the proverbial tree that falls in the forest with no one around: Does it make a sound? Students will read about the major media options available to advertisers today, the media-planning process, computer modeling in media planning, and the challenges that complicate the media-planning process.

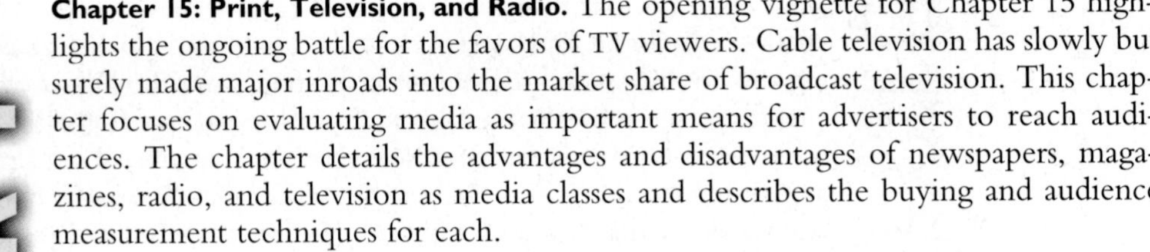

Chapter 15: Print, Television, and Radio. The opening vignette for Chapter 15 highlights the ongoing battle for the favors of TV viewers. Cable television has slowly but surely made major inroads into the market share of broadcast television. This chapter focuses on evaluating media as important means for advertisers to reach audiences. The chapter details the advantages and disadvantages of newspapers, magazines, radio, and television as media classes and describes the buying and audience measurement techniques for each.

Chapter 16: Advertising on the Internet. The first edition of *Advertising* was the first introductory advertising book to devote an entire chapter to advertising on the Internet, and this revision continues to set the standard for Internet coverage. Today's employers expect college advertising students to know about the Internet and the creative and selling opportunities it presents to advertisers as part of their IBP strategy. Chapter 16 presents a complete overview of advertising on the Internet and provides numerous Net activities to give students hands-on experience visiting and analyzing advertisers' Web sites. The chapter describes who's using the Internet today and the ways they are using it, identifies the advertising and marketing opportunities presented by the Internet, discusses fundamental requirements for establishing sites on the World Wide Web, and lays out the challenges inherent in measuring the cost effectiveness of the Internet versus other advertising media. This chapter doesn't assume that all students are already Internet gurus, but it won't insult those who are.

What is added to this chapter is that the Internet is not exclusively an advertising medium. Rather, it is emerging as a distribution system that carries advertising and communications of various sorts. The merging of Web site communication with sales transaction and fulfillment makes this a very different communications environment. There is an extensive new discussion of security and privacy issues and a very substantive discussion of measuring the effectiveness of using the Internet. We believe this is unique to our book.

Part 5: Integrated Brand Promotion

Chapter 17: Support Media, P-O-P Advertising, and Event Sponsorship. The story of Procter & Gamble's innovative poster campaign to promote Noxzema is exceptional—don't

miss it. With P&G's posters as introduction, Chapter 17 makes students aware of the vast number of support media options available to advertisers: event sponsorship, signage, outdoor billboards, transit advertising, aerial advertising, point-of-purchase displays, directories, and specialty items. If students do not already appreciate the challenge of integrating marketing communications before they get to this chapter, they certainly will afterward!

Chapter 18: Sales Promotion. Sales promotion is a multibillion-dollar business in the United States and is emerging as a global force as well. Chapter 18 explains the rationale for different types of sales promotions. It differentiates between consumer and trade sales promotions and highlights the risks and coordination issues associated with sales promotions—a consideration overlooked by other texts. All of the following are discussed: coupons, price-off deals, premiums, contests, sweepstakes, sampling, trial offers, brand (formerly product) placements, refunds, rebates, frequency programs, point-of-purchase displays, incentives, allowances, trade shows, and cooperative advertising.

This chapter has two new, extensive sections. The first is sales promotion techniques for the business market (added to the original discussions of the consumer market and the trade market). The second new section, "Sales Promotion, the Internet, and New Media," talks about using new distribution and communication techniques for sales promotion.

Chapter 19: Direct Marketing. Chapter 19 opens with an example of "high tech" direct marketing from NextCard and then moves quickly on to L. L. Bean and the well-known L. L. Bean mail-order catalog. Students quickly learn about Bean's emphasis on building an extensive mailing list, which serves as a great segue to database marketing. Students will learn why direct marketing continues to grow in popularity, what media are used by direct marketers to deliver their messages, and how direct marketing creates special challenges for achieving integrated brand promotion.

Chapter 20: Public Relations and Corporate Advertising. Chapter 20 begins with the story of Microsoft's ongoing problems with the Justice Department and how the press coverage of the case represents a public relations disaster for the firm. It illustrates the point that while some public relations crises are beyond the control of the organization, some are of the company's own doing. This dynamic and engaging chapter explains the role of public relations as part of an organization's overall IMC strategy and details the objectives and tools of public relations in a way that attracts and holds student interest. The chapter differentiates between proactive and reactive public relations and the strategies associated with each. The chapter goes on to discuss the various forms of corporate advertising and the way each can be used as a means for building the reputation of an organization in the eyes of key constituents.

Inside Every Chapter. Inside every chapter of *Advertising and Integrated Brand Promotion* you will find features that make this new book eminently teachable and academically solid, while at the same time fun to read. As we said earlier, this text was written and the examples were chosen to facilitate an effective meeting place for student and teacher. Who said learning has to be drudgery? It doesn't have to be and it shouldn't.

Dynamic Graphics and over 400 Ads and Exhibits. Ask any student and almost any instructor what an advertising book must include, and you will get as a top response—lots of ads. As you will see by quickly paging through *Advertising*, this book is full of ads. Over 400 ads are used to illustrate important points made in the chapters. Each ad is referenced in the text narrative, tying the visual to the concept being discussed.

As you can see, the book's clean, classic, graphic layout invites you to read it; it dares you to put it down without reading just one more caption or peeking at just the next chapter.

Opening Vignettes. Every chapter includes a classic or current real-world advertising story to draw students into the chapter and to stimulate classroom discussions. Each vignette illustrates important concepts that will be discussed in the chapter. The chapters throughout the book continue with these types of lively introductions, ensuring that students get off to a good start with every chapter.

In-Chapter Boxes. Every chapter contains boxed material that highlights interesting, unusual, or just plain entertaining information as it relates to the chapter. The boxes are not diversions unrelated to the text; rather, they provide information that can be fully integrated into classroom lectures. The boxes are for teaching, learning, and reinforcing chapter content. Three types of boxes are included in the text: E-Commerce, Global Issues, and IBP. Let's take a look at each.

E-Commerce. Much of the coverage in the E-Commerce boxes focuses on issues related to advertising and the Internet. Following is a sampling of the issues discussed in the E-Commerce boxes:

- *The Internet Is Big—But Not As Big As Seinfeld,* Chapter 1
- *Start the Evolution without Me,* Chapter 3
- *Diversity Comes to the Digital World,* Chapter 6
- *The Fundamentals Never Go Out of Style,* Chapter 8
- *News Flash: World Wide Web NOT Worldwide,* Chapter 9
- *Writing Cybercopy—Don't Abandon All the Old Rules,* Chapter 12
- *Myth: The Web Will Dominate Classified Advertising. Reality: Newspapers Don't Have to Worry,* Chapter 15
- *E-Commerce: It Takes a Warehouse . . .,* Chapter 19

Global Issues. The Global Issues boxes provide an insightful real-world look at the numerous challenges advertisers face internationally. Many issues are discussed in these timely boxes, including the development of more standardized advertising across cultures with satellite-based television programming, how U.S.-based media companies such as MTV and Disney/ABC are pursuing the vast potential in global media, obstacles to advertising in emerging markets, and cross-cultural global research. The following is a sampling of the Global Issues boxes you'll find in *Advertising:*

- *Motorola's Global Campaign Takes Flight—Then Comes Back to Earth,* Chapter 1
- *This Is Absolut-ly the Best Place to Reach Consumers,* Chapter 3
- *Japan's Marketing Bellwether? The Teenage Girl,* Chapter 7
- *From Salsa to Cinco de Mayo,* Chapter 9
- *Europe: The Birthplace of the 30-Minute Ad?,* Chapter 10
- *You Know That Kissing Thing—It Works for Global Ads, Too,* Chapter 12
- *Using the Net to Take a Brand Global,* Chapter 16
- *Bring on the World,* Chapter 18

IBP. As we said earlier, we are committed to students' awareness of IBP activities in the industry and the role advertising plays in the process. The IBP boxes in each chapter highlight interesting and important IBP programs or issues. Here are some of the titles of IBP boxes in the text:

- *Going Out and Finding the Market,* Chapter 1

- *Not Snake Oil—But Still Pretty Slick,* Chapter 3
- *Take Special Care with Promotions to Kids,* Chapter 6
- *Jaguar Looks to Spike for Answers,* Chapter 8
- *It's Not Easy Being Green,* Chapter 13
- *IBP in B to B,* Chapter 18
- *Where Is the Spin Control?,* Chapter 20

e-Sightings. In keeping with the new media distinctiveness of this book, you will find all new "e-Sightings" in each chapter. You can spot these e-Sightings by looking for the e-Sighting binoculars found above selected exhibits in each chapter. Students are asked to go to the Web site addresses provided to explore the advertiser's home page, bringing the ad in the book online and into real time. Questions are provided to prompt students to explore, explain, describe, compare, contrast, summarize, rethink, or analyze the content or features of the advertiser's home page. You can think of these e-Sightings as in-chapter experiential exercises and real-time cases. Instructors can assign these e-Sightings as individual or group activities. They are also excellent discussion starters. A note: Most Web sites are listed with the prefix *http://.* While this is the technical address, most Web browsers don't require the user to type out this prefix, so it has been dropped from the URLs in this book.

Concise Chapter Summaries. Each chapter ends with a summary that distills the main points of the chapter. Chapter summaries are organized around the learning objectives so that students can use them as a quick check on their achievement of learning goals.

Key Terms. Each chapter ends with a listing of the key terms found in the chapter. Key terms also appear in boldface in the text. Students can prepare for exams by scanning these lists to be sure they can define or explain each term.

Questions. These end-of-chapter questions, written by the authors, are designed to challenge students' thinking and to go beyond the "read, memorize, and regurgitate" learning process. The Questions for Review and Critical Thinking sections require students to think analytically and to interpret data and information provided for them in the text. Detailed responses to these questions are provided in the Instructor's Manual.

Below is a sampling of the types of critical-thinking questions found in *Advertising*:

- If a firm developed a new line of athletic shoes, priced them competitively, and distributed them in appropriate retail shops, would there be any need for advertising? Is advertising really needed for a good product that is priced right?
- The 1950s were marked by great suspicion about advertisers and their potential persuasive powers. Do you see any lingering effects of this era of paranoia in attitudes about advertising today?
- Some contend that self-regulation is the best way to ensure fair and truthful advertising practices. Why would it be in the best interest of the advertising community to aggressively pursue self-regulation?
- Identify several factors or forces that make consumers around the world more similar to one another. Conversely, what factors or forces create diversity among consumers in different countries?
- Explain the two basic strategies for developing corporate home pages, exemplified in this chapter by Saturn and Absolut.
- Visit some of the corporate home pages described in this chapter, or think about corporate home pages you have visited previously. Of those you have encountered, which would you single out as being most effective in giving the visitor a

reason to come back? What conclusions would you draw regarding the best ways to motivate repeat visits to a Web site?

- Everyone has an opinion on what makes advertisements effective or ineffective. How does this fundamental aspect of human nature complicate a copywriter's life when it comes to winning approval for his or her ad copy?

Experiential Exercises. At the end of each chapter, Experiential Exercises require students to apply the material they have just read by researching topics, writing short papers, preparing brief presentations, or interacting with professionals from the advertising industry. They require students to get out of the classroom to seek information not provided in the text. A number of these exercises are especially designed for teamwork, and many are classroom tested. Additional Experiential Exercises can be found in the Instructor's Manual.

Using the Internet. This unique set of Internet exercises is designed to get students on the Internet to examine the nature of the advertising that is there, to analyze the effectiveness of what they find, and to apply the Internet to fundamental advertising concepts presented in the text. Because the focus of these exercises is hands-on in nature, students will spend time accessing home pages using the Web site addresses provided and evaluating what they find. Application questions are provided for each exercise for students to answer after their Web site excursions. The application questions require students to apply the concepts taught in each chapter, making these surfing-the-Net exercises worthwhile and focused, not just browsing time. Additional Internet exercises can be found in the Instructor's Manual—for real diehard cyberhounds! Suggested answers to all of the Internet exercises can be found in the Instructor's Manual. Additionally, *Advertising*'s appendix provides the Web address of nearly every major advertiser that appears in the text.

Learning Objectives and a Built-In Integrated Learning System. The text and test bank are organized around the learning objectives that appear at the beginning of each chapter, to provide you and your students with an easy-to-use, integrated learning system. A numbered icon like the one shown here identifies each chapter objective and appears next to its related material throughout the chapter. This integrated learning system can provide you with a structure for creating lesson plans as well as tests. A correlation table at the beginning of every chapter in the test bank enables you to create tests that fully cover every learning objective or that emphasize the objectives you feel are most important.

The integrated system also gives structure to students as they prepare for tests. The icons identify all the material in the text that fulfill each objective. Students can easily check their grasp of each objective by reading the text sections and reviewing the corresponding summary sections. They can return to appropriate text sections for further review if they have difficulty with end-of-chapter questions.

End-of-Part IBP Case History: Cincinnati Bell℠ Wireless. No advertising text would be complete without giving special attention to integrated brand promotion. At the end of each of the five parts of this text is an ongoing case study of Cincinnati Bell and its Cincinnati Bell Wireless IBP campaigns. These sections will help students better understand IBP by examining the topic in two ways. First, each section begins by discussing the basics of IBP and methods for creating effective, integrated communications. Second, each section illustrates the basic principles of IBP in campaigns developed for Cincinnati Bell Wireless. As students will discover, Cincinnati Bell

used a wide range of communication tools to support its goal of introducing and growing its brand. Of course, these IBP sections are fully and colorfully illustrated. And, as with a lot of the features that distinguish this book, we were in the right place at the right time. Cincinnati Bell Wireless' campaigns have been remarkably successful in an increasingly competitive marketplace.

A Full Array of Teaching/Learning Supplementary Materials.

Instructor's Manual (0-324-11381-1). Prepared by Debra A. Laverie of Texas Tech University, the Instructor's Manual, originally prepared by the main text authors, has been thoroughly revised to complement the current edition. The Instructor's Manual consists of comprehensive lecture outlines for each chapter that include suggestions for using other ancillary products that accompany the text, thereby offering a complete and structured approach for preparing lesson plans and lectures. Also included in the instructor's manual are suggested answers for all exercises found within the text. These include the e-Sightings exercises found throughout the text, as well as the end-of-chapter questions including the Experiential Exercises, and Using the Internet exercises. The Instructor's Manual also includes a complete set of transparency masters derived from the PowerPoint slide presentation.

PowerPoint Slide Presentation (0-324-11762-0). Prepared by Michael Weigold of the University of Florida, the PowerPoint slide presentation has been improved with the current edition to add more variety, visual appeal, and coverage of material. The slides have been created with the intention of holding students' interest while assuring that all main concepts and terms are reinforced to improve student's learning of each chapter's material.

Test Bank (0-324-11382-X). Prepared by Edward E. Ackerly of the University of Arizona, this comprehensive test bank is organized around the main text's learning objectives. Each question is labeled according to the learning objective that is covered, the page number on which the answer can be found, and the type of question (definitional, conceptual, or application). With this edition, we have added more application-oriented questions in response to current user feedback. Grouping the questions according to type allows the instructor maximum flexibility in creating tests that are customized to individual classroom needs and preferences. The test bank includes true/false, multiple-choice, scenario application, and essay questions. There are a total of 2,000 questions. All questions have been carefully reviewed for clarity and accuracy.

ExamView Testing Software (0-324-11765-5). The electronic test bank allows instructors to easily manipulate the content found in our printed test bank supplement and create customized tests to suit varying student levels and classroom needs.

WebTutor Advantage on Blackboard (0-324-13060-0) and WebCT (0-324-13061-9). The WebTutor and WebCT include reviews of main concepts, flashcards, links to the Internet, discussion questions, and quizzes.

Award-Winning Video Package—Nobody Else Has the Clios!

The Best of 2001: The Clio Gold Winners (0-324-16195-6). Our award-winning video package is designed to show students how advertising works in the real world, from the perspective of both the ad agency and the client, and to demonstrate for students some of the most current and creative examples of advertising worldwide. It's a dynamic, attention-getting, and engaging package you'll enjoy using in your classes. Our video package brings life to the advertising principles presented in the text. This edition's Clio video presents the Clio gold winners for the year 2001. Entries include Budweiser's "What Are You Doing?"; Nike's "Train To Win" and "Beatboxer"; ESPN's "Swimming Pool," "Pottery Class," and "Piñata"; Orange mobile phone network's "Hold Up"; John West's "Bear"; Peugeot 406's "Upside Down"; Eatons' "Big Finish"; Companion Animal Placement's "Park"; Revista E'Poca's "The Week"; and Fox Sports' "Baby," "Nature Channel," "Milk," "India," "China," and "Turkey."

Other video support materials will also be available by the time of publication.

IMC: An Integrated Marketing Communications Exercise, 2nd Edition (0-324-01483-X). This comprehensive supplementary workbook puts students in the role of a client services manager at a major, full-service integrated marketing communications agency. The client, the Republic of Uruguay, wants the agency to create and manage a total marketing program for a new resort in Uruguay called Punta del Este. In approximately 80 pages, this semester-long project workbook includes step-by-step directions for students to follow. In addition to the traditional IMC mix, this exercise also takes students into the world of interactive media, because any successful presentation in the real world today will have to include a proposal integrating the Internet and other interactive media.

To begin the exercise, students are briefed on all aspects of the new resort: facts and details about Punta del Este, competition, research data, and the lore surrounding the resort. After the briefing, students are guided through the development of a four-part campaign recommendation for their client. They will create (1) a generalized communications statement complete with objectives and a strategy for segmentation, targeting, and product positioning; (2) a copy platform with their recommendations for TV and magazine ads; (3) a media plan, including interactive media; and (4) a promotion plan for travel industry intermediaries and travel consumers.

The correlating Instructor's Manual contains numerous suggestions and guidelines for the smooth implementation of this exercise into your course. It also offers suggestions for condensing the material, if you prefer a shorter exercise or one that focuses exclusively on advertising without the IMC topics.

This outstanding supplement was written by Bernard C. Jakacki of Ramapo College. In additional to writing this exercise, Professor Jakacki has tested it for years with many college students and advertising agency trainees. The response from users has been spectacular in terms of both its comprehensive content and the fun they have promoting Punta del Este. This tested and proven package is truly real-world in both orientation and design.

Campaign Planner for Promotion and IMC, 2nd Edition (0-324-15197-7). Developed by Shay Sayre, this text is designed to help students prepare and present a professional campaign in conjunction with *Advertising and Integrated Brand Promotion.* Using a 10-step guide, the Campaign Planner clearly explains the process of planning and executing a successful campaign. Acting as a simulated agency, students provide solutions for a chosen client's promotional problem. Problem solutions involve advertising, public relations, and promotional aspects to deliver a truly integrated marketing communications plan. Enhancements to the second edition include the following:

- Starbucks Coffee: A case synopsis featuring Starbucks Coffee is included to aid you in the development of your campaign objectives, strategies, and tactics.
- Theory in Action: Simulating the real-life process agencies use to develop a campaign, the exercises allow you to see how objectives translate into strategies, and how strategies are then developed into usable tactics.
- Student Resources: A tally sheet, sample surveys, and directions on how to conduct informational interviews are included to help students complete the research process.
- Guided Plans Book Development: Instructions on how to prepare and assemble a plans book provide you with important information needed to complete an end-of-term written proposal. A sample plans book appears at the back of the workbook.

oguinn.swcollege.com. Go online at oguinn.swcollege.com for additional resources, ideas, content, and lots and lots of links to great Web sites.

ACKNOWLEDGMENTS

The most pleasant task in writing a textbook is the expression of gratitude to people and institutions that have helped the authors. We appreciate the support and encouragement we received from many individuals, including the following:

- **Steve Hazelwood,** Acquisitions Editor, who oversaw the third edition; **Leslie Kauffman,** a truly great editor, who saw us 95 percent of the way through this edition; and **Tamborah Moore,** Production Editor, and **Mardell Toomey,** Developmental Editor, who took us the rest of the way and oversaw the ancillary products. We express gratitude, also, to our publisher's professional and committed sales force for the critically important customer feedback that we received all along the way.
- A very big thank you to the incomparable **Grace M. Davidson,** Project Manager, Lachina Publishing Services.
- For the three editions' worth of GREAT internal art and design: **Craig Ramsdell.**
- For great cover art: **Lou Beach**: Lou has created art for *The New York Times, Time, David Bowie, Brian Eno, The Big Lebowski,* and on and on. Lou is the hottest designer around. Thanks for the cover.
- For timely, patient, and expert computer support: **Barlow LeVold.**
- **Everyone at Cincinnati Bell and Northlich** who gave us tremendous help and support in creating the IBP case. We especially want to thank Cincinnati Bell's President **Jack Cassidy** and CBW Director of Marketing **Mike Vanderwoude,** as well as the following people from Northlich: **Mark Serrianne**, President and CEO; **Don Perkins,** Senior Vice President and Executive Creative Director; **Mandy Reverman,** Account Supervisor; **Scott Aaron,** Account Supervisor; **Susan Cheney,** Direct Marketing Account Supervisor; **Mike Swainey,** Account Manager; and **Jay Pioch,** Assistant Account Manager.

- **Marty Horn,** Senior Vice President, Group Director—Strategic Planning & Research, DDB-Chicago, for his thoughts and expert advice on our research chapter.
- **David Moore,** Vice President/Executive Producer at Leo Burnett, who gave us invaluable insights on the broadcast production process and helped us secure key materials for the text.
- **Kent Lancaster,** University of Florida, for his assistance with our media chapter.
- **Kimberly Paul,** University of Texas at Austin and Intensity Designs, Austin, Texas, for her help with the creative chapters.
- **Bernard C. Jakacki,** Ramapo College, for providing a truly excellent IMC supplement. The timing of his work was serendipitous, and we're glad to have it as part of the *Advertising and IBP* package.
- **Shay Sayre,** California State University, Fullerton, for creating an ad campaign planner of exceptional quality.
- **Mike Wiegold,** University of Florida, for putting in the extra care and effort to create truly outstanding PowerPoint slides, which serve as a very useful lecture aid.
- **Ross Stapleton-Gray,** of TeleDiplomacy, Inc., and Georgetown University, for his fine efforts in preparing the Using the Internet exercises and the e-Sightings.
- **Ed Ackerly,** University of Arizona, for revising the test bank, assuring its accuracy and usefulness.
- **Debra A. Laverie,** for creating an exceptional instructor's manual.
- The authors would like to recognize the outstanding efforts of **James Davis,** who was able to locate and secure permission for literally hundreds of ads and exhibits that appear in this edition.
- **Matt Smith** of Arnold, Finnegan & Martin, for providing us with the Watermark ad and sketches in Chapter 13.
- **Peter Sheldon,** University of Illinois: Chief Exhibitionist (yes, he made us say this). Peter is the creative heart and soul of this book. He picked many of the ads for this book, and provided substantive editorial material and comments. Everybody says this, but in Peter's case it is really true: Without him, we couldn't have done it. He made the book a reality. His vision, talent, and wonderful humor was our daily blessing. Thanks, Peter.
- **Brett Wilcoxson, Deborah Brown,** and **Emily Grissom,** University of Illinois, for help locating ads and data when we needed it *right now.*
- **Professors Gray Swicegood** and **Gillian Stevens,** University of Illinois, for their help with consumer demography.
- **Cinda Robbins-Cornstubble** and **Janette Bradley Wright** for their wonderful support and incredible competence.
- **Caitlin Ryus, Eliza Ryus,** and **Linda Scott** for their support, advice, and their incredible jobs as consumers.
- **Whitley Scott** for her constant affection and silent consent.
- **Connie M. Johnson** for years of great observations about the human condition.
- **Patrick Gavin Quinlan,** for years of great advice and friendship.
- **Susan E. Hunter,** Senior Associate of Social Marketing, Medical Review of North Carolina, for her creativity, affection, and support.
- **David Bryan Teets,** University of Illinois, for help with the TV commercial director becomes movie director lists and references. Dave knows film.
- **Mildred O'Guinn** (Tom's mom), who actually read every single word of the first edition and found the only misspelled word, one missed by countless computers, editors, authors, proofers, and so on: "Restritions," in Exhibit 9.16 on page 252. Very good job. Thanks.
- **Professor John Murphy II,** Joe C. Thompson Centennial Professor in Advertising at the University at Austin, who has given us great feedback and continued support. We ran our ideas past John for the third edition before we even started this revision.

- **Steve Hall,** who supports, critiques and gives his all to his students at The University of Illinois. Thanks for the support and advice.

We are particularly indebted to our reviewers—past and present—and the following individuals whose thoughtful comments, suggestions, and specific feedback shaped the content of *Advertising and Integrated Brand Promotion.* Our thanks go to:

Priscilla LaBarbera
New York University

Lynne Boles
Procter & Gamble

Anne Cunningham
University of Tennessee

Robert Dwyer
University of Cincinnati

Jon Freiden
Florida State University

Cynthia Frisby
University of Missouri–Columbia

Corliss L. Green
Georgia State University

Scott Hamula
Keuka College

Wayne Hilinski
Penn State University

Karen James
Louisiana State University–Shreveport

Donald Jugenheimer
Southern Illinois University

James Kellaris
University of Cincinnati

Patricia Kennedy
University of Nebraska–Lincoln

Robert Kent
University of Delaware

William LaFief
Frostburg State University

Tina M. Lowrey
Rider University

Nancy Mitchell
University of Nebraska–Lincoln

Darrel Muehling
Washington State University

John Purcell
Castleton State College

Joe Regruth
Procter & Gamble

Debra Scammon
University of Utah

Kim Sheehan
University of Oregon

Alan Shields
Suffolk County Community College

Jan Slater
Syracuse University

Patricia Stout
University of Texas–Austin

Lynn Walters
Texas A&M

Brian Wansink
University of Illinois

Marc Weinberger
University of Massachusetts–Amherst

Gary B. Wilcox
University of Texas–Austin

Kurt Wildermuth
University of Missouri–Columbia

Christine Wright-Isak
Young & Rubicam

Molly Ziske
Michigan State University

Thomas C. O'Guinn
Chris T. Allen
Richard J. Semenik

Preface vi
Acknowledgments xxii

Part One
The Process: Advertising in Business and Society 2
1 Advertising as a Process 4
2 The Structure of the Advertising Industry: Advertisers, Advertising Agencies, and Support Organizations 42
3 The Evolution of Advertising 74
4 Social, Ethical, and Regulatory Aspects of Advertising 114
Integrated Brand Promotion Part 1: From Principles to Practice: An Integrated Brand Promotion Case 148

Part Two
Planning: Analyzing the Advertising Environment 158
5 Advertising and Consumer Behavior 160
6 Market Segmentation, Positioning, and the Value Proposition 208
7 Advertising and Promotion Research 240
8 The Advertising Plan 270
9 Advertising Planning: An International Perspective 298
Integrated Brand Promotion Part 2: From Principles to Practice: Planning Advertising and IBP 326

Part Three
Preparing the Message 336
10 Creativity and Advertising 338
11 Message Strategy 362
12 Copywriting 400
13 Art Direction and Production 434
Integrated Brand Promotion Part 3: From Principles to Practice: Preparing Advertising and IBP 476

Part Four
Placing the Message in Conventional and "New" Media 484
14 Media Planning, Objectives, and Strategy for Advertising and Promoting the Brand 486
15 Media Planning: Print, Television, and Radio 522
16 Media Planning: Advertising and the Internet 558
Integrated Brand Promotion Part 4: From Principles to Practice: Cincinnati Bell Wireless: The Launch Campaign 596

Part Five
Integrated Brand Promotion 604
17 Support Media, P-O-P Advertising, and Event Sponsorship 606
18 Sales Promotion 634
19 Direct Marketing 668
20 Public Relations and Corporate Advertising 694
Integrated Brand Promotion Part 5: From Principles to Practice: Sustaining and Growing the Brand after Launch 718

Glossary 727
Name/Brand/Company Index 741
Subject Index 750
Credits 766

CONTENTS

Preface vi
Acknowledgments xxii

PART ONE
The Process: Advertising in Business and Society 2

1 Advertising as a Process 4

Introductory Scenario: A Tale of Two Burgers 6

What Is Advertising? 8
Advertising, Advertisements, Advertising Campaigns, and Integrated Brand Promotion 11

Advertising as a Communication Process 13
A Model of Mass-Mediated Communication 13

The Audiences for Advertising 15
Audience Categories 15
Audience Geography 17
Global Issues: Motorola's Global Campaign Takes Flight–Then Comes Back to Earth 19

Advertising as a Business Process 19
The Role of Advertising in Marketing and Brand Promotion 19
The Role of Advertising in the Marketing Mix • The Role of Advertising in Brand Development and Management • The Role of Advertising Market Segmentation, Differentiation, and Positioning • The Role of Advertising in Revenue and Profit Generation
E-Commerce: The Internet *Is* Big–It's Even Bigger Than Seinfeld 27

Types of Advertising 29

The Economic Effects of Advertising 33
Advertising's Effect on Gross Domestic Product 33
Advertising's Effect on Business Cycles 33
Advertising's Effect on Competition 33
Advertising's Effect on Prices 33
Advertising's Effect on Value 34

From Integrated Marketing Communications to Integrated Brand Promotion 37
IBP: Going Out and Finding the Market 38

Summary 39
Key Terms 40
Questions 40
Experiential Exercises 41
Using the Internet 41

2 The Structure of the Advertising Industry: Advertisers, Advertising Agencies, and Support Organizations 42

The Advertising Industry in Transition 45

Trends Affecting the Advertising Industry 46
IBP: See the Brand, Join the Club 48

The Scope and Structure of the Advertising Industry 48
Advertisers 50
Manufacturers and Service Firms • Trade Resellers • Federal, State, and Local Governments • Social Organizations
Agencies 54
Advertising Agencies • Promotion Agencies
Agency Services 59
Account Services • Marketing Research Services • Creative and Production Services • Media Planning and Buying Services • Administrative Services
E-Commerce: You Have E-Mail (as a Promotion Option) 59
Agency Compensation 62
Commissions • Markup Charges • Fee Systems • Pay-for-Results
External Facilitators 64
Marketing and Advertising Research Firms • Consultants • Production Facilitators • Information Intermediators • Software Firms
Controversy: So How Does It Feel to Have a Big Brother? 66

Media Organizations 66
Audiences 67

Summary 70
Key Terms 71
Questions 71
Experiential Exercises 72
Using the Internet 73

3 The Evolution of Advertising 74

Fundamental Influences on the Evolution of Advertising 76
The Rise of Capitalism 77
The Industrial Revolution 77
Manufacturers' Pursuit of Power in the Channel of Distribution 78
The Rise of Modern Mass Media 78

Advertising in Practice 79

The Preindustrialization Era (pre-1800) 79
The Era of Industrialization (1800 to 1875) 79
The "P.T. Barnum Era" (1875 to 1918) 80
The 1920s (1918 to 1929) 81
The Depression (1929 to 1941) 85
World War II and the Fifties (1941 to 1960) 87
IBP: Not Snake Oil–But Still Pretty Slick 89
Peace, Love, and the Creative Revolution (1960 to 1972) 90
The 1970s (1973 to 1980) 94
The Designer Era (1980 to 1992) 96
The Second Nineties (1993 to 2000) 98
The 00s: The Interactive/Wireless/Broadband Revolution (2001-present) 99

Reinventing the Advertising Process? 106
E-Commerce: Start the Evolution without Me 106
Global Issues: This Is Absolut-ly the Best Place to Reach Consumers 108

The Value of an Evolutionary Perspective 109

Summary 110
Key Terms 111
Questions 111
Experiential Exercises 112
Using the Internet 113

4 Social, Ethical, and Regulatory Aspects of Advertising 114

The Social Aspects of Advertising 117
Advertising Educates Consumers 117
Pro: Advertising Informs • Con: Advertising Is Superficial
IBP: Tackling Alcohol Abuse through Integrated Brand Promotion 119
Advertising Improves the Standard of Living 119
Pro: Advertising Lowers the Cost of Products • Con: Advertising Wastes Resources and Raises the Standard of Living Only for Some
Advertising Affects Happiness and General Well-Being 120
Con: Advertising Creates Needs • Pro: Advertising Addresses a Wide Variety of Basic Human Needs • Con: Advertising Promotes Materialism • Pro: Advertising Only Reflects Society's Priorities
Advertising: Demeaning and Deceitful, or Liberating and Artful? 122
Con: Advertising Perpetuates Stereotypes • Pro: Advertisers Are Showing Much More Sensitivity • Con: Advertising Is Often Offensive • Pro: Advertising Is a Source of Fulfillment and Liberation • Con: Advertisers Deceive via Subliminal Stimulation • Pro: Advertising Is Democratic Art
Advertising Has a Powerful Effect on the Mass Media 126
Pro: Advertising Fosters a Diverse and Affordable Mass Media • Con: Advertising Affects Programming

The Ethical Aspects of Advertising 126
Truth in Advertising 126
Advertising to Children 127
Advertising Controversial Products 128

The Regulatory Aspects of Advertising 129
Areas of Advertising Regulation 130
Deception and Unfairness • Competitive Issues • Advertising to Children
Regulatory Agents 133
Government Regulation • Industry Self-Regulation • Consumers as Regulatory Agents
Global Issues: Self-Regulation–with Full Government Approval 139

The Regulation of Other Promotional Tools 140
Regulatory Issues in Direct Marketing and E-Commerce • Regulatory Issues in Sales Promotion • Regulatory Issues in Public Relations
E-Commerce: Privacy? What Privacy? 141

Summary 144
Key Terms 145
Questions 146
Experiential Exercises 146
Using the Internet 147

Integrated Brand Promotion Part 1
From Principles to Practice: An Integrated Brand Promotion Case Background and Participants 148

From IMC to IBP 148
Factors Contributing to the Need for an Integrated Approach 149
Sounds Great . . . So What's So Hard about Advertising and Integrated Brand Promotion? 150

An Agency in Pursuit of Integrated Brand Promotion . . . 152
Northlich, www.northlich.com 152

A Client in Pursuit of Integrated Brand Promotion . . . 155
Cincinnati Bell Enterprises, www.cincinnatibell.com 155

IBP Exercises 157

PART TWO
Planning: Analyzing the Advertising Environment 158

5 Advertising and Consumer Behavior 160

Perspective One: The Consumer as Decision Maker 164
The Consumer Decision-Making Process 164
Need Recognition • Information Search and Alternative Evaluation • Postpurchase Use and Evaluation
Four Modes of Consumer Decision Making 169
Sources of Involvement • Extended Problem Solving • Limited Problem Solving • Habit or Variety Seeking • Brand Loyalty
E-Commerce: Digital Storytelling Unleashes the Power of Emotion 174
Key Psychological Processes 174
Multi-Attribute Attitude Models (MAAMs) • Information Processing and Perceptual Defense • The Elaboration Likelihood Model (ELM)

Perspective Two: The Consumer as Social Being 181
Advertising in a Sociocultural Consumption Context 183
Culture • Values • Rituals
Social Class 187
Family • Reference Groups • Cool • Race and Ethnicity • Gender • Community • Object Meaning and the Social Life of Brands
Global Issues: Rituals Drive Market Opportunities around the World 188
Advertising as Social Text 201
Ads Transmit Sociocultural Meaning
IBP: Coming Together . . . Over Saturn 203

Summary 205
Key Terms 206

Questions 206
Experiential Exercises 207
Using the Internet 207

6 Market Segmentation, Positioning, and the Value Proposition 208

STP Marketing and the Evolution of Marketing Strategies 212
Beyond STP Marketing 213

Identifying Target Segments 215
Usage Patterns and Commitment Levels 215
E-Commerce: Diversity Comes to the Digital World 216
Demographic Segmentation 217
IBP: Take Special Care with Promotions to Kids 218
Geographic Segmentation 218
Psychographics and Lifestyle Segmentation 220
Benefit Segmentation 221
Segmenting Business-to-Business Markets 222

Prioritizing Target Segments 224

Formulating the Positioning Strategy 226
Essentials for Effective Positioning Strategies 227
Fundamental Positioning Themes 229
Repositioning 233

Capturing Your Strategy in a Value Proposition 234
Controversy: Avoid Targeting's Dark Side 236

Summary 237
Key Terms 238
Questions 238
Experiential Exercises 239
Using the Internet 239

7 Advertising and Promotion Research 240

Advertising and Promotion Research 242

Developmental Advertising Research 243
Controversy: P2P or Not to P2P 244
Purposes of Developmental Advertising Research 244
Idea Generation • Concept Testing • Audience Definition • Audience Profiling
Developmental Advertising Research Methods 246
Global Issues: Japan's Marketing Bellwether? The Teenage Girl 246
Focus Groups • Other Methods • Field Work • Internal Company Sources • Government Sources • Commercial Sources

Copy Research 249
Evaluative Criteria 253
"Getting It" • Knowledge • Attitude Change • Feelings and Emotions • Physiological Changes • Behavior
Copy Research Methods 256
E-Commerce: What's in a Name? 256
Communication Tests • Resonance Tests • Thought Listings • Recall Tests • Recognition Tests • Attitude-Change Studies • Physiological Tests • Pilot Testing • Tracking Studies • Direct Response • Single-Source Data • Frame-by-Frame Tests • Account Planning versus Advertising Research

Another Thought on Message Testing 265

What We Need 266

Summary 267
Key Terms 267
Questions 268
Experiential Exercises 268
Using the Internet 269

8 The Advertising Plan 270

The Advertising Plan and Its Marketing Context 276
Introduction 277
Situation Analysis 278
Historical Context • Industry Analysis • Market Analysis • Competitor Analysis
Objectives 281

Communications versus Sales Objectives 283
Characteristics of Workable Advertising Objectives • Budgeting • Percentage of Sales • Share of Market/Share of Voice • Response Models • Objective and Task • Implementing the Objective-and-Task Budgeting Method
Global Issues: McDonald's Won't Back Down from Mad Cow 283
IBP: Jaguar Looks to Spike for Answers 290
Strategy 290
Execution 290
Copy Strategy • Media Plan • Integrated Brand Promotion
Evaluation 292

The Role of the Advertising Agency in Advertising Planning 293
E-Commerce: The Fundamentals Never Go Out of Style 294

Summary 295
Key Terms 296
Questions 296
Experiential Exercises 297
Using the Internet 297

9 Advertising Planning: An International Perspective 298

Overcoming Cultural Barriers 303
Barriers to Successful International Advertising 303
Global Issues: From Salsa to Cinco de Mayo 305
Cross-Cultural Audience Research 305
Economic Conditions • Demographic Characteristics • Values • Custom and Ritual • Product Use and Preferences

The Challenges in Executing Advertising Worldwide 311
The Creative Challenge 311
The Media Challenge 313
Media Availability and Coverage • Media Costs and Pricing
E-Commerce: News Flash: World Wide Web Not Worldwide 315
The Regulatory Challenge 316

Advertising Agencies around the World 316
IBP: Releasing That Pent-Up Urge to Clip Coupons 317
The Global Agency 317
The International Affiliate 317
The Local Agency 318

Globalized versus Localized Campaigns 319

Summary 323
Key Terms 323
Questions 324
Experiential Exercises 324
Using the Internet 325

Integrated Brand Promotion Part 2
From Principles to Practice: An Integrated Brand Promotion Case
Cincinnati Bell Wireless: Planning Advertising and Integrated Brand Promotion 326

A Model for Planning Advertising and Integrated Brand Promotion 326

Assessing CBW's Situation Prior to Launch 327
Historical Context 327
Industrial Analysis 328
Local Competition 330
Market Analysis 330

Pinpointing the Target Segment for Launch 331

Launch Strategy and the CBW Value Proposition 333
Objectives and Budget 333
The Mix of Persuasion Tools 334

IBP Exercises 335

PART THREE
Preparing the Message 336

10 Creativity and Advertising 338

Creating Brands 343

Creativity in General 343

Creativity across Domains 344
E-Commerce: Online Advertising: Creativity Takes a Back Seat 345
Can One Become Creative? 346
Creativity in the Business World 346
Against Stereotype 346

Advertising Agencies, the Creative Process, and the Product 348
Oil and Water: The Essential Organizational Behavior of the Creative/Management Interface 348
Global Issues: Europe: The Birthplace of the 30-Minute Ad? 349

Why Does Advertising Need Creativity 354
IBP: Crafting the Message in the Face of Tragedy 358

Summary 359
Key Terms 359
Questions 360
Experiential Exercises 360
Using the Internet 361

11 Message Strategy 362

Message Strategy 366
Objective #1: Promote Brand Recall 367
Method A: Repetition • Method B: Slogans and Jingles

IBP: Clock Running Out on Branding Strategies 367
Objective #2: Link Key Attributes to the Brand Name 369
Objective #3: Persuade the Consumer 369
Method A: Reason-Why Ads • Method B: Hard-Sell Ads • Method C: Comparison Ads • Method D: Testimonials • Method E: Demonstration • Method F: Advertorials • Method G: Infomercials
Objective #4: Instill Brand Preference 377
Method A: Feel-Good Ads • Method B: Humor Ads • Method C: Sexual Appeal Ads
Creativity: Iconic Ads Better Second Time Around? 378
Objective #5: Scare the Consumer into Action 386
Method: Fear-Appeal Ads
Objective #6: Change Behavior by Inducing Anxiety 387
Method A: Anxiety Ads • Method B: Social Anxiety Ads
Objective #7: Transform Consumption Experiences 390
Method: Transformational Ads
Objective #8: Situate the Brand Socially 390
Method A: Slice-of-Life Ads • Method B: Product Placement/Short Internet Films • Method C: Light Fantasy
Controversy: Harry Potter: Controversial Marketing Wizard 394
Objective #9: Define the Brand Image 394
Method: Image Ads
Objective #10: Invoke a Direct Response 396
Method: Call-or-Click-Now Ads
In the End 397

Summary 397
Key Terms 398
Questions 398
Experiential Exercises 399
Using the Internet 399

12 Copywriting 400

Copywriting and the Creative Plan 404
Global Issues: You Know That Kissing Thing–It Works for Global Ads, Too 408

Copywriting for Print Advertising 408
The Headline 408
Creativity: Advertising Sells Itself 409
Purposes of a Headline • Guidelines for Writing Headlines
The Subhead 414
The Body Copy 414
Guidelines for Writing Body Copy

Copywriting for Cyberspace 416

Copywriting for Broadcast Advertising 416
Writing Copy for Radio 417
E-Commerce: Writing Cybercopy: Don't Abandon All the Old Rules 418
Radio Advertising Formats • Guidelines for Writing Radio Copy • The Radio Production Process
Writing Copy for Television 424
Television Advertising Formats • Guidelines for Writing Television Copy

Slogans 428

Common Mistakes in Copywriting 429

The Copy Approval Process 430

Summary 431
Key Terms 432
Questions 432
Experiential Exercises 433
Using the Internet 433

13 Art Direction and Production 434

Illustration, Design, and Layout 436
Illustration 436
Illustration Purposes • Illustration Components • Illustration Formats •The Strategic and Creative Impact of Illustration
Creativity: We Could Be Heroes 438
Design 442
Principles of Design
Layout 447
Thumbnails • Rough Layout • Comprehensive • Mechanicals

Production in Print Advertising 449
The Print Production Schedule 449
Print Production Processes 451
Computer Print Production
Typography in Print Production 452
Categories of Type • Type Measurement • Readability

Art Direction and Production in Cyberspace 454

Art Direction and Production in Television Advertising 454
Art Direction in Television Advertising 456
The Creative Team in Television Advertising 457
Creative Guidelines for Television Advertising 457
Global Issues: Ad Queen to Boost USA's Global Image 457
The Production Process in Television Advertising 459
Preproduction • Production • Postproduction
IBP: It's Not Easy Being Green 464
Production Options in Television Advertising 471

Summary 472
Key Terms 473
Questions 473
Experiential Exercises 474
Using the Internet 475

Integrated Brand Promotion Part 3
From Principles to Practice: An Integrated Brand Promotion Case
Cincinnati Bell Wireless: Preparing Advertising and Integrated Brand Promotion 476

Making Beautiful Music Together: Coordination, Collaboration, and Creativity 476
What We Know About Teams 477
Teams Rule! • It's All about Performance • Synergy through Teams • The Demise of Individualism? • Teams Promote Personal Growth
Leadership in Teams 478

Teams as the Engine for Coordination, Collaboration, and Creativity in the Launch of Cincinnati Bell Wireless 479
The Account Team 479
Teams Moderate Tension in the Copy Approval Process 480
Teams Liberate Decision Making 480
More about Teams and Creativity 481

To Ensure the Uniform Look, Turn to Teams 482

IBP Exercises 483

PART FOUR
Placing the Message in Conventional and "New" Media 484

14 Media Planning, Objectives, and Strategy for Advertising and Promoting the Brand 486

IBP: Windows XP: A Ray of Light 488

The Media-Planning Process 491

Media Objectives 493

Media Strategies 497

Reach and Frequency • Continuity • Length or Size of Advertisements

Media Choices 500

Media Mix • Media Efficiency • Internet Media • Competitive Media Assessment

Controversy: Magazine Mogul: "Business Sucks" 503

Media Scheduling and Buying 508

Computer Media-Planning Models 509

Other Ongoing Challenges in the Media Environment 512

The Proliferation of Media Options 512

Insufficient and Inaccurate Information 514

Escalating Media Costs 515

Interactive Media 516

E-Commerce: Absolut Value 517

Media Choice and Integrated Brand Promotions 517

Summary 519

Key Terms 520

Questions 520

Experiential Exercises 521

Using the Internet 521

15 Media Planning: Print, Television, and Radio 522

Which Media: Strategic Planning Considerations 524

Print Media 525

Newspapers 526

Advantages of Newspapers • Disadvantages of Newspapers • Types of Newspapers • Categories of Newspaper Advertising • Costs and Buying Procedures for Newspaper Advertising • Measuring Newspaper Audiences • The Future of Newspapers

E-Commerce: Myth: The Web Will Dominate Classified Advertising. Reality: Newspapers Don't Have to Worry 530

Magazines 533

Advantages of Magazines • Disadvantages of Magazines • Types of Magazines • Costs and Buying Procedures for Magazine Advertising • Measuring Magazine Audiences • The Future of Magazines

Television: Strategic Planning Considerations 541

Television 541

Television Categories • Advantages of Television • Disadvantages of Television • Buying Procedures for Television Advertising • Measuring Television Audiences • The Future of Television

IBP: Using Cable (and the Web) to Reach Tight Markets 545

Radio 549

Radio Categories • Types of Radio Advertising • Advantages of Radio • Disadvantages of Radio • Buying Procedures for Radio Advertising • Measuring Radio Audiences • The Future of Radio

Controversy: The Death of Radio? 553

Summary 554
Key Terms 555
Questions 556
Experiential Exercises 556
Using the Internet 557

16 Media Planning: Advertising and the Internet 558

The Role of the Internet in the Advertising Process 560

The (R)evolution of the Internet 561

An Overview of Cyberspace 562

The Basic Parts 562
Internet Media 564

E-Mail • Usenet • The World Wide Web

IBP: Chatting a Star up the Charts 567
Surfing the World Wide Web 567
Hierarchical Search Engines 567

Collection Search Engines • Concept Search Engines • Robot Search Engines • Portals • Other Ways to Find Sites

Advertising on the Internet 570

The Advantages of Internet Advertising 570

Target Market Selectivity • Tracking • Deliverability and Flexibility • Interactivity • Cost • Integration

Who Advertises on the Internet 572
The Cost of Internet Advertising 574
Types of Internet Advertising 575

Banner Ads •Pop-Up Ads • E-Mail Communication • Streaming Video and Audio • Corporate Home Pages • Virtual Malls

Establishing a Site on the World Wide Web 579

Global Issues: Using the Net to Take a Brand Global 580
Getting Surfers to Come Back 580
Purchasing Keywords and Developing a Domain Name 582
Promoting Web Sites 583
Security and Privacy Issues 584

Measuring the Effectiveness of Internet Advertising 585

Technical Aspects of the Internet Measurement Problem 587
The Caching Complication in Internet Measurement 588
Internet Measurement and Payment 589

Managing the Brand in an E-Community 589

The Future of Advertising and the Internet 591

Creativity: Skipping Sales in Favor of Community 592

Summary 593
Key Terms 594
Questions 594
Experiential Exercises 595
Using the Internet 595

Integrated Brand Promotion Part 4
From Principles to Practice: An Integrated Brand Promotion Case
Cincinnati Bell Wireless: The Launch Campaign 596

An Overview of the CBW Launch Campaign 596
Public Relations 596
Television 597
Print, Radio, and Outdoor 597
Promotions and Events 600
Direct Marketing 600
P-O-P Advertising, Collateral, and Sales Support 602

Gauging the Impact of the CBW Launch Campaign 602

IBP Exercises 603

PART FIVE
Integrated Brand Promotion

17 Support Media, P-O-P Advertising, and Event Sponsorship 606

Traditional Support Media 609
Outdoor Signage and Billboard Advertising 610
Transit and Aerial Advertising 613
Specialty Advertising 616
Creativity: Brand Building by Way of the Moon 617
Directory Advertising 618
When Support Media Are More Than Support Media 620

Point-of-Purchase (P-O-P) Advertising 620

Event Sponsorship 623
Who Else Uses Event Sponsorship? 623
The Appeal of Event Sponsorship 624
Global Issues: Event Sponsorship Hits China 625
Seeking a Synergy around Event Sponsorship 627

The Coordination Challenge 628
IBP: Stop, Look, and Listen 629

Summary 631
Key Terms 631
Questions 632
Experiential Exercises 632
Using the Internet 633

18 Sales Promotion 634

Sales Promotion Defined 637

The Importance and Growth of Sales Promotion 637
The Importance of Sales Promotion 638
Growth in the Use of Sales Promotion 638
Demand for Greater Accountability • Short-Term Orientation • Consumer Response to Promotions • Proliferation of Brands • Increased Power of Retailers • Media Clutter

Sales Promotion Directed at Consumers 641
Creativity: This Is Fun? 642
Objectives for Consumer-Market Sales Promotion 642

Consumer-Market Sales Promotion Techniques 644

Coupons • Price-Off Deals • Premiums and Advertising Specialties • Contests and Sweepstakes • Samples and Trial Offers • Phone and Gift Cards • Brand Placement • Rebates • Frequency (Continuity) Programs • Event Sponsorship

Sales Promotion Directed at the Trade and Business Buyers 652

Objectives for Promotions in the Trade Market 652

Global Issues: Bring On the World 653

Trade-Market Sales Promotion Techniques 654

Point-of-Purchase Displays • Incentives • Allowances • Sales Training Programs • Cooperative (Co-Op) Advertising

Business Market Sales Promotion Techniques 656

Trade Shows • Business Gifts • Premiums and Advertising Specialties • Trial Offers • Frequency Programs

Sales Promotion, the Internet, and New Media 658

The Use of Sales Promotion by Internet and New Media Organizations 658

The Use of the Internet and New Media to Implement Sales Promotions 660

IBP: IBP in B to B 660

The Risks of Sales Promotion 661

Creating a Price Orientation 661

Borrowing from Future Sales 661

Alienating Customers 662

Time and Expense 662

Legal Considerations 662

The Coordination Challenge-Sales Promotion and IBP 662

Message Coordination 662

Media Coordination 663

Conclusions from Research 663

Summary 664

Key Terms 665

Questions 666

Experiential Exercises 666

Using the Internet 667

19 Direct Marketing 668

The Evolution of Direct Marketing 670

Direct Marketing–A Look Back 671

Direct Marketing Today 674

What's Driving the Growing Popularity of Direct Marketing? 675

Database Marketing 677

Mailing Lists 677

E-Commerce: It Takes a Warehouse . . . 677

List Enhancement 678

The Marketing Database 679

Marketing Database Applications 680

The Privacy Concern 681

Global Issues: Loyalty Programs Know No Boundaries 682

Media Applications in Direct Marketing 683

Direct Mail 684

Telemarketing 685

E-Mail 685

IBP: Nike Marketers Decide to Do E-Mail 686

Direct Response Advertising in Other Media 687
Infomercials 688

The Coordination Challenge Revisited 689

Summary 691
Key Terms 692
Questions 692
Experiential Exercises 693
Using the Internet 693

20 Public Relations and Corporate Advertising 694

Public Relations 698
Objectives of Public Relations 699
Tools of Public Relations 700
Press Releases • Feature Stories • Company Newsletters • Interviews and Press Conferences • Sponsored Events • Publicity
Creativity: Pepsi's School Effort Makes Sweet Music 702
Public Relations and New Media 705
Basic Public Relations Strategies 705
Proactive Public Relations Strategy • Reactive Public Relations Strategy
IBP: Where Is the Spin Control? 707

Corporate Advertising 708
Global Issues: Good Humor Is a Good Cause 709
The Scope and Objectives of Corporate Advertising 709
Types of Corporate Advertising 711
Corporate Image Advertising • Advocacy Advertising • Cause-Related Advertising

Summary 714
Key Terms 715
Questions 716
Experiential Exercises 716
Using the Internet 717

Integrated Brand Promotion Part 5
From Principles to Practice: An Integrated Brand Promotion Case
Cincinnati Bell Wireless: Sustaining and Growing the Brand after Launch 718

Refining the CBW Advertising and IBP Plan for 1999 718
Target Segment Identification 719
Consolidating the Value Proposition for the CBW Brand 719

Building the Brand and Growing the Business 719
Equity Building 719
Closing the Sale 721
Nurturing Relationships with Customers 723

Measuring Up in 1999 724

When Opportunity Comes Knockin' 724

IBP Exercises 725

Glossary 727
Name/Brand/Company Index 741
Subject Index 750
Credits 766

ADVERTISING

and Integrated Brand Promotion, 3e

PART ONE

The Process: Advertising in Business and Society

The first part of the book, "The Process: Advertising in Business and Society," sets the tone for our study of advertising. The chapters in this part of the book emphasize that advertising is much more than a wonderfully creative interpretation of important corporate marketing strategies. While it certainly serves that purpose, advertising is not just a corporate process, but is also a societal process that has evolved over time with culture, technology, and industry traditions.

To appreciate the true nature of advertising, we must first understand advertising as the complete dynamic business and social process it is. In this first part of the text, the roots of the advertising process are revealed. Advertising is defined as both a business *and* a communications process, and the structure of the industry through which modern-day advertising exists is described. The evolution of advertising is traced from modest beginnings through periods of growth and maturation. The complex and controversial social, ethical, and regulatory aspects of advertising conclude this opening part of the text.

Advertising as a Process Chapter 1, "Advertising as a Process," defines advertising and the role it fulfills within a firm's overall marketing and communications programs. This chapter also analyzes advertising as a basic communications tool and as a marketing communications *process.* We introduce the concept of integrated brand promotion (IBP), which provides a new perspective on the way in which a full range of communications options beyond advertising—sales promotion, sponsorship, point-of-purchase, the Internet, and public relations—are used to compete effectively, develop customer loyalty, and generate profits. Advertising has become a key factor in creating brand identity and ultimately a strong market position for a brand. 1

The Structure of the Advertising Industry: Advertisers, Agencies, and Support Organizations
Chapter 2, "The Structure of the Advertising Industry: Advertisers, Agencies, and Support Organizations," shows that effective advertising requires the participation of a variety of organizations, not just the advertiser. Advertising agencies, research firms, special production facilitators, designers, media companies, Web site developers, and Internet portals are just some of the organizations that form the structure of the industry. Each plays a different role, and billions of dollars are spent every year for the services of various participants. This chapter also highlights that the structure of the industry is in flux. New media options and advertisers interested in integrated brand promotion are forcing change in the industry. This chapter looks at the basic structure of the industry, the participants, and how the structure and participants are evolving with the new challenges of the marketplace. Special attention is given to the rising prominence of promotion agencies as counter-parts to advertising agencies. 2

The Evolution of Advertising Chapter 3, "The Evolution of Advertising," sets the process of advertising into both a historical and contemporary context. Advertising has evolved and proliferated because of fundamental influences related to free enterprise, economic development, and tradition. Advertising as a business process and a reflection of social values has experienced many evolutionary periods of change as technology, business management practices, and social values have changed. Special attention is given to the evolution of technology and how new technologies are changing the development and delivery of advertising. 3

Social, Ethical, and Regulatory Aspects of Advertising Chapter 4, "Social, Ethical, and Regulatory Aspects of Advertising," examines the broad societal aspects of the advertising process. From a social standpoint, we must understand that advertising has positive effects on the standard of living, addresses lifestyle needs, supports the mass media, and is a contemporary art form. Critics argue, though, that advertising wastes resources, promotes materialism, is offensive, and perpetuates stereotypes, or can make people do things they don't want to do. The ethical issues in advertising focus on truth in advertising, advertising to children, and the advertising of controversial products. 4

CHAPTER 1

After reading and thinking about this chapter, you will be able to do the following:

Know what advertising is and what it can do.

Discuss a basic model of advertising communication.

Describe the different ways of classifying audiences for advertising.

Explain the key roles of advertising as a business process.

Understand the concept of integrated brand promotion (IBP) and the role advertising plays in the process.

CHAPTER 1
Advertising as a Process

CHAPTER 2
The Structure of the Advertising Industry: Advertisers, Advertising Agencies, and Support Organizations

CHAPTER 3
The Evolution of Advertising

CHAPTER 4
Social, Ethical, and Regulatory Aspects of Advertising

Introductory Scenario: A Tale of Two Burgers.

One uses movie stars and hip-hop musicians in its advertising. The other uses the kindly company owner who delivers a down-home, aw-shucks kind of message. One has changed advertising agencies seven times in 15 years.[1] The other has had the same agency and same basic advertising theme for 13 straight years. One has gained three points in market share in the last three years, while the other has lost two points in market share.[2] One has seen sales decline by 6.2 percent in the most recent quarter, while the other enjoyed an 8 percent sales increase.[3]

e-SIGHTINGS

ARE WE NOT MEN?

Indulge in a fresh, hot 'n juicy Wendy's Classic Hamburger. It's Hamburger Bliss.

Wendy's OLD FASHIONED HAMBURGERS

EXHIBIT 1.1

Wendy's has used simple, value-focused brand advertising to consistently build market share and grow revenues. While there is nothing flashy about advertisements like this one, the emphasis on the brand and a simple message has worked well for Wendy's. Compare the Wendy's site (www.wendys.com) with the Hardee's site (www.hardees.com). Which do you think is more successful at building the brand's image? Do these sites appear to be integrated with the message of recent advertisements you have seen for these restaurant chains?

Which set of facts describes the Hardee's hamburger chain and which describes Wendy's International? Well, here is a hint: The one with the kindly owner doing the aw-shucks ads that has kept the same theme and ad agency for 13 years is the one that has gained three points of market share and realized the 8 percent sales increase. You probably guessed that Wendy's, with its founder, Dave Thomas doing the ads, is the chain with the outstanding results. Hardee's, even with flashy advertising and new ideas year after year, has had a lack of focus for its brand as well as declining market share and sales.

Guessing Dave Thomas and Wendy's might have been pretty easy. What is not so easy to guess is why advertising that seems so ordinary can be so successful. Instead of flashy, big productions, Wendy's formula for success is built on the concept of keeping "ideas simple and easily communicated," according to Wendy's senior vice president of marketing, Don Calhoon.[4] An example of the simple, straightforward approach to Wendy's communications is shown in Exhibit 1.1. This ad is simple and direct and highlights Wendy's advertising focus on delivering value. Analysts are a bit more elaborate in explaining Wendy's success compared not just to Hardee's, but to fast-food chains in general. While chains like Hardee's have been "wilting after continually fiddling with its ads and focus, Wendy's reaps rewards by staying the course."[5] And the rewards for "staying the course" go beyond simply increasing sales. The down-to-earth commercials with a tight focus on value have resulted in consumers trusting the Wendy's brand.[6] What is even more impressive is that Wendy's has been gaining market share with an advertising budget that is only about one-third of industry leader McDonald's.

As this example of Hardee's versus Wendy's highlights, advertising does not have to be flashy or expensive. What advertising does need to be, whether it is flashy or not, is an essential part of the brand-building process for a firm. And the role of advertising in communicating brand values is not reserved for big national or multinational companies. Marketers in firms of all sizes and in all industries recognize and

1. Bob Garfield, "Burger King's New Whopper Effort Worthy of the Crown," *Advertising Age,* March 5, 2001, 39.
2. Kate MacArthur, "Regional Chains Get McDonald's, BK Attention," *Advertising Age,* September 25, 2000, S10.
3. News release dated October 4, 2000, www.investquest.com, accessed November 17, 2000; Kate MacArthur, "Brands in Trouble—in Demand," *Advertising Age,* August 7, 2000, 22.
4. MacArthur, "Brands in Trouble—in Demand," 22.
5. Ibid.
6. News release dated July 18, 2000, www.investquest.com, accessed November 19, 2000.

invest in advertising as a potent competitive tool. Industry experts point to the fact that company leaders appreciate that advertising is key to driving sales and building brand value and market share.[7] To the average person, however, advertising is much less clearly understood or valued. Most people have significant misperceptions about the process of advertising and what it's supposed to do, what it can do, and what it can't do.

The general public's attitude toward advertising is ambivalent—most people like some of the ads they see or hear, but they may also say that they don't like advertising in general. Many think advertising deceives others, but rarely themselves. Most think it's a semiglamorous profession, but one in which people are either morally bankrupt con artists or pathological liars. At worst, advertising is seen as hype, unfair capitalistic manipulation, banal commercial noise, mind control, postmodern voodoo, or outright deception. Some believe it is the clearest marker of the decline of civilization and the undoing of meaning in the lives of ordinary people. Some of these descriptions of advertising reflect suspicions, biases, and superstitions that have long surrounded the industry. Yet some of these descriptions are, on occasion, regrettably true and precise.

At best, the average person sees advertising as amusing, informative, helpful, and occasionally hip. Advertising often helps consumers see possibilities and meanings in the things they buy and in the services they use. It can connect goods and services to the culture and liberate meanings that lie below the surface. It can turn mere products into meaningful brands and important possessions. For example, the advertising of Doyle Dane Bernbach for Volkswagen (see Exhibit 1.2) helped turn an unlikely automobile into a mobile social statement. The ads for the launch of the New Beetle (Exhibit 1.3) trade upon these roots, but deliver new looks and new meanings. Decades of advertising by Coca-Cola (an example is shown in Exhibit 1.4) have

7. MacArthur, "Advertising Sells Itself as AAF Sets Push to Marketing Execs," *Advertising Age,* October 9, 2000, 6.

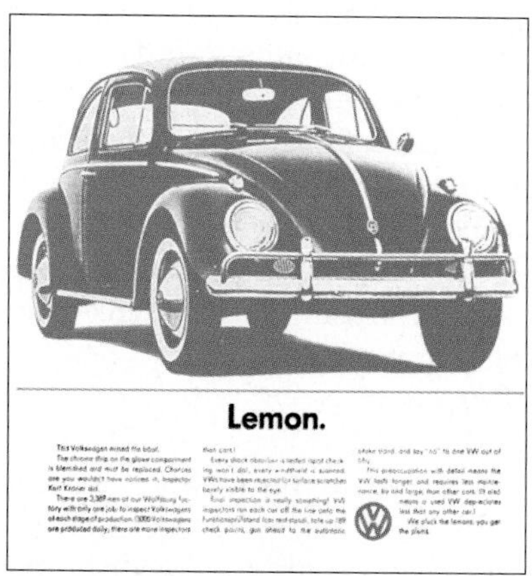

EXHIBIT 1.2

Advertising helps shape a product's image in the minds of consumers. Volkswagen used this ad from the 1960s to get consumers to replace the image of cars as "lemons" with the image of thrifty, dependable VWs. www.vw.com

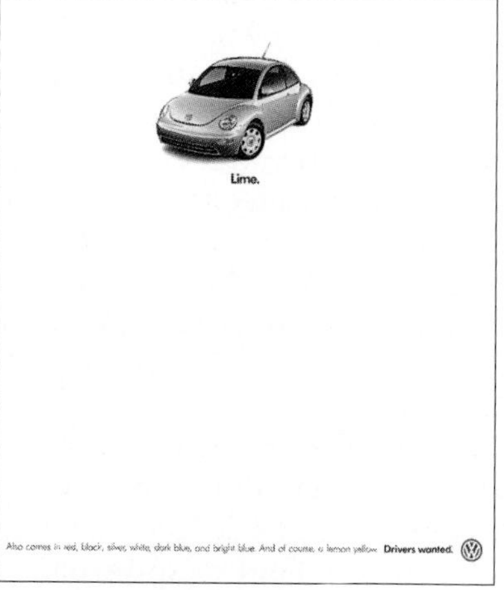

EXHIBIT 1.3

In 1998, Volkswagen launched its celebrated New Beetle model with a series of ads recalling the original Beetle and evoking imagery from its target audience's past (www.vw.com). *Compare VW's campaign for the New Beetle with that of Apple Computer's iMac* (www.apple.com), *the most successful new product in Apple's history.*

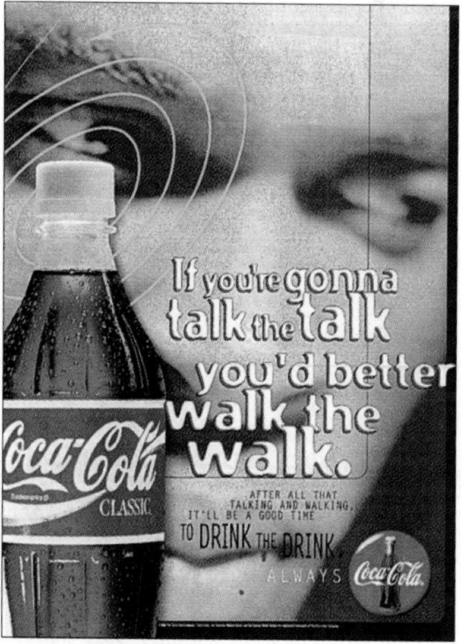

EXHIBIT 1.4

Decades of consistent, high-quality advertising have made Coca-Cola one of the most recognizable brand names in the world. www.cocacola.com

EXHIBIT 1.5

Advertising helps marketers attract attention to their brands and a brand's features. This ad for PowerQuest attracts attention with interesting photography. www.powerquest.com

helped turn this brand of soft drink into a nearly universally recognized cultural icon. Coke is much more than a sweet, fizzy drink; it has enormous cultural capital and meaning. There are, of course, many less-dramatic and less well-known examples of the way advertising helps attract attention to brands and serves marketers as an effective competitive tool, such as the PowerQuest ad in Exhibit 1.5.

The truth about advertising lies somewhere between the extremes. Sometimes advertising is hard-hitting and powerful; at other times, it is boring and ineffective. Advertising can be enormously creative and entertaining, and it can be simply annoying. One thing is for sure: advertising is anything but unimportant. Advertising plays a pivotal role in world commerce and in the way we experience and live our lives. It is part of our language and our culture. It reflects the way we think about things and the way we see ourselves. It is both a complex communication process and a dynamic business process. Advertising is an important topic for you to study.

1 What Is Advertising?

Advertising means different things to different people. It's a business, an art, an institution, and a cultural phenomenon. To the CEO of a multinational corporation, such as Dave Thomas at Wendy's International, advertising is an essential marketing tool that helps create brand awareness and loyalty and stimulates demand. To the owner of a small retail shop, advertising is a way to bring people into the store. To the art director in an advertising agency, advertising is the creative expression of a concept. To a media planner, advertising is the way a firm uses the mass media to communicate to current and potential customers. To scholars and museum curators, advertising is an important cultural artifact, text, and historical record. Advertising means something different to all these people. In fact, sometimes determining just what is and what is not advertising is a difficult task. Keeping that in mind, we offer this straightforward definition:

Advertising *is a paid, mass-mediated attempt to persuade.*

As direct and simple as this definition seems, it is loaded with distinctions. Advertising is *paid* communication by a company or organization that wants its information disseminated. In advertising language, the company or organization that pays for advertising is called the **client** or **sponsor.**

First, if communication is not *paid for,* it's not advertising. For example, a form of promotion called *publicity* is not advertising because it is not paid for. Let's say Bruce Willis appears on the *Late Show with David Letterman* to promote his newest movie. Is this advertising? No, because the producer or film studio did not pay the *Late Show with David Letterman* for airtime. In this example, the show gets an interesting and popular guest, the guest star gets exposure, and the film gets plugged. Everyone is happy, but no advertising took place. But when the film studio produces and runs ads for the newest Bruce Willis movie on television and in newspapers across the country, this communication is paid for by the studio, and it most definitely is advertising.

For the same reason, public service announcements (PSAs) are not advertising either. True, they look like ads and sound like ads, but they aren't ads. They are not commercial in the way an ad is because they are not paid for like an ad. They are offered as information in the public (noncommercial) interest. When you hear a message on the radio that implores you to "Just Say No" to drugs, this sounds very much like an ad, but it is a PSA. Simply put, PSAs are excluded from the definition of advertising because they are unpaid communication.

Consider the two messages in Exhibits 1.6 and 1.7. These two messages have similar copy and offer similar advice. Exhibit 1.6 has persuasive intent, is paid-for communication, and appears in the mass media. It is an advertisement. Exhibit 1.7 also has persuasive intent and appears in mass media outlets, but it is not advertising because it is not paid-for communication. PSAs are important and often strongly imitate their commercial cousins. For example, the Partnership for a Drug-Free America is taking on the "heroin chic" images of certain high-fashion advertising with a public service advertising campaign that takes the glamour out of heroin use.[8]

Second, advertising is *mass mediated.* This means it is delivered through a communication medium designed to reach more than one person, typically a large number—or mass—of people. Advertising is widely disseminated through familiar means—television, radio, newspapers, and magazines—and other media such as direct mail, billboards, the Internet, and CD-ROMs. The mass-mediated nature of advertising creates a communication environment where the message is not delivered in a face-to-face manner. This distinguishes advertising from personal selling as a form of communication.

Third, all advertising includes an *attempt to persuade.* To put it bluntly, ads are communication designed to get someone to do something. Even an advertisement with a stated objective of being purely informational still has persuasion at its core. The ad informs the consumer for some purpose, and that purpose is to get the consumer to like the brand and because of that liking to eventually buy the brand. In the absence of this persuasive intent, a communication might be news, but it would not be advertising.

At this point, we can say that for a communication to be classified as advertising, three essential criteria must be met:

1. The communication must be *paid for.*
2. The communication must be delivered to an audience via *mass media.*
3. The communication must be *attempting persuasion.*

It is important to note here that advertising can be persuasive communication not only about a product or service but also about an idea, a person, or an entire organization. When Colgate and Honda use advertising, this is product advertising and meets all three criteria. Likewise, when Dean Witter, Delta Air Lines, Terminix, or your dentist runs advertisements, it is service advertising and meets all three criteria.

But what about political advertising? Political ads "sell" candidates rather than commercial goods or services. Political advertisements may seem special because they are the only completely unregulated form of advertising; they are viewed as "political speech" and thus enjoy complete First Amendment protection. Still, political advertising meets our definition because it is paid-for communication, is mass mediated, and has a persuasive intent. Not only does political advertising pass the

8. Mercedes M. Cardona, "Drug Partnership Ads Tackle Heroin Use by Youth," *Advertising Age,* November 3, 1997, 8.

EXHIBITS 1.6 AND 1.7

The messages in Exhibits 1.6 and 1.7 communicate nearly identical information to the audience, but one is an advertisement and one is not. The message in Exhibit 1.6, sponsored by Trojan, is an advertisement because it is paid-for communication. The message in Exhibit 1.7, sponsored by the U.K.'s Health Education Authority, has a persuasive intent similar to the Trojan ad, but it is not advertising—Exhibit 1.7 is a PSA. Why isn't the Health Education Authority PSA message an ad? www.trojancondoms.com

definition test, but strategists also see advertising as a "brand"-building process for political candidates.[9]

Beyond the familiar political candidate campaign advertising, political advertising is often undertaken in conjunction with lobbying efforts. Critics of a health care plan used political advertising to sway lawmakers and defeat a pending change in government health care coverage.[10] Political advertising can be for a candidate, as shown

9. Erin Strout, "The Branding of a President," *Sales & Marketing Management,* October 2000, 54–62.
10. Ira Teinowitz, "Ad Campaigns Take Hold in Public-Policy Lobbying," *Advertising Age,* December 22, 1997, 14.

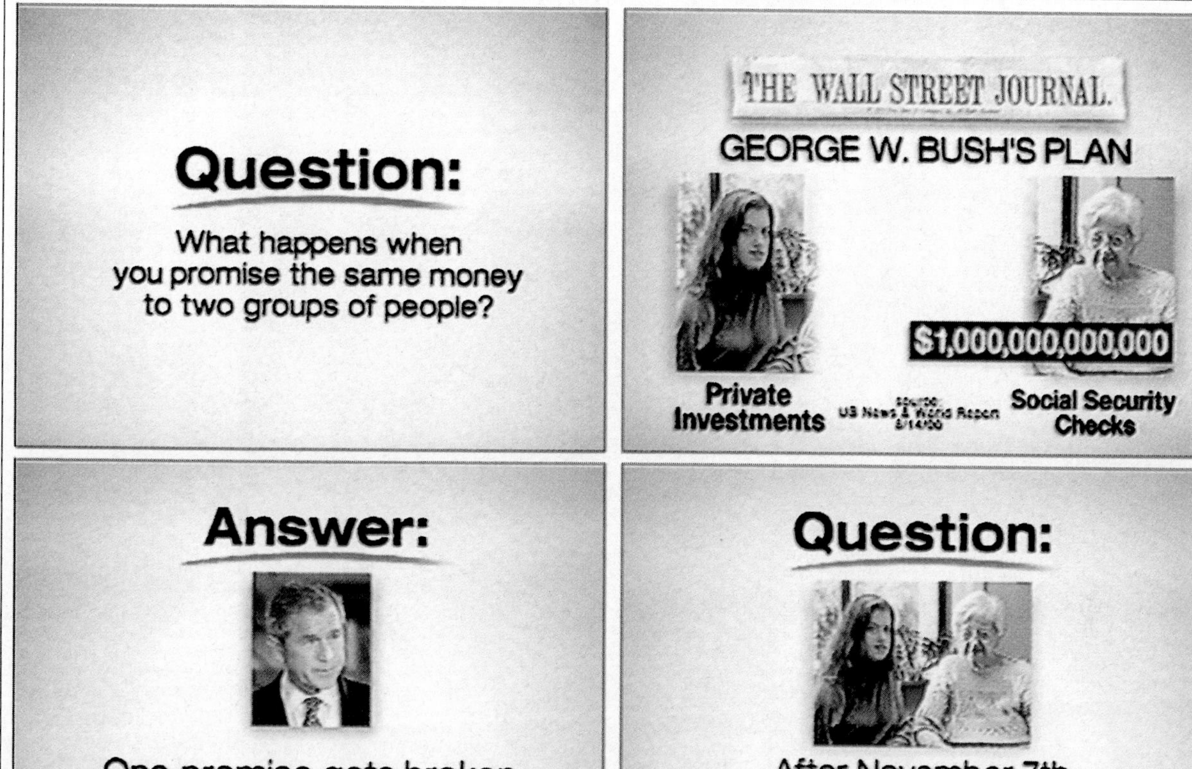

EXHIBIT 1.8

While this political message for Al Gore during the 2000 presidential campaign is promoting ideas, it meets the definitional test for advertising in general—it is paid-for communications, is placed in mass media, and has a persuasive intent. Check out www.democrats.org and www.rnc.org.

in Exhibit 1.8, or for a political organization, such as the National Rifle Association (NRA).

Although the Gore campaign ad does not ask anyone to buy anything (in terms of money), it is (1) paid for, (2) placed in a mass medium, and (3) an attempt to persuade members of the electorate to view Al Gore and his agenda favorably. It represents another way advertising can persuade beyond the purchase of products and services. Many political candidates, environmental groups, human rights organizations, and political groups buy advertising and distribute it through mass media to persuade people to accept their way of thinking. They, too, are selling something.

Advertising, Advertisements, Advertising Campaigns, and Integrated Brand Promotion. Now that we have a working definition of advertising, we turn our attention to other important distinctions in advertising. An **advertisement** refers to a specific message that someone or some organization has placed to persuade an audience. An **advertising campaign** is a series of coordinated advertisements and other promotional efforts that communicate a reasonably cohesive and integrated theme. The theme may be made up of several claims or points but should advance an essentially singular theme. Successful advertising campaigns can be developed around a single advertisement placed in multiple media, or they can be made up of several different advertisements (more typically) with a similar look, feel, and message. The Lee

EXHIBIT 1.9 THROUGH 1.12

A well-conceived and well-executed advertising campaign offers consumers a series of messages with a similar look and feel. This series of ads for Lee Casuals is an excellent example of a campaign that communicates with similar images to create a unified look and feel. www.leejeans.com

Casuals ads in Exhibits 1.9 through 1.12 represent an excellent use of similar look and feel to create an advertising campaign. Advertising campaigns can run for a few weeks or for many years. The advertising campaign is, in many ways, the most challenging aspect of advertising execution. It requires a keen sense of the complex environments within which an advertiser must communicate to different audiences and of how these messages interact with one another and an audience. The vast majority of ads you see each day are part of broader campaigns.

Furthermore, most individual ads would make little sense without the knowledge that audience members have about ads for this particular brand or for the product category in general. Ads are interpreted by consumers through their experiences with a brand and previous ads for the brand. When you see a new Nike ad, you make sense of the ad through your history with Nike and its previous advertising. Even ads for a new brand or a new product are situated within audiences' broader knowledge of products, brands, and advertising. After years of viewing ads and buying brands, audiences bring a rich history and knowledge base to every communications encounter.

Integrated brand promotion (IBP) is the use of various promotional tools, including advertising, in a coordinated manner to build and maintain brand awareness, identity, and preference. When marketers combine contests, a Web site, event sponsorship, and point-of-purchase displays with advertising, this creates an integrated brand promotion. Note that the word *coordinated* is central to this definition. Without coordination among these various promotional efforts, there is not an integrated brand promotion. Rather, the consumer will merely encounter a series of unrelated (and often confusing) communications about a brand.

Integrated brand promotion will be a key concept throughout our discussion of advertising. The fact that this phrase is included in the title of the book signals its importance to the contemporary advertising effort. Make no mistake, all of marketing, including the advertising effort, is about brand building. As consumers encounter a daily blitz of commercial messages and appeals, brands and brand identity offer a way to cope. Brands and the images they project allow consumers to quickly identify and evaluate the relevance of a brand to their lives and value systems. The folksy image of Wendy's is clearly distinguished from the hip, contemporary image being pursued by Hardee's. The marketer who does not use advertising and integrated brand promotion as a way to build brand meaning for consumers will, frankly, be ignored. We will develop this concept of integrated brand promotion throughout the text and demonstrate how advertising is central to the process. The encounters between consumers and advertisements, advertising campaigns, and integrated brand promotion underlie the discussion of our next topic.

2 Advertising as a Communication Process.

Communication is a fundamental aspect of human existence, and advertising is communication. To understand advertising at all, you must understand something about communication in general and about mass communication in particular. At the outset, you must understand the basic aspects of how advertising works as a means of communication. To this end, let's consider a contemporary model of mass communication. We will apply this basic model of communication as a first step in understanding advertising.

A Model of Mass-Mediated Communication.

As we said earlier, advertising is mass-mediated communication; it occurs, not face-to-face, but through a medium (such as radio, magazines, television, or a computer). While there are many valuable models of mass communication, a contemporary model of mass-mediated communication is presented

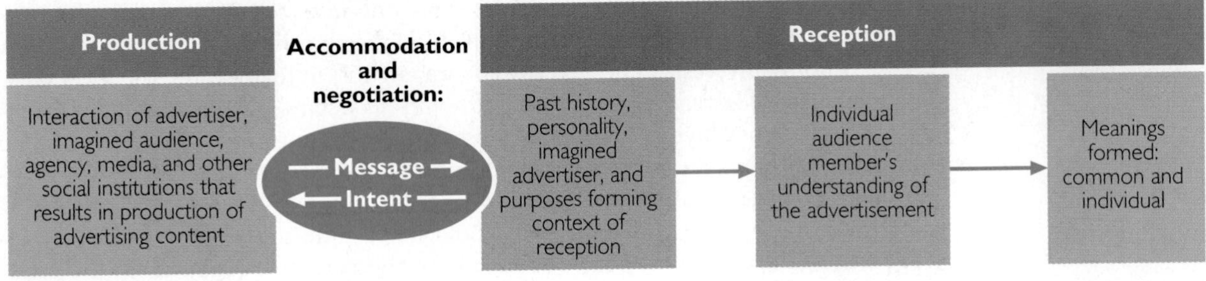

EXHIBIT 1.13

A model of mass-mediated communication.

in Exhibit 1.13. This model shows mass communication as a process of interacting individuals and institutions. It has two major components, each representing quasi-independent processes: production and reception. Between production and reception are the mediating (interpretation) processes of accommodation and negotiation. It's not as complex as it sounds. Let's investigate each part of the model.

Moving from left to right in the model, we first see the process of communication production, where the content of any mass communication is produced. An advertisement, like other forms of mass communication, is the product of institutions (such as networks, corporations, advertising agencies, and governments) interacting to produce content (what physically appears on a page as a print ad, or on a videotape as a television ad, or on a computer screen at a company's Web site). The creation of the advertisement is a complex interaction of the advertiser's message content; the advertiser's expectations regarding the target audience's desire for information; the advertiser's assumptions about how the audience will interpret the words and images in an ad; and the conventions, rules, and regulations of the medium that transmits the message. Advertising is rarely (if ever) the product of an individual; rather, it is a collaborative (social) product.

Moving to the right, we see that the mediating processes of accommodation and negotiation lie between the production and reception phases. Accommodation and negotiation are the ways in which consumers interpret ads. Audience members have some ideas about how the advertiser wants them to interpret the ad. Consumers also have their own needs, agendas, and preferred interpretations. They also know about the way other consumers think about this product and this message. Given all this, they arrive at an interpretation of the ad that makes sense, serves their needs, fits their personal history with a product category and the brand, and is not usually wholly incompatible with the way the advertiser wanted consumers to see the ad. In other words, the receivers of the ad must *accommodate* these competing forces, meanings, and agendas and then *negotiate* a meaning, or an interpretation, of the ad. That's why we say that communication is inherently a *social* process: what a message means to any given consumer is a function, not of an isolated solitary thinker, but of an inherently social being responding to what he or she knows about the producers of the message, other receivers of it, and the social world in which the good or service and the message about it resides. Now, admittedly, all this interpretation happens very fast and without much contemplation. Still, it happens. The level of conscious interpretation might be minimal (mere recognition) or it might be extensive (thoughtful, elaborate processing of an ad), but there is always interpretation.

We say that the processes of production and reception are partially independent because, although the producers of a message can control the placement of an ad in a medium, they cannot control or even closely monitor the actual reception and interpretation of the ad. Audience members are exposed to advertising outside the direct observation of the advertiser and are capable of interpreting advertising any

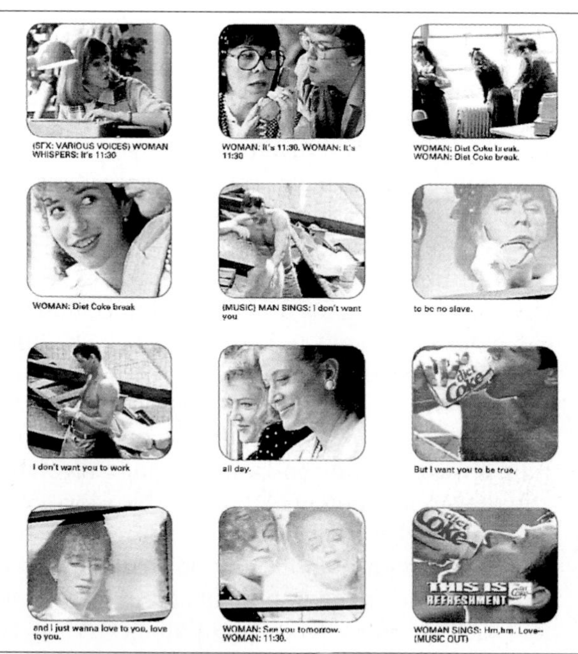

EXHIBIT 1.14

This ad is a good example of how the meaning of an ad can vary for different people. How would you interpret the meaning of this ad? Think of someone very different from you. What meaning might that person give this ad? www.cocacola.com

way they want. (Of course, most audience interpretations are not completely off the wall, either.) Likewise, audience members have little control over or input into the actual production of the message. Because of these aspects of communication, the model shows that both producers and receivers are thus "imagined," in the sense that the two don't have significant direct contact with one another but have a general sense of what the other is like.

The communication model in Exhibit 1.13 underscores the critical point that no ad contains a single meaning for all audience members. An ad for a pair of women's shoes means something different for women than it does for men. An ad that achieved widespread popularity (and controversy) is the ad for Diet Coke shown in Exhibit 1.14, which may be interpreted differently by men and women. For example, does the ad suggest that men drink Diet Coke so they can be the object of intense daily admiration by a group of female office workers? Or does the ad suggest that Diet Coke is a part of a modern woman's lifestyle, granting her "permission" to freely admire attractive men in the same way women have been eyed by male construction workers (or executives) for years? The audience decides. Keep in mind that although individual audience members' interpretations will differ to some extent, they may be close enough to the advertiser's intent to make the ad effective. When members of an audience are similar in their background, social standing, and goals, they generally yield similar enough meaning from an ad for it to accomplish its goals.

3 The Audiences for Advertising.

In the language of advertising, an **audience** is a group of individuals who receive and interpret messages sent from advertisers through mass media. In advertising, audiences are often targeted. A **target audience** is a particular group of consumers singled out for an advertisement or advertising campaign. Target audiences are *potential* audiences because advertisers can never be sure that the message will actually get through to them as intended. While advertisers can identify dozens of different target audiences, five broad audience categories are commonly described: household consumers, members of business organizations, members of a trade channel, professionals, and government officials and employees.

Audience Categories.

Household consumers are the most conspicuous audience in that most mass media advertising is directed at them. Unilever, Miller Brewing, Saturn, The Gap, and Nationwide Insurance have products and services designed for the consumer market, and so their advertising targets household consumers. The most recent information indicates that there are about 103 million households in the United States and approximately 275 million household consumers.[11] Total yearly retail spending

11. "2000 Survey of Buying Power," *Sales and Marketing Management* (2000), 10.

by these households is about \$3.4 trillion.[12] This huge audience is typically where the action is in advertising. Under the very broad heading of "consumer advertising," very fine audience distinctions are made by advertisers. Target audience definitions—such as men, 25 to 45, living in metropolitan areas, with incomes greater than \$50,000 per year—are common.

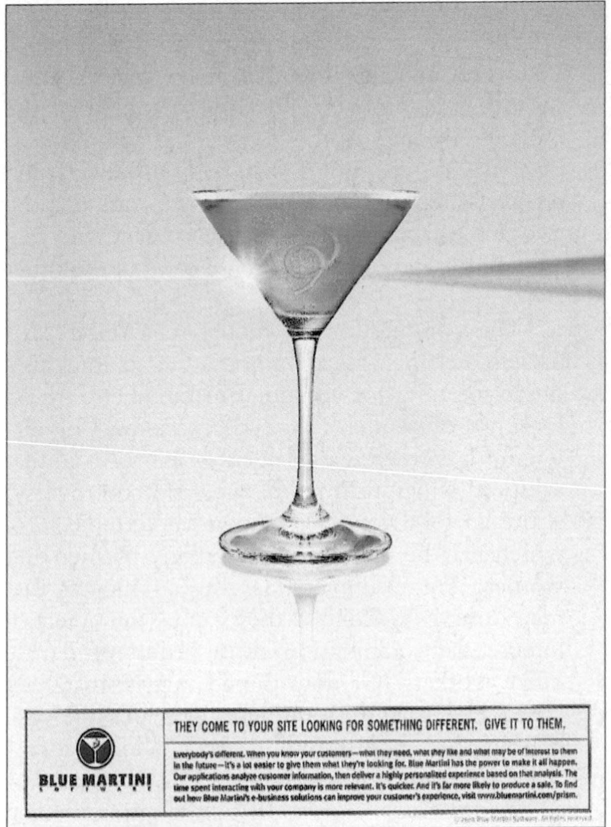

EXHIBIT 1.15

When members of business organizations use advertising to communicate, the ads often emphasize creating awareness of the company's brand name. Blue Martini, a software development firm, is using high visual appeal to accomplish brand name recognition.
www.bluemartini.com/prism

Members of business organizations are the focus of advertising for firms that produce business and industrial goods and services, such as office equipment, production machinery, supplies, and software. While products and services targeted to this audience often require personal selling, advertising is used to create an awareness and a favorable attitude among potential buyers. Not-for-profit businesses such as universities, some research laboratories, philanthropic groups, and cultural organizations represent an important and separate business audience for advertising. Exhibit 1.15 is an example of an ad directed at members of business organizations. Blue Martini is a software development firm that helps marketers analyze customer information.

Members of a trade channel include retailers, wholesalers, and distributors; they are an audience for producers of both household and business goods and services. Unless a producer can obtain adequate retail and wholesale distribution through a trade channel, the firm's products will not reach customers. Therefore, it is important to direct advertising at the trade level of the market. Various forms of advertising and promotion are instrumental in cultivating demand among members of a trade channel. Generally, the major promotional tool used to communicate with this group is personal selling. This is because this target audience represents a relatively small, easily identifiable group that can be reached with personal selling. When advertising is also directed at this audience, it can serve an extremely useful purpose, as we will see later in the section on advertising as a business process.

Professionals form a special target audience and are defined as doctors, lawyers, accountants, teachers, or any other professionals who have received special training or certification. This audience warrants separate classification because its members have specialized needs and interests. Advertising directed at professionals thus highlights products and services often uniquely designed to serve their more narrowly defined needs. In addition, the language and images used in advertising to this target audience rely on the esoteric terminology and unique circumstances that members of professions readily recognize. Advertising to professionals is predominantly carried out through trade publications. The ad for Prevacid in Exhibit 1.16 is an example of advertising directed to doctors.

Government officials and employees constitute an audience in themselves due to the large dollar volume of buying that federal, state, and local governments do. Government organizations such as schools and road maintenance operations buy huge amounts of various products. Producers of items such as furniture, construction materials, vehicles, fertilizers, computers, and business services all target this

12. Ibid., 19.

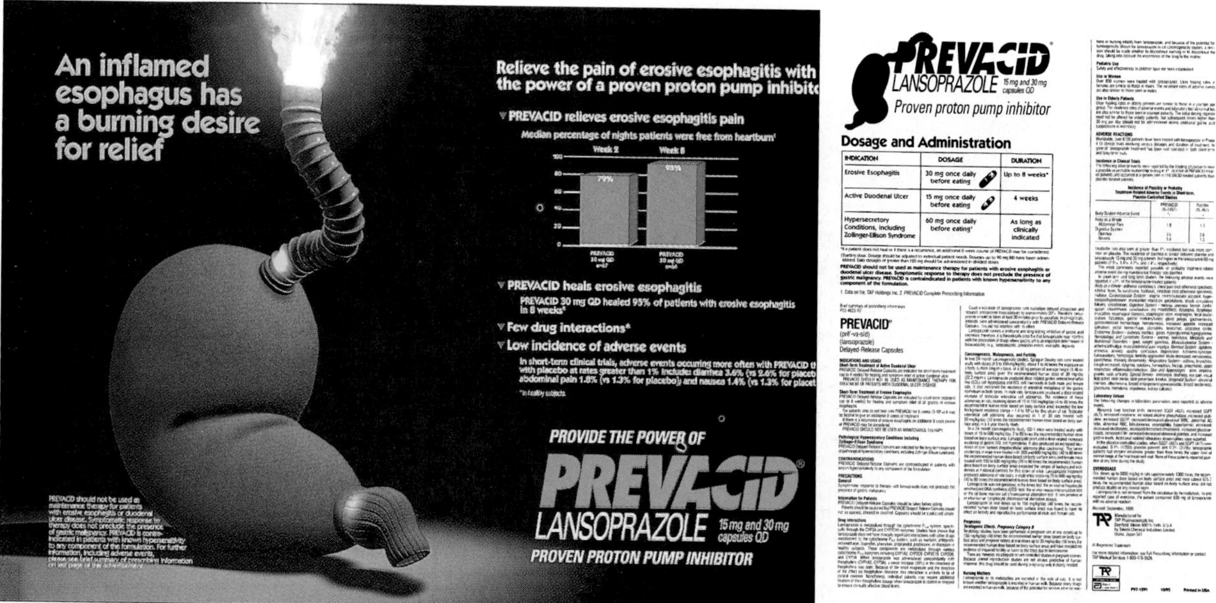

EXHIBIT 1.16

Professional audiences for advertising, such as doctors, lawyers, and engineers, have special needs and interests. This ad for Prevacid was run in a trade publication and offers medical doctors the kind of specialized information they desire about pharmaceutical products.
www.prevacid.com

group with their advertising. Advertising to this audience group is dominated by direct mail advertising.

Audience Geography. Audiences can also be thought of in geographic terms. Because of cultural differences, very few ads can be effective for all consumers worldwide. However, so-called **global advertising** can be used for some brands. These are typically brands that are considered citizens of the world and whose manner of use does not vary tremendously by culture. Even though cultures vary significantly in their view of time and men's jewelry, Exhibits 1.17 and 1.18 show extremely similar appeals in two different ads for Rolex watches. Firms that market brands with global appeal, such as Singapore Airlines, IBM, Levi's, Sony, and Pirelli, attempt to develop and place advertisements with a common theme and presentation in all markets around the world where the firm's brands are sold. Global placement is possible only when a brand and the messages about that brand have a common appeal across diverse cultures. Travelers in Asia seek the same benefits from an airline as travelers in the United States. Men in Europe want the same comfort from a razor when they shave that men in South America do. Motorola had its agency, McCann-Erickson Worldwide, prepare global ads for its cell phones and pagers; their strategy is discussed in the Global Issues box on page 19.

International advertising occurs when firms prepare and place different advertising in different national markets. Each international market often requires unique or original advertising due to product adaptations or message appeals tailored specifically for that market. Unilever prepares different versions of ads for its laundry products for nearly every international market due to differences in the way consumers in different cultures approach the laundry task. Consumers in the United States use

EXHIBITS 1.17 AND 1.18

No surprise—companies can tailor their advertising to target audiences and routinely do when the target is clear. The obvious audience difference here is language (German versus Italian), while other aspects—Rolex's appeal to an affluent elite who likely follow tennis, not NASCAR, and the Rolex brand imagery—remain the same. In cyberspace, everywhere can be "local," and advertising on the Web seems more attuned to lifestyle than to geography, with English as the most common lingua franca. *Although Rolex doesn't yet use the Web to advertise its products, a Web search at Yahoo!* (www.yahoo.com) *turns up a variety of retailers. Is the Web likely to be Rolex's best advertising channel anyway?*

large and powerful washers and dryers and lots of hot water. Households in Brazil use very little hot water and hang clothes out to dry. Very few firms enjoy the luxury of having a brand with truly cross-cultural appeal and global recognition. Since this is true, most firms must pursue other-nation markets with international advertising rather than global advertising.

National advertising reaches all geographic areas of one nation. National advertising is the term typically used to describe the kind of advertising we see most often in the mass media in the domestic U.S. market.

Regional advertising is carried out by producers, wholesalers, distributors, and retailers that concentrate their efforts in a relatively large, but not national, geographic region. Best Buy, a regional consumer electronics and appliance chain, has distribution confined to a few states. Because of the nature of the firm's market, it places advertising only in regions where it has stores.

Local advertising is much the same as regional advertising. **Local advertising** is directed at an audience in a single trading area, either a city or state. Exhibit 1.19 shows an example of this type of advertising. Retail shopkeepers of all types rely on local media to reach customers. Under special circumstances, national advertisers will share advertising expenses in a market with local dealers to achieve specific advertising objectives. This sharing of advertising expenses between national advertisers and local merchants is called **cooperative advertising** (or **co-op advertising**). Exhibit 1.20 illustrates a co-op advertisement run by TUMI luggage and one of its retailers, Shapiro. General Motors has recently redesigned its co-op advertising program with dealers in an attempt to create a more fully coordinated integrated brand promotion.[13]

GLOBAL ISSUES

Motorola's Global Campaign Takes Flight—Then Comes Back to Earth

As successful and astute as Motorola has been in reinventing itself as a corporation, it did miss one major market trend—the rush by consumers to go digital with cell phone technology. As a result, Motorola's share of the U.S. market for cellular handset technology dropped from 55 percent in 1995 to just 34.1 percent in 1998. The beneficiaries of Motorola's hesitancy were Nokia, whose 13.6 percent share increased to 24.4 percent, and Ericsson, whose share rocketed from merely 2 percent to over 14 percent.

Motorola clearly needed a lift and a global ad campaign was conceived. Motorola challenged its advertising agency, McCann-Erickson Worldwide, to "find the friendliest means of telling consumers about the wealth of benefits Motorola technology brings." The challenge was to develop a global advertising campaign that would feature technology as the universal appeal across geographic and cultural boundaries. The campaign needed to be a corporate image campaign. The Motorola name was known in the market but not preferred.

These conditions were classic prerequisites for a global image campaign that focused on creating a relationship with a brand rather than relying on product feature appeals, as competitors often do. So a new campaign took flight—literally. Motorola launched a $100 million global campaign called "Wings," which featured its batwinglike corporate logo. The images in the campaign highlighted a squadron of flight-related images: a nun pedaling a bike with a dove at her side; a woman in a chapel wearing giant feathered wings; a man tossing a paper airplane. In the background, Mick Jagger sings "You Can't Always Get What You Want."

The campaign worked beautifully through 1999, when strategists at Motorola decided that yet another global unification of the brand image was needed. Motorola's three ad agencies have been charged with creating a "unified Motorola brand presence." The new effort will be focused on creating an integrated global image that extends across the company's various businesses: semiconductors, wireless handsets, cable and broadband, and computer networking. A tall order indeed for a brand campaign. But the focus on global unification highlights once again how important the brand focus is to the process of effective advertising.

Sources: Bradley Johnson and Mercedes M. Cardona, "Motorola Seeks Unifying Elements for Global Ads," *Advertising Age,* August 18, 1997, 8; Sally Goll Beaty, "Motorola's Image Campaign Set to Fly," *Wall Street Journal,* April 18, 1998, B14; Tobi Elkin, "Motorola Seeking Unity for Global Brand Image," *Advertising Age,* July 31, 2000, 19; Tobi Elkin, "Motorola's Mandate: Develop Digital Image," *Advertising Age,* September 25, 2000, 118.

4 Advertising as a Business Process.

So far we have talked about advertising as a communication process and as a way companies reach diverse audiences with persuasive brand information. But we need to appreciate another aspect of advertising. Advertising is very much a business process as well as a communication process. For multinational organizations like IBM, as well as for small local retailers, advertising is a basic business tool that helps them communicate with current and potential customers. We need to understand advertising as a business process in three ways. First, we will consider the role advertising plays in the overall marketing and brand promotion programs in firms. Second, we will look at the types of advertising used by firms. Finally, we will take a broader look at advertising by identifying the economic effects of the process.

The Role of Advertising in Marketing and Brand Promotion. To truly appreciate advertising as a business process, we have to understand the role advertising plays in a firm's marketing and brand promotion effort. As the introductory scenario so clearly demonstrated, effective advertising as part of an overall integrated brand promotion can be a key factor in the success of a brand. Every organization must make marketing decisions. These decisions involve identifying market opportunities and

13. Joe Miller, "Dealers Regain Ad Input as GM Revives Program," *Advertising Age,* October 16, 2000, 80.

EXHIBIT 1.19

Daffy's is a clothing retailer with just two shops in New York City; it services a local geographic market. Retailers that serve a small geographic area use local advertising to reach their customers.

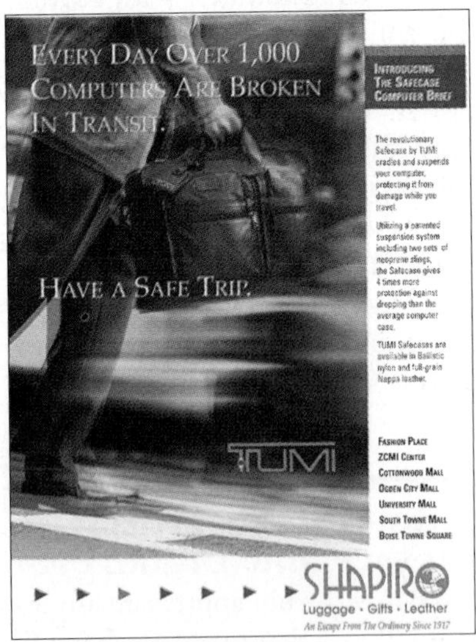

EXHIBIT 1.20

National advertisers will often share advertising expenses with local retail merchants if the retailer features the advertiser's brand in local advertising. This sharing of expenses is called co-op advertising. Here a local retailer, Shapiro, is featuring TUMI brand luggage in this co-op ad.
www.tumi.com

then developing, pricing, promoting, and distributing products and services for some target audience. The role of advertising in marketing and brand promotion relates to four important aspects of the marketing process: (1) the marketing mix; (2) brand development and management; (3) achieving effective market segmentation, differentiation, and positioning; and (4) contributing to revenue and profit generation.

The Role of Advertising in the Marketing Mix. A formal definition of marketing reveals that advertising (as a part of overall promotion) is one of the primary marketing tools available to any organization:

Marketing *is the process of planning and executing the conception, pricing, promotion, and distribution of ideas, goods, and services to create exchanges that satisfy individual and organizational objectives.*[14]

Marketing assumes a wide range of responsibilities related to the conception, pricing, promotion, and distribution of ideas, goods, or services. Many of you know that these four areas of responsibility and decision making in marketing are referred to as the **marketing mix.** The word *mix* is used to describe the blend of strategic emphasis on the product, its price, its promotion (including advertising), and its distribution when a brand is marketed to consumers. This blend, or mix, results in the overall marketing program for a brand. Advertising is important, but it is only one of the major areas of marketing responsibility *and* it is only one of many different promotional tools relied on in the marketing mix.

Generally speaking, the role of advertising in the marketing mix is to focus on the ability of the advertising effort to communicate to a target audience the value a

14. The American Marketing Association definition, given here, is still widely accepted and appeared in *Marketing News*, March 1, 1985, 1.

brand has to offer—precisely the role played by advertising for Wendy's. Value consists of more than simply the tangible aspects of the brand itself, though. Indeed, consumers look for value in the brand, but they also demand such things as convenient location, credit terms, warranties and guarantees, and delivery. In addition, a wide range of emotional values such as security, belonging, affiliation, and prestige can also be pursued in the brand choice process. Because of consumers' search for such diverse values, marketers must determine which marketing mix ingredients to emphasize and how to blend the mix elements in just the right way to attract and satisfy customers. These marketing mix decisions play a significant role in determining the message content and media placement of advertising.

Exhibit 1.21 lists factors typically considered in each area of the marketing mix. You can see that decisions under each of the marketing mix areas can directly affect the advertising message. The important point is that a firm's advertising effort must be consistent with and complement the overall marketing mix strategy being used by a firm.

The Role of Advertising in Brand Development and Management. Perhaps the most obvious effect of advertising in the marketing mix has to do with brand development and management. We have been referring to the brand throughout our discussion of the process of advertising. All of us have our own understanding of what a brand is. A formal definition of a **brand** is a name, term, sign, symbol, or any other feature that identifies one seller's good or service as distinct from those of other sellers.[15] Advertising plays a significant role in brand development and management. A brand is in many ways the most precious business asset owned by a firm. It allows a firm to communicate consistently and efficiently with the market.

Interbrand, a marketing analysis and consulting firm, has actually attached a dollar value to brand names. The 20 most valuable brands in the world in 2001 are shown in Exhibit 1.22 on page 23. Often, the brand name is worth much more than the annual sales of the brand. Coca-Cola, the most valuable brand in the world, is estimated to be worth about $68.95 billion even though sales of branded Coca-Cola products are only about $17.8 billion a year.

A brand would be at a serious competitive disadvantage without effective communication provided by advertising. In fact, managers at ConAgra came to the startling realization that while they were doing a good job of using advertising to develop and manage the Marie Callender line of frozen entrées, they had "let the Healthy Choice brand wither on the vine."[16] The firm is in the process of rectifying that mistake and is investing $40 million in advertising for the more than 300 items in the Healthy Choice product line. For all kinds of companies, advertising effects brand development and management in five important ways:

1. *Information and persuasion.* Target audiences learn about a brand's features and benefits through the communications transmitted by advertising and, to a lesser extent, other promotional tools being used in the integrated brand promotion effort. But advertising has the best capability to inform or persuade target audiences about the values a brand has to offer. No other variable in the marketing mix is designed to accomplish this communication. As an example, persuasive communication in the branding effort is particularly competitive in the credit card market, where consumers often perceive no difference between services offered by one firm and another. Analysts point out that "branding is becoming crucially important in the $1.3 trillion credit card market" as Visa, MasterCard, and American Express offer new products for a wider range of consumer groups.[17]

15. Peter D. Bennett, *Dictionary of Marketing Terms,* 2nd ed. (Chicago: American Marketing Association, 1995), 4.
16. Stephanie Thompson, "ConAgra Cooks Up Stronger Identity," *Advertising Age,* November 6, 2000, 42.
17. Kate Fitzgerald, "Branding Efforts Surge as Financial Services Take Share Fight Upscale," *Advertising Age,* September 25, 2000, S18.

EXHIBIT 1.21

Factors considered in creating a marketing mix. Advertising messages and media placement must be consistent with and complement strategies in all areas of the marketing mix.

Product	Promotion
Functional features	Amount and type of advertising
Aesthetic design	Number and qualifications of salespeople
Accompanying services	Extent and type of personal selling program
Instructions for use	Sales promotion—coupons, contests, sweepstakes
Warranty	Trade shows
Product differentiation	Public relations activities
Product positioning	Direct mail or telemarketing
	Event sponsorships
	Internet communications

Price	Distribution
Level:	Number of retail outlets
Top of the line	Location of retail outlets
Competitive, average prices	Types of retail outlets
Low-price policy	Catalog sales
Terms offered:	Other nonstore retail methods—Internet
Cash only	Number and type of wholesalers
Credit:	Inventories—extent and location
Extended	Services provided by distribution:
Restricted	Credit
Interest charges	Delivery
Lease/rental	Installation
	Training

2 *Introduction of new brand or brand extensions.* Advertising is essential when firms introduce a new brand or extensions of existing brands. A **brand extension** is an adaptation of an existing brand to a new product area. For example, the Snickers ice cream bar is a brand extension of the original Snickers candy bar, and Ivory shampoo is a brand extension of Ivory dishwashing liquid. When new brands or extensions are brought to market, the advertising and integrated brand promotion process bears large responsibility for attracting attention to the new market offering. This is often accomplished with advertising working in conjunction with other promotional activities such as sales promotions and point-of-purchase displays. Mars (famous for candy) is investing heavily in extending the Uncle Ben's Rice brand into Rice Bowls of all varieties, including Italian, Mexican, and Chinese.[18] Exhibit 1.23 on page 24, shows another example of advertising being used to extend a famous brand name into a totally different product category.

Again, trade buyers are key to the success of new brands or brand extensions. Marketers have little hope of successfully introducing a brand if there is no coop-

18. Stephanie Thompson, "The Bowl Is Where It's at for New Frozen Meal Lines," *Advertising Age,* August 14, 2000, 4.

EXHIBIT 1.22

The world's 20 most valuable brands, 2000 (U.S. dollars in millions).

Rank	Brand	Brand Value 2000 (billions)	Brand Value 2001 (billions)	% Change
1	Coca Cola	$72.53	$68.95	–5%
2	Microsoft	70.19	65.07	–7
3	IBM	53.18	52.75	–1
4	GE	42.40	38.13	–11
5	Nokia	38.52	35.04	–9
6	Intel	39.05	34.67	–11
7	Disney	33.55	32.59	–3
8	Ford	36.37	30.09	–17
9	McDonald's	27.86	25.29	–9
10	AT&T	25.54	22.83	–11
11	Marlboro	22.11	22.05	0
12	Mercedes	21.10	21.73	3
13	Citibank	18.88	19.01	1
14	Toyota	18.82	18.58	–1
15	Hewlett-Packard	20.57	17.98	–13
16	Cisco	20.01	17.21	–14
17	American Express	16.12	16.92	5
18	Gillette	17.36	15.30	–12
19	Merrill-Lynch	N/A	15.02	N/A
20	Sony	16.41	15.01	–9

Source: "The Top 100 Brands," *Business Week*, August 6, 2001, 60–61.

eration in the trade channel among wholesalers and retailers. This is where integrated brand promotion is key. The trade is less affected by advertising than by other forms of promotion. Direct support to the trade in terms of displays, contests, and other incentives combined with advertising in an IBP program help ensure the success of a brand.

3. *Building and maintaining brand loyalty among consumers.* Loyalty to a brand is one of the most important assets a firm can have. **Brand loyalty** occurs when a consumer repeatedly purchases the same brand to the exclusion of competitors' brands. This loyalty can result from habit, brand names that are prominent in the consumer's memory, barely conscious associations with brand images, or some fairly deep meanings consumers have attached to the brands they buy. While brand features are the most important influence on building and maintaining brand loyalty, advertising plays a key role in the process as well. Advertising reminds consumers of the values—tangible and intangible—of the brand. Advertising and integrated brand promotions often provide an extra incentive to consumers to remain brand loyal. Direct marketing can tailor communications to existing customers. Other promotional tools can also offer similarly valuable communications that will help build and strengthen lasting and positive associations with a brand—such as a frequent-flyer or frequent-buyer program. When a firm creates and maintains positive associations with the brand in the mind of consumers, the

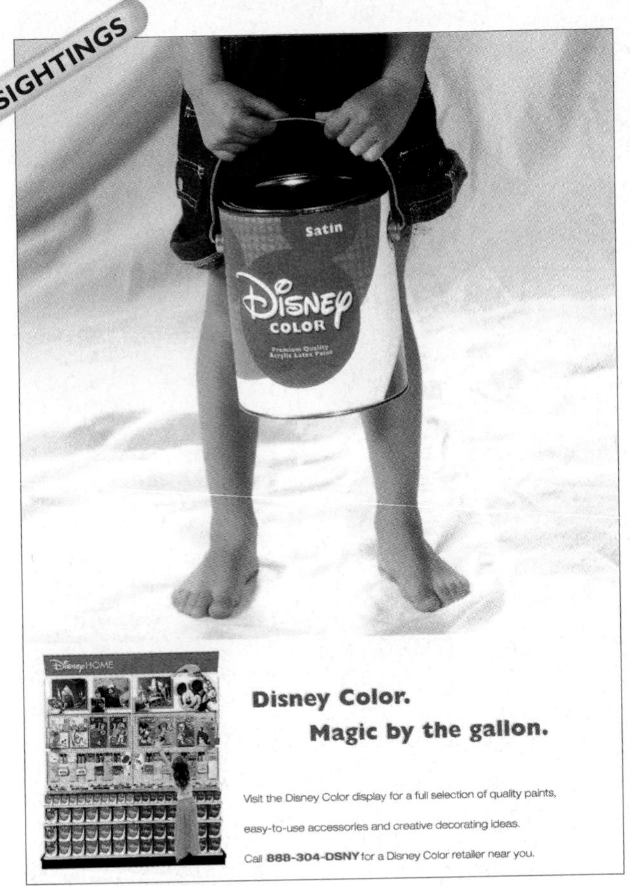

EXHIBIT 1.23

Advertising helps companies with brand extension strategies. Here, the famous Disney brand name is being used as the company extends the brand name into paint products. Explain how Monstermoving.com (www.monstermoving.com) is a similar example of brand extension. What value do the brand names lend to these products and services?

firm has developed **brand equity.**[19] While brand equity occurs over long periods of time, short-term advertising and promotional activities are key to long-term success.[20] This advertising fact of life became clear to strategists at the cosmetics firm Coty. The firm's 40-year-old Calgon brand needed to be refreshed and rejuvenated. A new $2 million print campaign was conceived to tout the soothing effects of the bath additive in a hectic, urban world.[21]

4. *Creating an image and meaning for a brand.* As we have determined, advertising can communicate how a brand addresses certain needs and desires and therefore plays an important role in attracting customers to brands they feel will be useful and satisfying. But advertising can go further. It can help link a brand's image and meaning to a consumer's social environment and to the larger culture, and it can thus deliver a sense of personal connection for the consumer.

   The Schiff ad for prenatal vitamins in Exhibit 1.24 is a clear example of how advertising can create an image and deeper meaning. The message in this ad is not just about the health advantages of using a nutritional supplement during pregnancy. The message mines associations related to love and caring for an unborn or recently born child. Even the slogan for the brand, "Benefits Beyond Your Daily Requirements," plays on the sense that a vitamin is more than a vehicle for dosing up on folic acid. Other promotional tools in the integrated brand promotion process, such as personal selling, sales promotions, and event sponsorship, simply cannot achieve such creative power or communicate all the potential meanings a brand can have to a consumer.

5. *Building and maintaining brand loyalty within the trade.* It might not seem as if wholesalers and retailers can be brand loyal, but they will favor one brand over others given the proper support from a manufacturer. Advertising and particularly advertising integrated with other brand promotions is an area where support can be given. Marketers can provide the trade with sales training programs, collateral advertising materials, point-of-purchase advertising displays, and traffic-building special events. Procter & Gamble is one firm that has determined that special interactive kiosk displays, combined with media advertising, are effective in attracting attention to P&G brands. The new displays will be placed in department stores and in shopping malls. The kiosks feature touch-screen technology and support sales clerks by providing information about as many as four P&G brands.[22]

19. Kevin L. Keller, *Strategic Brand Management: Building, Measuring, and Managing Brand Equity* (Upper Saddle River, N.J.: Prentice-Hall, 1998), 2.
20. Keller, "Conceptualizing, Measuring, and Managing Customer-Based Brand Equity," *Journal of Marketing,* vol. 57 (January 1993), 4.
21. Cardona, "Calgon Ads Refresh Brand Image," *Advertising Age,* November 6, 2000, 34.
22. Jack Neff, "P&G Goes Viral with Test of Innovative Locations," *Advertising Age,* September 4, 2000, 4.

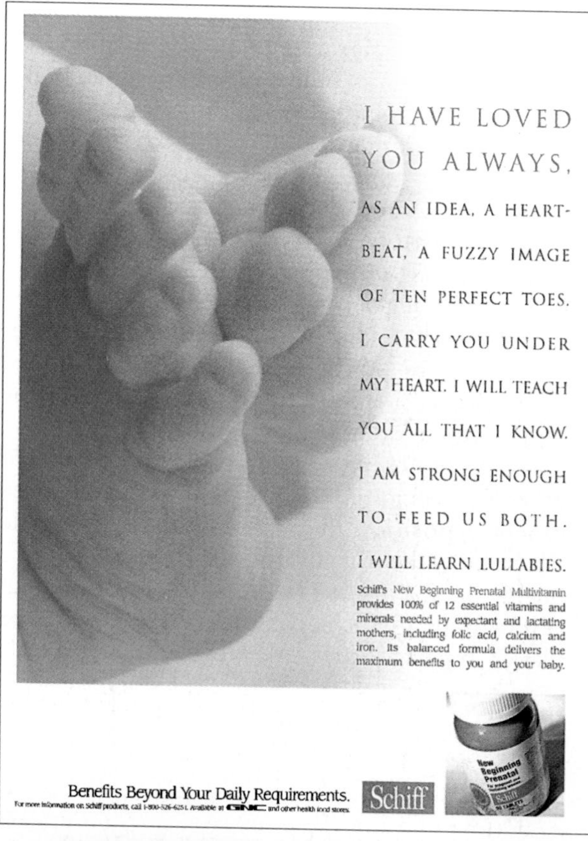

EXHIBIT 1.24

The message in this Schiff ad creates meaning for vitamins that goes beyond the daily nutrition role vitamins can play. What are the many meanings in this message offered to consumers?
www.schiffvitamins.com

The Role of Advertising Market Segmentation, Differentiation, and Positioning. For advertising to be effective, it must work to support the organization's basic marketing strategies. The most basic and important strategies for cultivating customers are market segmentation, differentiation, and positioning. Advertising plays an important role in helping a firm execute these marketing strategies.

Market segmentation is the process of breaking down a large, widely varied (*heterogeneous*) market into submarkets, or segments, that are more similar than dissimilar (*homogeneous*) in terms of what the consumer is looking for or is presumed to be looking for. Underlying the strategy of market segmentation are the facts that consumers differ in their wants and that the wants of one person can differ under various circumstances. The market for automobiles can be divided into submarkets for different types of automobiles based on the needs and desires of various groups of buyers. Identifying those groups, or segments, of the population who want and will buy large or small, luxury or economy, or sport or sedan or minivan models is an important part of basic marketing strategy. Larger markets are, however, often broken up by more indirect criteria, such as age, marital status, gender, and income, since these data are widely collected and widely available and tend to be reasonably related to product and usage. Advertising's role in the market segmentation process is to develop messages that appeal to the wants and desires of different segments and then to transmit those messages via appropriate media. At present, advertisers are struggling with decisions concerning how much to invest in new media vehicles for reaching target segments. The difficulty of these decisions is highlighted in the E-Commerce box on page 27.

Differentiation is the process of creating a perceived difference, in the mind of the consumer, between an organization's brand and the competition's. Notice that this definition emphasizes that brand differentiation is based on *consumer perception*. The perceived differences can be tangible differences, or they may be based on image or style factors. Consider the Fendi watch ad in Exhibit 1.25. A $20 Timex and a $12,000 Fendi keep time in exactly the same way. But the two brands are differentiated on intangible perceptions of style and the deeper meaning brands can have, as discussed earlier. The critical issue in differentiation is that consumers *perceive* a difference between brands. If consumers do not perceive a difference, then whether real differences exist does not matter. Differentiation is one of the most critical of all marketing strategies. If a firm's brand is not perceived as distinctive and attractive by consumers, then consumers will have no reason to choose that brand over one from the competition or to pay higher prices for the "better" or "more meaningful" brand.

Advertising can help create a difference in the mind of the consumer between an organization's brand and its competitors' brands. The advertisement may emphasize performance features, or it may create a different image of the brand. The essential task for advertising is to develop a message that is distinctive and unmistakably linked to the organization's brand. The ads in Exhibits 1.26 and 1.27 are distinctive and pursue product differentiation with both function and image.

Positioning is the process of designing a brand so that it can occupy a distinct and valued place in the target consumer's mind relative to other brands and then communicating this distinctiveness through advertising. Positioning, like differentiation, depends on a perceived image of tangible or intangible features. The importance of positioning can be understood by recognizing that consumers create a *perceptual space* in their minds for all the brands they might consider purchasing. A perceptual space is how one brand is seen on any number of dimensions—such as quality, taste, price, or social display value—in relation to those same dimensions in other brands.

The positioning decision really comprises two different decisions. A firm must decide on the **external position** for a brand—that is, the niche the brand will pursue relative to all the competitive brands on the market. Additionally, an **internal position** must be achieved with regard to the other similar brands a firm markets. With the external-

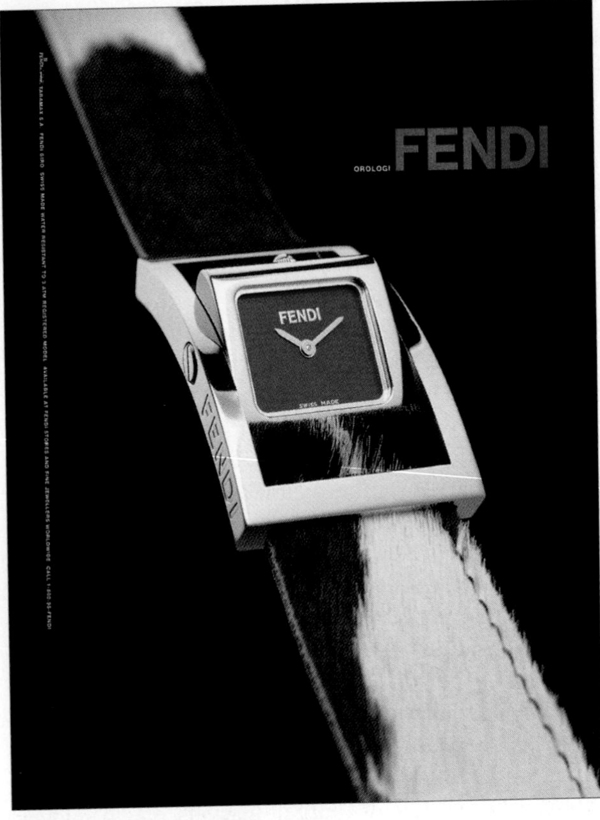

EXHIBIT 1.25

Advertising is key to the marketing strategy of differentiation. This very expensive Fendi watch keeps time just like a $20 Timex. But you won't see an ad like this for a Timex. What is it about this ad that differentiates the Fendi brand from the Timex brand? www.fendi.it

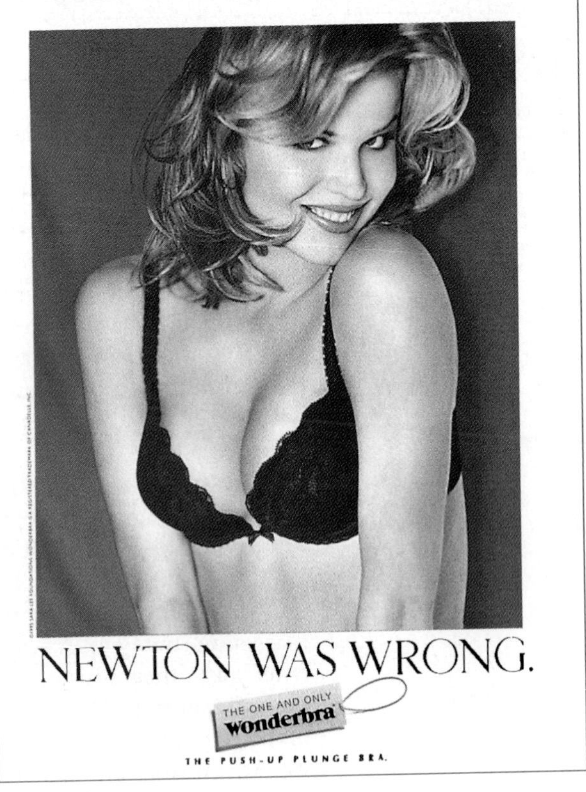

EXHIBITS 1.26 AND 1.27

An important role for advertising is to help a firm differentiate its brand from the competition with distinctive presentations. The Honda del Sol ad in Exhibit 1.26 draws attention to the car's removable roof as a basis for differentiation. The Wonderbra ad in Exhibit 1.27 also highlights this brand's superior design as a basis for differentiation. www.honda.com *and* www.wonderbra.com

positioning decision, a firm must achieve a distinctive competitive position based on design features, pricing, distribution, or promotion or advertising strategy. Some brands are positioned at the very top of their product category, such as BMW's 740i, priced around $75,000. Other brands seek a position at the low end of all market offerings, such as the Chevrolet Metro, whose base price is $10,000.[23]

Effective internal positioning is accomplished by either developing vastly different products within a product line (Ben & Jerry's ice cream, for example, offers plenty of distinctive flavors, as shown in Exhibit 1.28) or creating advertising messages that appeal to different consumer needs and desires. Procter & Gamble successfully positions its laundry detergent brands both internally and externally using a combination of product design and effective advertising. While some of these brands assume different positions within P&G's own line due to substantive differences (a liquid soap versus a powder soap, for example), others with minor differences achieve distinctive positioning through advertising. One P&G brand is advertised as being effective on kids' dirty clothes, while another brand is portrayed as effective for preventing colors from running (see Exhibit 1.29). In this way, advertising helps create a distinctive position, both internally and externally.

The methods and strategic options available to an organization with respect to market segmentation, product differentiation, and positioning will be fully discussed in Chapter 6. For now, recognize that advertising plays an important role in helping an organization put these essential market strategies into operation.

E-COMMERCE

The Internet *Is* Big—It's Even Bigger Than Seinfeld

The Internet is posing some difficult problems for advertisers. Traditional media—television, radio, newspapers, magazines—have demonstrated their ability, over decades, to reach targeted audiences with persuasive and informative communications. But then along comes this new medium—the Internet—with all kinds of special potential: It's huge! It's hot! It's interactive! Grandmothers are online! Every school in America is getting wired!

But really, just how big is the Internet? Well, we can finally say that the Internet is *really* big—now that it has surpassed the viewership of the final episode of *Seinfeld.* You see, up until now, traditional media were much bigger than the Internet. The symbol of major media size was the fact that over 80 million people watched the final episode of *Seinfeld* in 1998. But in 2001, the Internet surpassed even that huge audience. By August 2001, more than 163 million people in the United States were online—or about 58 percent of the U.S. population. Now that is still a lot smaller than the percentage of U.S. residents that use television (98 percent) or radio (99.9 percent), but the numbers are getting pretty compelling.

Before we get carried away believing that the Internet will take over the advertising world, let's consider some back-to-earth realities. Currently, advertisers invest about $4.3 billion in Internet advertising compared to $243 billion invested in television, radio, newspapers, magazines, and other advertising media. In other words, the Internet represents only about 2 percent of traditional media from an advertising standpoint. Is the Internet exciting, dynamic, entertaining, informative? Yes. Will it take over the advertising world? Probably not.

Sources: Thomas E. Weber, "Who, What, Where: Putting the Internet in Perspective," *Wall Street Journal*, April 16, 1998, B10; R. Craig Endicott, "100 Leading National Advertisers," *Advertising Age*, September 24, 2001, S12; NUA Internet Surveys, www.nua.ie, accessed October 19, 2001.

The Role of Advertising in Revenue and Profit Generation. The fundamental purpose of marketing can be stated quite simply: to generate revenue. No other part of an organization has this primary purpose. In the words of highly regarded management consultant and scholar Peter Drucker, "Marketing and innovation produce results: all the rest are 'costs.' "[24] The results Drucker is referring to are revenues. The marketing process is designed to generate sales and therefore revenues for the firm.

23. Pricing information at www.bmwusa.com and www.chevrolet.com, accessed November 20, 2000.
24. Peter F. Drucker, *People and Performance: The Best of Peter Drucker* (New York: HarperCollins, 1997), 90.

EXHIBIT 1.28

Firms with multiple brands in a single product category have to internally position these brands to differentiate them from each other in the minds of consumers. Ben & Jerry's achieves its product positioning by emphasizing the distinctly different flavors of each of its ice creams.
www.benjerry.com

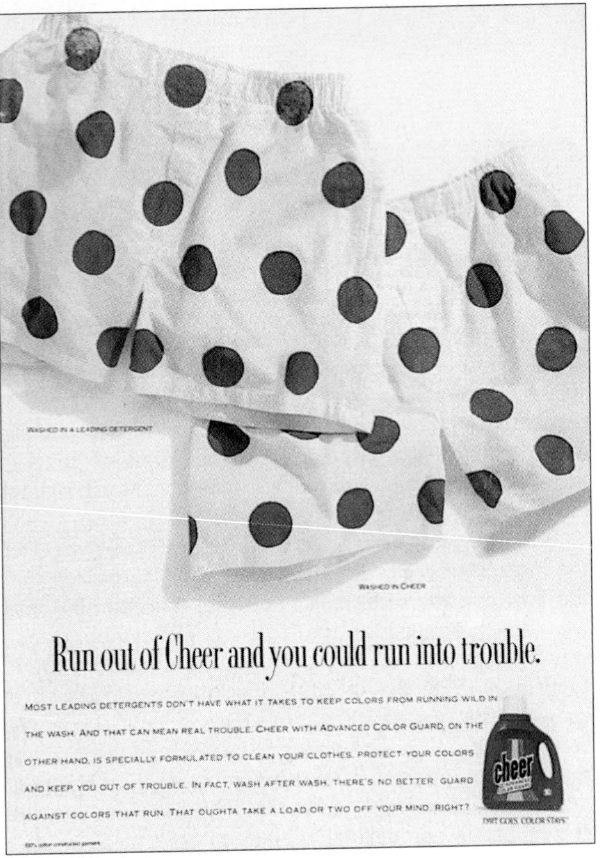

EXHIBIT 1.29

When a firm has multiple brands in a product category, it must be careful to position these brands distinctively so as to avoid cannibalization of one brand's sales by another. Procter & Gamble successfully achieves both a competitive external position and a distinctive internal product line position for Cheer laundry detergent by advertising the brand as the leader in preventing colors from running.
www.pg.com

The contribution to creating sales as part of the revenue-generating process is where advertising plays a significant role. As we have seen, advertising communicates persuasive information to audiences based on the values created in the marketing mix. This communication, which can highlight brand features, price, or availability through distribution, attracts customers. When a brand has the *right* features, the *right* price, the *right* distribution, and the *right* communication, sales will likely occur, and the firm generates revenue. In this way, advertising makes a direct contribution to the marketing goal of revenue generation. Notice that advertising *contributes* to the process of creating sales and revenue—it cannot be viewed as solely responsible for creating sales and revenue. Some organizations mistakenly see advertising as a panacea—the salvation for an ambiguous marketing mix strategy. Advertising alone cannot be held responsible for sales. Sales occur when a brand has a well-conceived and complete marketing mix—including good advertising.

The effect of advertising on profits is a bit more involved. This effect comes about when advertising can help give a firm greater flexibility in the price it charges for a product or service. Advertising can help create pricing flexibility by (1) contributing to economies of scale and (2) creating inelasticity of demand. When a firm creates large-scale demand for its product, the quantity of product produced is increased. As production reaches higher and higher levels, fixed costs (such as rent and equipment costs) are spread over a greater number of units produced. The result of this large-scale production is that the cost to produce each item is reduced. Lowering the cost of each item produced because of high-volume production is known as **economies of scale.**

When Colgate manufactures hundreds of thousands of tubes of its Colgate Total toothpaste and ships them in large quantities to warehouses, the fixed costs of production and shipping per unit are greatly reduced. With lower fixed costs per unit, Colgate can realize greater profits on each tube of toothpaste sold. Advertising contributes to demand stimulation by communicating to the market about the features and availability of a brand. By contributing to demand stimulation, advertising contributes to the process of creating economies of scale, which ultimately translates into higher profits per unit.

Remember the concept of brand loyalty discussed earlier? Well, brand loyalty and advertising work together to create another important economic effect. When consumers are brand loyal, they are generally less sensitive to price increases for the brand. In economic terms, this is known as **inelasticity of demand.** When consumers are less price sensitive, firms have the flexibility to raise prices and increase profit margins. Advertising contributes directly to brand loyalty, and thus to inelasticity of demand, by persuading and reminding consumers of the satisfactions and values related to a brand.

Types of Advertising.

Advertisers develop and place advertisements for many reasons. Some of the most basic types of advertising are based on functional goals, that is, on what the advertiser is trying to accomplish. The functional goals for advertising include primary and selective demand stimulation, direct- and delayed-response advertising, and corporate advertising.

One potential function for advertising is primary demand stimulation, although this role is quite limited. In **primary demand stimulation,** an advertiser is seeking to create demand for a new product category in general. In its pure form, the purpose of this type of advertising is to educate potential buyers about the fundamental values of an entire product category rather than to emphasize the values of a specific brand within the product category.

Primary demand stimulation is challenging and costly, and research evidence suggests that it is likely to have a perceivable impact only for new products on the market—such as when the VCR was first developed and introduced to the market. With a product that is totally new to the market, consumers need to be convinced that the product category itself is available and valuable. When the VCR was first introduced in the United States, RCA, Panasonic, and Quasar (see Exhibit 1.30) ran primary demand stimulation advertising to explain to household consumers the value and convenience of taping television programs with this new product called a VHS video recorder—something almost no one had ever done before at home.

For organizations that have tried to stimulate primary demand in mature product categories, typically trade associations, the results have been dismal. Both the National Fluid Milk Processor Promotion Board and the Florida Department of Citrus have tried to use advertising to stimulate primary demand for the entire product categories of milk and orange juice. Examples of these campaigns are shown in Exhibits 1.31 and 1.32. While the "mustache" campaign is very popular and gets widespread recognition, milk consumption has *declined* every year during the time of this campaign.[25] This is despite the fact that more than $1 billion in spending has

25. U.S. Bureau of the Census, *Statistical Abstract of the United States: 1995,* 115th ed. (Washington, D.C.: U.S. Government Printing Office, 1995); "Got Results?" *Marketing News,* March 2, 1998, 1.

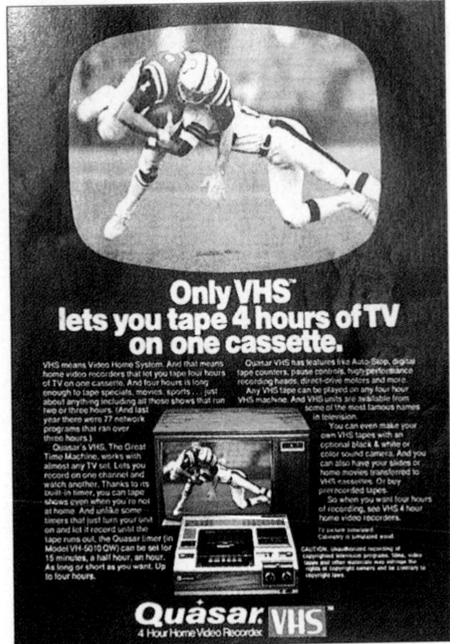

EXHIBIT 1.30

When new, innovative products are first introduced to the market, a type of advertising called primary demand stimulation is often used. Primary demand stimulation attempts to stimulate demand for the entire product category by educating consumers about the values of the product itself, rather than a brand. This ad from the early days of the VHS video cassette recorder is a classic example of primary demand stimulation in a new, innovative product category.

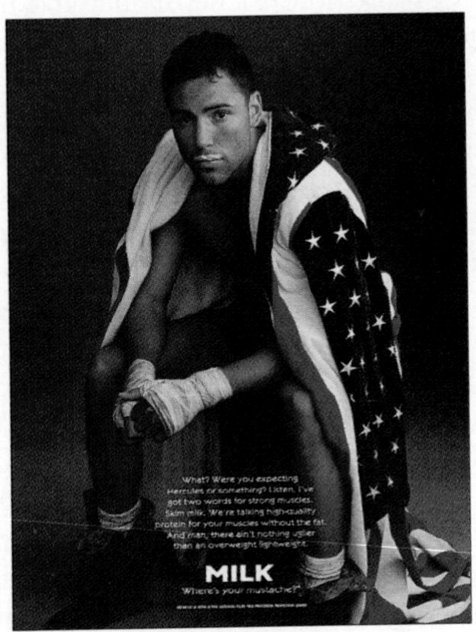

EXHIBIT 1.31

Advertising that attempts to stimulate primary demand is often tried by industry associations and advocacy groups, such as the National Fluid Milk Processor Promotion Board, rather than by specific manufacturers. Trouble is, it doesn't work. Primary demand stimulation has been shown to be ineffective in mature product categories, such as milk, but rather is appropriate for brand promotion. www.gotmilk.org *and* www.elsie.com

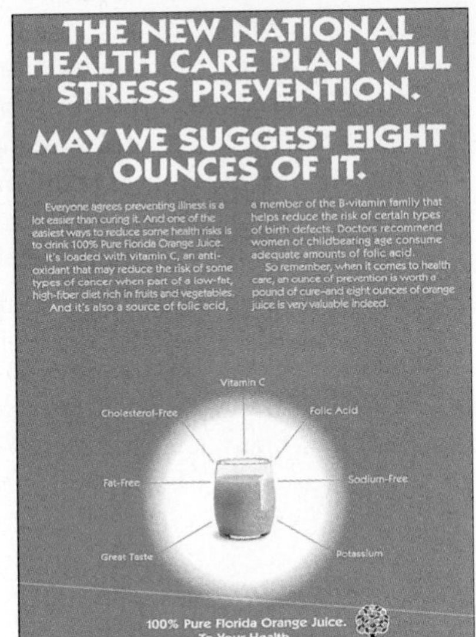

EXHIBIT 1.32

This ad promoting orange juice also attempts to stimulate primary demand, or demand for a product category rather than demand for a particular brand. Decades of literature demonstrate no relationship between aggregate levels of advertising in an industry and overall demand in an industry. It appears that advertising is indeed suited only to selective (brand) demand stimulation. www.floridajuice.com

been invested in the campaign. Even if the attempts at primary demand have reduced the overall decline, it is still not a very impressive result. This should come as no surprise, though. Research has clearly indicated that attempts at primary demand stimulation in mature product categories have never been successful.[26]

While some corporations have tried primary demand stimulation, the true power of advertising is shown when it functions to stimulate demand for a particular company's brand. This is known as selective demand stimulation. The purpose of **selective demand stimulation** advertising is to point out a brand's unique benefits compared to the competition. For example, examine the Tropicana ad in Exhibit 1.33—it touts this *brand's* superiority (contrast this brand ad with the primary demand stimulation ad in Exhibit 1.32). Likewise, now that the VCR is past the stage of primary demand stimulation and is a mature product category, households accept the value of this product and each brand selectively appeals to different consumer needs. Current advertising for VCRs emphasizes brand features such as hi-fi sound, remote control, and voice recognition programming, as Exhibit 1.34 illustrates. This is selective demand stimulation.

Another important type of advertising involves goals related to the immediacy of consumer response. **Direct response advertising** asks the receiver of the message

26. For an excellent summary of decades of research on the topic, see Mark S. Abion and Paul W. Farris, *The Advertising Controversy: Evidence of the Economic Effects of Advertising* (Boston: Auburn House, 1981); J. C. Luik and M. S. Waterson, *Advertising and Markets* (Oxfordshire, England: NTC Publications, 1996).

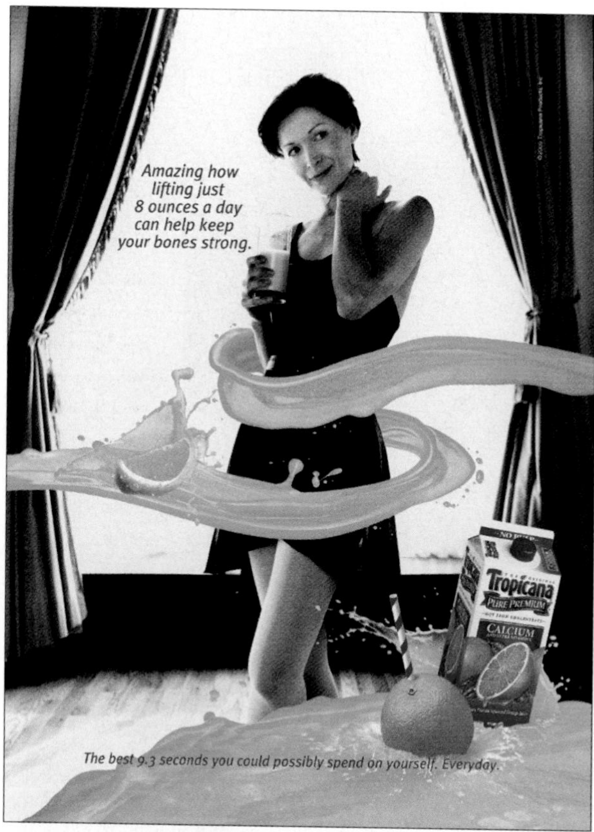

EXHIBIT 1.33

Selective demand stimulation advertising highlights a brand's superiority in providing satisfaction. In this ad, Tropicana touts its superiority as a brand of orange juice. Compare this ad to the primary demand ad in Exhibit 1.32. www.tropicana.com

EXHIBIT 1.34

Once the VHS video cassette recorder became widely adopted, there was no longer a need for primary demand stimulation. Companies turned to the selective brand stimulation process represented by this Toshiba ad. How is this ad different in its message content from the ad in Exhibit 1.30? www.toshiba.com

to act immediately. An ad that suggests that you "call this toll-free number" or "mail your $19.95 before midnight tonight" is an example of direct response advertising. The ad in Exhibit 1.35 is a good example. Here, the company implores consumers to act quickly in order to obtain the Frank Sinatra collector's plate. That's direct response advertising.

While exceptions exist, direct response advertising is most often used for products that consumers are familiar with, that do not require inspection at the point of purchase, and that are relatively low-cost. The proliferation of toll-free numbers and the widespread use of credit cards have been a boon to direct response advertisers.

Delayed response advertising relies on imagery and message themes that emphasize the benefits and satisfying characteristics of a brand. Rather than trying to stimulate an immediate action from an audience, delayed response advertising attempts to develop recognition and approval of a brand over time. In general, delayed response advertising attempts to create brand awareness, reinforce the benefits of using a brand, develop a general liking for the brand, and create an image for a brand. When a consumer enters the purchase process, the information from delayed response advertising comes into play. Most advertisements we see on television and

EXHIBIT 1.35

Direct response advertising asks consumers to take some immediate action. Direct response advertising is most often used with low-price products with which consumers have extensive experience.

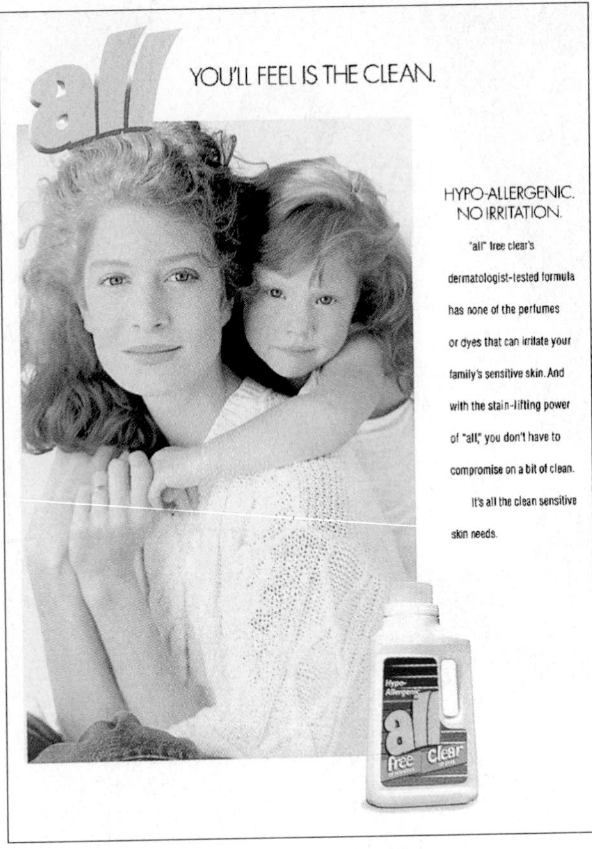

EXHIBIT 1.36

Delayed response advertising attempts to reinforce the benefits of using a brand and create a general liking for the brand. This ad for "all" detergent is an example of delayed response advertising.

in magazines are of the delayed response type. Exhibit 1.36, an ad for hypo-allergenic detergent, provides an example of this common form of advertising. In this ad, the message has as much to do with being a good parent (an image and delayed response message) than with the features of the brand.

Corporate advertising is not designed to promote a specific brand, but rather functions to establish a favorable attitude toward the company as a whole. Prominent users of corporate advertising are Phillips Petroleum, Xerox, and IBM. These firms have long-established corporate campaigns aimed at generating favorable public opinion toward the corporation and its products. This type of advertising can also have an effect on the shareholders of a firm. When shareholders see good corporate advertising, it instills confidence and, ultimately, long-term commitment to the firm and its stock. We'll consider this type of advertising in great detail in Chapter 20.

Another form of corporate advertising is carried out by members of a trade channel. Often, corporate advertising within a trade channel is referred to as *institutional advertising*. Retailers such as Nordstrom, County Seat, and Wal-Mart advertise to persuade consumers to shop at their stores. While these retailers may occasionally feature a particular manufacturer's brand in the advertising (County Seat often features Levi's, in fact), the main purpose of the advertising is to get the audience to shop at their store. Federated Department Stores, for example, invested $160 million in a campaign featuring the retailer's private-label clothing lines—available only at

Federated stores such as Charter Club and INC—that would encourage consumers to shop at Federated outlets.[27]

The Economic Effects of Advertising.

Our discussion of advertising as a business process has focused strictly on the use of advertising by individual business organizations. However, some aspects of advertising relate to broad effects across an entire economic system of a country and beyond.

Advertising's Effect on Gross Domestic Product.

Gross domestic product (GDP) is a measure of the total value of goods and services produced within an economic system. Earlier, we discussed advertising's role in the marketing mix. Recall that, as advertising contributes to marketing mix strategy, it can contribute to sales—along with the right product, the right price, and the right distribution. Because of this role, advertising is related to GDP in that it can contribute to levels of overall consumer demand when it plays a key role in introducing new products, such as VCRs, microcomputers, the Internet, or alternative energy sources. As demand for these new products grows, the resultant consumer spending fuels retail sales, housing starts, and corporate investment in finished goods and capital equipment. Consequently, GDP is affected by sales of products in new, innovative product categories.[28]

Advertising's Effect on Business Cycles.

Advertising can have a stabilizing effect on downturns in business activity. There is evidence that many firms increase advertising during times of recession in an effort to spend their way out of a business downturn. Similarly, there is research to suggest that firms that maintain advertising during a recession perform better afterward, relative to firms that cut advertising spending.[29]

Advertising's Effect on Competition.

Advertising is alleged to stimulate competition and therefore motivate firms to strive for better products, better production methods, and other competitive advantages that ultimately benefit the economy as a whole. Additionally, when advertising serves as a way to enter new markets, competition across the economic system is fostered. For example, Exhibit 1.37 shows an ad in which plastics manufacturers present themselves as competitors to manufacturers of other packaging materials.

Advertising is not universally hailed as a stimulant to competition. Critics point out that the amount of advertising dollars needed to compete effectively in many industries is often prohibitive. As such, advertising can act as a barrier to entry into an industry—that is, a firm may have the capability to compete in an industry in every regard *except* that the advertising expenditures needed to compete are so great that the firm cannot afford to get into the business. In this way, advertising can actually serve to decrease the overall amount of competition in an economy.[30]

Advertising's Effect on Prices.

One of the widely debated effects of advertising has to do with its effect on the prices consumers pay for products and services. Since advertising is a relatively costly process, then products and services would surely cost much less if firms did no advertising. Right? Wrong!

27. Alice Z. Cuneo, "Federated Sets Big Private Label Push," *Advertising Age*, February 16, 1998, 8.

28. There are several historical treatments of how advertising is related to demand. See, for example, Neil H. Borden, *The Economic Effects of Advertising* (Chicago: Richard D. Irwin, 1942), 187–189; and John Kenneth Galbraith, *The New Industrial State* (Boston: Houghton Mifflin, 1967), 203–207.

29. See, for example, Marion L. Elmquist, "100 Leaders Parry Recession with Heavy Spending," *Advertising Age*, September 8, 1983, 1.

30. This argument was well articulated many years ago by Colston E. Warn, "Advertising: A Critic's View," *Journal of Marketing*, vol. 26, no. 4 (October 1962), 12.

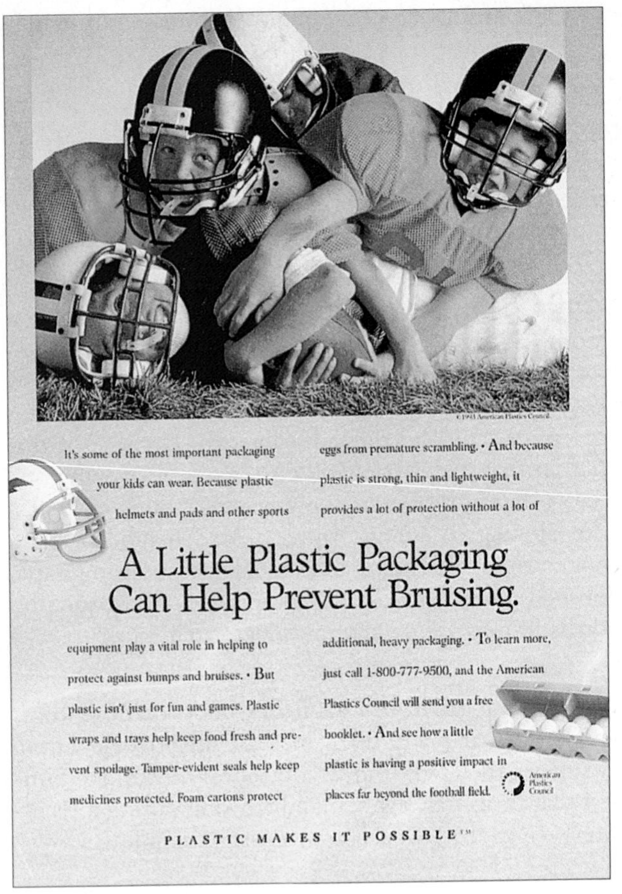

EXHIBIT 1.37

Advertising affects the competitive environment in an economy. This ad by a plastics manufacturers council is fostering competition with manufacturers of other packaging materials.
www.americanplastics-council.org

First, across all industries, advertising costs incurred by firms range from about 1 percent of sales in the automobile and retail industries to about 15 percent of sales in the personal care and luxury products businesses. Exhibit 1.38 shows the ratio of advertising to sales for various firms in selected industries. Notice that there is no consistent and predictable relationship between advertising spending and sales. Honda spent $1,035 million in advertising to generate about $31 billion in sales; L'Oréal spent $987 million on advertising, about $50 million less than Honda, but generated only $3.4 billion in sales; and Wal-Mart spent only $498 million on advertising to generate over $159 billion in sales! Different products and different market conditions demand that firms spend different amounts of money on advertising. These same conditions make it difficult to identify a predictable relationship between advertising and sales.

It is true that the costs for advertising are built into the costs for products, which are ultimately passed on to consumers. But this effect on price must be judged against how much time and effort a consumer would have to spend in searching for a product or service without the benefit of advertising.

Second, the effect of economies of scale, discussed earlier, has a direct impact on prices. Recall that economies of scale serve to lower the cost of production by spreading fixed costs over a large number of units produced. This lower cost can be passed on to consumers in terms of lower prices, as firms search for competitive advantage with lower prices. Nowhere is this effect more dramatic than the price of personal computers. In the early 1980s, an Apple IIe computer that ran at about 1 MHz and had 64K of total memory cost over $3,000. Today, you can get a computer that is several hundred times faster with vastly increased memory and storage for less than $1,000. And it is likely that companies such as Gateway and Dell are spending more today on advertising than Apple did back in the 1980s.

Advertising's Effect on Value. *Value* is the password for successful marketing in the current era. **Value** refers to a perception by consumers that a brand provides satisfaction beyond the cost incurred to acquire that brand. The value perspective of the modern consumer is based on wanting every purchase to be a "good deal." Value is added to the consumption experience by advertising. Recall the discussion of Hardee's versus Wendy's advertising at the beginning of the chapter. Analysts credit the market success of Wendy's over the last several years to the firm's unwavering dedication to the "value" theme. Another argument suggests that advertising contributes to consumer perception of value in an additional but very different way. For example, many advertising professionals and academic researchers believe that the experience of driving a Saab or using L'Oréal cosmetics is significantly enhanced by the expectations advertising has first created and then reinforced within the consumer.

Industry	Advertiser	2000 U.S. Ad Spending (millions)	2000 U.S. Sales (millions)	Advertising Spending as % of Sales
Automobiles				**2.70%**
	General Motors	$3,935	$136,399	2.88
	Ford	2,345	118,373	1.98
	Volkswagen	551	15,749	3.49
	Honda	1,035	31,604	3.27
Computers				**4.90**
	IBM	1,189	37,216	3.19
	Dell	430	21,428	2.00
	Microsoft	855	15,700	5.44
	Intel	773	13,912	5.55
Drugs				**12.50**
	Bristol-Myers Squibb	1,191	12,114	9.80
	Johnson & Johnson	1,601	17,000	9.41
	Bayer	649	8,961	7.24
Food				**11.00**
	ConAgra	578	23,194	2.49
	Nestlé S.A.	638	15,103	4.22
	Kellogg	455	4,067	11.18
	Campbell Soup	331	4,668	7.09
Personal Care				**12.80**
	Procter & Gamble	2,364	20,334	11.62
	Gillette	466	3,756	12.40
	Estée Lauder	717	2,659	26.96
	L'Oréal	987	3,473	28.41
Retail				**5.90**
	JCPenney	1,011	31,846	3.17
	Circuit City Stores	479	12,959	3.69
	Wal-Mart	498	159,229	0.31

Sources: Industry averages were obtained from "2000 Advertising to Sales Ratios for the 200 Largest Ad Spending Industries," *Advertising Age*, July 24, 2000, 44. Advertising spending and sales for individual firms was obtained from "100 Leading National Advertisers," *Advertising Age*, September 24, 2001, S2, S14. Reprinted with permission from the July 29, 2000, and September 24, 2001, issues of *Advertising Age*, Crain Communications Inc., 2000, 2001.

EXHIBIT 1.38

Advertising spending as a proportion of sales in selected industries, 2000 (U.S. dollars in millions).

Advertising also affects a consumer's perception of value by contributing to the symbolic value and the social meaning of a brand. **Symbolic value** refers to what a product or service means to consumers in a nonliteral way. For example, branded clothing such as Guess? jeans or Doc Martens shoes has been said to symbolize self-concept for some consumers. Exhibits 1.39 and 1.40 show examples of ads seeking to create symbolic value for two well-known brands. In reality, all branded products rely to some extent on symbolic value; otherwise they would not be brands, but unmarked commodities.

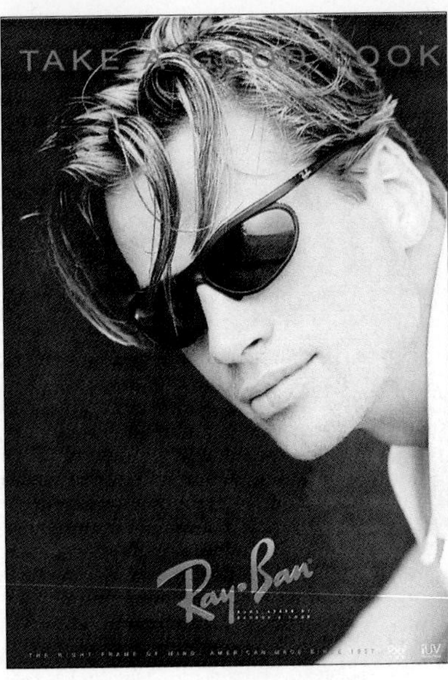

EXHIBITS 1.39 AND 1.40

Advertising contributes to the symbolic value that brands have for consumers. What is it about the ad for Levi's jeans in Exhibit 1.39 and the ad for Ray-Ban sunglasses in Exhibit 1.40 that contribute to the symbolic value of these brands? www.levi.com *and* www.ray-ban.com

EXHIBIT 1.41

Ads communicate social meaning to consumers, as a product or service carries meaning in a societal context beyond its use or purpose. This ad for United Airlines puts the company's service into such a context. www.ual.com

EXHIBITS 1.42 AND 1.43

*Waterford crystal and Gucci watches are two advertised products that consumers will pay premium prices to own. Both products have value in that they epitomize the highest levels of quality craftsmanship. Such craftsmanship, in itself, may not be enough to command premium prices in the marketplace. Advertising that creates an image of exclusivity may also be needed. In what way does the Gucci site (*www.gucci.com*) contribute directly to consumers' perceptions of brand's value? Compare this site to Waterford's site (*www.waterford.com*) and determine which communicates its brand's social meaning most effectively.*

Social meaning refers to what a product or service means in a societal context. For example, social class is marked by any number of products used and displayed to signify class membership, such as cars, beverages, and clothes. Exhibit 1.41 shows an ad for a service with clear social-class connections. Often, the product's connection to a social class addresses a need within consumers to move up in class.

Researchers from various disciplines have long argued that objects are never just objects. They take on meaning from culture, society, and consumers.[31] It is important to remember that these meanings often become just as much a part of the product as some physical feature. Since advertising is an essential way in which the image of a brand is developed, it contributes directly to consumers' perception of the value of the brand. The more value consumers see in a brand, the more they are willing to pay to acquire the brand. If the image of a Gucci watch, a Lexus coupe, or a Four Seasons hotel is valued by consumers, then consumers will pay a premium to acquire that value. Waterford crystal and Gucci watches, shown in Exhibits 1.42 and 1.43, are examples of products that consumers pay premiums to own.

5 **From Integrated Marketing Communications to Integrated Brand Promotion.** As we discussed in the section on advertising's role in the marketing mix, it is important to recognize that advertising is only one of many promotional tools available. It is not always the main choice of companies because in many situations, another tool, such as targeted e-mail, event sponsorship, or direct mail, is better suited to the task at hand. Firms such as Levi Strauss, featured in the IBP box on page 38, often employ a wide range of promotional tools to achieve desired communications coverage and results. Another example is PepsiCo. PepsiCo spends over $2.1 billion a year in advertising.[32] But the firm also spends tens of millions of dollars a year giving away samples to urban youth. Their promotions feature UPS-style vans that visit urban areas such as Philadelphia, Cleveland, and San Francisco, blasting music and giving away samples of Mountain Dew as a way to support the advertising effort.[33]

For the last 10 years or so, the concept of mixing various promotional tools has generally been referred to as integrated marketing communications.[34] **Integrated marketing communications (IMC)** is the process of using promotional tools in a unified way so that a synergistic communication effect is created. But as the discussion earlier in the chapter highlighted, the current thinking is that the emphasis on communication is not as important as the emphasis on the brand. The result is that there has been a recent evolution from an integrated marketing communications perspective to an integrated brand promotion perspective.[35]

Recall from the definition earlier in the chapter that integrated brand promotion (IBP) is the use of various communication tools, including advertising, in a coordinated manner to build and maintain brand awareness, identity, and preference. The distinction between IBP and IMC is pretty obvious. IMC emphasizes the communication effort, per se, and the need for coordinated and synergistic messages. IBP retains the emphasis on coordination and synergy, but goes beyond the parameters of IMC. In integrated brand promotion, the emphasis is on the brand and not just the communication. With a focus on building brand awareness, identity, and ultimately preference, the IBP perspective recognizes that coordinated promotional messages need to have brand-building effects and not just communication effects.

31. For a historical perspective, see Ernest Ditcher, *Handbook of Consumer Motivations* (New York: McGraw-Hill, 1964), 6. For a contemporary view, see David Glenn Mic and Claus Buhl, "A Meaning-Based Model of Advertising Experiences," *Journal of Consumer Research,* vol. 19 (December 1992), 312–338.

32. "100 Leading National Advertisers," *Advertising Age,* September 24, 2001, S14.

33. Kate MacArthur and Hillary Chura, "Urban Warefare," *Advertising Age,* September 4, 2000, 16–17.

34. Don E. Schultz, Stanley Tannenbaum, and Robert Lauterborn, *Integrated Marketing Communications* (Lincolnwood, Ill.: NTC Books, 1993).

35. A signal of this change is the most recent edition of Don Schultz's IMC book, which is no longer called IMC. Schultz has changed the name to *Strategic Brand Communication Campaigns.* The full citation is Don E. Schultz and Beth E. Barnes, *Strategic Brand Communication Campaigns,* (Lincolnwood, Ill.: NTC Books, 1999).

Because of the growing importance of IBP to the advertising industry, IBP issues are raised throughout this book in special boxes that highlight the strategy and coordination challenges of every aspect of advertising. In addition, five distinct sections of this book are devoted to a rich case history that features a real-life application of IBP. These five sections conclude each of the major parts of the book, parallel the emphasis of the text, and feature the complete story of the application of IBP concepts by Cincinnati Bell in its marketing of a new, wireless phone service:

- Part 1—*Cincinnati Bell Wireless*: From IMC to IBP
- Part 2—*Cincinnati Bell Wireless*: Planning Advertising and Integrated Brand Promotion
- Part 3—*Cincinnati Bell Wireless*: Preparing Advertising and Integrated Brand Promotion
- Part 4—*Cincinnati Bell Wireless*: The Launch Campaign
- Part 5—*Cincinnati Bell Wireless*: Sustaining and Growing the Brand after Launch

These special IBP sections are easy to find because each begins with the distinctive color scheme that designates our Cincinnati Bell Wireless case. These sections focus on the real-world challenges faced by Cincinnati Bell during the planning, development, and execution of nearly two years of brand-building activity for Cincinnati Bell Wireless. Cincinnati Bell, a Broadwing Company, and its advertising agency, Northlich, have generously provided their advertising and other brand promotion materials for use in this text. We believe that IBP is an important enough consideration in contemporary communications and promotion that its role alongside the advertising effort deserves comprehensive assessment. The materials and expertise gained in working with our corporate partners allow us to provide a comprehensive case history that offers a truly unique learning opportunity on the forefront of advertising and integrated brand promotion.

IBP

Going Out and Finding the Market

For a brand that has been associated for decades with youthful rebellion, Levi's has an interesting problem: teenage indifference. While Levi's has successfully followed baby boomers into adulthood and middle age with jeans tailored to a changing body and new "casual" clothes like Dockers, the firm has lost its grip on teenagers. The firm completely missed the baggy rebellion of youth—including the droopy shorts.

The problem is not minimal. Levi's market share among kids is down from 33 percent to 26 percent. What is worse is the way kids talk about Levi's. Company executives were forced to endure video after video of focus group sessions in which teens talked about Levi Strauss as if it were a has-been—saying the jeans were uncool or only suited for their parents or older brothers and sisters. Meanwhile, competitors were attacking kids from the top and bottom—Tommy Hilfiger and Ralph Lauren on the top and JCPenney and Sears on the bottom. As one consultant put it, Levi Strauss was zagging while the world was zigging. But Levi Strauss does have a response. The company's SilverTab brand is very popular among more stylish young consumers. The brand has a median age of 18 for purchasers. It has a baggier fit and is on the right side of the fashion line.

So how does Levi's take advantage of this brand opportunity? By developing an exciting and effective integrated brand promotion (IBP) program. Along with traditional magazine and television advertising—the mainstays of marketing clothes to teens—the firm has a wide array of new and different ways to reach teens. One of the key tactics in the IBP program is a partnership with SFX Entertainment—the $1.7-billion-a-year entertainment giant that owns the largest network of live-event venues in the United States. In partnership with SFX, Levi's launched a sponsorship program called 1st Stage. Through the sponsorship, local bands will perform on permanent stages at 26 SFX-owned amphitheaters: the perfect vehicle for reaching the youth market. In addition, Levi's gets double coverage at the venues when it sponsors one of the major SFX touring shows such as Christina Aguilera. As Sheri Timmons, Levi's director of sponsorships, put it, "They let us bring the program to a much wider audience."

The use of various tools, such as sponsorships, beyond major advertising is a way to reinforce the brand advertising themes and reach teens in different and interesting ways—classic integrated brand promotion. The trick will be to keep the company name viable among the Bob Dylan set.

Source: Linda Himelstein, "Levi's Is Hiking Up Its Pants," *Business Week*, December 1, 1997, 70, 75; Peter Breen, "All Access Pass," *PROMO Magazine*, September 2000, 70–73.

SUMMARY

Know what advertising is and what it can do.

Since advertising has become so pervasive, it would be reasonable to expect that you might have your own working definition for this critical term. But an informed perspective on advertising goes beyond what is obvious and can be seen on a daily basis. Advertising is distinctive and recognizable as a form of communication by its three essential elements: its paid sponsorship, its use of mass media, and its intent to persuade. An advertisement is a specific message that an advertiser has placed to persuade or inform an audience. An advertising campaign is a series of ads with a common theme also placed to persuade or inform an audience over a specified period of time.

Discuss a basic model of advertising communication.

Advertising cannot be effective unless some form of communication takes place between the advertiser and the audience. But advertising is about mass communication. There are many models that might be used to help explain how advertising works or does not work as a communication platform. The model introduced in this chapter features basic considerations such as the message-production process versus the message-reception process, and this model says that consumers create their own meanings when they interpret advertisements.

Describe the different ways of classifying audiences for advertising.

While it is possible to provide a simple and clear definition of what advertising is, it is also true that advertising takes many forms and serves different purposes from one application to another. One way to appreciate the complexity and diversity of advertising is to classify it by audience category or by geographic focus. For example, advertising might be directed at households or government officials. Using another perspective, it can be global or local in its focus.

Explain the key roles of advertising as a business process.

Many different types of organizations use advertising to achieve their business purposes. For major multinational corporations, such as Procter & Gamble, and for smaller more localized businesses, such as the San Diego Zoo, advertising is one part of a critical business process known as marketing. Advertising is one element of the marketing mix; the other key elements are the firm's products, their prices, and the distribution network. Advertising must work in conjunction with these other marketing mix elements if the organization's marketing objectives are to be achieved. It is important to recognize that of all the roles played by advertising in the marketing process, none is more important than contributing to building brand awareness and brand equity. Similarly, firms have turned to more diverse methods of communication beyond advertising that we have referred to as integrated brand promotion. That is, firms are using communication tools such as public relations, sponsorship, direct marketing, sales promotion, and others along with advertising to achieve communication goals.

Understand the concept of integrated brand promotion (IBP) and the role advertising plays in the process.

Integrated brand promotion (IBP) is the use of various promotional tools, including advertising, in a coordinated manner to build and maintain brand awareness, identity, and preference. When marketers use advertising in conjunction with other promotional tools, this creates an integrated brand promotion that highlights brand features and value. Note that the word *coordinated* is central to this definition. Over the last 30 years, the advertising and promotion industry has evolved to recognize that integration and coordination of promotional elements is key to effective communication and lasting brand identity.

KEY TERMS

advertising
client, or sponsor
advertisement
advertising campaign
integrated brand promotion (IBP)
audience
target audience
household consumers
members of business organizations
members of a trade channel
professionals
government officials and employees
global advertising
international advertising
national advertising
regional advertising
local advertising
cooperative advertising, or co-op advertising
marketing
marketing mix
brand
brand extension
brand loyalty
brand equity
market segmentation
differentiation
positioning
external position
internal position
economies of scale
inelasticity of demand
primary demand stimulation
selective demand stimulation
direct response advertising
delayed response advertising
corporate advertising
gross domestic product (GDP)
value
symbolic value
social meaning
integrated marketing communications (IMC)

QUESTIONS

1. What does it mean when we say that advertising is intended to persuade? How do different ads persuade in different ways?

2. Explain the differences between regional advertising, local advertising, and cooperative advertising. What would you look for in an ad to identify it as a cooperative ad?

3. How do the goals of direct response and delayed response advertising differ? How would you explain marketers' growing interest in direct response advertising?

4. When can a firm use global advertising? How does global advertising differ from international advertising?

5. Give an example of an advertising campaign that you know has been running for more than one year. Why do some advertising campaigns last for years, whereas others come and go in a matter of months?

6. If a firm developed a new line of athletic shoes, priced them competitively, and distributed them in appropriate retail shops, would there be any need for advertising? Is advertising really needed for a good product that is priced right?

7. Many companies now spend millions of dollars to sponsor and have their names associated with events such as stock-car races or rock concerts. Do these event sponsorships fit the definition for advertising given in this chapter?

8. How does the process of market segmentation lead an organization to spend its advertising dollars more efficiently and more effectively?

9. What does it mean to say that a brand has symbolic value? Is there any good reason to believe that consumers will actually pay higher prices for brands with the right symbolic value?

10. What is the concept of integrated brand promotion (IBP)? How are IBP and advertising related?

EXPERIENTIAL EXERCISES

1. In this chapter, audiences for advertising were divided into five broad audience categories. For each, find one ad that appears to be targeted to members of that audience. Analyze the message and style of each ad and determine whether the message seems effective, given the intended audience category. Why was the ad effective or ineffective? Did you have difficulty locating ads for any specific audience category? If so, explain why you think that might have occurred and what it reveals about the nature and methods of advertising to that audience category.

2. Very few advertisements or brands have the same appeal to all consumers worldwide. Advertisers must therefore strategically place ads based on geographic regions. List four favorite products or brands that you use in your everyday life. For each, decide whether it is appropriate to advertise the product at the global, international, national, regional, local, or cooperative level. Explain your answer.

USING THE INTERNET

1-1 What Is Advertising?

As a part of the recent settlement between the tobacco industry and attorneys general in 46 states, the Truth campaign is dedicated to distributing facts about the harmful effects of tobacco use, especially among young people. Run by the nonprofit American Legacy Foundation, the campaign gets its message out through TV, radio, magazines, and the Internet in the hopes of preventing the spread of tobacco use among its target audience while encouraging higher ethical standards for tobacco advertisers.

Truth: www.thetruth.com

1. Browse around the Truth Web site and describe its features. What audience category does the Truth campaign appear to be targeting?

2. What criteria need to be met for the Truth campaign to be considered advertising? Based on these criteria, should this campaign be classified as advertising?

3. List an advertising campaign that you have seen or heard recently that cannot be considered advertising and explain why.

1-2 Advertising as a Business Process

The wireless revolution is bringing about a whole new communications network based on computing devices that keep people connected to their work and lifestyle from almost any location. The race to supply consumers with instant e-mail and Internet access on handheld devices has increased the importance of advertising in the overall marketing and brand promotion programs of wireless-product manufacturers.

Palm: www.palm.com

1. What is a brand? Give reasons why the Palm brand name is so significant to the successful marketing of the company's computing products.

2. Using the text, list one of the ways advertising affects brand development and management, and give an example of how the Palm site accomplishes this.

3. Explain how the term *value* relates to the popularity of wireless computing products among your peer groups. Be sure to use the concepts of symbolic value and social meaning in your answer.

CHAPTER 1
Advertising as a Process

CHAPTER 2
The Structure of the Advertising Industry: Advertisers, Advertising Agencies, and Support Organizations

CHAPTER 3
The Evolution of Advertising

CHAPTER 4
Social, Ethical, and Regulatory Aspects of Advertising

CHAPTER 2

After reading and thinking about this chapter, you will be able to do the following:

Discuss six important trends transforming the advertising industry.

Describe the size, structure, and participants in the advertising industry.

Discuss the role played by advertising and promotion agencies, the services provided by these agencies, and how they are compensated.

Identify key external facilitators who assist in planning and executing advertising and integrated brand promotion campaigns.

Discuss the role played by media organizations in executing effective advertising and integrated brand promotion campaigns.

I am blue
How fast is online advertising changing? Whoops, you just lost ground to your biggest competitor. Yet the demands to provide rich, versatile, accountable, on-time solutions never seem to lessen. So you have a choice: Stay ahead, or you're toast. Whoops, they just did it to you again. That's why I am blue. JONN BEHRMAN CEO BEYOND INTERACTIVE
bluestreak
Get Results. Get Serious. | www.bluestreak.com | 401-341-3300

This was just the kind of situation that Madison Avenue veterans had come to hate. A "hot" new dot-com ad agency was getting the chance to pitch for the business of a well-established brand marketed by a traditional consumer products firm. The brand was Lipton Brisk—America's best-selling ready-to-drink iced tea. The advertiser was Pepsi-Lipton Tea Partnership (a joint venture between PepsiCo and Unilever). The Madison Avenue veteran (at 32 years old) was Kevin Wassong. Wassong was in charge of the Web marketing unit for J. Walter Thompson (JWT). JWT, a 136-year-old, full-service agency, had been handling all aspects of the Lipton Brisk account for its client, the Pepsi-Lipton Partnership. But the word on the street was that executives at Pepsi-Lipton weren't sure that their traditional full-service agency was up to the task of taking the Lipton Brisk brand effectively to the Web—Web marketing unit or not. Wassong's job was to convince the client that JWT could do more than produce effective television spots for the brand and that it could provide a seamless marketing and advertising strategy across all media—including the Web. Wassong was anxious about the pitch, but not pessimistic. After all, it was JWT that had created the popular, lovable, and widely recognized wisecracking Claymation puppet versions of Frank Sinatra, Elvis, James Brown, Babe Ruth, and Bruce Willis that had honed Lipton Brisk's contemporary and sassy image (see Exhibit 2.1).

The day of the competition for the account, Wassong presented a broad, integrated brand promotion campaign concept to the Lipton Brisk marketing team and an Internet marketing specialist from Unilever. Joint promotions were a key ingredient. As an example, the brand would be featured on the entertainment Web site E Online. The Frank Sinatra or Elvis Claymation puppet would appear on the site at key times, such as during the Oscars or the MTV music awards. But Wassong made a key tactical error. His proposal did not include a Web site for the brand—something he considered superfluous to the brand-building effort.

After the JWT pitch, two young executives from Agency.com Ltd. strode confidently into the conference room. They immediately launched into a high-energy presentation that showcased Web sites the firm had designed for high-profile clients such as British Airways, Compaq, Sprint, and 3M. The Agency.com team continued to emphasize their "e-savvy" throughout the pitch. Pepsi-Lipton executives commented at the time that the Agency.com presentation offered options and scenarios for using the Web that were easy for them to understand.[1] A week later, Kevin Wassong learned that Agency.com won the assignment.

But early in this new relationship with a hot e-agency, Brisk marketing strategists learned that this might not be as easy as it seemed during the campaign pitch. The Brisk advertisers were intent on translating the highly successful Brisk offline brand image to the Web. This is the image, created largely by the mouthy Claymation characters, that had earned the brand an industry-leading 25.8 percent market share. The marketing team leader for Brisk showed the Agency.com team the brand's TV spots and explained that this was a "fun" brand. Agency.com had other ideas. It wanted to bring its "new economy," e-agency irreverence to the process. For example, a key feature of the Web site would be a game that locked the Claymation puppets in mortal combat with each other. That was Agency.com's idea of fun. The Lipton Brisk executives were taken aback by the prospect. Yes, it was edgy and very dot-com. But the idea of a gladiator battle between Brisk's hallowed icons was unthinkable. "We're not mean-spirited toward the heroes," pleaded Michael Hartman, Lipton's marketing director. "We're a gentle parody."[2]

From the mortal combat idea, it continued to go downhill. The Brisk team felt that Agency.com continued to come back with ideas that were inappropriate for the Lipton Brisk image and showed a lack of real understanding of the brand.

1. Kathryn Kranhold, "Iced-Tea Bottler Finds Silicon Alley Ad Firm Too Cool for Its Taste," *Wall Street Journal,* July 21, 2000, A1.
2. Ibid., A4.

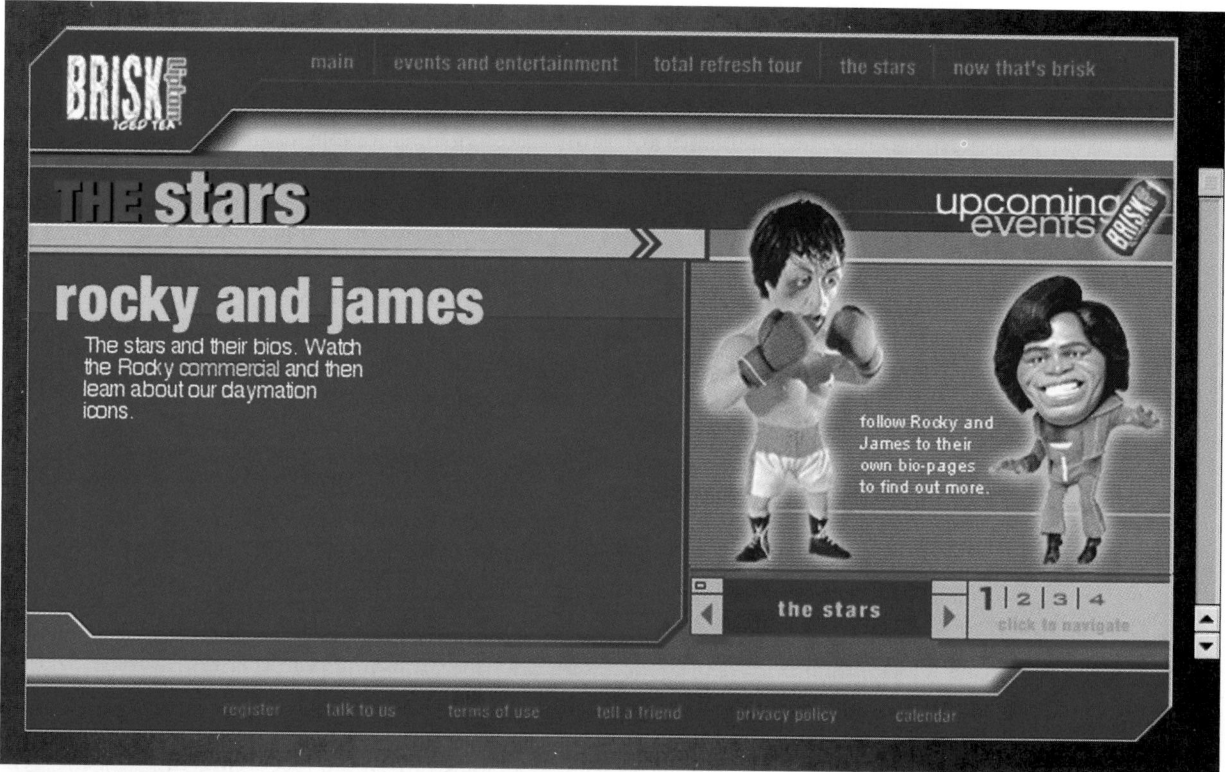

EXHIBIT 2.1

JWT created the popular, lovable, and widely recognized wisecracking Claymation puppet versions of Frank Sinatra, Elvis, James Brown, Babe Ruth, and Bruce Willis that were highly successful in developing Lipton Brisk's contemporary and sassy image. www.lipton.com

After four turbulent months during which Agency.com rotated various personnel in and out of the Brisk account, signed a deal with Coca-Cola (advertisers of Nestea and Pepsi's arch rival), and showed vacillating interest in Brisk brand work, Agency.com and Pepsi-Lipton mutually agreed to a parting of ways. The Brisk team leader called Kevin Wassong and asked if he would be willing to discuss the account again. Six months later, JWT launched an integrated campaign for Lipton Brisk featuring new TV spots and Babe Ruth as the host of a trivia quiz on ESPN.com. A month later, the full lineup of Claymation characters appeared on Sony's Web site partaking in a lively game of Jeopardy. Essentially, this campaign was a comprehensive integrated brand promotion led by television advertising supported by Web-based joint promotions—the original idea presented by JWT 18 months earlier.

The Advertising Industry in Transition.

The story of Lipton-Brisk signals the dynamic, complex, and changing nature of the advertising industry. We will examine the full range of these changes throughout the chapter. But first we need to realize that the fundamental process of advertising and the role it plays in organizations remains steadfastly rooted in persuasive communications directed at target audiences. This cannot change and has not changed.

But we need to appreciate that the advertising industry is in a state of constant transition, and is an industry with great breadth and complexity. Central to this complexity is the fact that we are dealing with communications. This is where we will turn our attention now—to understanding how advertising and other promotional tools are managed in a communications industry to create brand relationships. First, we will look at the advertising industry as a fairly well-structured communications industry. Then, we will consider all the different participants—particularly the advertisers and their advertising agencies—and the role they play in creating and executing advertising and integrated brand promotions.

1 Trends Affecting the Advertising Industry. What has changed over the last 10 years and what strategists at Pepsi-Lipton were struggling with is that the structure of the advertising industry is (again) in transition. How has the industry changed, and how is it continuing to change? Interactive media options, agency structure, client demands for immediate and measurable results, and creative techniques are just a few of the aspects of the industry undergoing significant and fundamental change. These changes were highlighted by the difficulty Pepsi-Lipton decision makers had with the choice between using J. Walter Thompson's interactive unit versus a hot e-agency like Agency.com. But in the end what was important was not the Web itself or the technology it had to offer, but rather the critical need to focus on the Brisk brand image and a persuasive, integrated presentation of the brand to the target market of consumers.

The central issues in the Lipton Brisk story, however, highlight just a few of the key aspects of change that are affecting the structure of the advertising industry. The structure of the advertising industry and key processes in the industry are being altered by six important trends:

1. *Consolidation and globalization.* The advertising industry has entered a period of extreme consolidation, which is occurring in two ways. Full-service agencies are acquiring and merging with other full-service agencies and interactive shops. One such merger was Leo Burnett with the MacManus group, which created a $1.7-billion-a-year agency with 500 operating units in 90 countries with 16,000 employees (now known as Bcom3 Group).[3] To add globalization to the Burnett/MacManus merger, the Japanese agency Dentsu took a partnership position in the agreement as well. Globalization is also occurring through mergers and acquisitions as well. In 2000, over $7 billion was paid in mergers and acquisitions for agencies in France, England, and Germany.[4]
2. *Budget fragmentation.* As Chapter 1 highlighted, a high degree of integration across all brand advertising and promotional efforts is being sought by advertisers. By virtue of this integration, fragmentation of marketing budgets within companies has occurred, with a greater proportion of these budgets going to other forms of promotion. One result of this trend is that agencies are becoming more diversified in the services offered to clients. The pure "ad agency" is, in many ways, a thing of the past. For example, in the last six years, the Interpublic Group has acquired public relations firms, event planning companies, and direct marketing companies, and has invested in 16 interactive companies.[5] Similarly, diversification to serve a broader range of client needs is occurring among promotion agencies. As an example, the Lake Capital investment group acquired the promotions firm DVC Group with the intention of developing a global network of promotion shops in the areas of direct marketing, events, and Internet programs.[6]
3. *Interactivity.* Historically, advertisers have controlled information and the flow of information—it was a one-way communication Now consumers are in greater control of the information they receive about product categories and the brands within those categories. And they also give information back to the firm. E-mail and tracking of Internet surfing behavior are two examples. This has helped create a brand relationship between advertisers and consumers where advertising communication needs to be sensitive to the interactive nature of the communication environment.[7] Perhaps "sensitive" is putting it too mildly. One research firm estimates that just one interactive device, personal video recorders (PVRs),

3. Laura Petrecca and Hillary Chura, "Merged Leo-MacManus Could Be Valued at $5 Billion," *Advertising Age,* November 8, 1999, 3.
4. Wendy Davis and Laura Q. Hughes, "Deutsch Now Part of Interpublic Empire," *Advertising Age,* December 4, 2000, 58.
5. Kathryn Kranhold, "Interpublic Group Agrees to Buy 40% of Caribiner," *Wall Street Journal,* March 14, 2000, B10.
6. Kerry E. Smith, "Consolidators Come, Maybe Go," *PROMO Magazine,* December 2000, 49.
7. Tom Duncan and Sandra Moriarty, "Brand Relationships Key to the Agency of the Future," *Advertising Age,* October 18, 1999, 44.

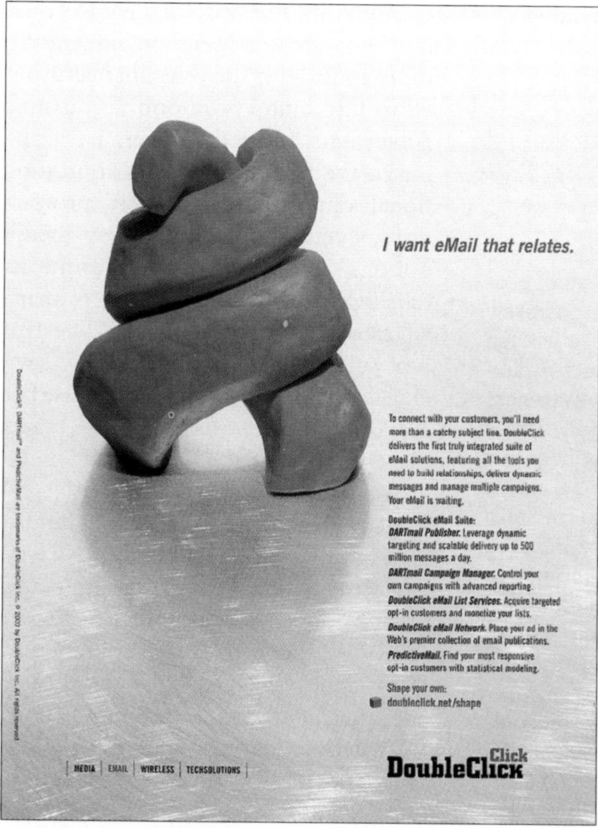

EXHIBIT 2.2

The proliferation of media alternatives has caused media fragmentation in the advertising industry. One effect of this change in the industry is that new specialized media organizations have emerged to sell and manage new media options. DoubleClick is one of these new media companies that manages targeted e-mail messages. www.doubleclick.net

which allow TV viewers to essentially "skip" broadcast advertising, will reduce ad viewership by as much as 30 percent by 2005. That translates into taking approximately $18 billion out of advertising industry revenue.[8] Advertisers will need to adapt to the concept that interactivity allows consumers greater control over the information they choose to receive.

4. *Media evolution.* The proliferation of cable television, direct marketing technology, and alternative new media has caused media fragmentation. Media fragmentation has spawned new specialized agencies to sell and manage the new media options (see Exhibit 2.2). But fragmentation is only one aspect of the media evolution. The really big news is the emergence of broadband as a reality. **Broadband** (actually short for *broad bandwidth*) is a high-speed network providing the capability of transmitting video as well as voice transmission over the Internet. What this means for advertisers is that "the emotional experiences that come naturally in TV will pervade the Internet, so you'll start to see broadband and interactive TV becoming one and the same thing."[9] By 2004, it is estimated that 15 percent of U.S. households (about 16 million households and 40 million people) will have broadband connections.[10] Because they are innovators, this is not a group that advertisers can take lightly.
5. *Media clutter.* A growing investment in advertising, from television ads to billboards to banner ads on the Internet, has resulted in so much clutter that the probability of any one advertisement breaking through and making a real difference continues to diminish. With a lack of faith in advertising alone, promotion options such as online communication, brand placement in film and television, point-of-purchase displays, and sponsorships are more attractive to advertisers. For example, advertisers on the Super Bowl, notorious for its clutter and outrageous ad prices ($2.5 to $3 million for a 30-second spot), have turned to promotional tie-ins to enhance the effect of the advertising. Miller Brewing distributed thousands of inflatable Miller Lite chairs by game day for Super Bowl 2001. The chairs were a tie-in with a national advertising campaign that began in November 2000.[11]
6. *Communication/distribution channels.* New communication/distribution channels are emerging in the context of e-commerce. These new communication/distribution links include catalogs, TV shopping networks, and especially the online shopping and interactive television cited earlier. Consumers do not just want a communications experience, they want a "commerce experience."[12] This topic is covered in detail in Chapter 19.

8. Russ Banham, "Advertising's Future," *Forbes Critical Mass,* Fall 2000, 54.
9. Ibid., 58.
10. Anna Bernasek, "How Broadband Adds Up," *Fortune,* October 9, 2000, 28–29.
11. Betsy Spethmann, "Pre-Game Warmups," *PROMO Magazine,* December 2000, 33–34.
12. Lauren Barack, "Chiat's New Day," *Business 2.0,* December 1999, 130–132.

As a result of these changes, advertisers are rethinking the way they try to communicate with consumers. Fundamentally, there is a greater focus on integrating more tools with the overall advertising effort into brand promotion programs. Advertisers, more than ever, are looking to the full complement of promotional opportunities in sales promotions, event sponsorships, new media options, and public relations as means to support and enhance the primary advertising effort for brands. The IBP box on this page highlights how several firms in the luxury brand market are using public relations and brand placements in celebrity settings to grow brand visibility and value.

For years to come, these fundamental changes will affect the way advertisers think about advertising and promotional communications. In response, advertising agencies will think about the way they serve their clients, and the way communications are delivered to audiences. Big spenders such as Procter & Gamble, Nestlé, and General Motors are already demanding new and innovative programs to enhance the impact of their promotional dollars. While the goal of persuasive communication remains intact—attract attention and develop preference for a brand—the dynamics of the marketplace and the changes it is causing in the structure of the advertising industry are the central topic of this chapter.

IBP

See the Brand, Join the Club

Most advertisers have embraced the concept that a wide range of promotional tools is essential for reaching target markets and positively affecting brand awareness and image. But few advertisers have needed the full range of integrated brand promotion strategies as much as luxury brand marketers, who need to not only maintain brand awareness but also to protect their brands from counterfeit brands. These "knockoffs" of luxury brands like Gucci, Hermes, and Rolex continue to be a problem. In the summer of 2000, "Power Beads" became a nationwide craze. The bead bracelet from New York design firm Stella Pace was the must-have accessory for the fashion conscious. But Zoe Metro, who conceived the bead designs and founded the company, lamented, "I've been a case study for these knockoffs." While the real thing, made from semi-precious stones, sold for $35 in upscale jewelry stores, knockoffs of the Power Beads were showing up in discount stores for as little as $5.

The answer to the knockoff problem? Experts say that the only solution is to continue to make the brand itself, not the object, the thing consumers covet. That, the experts continue, requires advertising plus a heavy investment in public relations, merchandising, and brand placements. The president of a brand consulting firm in New York argues, "There's a three dimensionality that builds these brands. It's not just advertising. Everything builds the brand from the advertising to the store experience to the Web site." The vice president of marketing for Louis Vuitton adds, "It's a top-to-bottom brand concept. PR is very important in helping these brands establish themselves. People are always trying to place their products in the right programs and with the right people because it adds validity to the brand." Ms. Metro credits the original success of Power Beads to celebrity plugs and coverage of the brand's popularity in the fashion media.

The formula of advertising plus integrated brand promotion strategies must be working for these luxury brand marketers. Despite the aggressiveness of the counterfeiters, Interbrand research found that luxury brands like Louis Vuitton and Chanel have been enjoying 30 to 60 percent growth, while the Gap and Nike have shown little or no growth in the last few years.

Source: Mercedes M. Cardona, "Trendsetting Brands Combat Knockoffs," *Advertising Age*, August 21, 2000, 20.

2 The Scope and Structure of the Advertising Industry.

To fully appreciate the structure of the advertising industry, let's first consider the size of the advertising industry. Remember from Chapter 1 that the advertising industry is huge—about $250 billion spent in the U.S. alone on various categories of advertising, with over $450 billion spent worldwide.[13]

Another indicator of the scope of advertising is the investment made by individual firms. Exhibit 2.3 shows spending for 1999 and 2000 among the top 20 U.S. advertisers. Hundreds of millions of dollars—and in the case of the largest spenders, even billions of dollars—is truly a huge amount of money to spend annually on advertising. But we have to realize that the $3.9 billion spent by General Motors on

13. R. Craig Endicott, "100 Leading National Advertisers," *Advertising Age*, September 24, 2001, S12.

EXHIBIT 2.3

The 20 largest advertisers in the United States in 2000 (U.S. dollars in millions).

Company	2000 Ad Dollars (millions)	1999 Ad Dollars (millions)	% Change
General Motors	$3,934	$4,118	–4.5%
Philip Morris	2,602	2,527	3.0
Procter & Gamble	2,363	2,694	–12.3
Ford Motor Co.	2,345	2,111	11.1
Pfizer	2,265	2,142	5.7
PepsiCo.	2,100	2,010	4.5
DailmerChrysler	1,984	1,801	10.1
AOL Time Warner	1,770	1,523	16.2
Walt Disney Co.	1,757	1,545	13.7
Verizon Communications	1,612	977	65.0
Johnson & Johnson	1,601	1,666	–3.9
Sears Roebuck & Co.	1,455	1,460	–0.3
Unilever	1,453	1,225	18.6
AT&T	1,415	1,430	–1.0
General Electric	1,310	1,111	17.9
Toyota Motor	1,273	1,124	13.3
McDonald's	1,273	1,203	5.8
U.S. Government	1,246	1,010	23.3
Sprint Corp.	1,227	932	31.6
ViaCom	1,220	1,189	2.6

Source: "100 Leading National Advertisers," *Advertising Age*, September 24, 2001, S2.

advertising was just 3 percent of GM's sales. Similarly, Sears spent $1.5 billion, but this amount represented only about 3 percent of its sales. So, while the absolute dollars are large, the relative spending is much more modest. Overall, the 100 leading advertisers in the United States spent $83 billion on advertising in 2000, which was a healthy 7.6 percent increase over 1999.[14] Still, there is no doubt that this rapidly increasing spending is related to increased clutter. Advertising may be quickly becoming its own worst enemy. Exhibit 2.4 shows the increase in advertising across the 20th century.

Beyond the scope of spending, the structure of the industry is really the key issue. When we understand the structure of the advertising industry, we know *who* does *what, in what order,* during the advertising process. The advertising industry is actually a collection of a wide range of talented people, all of whom have specialized expertise and perform necessary tasks in planning, preparing, and placing of advertising. Exhibit 2.5 shows the structure of the advertising industry by showing who the different participants are in the process.

Exhibit 2.5 demonstrates that *advertisers* (such as Kellogg) can employ the services of *advertising agencies* (such as Grey Advertising) that may (or may not) contract for

14. Ibid., S2.

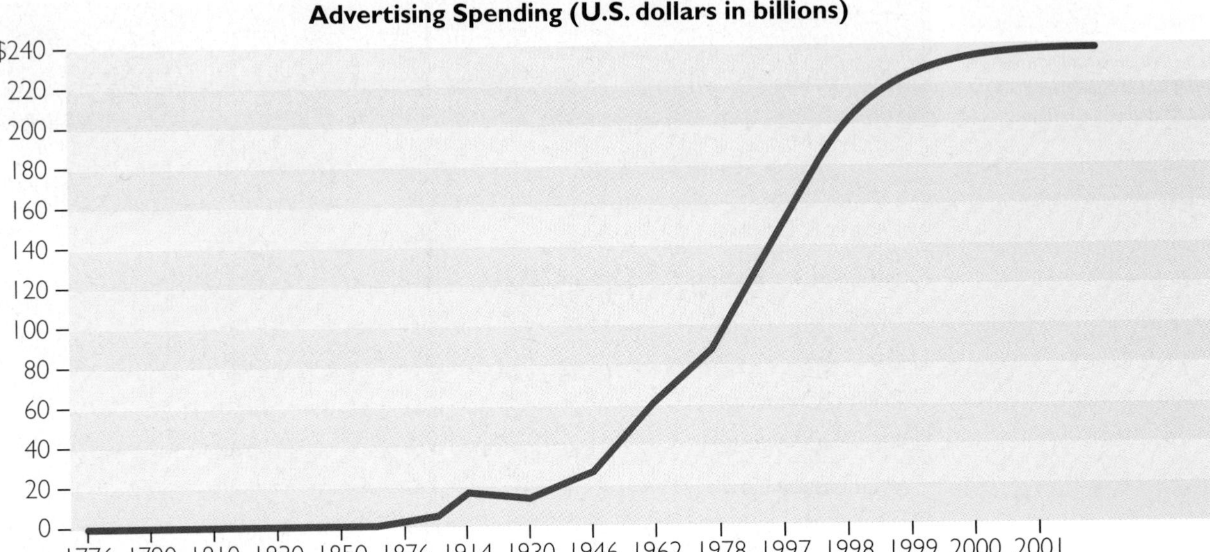

Source: "100 Leading National Advertisers," *Advertising Age*, annual estimates.

EXHIBIT 2.4

A graph of advertising spending throughout the 20th century.

specialized services with various *external facilitators* (such as Simmons Market Research), which results in advertising being transmitted with the help of various *media organizations* (such as the Nickelodeon cable network) to one or more *target audiences* (such as you).

Note the dashed line on the left side of Exhibit 2.5. This line indicates that advertisers do not always employ the services of advertising agencies. Nor do advertisers or agencies always seek the services of external facilitators. Some advertisers deal directly with media organizations for placement of their advertisements or implementation of their promotions. This happens either when an advertiser has an internal advertising/promotions department that prepares all the materials for the process, or when media organizations (especially radio, television, and newspapers) provide technical assistance in the preparation of materials. The new interactive media formats also provide advertisers the opportunity to work directly with entertainment programming firms, such as Walt Disney, Sony, and SFX Entertainment to provide integrated programming that features brand placements in films and television programs or at entertainment events. And, as you will see, many of the new media agencies provide the creative and technical assistance advertisers need to implement campaigns through new media.

Each level in the structure of the industry is complex. Let's take a look at each level, with particular emphasis on the nature and activities of agencies. When you need to devise advertising or a fully integrated brand promotion, no source will be more valuable than the advertising or promotion agency you work with. Advertising and promotion agencies provide the essential creative firepower to the process and represent a critical link in the structure.

Advertisers. A wide range of organizations—from your local pet store to multinational corporations—seek to benefit from the effects of advertising. Different types of advertisers each use advertising somewhat differently, depending on the type of product or service they sell. The following categories describe the different types of advertisers and the role advertising plays for them.

Manufacturers and Service Firms. Large national manufacturers of consumer products and services are the most prominent users of promotion, often spending hundreds of millions of dollars annually. Procter & Gamble, General Foods, MCI,

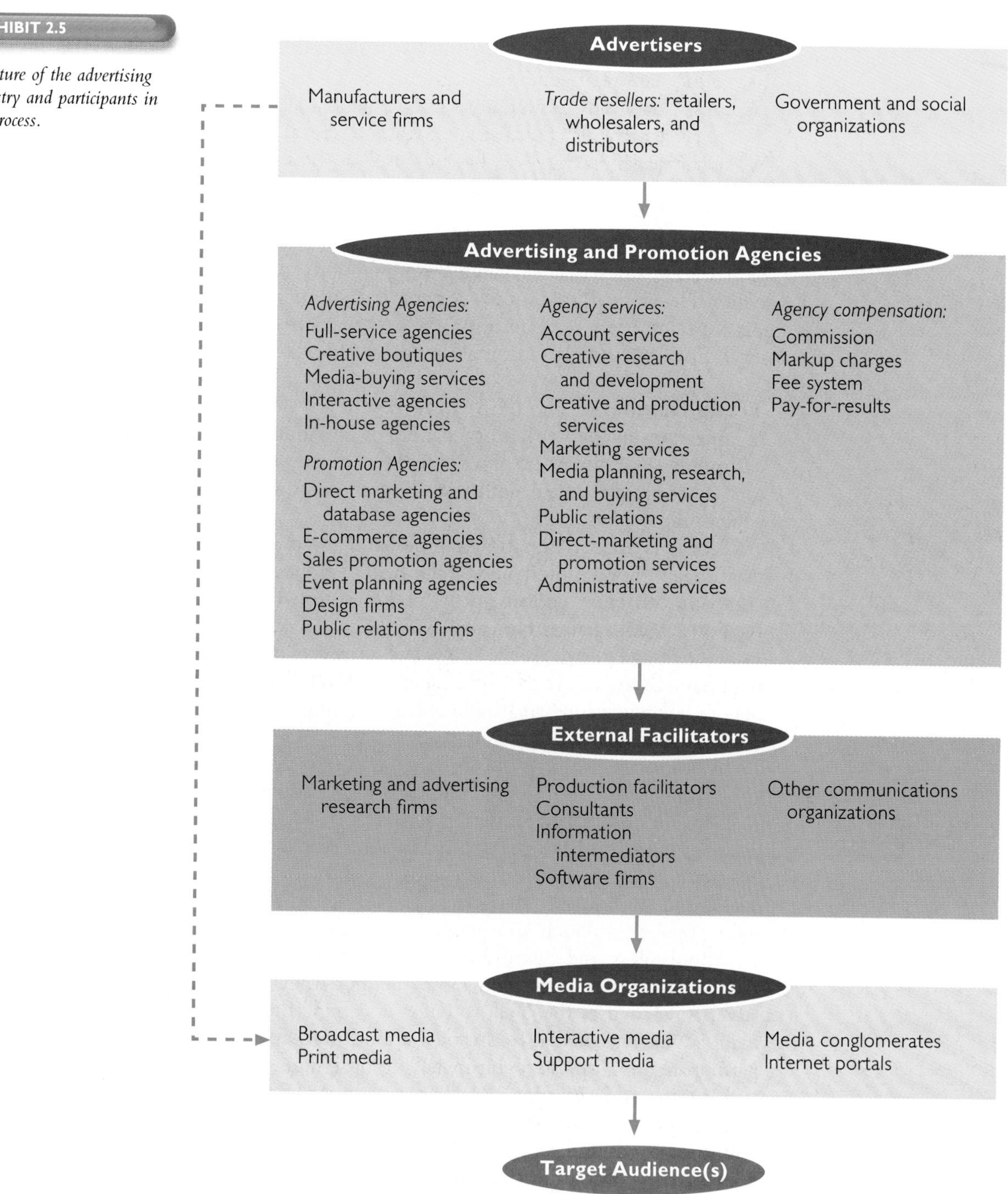

EXHIBIT 2.5

Structure of the advertising industry and participants in the process.

and Merrill Lynch all have national or global markets for their products and services. The use of advertising, particularly mass media advertising, by these firms is essential to creating awareness and preference for their brands. But advertising is not useful just to national or multinational firms; regional and local producers of household goods and services also rely heavily on advertising. For example, regional dairy companies sell milk, cheese, and other dairy products in regions usually comprising a few states. These firms often use ads placed in newspapers and regional editions of magazines. Further, couponing and sampling are ways to communicate with target markets with integrated brand promotions that are well suited to regional application. Several breweries and wineries also serve only regional markets. Local producers of products are relatively rare, but local service organizations are common. Medical facilities, hair salons, restaurants, auto dealers, and art organizations are examples of local service providers that use advertising to create awareness and stimulate demand. What car dealer in America has not used a "holiday event" advertising them or a remote local radio broadcast to attract attention!

Firms that produce business goods and services also use advertising on a global, national, regional, and local basis. IBM and PricewaterhouseCoopers are examples of global companies that produce business goods and services. At the national and regional level, firms that supply agricultural and mining equipment and repair services are common users of promotion, as are consulting and research firms. At the local level, firms that supply janitorial, linen, and bookkeeping services use advertising.

Trade Resellers. The term **trade reseller** is simply a general description for all organizations in the marketing channel of distribution that buy products to resell to customers. As Exhibit 2.5 shows, resellers can be retailers, wholesalers, or distributors. These resellers deal with both household consumers and business buyers at all geographic market levels.

Retailers that sell in national or global markets are the most visible reseller advertisers. Sears, The Limited, and McDonald's are examples of national and global retail companies that use various forms of promotion to communicate with customers. Regional retail chains, typically grocery chains such as Albertson's or department stores such as Dillards, serve multistate markets and use advertising suited for their regional customers. At the local level, small retail shops of all sorts rely on newspaper, radio, television, and billboard advertising and special promotional events to reach a relatively small geographic area.

Wholesalers and distributors, such as American Lock & Supply (which supplies contractors with door locks and hardware), are a completely different breed of reseller. Technically, these two groups deal with business customers only, since their position in the distribution channel dictates that they sell products either to producers (who buy goods to produce other goods) or to retailers (who resell goods to household consumers). Occasionally, an organization will call itself a wholesaler and sell to the public. Such an organization is actually operating as a retail outlet.

Wholesalers and distributors have little need for mass media advertising over media such as television and radio. Rather, they use trade publications, directory advertising such as the Yellow Pages and trade directories, and direct mail as their main advertising media. In this new era of Internet communications, these firms also participate in business-to-business "vertical trade communities," like VerticalNet and Buzzsaw (see Exhibit 2.6). These vertical trade communities act as comprehensive sources of information, interaction, and electronic commerce: the buying and selling of goods and services over the Internet. These trade communities are at the core of the communications/distribution channels discussed earlier as one of the important trends affecting the advertising industry.

Federal, State, and Local Governments. At first, you might think it is odd to include governments as advertising users, but government bodies invest millions of dollars in advertising annually. In fact, in 2000 the U.S. government was the 18th largest spender on advertising in the U.S., with expenditures exceeding $1.2 billion.[15] And that was just on advertising. If you add in the expense of brochures, recruiting fairs, and the personal selling expense of recruiting offices, the U.S. government spends well over $2 billion annually. The federal government's spending on advertising and promotion is concentrated in two areas: armed forces recruiting and

15. Ibid.

e-SIGHTINGS

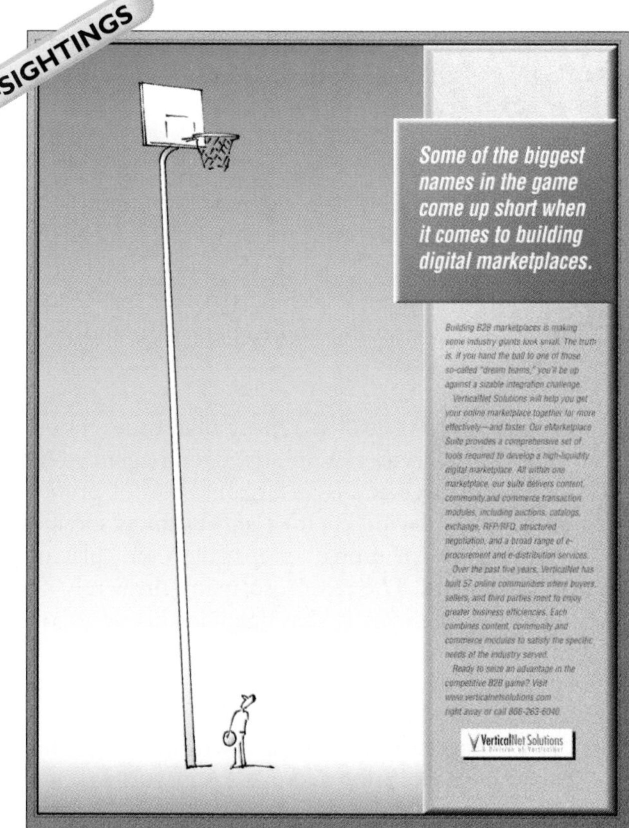

EXHIBIT 2.6

Internet trade communities like VerticalNet provide wholesalers with a medium through which they can both communicate about their brands and actually bring about a transaction with target customers. Visit the VerticalNet site (www.verticalnet.com) *and list the various advertising and promotion opportunities available to advertisers through this business-to-business trade community. How does VerticalNet compare with Yahoo! B2B Marketplace* (b2b.yahoo.com)*?*

social issues. As an example, the U.S. government regularly uses broad-based advertising campaigns for military recruiting. A recently launched National Guard recruiting effort will invest $400 million in advertising over a five-year period. Traditional television and radio ads will dominate the campaign, but the Internet will also be used.[16]

The other big promotion expense for government is in direct marketing. Each year, dozens of government publications are mailed to millions of business and individuals, particularly small businesses, to alert them to government programs or regulations and tax law changes. State and local government agencies, especially health care and welfare organizations, attempt to shape behaviors (reduce child abuse, for example) or communicate with citizens who can use their services, such as potential Social Security and Medicare recipients. State governments also invest millions of dollars in promoting state lotteries and tourism.

The U.S. government has also learned the value of integrated brand promotion. The U.S. Mint used a $40 million integrated campaign to introduce the Sacagawea "Golden Dollar" to the market. The campaign featured traditional advertising as well as partnerships with Wal-Mart, General Mills, and entertainment organizations. One of the key strategies was a promotion with SFX Entertainment in which concertgoers in 10 SFX venues got free tickets if they spent a certain number of the new dollars on tickets. The SFX venues also gave change in Golden Dollars. Broad-based consumer awareness was accomplished with TV and radio spots that featured George Washington spending the dollars in a vending machine, on a subway, and at a diner.[17]

Social Organizations. Advertising by social organizations at the national, state, and local level is common. The Nature Conservancy and the United Way promote their programs, seek donations, and attempt to shape behavior (deter drug use or encourage breast self-examination procedures, for example). National organizations such as these use both the mass media and direct mail to promote their causes and services. Every state has its own unique statewide organizations, such as Citizens against Hunger, a state arts council, a tourism office, an economic development office (see Exhibit 2.7), or a historical society. Social organizations in local communities represent a variety of special interests, from computer clubs to fraternal organizations to neighborhood child care organizations. The advertising used by social organizations has the same fundamental purpose as the advertising carried out by major multinational corporations: to stimulate demand and disseminate information. While big multinationals might use national or even global advertising, local organizations rely on advertising through local media to reach local audiences.

Few of the advertisers just discussed have the in-house expertise or resources to strategically plan and then prepare effective advertising. This is where advertising

16. Laura Q. Hughes and Wendy Davis, "Agencies Will Troop In to Fight for National Guard," *Advertising Age,* September 6, 2000, 6, 108.

17. Betsy Spethmann, "Mint Condition," *PROMO Magazine,* September 2000, 37.

NOT ONLY IS LIFE LESS TAXING IN IDAHO. . . IT'S LITERALLY LESS TAXING.

You've probably heard about the great recreational opportunities, impressive natural beauty, and outstanding lifestyle Idahoans enjoy. But you might not know Idaho has the 13th lowest overall per capita tax burden in the country and the second lowest tax burden among western states. Our state tax revenues come from a balanced mix of personal income, corporate income, sales, and property taxes which generate stable funding for needed public services without unfairly burdening any sector. In fact, the Corporation for Enterprise Development ranked Idaho's tax and fiscal system as the second best in the nation. One positive result is that Idaho's per capita debt continues to be the lowest in the nation.

Companies in Idaho are finding our tax structure very business-friendly.

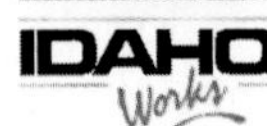

Idaho Department of Commerce • 700 West State Street • P.O. Box 83720 • Boise, Idaho 83720-0093
1-800-842-5858 • www.idoc.state.id.us

EXHIBIT 2.7

Government and social organizations can use advertising as effectively as corporations. Here the state of Idaho is using advertising to attract businesses with the appeal of lower personal and corporate taxes.
www.state.id.us

(and promotion) agencies play such an important role in the structure of the advertising industry.

3 Agencies.

Advertisers are fortunate to have a full complement of agencies that specialize in literally every detail of every advertising and promotional tool. Let's take a closer look at the types of agencies advertisers rely on to help create their advertising and integrated brand promotion campaigns.

Advertising Agencies.

Most advertisers choose to enlist the services of an advertising agency. An **advertising agency** is an organization of professionals who provide creative and business services to clients in planning, preparing, and placing advertisements. The reason so many firms rely on advertising agencies is that agencies house a collection of professionals with very specialized talent, experience, and expertise that simply cannot be matched by in-house talent.

Most big cities and small towns in the United States have advertising agencies. Advertising agencies often are global businesses as well. As discussed in the trends affecting the advertising industry, megamergers between agencies have been occurring for several years. Exhibit 2.8 shows the world's 10 largest advertising organizations and their worldwide gross income. The top 500 advertising agencies had worldwide income of more than $32.5 billion on gross billings of nearly $260 billion in 2000.[18] This 12.4 percent increase over 1999 shows the strength of investment in advertising from small American towns to centers of commerce worldwide.

The types of agency professionals who help advertisers in the planning, preparation, and placement of advertising and other promotional activities include the following:

- Account planners
- Account supervisors
- Art directors
- Creative directors
- Copywriters
- Radio and television producers
- Researchers
- Artists
- Technical staff—printing, film editing, and so forth
- Marketing specialists
- Media buyers
- Public relations specialists
- Sales promotion and event planners
- Direct marketing specialists
- Web developers
- Interactive media planners

As this list suggests, some advertising agencies can provide advertisers with a host of services, from campaign planning through creative concepts to e-strategies to measuring effectiveness. Several different types of agencies are available to the advertiser. Be aware that there are all sorts of ad agencies. A short description of the major types of agencies follows:

18. "57th Annual Agency Report," *Advertising Age,* April 23, 2001, S1.

Rank 2000	Rank 1999	Company	Headquarters	Worldwide Gross Income, 2000 (millions)	%Change
1	1	WPP Group	London	$7,971.0	19.9
2	2	Omnicom Group	New York	6,986.2	11.9
3	3	Interpublic Group	New York	6,595.9	16.9
4	5	Dentsu	Tokyo	3,089.0	22.2
5	4	Havas Advertising	Levallois-Perret, France	2,757.3	7.8
6	6	Publicis Groupe	Paris	2,479.1	7.8
7	7	BCom3 Group	Chicago	2,215.9	16.0
8	8	Grey Global Group	New York	1,863.2	18.7
9	9	True North Communications	Chicago	1,539.1	11.6
10	10	Cordiant Communications Group	London	1,254.8	16.5

Source: "57th Annual Agency Report," *Advertising Age*, April 23, 2001, S18.

EXHIBIT 2.8

The world's top 10 advertising organizations (ranked by worldwide gross income, U.S. dollars in millions).

Full-Service Agency. A **full-service agency** typically includes an array of advertising professionals to meet all the promotional needs of clients. Often, such an agency will also offer a client global contacts. Young & Rubicam and McCann-Erickson Worldwide are examples. Full-service agencies are not necessarily large organizations employing hundreds or even thousands of people. Small local and regional shops can be full service with just a few dozen employees. When American Honda put its Acura account up for review recently, it wanted "outstanding creative talent" no matter what size agency did the work. The account went to midsize agency Suissa Miller in Santa Monica, California.[19] Similarly, not every full-service agency is built on giant accounts worth hundreds of millions of dollars. Cramer-Krasselt, a midsize international agency, is building a stable of international clients one small account at a time. The agency rarely has accounts billing over $20 million. But by serving small accounts from clients such as Zenith Electronics, Kemper Insurance, and Ski-Doo, the agency has now reach $500 million in billings.[20]

Creative Boutique. A **creative boutique** typically emphasizes creative concept development, copywriting, and artistic services to clients. An advertiser can employ this alternative for the strict purpose of infusing greater creativity into the message theme or individual advertisement. As one advertising expert put it, "If all clients want is ideas—lots of them, from which they can pick and mix to their hearts' delight—they won't want conventional, full-service agencies. They'll want fast, flashy fee-based idea factories."[21] Creative boutiques are these "idea factories." Some large global agencies such as McCann-Erickson Worldwide have set up "creative-only" project shops that mimic the services provided by creative boutiques.

Interactive Agencies. As we saw in the chapter opening scenario, the era of new media has created a new form of agency—the interactive agency. **Interactive agencies** help

19. Advertising Age Viewpoint editorial, "Why Mid-Size Shops Survive," *Advertising Age,* October 28, 1998, 26.
20. Hillary Chura and Kate MacArthur, "Cramer-Krasselt Thinks Small," *Advertising Age,* September 11, 2000, 32.
21. Martin Sorell, "Agencies Face New Battle Grounds," *Advertising Age,* April 13, 1998, 22.

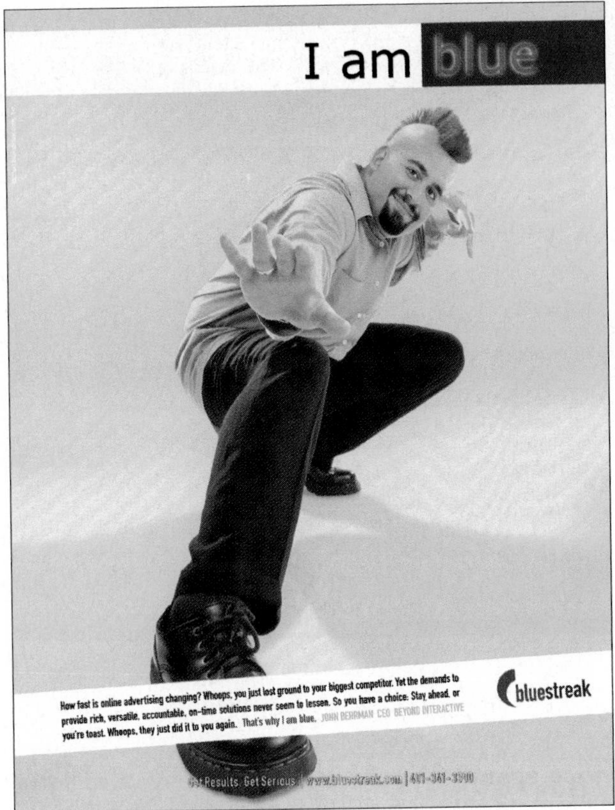

EXHIBIT 2.9

The era of new media has spawned new interactive advertising agencies that specialize in developing banner ads and corporate Web sites. Bluestreak is an agency with the stated purpose of providing "the infrastructure for marketers and agencies to create results-driven campaigns that generate dramatically higher click-throughs, conversion and transaction rates." Check out their philosophy and purpose at www.bluestreak.com.

advertisers prepare communications for new media such as the Internet, interactive kiosks, CD-ROMs, and interactive television. Interactive agencies for the most part focus on banner ads and Web site development (see Exhibit 2.9). Other "cyberagencies," which we will talk about shortly, specialize in online promotions. One of the best interactive agencies is Red Sky Interactive. They have prepared corporate Web sites for Nike, Levi Strauss, Absolut Vodka, and Altoids. Check out their work at www.redsky.com.

In-House Agencies. An **in-house agency** is often referred to as the advertising department in a firm and takes responsibility for the planning and preparation of advertising materials. This option has the advantage of greater coordination and control in all phases of the advertising and promotion process. The advertiser's own personnel have control over and knowledge of marketing activities, such as product development and distribution tactics. Another advantage is that the firm can essentially keep all the profits from commissions an external agency would have earned. As the senior VP for advertising and corporate communications at NEC explained about the firm's prospects for moving much of its $40 million Packard Bell account in-house, "We're certainly looking at taking some of the work in-house because it's more efficient."[22] While the advantages of doing advertising work in-house are attractive, there are two severe limitations. First, there may be a lack of objectivity, thereby constraining the execution of all phases of the advertising process. Second, it is highly unlikely that an in-house agency could ever match the breadth and depth of talent available in an external agency.

Media Buying and Planning Services. While not technically an agency, a **media buying and planning service** is an independent organization that specializes in buying media time and space and offers media planning advice as a service to advertising agencies and advertisers. The task of buying media space has become more complex because of the proliferation of media options. One additional advantage of using a media buying and planning service is that since it buys media in large quantities, it often acquires media time at a much lower cost than an agency or advertiser could. Also, media buying services often have acquired time and space in "inventory" and offer last-minute placement to advertisers. Media buying services have been a part of the advertising industry structure for many years. In recent years, however, media planning has been added to the task of simply buying media space. As an example, Unilever decided to turn over its $575 million media buying and planning tasks to a specialized agency, MindShare.[23] Firms are finding that the firm that buys space can provide keen insights into the media strategy as well.

Promotion Agencies.

While advertisers often rely on an advertising agency as a steering organization for their promotional efforts, many specialized agencies often

22. Bradley Johnson, "NEC May Move $40 Mil In-House," *Advertising Age,* April, 6, 1998, 48.
23. Richard Linnett, "Unilever Win Affirms MindShare Strategy," *Advertising Age,* December 4, 2000, 4.

enter the process and are referred to as **promotion agencies.** This is because advertising agencies, even full-service agencies, will concentrate on the advertising process and often provide only a few key ancillary services for other promotional efforts. This is particularly true in the current era, in which new media are offering so many different ways to communicate to target markets. Promotion agencies can handle everything from sampling to event promotions to in-school promotional tie-ins. A description of the types of agencies and their services follows.

Direct Marketing and Database Agencies. **Direct marketing agencies** and **database agencies** (sometimes also called **direct response agencies**) provide a variety of direct marketing services. These firms maintain and manage large databases of mailing lists as one of their services. These firms can design direct marketing campaigns either through the mail, telemarketing, or direct response campaigns using all forms of media. These agencies help advertisers construct databases of target customers, merge databases, develop promotional materials, and then execute the campaign. In many cases, these agencies maintain **fulfillment centers,** which ensure that customers receive the product ordered through direct mail. Direct Media (www.directmedia.com) is the world's largest list management and list brokerage firm, providing clients with services in both the consumer and business-to-business markets across the country and around the world.

Many of these agencies are set up to provide creative and production services to clients. These firms will design and help execute direct response advertising campaigns using traditional media such as radio, television, magazines, and newspapers. Also, they can prepare **infomercials** for clients—a 5-minute to 60-minute "information" program that promotes a brand and offers direct purchase to viewers.

E-commerce Agencies. There are so many new and different kinds of e-commerce agencies that it is hard to categorize all of them. **E-commerce agencies** handle a variety of planning and execution activities related to promotions using electronic commerce. Note that these agencies are different from the interactive agencies discussed earlier. They do not create Web sites or banner ads, but rather help firms conduct all forms of promotion through electronic media—particularly the Internet. They can run sweepstakes, issue coupons, help in sampling, and do direct response campaigns.[24] A firm like Netcentives (www.netcentives.com) offers advertisers the option of providing consumers with online coupons and loyalty programs (see Exhibit 2.10). Old Navy, American Airlines, The World Wildlife Fund, Cisco, and 3M are a few of the firms that have signed on with Netcentives. Another specialized firm is MessageMedia (www.messagemedia.com). MessageMedia (featured in the E-Commerce Box on page 59) provides advertisers with e-mail messaging services and database management to direct those messages to highly targeted audiences. Another of these new media e-commerce organizations is DoubleClick (featured in Exhibit 2.2 earlier in the chapter; www.doubleclick.net) which provides services related to Internet advertising, targeting technology, complete advertising management software solutions, direct response Internet advertising, and Internet advertising developed for regional and local businesses. The best way to view these new e-commerce agencies is to understand that they can provide all forms of promotion using new media technology usually specializing in Internet solutions.

Sales Promotion Agencies. These specialists design and then operate contests, sweepstakes, special displays, or coupon campaigns for advertisers. It is important to recognize that these agencies can specialize in **consumer sales promotions** and will

24. Al Urbanski, "Off-the-Rack Web Programs," *PROMO Magazine,* December 1999, i.4.

EXHIBIT 2.10

New e-commerce agencies are popping up faster than pop-up screens. This agency, Netcentives, helps advertisers use the Internet to send e-mail messages, develop loyalty programs, and distribute coupons to highly targeted audiences. Compare and contrast Netcentives (www.netcentives.com) and XactMail (www.xactmail.com). While there are similarities, how do they differ and why might advertisers choose one over the other?

focus on price-off deals, coupons, sampling, rebates, and premiums. Other firms will specialize in **trade sales promotions** designed to help advertisers use promotions aimed at wholesalers, retailers, vendors, and trade resellers. These agencies are experts in designing incentive programs, trade shows, sales force contests, in-store merchandising, and point-of-purchase materials.

Event-Planning Agencies. Event sponsorship can also be targeted to household consumers or the trade market. **Event-planning agencies** and organizers are experts in finding locations, securing dates, and putting together a "team" of people to pull off a promotional event—audio/visual people, caterers, security experts, entertainers, celebrity participants, or whoever is necessary to make the event come about. The event-planning organization will also often take over the task of advertising the event and making sure the press provides coverage (publicity) of the event. When an advertiser sponsors an entire event, such as a PGA golf tournament, managers will work closely with the event-planning agencies. If an advertiser is just one of several sponsors of an event, such as a NASCAR race, then it has less control over planning.

Design Firms. Designers and graphics specialists do not get nearly enough credit in the advertising and promotion process. If you take a job in advertising or promotion, your designer will be one of your first and most important partners. While designers are rarely involved in strategy planning, they are intimately involved in the execution of the advertising or IBP effort. In the most basic sense, **designers** help a firm create a **logo**—the graphic mark that identifies a company and other visual representations that promote an identity for a firm. This mark will appear on everything from advertising to packaging to the company stationery, business cards, and signage. But beyond the logo, graphic designers will also design most of the materials used in supportive communications such as coupons, phonecards, in-store displays, brochures, outdoor banners for events, newsletters, and direct mail pieces. They are key, although somewhat anonymous, participants in the process.

Public Relations Firms. **Public relations firms** manage an organization's relationships with the media, the local community, competitors, industry associations, and government organizations. The tools of public relations include press releases, feature stories, lobbying, spokespersons, and company newsletters. Most advertisers do not like to handle their own public relations tasks for two reasons. First, public relations takes highly specialized skills and talent not normally found in a firm. Second, managers are too close to public relations problems and may not be capable of handling a situation—particularly a negative situation—with measured public responses. For these reasons, advertisers, and even advertising agencies, turn to outside public relations firms. In keeping with the movement to incorporate the Internet across all forms of promotion, there are even organizations that will handle putting all of a firm's news releases online. One such firm is called PR Newswire (www.prnewswire.com).

Agency Services. Advertising and promotion agencies offer a wide range of services. The advertiser may need a large, global, full-service advertising agency to plan, prepare, and execute its advertising and integrated brand promotion campaigns. On the other hand, a creative boutique may offer the right combination of services. Similarly, a large promotions firm might be needed to manage events and promotions while a design firm is enlisted for design work, but nothing else. The most important issue, however, is for the advertiser and the agency to negotiate and reach agreement on the services being provided before any agency is hired. Exhibit 2.11 shows the typical organizational structure of a full-service advertising agency that also provides a significant number of IBP services. The types of services commonly offered by advertising and promotion agencies are discussed in the following sections.

Account Services. **Account services** includes managers who have titles such as account executive, account supervisor, or account manager, and work with clients to determine how the brand can benefit most from promotion. Account services entail identifying the benefits a brand offers, its target audiences, and the best competitive positioning, and then developing a complete promotion plan. In some cases, account services in an agency can provide basic marketing and consumer behavior research, but the client should really bring this information to the table. Knowing the target segment, the brand's values, and the positioning strategy are really the responsibility of the advertiser (more on this in Chapters 5 and 6).

Account services managers also work with the client in translating cultural and consumer values into advertising and promotional messages through the creative services in the agency. Finally, they work with media services to develop an effective media strategy for determining the best vehicles for reaching the targeted audiences. One of the primary tasks in account services is to keep the various agency teams—creative, production, media—on schedule and within budget (more about this in Chapter 8).

E-COMMERCE

You Have E-Mail (as a Promotion Option)

Most of us know e-mail as that useful but sometimes burdensome new technology for professional communications and keeping in touch with relatives in remote places. Well, one firm has emerged that will help advertisers use e-mail as another form of promotional communications: MessageMedia (www.messagemedia.com). The firm intends to distinguish itself among e-commerce agencies by offering synchronized marketing communications through e-mail, the Web, and offline media.

The company will handle a firm's inbound and outbound e-mail campaigns based on database technology. The applications available from the firm will include customer service and sales messages. But the founder, Larry Jones, is quick to point out that MessageMedia is not a "spamming" organization that sends millions of unsolicited e-mails to unsuspecting and unappreciative Web users. MessageMedia prepares and sends messages only to current customers of his clients—a true relationship-building component of the promotional process.

This is a fast-growing market if you can get the right offer, to the right customer, at the right time, based on the right database. According to Jones, highly targeted e-mail messages draw a 10 percent response rate, while "click-throughs" on Web banner ads are below 1 percent. The key to success for MessageMedia is in the philosophy of the founder, who believes that its not about sending e-mails, it's about understanding the recipient. If MessageMedia's knowledge of the recipients is as good as it's advertising suggests, this company can't miss.

Source: Dana Blankenhorn, "Message Media Vision Extends Beyond E-Mail," *Advertising Age*, August 16, 1999, 44.

Marketing Research Services. Research conducted by an agency for a client usually consists of the agency locating studies (conducted by commercial research organizations) that have bearing on a client's market or advertising and promotion objectives. The research group will help the client interpret the research and communicate these interpretations to the creative and media people. If existing studies are not sufficient, research may actually be conducted by the agency. As mentioned in the account services discussion, some agencies can assemble consumers from the target audience to

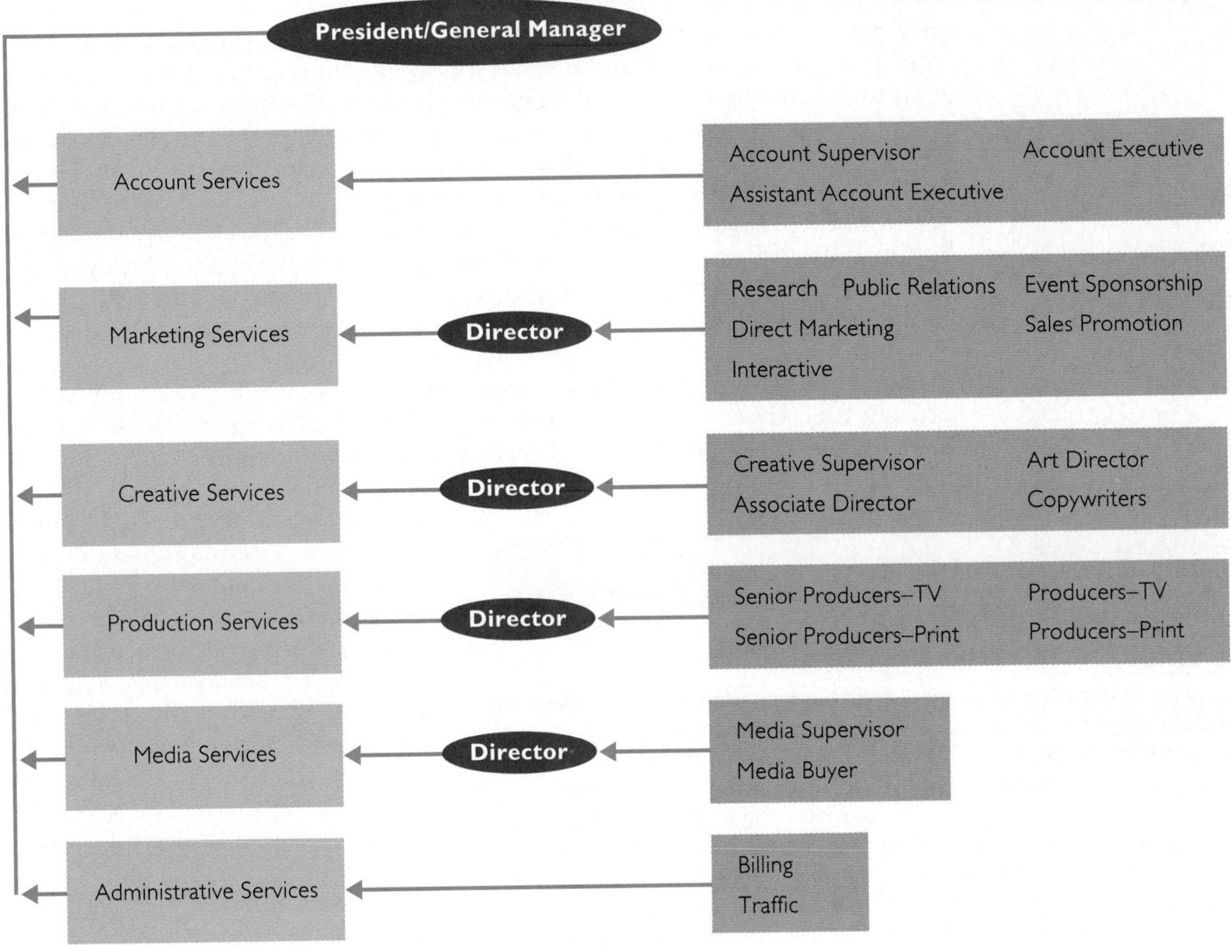

EXHIBIT 2.11

The typical structure of a full-service advertising agency. Note that this structure includes significant integrated brand promotion services as well as advertising services.

evaluate different versions of proposed advertising and determine whether messages are being communicated effectively.

Many agencies have established the position of account planner to coordinate the research effort. An **account planner** is an individual assigned to clients whose stature in the organization is on par with an account executive. The account planner will ensure that research input is included at each stage of development of campaign materials. Some agency leaders, like Jay Chiat of Chiat/Day, think that account planning is "the best new business tool ever invented."[25] Others are a bit more measured in their assessment. Jon Steel, director of account planning at Goody, Silverstein and Partners, described account planning this way: "[account] planning, when used properly, is the best *old* business tool ever invented."[26] Either way, agencies are understanding that research, signaled by the appointment of an account planner, is key to successful promotional campaigns. The advertising research issue is considered in detail in Chapter 7.

Creative and Production Services. The **creative services** group in an agency comes up with the concepts that express the value of a company's brand in interesting and memorable ways. In simple terms, the creative services group develops the

25. John Steel, *Truth, Lies & Advertising: The Art of Account Planning* (New York: John Wiley & Sons, 1998), 42.
26. Ibid., 43.

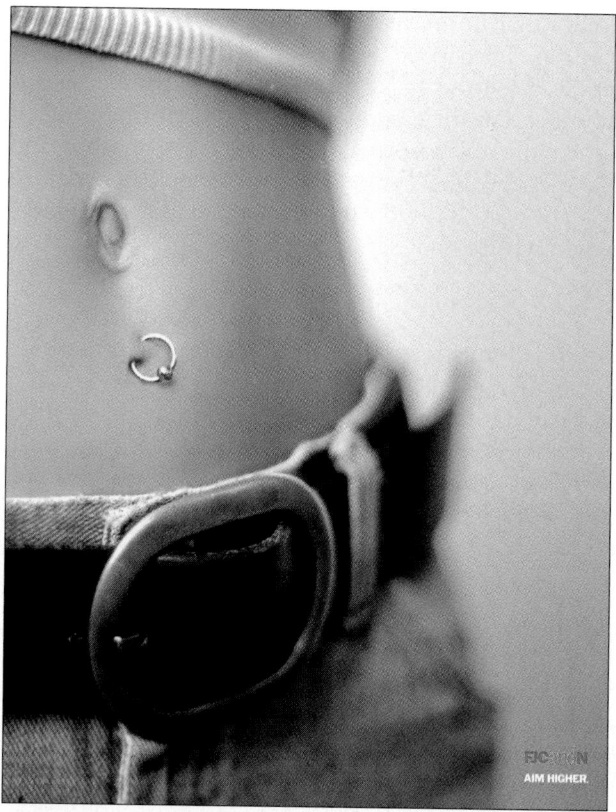

EXHIBIT 2.12

Advertising agencies, from large global agencies to smaller regional shops, provide a wide range of services for clients. Their greatest contribution to the process, perhaps, is their creative prowess. Here, FJCandN, a regional agency, is imploring advertisers to "aim higher." A nice bit of creativity to tout the agency's creative talents.
www.fjcn.com

message that will be delivered though advertising, sales promotion, direct marketing, event sponsorship, or public relations. Howard Davis, retired CEO of the full-service advertising agency Tracy-Locke, refers to this process in the industry as the "art of commerce."[27] Clients will push the agency hard to come up with interesting and expressive ways to represent the brand. Geoffrey Frost, vice president of consumer communications for Motorola's Personal Communications Sector, expressed his company's approach to demanding creative excellence by saying, "What we've challenged the agencies to do was to help us to figure out how to position Motorola as the company that has really figured out the future. . . ."[28] That seems like a pretty tall creative order, indeed. The creative group in an agency will typically include a creative director, art director, illustrators or designers, and copywriters. In specialized promotion agencies, event planners, contest experts, and interactive media specialists will join the core group. Exhibit 2.12 shows how advertising agency FJC and N promotes its creative services.

Production services includes producers (and sometimes directors) who take creative ideas and turn them into advertisements, direct mail pieces, or events materials. Producers generally manage and oversee the endless details of production of the finished advertisement or other promotion material. Advertising agencies maintain the largest and most sophisticated creative and production staffs.

Media Planning and Buying Services. This service was discussed earlier as a specialized agency through which advertisers can contract for media buying and planning. Advertising agencies themselves provide **media planning and buying services** similar to those of the specialized agencies. The central challenge is to determine how a client's message can most effectively and efficiently reach the target audience. Media planners and buyers examine an enormous number of options to put together an effective media plan within the client's budget. But media planning and buying is much more than simply buying ad space, timing a coupon distribution, or scheduling an event. A wide range of media strategies can be implemented to enhance the impact of the message. Agencies are helping clients sort through the blizzard of new media options such as CD-ROMs, videocassettes, interactive media, and the Internet. As we saw in the J. Walter Thompson story at the beginning of the chapter, most large agencies, such as JWT, Chiat/Day, and Fallon McElligott, set up their own interactive media groups years ago in response to client demands that the Internet media option be made available to them.[29] The three positions typically found in the media area are media planner, media buyer, and media researcher. This is where most of the client's money is spent; it's very important.

27. Howard Davis referenced his views in this regard during a speech at the Montana State University College of Business delivered on December 13, 2000.

28. Tobi Elkin, "Motorola Tenders Brand Challenge," *Advertising Age,* August 14, 2000, 14.

29. Kevin Goldman, "Ad Agencies Slowly Set Up Shop at New Addresses on the Internet," *Wall Street Journal,* December 29, 1994, B5.

Administrative Services. Like other businesses, agencies have to manage their business affairs. Agencies have personnel departments, accounting and billing departments, and sales staffs that go out and sell the agency to clients. Most important to clients is the traffic department, which has the responsibility of monitoring projects to be sure that deadlines are met. Traffic managers make sure the creative group and media services are coordinated so that deadlines for getting promotional materials to printers and media organizations are met. The job requires tremendous organizational skills and is critical to delivering the other services to clients.

Agency Compensation.

The way agencies get paid is somewhat different from the way other professional organizations are compensated. While accountants, doctors, lawyers, and consultants often work on a fee basis, advertising agencies often base compensation on a commission or markup system. Promotion agencies occasionally work on a commission basis, but more often work on a fee or contract basis. We will examine the four most prevalent agency compensation methods: commissions, markup charges, fee systems, and newer pay-for-results plans.

Commissions. The traditional method of agency compensation is the **commission system,** which is based on the amount of money the advertiser spends on media. Under this method, 15 percent of the total amount billed by a media organization is retained by the advertising or promotion agency as compensation for all costs in creating advertising/promotion for the advertiser. The only variation is that the rate typically changes to 16⅔ percent for outdoor media. Exhibit 2.13 shows a simple example of how the commission system works.

Over the past 10 years, the wisdom of the commission system has been questioned by both advertisers and agencies themselves. As the chairman of a large full-service agency put it, "It's incenting us to do the wrong thing, to recommend network TV and national magazines and radio when other forms of communication like direct marketing or public relations might do the job better."[30] About half of all advertisers compensate their agencies using a commission system based on media cost. But only about 14 percent of advertisers responding to a recent survey still use the traditional 15 percent commission. More advertisers are using other percentage levels of commission—often negotiated levels—as the basis for agency compensation. Unilever, the Dutch consumer products company with extensive U.S. revenues, has some agencies on rates as low as 10.75 percent, depending on the agreement negotiated.[31]

Markup Charges. Another method of agency compensation is to add a percentage **markup charge** to a variety of services the agency purchases from outside sup-

EXHIBIT 2.13

Calculation of agency compensation using a traditional commission-based compensation system.

30. Patricia Sellers, "Do You Need Your Ad Agency?" *Fortune,* November 15, 1993, 148.
31. Pat Sloan and Laura Petrecca, "Unilever Panel to Propose Hike in Fees for Agencies," *Advertising Age,* November 3, 1997, 2.

pliers. In many cases, an agency will turn to outside contractors for art, illustration, photography, printing, research, and production. The agency then, in agreement with the client, adds a markup charge to these services. The reason markup charges became prevalent in the industry is that many promotion agencies were providing services that did not use traditional media. Since the traditional commission method was based on media charges, there was no way for these agencies to receive payment for their work. This being the case, the markup system was developed. A typical markup on outside services is 17.65 to 20 percent.

Fee Systems. A **fee system** is much like that used by consultants or attorneys, whereby the advertiser and the agency agree on an hourly rate for different services provided. The hourly rate can be based on average salaries within departments or on some agreed-upon hourly rate across all services. This is the most common method for promotion agencies to get compensated. GM, the largest U.S. advertiser, agreed to a fee system in which compensation will be based on agency work and its thinking.[32] Recently agencies have been inundated with requests from dot-com companies to prepare campaigns and, as a result, have initiated a fee system that requires an "up-front" payment for anticipated expenses plus a "fair profit margin."[33] Some agencies felt that some dot-coms wouldn't be around long enough to make a commission system work. The agencies that went to a fee system turned out to be right in two ways: many dot-com firms did go bankrupt, and the vast majority of the new Internet firms that survived have dramatically curtailed their offline advertising expenditures from their peak spending in early 2000.[34]

Another version of the fee system is a fixed fee, or contract, set for a project between the client and the agency. It is imperative that the agency and the advertiser agree on precisely what services will be provided, by what departments in the agency, over what specified period of time. In addition, the parties must agree on which supplies, materials, travel costs, and other expenses will be compensated beyond the fixed fee. Fixed-fee systems have the potential for causing serious rifts in the client-agency relationship because out-of-scope work can easily spiral out of control when so many variables are at play.

Pay-for-Results. Recently, many advertisers and agencies alike have been working on compensation programs called **pay-for-results** that base the agency's fee on the achievement of agreed-upon results.[35] Historically, agencies have not agreed to be evaluated on "results" because "results" have often been narrowly defined as sales. The key effect on a sales result is based on factors outside the agency's control such as product features, pricing strategy, and distribution programs (that is, the overall marketing mix, not just advertising or IBP). These newer pay-for-results compensation plans tie the advertising or promotion agency compensation to a previously agreed-upon achievement of specified objectives. An agency may agree to be compensated based on achievement of sales levels, but more often (and more appropriately) communications objectives such as awareness, brand identification, or brand feature knowledge among target audiences will serve as the results criteria. A recent mandate by Procter & Gamble has all 200 of its brands and the agencies that handle them on a percentage-of-sales model.[36]

32. Jean Halliday, "GM to Scrap Agency Commissions," *Advertising Age,* November 16, 1998, 1, 57.
33. Alice Z. Cuneo, "Dot-Compensation: Ad Agencies Feel the Net-Effect," *Advertising Age,* February 7, 2000, 1.
34. Jennifer Gilbert, "Dot-Com Shift," *Advertising Age,* September 25, 2000, 1, 24.
35. Laura Petrecca, "Pay-for-Results Plans Can Boost Agencies: Execs," *Advertising Age,* September 8, 1997, 18, 20.
36. Betsy Spethmann, "Pay Day," *PROMO Magazine,* November 1999, 47–50; Kathryn Kranhold, "P&G Expands Its Program to Tie Agency Pay to Brand Performance," *Wall Street Journal,* September 16, 1999, B12; AdAge.com, Special Reports, "P&G to Base Agency Pay on Sales," www.adage.com, accessed November 19, 2000.

One of the most difficult tasks in the compensation system is coordinating all the agencies and coordinating how they get paid. As you have seen, more advertisers are using more different forms of promotion and enlisting the help of multiple agencies. A key to IBP here is integrated agency communication. When all of an advertiser's agencies are working together and coordinating their efforts, not only is integrated brand promotion achieved, but better relations between agencies are achieved.[37]

As if this long list of agencies and intricate compensation schemes weren't complicated enough, let's complicate things a bit more and consider a fairly long list of external facilitators and what their agencies rely on to create and execute promotional campaigns.

4 **External Facilitators.** While agencies offer clients many services and are adding more, advertisers often need to rely on specialized external facilitators in planning, preparing, and executing promotional campaigns. **External facilitators** are organizations or individuals that provide specialized services to advertisers and agencies. The most important of these external facilitators are discussed in the following sections.

Marketing and Advertising Research Firms. Many firms rely on outside assistance during the planning phase of advertising. Research firms such as Burke International and Simmons can perform original research for advertisers using focus groups, surveys, or experiments to assist in understanding the potential market or consumer perceptions of a product or services. Other research firms, such as SRI International, routinely collect data (from grocery store scanners, for example) and have these data available for a fee.

Advertisers and their agencies also seek measures of promotional program effectiveness after a campaign has run. After an advertisement or promotion has been running for some reasonable amount of time, firms such as Starch INRA Hooper will run recognition tests on print advertisements. Other firms such as Burke offer day-after recall tests of broadcast advertisements. Some firms specialize in message testing to determine whether consumers find advertising messages appealing and understandable.

Consultants. A variety of **consultants** specialize in areas related to the promotional process. Advertisers can seek out marketing consultants for assistance in the planning stage. Creative and communications consultants provide insight on issues related to message strategy and message themes. Consultants in event planning and sponsorships offer their expertise to both advertisers and agencies. Public relations consultants often work with top management. Media experts can help an advertiser determine the proper media mix and efficient media placement.

Two new types of consultants have emerged in recent years. One is a database consultant, who works with both advertisers and agencies. Organizations such as Shepard Associates help firms identify and then manage databases that allow for the development of integrated marketing communications programs. Diverse databases from research sources discussed earlier can be merged or cross-referenced in developing effective communications programs. The other new type of consultant specializes in Web site development and management. These consultants typically have the creative skills to develop Web sites and corporate home pages and the technical skills to advise advertisers on managing the technical aspects of the user interface.

Production Facilitators. External **production facilitators** offer essential services both during and after the production process. Production is the area where advertisers and their agencies rely most heavily on external facilitators. All forms of

37. Allen Winneker, "Avoiding Bonus Envy," *PROMO Magazine,* November 1999, 35–37.

media advertising require special expertise that even the largest full-service agency, much less an advertiser, typically does not retain on staff. In broadcast production, directors, production managers, songwriters, camera operators, audio and lighting technicians, and performers are all essential to preparing a professional, high-quality radio or television ad. Production houses can provide the physical facilities, including sets, stages, equipment, and crews, needed for broadcast production. Similarly, in preparing print advertising, brochures, and direct mail pieces, graphic artists, photographers, models, directors, and producers may be hired from outside the advertising agency or firm to provide the specialized skills and facilities needed in preparing advertisements. In-store promotions is another area where designing and producing materials requires the skills of a specialty organization.

The specific activities performed by external facilitators and the techniques employed by the personnel in these firms will be covered in greater detail in Part 3 of the text. For now, it is sufficient to recognize the role these firms play in the advertising and promotions industry.

Information Intermediators. This form of external facilitator has emerged as a result of new technology and the desire on the part of advertisers to target audiences more precisely. An **information intermediator** collects customer purchase transaction histories, aggregates them across many firms that have sold merchandise to these customers, and then sells the customer names and addresses back to the firms that originally sold to these customers. Firms such as American Express, AT&T, and regional telephone companies are uniquely situated in the information management process to accumulate and organize such data, and they will likely emerge as information intermediators. These firms will gather and organize information on consumer transaction histories across a variety of different firms selling goods and services. Once this information is organized by an intermediator, it allows an advertiser to merge information about important target segments—what they buy, when they buy, and how they buy. With this information, both message themes and media placement can be more effectively and efficiently developed.

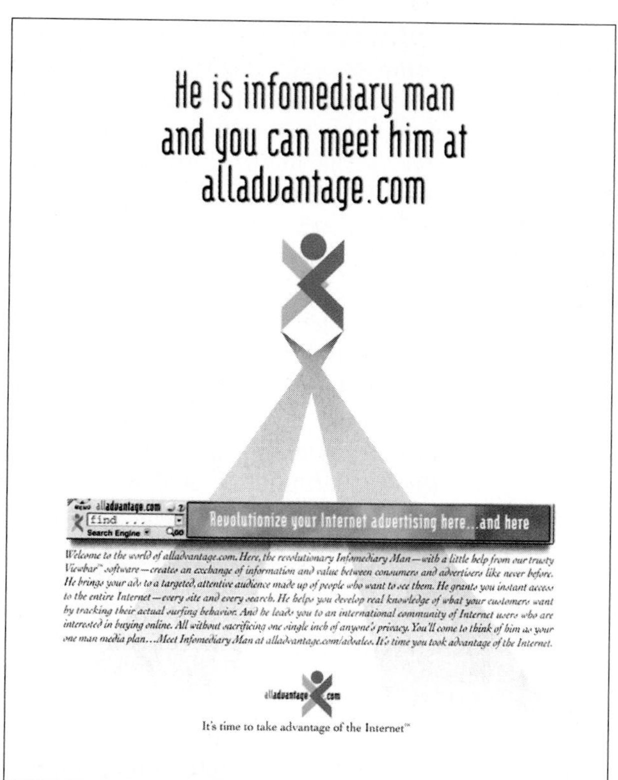

EXHIBIT 2.14

Information intermediators like AllAdvantage.com play an important role in providing advertisers with both media access and information about consumers. www.alladvantage.com

A variety of firms have emerged as specialty information intermediators for the Internet. The way the Internet works is uniquely suited to track the Web surfing behavior and also the purchase behavior of users (a point we will discuss as an ethical issue in Chapter 4). Exhibit 2.14 features one of the new breed of Internet infomediary firms, AllAdvantage.com (www.alladvantage.com)—which uses a brand mascot called "Infomediary Man." AllAdvantage has a unique system for attracting and then tracking consumers for advertisers. This company "pays" Web surfers to join their system (there is an hourly and referral rate for surfing) for the right to post advertising and promotional messages on members' computer screens as they surf. The company describes its service to advertisers in this way:

A leader in the emerging "infomediary" field, AllAdvantage.com is re-inventing the way consumers and advertisers communicate and do business together. We create value for consumers by providing them a way to profit from their time online. Active AllAdvantage.com members can be paid monthly simply for surfing the Web and receive membership benefits that include sponsor discounts and rebates. In addition, we provide a major incentive for advertisers to build one-on-one relationships with AllAdvantage.com members in an environment of accuracy, privacy and trust. In less than eleven months, more than 5 million consumers have signed up to receive the AllAdvantage.com service. And we're quickly growing.[38]

This important issue of consumers "controlling information" was raised at the outset of the chapter as one of the trends affecting the advertising industry. Once again, the importance of the issue is that the communications environment is much more than an interactive system, where consumers are controlling the information flow more than ever before.[39] But while this interactivity can mean good things for both consumers and advertisers, there is a price consumers have to pay, as the Controversy box on this page describes.

Software Firms. An interesting and complex new category of facilitator in advertising and promotion is composed of software firms. The technology in the industry, particularly new media technology, has expanded so rapidly that a variety of software firms facilitate the process. Some of these firms are well established and well known, such as Microsoft, Novell, and Oracle. But others, such as Hyperion (see Exhibit 2.15), L90, SAS, and Infinium, are new to the scene. These firms provide software ranging from the gathering and analysis of Web surfer behavior to broadband streaming audio and video to managing relationships with trade partners. These firms provide the kind of expertise that is so esoteric that even the most advanced full-service or e-commerce agency would have to seek their assistance.

CONTROVERSY

So How Does It Feel to Have a Big Brother?

Most consumers feel empowered by the Internet. After all, the freedom to log on anytime and nearly anywhere and accept and reject information offers much more control than the intrusive world of television and radio. And what about shopping anytime you want without fighting the crowds or overbearing salespeople? Yes, the interactive world of the Internet certainly is empowering. But the world of e-commerce comes with a price most consumers are just now beginning to understand and consider. That price is sacrificing privacy.

The online e-commerce privacy issue focuses on the "cookies" (online tracking devices) that advertisers place on a Web surfer's hard drive to track that person's online behavior. This alone is annoying and feels like an invasion of privacy. But it is nothing compared to the emerging possibilities. You see, cookies do not reveal a person's name or address. What is looming as a real possibility is that offline databases that do include a consumer's name, address, phone number, credit card accounts, medical records, credit records, and Social Security number can be *merged* with the online tracking data. This combination of online behavior with offline data represents the potential for an invasion of privacy that many consumers might find too great a cost for the freedom of the Internet. You see, the following could easily happen: You are browsing a Web page on mutual funds trying to decide how you want to make changes in your investment portfolio. Literally seconds later, you get a phone call from a telemarketer trying to sell you financial services! Now that feels like an invasion of privacy. While all of us might really like the convenience and control of online surfing, is it worth having a Big Brother watching our every move? The question is serious enough that Congress and the FTC are carefully scrutinizing mergers of firms that would create such comprehensive online and offline databases.

Marcia Stepanek, "Protecting E-Privacy: Washington Must Step In," *Business Week E. Biz*, July 26, 1999, EB30; Michael Krauss, "Get a Handle on the Privacy Wild Card," *Marketing News*, February 28, 2000, 12; Jennifer Gilbert and Ira Teinowitz, "Privacy Debate Continues to Rage," *Advertising Age*, February 7, 2000, 44.

5 **Media Organizations.** The next level in the industry structure, shown in Exhibit 2.16, comprises media available to advertisers. The media available for placing advertising, such as broadcast and print media, are well known to most of us simply because we're exposed to them daily. In addition, the Internet has created media organizations

38. Quote taken from "Advertisers" page of the AllAdvantage Web site, www.alladvantage.com, accessed December 26, 2000.

39. Don Schultz and Beth Barnes make very strong statements about the interactive nature of information in the 21st-century marketplace. For their basic premise, see Don E. Schultz and Beth E. Barnes, *Strategic Brand Communications Campaigns* (Lincolnwood, Ill.: NTC Business Books, 1999), 12.

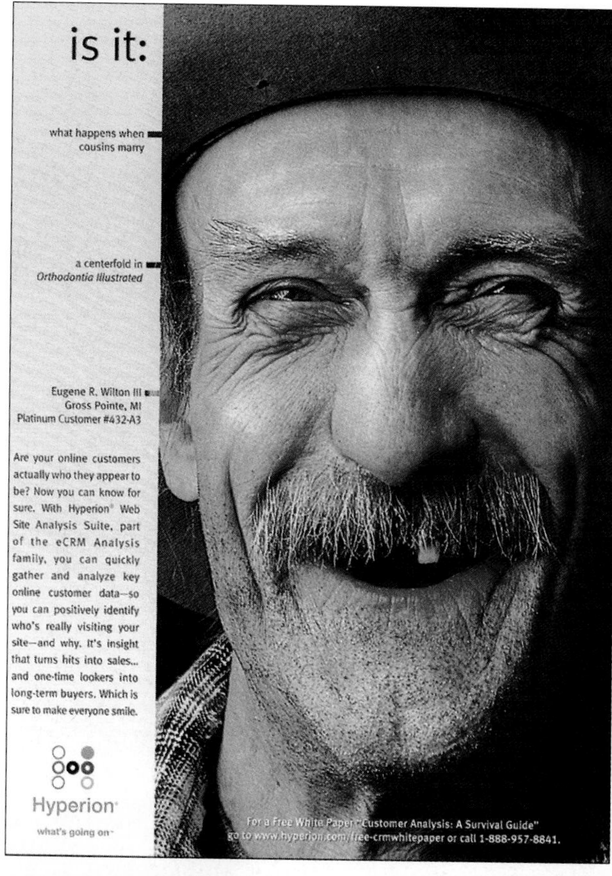

EXHIBIT 2.15

Software firms like Hyperion are providing advertisers with key assistance in the areas of audience analysis or broadband communications. Hyperion specializes in gathering and analyzing online customer data from Web site visits.
www.hyperion.com

through which advertisers can direct and distribute their advertising and promotional messages.

Advertisers and their agencies turn to media organizations that own and manage the media access to consumers. In traditional media, major television networks such as NBC or Fox, as well as national magazines such as *U.S. News & World Report* or *People,* provide advertisers with time and space—at considerable expense—for their messages.

Other media options are more useful for reaching narrowly defined target audiences. Specialty programming on cable television, tightly focused direct mail pieces, and a well-designed Internet campaign may be better ways to reach a specific audience. One of the new media options, broadband, offers advertisers the chance to target very specific audiences. Broadband allows Internet users to basically customize their programming by calling on only specific "broadcasts" from various providers. For example, The FeedRoom (www .feedroom.com) is an interactive broadband television news network that allows Web users to customize their news broadcasts to their personal preference. Advertisers can target different types of audiences using the broadband for interactive broadcasts. The next step in broadband communications is wireless broadband; firms are already developing technology and access for consumers (see Exhibit 2.17).

Note the inclusion of "Media Conglomerates" in the list shown in Exhibit 2.16. This category is included because organizations such as AOL Time Warner and Viacom own and operate companies in broadcast, print, and interactive media. Viacom brings you cable networks such as Nickelodeon, VH1, and TV Land. The recent merger of AOL and Time Warner has created the world's largest mega–media conglomerate that provides broadcasting, cable, music, film, print publishing, and a dominant Internet presence. One analyst described the media environment as "AOL Time Warner Anywhere, Anytime, Anyhow."[40] Not far behind AOL Time Warner is Disney. Disney has vastly expanded its media presence with the purchase of the ABC television network and partial or total ownership of multiple Web sites, including ESPN.com, ABCnews.com., movies.com, and GoTo.com.[41]

The support media organizations indicated in Exhibit 2.16 include all those places that advertisers want to put their messages but are not mainstream traditional or interactive media. Often referred to as "out-of-home" media, these support media organizations include transit companies (bus and taxi boards), billboard organizations, specialized directory companies, and sports and performance arenas for sponsorships, display materials, and premium items.

Audiences. The structure of the promotion industry (check Exhibit 2.5 again) and the flow of communication would obviously be incomplete without an audience—no audience, no communication. One interesting thing about the audiences for promotional communications—with the exception of household consumers—is that they are also the

40. Frank Gibney Jr., "Score One for AOLTW," *Time,* December 25, 2000–January 1, 2001, 138.
41. Chuck Ross, "Disney Eyes Stake in Excite as Part of Bold Web Strategy," *Advertising Age,* June 1, 1998, 1, 52.

EXHIBIT 2.16

Advertisers have an array of media organizations available to them. Notice that the choices range from traditional print and broadcast media to broadband and media conglomerates.

Broadcast

Television
Major network
Independent station
Cable
Broadband

Radio
Network
Local

Print

Magazines
By geographic coverage
By content

Direct Mail
Brochures
Catalogs
Videos

Newspapers
National
Statewide
Local

Specialty
Handbills
Programs

Interactive Media

Online Computer Services

Home-Shopping Broadcasts

Interactive Broadcast Entertainment Programming

Kiosks

CD-ROMs

Internet

Support Media

Outdoor
Billboards
Transit
Posters

Directories
Yellow Pages
Electronic directories

Premiums
Keychains
Calendars
Logo clothing
Pens

Point-of-Purchase Displays

Film and Program Brand Placement

Event Sponsorship

Media Conglomerates

Multiple Media Combinations
AOL Time Warner
Viacom
Turner Broadcasting
Comcast
AT&T

EXHIBIT 2.17

Broadband promises advertisers the opportunity to send audio and video through the Internet in a way that lets Web users customize their viewing and listening experiences. To learn more about various streaming services and media-rich content being developed for broadband, visit Akamai (www.akamai.com). www.starband.com

EXHIBIT 2.18

Businesses represent a large and lucrative target audience for business-to-business advertisers. Here Instinet, the world's largest agency brokerage firm, targets a professional audience. www.instinet.com

advertisers who use advertising and IBP communications. We are all familiar with the type of advertising directed at us in our role as consumers—toothpaste, window cleaner, sport-utility vehicles, soft drinks, insurance, and on and on. The text is full of advertising by firms targeting household consumers.

But business and government audiences are key to the success of a large number of firms that sell only to business and government buyers. While many of these firms rely heavily on personal selling in their promotional mix, many also use a variety of advertising and IBP tools. KPMG Consulting uses high-profile television and magazine advertising and sponsors events. Many business and trade sellers regularly need public relations, and most use direct mail to communicate with potential customers as a prelude to a personal selling call. Throughout the chapter, we have discussed the use of corporate Web sites as a way to communicate detailed information about a firm's offering in the business-to-business and business-to-government markets. Exhibit 2.18 is an example of a business organization, Instinet (www.instinet.com), communicating with its business market, securities brokers, by using magazine advertising.

SUMMARY

Discuss six important trends transforming the advertising industry.

Recent years have proven to be a period of dramatic change for the advertising industry. Many factors have propelled this change. Consumers' access to and greater control over information has made the communication process much more interactive between advertisers and consumers. Cable television has increased its reach, and the growing popularity of direct marketing programs and home shopping has diluted the impact of advertising delivered via mass media. Internet aggregators of radio and TV broadcasts and streaming video offer new hybrid media options, including the emerging broadband technology, for advertisers to consider. In addition to the growth and diversity of media, many advertisers have altered their budget allocations, with more funding going to sales promotion, public relations, and event sponsorship, and less money allocated for conventional advertising. These changes have contributed to the emphasis on integrated brand promotion (IBP).

Describe the size, structure, and participants in the advertising industry.

Many different types of organizations make up the industry. To truly appreciate what advertising is all about, one must understand who does what and in what order in the creation and delivery of an advertising or IBP campaign. The process begins with an organization that has a message it wishes to communicate to a target audience. This is the advertiser. Next, advertising and promotion agencies are typically hired to launch and manage a campaign, but other external facilitators are often brought in to perform specialized functions, such as assisting in the production of promotional materials or managing databases for efficient direct marketing campaigns. These external facilitators also include consultants with whom advertisers and their agencies may confer regarding advertising and IBP strategy decisions. All advertising and promotional campaigns must use some type of media to reach target markets. Advertisers and their agencies must therefore also work with companies that have media time or space.

Discuss the role played by advertising and promotion agencies, the services provided by these agencies, and how they are compensated.

Advertising and promotion agencies come in many varieties and offer diverse services to clients with respect to planning, preparing, and executing advertising and IBP campaigns. These services include market research and marketing planning, the actual creation and production of ad materials, the buying of media time or space for placement of the ads, and traffic management—keeping production on schedule. Some advertising agencies appeal to clients by offering a full array of services under one roof; others—such as creative boutiques—develop a particular expertise and win clients with their specialized skills. Promotion agencies specialize in one or more of the other forms of promotion beyond advertising. New media agencies are proliferating to serve the Internet and other new media needs of advertisers. The four most prevalent ways to compensate an agency for services rendered are commissions, markups, fee systems, and the new pay-for-results programs.

Identify key external facilitators who assist in planning and executing advertising and integrated brand promotion campaigns.

Marketing and advertising research firms assist advertisers and their agencies in understanding the market environment. Consultants of all sorts from marketing strategy through event planning and retail display are another form of external facilitator. Perhaps the most widely used facilitators are in the area of production of promotional materials. In advertising, a wide range of outside facilitators are used in the production of both broadcast and print advertising. In promotions, designers and planners are called on to assist in creation and execution of promotional mix tools. Information intermediators fill a new role in the structure of the industry. These firms help manage the vast information on consumer preferences and purchasing behavior, particularly with respect to the Internet.

Discuss the role played by media organizations in executing effective advertising and integrated brand promotion campaigns programs.

Media organizations are the essential link in delivering advertising and IBP communications to target audiences. There are traditional media organizations such as television, radio, newspaper, and magazines. Interactive media options include not just the Internet but CD-ROMs, electronic kiosks, and less widely known communications companies. Media conglomerates such as AT&T, AOL Time Warner, and Viacom control several different aspects of the communications system, from cable broadcast to Internet connections and emerging broadband communications technologies.

KEY TERMS

broadband
trade reseller
advertising agency
full-service agency
creative boutique
interactive agency
in-house agency
media buying and planning service
promotion agencies
direct marketing agency
database agency
direct response agency
fulfillment center
infomercial
e-commerce agency
consumer sales promotion
trade sales promotion
event-planning agency
designers
logo
public relations firm
account services
account planner
creative services
production services
media planning and buying services
commission system
markup charge
fee system
pay-for-results
external facilitator
consultants
production facilitator
information intermediator

QUESTIONS

1. What was it that ultimately won the Lipton Brisk account back for the interactive unit of the JWT agency? How had the new cyberagency failed and why?

2. As cable-TV channels continue to proliferate and Web TV becomes a reality, how would you expect the advertising industry to be affected?

3. The U.S. government spends millions of dollars each year trying to recruit young men and women into the armed services. What forms of advertising and IBP communication would be best suited to this recruiting effort?

4. Huge advertisers such as Procter & Gamble spend billions of dollars on advertising every year, yet they still rely on advertising agencies to prepare most of their advertising. Why doesn't a big company like this just do all its own advertising in-house?

5. As advertisers become more enamored with the idea of integrated brand promotion, why would it make sense for an advertising agency to develop a reputation as a full-service provider?

6. Explain the viewpoint that a commission-based compensation system may actually give ad agencies an incentive to do the wrong things for their clients.

7. What makes production of promotional materials the area where advertisers and their agencies are most likely to call on external facilitators for expertise and assistance?

8. Give an example of how the skills of a public relations firm might be employed to reinforce the message that a sponsor is trying to communicate through other forms of promotion.

EXPERIENTIAL EXERCISES

1. Break up into groups and simulate a small business planning to advertise a new or innovative product. Once you have chosen a general industry and a product to advertise, perform the following tasks and present your answers to the class.

a. Pick one of the main trends in the advertising industry and explain why you think that trend would have the greatest effect on advertising your product.

b. Determine what advertiser category your business is classified under, and explain the role advertising plays for organizations in that category. How does this apply to your campaign?

c. Select one advertising or promotion agency that would be the most effective in providing appropriate services to achieve your advertising or promotion goals. Explain your choice.

d. Select one external facilitator that would provide specialization services to help ensure the success of your campaign and explain your reasoning.

e. Choose an available media organization that would be best suited for advertising and promoting your brand's identity. What makes it the best choice?

2. Choose a popular brand from a local or national advertiser and try to determine what media organizations the advertiser is using to target its audience. Does the brand have a special site on the Internet? Can you find television or billboard ads for your product? Are there media organizations you couldn't find that you believe would be suitable or innovative for advertising this brand? Explain.

USING THE INTERNET

2-1 The Advertising Industry in Transition

The advertising industry is in a state of constant transition, and numerous trends are forcing advertisers to rethink the way they communicate with consumers. In general, greater focus is being placed on the importance of integrating multiple tools with the overall advertising effort for effective brand promotion. As one of the world's leading communications services providers, XO Communications develops Internet applications and Web media tools that ultimately influence the methods and structure of the advertising industry.

XO Communications: www.xo.com

1. Of the six important trends that are altering the structure and processes of the advertising industry, which are most closely associated with the services of XO Communications? Explain your answer.

2. What is broadband, and how does it relate to XO Communications? What effect do you think broadband will have on advertising?

3. What adjustments might advertising agencies need to make to accommodate emerging trends in the industry?

2-2 Agencies

Advertisers have a broad pool of agencies from which to choose that help execute the details of advertising and promotion strategies. Each type of agency has its own specialized services that enable advertisers to effectively target audiences and build brand recognition.

24/7 Media: www.247media.com

1. Is 24/7 Media a type of advertising agency or a promotion agency? What are the main differences?

2. Explain some of the services 24/7 Media provides to e-commerce companies, advertisers, and publishers. How do these services help attract and retain customers using the Internet?

3. Would 24/7 Media be considered an interactive agency? Why or why not?

CHAPTER 3

After reading and thinking about this chapter, you will be able to do the following:

Explain why advertising is an essential feature of capitalistic economic systems.

Describe manufacturers' dependence on advertising, promotion, and branding in achieving balanced relationships with retailers.

Discuss several important eras in the evolution of advertising in the United States, and relate important changes in advertising practice to more fundamental changes in society and culture.

Identify forces that may make the next decade a period of dramatic change for the advertising industry.

CHAPTER 1
Advertising as a Process

CHAPTER 2
The Structure of the Advertising Industry: Advertisers, Advertising Agencies, and Support Organizations

CHAPTER 3
The Evolution of Advertising

CHAPTER 4
Social, Ethical, and Regulatory Aspects of Advertising

—and he wonders why she said "NO!"

Could he have read her thoughts he would not have lost her. A picture of neatness herself, she detested slovenliness. And not once, but many times, she had noticed his ungartered socks crumpling down around his shoe tops. To have to apologize to her friends for a husband's careless habits was too much to ask. So she had to say "NO"—and in spite of his pleading couldn't tell him WHY.

No SOX Appeal Without

PARIS GARTERS

SINGLE GRIP

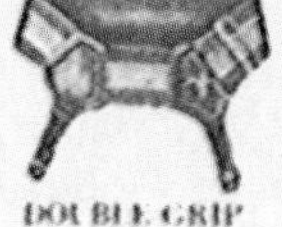

DOUBLE GRIP

NO METAL CAN TOUCH YOU

25c to $2

Dress Well and Succeed

EXHIBIT 3.1

While this ad for Lux laundry powder may seem curious to us today, it reflected the anxiety of the 1930s, during the Great Depression. Just as today's advertising reflects the values of contemporary society, this ad emphasized some very real concerns of the time—the economic well-being and status of women.

The 1935 Lux advertisement shown in Exhibit 3.1 is undoubtedly curious to contemporary audiences. It is, however, typical of its time and very likely made perfect sense to its original audience. In the 1930s, in the middle of the Great Depression, anxiety about losing one's husband—and thus one's economic well-being—to divorce was not unfounded. Targeted to a new generation of stay-at-home housewives anxious about their exclusion from the modern world of their husbands, during a period when losing one's source of income could mean abject poverty or worse, in a society where daily bathing was still rare but where self-doubt about personal hygiene was on the rise, such an ad may have pushed just the right buttons. If Lux can "remove perspiration odor from underthings," it might save more than colors and fabrics. It might save marriages. If Bob's romantic indifference continues, Sally may soon be back home with Mom or on the street. But with Lux on the scene, Bob goes home for dinner.

While some ads today use the same general technique to sell deodorants, soaps, and feminine-hygiene products, this ad is certainly not read the same way today as it was in 1935. Ads are part of their times. Today, Sally would likely have a job and be far less economically vulnerable and socially isolated—not to mention that Sally and Bob would both be bathing more. So we see the 1930s in this ad in the same way that students of the future will view ads of our time: as interesting, revealing, but still distorted reflections of daily life in the early 21st century. Even in the 1930s, consumers knew that ads were ads; they knew that ads exaggerated, they knew that ads tried to sell things, and they knew that ads didn't exactly mirror everyday life. But ads look enough like life to work, sometimes.

This chapter is about the evolution of advertising. Over the decades, advertisers have tried many different strategies and approaches, and you can learn a lot from their successes and failure. Studying them will allow you to know when a given advertising technique is really something new or just reheated retro. Besides being interesting, history is very practical.

Fundamental Influences on the Evolution of Advertising.

In many discussions of the evolution of advertising, the process is often portrayed as having its origins in ancient times, with even primitive peoples practicing some form of advertising. This is incorrect. Whatever those ancients were doing, they weren't advertising. Remember, advertising exists only as mass-mediated communication. As far as we know, there was no *Mesopotamia Messenger* or "Rome: Live at Five." So, while cavemen and cavewomen certainly were communicating with one another with persuasive intent, and maybe even in an exchange context, they were not using advertising. Advertising is a product of modern times and mass media.

Before offering a brief social history of American advertising, we will first discuss some of the major factors that gave rise to it. Advertising, as we have defined it, came into being as a result of at least four major developments:

1. The rise of capitalism
2. The Industrial Revolution
3. Manufacturers' pursuit of power in the channel of distribution
4. The rise of modern mass media

I **The Rise of Capitalism.** For advertising to become prominent in a society, the society must rely on aspects of capitalism in its economic system. The tenets of capitalism warrant that organizations compete for resources, called *capital,* in a free market environment. Part of the competition for resources involves stimulating demand for the organization's goods or services. When an individual organization successfully stimulates demand, it attracts capital to the organization in the form of money (or other goods) as payment. One of the tools used to stimulate demand is advertising.

The Industrial Revolution. The **Industrial Revolution** produced a need for advertising. Beginning about 1750 in England, the revolution spread to the United States and progressed slowly until the early 1800s, when the War of 1812 boosted domestic production. The emergence of the principle of interchangeable parts and the perfection of the sewing machine, both in 1850, coupled with the Civil War a decade later, laid the foundation for widespread industrialization. The Industrial Revolution took American society away from household self-sufficiency as a method of fulfilling material needs to marketplace dependency as a way of life. The Industrial Revolution was a basic force behind the rapid increase in a mass-produced supply of goods that required stimulation of demand, something that advertising can be very good at. By providing a need for advertising, the Industrial Revolution was a basic influence in its emergence.

Other equally revolutionary developments were part of the broad Industrial Revolution. First, there was a revolution in transportation, most dramatically symbolized by the east-west connection of the United States in 1869 by the railroad. This connection represented the beginnings of the distribution network needed to move the mass quantities of goods for which advertising would help stimulate demand. In the 1840s, the **principle of limited liability,** which restricts an investor's risk in a business venture to only his or her shares in a corporation rather than all personal assets, gained acceptance and resulted in the accumulation of large amounts of capital to finance the Industrial Revolution. Finally, rapid population growth and urbanization began taking place in the 1800s. From 1830 to 1860, the population of the United States increased nearly threefold, from 12.8 million to 31.4 million. During the same period, the number of cities with more than 20,000 inhabitants grew to 43. Historically, there is a strong relationship between per capita outlays for advertising and an increase in the size of cities.[1] Overall, the growth and concentration of population provided the marketplaces essential to the widespread use of advertising. As the potential grew for goods to be produced, delivered, and introduced to large numbers of people residing in concentrated areas, the stage was set for advertising to emerge and flourish.

1. Julian Simon, *Issues in the Economics of Advertising* (Urbana, Ill.: University of Illinois Press, 1970), 41–51.

2 **Manufacturers' Pursuit of Power in the Channel of Distribution.** Another fundamental influence on the emergence and growth of advertising relates to manufacturers' pursuit of power in the channel of distribution. If a manufacturer can stimulate sizable demand for a brand, then that manufacturer can develop power in the distribution channel and essentially force wholesalers and retailers to sell that particular brand. Demand stimulation among consumers causes them to insist on the item at the retail or wholesale level; retailers and wholesalers have virtually no choice but to comply with consumers' desires and carry the desired item. Thus, the manufacturer has power in the channel of distribution and not only can force other participants in the channel to stock the brand, but also is in a position to command a higher price for the item. The marketing of Intel's Pentium chip is an excellent example of how one manufacturer, Intel, has developed considerable power in the computer distribution channel, establishing its product, the Pentium chip, as a premium brand.

A factor that turned out to be critical to manufacturers' pursuit of power was the strategy of **branding** products. Manufacturers had to develop brand names so that consumers could focus their attention on a clearly identified item. Manufacturers began branding previously unmarked commodities, such as work clothes and package goods, by the late 1800s, with Levi's (1873), Maxwell House (1873), Budweiser (1876), Ivory (1879), and Coca-Cola (1876) being among the first branded goods to show up on shopkeepers' shelves. Once a product had a brand mark and name that consumers could identify, the process of demand stimulation could take place. Of course, the essential tool in stimulating demand for a brand is advertising. Even today, when Procter & Gamble and Philip Morris spend many billions of dollars each year to stimulate demand for such popular brands as Crest, Charmin, Velveeta, and Miller Lite, wholesalers and retailers carry these brands because advertising has stimulated demand and brought consumers into the retail store looking for and asking for the brands.

Manufacturers' pursuit of power in the distribution channel is a standard facet of capitalistic economic systems. Generally, the economic system also needs to be advanced enough to feature a national market and a sufficient communication and distribution infrastructure through which power in the channel is pursued. It is just this sort of pursuit of power by manufacturers that is argued to have caused the widespread use of advertising in the United States.[2]

The Rise of Modern Mass Media. Advertising is also tied to the rise of mass communication. With the invention of the telegraph in 1844, a communication revolution was set in motion. The telegraph not only allowed the young nation to benefit from the inherent efficiencies of rapid communication, but also did a great deal to engender a sense of national identity and community. People began to know and care about people and things going on thousands of miles away. This changed not only commerce, but social consciousness as well.[3] Also, during this period, many new magazines designed for larger and less socially privileged audiences made magazines both a viable mass advertising medium and a democratizing influence on American society.[4] Through advertising in these mass-circulation magazines, national brands could be projected into national consciousness. National magazines made national advertising possible; national advertising made national brands possible. Without the rise of mass media, there would be no national brands, and no advertising.

It is critical to realize that for the most part, mass media in the United States are supported by advertising. Television networks, radio stations, newspapers, and mag-

2. Vincent P. Norris, "Advertising History—According to the Textbooks," *Journal of Advertising*, vol. 9, no. 3 (1980), 3–12.
3. Carey, James W. *Communication as Culture: Essays on Media and Society* (Winchester, Mass.: Unwin Hyman, 1989).
4. Christopher P. Wilson, "The Rhetoric of Consumption: Mass-Market Magazines and the Demise of the Gentle Reader, 1880–1920," in *The Culture of Consumption: Critical Essays in American History*, 1880–1980, ed. Richard Weightman Fox and T. J. Jackson Lears (New York: Pantheon, 1983), 39–65.

azines produce shows, articles, films, and programs, not for the ultimate goal of entertaining or informing, but to make a healthy profit from the sale of advertising. Media vehicles sell audiences. If this really bothers you, become a journalist.

3 Advertising in Practice.

So far, our discussion of the evolution of advertising has identified the fundamental social and economic influences that fostered its rise. Now we'll turn our focus to the evolution of advertising in practice. Several periods in this evolution can be identified to give us various perspectives on the process of advertising.

The Preindustrialization Era (pre-1800).

In the 17th century, printed advertisements appeared in newsbooks (the precursor to the newspaper).[5] The messages were informational in nature and appeared on the last pages of the tabloid. In America, the first newspaper advertisement is said to have appeared in 1704 in the *Boston News Letter.* Two notices were printed under the heading "Advertising" and offered rewards for the return of merchandise stolen from an apparel shop and a wharf.[6]

Advertising grew in popularity during the 18th century both in Britain and the American colonies. The *Pennsylvania Gazette* printed advertisements and was the first newspaper to separate ads with lines of white space.[7] As far as we know, it was also the first newspaper to use illustrations in advertisements. But advertising changed little over the next 70 years. While the early 1800s saw the advent of the penny newspaper, which resulted in widespread distribution of the news medium, advertisements in penny newspapers were dominated by simple announcements by skilled laborers. As one historian notes, "Advertising was closer to the classified notices in newspapers than to product promotions in our media today."[8] Advertising was about to change dramatically, however.

The Era of Industrialization (1800 to 1875).

In practice, users of advertising in the mid- to late 1800s were trying to cultivate markets for growing production in the context of a dramatically increasing population. A middle class, spawned by the economic windfall of regular wages from factory jobs, was beginning to emerge. This newly developing populace with economic means was concentrated geographically in cities more than ever before.

By 1850, circulation of the **dailies,** as newspapers were then called, was estimated at 1 million copies per day. The first advertising agent—thought to be Volney Palmer, who opened shop in Philadelphia—basically worked for the newspapers by soliciting orders for advertising and collecting payment from advertisers.[9] This new opportunity to reach consumers was embraced readily by merchants, and at least one newspaper doubled its advertising volume from 1849 to 1850.[10]

With the expansion of newspaper circulation fostered by the railroads, a new era of opportunity emerged for the advertising process. Advertising was not universally hailed as an honorable practice, however. Without any formal regulation of advertising, the process was considered an embarrassment by many segments of society, including some parts of the business community. At one point, firms even risked their credit ratings if they used advertising—banks considered the practice a sign of financial weakness. This image wasn't helped much by advertising for patent medicines,

5. Frank Presbrey, *The History and Development of Advertising* (Garden City, N.Y.: Doubleday, Doran & Company, 1929), 7.
6. Ibid., 11.
7. Ibid., 40.
8. James P. Wood, *The Story of Advertising* (New York: Ronald Press, 1958), 45–46.
9. Daniel Pope, *The Making of Modern Advertising and Its Creators* (New York: William Morrow, 1984), 14.
10. Cited in Stephen Fox, *The Mirror Makers: A History of American Advertising and Its Creators* (New York: William Morrow, 1984), 14.

EXHIBIT 3.2

The expansion of newspaper circulation fostered more widespread use of advertising. Unfortunately, some of this new advertising did not contribute positively to the image of the practice. Ads like this one for a patent medicine carried bold claims, such as "Keep the blood pure."

which were the first products heavily advertised on a national scale. These advertisements promised a cure for everything from rheumatism and arthritis to "consumption" and respiratory affliction, as Exhibit 3.2 shows.

The "P. T. Barnum Era" (1875 to 1918).

The only one who could ever reach me was the son of a preacher man.

—John Hurley and Ronnie Wilkins,
"Son of a Preacher Man"; most
notably performed by Dusty Springfield[11]

Shortly after the Civil War in the United States, modern advertising began. This is advertising that we would begin to recognize as advertising. While advertising existed during the era of industrialization, it wasn't until America was well on its way to being an urban, industrialized nation that advertising became a vital and integral part of the social landscape. From about 1875 to 1918, advertising ushered in what has come to be known as **consumer culture,** or a way of life centered on consumption. True, consumer culture was advancing prior to this period, but during this age it really took hold, and the rise of modern advertising had a lot to do with it. Advertising became a full-fledged industry in this period. It was the time of advertising legends: Albert Lasker, head of Lord and Thomas in Chicago, possibly the most influential agency of its day; Francis W. Ayer, founder of N. W. Ayer; John E. Powers, the most important copywriter of the period; Earnest Elmo Calkins, champion of advertising design; Claude Hopkins, influential in promoting ads as "dramatic salesmanship"; and John E. Kennedy, creator of "reason why" advertising.[12] These were the founders, the visionaries, and the artists who played principal roles in the establishment of the advertising business. One interesting sidebar is that several of the founders of this industry had fathers with the exact same occupation: minister. This very modern and controversial industry was founded in no small part by the sons of preachers.

By 1900, total sales of patent medicines had reached $75 million—providing an early demonstration of the power of advertising.[13] This demonstration sent advertising in a new direction and set the stage for its modern form. During this period, the first advertising agencies were founded and the practice of branding products became the norm. Advertising was motivated by the need to sell the vastly increased supply of goods brought on by mass production and by the demands of an increasingly urban population seeking social identity through (among other things) branded products. In earlier times, when shoppers went to the general store and bought soap sliced from a large locally produced cake, advertising had little or no place. But with advertising's ability to create enormous differences between near-identical soaps, advertising suddenly held a very prominent place in early consumer culture. Advertising made unmarked commodities into social symbols and identity markers, and it allowed them to charge far more money for them. Consumers are much more will-

11. John Hurley and Ronnie Wilkins, "Son of a Preacher Man," Atlantic Recording Group, 1968.
12. Fox, *The Mirror Makers,* op. cit.
13. Presbrey, *The History and Development of Advertising,* 16.

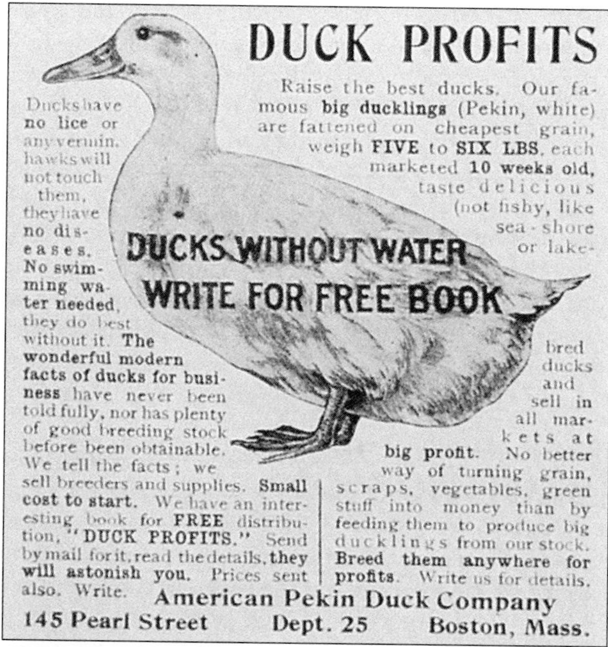

EXHIBIT 3.3

Ads from the "P. T. Barnum era" were often densely packed with fantastic promises. This 1902 Saturday Evening Post *advertisement featured many reasons why potential customers should get into the duck-raising business.*

ing to pay more money for brands (for example, Ivory) than for unmarked commodities (generic soap wrapped in plain paper).

The advertising of this period was, until 1906, completely unregulated. In that year, Congress passed the **Pure Food and Drug Act,** which required manufacturers to list the active ingredients of their products on their labels. Still, its effect on advertising was minimal; advertisers could continue to say just about anything—and usually did. Many advertisements took on the style of a sales pitch for snake oil. The tone and spirit of advertising owed more to P. T. Barnum—"There's a sucker born every minute"—than to any other influence. The ads were bold, carnivalesque, garish, and often full of dense copy that hurled fairly incredible claims at prototype "modern" consumers. A fairly typical ad from this era is shown in Exhibit 3.3.

Several things are notable about these ads: lots of copy (words); the prominence of the product itself and the corresponding lack of surrounding social space, or context in which the product was to be used; small size; little color; few photographs; and plenty of hyperbole. Over this period there was variation, and some evolution, but this style was fairly consistent up until World War I.

Consider also the social context of these ads. It was a period of rapid urbanization, massive immigration, labor unrest, and significant concerns about the abuses of capitalism. Some of capitalism's excesses and abuses, in the form of deceptive and misleading advertising, were the targets of early reformers. It was also the age of suffrage, the progressive movement, motion pictures, and mass culture. The world changed rapidly in this period, and it was no doubt disruptive and unsettling to many—but advertising was there to offer solutions to the stresses of modern life, no matter how real, imagined, or suggested.

The 1920s (1918 to 1929). In many ways, the Roaring Twenties really began a couple of years early. After World War I, advertising found respectability, fame, and glamour. It was the most modern of all professions; it was, short of being a movie actor or actress, the most fashionable. According to popular perception, it was where the young, smart, and sophisticated worked and played. During the 1920s, it was also a place where institutional freedom rang. The prewar movement to reform and regulate advertising was completely dissipated by the distractions of the war and advertising's role in the war effort. During World War I, the advertising industry learned a valuable lesson: donating time and personnel to the common good is not only good civics but smart business.

The 1920s were prosperous times. Most Americans enjoyed a previously unequaled standard of living. It was an age of considerable hedonism; the pleasure principle was practiced and appreciated, openly and often. The Victorian Age was over, and a great social experiment in the joys of consumption was underway. Victorian sexual repression and modesty gave way to a more open sexuality and a love affair with modernity. Advertising was made for this burgeoning sensuality; advertising gave people permission to enjoy. Ads of the era exhorted consumers to have a good time and instructed them how to do it. Consumption was not only respectable, but expected. Being a consumer became synonymous with being a citizen.

During this post–World War I economic boom, advertising instructed consumers how to be thoroughly modern and how to avoid the pitfalls of this new age. Consumers learned of halitosis from Listerine advertising and about body odor from Lifebuoy advertising (see Exhibit 3.4, a Lifebuoy ad from 1926). Not too surprisingly, there just happened to be a product with a cure for just about every social anxiety and personal failing one could imagine, many of which had supposedly been brought on as side effects of modernity. This was perfect for the growth and entrenchment of advertising as an institution: Modern times bring on many wonderful new things, but the new way of life has side effects that, in turn, have to be fixed by even more modern goods and services. Thus, a seemingly endless chain was created: Needs lead to products, new needs are created by new products, newer products solve newer needs, and on and on. This chain of needs is essential to a capitalist economy, which must continue to expand in order to survive. It also makes a necessity of advertising.

Other ads from the 1920s emphasized other modernity themes, such as the division between public workspace, the male domain of the office (see Exhibit 3.5), and the private, "feminine" space of the home (see Exhibit 3.6). Thus, two separate consumption domains were created, with women placed in charge of the latter, more economically important one. Advertisers soon figured out that women were responsible for as much as 80 percent of household purchases. While 1920s men were out in the "jungle" of the work world, women made most purchase decisions. So, from this time forward, advertising's primary target became women.

Another very important aspect of 1920s advertising, and beyond, was the role that science and technology began to play. Science and technology were in many ways the new religions of the modern era. The modern way was the scientific way.

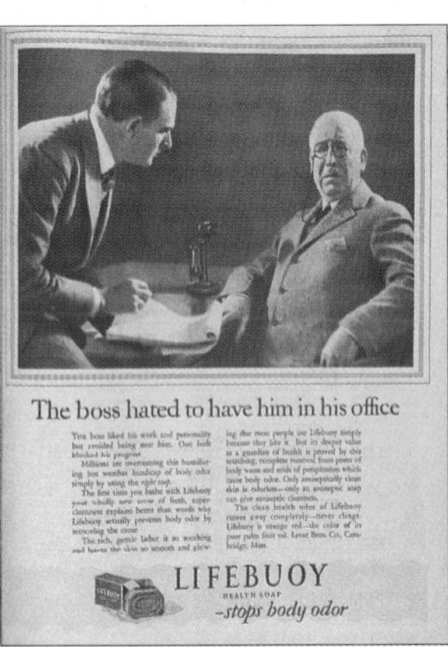

EXHIBIT 3.4

Many ads from the 1920s promised to relieve just about any social anxiety imaginable. Here, Lifebuoy offered a solution for people concerned that body odor could be standing in the way of career advancement.

EXHIBIT 3.5

This 1920s-era Gulf advertisement focuses on technological progress and the male prerogative in promoting its advancement. With the wonders of technology now found in every living room, selling gasoline aims more at individual gratification than at social uplift: Appeals to convenience, cost-consciousness, and environmental friendliness are all in evidence.

EXHIBIT 3.6

Ads from the 1920s often emphasized modernity themes, like the division between public and private workspace. This Fels-Naptha ad shows the private, "feminine" space of the home.

So one saw ads appealing to the popularity of science in virtually all product categories of advertising during this period. Ads even stressed the latest scientific offerings for child rearing and "domestic science," as Exhibits 3.7 and 3.8 demonstrate.

The style of 1920s ads was much more visual than in the past. Twenties ads showed slices of life, or carefully constructed "snapshots" of social life with the product. In these ads, the relative position, background, and dress of the people using or needing the advertised product were carefully crafted. These visual lessons were generally about how to fit in with the "smart" crowd, how to be urbane and modern by using the newest conveniences, and how not to fall victim to the perils and pressure of the new fast-paced modern world. The social context of product use became critical, as one can see in Exhibits 3.9, 3.10, and 3.11.

Advertising during the 1920s chronicled the state of technology and styles for clothing, furniture, and social functions. Advertising specified social relationships between people and products by depicting the social settings and circumstances into which products fit. Some of the best illustrators, artists, and writers in the world worked on advertisements during this period, and some of the ads from this period are now being collected and sold as art. Also note the attention to the social setting into which plumbing fixtures were to fit. Is the ad really about plumbing? Yes, in a very important way, because it demonstrates plumbing in a social context that works for both advertiser and consumer. Advertising was becoming sophisticated and had discovered social context in a major way.

In terms of pure art direction, the ads in Exhibits 3.12, 3.13, and 3.14 are examples of the beauty of the period's look. The J. Walter Thompson advertising agency was the dominant agency of the period. Stanley and Helen Resor and James Webb

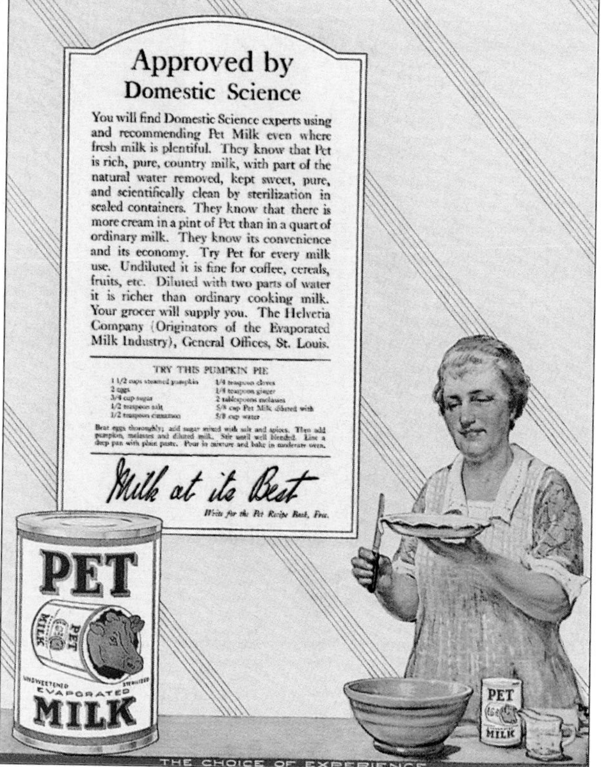

EXHIBITS 3.7 AND 3.8

The cultural theme of modernity in the 1920s emphasized science and technology. These ads for General Foods (Exhibit 3.7) and Pet Milk (Exhibit 3.8) tout the "domestic science" these brands brought to the home.

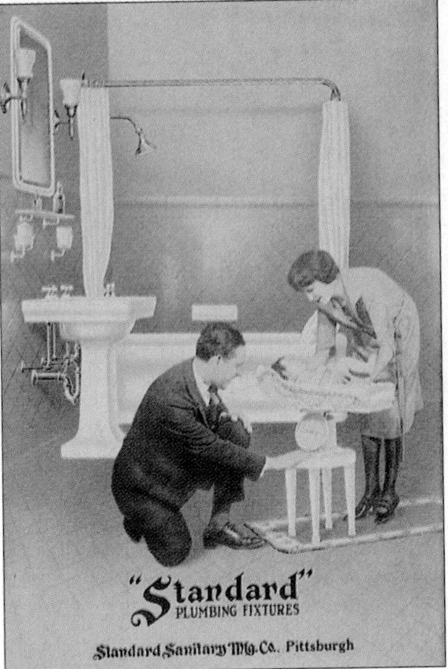

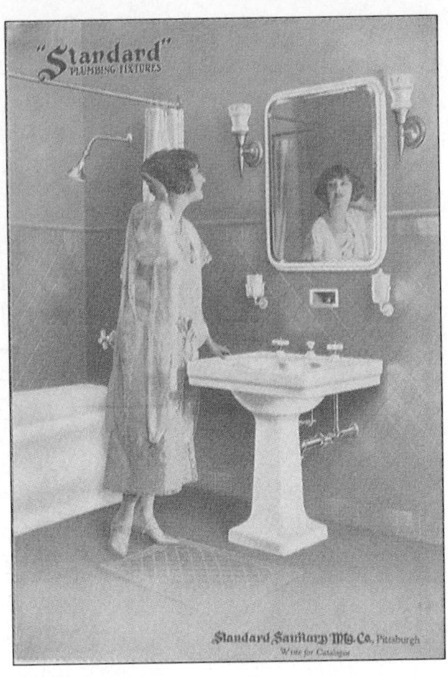

EXHIBITS 3.9, 3.10, AND 3.11

As the Kodak (Exhibit 3.9) and Standard Sanitary (Exhibits 3.10 and 3.11) ads illustrate, ads from the 1920s often showed carefully constructed "snapshots" of social life with the products. In an effort to make their advertising depict the technology and style of the era, advertisers in the 1920s enlisted the services of some of the best illustrators and artists of the time. So fine were the illustrations that some of them are now prized by some as works of art.

EXHIBITS 3.12, 3.13, AND 3.14

These 1920s ads are more examples of the beautiful and stylish art direction of the period.

Young brought this agency to a leadership position through intelligent management, vision, and great advertising. Helen Resor was the first prominent female advertising executive and was instrumental in J. Walter Thompson's success. Still, the most famous ad person of the era was a very interesting man named Bruce Barton. He was

EXHIBIT 3.15

The very tough times of the Great Depression, depicted in this 1936 photo by Walker Evans, gave Americans reason to distrust big business and its tool, advertising.

not only the leader of BBDO, but also a best-selling author, most notably of a 1924 book called *The Man Nobody Knows*.[14] The book was about Jesus and portrayed him as the archetypal ad man. This blending of Christian and capitalist principles was enormously attractive to a people struggling to reconcile traditional religious thought, which preached against excess, and the new religion of consumption, which preached just the opposite.

The Depression (1929 to 1941).

By 1932 a quarter of American workers were unemployed. But matters were worse than this suggests, for three quarters of those who had jobs were working part-time—either working short hours, or faced with chronic and repeated layoffs. . . . Perhaps half the working population at one time or another knew what it was like to lose a job. Millions actually went hungry, not once but again and again. Millions knew what it was like to eat bread and water for supper, sometimes for days at a stretch. A million people were drifting around the country begging, among them thousands of children, including numbers of girls disguised as boys. People lived in shanty towns on the fields at edges of cities, their foods sometimes weeds plucked from the roadside.[15]

If you weren't there, you have no idea how bad it was. We don't, but our parents and grandparents did. It was brutal, crushing, and mean. It killed people; it broke lives. Those who lived through it and kept their dignity are to be deeply admired. It forever changed the way Americans thought about a great many things: their government, business, money, and, not coincidentally, advertising.

Just as sure as advertising was glamorous in the 1920s, it was villainous in the 1930s. It was part of big business, and big business, big greed, and big lust had gotten

14. Bruce Barton, *The Man Nobody Knows* (New York: Bobbs-Merrill, 1924).
15. James Lincoln Collier, *The Rise of Selfishness in America* (New York: Oxford University Press, 1991), 162.

America into the great economic depression beginning in 1929—or so the story goes. The public now saw advertising as something bad, something that had tempted and seduced them into the excesses for which they were being punished.

Advertisers responded to this feeling by adopting a tough, no-nonsense advertising style. The stylish and highly aesthetic ads of the 1920s gave way to harsher and more cluttered ads. As one historian said, "The new hard-boiled advertising mystique brought a proliferation of 'ugly,' attention-grabbing, picture-dominated copy in the style of the tabloid newspaper."[16] Clients wanted their money's worth, and agencies responded by cramming every bit of copy and image they could into their ads. This type of advertising persisted, quite likely making the relationship between the public and the institution of advertising even worse. The themes in advertisements traded on the anxieties of the day; losing one's job meant being a bad provider, spouse, or parent, unable to give the family what it needed (as seen in Exhibits 3.16 and 3.17). The cartoon-strip style also became very popular during this period. (See Exhibit 3.18 for this style as well.)

Another notable event during these years was the emergence of radio as a significant advertising medium. During the 1930s, the number of radio stations rose to 814, and the number of radio sets in use more than quadrupled to 51 million. Radio was in its heyday as a news and entertainment medium, and it would remain so until the 1950s when television emerged. An important aspect of radio was its ability to create a new sense of community in which people thousands of miles apart listened to and became involved with their favorite radio soap opera, so named in reference to the soap sponsors of these shows.

Advertising, like the rest of the country, suffered dark days during this period. Agencies cut salaries and forced staff to work four-day weeks without being paid for the mandatory extra day off. Clients demanded frequent review of work, and agen-

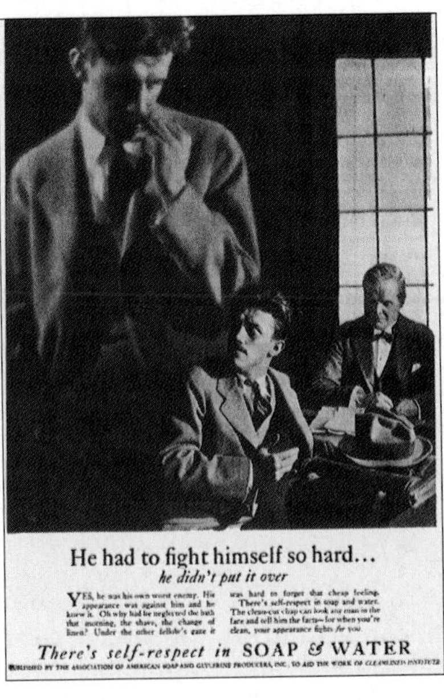

EXHIBITS 3.16 AND 3.17

The themes in advertising during the 1930s traded on the anxieties of the day, as these ads for Paris Garters (Exhibit 3.16) and the Association of American Soap and Glycerine Producers, Inc. (Exhibit 3.17) illustrate.

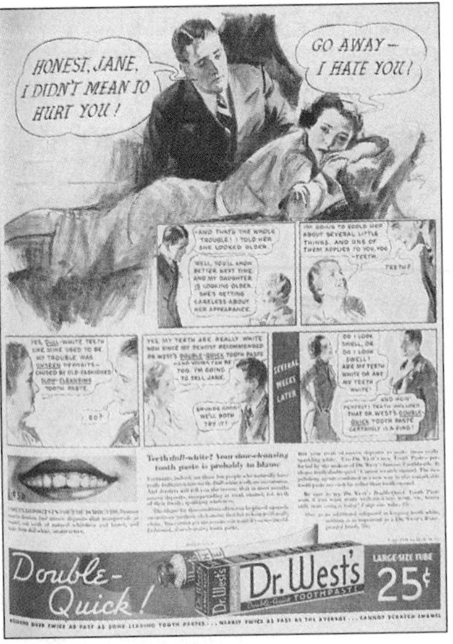

EXHIBIT 3.18

Another notable feature of 1930s advertising was the increasing use of the cartoon-strip style.

16. Ibid., 303–304.

cies were compelled to provide more and more free services to keep accounts. Advertising would emerge from this depression, just as the economy itself did, during World War II. However, it would never again reach its predepression status. It became the subject of a well-organized and angry consumerism movement. Congress passed real reform in this period. In 1938 the Wheeler-Lea Amendments to the Federal Trade Commission Act deemed "deceptive acts of commerce" to be against the law; this was interpreted to include advertising. Between 1938 and 1940, the FTC issued 18 injunctions against advertisers, including "forcing Fleischmann's Yeast to stop claiming that it cured crooked teeth, bad skin, constipation and halitosis."[17] These agencies soon used these new powers against a few large national advertisers, including Fleischmann's Yeast (consumers were being advised to eat yeast cakes for better health and vitality) and Lifebuoy and Lux soaps.

World War II and the Fifties (1941 to 1960).

Almost one-half of all women married while they were still teenagers. Two out of three white women in college dropped out before they graduated. In 1955, 41 percent of women "thought the ideal number of children was four."[18]

Many people mark the end of the depression with the start of America's involvement in World War II in December 1941. During the war, advertising often made direct reference to the war effort, as the ad in Exhibit 3.19 shows, linking the product with patriotism and helping to rehabilitate the tarnished image of advertising. During the war, advertisers sold war bonds and encouraged conservation. In addition, they encouraged women to join the workforce, as seen in the so-called Rosie the Riveter ads. The ad in Exhibit 3.20 for the Penn Railroad is a good example. During the war years, many women joined the workforce; of course, many left it (both voluntarily and involuntarily) after the war ended in 1945.

Following World War II, the economy continued to improve, and the consumption spree was on again. This time, however, public sentiment toward advertising was fundamentally different from what it had been in the 1920s. During the 1950s, when there was great concern about the rise of communism, the issue of "mind control" became an American paranoia, and many people suspected that advertising was involved. The country was filled with suspicion related to McCarthyism, the bomb, repressed sexual thoughts, and aliens from outer space. Otherwise normal people were building bomb shelters in their backyards (see Exhibit 3.21 on page 90) and wondering whether their neighbors were communists and whether listening to "jungle music" (a.k.a. rock-and-roll) would make their daughters less virtuous.

In this environment of fear, stories began circulating in the 1950s that advertising agencies were doing motivation research and using the psychological sell, which served only to fuel an underlying suspicion of advertising. It was also during this period that Americans began to fear they were being seduced by **subliminal advertising** (subconscious advertising) to buy all sorts of things they didn't really want or need. There had to be a reason that homes and garages were filling up with so much stuff; it must be all that powerful advertising—a great excuse for lack of self-control was born. In fact, a best-selling 1957 book, *The Hidden Persuaders,* offered the answer: slick advertising worked on the subconscious.[19] Suspicions about slick advertising still persist, and is still a big business for the "aren't consumers dumb/aren't advertisers evil" propagandists such as Jean Killbourne. Selling unfounded fears has always been good business. (See the IBP box on page 89.)

17. Fox, *The Mirror Makers,* 168.
18. Brienes, Wini, *Young, White and Miserable: Growing Up Female in the Fifties* (Boston: Beacon, 1992).
19. Vance Packard, *The Hidden Persuaders* (New York: D. McKay, 1957).

EXHIBIT 3.19

Advertisers often used America's involvement in World War II as a way to link their products with patriotism. This link provides advertising with a much-needed image boost after the dark period of the late 1930s. www.cocacola.com

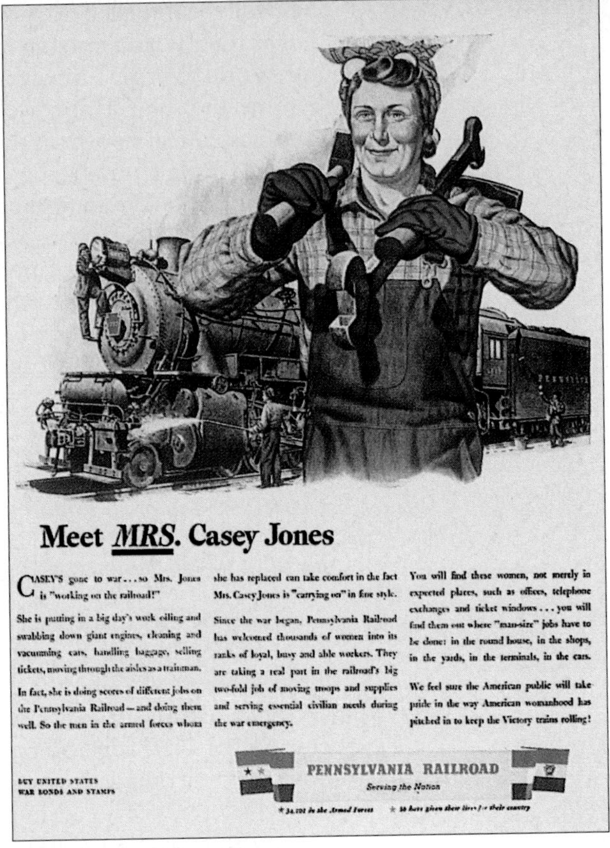

EXHIBIT 3.20

During the war, advertisers encouraged women to join the workforce, as this ad for Penn Railroad illustrates.

The most incredible story of the period involved a man named James Vicary. According to historian Stuart Rogers, in 1957 Vicary convinced the advertising world, and most of the U.S. population, that he had successfully demonstrated a technique to get consumers to do exactly what advertisers wanted. He claimed to have placed subliminal messages in motion picture film, brought in audiences, and recorded the results. He claimed that the embedded messages of "Eat Popcorn" and "Drink Coca-Cola" had increased sales of popcorn by 57.5 percent and Coca-Cola by 18.1 percent. He held press conferences and took retainer fees from advertising agencies. Later, he skipped town, just ahead of reporters who had figured out that none of this had ever happened. He completely disappeared, leaving no bank accounts and no forwarding address. He left town with about $4.5 million ($22.5 million in today's dollars) in advertising agency and client money.[20]

Wherever you are, Jim, it appears that you pulled off the greatest scam in advertising history. The big problem is that a lot of people, including regulators and members of Congress, still believe in the hype you were selling and that advertisers can actually do such things. That's the real crime.

20. Stuart Rogers, "How a Publicity Blitz Created the Myth of Subliminal Advertising," *Public Relations Quarterly,* Winter 1992–1993, 12–17.

The 1950s were also about sex, youth culture, rock-and-roll, and television. In terms of sex, volumes could be written about the very odd and paradoxical fifties. On one hand, this was the time of neo-Freudian pop psychology and *Beach Blanket Bingo,* with sexual innuendo everywhere; at the same time, very conservative pronouncements about sexual mores were giving young Americans very contradictory messages. What's more, they would be advertised to with a singular focus and force never seen before, becoming, as a result, the first "kid" and then "teen" markets. Because of their sheer numbers, they would ultimately constitute an unstoppable youth culture—one that everyone else had to deal with and try to please—the baby boomers. They would, over their parents' objections, buy rock-and-roll records in numbers large enough to revolutionize the music industry. Now they buy golf clubs, cell phones, and mutual funds.

And then there was TV (Exhibit 3.22). Nothing like it had happened before. Its rise from pre–World War II science experiment to 90 percent penetration in U.S. households occurred during this period. At first, advertisers didn't know what to do with it, and did two- and three-minute commercials, typically demonstrations. Of course, they soon began to learn TV's look and language.

This era also saw growth in the U.S. economy and in household incomes. The suburbs emerged, and along with them there was an explosion of consumption. Technological change was relentless, and it fascinated the nation. The television, the telephone, and the automatic washer and dryer became common to the American lifestyle. Advertisements of this era were characterized by scenes of modern life, social promises, and a reliance on science and technology.

Into all of this, 1950s advertising projected a confused, often harsh, at other times sappy presence. It is rarely remembered as advertising's golden age. Two of the most significant advertising personalities of the period were Rosser Reeves of the Ted Bates agency, who is best remembered for his ultra-hard-sell style, and consultant Ernest Dichter, best remembered for his motivational research, which focused on the subconscious and symbolic elements of consumer

IBP

Not Snake Oil—But Still Pretty Slick

Marketers and advertisers long ago gave up the snake-oil—"it cures all"—claims of eras past. But modern technology enables advertisers to use multiple media to integrate their marketing communications in a way that is, well, pretty slick.

Let's say your grandmother suffers from arthritis and really needs to take medication to relieve her pain, but all the prescription arthritis pain medications upset her stomach. Magically, a coupon for $1.00 off Zantac antacid shows up in her mailbox. The reason? Glaxo Wellcome PLC, the makers of Zantac, know that various forms of prescription arthritis medication lead to nausea in a high percentage of cases. It just so happens that Granny is in a Glaxo Wellcome database of arthritis medication users and—*voilà*—the coupon gets sent out for Zantac.

Until recently, pharmaceutical marketers did not know, and could not know, who their prescription customers were. Doctors and pharmacists were sworn to keep the names of patients confidential. But recent changes in advertising regulations have relaxed restrictions. Now, about 300 new database marketing programs are available that track drug use. With this information, direct mail campaigns, magazine placement of ads, and even certain television media placements can be made with greater efficiency in reaching target customers.

Acquiring names and other vital information about target customers is not a matter of doctors and pharmacists violating confidentiality, though. In many cases, drug companies get the names of people who suffer from such sensitive conditions as depression and impotence from an unlikely source—the patients themselves. Many people give out their names and addresses when they call toll-free numbers, subscribe to magazines, or fill out pharmacy questionnaires. For example, *Reader's Digest* sent a survey to 15 million of its subscribers asking them about their health problems. More than 3 million subscribers responded, and now *Reader's Digest* can target mailings to people with high cholesterol, to smokers, and to arthritis suffers. Many patients are outraged at the invasion of privacy, even though they gave out their names freely.

For the time being, firms such as Glaxo Wellcome are trying to understand the best way to use database information to the benefit of both the firm and the patient without violating the patient's sense of privacy and confidentiality.

Sources: William M. Bulkeley, "Prescriptions, Toll-Free Numbers Yield a Gold Mine for Marketers," *Wall Street Journal,* April 17, 1998, B1; Sally Beatty, "*Reader's Digest* Targets Patients by Their Ailments," *Wall Street Journal,* April 17, 1998, B1.

EXHIBIT 3.21

During the 1950s, with McCarthyism—and advertising—contributing to American paranoia, frightened people were building bomb shelters in their backyards.

EXHIBIT 3.22

At first, advertisers didn't know what to do with television, the pre–World War II science experiment that reached 90 percent of U.S. households by 1960.

desire. Exhibits 3.23 through 3.26 are representative of the advertising from this contradictory and jumbled period in American advertising.

These ads show what were becoming (or already were) mythic nuclear families, well-behaved children, our "buddy" the atom, the last days of unquestioned faith in science, and rigid gender roles. In a few short years, the atom would no longer be our friend; we would question science; youth would rebel; and women and African-Americans would demand inclusion and fairness.

Peace, Love, and the Creative Revolution (1960 to 1972).

You say you want a revolution, well, you know, we all want to change the world.

—John Lennon and Paul McCartney, "Revolution"[21]

Advertising in the United States during the 1960s was slow to respond to the massive social revolution going on all around it. While the nation was struggling with civil rights, the Vietnam War, and the sexual revolution, advertising was often still portraying women and minorities in subservient roles. Based on the ads of the day, one would conclude that only white people bought and used products, and that women had few aspirations beyond service in the kitchen and the bedroom.

The only thing really revolutionary about 1960s advertising was the **creative revolution.** This revolution was characterized by the "creatives" (art directors and copywriters) having a bigger say in the management of their agencies. The emphasis in advertising turned "from ancillary services to the creative product; from science and research to art, inspiration, and intuition."[22] The look of advertising during this period was clean, minimalist, and sparse, with simple copy and a sense of self-effacing humor. The creative revolution, and the look it produced, is most often associated with four famous advertising agencies: Leo Burnett in Chicago; Ogilvy & Mather in New York; Doyle Dane Bernbach in New York, and Wells Rich and Green in New York. They were led in this revolution by agency heads Leo Burnett, David Ogilvy, Bill Bernbach, and Mary Wells. The Kellogg's Special K cereal,

21. John Lennon and Paul McCartney, "Revolution," Northern Songs, 1968.
22. Fox, *The Mirror Makers,* 218.

EXHIBITS 3.23 THROUGH 3.26

Advertising during the 1950s offered consumers contradictory messages. On one hand, technological change and economic progress created the widespread enthusiasm reflected in the Ford, IBM, and Atlas Tires ads in Exhibits 3.23, 3.24, and 3.25. On the other hand, consumer suspicions about slick advertising that worked on the subconscious led some advertisers to use hard-sell messages, like the one in the Serta ad shown in Exhibit 3.26 (lower left). www.ibm.com *and* www.ford.com

Rolls-Royce, Volkswagen, and Braniff ads pictured in Exhibits 3.27 through 3.30 are 1960s ads prepared by these four famous agencies, respectively.

Of course, it would be wrong to characterize the entire period as a creative revolution. Many ads in the 1960s still reflected traditional values and relied on relatively uncreative executions. Typical of many of the more traditional ads during the era is the Goodyear ad in Exhibit 3.31. And it was certainly the case that a wide range of products, notably Pepsi (Exhibit 3.32), traded on youth and the idea of youth.

A final point that needs to be made about the era from 1960 to 1972 is that this was a period when advertising became generally aware of its own role in consumer culture—that is, advertising was an icon of a culture fascinated with consumption. While advertising played a role in encouraging consumption, it had become a symbol of consumption itself. While the creative revolution did not last long, advertising would always be different as a result. After the 1960s it would never again be quite as naive about its own place in society; it has since become much more self-conscious. In a very significant way, the 1960s changed advertising for real, and forever.

Every few years, it seems, the cycles of the sixties repeat themselves on a smaller scale, with new rebel youth cultures bubbling their way to a happy replenishing of the various culture

EXHIBITS 3.27 AND 3.28

The new era of advertising in the 1960s was characterized by the creative revolution, during which the creative side of the advertising process rose to new prominence. The ads in Exhibits 3.27 and 3.28 reflect the advertising of the day—clean, minimalist, and sparse, with simple copy. These ads were developed by two advertising agencies closely associated with the creative revolution of the sixties: Leo Burnett in Chicago and Ogilvy & Mather in New York. www.kelloggs.com *and* www.rollsroyce.com

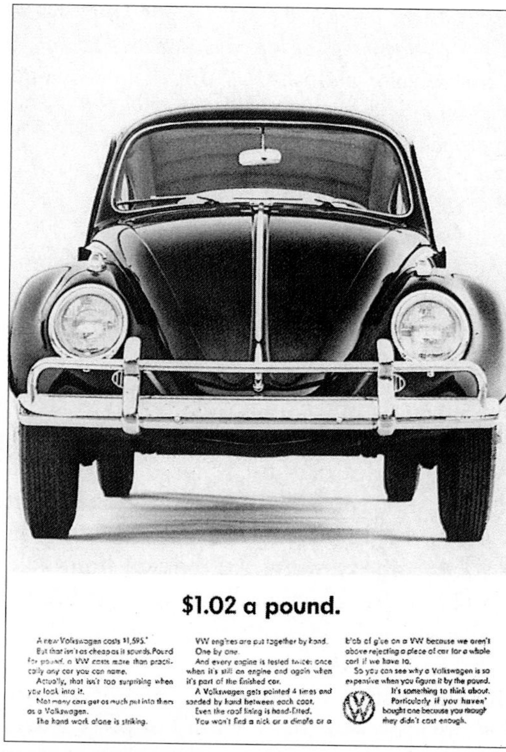

EXHIBIT 3.29

Through innovative advertising, Volkswagen has, over the years, been able to continually refuel its original message that its cars aren't expensive luxuries but as much a household staple as broccoli and ground round (and, at $1.02 a pound, cheaper than either!). www.vw.com

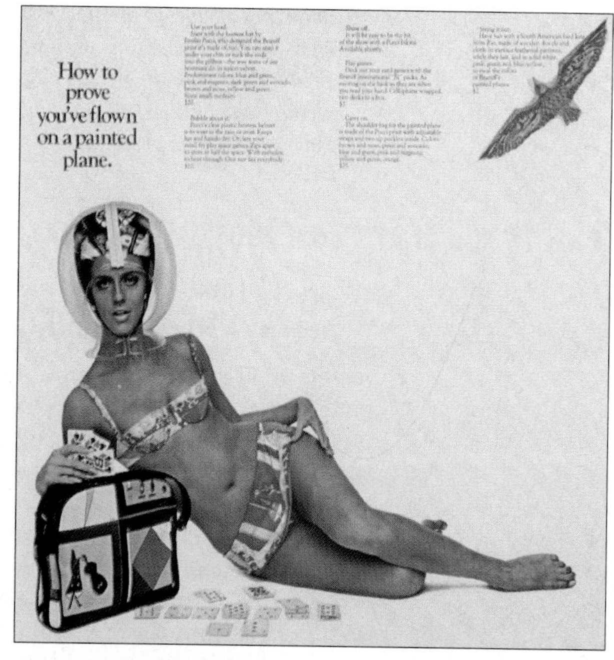

EXHIBIT 3.30

This is one of Mary Wells's famous ads.

EXHIBIT 3.31

Not all the advertising in the 1960s was characterized by the spirit of the creative revolution. The ad in Exhibit 3.31 relies more on traditional styles and values. www.goodyear.com

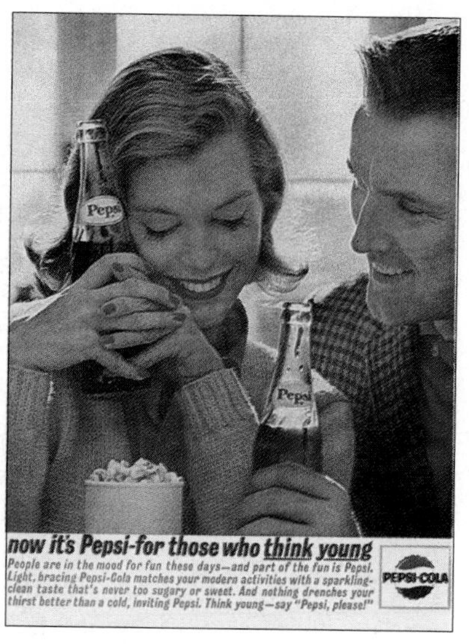

EXHIBIT 3.32

Pepsi "created" a generation and traded on the discovery of the vast youth market. They claimed youth as their own. www.pepsiworld.com

industries' depleted arsenal of cool. New generations obsolete the old, new celebrities render old ones ridiculous, and on and on in an ever-ascending spiral of hip upon hip. As adman Merle Steir wrote back in 1967, "Youth has won. Youth must always win. The new naturally replaces the old." And we will have new generations of youth rebellion as certainly as we will have generations of mufflers or toothpaste or footwear.[23]

The 1970s (1973 to 1980).

Mr. Blutarski, fat, drunk, and stupid is no way to go through life.

—Dean Vernon Wormer (John Vernon) in *National Lampoon's Animal House,* 1978

Dean Wormer's admonition to John Belushi's character in *Animal House* captured essential aspects of the 1970s, a time of excess and self-induced numbness. This was the age of polyester, disco, and driving 55. The re-election of Richard Nixon in 1972 marked the real start of the 1970s. America had just suffered through its first lost war, four student protesters had been shot and killed by the National Guard at Kent State University in the spring of 1970, Mideast nations appeared to be dictating the energy policy of the United States, and we were, as President Jimmy Carter said late in this period, in a national malaise. In this environment, advertising again retreated into the tried-and-true but hackneyed styles of decades before. The creative revolution of the 1960s gave way to a slowing economy and a return to the hard sell. This period also marked the beginning of the second wave of the American feminist movement. In the 1970s, advertisers actually started to present women in "new" roles and to include people of color, as the 1978 Polaroid OneStep ad in Exhibit 3.33 shows.

The seventies was also the end of the sixties, and the end of whatever revolution one wished to speak of. This period became known as the era of self-help and selfishness. "Me" became the biggest word in the 1970s. What a great environment for advertising. All of society was telling people that it was not only OK to be selfish, but it was the right thing to do. Selfishness was said to be natural and good. A refrain similar to "Hey babe, I can't be good to you, if I'm not good to me," became a seventies mantra. Of course, being good to one's self often meant buying stuff . . . always good for advertising. Funny how that worked out.

Somewhat surprisingly, the seventies also resulted in added regulation and the protection of special audiences. Advertising encountered a new round of challenges on several fronts. First, there was growing concern over what effect $200 million a year in advertising had on children. A group of women in Boston formed **Action for Children's Television (ACT),** which lobbied the government to limit the amount and content of advertising directed at children. Established regulatory bodies, in particular the **Federal Trade Commission (FTC)** and the industry's **National Advertising Review Board,** demanded higher standards of honesty and disclosure from the advertising industry. Several firms were subject to legislative mandates and fines because their advertising was judged to be misleading. Most notable among these firms were Warner-Lambert (for advertising that Listerine mouthwash could cure and prevent colds), Campbell's (for putting marbles in the bottom of a soup bowl to bolster its look), and Anacin (for advertising that its aspirin could help relieve tension).

While advertising during this period featured more African-Americans and women, the effort to adequately represent and serve these consumers was minimal; advertising agency hiring and promotion practices with respect to minorities were formally challenged in the courts. Two important agencies owned and managed by African-Americans emerged and thrived: Thomas J. Burrell founded Burrell Adver-

23. Thomas Frank, *The Conquest of Cool: Business Culture, Counterculture, and the Rise of Hip Consumerism* (Chicago: University of Chicago Press, 1997), 235.

EXHIBIT 3.33

While a bad economy and a national malaise caused a retreat to the tried-and-true styles of decades before, a bright spot of 1970s advertising was the portrayal of people of color. This Polaroid ad is from 1978. www.polaroid.com

EXHIBIT 3.34

Thomas Burrell created ads that portrayed African-Americans with "positive realism."

tising and Byron Lewis founded Uniworld. Burrell is perhaps best known for ads that rely on two principles: "positive realism" and "psychological distance." Optimistic realism is "people working productively; people engaging in family life . . . people being well-rounded . . . and thoughtful; people caring about other people; good neighbors, good parents . . . people with dreams and aspirations; people with ambition." Psychological distance is "a feeling of separation between the black consumer and a mainstream product." One of Burrell's well-known ads is shown in Exhibit 3.34. (You should also go to http://www.littleafrica.com/resources/advertising.htm for a current list of major African-American advertising agencies and resources.)

The 1970s also signaled a period of growth in communications technology. Consumers began to surround themselves with devices related to communication. The development of the VCR, cable television, and the laserdisc player all occurred during the 1970s. Cable TV claimed 20 million subscribers by the end of the decade. Similarly, cable programming grew in quality, with viewing options such as ESPN, CNN, TBS, and Nickelodeon. As cable subscribers and their viewing options grew, advertisers learned how to reach more specific audiences through the diversity of programming on cable systems.

The process of advertising was being restricted by both consumer and formal regulatory challenges, yet technological advances posed unprecedented opportunities. It was the beginning of the merger mania that swept the industry throughout the end of the decade and into the next, a movement that saw most of the major agencies merge with one another and with non-U.S. agencies as well. This period in the evolution of advertising presented enormous challenges.

EXHIBITS 3.35 AND 3.36

One of the significant differences between advertising prepared in the 1960s and in the 1970s is that ads began focusing on the product itself, rather than on creative techniques. The Alpo ad in Exhibit 3.35 and the Spirit ad in Exhibit 3.36 represent this product-focused feature of 1970s advertising, which reflects the fact that management had taken control of agency activities during this era. Does 7-Up's recent campaign (www.7up.com) reflect a similar focus on the product itself, or on creative techniques? What do current advertising trends tell us about the role of management in today's agencies? www.alpo.com

In all of this, the look of advertising was about as interesting as it was in the 1950s. Often, advertisements focused on the product itself, rather than on creative technique, as illustrated in the product-focused Alpo and Spirit ads in Exhibits 3.35 and 3.36. During this period, management took control and dominated agency activities. The MBA age was upon us. A very famous 1970s and 1980s CEO of a very large New York advertising agency, himself an ex-copywriter, was fond of saying that the worst thing that ever happened to advertising was the MBA. In agencies used to creative control, the idea of "bottom-liners" struck deep at the soul. Of course, all that money they made in the 1980s made them feel much better about the whole thing.

The Designer Era (1980 to 1992).

Greed, for a lack of a better word, is good.

—Gordon Gekko (Michael Douglas) in *Wall Street,* 1987

"In 1980, the average American had twice as much real income as his parents had had at the end of WWII."[24] The political, social, business, and advertising landscape changed again around 1980 with the election of Ronald Reagan. The country made

24. Collier, *The Rise of Selfishness in America,* 230.

a sharp right, and conservative politics was the order of the day. There was, of course, some backlash and many countercurrents, but the conservatives were in the mainstream.

Many ads from the Republican era are particularly social-class and values conscious. They openly promote consumption, but in an understated and conservative way. The quintessential 1980s ad may be the 1984 television ad for President Ronald Reagan's reelection campaign called "Morning in America." The storyboard for this ad is shown in Exhibit 3.37. This ad is soft in texture, but it gives an impression of firm reaffirmation of family and country. Other advertisers quickly followed with ads that looked similar to "Morning in America." The 1980s were also about designer labels and social-class consciousness, as the ad in Exhibit 3.38 demonstrates.

At the same time, several new, high-technology trends were emerging in the industry, which led to more-creative, bold, and provocative advertising. Television advertising of this period was influenced by the rapid-cut editing style of MTV, and some advertising near the end of the period played to at least someone's idea of Generation X, as the Pepsi ad in Exhibit 3.39 illustrates.

This was also the age of the **infomercial,** a long advertisement that looks like a talk show or a half-hour product demonstration. If you watch late-night cable television, you've probably seen some guy lighting his car on fire as part of a demonstration for car wax. These very long ads initially aired in late-night television time slots, when audiences were small in number and airtime was relatively inexpensive. Infomercials have since spread to other off-peak time slots, including those with somewhat larger audiences, and they have gained respect along the way. The Psychic Friends Network, Bowflex, and a wide assortment of automotive, weight loss,

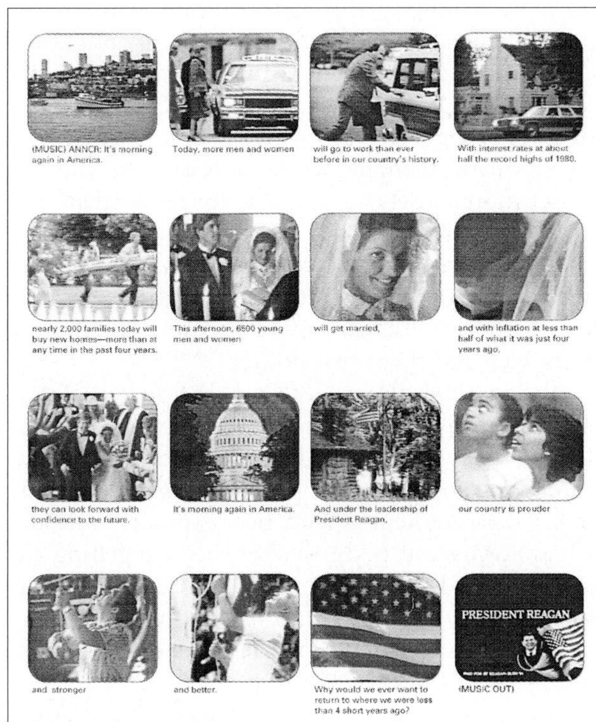

EXHIBIT 3.37

An ad that embodied the tone and style of 1980s advertising was Ronald Reagan's 1984 re-election campaign ad "Morning in America." The ad is soft in texture but firm in its affirmation of the conservative values of family and country.

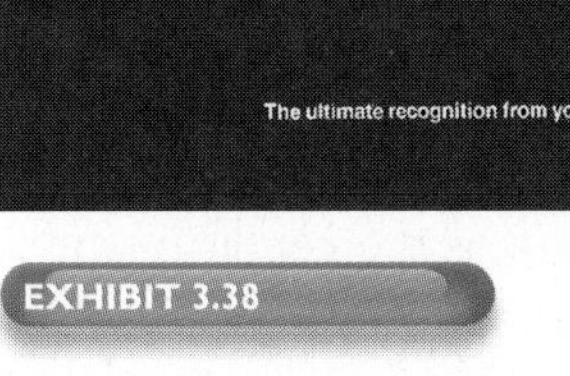

EXHIBIT 3.38

This MasterCard ad demonstrates the social-class and design consciousness of the 1980s.

and hair care products are all examples of products and services recently promoted on infomercials. You might check out http://www.as-on-tv-ads.com.

The Second Nineties (1993 to 2000).

Modern advertising had entered its second century, and it was more self-conscious than ever before. Winks and nods to the media-savvy audience were common. It was fast, and it was everywhere. It was being challenged by the World Wide Web and other new media, reshaped, and reinvented, but was still advertising.

The going for advertising got pretty rough in the mid-1990s. In May 1994, Edwin L. Artzt, then chairman and CEO of Procter & Gamble, the $40-billion-a-year marketer of consumer packaged goods, dropped a bomb on the advertising industry. During an address to participants at the American Association of Advertising Agencies (4As) annual conference, he warned that agencies must confront a "new media" future that won't be driven by traditional advertising. While at that time P&G was spending about $1 billion a year on television advertising, Artzt told the 4As audience, "From where we stand today, we can't be sure that ad-supported TV programming will have a future in the world being created—a world of video-on-demand, pay-per-view, and subscription TV. These are designed to carry no advertising at all."[25] Then, just when the industry had almost recovered from Artzt's blast, William T. Esrey, chairman and CEO of Sprint, fired another volley almost exactly a year later at the same annual conference. Esrey's point was somewhat different but equally challenging to the industry. He said that clients are "going to hold ad agencies more closely accountable for results than ever before. That's not just because we're going to be more demanding in getting value for our advertising dollars. It's also because we know the technology is there to measure advertising impact more precisely than you have done in the past."[26] Esrey's point: Interactive media will allow direct measurement of ad exposure and impact, quickly revealing those that perform well and those that do not.

e-SIGHTINGS

EXHIBIT 3.39

While the success of the Republican era in using advertising to create political images led to many imitations, the Pepsi ad here marked a countercurrent of rebellion that appealed to the younger markets. Is there evidence that this cultivated, youth-oriented image for Pepsi still drives the company's advertising? Visit Pepsi's home page (www.pepsiworld.com) *and see if you can draw direct comparisons to the past campaign illustrated in this exhibit. Compare Pepsi's site with that of its competitor Coca-Cola* (www.cocacola.com). *How might advertising's commodification of counterculture blur its distinctiveness with mainstream pop culture?*

Four years down the road, in August 1998, Procter & Gamble hosted an Internet "summit," due to "what is widely perceived as the poky pace of efforts to eliminate the difficulties confronted by marketers using on-line media to pitch products."[27] Some of these problems are technological: incompatible technical standards; limited bandwidth, and disappointing measurement of audience, exposure, and subsequent behavior. Advertisers such as P&G want to know what they are getting and what it costs when they place an Internet ad. Does anyone notice these ads, or do people click right past them? What would "exposure" in this environment mean? How do you use this medium to build brand relationships? At the end of this summit, P&G reaffirmed its commitment to the Internet. We'll see.

Another change has come in the form of a significant challenge on New York's claim as the center of the advertising universe. In the United States, the center has

25. This quote and information from this section can be found in Steve Yahn, "Advertising's Grave New World," *Advertising Age,* May 16, 1994, 53.

26. Kevin Goodman, "Sprint Chief Lectures Agencies on Future," *Wall Street Journal,* April 28, 1995, B6.

27. Stuart Elliot, "The Media Business: Advertising; Procter and Gamble Calls Internet Marketing Executive to Cincinnati for a Summit Meeting," *New York Times,* Business and Financial Section, New York Times on the Web, accessed February 20, 1999.

moved west, with the ascendency of the California, Oregon, and Washington agencies. These agencies tend to be more creatively oriented and less interested in numbers-oriented research than those in New York. Other hot or nearly hot markets include Minneapolis and Austin. Outside the United States, London and Singapore emerged as trendsetters (Exhibits 3.40, 3.41, and 3.42). Nineties ads were generally more visually oriented and much more self-aware. They said "this is an ad" in their look and feel. They tended to have a young and ironic flavor. Some call them "post-modern." Exhibits 3.43, 3.44, and 3.45 are good examples of 1990s advertising.

4 The 00s: The Interactive/Wireless/Broadband Revolution (2001–present).

As you might imagine, the perspectives offered by the heads of Procter & Gamble and Sprint did send shock waves through the advertising industry during that era of the mid- to late 1990s. The technological changes that occurred during those years were intoxicating. But at the outset of the 21st century, some harsh realities of the complexity of global commerce landed squarely on many dot-coms. In a phenomenon often referred to as a "shake-out," many Internet firms declared bankruptcy—such as Pets.com and Brandwise.com (see the E-commerce box on page 106)—that once had billion-dollar valuations and many believers (Exhibit 3.46).

The demise of Web sites that were totally dependent on online advertising for their revenues does not mean that online advertising is dead (although it's not feeling too well today). It's just not going to be as all-encompassing as those early predictions at P&G and Sprint (and others) might have suggested. From 1999 to 2000, online advertising grew from $4.6 billion to $6.1 billion—a more-than-healthy 32.6 percent. But 90 percent of that spending came in the first three quarters of 2000, and the fourth quarter showed a 6.5 percent rate indicating a significant slowdown in spending.[28] Despite the slowdown, predictions for growth in online ad spending are still highly optimistic (probably way too optimistic) for the future, with estimates ranging from 15 to 40 percent annual growth.[29]

The main impetus for such spending is focused on three aspects of technology that will foster further growth—interactive, wireless, and broadband technologies. We are living now with significant interactive capability. The Web is the most obvious example; for instance, P&G has developed and maintains 70 different Web sites for the company's 300 brands to serve and interact with customers.[30] But aside from the obvious, the crux of the real turmoil caused by interactive technology is **interactive media.** With interactive media, consumers can call up games, entertainment, shopping opportunities, and educational programs on a subscription or pay-per-view basis. The belief is that consumers want the wide range of choices, the convenience, and the control such programming provides. To reach consumers through this new technology, Procter & Gamble has set up partnerships with sites like Women.com and Bolt.com. In addition, P&G has gone beyond just product-oriented sites and has launched "relationship building" sites like beinggirl.com—a teen community site (Exhibit 3.47). With such a site, the firm can gather data, test new product ideas, and experiment with interactivity. For example, if a visitor wants to know what nail polish will match the lipstick she just saw in a commercial, she can go to the Web site and get an immediate answer. Thus, target audiences do not have to be broadly defined by age or geographic groups—individual households can be targeted through direct interaction with the audience member. Of course, there are those who believe that, at least in the case of television, consumers *do not* want to be interactive but passive. When they watch TV, they just want to watch TV and be left alone. The "audience" involvement of computers and the passivity of TV viewing may prove incompatible. We'll have to wait and see.

28. Patricia Riedman, "Net Ad Sector Moderates," *Advertising Age,* January 1, 2001, 17.

29. William Spain, "Hope Springs Eternal for Online Ads," CBS MarketWatch, www.adzoneinteractive.com, accessed January 8, 2001.

30. Beth Snyder Bulik, "Procter & Gamble's Great Web Experiment," *Business 2.0,* November 28, 2000, 48–54.

EXHIBITS 3.40 THROUGH 3.42

Outside the United States, London and Singapore have emerged as advertising trendsetters.

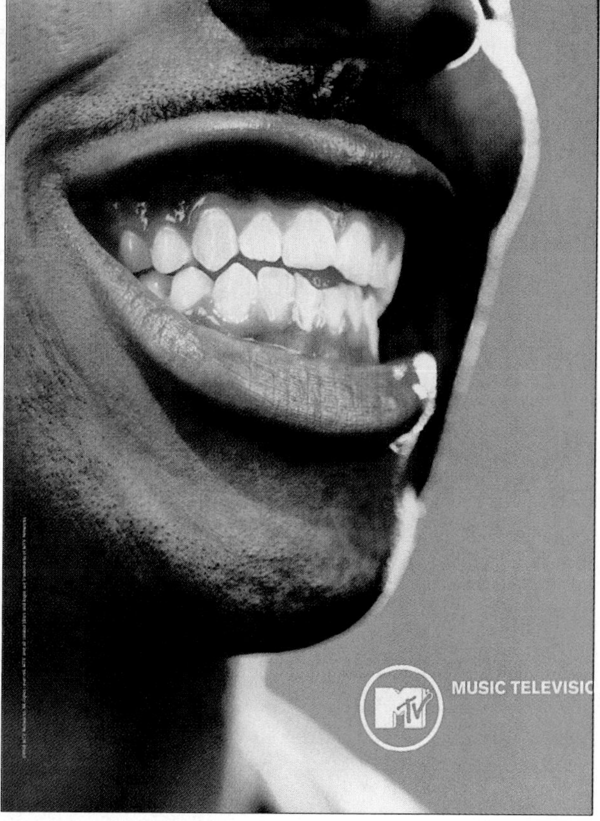

EXHIBITS 3.43 THROUGH 3.45

Exhibits 3.43 through 3.45 are good examples of 1990s advertising. They are visual, self-aware, young-feeling, and spiced with irony.

EXHIBIT 3.46

The lovable, but now unemployed, sock puppet for Pets.com.

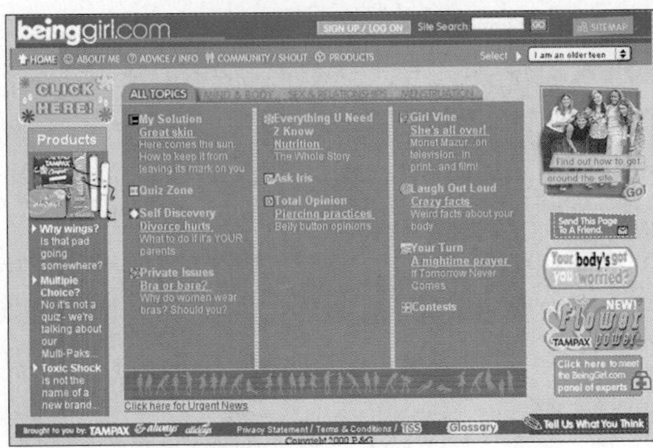

EXHIBIT 3.47

P&G's communal Web site beinggirl.com is a good example of online brand community building. www.beinggirl.com

Chapter 2 raised the issues of wireless and broadband technologies as trends that will be affecting the future of advertising (Exhibit 3.48). To follow up on that discussion, wireless penetration into U.S. households is poised for tremendous growth. In countries that have significant penetration of households with the Internet, wireless penetration is growing rapidly. With mobile phone subscribers worldwide estimated to be about 600 *million* in 2000 and estimated to grow to more than 1 billion people by 2003, the ability to go wireless would seem to be in place and developing rapidly.[31] These estimates seem credible given the declining cost and proliferation of wireless devices (see Exhibits 3.49 through 3.51).

Key to delivery is the broadband capability discussed in Chapter 2. Recall that broadband is a high-speed network for sending video and audio transmission over the Internet. The growth of broadband access parallels the growth of wireless use. By 2004, it is estimated that 15 percent of U.S. households (about 16 million households and 40 million people) will have broadband connections.[32] Advertisers will have to seriously consider the implications of this mode of communication and how well it will serve as a way to send persuasive communications.

In terms of the look, ads of the 00s have become even more self-aware and self-referential. They are ads that are very aware of being ads. Everyone is in on it. (See Exhibits 3.52 through 3.55.) It is also the period in which the biggest regulatory story of all ad history is being played out: the tobacco settlement in which the tobacco industry and the government worked out a settlement (after intense litigation). Under the terms of this settlement, tobacco advertising is highly restricted, and the industry pays for ads that are extremely critical of itself.

31. Will Daugherty, "The Growth of Wireless Mobile," *Business 2.0,* December 12, 2000, 276.
32. Anna Bernasek, "How Broadband Adds Up," *Fortune,* October 9, 2000, 28–29.

Say it's Tuesday. You've had a hard day at work and don't feel like joining your friends at the gym. Your Nokia communicator flashes a message that the latest Aki Kaurismäki movie is playing tonight at the local art house – the HVV system knows you might be interested because you went to see *Leningrad Cowboys Meet Moses* by the same director last week. So you message a friend who might want to go, too. She replies that she's already bought a ticket. With the aid of a seating plan that appears on your communicator screen, you not only book your admission but rebook hers, picking two seats in the middle of a row. The system alerts your friends that you won't be working out tonight and your home heating system that you'll be returning later than usual. Then it adds the fact that you're clearly nuts about Finnish auteurs to its ever-evolving list of your tastes and habits – maybe even notifying you that a movie club has formed in your apartment building. Would you like to join? Meanwhile, you haven't returned the message your mom left you at work; she wants to discuss her plans for Dad's surprise birthday party. Because she lives in Arabianranta and you've allowed her access to some parts of your HVV profile, she can see that you've gone to the movies tonight, sparing you a "Where *are* you?" scold on your voicemail.

Source: William Shaw, "In Helsinki Virtual Village . . . ," *Wired*, March 9, 2001, 158.

EXHIBIT 3.48

This excerpt from Wired *is a good discussion of technology's impact on advertising.*

EXHIBITS 3.49 THROUGH 3.51

Wireless devices come in all sizes, shapes, and capabilities, and they just keep coming.

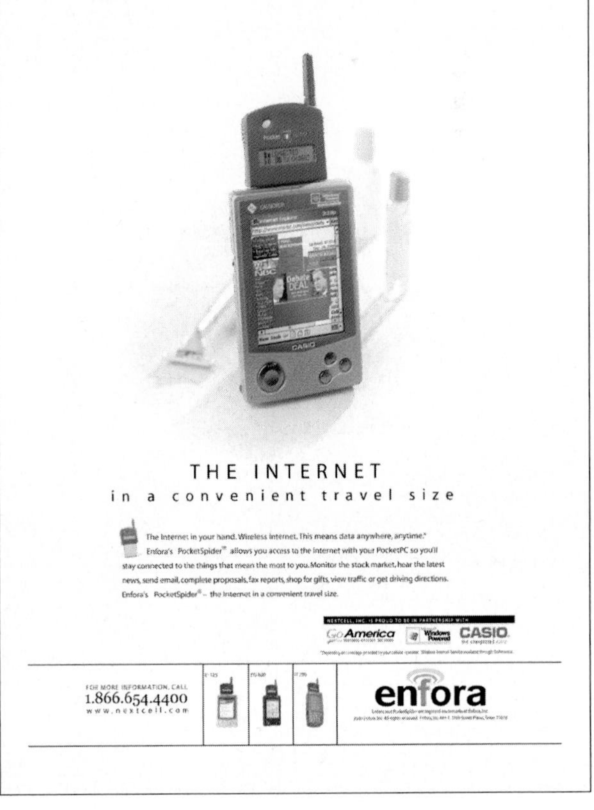

VENTED ZIP PANT

CHECK LONGNECK

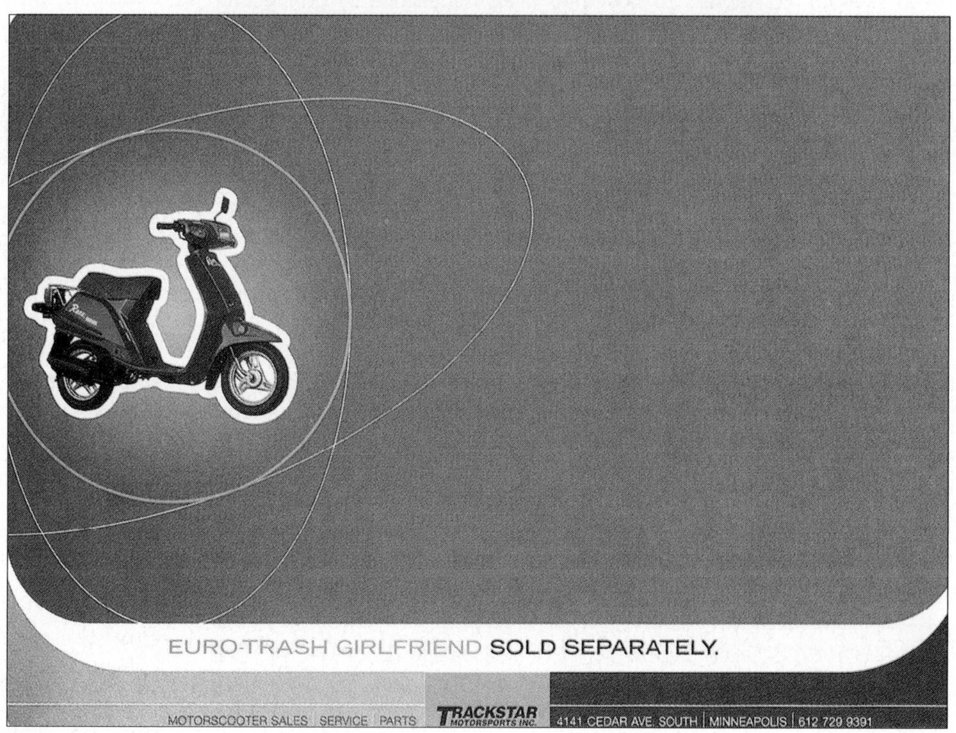

EXHIBITS 3.52 THROUGH 3.55

00s ads are even more self-aware, retro, and ironic.

Reinventing the Advertising Process?

As intriguing as new technology is and the new communications options it may present, we shouldn't jump to the conclusion that the very nature of advertising as a process will change. So far, it hasn't. Advertising will still be a paid, mass-mediated attempt to persuade. As a business process, advertising will still be one of the primary marketing mix tools that contribute to revenues and profits by stimulating demand and nurturing brand loyalty. Even though the executives at P&G believe there is a whole new world of communication and have developed 70 Web sites (Exhibit 3.56), the firm still spends almost $3 billion a year on traditional advertising through traditional media.[33] It is also safe to argue that consumers will still be highly involved in some product decisions and not so involved in others, so that some messages will be particularly relevant and others will be completely irrelevant to forming and maintaining attitudes about brands. To this date, technology (particularly e-commerce) has changed the way people shop, gather information, and purchase. E-advertising, on the other hand, has been pretty insignificant, an outright disappointment so far. So far the big winners have been traditional media (such as television), not e-advertising. Maybe things will change, maybe not.

If advertising retains its character as both a business and a communication process, then how would the process be reinvented in the context of new technology—if at all? Of course, there is no absolute answer to that question, but we can engage in some speculation. Some believe that e-commerce will force a change toward e-advertising. They believe this will be seen in the way advertising is prepared and delivered to target audiences. The scenario for the integrated, interactive advertisement of the future goes something like this: Prospective car buyers, from the comfort of their home, consider a variety of cars on their television screen. They change the model, position, color, and options on the

E-COMMERCE

Start the Evolution without Me

During the latter part of the 1990s and the early days of the 2000s, nearly every advertiser made a commitment to the Internet. The (fairly sound) logic was that this new medium was gaining more and more favor with consumers and more households were getting "wired" every day. Surely, this would be an ideal opportunity to reach a large number of consumers, through a new medium and in a much more personalized way.

Whirlpool was just the sort of company to use that logic. As one of the oldest U.S. companies and one that held a leading market share, not to mention a great brand image, Whirlpool wanted to be sure the opportunities to use the Internet effectively were not overlooked. Managers' thinking went something like this. Millions of people were scouring the Web in search for the best deals on books, air travel, and even cars. Surely, some of these millions of people would want to search the Web for a deal on a refrigerator or washing machine.

With that strategic orientation, Whirlpool launched Brandwise.com—the first comparative-shopping Web site for appliances. Brandwise.com would be consumers' trusted source for up-to-the-minute product information and reviews of all kinds of appliances made by all kinds of manufacturers. And Brandwise could make arrangements, right there on the Web site, for consumers to buy their dream appliance by connecting them to a nearby retailer. Whirlpool was so certain that Brandwise.com would be a runaway hit with consumers, that the firm hired Kathy Misunas, former CEO of American Airlines' Sabre Reservations Group. At Brandwise.com's launch, Misunas crowed, "Brandwise.com represents the next step in the evolution of e-commerce."

Wrong. Within eight months, Brandwise.com was shut down. The site attracted so few visitors—less than 200,000 per month—that Media Metrix wouldn't even follow it on its Web traffic–counting system. What went wrong and how could it go wrong so fast? The answer is actually painfully simple. Brandwise was conceived and executed with the attitude that the Web is so hot and hip that anything on the Web will not just survive but flourish. But what happened was that Whirlpool botched the marketing effort, failed to establish good relations with retailers, and underestimated the difficulty in setting up and maintaining a good Web site. In addition, the consumer behavior analysis was botched as well. Eighty percent of appliance purchasers are replacing something that broke. They don't want to go to a Web site, they want to go to a store and get a new appliance—now. In the end, what wrecked this new economy idea was an old economy challenge—execution.

Source: Amy Kover, "Brandwise Was Brand Foolish," *Fortune*, November 13, 2000, 201–208.

33. "100 Leading National Advertisers," *Advertising Age*, September 25, 2000, S2.

This is just one of P&G's 70 Web sites.

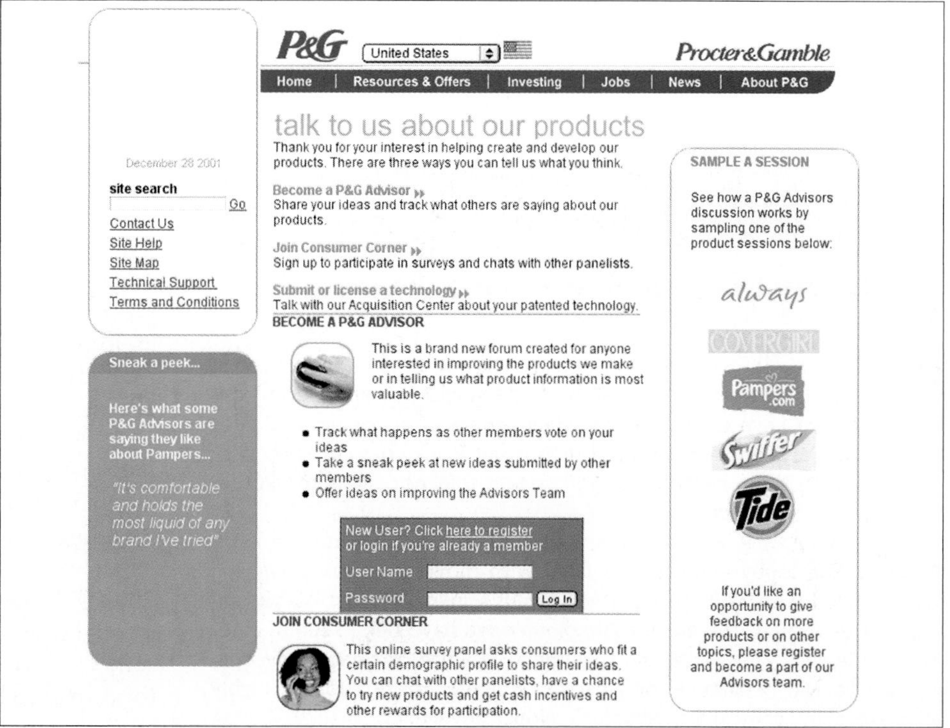

vehicle with a click of a mouse. Then, having constructed one or more appealing versions of the desired vehicle, another click of the mouse sets an appointment for a test drive with a nearby dealer. The dealer brings the requested car to prospective buyers. If a buyer is ready to take action, the dealer representative can go online with a laptop computer to check inventory and leasing programs and then signal the dealership to prepare the necessary paperwork.[34] Under this very optimistic scenario, e-commerce and e-advertising become indistinguishable.

Some organizations are already promoting interactive advertising and promotion. Consider the program available through Yahoo! Broadcast. Yahoo! Broadcast provides Internet broadcasting and support tools for businesses and content providers to deliver corporate communications messages via audio and video streaming. Applications include product launches, press conferences, e-learning, seminars, keynote addresses, annual shareholder meetings, quarterly earnings calls, and corporate TV channels. The program offers rich audio and video content and services through a digital distribution network designed to deliver high-quality audio and video to Yahoo!'s 166 million users worldwide via the Internet through both dial-up and broadband connections. The services of this Internet broadcast portal include the following:

- Live continuous broadcasts of more than 500 radio stations and networks
- Broadcasts of 70 television stations and cable networks
- Game broadcasts and other programming of more than 475 college and professional sports teams
- Live and on-demand corporate and special events from Yahoo!'s Business Services customers
- Live music, including concerts and club performances
- 3,100 full-length CDs on demand in the CD Jukebox
- 1,600 full-length audio books

34. Jonathan Berry and Kathy Rebello, "What Is an Ad in the Interactive Future?" *Business Week,* May 2, 1994, 103.

- 1,500 video titles, classic movies, documentaries, and independent films
- 15 million hours of "streaming" content[35]

Of course, for all this to happen, someone is going to actually have to make money . . . this is far from certain.

Another medium for interactive/wireless communication that is not as elaborate as broadband but certainly fulfills the objective of reaching target audiences with new technology is e-mail. While this may not seem like an important communication medium for advertising, advertisers invested $97 million in e-mail communications in 1999 to send an astounding 40 *billion* permission-based e-mails and another 38 *billion* spam e-mails. The spending on e-mail communication is expected to grow to $4.8 billion by 2004.[36] **Permission-based e-mail** is an advertiser originated e-mail to consumers who have granted permission for e-mail to be sent to them. **Spam** is advertiser-originated e-mail to consumers who have not granted permission for e-mail to be sent to them. E-mail is emerging as an important new interactive method for the advertising process for several reasons:

- Traditional direct mail methods such as letters, fliers, and coupons can cost from 50 cents to $2.00 per item.
- The message can be customized to individual users, creating a better opportunity for relationship building with the communication effort.
- The timing of the delivery of the message can be controlled more precisely than with traditional direct marketing media.

The world of new media and the effects on the advertising process will be covered throughout the text in E-Commerce boxes and in several chapters, including Chapter 10 on creativity; all the media chapters in Part Four of the text; Chapter 17, which covers supportive communications; and Chapter 19, which covers e-commerce in detail.

GLOBAL ISSUES

This Is Absolut-ly the Best Place to Reach Consumers

Advertisers worldwide are always searching for unique and effective ways to reach consumers with IBP tools. Advertising is still a dominant force, and we have discussed the effectiveness of sponsorships, sales promotions, and public relations. But Absolut Vodka has come up with a way it feels it can reach its target market that not many marketers have tried—the movies.

When you walk into a modern multiplex movie theater in Latin America, the lobby will likely be filled with movie posters, but it will also be filled with 3-D cutouts for Absolut Cinema's latest 60-second production. So far, the ads for Absolut Vodka have been seen in cinemas in Mexico, Venezuela, and Columbia. The use of cinema advertising is a radical departure for Absolut, which is famous for its highly effective print campaigns. Absolut's global advertising agency, TBWA Worldwide, convinced the distiller that print was not the way to go in Latin America. First, in many Latin American markets, consumers don't read much. Second, they go to the movies a lot. For example, Mexicans go the movies on average 2.5 times a week now that dumpy movie houses have been replaced by plush cinema complexes. Another plus for Absolut is that the new multiplex complexes are attracting young, upscale Mexicans—precisely Absolut's target market.

The use of various promotional tools other than advertising is gaining more favor for Absolut campaigns outside the United States. Aside from the cinema ads, two years ago "Absolut Summer" bloomed in Chile, the brainchild of Ann Stokes, TBWA's communications manager based in Sweden. Absolut Summer is a field of flowers planted in the shape of an Absolut bottle. Absolut will be sprouting all over Latin America before too long. Another "new media" effort was to place rotating signs *inside* bottles of Absolut to attract attention in the duty-free shop in Puerto Rico.

While the flashy and innovative print campaign for Absolut continues to be a winner in the United States, a wide range of IBP tools are being tried in the Latin American market to not only reach consumers but also attract and hold their attention.

Source: Laurel Wentz, "Absolut Goes to the Movies with Latin American Ads," *Advertising Age*, October 16, 2000, 19.

35. Information on Yahoo! Broadcast obtained from the Yahoo! Broadcast Web site, http://fusion.Yahoo.com/broadcast, accessed January 14, 2001.
36. Evantheia Schibsted, "E-mail Takes Center Stage," *Business 2.0*, December 26, 2000.

The Value of an Evolutionary Perspective. In this chapter, we have tried to offer an evolutionary perspective on advertising. We strongly believe that to understand advertising in an evolutionary perspective is to appreciate the reasons for advertising's use in a modern industrialized society. Advertising was spawned by a market-driven system and grew through self-interest in capitalistic, free enterprise market economies. Efficient methods of production made advertising essential as a demand stimulation tool. Urbanization, transportation expansion, and communications advancements all facilitated the use and growth of advertising. The result is that advertising has become firmly entrenched as a business function, with deeply rooted economic and cultural foundations. This evolutionary perspective allows us to understand the more basic aspects of the role and impact of advertising. An interesting correlate to any discussion of the evolution of advertising is, of course, the evolution of integrated brand promotion. While the advances in technology have taken center stage in our discussion of the latest era in advertising, IBP strategies and tactics evolve as well. Remember from Chapter 2 that more and more money is being allocated to IBP tools other than advertising. And the evolution of IBP is truly a global evolution as the Global Issues box highlights.

Corporate leaders such as Artzt from Procter & Gamble and Esrey from Sprint have issued a challenge to traditional advertising methods and media. New technologies and the interactive media options they present are an important issue, as we have discussed. But this should not be interpreted as the death of advertising, as some have argued.[37] In fact, paraphrasing Mark Twain, the death of advertising has been greatly exaggerated. Back in 1995, just when people were starting to describe advertising's sorrowful death at the hands of new media, we witnessed a surge in demand for traditional mass media space that set off a bidding war and the prospect of rationing time slots during the 1995–1996 prime-time network television season![38] A record $10 billion in advance media time was purchased then, and advertisers were scrambling for airtime. Now, in the early years of the 21st century, even though network television audiences appear to be shrinking somewhat, and virtually all broadcasters have purchased Internet services, they seem less worried about the survival of broadcast as a medium of traditional advertising than they were a short time ago. The death of advertising at the hands of interactive media does, indeed, seem to have been greatly exaggerated. Echoing and extending the recent sentiments of one Wall Street analyst: We have to look back at failure after failure in the interactive media realm, and wonder if consumers really want to be that engaged, that much of the time. We'll see. Passivity has its fans. Just because we can be more interactive doesn't mean we will choose to be.

37. Roland Rust and Richard W. Oliver, "The Death of Advertising," *Journal of Advertising,* vol. 23, no. 4 (December 1994), 71–77.
38. Joe Mandese, "Sizzling TV Ad Sales May Spark Rationing," *Advertising Age,* May 15, 1995, 1.

SUMMARY

Explain why advertising is an essential feature of capitalistic economic systems.

Although some might contend that the practice of advertising began thousands of years ago, it is more meaningful to connect advertising as we know it today with the emergence of capitalistic economic systems. In such systems, business organizations must compete for survival in a free market setting. In this setting, it is natural that a firm would embrace a tool that assists it in persuading potential customers to choose its products over those offered by others. Of course, advertising is such a tool. The explosion in production capacity that marked the Industrial Revolution gave demand-stimulation tools added importance.

Describe manufacturers' dependence on advertising, promotion, and branding in achieving balanced relationships with retailers.

Advertising and branding play a key role in the ongoing power struggle between manufacturers and their retailers. U.S. manufacturers began branding their products in the late 1800s. Advertising could thus be used to build awareness of and desire for the various offerings of a particular manufacturer. Retailers have power in the marketplace deriving from the fact that they are closer to the customer. When manufacturers can use advertising to build customer loyalty to their brands, they take part of that power back. Of course, in a capitalistic system, power and profitability go hand in hand.

Discuss several important eras in the evolution of advertising in the United States, and relate important changes in advertising practice to more fundamental changes in society and culture.

Social and economic trends, along with technological developments, are major determinants of the way advertising is practiced in any society. Before the Industrial Revolution, advertising's presence in the United States was barely noticeable. With an explosion in economic growth around the turn of the century, modern advertising was born: The "P. T. Barnum era" and the 1920s established advertising as a major force in the U.S. economic system. With the Great Depression and World War II, cynicism and paranoia regarding advertising began to grow. This concern led to refinements in practice and more careful regulation of advertising in the 1960s and 1970s. Consumption was once again in vogue during the designer era of the 1980s. The new communication technologies that emerged in the 1990s era may effect significant changes in future practice. Finally, the interactive, wireless, and broadband technologies that are leading advertising into the 21st century hold great promise but a hard-to-predict future.

Identify forces that may make the next decade a period of dramatic change for the advertising industry.

Integrated, interactive, and *wireless* have become the advertising buzzwords of the nineties. These words represent notable developments that may reshape advertising practice. Integrated marketing communications may grow in importance as advertisers work with more-varied media options to reach markets that are becoming even more fragmented. A variety of advertisers are now experimenting with interactive media to learn how to make effective use of this new tool. Advertising in the next decade will continue to be a vibrant and challenging profession.

KEY TERMS

Industrial Revolution
principle of limited liability
branding
dailies
consumer culture
Pure Food and Drug Act
subliminal advertising
creative revolution
Action for Children's Television (ACT)
Federal Trade Commission (FTC)
National Advertising Review Board
infomercial
interactive media
permission-based e-mail
spam

QUESTIONS

1. As formerly communist countries make the conversion to free market economies, advertising typically becomes more visible and important. Why would this be the case?

2. Explain why there is a strong relationship between increasing urbanization and per capita spending.

3. Why are manufacturers such as Nabisco and First Brands losing power in their channels of distribution? To whom, exactly, are they losing this power?

4. Describe the various factors that produced an explosion of advertising activity in the "P. T. Barnum era."

5. The 1950s were marked by great suspicion about advertisers and their potential persuasive powers. Do you see any lingering effects of this era of paranoia in attitudes about advertising today?

6. There were many important developments in the seventies that set the stage for advertising in the Reagan era. Which of these developments are likely to have the most enduring effects on advertising practice in the future?

7. Ed Artzt, then chairman and CEO of Procter & Gamble, made a speech in May 1994 that rattled the cages of many advertising professionals. What did Artzt have to say that got people in the ad business so excited?

8. Review the technological developments that have had the greatest impact on the advertising business. What new technologies are emerging that promise more profound changes for advertisers in the next decade?

EXPERIENTIAL EXERCISES

1. In this chapter, manufacturers' pursuit of power in the channel of distribution is listed as an important influence on the emergence and growth of advertising. Manufacturers depend on other members of the distribution channel (such as retailers and wholesalers) for the success of their brands. Hoping to pressure channel members to purchase manufacturers' brands, advertisers use ads to stimulate demand for their products at the consumer level, which in turn spurs retailers to purchase from manufacturers to meet that demand.

Contact a local retail store and set up a brief phone interview with the manager or retail buyer. Ask the manager what role customer requests and fashion trends play in determining the store's product offerings. Find out how they keep track of those requests and trends and how they respond to them. Finally, ask the manager to describe the role of advertisers in stimulating consumer demand and how that places leverage on them to carry certain brands. Ask for real-world examples.

2. During the period from 1980 to 1992, half-hour television product demonstrations known as infomercials emerged and became popular. Infomercials sell a variety of popular products—from diets and cosmetics to housewares and body training—and are designed to prompt a direct response from viewers. While many viewers question the integrity of these advertising programs, they have earned respect for their success in eliciting spontaneous purchases from broad target audiences.

The Carlton Sheets infomercial for his No Money Down Real Estate System is seen all over the country on late-night television. Go to a search engine and search for the Carlton Sheets Internet site. Compare and contrast the message of the infomercial with the message of the site. Do you think these two media reach the same target audience? Which medium do you think is more persuasive for this particular kind of product advertisement? Why? What social and economic conditions of the 1980s produced the advertising method known as the infomercial? If you are not familiar with Carlton Sheets, pick any infomercial and answer these same questions.

USING THE INTERNET

3-1 Reinventing the Advertising Process

While many aspects of advertising have remained constant over the course of its evolution, other aspects have changed dramatically. Emerging forces in technology and globalization have challenged advertisers to develop and promote brands in widely fragmented markets. As the evolutionary perspective of the history of advertising demonstrates, social, cultural, and economic shifts of the past have radically influenced the overall progression of the industry. As we would expect, many of today's important trends will guide the future evolution of advertising.

InfoWorld: http://www.infoworld.com

1. The final sections of the chapter examine some of the forces that will shape the next decade of advertising. What changes can be expected for the advertising industry, and why? What aspects of advertising are likely to remain constant?

2. Since new technologies will continue to play an important role in shaping the evolution of advertising, choose a relevant news story from InfoWorld and explain how you think the news might relate to the future evolution of the industry.

3-2 Important Eras in the Evolution of Advertising

The practice of advertising has emerged in modern times, owing its development largely to the social and economic changes of recent centuries and the rise of modern mass media. During the history of the United States, 11 important advertising eras evolved, each reflecting fundamental changes in society and culture. One of the world's largest searchable databases of classic print ads, adflip.com, features ads from the 1940s to the present. Fans of advertising history visit adflip.com to enjoy these retro ads and the evolution of pop culture they represent.

adflip: http://www.adflip.com

1. Browse adflip and select two ads from various decades of advertising history. Briefly describe the ads and explain how they fit the general characteristics of advertisements for their era as defined in the chapter.

2. Select an ad from the site that does not seem to reflect the general characteristics of its era. How does it differ from ads typical to this period? Would it fit better in a different general era of advertising history? Explain.

CHAPTER 4

After reading and thinking about this chapter, you will be able to do the following:

Assess the benefits and problems of advertising in a capitalistic society and debate a variety of issues concerning advertising's effects on society's well-being.

Explain how ethical considerations affect the development of advertising campaigns.

Discuss the role of government agencies in the regulation of advertising.

Explain the meaning and importance of self-regulation for an advertising practitioner.

Discuss the regulation of other promotional tools in the integrated brand promotion process.

CHAPTER 1
Advertising as a Process

CHAPTER 2
The Structure of the Advertising Industry: Advertisers, Advertising Agencies, and Support Organizations

CHAPTER 3
The Evolution of Advertising

CHAPTER 4
Social, Ethical, and Regulatory Aspects of Advertising

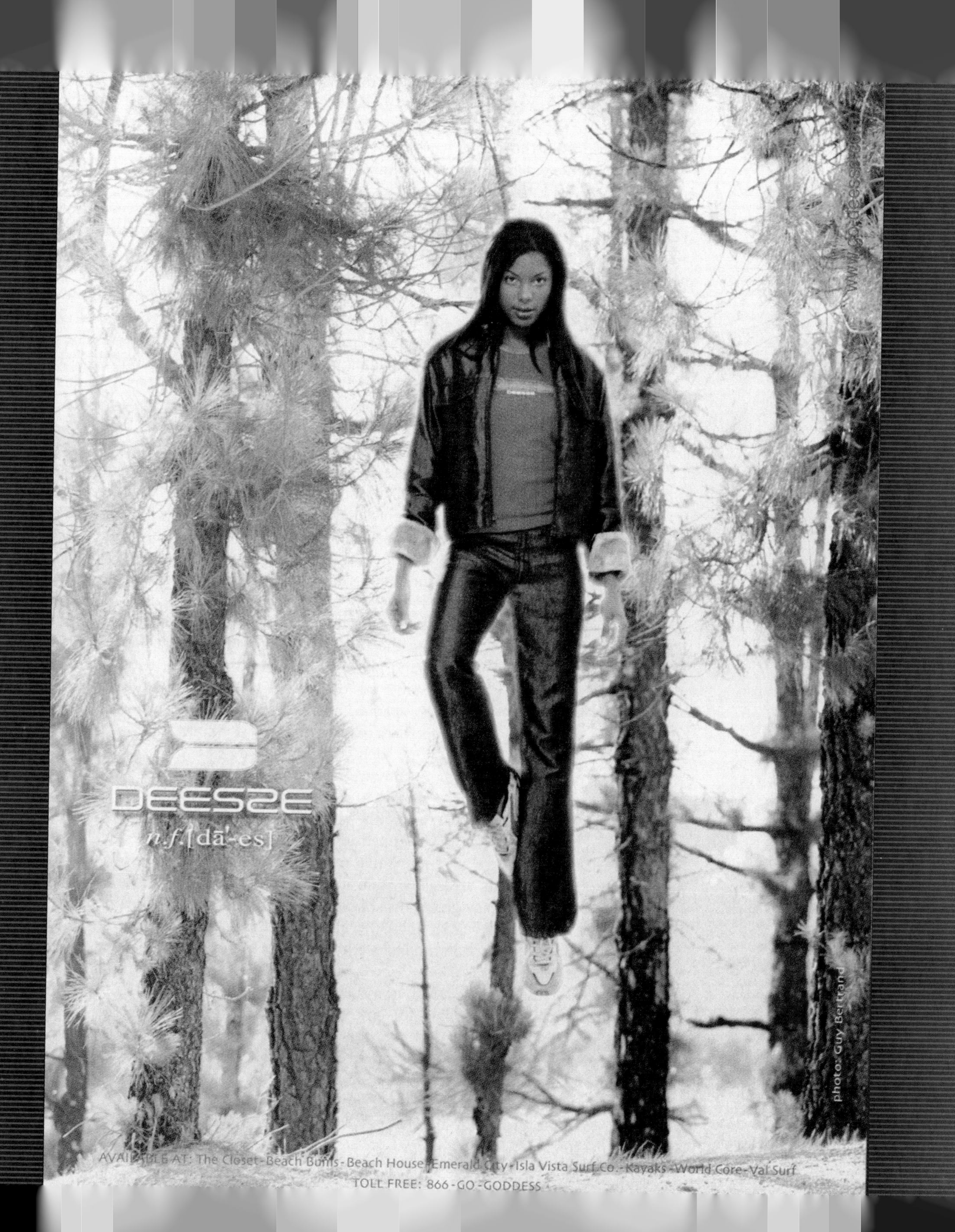
DEESSE
n.f. [dā'-es]
photo: Guy Bertrand
The Closet - Beach Bums - Beach House - Emerald City - Isla Vista Surf Co. - Kayaks - World Core - Val Surf
TOLL FREE: 866-GO-GODDESS

Has this ever happened to you? You see an ad in a magazine or the newspaper that announces a "Big Sweepstakes" where you can win a fabulous vacation to Hawaii, a killer speedboat, or $1 million in a drawing. You fill in the entry form, mail it, and wait. After a few months, it dawns on you that you haven't won the sweepstakes, but what you have won is a mailbox full of stuff from advertisers who got your name from the outfit that ran the sweepstakes!

This is exactly what happened to Anne Marie when she saw the Eddie Bauer edition of the Ford Explorer as a sweepstakes giveaway. It was her dream car and she entered the sweepstakes. But in the end, she decided that entering the sweepstakes created a nightmare. "Every Jeep dealer in the Galaxy was calling me after that," she said. "There was a span of about two weeks that a different car dealer called or mailed something about me coming in to test drive a car. I was furious."[1]

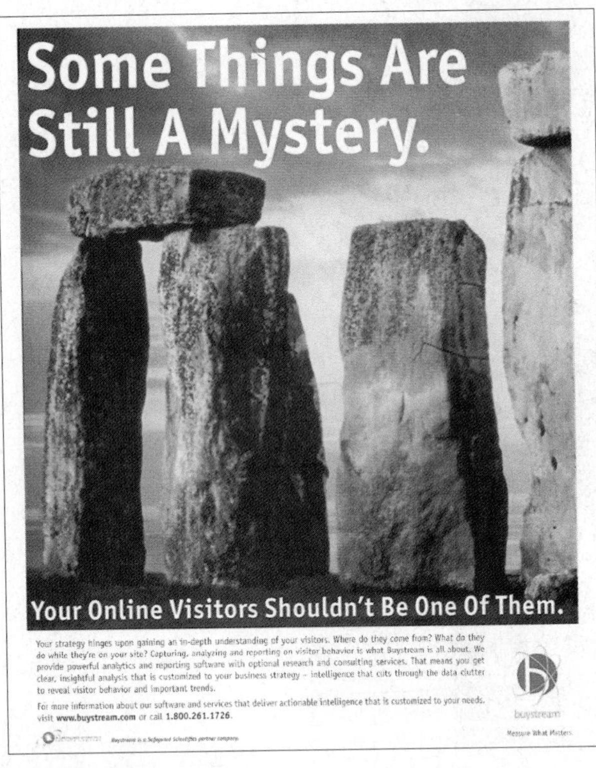

EXHIBIT 4.1

Many firms are in the business of providing information for advertisers to effectively and efficiently deliver advertising and integrated brand promotion messages to target audiences. While some firms sell consumers names and addresses creating privacy problems, Buystream helps its clients in a different way. Buystream helps a company gain an understanding of visitors to the company's Web site by gathering information on where the visitors come from and what behavior they exhibit at the site and providing summary reports.

What happened to Anne Marie happens to millions of Americans every day. Advertisers call it "database marketing." Contests, sweepstakes, supermarket discount cards, and product warranty cards are common methods used by marketers to gather information about customers and create a database to be used for advertising and integrated brand promotion strategies.[2] Big data "warehouse" companies such as Metromail, Acxiom, and R. L. Polk specialize in collecting massive amounts of consumer information. They then sell the data—including names, addresses, and phone numbers—to companies that use direct marketing, such as catalog publishers, Internet companies, charities, book clubs, and music clubs—you know, the ones who send you all the stuff in the mail. With the data, these firms can put together highly targeted advertising and integrated brand promotions using direct mail, telemarketing, banner ads on Web pages, and magazine ads. Some companies, however, do not infringe on customer privacy because they do not collect individual data. One such company is Buystream (see Exhibit 4.1). At Buystream, the firm provides aggregate data on visitors to a company's Web site with respect to where the visitor came from and what behavior they exhibited while at the site.

While marketers call this process database marketing, consumer advocates are calling it an invasion of privacy. The leader of Junkbusters, a consumer advocacy group that opposes invasions of consumer privacy, calls the practice of database development "Orwellian" because "George Orwell's *1984* described a world where each home had a television-like device that actually watched what individuals were doing."[3]

But advertisers defend the practice as good marketing research, which leads to greater efficiency and more value for customers. The information gathered about consumers is stored in a giant database, then "mined" or scrutinized for meaning. Once it is mined, consumers can be targeted with products or discount offers that match their previous buying patterns. As one direct marketer put it, "The more effective direct marketers get, the more they know about you, the better they can serve you."[4] For example, grocers argue that with the databases they can target coupons and

1. Teena Massingill, "Buyer Beware: Retailers Sharing Data," Knight Ridder News Service, September 17, 1999.
2. Alissa Quart, "Ol' College Pry," Business 2.0, April 3, 2001, 68.
3. Bradley Johnson, "Gov't Agencies Eye Online Profiling," *Advertising Age,* November 8, 1999, 102.
4. Erika Rasmusson, "What Price Knowledge?" *Sales and Marketing Management,* December 1998, 56.

other special advertised offers to the people most likely to use them, instead of wasting money on coupons and mailings that are never used. Consumer advocates are arguing for "permission marketing," in which marketers can direct advertising and promotions only to people who give them express permission to do so. Groups like the Privacy Rights Clearing House are taking up the fight for consumers, and the issue is currently being debated in Federal Trade Commission hearings.

Nothing about database development is unethical or illegal. It is, however, often pointed to as one of the most annoying aspects of the marketing and advertising effort. We will need to wait and see whether any restrictions are placed on the database process by either government mandate or consumer pressure. Or, we could all do what some people do. They don't enter sweepstakes, they never shop on the Internet, they throw junk mail and surveys directly into the trash, and they have unlisted phone numbers.

The story of Anne Marie (and perhaps your own experience) highlights that the social, ethical, and regulatory aspects of advertising are as dynamic and controversial as any of the strategic or creative elements of the process. What is socially responsible or irresponsible, ethically debatable, politically correct, or legal? The answers are constantly changing. As a society changes, so too do its perspectives. Like anything else with social roots and implications, advertising will be affected by these changes.

Advertising history includes all sorts of social, ethical, and legal lapses on the part of advertisers. However, advertising has also had its triumphs, moral as well as financial. Whether justified or not, criticisms of advertising can be naive and simplistic, often failing to consider the complex social and legal environment in which contemporary advertising operates. Sometimes they are right on. In this chapter, we will consider a wide range of social, ethical, and legal issues related to advertising and the many tools of integrated brand promotion.

1 The Social Aspects of Advertising.

The social aspects of advertising are often volatile. For those who feel that advertising is intrusive and manipulative, the social aspects usually provide the most fuel for heated debate.

We can consider the social aspects of advertising in several broad areas. On the positive side, we will consider advertising's effect on consumers' knowledge, standard of living, feelings of happiness and well-being, and its potential effects on the mass media. On the negative side, we will examine a variety of social criticisms of advertising, ranging from the charge that advertising wastes resources and promotes materialism to the argument that advertising perpetuates stereotypes. Our approach will be to offer pros and cons on several issues that critics and advertisers commonly argue about. Be forewarned—these are matters of opinion, with no clear right and wrong answers. You will have to draw your own conclusions.

Advertising Educates Consumers.

Does advertising provide valuable information to consumers, or does it seek only to confuse or entice them? Here's what the experts on both sides have to say.

Pro: Advertising Informs. Supporters of advertising argue that advertising educates consumers, equipping them with the information they need to make informed purchase decisions. By regularly assessing information and advertising claims, consumers become more educated regarding the features, benefits, functions, and value of products. Further, consumers can become more aware of their own tendencies toward being persuaded and relying on certain types of product information. The argument has been offered that advertising is "clearly an immensely powerful instrument for the elimination of ignorance."[5] According to this argument, better-educated

5. George J. Stigler, "The Economics of Information," *Journal of Political Economy* (June 1961), 213–220.

consumers enhance their lifestyles and economic power through astute marketplace decision making.

A related argument is that advertising *reduces search time*—that is, the amount of time an individual must spend to search for desired products and services is reduced because of advertising. The large amount of information readily available through advertising allows consumers to easily assess the potential value of brands, without spending time and effort to evaluate each one in a retail setting. The information contained in an advertisement "reduces drastically the cost of search."[6]

Another aspect of informing the public has to do with the role advertising can play in communicating about important social issues. Advertisers such as Anheuser-Busch devote millions of dollars to promoting responsible drinking with advertisements like the one shown in Exhibit 4.2. As described in the IBP box on page 119, Anheuser-Busch has also launched a unique Web site at www.beeresponsible.com as part of an IBP campaign designed to combat drunk driving, underage drinking, and binge drinking. In addition, government organizations use advertising for many purposes, including the education of consumers about social programs, as illustrated in Exhibit 4.3.

Con: Advertising Is Superficial. Critics argue that advertising does not provide good product information at all. The basic criticism of advertising here is that it frequently carries little, if any, actual product information (see Exhibit 4.4). What it does carry is said to be hollow ad-speak. Ads are rhetorical; there is no pure "information." All information in an ad is biased, limited, and inherently deceptive.

Critics claim that ads should contain information on functional features and performance results. Advertisers argue in response that, in many instances, consumers

EXHIBIT 4.2

This ad represents time and money spent by Anheuser-Busch to project a positive social message, yet the ad doesn't explicitly attempt to sell its products. Why is this choice important in a social-responsibility ad? www.budweiser.com

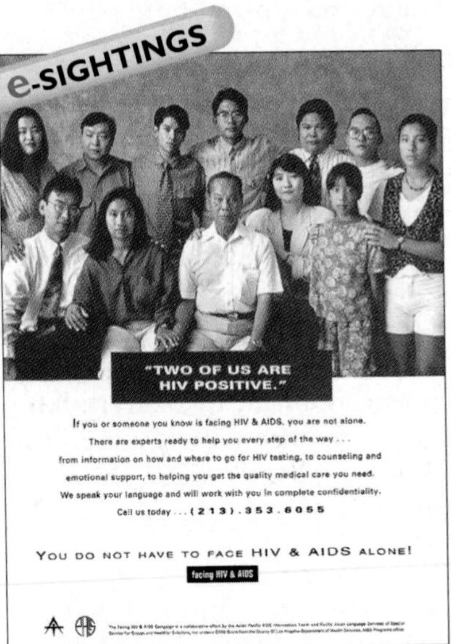

EXHIBIT 4.3

Many types of organizations use advertising to get their message out. In this case the message is very serious (www.youthhiv.org). *Social responsibility can be an essential part of corporate and brand identity. Click around Benetton's site and identify all the various ways it communicates and promotes social consciousness and multiculturalism.* www.benetton.com

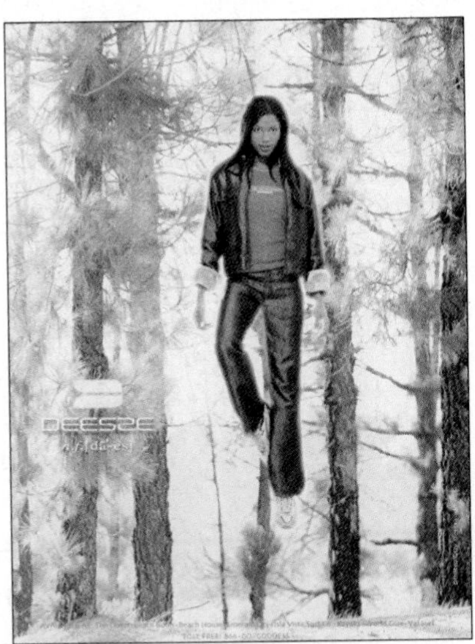

EXHIBIT 4.4

Critics of advertising complain that ads often carry little if any product information. Is this ad really devoid of product information?

6. Ibid., 220.

are interested in more than a physical, tangible material good with performance features and purely functional value. The functional features of a product may be secondary in importance to consumers in both the information search and the choice process. The advertisers' point is that critics often dismiss or ignore the totality of product benefits, including the hedonic (pleasure-seeking) aspects. The relevant information for the buyer relates to the criteria being used to judge the satisfaction potential of the product, and that satisfaction is quite often nonutilitarian. On the other hand, advertising apologists don't really understand how limited this "information" is. As evidence, they note how often the truth about products comes about only due to regulatory or legal action on this point. In truth, advertisers don't have the best record.

IBP

Tackling Alcohol Abuse through Integrated Brand Promotion

Why would the world's largest brewer and beer distributor also be a worldwide leader in the fight against alcohol abuse? Since 1982, when Anheuser-Busch launched its "Know When to Say When" ad campaign, it has spent over $350 million on advertising to promote responsible drinking among adults who choose to drink. In November 1997, Anheuser-Busch celebrated the 15-year anniversary of its campaign by launching the Web site www.beeresponsible.com to continue the fight against alcohol abuse "one person at a time." Over this time period, distributors of Anheuser-Busch's brands, such as Budweiser and Bud Light, have also made substantial contributions to the campaign. In 1996 alone, Anheuser-Busch's distributors placed more than 26,000 advertisements in local newspapers, on billboards, and on radio and television, reminding consumers to drink responsibly. Distributors also worked at the grassroots level to train 18,000 bartenders, waiters, and waitresses on responsible serving techniques to help discourage drunk driving, and they provided nearly 25,000 free cab rides to bar and restaurant patrons. All this effort has produced some positive results. For example, the number of high school seniors who reported having five or more drinks in a row dropped 32 percent from 1982 to 1999, and according to the U.S. Department of Transportation, the number of people killed in teenage drunk-driving crashes declined 64 percent between 1982 and 1999. While there is much more work to do in controlling alcohol abuse, the IBP campaign orchestrated by Anheuser-Busch appears to be having a desirable effect. As to the motives behind this effort, we choose to believe that the company just wants to do the right thing.

Source: www.beeresponsible.com, accessed October 21, 2001.

Advertising Improves the Standard of Living. Whether advertising raises or lowers the general standard of living is hotly debated. Opinions vary widely on this issue and go right to the heart of whether advertising is a good use or a waste of energy and resources.

Pro: Advertising Lowers the Cost of Products. First, supporters argue that due to the economies of scale produced by advertising, consumers actually realize less-expensive products. As broad-based demand stimulation results in lower production and administrative costs per unit, lower prices are passed on to consumers. Second, a greater variety of choice in products and services stems from the increased probability of success firms realize from being able to introduce new products with the assistance of advertising. Third, the pressures of competition and the desire to have fresh, marketable products stimulate firms to produce improved products. Fourth, the speed and reach of the advertising process aids in the diffusion of innovations. This means that new discoveries can be communicated to a large percentage of the marketplace very quickly. Innovations succeed when advertising communicates their benefits to the customer.

All four of these factors can contribute positively to the standard of living and quality of life in a society. Advertising may be instrumental in bringing about these effects because it serves an important role in demand stimulation and keeping customers informed.

Con: Advertising Wastes Resources and Raises the Standard of Living Only for Some. One of the traditional criticisms of advertising is that it represents an inefficient, wasteful process that channels monetary and human resources in a society to the "shuffling of existing total demand," rather than to the expansion of total demand.[7] Advertising thus brings about economic stagnation and a lower standard of living. Critics say that a society is no better off with advertising because it does not stimulate demand—it only shifts demand from one brand to another. Similarly, critics argue that brand differences are trivial and the proliferation of brands does not offer a greater variety of choice, but rather a meaningless waste of resources, with confusion and frustration for the consumer. Further, they argue that advertising is a tool of capitalism that just helps widen the gap between rich and poor.

Advertising Affects Happiness and General Well-Being. Critics and supporters of advertising differ significantly in their views about how advertising affects consumers' happiness and general well-being. As you will see, this is a complex issue with multiple pros and cons.

Con: Advertising Creates Needs. A common cry among critics is that advertising creates needs and makes people buy things they don't really need or even want. The argument is that consumers are relatively easy to seduce into wanting the next shiny bauble offered by marketers. Critics would say, for example, that a quick examination of any issue of *Seventeen* magazine reveals a magazine intent on teaching the young women of the world to covet slim bodies and a glamorous complexion. Cosmetics giant Estée Lauder spends nearly 30 cents from every dollar of sales to promote its brands as the ultimate solution for those in search of the ideal complexion.[8]

Pro: Advertising Addresses a Wide Variety of Basic Human Needs. A good place to start in discussing whether advertising can create needs is to consider the nature of needs. Abraham Maslow, a pioneer in the study of human motivation, conceived that human behavior progresses through the following hierarchy of need states:[9]

- *Physiological needs:* Biological needs that require the satisfaction of hunger, thirst, and basic bodily functions.
- *Safety needs:* The need to provide shelter and protection for the body and to maintain a comfortable existence.
- *Love and belonging needs:* The need for affiliation and affection. A person will strive for both the giving and receiving of love.
- *Esteem needs:* The need for recognition, status, and prestige. In addition to the respect of others, there is a need and desire for self-respect.
- *Self-actualization needs:* This is the highest of all the need states and is achieved by only a small percentage of people, according to Maslow. The individual strives for maximum fulfillment of individual capabilities.

It must be clearly understood that Maslow was describing *basic* human needs and motivations, not consumer needs and motivations. But in the context of an affluent society, individuals will turn to goods and services to satisfy needs. Many products are said to directly address the requirements of one or more of these need states. Food and health care products, for example, relate to physiological needs (see Exhibit 4.5). Home security systems and smoke detectors help address safety needs. Many personal-care products, such as the skin care system shown in Exhibit 4.6, promote feelings of self-esteem, confidence, glamour, and romance.

In the pursuit of esteem, many consumers buy products they perceive to have status and prestige; expensive jewelry, clothing, automobiles, and homes are exam-

7. Richard Caves, *American Industry: Structure, Conduct, Performance* (Englewood Cliffs, N.J.: Prentice-Hall, 1964), 102.
8. Nina Munk, "Why Women Find Lauder Mesmerizing," *Fortune,* May 25, 1998, 96–106.
9. A. H. Maslow, *Motivation and Personality* (New York: Harper & Row, 1970).

EXHIBIT 4.5

Many Johnson & Johnson products attempt to satisfy physiological needs. Does this ad provide motivation, need satisfaction, or both? www.jnj.com.

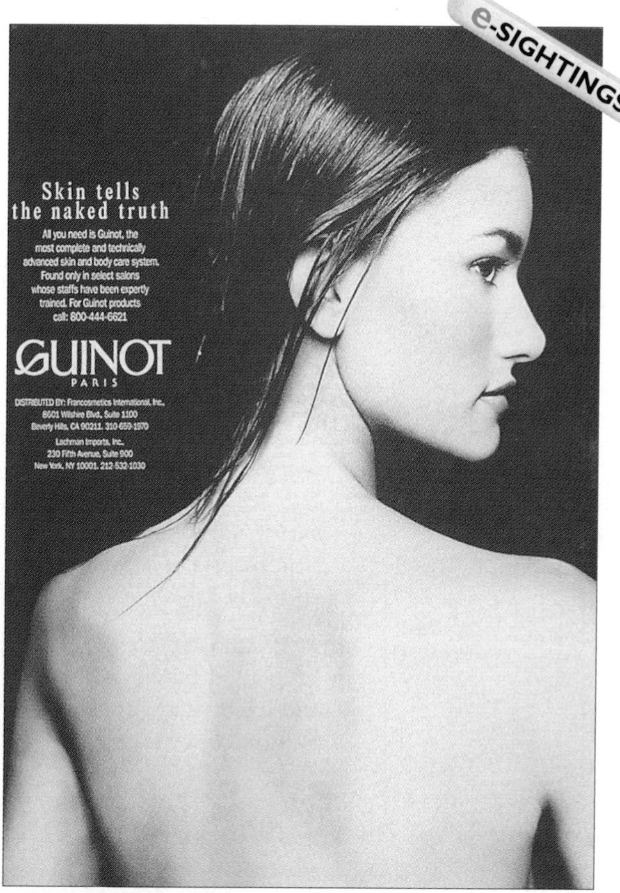

EXHIBIT 4.6

*"All you need is Guinot." In what sense might a person need Guinot? Does the Guinot site (*www.guinotusa.com*) tie in to consumers' happiness and general well-being? Click around the site and identify message and design elements that target consumers' various need states.*

ples. Though it may be difficult to buy self-actualization, educational pursuits and high-intensity leisure activities can certainly foster the feelings of pride and accomplishment that contribute to self-actualization. Supporters maintain that advertising may be directed at many different forms of need fulfillment, but it is of little use in creating new needs.

Con: Advertising Promotes Materialism. It is also claimed that individuals' wants and aspirations may be distorted by advertising. The long-standing argument is that in societies characterized by heavy advertising, there is a tendency for conformity and status-seeking behavior, both of which are considered materialistic and superficial.[10] Material goods are placed ahead of spiritual and intellectual pursuits. Advertising, which portrays products as symbols of status, success, and happiness, contributes to the materialism and superficiality in a society. It creates wants and aspirations that are artificial and self-centered. This results in an overemphasis on the production of private goods, to the detriment of public goods (such as highways,

10. Vance Packard, *The Status Seekers* (New York: David McKay, 1959).

parks, schools, and infrastructure).[11] It is also thought by some that long-term exposure to advertising will destroy your soul and blind you to what really matters in life.

Pro: Advertising Only Reflects Society's Priorities. Although advertising is undeniably in the business of promoting the good life, defenders of advertising argue that it did not create the American emphasis on materialism. For example, in the United States, major holidays such as Christmas (gifts), Thanksgiving (food), and Easter (candy and clothing) have become festivals of consumption. This is the American way. Stephen Fox concludes his treatise on the history of American advertising as follows:

One may build a compelling case that American culture is—beyond redemption—money-mad, hedonistic, superficial, rushing heedlessly down a railroad track called Progress. Tocqueville and other observers of the young republic described America in these terms in the early 1800s, decades before the development of national advertising. To blame advertising now for these most basic tendencies in American history is to miss the point. . . . The people who have created modern advertising are not hidden persuaders pushing our buttons in the service of some malevolent purpose. They are just producing an especially visible manifestation, good and bad, of the American way of life.[12]

While we clearly live in the age of consumption, goods and possessions have been used by all cultures to mark special events, to play significant roles in rituals, and to serve as vessels of special meaning, long before there was modern advertising. Still, have we taken it too far? Is excess what we do best in consumer cultures?

Advertising: Demeaning and Deceitful, or Liberating and Artful?

Without a doubt, advertisers are always on the lookout for creative and novel ways to grab and hold the attention of their audience. Additionally, many times an advertiser has a particular profile of the target customer in mind when an ad is being created. Both of these fundamental propositions about how ads get developed can spark controversy.

Con: Advertising Perpetuates Stereotypes. Advertisers often portray their target customer in advertisements, with the hope that individuals will relate to the ad and attend to its message. Critics charge that this practice yields a very negative effect—it perpetuates stereotypes. The portrayal of women, the elderly, and ethnic minorities is of particular concern. It is argued that women are still predominantly cast as homemakers or objects of desire (see Exhibit 4.7), despite the fact that women now hold top management positions and deftly head households. The elderly are often shown as helpless or ill, even though many active seniors enjoy a rich lifestyle. Critics contend that advertisers' propensity to feature African-American or Latin athletes in ads is simply a more contemporary form of stereotyping.

Pro: Advertisers Are Showing Much More Sensitivity. Much of this sort of stereotyping is becoming part of the past. Advertisements from prior generations do show a vivid stereotyping problem. The ad in Exhibit 4.8 shows that women can be featured as strong and feminine in contemporary advertising. Advertisers are realizing that a diverse world requires diversity in the social reality that ads represent and help construct. However, many remain dissatisfied with the pace of change; the Body Shop ad in Exhibit 4.9, promoting something other than the body of a supermodel as a valid point of reference for women, is still the exception, not the rule.

11. See, for example, George Katona, *The Mass Consumption Society* (New York: McGraw-Hill, 1964), 54–61; and John Kenneth Galbraith, *The Affluent Society* (Boston: Houghton Mifflin, 1958).

12. Stephen Fox, *The Mirror Makers: A History of American Advertising and Its Creators* (New York: William Morrow, 1984), 330.

EXHIBIT 4.7

What is the advertiser claiming in this ad? How about—a Versace gown is the ultimate in chic. www.versace.com

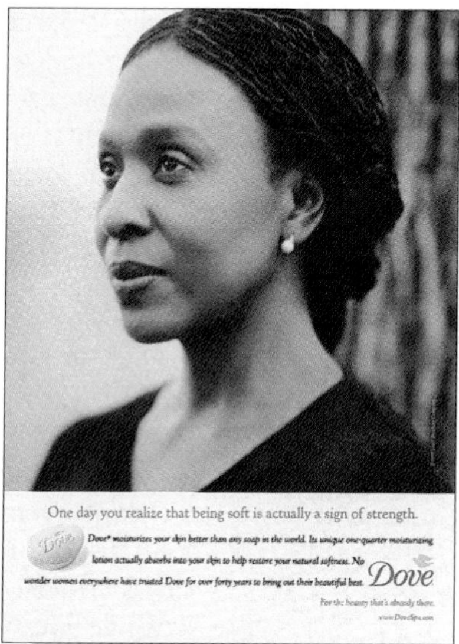

EXHIBIT 4.8

Advertisers today realize the diverse reality of consumers' lives. This Dove ad is a beautiful example of advertisers' efforts to represent diversity. www.dovespa.com

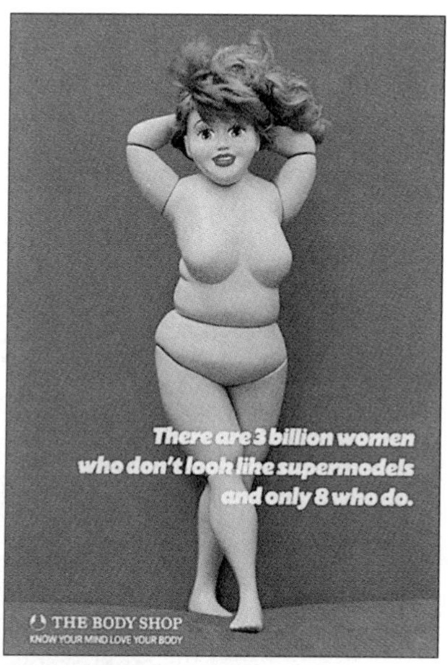

EXHIBIT 4.9

The Body Shop (www.bodyshop.com) is bucking trends by protesting the "supermodel" imagery often used in product advertising. While men's magazine sites, such as Playboy (www.playboy.com), triumphantly display airbrushed perfection and countless companies adorn everything from automobiles to breakfast cereal with the svelte and athletic, the Web is (currently) a rather low-fidelity medium for transmitting glossy photographs. Sex may sell, but simple, bold, and clever graphics may be as useful for "eye candy" as anything ever exhibited by Versace Couture.

Con: Advertising Is Often Offensive. A pervasive and long-standing criticism of advertising is that it is often offensive and the appeals are typically in poor taste. Moreover, some would say that the trend in American advertising is to be rude, crude, and sometimes lewd, as advertisers struggle to grab the attention of consumers who have learned to tune out the avalanche of advertising messages they are confronted with each day.[13] Of course, taste is just that, a personal and inherently subjective evaluation. What is offensive to one person is merely satiric to another. What should we call an ad prepared for the International Advertising Festival in Cannes, designed to show the durability of Kadu surfer shorts? The ad showed Kadu shorts emerging from the stomach of a gutted shark.[14] (By the way, the agency that conceived this ad is now defunct.) A television ad depicting Adolf Hitler as a reformed spokesperson for a brand of potato chips, complete with the Nazi swastika morphing into the brand's logo, caused a predictable outcry in Thailand. The agency that prepared this ad for the Thai market quickly withdrew it after protests from the Israeli embassy in Bangkok, and maintained the ad "was never intended to cause ill feelings."[15]

13. Stuart Elliott, "A New Pitch for U.S. Ads: Lewd, Crude and Rude," *Herald International Tribune,* June 20, 1998, 1, 4.
14. "Objection, Your Honor," *Advertising Age,* December 19, 1994, 19.
15. Pichayaporn Utumporn, "Ad with Hitler Causes a Furor in Thailand," *Wall Street Journal,* June 5, 1998, B8.

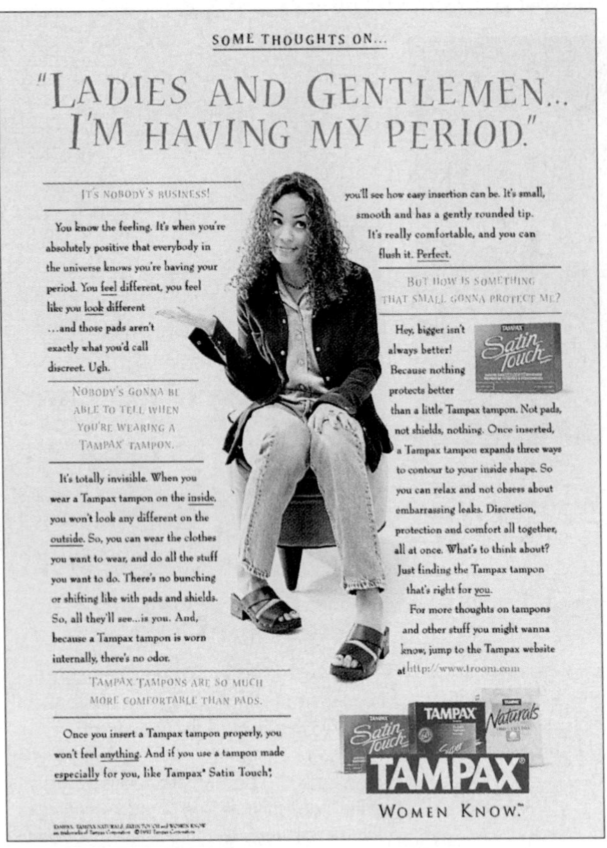

EXHIBIT 4.10

Oddly, frank talk about real-life issues is not all that common in advertising. Do you know anyone who would be put off by such frankness?
www.tampax.com

But not all advertising deemed offensive has to be as extreme as these examples. Many times, advertisers get caught in a firestorm of controversy because certain, and sometimes relatively small, segments of the population are offended. The AIDS prevention campaign run by the Centers for Disease Control (CDC) has been criticized for being too explicit. A spokesperson for the Family Research Council said about the ads, "They're very offensive—I thought I was watching *NYPD Blue*." A highly popular ad seen as controversial by some was the "People Taking Diet Coke Break" ad (see Exhibit 1.14 in Chapter 1). In this television spot, a group of female office workers is shown eyeing a construction worker as he takes off his T-shirt and enjoys a Diet Coke. Coca-Cola was criticized for using reverse sexism in this ad.[16] While Coca-Cola and the CDC may have ventured into delicate areas, consider these advertisers, who were caught completely by surprise in finding that their ads were deemed offensive:

- In a public service spot developed by Aetna Life & Casualty insurance for measles vaccine, a wicked witch with green skin and a wart resulted in a challenge to the firm's ad from a witches' rights group.
- A Nynex spot was criticized by animal-rights activists because it showed a rabbit colored with blue dye.
- A commercial for Black Flag bug spray had to be altered after a war veterans' group objected to the playing of "taps" over dead bugs.

It should be emphasized that most consumers probably did not find these ads particularly offensive.[17] Perhaps the spirit of political correctness causes such scrutiny, or maybe consumers are so overwhelmed with ads that they have simply lost their tolerance. Or maybe some people just have too much time on their hands. And sometimes they correctly point to insensitivity on the part of advertisers. Whatever the explanation, marketers today are well advised to take care in broadly considering the tastefulness of their ads. Expect the unexpected. An unpretentious ad like that in Exhibit 4.10, featuring frank copy about mundane aspects of menstruation, could be expected to breach some consumers' sensibilities. However, the marketer in this case is willing to take the risk in the hopes that the frank approach will get attention and ring true with the target customer.

Pro: Advertising Is a Source of Fulfillment and Liberation. On the other end of the spectrum, some argue that the consumption that advertising glorifies is actually quite good for members of society. Most people sincerely appreciate modern conveniences that liberate us from the more foul facets of the natural, such as body odor, close contact with dirty diapers, and washing clothes by hand. Furthermore, this view holds that consumption is more likely to set one free than the slavish worship of an unpleasant, uncomfortable, and likely odoriferous—but natural—

16. Kevin Goldman, "From Witches to Anorexics, Critical Eyes Scrutinize Ads for Political Correctness," *Wall Street Journal*, May 19, 1994, B1, B10.
17. Ibid.

condition. Some observers remind us that when the Berlin Wall came down, those in East Germany did not immediately run to libraries and churches—they ran to department stores and shops. Before the modern consumer age, the consumption of many goods was restricted by social class. Modern advertising has helped bring us a "democracy" of goods. Observers argue that there is a liberating quality to advertising and consumption that should be appreciated and encouraged.

Con: Advertisers Deceive via Subliminal Stimulation. There is much controversy, and almost a complete lack of understanding, regarding the issue of subliminal (below the threshold of consciousness) communication and advertising. Since there is much confusion surrounding the issue of subliminal advertising, perhaps this is the most appropriate point to provide some clarification: No one ever sold anything by putting images of breasts in ice cubes or the word *sex* in the background of an ad. Furthermore, no one at an advertising agency, except the very bored or the very eager to retire, has time to sit around dreaming up such things. We realize it makes for a great story, but hiding pictures in other pictures doesn't work to get anyone to buy anything. Although there is some evidence for some types of unconscious ad processing,[18] these effects are very short-lived and found only in laboratories, not the Svengali-type hocus-pocus that has become advertising mythology. If the rumors are true that advertisers are actually using subliminal messages in their ads (and they aren't), the conclusion should be that they're wasting their money.[19] As of yet, there is no practical application of subliminal advertising.

e-SIGHTINGS

EXHIBIT 4.11

Artist Andy Warhol demonstrated that the most accessible art was advertising. How does Intel connect advertising and art through its connection to the Blue Man Group (www.blueman.com)? What message does Intel seek to convey about its Pentium brand by associating it with this innovative, critically acclaimed theater troupe?

Pro: Advertising Is Democratic Art. Finally, some argue that one of the best aspects of advertising is its artistic nature. The pop art movement of the late 1950s and 1960s, particularly in London and New York, was characterized by a fascination with commercial culture. Some of this art critiqued consumer culture and simultaneously celebrated it. Above all, Andy Warhol (see Exhibit 4.11), himself a commercial illustrator, demonstrated that art was for the people and that the most accessible art was advertising. Art was not restricted to museum walls; it was on Campbell's soup cans, LifeSavers rolls, and Brillo pads. Advertising is anti-elitist, democratic art. As Warhol said about America, democracy, and Coke,

> *What's great about this country is that America started the tradition where the richest consumers buy essentially the same things as the poorest. You can be watching TV and see Coca-Cola, and you can know that the President drinks Coke, Liz Taylor drinks Coke, and just think, you can drink Coke, too. A Coke is a Coke and no amount of money can get you a better Coke than the one the bum on the corner is drinking. All the Cokes are the same and all the Cokes are good. Liz Taylor knows it, the President knows it, the bum knows it, and you know it.*[20]

18. Murphy, Monahan, and Zajonc, "Additivity of Nonconscious Affect: Combined Effects of Priming and Exposure," *Journal of Personality and Social Psychology,* 69 (1995), 589–602.
19. Timothy E. Moore, "Subliminal Advertising: What You See Is What You Get," *Journal of Marketing,* vol. 46 (Spring 1982), 38–47.
20. Andy Warhol, *The Philosophy of Andy Warhol: From A to B and Back Again* (New York: Harcourt Brace Jovanovich, 1975), 101.

Advertising Has a Powerful Effect on the Mass Media.

One final issue that advertisers and their critics debate is the matter of advertising's influence on the mass media. Here again, we find a very wide range of viewpoints.

Pro: Advertising Fosters a Diverse and Affordable Mass Media.

Advertising fans argue that advertising is the best thing that ever happened to an informed democracy. Magazines, newspapers, and television and radio stations are supported by advertising expenditures. In 2000, advertising expenditures in the United States reached nearly $250 billion.[21] Much of this spending went to support television, radio, magazines, and newspapers. With this sort of monetary support of the media, citizens have access to a variety of information and entertainment sources at low cost. Network television and radio broadcasts would not be free commodities, and newspapers would likely cost two to four times more, in the absence of advertising support.

Others argue that advertising provides invaluable exposure to issues. When noncommercial users of advertising rely on the advertising process, members of society receive information on important social and political issues. A dramatic example of the noncommercial use of advertising was the multimedia campaign launched in 1998 by the U.S. government, working in conjunction with the Partnership for a Drug-Free America.[22] At the campaign's launch in July 1998, President Clinton pledged to outspend major advertisers such as Nike and Sprint to remind the American public of the ruinous power of drugs such as heroin. Estimates at that time indicated that spending on the campaign over five years could approach $1 billion. A stockpile of nearly 400 ads was available for use in this comprehensive campaign. Some, like the one shown in Exhibit 4.12, involved the use of celebrities.

Con: Advertising Affects Programming.

Critics argue that advertisers who place ads in media have an unhealthy effect on shaping the content of information contained in the media. For example, if a magazine that reviews and evaluates stereo equipment tests the equipment of one of its large advertisers, the contention is that the publication will hesitate to criticize the advertiser's equipment.

Another charge leveled at advertisers is that they purchase airtime only on programs that draw large audiences. Critics argue that these mass market programs lower the quality of television because cultural and educational programs, which draw smaller and more selective markets, are dropped in favor of mass market programs. Additionally, television programmers have a difficult time attracting advertisers to shows that may be valuable, yet controversial. Programs that deal with abortion, sexual abuse, or AIDS may have trouble drawing advertisers who fear the consequences of any association with controversial issues.

2 The Ethical Aspects of Advertising.

Many of the ethical aspects of advertising border on and interact with both the social and legal considerations of the advertising process. **Ethics** are moral standards and principles against which behavior is judged. Honesty, integrity, fairness, and sensitivity are all included in a broad definition of ethical behavior. Much of what is judged as ethical or unethical comes down to personal judgment. We will discuss the ethical aspects of advertising in three areas: truth in advertising, advertising to children, and advertising controversial products.

Truth in Advertising.

While truth in advertising is a key legal issue, it has ethical dimensions as well. The most fundamental ethical issue has to do with **deception**—making false or mis-

21. R. Craig Endicott, "46th Annual Report, 100 Leading Advertisers," *Advertising Age,* September 24, 2001, S14.
22. B. G. Gregg, "Tax Funds Bankroll New Anti-Drug Ads," *Cincinnati Enquirer,* July 10, 1998, A1, A17.

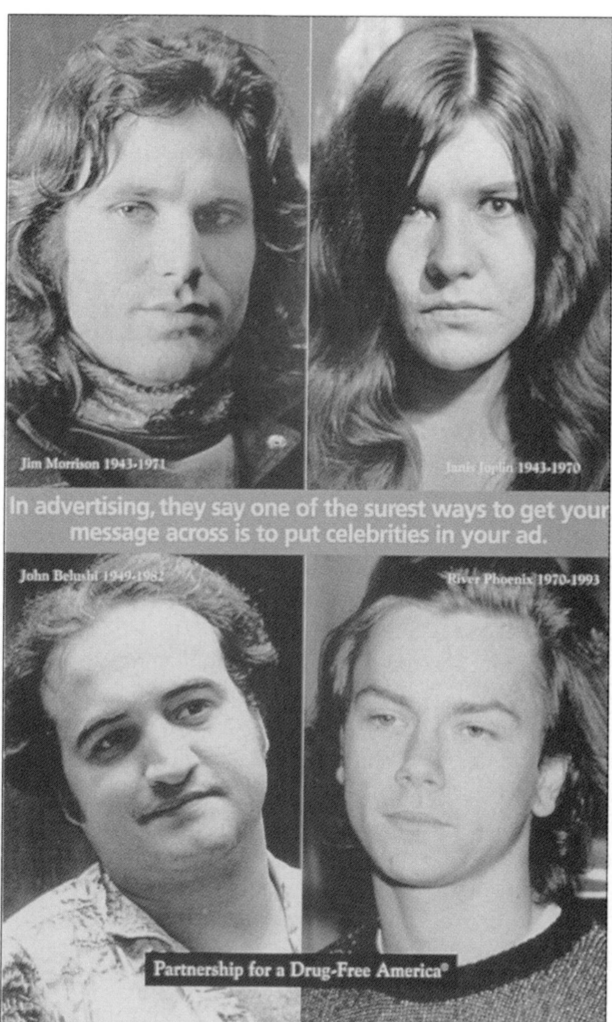

EXHIBIT 4.12

This ad both appeals to our fascination with celebrity and shocks the viewer with the realization that drug use can be fatal. At www.drugfreeamerica.org, the Partnership for a Drug-Free America hones its message that drug use is anything but glamorous. The Internet is rife with both authorized and (far more likely) unauthorized images of celebrities. This uncontrolled use of celebrity pics may dilute a message more compelling on TV or in magazines. Visit www.geocities.com/Hollywood/Studio/2487, a Web site dedicated to dead comedians, including John Belushi.

leading statements in an advertisement. The difficulty regarding this issue, of course, is in determining just what is deceptive. A manufacturer who claims a laundry product can remove grass stains is exposed to legal sanctions if the product cannot perform the task. Another manufacturer who claims to have "The Best Laundry Detergent in the World," however, is perfectly within its rights to employ superlatives. Just what constitutes "The Best" is a purely subjective determination; it cannot be proved or disproved. The use of absolute superlatives such as "Number One" or "Best in the World" is sometimes called **puffery** and is considered completely legal. The courts have long held that superlatives are understood by consumers as simply the standard language of advertising and are interpreted by consumers as such.

It is likewise impossible to legislate against emotional appeals such as those made about the beauty or prestige-enhancing qualities of a product, because these claims are unquantifiable. Since these types of appeals are legal, the ethics of such appeals fall into a gray area. Beauty and prestige, it is argued, are in the eye of the beholder, and such appeals are neither illegal nor unethical. Although there are some narrowly defined legal parameters for truth in advertising (as we will discuss shortly), the ethical issues are not as clear-cut.

Advertising to Children. The desire to restrict advertising aimed at children is based on a wide range of concerns. One concern is that advertising promotes superficiality and values founded in material goods and consumption—as we discussed earlier in the broader context of society as a whole. Another is that children are inexperienced consumers and easy prey for the sophisticated persuasions of advertisers. Advertising influences children's demands for everything from toys to snack foods. These demands create an environment of child-parent conflict. Parents find themselves having to say no over and over again to children whose desires are piqued by effective advertising. Most recently, child psychologists are contending that advertising advocates violence, is responsible for child obesity, creates a breakdown in early learning skills, and results in a destruction of parental authority.[23]

There is also concern that many programs aimed at children constitute program-length commercials. Many critics argue that programs featuring commercial products, especially products aimed at children, are simply long advertisements. In 1990, critics pointed out that 70 programs were based on commercial products such as He-Man, the Smurfs, and the Muppets.[24] More recent examples include elaborate, hour-long television productions such as *Treasure Island: The Adventure Begins.* Critics claim that a program such as this, which features a young boy's vacation at the Las Vegas resort Treasure Island, blurs the boundary between programming and advertising. The program was produced by the Mirage Resorts (owners of Treasure

23. Richard Linnett, "Psychologists Protest Kids' Ads," *Advertising Age,* September 11, 2000, 4.
24. Patrick J. Sheridan, "FCC Sets Children's Ad Limits," *1990 Information Access Company,* vol. 119, no. 20 (1990), 33.

Island), and the one-hour time slot was purchased from a major network, as advertising time, for an estimated $1.7 million.[25] While the program looks like an adventure show, critics argue that it merely promotes the theme park and casino to kids, without ever revealing its sponsor. There have been several attempts by special-interest groups to strictly regulate this type of programming aimed at children, but, to date, the Federal Communications Commission permits such programming to continue. But recently there has been movement to re-empower the FTC with broader controls over entertainment products aimed at children.[26]

Advertising Controversial Products. Some people question the wisdom of allowing the advertising of controversial goods and services, such as tobacco, alcoholic beverages, gambling and lotteries, and firearms. Most frequently criticized are the advertising of cigarettes and alcoholic beverages.

Critics charge that tobacco and alcoholic beverage firms are targeting adolescents with advertising and with making dangerous and addictive products appealing.[27] This is, indeed, a complex issue. Many medical journals have published survey research that claims that advertising "caused" cigarette and alcohol consumption—particularly among teenagers.[28] The main controversy in the tobacco debates swirled around the use of characters like "Joe Camel."

Interestingly, these recent studies contradicted the research since the 1950s carried out by marketing, communications, psychology, and economics researchers—including assessments of all the available research by the FTC.[29] These early studies (as well as several Gallup polls during the 1990s) found that family, friends, and peers—not advertising—are the primary influence on the use of tobacco and alcohol products. Studies published in the late 1990s and early in this decade have reaffirmed the findings of the earlier research.[30] While children at a very early age can, indeed, recognize tobacco advertising characters like "Joe Camel," they also recognize the Energizer Bunny, the Jolly Green Giant, and Snoopy—all characters associated with adult products. Kids are also aware that cigarettes cause disease and know that they are intended as an adult product.[31] Research in Europe offers the same conclusion: "Every study on the subject [of advertising effects on the use of tobacco and alcohol] finds that children are more influenced by parents and playmates than by the mass media."[32]

Why doesn't advertising cause people to smoke and drink? The simple answer is that advertising just isn't that powerful. Eight out of 10 new products fail and if advertising were so powerful, no new products would fail. The more detailed answer is that advertising cannot create primary demand in mature product cate-

25. Laura Bird, "NBC Special Is One Long Prime-Time Ad," *Wall Street Journal,* January 21, 1994, B1, B4.

26. Advertising Age "Forum," October 9, 2000, 58, 60.

27. Kathleen Deveny, "Joe Camel Ads Reach Children, Research Finds," *Wall Street Journal,* December 11, 1991, B1, B6.

28. See for example, Joseph R. DiFranza et al., "RJR Nabisco's Cartoon Camel Promotes Camel Cigarettes to Children," *Journal of the American Medical Association,* 266(22), 3168–3153.

29. For a summary of more than 60 articles that address the issue of alcohol and cigarette advertising and the lack of a relationship between advertising and cigarette and alcohol industry demand, see Mark Frankena et al., "Alcohol, Consumption, and Abuse," Bureau of Economics, Federal Trade Commission, March 5, 1985. A similar listing of research articles and the same conclusions were drawn during Congressional hearings on the topic; see "Advertising of Tobacco Products," Hearings before the Subcommittee on Health and the Environment, Committee on Energy and Commerce, House of Representatives, Ninety-Ninth Congress, July 18 and August 1, 1986, Serial No. 99–167.

30. For examples of the more recent studies that reaffirm peers and family rather than advertising as the basis for smoking initiation see Bruce Simons Morton, "Peer and Parent Influences on Smoking and Drinking Among Early Adolescents," *Journal of Health Education and Behavior,* February 2000; Karen H. Smith and Mary Ann Stutz, "Factors that Influence Adolescents to Smoke," *Journal of Consumer Affairs,* Winter 1999, vol. 33, no. 2, 321–357.

31. See, for example, Lucy L. Henke, "Young Children's Perceptions of Cigarette Brand Advertising: Awareness, Affect and Target Market Identification," *Journal of Advertising,* vol. 24, no. 4 (Winter 1995), 13–27; Richard Mizerski, "The Relationship between Cartoon Trade Character Recognition and Attitude toward the Product Category," *Journal of Marketing,* vol. 59 (October 1995), 58–70.

32. Jeffrey Goldstein, "Children and Advertising—the Research," *Commercial Communications,* July 1998, 4–8.

gories. **Primary demand** is demand for an entire product category (recall the discussion from Chapter 1). With mature products, advertising isn't powerful enough to have that effect. Research across several decades has demonstrated repeatedly that advertising does not create primary demand for tobacco or alcohol.[33]

No one has ever said that smoking or drinking is good for you. (Except for maybe that glass of wine with dinner.) That's not what we are saying here, either. The point is that these behaviors emerge in a complex social context, and the vast weight of research evidence suggests that advertising is not a significant causal influence on initiation behavior (e.g., smoking, drinking), but rather advertising plays its most important role in consumers' choice of brands (e.g., Camel, Coors) once they have decided to use a product category (e.g., cigarettes, beer).

Gambling and state-run lotteries represent another controversial product area with respect to advertising. What is the purpose of this advertising? Is it meant to inform gamblers and lottery players of the choices available? This would be selective demand stimulation. Or is such advertising designed to stimulate demand for engaging in wagering behavior? This would be primary demand stimulation. What of compulsive gamblers? What is the state's obligation to protect "vulnerable" citizens by restricting the placement or content of lottery advertising? When these vulnerable audiences are discussed, questions as to what is the basis for this vulnerability can become complex and emotionally charged. Those on one side of the issue argue that special audiences are among the "information poor," while those on the other side find such claims demeaning, patronizing, and paternalistic.

The issue of advertising controversial products is complex. But consider this as you contemplate the role advertising plays in people's decisions regarding these types of products. Currently, one in three children in the United States is diagnosed as clinically obese.[34] Will parents of these kids begin to sue McDonald's, Coca-Cola, Kellogg's, and General Mills because they advertise food products to children? Think this unbelievable? Think again. One critic of the food industry says that "we can't look any longer at blaming individuals."[35] Rather, there is a "toxic environment" that makes heavily advertised food available 24 hours a day. This critic has not proposed suing food companies (yet). Rather, he is proposing putting a tax on junk food (called the "Twinkie tax") as a way to deter consumption.

While we can group the ethical issues of advertising into some reasonable categories, it is not as easy to make definitive statements about the status of ethics in advertising. Ethics will always be a matter of personal values and personal interpretation.

3 The Regulatory Aspects of Advertising.

The term *regulation* immediately brings to mind government scrutiny and control of the advertising process. Indeed, various government bodies regulate advertising. But consumers themselves and several different industry organizations exert as much regulatory power over advertising as government agencies. Three primary groups—consumers, industry organizations, and government bodies—regulate advertising in the truest sense: Together they shape and restrict the process. The government relies on legal restrictions, while consumers and industry groups use less-formal controls. Like the other topics in this chapter, regulation of advertising can be controversial, and opinions about what does and doesn't need to be regulated can be highly variable. Moreover,

33. For research on this topic across several decades, see Richard Schmalensee, *The Economics of Advertising* (Amsterdam-London: North-Holland, 1972); Mark S. Albion and Paul W. Farris, *The Advertising Controversy* (Boston: Auburn House, 1981); Michael J. Waterson, "Advertising and Tobacco Consumption: An Analysis of the Two Major Aspects of the Debate," *International Journal of Advertising,* 9 (1990), 59–72.

34. Pat Wingert et al., "Generation XXL," *Newsweek,* July 3, 2000, 40–47.

35. Janet Rae Brooks, "'Toxic' Environment Plays Heavy Role in Obesity, Weight Expert Says," *Salt Lake Tribune,* August 1, 2000, www.sltrib.com, accessed August 2, 2000.

the topic of regulation could easily be an entire course of study in its own right, so here we present just an overview of major issues and major players.

First we will consider the areas of regulation pursued most ardently, whether it be by the government, consumers, or industry groups. Then we will examine the nature of the regulation exerted by these groups.

Areas of Advertising Regulation.

There are three basic areas of advertising regulation: deception and unfairness in advertising, competitive issues, and advertising to children. Each area is a focal point for regulation. Probably the majority of complaints against advertisers and their advertising efforts has to do with deception or unfair content in advertising. In general, critics and those who desire greater regulation of the advertising process feel that advertising does not provide enough information for consumers to make informed decisions. There are two main issues related to regulation of content: deception and unfairness.

Deception and Unfairness.

Agreement is widespread that deception in advertising is unacceptable. The problem, of course, is that it is as difficult to determine what is deceptive from a regulatory standpoint as from an ethical standpoint. The Federal Trade Commission's (FTC's) policy statement on deception is the authoritative source when it comes to defining deceptive advertising. It specifies the following three elements as essential in declaring an ad deceptive:[36]

1. There must be a representation, omission, or practice that is likely to mislead the consumer.
2. This representation, omission, or practice must be judged from the perspective of a consumer acting reasonably in the circumstance.
3. The representation, omission, or practice must be a "material" one. The basic question is whether the act or the practice is likely to affect the consumer's conduct or decision with regard to the product or service. If so, the practice is material, and consumer injury is likely because consumers are likely to have chosen differently if not for the deception.

If this definition of deception sounds like carefully worded legal jargon, that's because it is. It is also a definition that can lead to diverse interpretations when it is actually applied to advertisements in real life. Fortunately, the FTC now provides highly practical advice for anticipating what can make an ad deceptive (go to www.ftc.gov/bcp/guides/guides.htm under the section "Frequently Asked Advertising Questions"). One critical point about the FTC's approach to deception is that both implied claims and information that is missing from an ad can be bases for deeming an ad deceptive. Obviously, the FTC expects any explicit claim made in an ad to be truthful, but it also is on the lookout for ads that deceive through allusion and innuendo, or ads that deceive by not telling the whole story.

Many instances of deceptive advertising and packaging have resulted in formal government programs designed to regulate such practices. But as we discussed earlier, there can be complications in regulating puffery. Conventional wisdom has argued that consumers don't actually believe extreme claims and realize that advertisers are just trying to attract attention. There are those, however, who disagree with this view of puffery and feel that it actually represents "soft-core" deception, because some consumers believe these exaggerated claims.[37]

While the FTC and the courts have been reasonably specific about what constitutes deception, the definition of unfairness in advertising has been left relatively

36. For additional discussion of the FTC's definition of deception, see Gary T. Ford and John E. Calfee, "Recent Developments in FTC Policy on Deception," *Journal of Marketing,* vol. 50 (July 1986), 82–103.

37. Ivan Preston, *The Great American Blow Up* (Madison, Wis.: University of Wisconsin Press, 1975), 4.

vague until recently. In 1994, Congress ended a long-running dispute in the courts and in the advertising industry by approving legislation that defines **unfair advertising** as "acts or practices that cause or are likely to cause substantial injury to consumers, which is not reasonably avoidable by consumers themselves, and not outweighed by the countervailing benefits to consumers or competition."[38] This definition obligates the FTC to assess both the benefits and costs of advertising, and rules out reckless acts on the part of consumers, before a judgment can be rendered that an advertiser has been unfair.

Competitive Issues. Because the large dollar amounts spent on advertising may foster inequities that literally can destroy competition, several advertising practices relating to competition can result in regulation. Among them are cooperative advertising, comparison advertising, and using monopoly power.

Vertical cooperative advertising is an advertising technique whereby a manufacturer and dealer (either a wholesaler or retailer) share the expense of advertising. This technique is commonly used in regional or local markets where a manufacturer wants a brand to benefit from a special promotion run by local dealers. There is nothing illegal, per se, about the technique, and it is used regularly. The competitive threat inherent in the process, however, is that dealers (especially since the advent of department store chains) can be given bogus cooperative advertising allowances. These allowances require no effort or expenditure on the part of the dealer and thus represent hidden price concessions. As such, they are a form of unfair competition and are deemed illegal. If an advertising allowance is granted to a dealer, that dealer must demonstrate that the funds are applied specifically to advertising.

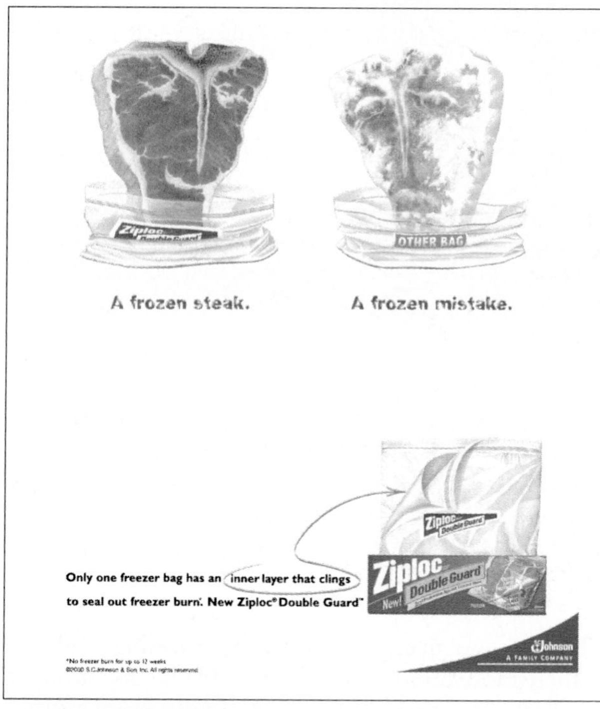

EXHIBIT 4.13

Comparison ads, like this one, that offer a straightforward and fair comparison between brands are completely legal.
www.scjohnson.com

The potential exists for firms to engage in unfair competition if they use comparison ads inappropriately. **Comparison advertisements** are those in which an advertiser makes a comparison between the firm's brand and competitors' brands. The comparison may or may not explicitly identify the competition. Again, comparison ads are completely legal and are used frequently by all sorts of organizations. The ad in Exhibit 4.13 is a example of straightforward and completely legal comparison advertising.

But the frequency of use of comparison ads has resulted in a large increase in complaints to the NAD (National Advertising Division of the Better Business Bureau [BBB]) from marketers who dispute the competitive comparative claims.[39] If an advertisement is carried out in such a way that the comparison is not a fair one, then there is an unfair competitive effect. The American Association of Advertising Agencies (4As) has issued a set of guidelines, shown in Exhibit 4.14, regarding the use of comparison ads. Further, the FTC may require a firm using comparison to substantiate claims made in an advertisement and prove that the claims do not tend to deceive.[40]

38. Christy Fisher, "How Congress Broke Unfair Ad Impasse," *Advertising Age,* August 22, 1994, 34. For additional discussion of the FTC's definition of unfairness, see Ivan Preston, "Unfairness Developments in FTC Advertising Cases," *Journal of Public Policy and Marketing,* vol. 14, no. 2 (1995), 318–321.
39. Jack Neff, "Household Brands Counter Punch," *Advertising Age,* November 1, 1999, 26.
40. Maxine Lans Retsky, "Lanham Have It: Law and Comparative Ads," *Marketing News,* November 8, 1999, 16.

EXHIBIT 4.14

American Association of Advertising Agencies guidelines for comparison advertising. www.aaaa.org

The Board of Directors of the American Association of Advertising Agencies recognizes that when used truthfully and fairly, comparative advertising provides the consumer with needed and useful information. However, extreme caution should be exercised. The use of comparative advertising, by its very nature, can distort facts and, by implication, convey to the consumer information that misrepresents the truth. Therefore, the Board believes that comparative advertising should follow certain guidelines:

1. The intent and connotation of the ad should be to inform and never to discredit or unfairly attack competitors.
2. When a competitive product is named, it should be one that exists in the marketplace as significant competition.
3. The competition should be fairly and properly identified, but never in a manner or tone of voice that degrades the competitive product or service.
4. The advertising should compare related or similar properties or ingredients of the product, dimension to dimension, feature to feature.
5. The identification should be for honest comparison purposes and not simply to upgrade by association.
6. If a competitive test is conducted, it should be done by an objective testing source, preferably an independent one, so that there will be no doubt as to the veracity of the test.
7. In all cases, the test should be supportive of all claims made in the advertising based on the test.
8. The advertising should never use partial results or stress insignificant differences to cause the consumer to draw an improper conclusion.
9. The property being compared should be significant in terms of value or usefulness of the product to the consumer.
10. Comparatives delivered through the use of testimonials should not imply that the testimonial is more than one individual's thought unless that individual represents a sample of the majority viewpoint.

Source: American Association of Advertising Agencies

Finally, some firms are so powerful in their use of advertising that **monopoly power** by virtue of the advertising can become a problem. This issue normally arises in the context of mergers and acquisitions. As an example, the U.S. Supreme Court blocked the acquisition of Clorox by Procter & Gamble because the advertising power of the two firms combined would (in the opinion of the Court) make it nearly impossible for another firm to compete.

Advertising to Children. Critics argue that continually bombarding children with persuasive stimuli can alter their motivation and behavior. While government organizations such as the FTC have been active in trying to regulate advertising directed at children, industry and consumer groups have been more successful in securing restrictions. The consumer group known as Action for Children's Television was actively involved in getting Congress to approve the Children's Television Act (1990). This act limits the amount of commercial airtime during children's programs to 10½ minutes on weekdays and 12 minutes on weekends. The Council of Better Business Bureaus established a Children's Advertising Review Unit and has issued a set of guidelines for advertising directed at children. These guidelines emphasize that advertisers should be sensitive to the level of knowledge and sophistication of children as decision makers. The guidelines also urge advertisers to make a constructive contribution to the social development of children by emphasizing positive social standards in advertising, such as friendship, kindness, honesty, and generosity. Similarly, the major television networks have set their own guidelines for advertising aimed at children. The guidelines restrict the use of celebrities, prohibit exhortive language (such as "Go ask Dad"), and restrict the use of animation to one-third of the total time of the commercial.

Regulatory Agents. Earlier in this chapter it was noted that consumer and industry groups as well as government agencies all participate in the regulation of advertising. We will now discuss examples of each of these agents along with the kinds of influence they exert. Given the multiple participants, this turns out to be a highly complex activity that we can only overview in this discussion. Additionally, our discussion focuses on regulatory activities in the United States, but advertising regulation can vary dramatically from country to country. Chapter 9 will provide additional insights on advertising regulation around the world, but we must emphasize that becoming an expert on the complex and dynamic topic of global ad regulation would literally require a lifetime of study.

Government Regulation. Governments have a powerful tool available for regulating advertising: the threat of legal action. In the United States, several different government agencies have been given the power and responsibility to regulate the advertising process. Exhibit 4.15 identifies the six agencies that have legal mandates concerning advertising, and their areas of regulatory responsibility.

Several other agencies have minor powers in the regulation of advertising, such as the Civil Aeronautics Board (advertising by air carriers), the Patent Office (trademark infringement), and the Library of Congress (copyright protection). The agencies listed in Exhibit 4.15 are the most directly involved in advertising regulation. Most active among these agencies is the Federal Trade Commission, which has the most power and is most directly involved in controlling the advertising process. The FTC has been granted legal power through legislative mandates and also has developed programs for regulating advertising.

The FTC's Legislative Mandates. The Federal Trade Commission was created by the FTC Act in 1914. The original purpose of the agency was to prohibit unfair methods of competition. In 1916, the FTC concluded that false advertising was one way in which a firm could take unfair advantage of another, and advertising was established as a primary concern of the agency.

It was not until 1938 that the effects of deceptive advertising on consumers became a key issue for the FTC. Until the passage of the Wheeler-Lea Amendment (1938), the commission was primarily concerned with the direct effect of advertising on competition. The amendment broadened the FTC's powers to include regulation of advertising that was misleading to the public (regardless of the effect on competition). Through this amendment, the agency could apply a cease-and-desist order, which required a firm to stop its deceptive practices. It also granted the agency specific jurisdiction over drug, medical device, cosmetic, and food advertising.

Several other acts provide the FTC with legal powers over advertising. The Robinson-Patman Act (1936) prohibits firms from providing phantom cooperative-advertising allowances as a way to court important dealers. The Wool Products Labeling Act (1939), the Fur Products Labeling Act (1951), and the Textile Fiber Products Identification Act (1958) provided the commission with regulatory power over labeling and advertising for specific products. Consumer protection legislation, which seeks to increase the ability of consumers to make more-informed product comparisons, includes the Fair Packaging and Labeling Act (1966), the Truth in Lending Act (1969), and the Fair Credit Reporting Act (1970). The FTC Improvement Act (1975) expanded the authority of the commission by giving it the power to issue trade regulation rules.

Recent legislation has expanded the FTC's role in monitoring and regulating product labeling and advertising. For example, the 1990 Nutrition Labeling and

EXHIBIT 4.15

Primary government agencies regulating advertising.

Government Agency	Areas of Advertising Regulation
Federal Trade Commission (FTC)	Most widely empowered agency in government. Controls unfair methods of competition, regulates deceptive advertising, and has various programs for controlling the advertising process.
Federal Communications Commission (FCC)	Prohibits obscenity, fraud, and lotteries on radio and television. Ultimate power lies in the ability to deny or revoke broadcast licenses.
Food and Drug Administration (FDA)	Regulates the advertising of food, drug, cosmetic, and medical products. Can require special labeling for hazardous products such as household cleaners. Prohibits false labeling and packaging.
Securities and Exchange Commission (SEC)	Regulates the advertising of securities and the disclosure of information in annual reports.
U.S. Postal Service	Responsible for regulating direct mail advertising and prohibiting lotteries, fraud, and misrepresentation. It can also regulate and impose fines for materials deemed to be obscene.
Bureau of Alcohol, Tobacco, and Firearms	Most direct influence has been on regulation of advertising for alcoholic beverages. This agency was responsible for putting warning labels on alcoholic beverage advertising and banning active athletes as celebrities in beer ads. It has the power to determine what constitutes misleading advertising in these product areas.

Education Act (NLEA) requires uniformity in the nutrition labeling of food products and establishes strict rules for claims about the nutritional attributes of food products. The standard "Nutrition Facts" label required by the NLEA now appears on everything from breakfast cereals to barbecue sauce. The NLEA is a unique piece of legislation from the standpoint that two government agencies—the FTC and the FDA—play key roles in its enforcement.

The law also provides the FTC and other agencies with various means of recourse when advertising practices are judged to be deceptive or misleading. The spirit of all these acts relates to the maintenance of an equitable competitive environment and the protection of consumers from misleading information. It is interesting to note, however, that direct involvement of the FTC in advertising practices more often comes about from its regulatory programs and remedies than from the application of legal mandates.

The FTC's Regulatory Programs and Remedies. The application of legislation has evolved as the FTC exercises its powers and expands its role as a regulatory agency. This evolution of the FTC has spawned several regulatory programs and remedies to help enforce legislative mandates in specific situations.

The **advertising substantiation program** of the FTC was initiated in 1971 with the intention of ensuring that advertisers make available to consumers supporting evidence for claims made. The program was strengthened in 1972 when the commission forwarded the notion of "reasonable basis" for the substantiation of advertising. This extension suggests not only that advertisers should substantiate their claims, but also that the substantiation should provide a reasonable basis for believing the claims are true.[41] Simply put, before a company runs an ad, it must have documented evidence that supports the claim it wants to make in that ad. The kind of evidence required depends on the kind of claim being made. For example, health and safety claims will require competent and reliable scientific evidence that has been examined and validated by experts in the field (go to www.ftc.gov for additional guidance).

The consent order and the cease-and-desist order are the most basic remedies used by the FTC in dealing with deceptive or unfair advertising. In a **consent order,** an advertiser accused of running deceptive or unfair advertising agrees to stop running the advertisements in question, without admitting guilt. For advertisers who do not comply voluntarily, the FTC can issue a **cease-and-desist order,** which generally requires that the advertising in question be stopped within 30 days so a hearing can be held to determine whether the advertising is deceptive or unfair. For products that have a direct effect on consumers' health or safety (for example, foods), the FTC can issue an immediate cease-and-desist order.

Affirmative disclosure is another remedy available to the FTC. An advertisement that fails to disclose important material facts about a product can be deemed deceptive, and the FTC may require **affirmative disclosure,** whereby the important material absent from prior ads must be included in subsequent advertisements. The absence of important material information may cause consumers to make false assumptions about products in comparison to the competition. Such was the case with Geritol; the FTC ordered the makers of the product to disclose that "iron-poor blood" was not the universal cause of tiredness.

The most extreme remedy for advertising determined to be misleading is **corrective advertising.**[42] In cases where evidence suggests that consumers have developed incorrect beliefs about a brand based on deceptive or unfair advertising, the firm may be required to run corrective ads in an attempt to dispel those faulty beliefs. The commission has specified not only the message content for corrective ads, but also the budgetary allocation, the duration of transmission, and the placement of the advertising. The goal of corrective advertising is to rectify erroneous beliefs created by deceptive advertising, but it hasn't always worked as intended.

Another area of FTC regulation and remedy involves **celebrity endorsements.** The FTC has specific rules for advertisements that use an expert or celebrity as a spokesperson for a product. In the case of experts (those whose experience or training allows a superior judgment of products), the endorser's actual qualifications must justify his or her status as an expert. In the case of celebrities (such as Michael Jordan as a spokesperson for McDonald's), FTC guidelines indicate that the celebrity must be an actual user of the product, or the ad is considered deceptive.

These regulatory programs and remedies provide the FTC a great deal of control over the advertising process. Numerous ads have been interpreted as questionable under the guidelines of these programs, and advertisements have been altered. It is likely also that advertisers and their agencies, who are keenly aware of the ramifications of violating FTC precepts, have developed ads with these constraints in mind.

41. For a discussion of the FTC advertising substantiation program and its extension to require reasonable basis, see Debra L. Scammon and Richard J. Semenik, "The FTC's 'Reasonable Basis' for Substantiation of Advertising: Expanded Standards and Implications," *Journal of Advertising,* vol. 12, no. 1 (1983), 4–11.

42. A history of the corrective-advertising concept and several of its applications are provided by Debra L. Scammon and Richard J. Semenik, "Corrective Advertising: Evolution of the Legal Theory and Application of the Remedy," *Journal of Advertising,* vol. 11, no. 1 (1982), 10–20.

Yet it is certainly fair to conclude that advertising regulation is a dynamic endeavor that will challenge regulators far into the future. Of course, the most notable new challenge that regulators around the world must learn to cope with is advertising on the Internet. For instance, while U.S. government agencies such as the FTC and FDA intend to extend their jurisdiction to the Internet, they clearly have a tiger by the tail.

4 **Industry Self-Regulation.** Advertisers have come far in terms of their self-control and restraint. Some of this improvement is due to tougher government regulation, and some to industry self-regulation. **Self-regulation** is the industry's attempt to police itself. Supporters say it is a shining example of how unnecessary government intervention is, while critics point to it as a joke, an elaborate shell game. According to the critics, meaningful self-regulation occurs only when the threat of government action is imminent. How you see this controversy largely depends on your own personal experience and level of cynicism.

Several industry and trade associations and public service organizations have voluntarily established guidelines for advertising within their industries. The reasoning is that self-regulation is good for the advertising community as a whole and promotes the credibility, and therefore the effectiveness, of advertising itself. Exhibit 4.16 lists some organizations that have taken on the task of regulating and monitoring advertising, and the year when each established a code by which to judge the acceptability of advertising.

The purpose of self-regulation by these organizations is to evaluate the content and quality of advertisements specific to their industries. The effectiveness of such organizations depends on the cooperation of members and the policing mechanisms used. Each organization exerts an influence on the nature of advertising in its industry. Some are particularly noteworthy in their activities and warrant further discussion.

The National Advertising Review Board. One important self-regulation organization is the National Advertising Review Board (NARB). The NARB is the operations arm of the National Advertising Division (NAD) of the Council of Better Business Bureaus. Complaints received from consumers, competitors, or local branches of the Better Business Bureau (BBB) are forwarded to the NAD. Most such complaints come from competitors. After a full review of the complaint, the issue may be forwarded to the NARB and evaluated by a panel. The complete procedure for dealing with complaints is detailed in Exhibit 4.17.

The NAD maintains a permanent professional staff that works to resolve complaints with the advertiser and its agency before the issue gets to the NARB. If no resolution is achieved, the complaint is appealed to the NARB, which appoints a panel made up of three advertiser representatives, one agency representative, and one public representative. This panel then holds hearings regarding the advertising in question. The advertiser is allowed to present the firm's case. If no agreement can be reached by the panel either to dismiss the case or to persuade the advertiser to change the advertising, then the NARB initiates two actions. First, the NARB publicly identifies the advertiser, the complaint against the advertiser, and the panel's findings. Second, the case is forwarded to an appropriate government regulatory agency (usually the FTC).

The NAD and the NARB are not empowered to impose penalties on advertisers, but the threat of going before the board acts as a deterrent to deceptive and questionable advertising practices. Further, the regulatory process of the NAD and the NARB is probably less costly and time-consuming for all parties involved than if every complaint were handled by a government agency.

State and Local Better Business Bureaus. Aside from the national Better Business Bureau (BBB), there are more than 140 separate local bureaus. Each local organiza-

EXHIBIT 4.16

Selected business organizations and industry associations with advertising self-regulation programs.

Organization	Code Established
Advertising Associations	
American Advertising Federation	1965
American Association of Advertising Agencies	1924
Association of National Advertisers	1972
Business/Professional Advertising Association	1975
Special Industry Groups	
Council of Better Business Bureaus	1912
Household furniture	1978
Automobiles and trucks	1978
Carpet and rugs	1978
Home improvement	1975
Charitable solicitations	1974
Children's Advertising Review Unit	1974
National Advertising Division/National Advertising Review Board	1971
Media Associations	
American Business Press	1910
Direct Mail Marketing Association	1960
Direct Selling Association	1970
National Association of Broadcasters	
Radio	1937
Television	1952
Outdoor Advertising Association of America	1950
Selected Trade Associations	
American Wine Association	1949
Wine Institute	1949
Distilled Spirits Association	1934
United States Brewers Association	1955
Pharmaceutical Manufacturers Association	1958
Proprietary Association	1934
Bank Marketing Association	1976
Motion Picture Association of America	1930
National Swimming Pool Institute	1970
Toy Manufacturers Association	1962

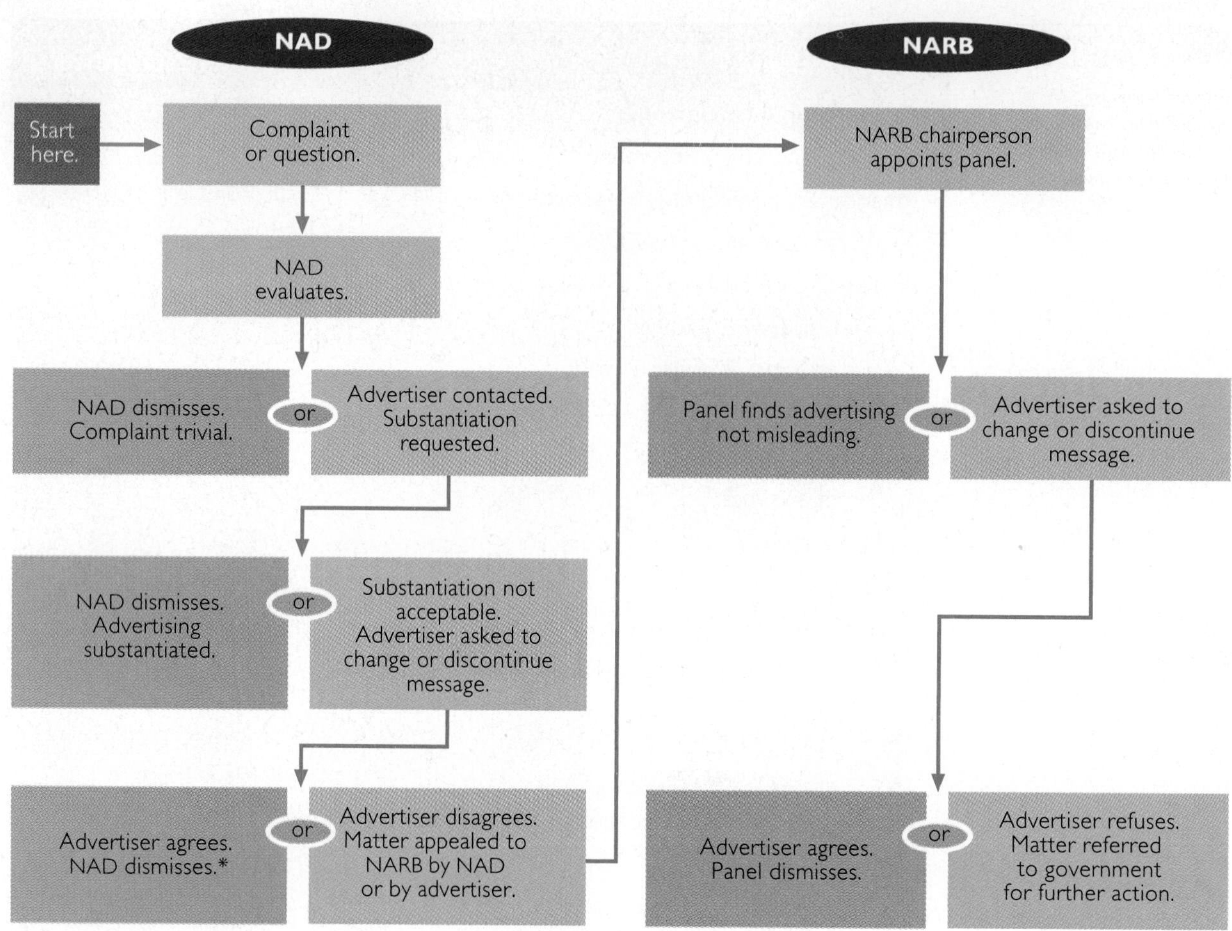

EXHIBIT 4.17

Flow diagram of the NAD and NARB regulatory process.

tion is supported by membership dues paid by area businesses. The three divisions of a local BBB—merchandise, financial, and solicitations—investigate the advertising and selling practices of firms in their areas. A local BBB has the power to forward a complaint to the NAD for evaluation.

Beyond its regulatory activities, the BBB tries to avert problems associated with advertising by counseling new businesses and providing information to advertisers and agencies regarding legislation, potential problem areas, and industry standards.

Advertising Agencies and Associations. It makes sense that advertising agencies and their industry associations would engage in self-regulation. An individual agency is legally responsible for the advertising it produces and is subject to reprisal for deceptive claims. The agency is in a difficult position in that it must monitor not only the activities of its own people, but also the information that clients provide to the agency. Should a client direct an agency to use a product appeal that turns out to be untruthful, the agency is still responsible.

The American Association of Advertising Agencies (4As) has no legal or binding power over its agency members, but it can apply pressure when its board feels that industry standards are not being upheld. The 4As also publishes guidelines for its members regarding various aspects of advertising messages. One of the most widely recognized industry standards is the 4As' Creative Code. The code outlines the responsibilities and social impact advertising can have and promotes high ethical standards of honesty and decency.

Media Organizations. Individual media organizations evaluate the advertising they receive for broadcast and publication. The National Association of Broadcasters (NAB) has a policing arm known as the Code Authority, which implements and interprets separate radio and television codes. These codes deal with truth, fairness, and good taste in broadcast advertising. Newspapers have historically been rigorous in their screening of advertising. Many newspapers have internal departments to screen and censor ads believed to be in violation of the newspaper's advertising standards. While the magazine industry does not have a formal code, many individual publications have very high standards.

Direct mail may have a poor image among many consumers, but its industry association, the Direct Marketing Association (DMA), is active in promoting ethical behavior and standards among its members. It has published guidelines for ethical business practices. In 1971, the association established the Direct Mail Preference Service, which allows consumers to have their names removed from most direct mail lists. And the direct mail industry's efforts at self-regulation have a global presence, as the Global Issues box discusses.

A review of all aspects of industry self-regulation suggests not only that a variety of programs and organizations are designed to monitor advertising, but also that many of these programs are effective. Those whose livelihoods depend on advertising are just as interested as consumers and legislators in maintaining high standards. If advertising deteriorates into an unethical and untrustworthy business activity, the economic vitality of many organizations will be compromised. Self-regulation can help prevent such a circumstance and is in the best interest of all the organizations discussed here.

GLOBAL ISSUES

Self-Regulation—with Full Government Approval

As the opening scenario to this chapter highlighted, consumers, marketers, and advocacy groups have been struggling with the issue of privacy when it comes to harvesting information about consumers' personal lives and shopping behavior. The controversy swirls around what data marketers could, should, or might obtain and how they might use it once they have it.

The controversy over privacy in direct marketing programs is raging in the United States and Europe, but the Australians seem to have come up with a solution that, for the time being, seems to be satisfying everyone. Termed "enhanced self-regulation" by Rob Edwards, CEO of the Australian Direct Marketing Association (ADMA) and one of the plan's architects, a code of behavior has been proposed for direct marketers that focuses on five aspects of the direct marketing process. An industry body called the Code Administration Authority will review consumer complaints related to these aspects:

- Compulsory use of the Do Not Mail/Do Not Call service, which gives consumers the right to limit the number of direct marketing solicitations they receive. Consumers request the service by calling a toll-free number.
- A seven-day cooling-off period during which consumer can cancel a direct marketing contract.
- Compulsory adoption of the National Privacy Principles as set down by the Federal Privacy Commissioner. The principles include an "opting out" clause so consumers can avoid getting any more direct marketing offers.
- An independent Code Authority made up of consumers and industry representatives. A negative ruling by this body could result in the expulsion of a member from the ADMA.
- A set of international "best practices" for e-commerce. The list would be distributed to the more than 400 members of the ADMA.

So while most of the world debates and consternates over privacy issues, the Australians have taken bold and specific steps to improve the industry and reassure consumers of direct marketers' professionalism.

Source: Don E. Schultz, "Australians 'It' When It Comes to Privacy," *Marketing News*, November 8, 1999, 18.

Consumers as Regulatory Agents. Consumers themselves are motivated to act as regulatory agents based on a variety of interests, including product safety, reasonable choice, and the right to information. Advertising tends to be a focus of consumer regulatory activities because of its conspicuousness. Consumerism and consumer organizations have provided the primary vehicles for consumer regulatory efforts.

Consumerism, the actions of individual consumers or groups of consumers designed to exert power in the marketplace, is by no means a recent phenomenon. The earliest consumerism efforts can be traced to 17th-century England. In the United States, there have been recurring consumer movements throughout the 20th century. *Adbusters* magazine is a recent example.

In general, these movements have focused on the same issue: Consumers want a greater voice in the whole process of product development, distribution, and information dissemination. Consumers commonly try to create pressures on firms by withholding patronage through boycotts. Some boycotts have been effective. Firms as powerful as Procter & Gamble, Kimberly-Clark, and General Mills all have historically responded to threats of boycotts by pulling advertising from programs consumers found offensive.[43]

Consumer Organizations. The other major consumer effort to bring about regulation is through established consumer organizations. The following are the most prominent consumer organizations and their prime activities:

- *Consumer Federation of America (CFA).* This organization, founded in 1968, now includes more than 200 national, state, and local consumer groups and labor unions as affiliate members. The goals of the CFA are to encourage the creation of consumer organizations, provide services to consumer groups, and act as a clearinghouse for information exchange between consumer groups.
- *Consumers Union.* This nonprofit consumer organization is best known for its publication of *Consumer Reports.* Established in 1936, Consumers Union has as its stated purpose "to provide consumers with information and advice on goods, services, health, and personal finance; and to initiate and cooperate with individual and group efforts to maintain and enhance the quality of life for consumers."[44] This organization supports itself through the sale of publications and accepts no funding, including advertising revenues, from any commercial organization.
- *Action for Children's Television (ACT).* ACT has been active in conjunction with the national Parent-Teacher Association (PTA) in initiating boycotts against the products of advertisers who sponsor programs that are violent in nature. On its own, ACT has lobbied government bodies to enact legislation restricting the use of premiums in advertising to children and the use of popular cartoon characters in promoting products.

These three consumer organizations are the most active and potent of the consumer groups, but there are hundreds of such groups organized by geographic location or product category. Consumers have proven that when faced with an organized effort, corporations can and will change their practices. In one of the most publicized events in recent times, consumers applied pressure to Coca-Cola and, in part, were responsible for forcing the firm to re-market the original formula of Coca-Cola (as Coca-Cola Classic). If consumers are able to exert such a powerful and nearly immediate influence on a firm such as Coca-Cola, one wonders what other changes they could effect in the market.

5 **The Regulation of Other Promotional Tools.** As firms broaden the scope of the promotional effort beyond advertising, the regulatory constraints placed on other IBP tools become relevant. We will consider the current and emerging regulatory environment for direct marketing, e-commerce, sales promotion, and public relations.

43. Alix M. Freedman, "Never Have So Few Scared So Many Television Sponsors," *Wall Street Journal,* March 20, 1989, B4.
44. This statement of purpose can be found inside the cover of any issue of *Consumer Reports.*

Regulatory Issues in Direct Marketing and E-Commerce. The most pressing regulatory issue facing direct marketing and e-commerce was actually discussed at the outset of the chapter—database development and the privacy debate that accompanies the practice. But that discussion just scratched the surface. The real privacy issue has to do with the developing ability of firms to merge offline databases with the online Web search and shopping behavior of consumers.

Privacy. The online e-commerce privacy issue focuses on *cookies* (online tracking devices), which advertisers place on a Web surfer's hard drive to track that person's online behavior. This alone is annoying and feels like an invasion of privacy. But it is nothing compared to the emerging possibilities. Cookies do not reveal a person's name or address. But what is looming as a real possibility is that offline databases that *do* include a consumer's name, address, phone number, credit cards, medical records, credit records, and Social Security number can be merged with the online tracking data.[45] With this combination of data, the following could easily happen: You are browsing a Web page on mutual funds and seconds later, you get a phone call from a telemarketer trying to sell you financial services! This scenario may not be too far in the future. The merger of DoubleClick with Abacus Direct created a database that contains transactional data from 1,700 cataloguers, retailers, and publishers—data that chronicles more than 3.6 *billion* transactions by 90 million U.S. households.[46] By the way, there are only about 102 million households in the United States.[47] Sure feels like an invasion of privacy. Firms are searching for ways to guarantee to consumers that their privacy will be preserved (see Exhibit 4.18). In the meantime, the concern is great enough that Congress and the FTC are carefully scrutinizing mergers of firms that would create such comprehensive online and offline databases.[48] We have to realize though that while this tracking of behavior seems pretty scary, many people don't really seem to care, as the E-Commerce box describes.

E-COMMERCE

Privacy? What Privacy?

What does it take to get 200 college students to surrender their e-mail addresses and other personal information to a company in a single day? Would you guess $50 each? $100 each? Maybe even $200 each? How about some mouse pads and t-shirts? That's all it took for Kangaroo.net to get a couple of college kids to sign up 200 other college kids for a Web-based research effort for its client The Magma Group, a youth marketing firm in Brighton, Massachusetts.

Despite all the hoopla and hand-wringing over the threat of privacy invasions that new technology may be bringing, over 46 percent of online shoppers *never* read a site's privacy statement and another 31 percent rarely read it. Only 6 percent of online shoppers say they always read the privacy policy of the merchants with whom they do business. If privacy were such a big deal, you would expect a lot more people to act a lot more carefully to protect their privacy.

With this little protest, you can be sure that firms will proceed post-haste with creating large and comprehensive databases—especially databases containing information on young adults in the United States. In 1999, U.S. teens spent $158 billion. In addition, college students spent another $60.8 billion on products from books to food and clothing to cell phones. But that's not the really good news. The really good news is that this "peer-to-peer" marketing, as it is called, costs peanuts. Peer programs, where kids sign up other kids, cost from $25,000 at the low end to $300,000 at the very top end—not a lot of money in today's world of marketing and advertising.

What may be driving this willing invasion of privacy, though, is the fact that there is usually something in it for the "invadee." In the simplest terms, one of Kangaroo.com's willing participants put it this way: "I don't have to give them any money, I get a free T-shirt, and if I am interested in the product, I'll get an e-mail about it and find out more." Well, there you have it—direct and personal, and not that big a deal for some people.

Sources: Alissa Quart, "Ol' College Pry," *Business 2.0,* April 3, 2001, 68; Business 2.0.com Snapshot, *Business 2.0,* January 23, 2001, 17.

45. Marcia Stepanek, "Protecting E-Privacy: Washington Must Step In," *Business Week E.Biz,* July 26, 1999, EB30; Michael Krauss, "Get a Handle on the Privacy Wild Card," *Marketing News,* February 28, 2000, 12.
46. G. Beato, "Big Data's Big Business," *Business 2.0,* February 2001, 62.
47. *2000 Survey of Buying Power, Sales and Marketing Management,* September 2000, 15.
48. Jennifer Gilbert and Ira Teinowitz, "Privacy Debate Continues to Rage," *Advertising Age,* February 7, 2000, 44.

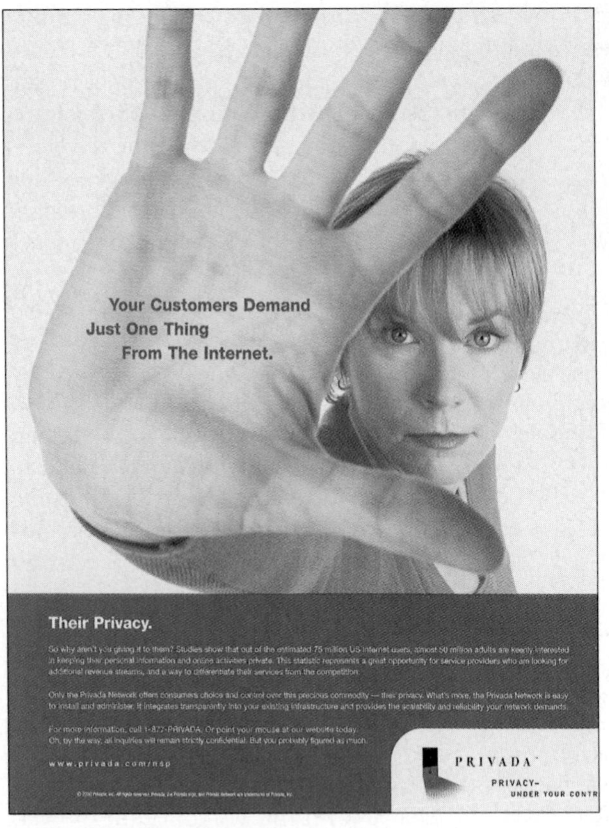

EXHIBIT 4.18

Consumer concerns over privacy have given rise to firms that can offer assurances that online behavior is kept confidential.

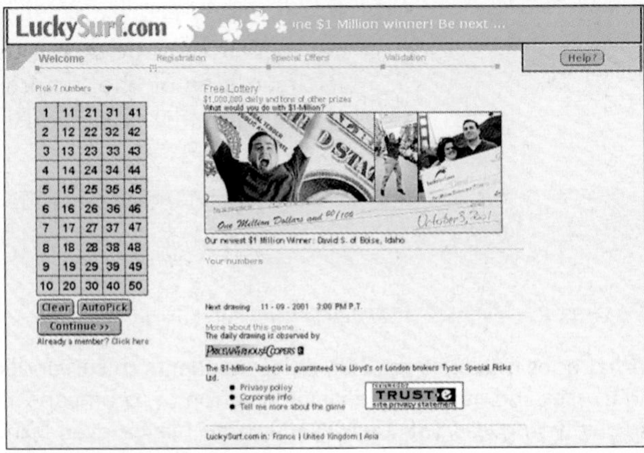

EXHIBIT 4.19

Online contests and sweepstakes are being monitored by government regulatory agents. luckysurf.com

Contests and Sweepstakes. While privacy is a huge direct marketing and e-commerce issue, it is not the only one. The next biggest legal issue has to do with sweepstakes and contests. Because of the success and widespread use of sweepstakes in direct marketing (such as the Publishers Clearing House sweepstakes), Congress has proposed limits on such promotions. The limits on direct mail sweepstakes include the requirement that the phrases "No purchase is necessary to win" and "A purchase will not improve an individual's chance of winning" must be repeated three times in letters to consumers and again on the entry form. In addition, penalties can be imposed on marketers who do not promptly remove consumers' names from mailing lists at the consumer's request.[49]

The online version of sweepstakes and contests also has the attention of the U.S. Congress. Sweepstakes, like the ones promoted at LuckySurf.com shown in Exhibit 4.19, play a lot like traditional sweepstakes, lotteries, games, or contests. At the LuckySurf site, you merely need to register (providing name, home address, e-mail address, and password), pick seven numbers, then click on one of four banner ads to activate your entry in a $1 million a day drawing—observed by Pricewaterhouse-

49. Ira Teinowitz, "Congress Nears Accord on Sweepstakes Limits," *Advertising Age,* August 9, 1999, 33.

Coopers. So far, these online games have avoided both lawsuits and regulation, but they have attracted the attention of policymakers.[50]

Telemarketing. Another legal issue in direct marketing has to do with telemarketing practices. The Telephone Consumer Fraud and Abuse Prevention Act of 1994 (later strengthened by the FTC in 1995) requires telemarketers to state their name, the purpose of the call, and the company they work for. The guidelines in the act prohibit telemarketers from calling before 8 A.M. and after 9 P.M., and they cannot call the same customer more than once every three months. In addition, they cannot use automatic dialing machines that contain recorded messages, and they must keep a list of consumers who do not want to be called.[51]

Regulatory Issues in Sales Promotion. Regulatory issues in sales promotion focus on three areas: premium offers, trade allowances, and contests and sweepstakes.

Premium Offers. With respect to **premiums** (an item offered for "free" or at a greatly reduced price with the purchase of another item), the main area of regulation has do with requiring marketers to state the fair retail value of the item offered as a premium.

Trade Allowances. In the area of trade allowances, marketers need to be familiar with the guidelines set forth in the Robinson-Patman Act of 1936. Even though this is an old piece of legislation, it still applies to contemporary trade promotion practices. The guidelines of the Robinson-Patman Act require marketers to offer similar customers similar prices on similar merchandise. This means that a marketer cannot use special allowances as a way to discount the price to highly attractive customers. This issue was raised earlier in the context of vertical cooperative advertising.

Contests and Sweepstakes. In the area of sweepstakes and contests, the issues discussed under direct marketing and e-commerce apply, but there are other issues as well. The FTC has specified four violations of regulations that marketers must avoid in carrying out sweepstakes and contests:

1. Misrepresentations about the value (for example, stating an inflated retail price) of the prizes being offered
2. Failure to provide complete disclosure about the conditions necessary to win (are there behaviors required on the part of the contestant?)
3. Failure to disclose the conditions necessary to obtain a prize (are there behaviors required of the contestant *after* the contestant is designated a "winner"?)
4. Failure to ensure that a contest or sweepstakes is not classified as a lottery, which is considered gambling—a contest or sweepstakes is a lottery if a prize is offered based on chance *and* the contestant has to give up something of value in order to play

Regulatory Issues in Public Relations. Public relations is not bound by the same sorts of laws as other elements of the promotional mix. Because public relations activities deal with public press and public figures, much of the regulation relates to these issues. The public relations activities of a firm may place it on either side of legal issues with respect to privacy, copyright infringement, or defamation through slander and libel.

50. James Heckman, "Online, But Not on Trial, though Privacy Looms Large," *Marketing News,* December 6, 1999, 8.
51. Ford and Calfee, "Recent Developments in FTC Policy on Deception," op. cit.

Privacy. The privacy problems facing a PR firm center on the issue of appropriation. **Appropriation** is the use of pictures or images owned by someone else without permission. If a firm uses a model's photo or a photographer's work in an advertisement or company brochure without permission, then the work has been appropriated without the owner's permission. The same is true of public relations materials prepared for release to the press or as part a company's public relations kit.

Copyright Infringement. Copyright infringement can occur when a public relations effort uses written, recorded, or photographic material in public relations materials. Much as with appropriation, written permission must be obtained to use such works.

Defamation. When a communication occurs that damages the reputation of an individual because the information in the communication was untrue, this is called **defamation** (you many have heard it referred to as "defamation of character"). Defamation can occur either through slander or libel. **Slander** is oral defamation and in the context of promotion would occur during television or radio broadcast of an event involving a company and its employees. **Libel** is defamation that occurs in print and would relate to magazine, newspaper, direct mail, or Internet reports.

The public relations practitioner's job is to protect clients from slanderous or libelous reports about a company's activities. Inflammatory TV "investigative" news programs are often sued for slander and libel, and are challenged to prove the allegations they make about a company and personnel working for a company. The issues revolve around whether negative comments can be fully substantiated.[52] Erroneous reports in major magazines and newspapers about a firm can result in a defamation lawsuit as well. Less frequently, public relations experts need to defend a client accused of making defamatory remarks.

52. One of the most widely publicized lawsuits of this time involved Philip Morris's $10 billion libel suit against ABC's news program *DayOne*. For a summary of this suit, see Steve Weinberg, "ABC, Philip Morris and the Infamous Apology," *Columbia Journalism Review*, November/December 1995, www.cjr.org, accessed December 7, 1999.

SUMMARY

1 Assess the benefits and problems of advertising in a capitalistic society and debate a variety of issues concerning advertising's effects on society's well-being.

Advertisers have always been followed by proponents and critics. Proponents of advertising argue that it offers benefits for individual consumers and society at large. At the societal level, proponents claim, advertising helps promote a higher standard of living by allowing marketers to reap the rewards of product improvements and innovation. Advertising also "pays for" mass media in many countries, and provides consumers with a constant flow of information not only about products and services, but also about political and social issues.

Over the years critics have leveled many charges at advertising and advertising practitioners. Advertising expenditures in the multi-billions are condemned as wasteful, offensive, and a source of frustration for many in society who see the lavish lifestyle portrayed in advertising, knowing they will never be able to afford such a lifestyle. Critics also contend that advertisements rarely furnish useful information but instead perpetuate superficial stereotypes of many cultural subgroups. For many years, some critics have been concerned that advertisers are controlling us against our will with subliminal advertising messages.

2 Explain how ethical considerations affect the development of advertising campaigns.

Ethical considerations are a concern when creating advertising, especially when that advertising will be targeted to children or will involve controversial products such as firearms, gambling, alcohol, or cigarettes. While ethical standards are a matter for personal reflection, it certainly is the case that unethical people can create unethical advertising. But there are also many safeguards against such behavior, including the corporate and personal integrity of advertisers.

Discuss the role of government agencies in the regulation of advertising.

Governments typically are involved in the regulation of advertising. It is important to recognize that advertising regulations can vary dramatically from one country to the next. In the United States, the Federal Trade Commission (FTC) has been especially active in trying to deter deception and unfairness in advertising. The FTC was established in 1914, and since then a variety of legislation has been passed to clarify the powers of the FTC. The FTC has also developed regulatory remedies that have expanded its involvement in advertising regulation, such as the advertising substantiation program.

Explain the meaning and importance of self-regulation for an advertising practitioner.

Some of the most important controls on advertising are voluntary; that is, they are a matter of self-regulation by advertising and marketing professionals. For example, the American Association of Advertising Agencies has issued guidelines for promoting fairness and accuracy when using comparative advertisements. Many other organizations, such as the Better Business Bureau, the National Association of Broadcasters, and Action for Children's Television, participate in the process to help ensure fairness and assess consumer complaints about advertising.

Discuss the regulation of other promotional tools in the integrated brand promotion process.

The regulation of other tools in the IBP process focuses on direct marketing, e-commerce, sales promotions, and public relations. In direct marketing and e-commerce, the primary concern has to do with consumer privacy. New technologies have enabled firms to match consumers' online behavior with offline personal information. Another aspect of e-commerce has to do with contests and sweepstakes and the potential for such games to actually be gambling opportunities.

In sales promotions, premium offers, trade allowances, and offline contests and sweepstakes are subject to regulation. Firms are required to state the fair value of "free" premiums, trade allowances must follow the guidelines of fair competition, and contests and sweepstakes must follow strict rules specified by the FTC.

The regulation of public relations efforts has to do with privacy, copyright infringement, and defamation. Firms must be aware of the strict legal parameters of these factors.

KEY TERMS

ethics
deception
puffery
primary demand
unfair advertising
vertical cooperative advertising
comparison advertisements
monopoly power
advertising substantiation program
consent order
cease-and-desist order
affirmative disclosure
corrective advertising
celebrity endorsements
self-regulation
consumerism
premiums
appropriation
defamation
slander
libel

QUESTIONS

1. Advertising has been a focal point of criticism for many decades. In your opinion, what are some of the key factors that make advertising controversial?

2. Proponents claim that because of mass media advertising, American consumers enjoy lower prices on a variety of products and services than would be the case if there were no mass media advertising. How could this be possible?

3. You have probably been exposed to hundreds of thousands of advertisements in your lifetime. In what ways does exposure to advertising make you a better or worse consumer?

4. Use Maslow's hierarchy of needs to address critics' concerns that too much advertising is directed at creating demand for products that are irrelevant to people's true needs.

5. What does it mean to suggest that an advertisement projects a stereotype? How might this problem of stereotyping relate to the process of market segmentation?

6. One type of advertising that attracts the attention of regulators, critics, and consumer advocates is advertising directed at children. Why is it the focus of so much attention?

7. What is comparison advertising, and why does this form of advertising need a special set of guidelines to prevent unfair competition?

8. Explain why a marketer might be tempted to misuse cooperative-advertising allowances to favor some kinds of retailers over others. What piece of legislation empowered the FTC to stop these bogus allowances?

9. The Nutrition Labeling and Education Act of 1990 is unique for a number of reasons. How has this act affected the day-to-day eating habits of many U.S. consumers? What makes this a special piece of legislation from an enforcement standpoint?

10. Some contend that self-regulation is the best way to ensure fair and truthful advertising practices. Why would it be in the best interests of the advertising community to aggressively pursue self-regulation?

EXPERIENTIAL EXERCISES

1. Cut out an ad from a magazine. Choose three pros or cons in the social aspects of advertising to demonstrate how advertising educates consumers, affects the standard of living, affects happiness, influences mass media, and is demeaning or artful.

2. List two product categories (other than cigarettes) that you think require some kind of advertising regulation and explain why. Do you think they require federal regulation, industry self-regulation, or consumer regulation? Explain. Based on your answer, list regulatory agents that might get involved in controlling the advertising process for these products. Finally, go to the Internet and do a search for one or more agency or watchdog sites that would be relevant to the regulatory process. How does the site encourage consumers to get involved, and what resources does the site offer to empower their participation in the process?

USING THE INTERNET

4-1 Social and Ethical Considerations of Advertising

Although all advertising has pros and cons, one particularly divisive issue in the past 50 years has been the promotion of cigarettes. Critics claim that cigarette manufacturers create ads that target children and make potentially dangerous or addictive products seem appealing. The ongoing clash between the industry and the federal government resulted in the 1998 Master Settlement Agreement. This legislation requires manufacturers to take down advertising from billboards and sports arenas and to stop using cartoon characters to sell cigarettes. The tobacco companies also agreed to not market or promote their products to young people. This strict regulatory environment is a far cry from the heyday of the tobacco advertising of past decades. Truth in Advertising, a site that contains historic ads for well-known cigarette products, is a virtual shrine to the *laissez-faire* days of tobacco advertising.

Truth in Advertising: www.chickenhead.com/truth

1. Go to this site and choose an ad from the 1940s or 1950s and describe how it reflects the priorities of society in that era. Is the advertisement guilty of promoting materialism? Explain.

2. In what way does the ad inform the consumer? In what way is the ad superficial?

3. What needs does the product claim to satisfy? How does the advertisement create artificial needs?

4. What do you think is the advertiser's ethical and social responsibility concerning the promotion of cigarettes? Apply relevant chapter concepts in your answer.

4-2 Advertising to Children

Protecting children's privacy online is a hot topic in advertising regulation. Advertisers routinely acquire important market information from Internet users, gathering data from consumer registration forms as well as from hidden browser cookie files. The Children's Online Privacy Protection Act of 1998 (COPPA) sets guidelines for Internet businesses, requiring full disclosure of the site's data-gathering procedures. Sites like LycosZone are a good example of how online brands seek to comply with regulatory standards and conduct socially responsible marketing and advertising practices.

LycosZone: www.lycoszone.com

Lycos Safety Cartoon (Flash 4 Player required): www.lycoszone.com/ftc.asp

1. Using the text, list some of the main concerns regarding advertising targeted to children.

2. Describe the purpose and features of LycosZone. What specific sections are designed to help protect children from the potentially harmful effects of advertising and marketing?

3. Click the links to the LycosZone privacy policy and describe the information disclosed about the site's data-gathering practices.

4. What is the purpose of the Lycos Safety Cartoon? What basic advice does it give to kids?

PART I
Cincinnati Bell Wireless: From IMC to IBP
Client: Cincinnati Bell Enterprises
Agency: Northlich

Background and Participants. In Chapter 1, we introduced the concept of integrated brand promotion (IBP) as an extension of conventional thinking about integrated marketing communication (IMC). The rise in prominence of IBP makes it essential that this evolving perspective on marketing communication be understood in conjunction with traditional mass media advertising. On the client side, sophisticated marketers such as Starbucks, Citibank, and Ford Motor Company are integrating communication tools such as direct marketing, event sponsorship, sales promotions, and public relations, with or without mass media advertising, to build their brands.[1] On the agency side, new organizational designs continue to evolve in search of just the right mix that will deliver clients the integrated expertise they need for building their brands.[2] Coordination and synergy in communication have become the key themes in a world where the advertiser with the strongest brand is the winner in the marketplace.

The five sections at the end of each part of this text will help you better understand advertising and integrated brand promotion by examining topics in two ways. First, each section will discuss IBP relative to each part of the text to provide more concepts and principles for understanding this important approach. Second, we will bring these concepts to life through an in-depth and ongoing case history. This in-depth case history features the working relationship between a client and an ad agency in pursuit of the initial launch and subsequent growth of a wireless phone-service brand (Cincinnati Bell Wireless). The featured client and agency are Cincinnati Bell Enterprises and Northlich. You will learn a great deal about these two organizations over the course of our five-part case history. More important, by closely examining the work of Northlich in launching and growing Cincinnati Bell Wireless, we can gain a concrete appreciation for the challenges and benefits of sophisticated advertising and IBP campaigns.

1. For discussions of how these and other marketers are using multiple communications options in an integrated way, see Robert Frank, "Pepsi Bets a Blue Can Will Spur Sales Abroad," *Wall Street Journal,* April 2, 1996, B8; Laura Petrecca, "Ikea Homes In on Office," *Advertising Age,* August 10, 1998, 16; and Betsy Spethmann, "Is Advertising Dead?" *PROMO Magazine,* September 1998, 32–36, 159–162.

2. For example, see Kate Fitzgerald, "Beyond Advertising," *Advertising Age,* August 3, 1998, 1, 14; Kathryn Kranhold, "FCB Makes Itself a New Economy Shop," *Wall Street Journal,* June 14, 2000, B8; Suzanne Vranica, "Y&R's Partilla Reshapes Ad Approach," *Wall Street Journal,* November 29, 2000, B6; Peter Breen, "Six Degrees of Integration," *PROMO Magazine,* October 2001, 75–80.

From IMC to IBP. There is always some risk in advancing new terminology to replace existing terminology, as we are doing here. As champions of advertising and integrated brand promotion, we are not arguing that integrated marketing communication is no longer a valid perspective. The emphasis on synergy and coordination that are at the heart of IMC are also at the heart of IBP. Moreover, we draw explicitly on the analysis of IMC provided by Esther Thorson and Jeri Moore in their 1996 book *Integrated Communication: Synergy of Persuasive Voices*. In their words,

IMC is the strategic coordination of multiple communication voices. Its aim is to optimize the impact of persuasive communication on both consumer and nonconsumer (e.g., retailers, sales personnel, opinion leaders) audiences by coordinating such elements of the marketing mix as advertising, public relations, promotions, direct marketing, and package design.[3]

However, Thorson and Moore also make it clear that achieving synergy and coordination must be based on an understanding of the brand. They note that the first task in planning an integrated communications campaign is to *define and understand in detail the brand itself and the "equity" it possesses . . . (one) must explore extensively the brand's essence—both current and intended.*[4] We concur with this view that a clear focus on a brand's current and desired brand equity is essential for creating effective, integrated campaigns. Branding gurus like Donald Schultz and Kevin Keller also endorse this position with their recommendations to *align all (marketing) actions with the brand's value proposition*[5] and *evaluate marketing communication options strategically to determine how they can contribute to brand equity.*[6] Without an explicit focus on brand building, there can be no integrated communication. Hence, the task at hand is not simply integrated marketing communication, but rather advertising and integrated brand promotion.

Factors Contributing to the Need for an Integrated Approach. Why have synergy and coordination of communication tools for brand-building purposes become a necessity? Several significant and pervasive changes in the communications environment have contributed to the need for an integrated approach:[7]

- *Fragmentation of media.* Media options available to marketers have proliferated at an astounding rate. Broadcast media now offer "narrowcasting" so specific that advertisers can reach consumers at precise locations, such as airports and supermarket checkout counters. The print media have proliferated dramatically as well. At one point, there were 197 different sports magazines on the market in the United States! The proliferation and fragmentation of media have resulted in less reliance on mass media and more emphasis on other promotional options, such as point-of-purchase promotions and event sponsorship.
- *Better audience assessment.* More sophisticated research methods have made it possible to more accurately identify and target specific market segments such as Asian-Americans, teenagers, Hispanics, and dual-income households with no kids (DINKs). This leads the marketer away from mass media to promotional tools that reach only the segment that has been targeted.
- *Consumer empowerment.* Consumers today are more powerful and sophisticated than their predecessors. Fostering this greater power are more single-person

3. Esther Thorson and Jeri Moore, *Integrated Communication: Synergy of Persuasive Voices* (Mahwah, N. J.: Lawrence Erlbaum, 1996), 1.
4. Thorson and Moore, *Integrated Communication: Synergy of Persuasive Voices,* 3.
5. Don E. Schultz, "A Boatload of Branders," *Marketing Management,* Fall 2000, 9.
6. Kevin Keller, *Strategic Brand Management* (Upper Saddle River, N.J.: Prentice-Hall, 1998), 263.
7. In the opening chapter of his influential book *Permission Marketing* (New York: Simon & Schuster, 1999), Seth Godin argues that increasing fragmentation of the mass media and rampant ad clutter are due to cause a cataclysmic decline in the effectiveness of conventional mass media advertising. Check it out at www.permission.com and see if you agree.

households, smaller families, higher education levels, and more experienced consumers. Empowered consumers are more skeptical of commercial messages and demand information tailored to their needs.

- *Increased advertising clutter.* Not only are consumers becoming more sophisticated, they are becoming more jaded as well. The proliferation of advertising stimuli has diluted the effectiveness of any single message. There is no end in sight to this "message" proliferation.
- *Database technology.* The ability of firms to generate, collate, and manage databases has created diverse communications opportunities beyond mass media. These databases can be used to create customer and noncustomer profiles. With this information, highly targeted direct response and telemarketing programs can be implemented. Growth of the Internet will foster more of this type of marketing activity.
- *Channel power.* In many product and market categories, there has been a shift in power away from big manufacturers toward big retailers. The new "power retailers," such as Wal-Mart and Home Depot, are able to demand promotional fees and allowances from manufacturers, which diverts funds away from advertising and into special events or other retail promotions.
- *Accountability.* In an attempt to achieve greater accountability, firms have reallocated marketing resources from advertising to more short-term and more easily measurable methods, such as direct mail and sales promotion.

All these factors have contributed to an increase in the diversity and complexity of the communication tools used by firms in building their brands. Mass media advertising still plays an important role for many companies, but the opportunity to use other communication and promotional tools makes coordination and integration ever more challenging. Learning to cope with this challenge is what our book and this case history is all about.

Sounds Great . . . So What's So Hard about Advertising and Integrated Brand Promotion?

Exhibit IBP 1.1 presents a hierarchy of participants that helps to illustrate the challenges that marketers will encounter when attempting to surround current or prospective customers with a "wall" of advertising and integrated brand promotion. Notice that the marketer typically brings to the process a marketing plan, goals and objectives, and perhaps a database that will identify current and prospective customers. The advertising agency will help research the market, suggest creative strategies, and produce persuasive messages. In addition, agencies can assist in placing these messages in outlets that range from conventional mass media to event sponsorship to Internet advertising. The exhibit also shows a number of specialized marketing communication organizations that may need to be hired in conjunction with or in place of the firm's ad agency to execute a comprehensive campaign. Back in Chapter 2 we referred to such specialists as promotion agencies and external facilitators. This is where the process starts to get messy.

Most ad agencies simply do not have all the internal expertise necessary to develop and manage every marketing communication tool. First and foremost, the ad agency is the expert in the development and placement of mass media advertising. This is especially the case for large advertising agencies. Mega-agencies such as those listed in Exhibit 2.8 became mega-agencies because of their prowess in mass media advertising. Because they have a lot invested in their mass media expertise, large ad agencies are often criticized for the tendency to push mass media as the best communication solution for any and all clients.[8]

8. For example, see Jim Osterman, "This Changes Everything," *Adweek,* May 15, 1995, 44–45; Fitzgerald, "Beyond Advertising"; Spethmann, "Is Advertising Dead?"

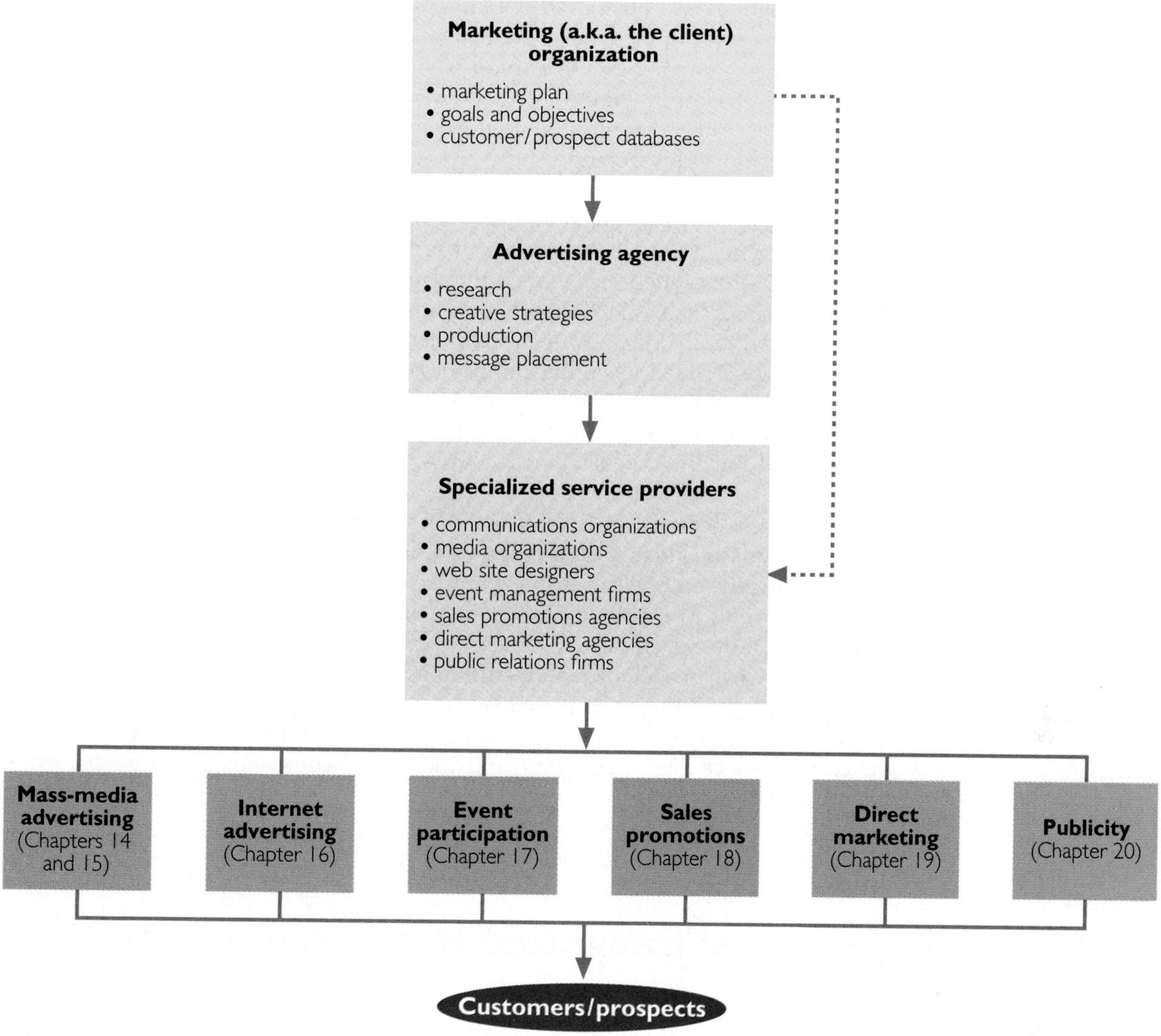

EXHIBIT IBP 1.1

The advertising and integrated brand promotion hierarchy.

Hence, when marketers want other communication options, they often must turn to specific types of promotion agencies to get the expertise they are looking for. For example, companies such as Avon and Ford's Lincoln Mercury division have retained Wunderman Cato Johnson–Chicago just to help them with event management, and Pepsi and Philip Morris have hired Cyrk-Simon Worldwide to design and run their Pepsi Stuff and Marlboro Miles branded-merchandise reward programs.[9] As reflected by the dashed line in Exhibit IBP 1.1, in many instances marketing organizations must bypass their traditional advertising agency to get the expertise they require for building their brands.

Coordination and integration of a marketing communications program becomes much more complex as various promotion agencies are brought into the picture. These diverse specialists often will view one another as competitors for clients' marketing dollars, and will most likely champion their particular specialty, be it event sponsorship, sales promotions, Web site development, direct marketing, or whatever. This is just human nature in a free enterprise system. But instead of ending up

9. Spethmann, "Is Advertising Dead?"

with coordination and integration, we now have a situation characterized by conflict and disintegration. Of course, conflict and disintegration are *not* what the marketer wants for his or her brand. As you saw in the example of Lipton Brisk at the beginning of Chapter 2, adding just one new player (in that case, Agency.com) to the process can cause considerable conflict, particularly when alignment about the meaning of the brand is lacking.

Advertising agencies of all sizes are well aware of these challenges, and as we noted in Chapter 2, many are attempting to redesign themselves to add more internal expertise that can foster the goals of IBP. Sometimes this redesign comes in the form of new cross-functional work units launched within the traditional agency under nifty names such as J. Walter Thompson's Total Solutions Group,[10] or Young & Rubicam's Brand Buzz—a unit totally devoted to guerrilla marketing.[11] Other times, expertise is added when big companies buy out smaller specialist firms to supplement their range of services.[12] As you can see, this whole business of advertising and IBP is about bringing together the right combination of expertise to serve a client's brand-building needs. This is always a complex undertaking with no easy answers.

The process depicted in Exhibit IBP 1.1 shows a complex array of participants and tools. Our Cincinnati Bell Wireless case history will bring this process to life for you. Additionally, each of the chapters in Parts Four and Five of the book will examine different tools to help you master the complexity of advertising and integrated brand promotion. Specifically, Chapters 14 and 15 will emphasize traditional mass media tools; Chapter 16 looks at advertising using the Internet; Chapter 17 will consider event sponsorship, support media, and point-of-purchase advertising; Chapter 18 reviews the array of possibilities in sales promotion; Chapter 19 provides a comprehensive look at direct marketing; and Chapter 20 completes the set by discussing the public relations function. So if Exhibit IBP 1.1 is not completely clear to you at this point, fear not. There's more to come on all this! But enough about what's to come. Now let's meet the participants in our comprehensive case history.

An Agency in Pursuit of Integrated Brand Promotion . . .

NORTHLICH

Northlich, www.northlich.com. Northlich Stolley LaWarre, based in Cincinnati, Ohio, was founded in 1949. As part of their 50-year birthday party, managers at the agency decided that their name was a bit unwieldy and inhibited efforts in cultivating their own brand identity. As an agency in the business of building brands, management at Northlich Stolley LaWarre decided they should pay more attention to building their own brand. As part of this commitment, they changed the agency's brand name to simply Northlich (pronounced "North-lick").

As of the year 2000, Northlich ranked #81 in *Adweek* magazine's ranking of the Top 100 U.S. agencies. In 2000 Northlich enjoyed a 14 percent increase in billings over the previous year to nearly $150 million, which generated revenues for the company of about $22 million. Northlich's client base is diverse and includes Ashland, Broadwing, Iams, Linens 'n Things, Mead Corporation, Procter & Gamble, Speedo International, StarKist Seafood Company, and Whirlpool, to name a few. Samples of Northlich's recent work on its own behalf and for some of its clients are shown in Exhibit IBP 1.2. Northlich became the agency of record for Cincinnati Bell two years prior to the launch of Cincinnati Bell Wireless.

10. Fitzgerald, "Beyond Advertising."
11. Vranica, "Y&R's Partilla Reshapes Ad Approach."
12. Spethmann, "Is Advertising Dead?"

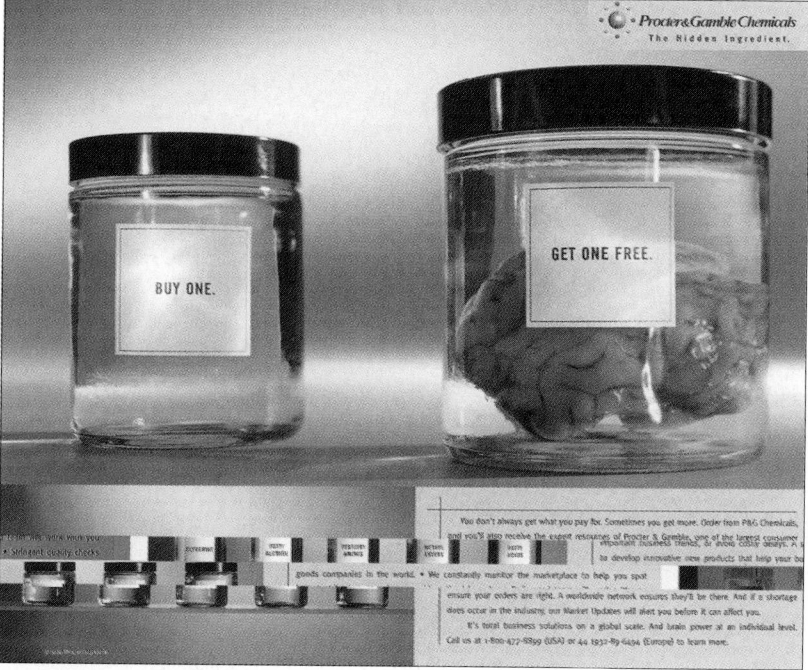

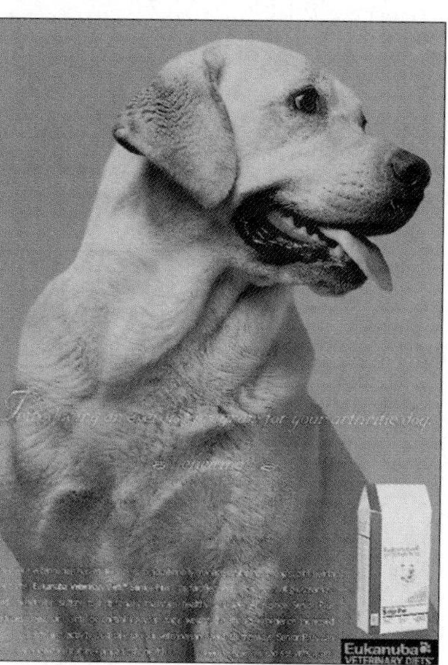

EXHIBIT IBP 1.2

Recent Northlich advertising samples.

Northlich executives attribute their success as a full-service communications agency to their people and their underlying values. The following six value statements are displayed proudly throughout the Northlich office complex:

1. A visceral connection to our clients' consumers and constituents.
2. A reverence for breakthrough ideas as the nourishment of growth.
3. Agility in our thinking and action.
4. A captivating work environment.
5. An independent spirit.
6. Great style, fine taste, and a big heart.

Other elements of the Northlich business model include the following:

- Relentless pursuit of audience insights that leads to distinctive and preemptive value propositions for clients' brands.
- Targeted programs that divide and conquer with each constituency.
- Provocative advertising that disrupts the category and causes a chain reaction.
- Compelling demos that deliver memorable visualization benefits.

- Integrated communications that drive home the essence of a brand's value proposition in every vehicle.

While the folks at Northlich usually refer to their company as an advertising agency, it is probably more accurate to think of them as an IBP agency. Integration at Northlich means using whatever marketing tools are appropriate for the brand-building problem at hand. That could mean that direct marketing must be used in conjunction with image-oriented advertising, or that PR alone is the best way to proceed. To truly leverage the power of a brand name and motivate consumers, it takes an intimate understanding of how to orchestrate different media and messages. The overriding goal is always to build the strength of the client's brand.

Northlich employs about 150 full-time people. The agency's leadership team, featured in Exhibit IBP 1.3, gives an indication of the range of expertise that Northlich can marshal to serve clients' communication needs. This starts with an extensive client-service capability that includes strategic marketing planning, product positioning, and market research expertise. Northlich also provides a full line of creative

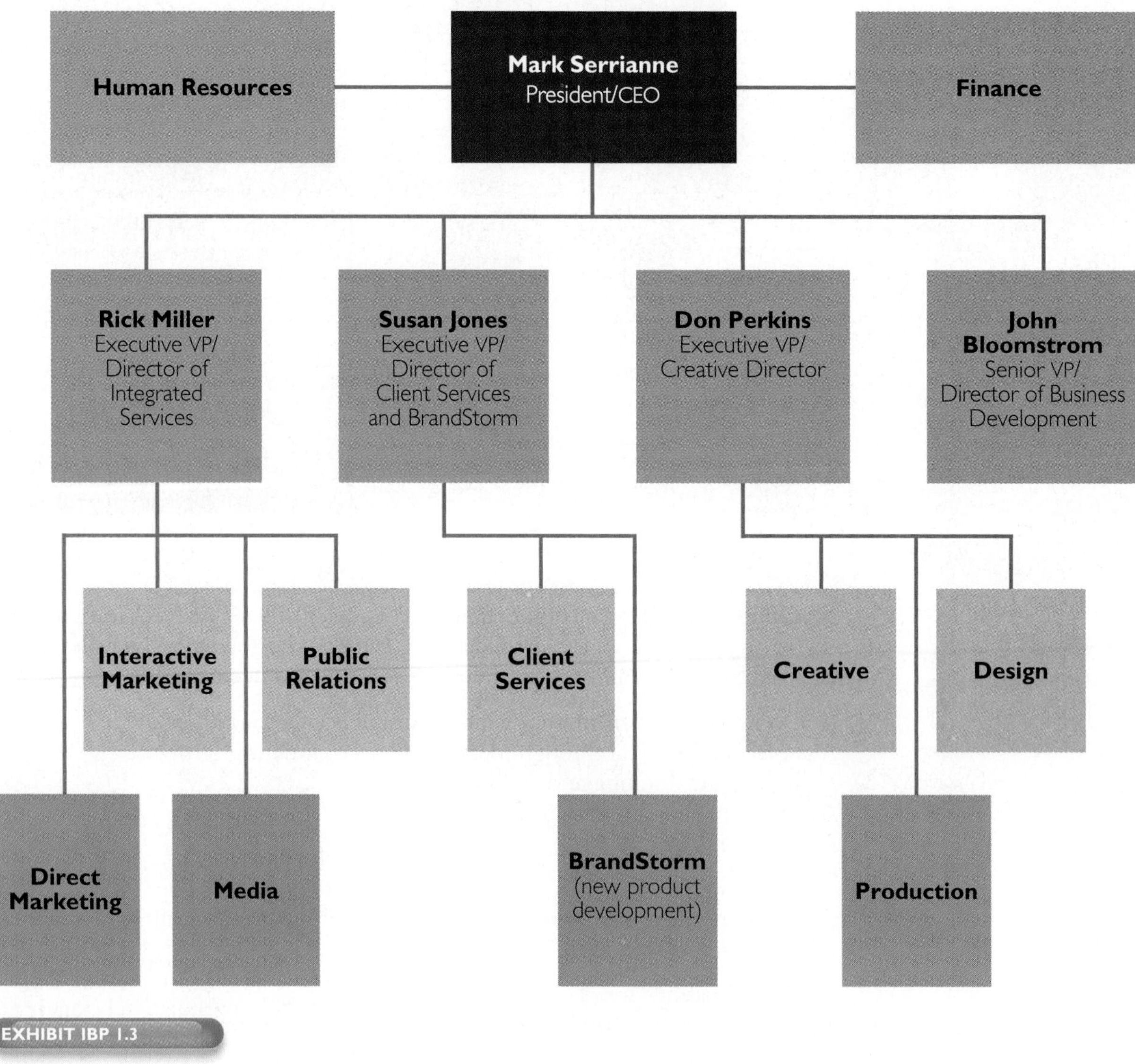

EXHIBIT IBP 1.3

The Northlich leadership team.

and production services for development of media advertising, collateral, packaging, point-of-purchase, direct marketing, and other IBP materials. The direct marketing department will assist clients with program design, strategy development, program oversight, measurement, and effectiveness evaluation. Northlich offers complete media planning, buying, and postbuy evaluation, and has additional expertise in interactive marketing with specific capabilities in Web site design and construction. The public relations group also has full-service capabilities including media and community relations, consumer promotion activities, employee relations, and crisis management. The combination of Northlich's value system, its manageable size, its collocation of diverse capabilities, a team-oriented work environment, and its excellent range and depth of expertise puts it in an excellent position to fulfill its promise of integrated brand builder.

In 1998, after 23 years with the agency, Mark Serrianne was named Northlich's president and CEO. He is clearly an advocate for IBP. As executive vice president in 1987, Serrianne began the redesign of Northlich from a conventional, mass media–oriented ad agency to a full-service marketing communications firm. One conclusion should be obvious: The transformation from conventional to integrated does not happen overnight. In Serrianne's view, Northlich has created an internal culture that embraces and rewards integration. Simple aspects of the daily work environment feed into the drive for integration. For example, no one, including the CEO, has a private office. In Serrianne's view, the open-office policy "has created more energy . . . culturally sends a good message to everyone . . . and breaks down barriers between departments." At the same time, Northlich's office complex is filled with numerous breakout rooms of various sizes that allow teams of employees to retreat and focus on clients' problems from a cross-departmental perspective. "Clients are convinced to buy integrated services," says Serrianne, "once you have some pretty good case histories and they have experience with our multidisciplinary teams."[13] We will see those multidisciplinary teams at work in the case history of the launch of Cincinnati Bell Wireless.

A Client in Pursuit of Integrated Brand Promotion . . .

Cincinnati Bell Enterprises, www.cincinnatibell.com. The other key player in our ongoing IBP case history is Cincinnati Bell, a diversified and innovative telecommunications company that began in 1873 as the City & Suburban Telegraph Association. Today, Cincinnati Bell supplies the Greater Cincinnati region with an array of services and business solutions that cannot be found anywhere else in the United States, such as local, long distance, wireless, Internet, and broadband services from a single source, billed together with one point of contact. Cincinnati Bell's residential customers routinely score the company among the highest in the country for customer service, as measured in the annual J. D. Power & Associates customer satisfaction survey. In addition, Cincinnati Bell's high-speed, asymmetrical digital subscriber line service, called ZoomTown, helps make Cincinnati one of the most wired communities in America, with service available to more than 70 percent of households, versus a 5 percent national average. Here we'd expect you to conclude that Cincinnati Bell is a lot more than just a sleepy little telephone service provider nestled on the banks of the Ohio River.

In November 1999, Cincinnati Bell acquired IXC Communications of Austin, Texas. This acquisition combined IXC's state-of-the-art, nationwide, fiber-optic communications network with Cincinnati Bell's regional telecommunications businesses to form a new company, Broadwing, Inc. The three primary subsidiaries of

13. Sue Fulton, "Local to National: One Agency's Strategy," *Ad Business Report,* June 1998, 1.

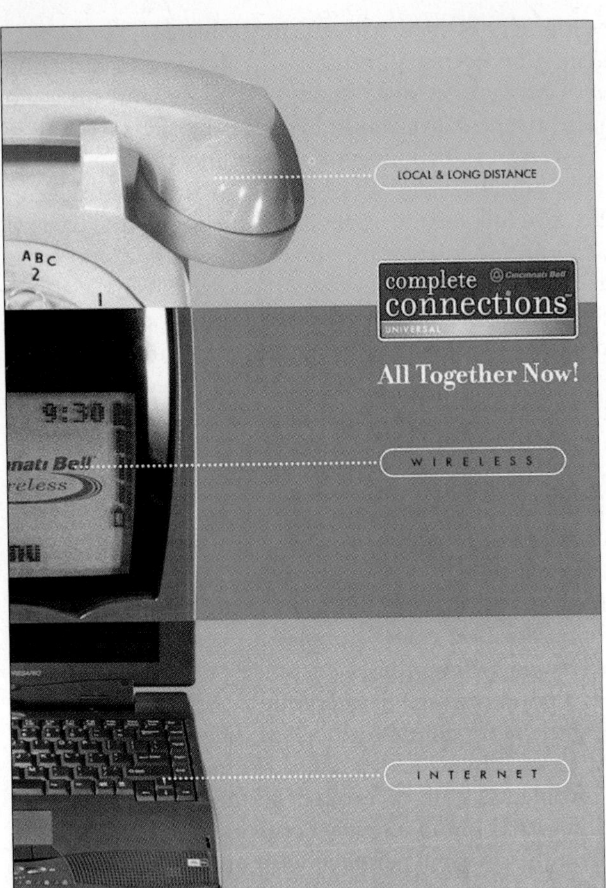

EXHIBIT IBP 1.4

Recent Cincinnati Bell advertising samples.

Broadwing, Inc. are Broadwing Communications, Cincinnati Bell Telephone, and Cincinnati Bell Enterprises. Of these, Cincinnati Bell Enterprises is our focal point, because here is housed the product innovation and brand-building capability for the Cincinnati metro market. From this unit innovative brands such as ZoomTown, Complete Connections, Fuse Internet Access, and Cincinnati Bell Any Distance have been launched. Sample ads for some of these branded services are displayed in Exhibit IBP 1.4. And most important, it is within Cincinnati Bell Enterprises where we find the star of our case history—*Cincinnati Bell Wireless*. Our case history officially begins in late fall, 1997.

In the fourth quarter of 1997, Cincinnati Bell signed a landmark agreement with AT&T Wireless Services that marked the birth of Cincinnati Bell Wireless (www.cbwireless.com). Previously, they had hired away John F. (Jack) Cassidy from Cantel Cellular Services in Canada to become the new president of Cincinnati Bell Wireless (CBW). The stage was set for a tumultuous six-month period in which Northlich and CBW would prepare to launch advanced personal communication services: voice, paging, and e-mail messaging, with other features and associated products. The strategy formulation that occurred in the period from November 1997 through the spring of 1998 will be described in the next installment of this IBP case history, at the end of Part Two.

IBP EXERCISES

1. What is it about integrated brand promotion that extends and better focuses the perspective previously referred to as integrated marketing communication? What do these two perspectives have in common? Explain where the conflict arose in the Lipton Brisk example (see Chapter 2) in terms of the IBP perspective.
2. A major challenge in executing advertising and integrated brand promotion is to speak to the customer via multiple communications tools in a single voice. What does *single voice* mean, and what's so hard about achieving a single voice in an IBP campaign?
3. Examine the Northlich organizational structure, shown in Exhibit IBP 1.3. How do you think this structure would compare to the structure of a more traditional advertising agency? How does the structure of Northlich lend itself to the execution of the Cincinnati Bell Wireless launch campaign?
4. Why would a regional company like Cincinnati Bell seek out an advertising agency with IBP capabilities to launch its new wireless service? Why might Cincinnati Bell not want to rely on mass media advertising alone to promote its new service? (*Hint:* Refer to the discussion of the factors contributing to the need for integration: fragmentation of media, better audience assessment, consumer empowerment, increased advertising clutter, database technology, channel power, and accountability.)

PART TWO

Planning: Analyzing the Advertising Environment

Successful advertising and integrated brand promotion rely on a clear understanding of how and why consumers make their purchase decisions. Successful campaigns are also rooted in sound marketing strategies and careful research about a brand's market environment. This understanding of the market, sound marketing strategy, and research are brought together in a formal advertising plan. Part Two, "Planning: Analyzing the Advertising Environment," discusses several important bases for the development of an advertising plan and concludes with a look at planning challenges in international markets.

Advertising and Consumer Behavior Chapter 5, "Advertising and Consumer Behavior," begins with an assessment of the way consumers make product and brand choices. These decisions depend on consumers' involvement and prior experiences with the product in question. This chapter also addresses consumer behavior and advertising from both psychological and sociological points of view. It concludes with a discussion of how culture affects consumer behavior and advertising. This includes a discussion of ads as social texts. 5

Market Segmentation, Positioning, and the Value Proposition Chapter 6, "Market Segmentation, Positioning and the Value Proposition," details how these three fundamental planning efforts are developed by an organization. With a combination of audience and competitive information, products and services are developed to provide benefits that are both valued by target customers and different from those of the competition. Finally, the way advertising contributes to communicating value to consumers is explained and modeled. 6

Advertising and Promotion Research Chapter 7, "Advertising and Promotion Research," discusses the types of research conducted by advertisers and the role information plays in planning an advertising effort. Advertisers do research before messages are prepared, during the preparation process, and after messages are running in the market. The new "account planning process" is also covered in this chapter. 7

The Advertising Plan Chapter 8, "The Advertising Plan," explains how formal advertising plans are developed. The inputs to the advertising plan are laid out in detail, and the process of setting advertising objectives—both communications and sales objectives—is described. The methods for setting an advertising budget are presented, including the widely adopted and preferred objective-and-task approach. 8

Advertising Planning: An International Perspective Chapter 9, "Advertising Planning: An International Perspective," introduces issues related to planning advertising targeted to international audiences. Global forces are creating more accessible markets. In the midst of this trend toward international trade, marketers are redefining the nature and scope of the markets for their goods and services while adjusting to the creative, media, and regulatory challenges of competing across national boundaries. 9

CHAPTER 5

CHAPTER 5
Advertising and Consumer Behavior

CHAPTER 6
Market Segmentation, Positioning, and the Value Proposition

CHAPTER 7
Advertising and Promotion Research

CHAPTER 8
The Advertising Plan

CHAPTER 9
Advertising Planning: An International Perspective

After reading and thinking about this chapter, you will be able to do the following:

Describe the four basic stages of consumer decision making.

Explain how consumers adapt their decision-making processes as a function of involvement and experience.

Discuss how advertising may influence consumer behavior through its effects on various psychological states.

Discuss the interaction of culture and advertising.

Discuss the role of sociological factors in consumer behavior and advertising response.

The Japanese marketplace is one of the toughest competitive arenas in the world. Japanese consumers are among the most affluent and educated in the world. Giant U.S. corporations such as Procter & Gamble often struggle in this challenging environment. Up until 1995, P&G—maker of dishwashing products such as Dawn, Joy, Ivory, and Cascade—did not sell any dish soap in Japan.[1] Soaps are P&G's core business; P&G aspires to market all its brands around the world; and P&G is one of the most sophisticated companies in the world when it comes to executing multimillion-dollar advertising campaigns. But how to get started in Japan?

P&G used a tried-and-true formula. They sent their managers into the field to talk to consumers and study Japanese dishwashing rituals. They watched the Japanese wash their dishes, videotaped them washing dishes, and talked to them before, during, and after dishwashing. As a result of this careful observation, P&G researchers discovered one critical habit: Japanese homemakers, one after another, squirted out more liquid than was called for, more than was needed, and more than was effective. P&G managers interpreted this as a clear sign of consumers' frustrations with existing products. Implicitly, these consumers wanted a more powerful cleaning liquid, and were trying to get it by simply using more of their current brand. But it wasn't working.

P&G's chemical engineers in Kobe, Japan, went to work on a new, highly concentrated soap formula just for the frustrated Japanese consumer. The marketing pitch would be simple and to the point: A little bit of Joy cleans better, yet is easier on the hands. Encouraged by positive results in test marketing, P&G prepared for a nationwide launch in Japan.

For its advertising campaign P&G settled on a documentary-style TV ad in which a famous Japanese comedian named Junji Takada dropped in on unsuspecting homemakers (see Exhibit 5.1), with his camera crew in tow, to test Joy on the household's dirty dishes. Television ads featured a shot of a grease slick in a sink full of dirty dishes. One squirt of Joy and the grease disappeared. With this simple visual demonstration the ad communicated to consumers that the new Joy was more potent than their old brand. It wasn't long before Joy began racking up impressive market share gains throughout Japan.

Of course, P&G's Japanese competitors were quick to notice the success of Joy. The Kao Corporation (think of Kao as the P&G of Japan) conducted research to better understand Joy's success. Kao's research showed that more than 70 percent of Joy's users began using it because the TV ads persuaded them that this new brand offered superior performance. Now that's effective advertising! Kao's management admitted: "We had mistakenly assumed Japanese didn't care much about grease-fighting power in dish soaps. The reality was that people were eating more meat and fried food and were frustrated about grease stains on their plastic dishes and storage containers."[2] Kao's lack of understanding of what was important to the customer led to a predictable outcome: Joy became Japan's best-selling dishwashing soap.

Many things must go right for a new brand to enter a crowded marketplace and achieve market leadership, as Joy did in Japan. The product's performance, its packaging, its pricing, and the advertising campaign must work synergistically to achieve this level of success. But success can commonly be traced back to understanding consumers, creating products that address their needs, and executing ad campaigns that persuade consumers that only one brand has just what they're looking for. As with Joy in Japan, insights about the behavior of consumers are crucial to advertising professionals. Before advertisers initiate campaigns for any product or service, they need a thorough understanding of what's important to the customer. This understanding greatly increases the advertiser's chance of effecting purchase behavior.

1. Norihiko Shirouzu, "P&G's Joy Makes an Unlikely Splash in Japan," *Wall Street Journal,* December 10, 1997, B1.
2. Ibid.

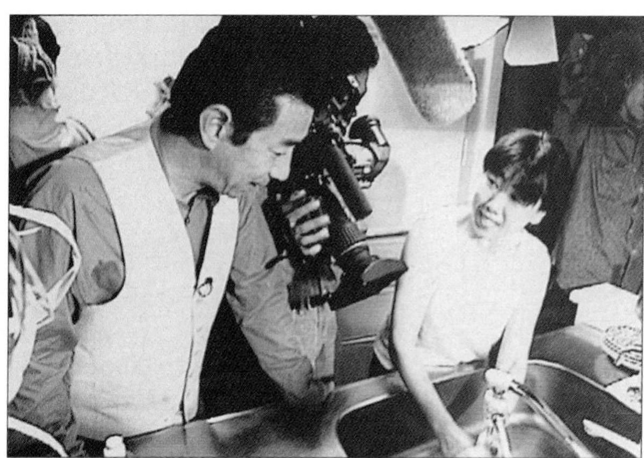

EXHIBIT 5.1

P&G used a documentary-style advertising campaign for its launch of Joy in Japan: on the road in search of greasy dishes. The interviewer is comedian Junji Takada. His celebrity status and sense of humor were important elements in creating likable and persuasive TV commercials.
www.pg.com

Chapters 1 through 4 provided important background and perspectives about the business of advertising. With this background in place, we are now ready to begin consideration of how one would actually go about planning for an advertising campaign. Where to begin? How does one get started? As you saw in the preceding success story about marketing dishwashing liquids in Japan, a great place to start is with unique insights about your consumers.

Consumer behavior is defined as the entire broad spectrum of things that affect, derive from, or form the context of human consumption. Like all human behavior, the behavior of consumers is complicated, rich, and varied. However, advertisers must make it their job to understand consumers if they want to experience sustained success in creating effective advertising. Sometimes this understanding comes in the form of comprehensive research efforts; other times in the form of years of experience and implicit theories; other times in the form of blind, dumb luck (rarely attributed as such). However this understanding comes about, it is a key factor for advertising success.

This chapter summarizes the concepts and frameworks we believe are most helpful in trying to understand consumer behavior. We will describe consumer behavior and attempt to explain it, in its incredible diversity, from two different perspectives. The first portrays consumers as reasonably systematic decision makers who seek to maximize the benefits they derive from their purchases. The second views consumers as active interpreters (meaning-makers) of advertising, whose membership in various cultures, societies, and communities significantly affects their interpretation and response to advertising. These two perspectives are different ways of looking at the exact same people and the exact same behaviors. Though different in essential assumptions, both of these perspectives offer something valuable to the task of actually getting the work of advertising done.

The point is that no one perspective can adequately explain consumer behavior. Consumers are psychological, social, cultural, historical, and economical at the same time. For example, suppose a sociologist and a psychologist both saw someone buying a car. The psychologist might explain this behavior in terms of attitudes, decision criteria, and the like, while the sociologist would probably explain it in terms of the buyer's social environment and circumstances (that is, income, housing conditions, social class, the social value or "cultural capital" the brand afforded, and so on). Both explanations may be valid, but each is incomplete. The bottom line is that all consumer behavior is complex and multifaceted. Why you or any other consumer buys a movie ticket rather than a lottery ticket, or Pepsi rather than Coke, or Duracell rather than Eveready, is a function of psychological, economic, sociological, anthropological, historical, textual, and other forces. No single explanation is sufficient. With this in mind, we offer two basic perspectives on consumer behavior.

1 Perspective One: The Consumer as Decision Maker.

One way to view consumer behavior is as a logical, sequential process culminating with the individual's reaping a set of benefits from a product or service that satisfies that person's perceived needs. In this basic view, we can think of individuals as purposeful decision makers who take matters one step at a time. All consumption episodes might then be conceived as a sequence of four basic stages:

1. Need recognition
2. Information search and alternative evaluation
3. Purchase
4. Postpurchase use and evaluation

The Consumer Decision-Making Process.

A brief discussion of what typically happens at each stage will give us a foundation for understanding consumers, and it can also illuminate opportunities for developing powerful advertising.

Need Recognition. The consumption process begins when people perceive a need. A **need state** arises when one's desired state of affairs differs from one's actual state of affairs. Need states are accompanied by a mental discomfort or anxiety that motivates action; the severity of this discomfort can be widely variable depending on the genesis of the need. For example, the need state that arises when one runs out of toothpaste would involve very mild discomfort for most people, whereas the need state that accompanies the breakdown of one's automobile on a dark and deserted highway in Minnesota in mid-February can approach true desperation.

One way advertising works is to point to and thereby activate needs that will motivate consumers to buy a product or service. For instance, nearly every fall, advertisers from product categories as diverse as autos, snowblowers, and footwear roll out predictions for another severe winter and encourage consumers to prepare themselves before it's too late. Such an appeal is very productive when the previous winter was especially severe and the advertiser does a good job of capturing the sights and sounds of last year's terrible storms.

Following an especially severe winter in the Northeast, Jeep dealers in New York State warned, "Last year's winter produced 17 winter storms. . . . This year, the *Old Farmer's Almanac* is predicting another winter with above-average snowfall." As a result of this campaign, Jeep dealers in the New York region sold every vehicle they could get their hands on.[3] Consumers in New York obviously responded to the advertiser's effort to activate a need state.

Many factors can influence the need states of consumers. For instance, Maslow's hierarchy of needs suggests that a consumer's level of affluence can have a dramatic impact on the types of needs he or she might perceive as relevant. The less fortunate are concerned with fundamental needs, such as food and shelter; more-affluent consumers may fret over which new piece of Williams-Sonoma kitchen gadgetry or other accoutrement to place in their uptown condo. The former's needs are predominantly for physiological survival and basic comfort, while the latter's may have more to do with seeking to validate personal accomplishments and derive status and

3. Fara Warner, "Relishing and Embellishing Forecasts for Frigid Winter," *Wall Street Journal*, December 1, 1994, B1.

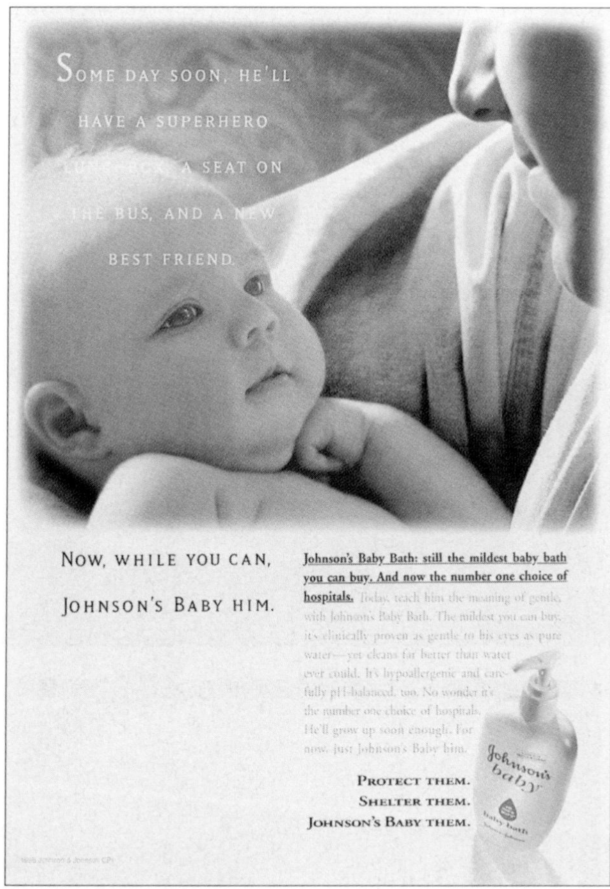

EXHIBIT 5.2

All parents want to be good to their child. This ad promises both functional benefits and emotional rewards for diligent parents.
www.jnj.com

recognition through consumption. While income clearly matters in this regard, it would be a mistake to believe that the poor have no aesthetic concerns, or that the rich are always oblivious to the need for basic essentials. The central point is that a variety of needs can be fulfilled through consumption, and it is reasonable to suggest that consumers are looking to satisfy needs when they buy products or services.

Products and services should provide benefits that fulfill consumers' needs; hence, one of the advertiser's primary jobs is to make the connection between the two for the consumer. Benefits come in many forms. Some are more functional—that is, they derive from the more objective performance characteristics of a product or service. Convenience, reliability, nutrition, durability, and economy are descriptors that refer to **functional benefits.**

Consumers may also choose products that provide **emotional benefits;** these are not typically found in some tangible feature or objective characteristic of a product. Emotional benefits are more subjective and may be perceived differently from one consumer to the next. Products and services help consumers feel pride, avoid guilt, relieve fear, and experience intense pleasure. These are powerful consumption motives that advertisers often try to activate. Can you find the emotional benefits promised in Exhibit 5.2?

Any advertiser must develop a keen appreciation for the kinds of benefits that consumers might derive from its product and brand. Even in the same product category, the benefits promised may be quite disparate. As shown in Exhibit 5.3, the makers of the Geo Metro portray their vehicle as the epitome of functional transportation. The Toyota Corolla offers dependable transportation along with a car that's more fun to drive, per Exhibit 5.4. The makers of the Mercedes-Benz SL 500 appeal to the emotional rewards of ownership with ads like that in Exhibit 5.5.

The ads for these three cars demonstrate the diversity of needs perceived by consumers, along with benefits offered by advertisers. If consumers do not know about or forget the benefits that a particular brand is supposed to provide, the maker's advertising effort is likely at fault.

Information Search and Alternative Evaluation. Given that a consumer has recognized a need, it is often not obvious what would be the best way to satisfy that need. For example, if you have a fear of being trapped in a blizzard in upstate New York, a condo on Miami Beach may be a much better solution than a Jeep or new snow tires. Need recognition simply sets in motion a process that may involve an extensive information search and careful evaluation of alternatives prior to purchase. Of course, during this search and evaluation, there are numerous opportunities for the advertiser to influence the final decision.

Once a need has been recognized, information for the decision is acquired through an internal or external search. The consumer's first option for information is to draw on personal experience and prior knowledge. This **internal search** for information may be all that is required. When a consumer has considerable prior experience with the products in question, attitudes about the alternatives may be

EXHIBIT 5.3

Functional benefits rule in this ad. Of course, the "tiny, little price tag" of the Geo Metro is a good place to start when promoting functionality. www.chevrolet.com

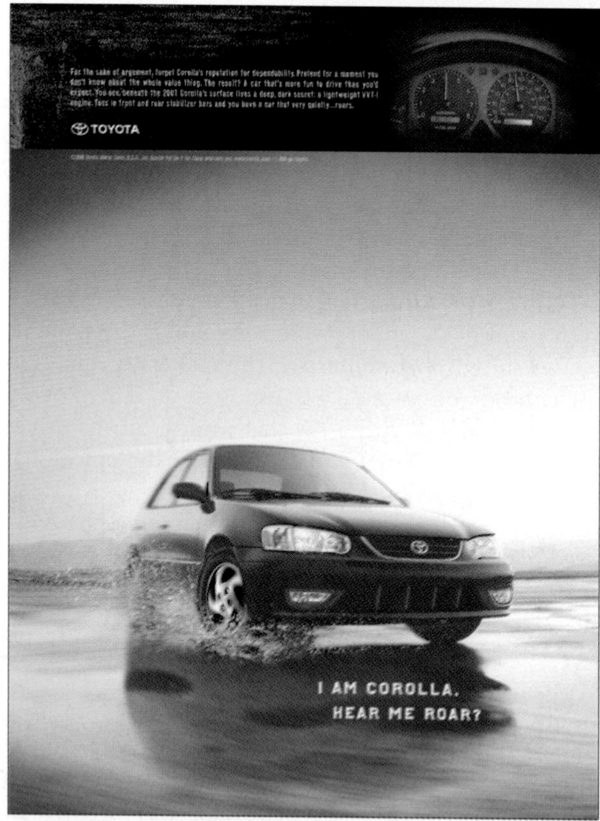

EXHIBIT 5.4

While the Toyota Corolla and Geo Metro both target youthful, first-time car buyers, Toyota's promise has a different twist. Is the Corolla promising just functional benefits? www.toyota.com

e-SIGHTINGS

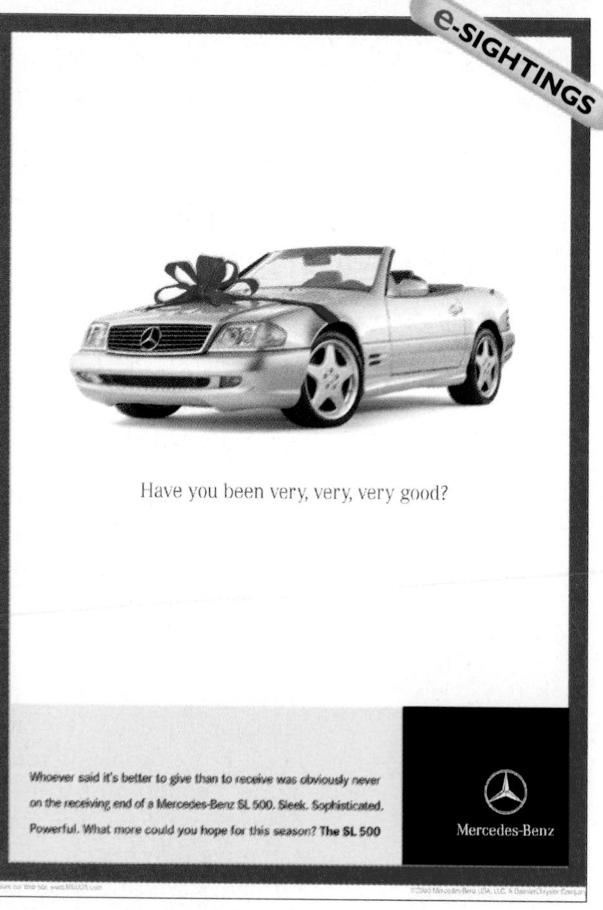

EXHIBIT 5.5

This ad makes no concession to functional benefits. Driving is about emotional rewards. But which emotional rewards? Does the Mercedes-Benz site (www.mbusa.com) effectively communicate these rewards? How does this site compare with competitor Lexus? (www.lexus.com)

EXHIBIT 5.6

For a cultural icon such as Campbell's soup, an advertiser can assume that consumers have some prior knowledge. Here the advertiser seeks to enhance that knowledge to lead people to use more canned soup. www.campbellsoups.com

well established and determine choice, as is suggested in the ad for Campbell's soup shown in Exhibit 5.6.

An internal search can also tap into information that has accumulated in one's memory as a result of repeated advertising exposures. Affecting people's beliefs about a brand before their actual use of it, or merely establishing the existence of the brand in the consumer's consciousness, is a critical function of advertising. As noted in Chapter 1, the purpose of delayed response advertising is to generate recognition of and a favorable predisposition toward a brand so that when consumers enter into search mode, that brand will be one they immediately consider as a possible solution to their needs. If the consumer has not used a brand previously and has no recollection that it even exists, then that brand probably will not be the brand of choice.

It is certainly plausible that an internal search will not turn up enough information to yield a decision. The consumer then proceeds with an **external search.** An external search involves visiting retail stores to examine the alternatives, seeking input from friends and relatives about their experiences with the products in question, or perusing professional product evaluations furnished in various publications such as *Consumer Reports* or *Car and Driver.* In addition, when consumers are in an active information-gathering mode, they may be receptive to detailed, informative advertisements delivered through any of the print media, or they may deploy a shopping agent or a search engine to help them find all there is to know about their product category on the World Wide Web.

During an internal or external search, consumers are not merely gathering information for its own sake. They have some need that is propelling the process, and their goal is to make a decision that yields benefits. The consumer searches and is simultaneously forming attitudes about possible alternatives. This is the alternative-evaluation component of the decision process, and it is another key phase for the advertiser to target.

Alternative evaluation will be structured by the consumer's **consideration set** and evaluative criteria. The consideration set is the subset of brands from a particular product category that becomes the focal point of the consumer's evaluation. Most product categories contain too many brands for all to be considered, so the consumer finds some way to focus the search and evaluation. For example, for autos, consumers may consider only cars priced less than $10,000, or only cars that have antilock brakes, or only foreign-made cars, or only cars sold at dealerships within a five-mile radius of their work or home. A critical function of advertising is to make consumers aware of the brand and keep them aware, so that the brand has a chance to be part of the consideration set. Virtually all ads try to do this.

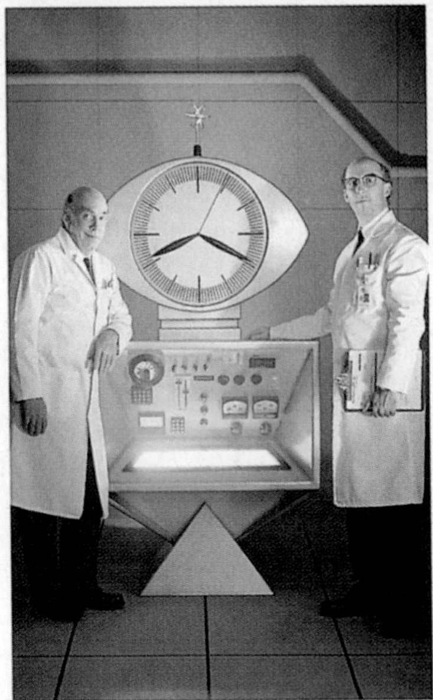

EXHIBIT 5.7

Advertisers must know the relevant evaluative criteria for their products. For an airline, on-time arrival is certainly an important matter.

www.nwa.com

As the search-and-evaluation process proceeds, consumers form evaluations based on the characteristics or attributes that brands in their consideration set have in common. These product attributes or performance characteristics are referred to as **evaluative criteria.** Evaluative criteria differ from one product category to the next and can include many factors, such as price, texture, warranty terms, color, scent, or fat content. As Exhibit 5.7 suggests, one traditional evaluative criterion for judging airlines has been on-time arrivals.

It is critical for advertisers to have as complete an understanding as possible of the evaluative criteria that consumers use to make their buying decisions. They must also know how consumers rate their brand in comparison with others from the consideration set. Understanding consumers' evaluative criteria furnishes a powerful starting point for any advertising campaign and will be examined in more depth later in the chapter.

Purchase. At this third stage, purchase occurs. The consumer has made a decision, and a sale is made. Great, right? Well, to a point. As nice as it is to make a sale, things are far from over at the point of sale. In fact, it would be a big mistake to view purchase as the culmination of the decision-making process. No matter what the product category, the consumer is likely to buy from it again in the future. So, what happens after the sale is very important to advertisers.

Postpurchase Use and Evaluation. The goal for marketers and advertisers must not be simply to generate a sale; it must be to create satisfied and, ultimately, loyal customers. The data to support this position are quite astounding. Research shows that about 65 percent of the average company's business comes from its present, satisfied customers, and that 91 percent of dissatisfied customers will never buy again from the company that disappointed them.[4] Thus, consumers' evaluations of prod-

4. Terry G. Vavra, *Aftermarketing: How to Keep Customers for Life through Relationship Marketing* (Homewood, IL.: Business One Irwin, 1992), 13.

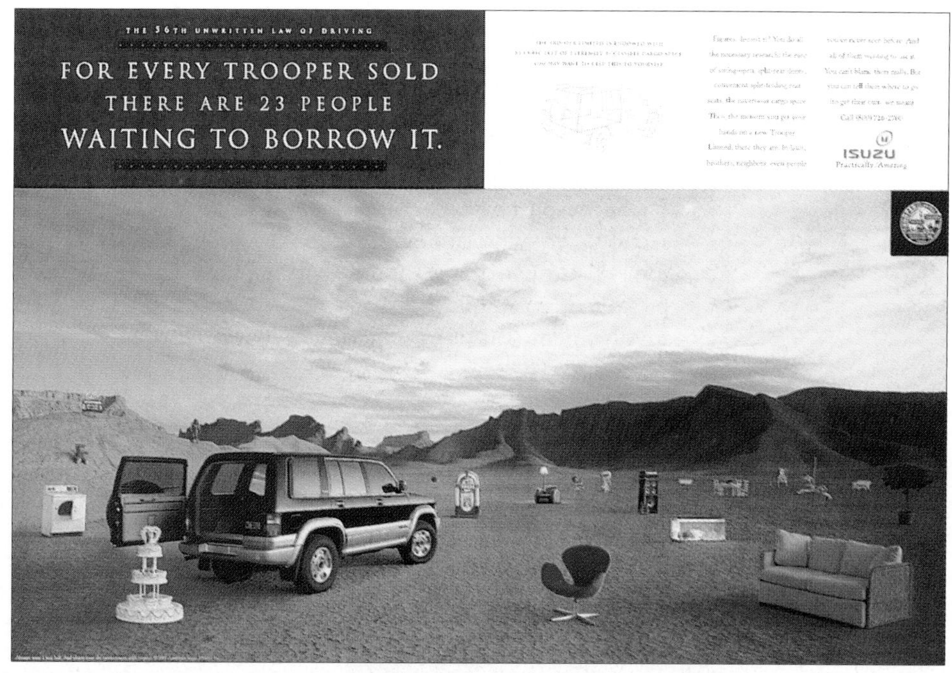

EXHIBIT 5.8

This ad offers lots of reassurance to those who buy an Isuzu Trooper. This vehicle not only will prove to be a great cargo hauler, but also will make purchasers the envy of their friends and family. www.isuzu.com/trooper.htm

ucts in use become a major determinant of which brands will be in the consideration set the next time around.

Customer satisfaction derives from a favorable postpurchase experience. It may develop after a single use, but more likely it will require sustained use. Advertising can play an important role in inducing customer satisfaction by creating appropriate expectations for a brand's performance, or by helping the consumer who has already bought the advertised brand to feel good about doing so.

Advertising plays an important role in alleviating the **cognitive dissonance** that can occur after a purchase. Cognitive dissonance is the anxiety or regret that lingers after a difficult decision. Often, rejected alternatives have attractive features that lead people to second-guess their own decisions. If the goal is to generate satisfied customers, this dissonance must be resolved in a way that leads consumers to conclude that they did make the right decision after all. Purchasing high-cost items or choosing from categories that include many desirable and comparable brands can yield high levels of cognitive dissonance.

When dissonance is expected, it makes good sense for the advertiser to reassure buyers with detailed information about its brands. Postpurchase reinforcement programs might involve direct mail, e-mail, or other types of personalized contacts with the customer. This postpurchase period represents a great opportunity for the advertiser to have the undivided attention of the consumer and to provide information and advice about product use that will increase customer satisfaction. It can also help marketers in getting consumers to think about their new purchase in the way advertisers want them to. For an example, see the ad for Isuzu shown in Exhibit 5.8.

2 **Four Modes of Consumer Decision Making.** As you may be thinking about now, consumers aren't always deliberate and systematic; sometimes they are hasty, impulsive, or even irrational. The search time that people put into their purchases can vary dramatically for different types of products. Would you give the purchase of a toothbrush the same amount of effort as the purchase of a new stereo system? Probably not, unless you've been chastised by your dentist recently. Why is that T-shirt you

bought at a concert more important to you than the brand of orange juice you had for breakfast this morning? Does buying a Valentine's gift from Victoria's Secret create different feelings than buying a newspaper for your father? When you view a TV ad for car batteries, do you carefully memorize the information being presented so that it will be there to draw on the next time you're evaluating the brands in your consideration set?

Some purchase decisions are just more engaging than others. In the following sections we will elaborate on the view of consumer as decision maker by explaining four decision-making modes that help advertisers appreciate the richness and complexity of consumer behavior. These four modes are determined by a consumer's involvement and prior experiences with the product or service in question.

e-SIGHTINGS

EXHIBIT 5.9

The emotional appeal in this Casio ad is just one of the many involvement devices. The play on water resistance also increases involvement as the reader perceives the double meaning. Describe how these devices work. How does Casio use involvement devices at its Web site, www.casio-usa.com, *to encourage visitors to further explore its products on the site? Describe the involvement devices used by competitor Timex at its home page,* www.timex.com.

Sources of Involvement. To accommodate the complexity of consumption decisions, those who study consumer behavior typically talk about the involvement level of any particular decision. **Involvement** is the degree of perceived relevance and personal importance accompanying the choice of a certain product or service within a particular context.[5] Many factors contribute to an individual's level of involvement with any given decision. People can develop interests and avocations in many different areas, such as cooking, photography, pet ownership, or exercise and fitness. Such ongoing personal interests can enhance involvement levels in a variety of product categories. Also, any time a great deal of risk is associated with a purchase—perhaps as a result of the high price of the item, or because the consumer will have to live with the decision for a long period of time—one should also expect elevated involvement.

Consumers can also derive important symbolic meaning from products and brands. Ownership or use of some products can help people reinforce some aspect of their self-image or make a statement to other people who are important to them. If a purchase carries great symbolic and real consequences—such as choosing the right gift for someone on Valentine's Day—it will be highly involving.

Some purchases can also tap into deep emotional concerns or motives. For example, many marketers, from Wal-Mart to Marathon Oil, have solicited consumers with an appeal to their patriotism. The ad for Casio watches (a Japanese product) in Exhibit 5.9 demonstrates that a product doesn't have to be American to wrap itself in the Stars and Stripes. For some individuals, this can be a powerful appeal that strikes an emotional chord. Here, the appeal to emotion influences the consumer's involvement with the decision.

Involvement levels vary not only among product categories for any given individual, but also among individuals for any given product category. For example, some pet owners will feed their pets only the expensive canned products that look and smell like people food. IAMS, whose ad is featured in Exhibit 5.10, understands this and made a special premium dog food for consumers who think of their pets as

5. James F. Engel, Roger D. Blackwell, and Paul W. Miniard, *Consumer Behavior,* (Fort Worth, TX: Dryden Press, 1993), Chapter 9.

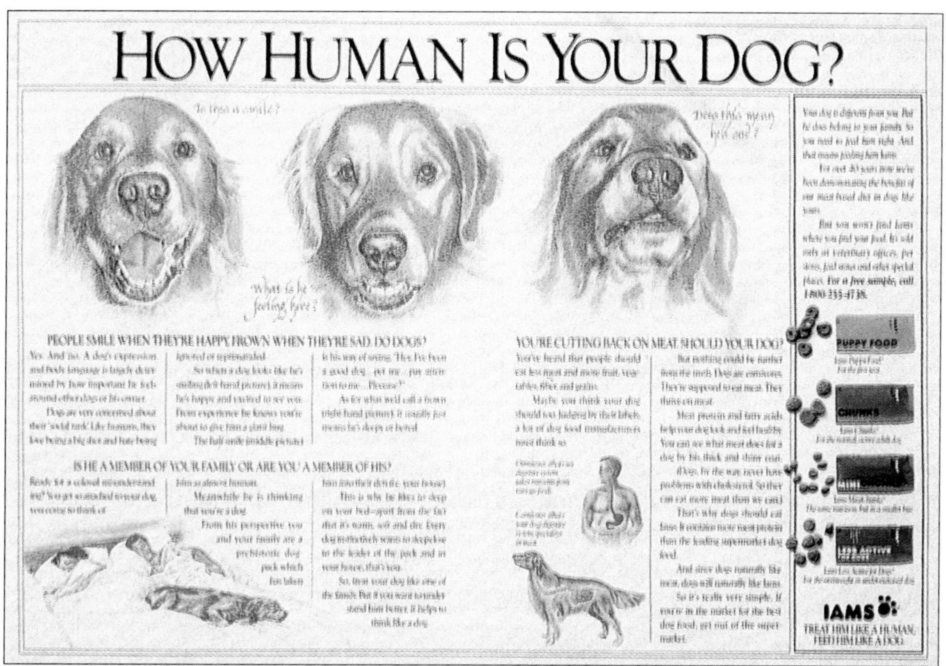

EXHIBIT 5.10

When people think of their pets as human beings, they take their selection of pet food very seriously. IAMS offers serious pet food for the serious dog owner. www.iams.com

humans. Many other pet owners, however, are perfectly happy with the 50-pound, economy-size bag of dry dog food.

Now we will use the ideas of involvement and prior experience to help conceive four different types of consumer decision making. These four modes are shown in Exhibit 5.11. Any specific consumption decision is based on a high or low level of prior experience with the product or service in question, and a high or low level of involvement. This yields the four modes of decision making: (1) extended problem solving; (2) limited problem solving; (3) habit or variety seeking; and (4) brand loyalty. Each is described in the following sections.

Extended Problem Solving. When consumers are inexperienced in a particular consumption setting yet find the setting highly involving, they are likely to engage in **extended problem solving.** In this mode, consumers go through a deliberate decision-making process that begins with explicit need recognition, proceeds with careful internal and external search, continues through alternative evaluation and purchase, and ends with a lengthy postpurchase evaluation.

Examples of extended problem solving come with decisions such as choosing a home or a diamond ring, as suggested by Exhibit 5.12. These products are expensive, are publicly evaluated, and can carry a considerable amount of risk in terms of making an uneducated decision. Selecting one's first new automobile or choosing a college are two other consumption settings that may require extended problem solving. Extended problem solving is the exception, not the rule.

Limited Problem Solving. In this decision-making mode, experience and involvement are both low. **Limited problem solving** is a more common mode of decision making. In this mode, a consumer is less systematic in his or her decision making. The consumer has a new problem to solve, but it is not a problem that is interesting or engaging, so the information search is limited to simply trying the first brand encountered. For example, let's say a young couple have just brought home a new baby, and suddenly they perceive a very real need for disposable diapers. At the hospital they received complimentary trial packs of several products, including Pampers

EXHIBIT 5.11

Four modes of consumer decision making.

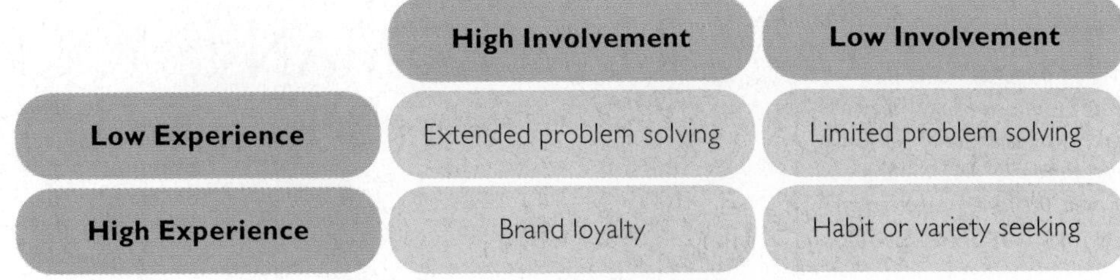

disposables. They try the Pampers, find them an acceptable solution to their messy new problem, and take the discount coupon that came with the sample to their local grocery, where they buy several packages. In the limited problem-solving mode, we often see consumers simply seeking adequate solutions to mundane problems. It is also a mode in which just trying a brand or two may be the most efficient way of collecting information about one's options. Of course, smart marketers realize that trial offers can be a preferred means of collecting information, and they facilitate trial of their brands through free samples, inexpensive "trial sizes," or discount coupons.

Habit or Variety Seeking. Habit and variety seeking occur in settings where a decision is uninvolving and a consumer repurchases from the category over and over again. In terms of sheer numbers, habitual purchases are probably the most common decision-making mode. Consumers find a brand of laundry detergent that suits their needs, they run out of the product, and they buy it again. The cycle repeats itself many times per year in an almost mindless fashion. Getting in the habit of buying just one brand can be a way to simplify life and minimize the time invested in "nuisance" purchases. When a consumer perceives little difference among the various competitive brands, it is easier to buy the same brand repeatedly. A lot of consumption decisions are boring but necessary. Habits help us minimize the inconvenience.

In some product categories where a buying habit would be expected, an interesting phenomenon called variety seeking may be observed instead. Remember, **habit** refers to buying a single brand repeatedly as a solution to a simple consumption problem. This can be very tedious, and some consumers fight the boredom through variety seeking. **Variety seeking** refers to the tendency of consumers to switch their selection among various brands in a given category in a seemingly random pattern. This is not to say that a consumer will buy just any brand; he or she probably has two to five brands that all provide similar levels of satisfaction to a particular consumption problem. However, from one purchase occasion to the next, the individual will switch brands from within this set, just for the sake of variety.

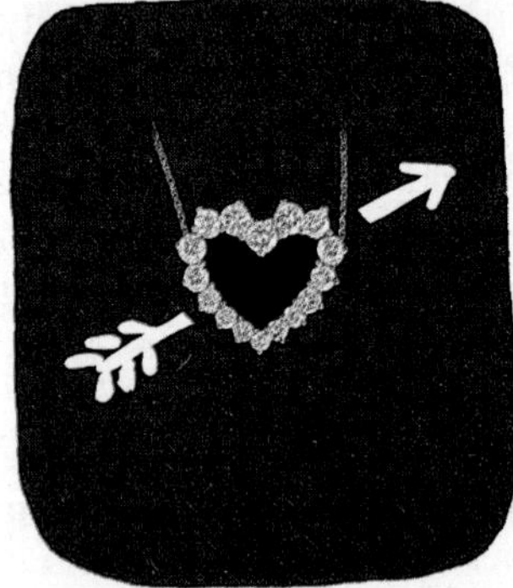

EXHIBIT 5.12

High involvement and low experience typically yield extended problem solving. Buying an engagement ring is a perfect example of this scenario. This ad offers lots of advice for the extended problem solver. www.adiamondisforever.com

Variety seeking is most likely to occur in frequently purchased categories where sensory experience, such as taste or smell, accompanies product use. Satiation will occur after repeated use and may leave the consumer looking for a fresh sensory

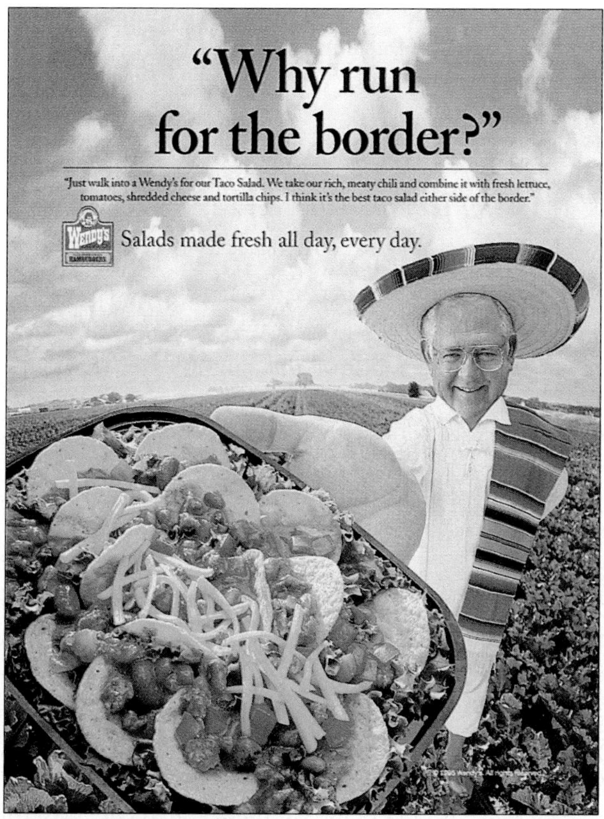

EXHIBIT 5.13

The late Dave Thomas of Wendy's combined the reliability of an easily recognizable celebrity with an appeal to variety-seeking behavior. How does this pairing encourage consumers to seek variety?
www.wendys.com

experience. Product categories such as soft drinks and alcoholic beverages, snack foods, breakfast cereals, and fast food are prone to variety seeking, as exemplified by the Wendy's ad in Exhibit 5.13.

Brand Loyalty. The final decision-making mode is typified by high involvement and rich prior experience. In this mode, **brand loyalty** becomes a major consideration in the purchase decision. Consumers demonstrate brand loyalty when they repeatedly purchase a single brand as their choice to fulfill a specific need. In one sense, brand-loyal purchasers may look as if they have developed a simple buying habit; however, it is important to distinguish brand loyalty from simple habit. Brand loyalty is based on highly favorable attitudes toward the brand and a conscious commitment to find this brand each time the consumer purchases from this category. Conversely, habits are merely consumption simplifiers that are not based on deeply held convictions. Habits can be disrupted through a skillful combination of advertising and sales promotions. Spending advertising dollars to persuade truly brand-loyal consumers to try an alternative can be a great waste of resources.

Brands such as Sony, Starbucks, Gerber, Coke, Heineken, Levi's, Disney, Harley-Davidson, FedEx, and Bath & Body Works have inspired loyal consumers. Brand loyalty is something that any marketer aspires to have, but in a world filled with more-savvy consumers and endless product proliferation, it is becoming harder and harder to attain. Brand loyalty may emerge because the consumer perceives that one brand simply outperforms all others in providing some critical functional benefit. For example, the harried business executive may have grown loyal to FedEx's overnight delivery service as a result of repeated satisfactory experiences with FedEx—and as a result of FedEx's advertising that has repeatedly posed the question, Why fool around with anyone else?

Perhaps even more important, brand loyalty can be due to the emotional benefits that accompany certain brands. One of the strongest indicators for brand loyalty has to be the tendency on the part of some loyal consumers to tattoo their bodies with the insignia of their favorite brand. While statistics are not kept on this sort of thing, it would be reasonable to speculate that the worldwide leader in brand-name tattoos is Harley-Davidson. What accounts for Harley's fervent following? Is Harley's brand loyalty simply a function of performing better than its many competitors? Or does a Harley rider derive some deep emotional benefit from taking that big bike out on the open road and leaving civilization far behind? To understand loyalty for a brand such as Harley, one must turn to the emotional benefits, such as feelings of pride, kinship, and nostalgia that attend "the ride." Owning a Harley—perhaps complete with tattoo—makes a person feel different and special. Harley ads are designed to reaffirm the deep emotional appeal of this product.

Strong emotional benefits might be expected from consumption decisions that we classify as highly involving, and they are major determinants of brand loyalty. Indeed, with so many brands in the marketplace, it is becoming harder and harder to create loyalty for one's brand through functional benefits alone. To break free of this brand-parity problem and provide consumers with enduring reasons to become or stay loyal, advertisers are investing more and more effort in communicating the emotional benefits that might be derived from brands in categories as diverse as soup (Campbell's—"Good for the Soul") to greeting cards (Hallmark—"When you care enough to send the very best").

In addition, as suggested by the E-Commerce box on this page, many companies are exploring ways to use the Internet to create dialogue and community with customers. To do this, one must look for means to connect with customers at an emotional level.

3 **Key Psychological Processes.** To complete our consideration of the consumer as a thoughtful decision maker, one key issue remains. We need to examine the explicit psychological consequences of advertising. What does advertising leave in the minds of consumers that ultimately may influence their behavior? For those of you who have previously taken psychology courses, many of the topics in this section will sound familiar.

As we noted earlier in the chapter, a good deal of advertising is designed to ensure recognition and create favorable predispositions toward a brand so that as consumers search for solutions to their problems, they will think of the brand immediately. The goal of any delayed-response ad is to effect some psychological state that will subsequently influence a purchase.

Two ideas borrowed from social psychology are usually the center of attention when discussing the psychological aspects of advertising. First is attitude. **Attitude** is defined as an overall evaluation of any object, person, or issue that varies along a continuum, such as favorable to unfavorable or positive to negative. Attitudes are learned, and if they are based on substantial experience with the object or issue in question, they can be held with great conviction. Attitudes make our lives easier because they simplify decision making; that is, when faced with a choice among several alternatives, we do not need to process new information or analyze the merits of the alternatives. We merely select the alternative we think is the most favorable. We all possess attitudes on thousands of topics, ranging from political candidates to underage drinking. Marketers and advertisers, however, are most interested in one particular class of attitudes—brand attitudes.

E-COMMERCE

Digital Storytelling Unleashes the Power of Emotion

The premise of interactive media seems ideally suited for brand development. After all, *interactive* by definition means a two-way communication between buyer and seller; communication builds relationships, and relationships translate into brand loyalty. Right? Well, the rules of online marketing are far from established, but the Internet may prove to be the most powerful tool ever in creating long-term relationships with brand-conscious consumers. And maybe, just maybe, it can be as simple as asking consumers to tell their own stories. Traditional brand builders such as Coca-Cola, McDonald's, and Ford Motor Company are determined to find out.

Digital StoryTelling (DST)—which combines the glamour and reach of the Internet with the emotional appeal of personal stories—is surely among the most innovative applications of the Web for brand-building purposes. While advertisers have always used stories in an effort to sell their products, this is not business as usual. Unlike conventional mass media, wherein company-created stories are told in an effort to persuade customers, DST seeks to build community around a brand by inviting consumers to share their experiences with the brand. This sharing leads to stories that are much more authentic and interactive than just another TV testimonial.

How does one foster this unique form of storytelling? Any number of ways. Coca-Cola hires the Web equivalent of a TV ad producer to seek out, record, and produce customer stories that are Web-ready. Coke also features the best of these stories at its DST exhibit inside its Atlanta headquarters. According to Coke's chief DST archivist, Phil Mooney, "You simply can't buy advertising as emotionally potent as a good customer story. DST helped us pop the lid on a lot of emotional ties that we just hadn't been able to capture in our marketing before the Internet." With no real prospects of differentiating its brand on the basis of functional benefits, it's easy to understand the enthusiasm of Coke execs for unleashing emotional ties.

Sources: "Secrets of the New Brand Builders," *Fortune*, June 22, 1998, 170; "Tell Me a (Digital) Story," *Business Week E.Biz*, May 15, 2000, EB92–EB94.

EXHIBIT 5.14

An example of two consumers' beliefs about Caddies.

Consumer 1	Consumer 2
Cadillacs are clumsy to drive	Cadillacs are sturdy and safe
Cadillacs are expensive	Cadillacs are a good investment
Cadillacs are gas guzzlers	Cadillacs are simple to maintain
Cadillacs are large	Cadillacs are good for long trips
Cadillacs are for senior citizens	Cadillacs are a symbol of one's success

Brand attitudes are summary evaluations that reflect preferences for various products and services. The next time you are waiting in a checkout line at the grocery, take a good look at the items in your cart. Those items are a direct reflection of your brand attitudes.

But what is the basis for these summary evaluations? Where do brand attitudes come from? Here we need a second idea from social psychology. To understand why people hold certain attitudes, we need to assess their specific beliefs. **Beliefs** represent the knowledge and feelings a person has accumulated about an object or issue. They can be logical and factual in nature, or biased and self-serving. A person might believe that Cadillacs are large, that garlic consumption promotes weight loss, and that pet owners are lonely people. For that person, all these beliefs are valid and can serve as a basis for attitudes toward Cadillacs, garlic, and pets.

If we know a person's beliefs, it is usually possible to infer attitude. Consider the two consumers' beliefs about Cadillacs summarized in Exhibit 5.14. From their beliefs, we might suspect that one of these consumers is a Cadillac owner, while the other will need a dramatic change in beliefs to ever make Cadillac part of his or her consideration set. It follows that the brand attitudes of the two individuals are at opposite ends of the favorableness continuum.

People have many beliefs about various features and attributes of products and brands. Some beliefs are more important than others in determining a person's final evaluation of a brand. Typically, a small number of beliefs—on the order of five to nine—underlie brand attitudes.[6] These beliefs are the critical determinants of an attitude and are referred to as **salient beliefs.**

Clearly, we would expect the number of salient beliefs to vary between product categories. The loyal Harley owner who proudly displays a tattoo will have many more salient beliefs about his bike than he has about his brand of shaving cream. Also, salient beliefs can be modified, replaced, or extinguished. Exhibit 5.15 is a two-page ad from a Sears campaign designed to modify the salient beliefs of its target audience.

Since belief shaping and reinforcement can be one of the principal goals of advertising, it should come as no surprise that advertisers make belief assessment a focal point in their attempts to understand consumer behavior.

Multi-Attribute Attitude Models (MAAMs). Multi-attribute attitude models (MAAMs) provide a framework and a set of research procedures for collecting information from consumers to assess their salient beliefs and attitudes about competitive brands. Here we will highlight the basic components of a MAAMs analysis and illustrate how such an analysis can benefit the advertiser.

6. Icek Ajzen and Martin Fishbein, *Understanding Attitudes and Predicting Social Behavior* (Englewood Cliffs, N. J.: Prentice-Hall, 1980), 63.

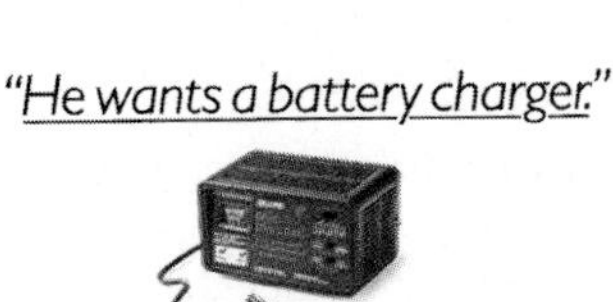

EXHIBIT 5.15

Belief change is a common goal in advertising. With its "Softer Side" campaign, Sears attempted to change beliefs about its stores as a source for women's fashions.
www.sears.com

Any MAAMs analysis will feature four fundamental components:

- *Evaluative criteria* are the attributes or performance characteristics that consumers use in comparing competitive brands. In pursuing a MAAMs analysis, an advertiser must identify all evaluative criteria relevant to its product category.
- *Importance weights* reflect the priority that a particular evaluative criterion receives in the consumer's decision-making process. Importance weights can vary dramatically from one consumer to the next; for instance, some people will merely want good taste from their bowl of cereal, while others will be more concerned about fat and fiber content.
- The *consideration set* is that group of brands that represents the real focal point for the consumer's decision. For example, the potential buyer of a luxury sedan might be focusing on Acuras, BMWs, and Saabs. These and comparable brands would be featured in a MAAMs analysis. Cadillac could have a model, such as its Seville, that aspired to be part of this consideration set, leading General Motors to conduct a MAAMs analysis featuring the Seville and its foreign competitors. Conversely, it would be silly for GM to include the Chevy Malibu in a MAAMs analysis with this set of imports.
- *Beliefs* represent the knowledge and feelings that a consumer has about various brands. In a MAAMs analysis, beliefs about each brand's performance on all relevant evaluative criteria are assessed. Beliefs can be matters of fact—Raisin Nut Bran has five grams of fat per serving, same as the six-inch Subway Club—or highly subjective—the Mercedes-Benz SL 500 is the sleekest, sexiest car on the road. It is common for beliefs to vary widely among consumers.

In conducting a MAAMs analysis, we must specify the relevant evaluative criteria for our category, as well as our direct competitors. We then go to consumers and

EXHIBIT 5.16

Here Sony tries to change the rules of digital videography with its introduction of an important new feature.
www.sony.com/di

let them tell us what's important and how our brand fares against the competition on the various evaluative criteria. The information generated from this survey research will give us a better appreciation for the salient beliefs that underlie brand attitudes, and it may suggest important opportunities for changing our marketing or advertising to yield more favorable brand attitudes.

Three basic attitude-change strategies can be developed from the MAAMs framework. First, a MAAMs analysis may reveal that consumers do not have an accurate perception of the relative performance of our brand on an important evaluative criterion. For example, consumers may perceive that Crest is far and away the best brand of toothpaste for fighting cavities, when in fact all brands with a fluoride additive perform equally well on cavity prevention. Correcting this misperception could become our focal point if we compete with Crest.

Second, a MAAMs analysis could uncover that our brand is perceived as the best performer on an evaluative criterion that most consumers do not view as very important. The task for advertising in this instance would be to persuade consumers that what our brand offers (say, more baking soda than any other toothpaste) is more important than they had thought previously.

Third, the MAAMs framework may lead to the conclusion that the only way to improve attitudes toward our brand would be through the introduction of a new attribute to be featured in our advertising. For example, the advertisement in Exhibit 5.16 makes the case that being able to burn your digital images directly onto a compact disc makes for a digital camera that is *intensely cool.* And this particular feature is only available on the Sony Mavica CD1000. Interested? Check it out at www.sony.com/di.

When marketers use the MAAMs approach, good things can result in terms of more-favorable brand attitudes and improved market share. When marketers carefully isolate key evaluative criteria, bring products to the marketplace that perform well on the focal criteria, and develop ads that effectively shape salient beliefs about the brand, the results can be dramatic—as we saw in the case of Joy in Japan.

Information Processing and Perceptual Defense. At this point you may have the impression that creating effective advertising is really a straightforward exercise. We carefully analyze consumers' beliefs and attitudes, construct ads to address any problems that might be identified, and choose various media to get the word out to our target customers. Yes, it would be very easy if consumers would just pay close attention and believe everything we tell them, and if our competition would kindly stop all of its advertising so that ours would be the only message that consumers had to worry about. Of course, these things aren't going to happen.

Why would we expect to encounter resistance from consumers as we attempt to influence their beliefs and attitudes about our brand? One way to think about this problem is to portray the consumer as an information processor who must advance through a series of stages before our message can have its intended effect. If we are skillful in selecting appropriate media to reach our target, then the consumer must (1) pay attention to the message, (2) comprehend it correctly, (3) accept the message exactly as we intended, and (4) retain the message until it is needed for a purchase decision. Unfortunately, problems can and do occur at any or all of these four stages, completely negating the effect of our advertising campaign.

There are two major obstacles that we must overcome if our message is to have its intended effect. The first—the **cognitive consistency** impetus—stems from the individual consumer. Remember, a person develops and holds beliefs and attitudes for a reason: They help him or her make efficient decisions that yield pleasing outcomes. When a consumer is satisfied with these outcomes, there is really no reason to alter the belief system that generated them. New information that challenges existing beliefs can be ignored or disparaged to prevent modification of the present cognitive system. The consumer's desire to maintain cognitive consistency can be a major roadblock for an advertiser that wants to change beliefs and attitudes.

The second obstacle—**advertising clutter**—derives from the context in which ads are processed. Even if a person wanted to, it would be impossible to process and integrate every advertising message that he or she is exposed to each day.[7] Pick up today's newspaper and start reviewing every ad you come across. Will you have time today to read them all? The clutter problem is further magnified by competitive brands making very similar performance claims. Was it Advil, Anacin, Aveda, Aleve, Avia, Aflexa, Motrin, Nuprin, or Tylenol Gelcaps that promised you 12 hours of relief from your headache? (Can you select the brands from this list that aren't a headache remedy?) The simple fact is that each of us is exposed to hundreds of ads each day, and no one has the time or inclination to sort through them all.

Consumers thus employ perceptual defenses to simplify and control their own ad processing. It is important here to see that the consumer is in control, and the advertiser must find some way to engage the consumer if an ad is to have any impact. Of course, the best way to engage consumers is to offer them information about a product or service that will address an active need state. Simply stated, it is difficult to get people to process a message about your headache remedy when they don't have a headache. **Selective attention** is certainly the advertiser's greatest challenge and produces tremendous waste of advertising dollars. Most ads are simply ignored by consumers. They turn the page, change the station, mute the sound, head for the refrigerator, or just daydream or doze off—rather than process the ad.

Advertisers employ a variety of tactics to break through the clutter. Popular music, celebrity spokespersons, sexy models, rapid scene changes, and anything that is novel are devices for combating selective attention. Remember, as we discussed in Chapter 4, advertisers constantly walk that fine line between novel and obnoxious in their never-ending battle for the attention of the consumer. They really don't want to insult you or anyone else; they just want to be noticed. Of course, they often step over the annoyance line.

The battle for consumers' attention poses another dilemma for advertisers. Without attention, there is no chance that an advertiser's message will have its desired impact; however, the provocative, attention-attracting devices used to engage consumers often become the focal point of consumers' ad processing. They remember seeing an ad featuring 27 Elvis Presley impersonators, but they can't recall what brand was being advertised or what claims were being made about the brand. If advertisers must entertain consumers to win their attention, they must also be careful that the brand and message don't get lost in the shuffle.

Let's assume that an ad gets attention and the consumer comprehends its claims correctly. Will acceptance follow and create the enduring change in brand attitude that is desired, or will there be further resistance? If the message is asking the consumer to alter beliefs about the brand, expect more resistance. When the consumer is involved and attentive and comprehends a claim that challenges current beliefs, the cognitive consistency impetus kicks in, and cognitive responses can be expected.

7. Seth Godin reports that the average consumer is exposed to about one million marketing messages per year and that this number will only continue to grow. See his analysis in *Permission Marketing* (New York, NY.: Simon & Schuster, 1999), Chapter 1.

Cognitive responses are the thoughts that occur to individuals at that exact moment in time when their beliefs and attitudes are being challenged by some form of persuasive communication. Remember, most ads will not provoke enough mental engagement to yield any form of cognitive response, but when they occur, the valence of these responses is critical to the acceptance of one's message. As we shall see in the next section, cognitive responses are one of the main components of an influential framework for understanding the impact of advertising labeled the **elaboration likelihood model (ELM).**

The Elaboration Likelihood Model (ELM). The ELM is another of those ideas that has been borrowed from social psychology and applied to advertising settings.[8] It is a model that pertains to any situation where a persuasive communication is being sent and received, and has particular relevance in this chapter because it incorporates ideas such as involvement, information processing, cognitive responses, and attitude formation, in a single, integrated framework. The basic premise of the ELM is that to understand how a persuasive communication may affect a person's attitudes, we must consider his or her motivation and ability to elaborate on the message during processing. For most advertising contexts, motivation and ability will be a function of how involved he or she is with the consumption decision in question. Involving decisions will result in active, mental elaboration during ad processing, whereas uninvolving decisions will implicate passive ad processing.

As indicated in Exhibit 5.17, the ELM uses the involvement dichotomy in spelling out two unique routes to attitude change. These are typically referred to as the central and peripheral routes to persuasion.

When involvement is high, we should expect the consumer to draw on prior knowledge and experience and scrutinize or elaborate on the message arguments that are central to the advertiser's case. The nature of the individual's effortful thinking about the issues at hand could be judged from the cognitive responses that the ad provokes. These cognitive responses may be positive or negative in tone, and can be reactions to specific claims or any executional element of the ad.

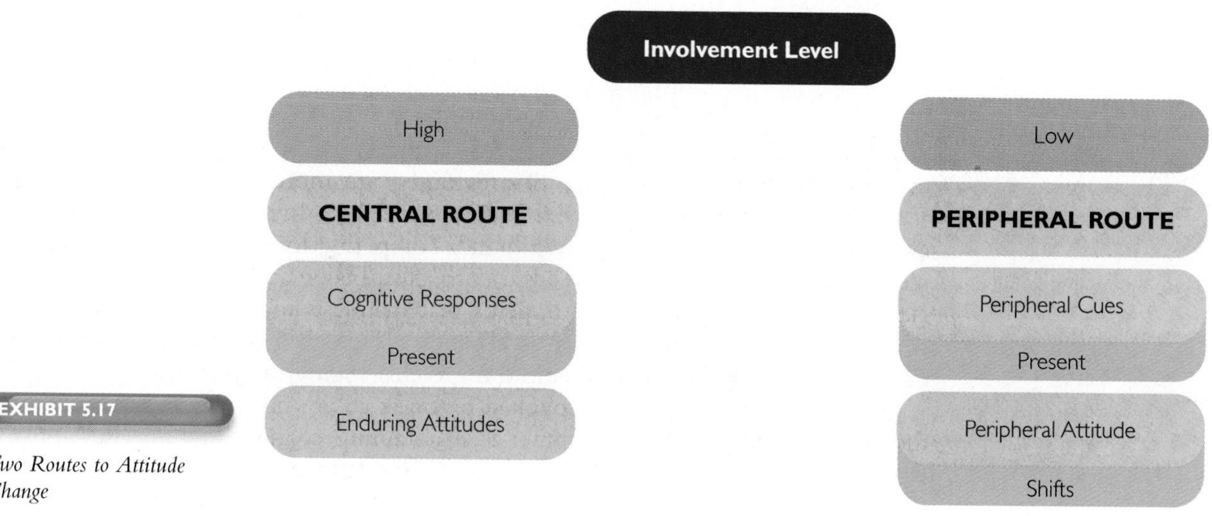

EXHIBIT 5.17

Two Routes to Attitude Change

8. For an expanded discussion of these issues, see Richard E. Petty, John T. Cacioppo, Alan J. Strathman, and Joseph R. Priester, "To Think or Not to Think: Exploring Two Routes to Persuasion," in *Persuasion: Psychological Insights and Perspectives,* ed. Sharon Shavitt and Timothy C. Brock (Boston: Allyn & Bacon, 1994), 113–147.

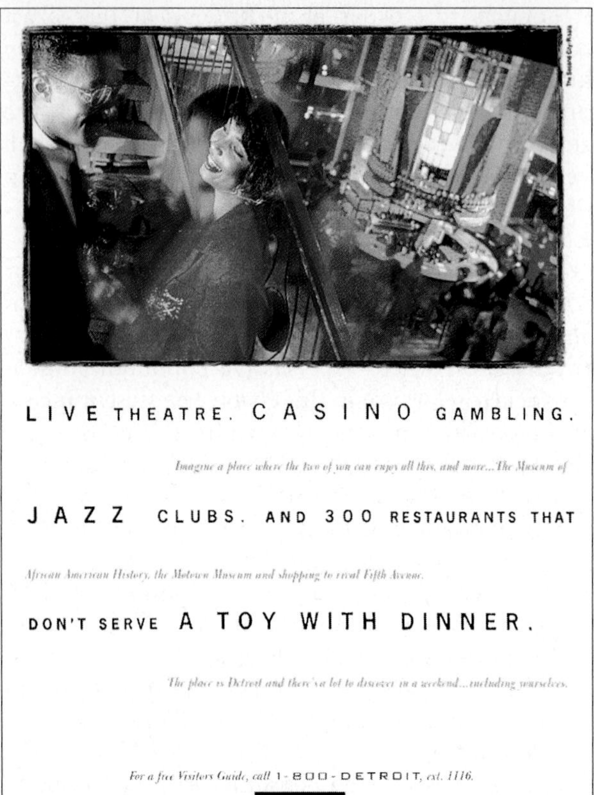

EXHIBIT 5.18

Cities can also engage in persuasive communications. Does this ad present an image of Detroit that is compatible with your prior beliefs? www.detroit.com

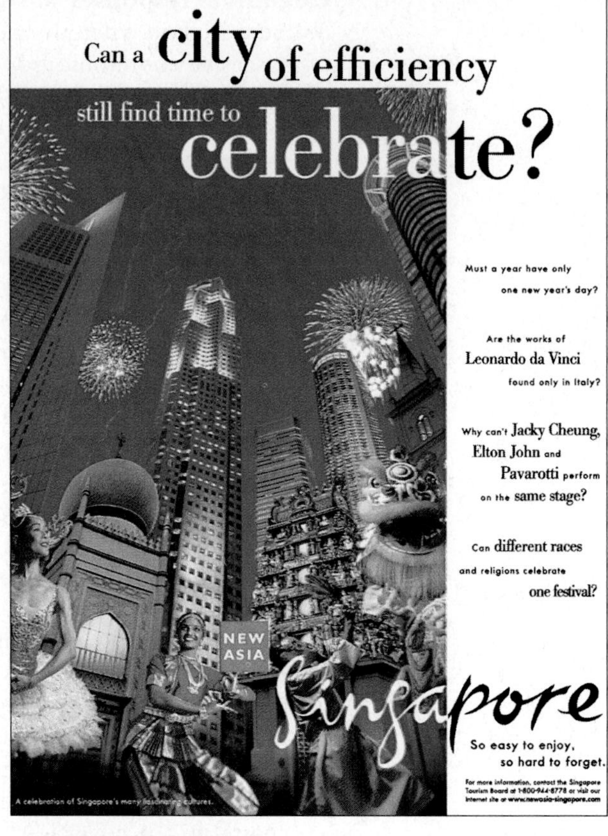

EXHIBIT 5.19

*Singapore's Tourism Board uses this ad to educate readers about its broad cultural diversity, and to tickle their curiosity (*www.newasia-singapore.com*). Is Singapore an Asian city? Yes, but with influences from many cultures. The ad invites the reader to break out of a conceptual box, just as the Florida orange growers did with their "Orange juice: It's not just for breakfast anymore" campaign.*

Messages designed to reinforce existing beliefs, or shape beliefs for a new brand that the consumer was unaware of previously, are more likely to win uncritical acceptance. Compare the ads in Exhibits 5.18 and 5.19. In this example, think of the cities Detroit and Singapore as two brands competing for a tourist's attention (and ultimately, dollars). Each of these ads tries to affect beliefs and attitudes about its focal city. The cognitive consistency impetus that manifests in cognitive responses will work against the city that is more well known, especially when the ad challenges existing beliefs. Which ad do you find more challenging to your beliefs?

If the cognitive responses provoked by one's ad are primarily negative in tone, the ad has backfired: The consumer is maintaining cognitive consistency by disparaging your ad, and that person's negative thoughts are likely to foster negative evaluation of your brand. However, when positive attitudes can be affected through the central route, they have very appealing properties. Because they are based on careful thought, central-route attitudes will (1) come to mind quickly for use in product selection, (2) resist the change efforts of other advertisers, (3) persist in memory without repeated ad exposures, and (4) be excellent predictors of behavior. These properties cannot be expected of attitudes that are formed in the peripheral route.

For low-involvement products, such as batteries or tortilla chips, cognitive responses to advertising claims are not expected.[9] In such situations, attitude formation will often follow a more peripheral route, and peripheral cues become the focal point for judging the ad's impact. **Peripheral cues** refer to features of the ad other than the actual arguments about the brand's performance. They include an attractive or comical spokesperson, novel imagery, humorous incidents, or a catchy jingle. Any feature of the ad that prompts a pleasant emotional response could be thought of as a peripheral cue.

In the peripheral route the consumer can still learn from an advertisement, but the learning is passive and typically must be achieved by frequent association of the peripheral cue (for example, the Eveready Energizer Bunny) with the brand in question. It has even been suggested that classical conditioning principles might be employed by advertisers to facilitate and accelerate this associative learning process.[10] As consumers learn to associate pleasant feelings and attractive images with a brand, their attitude toward the brand should become more positive.

What do Dave Thomas, LeAnn Rimes, George Foreman, Jerry Seinfeld, Junji Takada, the Pillsbury Doughboy, Shaq, the Budweiser "Waas Up" guys, Cindy Crawford, and the song "Instant Karma" by John Lennon have in common? They and many others like them have been used as peripheral cues in advertising campaigns. When all brands in a category offer similar benefits, the most fruitful avenue for advertising strategy is likely to be the peripheral route, where the advertiser merely tries to maintain positive or pleasant associations with the brand by constantly presenting it with appealing peripheral cues. This strategy can be especially important for mature brands in low-involvement categories where the challenge is to keep the customer from getting bored,[11] but it is expensive because any gains made along the peripheral route are short-lived. Expensive TV air time, lots of repetition, and a never-ending search for the freshest, most popular peripheral cues demand huge advertising budgets. When you think of the peripheral route, think of the advertising campaigns for high-profile, mature brands such as Coke, Pepsi, Budweiser, McDonald's, Nike, and Doritos. They entertain in an effort to keep you interested.

Perspective Two: The Consumer as Social Being. The view of the consumer as decision maker is a popular one. It is not, however, without its limitations or its critics. Certainly, it tells only part of the story. It gives us information concerning consumer psychology, or what goes on in the minds of consumers. But in its effort to isolate psychological mechanisms, this approach often takes consumer behavior out of its natural social context, and studies ads where ads may no longer even be ads (for example, in a laboratory). Further, by thinking of consumers as "information processors," this approach makes consumers appear to be something more akin to kitchen appliances than the human beings they are. Critics in industry and academia alike believe that much of the psychological research (most popular in the industry in the 1950s and then again in the 1970s) has significantly less to do with the advertising and consumption of real goods and services in the real world than with advancing psychological theory. Some critics say that whatever these psychologists are testing in their labs are not ads at all but have been reduced to experimental "stimulus material." They believe that ads really exist only in the social world and natural environment. When removed from that environment they are no longer ads in any meaningful sense.

9. Ibid.

10. For additional discussion of this issue, see Frances K. McSweeney and Calvin Bierley, "Recent Developments in Classical Conditioning," *Journal of Consumer Research,* vol. 11 (September 1984): 619–631.

11. The rationale for cultivating brand interest for mature brands is discussed more fully in Karen A. Machleit, Chris T. Allen, and Thomas J. Madden, "The Mature Brand and Brand Interest: An Alternative Consequence of Ad-Evoked Affect," *Journal of Marketing,* vol. 57 (October 1993), 72–82.

EXHIBIT 5.20

Consuming at Crispy Corn. Consumers are social beings. Just think about all the things that are going on in the scene to the right. Think about it.

The move away from purely psychological approaches had been going in the industry for quite some time. It gathered momentum, and never looked back, in the mid-1980s. At that time U.S. West Coast agencies began adopting what they called "British research," which was really just qualitative research as has been practiced by anthropologists, sociologists, and others for well over a century. The only thing really "British" about it at all is that some very hot London agencies had been doing research this way all along. (Actually, many had been, but these agencies used it as a point of differentiation.) This industry trend also resonated with a similar move in universities toward more interpretive, qualitative, and humanistic approaches to the study of human behavior, including consumer behavior. People began to see consumers as more than information processors and ads as more than static attempts at attitude manipulation. Consumers do process information, but they also do a whole lot more. Furthermore, "information" itself is a rich and complex socioculturally bound textual product, interpreted in very sophisticated ways by very human beings. It is not the same as counting kilos of sulfur, concentrations of acids, or stars in a galaxy. "Information" is more than that. We will talk more about this in Chapter 7 when we turn our attention to advertising research.

In this section we present a second perspective on consumer behavior, a perspective concerned with social and cultural processes. It draws on basic ideas from anthropology, sociology, and communications, and it should be considered another part of the larger story of how advertising works. But, remember, this is just another perspective. We are still talking about the same consumers discussed in the preceding section; we are just viewing their behavior from a different vantage point. When it comes to the complexities of consumer behavior, we really can't have too many perspectives.

We are going to divide our discussion of this perspective in two: (1) the sociocultural environment in which consumers consume, and (2) one in which the ad itself is viewed as a sociocultural text. There we will think about how ads work as a piece of advertising created, delivered, and interpreted through sociocultural processes. This division also reflects the way that consumer behavior research is typically practiced in the advertising industry: In one domain it is concerned with how and why consumers consume (or don't consume) an advertised brand; in another, it focuses on studying (and evaluating) the advertisement itself (sometimes called copy research).

4 **Advertising in a Sociocultural Consumption Context.** Consumers consume in a sociocultural context. To have any hope of understanding how they will respond to ads, you must first consider how they come to consume (or not consume) your brand. Some major components of this context are discussed next.

Culture. **Culture** is what a people do, or "the total life ways of a people, the social legacy the individual acquires from his (her) group."[12] It is the way we eat, groom ourselves, celebrate, and mark our space and position. It is the way things are done. Cultures are often thought of as large and national, but in reality cultures are usually smaller, but not necessarily geographic, such as urban hipster culture, teen tech-nerd culture, Junior League culture, and so on. It's usually easier to see and note culture when it's more distant and unfamiliar. For most people, this is when they travel to another place. For example, if you've traveled beyond your own country, you have no doubt noticed that people in other cultures do things differently. If you were to point this out to one of the locals—for example, to a Parisian—and say something like, "Boy, you guys sure do things funny over here in France," you would no doubt be struck (perhaps literally) with the locals' belief that it is not they, but you, who behave oddly. This is a manifestation of culture and points out that members of a culture find the ways they do things to be perfectly natural. Culture is thus said to be invisible to those who are immersed in it. Everyone around us behaves in a similar fashion, so we do not think about the existence of some large and powerful force acting on us all. But it's there; this constant background force is culture. Make no mistake, culture is real, and it affects every aspect of human behavior, including consumer behavior and response to advertising. Culture surrounds the creation, transmission, reception, and interpretation of ads, just as it touches every aspect of consumption.

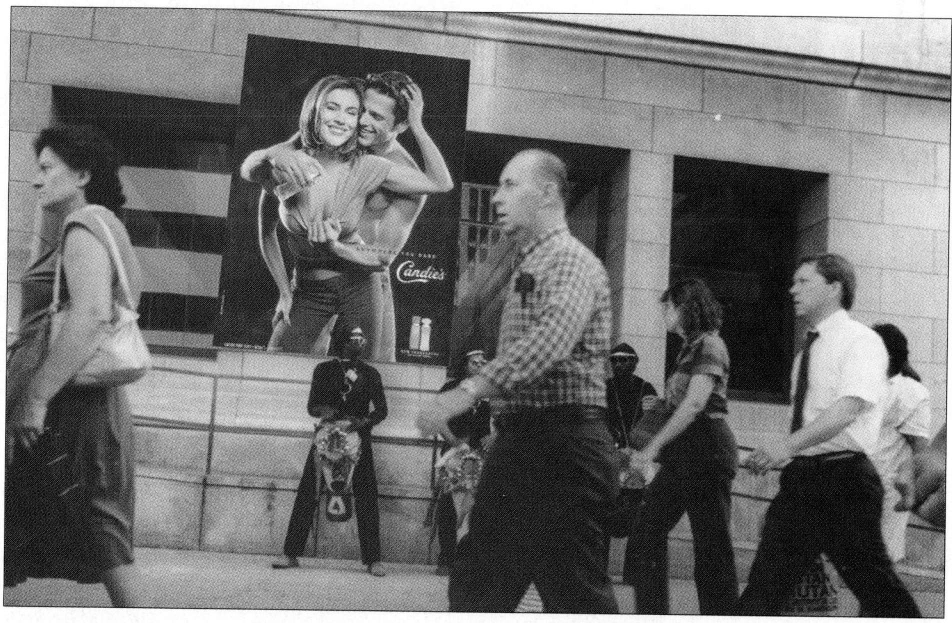

12. Gordon Marshall, ed., *The Concise Oxford Dictionary of Sociology* (New York: Oxford University Press, 1994), 104–105.

EXHIBITS 5.21 THROUGH 5.23

Three advertisers incorporate Easter rituals.

When advertisers consider just why consumers consume certain goods or services, or why they consume them in a certain way, they are considering culture itself. Culture informs consumers' views about food, the body, gifts, possessions, a sense of self versus others, mating, courtship, death, religion, family, jobs, art, holidays, leisure, satisfaction, work . . . just about everything. For example, if you are Ocean Spray, you want to understand how the cultural ritual of Thanksgiving works so that you can sell more cranberries. What is Thanksgiving? Why do we value it? Why do we have the particular rituals we perform on that day? Or who makes up the rules of gift giving? If you are Tiffany, Barnes & Noble, or Hallmark, you have a very good reason to understand why people do things a certain way (for example, buy things for one holiday but not for another). The list is endless. When you're in the advertising business, you're in the culture business. In Exhibits 5.21, 5.22, and 5.23 we see three advertisers trying to incorporate their brands and stores into Easter rituals.

Values. **Values** are the defining expressions of culture. They express in words and deeds what is important to a culture. For example, some cultures value individual freedom, while others value duty to the society at large. Some value propriety and restrained behavior, while others value open expression. Values are cultural bedrock. Values are enduring. They cannot be changed quickly or easily. They are thus different from attitudes, which advertisers believe can be changed through a single advertising campaign or even a single ad. Think of cultural values as the very strong and rigid foundation on which much more mutable attitudes rest. Exhibit 5.24 illustrates this relationship. Values are the foundation of this structure. Attitudes are, in turn, influenced by values, as well as by many other sources. Advertising has to be consistent with, but cannot easily or quickly change, values. It is thus senseless for an advertiser to speak of using advertising to change values in any substantive way. Advertising influences values in the same way a persistent drip of water wears down a granite slab—very slowly and through cumulative impact, over years and years. It is also the case that cultural values change advertising.

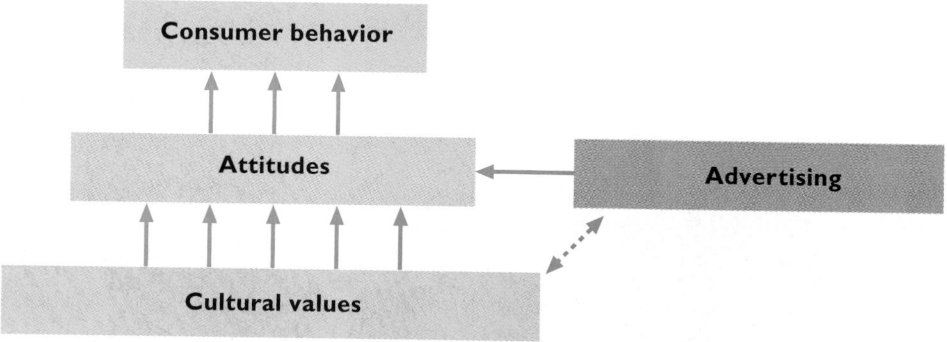

EXHIBIT 5.24

Cultural values, attitudes, and consumer behavior. Some believe that advertising can directly affect consumer behavior and, over time, cultural values as well.

Typically, advertisers try to either associate their product with a cultural value or criticize a competitor for being out of step with one. For example, in America, to say that a product "merely hides or masks odors" would be damning criticism indeed, because it suggests that anyone who would use such a product doesn't really value cleanliness and thus isn't like the rest of us.

Advertisements must be consistent with the values of a people. If they are not, they will likely be rejected. Many argue that the best (most effective) ads are those that best express and affirm core cultural values. For example, one core American value is said to be individualism, or the predisposition to value the individual over the group. This value has been part of American culture for a very long time. Some hold that advertisements that celebrate or affirm this value (all else being equal, which it rarely is) are more likely to succeed than ones that denigrate or ignore it. Exhibit 5.25 shows an ad that leans heavily on this value.

THE SONG ISN'T "BORN TO BE STATUS QUO."

We never did one like this before. Check out that rear fender and the stretched fuel tank. Note the immaculate front end, the chrome oil lines, the bullet turn signals. It's classic Harley. Yet it's unlike anything the road's ever seen. The Softail Deuce lives to push the limits. Maybe you should follow suit. 1-800-443-2153 or www.harley-davidson.com. **The Legend Rolls On.**

EXHIBIT 5.25

What could be more thoroughly individual?

Rituals. Rituals are "often-repeated formalized behaviors involving symbols."[13] Cultures participate in rituals. Cultures affirm, express, and maintain their values through rituals. Rituals are core elements of culture. They are a way in which individuals are made part of the culture, and a method by which the culture constantly renews and perpetuates itself. For example, ritual-laden holidays such as Thanksgiving, Christmas, and the Fourth of July help perpetuate aspects of American culture through their repeated re-enactment. Because they include consumption (for example, feasts and gift giving), they help intertwine national culture and consumption practices (see Exhibit 5.26). For example, Jell-O may have attained the prominence of a national food because of its regular usage as part of the Thanksgiving dinner ritual.[14] In the American South, it is common to eat black-eyed peas on New Year's Day to ensure good luck. In one sense it is "just done," but in another it is just done because it is a ritual embedded in a

13. Ibid., 452.

14. Melanie Wallendorf and Eric J. Arnould, "We Gather Together: Consumption Rituals of Thanksgiving Day," *Journal of Consumer Research*, vol. 18, no. 1 (June 1991), 13–31.

EXHIBIT 5.26

This ad promotes Kraft products as an integral part of family traditions. www.kraftfoods.com

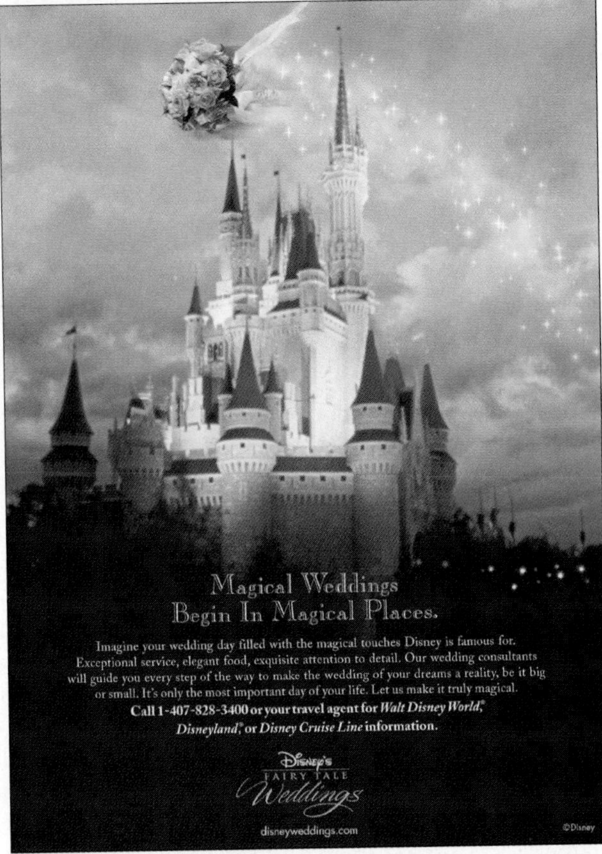

EXHIBIT 5.27

Do you think Disney does a good job here?

culture. If you are a canned-goods manufacturer, understanding this particular ritual is not a trivial concern at all. Clearly, there are incredible opportunities for marketers who can successfully link their products to consumption rituals (see Exhibit 5.27).

Rituals also occur every day in millions of other contexts. For example, when someone buys a new car or a new home, they do all sorts of "unnecessary" things to make it theirs. They clean the carpets even if they were just cleaned, they trim trees that don't need trimming, they hang things from the mirror of the used car they just bought, they change oil that was just changed . . . all to make the new possession theirs and "remove" any trace of the former owner. These behaviors are not only important to anthropologists, they are also important to those making and trying to sell products such as paint, rug shampoos, household disinfectants, lawn and garden equipment, auto accessories, and on and on.

Rituals don't have to be the biggest events of the year. There are also everyday rituals, such as the way we eat, clean ourselves, and groom. Think about all the habitual things you do from the time you get up in the morning until you crawl into bed at night. These things are done in a certain way; they are not random. Members of a common culture tend to do them one way, and members of other cultures do them other ways. Again, if you've ever visited another country, you have no doubt noticed significant differences. An American dining in Paris might be surprised to have sorbet to begin the meal and a salad to end it.

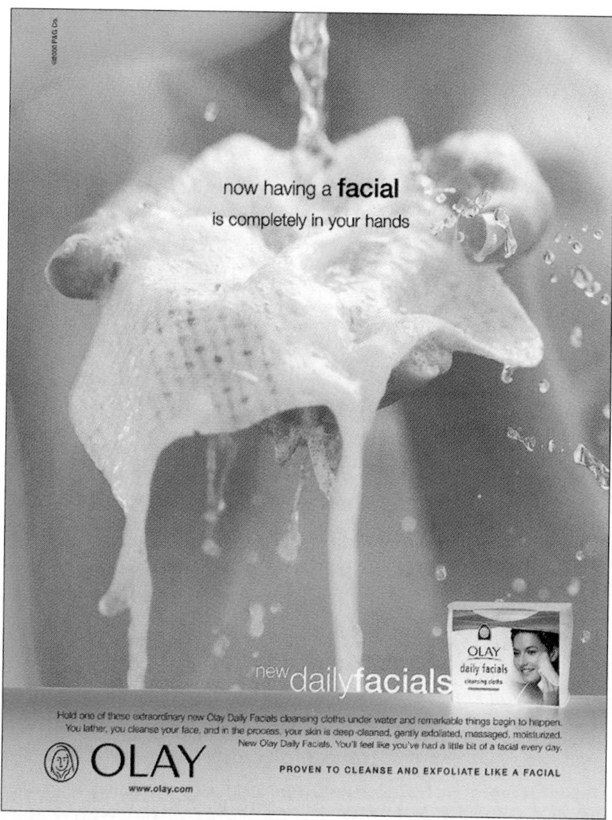

EXHIBIT 5.28

This ad helps Olay become part of an already existing ritual.

Daily rituals seem inconsequential because they are habitual and routine. If, however, someone tried to get you to significantly alter the way you do these things, he or she would quickly learn just how important and resistant to change these rituals are. If a product or service cannot be incorporated into an already-existing ritual, it is very difficult and expensive for advertisers to effect a change. If, on the other hand, an advertiser can successfully incorporate the consumption of its good or service into an existing ritual, then success is much more likely (see Exhibit 5.28). Think about how grooming rituals are vital to the global beauty industry, as discussed in the Global Issues box on page 188.

5 Social Class. **Social class** refers to a person's relative standing in a social hierarchy resulting from systematic inequalities in the social system. (These systematic inequalities are also known as social stratification.) Social class is a type of social stratification. Wealth, power, prestige, and status are not distributed equally within any society. People are rich or poor, are powerful or powerless, possess low status or high status, and so on. Race and gender are likewise unequally distributed within classes of power, income, and status. Thus a cross-section, or slice, of American society would reveal many different levels (or strata) of the population along these different dimensions.

Social class has historically been a fairly slippery concept. Some sociologists actually reject the idea altogether, arguing that societal groupings are less stable than the term implies. We tend to disagree, but we get the point. For example, some individuals possess higher social class than their income indicates, and vice versa. Successful plumbers often have higher incomes than college professors, but their occupation is (perhaps) less prestigious. Education also has something to do with social class, but a person with a little college experience and a lot of inherited wealth will probably rank higher than an insurance agent with an MBA. Thus income, education, and occupation are three important variables for indicating social class, but are still individually, or even collectively, inadequate at capturing its full meaning. Clearly, "complex combinations of social rewards and social opportunities compose social class."[15] Others have argued that the emergence of the New Class, a class of technologically skilled and highly educated individuals with great access to information and information technology, will change the way we define social class: "Knowledge of, and access to, information may begin to challenge property as a determinant of social class."[16]

Here, we use the term *social class* in a very inclusive sense. To us, social class includes not only economic criteria (such as income and property), but prestige, status, mobility, and a felt sense of similarity or communal belonging. Members of a social class tend to live in a similar way, have similar views and philosophies, and, most critically, tend to consume in similar ways. Markers of social class include what

15. James R. Kluegal and Eliot R. Smith, *Beliefs about Inequality: Americans' View of What Is and What Ought to Be* (New York: Aldine de Gruyter, 1986).

16. Alvin W. Gouldner, "The Future of Intellectuals and the Rise of the New Class," in *Social Stratification in Sociological Perspective: Class, Race and Gender,* ed. David B. Grusky (San Francisco: Westview Press, 1994), 711–729.

one wears, where one lives, and how one talks. In a consumer society, consumption marks or indicates social class in a myriad of ways. In fact, some believe that social class is the single biggest predictor of consumer behavior and consumer response to advertising. Social-class-related consumption preferences reflect class-related value differences and different ways of seeing the world and the role of things in it; they reflect taste. **Taste** refers to a generalized set or orientation to consumer preferences. Social class impacts consumption through tastes, including media habits, and thus exposure to various advertising media vehicles—for example, *RV Life* versus *Wine Spectator*. We think of tennis more than bowling as belonging to the upper classes, chess more than checkers, and Brie more than Velveeta. Ordering wine instead of beer has social significance, as does wearing Tommy Hilfiger rather than Lee jeans, or driving a Volvo rather than a Chevy. Social class and consumption are undeniably intertwined; they go hand in hand. In fact, cultural theorist Pierre Bourdieu argues that social class is such a powerful socializing factor that it "structures the whole experience of subjects," particularly when it comes to consumption.[17] This has to do with the relationship between social class and taste.

Cultural capital describes the value that cultures place on certain consumption practices. For example, a certain consumption practice, say in-line skating, has a certain capital or social value (like money) for some segment of the population. If you own in-line skates (a certain amount of cultural capital) and can actually use them (more cultural capital), and look good while using them (even more capital), then this activity is like cultural currency or money in the bank. A Porsche has a certain cultural capital among some groups, as does wearing khakis, drinking Bud, ordering the right Pinot Noir, knowing how to hail a cab, flying first class, or knowing the latest alternative band. This capital may be situated within a hipster culture, or a 40-something wine snob culture, or redneck culture. These are all cultures, and certain consumer practices are favored or valued more in each. Advertisers need to figure out which ones are valued more, and why, and how to make their product sought after because it has higher cultural capital. This is what "taste" is all about. These ads try to emphasize the cultural capital, style, and taste to be found in the product (see Exhibits 5.29 and 5.30), and then on to the consumer.

GLOBAL ISSUES

Rituals Drive Market Opportunities around the World

There are few rituals as curious as the beauty pageant. Recent globalization of this ritual provides a vivid illustration of the connections among rituals, values, and consumption behavior. Just ask the young women of India.

If rituals are about a culture affirming and expressing its values, then the values embedded in a beauty pageant are probably pretty obvious, and some would argue pretty superficial as well. Be that as it may, when Lara Dutta was crowned Miss Universe in May 2000, many young women in India took notice and apparently approved of the outcome. The beauty pageant ritual and Miss Dutta's subsequent emergence as a role model for women in India changed the way these women thought about themselves. With this change came a new set of values concerning personal appearance that no longer was restricted to traditional ways, but instead reflected a more international concept of beauty.

Is there hard evidence from the marketplace that values have shifted in India? Without a doubt. Analysts estimate that India's "beauty market" is worth in excess of $1.5 billion and is growing 20 percent each year—which is twice as fast as this market's growth in the United States and Europe. The cosmetics business in India is booming with familiar players like L'Oréal, Revlon, and Clarins in hot pursuit of the opportunity. Additionally, Indian women are participating in health and fitness activities as never before. Gyms are opening from Bombay to Calcutta—and to do the gym thing the right way, one also needs all the appropriate workout gear. Even cosmetic surgeons in India have seen their businesses benefit from the new passion for beauty. When values shift in a culture, consumption shifts are sure to follow. Look to rituals as a way to better comprehend when and where these powerful forces are likely to manifest in the marketplace.

Source: "From the Runway to Runaway Sales," *Business Week*, June 19, 2000, 68.

17. Pierre Bourdieu, "Distinction: A Social Critique of the Judgement of Taste," in *Social Stratification in Sociological Perspective: Class, Race and Gender*, ed. David B. Grusky (San Francisco: Westview Press, 1994), 404–429.

EXHIBITS 5.29 AND 5.30

These two ads do a good job of pointing to the high cultural capital of the products.

Consider some examples. Think about the purchases of equivalently priced cars, say a Saab and a Cadillac. The Saab is owned by a young architect, the Cadillac by the owner of a small construction company. These two consumers don't frequent the same restaurants, drink in the same bars, or eat the same kinds of foods. They don't belong to the same social class, and it is evident in their consumption. Think about the contents of the living rooms of those in various social classes. The differences are not due to money only, or the lack of it. Clearly, there is another dynamic at work here.

Class also becomes apparent when a person moves from one class into another. Consider the following example: Bob and Jill move into a more expensive neighborhood. Both grew up in lower-middle-class surroundings and moved into high-paying jobs after graduate school. They have now moved into a fairly upscale neighborhood, composed mostly of "older money." On one of the first warm Sundays, Bob goes out to his driveway and begins to do something he has done all his life: change the oil in his car. One of Bob's neighbors comes over and chats, and ever so subtly suggests to Bob that people in this neighborhood have "someone else" do "that sort of thing." Bob gets the message: It's not cool to change your oil in your own driveway. This is not how the new neighbors behave. It doesn't matter whether you like to do it or not; it is simply not done. To Bob, paying someone else to do this simple job seems wasteful and uppity. He's a bit offended, and a little embarrassed. But, over time, he decides that it's better to go along with the other people in the neighborhood. Over time, Bob begins to see the error of his ways and changes his attitudes and his behavior.

e-SIGHTINGS

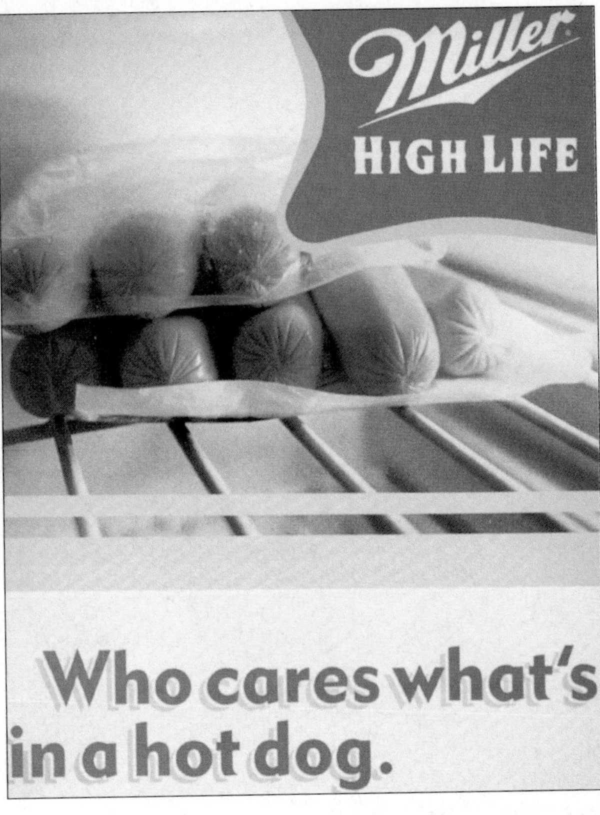

EXHIBITS 5.31 AND 5.32

These ads speak to two different social classes. Compare the sites of Chivas (www.chivas.com) and Miller Lite (www.millerlite.com). What activities and interests are featured at each? How does leisure-oriented content at each site create a context of social class that reinforces each brand's image? Which brand image appeals to you most?

This is an example of the effect of social class on consumer behavior. Bob will no longer be a good target for Fram, Purolator, AutoZone, or any other product or service used to change oil at home. On the other hand, Bob is now a perfect candidate for quick oil change businesses such as Jiffy Lube. Consider the ads in Exhibits 5.31 and 5.32 in terms of social-class considerations. Which social classes do you believe are being targeted by these ads?

Family. The consumer behavior of families is also of great interest to advertisers. Advertisers want not only to discern the needs of different kinds of families, but also to discover how decisions are made within families. The first is possible; the latter is much more difficult. For a while, consumer researchers tried to determine who in the traditional nuclear family (that is, Mom, Dad, and the kids) made various purchasing decisions. This was largely an exercise in futility. Due to errors in reporting and conflicting perceptions between husbands and wives, it became clear that the family purchasing process is anything but clear. While some types of purchases are handled by one family member, many decisions are actually diffuse nondecisions, arrived at through what consumer researcher C. W. Park aptly calls a "muddling-through" process.[18] These "decisions" just get made, and no one is really sure who made them, or even when. For an advertiser to influence such a diffuse and vague

18. C. Whan Park, "Joint Decisions in Home Purchasing: A Muddling-Through Process," *Journal of Consumer Research*, vol. 9 (September 1982), 151–162.

EXHIBIT 5.33

Who are the Cleavers?

process is indeed a challenge. The consumer behavior of the family is a complex and often subtle type of social negotiation. One person handles this, one takes care of that. Sometimes specific purchases fall along gender lines, but sometimes they don't.[19] While they may not be the buyer in many instances, children can play important roles as initiators, influencers, and users in many categories, such as cereals, clothing, vacation destinations, fast-food restaurants, and even computers. Still, some advertisers capitalize on the flexibility of this social system by suggesting in their ads who should take charge of a given consumption task, and then arming that person with the appearance of expertise so that whoever wants the job can take it and defend his or her purchases.

We also know that families have a lasting influence on the consumer preferences of family members. One of the best predictors of the brands adults use is the ones their parents used. This is true for cars, toothpaste, household cleansers, and many more products. Say you go off to college. You eventually have to do laundry, so you go to the store, and you buy Tide. Why Tide? Well, you're not sure, but you saw it around your house when you lived with your parents, and things seemed to have worked out okay for them, so you buy it for yourself. The habit sticks, and you keep buying it. This is called an **intergenerational effect.**

Advertisers often focus on the major or gross differences in types of families, because different families have different needs, buy different things, and are reached by different media. Family roles often change when both parents (or a single parent) are employed outside the home. For instance, a teenage son or daughter may be given the role of initiator and buyer, while the parent or parents serve merely as influences. Furthermore, we should remember that Ward, June, Wally, and the Beaver (Exhibit 5.33) are not (if they ever were) the norm (see Exhibit 5.34). There are a lot of single parents and second and third marriages. *Family* is a very open concept. In addition to the "traditional" nuclear family and the single-parent household, there is the extended family (nuclear family plus grandparents, cousins, and others) and the so-called alternative family (single and never-married mothers and gay and lesbian households with and without children, for example).

Beyond the basic configuration, advertisers are often interested in knowing things such as the age of the youngest child, the size of the family, and the family income. The age of the youngest child living at home tells an advertiser where the family is in terms of its needs and obligations (that is, toys, investment instruments for college savings, clothing, and vacations). When the youngest child leaves home, the consumption patterns of a family radically change. Advertisers love to track the age of the youngest child living at home and use it as a planning criterion.

Reference Groups. Obviously, other people and their priorities can have a dramatic impact on our consumption priorities, as suggested by the MasterCard ad in Exhibit 5.35 on page 193. A **reference group** is any configuration of other people

19. For an excellent article on this topic, see Craig J. Thompson, William B. Locander, and Howard R. Pollio, "The Lived Meaning of Free Choice: An Existential-Phenomenological Description of Everyday Consumer Experiences of Contemporary Married Women," *Journal of Consumer Research,* vol. 17 (December 1990), 346–361.

Characteristics	All households	Family households				Nonfamily households		
				Other families				
		Total	Married couple	Female householder	Male householder	Total	Female householder	Male householder
All households	104,705	72,025	55,311	12,687	4,028	32,680	18,039	14,641
Race and Hispanic origin								
White	87,671	60,251	48,790	8,380	3,081	27,420	15,215	12,204
White not Hispanic	78,819	53,066	43,865	6,732	2,468	25,753	14,475	11,278
Black	12,849	8,664	4,144	3,814	706	4,185	2,309	1,876
Hispanic	9,319	7,561	5,133	1,769	658	1,758	783	974
Size of household								
1 person	26,724	N/A	N/A	N/A	N/A	26,724	15,543	11,181
2 people	34,666	29,834	22,899	5,206	1,730	4,832	2,225	2,607
3 people	17,152	16,405	11,213	4,086	1,106	746	177	570
4 people	15,309	15,064	12,455	1,927	682	245	66	179
5 people	6,981	6,894	5,723	864	307	87	17	70
6 people	2,445	2,413	1,916	366	130	32	6	26
7 or more people	1,428	1,415	1,105	237	73	13	5	8
Average size	2.62	3.24	3.26	3.17	3.16	1.25	1.17	1.34
Presence of own children under 18	34,605	34,605	25,248	7,571	1,786	N/A	N/A	N/A

Note: Data are not shown separately for the American Indian and Alaska Native population because of the small size in the Current Population Survey in March 2000.

Source: U.S. Census Bureau, Current Population Survey, March 2000.

EXHIBIT 5.34

American households by type and selected characteristics, 2000. Numbers are in thousands, except averages and percentages.

that a particular individual uses as a point of reference in making his or her own consumption decisions.

Reference groups can be small and intimate (you and the people sharing your neighborhood) or large and distant (you and all other people taking an advertising course). Reference groups can also vary in their degree of formal structure. They can exist as part of some larger organization—such as any business or employer—with formal rules for who must be part of the group and what is expected of the group in terms of each day's performance. Or they may be informal in their composition and agenda, such as a group of casual friends who all live in the same apartment complex.

Another way of categorizing reference groups involves the distinction between membership groups and aspirational groups.[20] **Membership groups** are those that we interact with in person on some regular basis; we have personal contact with the group and its other members. **Aspirational groups** are made up of people we admire or use as role models, but it is likely we will never interact with the members of this group in any meaningful way. However, because we aspire to be like the members of this group, they can set standards for our own behavior. Professional athletes, movie stars, rock-and-roll bands, and successful business executives become role models whether they like it or not. Of course, advertisers are keenly aware of the potential influence of aspirational groups, and they commonly employ celebrities, from Grant Hill to Hanson, as endorsers for their products. After all, who

20. For additional explanation of this distinction, see Michael R. Solomon, *Consumer Behavior* (Upper Saddle River, NJ: Prentice-Hall, 1996), 342–344.

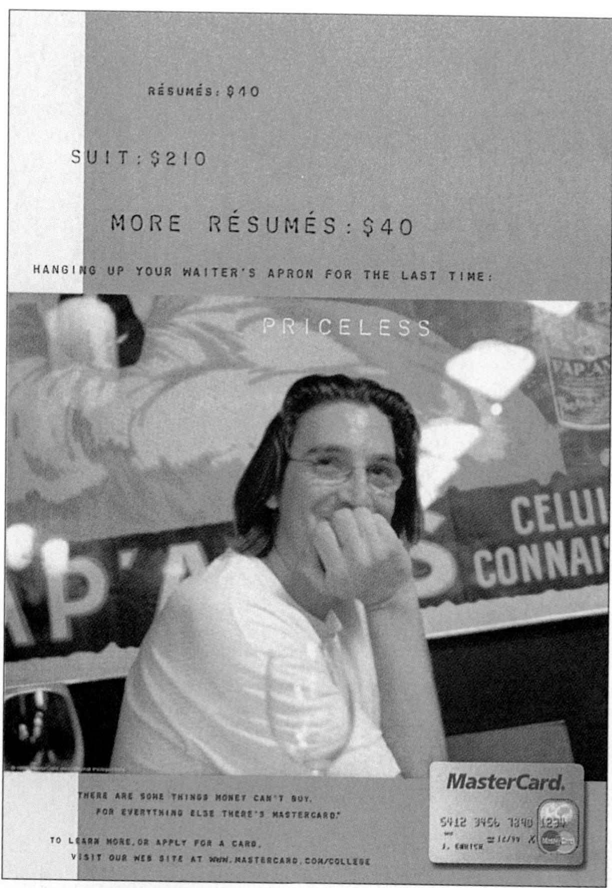

EXHIBIT 5.35

Aspirations play a large part in the message of this MasterCard ad.
www.mastercard.com

wouldn't want to be, to paraphrase another ad, like Michael Jordan?

Reference groups affect our consumption in a variety of ways. At the simplest level, they can furnish information that helps us evaluate products and brands, and if we will actually consume a particular product (for example, tonight's dinner) with the group, the group's preferences may become hard to distinguish from our own. Additionally, reference groups play an important role in legitimizing the symbolic value of some forms of consumption—that is, individuals choose some brands because they perceive that using these products will enhance their image with a reference group, signal to others the particular reference group they belong to, or serve as a gift to another member of the group to let that person know how special he or she is. In this way products and brands end up offering consumers important **self-expressive benefits.** And where do products and brands get their symbolic meaning that makes them valuable as props for communicating with others? How did Cadillac become a symbol of status and Nike become a symbol of devotion to performance? Such symbolism is shaped and reaffirmed by years of consistent advertising, as long as the status conferred is consistent with the other coexisting social forces. Even great advertising will not succeed against the tide. And remember, much of what a brand means is determined by consumers, not just handed down by marketers.

Celebrity is a unique sociological category, and it matters a great deal to advertisers. Twenty-first-century society is all about celebrity. While there are all sorts of celebrities, they can be both self-expressive and aspirational for consumers. Current thinking is that in a celebrity-based culture, celebrities help contemporary consumers with identity. Identity in a consumer culture becomes a "fashion accessory" prop for a day—lesbian chic, head banger, corporate slave at work, and so forth. The idea is that contemporary (postmodern) consumers are very good at putting on and taking off, trying on, switching, and trading various identities, in the same way that they have clicked through the channels since they could reach the remote. E-generation children have become who they are through celebrity-inspired identities—the way they surf the net, the way they change clothes to go out. This means that celebrities and images of them are used moment to moment to help in a parade of identity. For this reason, the understanding of the celebrity is much more complex and vital than merely thinking in terms of similar attitudes and behaviors. It's who we are, minute to minute, ad to ad, mall to mall, purchase to purchase (Exhibits 5.36 through 5.39).

Cool. A lot of what advertising is all about is figuring out what is cool, and then transmitting that meaning onto the brand. What is cool is determined through a social process. Consumers have a great deal of power in this way, because they along with advertisers determine the meaning of cool. Sometimes the last person to know what is cool (or not) is the advertiser. These days some marketers actually go out into various areas known for the hot spot on the cool map (like certain urban settings), and see what the kids are wearing, and doing, and saying. These "coolhunts" are then translated into brands and ads (see Exhibits 5.40 and 5.41).

EXHIBITS 5.36 THROUGH 5.39

These ads use a very sophisticated approach to celebrity and consumer identity.

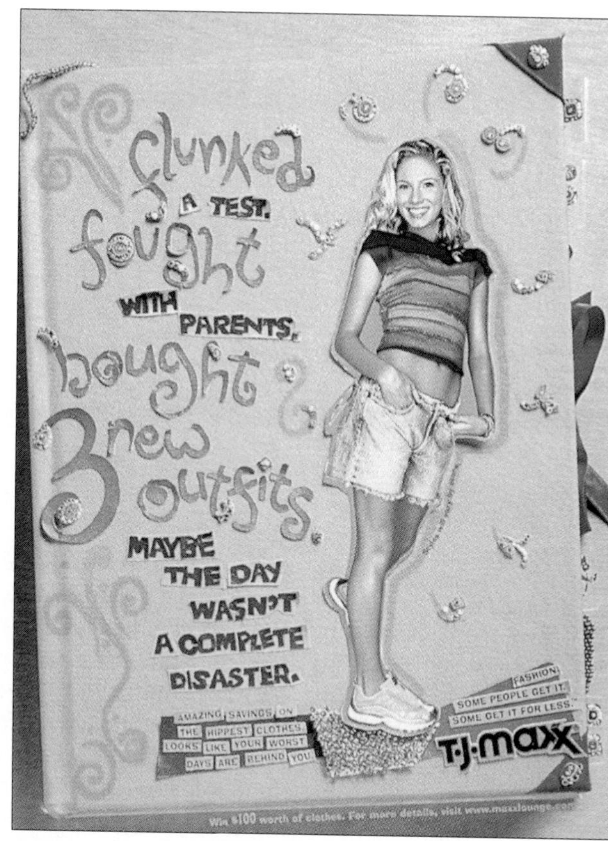

EXHIBITS 5.40 AND 5.41

Do you see the evidence of coolhunting in these two ads?

ROCK MECCA.
GET DAP.

Year	White	Black	Hispanic	Asian	American Indian
1996	194.4 (73.3%)	32.0 (12.1%)	27.8 (10.5%)	9.1 (3.4%)	2.0 (0.7%)
2000	197.1 (71.8%)	33.6 (12.2%)	31.4 (11.4%)	10.6 (3.9%)	2.1 (0.7%)
2010	202.4 (68.0%)	37.5 (12.6%)	41.1 (13.8%)	14.4 (4.8%)	2.3 (0.8%)
2020	207.4 (64.3%)	41.5 (12.9%)	52.7 (16.3%)	18.6 (5.7%)	2.6 (0.8%)
2030	210.0 (60.5%)	45.4 (13.1%)	65.6 (18.9%)	23.0 (6.6%)	2.9 (0.8%)
2040	209.6 (56.7%)	49.4 (13.3%)	80.2 (21.7%)	27.6 (7.5%)	3.2 (0.9%)
2050	207.9 (52.8%)	53.6 (13.6%)	96.5 (24.5%)	32.4 (8.2%)	3.5 (0.9%)

Source: U.S. Census Bureau.

EXHIBIT 5.42

Ethnic diversity in America: projected U.S. population by race in millions (and percentage of total population by race).

Race and Ethnicity. Race and ethnicity provide other ways to think about important social groups. Answering the question of how race figures into consumer behavior is difficult. Our discomfort stems from having, on the one hand, the desire to say, "Race doesn't matter, we're all the same," and on the other hand not wanting (or not being able) to deny the significance of race in terms of reaching ethnic cultures and influencing a wide variety of behaviors, including consumer behavior. Obviously, a person's pigmentation, in and of itself, has almost nothing to do with preferences for one type of product over another. But because race has mattered in culture, it does matter in consumer behavior. To the extent that race is part of culture, it matters. Race clearly affects cultural and social phenomena. The United States is becoming an increasingly diverse culture (Exhibit 5.42). But how do we (and should we) deal with this reality?

There probably isn't an area in consumer behavior where research is more inadequate. We simply know next to nothing about the role of race in consumer behavior. This is probably because everyone is terrified to discuss it, and because most of the findings we do have are suspect. What is attributed to race is often due to another factor that is itself associated with race. For example, consumer behavior textbooks commonly say something to the effect that African-Americans and Hispanics are more brand loyal than their Anglo counterparts. Data on the frequency of brand switching is offered, and lo and behold, it does appear that white people switch brands more often. But why? Some ethnic minorities live in areas where there are fewer retail choices. When we statistically remove the effect of income disparities between white people and people of color, we see that the brand-switching effect often disappears. This suggests that brand loyalty is not a function of race, but of disposable income and shopping options.

Still, race does inform one's social identity to varying degrees. One is not blind to one's own ethnicity. African-Americans, Hispanics, and other ethnic groups have culturally related consumption preferences. It is not enough, however, for advertisers to say one group is different from another group. If they really want a good, long-term relationship with their customers, they must acquire, through good consumer research, a deeper understanding of who their customers are and how this identity is informed by culture, felt ethnicity, and race. In short, advertisers must ask why groups of consumers are different, and not settle for an easy answer. It wasn't until the mid- to late 1980s that most American corporations made a concerted effort to court African-American consumers, or even to recognize their existence.[21] Efforts

21. Jannette L. Dates, "Advertising," in *Split Image: African Americans in the Mass Media,* ed. Jannette L. Dates and William Barlow (Washington, D.C.: Howard University Press, 1990), 421–454.

EXHIBITS 5.43 AND 5.44

These two ads target Asian and Hispanic consumers.

to serve the Hispanic consumer have been intermittent and inconsistent. This, coupled with a very sad historical corporate record, is simply shameful. Sample ads directed at diverse audiences are shown in Exhibits 5.43 and 5.44.

Gender. **Gender** is the social expression of sexual biology, sexual choice, or both. Obviously, gender matters in consumption. But are men and women really that different in any meaningful way in their consumption behavior, beyond the obvious? Again, to the extent that gender informs a "culture of gender," the answer is yes. As long as men and women are the products of differential socialization, then they will continue to be different in some significant ways. There is, however, no definitive list of gender differences in consumption, because the expression of gender, just like anything else social, depends on the situation and the social circumstances. In the 1920s, advertisers openly referred to women as less logical, more emotional, the cultural stewards of beauty.[22] (Some say that the same soft, irrational, emotional feminine persona is still invoked in 1990s advertising.) Advertising helps construct a social reality, with gender a predominant feature. Not only is it a matter of conscience and social responsibility to be aware of this construction, but it is good business as well. Advertisers must keep in mind, though, that it's hard to do business with people you patronize, insult, or ignore.

22. Roland Marchand, *Advertising: The American Dream* (Berkeley, Calif.: University of California Press, 1984), 25; Laura Koss-Feder, "Out and About: Firms Introduce Gay-Specific Ads for Mainstream Products, Services," *Marketing News,* May 25, 1998, 1, 20.

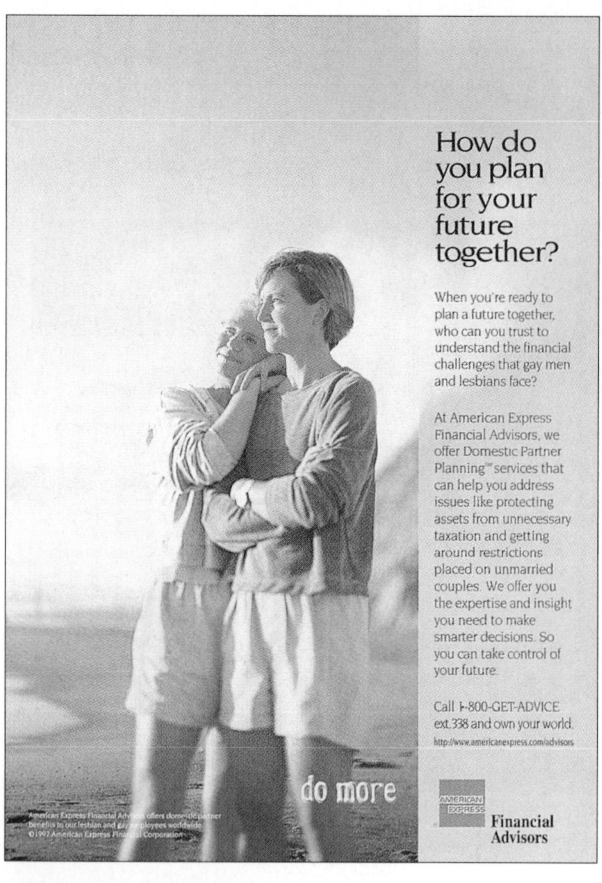

EXHIBIT 5.45

Some advertisers are beginning to recognize the advantages of marketing to gay and lesbian consumers. Here, American Express recognizes the special financial challenges faced by lesbian couples.
www.americanexpress.com.

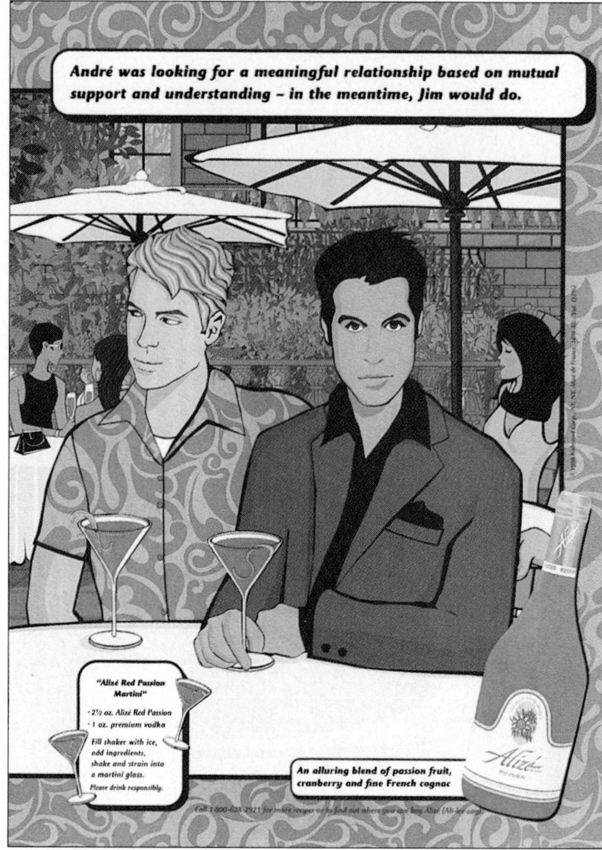

EXHIBIT 5.46

Here, Alizé attempts to represent and appeal to gay consumers.

Obviously, gender's impact on consumer behavior is not limited to heterosexual men and women. Gay men and lesbian women are large and significant markets. Of late, these markets have been targeted by corporate titans such as IBM, United Airlines, and Citibank.[23] Again, these are markets that desire to be acknowledged and served, but not stereotyped and patronized. Exhibits 5.45 and 5.46 are ads targeted at lesbian and gay audiences.

In the late 1970s, advertisers discovered working women. In the 1980s, marketers discovered African-American consumers, about the same time they discovered Hispanic consumers. Later they discovered Asian-Americans, and just lately they discovered gays and lesbians. Of course, these people weren't missing. They were there all along. These "discoveries" of forgotten and marginalized social groups create some interesting problems for advertisers. Members of these groups, quite reasonably, want to be served just like any other consumers. To serve these markets, consider what Wally Snyder of the American Advertising Federation said:

Advertising that addresses the realities of America's multicultural population must be created by qualified professionals who understand the nuances of the disparate cultures. Otherwise,

23. Koss-Feder, "Out and About," op cit.

agencies and marketers run the risk of losing or, worse, alienating millions of consumers eager to buy their products or services. Building a business that "looks like" the nation's increasingly multicultural population is no longer simply a moral choice, it is a business imperative.[24]

Attention and representation without stereotyping from a medium and a genre that is known for stereotyping might be a lot to expect, but it's not that much.

Community. **Community** is a powerful and traditional sociological variable, considered by some to be the fundamental concept in sociology. It is defined as a "wide-ranging relationship of solidarity over a rather undefined area of life and interests."[25] Its meaning extends well beyond the idea of a specific geographic place. Communities can be imagined or even virtual.[26]

Advertisers are becoming increasingly aware of the power of community. It is important in at least two major ways. First, it is where consumption is grounded, where consumption literally lives. Products have social meanings, and community is the quintessential social domain, so consumption is inseparable from the notion of where we live. Communities may be the fundamental reference group, and they exhibit a great deal of power. A community may be your neighborhood, or it may be people like you with whom you feel a kinship, such as members of social clubs, other consumers who collect the same things you do, or people who have the same interests you do. In a consumer society, goods and services figure prominently in the symbolic fabric of communities. Communities may exist through a common text (such as an ad) or a product.

Second, the extent to which brands can derive power is determined in part by brand community. **Brand communities** are groups of consumers who feel a commonality and a shared purpose grounded or attached to a consumer good or service.[27] When owners of Doc Martens, Saabs, Mountain Dews, or Saturns experience a sense of connectedness by virtue of their common ownership or usage, a brand community exists. When two perfect strangers stand in a parking lot and act like old friends simply because they both own Saturns, a type of community is revealed. Indeed, Saturn's Spring Hill Homecoming, described in the IBP box on page 203, is considered a great marketing success story in the area of cultivating brand community. Exhibit 5.47 reinforces the communal appeal of Saturn.

Object Meaning and the Social Life of Brands. The things we buy, the things we consume, have meaning. All consumed objects (in fact, all material things) have sociocultural meaning. They are not just things. Look around you: The things in your home, the things in your room, the things in your car, your car itself, all things material, derive their meaning from society and culture. A Fender Stratocaster is not just a piece of wood with some wires and strings. It is also not just a fine musical instrument. It is an electric guitar. It is a Fender. It is the kind of guitar that Stevie Ray Vaughan, Eric Clapton, Kurt Cobain, Jimi Hendrix, and other famous guitarists have played (Exhibit 5.48). It is social history. What others think about it makes it something other than wood and wire. People give it meaning. A tuxedo is not just a coat and pants combo. It is worn on certain social occasions. Paper plates (not even Chinette) are not just plates made of paper. If you serve your guests a fine meal on them, they will notice. A Tag Heuer watch is not just a timepiece; neither is a Timex or a $20 Casio. They all mean something, and this meaning is derived socially. Advertisers try to influence this process. Sometimes they succeed; other times they don't. A lot of good research lately has demonstrated these observations.

24. Wally Snyder, "Advertising's Ethical and Economic Imperative," *American Advertising* (Fall 1992), 28.
25. Marshall, *Concise Oxford Dictionary of Sociology*, 72–73.
26. Benedict Anderson, *Imagined Community* (London: Verso, 1983).
27. Albert Muniz Jr. and Thomas O'Guinn, *Brand Community* (Berkeley, Calif.: unpublished manuscript).

EXHIBIT 5.47

GM's Saturn division has been a leader in promoting a sense of community among its owners. In this ad, that sense of community is cultivated through photographs from the Spring Hill Homecoming. Savvy Saturn marketers used the homecoming as a feature in advertising campaigns to show that the bond between Saturn owners and their cars is something special. www.saturncars.com

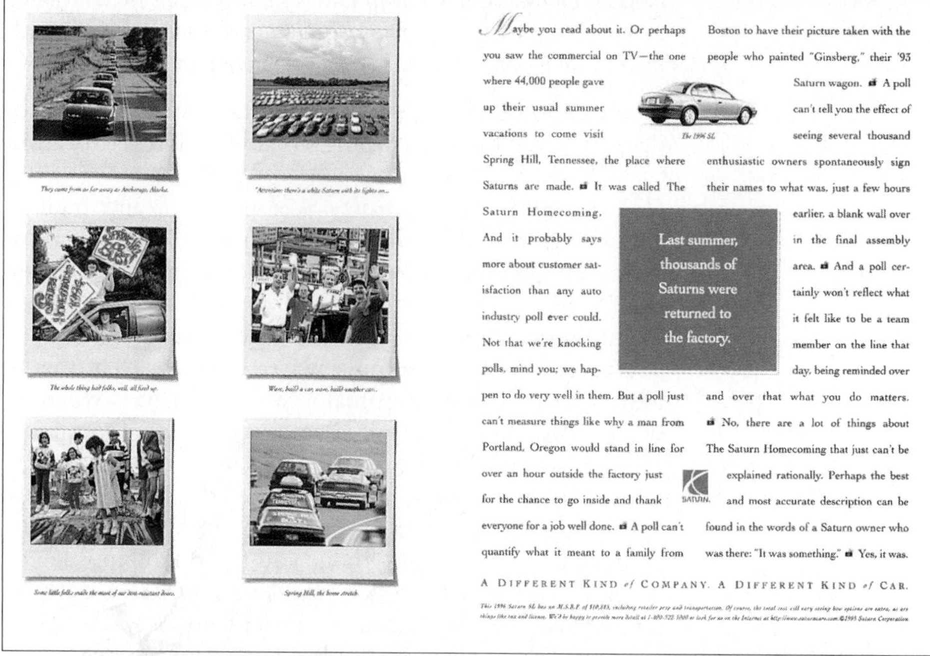

EXHIBIT 5.48

Hubert Sumlin's Strat is hardly just wood and wire. How does Fender (www.fender.com) *promote object meaning for its products at its site? Does the Fender Museum also utilize this powerful emotional connection between consumers and products?* (www.fendermuseum.com)

e-SIGHTINGS

Some researchers have looked at more "ordinary" or "everyday" social meaning; others have delved into deeper meanings: the meanings of our most prized possessions, the things we could hardly stand to lose, something our parents or grandparents gave us, something that reminds us of someone dear, or something that would really be hard to explain just why it means so much. Just remember, all material

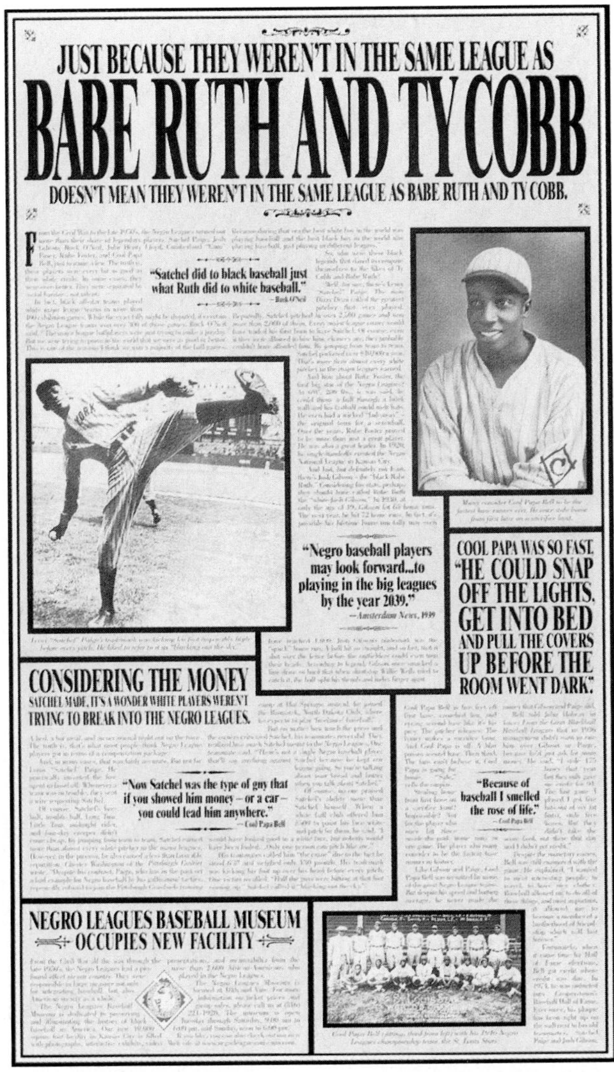

EXHIBIT 5.49

The consumer's cultural background often contributes to his or her interpretation of a text. Can you identify the cultural references in this ad?

things have meaning, as do activities. Smart advertisers must hope to understand relevant and widely shared social meaning in order to get consumers to appreciate their brand.

Advertising as Social Text. Advertising is a sociocultural object. It is created, in a very real way, by society and culture. Individuals and groups of advertising professionals may actually physically craft ads, but the sociocultural environment "creates" them.

Advertising is also a text. It is "read" and interpreted by consumers. You can think of it as being like other texts, books, movies, posters, paintings, and so on. In order to "get" ads, you have to know something of the cultural code, or they would make no sense. In order to really understand a movie, to really get it, you have to know something about the culture that created it. Sometimes when you see a foreign film (even in your native tongue), you just don't quite get all the jokes and references, because you are not really good at reading the text. You don't possess the cultural knowledge necessary to really effectively "read" the text. So ads are, just like these other forms, sociocultural texts (see Exhibit 5.49).

Ads Transmit Sociocultural Meaning. The link between culture and advertising is key. Anthropologist Grant McCracken has offered the model in Exhibit 5.50 to explain how advertising (along with other cultural agents) functions in the transmission of meaning. To understand advertising as a mechanism of meaning transfer is to understand a great deal about advertising. In fact, one could legitimately say that advertisers are really in the meaning-transfer business.

Think about McCracken's model as you examine the ad for Johnston and Murphy in Exhibit 5.51. The product—in this case, shoes—exists "out there" in the culturally constituted world, but it needs advertising to link it to certain social representations, certain slices of life. The advertiser places the advertised product and the slice of social life in an ad to get the two to rub off on each other, to intermingle, to become part of the same social reality. In other words, the product is given social meaning by being placed within an ad that represents some social reality. This slice of life, of course, is the type of social setting in which potential customers might find, or desire to find, themselves. According to McCracken's model, meaning has moved from the world to the product (shoes) by virtue of its sharing space within the social frame of the advertisement. When a consumer purchases or otherwise incorporates that good or service into his or her own life, the meaning is transferred to the individual consumer. Meaning is thus moved from the world to the product (via advertising) to the individual. When the individual uses the product, that person conveys to others the meaning he or she and the advertisement have now given it. Their use incorporates various rituals that facilitate the movement of meaning from good to consumer.

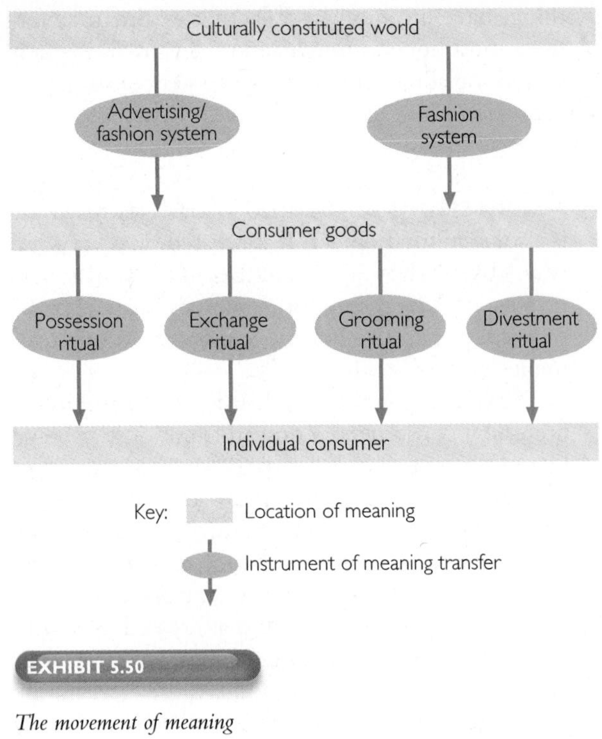

EXHIBIT 5.50

The movement of meaning

EXHIBIT 5.51

A Johnston & Murphy shoe is not just any shoe. One goal of this advertisement is to create a special meaning for this brand of men's shoes. www.johnstonmurphy.com

Remember, the meaning of an ad does not exist inviolate and immutable within its borders. In fact, it doesn't exist there at all. Meaning is constructed in the minds of consumers, not delivered by advertisements. What an ad means is determined through a subtle but powerful process of meaning construction by consumers. What something means depends on who the consumer is, the strategy or motivation with which he or she receives the ad, and the ad itself. Consider texts in general: For some African-Americans, reading *Huckleberry Finn* is a very different experience than it is for white suburban middle-class kids. In fact, if the experience is so entirely different, then so is the text for these two groups. In other words, there is no single text. Since what a text means is really up to the reader, then we must acknowledge that who the reader is, in terms of major sociological factors, matters as well.[28]

28. Stanley Fish, *Is There a Text in This Class?* (Cambridge, Mass.: Harvard University Press, 1980).

Textual meaning is created through the interaction of sociological, cultural, and individual factors. So it is for ads. Ads are no less texts than is *Huckleberry Finn.* Consumers determine what ads mean, and since they are socially situated within significant groups, their interpretations will be affected by those group memberships.[29] Ads are created by organizations (social entities) through social processes, all affected by social actions. They are then interpreted according to social conventions and have their meanings determined through social interpretive processes.

Think about how different individuals might interpret the ads shown in Exhibits 5.52 and 5.53. Of course, the different meanings will not be random. While there will be variations, the meanings will have a certain commonality about them, because members of the same culture tend to bring similar cultural baggage to the interpretive event (reading the ad) and thus render similar interpretations. When advertisers include social and cultural factors in their analysis of consumer behavior, they dramatically enhance their chances of anticipating the meaning consumers will draw from advertisements.

Ads also become part of consumers' everyday language and conversation.[30] Characters, lines, and references all become part of conversations, thoughts, and—coming full circle—the culture. Children, co-workers, family members, and talk show hosts all pick up things from ads, and then replay them, adapt them, and recirculate them just like things from movies, books, and other texts. Ads, in many ways, don't exist just within the sociocultural context; they are the sociocultural context of our time.

IBP

Coming Together . . . Over Saturn

It sounded like a goofy idea: Invite every Saturn owner (about 600,000) to a "homecoming" at the Spring Hill, Tennessee, plant where their cars were "born." After all, who in their right mind would plan their vacation around a remote manufacturing facility? About 44,000 Saturn owners, that's who. Owners came from as far away as Alaska and Taipei; one couple ended up getting married by a United Auto Workers chaplain, with the Saturn president there to give away the bride. Another 100,000 Saturn owners participated in related, dealer-sponsored programs all over the United States. Add in the national publicity provided from the news media and ensuing Saturn ads depicting the event, and the idea isn't so goofy anymore. It's a masterful integrated brand promotion campaign that has helped build an allegiance to the Saturn brand that is the envy of the automotive industry.

The genius of the Spring Hill Homecoming (and subsequent ads, such as Exhibit 5.47) is that Saturn's primary marketing strategy revolves around strong customer relations and service. The four-day event at the Tennessee plant rewarded customers for their purchase behavior and provided reassurance for new-car shoppers seeking the trust and relationships that allay service-related fears and the general mystery of new-car buying. Saturn's innovative approach is also integral to the overall strategy of its parent company, General Motors: The overwhelming majority of Saturn sales come from previous import owners, and not at the expense of other GM divisions. Actually, Saturn's retention programs just may be the greatest tangible benefit to arise from GM's earth-shaking $5 billion initial investment in the Saturn project.

Sources: "Savvy Companies Hold Customer," *Sales & Marketing Management,* December 1994, 15; Kevin L. Keller, *Strategic Brand Management* (Upper Saddle River, NJ: Prentice-Hall: 1998), 244–245; for an in-depth analysis of Saturn's brand-building programs, see David Aaker, *Building Strong Brands* (New York: Free Press, 1996), Chapter 2.

29. Linda M. Scott, "The Bridge from Text to Mind: Adapting Reader Response Theory for Consumer Research," *Journal of Consumer Research,* vol. 21 (December 1994): 461–486; David Glenn Mick and Claus Buhl, "A Meaning-Based Model of Advertising Experiences," *Journal of Consumer Research,* vol. 19 (December 1992): 312–338.

30. Richard Eliot and Mark Ritson, unpublished manuscript.

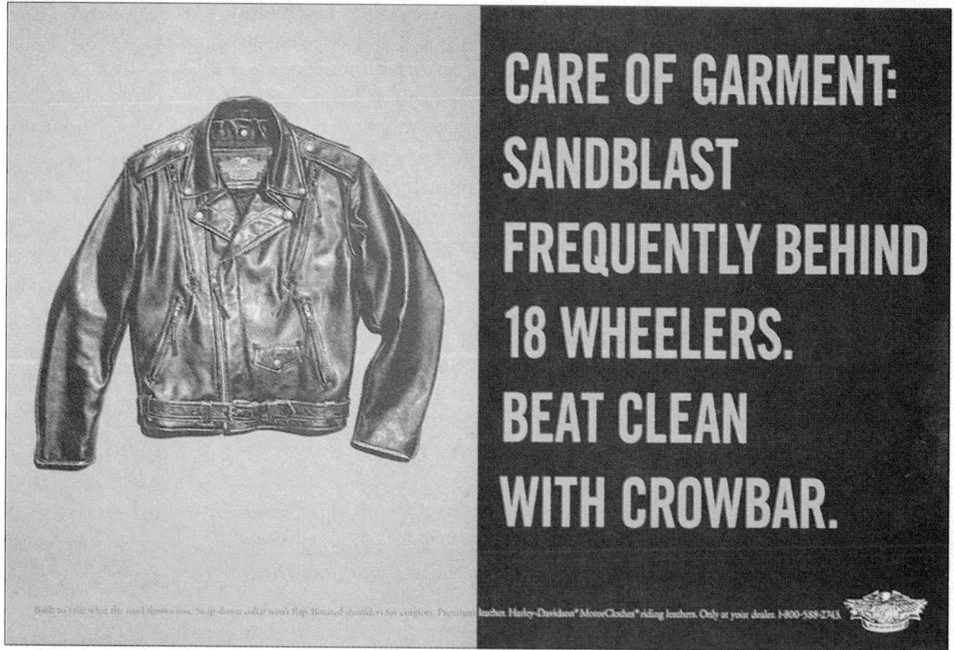

EXHIBITS 5.52 AND 5.53

How might different people interpret these ads, based on their differing social and cultural backgrounds? www.joeboxer.com *and* www.harley-davidson.com

SUMMARY

Describe the four basic stages of consumer decision making.

Advertisers need a keen understanding of their consumers as a basis for developing effective advertising. This understanding begins with a view of consumers as systematic decision makers who follow a predictable process in making their choices among products and brands. The process begins when consumers perceive a need, and it proceeds with a search for information that will help in making an informed choice. The search-and-evaluation stage is followed by purchase. Postpurchase use and evaluation then become critical as the stage in which customer satisfaction is ultimately determined.

Explain how consumers adapt their decision-making processes as a function of involvement and experience.

Some purchases are more important to people than others, and this fact adds complexity to any analysis of consumer behavior. To accommodate this complexity, advertisers often think about the level of involvement that attends any given purchase. Involvement and prior experience with a product or service category can lead to four diverse modes of consumer decision making. These modes are extended problem solving, limited problem solving, habit or variety seeking, and brand loyalty.

Discuss how advertising may influence consumer behavior through its effects on various psychological states.

Advertisements are developed to influence the way people think about products and brands. More specifically, advertising is designed to affect consumers' beliefs and brand attitudes. Advertisers use multi-attribute attitude models to help them ascertain the beliefs and attitudes of target consumers. However, consumers have perceptual defenses that allow them to ignore or distort most of the commercial messages to which they are exposed. When consumers are not motivated to thoughtfully process an advertiser's message, it may be in that advertiser's best interest to feature one or more peripheral cues as part of the message.

Discuss the interaction of culture and advertising.

Advertisements are cultural products, and culture provides the context in which an ad will be interpreted. Advertisers who overlook the influence of culture are bound to struggle in their attempt to communicate with the target audience. Two key concepts in managing the impact of culture are values and rituals. Values are enduring beliefs that provide a foundation for more-transitory psychological states, such as brand attitudes. Rituals are patterns of behavior shared by individuals from a common culture. Violating cultural values and rituals is a sure way to squander advertising dollars.

Discuss the role of sociological factors in consumer behavior and advertising response.

Consumer behavior is an activity that each of us undertakes before a broad audience of other consumers. Advertising helps the transfer of meaning. Reference groups of various types have a dramatic influence on the consumption behavior of their individual members. Reference groups can be either groups we merely aspire to be part of, or groups, such as our families, that count us as members.

KEY TERMS

consumer behavior
need state
functional benefits
emotional benefits
internal search
external search
consideration set
evaluative criteria
customer satisfaction
cognitive dissonance
involvement
extended problem solving
limited problem solving
habit
variety seeking
brand loyalty
attitude
brand attitudes
beliefs
salient beliefs
multi-attribute attitude models (MAAMs)
cognitive consistency
advertising clutter
selective attention
cognitive responses
elaboration likelihood model (ELM)
peripheral cues
culture
values
rituals
social class
taste
intergenerational effect
reference group
membership groups
aspirational groups
self-expressive benefits
celebrity
gender
community
brand communities

QUESTIONS

1. When consumers have a well-defined consideration set and a list of evaluative criteria for assessing the brands in that set, they in effect possess a matrix of information about that category. Drawing on your experiences as a consumer, set up and fill in such a matrix for the category of fast-food restaurants.

2. Is cognitive dissonance a good thing or a bad thing from an advertiser's point of view? Explain how and why advertisers should try to take advantage of the cognitive dissonance their consumers may experience.

3. Most people quickly relate to the notion that some purchasing decisions are more involving than others. What kinds of products or services do you consider highly involving? What makes these products more involving from your point of view?

4. Explain the difference between brand-loyal and habitual purchasing. When a brand-loyal customer arrives at a store and finds her favorite brand out of stock, what would you expect to happen next?

5. Describe three attitude-change strategies that could be suggested by the results of a study of consumer behavior using multi-attribute attitude models. Provide examples of different advertising campaigns that have employed each of these strategies.

6. Watch an hour of prime-time television and for each commercial you see, make a note of the tactic the advertiser employed to capture and hold the audience's attention. How can the use of attention-attracting tactics backfire on an advertiser?

7. What does it mean to say that culture is invisible? Explain how this invisible force serves to restrict and control the activities of advertisers.

8. Give three examples of highly visible cultural rituals practiced annually in the United States. For each ritual you identify, assess the importance of buying and consuming for effective practice of the ritual.

9. Are you a believer in the intergenerational effect? Make a list of the brands in your cupboards, refrigerator, and medicine cabinet. Which of these brands would you also expect to find in your parents' cupboards, refrigerator, and medicine cabinet?

10. "In today's modern, highly educated society, there is simply no reason to separate men and women into different target segments. Gender just should not be an issue in the development of marketing and advertising strategies." Comment.

EXPERIENTIAL EXERCISES

1. This chapter discussed the importance of understanding advertising and consumer behavior within a larger sociocultural context. To have any hope of forecasting how audiences will respond to their ads, advertisers must grasp the sociocultural forces that largely determine consumer behavior. If advertisers understand the values and rituals shared by members of the same sociocultural contexts, they will be more likely to produce effective advertising messages and strategies.

2. Visit a friend or family member and identify the types of products they use. Examine apparel, bath and personal care products, foods and beverages, or any other product category of your choosing. Based on what you've learned about sociocultural consumption contexts, describe what their preferred products reveal about their values and rituals. Be sure to identify how their consumer choices are related to concepts such as social class, cultural capital, reference groups, cool, race and ethnicity, gender, and brand meaning. Based on your analysis, suggest two or three new brands that your friend might be inclined to try out or use on a regular basis, and support your reasoning.

3. Find ads that address the following four modes of decision making: extended problem solving, limited problem solving, habit or variety seeking, and brand loyalty. Explain why each ad fits with that particular decision-making mode and state whether you think the ad is effective in persuading consumers. Be sure to include the concepts of involvement and prior experience in your answer.

USING THE INTERNET

5-1 Comparison Shopping: Evaluating Prices and Products

Once a consumer has recognized a need, a process is set in motion involving an extensive product-information search and a careful evaluation of alternatives prior to purchase. Consumers usually conduct searches by comparison shopping, choosing between brands in a certain product category as they focus in on individual product attributes. In the real world, this information search and evaluation takes place in an interactive environment where consumers can consult the opinions of others as well as test products. But how does this process take place on the Web? Dozens of sites have emerged on the Internet to aid consumers, re-creating the real-world decision-making process on the Web.

Epinions: http://www.epinions.com

mySimon: http://www.mysimon.com

1. Briefly describe the purpose of these sites. How are they similar? How are they different?

2. Do these sites help consumers with an internal search or an external search? What's the difference between the two? Can an internal search be conducted online? Explain.

3. Compare online product evaluation with the traditional brick-and-mortar evaluation process. What advantage does each have in terms of convenience and usefulness?

5-2 Two Perspectives on Consumer Behavior

This chapter attempts to explain consumer behavior from two basic perspectives. The consumer can be understood as a decision maker walking through a logical process of analyzing needs and evaluating products to meet those needs at the cost-to-rewards level of consciousness. Another valuable perspective views the consumer as a product of social surroundings and forces that invariably lead to the purchase of products consistent with that consumer's culture, values, and beliefs. While no one perspective can fully explain the complicated and multifaceted phenomenon of consumer behaviors, these broad perspectives help advertisers create ads that are more likely to be effective in promoting brands and persuading audiences.

360 Hip Hop: http://www.360hiphop.com

CCS: http://www.ccs.com

1. Describe the characteristics of these two shopping sites. Which of the two perspectives on consumer behavior do they appear to represent?

2. Describe the role of values and rituals as they relate to the consumer culture of 360 Hip Hop and CCS. How do advertisers accommodate—and even create—sociocultural consumption contexts to benefit the promotion of brands?

3. What is cultural capital and why is it important to advertisers? Explain the role of membership groups and aspirational groups in creating cultural capital. Give a real-world example of this from one of these sites.

CHAPTER 5
Advertising and Consumer Behavior

CHAPTER 6
Market Segmentation, Positioning, and the Value Proposition

CHAPTER 7
Advertising and Promotion Research

CHAPTER 8
The Advertising Plan

CHAPTER 9
Advertising Planning: An International Perspective

CHAPTER 6

After reading and thinking about this chapter, you will be able to do the following:

Explain the process known as STP marketing.

Describe different bases that marketers use to identify target segments.

Discuss the criteria used for choosing a target segment.

Identify the essential elements of an effective positioning strategy.

Review the necessary ingredients for creating a brand's value proposition.

GG2652/S
GUCCI
sunglasses

It would be fair to say that executives at The Gillette Company in Boston, Massachusetts, have become prisoners of their own success. King C. Gillette invented the safety razor in 1903, and since that time male grooming habits and the "wet shave" have been the company's obsession. Few companies can demonstrate the growth rates and global success that Gillette achieved in the 20th century. By the end of the century Gillette was able to claim that roughly two-thirds of all wet shaves around the world involved one of its razors, and that the company's profit growth was averaging nearly 15 percent annually.[1] Its advertising slogan—"Gillette: The Best a Man Can Get"—and products such as its SensorExcel and Mach3 shaving systems were ubiquitous. Thus, the challenge for Gillette executives was how to maintain their company's success at growing sales and profits around the world. They could keep introducing more expensive (and more profitable) shaving systems like the Mach3, and try to reach every last wet-shaving male on the face of the planet, but at some point they literally would run out of new faces.

Many companies large and small share Gillette's problem: How do you keep growing when there are always natural limits to growth? Or, how do you keep growing in the face of effective competitors who also want to grow just as much as you do? Companies anticipate and address this problem through a process we will refer to as STP marketing. It is a critical process from an advertising standpoint because it leads to decisions about to whom we need to advertise, and the value proposition we will want to present to them.

To find sources for new growth, Gillette would need to identify new markets—someone other than wet-shaving males—to target with its new products and advertising campaigns. To make a long story short, Gillette decided to target wet-shaving females. The quintessential male-focused company would finally devote some of its considerable resources to address the unique shaving needs of women. And not just men's razors with pink handles (like the Daisy disposable razor, a failed Gillette product in the mid-1970s), but a complete line of products developed by women for women. When the strategy was announced, one competitor quipped, "What's your headline—Gillette discovers women?"[2]

In effect, Gillette had discovered women as a focal point for its considerable marketing and advertising efforts. But not all women; more specifically, Gillette would emphasize women in the 15-to-24-year-old range—a new target segment for Gillette. The thinking was that winning over youthful, wet-shaving females would create customers for life. Additionally, Gillette had the global marketplace in mind when it launched its "Gillette for Women: Are You Ready?" campaign. While women around the world are less likely to remove body hair than their counterparts in the United States (for example, Gillette estimates that 84 percent remove body hair in the United States versus 18 percent in Germany), younger women worldwide are most receptive to the idea. Gillette set out to tap the growth potential represented by the target segment of 15-to-24-year-old females around the world.

The program Gillette launched for these young women was multifaceted. It started with the Sensor shaving system for women, created by a female industrial designer, which featured a flat, wafer-shaped handle to give women better control while shaving. Other products followed, such as a high-end disposable razor named Agility and a line of shaving creams and after-shave products marketed under the brand name Satin Care. More money was allocated for global ad campaigns featuring ads such as those shown in Exhibits 6.1 and 6.2. This advertising, with the theme "Gillette for Women: Are You Ready?," was based on market research showing that most women perceive shaving as a nuisance or chore. Hence, they treat razors as a commodity item and are satisfied with inexpensive disposables. Gillette's advertising

1. Mark Maremont, "Gillette Finally Reveals Its Vision of the Future, and It Has 3 Blades," *Wall Street Journal,* April 14, 1998, A1, 10.

2. Mark Maremont, "Gillette's New Strategy Is to Sharpen Pitch to Women," *Wall Street Journal,* May 11, 1998, B1, B16.

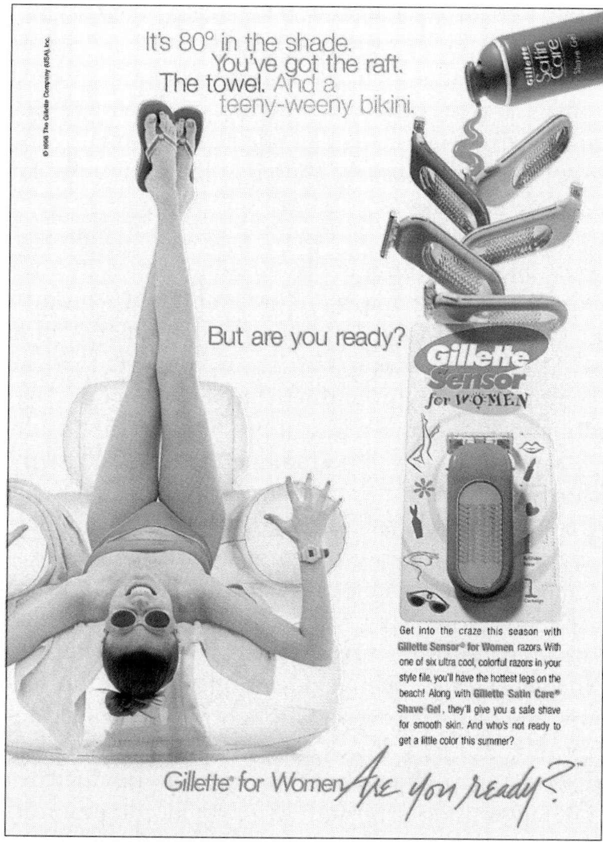

EXHIBIT 6.1

This was one of the first ads featured in Gillette's aggressive marketing program to young women. As suggested by the ad, most of each year's ad budget was concentrated on the peak season—summertime.
www.gillette.com

EXHIBIT 6.2

Gillette marketing executives were intent on elevating the role of shaving from the practical realm to the emotional realm. Would you agree that emotional benefits are promised by this ad?
www.gillette.com

was designed to make this routine grooming chore more important and more glamorous, and, in the words of Gillette's VP of female shaving, "elevate the role of shaving beyond the practical to a more emotional realm."[3] In this "emotional realm," Gillette's hopes were that more women would be willing to pay a bit extra for products such as Sensor and Satin Care.

By targeting wet-shaving young women, Gillette executives found a way to keep the company's sales and profits growing. Annual growth rates for women's products hovered around 20 percent, outperforming the men's division. This success convinced Gillette management that distinctive brands just for females were critical to the future of the company, and product development efforts were intensified to perfect the wet shave for women. This culminated in another high-profile, global product launch in the spring of 2001. Gillette for Women's next generation wet-shaving system would be branded "*Venus: to Reveal the Goddess in You.*"[4]

3. Ibid.
4. Betsy Spethmann, "Venus Rising," *PROMO Magazine,* April 2001, 52–61.

1 **STP Marketing and the Evolution of Marketing Strategies.** The Gillette example illustrates the process that marketers use to decide whom to advertise to and what to say in that advertising. Gillette executives started with the diverse market of all women, and they broke the market down by age segments. They then selected 15-to-24-year-old females as their target segment. The **target segment** is the subgroup (of the larger market) chosen as the focal point for the marketing program and advertising campaign.

While markets are segmented, products are positioned. To pursue the target segment, a firm organizes its marketing and advertising efforts around a coherent positioning strategy. **Positioning** is the act of designing and representing one's product or service so that it will occupy a distinct and valued place in the consumer's mind. **Positioning strategy** involves the selection of key themes or concepts that the organization will feature when communicating this distinctiveness to the target segment. In Gillette's case, its executives first designed a line of products for the youthful female wet-shaver. They then came up with the positioning theme "Gillette for Women: Are You Ready?" to clearly distinguish this new line from their traditional male-oriented shaving systems. Finally, through skillful advertising, they communicated distinctive functional and emotional benefits to the target segment.

Notice the specific sequence, illustrated in Exhibit 6.3, that was played out in the Gillette example: the marketing strategy evolved as a result of segmenting, targeting, and positioning. This sequence of activities is often referred to as **STP marketing,** and it represents a sound basis for generating effective advertising.[5] While no formulas or models guarantee success, the STP approach is strongly recommended for markets characterized by diversity in consumers' needs and preferences. In markets with any significant degree of diversity, it is impossible to design one product that would appeal to everyone, or one advertising campaign that would communicate with everyone. Organizations that lose sight of this simple premise often run into trouble.

EXHIBIT 6.3

Laying the foundation for effective advertising campaigns through STP marketing.

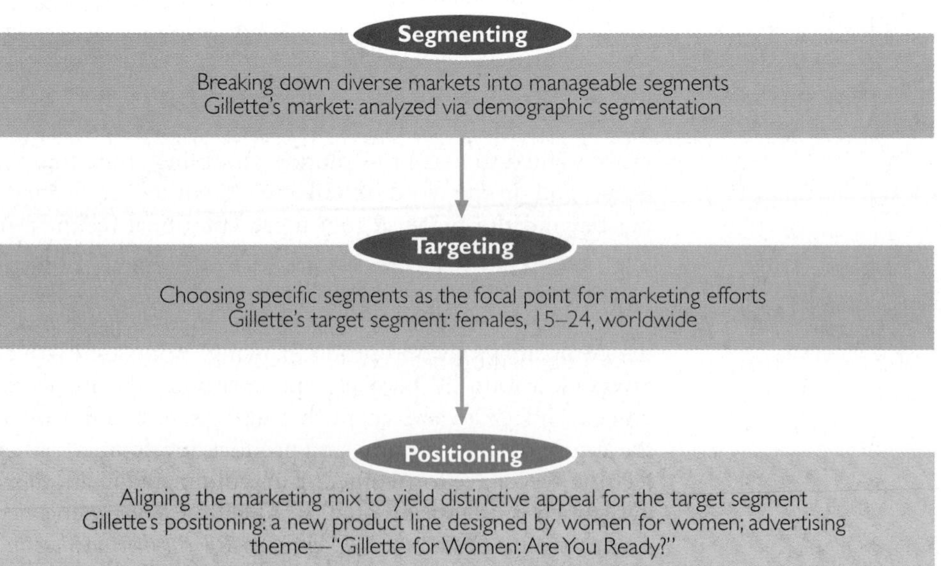

5. For a more extensive discussion of STP marketing, see Philip Kotler, *Marketing Management* (Englewood Cliffs, N.J.: Prentice-Hall, 1994), Chapters 11 and 12.

Indeed, in most product categories one finds that different consumers are looking for different things, and the only way for a company to take advantage of the sales potential represented by different customer segments is to develop and market a different brand for each segment. No company has done this better than cosmetics juggernaut Estée Lauder. Lauder has more than a dozen cosmetic brands, each developed for a different target segment of women.[6] For example, there is the original Estée Lauder brand, for women with conservative values and upscale tastes. Then there is Clinique, a no-nonsense brand that represents functional grooming for Middle America. Bobbi Brown Essentials are for the working mom who skillfully manages a career and her family and manages to look good in the process. M.A.C. is a brand for those who want to make a bolder statement: its spokespersons have been RuPaul, a 6-foot 7-inch drag queen, and k. d. lang, the talented lesbian vocalist. Prescriptives is marketed to a hip, urban, multiethnic target segment, and Origins, with its earthy packaging and natural ingredients, is for consumers who are concerned about the environment. These are just some of the cosmetics brands that Estée Lauder has marketed to appeal to diverse target segments.

We offer the Estée Lauder example to make two key points before we move on. First, the Gillette example may have made things seem too simple: STP marketing is a lot more complicated than just deciding to target women or men. Gender alone is rarely specific enough to serve as a complete identifier of a target segment. Second, the cosmetics example shows that many factors beyond just age and gender can come into play when trying to identify valid target segments. For these diverse cosmetics brands we see that considerations such as attitudes, lifestyles, and basic values all may play a role in identifying and describing customer segments.

To illustrate these two points, examine the three ads in Exhibits 6.4, 6.5, and 6.6. All three of these ads ran in *Seventeen* magazine, so it is safe to say that in all cases the advertiser was trying to reach adolescent females. But as you compare these exhibits, it should be pretty obvious that the advertisers were really trying to reach out to very different segments of adolescent females. To put it bluntly, it is hard to imagine a marine captain wearing either Clinique lipstick in Red Kiss or Hard Candy lip gloss. These ads were designed to appeal to different target segments, even though the people in these segments would seem the same if we considered only their age and gender.

Beyond STP Marketing. If an organization uses STP marketing as its framework for strategy development, at some point it will find the right strategy, develop the right advertising, make a lot of money, and live happily ever after. Right? As you might expect, it's not quite that simple. Even when STP marketing yields profitable outcomes, one must presume that success will not last indefinitely. Indeed, an important feature of marketing and advertising—a feature that can make these professions both terribly interesting and terribly frustrating—is their dynamic nature. To paraphrase a popular saying, shifts happen—consumer preferences shift. Competitors improve their marketing strategies, or technology changes and makes a popular product obsolete. Successful marketing strategies need to be modified or may even need to be reinvented as shifts occur in the organization's competitive environment.

To maintain the vitality and profitability of its products or services, an organization has two options. The first entails reassessment of the segmentation strategy. This may come through a more detailed examination of the current target segment to develop new and better ways of meeting its needs, or it may be necessary to adopt new targets and position new products to them, as was the case with Gillette for Women.

6. Nina Munk, "Why Women Find Lauder Mesmerizing," *Fortune,* May 25, 1998, 96–106.

EXHIBIT 6.4

The U.S. Armed Forces, including the Marines, are very aggressive and sophisticated advertisers. Here the Marines direct a message to basically the same target segment (from an age and gender standpoint) that was the focal point in Gillette's "Are You Ready?" campaign. www.usmc.mil

EXHIBIT 6.5

The Clinique brand is positioned as elegant but sensible. Its Superlast Cream Lipstick doesn't even leave a smudge! www.clinique.com

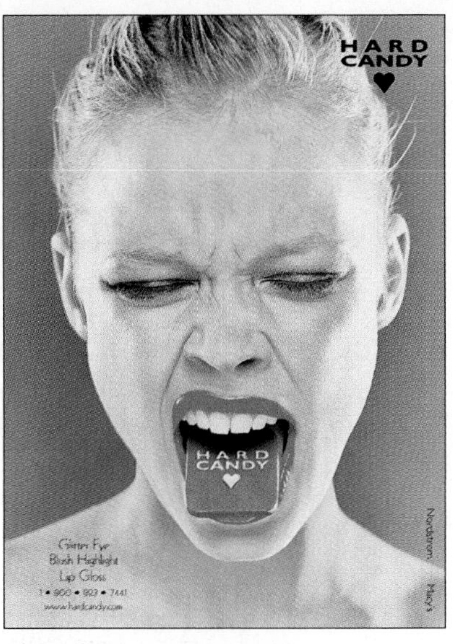

EXHIBIT 6.6

Hard Candy comes by its hip style, perhaps in large part, because of its uninhibitedly energetic founding by Gen X twentysomething Dineh Mohajer, who was unhappy with the choices traditional cosmetics firms offered her (www.hardcandy.com) *and her market demographic. There must be something in that California air. Internet technology company Cisco co-founder Sandy Lerner created Urban Decay* (www.urbandecay.com)*—another alternative for the fashion-mad—out of a similar dissatisfaction with the offerings of companies like Lancôme* (www.lancome.com).

The second option is to pursue a product differentiation strategy. As defined in Chapter 1, product differentiation focuses the firm's efforts on emphasizing or even creating differences for its brands to distinguish them from the offerings of established competitors. Advertising plays a critical role as part of the product differentiation strategy because often the consumer will have to be convinced that the intended difference is meaningful. Product differentiation strategies try to make a brand appear different from competing brands, but it is consumers' perceptions of the difference that will determine the success of the strategy.

For example, when Church & Dwight Company introduced its Arm & Hammer Dental Care baking soda toothpaste, major toothpaste marketers such as Procter & Gamble and Colgate-Palmolive were not impressed. The product had a distinctive difference from traditional brands like Crest and Colgate, but would consumers find this difference meaningful? The answer turned out to be yes—the slightly salty taste and gritty texture of the Arm & Hammer brand proved popular with consumers; in no time, sales of baking soda toothpastes approached $300 million annually.[7]

The basic message is that marketing strategies and the advertising that supports them are never really final. Successes realized through proper application of STP

7. Kathleen Deveny, "Anatomy of a Fad: How Clear Products Were Hot and Then Suddenly Were Not," *Wall Street Journal*, March 15, 1994, B1.

marketing can be short-lived in highly competitive markets where any successful innovation is almost sure to be copied by competitors. Thus, the value creation process for marketers and advertisers is continuous; STP marketing must be pursued over and over again and may be supplemented with product differentiation strategies.

Virtually every organization must compete for the attention and business of some customer groups while de-emphasizing or ignoring others. In this chapter we will examine in detail the way organizations decide whom to target and whom to ignore in laying the foundation for their marketing programs and advertising campaigns. The critical role of advertising campaigns in executing these strategies is also highlighted.

2 Identifying Target Segments.

The first step in STP marketing involves breaking down large, heterogeneous markets into more manageable submarkets or customer segments. This activity is known as **market segmentation.** It can be accomplished in many ways, but keep in mind that advertisers need to identify a segment with common characteristics that will lead the members of that segment to respond distinctively to a marketing program. For a segment to be really useful, advertisers also must be able to reach that segment with information about the product. Typically this means that advertisers must be able to identify media the segment uses that will allow them to get an advertising message to the segment. For example, teenage males can be reached efficiently through media such as MTV; selected rap, contemporary rock-and-roll, or alternative radio stations; and the Internet. As described in the E-Commerce box on page 216, one of the most appealing aspects of the Internet for advertisers is the way it allows them to reach increasingly diverse target segments.

In this section we will review several ways that consumer markets are commonly segmented. Markets can be segmented on the basis of usage patterns and commitment levels, demographic and geographic information, psychographics and lifestyles, or benefits sought. Many times, segmentation schemes evolve in such a way that multiple variables are used to identify and describe the target segment. Such an outcome is desirable because more knowledge about the target will usually translate into better marketing and advertising programs.

Usage Patterns and Commitment Levels.

One of the most common ways to segment markets is by consumers' usage patterns or commitment levels. With respect to usage patterns, it is important to recognize that for most products and services, some users will purchase much more frequently than others. It is common to find that **heavy users** in a category account for the majority of a product's sales and thus become the preferred or primary target segment. For example, Campbell Soup Company has discovered what it refers to as its extra-enthusiastic core users: folks who buy nearly 320 cans of soup per year.[8] That's enough soup to serve Campbell's at least six days a week every week. To maintain this level of devotion to the product, standard marketing thought holds that it is in Campbell's best interest to know these heavy users in great detail and make them a focal point of the company's marketing strategy.

While being the standard wisdom, the heavy-user focus has some potential downsides. For one, devoted users may need no encouragement at all to keep consuming. In addition, a heavy-user focus takes attention and resources away from those who do need encouragement to purchase the marketer's brand. Perhaps most important, heavy users may be significantly different in terms of their motivations to consume, their approach to the product, or their image of the product.

8. Rebecca Piirto, *Beyond Mind Games: The Marketing Power of Psychographics* (Ithaca, N.Y.: American Demographics Books, 1991), 230.

Another segmentation option combines prior usage patterns with commitment levels to identify four fundamental segment types—brand-loyal customers, switchers (or variety seekers), nonusers, and emergent consumers.[9] Each segment represents a unique opportunity for the advertiser. **Nonusers** offer the lowest level of opportunity relative to the other three groups. **Brand-loyal users** are a tremendous asset if they are the advertiser's customers, but they are difficult to convert if they are loyal to a competitor.

Switchers, or **variety seekers,** often buy what is on sale or choose brands that offer discount coupons or other price incentives. Whether they are pursued through price incentives, high-profile advertising campaigns, or both, switchers turn out to be a costly target segment. Much can be spent in getting their business merely to have it disappear just as quickly as it was won.

Emergent consumers, however, offer the organization an important business opportunity. In most product categories, there is a gradual but constant influx of first-time buyers. The reasons for this influx vary by product category and include purchase triggers such as puberty, college graduation, marriage, birth of a child, divorce, job promotions, and retirement. Immigration can also be a source of numerous new customers for many product categories. Generation X has attracted the attention of marketers and advertisers because it is a large group of emergent adult consumers. But inevitably, Generation X will lose its emergent status and be replaced by a new age cohort—you guessed it, Generation Y—who will take their turn as advertisers' darlings.[10]

Emergent consumers are motivated by many different factors, but they share one important characteristic: Their brand preferences are still under development. Targeting emergents with messages that fit their age or social circumstances may produce modest effects in the short run, but it eventually may yield a brand loyalty that pays handsome rewards for the discerning organization. Of course, this was part of Gillette's rationale in targeting youthful females. As another example, banks actively recruit college students who have limited financial resources in the short term, but excellent potential as long-

E-COMMERCE

Diversity Comes to the Digital World

Now that Internet access is diffusing broadly throughout many countries, it would be a mistake to hold on to the old cliché that WWW stands for "World White Web." Yes, a digital divide remains. That is, there is a gap between technology haves and have-nots, and those on the "haves" side are disproportionately Caucasian. But in the United States, Internet access is expanding rapidly across all segments of society, and if projections for what's to come are realized, the Web will only become more useful as a tool for reaching ethnically diverse audiences. For example, according to New York's eMarketer, African-American, Latino, and Asian-American households spent $5.7 billion shopping online in 2000, and will spend $24.5 billion by 2004, an increase of 330 percent! Jupiter research estimates that by 2005, Internet use among African-American and Latino households will rival that for white households, and Asian-Americans will surpass all groups, with 84 percent of their households projected to have access to the World Wide Web.

Already, some astute marketers have come to appreciate the power of the Web for reaching diverse audiences. Whom do we find on the cutting edge of this Web application? You probably never would have guessed the U.S. Army. Or perhaps you would, since they may have already contacted you. Col. Rodney Davis, director of marketing and public affairs for the Army ROTC, is already a heavy user of the Web. In his estimation, "We want to reach the entire ethnic spectrum. The Web is a cost-effective way to target all groups." In 2001 Davis committed about 6 percent of his advertising budget to online initiatives, with a majority of those dollars being directed at programs to appeal to minorities. Davis sees a larger and larger share of his budget being allocated to Internet marketing over time. He plans to stay on the cutting edge when it comes to use of the Internet for reaching his target audiences, and offers this advice: "Clearly, if you're marketing in this day and time, you've got to use the Web, particularly when you consider the demographic trends online." Avoid cliché, know the facts, and like Colonel Davis, you may become an advocate for reaching customers in the digital world.

Source: Evantheia Schibsted, "Creating the Digital Dividend," *Business 2.0,* March 6, 2001, 60–63.

9. Further discussion of this four-way scheme is provided by David W. Stewart, "Advertising in Slow-Growth Economies," *American Demographics* (September 1994), 40–46.
10. Bonnie Tsui, "Generation Next," *Advertising Age,* January 15, 2001, 14, 16.

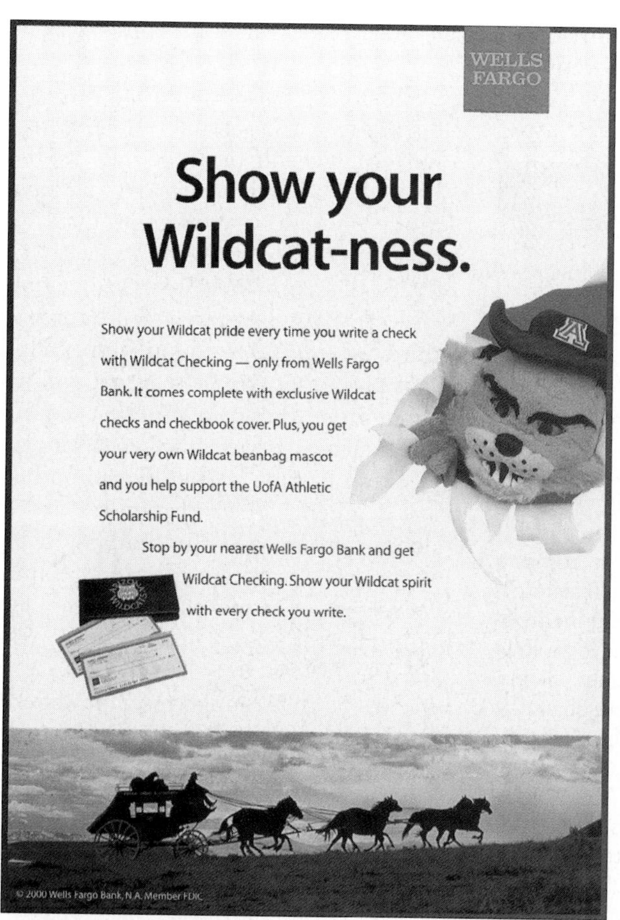

EXHIBIT 6.7

Emergent consumers represent an important source of long-term opportunity for many organizations. Have you ever thought of yourself as an emergent consumer?
www.wellsfargo.com

term customers. Exhibit 6.7 shows an ad from Wells Fargo Bank with an appeal to emergent consumers at the University of Arizona.

Demographic Segmentation. **Demographic segmentation** is widely used in selecting target segments and includes basic descriptors such as age, gender, race, marital status, income, education, and occupation. Demographic information has special value in market segmentation because if an advertiser knows the demographic characteristics of the target segment, choosing media to efficiently reach that segment is much easier.

Demographic information has two specific applications. First, demographics are commonly used to describe or profile segments that have been identified with some other variable. If an organization had first segmented its market in terms of product usage rates, the next step would be to describe or profile its heavy users in terms of demographic characteristics such as age or income. In fact, one of the most common approaches for identifying target segments is to combine information about usage patterns with demographics.

Mobil Oil Corporation used such an approach in segmenting the market for gasoline buyers and identified five basic segments: Road Warriors, True Blues, Generation F3, Homebodies, and Price Shoppers.[11] Extensive research on more than 2,000 motorists revealed considerable insight about these five segments. At the one extreme, Road Warriors spend at least $1,200 per year at gas stations; they buy premium gasoline and snacks and beverages and sometimes opt for a car wash. Road Warriors are generally more affluent, middle-aged males who drive 25,000 to 50,000 miles per year. (Note how Mobil combined information about usage patterns with demographics to provide a detailed picture of the segment.) In contrast, Price Shoppers spend no more than $700 annually at gas stations, are generally less affluent, rarely buy premium, and show no loyalty to particular brands or stations. In terms of relative segment sizes, there are about 25 percent more Price Shoppers on the highways than Road Warriors. If you were the marketing vice president at Mobil, which of these two segments would you target? Think about it for a few pages—we'll get back to you.

Second, demographic categories are used frequently as the starting point in market segmentation. This was the case in the Gillette example, where teenage females turned out to be the segment of interest. Demographics will also be a major consideration in the travel industry, where families with young children are often the marketer's primary target. To boost tourism, the Bahamian government launched a program in 2001 to attract families to their island paradise. But instead of reaching out to mom and dad, Bahamian officials made their appeal to kids by targeting the 2-to-11-year-old viewing audience of Nickelodeon's cable television channel.[12] Marketing to and through children is always complex, and as we saw in Chapter 4, is often

11. Allanna Sullivan, "Mobil Bets Drivers Pick Cappuccino over Low Prices," *Wall Street Journal,* January 30, 1995, B1.
12. Sally Beatty, "Nickelodeon Sets $30 Million Ad Deal with the Bahamas," *Wall Street Journal,* March 14, 2001, B6.

controversial as well. The IBP box on this page offers some guidelines for approaching young consumers in a professional manner.

Another demographic group that will receive increasing attention from advertisers in the years to come is the "woopies," or well-off older people. In the United States, consumers over 50 have more discretionary income than all other age segments combined. By 2025, the number of people over 50 will grow by 80 percent to become a third of the U.S. population. This growth in the woopie segment will be even more dramatic in other countries, such as Japan and the nations of Western Europe.[13] Still, like any other age segment, older consumers are a diverse group, and the temptation to stereotype must be resisted. Some marketers advocate partitioning older consumers into groups aged 50–64, 65–74, 75–84, and 85 or older, as a means of reflecting important differences in needs. Still, more thorough knowledge of this population is clearly needed.

IBP

Take Special Care with Promotions to Kids

Kids' discretionary income grows as societies become more affluent. Kids also exert significant influence in purchasing decisions made by moms, dads, grandmas, grandpas, aunts and uncles, and so forth and so on. When you add it all up, kids either control or influence the expenditure of hundreds of billions of dollars every year. So it is logical that in many instances, tykes, tweens, and/or teens are identified as primary target markets for planning special promotions. When targeting kids for special promotions, here are three good principles to live by.

- *Play by their tools.* When targeting a generation that takes computers, high-tech video games, and the Internet for granted, marketers must learn how to play by their tools. This will usually mean incorporating the Internet as part of the promotion. For example, even a low-tech baseball card giveaway can be moved to the Internet. Skippy peanut butter developed such a promotion featuring its baseball star spokesperson—Derek Jeter of the New York Yankees. Skippy jar tops directed kids to peanutbutter.com, where they entered "the secret code" to receive downloadable cards known as Digibles. These digital baseball cards provided both sound and video featuring baseball's MVP.
- *Treat them like family.* When moving your promotions to the Internet, privacy should always be a concern, and this goes double for promotions to kids. We encourage you to respect young consumers' privacy because it is the right thing to do, and because there are numerous laws that require it. The Children's Online Privacy Protection Act (COPPA), which is enforced by the FTC, restricts kid-focused Web sites in the areas of data collection, spamming, sweepstakes, and contests. According to Susan Bennett, director of promotions for foxkids.com, "If you're in the kids marketplace, you better know what COPPA is."
- *Look for the high road.* Something really cool is happening among young people. Kids are less likely to be ridiculed by their peers for being interested in learning about math, science, reading, and especially the environment and all living things. In other words, it's hip to be smart. Thus, educationally themed promotions are increasingly common among kids' brands, and there are abundant opportunities to build on the premise of engaging kids through participative learning. For instance, in the case of the Bahamas' campaign directed at kids and their families, a featured element was learning about a coral reef in the Bahamas and identifying actions that children can take to help protect endangered waterways. Giveaways are nice, but don't forget to look for the high road.

Sources: John Palmer, "Connecting to Kids," *PROMO Magazine*, March 2001, 21–33; and Sally Beatty, "Nickelodeon Sets $30 Million Ad Deal with the Bahamas," *Wall Street Journal*, March 14, 2001, B6.

Geographic Segmentation.

Geographic segmentation needs little explanation other than to emphasize how useful geography is in segmenting markets. Geographic segmentation may be conducted within a country by region (for example, the Pacific Northwest versus New England in the United States), by state or province, by city, or even by neighborhood. Climate and topographical features yield dramatic differences in consumption by region for products such as snow tires and surfboards, but geography can also correlate with other differences that are not so obvious. Eating and food preparation habits, entertainment preferences, recreational activities, and other aspects of lifestyle have been shown to vary along geographic lines. Exhibits 6.8 and 6.9 show U.S. consumption patterns for Twinkies and for Obsession versus Old Spice. As you can see, where one lives does seem to affect preferences.

13. "The Rich Autumn of a Consumer's Life," *The Economist*, September 5, 1992, 67–68.

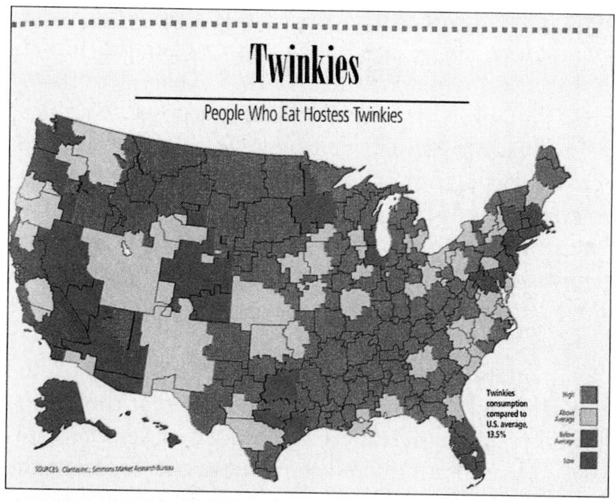

EXHIBIT 6.8

People who eat Hostess Twinkies.

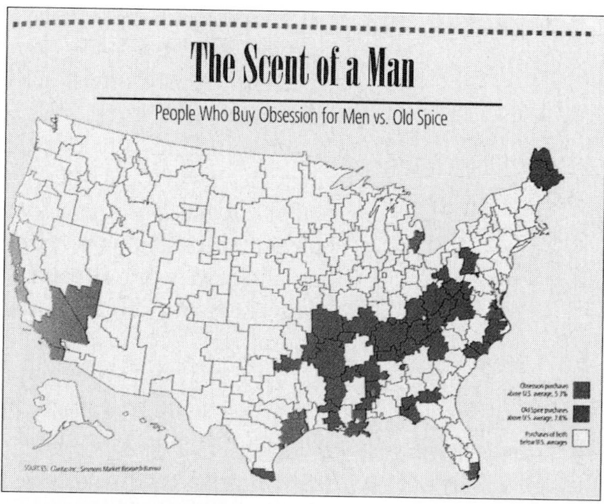

EXHIBIT 6.9

People who buy Obsession for Men versus Old Spice.

In recent years, skillful marketers have merged information on where people live with the U.S. Census Bureau's demographic data to produce a form of market segmentation known as geodemographic segmentation. **Geodemographic segmentation** identifies neighborhoods (by ZIP codes) around the country that share common demographic characteristics. One such system, known as PRIZM (potential rating index by ZIP marketing), identifies 62 market segments that encompass all the ZIP codes in the United States.[14] Each of these segments has similar lifestyle characteristics and can be found throughout the country.

For example, the American Dreams segment is found in many metropolitan neighborhoods and comprises upwardly mobile ethnic minorities, many of whom were foreign-born. This segment's product preferences are different from those of people belonging to the Rural Industria segment, who are young families with one or both parents working at low-wage jobs in small-town America. Systems such as PRIZM are very popular because of the depth of segment description they provide, along with their ability to precisely identify where the segment can be found.

Given PRIZM's success, it was logical to expect the same methods and technology to be applied on an international scale, and Experian, based in Nottingham, England, and Orange, California, has done just that.[15] Experian has developed a geodemographic segmentation system for 18 countries (accounting for about 800 million consumers), including most of Western Europe, Australia and New Zealand, Japan, South Africa, and the United States. Such a system can prove very powerful for marketers with global aspirations, because it can tell them whether the segment they are pursuing in one country also exists in others. When a common customer segment exists in many countries (for example, middle-income, urban office workers), one marketing and advertising campaign can sometimes be used to appeal to them across national borders. Expect these systems to grow in popularity as the tools and technology spread around the world.

14. Christina Del Valle, "They Know Where You Live—and How You Buy," *Business Week,* February 7, 1994, 89; Amy Merrick, "Counting on the Census," *Wall Street Journal,* February 14, 2001, B1.

15. Susan Mitchell, "Parallel Universes," *Marketing Tools,* November/December 1997, 14–17.

Psychographics and Lifestyle Segmentation. **Psychographics** is a term that advertisers created in the mid-1960s to refer to a form of research that emphasizes the understanding of consumers' activities, interests, and opinions (AIOs).[16] Many advertising agencies were using demographic variables for segmentation purposes, but they wanted insights into consumers' motivations, which demographic variables did not provide. Psychographics were created as a tool to supplement the use of demographic data. Because a focus on consumers' activities, interests, and opinions often produces insights into differences in the lifestyles of various segments, this approach usually results in a **lifestyle segmentation.** Knowing details about the lifestyle of a target segment can be valuable for creating advertising messages that ring true to the consumer.

Lifestyle, or psychographic, segmentation can be customized with a focus on the issues germane to a single product category, or it may be pursued so that the resulting segments have general applicability to many different product or service categories. An example of the former is research conducted for Pillsbury to segment the eating habits of American households.[17] This "What's Cookin'" study involved consumer interviews with more than 3,000 people and identified five segments of the population, based on their shared eating styles:

- *Chase & Grabbits,* at 26 percent of the population, are heavy users of all forms of fast food. These are people who can make a meal out of microwave popcorn; as long as the popcorn keeps hunger at bay and is convenient, this segment is happy with its meal.
- *Functional Feeders,* at 18 percent of the population, are a bit older than the Chase & Grabbits but no less convenience-oriented. Since they are more likely to have families, their preferences for convenient foods involve frozen products that are quickly prepared at home. They constantly seek faster ways to prepare the traditional foods they grew up with.
- *Down-Home Stokers,* at 21 percent of the population, involve blue-collar households with modest incomes. They are very loyal to their regional diets, such as meat and potatoes in the Midwest versus clam chowder in New England. Fried chicken, biscuits and gravy, and bacon and eggs make this segment the champion of cholesterol.
- *Careful Cooks,* at 20 percent of the population, are more prevalent on the West Coast. They have replaced most of the red meat in their diet with pastas, fish, skinless chicken, and mounds of fresh fruit and vegetables. They believe they are knowledgeable about nutritional issues and are willing to experiment with foods that offer healthful options.
- *Happy Cookers* are the remaining 15 percent of the population but are a shrinking segment. These cooks are family-oriented and take substantial satisfaction from preparing a complete homemade meal for the family. Young mothers in this segment are aware of nutritional issues but will bend the rules with homemade meat dishes, casseroles, pies, cakes, and cookies.

Even these abbreviated descriptions of Pillsbury's five psychographic segments should make it clear that very different marketing and advertising programs are called for to appeal to each group. Exhibits 6.10 and 6.11 show ads from Pillsbury. Which segments are these ads targeting?

As noted, lifestyle segmentation studies can also be pursued with no particular product category as a focus, and the resulting segments could prove useful for many different marketers. A notable example of this approach is the VALS™ (for values and lifestyles) system developed by SRI International and marketed by SRI Consult-

16. Pirto, *Beyond Mind Games,* 21–23.
17. Ibid., 222–23.

e-SIGHTINGS

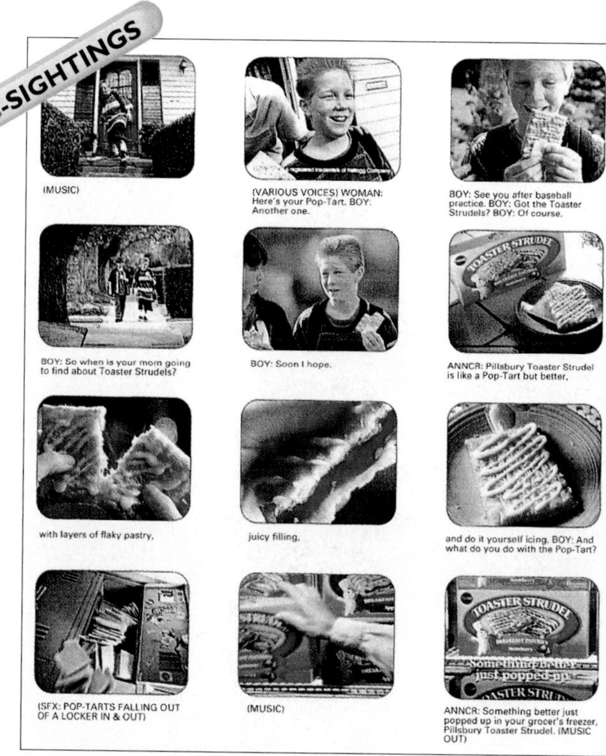

EXHIBIT 6.10

Which lifestyle segment is Pillsbury targeting with this ad? It looks like a toss-up between Chase & Grabbits and Functional Feeders. Does Pillsbury's site (www.pillsbury.com) *target the same lifestyle segment as the ads? What features at the site are designed to build customer loyalty? Based on the site's message and design, what lifestyle choices does Pillsbury seem to assume that its target segment has made?*

EXHIBIT 6.11

The convenience-oriented Functional Feeders seem the natural target for this novel ad. That Pillsbury Doughboy sure gets around!
www.pillsbury.com

ing Business Intelligence of Menlo Park, California.[18] The VALS™ framework was first introduced in 1978 with nine potential segments, but in recent years it has been revised as VALS 2 with eight market segments.

As shown in Exhibit 6.12, these segments are organized in terms of resources (which includes age, income, and education) and personal orientation. For instance, the Experiencer is relatively affluent and action-oriented. This enthusiastic and risk-taking group has yet to establish predictable behavioral patterns. Its members look to sports, recreation, exercise, and social activities as outlets for their abundant energy. SRI Consulting Business Intelligence sells detailed information and marketing recommendations about the eight segments to a variety of marketing organizations.

Benefit Segmentation. Another segmentation approach developed by advertising researchers and used extensively over the past 30 years is **benefit segmentation.** In benefit segmentation, target segments are delineated by the various benefit packages that different consumers want from the same product category. For instance, different people want different benefits from their automobiles. Some consumers want efficient and reliable transportation; others want speed, excitement, and glamour; and still others want luxury, comfort, and prestige. One product could not possibly serve

18. Ibid.; see Chapters 3, 5, and 8 for an extensive discussion of the VALS system.

EXHIBIT 6.12

The eight VALS™ segments. www.sri.com

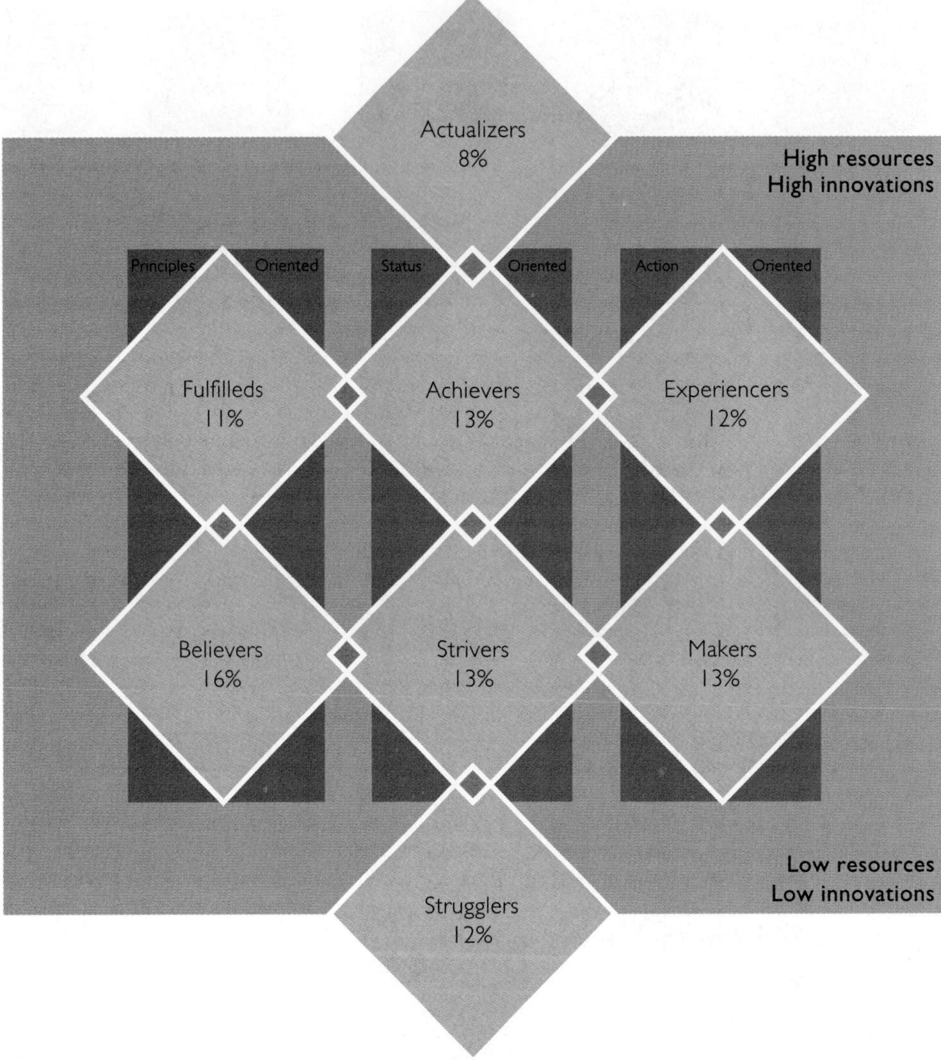

Source: SRI Consulting Business Intelligence. All rights reserved. © 2001.

such diverse benefit segments. Exhibits 6.13 and 6.14 show two car ads that are appealing to very different benefit segments.

This notion of attempting to understand consumers' priorities and assess how different brands might perform based on criteria deemed important by various segments should have a familiar ring. If not, turn back to Chapter 5 and revisit our discussion of multi-attribute attitude models (MAAMs). The importance weights collected from individual consumers in MAAMs research often provide the raw material needed for identifying benefit segments.

Segmenting Business-to-Business Markets. Thus far, our discussion of segmentation options has focused on ways to segment **consumer markets.** Consumer markets are the markets for products and services purchased by individuals or households to satisfy their specific needs. Consumer marketing is often compared and contrasted with business-to-business marketing. **Business markets** are the institutional buyers who purchase items to be used in other products and services or to be resold to other businesses or households. Although advertising is more prevalent in consumer markets, products and services such as fax machines, wireless phones, Web hosting, and

EXHIBIT 6.13

Benefit segmentation really comes to life in the automobile market. Honda's distinctive package of benefits includes its designation by the Union of Concerned Scientists as the cleanest car company in the world. www.honda.com

EXHIBIT 6.14

Included in the package of benefits of the Sebring LXi Convertible is the chance to enjoy all that clean air that Honda drivers leave behind. www.chrysler.com

a wide array of consulting and package-delivery services (see Exhibits 6.15 and 6.16) are commonly promoted to business customers. Hence, segmentation strategies are also valuable for business-to-business marketers.

Business markets can be segmented using several of the options already discussed.[19] For example, business customers differ in their usage rates and geographic locations, so these variables may be productive bases for segmenting business markets. Additionally, one of the most common approaches uses the Standard Industrial Classification (SIC) codes prepared by the U.S. Census Bureau. SIC information is helpful for identifying categories of businesses and then pinpointing the precise locations of these organizations.

Some of the more sophisticated segmentation methods used by firms that market to individual consumers do not translate well to business markets.[20] For instance, rarely would there be a place for psychographic or lifestyle segmentation in the business-to-business setting. In business markets, advertisers fall back on simpler strategies that are easier to work with from the perspective of the sales force. Segmentation by a potential customer's stage in the purchase process is one such strategy. It turns out that first-time prospects, novices, and sophisticates want very different packages of benefits

19. Kotler, *Marketing Management,* 278.

20. Thomas S. Robertson and Howard Barich, "A Successful Approach to Segmenting Industrial Markets," *Planning Forum* (November/December 1992), 5–11.

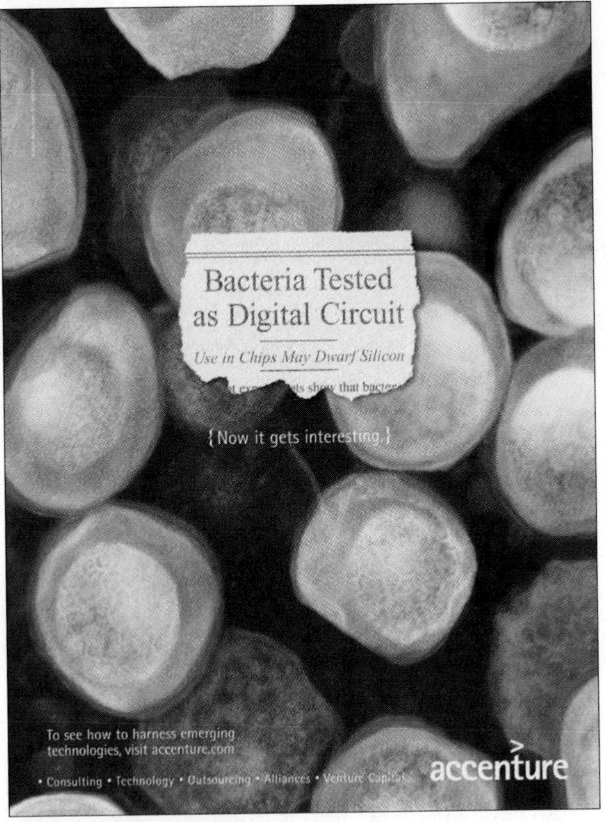

EXHIBIT 6.15

Here we see Accenture (formerly Andersen Consulting) touting its expertise in the emerging field of biotech. www.accenture.com

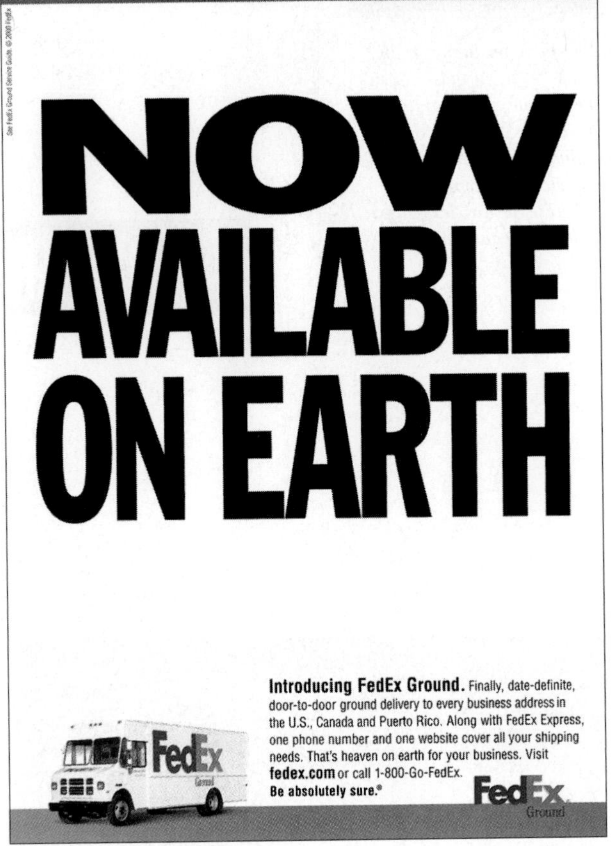

EXHIBIT 6.16

If you have a package that needs to be there on time, FedEx has always been a good choice. FedEx Ground promises date-definite, door-to-door delivery to any and all business addresses in the United States, Canada, and Puerto Rico. fedex.com

from their vendors, and thus they should be targeted separately in advertising and sales programs.

3 Prioritizing Target Segments.

Whether it is done through usage patterns, demographic characteristics, geographic location, benefit packages, or any combination of options, segmenting markets typically yields a mix of segments that vary in their attractiveness to the advertiser. In pursuing STP marketing, the advertiser must get beyond this potentially confusing mixture of segments to a selected subset that will become the target for its marketing and advertising programs. Recall the example of Mobil Oil Corporation and the segments of gasoline buyers it identified via usage patterns and demographic descriptors. What criteria should Mobil use to help decide between Road Warriors and Price Shoppers as possible targets?

Perhaps the most fundamental criteria in segment selection revolve around what the members of the segment want versus the organization's ability to provide it. Every organization has distinctive strengths and weaknesses that must be acknowledged when choosing its target segment. The organization may be particularly strong in some aspect of manufacturing, like Gillette, which has particular expertise in mass production of intricate plastic and metal products. Or perhaps its strength lies in well-trained and loyal service personnel, like those at FedEx, who can effectively implement new service programs initiated for customers, such as next-day delivery "absolutely, positively by 10:30 A.M." To serve a target segment, an organization may have to commit substantial resources to acquire or develop the capabilities to provide what that segment wants. If the price tag for these new capabilities is too high, the organization must find another segment.

Another major consideration in segment selection entails the size and growth potential of the segment. Segment size is a function of the number of people, households, or institutions in the segment, plus their willingness to spend in the product category. When assessing size, advertisers must keep in mind that the number of people in a segment of heavy users may be relatively small, but the extraordinary usage rates of these consumers can more than make up for their small numbers. In addition, it is not enough to simply assess a segment's size as of today. Segments are dynamic, and it is common to find marketers most interested in devoting resources to segments projected for dramatic growth. As we have already seen, the purchasing power and growth projections for people age 50 and older have made this a segment that many companies are targeting.

So does bigger always mean better when choosing target segments? The answer is a function of the third major criterion for segment selection. In choosing a target segment, an advertiser must also look at the **competitive field**—companies that compete for the segment's business—and then decide whether it has a particular expertise, or perhaps just a bigger budget, that would allow it to serve the segment more effectively.

When an advertiser factors in the competitive field, it often turns out that smaller is better when selecting target segments. Almost by definition, large segments are usually established segments that many companies have identified and targeted previously. Trying to enter the competitive field in a mature segment isn't easy because established competitors can be expected to respond aggressively with advertising campaigns or price promotions in an effort to repel any newcomer.

Alternatively, large segments may simply be poorly defined segments; that is, a large segment may need to be broken down into smaller categories before a company can understand consumers' needs well enough to serve them effectively. Again, the segment of older consumers—age 50 and older—is huge, but in most instances it would simply be too big to be valuable as a target. Too much diversity exists in the needs and preferences of this age group, so further segmentation based on other demographic variables, or perhaps via psychographics, is called for before an appropriate target can be located.

The smaller-is-better principle has become so popular in choosing target segments that it is now referred to as niche marketing. A market niche is a relatively small group of consumers who have a unique set of needs and who typically are willing to pay a premium price to the firm that specializes in meeting those needs.[21] The small size of a **market niche** often means it would not be profitable for more than one organization to serve it. Thus, when a firm identifies and develops products for market niches, the threat of competitors developing imitative products to attack the niche is reduced. Exhibit 6.17 is an example of an ad directed toward a very small niche, those who prefer imported Russian tubes for their high-end tube stereo amplifiers.

Niche marketing will continue to grow in popularity as the mass media splinter into a more and more complex and narrowly defined array of specialized vehicles. Specialized programming—such as the Health & Fitness Channel, the Cooking

21. Kotler, *Marketing Management,* 267.

EXHIBIT 6.17

Niche marketers are usually able to charge a premium price for their distinctive products. If you decide to go with Svetlana the next time you are buying amplifier tubes, expect to pay a little extra. www.svetlana.com

Channel, or the 24-hour Golf Channel—attracts small and very distinctive groups of consumers, providing advertisers with an efficient way to communicate with market niches.[22] Additionally, perhaps the ideal application of the Internet as a marketing tool is in identifying and accessing market niches.[23]

But now let's return to the question faced by Mobil Oil Corporation. Whom should it target—Road Warriors or Price Shoppers? Hopefully you will see this as a straightforward decision. Road Warriors are a more attractive segment in terms of both segment size and growth potential. Although there are more Price Shoppers in terms of sheer numbers, Road Warriors spend more at the gas station, making them the larger segment from the standpoint of revenue generation. Road Warriors are much more prone to buy those little extras, such as a sandwich and a car wash, that could be extremely profitable sources of new business. Mobil also came to the conclusion that too many of its competitors were already targeting Price Shoppers. Mobil thus selected Road Warriors as its target segment and developed a positioning strategy it referred to as "Friendly Serve." Gas prices went up at Mobil stations, but Mobil also committed new resources to improving all aspects of the gas-purchasing experience.[24] Cleaner restrooms and better lighting alone yielded sales gains between 2 percent and 5 percent. Next, more attendants were hired to run between the pump and the snack bar to get Road Warriors in and out quickly—complete with their sandwich and beverage. Early results indicated that helpful attendants boosted station sales by another 15 to 20 percent. The Mobil case is a good example of how the application of STP marketing can rejuvenate sales, even in a mundane product category such as gasoline.

4 Formulating the Positioning Strategy.

Now that we have discussed the ways markets are segmented and the criteria used for selecting specific target segments, we turn our attention to positioning strategy. If a firm has been careful in segmenting the market and selecting its targets, then a positioning strategy—such as Mobil's "Friendly Serve" or Gillette's "The Best a Man Can Get"—should occur naturally. In addition, as an aspect of positioning strategy, we will begin to entertain ideas about how a firm can best communicate to the target segment what it has to offer. This is where advertising plays its vital role. A positioning strategy will include particular ideas or themes that must be communicated effectively if the marketing program is to be successful.

22. Patricia Sellers, "The Best Way to Reach Your Buyers," *Fortune,* Autumn/Winter 1993, 14–17.
23. Heather Green, "How to Reach John Q. Public," *Business Week,* March 26, 2001, 132, 133.
24. Chad Rubel, "Quality Makes a Comeback," *Marketing News,* September 23, 1996, 10.

Essentials for Effective Positioning Strategies. Any sound positioning strategy includes several essential elements. Effective positioning strategies are based on meaningful commitments of organizational resources to produce substantive value for the target segment. They also are consistent internally and over time, and they feature simple and distinctive themes. Each of these essential elements is described and illustrated in this section.

Let's begin with the issue of substance. For a positioning strategy to be effective and remain effective over time, the organization must be committed to creating substantive value for the customer. Take the example of Mobil Oil Corporation and its target segment, the Road Warriors. Road Warriors are willing to pay a little more for gas if it comes with extras such as prompt service or fresh coffee. So Mobil must create an ad campaign that depicts its employees as the brightest, friendliest, most helpful people you'd ever want to meet. The company asks its ad agency to come up with a catchy jingle that will remind people about the great services they can expect at a Mobil station. It spends millions of dollars running these ads over and over and wins the enduring loyalty of the Road Warriors. Right? Well, maybe, and maybe not. Certainly, a new ad campaign will have to be created to make Road Warriors aware of what the company has to offer, but it all falls apart if they drive in with great expectations and the company's people do not live up to them.

Effective positioning begins with substance. In the case of Mobil's "Friendly Serve" strategy, this means keeping restrooms attractive and clean, adding better lighting to all areas of the station, and upgrading the quality of the snacks and beverages available in each station's convenience store. It also means hiring more attendants, outfitting them in blue pants, blue shirts, ties, and black Reeboks, and then training and motivating them to anticipate and fulfill the needs of the harried Road Warrior.[25] Effecting meaningful change in service levels at its 8,000 stations nationwide is an expensive and time-consuming process for Mobil, but without some substantive change, there can be no hope of retaining the Road Warrior's lucrative business.

A positioning strategy also must be consistent internally and consistent over time. Regarding internal consistency, everything must work in combination to reinforce a distinct perception in the consumer's eyes about what a brand stands for. If we have chosen to position our airline as the one that will be known for on-time reliability, then we certainly would invest in things like extensive preventive maintenance and state-of-the-art baggage-handling facilities. There would be no need for exclusive airport lounges as part of this strategy, nor would any special emphasis need to be placed on in-flight food and beverage services. If our target segment wants reliable transportation, then this and only this should be the obsession in running our airline. This particular obsession has made Southwest Airlines a very formidable competitor, even against much larger airlines, as it has expanded its routes to different regions of the United States.[26]

A strategy also needs consistency over time. As we saw in Chapter 5, consumers have perceptual defenses that allow them to screen or ignore most of the ad messages they are exposed to. Breaking through the clutter and establishing what a brand stands for is a tremendous challenge for any advertiser, but it is a challenge made easier by consistent positioning. If year in and year out an advertiser communicates the same basic themes to the target segment, then the message may get through and shape the way consumers perceive the brand. An example of a consistent approach is the long-running "Good Neighbor" ads of State Farm Insurance. While the specific copy changes, the thematic core of the campaign does not change. Exhibit 6.18 shows a contemporary ad from this long-running campaign.

25. Ibid.
26. Scott McCartney, "Southwest Airlines Lands Plenty of Florida Passengers," *Wall Street Journal,* November 11, 1997, B4.

e-SIGHTINGS

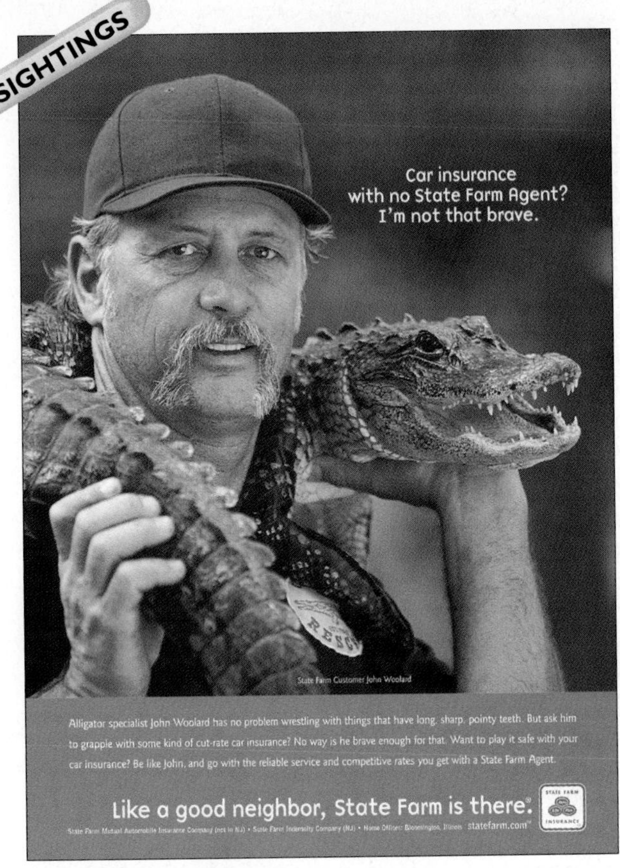

EXHIBIT 6.18

Consistency is a definite virtue in choosing and executing a positioning strategy. State Farm's "Good Neighbor" theme has been a hallmark of its advertising for many years. Does State Farm's site (www.statefarm.com) produce substantive value for its target segment? How? What simple and distinctive themes can you find? Why are these elements essential to State Farm's positioning strategy?

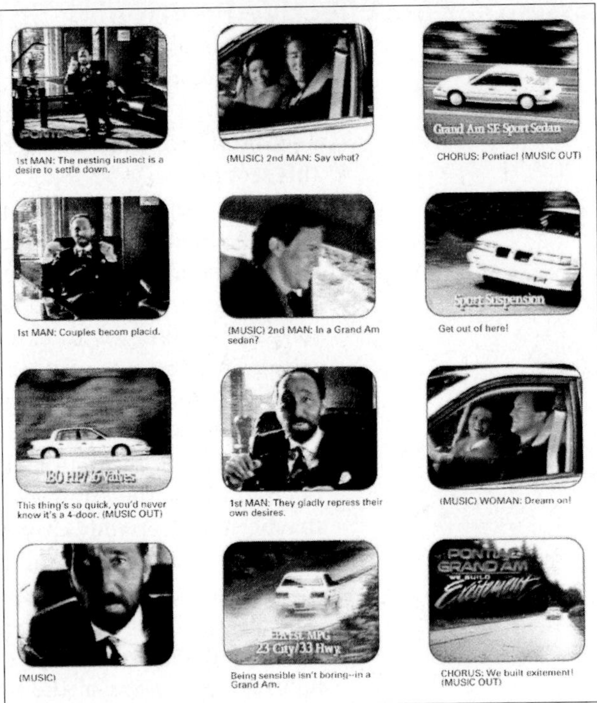

EXHIBIT 6.19

"We Build Excitement" is a perfect example of a single-benefit positioning theme. Pontiac has used this theme, with recent adaptations (for example, "We Are Driving Excitement"), for nearly two decades. www.pontiac.com

Finally, there is the matter of simplicity and distinctiveness. Simplicity and distinctiveness are essential to the advertising task. No matter how much substance has been built into a product, it will fail in the marketplace if the consumer doesn't perceive what the product can do. Keep in mind, in a world of harried consumers who can be expected to ignore, distort, or completely forget most of the ads they are exposed to, complicated, imitative messages simply have no chance of getting through. The basic premise of a positioning strategy must be simple and distinctive if it is to be communicated effectively to the target segment.

The value of simplicity and distinctiveness in positioning strategy is nicely illustrated by the success of GM's Pontiac division starting in the mid-1980s. This was a period when Japanese automakers were taking market share from their U.S. counterparts, and no American car company was being hit harder than General Motors. Pontiac, however, grew its market share in this period with a positioning strategy that involved a return to Pontiac's heritage from the 1960s as a performance car.[27] Pontiac's positioning strategy, which was communicated with a relentless barrage of advertisements like that shown in Exhibit 6.19, was "We Build Excitement."

27. Paul Ingrassia, "Pontiac Revives 'Sporty' Image, Setting a Marketing Example for Other GM Units," *Wall Street Journal,* August 15, 1986, 13.

This was certainly a distinctive claim relative to GM's other stodgy divisions of the mid-1980s, and its beauty was its simplicity. Pontiac's Grand Am featured distinctive styling and mechanics that furnished the substance to support its advertising claim, which in a more recent variation was articulated as "*Grand Am—Excitement Well Built.*" In 2001, the Pontiac division celebrated its 75th birthday around the theme "*Excitement Matters,*" and to commemorate the occasion, offered excitement that really matters in the form of cash-back deals on popular Grand Am models. Pontiac's relentless commitment to the "excitement mentality" over the past two decades is precisely the kind of commitment that gets your message across in an increasingly cluttered marketplace. Indeed, in this Pontiac positioning strategy we see substance, consistency, simplicity, and distinctiveness—all the essential elements for effective positioning.

Fundamental Positioning Themes. Positioning themes that are simple and distinctive help an organization make internal decisions that yield substantive value for customers, and they assist in the development of focused ad campaigns to break through the clutter of competitors' advertising. Thus, choosing a viable positioning theme is one of the most important decisions faced by marketers and advertisers. In many ways, the *raison d'être* for STP marketing is to generate viable positioning themes.

Positioning themes take many forms, and like any other aspect of marketing and advertising, they can benefit from creative breakthroughs. Yet while novelty and creativity are valued in developing positioning themes, some basic principles should be considered when selecting a theme. Whenever possible, it is helpful if the organization can settle on a single premise—such as "Good Neighbor" or "We Build Excitement" or "Friendly Serve" or "Gillette for Women: Are You Ready?"—to reflect its positioning strategy.[28] In addition, three fundamental options should always be considered in selecting a positioning theme: benefit positioning, user positioning, and competitive positioning.[29]

"We Build Excitement" and "Friendly Serve" are examples of **benefit positioning.** Notice in these premises that a distinctive customer benefit is featured. This single-benefit focus is the first option that should be considered when formulating a positioning strategy. As we saw in Chapter 5, consumers purchase products to derive functional, emotional, or self-expressive benefits, so an emphasis on the primary benefit they can expect to receive from a brand is fundamental. While it might seem that more compelling positioning themes would result from promising consumers a wide array of benefits, keep in mind that multiple-benefit strategies are hard to implement. Not only will they send mixed signals within an organization about what a brand stands for, but they will also place a great burden on advertising. Exhibit 6.20 shows an ad that executes a functional benefit positioning: Here the benefit is simply the capacity to create.

Functional benefits are the place to start in selecting a positioning theme, but in many mature product categories, the functional benefits provided by the various brands in the competitive field are essentially the same. In these instances the organization may turn to emotion in an effort to distinguish its brand. Emotional benefit positioning may involve a promise of exhilaration, like "Exciting Armpits," per Exhibit 6.21, or may feature a way to avoid negative feelings—such as the embarrassment felt in social settings due to bad breath, dandruff, or, as we see in Exhibit 6.22, those ghastly metal braces.

28. A more elaborate case for the importance of a single, consistent positioning premise is provided in Al Ries and Jack Trout, *Positioning: The Battle for Your Mind* (New York: Warner Books, 1982).

29. Other positioning options are discussed in Philip Kotler, *Kotler on Marketing: How to Create, Win, and Dominate Markets* (New York: Free Press, 1999), Chapter 4.

EXHIBIT 6.20

In this no-nonsense ad we see the storage capacity of a Zip disk being highlighted. What specific features of this ad are designed to reinforce the message that a Zip disk enhances your capacity? www.iomega.com

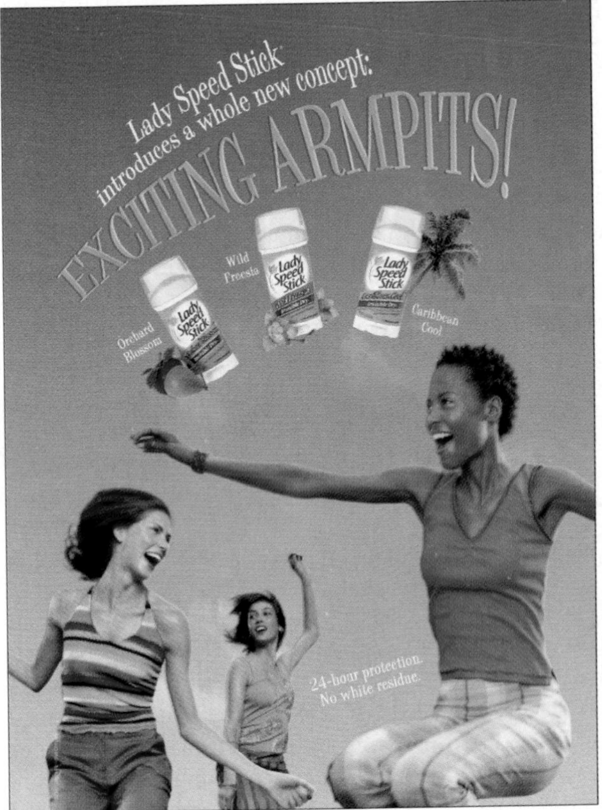

EXHIBIT 6.21

When the functional benefits of 24-hour protection and no white residue become old hat, then the advertiser may have no choice but to try to engage consumers through a promise of emotional benefits, as we see in this ad for Lady Speed Stick. www.mennen.com

EXHIBIT 6.22

Avoiding embarrassment in social settings can be a powerful motivator. Here we see an ad that offers a way to avoid embarrassment and achieve a desirable outcome in an important social context. The choice is clear: ditch the metal, get the guy. www.invisalign.com

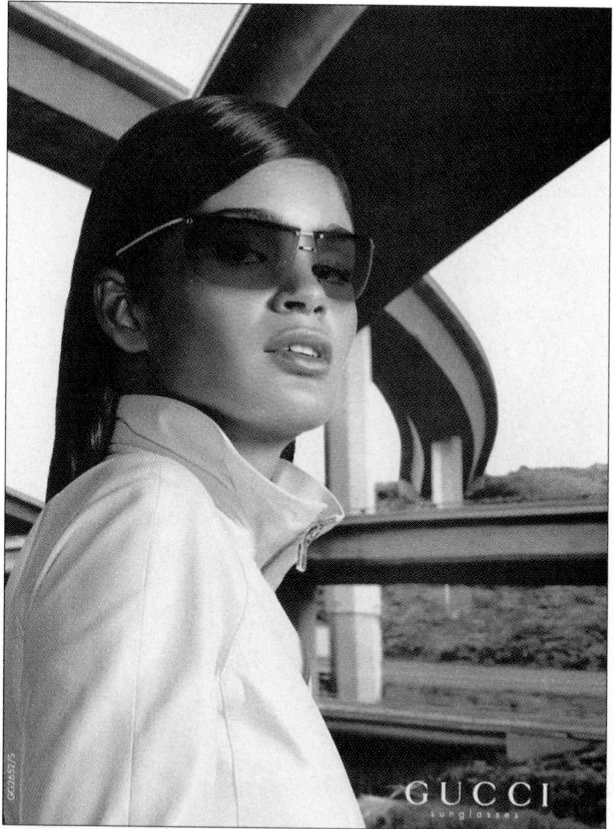

EXHIBIT 6.23

Gucci's benefit promise is one of distinctive self-expression. Even in the urban jungle, Gucci delivers elegance and a sophisticated sense of style.

Another sometimes controversial way to add emotion to one's positioning is by linking a brand with important causes that provoke intense feelings. Avon Products' former CEO, James E. Preston, has insisted that tie-ins with high-profile social issues can cut through the clutter of rivals' marketing messages.[30] His company supported breast cancer research in the United States and child nourishment programs in China. Likewise, Sears helped raise money for the homeless, Star-Kist has promoted dolphin-safe fishing practices, Coors Brewing has funded public literacy programs, and Bestfoods' Popsicle brand generates donations for the World Wildlife Fund—all as ways of offering a distinctive emotional benefit to customers. There's a notable trend here: In a recent survey of executives from 211 companies, 69 percent indicated that their companies planned to increase participation in cause-related marketing, as a way to build emotional bonds with their consumers.[31]

Self-expressive benefits can also be the bases for effective positioning strategies. With this approach, the purpose of an advertising campaign is to create distinctive images or personalities for brands, and then invite consumers into brand communities.[32] These brand images or personalities can be of value to individuals as they use the brands to make statements about themselves to other people. For example, feelings of status, pride, and prestige might be derived from the imagery associated with brands such as BMW, Rolex, and Gucci (see Exhibit 6.23). Brand imagery can also be valued in gift-giving contexts. A woman who gives a man Romance by Ralph Lauren is expressing something very different than the woman who gives Old Spice. Advertisers help brands have meaning and self-expressive benefits to distinguish them beyond their functional forms.

Besides benefit positioning, another fundamental option is **user positioning.** Instead of featuring a benefit or attribute of the brand, this option takes a specific profile of the target user as the focal point of the positioning strategy. For example, the Aqueous 9H2O by Rykä is positioned as the aquatic aerobic shoe for women. This focused positioning strategy is apparent in the ad in Exhibit 6.24. It should be obvious from Exhibit 6.25 that makers of the Merrell Chameleon Ventilator have a very different user in mind.

The third option for a positioning theme is **competitive positioning.** This option is sometimes useful in well-established product categories with a crowded competitive field. Here, the goal is to use an explicit reference to an existing competitor to help define precisely what your brand can do. Many times this approach is used by smaller brands to carve out a position relative to the market share leader in their category. For instance, in the analgesics category, many competitors have used market leader Tylenol as an explicit point of reference in their positioning strategies. Excedrin, for one, has attempted to position itself as the best option to treat a simple headache, granting that Tylenol might be the better choice to treat the

30. Geoffrey Smith and Ron Stodghill, "Are Good Causes Good Marketing?" *Business Week,* March 21, 1994, 64–65.
31. Stephanie Thompson, "Good Humor's Good Deeds," *Advertising Age,* January 8, 2001, 6.
32. Albert M. Muniz, Jr. and Thomas C. O'Guinn, "Brand Community," *Journal of Consumer Research,* vol. 27 (2001), 412–432.

e-SIGHTINGS

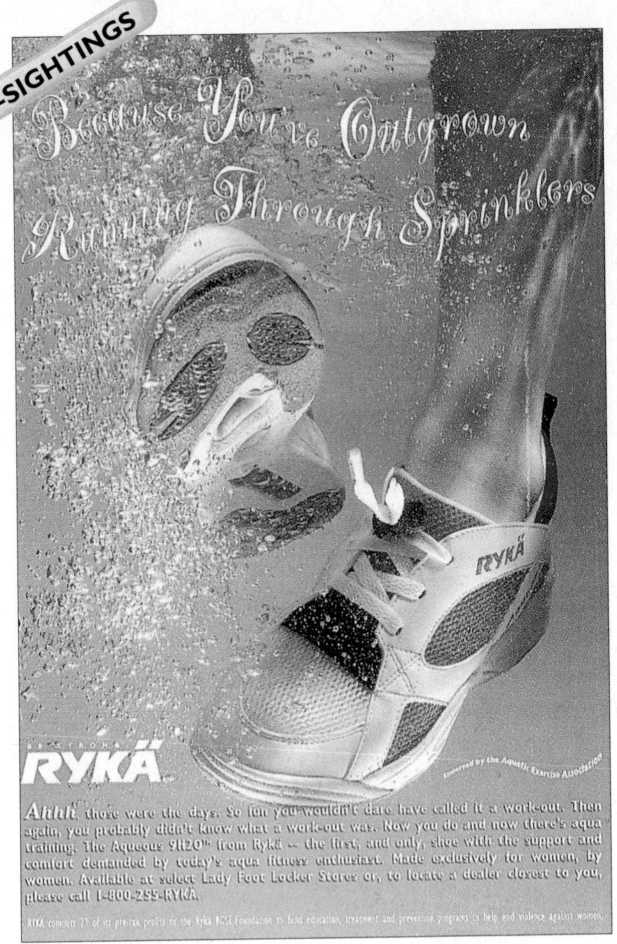

EXHIBIT 6.24

The Aqueous 9H2O from Rykä is made for the female aqua fitness enthusiast. This is a nice example of user positioning. In what ways does the site (www.ryka.com) reinforce Rykä's positioning in the aquatic aerobic shoe only for women? How does the site's message appeal to the assumed interests, activities, and opinions of this target segment?

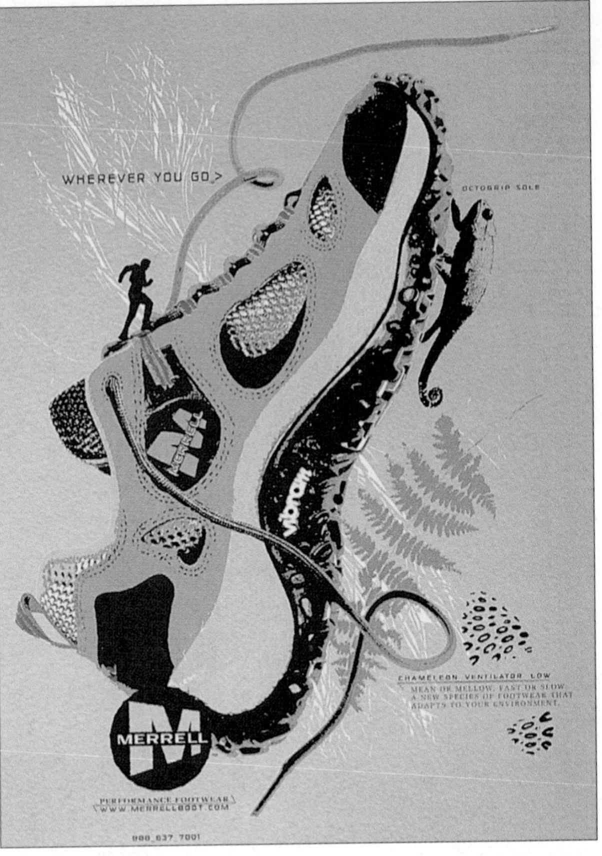

EXHIBIT 6.25

Can you find the cues in this ad that indicate that Merrell Performance Footwear is meant to be a "guy thing"? Does their Web site (www.merrellboot.com) do anything to refute or support this male-oriented positioning?

various symptoms of a cold or the flu. As shown in Exhibit 6.26, Excedrin's strategy must have been effective, because Tylenol came back with a very pointed reply.

Now that you've seen the three fundamental options for creating a positioning strategy, we need to make matters a bit more messy. There is nothing that would prevent a person from combining these various options to create a hybrid involving two or more of them working together. The combination of benefit and user, and benefit and competitive, are quite common in creating positioning strategies. For example, the two Gillette ads you examined at the beginning of the chapter are hybrids involving the benefit/user combination. And if you look carefully at the ad in Exhibit 6.20, you'll see that it has a small element of competitive positioning to enhance its primary emphasis on benefit positioning. The Xootr ad in Exhibit 6.27 is a superb example of user and competitive positioning combined. Do keep in mind that we're looking for a strategy that reflects substance, consistency, simplicity, and distinctiveness. But the last thing we'd want to do is give you guidelines that would shackle your creativity. So don't be shy about looking for creative combinations.

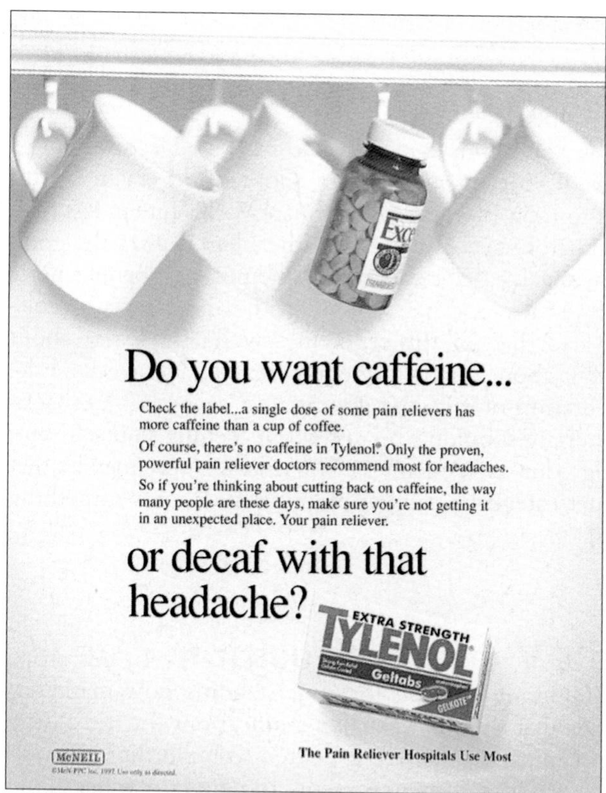

EXHIBIT 6.26

In mature saturated markets where the performance features of brands don't change much over time, it is common to see competitors making claims back and forth in an effort to steal market share from one another. Powerhouse brands such as Tylenol usually don't initiate these exchanges, because they have the most to lose. This ad is a reply from the makers of Tylenol, responding to a campaign of a smaller competitor. www.tylenol.com

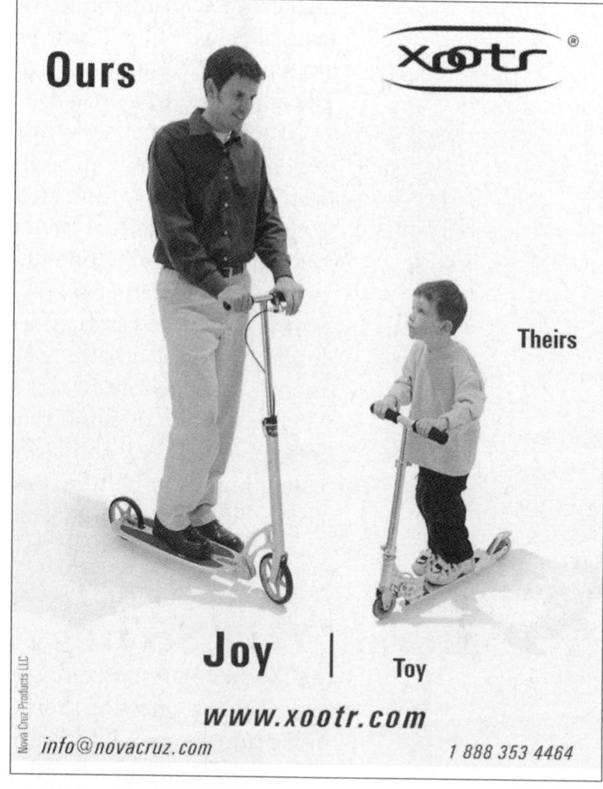

EXHIBIT 6.27

The beauty of this ad for Xootr is its simple, unequivocal message. Ours versus Theirs equates to Joy versus Toy. www.xootr.com

Repositioning. STP marketing is far from a precise science, so marketers do not always get it right the first time.[33] Furthermore, markets are dynamic. Things change. Even when marketers do get it right, competitors can react, or consumers' preferences may shift for any number of reasons, and what once was a viable positioning strategy must be altered if the brand is to survive. One of the best ways to revive an ailing brand or to fix the lackluster performance of a new market entry is to redeploy the STP process to arrive at a revised positioning strategy. This type of effort is commonly referred to as **repositioning.**

While repositioning efforts are a fact of life for marketers and advertisers, they present a tremendous challenge. When brands that have been around for some time are forced to reposition, perceptions of the brand that have evolved over the years must be changed through advertising. This problem is common for brands that become popular with one generation but fade from the scene as that generation ages and emergent consumers come to view the brand as passé. So, for several years, the

33. Michael Gershman, *Getting It Right the Second Time* (Reading, Mass.: Addison-Wesley, 1990).

makers of Oldsmobile tried to breathe new life into their brand with catchy ad slogans such as "This is not your father's Oldsmobile," "Demand better," and "Defy convention." Ultimately, none of these efforts were able to save a brand that had become passé in a crowded marketplace.[34]

Faced with fierce competition and plummeting market share, Nabisco set out to reposition its "new and improved" line of SnackWell's cookies and crackers.[35] In fact, this was the second attempt to reposition the failing SnackWell's line in less than a year, a sure sign that the brand had lost its luster. And rather than feature the good taste or the low-fat content of its snacks, Nabisco attempted emotional benefit positioning. Their target segment was baby-boomer women with a high sense of self-worth. Their research had revealed that for this segment, "wellness" is not about looking good in a bathing suit, but about celebrating competencies and accomplishments. To "feed into" this celebration of self, one commercial opined: "At SnackWell's, we like to think that snacking shouldn't be just about feeding yourself, but, in some small way, about feeding your self-esteem."[36] The message here may be that failing brands in cluttered product categories can get pretty desperate for something compelling to say to consumers.

5 Capturing Your Strategy in a Value Proposition.

In this chapter we have presented several important concepts for understanding how marketers develop strategies for their brands that then have major implications for the advertising and integrated promotion campaigns that are executed to build those brands. One needs to think about and research customer segments and target markets along with the competitive field to make decisions about various kinds of positioning themes that might be appropriate in guiding the creation of a campaign. Yes, as noted up front, it can get complicated. Furthermore, as time passes, and as new people from both the client and agency side are brought in to work on the brand team, it can be easy to lose sight of what the brand used to stand for in the eyes of the target segment. Of course, if the people who create the advertising and promotion programs for a brand get confused about the brand's desired identity, then the consumer is bound to get confused as well. This is a recipe for disaster. Thus, we need a way to capture and keep a record of what our brand is supposed to stand for in the eyes of the target segment. While there are many ways to capture one's strategy on paper, we recommend doing just that by articulating the brand's value proposition. If we are crystal clear in our own minds on what value we believe our brand offers to consumers, and everyone on the brand team shares that clarity, the foundation is in place for creating effective advertising and integrated brand promotion.

At this point you should find the following definition of a **value proposition** a natural extension of concepts that are already familiar; it simply consolidates the emphasis on customer benefits that has been featured in this and the previous chapter:

A brand's value proposition is a statement of the functional, emotional, and self-expressive benefits delivered by the brand that provide value to customers in the target segment. A balanced value proposition is the basis for brand choice and customer loyalty, and is critical to the ongoing success of a firm.[37]

34. Vanessa O'Connell and Joe White, "After Decades of Brand Bodywork, GM Parks Oldsmobile—For Good," *Wall Street Journal,* December 13, 2000, B1, B4.
35. Vanessa O'Connell, "Nabisco Ads Push Cookies for Self-Esteem," *Wall Street Journal,* July 10, 1998, B5.
36. Ibid.
37. This definition is adapted from David Aaker, *Building Strong Brands* (New York: Free Press, 1996), Chapter 3.

EXHIBIT 6.28

Don't let your value proposition get out of balance!

Exhibit 6.28 emphasizes the point in our definition that we must have a balanced value proposition to be successful in the marketplace. On the one hand, if the set of benefits provided by the brand does not justify its price relative to competitive brands, then we've obviously got a problem. On the other hand, if our price is too low relative to the benefits the brand offers, then we are essentially giving away profits. Balance is optimal.

Here are the extensive value propositions for two global brands that are likely familiar to you.[38]

McDonald's Value Proposition

Functional benefits: Good-tasting hamburgers, fries, and drinks served fast; extras such as playgrounds, prizes, premiums, and games.

Emotional benefits: Kids—fun via excitement at birthday parties; relationship with Ronald McDonald and other characters; a feeling of special family times. Adults—warmth via time spent enjoying a meal with the kids; admiration of McDonald's social involvement such as McDonald's Charities and Ronald McDonald Houses.

Nike's Value Proposition

Functional benefits: High-technology shoe that will improve performance and provide comfort.

Emotional benefits: The exhilaration of athletic performance excellence, feeling engaged, active, and healthy; exhilaration from admiring professional and college athletes as they perform wearing "your brand"—When they win, you win a little bit too.

Self-expressive benefits: Using the brand endorsed by high-profile athletes lets one's peers know your desire to compete and excel.

Notice from these two statements that over time many different aspects can be built into the value proposition for a brand. Brands like Nike may offer benefits in all three benefit categories, McDonald's from two of the three. Benefit complexity of this type is extremely valuable when the various benefits reinforce one another. In these examples, this cross-benefit reinforcement is especially strong for Nike, with all levels working together to deliver the desired state of performance excellence. The job of advertising is to carry the message to the target segment about the value

38. These examples are adapted from David Aaker, *Building Strong Brands* (New York: Free Press, 1996), Chapter 3.

CONTROVERSY

Avoid Targeting's Dark Side

Targeting is all about finding your best prospects and appealing to them very directly to attract their business. As we've noted before, it is often true that a small group of heavy users will drive the success of your business, if you come to know them and are able to reach them efficiently. But sometimes the heavy user can be attracted to your product or service for the wrong reason. That reason may entail a physical or psychological addiction, or may be based in a lack of education that yields misunderstanding about the real benefits of your product. In such instances, you face an ethical dilemma that can't be ignored.

Let's take a concrete example. If you are in the casino and gaming business (and this is very big business, and not just in Las Vegas), you will need to make an explicit decision on whether you will deploy marketing tactics to attract pathological gamblers. These are folks who in a very real sense are addicted to the rush that comes when they put their money on the line in hopes of scoring that next big win. They are the ultimate heavy user who lacks the ability to say no, even if it means blowing an entire paycheck. A common tactic for attracting these people is the payday bonanza. Offering special jackpots, free food, and show tickets for gamblers who bring their paychecks or welfare or Social Security checks right to the casino to be cashed appeals to the pathological gambler. And once in the casino with that cash in their pocket, there is little chance that they will take any of it home.

The good news is that major players such as Harrah's Entertainment are coming forth with codes of conduct that ban advertising that could appeal to pathological gamblers and other vulnerable market segments such as young consumers. Harrah's has banned all promotions in college newspapers and in any media that could reach children, and it explicitly bans paycheck promotions that appeal to the addicted gambler. Instead, Harrah's targets people between ages 45 and 70 who spend $1,000 to $2,000 a year on gambling. While these may be thought of as heavy users, Harrah's executives believe that this spending level is far less than what could be expected from a pathological gambler. The thoughtfulness and thoroughness reflected in Harrah's code of conduct nicely illustrates what we mean by the phrase *avoid targeting's dark side.*

Source: Christina Binkley, "Harrah's New Code to Restrict Marketing," *Wall Street Journal,* October 19, 2000, B16.

that is offered by the brand. However, for brands with complex value propositions such as McDonald's and Nike, no single ad could be expected to reflect all aspects of the brand's value. However, if any given ad is not communicating some selected aspects of the brand's purported value, then we have to ask, why run that ad?

So from now on, every time you see an ad, ask yourself, what kind of value or benefits is that ad promising the target customer? What is the value proposition underlying this ad? We very definitely expect you to carry forward an ability to select target segments and isolate value propositions.

One gains tremendous leverage from the process of STP marketing because it is all about anticipating and servicing customers' wants and needs. But targeting groups for focused advertising and promotion efforts has a controversial side, as do many things in today's complex marketplace. So we end here with another appeal to your ethical sensibilities, which hopefully will be heightened by the Controversy box on this page.

SUMMARY

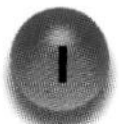

Explain the process known as STP marketing.

The term STP marketing refers to the process of segmenting, targeting, and positioning. Marketers pursue this set of activities in formulating marketing strategies for their brands. STP marketing also provides a strong foundation for the development of advertising campaigns. While no single approach can guarantee success in marketing and advertising, STP marketing should always be considered when consumers in a category have heterogeneous wants and needs.

Describe different bases that marketers use to identify target segments.

In market segmentation, the goal is to break down a heterogeneous market into more manageable subgroups or segments. Many different bases can be used for this purpose. Markets can be segmented on the basis of usage patterns and commitment levels, demographics, geography, psychographics, lifestyles, benefits sought, SIC codes, or stage in the decision process. Different bases are typically applied for segmenting consumer versus business-to-business markets.

Discuss the criteria used for choosing a target segment.

In pursuing STP marketing, an organization must get beyond the stage of segment identification and settle on one or more segments as a target for its marketing and advertising efforts. Several criteria are useful in establishing the organization's target segment. First, the organization must decide whether it has the proper skills to serve the segment in question. The size of the segment and its growth potential must also be taken into consideration. Another key criterion involves the intensity of the competition the firm is likely to face in the segment. Often, small segments known as market niches can be quite attractive because they will not be hotly contested by numerous competitors.

Identify the essential elements of an effective positioning strategy.

The P in STP marketing refers to the positioning strategy that must be developed as a guide for all marketing and advertising activities that will be undertaken in pursuit of the target segment. As exemplified by Pontiac's "We Build Excitement" campaign, effective positioning strategies are rooted in the substantive benefits offered by the brand. They are also consistent internally and over time, and they feature simple and distinctive themes. Benefit positioning, user positioning, and competitive positioning are options that should be considered when formulating a positioning strategy.

Review the necessary ingredients for creating a brand's value proposition.

Many complex considerations underlie marketing and advertising strategies, so some device is called for to summarize the essence of one's strategy. We advance the idea of the value proposition as a useful device for this purpose. A value proposition is a statement of the various benefits (functional, emotional, and self-expressive) offered by a brand that create value for the customer. These benefits as a set justify the price of the product or service. Clarity in expression of the value proposition is critical for development of advertising that sells.

KEY TERMS

target segment
positioning
positioning strategy
STP marketing
market segmentation
heavy users
nonusers
brand-loyal users
switchers, or variety seekers
emergent consumers
demographic segmentation
geodemographic segmentation
psychographics
lifestyle segmentation
benefit segmentation
consumer markets
business markets
competitive field
market niche
benefit positioning
user positioning
competitive positioning
repositioning
value proposition

QUESTIONS

1. While STP marketing often produces successful outcomes, there is no guarantee that these successes will last. What factors can erode the successes produced by STP marketing, forcing a firm to reformulate its marketing strategy?

2. Why does the persuasion required with a product differentiation strategy present more of a challenge than the persuasion required with a market segmentation strategy?

3. Explain the appeal of emergent consumers as a target segment. Identify a current ad campaign targeting an emergent-consumer segment.

4. It is often said that psychographics were invented to overcome the weaknesses of demographic information for describing target segments. What unique information can psychographics provide that would be of special value to advertisers?

5. What criteria did Mobil Oil Corporation weigh most heavily in its selection of Road Warriors as a target segment? What do you think will be the biggest source of frustration for Mobil in trying to make this strategy work?

6. Explain why smaller can be better when selecting segments to target in marketing strategies.

7. What essential elements of a positioning strategy can help overcome the consumer's natural tendency to ignore, distort, or forget most of the advertisements he or she is exposed to?

8. Identify examples of current advertising campaigns featuring benefit positioning, user positioning, and competitive positioning.

9. Carefully examine the Gillette ads displayed in Exhibits 6.1 and 6.2. What positioning theme (benefit, user, or competitive) is the basis for these ads? If you say benefit positioning, what form of benefit promise (functional, emotional, or self-expressive) is being made in these ads? Write a statement of the value proposition that you believe is reflected by these two ads.

10. Look around your room or apartment and find a product that you consider one of your favorite brands. Consider what it is about this brand that makes it a personal favorite for you. Is it functional, emotional, self-expressive, or some combination of these different types of benefits that you particularly value about this brand?

EXPERIENTIAL EXERCISES

1. Kmart, the nation's third-largest discount retailer, is striving to stay competitive in challenging markets where e-businesses and savvy young retailers like Target seem to have competitive advantage. While Kmart's image has suffered at times from poor customer service and a lack of consumer enthusiasm toward its brands, the company is currently repositioning itself in new markets in the hope of recovering from lackluster sales. Visit Kmart's special e-tail site (www.bluelight.com) and list ways the company seeks to reconnect with consumers through new brands and innovative services. Be sure to touch on new initiatives such as Kmart's exclusive line of Martha Stewart housewares products, free Internet service, bluelight.com, and other features you may find. Interview someone who is older and ask that person to describe his or her perception of Kmart over the last couple decades. How do those perceptions compare to the perceptions you are gathering through your analysis? Do you think Kmart will be successful in its repositioning strategy given its previous track record with consumers?

2. Break up into teams and imagine you are creating an e-business. Choose your business and then identify and break down relevant heterogeneous markets into manageable subgroups. Identify your target segment. Which criteria did you use to identify your target and why? Choosing from among the benefit, user, and competitive positioning options, select your positioning theme. Why will this theme be most effective for your advertising and marketing efforts? Formulate your brand's value proposition. Present your answers and reasoning to the class.

USING THE INTERNET

6-1 Segmentation

Community sites are popular Internet hangouts for Web users who share common interests, hobbies, and lifestyles. The enhanced technology features of these sites allow for live interaction with others via message boards, chat rooms, personal home pages, clubs, Web-based e-mail, and instant messaging services. In addition, interactive games, polls, and streaming broadcasts engage users and promote user loyalty, making community sites powerful entities that deliver ready-made audiences for savvy marketers.

Bolt.com: www.bolt.com

Talk City: www.talkcity.com

gURL.com: www.gurl.com

1. What broad consumer market do these sites share in common?

2. Describe the target segment for each of these sites. On what basis are these markets segmented (user pattern, psychographics, etc.)?

3. How does the positioning reflected in each Web site match with the target segment?

4. For each site, list one advertiser or corporate sponsor. Why might it be more beneficial for advertisers to place ads at these sites instead of high-traffic portal sites like Yahoo or Lycos?

6-2 Positioning

Once a firm has carefully segmented it market and selected target segments, a positioning strategy should evolve naturally. The positioning strategy includes particular ideas and themes that must be communicated effectively if the marketing program is to be successful.

Match.com: www.match.com

Metrodate.com: www.metrodate.com

AfroConnections.com: www.afroconnections.com

1. What are the essential elements of an effective positioning strategy? Which do you think is most important for these sites? Explain.

2. Which of these three positioning themes do these sites use? In what sense can they be viewed as having a hybrid of these three positioning options?

3. Pick one of these sites and define, in your own words, its value proposition. What is the importance of a brand's value proposition in creating effective advertising and integrated brand promotion?

CHAPTER 5
Advertising and
Consumer Behavior

CHAPTER 6
Market Segmentation,
Positioning, and the
Value Proposition

CHAPTER 7
Advertising and
Promotion Research

CHAPTER 8
The Advertising Plan

CHAPTER 9
Advertising Planning:
An International
Perspective

CHAPTER 7

After reading and thinking about this chapter, you will be able to do the following:

Explain the purposes served by and methods used in developmental advertising research.

Identify sources of secondary data that can aid the IBP planning effort.

Discuss the purposes served by and methods used in copy research.

Diet
Coke

that one of the most liberating forces of social justice on the scene today was a "new form of advertising research: account planning.[1] OK, let's get this straight. . . . Advertising account planners will be the next social revolutionaries; they will feed the poor, fight social injustice, and bring one universal peace, love, and understanding? Yeah, right.

Advertising professionals do go on, don't they?

But that is the kind of rhetoric that some people actually use to describe account planning: the "new" thing in advertising and promotion management/research. Some agencies are adopting this system (described later), and many more are celebrating it in theory. While it may or may not be any big deal in reality, some of the thinking surrounding it is different.

The **account planning** way of thinking merges the research and brand management business. It says that figuring out what's cool, projecting that in your brand, and keeping it cool is all one brand management function. The advertising and promotion agency's share of the brand management business has to do with not only creating, but constantly maintaining the brand.

Good research can play an important role in this; it can be very helpful or an enormous hindrance, as advertisers are realizing more and more. Top-down delivered marketing is not considered realistic by many in the industry. With this new realization comes new terms. One is the idea of account planning as a substitute for the traditional research efforts of an agency. There has been a very recent, but very significant turn in thinking about research and its role in advertising, promotion, and brand management. There has also been a very recent but strong recognition that advertising is really about chasing cool.

Advertising and Promotion Research.

Advertising research is better defined by history and practice than anything else. Research comes into the advertising process at several points. Early in the process, it is sometimes used to help a marketer determine which segment of the market to target. Throughout, research plays a role in helping the creatives (the people who actually make the ads) understand their audience members. Later, it is sometimes used to make go/no go decisions, to estimate the effect of an ad campaign, and to evaluate the performance of an ad agency. Unfortunately, it is also commonly misused. At the end of this chapter, we will suggest what we wish it could be.

As you can see, advertising research is used to judge advertising, but who judges advertising research, and how? First of all, not enough people, in our opinion, question and judge advertising research. Research is not magic or truth, and it should never be confused with such. Issues of reliability, validity, trustworthiness, and meaningfulness should be seriously considered when research is used to make important decisions. Otherwise, you're just using research as some sort of mystical ritual that you know really has no meaning, mouthing the words, faithfully uttering the chant, too afraid to think about the reality of the naked emperor.

Here are a few helpful concepts. *Reliability* means that the method generates generally consistent findings over time. *Validity* means that the information generated is relevant to the research questions being investigated. In other words, the research investigates what it seeks to investigate. *Trustworthiness* is a term usually applied to qualitative data, and it means exactly what it implies: Can one, knowing how the

1. Thomas Frank, "What Is This Thing Called Brand, Book Excerpt: A 'New Economy' Critic Explores the Mysteries of Branding and Account Planners," *Advertising Age,* November 6, 2000, 48–52.

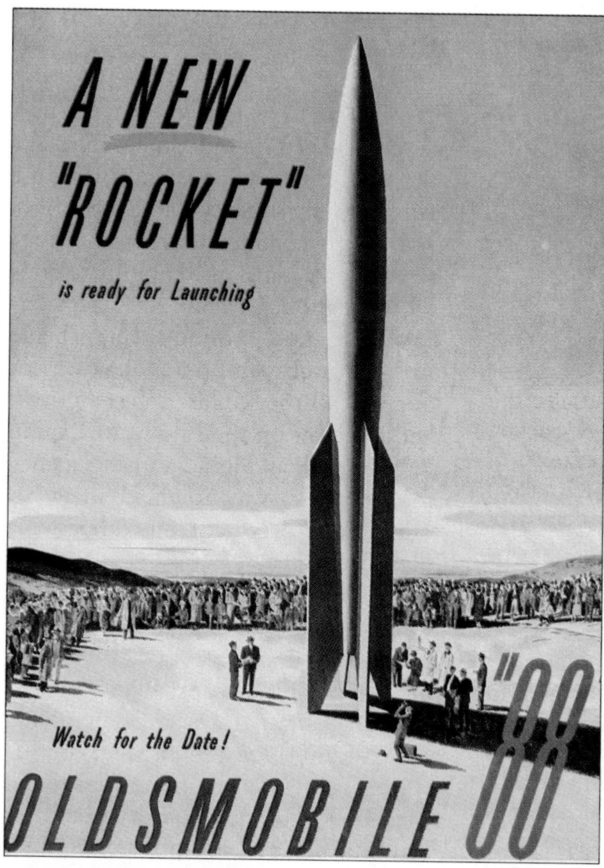

EXHIBIT 7.1

People really loved science in the 1950s. In fact, this love affair has influenced advertising research ever since . . . not for the better.

data were collected, trust them, and to what extent? Most difficult of all is the notion of *meaningfulness*. Just what does a piece of research really mean (if anything)? It is important for advertising professionals to take a moment (or several) and consider the limitations inherent in their data and in their interpretations. Too few take the time, and way too much advertising research is misapplied, misguided, misleading, irrelevant, wrong, or just plain silly. It can actually help make better decisions involving ads, and maybe (although we are not entirely convinced) better ads. Consider, for instance, the impact of Internet peer-to-peer (P2P) file swapping to advertisers, as discussed in the Controversy box on page 244.

The history of advertising research tells us quite a bit about its current status. Although some advertising agencies have had research departments for 80 years or more, the real boom days came between the 1930s and the 1970s. During this period, agencies adopted research departments for two basic reasons: (1) The popularization of science in the culture during this period suggested its necessity, and (2) other agencies had research departments. The need to actually know more about the consumer and the message probably ran a distant third. The most critical moment in this story was the 1950s. During this time, our adoration of science was at its height; the books, the plays, the movies, and the ads (Exhibit 7.1) of this period are full of pop science. There was a popular belief in hidden persuasion accompanied by a pop-culture version of Freud and his obsession with the repressed subconscious (typically sexual in flavor). It was a period of paranoia about communist mind control, seduction, and subversion. This social environment gave researchers ammunition to argue for more resources and "scientific methods" to study advertising. The reason advertising research is what it is today (and the reason many ads look the way they do) is because of this turn of history. However, over the last 15 to 20 years, much of the science worship diminished. Still, it would be a mistake to think that social science has no place in advertising research. It should, and it does; it's just that we are now more balanced and realistic in our beliefs and expectations regarding the social science application to advertising.

A lot of things are called "advertising research." Not all of it is done on the actual ads themselves. Quite a bit of advertising research is really done in preparation for making the ads. This reality yields a helpful distinction between developmental research and copy research.

1 Developmental Advertising Research.

Developmental advertising research is used to generate advertising opportunities and messages. It helps the creatives and the account team figure out things such as the target audience's identity, "street language," usage expectations, history, and context. It provides critical information used by creatives in actually producing ads. It is conducted early in the process so there is still an opportunity to influence the way the ads come out. Because of this, many consider it the most valuable kind of advertising research.

Purposes of Developmental Advertising Research. The purposes served by developmental research include the following:

Idea Generation. Sometimes an ad agency is called on to invent new ways of presenting an advertised good or service to a target audience. The outcome might take the form of a new product launch or a repositioning strategy for an advertiser. For example, after many years of representing its parks as the ultimate family destination, Disney and its ad agencies have now positioned its theme parks as adult vacation alternatives for couples whose children have grown and gone off on their own. In Exhibit 7.2, Windex and its advertising agency found a new way to differentiate its old familiar product from other window cleaners.

Where does an advertiser get ideas for new and meaningful ways to portray a brand? Direct contact with the customer can be an excellent place to start. Qualitative research involving observation of customers, brainstorming sessions with customers, and extended interviews with customers can be great devices for fostering fresh thinking about a brand. (Disney probably got its idea for repositioning by simply observing how many older couples were visiting its parks without children in tow!) Direct contact with and aggressive listening to the customer can fuel the creative process at the heart of any great advertising campaign. It can also be a great way to anticipate and shape marketplace trends, as seen in the Global Issues box on page 246.

CONTROVERSY

P2P or Not to P2P

While Napster's popularity has been muted by ongoing lawsuits, the demand for free music on the Internet continues to skyrocket. According to research by Jupiter Media Metrix, the number of users of file-swapping applications other than Napster jumped from 1.2 million to 6.9 million from March to August 2001. With the steady demise of Napster's trademark service, netizens are flocking to alternatives like Morpheus, Kazaa, and Winmx.

This research presents a controversy for record companies that aim to shut down peer-to-peer (P2P) music networks. It is apparent that the former Napster audience wants the ability to swap files in a peer-to-peer setting. Record companies, however, imagine a future of digital music contrary to current market impulses—major record labels expect audiences to pay for music through a central standardized system. Furthermore, while it is true that most Internet media piracy is committed using peer networks, a P2P system reduces bandwidth costs for music distribution as much as 90 percent compared to a central network server. This means that current lawsuits might not hurt only Napster—the future of the entire ingenious P2P system is at risk.

What's at stake for advertisers is access to a vital youth demographic. Collectively, 31 percent of the users of file-sharing alternatives are between 12 and 17 years old; 43 percent are males age 18 and older; and 26 percent are females age 18 and older. In championing the rights of artists and enforcing copyright laws, music industry executives are potentially painting themselves into a corner. Resisting market forces and litigating against the most cost-effective system of distribution could be a no-win situation. If the music industry has its way in the courts, all parties—consumers, advertisers, marketers, and musicians—could squander a grand opportunity afforded by advances in technology.

Sources: Michael Pastore, "Little Has Changed on Digital Music Front," www.cyberatlas.com, accessed September 27, 2001; Jupiter Media Metrix research cited by Michael Pastore, "Net Users Finding P2P Music Alternatives," accessed October 12, 2001.

Concept Testing. Many times advertisers also need feedback about new ideas before they spend a lot of money to turn the idea into a new marketing or advertising initiative. A **concept test** seeks feedback designed to screen the quality of a new idea, using consumers as the final judge and jury. Concept testing may be used to screen new ideas for specific advertisements or to assess new product concepts. How the product fits current needs and how much consumers are willing to pay for the new product are questions a concept test attempts to answer. For example, are consumers willing to cover their teeth with white flexible strips in order to brighten up their smiles? Crest certainly hopes so (see Exhibit 7.3). Concept tests of many kinds are commonly included as part of the agenda of focus groups to get quick feedback on new product or advertising ideas. Concept testing is also executed via survey research when more generalizable feedback is desired.

EXHIBIT 7.2

Ideas sometimes turn into products. Research can reveal the good ideas consumers have. www.scjohnson.com

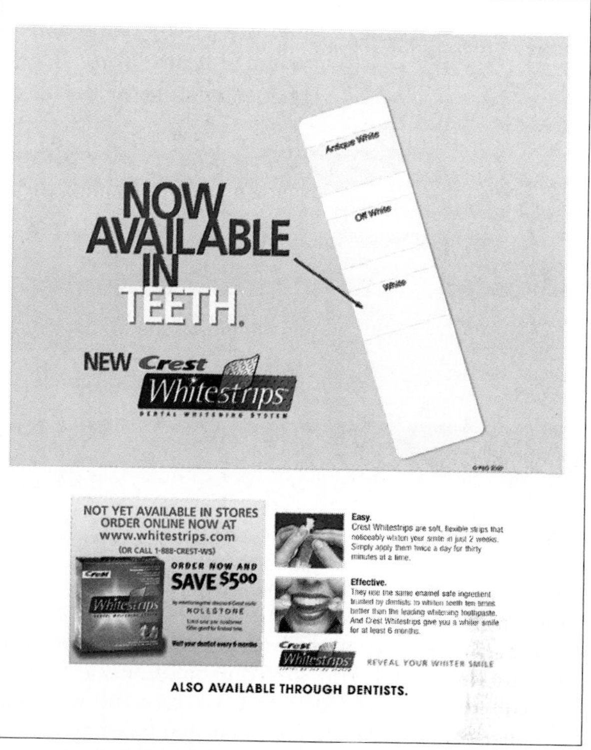

EXHIBIT 7.3

Concept testing allows advertisers to see what consumers think of new ideas. Sometimes these ideas then become real products. www.whitestrips.com

Audience Definition. Market segmentation and targeting are among the first and most important marketing decisions a firm must make. As discussed in the previous chapter, the goal of market segmentation is to identify target audiences that represent the best match between the firm's market offering and consumers' needs and desires, and then target them with effective advertising. Basic data about audience sizes along with their demographic profiles are absolutely critical in this process. Furthermore, new market opportunities are commonly discovered when you get to know your audience.

Audience Profiling. Perhaps the most important service provided by developmental advertising research is the profiling of target audiences for the creatives. Creatives need to know as much as they can about the people to whom their ads will speak. This research is done in many ways. One of the most popular is through lifestyle research. Lifestyle research, also known as AIO (activities, interests, and opinions) research, uses survey data from consumers who have answered questions about themselves. From the answers to a wide variety of such questions, advertisers can get a pretty good profile of the consumers they are most interested in talking to. Since the data also contain other product usage questions, advertisers can account for a consumption lifestyle as well. For example, it may turn out that the target for a brand of roach killer consists of male consumers, age 35 to 45, living in larger cities, who are more afraid of "unseen dirt" than most people and who think of themselves as extremely organized and bothered by messes. Maybe they also tend to enjoy hunting more than average, and tend to be gun owners. They read *Guns and Ammo* and watch *America's Most Wanted*. Profiles like this present the creative staff with a finer-grained picture of the target audience and their needs, wants, and motivations. Of course, the answers to these questions are only as valuable as the questions are valid. In-depth interviews with individual consumers provide an excellent source of information to supplement the findings from AIO research.

Developmental Advertising Research Methods. Several methods are used in developmental advertising research; they will be discussed next.

Focus Groups. A **focus group** is a brainstorming session with 6 to 12 target customers who have been brought together to come up with new insights about the good or service. With a professional moderator guiding the discussion, the consumers are first asked some general questions; then, as the session progresses, the questioning becomes more focused and moves to detailed issues about the brand in question. Advertisers tend to like focus groups because they can understand them and observe the data being collected. While focus groups provide an opportunity for in-depth discussion with consumers, they are not without limitations. Even multiple focus groups represent a very small sample of the target audience, and advertisers must remember that generalization is not the goal. The real goal is to get or test a new idea and gain depth of information. Greater depth of information allows for a greater understanding of the context of actual usage and its subtleties.

It also takes great skill to lead a focus group effectively. If the group does not have a well-trained and experienced moderator, some individuals will completely dominate the others. Focus group members also feel empowered and privileged; they have been made experts by their selection, and they will sometimes give the moderator all sorts of strange answers that may be more a function of trying to impress other group members than anything having to do with the product in question.

GLOBAL ISSUES

Japan's Marketing Bellwether? The Teenage Girl

For many marketers in Japan, aggressive listening to the customer begins and ends with adolescent females. It seems that high school girls in Japan have an unusual ability to predict consumer product successes, and, when targeted with special promotions, are also able to create favorable hype for products that can turn those products into family favorites. For example, Coca-Cola used focus groups of teenage girls to help fine-tune the marketing program for its fermented-milk drink Lactia. The girls suggested a light and smooth consistency for the product, and a short, stubby bottle with a pink label. Coke followed this advice and then handed out 30,000 of the stubby bottles to high school girls to help generate favorable word-of-mouth during the brand's launch. Lactia is now one of Japan's most popular beverages.

What could account for this special status of young women as a focal point in market research? Japanese marketing executives say that the girls are simply much more open and honest than their modest and tradition-bound elders. Additionally, these young women are very value-conscious consumers, and thus have good insights when inexpensive products are the focal point of the research. And they often have a substantial say in their mothers' selections of food items for the entire family. When Meiji Milk Products of Japan introduced its breath-cleansing Chinese tea under the brand name Oolong Socha, it did so with the advice of teenage girls. It soon became a family favorite. Yasuo Olo, a Meiji Milk brand manager, commented: "We were flabbergasted. We didn't think high school girls were that close with their parents these days."

And what about teenage boys? One market research consultant in Tokyo put it this way: "Most Japanese high school boys have trouble articulating. They're no help for our purposes."

Source: Norihiko Shirouzu, "Japan's High-School Girls Excel in Art of Setting Trends," *Wall Street Journal*, April 24, 1998, B1.

Other Methods. Projective techniques are designed to allow consumers to project thoughts and feelings (conscious or unconscious) in an indirect and unobtrusive way onto a theoretically neutral stimulus. (Seeing zoo animals in clouds, or faces in ice cubes, is an example of projection.) Projective techniques share a history with Freudian psychology and depend on notions of unconscious or even repressed thoughts. Projective techniques often consist of offering consumers fragments of pictures or words and asking them to complete the fragment. The most common projective techniques are association tests, sentence or picture completion, dialogue balloons, and story construction. While there is little doubt that people can, and do, project, the trustworthiness, validity, and usefulness of these techniques are often suspect.

Association tests ask consumers to express their feelings or thoughts after hearing a brand name or seeing a logo. In **sentence and picture completion,** a researcher presents consumers with part of a picture or a sentence with words deleted and then asks that the stimulus be completed. The picture or sentence relates to one or several brands of products in the category of interest. For example, a sentence completion task might be: *Most American-made cars are* __________. The basic idea is to elicit honest thoughts and feelings. Of course, consumers usually have some idea of what the researcher is looking for. Still, one can get some reasonably good data from this method.

Sometimes **dialogue balloons** offer consumers the chance to fill in the dialogue of cartoonlike stories, much like those in the comics in the Sunday paper. The story usually has to do with a product use situation. **Story construction** asks consumers to tell a story about people depicted in a scene or picture. Respondents might be asked to tell a story about the personalities of the people in the scene, what they are doing, what they were doing just before this scene, what type of car they drive, and what type of house they live in. Again, the idea is to use a less direct method to less obtrusively bring to the surface some often unconscious mapping of the brand and its associations.

One specific method that has enjoyed growing popularity in developmental applications is the **Zaltman Metaphor Elicitation Technique (ZMET).**[2] This technique claims to draw out people's buried thoughts and feelings about products and brands by encouraging participants to think in terms of metaphors. A metaphor simply involves defining one thing in terms of another. ZMET draws metaphors from consumers by asking them to spend time thinking about how they would visually represent their experiences with a particular product or service. Participants are asked to make a collection of photographs and pictures from magazines that reflect their experience. For example, in research conducted for DuPont, which supplies raw material for many pantyhose marketers, one person's picture of spilled ice cream reflected her deep disappointment when she spots a run in her hose. In-depth interviews with several dozen of these metaphor-collecting consumers can often reveal new insights about consumers' consumption motives, which then may be useful in the creation of products and ad campaigns to appeal to those motives.

Field Work. **Field work** is conducted outside the agency (i.e., in the "field"), usually in the home or site of consumption. Its purpose is to learn from the experiences of the consumer and from direct observation. Consumers live real lives, and their behavior as consumers is intertwined throughout these real lives. More and more, researchers are attempting to capture more of the real experiences of consumers.[3] Advertising researchers can make better messages if they understand the lives of their target audience, and understand it in some rich context. Various types of qualitative research attempt to do this. This general type of research uses prolonged observation and in-depth study of individuals or small groups of consumers, typically in their own social environment. This work is usually accomplished

2. For three different viewpoints on ZMET, compare Kevin Lane Keller, *Strategic Brand Management* (Upper Saddle River, N. J.: Prentice-Hall, 1998), 317–320; Ronald B. Lieber, "Storytelling: A New Way to Get Close to Your Customer," *Fortune,* February 3, 1997, 102–108; and Gerald Zaltman, "Rethinking Market Research: Putting People Back In," *Journal of Marketing Research,* vol. 34 (November 1997), 424–437.

3. Craig J. Thompson, William B. Locander, and Howard Pollio, "Putting Consumer Experience Back into Consumer Research: The Philosophy and Method of Existential Phenomenology," *Journal of Consumer Research,* vol. 16 (June 1989), 133–147.

through field work, or going to where the consumer lives and consumes. The advertising industry has long appreciated the value of qualitative data and is currently moving to even more strongly embrace extended types of fieldwork. **Coolhunts** do this by getting researchers to actually go to the site where they believe cool resides, stalk it, and bring it back to be used in the product and its advertising. Exhibit 7.4 on pages 250–251 gives an example of coolhunting.

2 **Internal Company Sources.** Some of the most valuable data are available within a firm itself and are, therefore, referred to as internal company sources of secondary data. Commonly available information within a company includes strategic marketing plans, old research reports, customer service records, warranty registration cards, letters from customers, customer complaints, and various sales figures (by region, by customer type, by product line). All provide a wealth of information relating to the proficiency of the company's advertising programs and, more generally, changing consumer tastes and preferences.

Government Sources. Various government organizations generate data on factors of interest to advertising planners; information on population and housing trends, transportation, consumer spending, and recreational activities in the United States is available through government documents.[4] Go to www.lib.umich.edu/govdocs/federal.html for 140 or so pages of great links to data from federal, state, and international government sources. The Census of Population and Housing is conducted every 10 years in years ending in 0. The data (actually tables, not the data itself, unfortunately) are released at various times over the following handful of years after the census. The census tabulations are not really "published" any more in (print) volumes. Instead the Census Bureau has a great Web site with access to numerous tables and papers (www.census.gov/).

The new up-and-coming source of data is the *American Community Survey,* which the Census Bureau actually hopes will replace almost all aspects of the census in 2010. The ACS is a new approach for collecting accurate, timely information. It is designed as an ongoing survey that will replace the so-called long form in the 2010 census. Full implementation of the ACS is planned for 2003. The ACS will provide estimates of demographic, housing, social, and economic characteristics every year for states, cities, counties, metropolitan areas, and population groups of 65,000 people or more (factfinder.census.gov/home/en/acsdata.html). There is also the commonly used *Current Population Survey,* which is a national survey that has been conducted monthly since 1940 by the Bureau of the Census for the Department of Labor Statistics. It provides information on unemployment, occupation, income, and sources of income, as well as a rotating set of topics such as health, work schedules, school enrollment, fertility, households, immigration, and language (www.bls.census.gov/cps/cpsmain.htm).

You might also check out the International Social Survey Programme at www.issp.org. Another very cool site is the National Archives and Records Administration, www.nara.gov. The array of consumer data available from government sources is a particularly useful starting place in advertising planning for businesses of all sizes. These publications are reasonably current, and many print versions are available at public libraries. This means that even a small business owner can access large amounts of information for advertising planning purposes at little cost.

Commercial Sources. Since information has become such a critical resource in marketing and advertising decision making, commercial data services have emerged to provide data of various types. Firms specializing in this sort of information tend to concentrate their data-gathering efforts on household consumers. Prizm is a good

4. We would like to thank Professor Gillian Stevens of the University of Illinois for her assistance with government data sources.

example. Prizm's owner, Claritas, collects data at the zip-code level on consumption. This way, a marketer can see a pretty interesting profile of who is most likely to consume a given good or service, and also *where*. This is based on the assumption that most consumers within a given zip code are more alike than different in their consumption habits. However, this assumption is not accepted universally. Sometimes there are significant variations in consumer practices within a given geographic area. But that is the exception. More often than not, people living in close proximity to one another are more like each other (in consumption practices) than people living in different geographic areas. That simple reality is what makes geographic clustering research methods work at all.

Information from commercial data sources is reasonably comprehensive and is normally gathered using reasonably sound methods. The cost of information from these sources is greater than information from government sources. Despite the greater expense, information from commercial sources still generally costs less than primary data generation.

Professional Publications. Another secondary data source is professional publications. Professional publications are periodicals in which marketing and advertising professionals report significant information related to industry trends or new research findings. Exhibit 7.5 on page 252 provides a listing of publications that frequently contain secondary data for advertising planning, along with their Web addresses.

It probably goes without saying for today's Web-savvy college student that the Internet can be an advertiser's best friend when looking for secondary data of almost any kind. The Internet has revolutionized developmental research, particularly for smaller agencies. Common search engines allow the search of enormous amounts of data previously available only to the wealthiest agencies. Human search costs have been slashed. Beyond commonly available engines, some companies buy customized engines to search the Web for their own particular needs. Of particular value is Usenet, a collection of over 80,000 discussion groups, many of them consumer- and brand-based. There, advertisers can gain incredibly rich and unobtrusive data from real consumers at virtually no cost. Sophisticated newsreader programs can quickly search and organize these data. The E-Commerce box on page 256 discusses the phenomenon of online gathering of ad-tracking data.

3 **Copy Research.** Copy research, also called *evaluative research,* is the second major type of advertising research. It is the kind that people usually think of when one says "advertising research." It is research on the actual ads themselves, finished or unfinished. It is used to judge or evaluate the ads in one way or another. Even though most contemporary ads are mostly visuals with few words (copy), the name still reflects the time when it was the effect of advertising copy (words) that was supposed to be measured by these tests. Much copy research is most typically driven as much by custom as by present realities. In the best case, reliable, valid, trustworthy, and meaningful tests are appropriately applied. In the worst case, tests in which few still believe continue to survive because they represent "the way we have always done things." Typically, industry practice falls somewhere in between. The pressure of history and the felt need for normative data (which allows comparisons with the past) significantly obscure questions of appropriateness. This makes for an environment in which the best test is not always done, and the right questions are not always asked.

This brings us to motives and expectations of the agency and the client. Just what is it that advertising people want out of their copy research? The answer, of course, depends on who you ask. Generally speaking, the account team wants some assurance that the ad does essentially what it's supposed to do. Many times, the team simply wants whatever the client wants. The client typically wants to see some numbers,

COOLHUNT

Baysie Wightman met DeeDee Gordon, appropriately enough, on a coolhunt. It was 1992. Baysie was a big shot for Converse, and DeeDee, who was barely twenty-one, was running a very cool boutique called Placid Planet, on Newbury Street in Boston. Baysie came in with a camera crew—one she often used when she was coolhunting—and said, "I've been watching your store, I've seen you, I've heard you know what's up," because it was Baysie's job at Converse to find people who knew what was up and she thought DeeDee was one of those people. DeeDee says that she responded with reserve—that "I was like, 'Whatever' "—but Baysie said that if DeeDee ever wanted to come and work at Converse she should just call, and nine months later DeeDee called. This was about the time the cool kids had decided they didn't want the hundred-and-twenty-five-dollar basketball sneaker with seventeen different kinds of high-technology materials and colors and air-cushioned heels anymore. They wanted simplicity and authenticity, and Baysie picked up on that. She brought back the Converse One Star, which was a vulcanized, suede, low-top classic old-school sneaker from the nineteen-seventies, and, sure enough, the One Star quickly became the signature shoe of the retro era. Remember what Kurt Cobain was wearing in the famous picture of him lying dead on the ground after committing suicide? Black Converse One Stars. DeeDee's big score was calling the sandal craze. She had been out in Los Angeles and had kept seeing the white teenage girls dressing up like cholos, Mexican gangsters, in tight white tank tops known as "wife beaters," with a bra strap hanging out, and long shorts and tube socks and shower sandals. DeeDee recalls, "I'm like, 'I'm telling you, Baysie, this is going to hit. There are just too many people wearing it. We have to make a shower sandal.' " So Baysie, DeeDee, and a designer came up with the idea of making a retro sneaker-sandal, cutting the back off the One Star and putting a thick outsole on it. It was huge, and amazingly, it's still huge.

Today, Baysie works for Reebok as general-merchandise manager—part of the team trying to return Reebok to the position it enjoyed in the mid-nineteen-eighties as the country's hottest sneaker company. DeeDee works for an advertising agency in Del Mar called Lambesis, where she puts out a quarterly tip sheet called the L Report on what the cool kids in major American cities are thinking and doing and buying. Baysie and DeeDee are best friends. They talk on the phone all the time. They get together whenever Baysie is in L.A. (DeeDee: "It's, like, how many times can you drive past O.J. Simpson's house?"), and between them they can talk for hours about the art of the coolhunt. They're the Lewis and Clark of cool.

What they have is what everybody seems to want these days, which is a window on the world of the street. Once, when fashion trends were set by the big couture houses—when cool was trickle-down—that wasn't important. But sometime in the past few decades things got turned over, and fashion became trickle-up. It's now about chase and flight—designers and retailers and the mass consumer giving chase to the elusive prey of street cool—and the rise of coolhunting as a profession shows how serious the chase has become. The sneakers of Nike and Reebok used to come out yearly. Now a new style comes out every season. Apparel designers used to have an eighteen-month lead time between concept and sale. Now they're reducing that to a year, or even six months, in order to react faster to new ideas from the street. The paradox, or course, is that the better coolhunters become at bringing the mainstream close to the cutting edge, the more elusive the cutting edge becomes. This is the first rule of the cool: The quicker the chase, the quicker the flight. The act of discovering what's cool is what causes cool to move on, which explains the triumphant circularity of coolhunting: because we have coolhunters like DeeDee and Baysie, cool changes more quickly, and because cool changes more quickly, we need coolhunters like DeeDee and Baysie.

One day last month, Baysie took me on a coolhunt to the Bronx and Harlem, lugging a big black canvas bag with twenty-four different shoes that Reebok is about to bring out, and as we drove down Fordham Road, she had her head out the window like a little kid, checking out what everyone on the street was wearing. We went to Dr. Jay's, which is the cool place to buy sneakers in the Bronx, and Baysie crouched down on the floor and started pulling the shoes out of her bag one by one, soliciting opinions from customers who gathered around and asking one question after another, in rapid sequence. One guy she listened closely to was maybe eighteen or nineteen, with a diamond stud in his ear and a thin beard. He was wearing a Polo baseball cap, a brown leather jacket, and the big, oversized leather boots that are everywhere uptown right now. Baysie would hand him a shoe and he would hold it, look at the top, and move it up and down and flip it over. The first one he didn't like: "Oh-kay." The second one he hated: he made a growling sound in his throat even before Baysie could give it to him, as if to say, "Put it back in the bag—now!" But when she handed him a new DMX RXT—a low-cut run/walk shoe in white and blue and mesh with a translucent "ice" sole, which retails for a hundred and ten dollars—he looked at it long and hard and shook his head in pure admiration and just said two words, dragging each of them out: "No doubt."

Baysie was interested in what he was saying, because the DMX RXT she had was a girls' shoe that actually hadn't been doing all that well. Later, she explained to me that the fact that the boys loved the shoe was critical news, because it suggested that Reebok had a potential hit if it just switched the shoe to the men's section. How

Continued

she managed to distill this piece of information from the crowd of teenagers around her, how she made any sense of the two dozen shoes in her bag, most of which (to my eyes, anyway) looked pretty much the same, and how she knew which of the teens to really focus on was a mystery. Baysie is a Wasp from New England, and she crouched on the floor in Dr. Jay's for almost an hour, talking and joking with the homeboys without a trace of condescension or self-consciousness.

Near the end of her visit, a young boy walked up and sat down on the bench next to her. He was wearing a black woolen cap with white stripes pulled low, a blue North Face pleated down jacket, a pair of baggy Guess jeans, and on his feet, Nike Air Jordans. He couldn't have been more than thirteen. But when he started talking you could see Baysie's eyes light up, because somehow she knew the kid was the real thing.

"How many pairs of shoes do you buy a month?" Baysie asked.

"Two," the kid answered. "And if at the end I find one more I like I get to buy that, too."

Baysie was on to him. "Does your mother spoil you?"

The kid blushed, but a friend next to him was laughing. "Whatever he wants, he gets."

Baysie laughed, too. She had the DMX RXT in his size. He tried them on. He rocked back and forth, testing them. He looked back at Baysie. He was dead serious now: "Make sure these come out."

Baysie handed him the new "Rush" Emmitt Smith shoe due out in the fall. One of the boys had already pronounced it "phat," and another had looked through the marbleized-foam cradle in the heel and cried out in delight, "This is bug!" But this kid was the acid test, because this kid knew cool. He paused. He looked at it hard. "Reebok," he said, soberly and carefully, "is trying to get butter."

When Baysie comes back from a coolhunt, she sits down with marketing experts and sales representatives and designers, and reconnects them to the street, making sure they have the right shoes going to the right places at the right price. When she got back from the Bronx, for example, the first thing she did was tell all these people they had to get a new DMX RXT out, fast, because the kids on the street loved the women's version. "It's hotter than we realized," she told them. The coolhunter's job in this instance is very specific. What DeeDee does, on the other hand, is a little more ambitious. With the L Report, she tries to construct a kind of grand matrix of cool, comprising not just shoes but everything kids like, and not just kids of certain East Coast urban markets but kids all over. DeeDee and her staff put it out four times a year, in six different versions—for New York, Los Angeles, San Francisco, Austin-Dallas, Seattle, and Chicago—and then sell it to manufacturers, retailers, and ad agencies (among others) for twenty thousand dollars a year. They go to each city and find the coolest bars and clubs, and ask the coolest kids to fill out questionnaires. The information is then divided into six categories—You Saw It Here First, Entertainment and Leisure, Clothing and Accessories, Personal and Individual, Aspirations, and Food and Beverages—which are, in turn, broken up into dozens of subcategories, so that Personal and Individual, for example, include Cool Date, Cool Evening, Free Time, Favorite Possession, and on and on. The information in those subcategories is subdivided again by sex and by age bracket (14–18, 19–24, 25–30), and then, as a control, the L Report gives you the corresponding set of preferences for "mainstream kids."

What DeeDee argues, though, is that cool is too subtle and too variegated to be captured with these kind of road strokes. Cool is a set of dialects, not a language. The L Report can tell you, for example, that nineteen-to-twenty-four-year-old male trendsetters in Seattle would most like to meet, among others, King Solomon and Dr. Seuss, and that nineteen-to-twenty-four-year-old female trendsetters in San Francisco have turned their backs on Calvin Klein, Nintendo Game Boy, and sex. What's cool right now? Among male New York trendsetters: North Face jackets, rubber and latex, khakis, and the rock band Kiss. Among female trendsetters: ska music, old-lady clothing, and cyber tech. In Chicago, snowboarding is huge among trendsetters of both sexes and all ages. Women over nineteen are into short hair, while those in their teens have embraced mod culture, rock climbing, tag watches, and bootleg pants. In Austin-Dallas, meanwhile, twenty-five-to-thirty-year-old women trendsetters are into hats, heroin, computers, cigars, Adidas, and velvet, while men in their twenties are into video games and hemp. In all, the typical L Report runs over one hundred pages. But with the flood of data comes an obsolescence disclaimer: "The fluctuating nature of the trendsetting market makes keeping up with trends a difficult task." By the spring, in other words, everything may have changed.

The key to coolhunting, then, is to look for cool people first and cool things later, and not the other way around. Since cool things are always changing, you can't look for them, because the very fact they are cool means you have no idea what to look for. What you would be doing is thinking back on what was cool before and extrapolating, which is about as useful as presuming that because the Dow rose ten points yesterday it will rise another ten points today. Cool people, on the other hand, are a constant.

Source: From Malcolm Gladwell, "The Coolhunt," in *The Consumer Society Reader*, Juliet B. Schor and Douglas B. Holt, eds. (New York: New Press, 2000), 360–374.

EXHIBIT 7.4

This is a description of coolhunting.

Commercial Information Source	Type of Information
Dun & Bradstreet Market Identifiers	DMI is a listing of 4.3 million businesses that is updated monthly. Information includes number of employees, relevant SIC codes that relate to the businesses' activities, location, and chief executive. Marketing and advertising managers can use the information to identify markets, build mailing lists, and specify media to reach an organization. www.dnb.com/
Nielsen Retail Index	Nielsen auditors collect product inventory turnover data from 1,600 grocery stores, 750 drugstores, and 150 mass merchandise outlets. Information is also gathered on retail prices, in-store displays, and local advertising. Data from the index are available by store type and geographic location. www.nielsenmedia.com/
National Purchase Diary Panel	With more than 13,000 families participating, NPD is the largest diary panel in the United States. Families record on preprinted sheets their monthly purchases in 50 product categories. Information recorded includes brand, amount purchased, price paid, use of coupons, store, specific version of the product (flavor, scent, etc.), and intended use.
Roper Starch Advertisement Readership	The Roper Starch service tracks readership of more than 70,000 advertisements appearing in 1,000 consumer and farm publications, newspapers, and business periodicals. More than 100,000 personal interviews are conducted each year to determine the readership of the ads. Starch uses a recognition approach, which rates each ad on the extent of readership it was able to stimulate. Data on headlines, copy, and other component parts of an ad are also recorded. www.roper.com
Nielsen Television Index	This is one of the most familiar commercial services, since the Nielsen ratings receive so much popular press. The index provides estimates of the size and characteristics of the audience for television programs. Data are gathered through an electronic device attached to participating households' television sets. The device records the times the TV is on and what channel is tuned in. Reports on viewership are published biweekly. www. acnielsen.com
Consumer Mail Panel	This panel is operated by a firm called Market Facts. There are 45,000 active participants at any point in time. Samples are drawn in lots of 1,000. The overall panel is said to be representative of different geographic regions in the United States and Canada, then broken down by household income, urbanization, and age of the respondent. Data are provided on demographic and socioeconomic characteristics as well as type of dwelling and durable goods ownership. www.marketfacts.com
Information Resources	One of the leading organizations in single-source research, where all phases of a consumer's media exposure and, ultimately, purchase behavior are tracked. This firm is also recognized for its research on the impact of grocery store promotional programs (PromotioScan) and coupon redemption.

EXHIBIT 7.5

Examples of the secondary data sources available to advertisers.

generally meaning **normative test scores.** In other words, the client wants to see how well a particular ad scored against average commercials of its type that were tested previously. The creatives who produced the ad often believe there is no such thing as the average commercial, and they are quite sure that if there are average

EXHIBIT 7.6

Creative pumps up DAR numbers.

Bob, a creative at a large agency, has learned from experience how to deal with lower-than-average day-after recall (DAR) scores. As he explains it, there are two basic strategies: (1) Do things that you know will pump up the DAR. For example, if you want high DARs, never simply super (superimpose) the brand name or tag at the end of the ad. Always voice it over as well, whether it fits or not. You can also work in a couple of additional mentions in dialogue; they may stand out like a sore thumb and make consumers think, "Man, is that a stupid commercial," because people don't talk that way. But it will raise your DARs. (2) Tell them (the account executive or brand manager and other suits) that this is not the kind of product situation that demands high DARs. In fact, high DARs would actually hurt them in the long run due to quick wearout and annoyance. Tell them, "You're too sophisticated for that ham-handed kind of treatment. It would never work with our customers." You can use the second strategy only occasionally, but it usually works. It's amazing.

commercials, theirs are not among them. Besides benefiting the sales of the advertised product or service, the creatives wouldn't mind another striking ad on their reel or in their book, another Addy or Clio on their wall. Message testing tools also generate a type of report card, and some people, particularly on the creative side of advertising, resent getting report cards from people in suits. (Who wouldn't?) Creatives also argue that these numbers are often misleading and misapplied. More often than not, they're right. Because of these problems, and the often conflicting agenda of creatives (awards, career as a filmmaker) and account managers (keep your job, sell more stuff, maybe get to move to the brand side), copy research is often the center of agency tensions.

Whenever people begin looking at the numbers, there is a danger that trivial differences can be made monumental. Other times, the mandatory measure is simply inappropriate. Still other times, creatives wishing to keep their jobs simply give the client what he or she wants, as suggested in Exhibit 7.6. If simple recall is what the client wants, then increasing the frequency of brand mentions might be the answer. It may not make for a better commercial, but it may make for a better score and, presumably, a happy client in the short run. A lot of games are played with copy tests.

Despite the politics involved, message testing research is probably a good idea, at least some of the time. Properly conducted, such research can yield important data that management can then use to determine the suitability of an ad.

Evaluative Criteria. There are many standards against which ads are judged. Of course, picking the right criterion is not always an easy task, but it is vital to the effective message evaluation. An ad like that in Exhibit 7.7 could be judged along many dimensions and with several criteria. Several of the purposes served by evaluative advertising research are reviewed in the following sections.

"Getting It." Sometimes advertisers just want to know if audience members "get" the ad. Do they generally understand it, get the joke, see the connection? This is really a hugely important criterion. Do you get the ads in Exhibits 7.8 and 7.9?

Knowledge. It is commonly assumed that advertising generates thoughts, some of which are at some point retrieved to then influence purchase. Some ads are judged effective if they leave this cognitive residue, or knowledge, about the brand. This knowledge may take many different forms. It could be a jingle, a tag line, or merely the recognition of a brand name or product symbol (Exhibit 7.10). Generally, tests

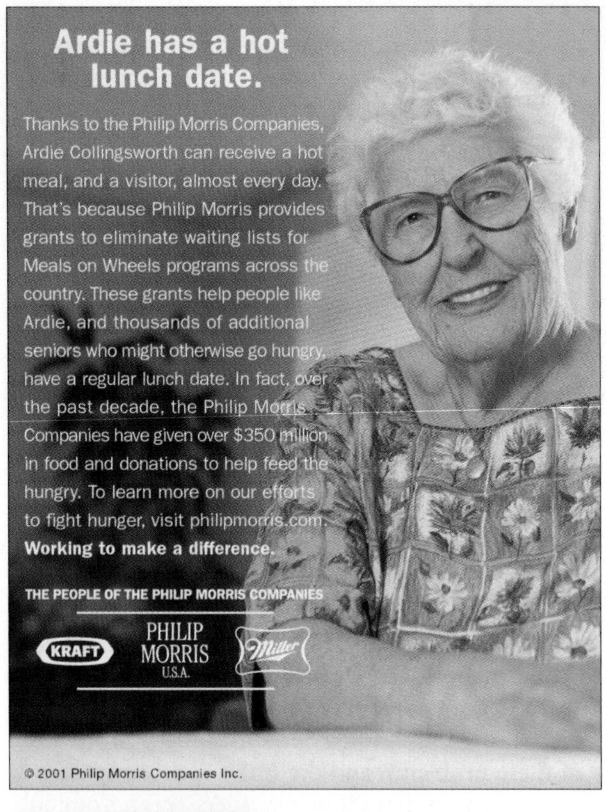

EXHIBIT 7.7

How should this ad be judged? What should be evaluated here? www.philipmorris.com

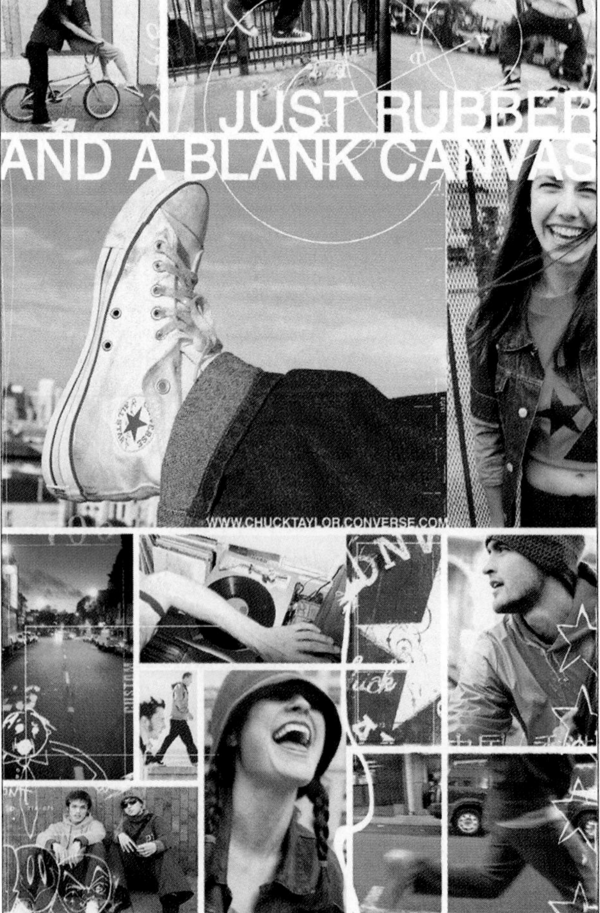

EXHIBITS 7.8 AND 7.9

Do you get it? www.cocacola.com *and* www.converse.com

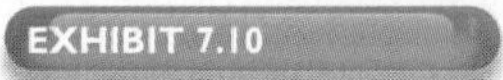

EXHIBIT 7.10

Some ads are judged on the knowledge they leave in the mind of the consumer. www.pringles.com

EXHIBIT 7.11

Some ads are all about feelings. www.majorica.com

of recall and recognition are featured when knowledge generation is the advertiser's primary concern.

Attitude Change. Attitudes suggest where a brand stands in the consumer's eyes. Attitudes can be influenced both by what people know and by what people feel about a brand. In this sense, attitude or preference is a summary evaluation that ties together the influences of many different factors. Advertisers thus may view attitude shaping or attitude change as a key dimension for assessing advertising effectiveness.

Feelings and Emotions. Advertisers have always had a special interest in feelings and emotions. Ever since the "atmospheric" ads of the 1920s, there has been the belief that feelings may be more important than thoughts as a reaction to certain ads. For example, the way a consumer feels about the imagery in the ad in Exhibit 7.11 may be far more important than any cognitive component of the communication. While the popularity of this philosophy waxes and wanes, there has been a renewed interest in developing better measures of the feelings and emotions generated by advertising.[5] This has included better paper-and-pencil measures as well as dial-turning devices with which those watching an ad turn a dial in either a positive or negative direction to indicate their emotional response to the ad. Participants' responses are tracked by computer and can be aggregated and superimposed over the ad during playback to allow account executives and brand managers to see the pattern of affective reactions generated by the ad.

5. Stuart J. Agres, Julie A. Edell, and Tony M. Dubitsky, eds., *Emotion in Advertising* (Westport, Conn.: Quorum Books, 1990). See especially Chapters 7 and 8.

E-COMMERCE

What's in a Name?

With rapid-fire changes in technology come rapid shifts for technology-based research firms. One online advertising tracking company, Leading Web Advertisers (LWA), recently changed its name to Evaliant Media Resources in an attempt to keep up with the progression of advertising beyond the Web and into all electronic media advertising such as wireless and digital. The firm's former identity, based solely on Web advertising, has become outmoded by the emergence of promising new media such as iDTV, digital cellular services, and wireless handheld devices. The firm's new name reflects the demand for advertising tracking across all forms of electronic media.

While conventional wisdom has it that new-media advertising is either on the critical list or dead altogether, there are signs that quite the opposite is true. One way of gauging the popularity of Internet advertising is to find out how many new brands are being advertised. Evaliant has tracked new brands to the Web since April 1999, when there were less than 200 new brands each week. By July 1999, the number approached 600 and has remained at that level ever since. Evaliant co-CEO Michael Kubin stated, "Even during the past six months, when everyone's been talking about the gloom and doom of the Web, the growth has been pretty consistent."

Marketers are beginning to understand several critical facts about digital and Internet media. While companies quote a variety of Web-related research statistics, the validity of these numbers is still in question. The Web is a complicated medium to measure, and for marketers the best source of information on Web usage is their own direct experience. Furthermore, advertisers realize that the Web is not a straightforward advertising medium—new technology is evolving constantly, and advertisers must take the effort and expense to unlock its full potential. Experiments in branding, promotions, and direct marketing yield excellent information that can be used for integrated brand promotion in ways never before imagined.

Evaliant expects continued growth, and the firm's acquisition of Forrester's Internet AdWatch service is a sign of good things to come. "To put it simply, LWA just outgrew its name," said Kubin. "Looking to the future, we want to be the authoritative source for ad-tracking data in all electronic media."

Sources: Ken Liebeskind, "New Brands Advertising Online," *MediaPost*, January 24, 2001; "Forrester Sells Internet AdWatch to Evaliant," www.forrester.com, accessed on October 3, 2001.

Physiological Changes. Some advertisers look for changes in the bodies of people exposed to their ads. Typically this is in terms of eye movement or dimensions measured by lie-detector-like devices such as skin conductivity, respiration, and pulse.

Behavior. Other advertisers really want to see evidence that the new ads will actually get people to do something: generally, to buy their product.

Copy Research Methods.

In pursuit of assessing the ad's impact on the dimensions listed earlier, several methods are employed.

Communication Tests. These test the "getting it" dimension more than anything else. A **communication test** simply seeks to discover whether a message is communicating something close to what is desired. Communication tests are usually done in a group setting, with data coming from a combination of pencil-and-paper questionnaires and group discussion. They are done with one major thought in mind: to prevent a major disaster, to prevent communicating something the creators of the ad are too close to see but that is entirely obvious to consumers first seeing the ad. This could be an unintended double entendre or an unseen sexual allusion. It could be an unexpected interpretation of the imagery in an ad as that ad is moved from country to country around the world. Remember, if the consumer sees unintended things, it doesn't matter whether they're intended or not—to the consumer, they're there. However, advertisers should balance this against the fact that communication test members feel privileged and special, and thus they may try too hard to see things. This is another instance where well-trained and experienced researchers must be counted on to draw a proper conclusion from the testing.

Resonance Tests. In a **resonance test,** the goal is to determine to what extent the message resonates or rings true with target-audience members.[6] The question becomes,

6. David Glenn Mick and Claus Buhl, "A Meaning-Based Model of Advertising Experiences," *Journal of Consumer Research,* vol. 19 (December 1992), 317–338.

EXHIBIT 7.12

Some ads are judged by their resonance, or how true they ring. www.wisk.com

Does this ad match consumers' own experiences? Does it produce an affinity reaction? Do consumers who view it say, "Yeah, that's right; I feel just like that" (Exhibit 7.12)? Do consumers read the ad and make it their own?[7] In the view of some, this is the direction in which copy research needs to move. The assessment dimension here reflects knowledge, emotions, and feelings, as well as the "getting it" dimension.

Thought Listings. It is commonly assumed that advertising generates thoughts, or cognitions, during and following exposure. Copy research that tries to identify specific thoughts that may be generated by an ad is referred to as **thought listing,** or cognitive response analysis. Here the researcher is interested in the thoughts that a finished or near-finished ad generates in the mind of the consumer. Typically, cognitive responses are collected by having individuals watch the commercial in groups and, as soon as it is over, asking them to write down all the thoughts that were in their minds while watching the commercial. The hope is that this will capture what the potential audience members made of the ad and how they responded, or talked back, to it.

These verbatim responses can then be analyzed in a number of ways. Usually, simple percentages or box scores of word counts are used. The ratio of favorable to unfavorable thoughts may be the primary interest of the researcher. Alternatively, the number of times the person made a self-relevant connection—that is, "That would be good for me" or "That looks like something I'd like"—could be tallied and compared for different ad executions. This method gets at several things: "getting it," knowledge acquired, attitude shifts, and emotions and feelings. The idea itself is very appealing: getting at people's stream of thoughts about an ad at time of exposure. It is in the actual execution of the test that problems arise, because these thoughts are in reality retrospective, highly edited, and obtained in environments and mental states completely unlike anything resembling how people actually are exposed to ads, such as sitting in their living room, talking, half-listening to the TV, and so on. It is also feared that these thoughts are really only created retrospectively for the researcher, and that in a real setting the consumer may be thinking about something or someone else, or may be "zoned out" entirely. But the researchers asked; you have to tell them something.

Recall Tests. These commonly employed tests are performed to get at the knowledge dimension. The basic idea is that if the ad is to work, it has to be remembered. Following on this premise is the further assumption that the ads best remembered are the ones most likely to work. Thus the objective of these tests is to see just how much, if anything, the viewer of an ad remembers of the message. Recall is used in the testing of print and television advertising.

7. Linda Scott, "The Bridge from Text to Mind: Adapting Reader Response Theory for Consumer Research," *Journal of Consumer Research,* vol. 21 (December 1994), 461–486.

In television, the basic procedure is to recruit a group of individuals from the target market who will be watching a certain channel during a certain time on a test date. They are asked to participate ahead of time, and simply told to watch the show. A day after exposure, the testing company calls the individuals on the phone and determines, of those who actually saw the ad, how much they can recall. The day-after-recall (DAR) procedure generally starts with questions such as, "Do you remember seeing a commercial for any laundry detergents? If not, do you remember seeing a commercial for Tide?" If the respondent remembers, he or she is asked what the commercial said about the product: What did the commercial show? What did the commercial look like? The interview is recorded and transcribed. The verbatim interview is coded into various categories representing levels of recall, typically reported as a percentage. *Unaided recall* is when the respondent demonstrates that he or she saw the commercial and remembered the brand name without having the brand name mentioned. If the person had to be asked about a Tide commercial, it would be scored as *aided recall*. Burke Marketing Service and Gallup and Robinson's In-View Service (see Exhibit 7.13) are the two major suppliers of these tests.

In a typical print recall test, a consumer is recruited from the target market, generally at a shopping mall. He or she is given a magazine to take home. Many times the magazine is an advance issue of a real publication; other times it is a fictitious magazine created only for testing purposes. The ads are "tipped in," or inserted, into the vehicle. Some companies alter the mix of remaining ads; others do not. Some rotate the ads (put them in different spots in the magazine) so as not to get effects

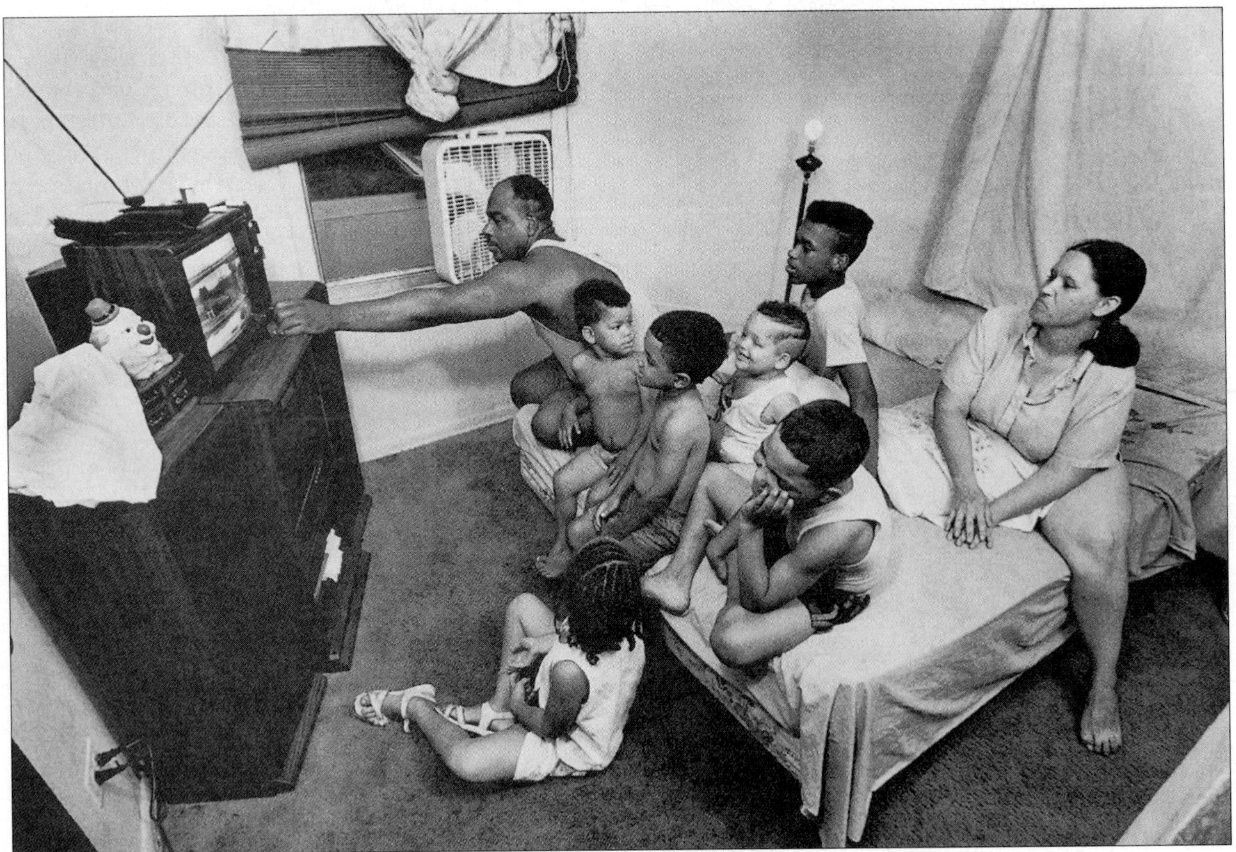

EXHIBIT 7.13

Tapping the thought processes of people in a highly controlled lab setting is a little different than what goes on in real life.

due to either editorial context or order. The participants are told that they should look at the magazine and that they will be telephoned the following day and asked some questions. During the telephone interview, aided recall is assessed. This involves a product category cue, such as, "Do you remember seeing any ads for personal computers?" The percentage who respond affirmatively and provide some evidence of actually remembering the ad are scored as exhibiting aided recall. Other tests go into more detail by actually bringing the ad back to the respondent and asking about various components of the ad, such as the headline and body copy. Sometimes a deck of cards with brand names is given to consumers, and they are asked to stop if they can remember any ads from the brands on the cards. If they can, then they are asked to describe everything they can remember about the ad. These are scored in a manner similar to television day-after recall (DAR) tests.

Considerable research indicates there is little relation between recall scores and sales effectiveness.[8] But doesn't it make sense that the best ads are the ads best remembered? Well, the evidence for that is simply not there. This seeming contradiction has perplexed academics and practitioners for a long time. And as ads become more and more visual, recall of words and claims is more and more irrelevant. The fact is that, as measured, the level of recall for an ad seems to have relatively little (if anything) to do with sales. This may be due to highly inflated and artificial recall scores.

e-SIGHTINGS

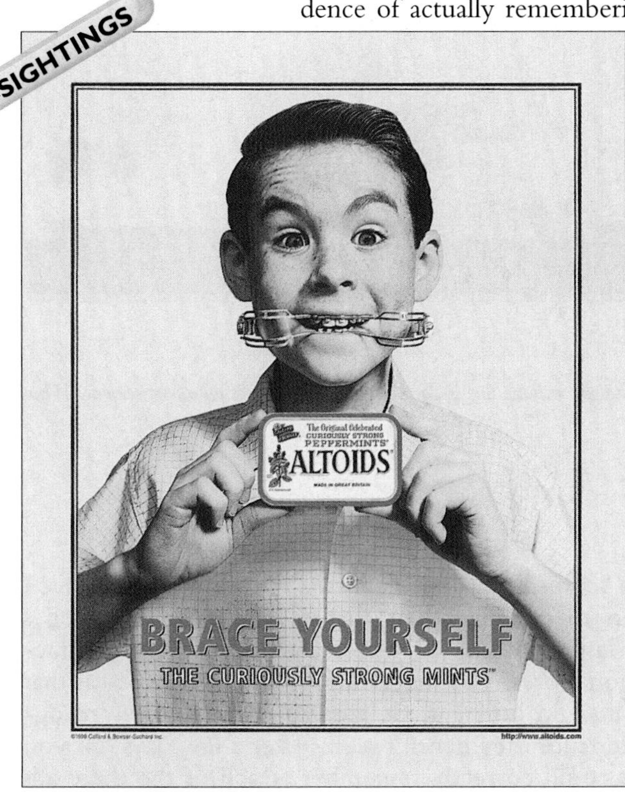

EXHIBIT 7.14

Recognition testing uses the ad itself to test whether consumers remember it and can associate it with its brand and message. This unusual, comically fanciful image would likely make this ad easy to recognize. But imagine this ad with the Altoids brand name blacked out. If consumers remember the ad, will they also remember the Altoids brand name? Novel imagery sometimes actually distracts readers, enticing them to overlook brand names. Visit the Altoids site (www.altoids.com) and evaluate how it reinforces or dilutes recognition in the minds of consumers. Are the interactive features useful or distracting? Does the site achieve "cool," or is it too over-the-top to reinforce brand recognition?

Recognition Tests. This type of testing also attempts to get at little more than evidence of exposure and some knowledge gain. Recognition tests ask magazine readers and television viewers whether they remember having seen particular advertisements and whether they can name the company sponsoring the ad. For print advertising, the actual advertisement is shown to respondents, and for television advertising, a script with accompanying photos is shown. For instance, a recognition test might ask, "Do you remember seeing [the ad in Exhibit 7.14]?" This is a much easier task than recall in that respondents are cued by the very stimulus they are supposed to remember, and they aren't asked to do anything more than say yes or no. Do you think any complications might arise in establishing recognition of the ad displayed in Exhibit 7.15?

Companies that do this kind of research follow some general procedures. Subscribers to a relevant magazine are contacted and asked if an interview can be set up in their home. The readers must have at least glanced at the issue to qualify. Then each target ad is shown, and the readers are asked if they remember seeing the ad (if they *noted* it), if they read or saw enough of the ad to notice the brand name (if they *associated* it), and if they claim to have read at least 50 percent of the copy (if they read *most* of it). This testing is usually conducted just a few days after the current issue becomes available. The *noted, associated,* and *read most* scores are calculated. With print ads, Starch is the major supplier of recognition tests, and in television, Bruzzone is the leader.

8. Rajeev Batra, John G. Meyers, and David A. Aaker, *Advertising Management*, 5th ed. (Upper Saddle River, N.J.: Prentice-Hall, 1996), 469.

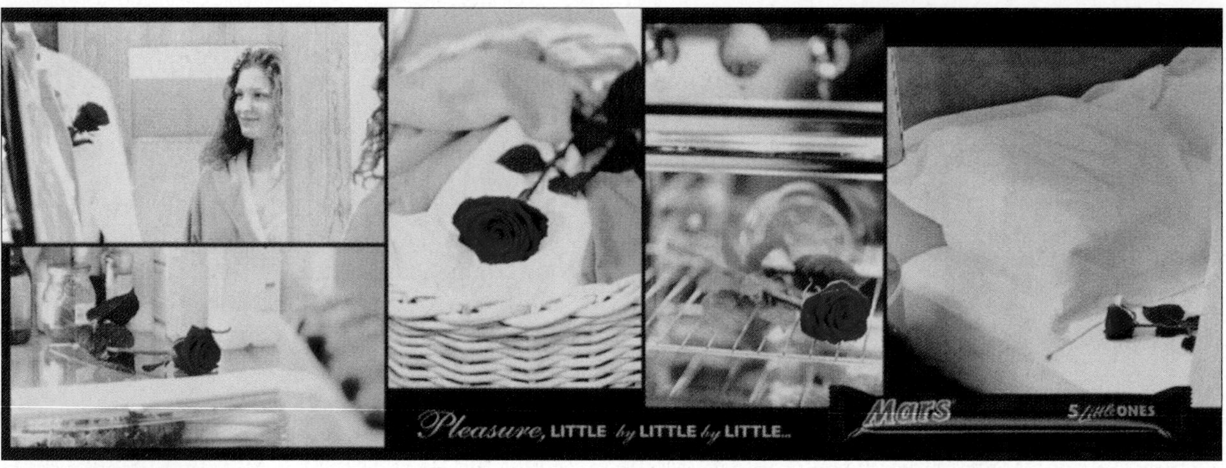

EXHIBIT 7.15

Though the correlation between seduction and candy is not new, consumers might mistake this imagery for a valentine, not an advertisement. What is the advantage to the product placement in this ad?

STARCH™ AD-AS-A-WHOLE		
Noted %	Associated %	Read Most %
W 55	50	23-

Recognition scores have been collected for a long time, which allows advertisers to compare their current ads with similar ones done last week, last month, or fifty years ago. This is a big attraction of recognition scores. The biggest problem with this test is that of a yea-saying bias. In other words, many people say they recognize an ad that in truth they haven't seen. After a few days, do you really think you could correctly remember which of the three ads in Exhibits 7.16, 7.17, and 7.18 you really saw, if you saw the ads under natural viewing conditions? Still, on a relative basis, they may tell which ads are way better or way worse than others.

Attitude-Change Studies. The typical **attitude-change study** uses a before-and-after ad exposure design. They may be either survey based or done in a theater or shopping mall setting. In the latter case, people from the target market are recruited, and their pre-exposure attitudes toward the advertised brand as well as toward competitors' brands are taken. Then they are exposed to the test ad, along with some other ads. Following this exposure, their attitudes are measured again. The goal, of course, is to gauge the potential of specific ad versions for changing brand attitudes. These studies are often conducted in a theater test setting. These tests often use a constant-sum measurement scale. A subject is asked to divide a sum (for example, 100 points) among several (usually three) brands. For example, they would be asked to divide 100 points among three brands of deodorants in relation to how likely they are to purchase each. They do this before and after ad exposure. A change score is then computed. Sometimes this change score is adjusted by the potential change, so as not to unfairly penalize established brands with high pre-exposure ratings since there's not much room for improvement. Simulated shopping trips can also be part of this research. In the survey version of this a survey is delivered before the ads are in the test market, and after. Various levels of "warning" are used to make sure the people with surveys see the ads.

EXHIBITS 7.16, 7.17, AND 7.18

*All of these ads, so strikingly similar, do little to (1) differentiate the product, (2) make it memorable for the consumer, or (3) promote the brand, though presumably GM and Ford had intended to do all three with these ads. Compare and contrast the new Cadillac models (*www.cadillac.com*) with the Ford luxury models (*www.lincolnvehicles.com*). Has either company broken any new ground in its approach to advertising these vehicles? Do you think in a few days you could distinguish between these models or remember the message of these Web sites?*

The reliability of these procedures is very dependent on sample size and appropriateness. Furthermore, their validity is premised on a single ad exposure (sometimes two) in an unnatural viewing environment (such as a theater). Many advertisers believe that commercials don't register their impact until after three, four, or more exposures. Still, a significant swing in scores with a single exposure suggests that something is going on, and that some of this effect might be expected when the ad reaches real consumers in the comfort of their homes. But this method is expensive and may be waning in popularity. It survives because they provide objective information, and in the political struggle that generally embroils advertising, this is something. It also provides the good old blame game: when the ad does poorly, the person who lobbied for it can always say that the numbers looked good. John Philip Jones of Syracuse University has conducted analyses on these data and his conclusions are very supportive.[9] He contends that even if this form of message pretesting yields some incorrect predictions

9. John Philip Jones, "Advertising Pre-Testing: Will Europe Follow America's Lead?," *Commercial Communications,* June 1997, 21–26.

about ads' potential effectiveness (as it surely will), an advertiser's success rate with this tool is bound to improve relative to that which would be realized without it. On the other hand, it is difficult to know whether the respondent is really expressing feelings toward the ad or the product advertised, given the artificial conditions.

To test attitude change in print ads, test ads can be dropped off at the participants' homes in the form of magazines. The test ads have been "tipped in," or inserted. Subjects are told that the researcher will return the next day for an interview. They are also told that as part of their compensation for participating, they are being entered in a drawing. At that point, they are asked to indicate their preferences on a wide range of potential prizes. The next day when the interviewer returns, he or she asks for these preferences a second time. This is the postexposure attitude measure.

Physiological Tests. **Physiological measures** detect how consumers react to messages, based on physical responses. **Eye-tracking systems** have been developed to monitor eye movements across print ads. With one such system, respondents wear a gogglelike device that records (on a computer system) pupil dilations, eye movements, and length of view by sectors within a print advertisement. Another physiological measure is a **psychogalvanometer,** which measures galvanic skin response (GSR). GSR is a measure of minute changes in perspiration, which suggest arousal related to some stimulus—in this case, an advertisement.

Voice response analysis is another high-tech research procedure. The idea here is that inflections in the voice when discussing an ad indicate excitement and other physiological states. In a typical application, a subject is asked to respond to a series of ads. These responses are tape-recorded and then computer analyzed. Deviations from a flat response are claimed to be meaningful. Other, less frequently used physiological measures record brain wave activity, heart rate, blood pressure, and muscle contraction.

All physiological measures suffer from the same drawbacks. While we may be able to detect a physiological response to an advertisement, there is no way to determine whether the response is to the ad or the product, or which part of the advertisement was responsible for the response. In some sense, even the positive-negative dimension is obscured. Without being able to correlate specific effects with other dimensions of an ad, physiological measures are of minimal benefit.

Since the earliest days of advertising, there has been a fascination with physiological measurement. Advertising's fascination with science is well documented, with early attempts at physiology being far more successful as a sales tool than as a way to actually gauge ad effectiveness. There is something provocative about scientists (sometimes even in white lab coats) wiring people up; it seems so precise and legitimate. Unfortunately—or fortunately, depending on your perspective—these measures tell us little beyond the simple degree of arousal attributable to an ad. For most advertisers, this minimal benefit doesn't justify the expense and intrusion involved with physiological measurement.

Pilot Testing. Before committing to the expense of a major campaign, advertisers often test their messages in the marketplace via **pilot testing.** There are three major types of pilot testing. **Split-cable transmission** allows testing of two different versions of an advertisement through direct transmission to two separate samples of similar households within a single, well-defined market area. This method provides exposure in a natural setting for heightened realism. Factors such as frequency of transmission and timing of transmission can be carefully controlled. The advertisements are then compared on measures of exposure, recall, and persuasion.

Split-run distribution uses the same technique as split-cable transmission, except the print medium is used. Two different versions of the same advertisement are placed in every other copy of a magazine. This method of pilot testing has the advantage of using direct response as a test measure. Ads can be designed with a reply card that can serve as a basis of evaluation. Coupons and toll-free numbers can also be used. The realism of this method is a great advantage in the testing process. Expense is, of course, a major drawback.

Finally, a **split-list experiment** tests the effectiveness of various aspects of direct mail advertising pieces. Multiple versions of a direct mail piece are prepared and sent to various segments of a mailing list. The version that *pulls* (produces sales) the best is deemed superior. The advantage of all the pilot testing methods is the natural and real setting within which the test takes place. A major disadvantage is that competitive or other environmental influences in the market cannot be controlled and may affect the performance of one advertisement without ever being detected by the researcher.

Tracking Studies. **Posttest message tracking** assesses the performance of advertisements during or after the launch of an advertising campaign. Common measures of an ad's performance are recall, recognition, awareness and attitude, and purchase behavior. Tracking studies measure the change in an audience's brand awareness and attitude before and after an advertising campaign. This common type of advertising research is almost always conducted as a survey. Members of the target market are surveyed on a fairly regular basis to detect any changes. Any change in awareness or attitude is usually attributed (rightly or wrongly) to the advertising effort. The problem with these types of tests is the inability to isolate the effect of advertising on awareness and attitude amid a myriad of other influences—media reports, observation, friends, competitive advertising, and so forth.

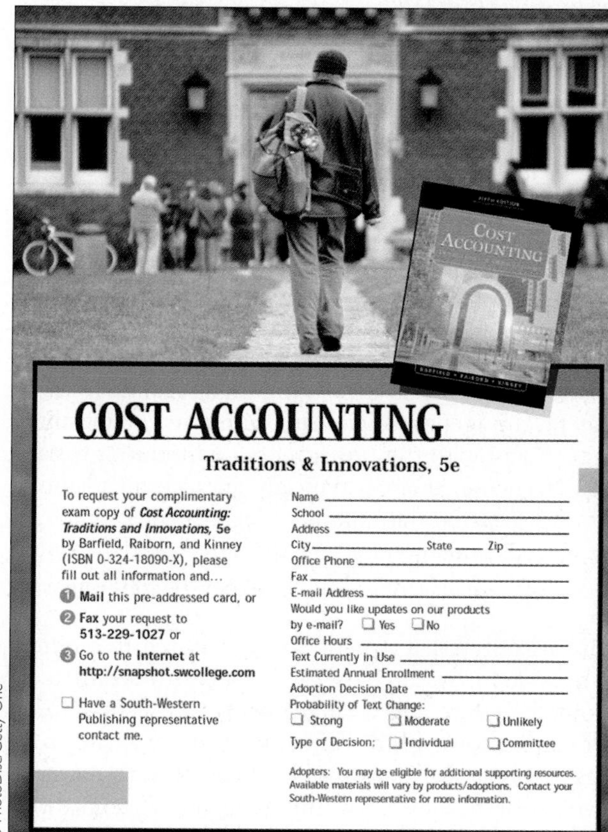

© PhotoDisc/Getty One

EXHIBIT 7.19

An ad like this allows for a very simple kind of advertising response management.

Direct Response. Advertisements in both print and broadcast media that offer the audience the opportunity to place an inquiry or respond directly through a Web site, reply card, or toll-free phone number produce **inquiry/direct response measures.** An example is displayed in Exhibit 7.19. These measures are quite straightforward in the sense that advertisements that generate a high number of inquiries or direct responses, compared to historical benchmarks, are deemed effective. Additional analyses may compare the number of inquiries or responses to the number of sales generated. For example, some print ads will use different 800 numbers for different versions of the ad so that the agency can compute which ad is generating more inquiries. These measures are not relevant for all types of advertising, however. Ads designed to have long-term image building or brand identity effects should not be judged using such short-term response measures.

Single-Source Data. With the advent of universal product codes (UPCs) on product packages and the proliferation of cable television, research firms are now able to engage in *single-source research* to document the behavior of individuals in a respondent pool by tracking their behavior from the television set to the checkout counter. **Single-source tracking measures** provide information from individual households about brand purchases, coupon use, and television advertising exposure by combining grocery store scanner data and data from devices (called *peoplemeters*) attached to the households' televisions, which monitor viewing behavior. These sophisticated measures are used to gauge the impact of advertising and promotions on consumers' actual purchases. The main problem with these measures is that it is impossible to determine what aspects of advertising had positive effects on consumers.

Frame-by-Frame Tests. These tests are usually employed for ads where the affective or emotional component is seen as key, although they may also be used to obtain thought listing as well. These tests typically work by getting consumers to turn dials (like/dislike) while viewing television commercials in a theater setting. The data from these dials is then collected, averaged, and superimposed over the commercial. The superimposed lines display interest in the ad. Where the line is higher represents a period of higher interest in the ad, and subsequently when the line dips, it shows less interest in that particular point of the ad. While some research companies do ask consumers what they were thinking or feeling at certain points along the trace, and sometimes these responses are diagnostic, others do not. In those cases (such as the ones shown in Exhibit 7.20), what the trace line really does then is measure the levels of interest at each specific moment in the execution—it does not explain why consumers reactions were positive or negative. Its downside involves somewhat higher costs than other methods, and some validity concerns . . . in that you are asking them to do something they do not normally do while watching television. On the other hand, the method has widespread application from television commercials to feature films to trial simulations with mock jurors. Most researchers, including academic ones, believe that useful data can be gathered in this way.

Account Planning versus Advertising Research. Jon Steel, director of account planning and vice chairman of Goodby, Silverstein and Partners (its clients include Anheuser-Busch, the California Fluid Milk Processors Board ("Got Milk?"), Nike, Porsche, and Hewlett-Packard), has called account planning "the biggest thing to hit American advertising since Doyle Dane Bernbach's Volkswagen campaign."[10] That is stretching it a bit, but account planning is a big story in the industry. What is it? Well, good question. (See Exhibit 7.21.)

Account planning is defined in contrast to traditional advertising research. It differs mostly in three ways. First, in terms of organization, agencies that use this system typically assign an "account planner" to work cooperatively with the account executive on a given client's business. Rather than depending on a separate research department's occasional involvement, the agency assigns the planner to a single client (just like an advertising executive) to stay with the projects on a continuous basis—even though, in this organizational scheme, there is typically an account planning department. In the more traditional system, the research department would get involved from time to time as needed, and members of the research department would work on several different clients' advertising. (There are several variations on this theme.)

Another difference is that this organizational structure puts research in a different, more prominent role. In this system, researchers (or "planners") seem to be more actively involved throughout the entire advertising process and seem to have a bigger impact on it as well. (Of course, some of the difference is more agency self-promotion than reality.) Agencies that practice "account planning" tend to do more developmental and less evaluative research. Third, "planning agencies" tend to do more qualitative and naturalistic research than their more traditional counterparts. But these differences, too, seem fairly exaggerated—even though Jay Chiat called planning "the best new business tool ever invented,"[11] there is another, more cynical side to this story: Many advertising agencies have decided that they simply cannot

10. Jon Steel, *Truth, Lies & Advertising: The Art of Account Planning* (New York: John Wiley & Sons, 1998), jacket.
11. Ibid., p. 42.

EXHIBIT 7.20

Here consumers interest levels are measured while watching the ads in real time.

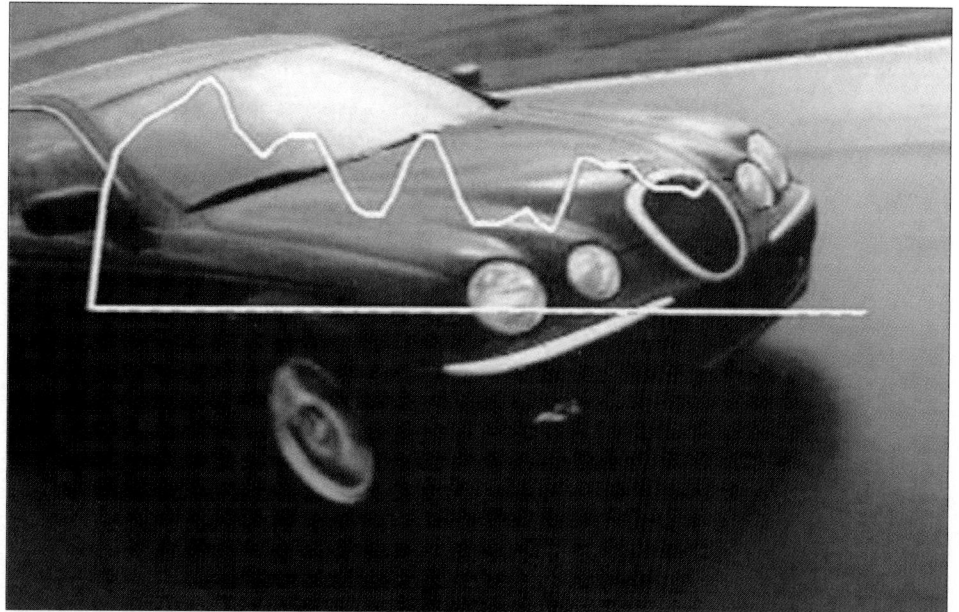

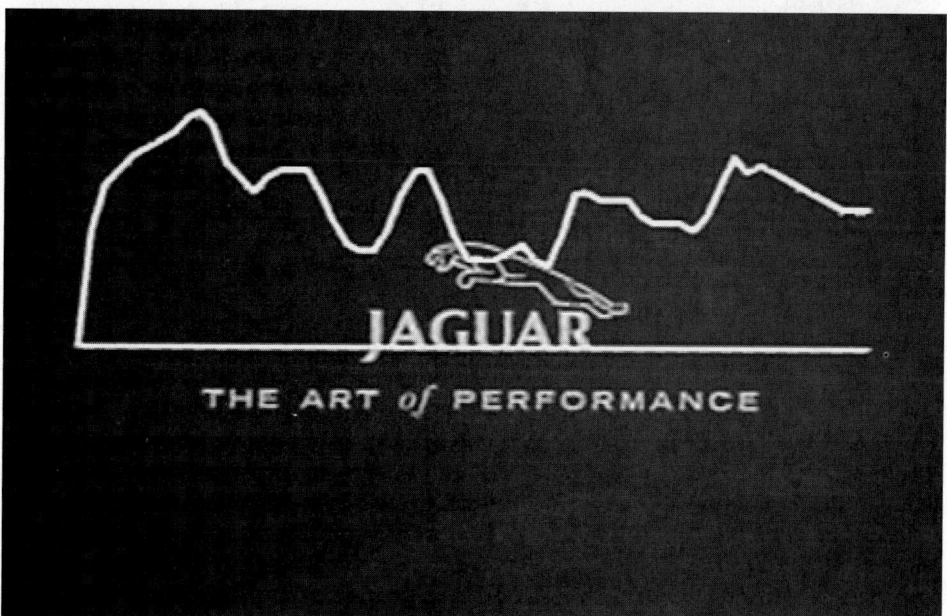

afford the cost of a full-time research staff. It's cheaper and maybe even better to outsource the work. But a quieter and more devious way of downsizing (or eliminating these expensive departments) is to go to the "account planning" system, in which a researcher will always be a part of the team. Then, there's no need for a centralized research department, and it appears as if the agency is actually demonstrating more commitment to research. Ah, the art of spin.

Another Thought on Message Testing. None of these methods are perfect. There are challenges to reliability, validity, trustworthiness, and meaningfulness with all of them. Advertisers sometimes think that consumers watch new television commercials the way they watch new, eagerly awaited feature films, or that they listen to radio spots like they listen to a symphony, or read magazine ads like a Steinbeck novel. Work by James Lull and other naturalistic researchers and ethnographers

EXHIBIT 7.21

Much ado is made about the account planner versus traditional advertising research.

demonstrate what we know: We watch TV while we work, talk, eat, and study; we use it as a night light, background noise, and babysitter.[12] Likewise, we typically thumb through magazines very, very quickly. While these traditional methods of message testing have their strengths, more naturalistic methods are clearly recommended. Still, it would be a mistake to throw the baby out with the bath water; good and appropriate social science can produce better advertising.

What We Need. Advertising research could do with some change. The way we think about ads is certainly changing. Many U.S. agencies on the west coast, as well as some British agencies, have embraced qualitative methods. These shops, known for their creativity, have been more attractive to hot creatives because of the lack of old-style quantitative copy research. In fact, across the industry, the view that ads are complex social texts rather than the equivalent of a high school debate has caught on. The move to an almost complete visual advertising style has also put into question the appropriateness of a set of tests that focus on the acceptance of message claims, as well as remembrance.[13]

12. James Lull, "How Families Select Television Programs: A Mass Observational Study," *Journal of Broadcasting,* vol. 26, no. 4 (1982), 801–811.

13. John W. Pracejus, G. Douglas Olsen, and Thomas C. O'Guinn, "Nothing is Something: The Production and Reception of Advertising Meaning Through the Use of White Space," *Journal of Marketing Research,* Alberta, Canada, 2001.

SUMMARY

Explain the purposes served by and methods used in developmental advertising research.

Advertising and promotion research can serve many purposes in the development of a campaign. There is no better way to generate fresh ideas for a campaign than to listen carefully to the customer. Qualitative research involving customers is essential for fostering fresh thinking about a brand. Audience definition and profiling are fundamental to effective campaign planning and rely on advertising research. In the developmental phase, advertisers use diverse methods for gathering information. Focus groups, projective techniques, association tests, the ZMET, and field work are trusted research methods that directly involve consumers and aid in idea generation and concept testing.

Identify sources of secondary data that can aid the IBP planning effort.

Since information is such a critical resource in the decision-making process, several sources of secondary data are widely used. Internal company sources such as old research reports, customer service records, and sales figures provide a wealth of information on consumer tastes and preferences. Government sources generate a wide range of census and labor statistics, providing key data on trends in population, consumer spending, employment, and immigration. Commercial data sources provide advertisers with a wealth of information on household consumers. Finally, secondary data sources such as professional publications share insider information on industry trends, and more and more advertisers use the Internet as a revolutionary research tool that delivers rich data at virtually no cost.

Discuss the purposes served by and methods used in copy research.

Copy research (evaluative research) aims to judge the effectiveness of actual ads. Advertisers and clients try to determine if audiences "get" the joke of an ad or retain key knowledge concerning the brand. Tracking changes in audience attitudes, emotions, behavior, and physiological response is important in gauging the overall success of an ad, and various methods are employed before and after the launch of a campaign to assess the impact on audiences. Communication tests, recall testing, and the thought-listing technique are a few of the methods that try to measure the persuasiveness of a message. Some agencies, attempting to bypass the high cost and inconclusive results of research, substitute account planning for traditional advertising and promotion research. Advocates of this trend believe an account planning system merges the best in research and brand management.

KEY TERMS

account planning
concept test
focus group
projective techniques
association tests
sentence and picture completion
dialogue balloons
story construction
Zaltman Metaphor Elicitation Technique (ZMET)
field work
coolhunts
normative test scores
communication tests
resonance test
thought listing
attitude-change study
physiological measures
eye-tracking systems
psychogalvanometer
pilot testing
split-cable transmission
split-run distribution
split-list experiment
posttest message tracking
inquiry/direct response measures
single-source tracking measures

QUESTIONS

1. What does it mean to profile the target audience? What is the value of audience profiling? Identify three different types of information commonly used in developing audience profiles.

2. Focus groups are one of the advertising researcher's most versatile tools. Describe the basic features of focus group research that could lead to inappropriate generalizations about the preferences of the target audience.

3. ZMET is a technique that advertisers may use in place of focus groups. What aspects of ZMET and focus groups are similar? What particular features of ZMET could foster richer understanding of consumers' motives than is typically achieved with focus groups?

4. List the sources and uses of secondary data. What are the benefits of secondary data? What are the limitations? Do you think primary data sources should always be given priority over secondary sources? Justify your answer.

5. Identify issues that could become sources of conflict between account managers and advertising creatives in the message-testing process. What could go wrong if people in an ad agency take the position that what the client wants, the client gets?

6. Criteria for judging ad effectiveness include "getting it," knowledge, attitude change, feelings and emotions, physiological changes, and behavior. Identify specific evaluative advertising research methods that could be used to test an ad's impact on each of these dimensions.

7. Normative test scores help the advertiser put test results for a new ad in proper context. Do you think it would be a good idea to compare scores for recognition versus recall tests as another way to "put things in context"? Explain your position.

8. How would you explain the finding that ads that achieve high recall scores don't always turn out to be ads that do a good job in generating sales? What does this say about the concept of meaningfulness? Can you name three ads you saw yesterday?

9. What is the meaning of the term *single-source research*? What is the connection between the UPCs one finds on nearly every product in the grocery store and this thing called single-source research?

10. Explain the industry trend of substituting account planning for traditional advertising and promotion research. Why do some agency directors claim that this trend is the biggest thing in advertising since the famous Bernbach Volkswagen campaign? Do you tend to believe the hype surrounding this trend, or are you cynical that forces of downsizing are driving it? Explain your reasoning.

EXPERIENTIAL EXERCISES

1. Break up into teams to plan and execute an advertising research test on a popular television commercial of your choice. First, determine the evaluative criteria you think would be most relevant for determining the ad's effectiveness. Next, plan and design a test for the commercial by choosing an evaluative advertising research method and typing up a short pencil-and-paper questionnaire to be answered by classmates. Each team of "researchers" should assign the simple questionnaire to another team to be filled out in response to watching the commercial. After answering the questionnaire, pass the forms back to the original research teams and let each team provide a brief report to the class concerning the research results. Be sure to explain what feedback the test was designed to produce, and give an evaluation of the commercial based on the results of the survey. Finally, be sure to discuss the reliability, validity, trustworthiness, and meaningfulness of your research.

2. Go to your favorite search engine and do a search on "advertising research." Surf until you find an organization that is related to the field of advertising research and browse its Web site. Type a one-page paper, explaining what information or services the organization provides and who would be likely to benefit from them. If the information is available at the site, list a specific advertiser that has worked with the organization, and explain the kind of research or information that the organization provided to guide the advertising and promotion initiatives of the advertiser.

USING THE INTERNET

7-1 Developmental Advertising Research

Developmental advertising research provides key information used by creatives in producing ads. A brand's optimal advertising and promotion effort depends on accurate information about trends, target audience, product usage expectations, and other data that are useful during the production of the advertising message.

Clairol delivers integrated brand promotion for many of its product lines, and develops effective campaigns based on important research. Clairol's research has led to the development of its Herbal Essences products, which target a very specific consumer niche within the broad category of personal care products.

Herbal Essences: http://www.herbalessences.com

1. Explain the role of "audience profiling" and how it guides the uses and message of the Herbal Essences Web site.

2. What is the main concept behind the Herbal Essences product line? Do you believe that concept testing played an important role for Clairol in the development of Herbal Essences? Explain.

3. What trends do you believe had to be measured quantitatively by trustworthy advertising research in order for Clairol to develop and advertise Herbal Essences? Identify the developmental advertising research method that you think would be the most important to guide Clairol's efforts to advertise and promote Herbal Essences. Explain why you picked this method.

7-2 Evaluative Research

Evaluative advertising research is used to help assure advertisers that ads actually accomplish the strategic goals set by the creative team and their clients. A variety of evaluative criteria are used to judge ads, and numerous methods can be employed to gather dependable response data. Perhaps one of the most consistent ads of recent years has been the repetitive campaign of 1-800-COLLECT, a long-distance service that is memorable for its use of Hollywood personalities in delivering the brand's message.

1-800-COLLECT: http://www.1800collect.com

1. List two of the evaluative criteria used to judge the effectiveness of ads and explain how they apply to the 1-800-COLLECT television ads or Web site.

2. Explain the concept of "recall testing" and describe how 1-800-COLLECT's ad message strategy is firmly based upon this concept. Have you ever remembered this 1-800-COLLECT service when you needed to make a collect phone call?

3. Why do advertisers use Hollywood personalities in ads to deliver the brand's message? Choose one evaluative criteria or evaluative research method and explain how it might be related to 1-800-COLLECT's decision to invest big money in order to use Hollywood personalities in every advertisement.

CHAPTER 5
Advertising and Consumer Behavior

CHAPTER 6
Market Segmentation, Positioning, and the Value Proposition

CHAPTER 7
Advertising and Promotion Research

CHAPTER 8
The Advertising Plan

CHAPTER 9
Advertising Planning: An International Perspective

CHAPTER 8

After reading and thinking about this chapter, you will be able to do the following:

Describe the basic components of an advertising plan.

Compare and contrast two fundamental approaches for setting advertising objectives.

Explain various methods for setting advertising budgets.

Discuss the role of the advertising agency in formulating an advertising plan.

What are you doing to save time?

Let quixi do what you don't have time to do. Reach us by phone or on the web and our live helpers will shop online for you, give you movie times, directions or connect you to the people you need to reach. **Help is standing by.**

www.quixi.com

. . *Think Different.*

This was the battle cry in all advertising for Apple Computer as the new millennium approached. But it seemed that no one was listening. The once high-flying computer manufacturer was floundering in an Intel/Windows onslaught. In June 1998 Apple's U.S. retail market share had fallen to a mere 2 percent.[1] The company that had once rocked the computer business with its innovative Macintosh computer and its provocative "1984" TV commercial was approaching virtual extinction. Could Apple be saved?

Apple found itself in a real mess. And we want to emphasize that the severity of its problems went well beyond what one might be able to fix with a fresh advertising campaign and a catchy slogan like "Think Different." To rebound, Apple would need inspired leadership and, most important, a series of innovative new products to capture the imagination of consumers around the world. The leadership would have to come from its celebrated founder and on-again/off-again CEO—Steve Jobs. The new product designed to salvage the company was the iMac personal computer.

Put yourself in the shoes of Steve Jobs. The company that you helped create was adrift and you desperately needed a major new product success to turn things around. You have decided to stake the future of your company on a new product called iMac. Launching a great new product via a comprehensive advertising and IBP campaign is your best hope for reviving the company. As you will see, Mr. Jobs held nothing back in his determined effort to save Apple.

The iMac was the first in a new generation of Internet appliances. It was a system designed first and foremost to get households hooked to the Net. As described by Steve Jobs, "iMac does for Internet computing what the original Macintosh did for personal computing. Macintosh let anyone use a computer and iMac lets anyone get on to the Internet quickly and easily." Regarding his advertising and IBP campaign, Jobs went on to say, "We're launching this campaign because we want the world to know that iMac is the computer for the tens of millions of consumers who want to get to the Internet easily, quickly, and affordably."[2] Jobs, of course, was not just grasping at straws: His market research at the time was telling him that one of consumers' primary motives for buying a personal computer was to hook up to the Internet.

While the iMac actually went on sale August 14, 1998, its launch campaign was initiated three months before at a surprise unveiling of the machine before an audience of media types in the same auditorium where the Macintosh was introduced. In other parallels with the 1984 launch of the Macintosh, Jobs departed from his usual dress code by wearing a suit and keeping the iMac prototype behind a veil on stage until he was ready to spring it on his unsuspecting audience. Mr. Jobs stated at the time: "We figured we'd have a surprise and then let people feed on it before they could get it."[3] In the weeks leading up to August 14, Jobs's sneak preview had the desired effect of creating an iMac buzz across Web sites frequently visited by loyal Mac users.

Mr. Jobs and his public relations machine continued to strut their stuff in the hours leading up to the first public sale of the iMac at 12:01 A.M. on August 14. Working with loyal retailers, Apple's PR people created 20-foot-high inflatable iMac balloons to fly above retail stores at the Midnight Madness event on August 14, 1998. A Cupertino, California, retailer added giant searchlights and scheduled part of its midnight iMac delivery using four new Volkswagen Beetles on loan from a local dealer. Of course, TV crews from every station in the Bay Area were there to cover the action and report it all to the world the next day. Summarizing the state of affairs on launch day, one salesperson at a CompUSA Superstore in San Francisco

1. Bradley Johnson, "Jobs Orchestrates Ad Blitz for Apple's New iMac PC," *Advertising Age,* August 10, 1998, 6.
2. "Apple Launches Its Largest Marketing Campaign Ever for iMac," www.apple.com/pr/library, accessed August 13, 1998.
3. Jim Carlton, "From Apple, a New Marketing Blitz," *Wall Street Journal,* August 14, 1998, B1.

said: "I don't think even Apple expected it to be this crazy; We're having trouble keeping iMacs on the shelves."[4]

And that was just for starters. As the new iMac was going on sale, Apple executives also announced the start of the largest advertising campaign in their history, where paid media advertising costs were expected to run more than $100 million between August 15 and December 31, 1998. (Yes, Mr. Jobs was betting the future of his company on the success of the iMac.) These are just some of the key elements of the campaign:[5]

- *Television advertising*—National TV ads began August 16 on *The Wonderful World of Disney* and continued on programs such as *NewsRadio* and *The Drew Carey Show,* and on cable shows such as *South Park* and *Larry King Live*. TV ads were also placed in the top 10 metro markets—Boston; Chicago; Los Angeles; New York; San Francisco; Philadelphia; Washington, D.C.; Seattle; Minneapolis; and Denver. TV ads began airing in Europe and Asia in September 1998.
- *Outdoor advertising*—Billboards also went up in the top 10 metro markets. As shown in Exhibit 8.1, they featured a photo of the iMac and one of the following copy lines: "Chic. Not Geek"; "Sorry, no beige"; "Mental floss"; and "I think, therefore iMac." This last copy line was attributed to Mr. Magic—Steve Jobs.
- *Magazine advertising*—An informative 12-page iMac insert was distributed through leading magazines such as *Time, People, Sports Illustrated,* and *Rolling Stone*. More than 15 million copies were put in consumers' hands in the first few weeks after launch. This more than doubled the amount of inserts ever distributed by Apple in any prior campaign. Four pages from this insert are displayed in Exhibit 8.2. In addition, the playfulness of the iMac launch campaign is nicely exemplified by the magazine ad in Exhibit 8.3.
- *Radio advertising*—A five-day countdown to the iMac launch was executed through a network of 20 nationwide radio companies. This promotion featured iMac giveaways each day of the week preceding Midnight Madness. Apple's was the most comprehensive radio campaign in the United States the week of August 10, 1998.

EXHIBIT 8.1

Apple's iMac launch used outdoor billboards like this one in the 10 top metro markets across the United States. What value proposition do you see being addressed by this billboard? Does this value proposition relate to a larger trend in the computer and technology industry? www.apple.com

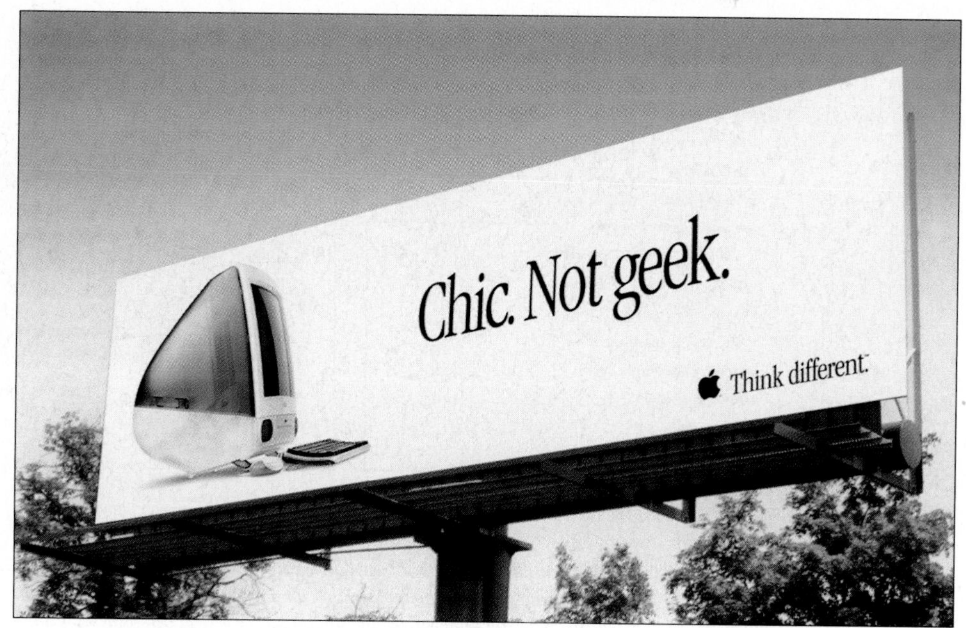

4. "iMac Makes a Midnight Debut," www.macweek.com. accessed August 15, 1998.
5. "Apple Launches its Largest Marketing Campaign Ever for iMac."

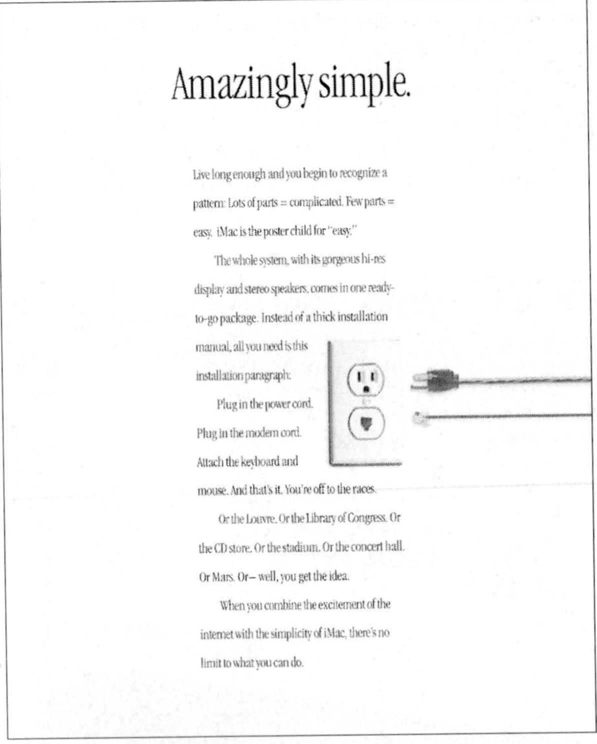

EXHIBIT 8.2

Apple (www.apple.com) has consistently broken new ground in its product advertising. Former Chairman John Sculley, who came to Apple from PepsiCo, contrasted the company with his former margin-focused employer, as an agent of incessant innovation and radical change. Apple ads certainly seem to find endless ways to herald the new, the innovative, the unordinary—better, perhaps, than any others. Prior to the iMac's release, Apple had already launched a "Think Different" campaign with images of famous iconoclasts, but "Think Different" continues to play a role in Apple's marketing of the iMac. (One wonders, though, at the "too beige" jab: While most PCs can be painted with that brush, so, too, could Apple's Macintosh product line!)

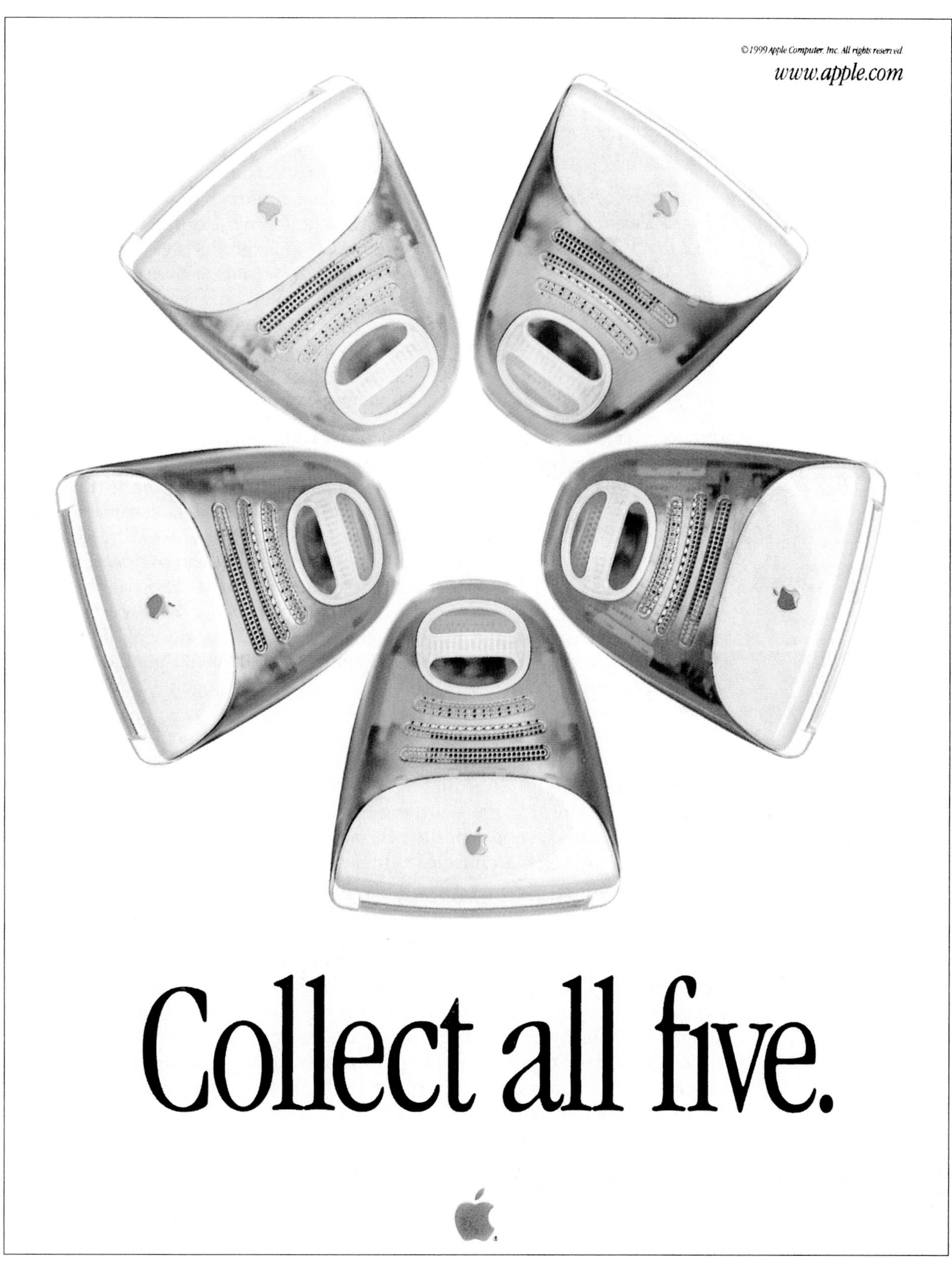

EXHIBIT 8.3

Funny how little things can become big things in the hands of a skillful marketer like Apple. Here we see Apple champion one of iMac's simple virtues: THEY COME IN COLORS! A related television spot featured the Rolling Stones' tune "She's A Rainbow" to further glorify the colorful iMac.

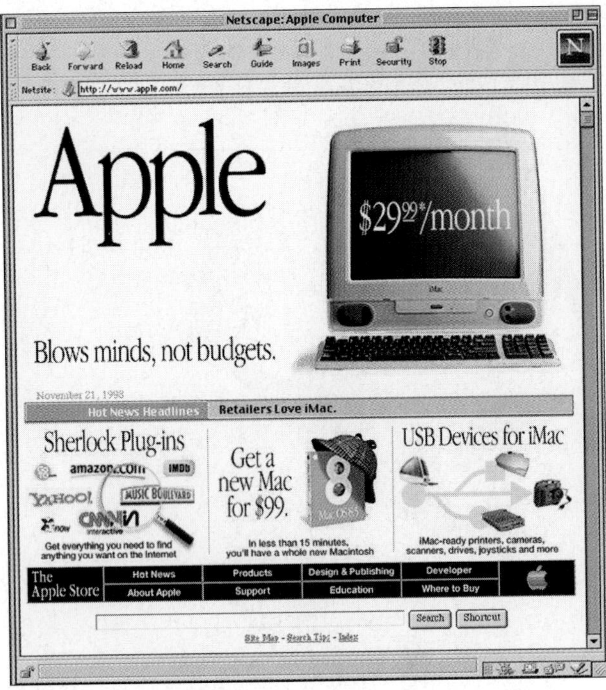

EXHIBIT 8.4

Of course, Apple's home page featured the iMac in November 1998. The interactivity of the Web makes it the perfect medium for anticipating and answering questions about the technical features of a product such as a new PC.

- *Cooperative advertising*—Apple also joined forces with its local retailers in cooperative-advertising efforts around the United States. For example, Apple worked with the New York dealer DataVisions Inc. to help sponsor iMac ads on movie screens in all 600 of Long Island's theaters. Other dealers participated in software and T-shirt giveaways, and CompUSA launched newspaper ads that for the first time promoted Apple products exclusively.
- *Web site features and promotions*—Of course, everything you could ever want to know about the iMac and the iMac product launch was available for the world to peruse at www.apple.com. Exhibit 8.4 shows the Apple home page as of November 1998.

The iMac launch campaign yielded the kind of results that Steve Jobs needed for reviving his company. In November 1998 the iMac was the best selling PC in the consumer market, with about a third of iMac buyers being first-time owners of any type of personal computer.[6] And it wasn't just a faddish success: the iMac would propel Apple Computer Inc. to 11 consecutive quarters of profitable growth. But just to illustrate the point that nothing in marketing and advertising is ever permanent, by the summer of 2000 media pundits of all kinds began asking questions like, "Yes, Steve, you fixed it. Congrats! Now what's Act Two?"[7]

As the high-profile CEO of Apple, Mr. Jobs received a good deal of the praise for iMac's provocative launch campaign. However, he quickly demurred and assigned the credit to his advertising agency—TBWA Chiat/Day of Venice, California. Said Jobs: "Creating great advertising, like creating great products, is a team effort. I am lucky to work with the best talent in the industry."[8] Indeed, it would be impossible to launch a campaign of this scale without great teamwork between agency and client.

While we have merely scratched the surface in describing all that was involved in the campaign that launched the iMac, we hope this example gives you a taste for the complexity that can be involved in executing a comprehensive advertising and IBP effort. You don't go out and spend $100 million promoting a new product that is vital to the success of a firm without giving the entire endeavor considerable forethought. Such an endeavor will call for a plan. As you will see in this chapter, Jobs, Apple, and Chiat/Day followed the process of building an advertising effort based on several key features of the advertising plan. An advertising plan is the culmination of the planning effort needed to create effective advertising.

1 The Advertising Plan and Its Marketing Context.

An ad plan should be a direct extension of a firm's marketing plan. As suggested in the closing section of Chapter 6, one device that can be used to explicitly connect the market-

6. "Apple Unveils Cheaper iMac," *Cincinnati Enquirer,* January 6, 1999, B10.
7. For a thorough debriefing on Apple's situation post-iMac, see Peter Burrows, "Apple," *Business Week,* July 31, 2000, 102–113; Jon Swartz, "After iMac, Pressure Mounts on Apple," *USA Today,* July 25, 2000, 3B; and Pui-Wing Tam, "Apple's Growth beyond Traditional Base Is Called into Question," *Wall Street Journal,* October 2, 2000, B26.
8. Johnson, "Jobs Orchestrates Ad Blitz for Apple's New iMac PC," op. cit.

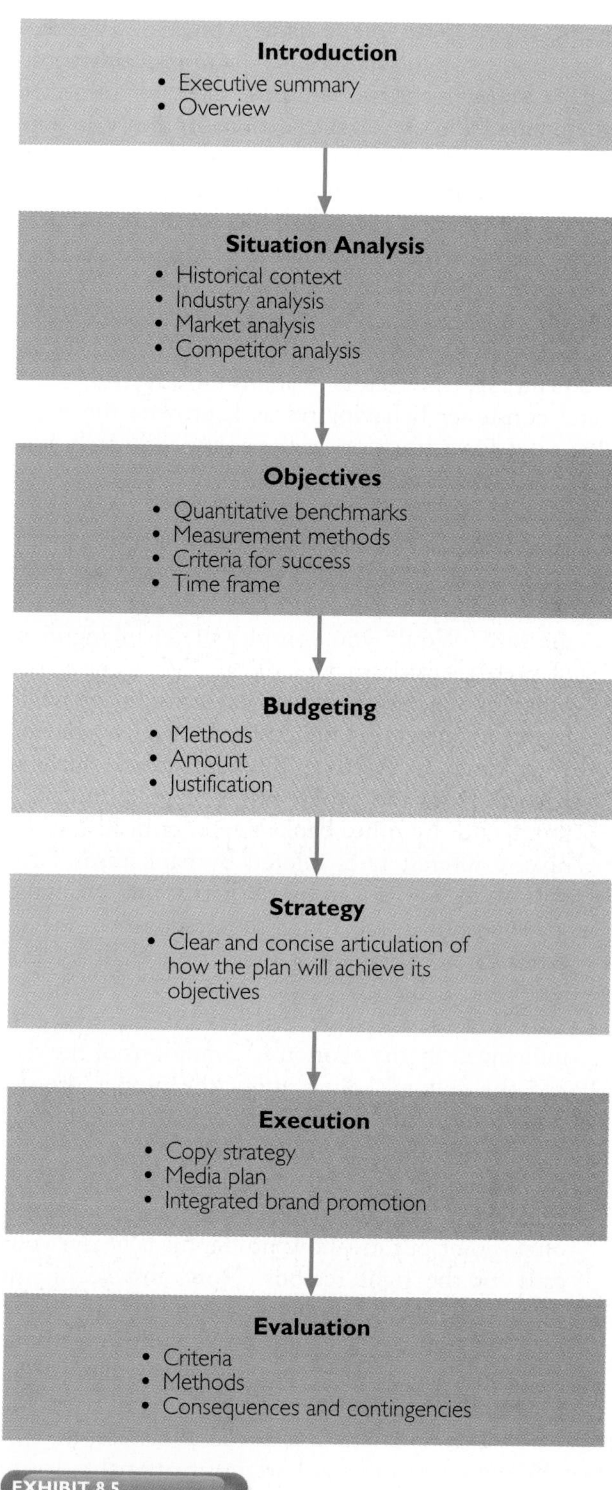

EXHIBIT 8.5

The advertising plan.

ing plan with the advertising plan is the statement of a brand's value proposition. A statement of what the brand is supposed to stand for in the eyes of the target segment derives from the firm's marketing strategy, and will guide all ad-planning activities. The advertising plan, including all integrated brand promotion, is a subset of the larger marketing plan. The IBP component must be built into the plan in a seamless and synergistic way. Everything has to work together, whether the plan is for Apple or for a business with far fewer resources. And as Steve Jobs noted about his iMac campaign, there is no substitute for good teamwork between agency and client in the development of compelling marketing and advertising plans.

An **advertising plan** specifies the thinking and tasks needed to conceive and implement an effective advertising effort. We particularly like the iMac example because it illustrates the wide array of options that can be deployed in creating interest and communicating the value proposition for a brand. Jobs and his agency choreographed public relations activities, promotions and giveaways, cooperative advertising, broadcast advertising, billboard advertising, Web site development, and more as part of the iMac launch. An advertising planner should review all the options before selecting an integrated set to communicate with the target audience. We wish to emphasize that advertising planners must think beyond traditional broadcast media when considering the best way to break through the clutter of the modern marketplace and get their message across to the focal customer.

Exhibit 8.5 shows the components of an advertising plan. It should be noted that there is a great deal of variation in advertising plans from advertiser to advertiser. Our discussion of the advertising plan will focus on the seven major sections shown in Exhibit 8.5: the introduction, situation analysis, objectives, budgeting, strategy, execution, and evaluation. Each of these advertising plan components is discussed in the following sections.

Introduction. The introduction of an advertising plan consists of an executive summary and an overview. An executive summary, typically two paragraphs to two pages in length, is offered to state the most important aspects of the plan. This is the take-away; that is, it is what the reader should remember from the plan. It is the essence of the plan.

As with many documents, an overview is also customary. An overview ranges in length from a paragraph to a few pages. It sets out what is to be covered, and it structures the context. All plans are different, and some require more of a setup than others. Don't underestimate the benefit of a good introduction. It's where you can make or lose a lot of points with your boss or client.

Situation Analysis. When someone asks you to explain a decision you've made, you may say something such as, "Well, here's the situation . . ." In what follows, you probably try to distill the situation down to the most important points and how they are connected in order to explain why you made the decision. An ad plan **situation analysis** is no different. It is where the client and agency lay out the most important factors that define the situation, and then explain the importance of each factor.

An infinite list of potential factors (for example, demographic, social and cultural, economic, and political/regulatory) define a situation analysis. Some books offer long but incomplete lists. We prefer to play it straight with you: There is no complete list of situational factors. The idea is not to be exhaustive or encyclopedic when writing a plan, but to be smart in choosing the few important factors that really describe the situation, and then explain how the factors relate to the advertising task at hand. Market segmentation and consumer behavior research provide the organization with insights that can be used for a situation analysis, but ultimately you have to decide which of the many factors are really the most critical to address in your advertising. This is the essence of management.

Let's say you represent American Express. How would you define the firm's current advertising situation? What are the most critical factors? What image has prior advertising, like that in Exhibit 8.6, established for the card? Would you consider the changing view of prestige cards to be critical? What about the problem of hanging onto an exclusive image while trying to increase your customer base by having your cards accepted at discount stores, such as Kmart? Does the proliferation of gold and platinum cards by other banks rate as critical? Do the diverse interest rates offered by bank cards seem critical to the situation? What about changing social attitudes regarding the responsible use of credit cards? What about the current high level of consumer debt?

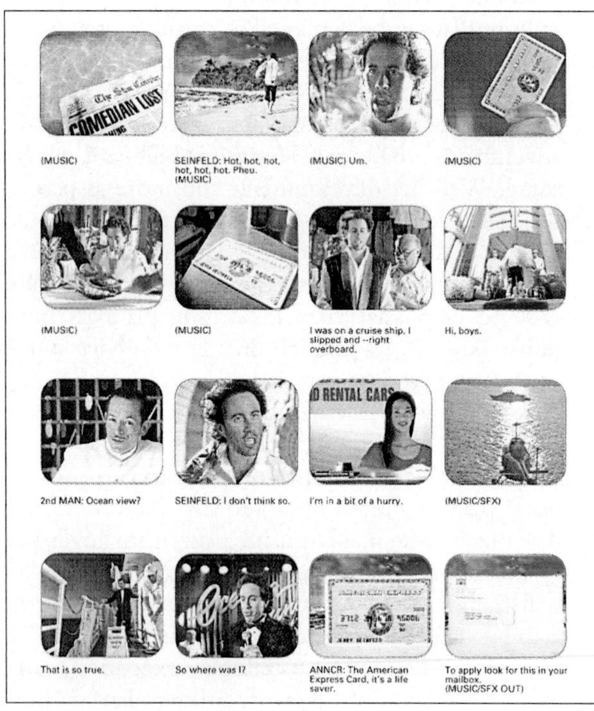

EXHIBIT 8.6

What is the image this ad establishes for the American Express card? How is this image a response to the company's situation analysis? Link your answer to a discussion of market segmentation and product positioning. Who is reached by this ad and how does reaching this segment fit into the overall strategy for American Express?
www.americanexpress.com

Think about how credit card marketing is influenced by the economic conditions of the day and the cultural beliefs about the proper way to display status. In the eighties, it was acceptable for advertisers to tout the self-indulgent side of plastic (for example, MasterCard's slogan "MasterCard, I'm bored"). Today, charge and credit card ads often point out just how prudent it is to use your card for the right reasons. Now, instead of just suggesting you use your plastic to hop off to the islands when you feel the first stirrings of a bout with boredom, credit card companies often detail functional benefits for their cards with a specific market segment in mind, as reflected by the American Express ad in Exhibit 8.7.

Basic demographic trends may be the single most important situational factor in advertising plans. Whether it's baby boomers or Generation X, Y, or Z, where the numbers are is usually where the sales are. As the population distribution varies with time, new markets are created and destroyed. The baby boom generation of post–World War II disproportionately dictates consumer offerings and demand simply because of its size. As the boomers age, companies that offer the things needed by tens of millions of aging boomers will have to devise new appeals. Think of the consumers of this generation needing long-term health care, geriatric products, and things to amuse themselves in retirement. Will they have the disposable income necessary to have the bountiful lifestyle many of them have had during their working

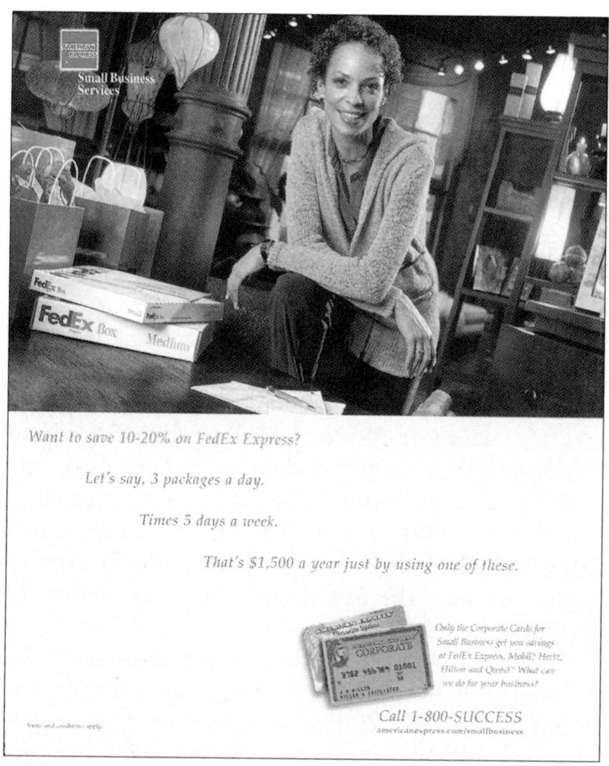

EXHIBIT 8.7

Here we see American Express offering a specific package of benefits to a well-defined target segment. Obviously, the folks at American Express understand STP marketing (per Chapter 6).

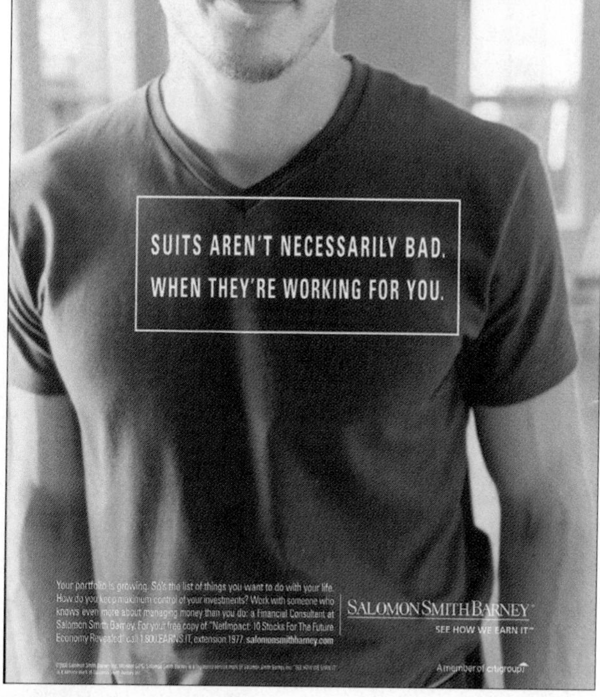

EXHIBIT 8.8

Are you ready for that phone call from Salomon Smith Barney? As suggested by this ad, it just might come sooner than you think. www.salomonsmithbarney.com

years? After all, they aren't the greatest savers. And what of the X'ers? Are the needs of the current twentysomethings fundamentally different from those of boomers? For instance, as X'ers age, will they develop an interest in the stock market to rival that of their parents' generation? From the looks of Exhibit 8.8, Salomon Smith Barney seems to think so.

Historical Context. No situation is entirely new, but all situations are unique. Just how a firm arrived at the current situation is very important. Before trying to design Apple's iMac campaign, an agency should certainly know a lot about the history of all the principal players, the industry, the brand, the corporate culture, critical moments in the company's past, its big mistakes and big successes. All new decisions are situated in a firm's history, and an agency should be diligent in studying that history. For example, would an agency pitch new business to Green Giant without knowing something of the brand's history and the rationale behind the Green Giant? The history of the Green Giant dates back decades, as the ad in Exhibit 8.9 shows. The fact is that no matter what advertising decisions are made in the present, the past has a significant impact.

Apart from history's intrinsic value, sometimes the real business goal is to convince the client that the agency knows the client's business, its major concerns, and its corporate culture. A brief history of the company and brand are included to demonstrate the thoroughness of the agency's research, the depth of its knowledge, and the scope of its concern.

e-SIGHTINGS

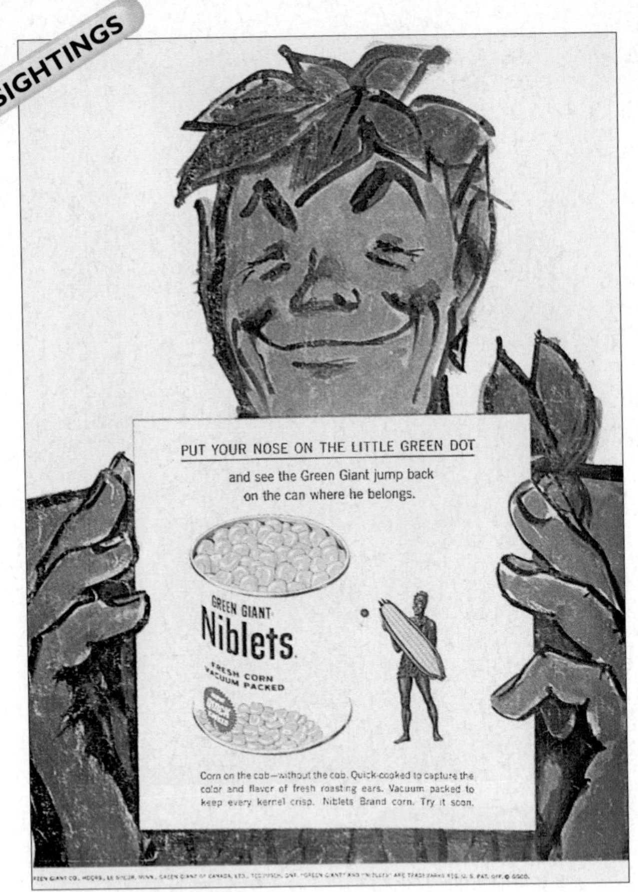

EXHIBIT 8.9

Knowing a brand's history can guide the development of future campaigns. Visit the Green Giant corporate site (www.greengiant.com) and read all about the history of the Green Giant character. Do a search for "Green Giant" at adflip (www.adFlip.com) and compare historic Green Giant ads to this one. How might this history determine future Green Giant ads? Can you think of brands that made drastic changes in their popular animated icons? What might motivate a company to modernize or change its animated character icons?

Industry Analysis. An **industry analysis** is just that; it focuses on developments and trends within an industry and on any other factors that may make a difference in how an advertiser proceeds with an advertising plan. An industry analysis should enumerate and discuss the most important aspects of a given industry, including the supply side of the supply-demand equation. For example, if you were designing advertising for Blockbuster Video, you would be concerned that movie rentals have been lower industry-wide. Are consumers watching fewer movies? No. In this particular industry, film studios are discovering that they can make more money by selling films directly to the public at deeply discounted prices. Also, on-demand distribution of movies is cutting into video and DVD rentals. Indeed, the threat posed by new technologies has motivated numerous predictions over the past decade about the demise of Blockbuster.

Industry trends have a major impact on the long-term future of companies like Blockbuster, but even in the short term they have meaning. If you're Blockbuster, you want someone to come up with some advertising that counteracts the threats to your business. You want your agency to figure out what is unique about going to a video store. Maybe it means more integrated promotion efforts, such as tie-ins with fast-food restaurants and toy stores, appearances by celebrities, or a chance to win tickets to a sporting event. One thing is clear—you can't ignore the trends in an industry. Obviously, the folks at Blockbuster know this, and with 75 percent of the U.S. population living within a 10-minute drive of one of its 5,000+ outlets, Blockbuster continues to find ways to anticipate and take advantage of the trends in its industry.[9]

Market Analysis. A **market analysis** is the flip side of industry analysis; it is the demand side of the equation. In a market analysis, an advertiser examines the factors that drive and determine the market for the firm's product or service. First, the advertiser needs to decide just exactly what the market is for the product. Most often, the market for a given good or service is simply defined as current users. The idea here is that consumers figure out for themselves whether they want the product or not and thus define the market for themselves, and for the advertiser. This approach has some wisdom to it. It's simple, easy to defend, and very conservative. Few executives get fired for choosing this target market. However, it completely ignores those consumers who might otherwise be persuaded to use the product.

A market analysis commonly begins by stating just who the current users are, and (hopefully) why they are current users. Consumers' motivations for using one product or service but not another may very well provide the advertiser with the means toward a significant expansion of the entire market. If the entire pie grows, the firm's slice usually does as well. The advertiser's job in a market analysis is to find out the most important market factors and why they are so important. It is at this stage in the situation analysis that account planning can play an important role.

9. Susan Orenstein, "Blockbuster's Long, Long Run," *Industry Standard,* April 16, 2001, 48–51.

Competitor Analysis. Once the industry and market are studied and analyzed, attention is turned to **competitor analysis.** Here an advertiser determines just exactly who the competitors are, discussing their strengths, weaknesses, tendencies, and any threats they pose.

Suppose you are creating advertising for Fuji 35-mm film. Who are your competitors? Is Kodak, with its dominant market share, your only real competitor? Are Agfa and Konica worth worrying about? Would stealing share from these fairly minor players amount to much? What has Kodak done in the past when Fuji has made a move? What are Kodak's advantages? For one, it may have successfully equated memories with photographs and with trusting the archiving of these memories to Kodak film. Does Kodak have any weaknesses? Is it as technologically advanced as Fuji? Japanese technologies are often thought to be superior to American. Could Kodak be characterized as stodgy and old-fashioned? What of recent product innovations? What about financial resources? Can Kodak swat Fuji like a fly? Or does Fuji have deep pockets, too? What would happen if Fuji tripled its advertising and directly compared its product to Kodak's? These are the kinds of questions that would be addressed in a thorough analysis of the competitive field.

Objectives.

Advertising objectives lay the framework for the subsequent tasks in an advertising plan and take many different forms. Objectives identify the goals of the advertiser in concrete terms. The advertiser, more often than not, has more than one objective for an ad campaign. An advertiser's objective may be (1) to increase consumer awareness of and curiosity about its brand, (2) to change consumers' beliefs or attitudes about its product, (3) to influence the purchase intent of its customers, (4) to stimulate trial use of its product or service, (5) to convert one-time product users into repeat purchasers, (6) to switch consumers from a competing brand to its brand, or (7) to increase sales. (Each of these objectives is discussed briefly in the following paragraphs.) The advertiser may have more than one objective at the same time. For example, a swimwear company may state its advertising objectives as follows: to maintain the company's brand image as the market leader in adult female swimwear and to increase revenue in this product line by 15 percent.

Creating or maintaining brand awareness and interest is a fundamental advertising objective. Brand awareness is an indicator of consumer knowledge about the existence of the brand and how easily that knowledge can be retrieved from memory. For example, a market researcher might ask a consumer to name five Internet shopping services. **Top-of-the-mind awareness** is represented by the brand listed first. Ease of retrieval from memory is important because for many goods or services, ease of retrieval is predictive of market share. Ads like those in Exhibits 8.10 and 8.11 are designed to promote top-of-the-mind awareness for two "new economy" businesses. The recent explosion of Internet-based businesses has made brand awareness critical to the survival of concerns like *Commerce One* and *quixi*. Exhibits 8.10 and 8.11 show their attempts to get noticed via a well-placed tattoo and a not-so-well-placed baby.

Beliefs are knowing with some degree of certainty that certain things are true. For example, you may believe that FedEx is the most reliable next-day delivery service or that Saturn has a no-pressure sales environment. You may believe that mad cow disease is the scourge of the Western world, and no one is safe from it. In the case of McDonald's or any mass marketer of beef-based products, beliefs about mad cow disease must be considered as part of advertising planning. As described in the Global Issues box on page 283, the French unit of McDonald's used a keen understanding of consumers' beliefs in developing advertising objectives to launch "Le 280 Grammes."

Creating or changing attitudes is another popular advertising objective. Per Chapter 5, one way to go about changing people's attitudes is to give them new

Commerce One provides services to help businesses build electronic marketplaces on the Internet. In new economy vernacular, this is known as operating in the B2B space. www.commerceone.com

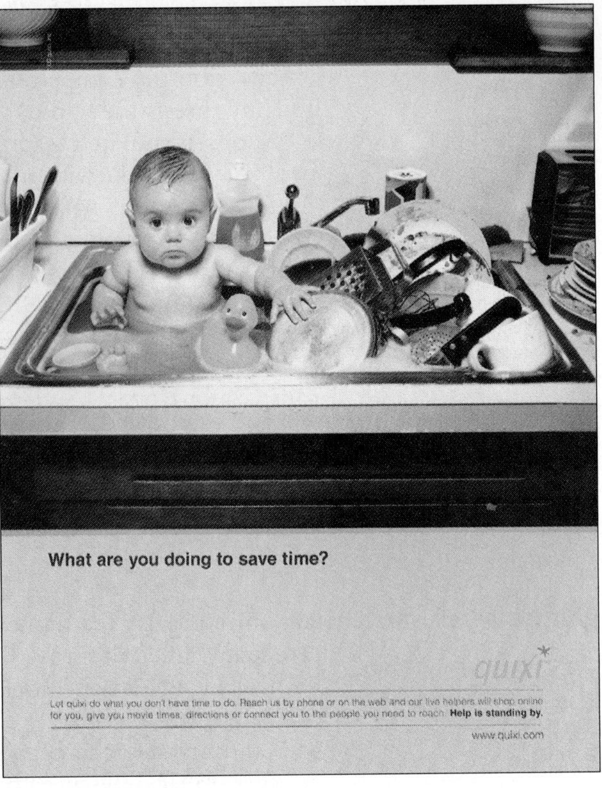

EXHIBIT 8.11

Quixi provides an Internet shopping service for consumers who are so busy that they can't find time to wash the baby. In new economy vernacular, this is known as operating in the B2C space. www.quixi.com

information designed to alter their beliefs (as in the Global Issues box). Alternatively, attitude change may be pursued by consistently associating one's brand with other likable objects or settings to effect a direct change in liking. Information-dense ads are designed to change attitudes by first altering beliefs, whereas entertaining ads are designed to influence attitudes through direct affect transfer. Even for an information-intensive service such as a mutual fund, there are times when the most prudent advertising goal is to build brand awareness and make your fund more likable by using entertaining or humorous advertising. At last count there were 8,900 different mutual funds being marketed to U.S. consumers.[10] In this sea of competitive clutter, if your advertising can't get you noticed and make your fund likable, you are destined to drown.

Purchase intent is another popular criterion in setting objectives. Purchase intent is determined by asking consumers whether they intend to buy a product or service in the near future. The appeal of influencing purchase intent is that intent is closer to actual behavior, and thus closer to the desired sale, than are attitudes. While this makes sense, it does presuppose that consumers can express their intentions with a reasonably high degree of reliability. Sometimes they can, sometimes they cannot. Purchase intent, however, is fairly reliable as an indicator of relative intention to buy, and it is, therefore, a worthwhile advertising objective.

10. Vanessa O'Connell, "Alliance Capital Tries to Spice Up Funds with Offbeat TV Spots," *Wall Street Journal,* March 25, 1998, B8.

Trial usage reflects actual behavior and is commonly used as an advertising objective. Many times, the best that we can ask of advertising is to encourage the consumer to try our brand once. At that point, the product or service must live up to the expectations created by our advertising. In the case of new products, stimulating trial usage is critically important. In the marketing realm, the angels sing when the initial purchase rate of a new product or service is high.

The **repeat purchase,** or conversion, objective is aimed at the percentage of consumers who try a new product and then purchase it a second time. A second purchase is reason for great rejoicing. The odds of long-term product success go way up when this percentage is high.

Brand switching is the last of the advertising objectives mentioned here. In some brand categories, switching is commonplace, even the norm. In others it is rare. When setting a brand-switching advertising objective, the advertiser must neither expect too much, nor rejoice too much, over a temporary gain. Persuading consumers to switch brands can be a long and arduous task.

2 **Communications versus Sales Objectives.** Some analysts argue that as a single variable in a firm's overall marketing mix, it is not reasonable to set sales expectations for advertising when other variables in the mix might undermine the advertising effort or be responsible for sales in the first place. In fact, some advertising analysts argue that communications objectives are the *only* legitimate objectives for advertising. This perspective has its underpinnings in the proposition that advertising is but one variable in the marketing mix and cannot be held solely responsible for sales. Rather, advertising should be held responsible for creating awareness of a brand, communicating information about product features or availability, or developing a favorable attitude that can lead to consumer preference for a brand. All of these outcomes are long term and based on communications impact.

Central to a strict communications perspective is the belief that since it is often impossible to judge sales impact directly from advertising, then sales objectives should not be part of advertising objectives. For a product such as the one being advertised in Exhibit 8.12, it is easy to appreciate the irrelevance of a sales objective. This ad is designed to get you to call 1-800-IBM-7080 and ask for a host, or visit www.ibm.com/e-business/hosting. At that point IBM's business sales force must do its job if a sale is to be secured.

GLOBAL ISSUES

McDonald's Won't Back Down from Mad Cow

Mad cow disease is a scary thing. That goes double if you make your living selling hamburgers. In Europe, consumers in France, Germany, Italy, and Spain have cut their beef consumption big-time, and sales at hamburger chains like McDonald's have plummeted. Where to go from here if you're in the hamburger business?

McDonald's can't afford to back down, so it launched its comeback with the introduction of *Le 280 Grammes,* a mammoth burger twice the size of the Big Mac. Posters inside its French restaurants challenged consumers with the tagline, "Can you handle it?" But a bigger burger with a catchy slogan isn't the answer for McDonald's, and they know it. So as part of the launch of *Le 280 Grammes,* McDonald's also embarked on a controversial ad campaign designed to educate French consumers with new facts about mad cow. McDonald's argued that the scientific evidence to date shows that burgers made from 100% muscle tissue pose a negligible risk of infecting people with mad cow. Specifically, it deployed advertising on French TV, in movie theaters, and in newspapers that carries the ghoulish message that McDonald's burgers are 100% muscle; they contain "no offal, no brain, no spinal cord, and no lymph nodes." Now doesn't that make you want to reach for a nice, big, muscle burger?

Early results from the muscle-message campaign and *Le 280 Grammes* launch were favorable for McDonald's. Burger sales in the first three months of the campaign increased by about 9%, reversing the downward spiral. We surely can't say whether McDonald's has the facts right when it comes to the science of mad cow disease, nor do we know the long-term effectiveness of its muscle-tissue message in calming the fears of European consumers. But if your business is beef, you must do something to confront the mad cow.

Source: John Carreyrou, "In France, McDonald's Takes Mad-Cow Fears by the Horns," *Wall Street Journal,* April 5, 2001, A17.

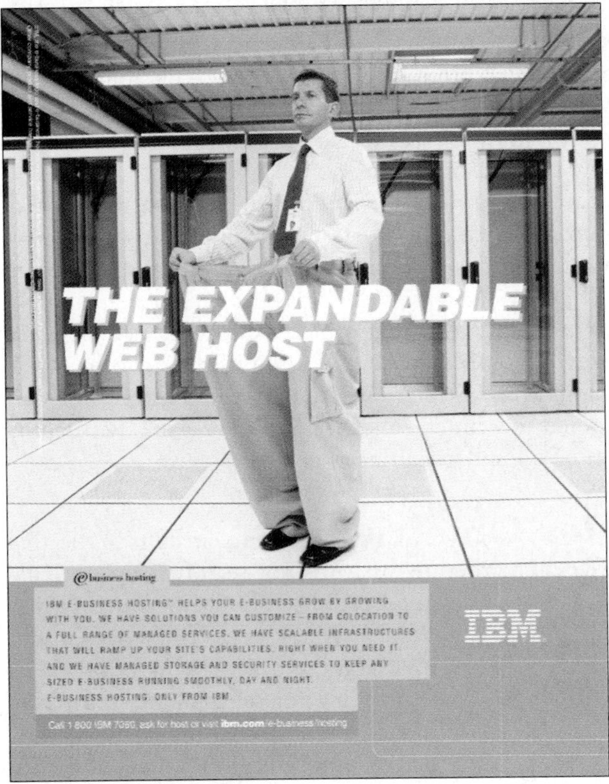

EXHIBIT 8.12

IBM has a long track record of using advertising as a lead-generating tool for its professional sales force. In a practice that is now standard in many industries, here we see IBM inviting the customer to make contact through an 800 number, or via www.ibm.com.

There are some major benefits to maintaining a strict communications perspective in setting advertising objectives. First, by viewing advertising as primarily a communications effort, marketers can consider a broader range of advertising strategies. Second, they can gain a greater appreciation for the complexity of the overall communications process. Designing an integrated communications program with sales as the sole objective neglects aspects of message design, media choice, public relations, or sales force deployment that should be effectively integrated across all phases of a firm's communication efforts. Using advertising messages to support the efforts of the sales force and/or drive people to your Web site (as in Exhibit 8.12) is an example of integrating diverse communication tools to build synergy that may ultimately produce a sale.

Nowhere is the tension between communication and sales objectives more apparent than in the annual debate about what advertisers really get for the tremendous sums of money they spend on Super Bowl ads. Every year great hoopla accompanies the ads that appear during the Super Bowl, and numerous polls are taken after the game to assess the year's most memorable ads. One such study showed that among the five most memorable ads (for Budweiser, Pepsi, VW, E * Trade, and Doritos) that ran during a recent Super Bowl, only the Doritos ad moved people to say that they were much more likely to purchase the product as a result of seeing the ad.[11] If a super-cool Pepsi ad featuring Britney Spears and Bob Dole doesn't affect consumers' purchase intentions, can it really be worth the millions of dollars it takes to produce and air it?

While there is a natural tension between those who advocate sales objectives and those who push communications objectives, nothing precludes a marketer from using both categories of objectives when developing an advertising plan. Indeed, combining sales objectives such as market share and household penetration with communication objectives such as awareness and attitude change can be an excellent means of motivating and evaluating an advertising campaign.[12]

Characteristics of Workable Advertising Objectives. Objectives that enable a firm to make intelligent decisions about resource allocation must be stated in an advertising plan in terms specific to the organization. Articulating such well-stated objectives is easier when advertising planners do the following:

1. *Establish a quantitative benchmark.* Objectives for advertising are measurable only in the context of quantifiable variables. Advertising planners should begin with quantified measures of the current status of market share, awareness, attitude, or other factors that advertising is expected to influence. The measurement of effectiveness in quantitative terms requires a knowledge of the level of variables of interest before an advertising effort, and then afterward. For example, a statement of objectives in quantified terms might be, "Increase the market share of heavy

11. Bonnie Tsui, "Bowl Poll: Ads Don't Mean Sales," *Advertising Age,* February 5, 2001, 33.
12. John Philip Jones, "Advertising's Crisis of Confidence," *Marketing Management,* vol. 2, no. 1 (1993), 15–24.

users of the product category using our brand from 22 to 25 percent." In this case, a quantifiable and measurable market share objective is specified.

2. *Specify measurement methods and criteria for success.* It is important that the factors being measured be directly related to the objectives being pursued. It is of little use to try to increase the awareness of a brand with advertising and then judge the effects based on changes in sales. If changes in sales are expected, then measure sales. If increased awareness is the goal, then change in consumer awareness is the only legitimate measure of success. This may seem obvious, but in a classic study of advertising objectives, it was found that claims of success for advertising were unrelated to the original statements of objective in 69 percent of the cases studied.[13] In this research, firms cited increases in sales as proof of success of advertising when the original objectives were related to factors such as awareness, conviction to a brand, or product use information. Yet another recent complication for measurement stems from vehicles such as the World Wide Web. The interactive media have presented a substantial challenge with respect to establishing success criteria.[14]
3. *Specify a time frame.* Objectives for advertising should include a statement of the period of time allowed for the desired results to occur. In some cases, as with direct response advertising, the time frame may be related to a seasonal selling opportunity like the Easter holiday period. For communications-based objectives, the measurement of results may not be undertaken until the end of an entire multiweek campaign. The point is that the time period for accomplishment of an objective and the related measurement period must be stated in advance in the ad plan.

These criteria for setting objectives help ensure that the planning process is organized and well directed. By relying on quantitative benchmarks, an advertiser has guidelines for making future decisions. Linking measurement criteria to objectives provides a basis for the equitable evaluation of the success or failure of advertising. Finally, the specification of a time frame for judging results keeps the planning process moving forward. As in all things, however, moderation is a good thing. A single-minded obsession with watching the numbers can be dangerous in that it minimizes or entirely misses the importance of qualitative and intuitive factors.

3 **Budgeting.** One of the most agonizing tasks is budgeting the funds for an advertising effort. Normally, the responsibility for the advertising budget lies with the firm itself. Within a firm, budget recommendations come up through the ranks, from a brand manager to a category manager and ultimately to the executive in charge of marketing. The sequence then reverses itself for the allocation and spending of funds. In a small firm, such as an independent retailer, the sequence just described may include only one individual who plays all the roles.

In some cases, a firm will rely on its advertising agency to make recommendations regarding the size of the advertising budget. When this is done, it is typically the account executive in charge of the brand who will analyze the firm's objectives and its creative and media needs and then make a recommendation to the company. The account supervisor's budget planning will likely include working closely with brand and product-group managers to determine an appropriate spending level.

To be as judicious and accountable as possible in spending money on advertising and IBP, marketers rely on various methods for setting an advertising budget. To appreciate the benefits (and failings) of these methods, we will consider each of them in turn.

13. Stewart Henderson Britt, "Are So-Called Successful Advertising Campaigns Really Successful?" *Journal of Advertising Research*, vol. 9 (1969), 5.

14. Terry Lefton, "The Great Flameout," *Industry Standard,* March 19, 2001, 75–78.

Percentage of Sales. A **percentage-of-sales approach** to advertising budgeting calculates the advertising budget based on a percentage of the prior year's sales or the projected year's sales. This technique is easy to understand and operationalize. The budget decision makers merely specify that a particular percentage of either last year's sales or the current year's estimated sales will be allocated to the advertising process. It is common to spend between 2 and 12 percent of sales on advertising.

While simplicity is certainly an advantage in decision making, the percentage-of-sales approach is fraught with problems. First, when a firm's sales are decreasing, the advertising budget will automatically decline. Periods of decreasing sales may be precisely the time when a firm needs to increase spending on advertising; if a percentage-of-sales budgeting method is being used, this won't happen. Second, this budgeting method can easily result in overspending on advertising. Once funds have been earmarked, the tendency is to find ways to spend the budgeted amount. Third, the most serious drawback from a strategic standpoint is that the percentage-of-sales approach does not relate advertising dollars to advertising objectives. Basing spending on past or future sales is devoid of analytical evaluation and implicitly presumes a direct cause-and-effect relationship between advertising and sales. But here, sales cause advertising.

A variation on the percentage-of-sales approach that firms may use is the **unit-of-sales approach** to budgeting, which simply allocates a specified dollar amount of advertising for each unit of a brand sold (or expected to be sold). This is merely a translation of the percentage-of-sales method into dollars per units sold. The unit-of-sales approach has the same advantages and disadvantages as the percentage-of-sales approach.

Share of Market/Share of Voice. With this method, employed by many firms, a firm monitors the amount spent by various significant competitors on advertising and allocates an amount equal to the amount of money spent by competitors or an amount proportional to (or slightly greater than) the firm's market share relative to the competition.[15] Exhibit 8.13 shows the relationship between share of market and share of voice for two fierce competitors: Coke and Pepsi.

With this method, an advertiser will achieve a **share of voice,** or an advertising presence in the market, equal to or greater than the competitors' share of advertising voice. This method is often used for advertising budget allocations in new-product introductions. Conventional wisdom suggests that some multiple, often 2.5 to 4 times the desired first-year market share, should be spent in terms of share-of-voice advertising expenditures. For example, if an advertiser wants a 2 percent first-year share, it would need to spend up to 8 percent of the total dollar amount spent in the industry (for an 8 percent share of voice). The logic is that a new product will need a significant share of voice to gain notice among a group of existing, well-established brands.[16] To achieve significant share of voice for its new toothpaste with baking soda and peroxide, Colgate-Palmolive spent $40 million in the first six months on advertising.[17] This sort of massive spending on a product launch can give a brand visibility in a crowded market but would be far out of line relative to competitors' spending.

Although this technique is sound in the sense that it shows a heightened awareness of competitors' activities, there is some question as to whether it can or should be used. First, it may be difficult to gain access to precise information on competitors' spending. Second, there is no reason to believe that competitors are spending their money wisely or in a way even remotely related to what the decision-making

15. The classic treatment of this method was first offered by James O. Peckham, "Can We Relate Advertising Dollars to Market-Share Objectives?" in Malcolm A. McGiven, ed., *How Much to Spend for Advertising* (New York: Association of National Advertisers, 1969), 24.

16. James C. Shroer, "Ad Spending: Growing Market Share," *Harvard Business Review* (January–February 1990), 44.

17. Pat Sloan, "Colgate Packs $40M behind New Toothpaste," *Advertising Age,* December 12, 1994, 36.

EXHIBIT 8.13

Share of market versus share of voice, 1992 cola market. Figures are in millions of U.S. dollars.

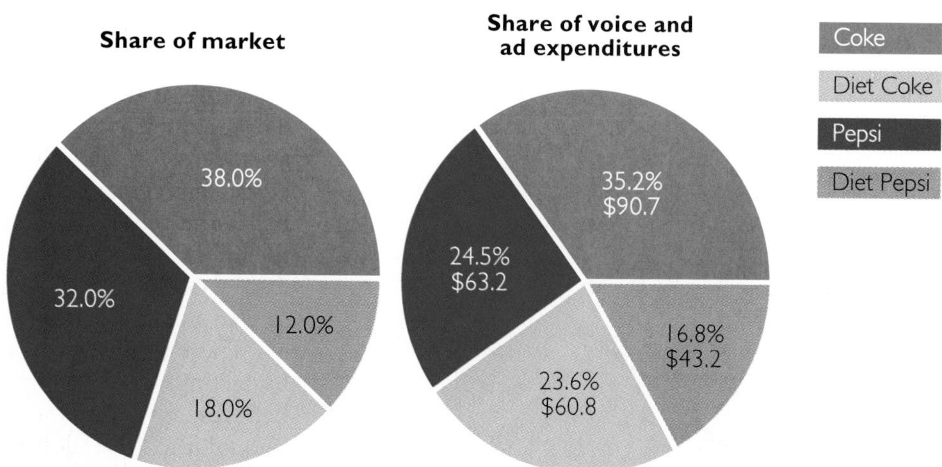

Source: Taken from *Market Share Reporter* (Detroit: Gale Research, 1994), 100. Share of voice/ad expenditures computed from January to December 1992 in LNA/Media Watch Multi-Media Service (New York: 1992), 186, 209, 392. Copyright ©1994, Gale Research, Inc. All rights reserved. Reproduced by permission.

firm wants to accomplish. Third, the flaw in logic in this method is the presumption that every advertising effort is of the same quality and will have the same effect from a creative execution standpoint. Nothing could be further from the truth. Multimillion-dollar advertising campaigns have been miserable failures, and limited-budget campaigns have been big successes.

Response Models. Using response models to aid the budgeting process is a fairly widespread practice among larger firms.[18] The belief is that greater objectivity can be maintained with such models. While this may or may not be the case, response models do provide useful information on what a given company's advertising response function looks like. An **advertising response function** is a mathematical relationship that associates dollars spent on advertising and sales generated. To the extent that past advertising predicts future sales, this method is valuable. Using marginal analysis, an advertiser would continue its spending on advertising as long as its marginal spending was exceeded by marginal sales. Marginal analysis answers the advertiser's question, "How much more will sales increase if we spend an additional dollar on advertising?" As the rate of return on advertising expenditures declines, the wisdom of additional spending is analyzed.

Theoretically, this method leads to a point where an optimal advertising expenditure results in an optimal sales level and, in turn, an optimal profit. The relationship between sales, profit, and advertising spending is shown in the marginal analysis graph in Exhibit 8.14. Data on sales levels, prior advertising expenditures, and consumer awareness are typical of the numerical input to such quantitative models.

Unfortunately, the advertising-to-sales relationship assumes simple causality, and we know that that assumption isn't true. Many other factors, in addition to advertising, affect sales directly. Still, some feel that the use of response models is a better budgeting method than guessing or applying the percentage-of-sales or other budgeting methods discussed so far.

Objective and Task. The methods for establishing an advertising budget just discussed all suffer from the same fundamental deficiency: a lack of specification of how

18. James E. Lynch and Graham J. Hooley, "Increasing Sophistication in Advertising Budget Setting," *Journal of Advertising Research* (February–March 1990), 72.

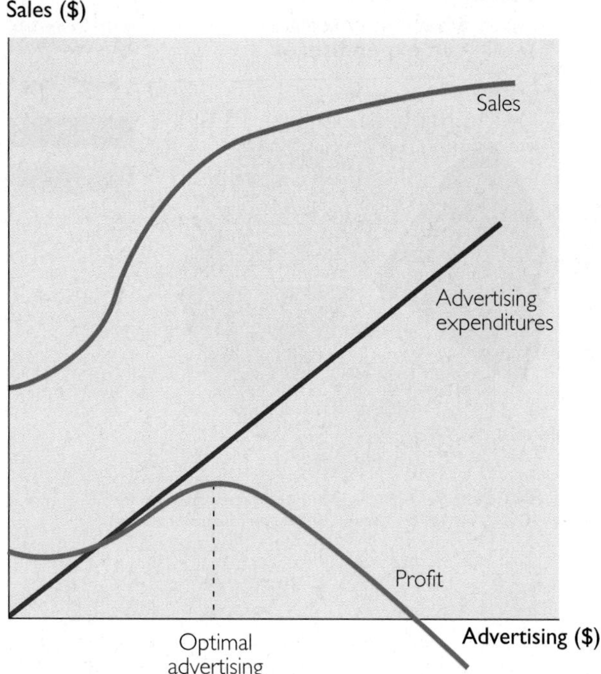

Source: David A. Aaker, Rajeev Batra, and John G. Meyers, *Advertising Management*, 4th ed. (Englewood Cliffs, N.J.: Prentice-Hall, 1992), 469. Reprinted by permission of Prentice-Hall, Inc., Upper Saddle River, N.J.

EXHIBIT 8.14

Sales, profit, and advertising curves used in marginal analysis.

expenditures are related to advertising goals. The only method of budget setting that focuses on the relationship between spending and advertising objectives is the **objective-and-task approach.** This method begins with the stated objectives for an advertising effort. Goals related to production costs, target audience reach, message effects, behavioral effects, media placement, duration of the effort, and the like are specified. The budget is formulated by identifying the specific tasks necessary to achieve different aspects of the objectives.

There is a lot to recommend this procedure for budgeting. A firm identifies any and all tasks it believes are related to achieving its objectives. Should the total dollar figure for the necessary tasks be beyond the firm's financial capability, then a reconciliation must take place. But even if a reconciliation and a subsequent reduction of the budget results, the firm has at least identified what *should* have been budgeted to pursue its advertising objectives.

The objective-and-task approach is the most logical and defensible method for calculating and then allocating an advertising budget. It is the only budgeting method that specifically relates advertising spending to the advertising objectives being pursued. It is widely used among major advertisers. For these reasons, we will consider the specific procedures for implementing the objective-and-task budgeting method.

Implementing the Objective-and-Task Budgeting Method. Proper implementation of the objective-and-task approach requires a data-based, systematic procedure. Since the approach ties spending levels to specific advertising goals, the process depends on proper execution of the objective-setting process described earlier. Once a firm and its agency are satisfied with the specificity and direction of stated objectives, a series of well-defined steps can be taken to implement the objective-and-task method. These steps are shown in Exhibit 8.15 and summarized in the following sections.

Determine costs based on build-up analysis. Having identified specific objectives, an advertiser can now begin determining what tasks are necessary for the accomplishment of those objectives. In using a **build-up analysis**—building up the expenditure levels for tasks—the following factors must be considered in terms of costs:

- *Reach:* The advertiser must identify the geographic and demographic exposure the advertising is to achieve.
- *Frequency:* The advertiser must determine the number of exposures required to accomplish desired objectives.
- *Time frame:* The advertiser must estimate when communications will occur and over what period of time.
- *Production costs:* The decision maker can rely on creative personnel and producers to estimate the costs associated with the planned execution of advertisements.
- *Media expenditures:* Given the preceding factors, the advertiser can now define the appropriate media, media mix, and frequency of insertions that will directly address objectives. Further, differences in geographic allocation, with special attention to regional or local media strategies, are considered at this point.

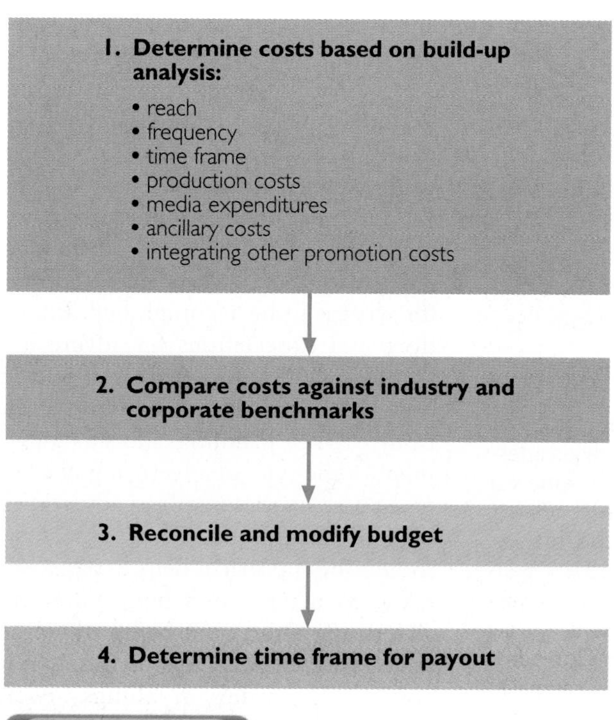

EXHIBIT 8.15

Steps in implementing the objective-and-task approach.

- *Ancillary costs:* There will be a variety of related costs not directly accounted for in the preceding factors. Prominent among these are costs associated with advertising to the trade and specialized research unique to the campaign.
- *Integrating other promotional costs:* In this era of advertising and integrated brand promotion, the budget must be considered in the context of spending on all promotional efforts.

Some of these promotional expenditures will directly support mass media advertising. Others will have distinct objectives, like those discussed in the IBP box on page 290. The goal should always be to deploy various communication tools in such a way that they support one another to produce desired outcomes for the brand, be it Jaguar or Jockey.

Compare costs against industry and corporate benchmarks. After compiling all the costs through a build-up analysis, an advertiser will want to make a quick reality check. This is accomplished by checking the percentage of sales that the estimated set of costs represents relative to industry standards for percentage of sales allocated to advertising. If most competitors are spending 4 to 6 percent of gross sales on advertising, how does the current budget compare to this percentage? Another recommended technique is to identify the share of industry advertising that the firm's budget represents. Another relevant reference point is to compare the current budget with prior budgets. If the total dollar amount is extraordinarily high or low compared to previous years, this variance should be justified based on the objectives being pursued. The use of percentage of sales on both an industry and internal corporate basis provides a reference point only. The percentage-of-sales figures are not used for decision making per se, but rather as a benchmark to judge whether the budgeted amount is so unusual as to need reevaluation.

Reconcile and modify the budget. It is always a fear that the proposed budget will not meet with approval. It may not be viewed as consistent with corporate policy related to advertising expense, or it may be considered beyond the financial capabilities of the organization. Modifications to a proposed budget are common. Having to make radical cuts in proposed spending is disruptive and potentially devastating. The objective-and-task approach is designed to identify what a firm will need to spend in order to achieve a desired advertising impact. To have the budget level compromised after such planning can result in a totally impotent advertising effort because necessary tasks cannot be funded.

Every precaution should be taken against having to radically modify a budget. Planners should be totally aware of corporate policy and financial circumstance *during* the objective-setting and subsequent task-planning phases. This will help reduce the extent of budget modification, should any be required.

Determine a time frame for payout. It is important that budget decision makers recognize when the budget will be available for funding the tasks associated with the proposed effort. Travel expenses, production expenses, and media time and space are tied to specific calendar dates. For example, media time and space are often acquired and paid for far in advance of the completion of finished advertisements. Knowing when and how much money is needed will usually increase the odds of the plan being carried out smoothly.

If these procedures are followed for the objective-and-task approach, an advertiser will have a defendable budget with which to pursue advertising objectives. One point to be made, however, is that the budget should not be viewed as the final word in funding an advertising effort. The dynamic nature of the market and rapid developments in media require flexibility in budget execution. This can mean changes in expenditure levels, but it can also mean changes in payout allocation.

Like any other business activity, a marketer must take on an advertising effort with clearly specified intentions for what is to be accomplished. Intentions and expectations for advertising are embodied in the process of setting objectives. Armed with information from market planning and an assessment of the type of advertising needed to support marketing plans, advertising objectives can be set. These objectives should be in place before steps are taken to determine a budget for the advertising effort, and before the creative work begins. Again, this is not always the order of things, even though it should be. These objectives will also affect the plans for media placement.

IBP

Jaguar Looks to Spike for Answers

Direct marketing, the focal point of Chapter 19, is a particularly potent communication tool when the objective is to deliver a detailed message to a well-defined target segment. Jaguar Cars North America deployed this tool in an effort to increase its success with affluent African-American auto buyers. Prior attempts to reach this market through media such as BET, *Essence,* and *Black Enterprise* had not generated the results Jaguar was looking for. And to assist them in crafting a message that would ring true for their target segment, Jaguar retained Spike Lee and his 40 Acres and a Mule Production Company.

Spike's message would be delivered through a direct mail campaign to nearly 700,000 households. The mailing included a lifestyle-oriented brochure and an eight-minute video featuring a black couple on the road from Harlem to Martha's Vineyard in their exquisite Jaguar. The name-and-address file for the mailing was derived from six sources, including *Essence*'s database, and specifically targeted consumers between ages 35 and 54 with annual incomes over $75,000 who currently drive a competitor's vehicle. Jaguar owners were excluded from the mailing. Mike Sachs, relationship marketing manager at Jaguar, expressed the challenge this way: "We recognize that the African-American target is a big market for us, but they don't really consider us, I think because the perception is we're too pricey." Spike Lee's task was to convince skeptical consumers that Jaguar luxury is worth the price. His message to the African-American audience: *It's not luck that got you where you are.* So reward yourself with a Jaguar.

Source: Jean Halliday, "Spike Lee's Jaguar Ads Begin First Test Mailing," *Advertising Age,* December 18, 2000, 18.

Strategy. Strategy represents the mechanism by which something is to be done. It is an expression of the means to an end. All of the other factors are supposed to result in a strategy. Strategy is what you do, given the situation and objectives. There are an infinite number of possible advertising strategies. For example, if you are trying to get more top-of-the-mind awareness for your brand of chewing gum, a simple strategy would be to employ a high-frequency, name-repetition campaign. Exhibit 8.16 presents an ad from Danskin's campaign designed to broaden the appeal of its products beyond dance accessories to the much larger fitness-wear market. Danskin's advertising strategy features unique "fitness" celebrities as implicit endorsers of the Danskin brand.

More sophisticated goals call for more sophisticated strategies. You are limited only by your resources: financial, organizational, and creative. Ultimately, strategy formulation is a creative endeavor. It is best learned through the study of what others have done in similar situations and through a thorough analysis of the focal consumer. To assist in strategy formulation, a growing number of ad agencies have created a position called the account planner (see Chapter 7). This person's job is to synthesize all relevant consumer research and draw inferences from it that will help define a coherent advertising strategy. As with so many things, experience counts in this crucial role.

Execution. The actual "doing" is the execution of the plan. It is the making and placing of ads across all media. To quote a famous bit of advertising copy from a tire manufacturer, this is

EXHIBIT 8.16

This ad provides an excellent example of repositioning. The slogan says it all: "DANSKIN—Not Just for Dancing." www.danskin.com

where "the rubber meets the road." There are two elements to the execution of an advertising plan: determining the copy strategy and devising a media plan.

Copy Strategy. A copy strategy consists of copy objectives and methods, or tactics. The objectives state what the advertiser intends to accomplish, while the methods describe how the objectives will be achieved. Part Three of this text will deal extensively with these executional issues.

Media Plan. The media plan specifies exactly where ads will be placed and what strategy is behind their placement. In an integrated communications environment, this is much more complicated than it might first appear. Back when there were just three broadcast television networks, there were already more than a million different combinations of placements that could be made. With the explosion of media and promotion options today, the permutations are almost infinite.

It is at this point—devising a media plan—where all the money is spent, and so much could be saved. This is where the profitability of many agencies is really determined. Media placement strategy can make a huge difference in profits or losses and is considered in great depth in Part Four of this text.

Integrated Brand Promotion. Many different forms of brand promotion may accompany the advertising effort in launching or maintaining a brand; these should

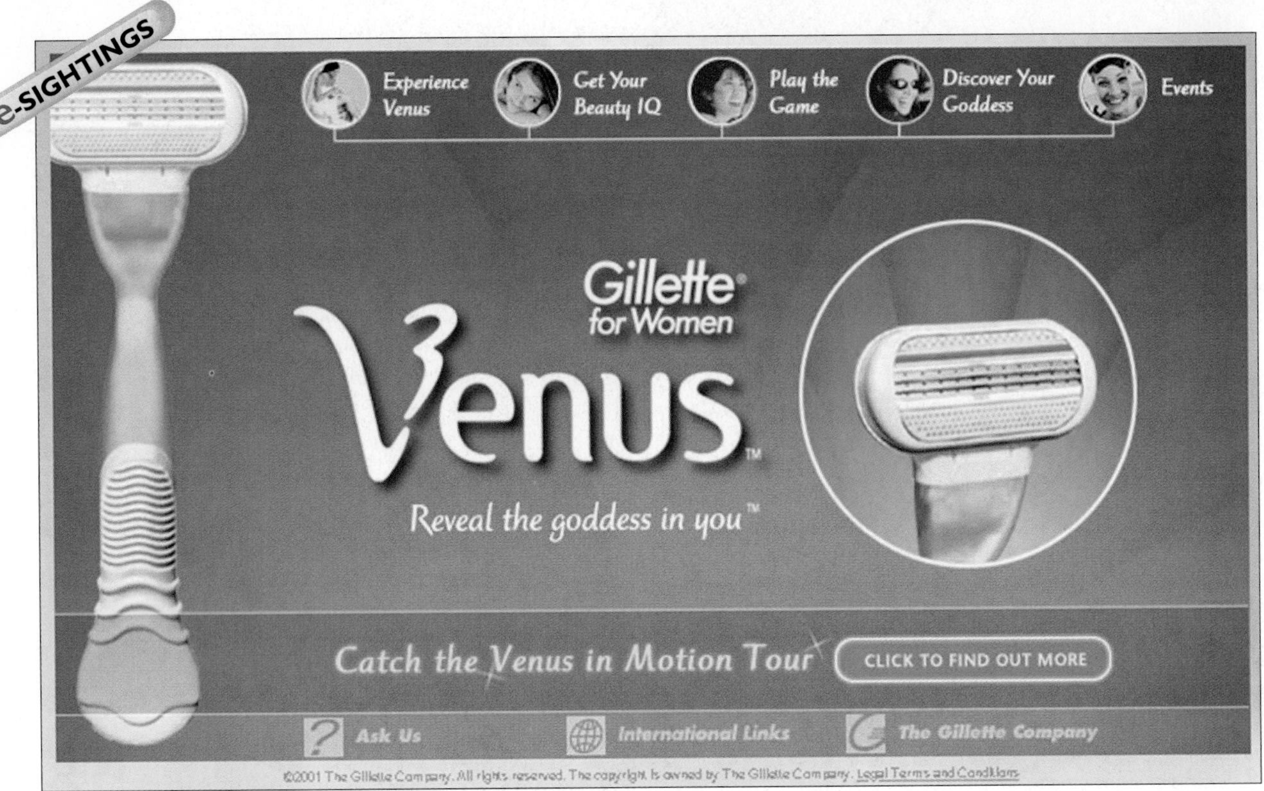

EXHIBIT 8.17

The Venus Web site has offered many possibilities, including the prospect of winning a great vacation, a beauty IQ test, and a way to "Reveal the goddess in you." Compare these examples of integrated brand promotion with attempts by competitors Norelco (www.norelco.com) and Schick (www.schick.com). Are these promotions integrated in a way that supports the image of the brand?

be spelled out as part of the overall plan. There should be a complete integration of all communication tools in working up the plan. For example, in the launch of its new Venus shaving system for women, Gillette had the usual multimillion-dollar budget allocation for traditional mass media. But along with its aggressive advertising effort, several other promotional tools were deployed.[19] At www.GilletteVenus.com, women could sign up for an online sweepstakes to win vacations in Hawaii, New York City, and Tuscany, and provide friends' e-mail addresses (a tactic known as viral e-mail) to increase their own chances of winning. Gillette also put a pair of 18-wheelers on the road (see Exhibit 8.18) to spread the word about Venus at beaches, concerts, colleges campuses, and store openings. So the launch of Venus integrated tools that ran the gamut from TV ads to the World Wide Web to Interstate 95. You'll learn much more about a variety of IBP tools in Part Five of this text.

Evaluation. Last but not least in an ad plan is the evaluation component. This is where an advertiser determines how the agency will be graded: what criteria will be applied and how long the agency will have to achieve the agreed-upon objectives. It's critically important for the advertiser and agency to align around evaluation criteria up front. John Wanamaker's classic line still captures the challenge associated with evaluation; he said, "I know half my advertising is wasted, I just don't know which half." In a

19. Betsy Spethmann, "Venus Rising," *PROMO Magazine,* April 2001, 52–61.

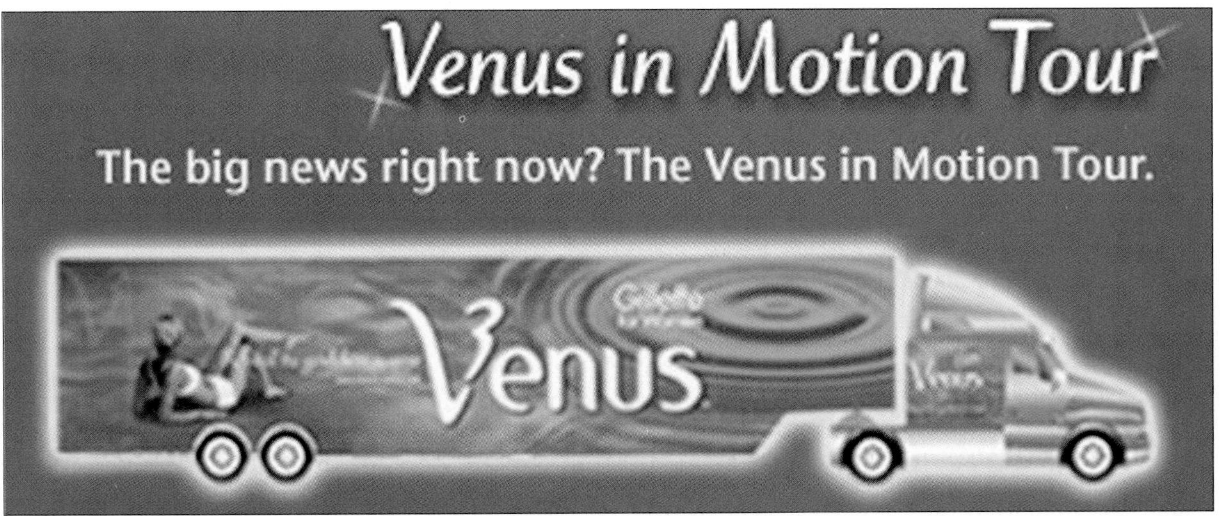

EXHIBIT 8.18

Hard to imagine goddesses going on the road in an 18-wheeler, but in today's world of integrated brand promotion, just about anything goes.

world where the pressures on companies to deliver short-term profitability continue to intensify, advertising agencies find themselves under increasing pressure to show quantifiable outcomes from all advertising and IBP activities.[20]

4 The Role of the Advertising Agency in Advertising Planning.

Now that we have covered key aspects of the advertising planning process, one other issue should be considered. Because many marketers rely heavily on the expertise of an advertising agency, understanding the role an agency plays in the advertising planning process is important. As implied by the E-Commerce box on page 294, various agencies will approach their craft with different points of emphasis. But while not everyone does it the same way, it is still important to ask: What contribution to the planning effort can and should an advertiser expect from its agency?

The discussion of advertising planning to this point has emphasized that the marketer is responsible for the marketing-planning inputs as a type of self-assessment that identifies the firm's basis for offering value to customers. This assessment should also clearly identify, in the external environment, the opportunities and threats that can be addressed with advertising. A firm should bring to the planning effort a well-articulated statement of a brand's value proposition and the marketing mix elements designed to gain and sustain competitive advantage. However, when client and agency are working in harmony, the agency may take an active role in helping the client formulate the more general marketing plan. Indeed, when things are going right, it can be hard to say exactly where the client's work ended and the agency's work began. This is the essence of teamwork, and as Steve Jobs noted in the case of iMac: "Creating great advertising, like creating great products, is a team effort."

20. Laura Q. Hughes, "Measuring Up," *Advertising Age,* February 5, 2001, 1, 34.

E-COMMERCE

The Fundamentals Never Go Out of Style

The dot-com debacle that marked the dawning of the new millennium sent shock waves through the ad agency business. Many high-profile agencies suffered from the demise of the dot-coms because they had built up large interactive units with catchy names like Darwin Digital and Zentropy Partners, in search of Internet advertising riches. These units then had to be downsized or discontinued after the dot-com crash. One agency that didn't follow the pack in search of Internet riches was Goodby, Silverstein & Partners, San Francisco (www.goodbysilverstein.com). You've seen their work: "Got Milk?," the Budweiser lizards, E*Trade's singing chimp, and many more.

But here's the irony. As the dust settled after all the interactive downsizing, Goodby, Silverstein's stable of clients included companies such as TiVo, eBay, eLuxury.com, and Loudcloud, some of the best performers in the Internet sector. Turns out that slow-moving, old-fashioned Goodby, Silverstein had timeless skills that marketers of all types need for building their brands, whether they are based in the physical or the digital world. Industry analysts claim that Goodby's lack of Internet hype and its enduring focus on brand building via breakthrough advertising campaigns are the things that won it loyal digital clients. Here are a few fundamental rules for creating great ad campaigns, inspired by Goodby, Silverstein & Partners:

- *Simplicity is key.* Complexity fuels confusion. Trying to say too much is the number one pitfall, even among advertising veterans.
- *Don't talk down.* Assume your audience is paying attention, is as smart as you are, and has a sense of humor. This is how you win their respect.
- *Don't be invisible.* Make your communication different. Take risks. Better to take risks and be noticed than to spend money on something that is technically correct, but practically invisible.
- *Refresh Yourself.* Nitpicking old ideas is a sure sign that you are creating tired advertising. When you find yourself in nitpicking mode, refresh yourself by starting over.

Source: Beth Snyder Bulik, "As Goodby as It Gets," *Business 2.0,* May 1, 2001, 58–60.

But the advertising agency's crucial role is to translate the current market and marketing status of a firm and its advertising objectives into advertising strategy and, ultimately, finished advertisements and IBP materials. An agency can serve its clients best by taking charge of the preparation and placement stages. Here, message strategies and tactics for the advertising effort and for the efficient and effective placement of ads in media need to be hammered out. At this point, the firm (as a good client) should turn to its agency for the expertise and talent needed for planning and executing at the stage where design and creative execution brings marketing strategies to life. There are two basic models for the relationship between agencies and their clients: adversarial or partnering. The former is too common; the latter is certainly preferred.

SUMMARY

Describe the basic components of an advertising plan.

An advertising plan is motivated by the marketing planning process and provides the direction that ensures proper implementation of an advertising campaign. An advertising plan incorporates decisions about the segments to be targeted, communications and/or sales objectives with respect to these segments, and salient message appeals. The plan should also specify the dollars budgeted for the campaign, the various communication tools that will be employed to deliver the messages, and the measures that will be relied on to assess the campaign's effectiveness.

Compare and contrast two fundamental approaches for setting advertising objectives.

Setting appropriate objectives is a crucial step in developing any advertising plan. These objectives are typically stated in terms of communications or sales goals. Both types of goals have their proponents, and the appropriate types of objectives to emphasize will vary with the situation. Communications objectives feature goals such as building brand awareness or reinforcing consumers' beliefs about a brand's key benefits. Sales objectives are just that: They hold advertising directly responsible for increasing sales of a brand.

Explain various methods for setting advertising budgets.

Perhaps the most challenging aspect of any advertising campaign is arriving at a proper budget allocation. Companies and their advertising agencies work with several different methods to arrive at an advertising budget. A percentage-of-sales approach is a simple but naive way to deal with this issue. In the share-of-voice approach, the activities of key competitors are factored into the budget-setting process. A variety of quantitative models may also be used for budget determination. The objective-and-task approach is difficult to implement, but with practice it is likely to yield the best value for a firm's advertising dollars.

Discuss the role of the advertising agency in formulating an advertising plan.

An advertising plan will be a powerful tool when firms partner with their advertising agencies in its development. The firm can lead this process by doing its homework with respect to marketing strategy development and objective setting. The agency can then play a key role in managing the preparation and placement phases of campaign execution.

KEY TERMS

advertising plan
situation analysis
industry analysis
market analysis
competitor analysis
top-of-the-mind awareness
purchase intent
trial usage
repeat purchase
brand switching
percentage-of-sales approach
unit-of-sales approach
share of voice
advertising response function
objective-and-task approach
build-up analysis

QUESTIONS

1. Review the materials presented in this chapter (and anything else you may be able to find) about Apple's launch of the iMac. Based on the advertising utilized, what do you surmise must have been the value proposition for iMac at the time of its launch?

2. Find an example of cooperative advertising in your local newspaper. Why would computer manufacturers such as Apple, IBM, or Compaq want to participate in cooperative advertising programs with their retailers?

3. Explain the connection between marketing strategies and advertising plans. What is the role of target segments in making this connection?

4. Describe five key elements in a situation analysis and provide an example of how each of these elements may ultimately influence the final form of an advertising campaign.

5. How would it ever be possible to justify anything other than sales growth as a proper objective for an advertising campaign? Is it possible that advertising could be effective yet not yield growth in sales?

6. What types of objectives would you expect to find in an ad plan that featured direct response advertising?

7. Write an example of a workable advertising objective that would be appropriate for a product like Crest Tartar Control toothpaste.

8. In what situations would share of voice be an important consideration in setting an advertising budget? What are the drawbacks of trying to incorporate share of voice in budgeting decisions?

9. What is it about the objective-and-task method that makes it the preferred approach for the sophisticated advertiser? Describe how build-up analysis is used in implementing the objective-and-task method.

10. Briefly discuss the appropriate role to be played by advertising agencies and their clients in the formulation of marketing and advertising plans.

EXPERIENTIAL EXERCISES

1. Five of the most common objectives for advertising are listed in this chapter: top-of-the-mind awareness, purchase intent, trial usage, repeat purchase, and brand switching. For each, find an ad in a magazine or newspaper that you think aims to accomplish this objective and give an analysis as to whether or not the ad is successful.

2. The advertising plan consists of seven basic components: the introduction, situation analysis, objectives, budgeting, strategy, execution, and evaluation. Break up into teams and choose a popular television advertising campaign familiar to everyone in the group. Analyze the commercial and explain how you think the goals of advertisement relate to each basic component of the advertising plan. Based on your analysis of the commercial, speculate on how each of the seven components might have been developed in the advertiser's original planning process.

USING THE INTERNET

8-1 Situation Analysis

A clear situation analysis is an important component of a strategic advertising plan. The situation analysis lays out the most important factors defining the current advertising situation and helps form the basis for an advertising strategy. It involves understanding the history of the market, identifying current industry and market trends, and analyzing the strengths and weaknesses of the competition.

Listen: http://www.listen.com

eMusic: http://www.emusic.com

1. Imagine you are conducting a situation analysis for a client that offers music downloads on the Internet. The client's competition is listen.com and emusic.com. Visit the sites and look up articles and information on this industry and list some of the important situational factors for your client's advertising plan. Be sure to identify how the factors relate to historical context, industry analysis, market analysis, or competitor analysis.

2. Of all the factors you listed, which one is the most critical for your client to address? List reasons to support your answer.

8-2 Communications versus Sales Objectives

Advertising objectives provide a framework for the advertising plan, defining the goals of the advertiser in concrete terms. Advertisers usually have multiple objectives at one time, and often set goals for effective communication as well as sales.

Xootr: http://www.xootr.com

1. What objectives do you think are most common for advertising in the scooter industry?

2. Briefly explain the difference between communications versus sales objectives. Does the Xootr site reflect sales objectives?

3. Describe how an advertisement for scooters might achieve both sales and communications objectives. Why do some analysts believe that communications objectives are the only legitimate objectives for advertising?

CHAPTER 9

After reading and thinking about this chapter, you will be able to do the following:

Explain the types of audience research that are useful for understanding cultural barriers that can interfere with effective communication.

Identify three distinctive challenges that complicate the execution of advertising in international settings.

Describe the three basic types of advertising agencies that can assist in the placement of advertising around the world.

Discuss the advantages and disadvantages of globalized versus localized advertising campaigns.

CHAPTER 5
Advertising and Consumer Behavior

CHAPTER 6
Market Segmentation, Positioning, and the Value Proposition

CHAPTER 7
Advertising and Promotion Research

CHAPTER 8
The Advertising Plan

CHAPTER 9
Advertising Planning: An International Perspective

Van Cleef & Arpels

International advertising blunders are a rich part of advertising lore. Cruise the Internet and you will find many examples:[1]

The name *Coca-Cola* in China was first rendered as "Ke-kou-ke-la." Unfortunately, Coke did not discover until after thousands of signs had been printed that the phrase means "bite the wax tadpole" or "female horse stuffed with wax," depending on the dialect. Coke then researched 40,000 Chinese characters and found a close phonetic equivalent, "ko-kou-ko-le," which can be loosely translated as "happiness in the mouth."

- In Taiwan, the translation of the Pepsi slogan "Come alive with the Pepsi generation" came out as "Pepsi will bring your ancestors back from the dead."
- Scandinavian vacuum manufacturer Electrolux used the following in an American ad campaign: "Nothing sucks like an Electrolux."
- When Parker Pen marketed a ballpoint pen in Mexico, its ads were supposed to say, "It won't leak in your pocket and embarrass you." Instead the ads said that "It won't leak in your pocket and make you pregnant."

Humorous or not, such episodes remind us that communicating with consumers around the world is a special challenge.

International advertising is advertising that reaches across national and cultural boundaries. Unfortunately, a great deal of international advertising in the past was nothing more than translations of domestic advertising. Often, these translations were at best ineffective, at worst offensive. The day has passed, however—if there ever was such a day—when advertisers based in industrialized nations could simply "do a foreign translation" of their ads. Today, international advertisers must pay greater attention to local cultures. While this chapter is written by Americans, we have tried hard to write about advertising from an international perspective. We argue that the real issue is not nations, but cultures.

As we said in Chapter 5, culture is a set of values, rituals, and behaviors that define a way of life. Culture is typically invisible to those who are immersed within it. Communicating *across* cultures is not easy. It is, in fact, one of the most difficult of all communication tasks, largely because there is no such thing as culture-free communication. Advertising is a cultural product; it means nothing outside of culture. Culture surrounds advertising, informs it, gives it meaning. To transport an ad across cultural borders, one must respect, and hopefully understand, the power of culture.

This chapter augments and extends the advertising planning framework offered in Chapter 8. We add some necessary international planning tools along with a discussion of the special challenges found in advertising around the world.

Ads depend on effective communication, and effective communication depends on shared meaning. The degree of shared meaning is significantly affected by cultural membership. When an advertiser in culture A wants to communicate with consumers in culture B, it is culture B that will surround the created message, form its cultural context, and significantly affect how it will be interpreted.

Some products and brands may belong to a global consumer culture more than to any one national culture. Such brands travel well, as do their ads, because there is already common cultural ground on which to build effective advertising. The Nike and Swatch ads in Exhibits 9.1 and 9.2 provide examples of products and brands with wide, if not "global,"appeal. Switzerland has long been associated with watchmaking, but over many years the Swatch brand has cultivated its global image as a moderately priced but fun fashion accessory. So, the ad for this Swiss-made product, which appeared in a German issue of *Elle* magazine, features copy entirely in English. Swatch nearly flaunts its status as a brand that cannot be confined to any one

1. These examples are quoted directly from Robert Kirby, "Kirby: Advertising Translates Into Laughs," *Salt Lake Tribune*, www.sltrib.com, accessed February 24, 1998.

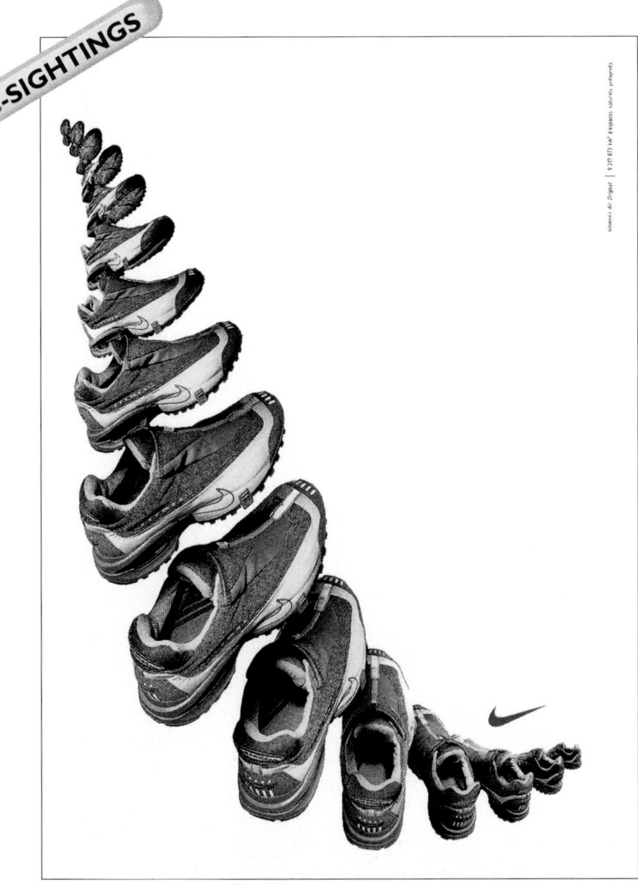

EXHIBIT 9.1

This graceful product array is a bit unusual for the Nike brand, but it is clearly an attempt to fit in with elegant company. That is, this ad for the Women's Air Drigoat appeared in the special year-end double issue of Vogue *magazine—Paris. The company's Web site* (www.nike.com) *contains links to various international sites. Visit some of these sites and compare and contrast them. What do the interactive and engaging site features say about Nike's global audience? Does the highly interactive content interfere with basic Internet functionality and ease of use?*

swatch
SKIN
THE ULTRAFLAT FROM SWATCH

EXHIBIT 9.2

The White Cape Ultraflat from Swatch says affordable chic in any language. Don't be fooled: While the copy here happens to be in English, the message is definitely intended for youthful consumers worldwide.

country. Nike, although clearly an American icon, has also become well known around the world, thus facilitating something of a global image. Such examples, however, are the exception rather than the rule, and as "global" as they may be, they are still affected by local culture as to their use and, ultimately, their meaning.

Advertising *is* a global business. The point was made in Chapter 2, but it bears repeating here: advertising as a business has truly become globalized. This can be illustrated in many ways. For example, Exhibit 9.3 presents a number of salient facts about ad spending in various countries. Among these top ten spenders, it probably comes as no surprise that the United States is the worldwide leader for advertising spending. Following Canada in the second ten among ad spenders are Mexico, China, Australia, the Netherlands, Hong Kong, Argentina, Switzerland, Colombia, Belgium, and Sweden. When you add it all up, spending on advertising around the world is fast approaching the $400 billion level. The dollars (or yen or marks or pounds or francs) involved, by definition, make this big business worldwide.

	Ad Spending (billions)	2000 Population (millions)	GNP per Capita	Top Ad Category	2000 Internet Ad Spending (millions)	Top TV Program	Ad Rate for Top Show (30 secs)
U.S.A.	$147.1	281.4	$26,980	Automotive	$5300.0	Survivor (reality show)	$200,000
Japan	39.7	127.9	38,000	Cosmetics and toiletries	517.5	Hero (law drama)	145,454.40 –159,090.75/ 2 30-sec spots
Germany	20.7	82.9	27,100	Mass media	700.0	Who Wants to Be a Millionaire?	72,463
U.K.	16.5	59.5	22,640	Finance	93.0	Coronation Street (soap opera)	146,600
France	10.7	59.7	25,900	Retail	140.0	Julie Lescaut (police drama)	83,000
Italy	8.4	57.9	21,800	Telecommunications and information	104.8	San Remo (music special)	59,048 –109,523
South Korea	6.4	47.7	10,800	Computers and information technology	106.8	Three Friends (sitcom)	5,102.04
Brazil	6.2	167.6	4,270	Retail	70.0	Jornal Nacional (news)	76,060
Spain	6.0	39.6	16,500	Telecommunications	48.6	Campanadas (a New Year's Eve special)	107,439 (20 secs)
Canada	5.2	30.7	23,300	Retail	125.1	Who Wants to Be a Millionaire?	18,400.97

Source: *Ad Age Global*, April 2001, 31–35.

EXHIBIT 9.3

Advertising around the world.

Television is a popular advertising medium around the world, and in countries as diverse as the United States, Japan, Italy, and Brazil, television attracts more advertising expenditures than any other medium. However, in Germany and the United Kingdom, newspaper advertising is the dominant expenditure category, while in France it is magazines, and in Canada it is radio. But among these heavy spending countries, a wide array of vehicles are deployed for carrying advertisers' messages. Regarding Internet advertising, Exhibit 9.3 shows that the United States led all countries, with $5.3 billion spent in 2000. Germany is a distant second, with $700 million spent for online advertising. Exhibit 9.3 also illustrates that advertising around the world involves just the kinds of things that all of us would expect—things like automobiles, cosmetics, wireless phone services, financial services, food products, and many different varieties of retailers.

Another way to illustrate the global nature of the advertising business is to consider the issue of creativity. As you will see in Chapter 10, serious creativity is at the heart of the advertising business. As a result, many different types of organizations around the world rate the ads and campaigns created by various advertising agencies on the basis of their creativity, and creativity awards (such as the Clios) are a fact of life in the advertising business. One such top ten list, which appeared in *Advertising Age,* is reproduced in Exhibit 9.4. In this particular year in this particular competi-

EXHIBIT 9.4

Top global networks ranked by creative awards.

2000 Ranking	1999 Ranking	Network	Most Award-Winning Offices
1	2	BBDO Worldwide	London, Sao Paulo
2	1	DDB Worldwide	Barcelona, Chicago
3	4	Saatchi & Saatchi	London, Sao Paulo
4	6	Leo Burnett Co.	Bangkok, Warsaw
5	3	TBWA Worldwide	Paris, Johannesburg
6	5	Lowe Lintas & Partners	London
7	7	Ogilvy & Mather Worldwide	Hong Kong
8	11	Euro RSCG Worldwide	Buenos Aires
9	8	Y & R Advertising	Buenos Aires
10	10	Dentsu	Tokyo, Osaka

Source: *Advertising Age*, November 20, 2000, 11.

tion, BBDO Worldwide was ranked #1 for creativity. However, the key point revealed by Exhibit 9.4 is not so much about who's #1, but rather where is the great creative work being done around the world. If you look at the right-hand column of Exhibit 9.4, you see award-winning offices identified in cities such as London, Sao Paulo, Paris, and Tokyo. Indeed, only one North American office appears among the top ten. We are not trying to suggest that there is no creative firepower in the United States; however, if you perceive that the advertising business is "housed in" or confined to North America, you really need to look around the world!

1 Overcoming Cultural Barriers.

Global trade initiatives such as the General Agreement on Tariffs and Trade (GATT) and the North American Free Trade Agreement (NAFTA) are designed to facilitate trade and economic development across national borders. These initiatives signal the emergence of international markets that are larger, more accessible, and perhaps more homogeneous. A couple nice examples of this emerging homogenization between two NAFTA trading partners are discussed in the Global Issues box on page 305. In the midst of this trend toward more and more international trade, marketers are redefining the nature and scope of the markets for their goods and services which in turn redefines the nature and scope of advertising and the advertising planning effort. This means that firms must be more sensitive to the social and economic differences of various international markets.

Exhibit 9.5 offers perspective on the kinds of companies that are most committed and successful in marketing and advertising around the world. Most of the firms listed in Exhibit 9.5 compete in either consumer products or the automotive markets. These are corporate titans such as Unilever, P&G, Coke, and General Motors. Today, however, most companies consider their markets to extend beyond national boundaries and across cultures. Hence, advertisers must come to terms with how they are going to effectively overcome cultural barriers in trying to communicate with consumers around the world.

Barriers to Successful International Advertising.

Adopting an international perspective is often difficult for marketers. The reason is that experiences gained over a career and

EXHIBIT 9.5

Top 15 global marketers by ad spending outside the United States (U.S. dollars).

Rank 1999	Advertiser (Parent Company)	Headquarters	Non-U.S. Ad Spending, 1999	U.S. Ad Spending, 1999
1	Unilever	Rotterdam/London	$3,110	$ 588
2	Procter & Gamble Co.	Cincinnati	2,988	1,704
3	Nestle	Vevey, Switzerland	1,580	329
4	Coca-Cola Co.	Atlanta	1,178	355
5	Ford Motor Co.	Dearborn, Mich.	1,150	1,272
6	General Motors Corp.	Detroit	1,148	2,960
7	L'Oreal	Paris	1,120	450
8	Volkswagen	Wolfsburg, Germany	1,009	372
9	Toyota Motor Corp.	Toyota City, Japan	1,007	718
10	PSA Peugeot Citroen	Paris	906	N/A
11	Sony Corp	Tokyo	886	590
12	Mars Inc.	McLean, Va.	841	298
13	Renault	Paris	809	N/A
14	Philip Morris Cos.	New York	767	1,358
15	Henkel	Duesseldorf	728	19

Source: *Advertising Age*, November 13, 2000, p. 21.

a lifetime create a cultural "comfort zone"—that is, one's own cultural values, experiences, and knowledge serve as a subconscious guide for decision making and behavior. International advertisers are particularly beset with this problem.

Managers must overcome two related biases to be successful in international markets. **Ethnocentrism** is the tendency to view and value things from the perspective of one's own culture. A **self-reference criterion (SRC)** is the unconscious reference to one's own cultural values, experiences, and knowledge as a basis for decisions. These two closely related biases are primary obstacles to success when conducting marketing and advertising planning that demands a cross-cultural perspective.

A decision maker's SRC and ethnocentrism can inhibit his or her ability to sense important cultural distinctions between markets. This in turn can blind advertisers to their own culture's "fingerprints" on the ads they've created. Sometimes these are offensive or, at a minimum, markers of "outsider" influence. Outsiders aren't always welcome; other times, they just appear ignorant.

For example, AT&T's "Reach Out and Touch Someone" advertising campaign was viewed as much too sentimental for most European audiences. Similarly, AT&T's "Call USA" campaign, aimed at Americans doing business in Europe, was negatively perceived by many Europeans. The ad featured a harried American businessman whose language skills were so poor that he could barely ask for assistance to find a telephone in a busy French hotel. European businesspeople are typically fluent in two or three languages and have enough language competence to ask for a telephone. This ad, with its portrayal of Americans as culturally inept and helpless, created a negative association for AT&T among European businesspeople. Granted, the target market was Americans in foreign assignments, but the perspective of the ad was still decidedly ethnocentric and offensive to Europeans.

The only way you can have any hope at all of counteracting the negative influences that ethnocentrism and SRC have on international advertising decision making is to be constantly sensitive to their existence and to the virtual certainty of important differences between cultures that will somehow affect your best effort. Even with the best cross-cultural analysis, it is still likely that problems will present themselves. However, without it, it is a virtual certainty.

GLOBAL ISSUES

From Salsa to Cinco de Mayo

When it comes to fast food in Mexico, the taco remains supreme. Steak, pork, chicken, and fish tacos are always available, broiled or steamed, with corn or flour tortillas, piled high with chilies and salsa. Vendors set up for the breakfast crowd and usually stay in place till about midnight. But sales of the taco in Mexico have been slumping of late. Why? Because Mexican fast-food consumers can now also choose from pizza at Domino's and Pizza Hut, hamburgers at McDonald's and Jack in the Box, and cold sandwiches at their local Subway. Hungry yet?

In the United States, "Americanized" Mexican food continues to grow in popularity. "Tex-Mex" has become a food genre that is popular around the world. U.S. consumers chow down on chili dogs, nachos, Doritos, Tostitos, and salsa brands such as Victoria and Ortega, to get their taste of Old Mexico. The irony, of course, is that products such as these are largely invented in the United States to appeal to the U.S. consumer's idealized sense of what Mexican food must be like.

The ultimate staple of the native Mexican diet is salsa and fresh chilies. They are at the table for breakfast, lunch, and dinner. Here we clearly observe the homogenization effect on consumer preferences that evolves between close trading partners. Salsa brands made in the United States now fill the shelves of grocery stores in Mexico, side by side with Mexican brands. Now Mexican consumers can choose the salsa with a taste of Old USA to spice up their fish tacos at breakfast.

Holiday exports/imports is another excellent example of this relentless cultural fusion. Cinco de Mayo, which commemorates a Mexican victory over French invaders on May 5, 1862, is not one of Mexico's major fiestas. However, it appears destined to take its place with other "ethnic" celebrations like Oktoberfest and St. Patrick's Day as cause for "shared" rejoicing. Turns out that Cinco de Mayo is timed perfectly for the U.S. celebrant: May 5 is ideally positioned about halfway between Easter and Memorial Day. And while few people from Mexico would recognize their fiesta as it is practiced in the United States, it has become a major point of emphasis in the marketing plan for Corona beer, Mexico's top-selling brand. Like it or not, commercialization of culture is a fact of life in today's global economy.

Sources: Ignacio Vazquez, "Mexicans Are Buying 'Made in USA' Food," *Marketing News*, August 31, 1998, 14; Joel Millman, "U.S. Marketers Adopt Cinco de Mayo as National Fiesta," *Wall Street Journal*, May 1, 2001, B1.

Cross-Cultural Audience Research. Analyzing audiences in international markets can be a humbling task. If firms have worldwide product distribution networks—as do Nestlé, Unilever, and Philip Morris—then international audience analysis will require dozens of separate analyses. There really is no way to avoid the task of specific audience analysis. This typically involves research in each different country, generally from a local research supplier. There are, however, good secondary resources that may provide broad-based information to advertisers about international markets. The U.S. Department of Commerce has an International Trade Administration (ITA) division, which helps companies based in the United States develop foreign market opportunities for their products and services. The ITA publishes specialized reports that cover most of the major markets in the world and provide economic and regulatory information. The United Nations' *Statistical Yearbook* is another source of general economic and population data. The yearbook, published annually, provides information for more than 200 countries. This type of source provides some helpful information for the international advertiser. Unfortunately, it's rarely enough.

An international audience analysis will also involve evaluation of economic conditions, demographic characteristics, values, custom and ritual, and product use and preferences.

Economic Conditions. One way to think about the economic conditions of a potential international audience is to break the world's markets into three broad classes of economic development: less-developed countries, newly industrialized countries, and highly industrialized countries. These categories provide a basic understanding of the economic capability of the average consumer in a market and thus help place consumption in the context of economic realities.

Less-developed countries represent nearly 75 percent of the world's population. Some of these countries are plagued by drought and civil war, and their economies lack almost all the resources necessary for development: capital, infrastructure, political stability, and trained workers. Many of the products sold in these less-developed economies are typically not consumer products, but rather business products used for building infrastructure (such as heavy construction equipment) or agricultural equipment.

Newly industrialized countries have economies defined by change; they are places where traditional ways of life that have endured for centuries are changing and modern consumer cultures have emerged in a few short years. This creates a very particular set of problems for the outside advertiser trying to hit a moving target, or a culture in rapid flux.

Rapid economic growth in countries such as Singapore, Malaysia, Taiwan, and South Korea has created a new middle class of consumers with radically different expectations than their counterparts of a mere decade ago. Asian consumers are relatively heavy users of media-based information. The latest global trends in fashion, music, and travel have shorter and shorter lag times in reaching this part of the world. Many U.S. firms already have a strong presence in these markets with both their products and their advertising, like the Tropicana brand shown in Exhibit 9.6.

The **highly industrialized countries** of the world are those with mature economies and high levels of affluence as indicated by data such as GNP per capita

EXHIBIT 9.6

This ad for Tropicana exemplifies the rapid changes occurring in many Asian countries. Traditional values are giving way to focus on consumption and consumer culture. www.tropicana.com

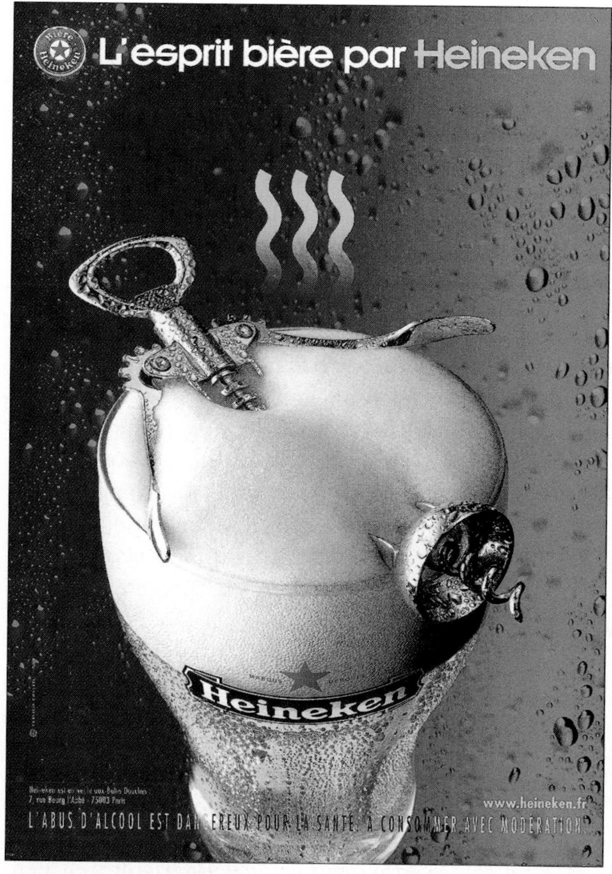

EXHIBIT 9.7

Heineken's distinctive Red Star is a logo known around the world. Here Heineken challenges partygoers in France to choose the bottle opener over the corkscrew in their next celebration.
www.heineken.com

EXHIBIT 9.8

Nokia—the quintessential global brand for the sophisticated global consumer. www.nokia.com

(see column three in Exhibit 9.3). These countries have also invested heavily over many years in infrastructure—roads, hospitals, airports, power-generating plants, educational institutions, and the Internet. Within this broad grouping, an audience assessment will focus on more-detailed analyses of the market, including the nature and extent of competition, marketing trade channels, lifestyle trends, and market potential. Firms pursuing opportunities in highly industrialized countries proceed with market analysis in much the same way it would be conducted in the United States. While the advertising in these countries will often vary based on unique cultural and lifestyle factors, consumers in these markets are accustomed to seeing a full range of creative appeals for goods and services. The Heineken and Nokia ads in Exhibits 9.7 and 9.8 provide vivid examples.

Demographic Characteristics. Information on the demographic characteristics of nations is generally available. Both the U.S. Department of Commerce and the United Nations publish annual studies of population for hundreds of countries. Advertisers must be sensitive to the demographic similarities and differences in international markets. Demographics, including size of population, age distribution, income distribution, education levels, occupations, literacy rates, and household size, can dramatically affect the type of advertising prepared for a market. Large-scale demographic trends are important to advertisers. For example, those thinking of entering international markets should keep in mind that roughly 20 percent of the world's population, generally residing in the highly industrialized countries, controls 75 percent of the world's wealth and accounts for 75 percent of all consumption.[2]

While much has been written about the graying of the U.S. population, other parts of the world do not follow this pattern. In the Middle East, Africa, and Latin America, roughly 40 percent of the population is under the age of 20.[3] Increases and decreases in the proportion of the population in specific age groups are closely related to the demand for particular products and services. As populations continue to increase in developing countries, new market opportunities emerge for products and services for young families and teens. Similarly, as advanced-age groups continue to increase in countries with stable population rates, the demand for consumer services such as health care, travel, and retirement planning will increase.

One of the most interesting demographic evolutions is taking place in Asian countries. By the year 2010, an additional 400 million people will be born in the Pacific Rim region. In addition, people are migrating from rural to urban areas in search of job and career opportunities. In just 30 years, South Korea's population has flip-flopped to 73 percent urban from 72 percent rural.[4] Advertising messages must accommodate the new experiences of an urban audience, and advertising strategists must place ads in media that efficiently reach these audiences.

Values. Cultural values are enduring beliefs about what is important to the members of a culture. They are the defining bedrock of a culture. They are an outgrowth of the culture's history and its collective experience. (Even though there are many cultures within any given nation, many believe that there are still enough shared values to constitute a meaningful "national culture," such as "American culture.") For example, the value of individualism enjoys a long and prominent place in American history and is considered by many to be a core American value. Other cultures seem to value the group or collective more. Even though a "collectivist" country like Japan may be becoming more individualistic, there is still a Japanese tradition that favors the needs of the group over those of the individual. In Japan, organizational loyalty and social interdependence are values that promote a group mentality. Japanese consumers are thus thought to be more sensitive to appeals that feature stability, longevity, and reliability, and they find appeals using competitive comparisons to be confrontational and inappropriate.[5]

Some researchers believe this continuum from individualism to collectivism to be a stable and dependably observed cultural difference among the peoples of the world. Exhibits 9.9 and 9.10 show two ads that appear to reflect this difference. The Scotch ad in Exhibit 9.9 shows an appeal to individualism; it ran in the United States. The IBM ad shown in Exhibit 9.10 reflects a collectivist approach; it is from Japan. Scotch whiskey certainly has a social component in actual use, and computers are not typically considered group products by Americans. But IBM appears to have adapted its message accordingly for advertising in a "collectivist" culture. Some researchers believe this continuum from individualism to collectivism to be a stable and dependably observed difference among the people of the world, or at least stable enough for crafting different ads for different cultures.[6]

2. Clive Cook, "Catching Up," *The Economist*, Winter 1993, 15–16.
3. Adapted from Richard Sookdeo, "The New Global Consumer," *Fortune*, Autumn/Winter 1993, 68–79.
4. Ford S. Worthy, "A New Mass Market Emerges," *Fortune*, Fall 1991.
5. Johny Johansson, "The Sense of Nonsense: Japanese TV Advertising," *Journal of Advertising* (March 1994), 17–26. Political advertising in Japan also emphasizes a nonconfrontational style, but there have been some recent exceptions. For an example, see Peter Landers, "The Japanese Get a Taste of American-Style Political Ads," *Wall Street Journal*, April 10, 2001, A16.
6. S. Han and S. Shavitt, "Persuasion and Culture: Advertising Appeals in Individualistic and Collectivistic Societies," *Journal of Experimental Social Psychology*, vol. 30 (1994), 326–350.

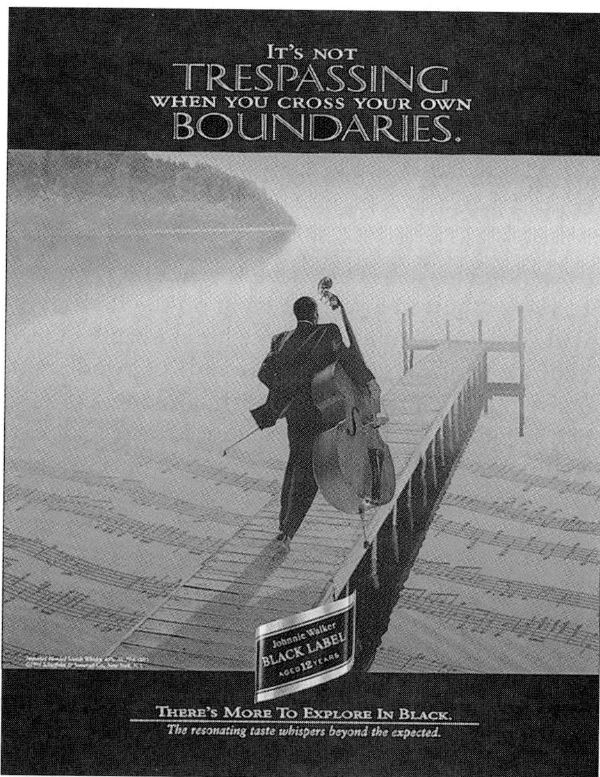

EXHIBIT 9.9

Individualism is a core value in U.S. culture and is reflected by the message of this Johnnie Walker ad. In contrast, the IBM ad in Exhibit 9.10 appeals to the collectivist nature of Asian culture.

e-SIGHTINGS

EXHIBIT 9.10

How does the IBM ad shown here underscore the collectivist values important to Japanese consumers? Even if you don't read Japanese, what is it about the ad that communicates these values right away? Does IBM (www.ibm.com) make an effort to communicate cultural values at its international sites? Compare and contrast this with competitor Hewlett-Packard and its international sites (www.hewlett-packard.com). Do you think ads for technology products are inherently global in their appeal, or do they need heavy customization across local markets?

Custom and Ritual. Among other things, rituals perpetuate a culture's connections to its core values. They seem perfectly natural to members of a culture, and they can often be performed without much thought (in some cases, hardly any) regarding their deeper meaning. Many consumer behaviors involve rituals, such as grooming, gift giving, or preparing food. To do a good job in cross-cultural advertising, the rituals of other cultures must be not only appreciated, but also understood. This requires in-depth and extended research efforts. Quick marketing surveys rarely do anything in this context, except invite disaster.

One of the most devastating mistakes an advertiser can make is to presume that consumers in one culture have the same rituals as those in another. Religion is an obvious expression of values in a culture. In countries adhering to the precepts of the Islamic religion, which includes most Arab countries, traditional religious beliefs restrict several products from being advertised at all, such as alcohol and pork. Other restrictions related to religious and cultural values include not allowing women to appear in advertising and restricting the manner in which children can be portrayed in advertisements.[7] Each market must be evaluated for the extent to which prevalent customs or values translate into product choice and other consumer behaviors.

Understanding values and rituals can represent a special challenge (or opportunity) when economic development in a country or region creates tensions between the old and the new. The classic example is the dilemma that advertisers face as more wives leave the home for outside employment, creating tensions in the home about who should do the housework. This tension over traditional gender assignments in household chores has been particularly acute in Asia, and advertisers there have tried to respond by featuring husbands as homemakers. For example, an ad for vacuum cleaners made by Korea's LG Electronics showed a woman lying on the floor exercising and giving herself a facial with slices of cucumbers, while her husband cleaned around her. The ad received mixed reviews from women in Hong Kong and South Korea, with younger women approving but their mothers disapproving.[8] (Sound familiar?) The advertiser's dilemma in situations like these is how to make ads that reflect real changes in a culture, without alienating important segments of consumers by appearing to push the changes. Not an easy task!

Product Use and Preferences. Information about product use and preferences is available for many markets. The major markets of North America, Europe, and the Pacific Rim typically are relatively heavily researched. In recent years, A. C. Nielsen has developed an international database on consumer product use in 26 countries. Also, Roper Starch Worldwide has conducted "global" studies on product preferences, brand loyalty, and price sensitivity in 40 different countries. The Roper Starch study revealed that consumers in India were the most brand loyal (34 percent of those surveyed), and that German and Japanese consumers showed the greatest tendency for price sensitivity (over 40 percent of survey consumers in each market).[9]

Studies by firms such as Nielsen and Roper Starch do not dispute that consumers around the world display vastly different product use characteristics and preferences. One area of great variation is personal-care products. There is no market in the world like the United States, where consumers are preoccupied with the use of personal-care products such as toothpaste, shampoo, deodorant, and mouthwash. Procter & Gamble, maker of brands such as Crest, Pert, Secret, and Scope, among others, learned the hard way in Russia with its Wash & Go shampoo. Wash & Go (comparable to Pert in the United States) was a shampoo and conditioner designed for the consumer who prefers the ease, convenience, and speed of one-step washing and conditioning. Russian consumers, accustomed to washing their hair with bar soap, didn't understand the concept of a hair conditioner, and didn't perceive a need to make shampooing any more convenient.

Other examples of unique and culture-specific product uses and preferences come from Brazil and France. In Brazil, many women still wash clothes by hand in metal tubs, using cold water. Because of this behavior, Unilever must specially formulate its Umo laundry powder and tout its effectiveness under these washing conditions.

In France, men commonly use cosmetics like those used by women in the United States. Advertising must, therefore, be specifically prepared for men and placed in media to reach them with specific male-oriented appeals. As another example, Exhibit 9.11 shows an ad directed toward French women—some of whom are relatively less accustomed (compared to women in the USA) to shaving their legs and underarms—for a razor designed for just such a purpose. The ad uses both pictures and text to promote the behavior. Perfume is another product category that inspires distinctive approaches around the world. As exemplified by Exhibit 9.12, the

7. Marian Katz, "No Women, No Alcohol: Learn Saudi Taboos before Placing Ads," *International Advertiser,* February 1986, 11; Barbara Sundberg Baudot, *International Advertising Handbook* (Boston: Lexington Books, 1989), 220–221.
8. Louise Lee, "Depicting Men Doing Housework Can Be Risky for Marketers in Asia," *Wall Street Journal,* August 14, 1998, B6.
9. Leah Rickard, "Ex-Soviet States Lead World in Ad Cynicism," *Advertising Age,* May 5, 1995, 3.

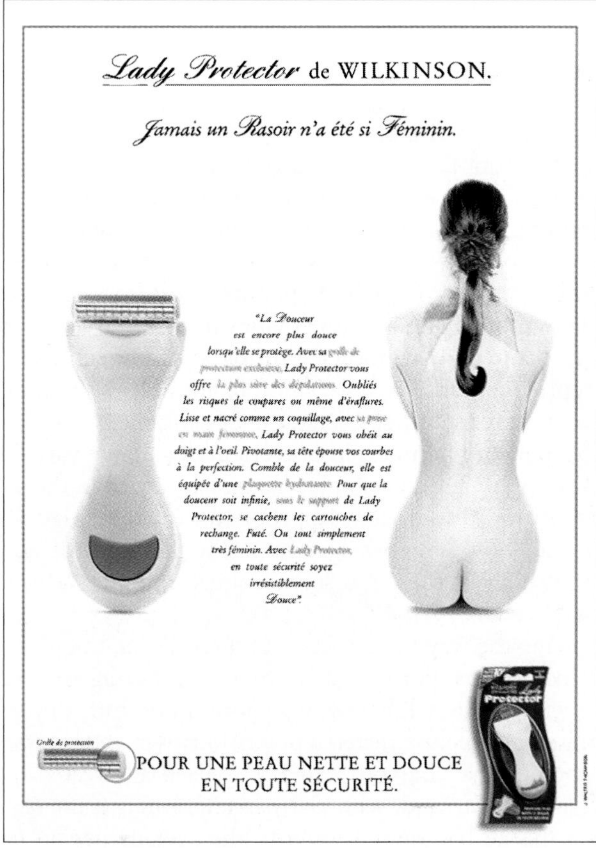

EXHIBIT 9.11

It's been said that "all politics are local," but so too is personal hygiene. The United Kingdom's Wilkinson might encounter difficulties in selling its Lady Protector, specifically designed for shaving women's legs and underarms, in France. The company's Web site (www.wilkinson-sword.com) is admirably multilingual, though, appealing to British, French, and Germans. Might Wilkinson have done better to have "Americanized" a Web site as well?

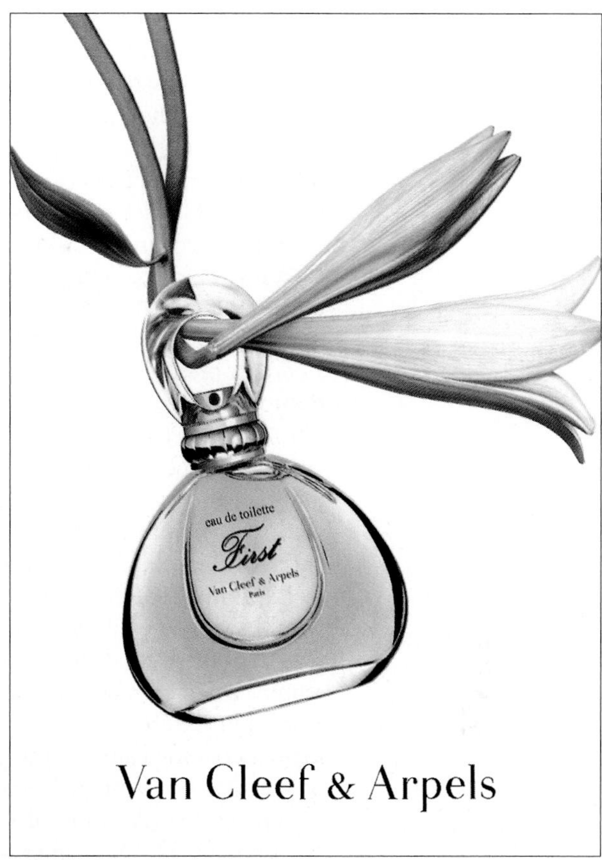

EXHIBIT 9.12

Thumb through a French fashion magazine and you'll appreciate both the passion for art and the passion for perfume that are hallmarks of French culture.

French have a passion for perfume that transforms their advertisements in this category to near works of art.

The Challenges in Executing Advertising Worldwide.

Cross-cultural audience research on basic economic, social, and cultural conditions is an essential starting point for planning international advertising. But even with excellent audience analysis, three formidable and unique challenges face the advertiser: the creative challenge, the media challenge, and the regulatory challenge.

2 The Creative Challenge.

Written or spoken language is a basic barrier to cross-cultural communication. Ads written in German are typically difficult for those who speak only Arabic—this much is obvious. We've all heard stories of how some literal translation of an ad said something very different than what was intended. For example, when Sunbeam introduced the Mist-Stick mixer into the German market, the firm ran into a fairly severe language problem. The word *Mist* spelled and pronounced precisely the same way in German means "manure." The word *Stick* translates roughly as "wand." Sunbeam was attempting to introduce a "manure wand" for use in German food preparation.[10]

What is less obvious, however, is the role of **picturing** in cross-cultural communication. There is a widely held belief that pictures are less culturally bound than are words, and that pictures can speak to many cultures at once. International advertisers are increasingly using ads that feature few words and rely on pictures to communicate. This is, as you might expect, a bit more complicated than it sounds.

First, picturing is culturally bound. Different cultures use different conventions or rules to create representations (or pictures) of things. Pictures, just like words, must be "read" or interpreted, and the "rules of reading" pictures vary from culture to culture. People living in Western cultures often assume that everyone knows what a certain picture means. This is not true and is another example of ethnocentrism. Photographic two-dimensional representations are not even recognizable as pictures to those who have not learned to interpret such representations. Symbolic representations that seem so absolute, common, and harmless in one culture can have varied, unusual, and even threatening meaning in another. A picture may be worth a thousand words, but those words may not mean something appropriate—or they may be entirely unintelligible or tasteless—to those in another culture. Think about the ads in Exhibits 9.13, 9.14, and 9.15. Which of these ads seem culture-bound? Which would seem to easily cross cultural borders? Why?

All of these ads depend on knowing the way to correctly interpret the ad, but some require more cultural knowledge than others. For U.S. consumers, the message of the Visa ad in Exhibit 9.13 is perfectly clear. Visa will help you acquire more stuff. But in less materialistic cultures, the premise of collecting material possessions as an expression of self may be completely incomprehensible. Exhibit 9.14 is a stylized ad created to present a romantic vision of a vacation in Thailand, with German consumers as the target segment. Do you suppose that this ad has any meaning to the average person in

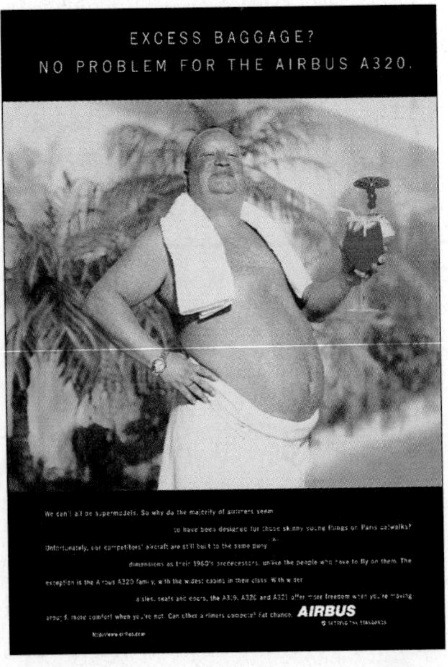

EXHIBITS 9.13 THROUGH 9.15

Which of these ads seem most bound to their national cultures, based on the pictures portrayed in the ads? Are any of them not culturally bound?

10. David Ricks, *Big Business Blunders: Mistakes in Multi-National Marketing* (Homewood, Ill.: Dow Jones–Irwin, 1983), 66.

Thailand? And check out the belly on that guy in Exhibit 9.15. Is a big bare belly going to reflect the same level of status in Austria, India, and Argentina? Work by Aaker[11] suggests that some of the actual markers of culture may make some ads easier to access (and perhaps store) from memory than other ads without those markers.

A few human expressions, such as a smile, are widely accepted to mean a positive feeling. Such expressions and their representations, even though culturally connected, have widespread commonality. But cultureless picture meanings do not exist. A much larger contributor to cross-cultural commonalities are those representations that are a part of a far-flung culture of commerce and have thus taken on similar meanings in many different nations. With sports playing an ever-larger role in international commerce, the sports hero is often used to symbolize common meaning across the world. What do you think? Is Tiger Woods Tiger Woods, no matter what he is selling, or where he is selling it? Can the Williams sisters revive the Avon cosmetics brand around the world? Janice Spector, Avon's senior director, global advertising, signed the tennis champs to a three-year contract to do just that.[12]

The Media Challenge.

Of all the challenges faced by advertisers in international markets, the media challenge may be the greatest. Exhibit 9.16 shows a sampling of traditional media options for reaching consumers around the world.

Media Availability and Coverage.

Some international markets simply have too few media options. In addition, even if diverse media are available in a particular international market, there may be severe restrictions on the type of advertising that can be done or the way in which advertising is organized in a certain medium.

Many countries have dozens of subcultures and language dialects within their borders, each with its own newspapers and radio stations. This complicates the problem of deciding which combination of newspapers or radio stations will achieve the desired coverage of the market. The presence of a particular medium in a country does not necessarily make it useful for advertisers if there are restrictions on accepting advertising. The most prominent example is the BBC networks in the United Kingdom, where advertising is still not accepted. While the UK does have commercial networks in both radio and television, the BBC stations are still widely popular. Or consider the situation with regard to television advertising in Germany and The Netherlands. On the German government-owned stations, television advertising is banned on Sundays and holidays and restricted to four five-minute blocks on other days. In The Netherlands, television advertising cannot constitute more than 5 percent of total programming time, and most time slots must be purchased nearly a year in advance. Similar circumstances exist in many markets around the world.

Newspapers are actually the most localized medium worldwide, and they require the greatest amount of local market knowledge to be used correctly as an advertising option. In Mexico, for example, advertising space is sold in the form of news columns, without any notice or indication that the "story" is a paid advertisement. This situation influences both the placement and layout of ads. Turkey has more than 350 daily national newspapers; The Netherlands has only three. Further, many newspapers (particularly regional papers) are positioned in the market based on a particular political philosophy. Advertisers must be aware of this, making certain that their brand's position with the target audience does not conflict with the politics of the medium.

The best news for advertisers from the standpoint of media availability and coverage is the emergence of several global television networks made possible by satellite

11. Aaker, Jennifer L., "The Influence of Culture on Persuasion and Attitudes: Diagnosticity or Accessibility?," *Journal of Consumer Research*, 26:4 (March 2000), 340–357.

12. Mercedes Cardona, "Venus and Serena Become Avon's New Leading Ladies," *Advertising Age*, January 22, 2001, 8.

EXHIBIT 9.16

Advertising Age's global media lineup.

Media	Ownership	Circulation or Number of Households
PRINT		
Business Week	The McGraw-Hill Cos.	1.08 million
Computerworld/InfoWorld	IDG	1.9 million
The Economist	The Economist Group	684,416
Elle	Hachette Filipacchi	5.1 million
Elle Deco	Hachette Filipacchi	1.5 million
Financial Times	Pearson PLC	363,525
Forbes Global Business & Finance	Forbes	860,000**
Fortune	Time Warner	915,000
Harvard Business Review	Harvard Business School Publishing	220,000
International Herald Tribune	The New York Times/ The Washington Post Co.	222,930
National Geographic	National Geographic Society	8.8 million
Newsweek Worldwide	The Washington Post Co.	4.2 million
PC World	IDG	3.6 million
Reader's Digest	Reader's Digest Association	26 million
Scientific American	Yerlagsgruppe Hoitzbrinck	562,150
TIME	Time Warner	5.6 million
USA Today International	Gannett Co.	2.2 million† (Mon.–Thurs.)
		2.6 million (Friday edition)
The Wall Street Journal	Dow Jones & Co.	4.3 million
TV		
Animal Planet	Discovery Communications/BBC	4.9 million*
BBC World	BBC Worldwide	60 million
Cartoon Network	Time Warner	125.5 million
CNBC	NBC/Dow Jones & Co. (only 100% NBC-owned in U.S.)	136 million**
CNN International	Time Warner	221 million
Discovery Networks International	Discovery Communications	144 million
ESPN	Walt Disney Co./Hearst Corp.	242 million
MTV Networks	Viacom	285 million
TNT	Time Warner	104.2 million

* Includes 45 million homes in the United States
** Excludes Latin America
† For international edition only

Source: *Advertising Age International,* February 8, 1999, 23. Reprinted with permission from the February 8, 1999, issue of *Advertising Age International.*

technology. Viacom bills its combined MTV Networks (MTVN) as the largest TV network in the world, with a capability to reach over 300 million households worldwide.[13] MTVN not only can provide media access, but also offers expertise in developing special promotions to Generations X, Y, and Z around the world. MTVN has facilitated international campaigns for global brands such as Pepsi, Swatch, Sega, and BMX Bikes.[14] CNN, the worldwide news network, can be seen in 100 countries and specifically offers newly acquired access to the vast Indian market.[15]

Another development affecting Europe and Asia is direct broadcast by satellite (DBS). DBS transmissions are received by households through a small, low-cost receiving dish. STAR TV, which stands for Satellite Televisions Asian Region, sends BBC and U.S. programming to millions of Asian households and hotels. Ultimately, STAR TV could reach 3 billion people, making it the most widely viewed medium in the world.[16] An ad for one of STAR TV's partners in the Asian market is shown in Exhibit 9.17.

Additionally, global expansion of the Internet may one day offer advertisers economical access to huge new markets. But that day has yet to arrive. As described in the E-Commerce box on this page, it would be inappropriate to presume that the Internet is equally accessible or equally important to consumers in various parts of the world.

E-COMMERCE

News Flash: World Wide Web Not Worldwide

Whereas once many thought the Internet would spread around the globe at the speed of light, we now can see clearly that the Internet is diffusing around the continents of the world at very different speeds. Good infrastructure and a PC in most homes and/or offices allowed the Internet to diffuse with lightning speed in the United States. This explains the large sums of money spent on Internet advertising in the United States as compared to other countries (see Exhibit 9.3). But poor infrastructure and slow diffusion of the personal PC has constrained the Internet's spread in many regions, such as Latin America.

Within Latin America, three countries house two-thirds of the region's Internet users. The "big three" are Brazil, Mexico, and Argentina, with 3.9 million, 1.5 million, and 1 million Internet users, respectively. Sound like a lot? Well, take Brazil. That's 3.9 million users out of a population of 168 million: just over 2 percent of Brazilian consumers have access to the Internet. By contrast, at the same point in time in the United States, there were 158 million users out of a population of 281 million, which comes out to about 56 percent. Internet users in Latin America are a very small market sliver; in North America, they are the majority. In Latin America, the Internet is used primarily as a communication tool. People there are still very skeptical about using the Web as a place to cybershop. In North America, e-shopping is now largely taken for granted as a convenient supplement to shopping in the physical world.

The point here is definitely not to try to build someone up or tear someone down because they do or don't have access to or shop on the Internet. Rather, the point is to encourage you to have your facts straight before you start thinking about the global potential of the Internet as an advertising tool. It is a valid tool in North America, but much less so in many other places around the world. And while the Web's influence continues to grow, the fact that we call it "World Wide" is a nice example of U.S. ethnocentrism. We see the world as we see ourselves . . .

Sources: Charles Dawson, "Latin America's Internet E-Volution," *adageglobal,* March 2001, 27–34; "Web's Heavy U.S. Accent Grates on Overseas Ears," *Wall Street Journal,* September 26, 1996, B4; "Internet at a Glance," *Business 2.0,* March 6, 2001, 102.

Media Costs and Pricing. Confounding the media challenge is the issue of media costs and pricing. As discussed earlier, some markets have literally hundreds of media options (recall the 350 Turkish newspapers). Whenever a different medium is chosen, separate payment and placement must be made. Additionally, in many markets, media prices are subject to negotiation—no matter what the official rate cards say. The time needed to negotiate these rates is a tremendous cost in and of itself.

Global coverage is an expensive proposition. For example, a four-color ad in *Reader's Digest* costs nearly half a million dollars.[17] Should the advertiser desire to achieve full impact in *Reader's Digest,*

13. "On-Air Opportunities," *Television Business International,* vol. 49 (January 1998), 1.
14. Ibid.
15. Todd Pruzan, "Global Media: Distribution Slows but Rates Climb," *Advertising Age International,* January 16, 1995, 1-19; "India Will Allow CNN Broadcasts," July 12, 1995, 9.
16. Thomas McCarroll, "New Star over Asia," *Time,* August 9, 1993, 53.
17. Pruzan, "Global Media," op. cit.

EXHIBIT 9.17

Direct broadcast by satellite allows households to receive television transmission via a small, low-cost receiving dish. This is an ad for Skyport TV promoting its satellite service in the Asian market.

then the ad should be prepared in all 20 of the different languages for the international editions—again, generating substantial expense. Both ad rates and the demand for ad space are on the increase. In some markets, advertising time and space are in such short supply that, regardless of the published rate, a bidding system is used to escalate the prices. As you will see in Chapter 14, media costs represent the majority of costs in an advertising budget. With the seemingly chaotic buying practices in some international markets, media costs are indeed a great challenge in executing cost-effective advertising campaigns.

The Regulatory Challenge. The regulatory restrictions on international advertising are many and varied, reflecting diverse cultural values, market by market. The range and specificity of regulation can be aggravatingly complex. Tobacco and liquor advertising are restricted (typically banned from television) in many countries, although several lift their ban on liquor after 9 or 10 P.M. With respect to advertising to children, Austria, Canada, Germany, and the United States have specific regulations. Other products and topics monitored or restricted throughout the world are drugs (Austria, Switzerland, Germany, Greece, and The Netherlands), gambling (United Kingdom, Italy, and Portugal), and religion (Germany, United Kingdom, and The Netherlands).

This regulatory complexity, if anything, continues to grow. For instance, the European Union has proposed restrictions for the placement of advertising on teleshopping, pay-per-view, and movie-on-demand channels.[18] Generally, advertisers must be sensitive to the fact that advertising regulations can, depending on the international market, impose limitations on the following:

- The types of products that can be advertised
- The types of appeals that can be used
- The times during which ads for certain products can appear on television
- Advertising to children
- The use of foreign languages (and talent) in advertisements
- The use of national symbols, such as flags and government seals, in advertisements
- The taxes levied against advertising expenditures

In short, just about every aspect of advertising can be regulated, and every country has its own peculiarities with respect to ad regulation. As explained in the IBP box on page 317, these restrictions and regulations may also apply to a host of common promotional tactics such as couponing and loyalty rewards programs.

3 Advertising Agencies around the World.

An experienced and astute agency can help an advertiser deal with the creative, media, and regulatory challenges just discussed. In Brazil, using a local agency is essential to get the creative

18. Bruce Crumley, "EU Proposal May Limit TV Spots," *Advertising Age*, January 9, 1995, 12.

style and tone just right. In Australia, Australian nationals must be involved in certain parts of the production process. And in China, trying to work through the government and media bureaucracy is nearly impossible without the assistance of a local agency.

Advertisers have three basic alternatives in choosing an agency to help them prepare and place advertising in other countries: They can use a global agency, an international affiliate, or a local agency.

IBP

Releasing That Pent-Up Urge to Clip Coupons

A few years ago, a court in Düsseldorf blocked a drugstore there from giving away 75-cent shopping bags in celebration of the anniversary of its opening. The bags featured a lovable penguin holding a birthday cake . . . pretty dangerous stuff! The German court ruled this was a violation of the Free Gift Act. The court reasoned that since most German retailers sell shopping bags, giving them away as a free gift was *verboten.* Half-price happy hour drinks didn't fare any better with the courts in Germany. Since the Discount Law there forbids price breaks of more than 3 percent off list, a half-price offer on drinks is strictly *verboten.* These are just two examples of a myriad of laws and regulations in Germany controlling many kinds of price promotions that American consumers take for granted.

Oftentimes laws like these are remnants of another era. Many such German regulations date back to the Nazi regime when the intent was to eliminate deals and discounting because these tactics were associated with the soft economic policies of the Marxist movement. The wild part of it is, 70 years later, these laws are still enforced aggressively. As hard as it may be to get laws passed in any culture, it is probably always harder to make them go away, even when it is not clear what purpose they are serving in modern times.

But fear not, there is hope for the German coupon clipper. Coupons and other familiar promotional tactics are on the way, thanks to the Internet. Even though less than 10 percent of German consumers shop via the Internet, there is a growing concern that the Internet will introduce discounting practices that will be hard for traditional retailers to match if they are shackled by regulations like the Free Gift Act and the Discount Law. So how will German consumers react to the prospect of free shopping bags, happy hour specials, coupons, or buy-one-get-one-free offers? They'll probably be pretty excited at first, given that these things will be something new and different. But it shouldn't take long for things to settle down, with coupon clipping becoming the tedious chore that many consumers around the world already know it to be.

Source: David Wessel, "German Shoppers Get Coupons," *Wall Street Journal,* April 5, 2001, 1.

The Global Agency. The consolidation and mergers taking place in the advertising industry are creating more and more **global agencies,** or worldwide advertising groups. Two of the global advertising giants are WPP Group and Omnicom Group. The line-up of companies affiliated with each of these multibillion-dollar businesses is detailed in Exhibit 9.18. Note how these gigantic companies have assembled a network of diverse service providers to deliver advertising and integrated brand promotion for clients who demand global reach.

The great advantage of a global agency is that it will know the advertiser's products and current advertising programs (presuming it handles the domestic advertising duties). With this knowledge, the agency can either adapt domestic campaigns for international markets or launch entirely new campaigns. Another advantage is the geographic proximity of the advertiser to the agency headquarters, which can often facilitate planning and preparation of ads. The size of a global agency can be a benefit in terms of economies of scale and political leverage.

Their greatest disadvantage stems from their distance from the local culture. Exporting meaning is never easy. This is no small disadvantage to agencies that actually believe they can do this. Most, however, are not that naive or arrogant, and they have procedures for acquiring local knowledge.

The International Affiliate. Many agencies do not own and operate worldwide offices, but rather have established foreign-market **international affiliates** to handle clients' international advertising needs. Many times these agencies join a network of foreign agencies or take minority ownership positions in several foreign agencies. The benefit of this arrangement is that the advertiser typically has access to a large number of international agencies that can provide local market expertise. These international agencies

	WPP Group, London	Omnicom Group, New York
2000 revenue	$6.6 billion (including the purchase of Young & Rubicam over the full year)	$6.15 billion
Major clients	Ford Motor, AT&T, International Business Machines, Nestle, American Express, Pfizer	DaimlerChrysler, Anheuser-Busch, PepsiCo, Tricon Global Restaurants, McDonald's, Nissan Motor
Advertising	Ogilvy & Mather Worldwide, J. Walter Thompson Company, Young & Rubicam Advertising, Red Cell	BBDO Worldwide, DDB Worldwide, TBWA Worldwide, Goodby Silverstein & Partners, GSD&M, Martin/Williams, Merkley Newman Harty
Media services	Mind Share, Media Edge	Optimum Media Direction (OMD), PhD Network
Public relations	Burson-Marsteller, Cohn & Wolfe, Hill and Knowlton, Ogilvy Public Relations Worldwide, Robinson Lerer & Montgomery	Brodeur Worldwide, Fleishman-Hillard, Gavin Anderson and Company, Ketchum, Porter Novelli International
Healthcare	CommonHealth, Ogilvy Healthcare, Sudler & Hennessey	Accel Healthcare, Cline Davis & Mann, Corbett HealthConnect
Digital & tech. services	Digital@jwt, Ogilvy Interactive	Agency.com and Razorfish (owns a minority stake), Atmosphere, Tribal DDB
Marketing services & specialty communications	Impiric, OgilvyOne Worldwide, Millward Brown, Knowledge Base Marketing, Research International	Rapp Collins Worldwide, Direct Partners, Millsport, TLP, M/A/R/C Research
Urban and ethnic marketing	Bravo Group, Kang & Lee, Mendoza Dillon & Asociados, UniWorld	Footsteps

Source: *Wall Street Journal*, March 19, 2001, B4.

EXHIBIT 9.18

Global advertising giants.

are usually well established and managed by foreign nationals, which gives the advertiser a local presence in the international market, while avoiding any resistance to foreign ownership. This was the reasoning behind Coca-Cola's decision to give local creative responsibility for advertising its Coke Classic brand in Europe to the French agency Publicis SA.[19] Although Coke Classic is a global brand, Coke felt that the French agency was better suited to adapt U.S. ad campaigns for European use.

The risk of these arrangements is that while an international affiliate will know the local market, it may be less knowledgeable about the advertiser's brands and competitive strategy. The threat is that the real value and relevance of the brand will not be incorporated into the foreign campaign.

The Local Agency. The final option is for an advertiser to choose a **local agency** in every foreign market where advertising will be carried out. Local agencies have the same advantages as the affiliate agencies just discussed: They will be knowledgeable about the culture and local market conditions. Such agencies tend to have well-established contacts for market information, production, and media buys. But the advertiser that chooses this option is open to administrative problems. There is less tendency for standardization of the creative effort; each agency in each market will feel compelled to provide a unique creative execution. This lack of standardization can be expensive, and potentially disastrous for brand imagery when the local agency seeks to

19. Daniel Tilles, "Publicist Gets a Sip of Coke Account," *International Herald Tribune*, July 7, 1995, 13.

make its own creative statement without a good working knowledge of a brand's heritage.[20] Finally, working with local agencies can create internal communication problems, which increases the risk of delays and errors in execution.

4 Globalized versus Localized Campaigns. One additional issue must be resolved. This key issue involves the extent to which a campaign will be standardized versus localized across markets. In discussions of this issue, the question is often posed as, How much can the advertiser globalize the advertising? **Globalized campaigns** use the same message and creative execution across all (or most) international markets. Exhibits 9.19 and 9.20 show ads from Jack Daniel's globalized campaign. By contrast, **localized campaigns** involve preparing different messages and/or creative executions for each market a firm has entered, as is illustrated by the Nikon ad in Exhibit 9.21.

The issue is more complex than simply a question of globalized versus localized advertising. Both the brand and its overall marketing strategy must be examined.

e-SIGHTINGS

EXHIBITS 9.19 AND 9.20

Globalized advertising campaigns maintain a highly similar look and feel across international markets. These Jack Daniel's ads from the United States and Japan demonstrate how a global brand can use a global campaign. Can you identify the common themes used in these two ads? The Jack Daniel's home page (www.jackdaniels.com) contains links to its international sites. Visit multiple sites (after giving your date of birth) and compare content and features. Does Jack Daniel's assume that its brand image and company history have global appeal? What communication context, if any, would a 21st-century consumer from South America or the Pacific Rim share with mid-1800s Tennessean distillery culture?

20. Leon E. Wynter, "Global Marketers Learn to Say No to Bad Ads," *Wall Street Journal*, April 1, 1998, B1.

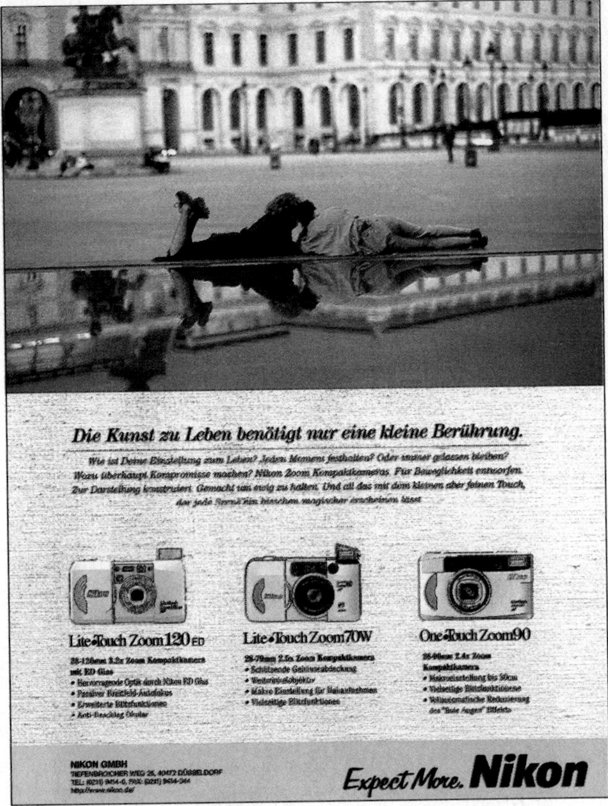

EXHIBIT 9.21

This ad for the Nikon Lite-Touch line has been tailored for its German audience. Nikon is certainly a global brand. Is this ad structured in such a way that it could be easily adapted for other countries around the world? What visual image would you choose to catch the eye of consumers in your country?
www.nikon.com

The marketer must first consider the extent to which the brand can be standardized across markets, and then the extent to which the advertising can be globalized across markets. The degree to which advertising in international markets can use a common appeal, versus whether the ads prepared for each market must be customized, has been a widely debated issue.

Those who favor the globalized campaign assume that similarities as well as differences between markets should be taken into account. They argue that standardization of messages should occur whenever possible, adapting the message only when absolutely necessary. For example, Mars's U.S. advertisements for Pedigree dog food have used golden retrievers, while poodles were deemed more effective for the brand's positioning and image in Asia. Otherwise, the advertising campaigns were identical in terms of basic message appeal.[21]

Those who argue for the localized approach see each country or region as a unique communication context, and they claim that the only way to achieve advertising success is to develop separate campaigns for each market.

The two fundamental arguments for globalized campaigns are based on potential cost savings and creative advantages. Just as organizations seek to gain economies of scale in production, they also look for opportunities to streamline the communication process. Having one standard theme to communicate allows an advertiser to focus on a uniform brand or corporate image worldwide, develop plans more quickly, and make maximum use of good ideas. Thus, while Gillette sells hundreds of different products in more than 200 countries around the world, its corporate philosophy of globalization is expressed in its "Gillette—the Best a Man Can Get" theme. This theme is attached to all ads for men's toiletry products, wherever they appear.[22]

In recent years, several aspects of the global marketplace have changed in such a way that the conditions for globalized campaigns are more favorable. Specifically, these conditions fostering the use of such campaigns are as follows:[23]

- *Global communications.* Worldwide cable and satellite networks have resulted in television becoming a truly global communications medium. MTV's 200 European advertisers almost all run English-language-only campaigns in the station's 28-nation broadcast area. These standardized messages will themselves serve to homogenize the viewers within these market areas.
- *The global teenager.* Global communications, global travel, and the demise of communism are argued to have created common norms and values among teenagers around the world. One advertising agency videotaped the rooms of teenagers from 25 countries, and it was hard to tell whether the room belonged to an

21. Zachary Schiller and Rischar A. Melcher, "Marketing Globally Thinking Locally," *International Business Week,* May 13, 1991, 23.
22. Bill Saporito, "Where the Global Action Is," *Fortune,* Autumn/Winter 1993, 63; Mark Maremont, "Gillette Finally Reveals Its Vision of the Future, and It Has 3 Blades," *Wall Street Journal,* April 14, 1998, A1, A10.
23. This list is adapted from Henry Assael, *Consumer Behavior and Marketing Action,* 5th ed. (Cincinnati, Ohio: South-Western/International Thomson Publishing, 1995), 491–494.

American, German, or Japanese teen. The rooms had soccer balls, Levi jeans, NBA jackets, and Sega video games.[24] Habits and practices among young people in South Korea suggest that they too are ready to embrace a globalized youth-oriented pop culture. Multiple earrings, blond hair dye, the omnipresent wireless phone, and hip-hop baggy pants are standard fare among teens on the streets of Seoul.[25]

- *Universal demographic and lifestyle trends.* Demographic and lifestyle trends that emerged in the 1980s in the United States are manifesting themselves in markets around the world. More working women, more single-person households, increasing divorce rates, and fewer children per household are now widespread demographic phenomena that are affecting lifestyles. The rising number of working women in Japan caused Ford Motor Company to prepare ads specifically targeted to this audience.
- *The Americanization of consumption values.* Perhaps of greatest advantage to U.S. advertisers is the Americanization of consumption values around the world. American icons are gaining popularity worldwide, especially due to the exportation of pop culture fueled by the U.S. entertainment industry. This trend has become so pervasive that some countries are seeking ways to shield themselves from U.S. entertainment exports. One meeting of culture ministers from 19 nations, including Canada, Britain, Mexico, and Sweden, discussed proposals for exempting cultural "products" from international free-trade pacts. The ultimate target of this discussion by these czars of local culture was undeniably "Made in the USA" entertainment products.[26]

All of these forces are creating an environment where a common message across national boundaries becomes more plausible. To the extent that consumers in various countries hold the same interests and values, "standardized" images and themes can be effective in advertising.

Arguments against globalization tend to center on issues relating to local market requirements and cultural constraints within markets. The target audiences in different countries must understand and place the same level of importance on brand features or attributes for a globalized campaign to be effective. In many cases, different features are valued at different levels of intensity, making a common message inappropriate. Also, if a globalized campaign defies local customs, values, and regulations, or if it ignores the efforts of local competition, then it has little chance of being successful.

It is sometimes the case that local managers do not appreciate the value of globalized campaigns. Since they did not help create the campaign, they may drag their feet in implementing it. Without the support of local managers, no globalized campaign can ever achieve its potential.

Developing global brands through standardized campaigns can be successful only when advertisers can find similar needs, feelings, or emotions as a basis for communication across cultures. Understanding consumers around the world is the critical success factor. As expressed by Bob Wehling, Procter & Gamble's former chief of global marketing: "When you bring consumers in every part of the world what they want and you present it in an arresting and persuasive manner, success will follow. And when you don't, the consumer will be the first to tell you to fix it."[27]

Finally, global marketers need to distinguish between strategy and execution when using a global approach to advertising. The basic need identified may well be universal, but communication about the product or service that offers satisfaction of the need may be strongly influenced by cultural values in different markets and thus

24. Shawn Tully, "Teens: The Most Global Market of All," *Fortune,* May 16, 1994, 90.
25. Louis Hau, "Korea's Pop Culture Breaks Out," *adageglobal,* March 2001, 17.
26. Terry Teachout, "Cultural Protectionism," *Wall Street Journal,* July 10, 1998, W11.
27. Jack Neff, "Rethinking Globalism," *Advertising Age,* October 9, 2000, 100.

EXHIBIT 9.22

Using standardized campaigns for global brands is difficult. This Italian Yokohama ad (www.yokohamatire.com) may suit Italian sensibilities, but how will it play in Peoria? Many American tire ads stress safety (for example, the ad showing a baby securely nestled in a solid, sensible tire) and performance in adverse weather, not a torrid romance with the road. Might this be a consequence of differences in who buys tires? When both mom and dad drive (and take for service) their own cars, the whole of the family's considerations come into play.

may work against globalization. Recall the example of AT&T's "Reach Out and Touch Someone" campaign. The campaign was highly successful in the United States in communicating the need to keep in touch with loved ones, but it was viewed by European audiences as too sentimental in style and execution. For another executional example, take a look at Exhibit 9.22. What do you think of this Italian ad for Yokohama tires? Would it play in Peoria?

SUMMARY

Explain the types of audience research that are useful for understanding cultural barriers that can interfere with effective communication.

All of us wear cultural blinders, and as a result we must overcome substantial barriers in trying to communicate with people from other countries. This is a major problem for international advertisers as they seek to promote their brands around the world. To overcome this problem and avoid errors in advertising planning, cross-cultural audience analysis is needed. Such analyses involve evaluation of economic conditions, demographic characteristics, customs, values, rituals, and product use and preferences in the target countries.

Identify three distinctive challenges that complicate the execution of advertising in international settings.

Worldwide advertisers face three distinctive challenges in executing their campaigns. The first of these is a creative challenge that derives from differences in experience and meaning among cultures. Even the pictures featured in an ad may be translated differently from one country to the next. Media availability, media coverage, and media costs vary dramatically around the world, adding a second complication to international advertising. Finally, the amount and nature of advertising regulation vary dramatically from country to country and may force a complete reformulation of an ad campaign.

Describe the three basic types of advertising agencies that can assist in the placement of advertising around the world.

Advertising agencies provide marketers with the expertise needed to develop and execute advertising campaigns in international markets. Marketers can choose to work with global agencies, local agencies in the targeted market, or an international affiliate of the agency they use in their home country. Each of these agency types brings different advantages and disadvantages on evaluative dimensions such as geographic proximity, economies of scale, political leverage, awareness of the client's strategy, and knowledge of the local culture.

Discuss the advantages and disadvantages of globalized versus localized advertising campaigns.

A final concern for international advertising entails the degree of customization an advertiser should attempt in campaigns designed to cross national boundaries. Globalized campaigns involve little customization among countries, whereas localized campaigns feature heavy customization for each market. Standardized messages bring tremendous cost savings and create a common brand image worldwide, but they may miss the mark with consumers in different nations. As consumers around the world become more similar, globalized campaigns may become more prevalent. Teenagers in many countries share similar values and lifestyles and thus make a natural target for globalized campaigns.

KEY TERMS

international advertising
ethnocentrism
self-reference criterion (SRC)
less-developed countries
newly industrialized countries
highly industrialized countries
picturing
global agencies
international affiliates
local agency
globalized campaigns
localized campaigns

QUESTIONS

1. From the various facts and figures presented throughout this chapter, which did you find most compelling in making the case for the global nature of the advertising business?

2. In this chapter we discuss the challenges advertisers face in Asia when it comes to representing husbands and wives in ads for products such as laundry detergents and vacuum cleaners. Why is this a challenging issue in Asia today? Would you expect that advertisers face this same challenge in other parts of the world? Where?

3. If you were creating a media strategy for a global advertising campaign, what emphasis would you put on newspapers in executing your strategy? What factors complicate their value for achieving broad market coverage?

4. Explain the appeal of new media options such as direct broadcast by satellite and the World Wide Web for marketers who have created globalized advertising campaigns.

5. Compare and contrast the advantages of global versus local ad agencies for implementing international advertising.

6. Identify several factors or forces that make consumers around the world more similar to one another. Conversely, what factors or forces create diversity among consumers in different countries?

7. Teens and retired people are two market segments found worldwide. If these two segments of European consumers were each being targeted for new advertising campaigns, which one would be most responsive to a globalized ad campaign? Why?

EXPERIENTIAL EXERCISES

1. This chapter discussed the various difficulties in international advertising. Many barriers must be anticipated and addressed for a brand's value to be successfully communicated in global markets.

With its headquarters in Madrid, Spain, Terra Networks (www.terra.com) is one of the largest international portals on the Internet. Its international sites target mostly Hispanic countries, with many sites in Central and South America. Create a hypothetical brand and then research terra.com for all the opportunities the site provides to advertise and promote your product. (Note: terra.com has a link so you can have the site translated into English.) Consider banner ads, the shopping section, and other opportunities Terra provides to advertisers as you think about advertising your brand. For research purposes, get information about Terra from the corporate site (www.terralycos.com), financial sites, or other relevant sources. Finally, outline a brief advertising strategy, making a list of all the relevant barriers that must be addressed for your brand to be advertised successfully in these predominantly Hispanic markets.

2. Conduct a study on the concept of "picturing" in cross-cultural communication. Go to a library and find any magazine for another country that has numerous ads with photographic representations. Based on what you learned about picturing in this chapter, analyze the photographic messages of the ads and compare them to the messages you would commonly find in ads targeted to your own culture. What contrasts or similarities did you find? What can you infer about the values of a culture based on the types of photographic images that are used?

USING THE INTERNET

9-1 Advertising Agencies around the World

As the international Web agency of choice for marketers such as Hyundai Motors, Microsoft, and Samsung, 24/7 Asia delivers interactive end-to-end solutions to advertisers and Web publishers for specific geographic regions. 24/7 Asia is a highly targeted ad-serving network for Greater China, the ASEAN nations, Australia, South Korea, and Japan that employs hundreds of seasoned media professionals. Click around the site to answer the following questions.

24/7 Asia: http://www.247asia.com

1. List a few of the various services 24/7 Asia offers clients.

2. Based on information given in the text, determine whether 24/7 is best characterized as a global agency, an international affiliate, or a local agency.

3. List some of the advantages and disadvantages of globalized versus localized advertising campaigns. Does 24/7 advise its clients on these kinds of campaign strategy issues?

9-2 Challenges in Executing Worldwide Advertising

Advertisers seeking to reach a global audience face distinctive challenges in executing their campaigns. Differences in meaning between cultures, availability of media, and advertising regulations across borders can cause a lot of headaches for advertisers. Nowhere is this more evident than on the Web, where quick access to international audiences is too tempting for advertisers to pass up. Maybelline, one of the leaders in the cosmetics industry, has produced numerous international sites to develop integrated brand promotion for its products. Visit the link and compare Maybelline's international sites by clicking on the links from the home page.

Maybelline: http://www.maybelline.com

1. What creative challenges do you think Maybelline is likely to encounter as it tries to promote its make-up products internationally? What is "picturing," and how essential is it to the success of Maybelline's global sites?

2. What are typical media challenges that companies have to overcome when advertising globally? Which of Maybelline's current international sites do you think has the most media challenges? Why?

3. List some of the promotional tactics employed by Maybelline at its sites. Does the company use the same promotions in every country? What regulatory challenges does Maybelline face with its sites and with its promotion strategies?

PART 2
Cincinnati Bell Wireless: Planning Advertising and Integrated Brand Promotion

It has become common for marketers to deploy a variety of communication tools to build their brands. Depending on a firm's objectives and resources, many different combinations of tools may be used. For example, TV advertising is relied on more heavily for establishing brand awareness; print advertising may carry specific information about terms or features of an offering; sales promotions are used to cause short-term spikes in demand; direct marketing is used to motivate action from a well-defined target audience; and public relations can help a firm manage media reports about its activities. We will see all these tools and more put in play in the launch of Cincinnati Bell Wireless.

This range of promotional devices and their application under different conditions is common. But achieving desired outcomes (for example, sales and brand loyalty) through sophisticated advertising and IBP campaigns will always require careful planning. Here we will thoroughly review the planning process that served as the platform for launching Cincinnati Bell Wireless.

A Model for Planning Advertising and Integrated Brand Promotion. There are many different models that one might use for direction in the process of planning a launch campaign. To put the Cincinnati Bell Wireless campaign in a proper context, and to be consistent with our discussion of planning issues in the last five chapters, we will frame this discussion using the strategic planning triangle proposed by advertising researchers Esther Thorson and Jeri Moore.[1] As reflected in Exhibit IBP 2.1, the apexes of the planning triangle entail the segment(s) selected as targets for the campaign, the brand's value proposition, and the array of persuasion tools that might be deployed to achieve campaign objectives.

In planning an IBP campaign, a firm starts with the customer or prospect and works backward, identifying what the customer deems important information. Hence, we place identification and specification of the target segment as the paramount apex in the triangle. Building a consensus between the client and the agency about which customer segments will be targeted is essential to the campaign's effectiveness. Complex IBP campaigns may end up targeting multiple segments; when this is so, it is critical to analyze if and how different target segments will interact to support or disparage the campaign. As suggested in Chapter 6, compelling advertising begins with descriptions and insights about one's target segment(s) that are both personal and precise.

1. Esther Thorson and Jeri Moore, *Integrated Communication: Synergy of Persuasive Voices* (Mahwah, N.J.: Erlbaum, 1996).

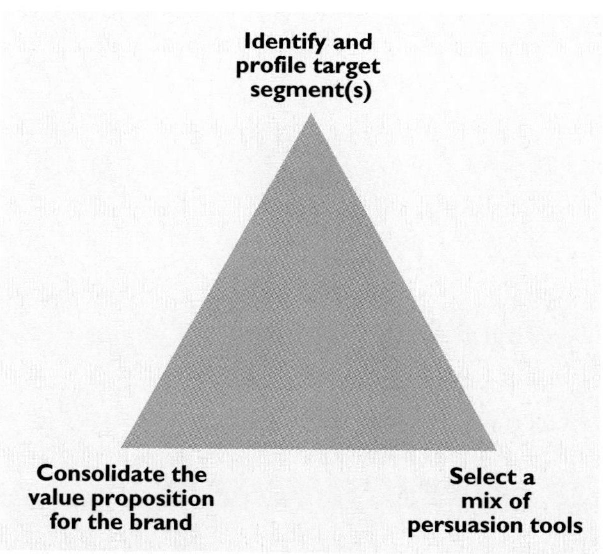

Adapted from Esther Thorson and Jeri Moore, *Integrated Communication: Synergy of Persuasive Voices* (Mahwah, N.J.: Erlbaum, 1996).

EXHIBIT IBP 2.1

Thorson and Moore's strategic planning triangle.

The second important apex in the planning triangle entails specification of the brand's value proposition. Per Chapter 6, a brand's value proposition is a statement of the functional, emotional, and self-expressive benefits delivered by the brand that provide value to customers in the target segment. In formulating the value proposition, one should consider both what a brand has stood for or communicated to consumers in the past, and what new types of value or additional benefits one wants to claim for the brand going forward. For mature and successful brands, reaffirming the existing value proposition may be the primary objective for any campaign. When launching a new brand, there is an opportunity to start from scratch in establishing the value proposition. For Cincinnati Bell Wireless (CBW), which was a combination of something old (Cincinnati Bell) and something new (wireless), the challenge was to draw on the strengths of the old as a foundation for claims about the new.

The final apex of the planning triangle considers the various persuasion tools that may be deployed in executing the campaign. A complete description of the tools is yet to come. Chapters 14 and 15 will emphasize traditional mass media tools; Chapter 16 looks at the Internet advertising option; Chapter 17 will consider support media, point-of-purchase advertising, and event sponsorship; Chapter 18 reviews the array of possibilities in sales promotion; Chapter 19 provides a comprehensive look at direct marketing; and Chapter 20 completes the set by discussing the public relations function. The mix of tools used will depend on the objectives that are set for the campaign in question. For example, building awareness of and excitement about a new brand such as CBW will be accomplished most effectively via mass media and event sponsorship, whereas bringing consumers into retail stores with an intent to purchase may require a sales promotion, delivered to the targeted customer via a direct mail offer, with a telemarketing follow-up. As you will see, one of the most admirable aspects of the IBP campaign designed by Northlich for the CBW launch was its skillful use of multiple persuasion tools working in harmony to sell the product. That's right, we want to emphasize: *to sell the product.* Marketers such as Cincinnati Bell fund IBP campaigns to get results that affect their companies' revenues and profitability. The campaign that launched CBW did just that.

Assessing CBW's Situation Prior to Launch. As described in Chapter 8, an effective campaign begins with a keen appreciation for the critical elements of one's situation. There is an infinite list of potential factors (for example, demographic, social and cultural, economic, political/regulatory) that may be considered in analyzing the situation. However, the idea is to be smart in choosing the few important factors that really describe the situation, and then explain how the factors relate to the task at hand. To appreciate the task that Northlich faced in planning the campaign to launch CBW requires an appreciation for several key elements of the situation.

Historical Context. Cincinnati Bell officially launched its wireless phone service on May 11, 1998. However, this particular launch was just one in a continuing series of new products

EXHIBIT IBP 2.2

Cincinnati Bell: Celebrating 125 years of innovation.

A Corporate Timeline . . .
1873—City & Suburban Telegraph Association (now Cincinnati Bell) founded
1876—Alexander Graham Bell invents the telephone
1877—First telephone installed in Cincinnati
1907—First Yellow Pages directory published
1975—911 emergency service activated
1984—First fiber optic cable installed
1990—Cincinnati Reds sweep Oakland in the World Series
1992—Cincinnati Bell pioneered the self-healing fiber optic network
1996—First telecommunication company to offer Internet access: Fuse
1997—1,000,000th access line installed
1997—Ranked one of the nation's top two providers of trouble-free local phone service
1998—First to offer Internet Call Manager
1998—Ranked highest independent telecommunications company for Web technology
1998—Cincinnati Bell: Celebrating 125 years of innovation

and services involving the Cincinnati Bell brand name. Moreover, in 1998 Cincinnati Bell celebrated its 125-year anniversary in the Greater Cincinnati metropolitan market under the banner "Celebrating 125 Years of Innovation." Some important milestones in the history of the company are listed in Exhibit IBP 2.2. In addition, as illustrated by the sample ads in Exhibit IBP 2.3, a common theme across ads for its various products and services was the slogan "People you know you can rely on." Obviously, the launch of CBW should not be viewed as an isolated event, and the Cincinnati Bell brand name carried with it equities that provided a sound foundation for the launch of a wireless service. Certainly, it was a name widely known in the local market, and one that connoted superior service, quality, innovation, and value. These types of connections to the Cincinnati Bell brand would of course be tremendous assets in the launch of CBW.

Industry Analysis. Telecommunications is a dynamic, technical, and complex business. Building a product and service network that would deliver good value to the wireless phone customer was the responsibility of Cincinnati Bell and its partners. Although it is beyond the scope of this discussion to explain the interworkings of the telecommunications business, some familiarity with key industry issues is essential for appreciating the business opportunity that CBW sought to capitalize on in May of 1998.

In the winter of 1998, the wireless phone marketplace in Cincinnati, and for that matter, nationwide, was on the brink of bedlam. As one writer put it at the time:

Well, the future of (wireless) is now. And while some of its promises are already being fulfilled, all of the new (and sometimes incompatible gear) and advanced services have had an unintended impact: It's wireless chaos out there.[2]

Executives at Cincinnati Bell realized that in a marketplace typified by chaos, the rewards would go to companies that offered consumers simple solutions and good value. Out of chaos often comes wonderful business opportunity.

2. Chris O'Malley, "Sorting Out Cellphones," *Popular Science,* February 1998, 55.

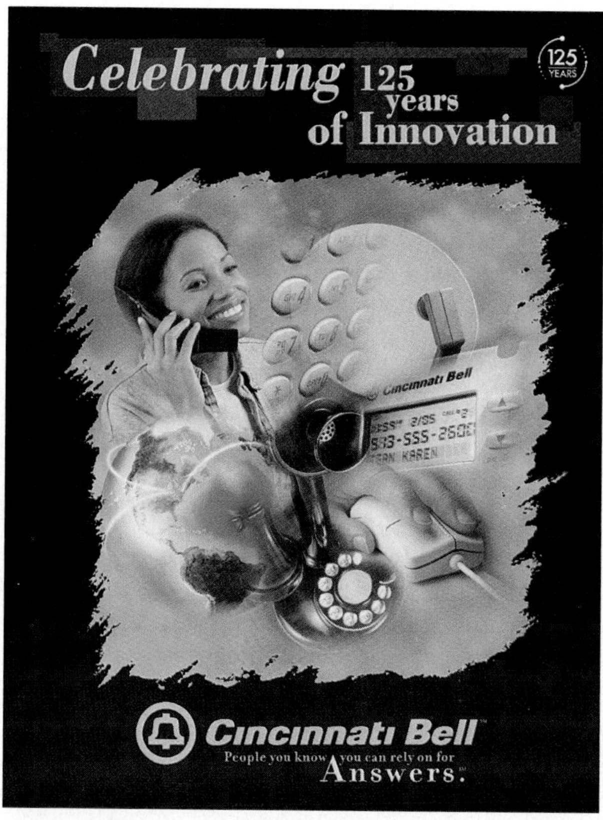

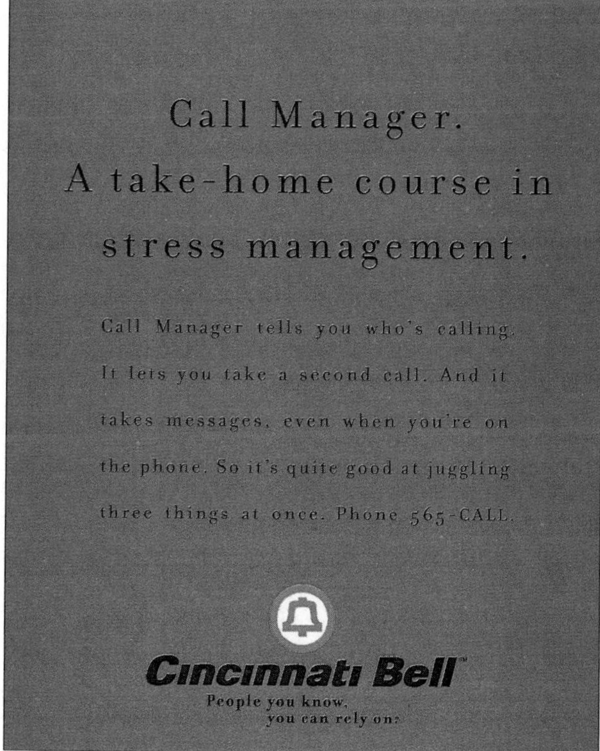

EXHIBIT IBP 2.3

Cincinnati Bell: Celebrating 125 years of innovation.

Critical to understanding this opportunity is the distinction between analog cellular and digital PCS (personal communication services) wireless phones. CBW would launch a new digital PCS offering to the Greater Cincinnati marketplace. Its primary competition at launch would be analog cellular providers. Analog cellular was the established technology that introduced most of us to the concept of a wireless phone. Across the United States, analog service providers all rely on the same transmission methods and thus can handle calls for each others' customers, for a heavy "roaming fee." Hence, you can make an analog cellular call almost anywhere in the United States. The common transmission standard for analog also meant that consumers could select from a wide variety of phone models, ranging from the low-cost Nokia 232 to the pricey ($800 to $1,200) but chic Motorola StarTAC 8600.[3]

Digital PCS was the new kid on the block, and offered some important advantages over analog. Digital PCS can be marketed at lower prices vis-à-vis analog because digital technology allows providers to expand capacity to handle calls much more easily than is the case for analog service. Also, because digital service always relies on a computer-mediated stream of ones and zeros, digital messages can be more easily encrypted, thus eliminating many forms of "cellular fraud" that plague analog systems. Digital technology also opens the door for add-on services such as e-mail and Internet access, and the sound quality for digital is superior to that of analog. Finally, the agreement that Cincinnati Bell Inc. signed with AT&T Wireless Services in the fourth quarter of 1997 made Cincinnati Bell Wireless part of a nationwide system that would allow CBW customers to use their phones in 400 cities across the United States. Opportunity was knocking, but only if CBW could get its value proposition in front of consumers before the competition.

Local Competition. In the winter of 1998 Cincinnati Bell worked closely with its ad agency in an effort to capitalize on the competitive advantages in digital PCS. At the time, only one other PCS provider existed in the Cincinnati market under the brand name GTE Wireless. However, GTE Wireless had not been aggressive in convincing Cincinnatians of the benefits of digital PCS, and was further hampered by a very limited calling area. More established competition came from analog cellular providers, and two of these—Ameritech Cellular and AirTouch Cellular—had strong brand identity in the local market. As part of the planning process, CBW and Northlich would have to resolve a fundamental dilemma created by the local competition. That is, should they concentrate the launch campaign on signing up first-time wireless phone users, or should they seek to steal customers away from entrenched analog competition? The resolution of this dilemma would come through a thorough segmentation analysis.

Market Analysis. CBW was preparing to launch its service in the face of surging demand for both digital PCS and analog cellular. Nationwide, the market for these services had more than doubled from 1995 to 1998, to over 60 million subscribers.[4] Market growth rates approaching 30 percent annually had several companies scrambling to take advantage of this opportunity (for example, Sprint would introduce its PCS service to the Cincinnati market in November 1998), so CBW executives pressed for their launch as soon as was humanly possible. The Federal Communications Commission estimates the Cincinnati marketplace to be about 1.9 million people. Given a national penetration rate of 25 percent,[5] this translates into a potential market of 475,000 wireless phone subscribers in Greater Cincinnati. Who among these should be tar-

3. Ibid.
4. Mike Boyer, "Wireless Wars," *Cincinnati Enquirer,* November 15, 1998, E1, E4.
5. Ibid.

geted in the CBW launch? How many of these could CBW hope to sign on to its service in the first 90 days after launch? These would be pivotal questions hotly debated by Northlich and CBW personnel leading up to their May 11 blastoff.

Pinpointing the Target Segment for Launch. Northlich and CBW would draw on various forms of market research in preparing for the spring launch. Both quantitative and qualitative research tools uncovered important consumer insights that benefited the planning process. For example, survey research established that the number one motivation for sign-up among new users was concern for safety of a family member. Hence, if the decision was to target non-users, alleviating concerns about safety when a family member is traveling or away from home would have to be the primary appeal. Additionally, focus group research established that many consumers felt confused and overwhelmed by the growing number of wireless phone deals and options. Consumers don't like marketplace chaos, so the supplier that can make things simple would have almost instant appeal. Moreover, in a finding that had to warm the hearts of executives at Cincinnati Bell, consumers also rated corporate identity and credibility as becoming increasingly important in the decision about which wireless service to choose.

Synthesizing the various market research studies and developing a consensus between client and agency about who should be the primary launch target for the campaign was achieved, as described in Chapter 6, via an in-depth segmentation analysis. The general framework that was developed to structure this analysis is summarized by the diagram in Exhibit IBP 2.4. As reflected there, usage considerations and demographic factors were combined to isolate a number of different market segments. Guided by this framework, an analysis was pursued that ultimately produced consensus about the primary launch target. In the discussion that follows, two specific segments will be profiled to provide an appreciation for the details that must be considered in planning for a major new product launch. As we noted earlier, compelling advertising begins with descriptions and insights about one's target segment(s) that are both personal and precise.

- *Midlevel executives—profile and motivations.* One market segment carefully assessed as the launch target was midlevel executives who were current users of another wireless service. This segment was primarily college-educated males who embraced technology and were early adopters of many advanced technologies, including the Internet. These individuals looked at their wireless phone as a productivity-enhancing device for their work, and were receptive to any features in a wireless phone, such as e-mail, voice mail, or text messaging, that could make them more productive. Most of these executives indicated that price was a key factor that would make them switch carriers, and many also acknowledged that they probably could find a better deal if they spent the time to comparison shop. Poor customer service, erratic sound quality, and restrictive calling zones were also concerns among those in this market segment.
- *Families with a child in college—profile and motivations.* Families with one or more children in college represented an important segment of non-users. Here, the purchase of the service would most likely be by the parent, whereas the primary user was projected to be the student. Both parents and students looked to a wireless phone as offering safety and security. Parents also wanted to be able to reach their student at a moment's notice and expressed a lack of confidence in roommates or other means of passing on important messages to their college student. However, parents expressed concerns about the phone being misused once it was out of their control; they wanted to realize the security and convenience of a wireless phone while controlling costs. Parents as primary purchasers did not represent early adopters of new technologies and thus were especially intimidated by

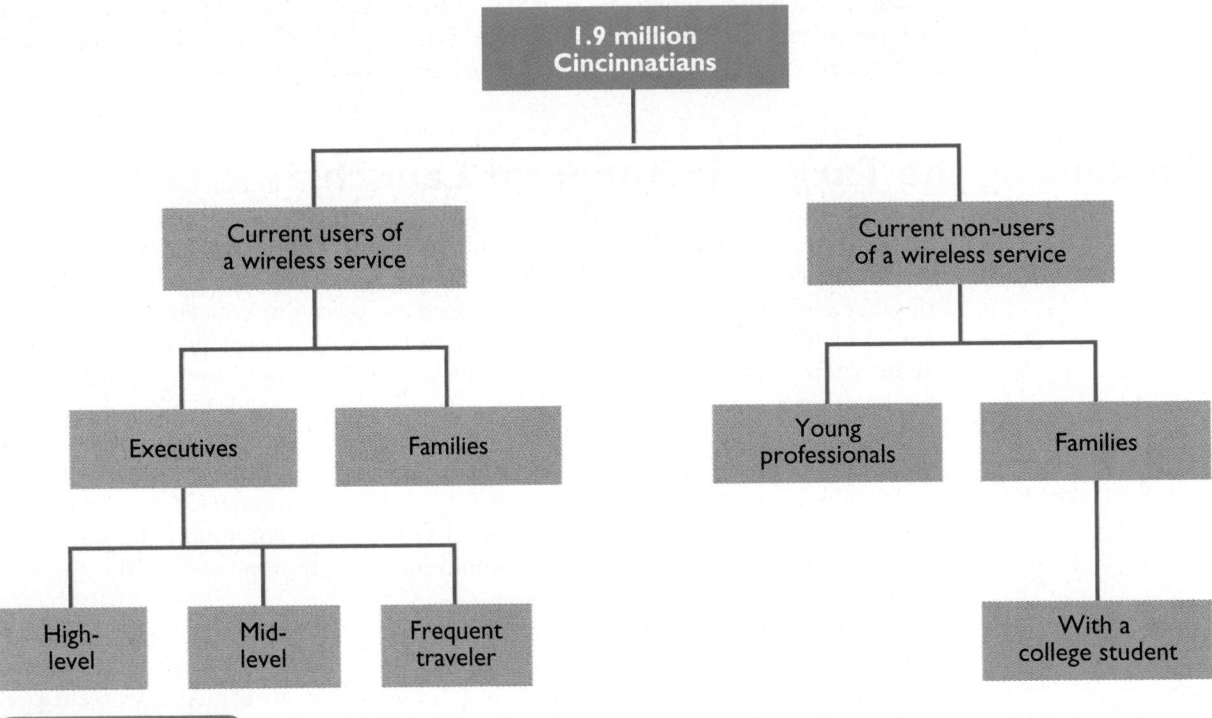

EXHIBIT IBP 2.4

The CBW/Northlich segmentation framework: Spring 1998.

various options regarding contracts, pricing, coverage zones, and add-on features. They just wanted an easy and safe way to get direct access to their son or daughter at college. Hence, for this market segment, a familiar brand name that parents already trusted would be a great asset in winning their new business.

The two market segments profiled here reflect the dilemma faced by CBW and Northlich as they approached the launch date in May 1998. Should they attempt to steal savvy customers from established competitors such as Ameritech Cellular and AirTouch Cellular, or appeal to the novice customer who had previously never used wireless? This is a tough choice because it can be hard to get savvy customers to switch when they already have a product or service that is filling their requirements, and it can be hard to get novice customers to take the plunge and sign on for something new, especially when that "something new" involves advanced technology such as PCS digital.

In either case, CBW would need a carefully orchestrated communications campaign to break through the clutter of the marketplace to convince the launch target that CBW did offer something special, just for them. And it should be clear that there is no way CBW could have it both ways. That is, the fast-track business executive and the concerned parent of a college student would require very different appeals and persuasion tools. CBW and Northlich had to choose one target segment for their launch, or risk coming to the marketplace with a diluted message that would leave all segments confused about CBW's value proposition. Value-proposition ambiguity would hand the opportunity of taking first-mover advantage in the Cincinnati PCS digital market to a competitor such as Sprint or GTE.

So, which would you choose—current users or non-users? Before you read on, stop and give this some thought. Reflecting on the example of Mobil Oil that was described back in Chapter 6 will help you make this call.

CBW and Northlich selected mid- and high-level executives who currently were using another wireless service as the primary targets for the their launch of PCS digital in Cincinnati. The rationale for this launch target was much like the one Mobil

Oil used in targeting Road Warriors. Recall that although Road Warriors were outnumbered by Price Shoppers, Road Warriors spend more at the gas station, making them the larger segment from the standpoint of revenue generation and profit potential. Likewise for MOPEs (managers, owners, professionals, and entrepreneurs) when it comes to use of a wireless phone: They make much heavier use of the wireless service in terms of minutes called per month, versus household users. And the way Cincinnati Bell makes money on a service like this is when customers are actually using the phone. Having a phone at home in the kitchen drawer that no one ever uses unless there is an unwanted emergency was not the usage scenario that excited CBW management. Hence, MOPEs became the launch target.

Launch Strategy and the CBW Value Proposition. The launch strategy was set: MOPEs using another wireless service would be targeted for conversion to PCS digital from Cincinnati Bell. The value proposition to be advanced through a diversified advertising and IBP campaign would feature the functional benefits of this new service. Various media and methods would be deployed to communicate a compelling value proposition around these benefit claims:

- *Simple pricing, better value.* No contracts to sign; subscribers choose a simple pricing plan, such as 500 minutes for $49/month or 1,600 minutes for $99/month.
- *Member of the AT&T Wireless Network.* As a member of AT&T's nationwide network, CBW offered customers complete wireless access in over 400 cities at one "hometown rate."
- *Worry-free security.* Digital PCS allows secure business transactions that may be compromised over analog cellular.
- *The coolest phone on the planet.* CBW launched its service with the feature-laden Nokia 6160 wireless phone. It really is a cool phone: The kind you want people to see you using.

Cincinnati Bell had several important benefit claims to make for its service in comparison to the analog cellular competition. In addition, it had a tremendous advantage from the standpoint of the combined brand equities of its strategic partners, which surely contributed to the credibility of all its claims. Specifically, its claim of a nationwide network was instantly validated by its association with AT&T, and the quality of its phone gear per se was supported by brand-building ads (see Exhibit IBP 2.5) and high-visibility event sponsorship (for example, the Nokia Sugar Bowl) that made Nokia one of the best-known portable phone brands at the time of launch. In combination, the Cincinnati Bell, AT&T, and Nokia brand names were an imposing triad that would establish instant credibility for Cincinnati Bell Wireless.

Objectives and Budget. With all this opportunity staring them in the face, Northlich was clearly challenged to produce dramatic results with the launch of CBW. Jack Cassidy, CBW's president at the time, stated the initial objective for launch simply and forcefully: "Get me activations!" Although activating a customer does not necessarily create a satisfied or profitable customer, everything starts with an activation. And while the distinction between communication and sales objectives discussed in Chapter 8 was not lost on Mr. Cassidy, he clearly was just interested in the sale. Since it is the client that pays the bills, it is the client's prerogative to determine a campaign's objectives. Northlich's work would be judged initially on the basis of the number of new customers who signed on for CBW's service. Mr. Cassidy and his associates at Cincinnati Bell specified as their goal 16,868 new CBW customers for the calendar year 1998. Given the estimate of 475,000 potential wireless customers in the Greater Cincinnati market, Mr. Cassidy was looking for an immediate market penetration in excess of 3.5 percent.

EXHIBIT IBP 2.5

Another asset in the CBW launch: The Nokia 6100 Series Digital Phone.

The initial thinking was that the first eight months of advertising for CBW would be supported by a $3 million budget. Starting in May 1998, all marketing communications would be directed at the Greater Cincinnati market, but about 90 days after launch the market space would be expanded to include the Dayton, Ohio, market, which would increase the scope of the overall market from 1.9 to 3.2 million people. This $3 million budget for May through December may not seem all that impressive on first glance, but if we project it to a year-long nationwide campaign we can immediately grasp the level of importance Cincinnati Bell was placing on this launch. Specifically, if such a campaign were to be executed for 12 months in the top 50 metro markets across the United States, the $3 million budget would translate into a $225 million program. Per Chapter 8, this would be a commitment on par with that made by Steve Jobs in launching his new iMac in the second half of 1998. Clearly, the folks at Cincinnati Bell were committed to making a "big-time" investment in their launch of CBW, and they were expecting "big-time" results. These expectations would create many sleepless nights for the Northlich personnel working on CBW.

The Mix of Persuasion Tools. Now, while the folks at Northlich knew that their work would be evaluated initially on the basis of Mr. Cassidy's "Get me activations!," they first conceived their challenge in terms of more fundamental communication objectives. To get new customers, the campaign would first have to create brand awareness, then generate interest in the brand, and finally bring people into retail outlets where they could buy their Nokia 6160 phone (at a special introductory price of $99) and activate their service. In Part 4 of this case history, substantial details will be provided about the various elements of the campaign that were deployed to launch CBW. For example, television, radio, and outdoor ads were created to build brand awareness for CBW; print ads were used to provide information about specific features; event sponsorships were placed to create excitement and visibility for the new service; and a sophisticated direct marketing effort was launched in conjunction with sales promotion to motivate MOPEs to visit retail stores and close the deal. Indeed, nearly all the persuasion tools discussed in Chapters 14 through 20 were considered as part of this comprehensive campaign. But would they really produce the kind of results that the client was looking for? Stay tuned . . .

IBP EXERCISES

1. Refer to Exhibit IBP 2.1, Thorson and Moore's planning triangle. Whom did Cincinnati Bell Wireless (CBW) identify as the primary market segments for its new wireless phone service? How did it profile each market segment? What was the value proposition CBW planned to communicate to its targeted market?
2. One of the ways Northlich and CBW gather data is through focus group research. Develop a list of 10 questions you would use in a focus group of potential wireless phone users to identify their preferences and values related to wireless phone use. If you are a wireless phone user, think back to the reasons why you decided to subscribe. Recalling your own reasons for subscribing will assist you in drafting your questions.
3. In Chapter 5, we learned that products and services should provide benefits that fulfill consumers' needs. List three functional and three emotional benefits a consumer might derive from subscribing to a wireless phone service.
4. What kinds of associations come to your mind when you think of the brand names Nokia and AT&T? In what ways did Cincinnati Bell hope to capitalize on the brand equity of its partners as part of the launch of CBW?

PART THREE

Preparing the Message

Part Three, "Preparing the Message," marks an important passage in our study of advertising. The topics to this point have raised the essential process and planning issues that make advertising what it is as a communication and business tool. Now we need to take the plunge into the actual *preparation* of advertising.

Creativity is the soul of advertising. Without the creative function, there is no advertising. It's the one thing advertising could not get by without. Yet most advertising books treat it as either a bunch of creative "rules," or dry lectures about the value of various fonts. We take a different approach. We first consider the idea of creativity itself: what is it, what distinguishes it, what is its beauty, what is its pain? What makes creative people creative? We then quickly present the organizational and managerial/creative interface. We honestly discuss what many textbooks don't mention at all: the problem of the competing reward systems of brand managers, account executives, and creatives. We then offer a chapter like no other: message strategy, where we detail ten time-honored message strategies and their strategic pluses and minuses. We then offer the best basic chapters on copywriting and art direction available. These chapters have been developed and refined with constant input from industry professionals. They are very good. If you read them carefully, you will know a lot about art direction and copywriting.

Creativity and Advertising A famous dancer once said, "If I could describe dancing, I wouldn't have to do it." Well, we feel the same way about creativity in advertising—it really is impossible to describe fully. But in Chapter 10, "Creativity and Advertising," we do our best to give you insights into the creative process by giving examples of how the creative process is worked out in an advertising context—how the "creatives" work with the "strategists." But we also try to provide insight into this wonderfully slippery thing called creativity. We do it by drawing on many sources and the examples of some of the most creative minds of the last century, from physics to painting. While creativity is creativity, we move from the general to discussing the particular context of advertising creativity and its unique opportunities and problems. Creativity is the soul of advertising, and this chapter tries to show the magic that is advertising. 10

Message Strategy Chapter 11, "Message Strategy: Objectives and Methods," is a chapter like no other anywhere. We take ten key and primary message objectives and their matching strategies and fully explore. We give you lots of specific real-world examples and walk you through each one. We discuss their advantages and disadvantages and tell you when they should be used and when they should not. This is a very cool chapter. 11

Copywriting Chapter 12, "Copywriting," explores the development of copy from the creative plan through dealing with the constraints and opportunities of the medium that will carry the message. This chapter also highlights guidelines for writing effective copy and common mistakes in copywriting. A full discussion of radio and television advertising formats, which provide the context for copy development, is also provided. At the end of this chapter is a discussion of a typical copy approval process used by advertisers and agencies. This chapter received enormous input from real live advertising professionals with years of copywriting experience in real advertising agencies. It's a very experience-driven chapter. Enjoy. 12

Art Direction and Production In Chapter 13, "Art Direction and Production," you will first learn about creating effective print advertisements destined for magazines, newspapers, and direct-marketing promotions. The nature of the illustration, design, and layout components of print advertising are considered. Then the exciting and complex process of creating broadcast advertising is discussed. This part of the chapter describes the people and techniques involved in creating television and radio ads. The emphasis in this chapter is on the creative team and how creative concepts are brought to life. The chapter follows a preproduction, production, and postproduction sequence. Also highlighted in this chapter are the large numbers of people outside the agency who facilitate the production effort. Again, this chapter was overseen by advertising professionals who have worked in art direction for years. This is experience talking. 13

CHAPTER 10

CHAPTER 10
Creativity and Advertising

CHAPTER 11
Message Strategy

CHAPTER 12
Copywriting

CHAPTER 13
Art Direction and Production

After reading and thinking about this chapter, you will be able to do the following:

1

Describe the core characteristics of great creative minds.

2

Contrast the role of an advertising agency's creative department with that of its business managers/account executives and explain the tensions between them.

e-SIGHTINGS

EXHIBIT 10.1

Nissan's "Mr. K" campaign pitted the poets against the killers (www.nissandriven.com). Compare Nissan's Web site to those of Mitsubishi (www.mitsubishi.com) and Honda (www.honda.com). Do these sites give off any signs of the behind-the-scenes creative battles that rage between the poets and the killers? Are these advertisers integrating their Internet initiatives with their most current ad campaigns?

This is the kind of conference room that can be very scary. When you enter the room, the lights come on like magic. But they don't burst on in a blaze. They come up very, very slowly. A spooky kind of slowly. When the lights are full, the room is perfectly lit—no shadows, no glare. Then there are the floor-to-ceiling windows—tall enough so that Shaq would need a ladder to clean them. What's more, this corner conference room on the 50th floor gives you a 120-degree view of Manhattan (or L.A., or Dallas, or Chicago, or Seattle). All very intimidating.

But not as intimidating as the meetings that go on here. You see, this is sort of a modern-day Colloseum. It's not supposed to be that way in this era of "relationships" and "partnering." But like the lions and the Christians, this is where the poets meet the killers.[1] There is no real bloodshed, but there are battered egos and bloodied relationships.

The poets are the creatives from the ad agency—the art directors, copywriters, graphic artists, and account planners who are dedicated to making advertising exciting, aesthetic, compelling, and edgy. The poets are dedicated to conceiving advertising that makes clients nervous enough to rise out of their seats, pace the floor, and jingle the change in their pockets.[2]

The killers are the clients—or, more specifically, the marketing and strategy-trained managers from the client who wield the anything-but-aesthetic bottom-line sword against the poets' creative prowess. It's not that the killers don't like the poets. It's not that they don't like advertising. It is that they like sales and want the poets to talk about sales. But the poets have a higher calling. Neither side means to wage a bloody battle, and the meetings never start with either side intending it to be that way. But these are tense times: new media, more old media, monster databases, astute audiences, shareholders clamoring for higher earnings per share.

No ad campaign in recent history has locked the poets against the killers in mortal battle like Nissan's "Mr. K" campaign (see Exhibit 10.1). Mr. K was the kindly guy who used to show up at the end of Nissan ads. The creative community loved the campaign, but the Nissan dealers were sitting on unmoved inventory. The result was the resignation of Nissan USA president Bob Thomas. The battle lines drawn around this campaign were so severe that ad agency types didn't even want to talk about it. One creative director said that talking about the Mr. K campaign with his clients "was kind of like the McCarthy hearings. You know, 'Are you now, or have you ever been, an admirer of Nissan's advertising.' "[3] The latest casualties of unmoved inventory were "Ads by Dick." These were the offbeat Miller Lite ads, like the one featured in Exhibit 10.2, that featured rampaging beavers and furry ani-

1. Anthony Vagnoni, "Creative Differences," *Advertising Age,* November 17, 1997, 1, 28, 30.
2. This description of clients' nervous reactions is credited to Mike Dunn, founder and principal of Dunn Communications, Salt Lake City, Utah.
3. Vagnoni, "Creative Differences," 28–30.

EXHIBIT 10.2

Miller Lite's "Ads by Dick" were popular among creatives, but left Miller with unmoved inventory.
www.millerlite.com

("Naked/Texas" :60 Radio)

(**SFX:** MILLER TIME MUSIC)
ANNCR.: Not long ago we asked Dick, the Creative Superstar behind Miller Lite advertising, to come up with a Miller Time radio concept just for beer-loving Texans. Dick said, "OK." Dick said he liked radio ads because you could get away with more naughty stuff than in TV. We weren't sure what Dick meant by this, so we asked him to explain. Dick said, for example, that you can't show naked people in TV commercials. But by merely saying the words "naked people" in a radio commercial, you force listeners to picture naked people in their minds. Here is what Dick wants you to picture in your mind while listening to his commercial. Naked people. Naked people in Texas. Naked Texans going to the refrigerator and getting a Miller Lite. Wearing nothing . . . except cowboy boots . . . with spurs, drinking Miller Lite. Naked. This has been a very naughty Miller Time presentation for Texas by Dick. Thank you for your time.
SINGERS: Miller Time.
ANNCR.: Miller Brewing Company, Fort Worth, Texas.

Fallon McElligott (Minneapolis, MN), ad agency
Miller Lite, client

mals living in armpits. The light-beer category grew 2.7 percent in 1998, while Miller Lite's volume grew only 2.4 percent—oops.[4]

Still not convinced that battles such as these are being fought every day through the halls of agencies and businesses? How about the great Chihuahua war? Surely you remember the campaign (Exhibit 10.3). Client Taco Bell and agency TBWA Chiat Day were trying to position Taco Bell as a cool place for teenagers and twentysomethings to eat. The themeline of the campaign, "Yo quiero Taco Bell" ("I want Taco Bell"), was on its way to becoming a national catchphrase.

We'll let the press coverage of the campaign tell the rest of the story. The headline on March 29, 1999? "Taco Bell Chihuahua is an advertising triumph."[5] A quote from the client? "If we keep it exciting, (the Chihuahua) can last forever."[6] And from the agency? "We never set out to create an icon for the company, but that's what it became."[7] Sales rose 3 percent over the year, and during the time period when Chihuahua plush toys were sold at franchises, sales were up 9 percent. Over time, 20 million of the fuzzy things were sold. Clearly, just about everyone was "yo quiero-ing" the little dog.

But then sales slowed. After rising 4 percent in the first quarter of 1999, they shrank to 1 percent growth in the second.[8] The killers began nipping at the Chihuahua's heels. A new headline announced a bit of a change in the role of the advertising icon. It read, "Top Dog No More."[9] Taco Bell indicated that the focus in its ads was shifting from the dog to the food. A spokesperson stated, "We'll use the dog in a different sense to draw attention to the food."[10] There was no reaction from the

4. Sally Beatty, "Remember Dick? He Was Miller's Attempt to Woo Cool Drinkers," *Wall Street Journal,* May 4, 1999, 1.
5. Greg Johnson, "Taco Bell Chihuahua Is an Advertising Triumph," *Lexington* [Kentucky] *Herald-Leader,* March 22, 1999, www.Kentuckyconnect.com, accessed June 16, 2001.
6. Ibid.
7. Ibid.
8. Associated Press, "Top Dog No More: Taco Bell Pushes Chihuahua to Side in New Campaign," ABC News Internet Ventures, October 11, 1999, www.abcnews.com, accessed June 16, 2001.
9. Ibid.
10. Ibid.

EXHIBIT 10.3

People liked the dog, but the doggie went away.

agency to the change in the article. Nine months later, the killers finished off the dog. Headline? "Taco Bell replaces top executive and Chihuahua, too."[11] It seems that the Chihuahua that "can last forever" couldn't. The president of Taco Bell was replaced. The agency was canned. According to the head of the agency, Taco Bell had clearly made an error. "People liked the dog," he said. "It's that simple."[12]

But the debate doesn't center on offbeat, unusual ads. The debate is much more central to the entire advertising process. It centers on the creative role of advertising. One side says you must sell with advertising, and selling means giving consumers facts they can use to make decisions. The other side says you have to build an emotional bond[13] between consumers and brands, and that process requires communicating much more than product attributes. Bob Kuperman, president and CEO of TBWA Chiat/Day North America, puts it quite simply: "Before you can be believed, you have to be liked."[14] The killers who favor selling—and believe that there are plenty of killer/rationalists on the agency side as well as the client side—point to the historic failures of emotional advertising: any Alka-Seltzer campaign, Joe Isuzu, Mr. K, and Ads by Dick. They say that such campaigns are creatively self-indulgent and grossly inefficient. Fortunately, the poets and killers are not always working at cross purposes.

While the killers call creative advertising inefficient, the poets are starting to lose their patience. In a speech to the European Association of Advertising Agencies, CEO of Saatchi & Saatchi Worldwide Kevin Roberts said, "[I]t seems like it's open season on attacking agencies nowadays, everyone's jumping on the bandwagon. Clients, management consultants, Silicon Valley hot shot technic nerds and even Rance Crain of *Ad Age*. Enough's enough! In the words of my New Zealand compatriot, Xena, Warrior Princess: 'Stop staring at me before I take your eyes out.' "[15]

11. Associated Press, "Taco Bell Replaces Top Executive and Chihuahua, Too," July 19, 2000, www.cnn.com, accessed June 16, 2001.
12. Ibid.
13. Marc Gobe, *Emotional Branding: The New Paradigm for Connecting Brands to People* (New York: Allworth, 2001).
14. Vagnoni, "Creating Differences," 1.
15. Kevin Roberts, "Making Magic," keynote address to the European Advertising Agencies Association Conference, Budapest, Hungary, October 16, 1998. Available online at www.saatchikevin.com/speeches/magic.html.

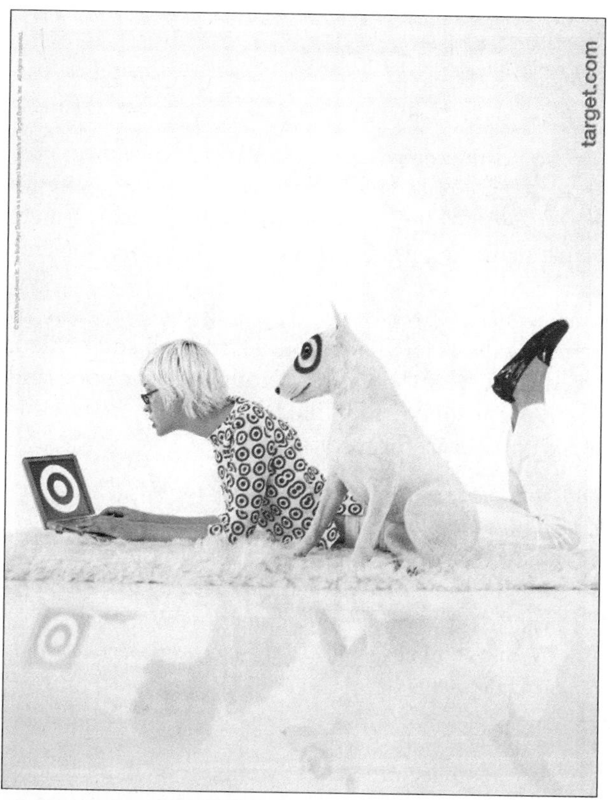

EXHIBIT 10.4

Advertising is about brands.
www.target.com

These scenarios are not unusual. There has been a tension between "poets" and "killers" for as long as there have been poets and killers. In the world of advertising and promotion, it happens all the time, even filtering into Web advertising, as evidenced in the E-Commerce box on page 345. The reasons are at once simple (often conflicting reward systems), and complex (the nature of creative professionals and those not so designated).

Creating Brands. Brands are all about creativity (Exhibit 10.4). They always have been. Marketers use advertising and promotion to invent and reinvent brands all the time. Remember, advertising and promotion professionals are in the brand-meaning creation and management business. The people who actually create the ads and shape the brand image can have a huge input into what the brand comes to mean. Making ads and promotions is one of the most important functions in the creation, growth, and survival of brands.

Advertisers try to get consumers to see the brand their way. But of course there are always those pesky consumers. They want to have a say in it too. A brand is not just some object; it is an incredibly complicated social creation. Advertisers and consumers themselves struggle with each other to make a brand mean what it means. Think about Mountain Dew, was it just the advertising that made it the official Gen-X soft drink, or Birkenstock the official counter-culture brand, or Tommy Hilfiger the official hip-hop brand . . . no, it was consumers, maybe more than advertisers. A lot of what Apple Macintosh, Coke, Skechers, Nike, Prada, Palm, Pepsi, Guinness . . . and on and on, are, is derived through a process of social meaning creation. Advertisers get a say, consumers get a say, then advertisers get another say, then consumers respond, on and on. So, a brand has to have a creative force behind it, or it is dead or lost at sea, the sea of thousands of ads a day, every day, trying to create meaning in a brand that will resonate with the consumer long enough to be purchased and repurchased. And all the while, the competition doesn't sleep. So, of course, creativity matters.

Creativity in General. To understand how the creative function plays out in the advertising and promotion world, it might be best to take a brief look at creativity in general.

Any book on advertising, promotion, and branding really needs some attention paid to creativity, the thing that most people think about when they think about advertising. And, in reality, it is the thing that makes the promotion and advertising world go round. Without it, there is really no promotion or advertising. There is no branding. Creativity is advertising's soul . . . it is branding's soul. Yet most textbooks say relatively little about it. They give you some technical information on typefaces, T-squares, and film production, but they tell you little about creativity itself. We will tell you more.

We will first discuss creativity in general, then creativity in the advertising and promotion world, and then the creative-management interface/friction zone. It's an entertaining story, but it doesn't always support the myth of orderly business. It's way too messy, way too human; avert your eyes if the sight of disorder makes you squeamish. But it is the way it is in that messy REAL WORLD out there.

1 Creativity across Domains.

The creative mind plays with the objects it loves.

—C. G. Jung[16]

Creativity, in its essence, is the same no matter what the domain. People who create, create, whether they write novels, take photographs, ponder the particle physics that drives the universe, craft poetry, write songs, play a musical instrument, dance, make films, design buildings, paint, or make ads. Great ads can be truly great creative accomplishments.

Creativity is generally seen as a gift, a special way of seeing the world. It is. Throughout the ages, creative people have been seen as special, revered and reviled, loved and hated. They have served as powerful political instruments (for good and evil), and they have been ostracized, imprisoned, and killed for their art. For example, creativity has been associated with various forms of madness:

Madness, provided it comes as the gift of heaven, is the channel by which we receive the greatest blessings. . . . [T]he men of old who gave their names saw no disgrace or reproach in madness; otherwise they would not have connected it with the name of the noblest of all arts, the art of discerning the future, and called by our ancestors, madness is a nobler thing than sober sense. . . . [M]adness comes from God, whereas sober sense is merely human.

—Socrates[17]

e-SIGHTINGS

EXHIBIT 10.5

Pablo Picasso, seen here in a self-portrait, was one of the greatest creative minds of the 20th century. Read about the life of Pablo Picasso at Artcyclopedia (www.artcyclopedia.com), or visit the official Pablo Picasso Web site (www.picasso.fr).

Creativity reflects early childhood experiences, social circumstances, and mental styles. In one of the best books ever written on creativity, *Creating Minds,* Howard Gardner examines the lives and works of seven of the greatest creative minds of the 20th century: Sigmund Freud, Albert Einstein, Pablo Picasso (see Exhibit 10.5), Igor Stravinsky, T. S. Eliot, Martha Graham, and Mahatma Gandhi.[18] His work reveals fascinating similarities among great creators. All seven of these individuals, from physicist to modern dancer, were

self confident, alert, unconventional, hardworking, and committed obsessively to their work. Social life or hobbies are almost immaterial, representing at most a fringe on the creators' work time.[19]

Apparently, total commitment to one's craft is the rule. While this commitment sounds positive, there is also a darker reflection:

[T]he self confidence merges with egotism, egocentrism, and narcissism: highly absorbed, not only wholly involved in his or her own projects, but likely to pursue them at costs of other individuals.[20]

16. Carl G. Jung, cited in Astrid Fitzgerald, *An Artist's Book of Inspiration: A Collection of Thoughts on Art, Artists, and Creativity* (New York: Lindisfarne, 1996), 58.
17. Socrates, cited in Plato, *Phaedrus and the Seventh and Eighth Letters,* Walter Hamilton, trans. (Middlesex, England: Penguin, 1970), 46–47, cited in Kay Redfield Jamison, *Touched with Fire: Manic-Depressive Illness and the Artistic Temperament* (New York: Free Press, 1993), 51.
18. Howard Gardner, *Creating Minds: An Anatomy of Creativity Seen through the Lives of Freud, Einstein, Picasso, Stravinsky, Eliot, Graham, and Gandhi* (New York: Basic Books, 1993).
19. Gardner, *Creating Minds,* 364.
20. Ibid.

E-COMMERCE

Online Advertising: Creativity Takes a Back Seat

While the promise of interactive advertising may still spark hopes for tech-minded creatives, the current reality of Web advertising is downright gloomy. Most people accept that advertising is necessary to support the content that they want, but the onslaught of online casino ads, X10 pop-ups, and other downscale advertising is quickly wearing out Net-advertising's welcome. Advertisers realize that they must do more than merely support valuable content—they have to provide value itself. Since Web ads are integrated into the Net's user experience, online ads need to do more than just get in the way.

Yet at this stage of the Web's development, creativity has suffered at the hands of account managers and impatient clients. While "poet" creatives may desire to make online advertising better, there are signs that "killer" brand managers are winning the day. The emphasis on the Internet's enhanced measurement capabilities has forced advertisers into a cutthroat competition over click-through and direct-response results. One prominent interactive service finds itself mired in the thick of the issue. E-commerce firm Gator.com is suing the Interactive Internet Advertising Bureau for asserting that its practices violate contract interests of Web publishers and advertisers. Gator is a plug-in application that makes browsing and online shopping more customizable for the end user. However, the technology also allows advertisers to advertise directly over a competing company's advertisement with banners, pop-ups, and other creative formats, effectively blocking the publisher's intended ad from being seen. Such advertising tricks and gizmos have devalued Web media and offended the sensibilities of users.

How are consumers responding to the Vegas-styled clutter of Web advertising? Boycott. Services that enable Web users to filter all unwanted advertising are gaining popularity. One service, Guidescope, uses patent-pending technology to filter advertisements and other unwanted graphics from Web pages; it even limits the ability of Web companies to track one's surfing. Another service, AdSubtract, lets you "subtract ads" by blocking pop-ups, cookies, daughter windows, and animation. Siemens AG's WebWasher service is designed to fight excessive advertising and claims more than a thousand corporate customers.

Whatever the future holds for online advertising, one thing is clear: As long as clients are mesmerized by the measurement and tracking capabilities of the Web, creativity will continue to take a back seat to crass marketing strategies inspired by the bottom line.

Sources: Kevin Featherly, "Gator Chomps First, Sues Interactive Advertising Bureau," Newsbytes, www.newsbytes.com, accessed August 28, 2001; Jeffrey Graham, "Why Online Advertising Has to Get Better," *ClickZ*, www.clickz.com, accessed October 17, 2001.

Let's be clear: One should not stand between a great creator and his or her work. It's not safe; you'll have tracks down your back. Or maybe the creator will just ignore you to death. Not coincidentally, these great creative minds had troubled personal lives and simply did not have time for the more ordinary people (such as their families). According to Gardner, they were generally not very good to those around them. This was true even of Gandhi.[21]

All seven of these great creatives were also great self-promoters.[22] Widely recognized creative people are not typically shy about getting exposure for their work. Apparently, fame in the creative realm rarely comes to the self-effacing and timid.

All seven of these great creators were, very significantly, childlike in a critical way. All of them had the ability to see things as a child does. Einstein spent much of his career revolutionizing physics by pursuing in no small way an idea he produced as a child: What would it be like to move along with a strand of pure light? Picasso commented that it ultimately was his ability to paint as a child (along with amazingly superior technical skills) that explained much of his greatness.[23] Freud's obsession with and interpretation of his childhood dreams had a significant role in what is one of his most significant works, *The Interpretation of Dreams*.[24] T. S. Eliot's poetry demonstrated imaginative abilities that typically disappear past childhood. The same is true of Martha Graham's modern dance. Even Gandhi's particular form of social action was formulated with a very simple and childlike logic at its base. These artists and creative thinkers never lost the ability to see the ordinary as extraordinary, to not have their particular form of imagination beaten out of them by the process of "growing up."

21. Ibid.
22. Ibid.
23. Ibid.
24. Gardner, *Creating Minds*, 145; Sigmund Freud, *The Interpretation of Dreams*, in A. A. Brill, ed., *The Basic Writings of Sigmund Freud* (New York: Modern Library, 1900/1938).

Of course, the problem with this childlike thinking is that these individuals also behaved as children throughout most of their lives. Their social behavior was egocentric and selfish. They expected those around them to be willing sacrifices at the altar of their gift. Gardner put it this way: "[T]he carnage around a great creator is not a pretty sight, and this destructiveness occurs whether the individual is engaged in solitary pursuit or ostensibly working for the betterment of humankind."[25] They can, however, be extraordinarily charming when it suits their ambitions. They could be monsters at home, and darlings when performing.

Apparently they actually desire marginality;[26] they love being outsiders. They revel in it. This marginality seems to have been absolutely necessary to these people, and provided them with some requisite energy.

Emotional stability did not mark these creative lives either. All but Gandhi had a major mental breakdown at some point in their lives, and Gandhi suffered from at least two periods of severe depression. Extreme creativity, just as the popular myth suggests, seems to come at some psychological price.

Can One Become Creative? This is a very big question. The popular answer in a democratic society would be to say, "Yes, sure; you too can be Picasso." Well, it's not quite that way. It really depends on what one means by *creativity*. For starters, determining creativity is about as simple as nailing Jell-O to a wall. Is a person creative because he or she can produce a creative result? Or is a person creative because of the way he or she thinks? Further, who gets to determine what is creative and what is not? When an elephant paints holding a brush with its trunk, and the paintings sell for thousands of dollars, does it mean that the elephant is creative? Or is the next teen-throb band creative because they sell a gazillion albums? Clearly, public acceptance may not be the best measuring stick. Yet is it inconsequential? No.

Creativity in the Business World. The difficulty of determining who is creative and who is not, or what is creative and what is not, in the artistic world is paralleled in the business world. Certainly, no matter how this trait is defined, creativity is viewed in the business world as a positive quality for employees.[27] It's been said that "creative individuals assume almost mythical status in the corporate world."[28] Everybody needs them, but no one is sure who or what they are. Furthermore, business types often expect that working with creative people will not be easy. Often, they are right.

Against Stereotype. While we are discussing the general traits of seven extraordinary creative people, a couple of notes of caution are in order. First, it should be understood that just because you are in a "creative" job, it doesn't always follow that you are creative. Conversely, just because you are on the account side (a.k.a. "a suit") does not mean you are not creative (see Exhibit 10.6). In fact, great strategy is all about creativity.

Some people who study creativity in business believe that everybody is creative, albeit in different ways. For example, *adaptation/innovation theory* maintains that the way people think when facing creative tasks places them on a continuum between being an adaptor and being an innovator.[29] **Adaptors** tend to work within the exist-

25. Ibid., p. 369.
26. Ibid.
27. Bernd H. Schmitt, *Experiential Marketing: How to Get Customers to Sense, Feel, Think, Act, and Relate to Your Company and Brands* (New York: Free Press, 1999).
28. T. A. Matherly and R. E. Goldsmith, "The Two Faces of Creativity," *Business Horizons*, 1985, 8–11.
29. M. Kirton, "Adaptors and Innovators: A Description and Measure," *Journals of Applied Psychology*, vol. 61, no. 5 (1976), 622–629.

EXHIBIT 10.6

Artist David Ross's Swimming Suits, *a view of corporate individuality and creativity that is often shared by art directors and copywriters.*

ing paradigm, whereas innovators treat the paradigm as part of the problem. In other words, adaptors try to do things better. **Innovators** try to do things differently.[30] It can be argued that adaptors and innovators are equally creative.[31] However, between and within organizations, one mode of creative problem solving may be more conducive to success than the other.[32] An example of this is presented in the Global Issues box on page 349.

This approach has a certain commonsense appeal. The CEO of an airline might reward and promote an employee who created a way to get customers through the ticket line faster using technology the airline was using in a different part of its operations. However, the same CEO might not respond as favorably to an employee who created a rising set of service expectations on the part of customers. The commonsense appeal has its limitations—especially if you were an employee at a bank in 1970 who figured out a way to keep customers out of the bank. You might have gotten laughed out of a job. Luckily, ten years later you could deposit your unemployment checks at the ATM around the corner.

Creativity is the ability to consider and hold together seemingly inconsistent elements and forces. This ability to step outside of everyday logic, to free oneself of thinking in terms of "the way things are" or "the way things have to be," apparently allows creative people to put things together in a way that, once we see it, makes sense, is interesting, is creative. To see love and hate as the same entity, to see "round squares," or to imagine time bending like molten steel is to have this ability. Ideas born of creativity reveal their own logic, and then we all say, "Oh, I see."

30. M. Kirton, "Adaptors and Innovators in Organizations," *Human Relations,* vol. 33, no. 4 (1980), 213–224.
31. Ibid.; Matherly and Goldsmith, "The Two Faces of Creativity."
32. Kirton, "Adaptors and Innovators in Organizations."

Advertising Agencies, the Creative Process, and the Product.

As an employee in an agency creative department, you will spend most of your time with your feet up on a desk working on an ad. Across the desk, also with his feet up, will be your partner—in my case, an art director. And he will want you to talk about movies.

In fact, if the truth be known, you will spend fully one-fourth of your career with your feet up talking about movies.

The ad is due in two days. The media space has been bought and paid for. The pressure's building. And your muse is sleeping off drunk behind a dumpster somewhere. Your pen lies useless. So you talk movies.

That's when the traffic person comes by. Traffic people stay on top of a job as it moves through the agency. Which means they also stay on top of you. They'll come by to remind you of the horrid things that happen to snail-assed creative people who don't come through with the goods on time.

So, you try to get your pen moving. And you begin to work. And working in this business, means staring at your partner's shoes.

That's what I've been doing from 9 to 5 for almost 20 years. Staring at the bottom of the disgusting tennis shoes on the feet of my partner, parked on the desk across from my disgusting tennis shoes. This is the sum and substance of life at an agency.

—Luke Sullivan[33]

Exhibit 10.7on page 350 is illustrative of many creative pursuits: lots of time trying to get an idea, or the right idea. You turn things over and over in your head, trying to see the light. You try to find that one way of seeing it that makes it all fall into place. Or, it just comes to you, real easy, just like that. Magic. Every creative pursuit involves this sort of thing. However, advertising and promotion, like all creative pursuits, are unique in some respects. Ad people come into an office and try to solve a problem, always under time pressure, given to them by some businessperson. Often this problem is poorly defined, and there are competing agendas. They work for people who seem not to be creative at all, and doing their best not to let them be creative. They are housed in the "creative department," which makes it seem as if it's some sort of warehouse where the executives keep all the creativity so they can find it when they need it, and so it won't get away. This implies that one can pick some up, like getting extra batteries at Wal-Mart.

2 **Oil and Water: The Essential Organizational Behavior of the Creative/Management Interface.** Here are some thoughts on management and creativity by two advertising greats:

The majority of businessmen are incapable of original thinking, because they are unable to escape from the tyranny of reason. Their imaginations are blocked.

—William Bernbach[34]

If you're not a bad boy, if you're not a big pain in the ass, then you are in some mush in this business.

—George Lois[35]

As you can see, this topic rarely yields tepid, diplomatic comments. Advertising is produced through a social process. As a social process, however, it's marked by struggles for control and power that occur within departments, between departments, and between the agency and its clients on a daily basis.

33. Luke Sullivan, "Staring at Your Partner's Shoes," in *Hey Whipple, Squeeze This: A Guide to Creating Great Ads* (New York: Wiley, 1998), 20–22.

34. William Bernbach, cited in Thomas Frank, *The Conquest of Cool: Business Culture, Consumer Culture, and the Rise of Hip Consumerism* (Chicago: University of Chicago Press, 1997).

35. George Lois, cited in Randall Rothenberg, *Where the Suckers Moon* (New York: Knopf, 1994), 135–172.

Most research concerning the contentious environment in advertising agencies places the creative department in a central position within these conflicts. We know of no research that has explored conflict within or between departments in an advertising agency that doesn't place the creative department as a focus of the conflict. One explanation hinges on reactions to the uncertain nature of the product of the creative department. What is it they do? From the outside it sometimes appears that they are having a lot of fun and just screwing around while everyone else has to wear a suit to the office and try to sell more stuff for their client. But you really can't replace them . . . you need them. This creates a great deal of tension between the creative department and the account service department. In addition, individuals in the account service department and in the creative department of an advertising agency do not always share the same ultimate goals for advertisements. Individuals in the creative department see an advertisement as a vehicle to communicate a personal creative ideology that will further their careers. (See Exhibits 10.8 and 10.9.) The account manager, serving as liaison between client and agency, sees the goal of the communication as achieving some predetermined objective in the marketplace.[36] Another source of conflict is attributed to differing perspectives due to differing background knowledge of the members of creative groups and the account service team. Account managers must be generalists with broad knowledge, whereas creatives (copywriters and art directors) are specialists who must possess great expertise in a single area.[37]

Regardless of its role as a participant in conflict, the creative department is recognized as an essential part of an advertising agency's success. It is the primary consideration of potential clients when they select advertising

GLOBAL ISSUES

Europe: The Birthplace of the 30-Minute Ad?

Creatives have their work cut out for them in the next five years. The emergence of interactive digital television (iDTV) as Europe's "next big thing" is sending major reverberations to the heads of global advertising agencies. A recent research study says that within the next few years, most Europeans will use televisions instead of PCs as their main points of Internet access. Researchers predict that by 2005, 50 percent of European households will use iDTV. Current iDTV services are offered on private networks operated by broadcasters such as BSkyB's SkyDigital TV, and technology giants such as AOL/Time Warner and Microsoft are set to lead the expansion of this new medium around the globe.

iDTV's interactive capabilities are changing the way advertisers think of creativity, and agency conglomerates such as Bcom3 are getting positioned to pioneer the interactive ads of the future. The group announced its strategic investment in Spring Communications, a London-headquartered agency dedicated to offering brand owners best-of-breed iDTV marketing services. Marcus Vinton, chief creative officer of Spring, said, "Interactivity at the brand level will only extend the advertising experience beyond mainstream media opportunities. The next five years are about the birth of the 30-minute ad, not the demise of the 30-second spot."

Exactly how will iDTV influence the creative capabilities of advertisers? Advertising is likely to become more varied as it becomes more targeted. Pundits generally agree that it will carry more content. There will be less focus on 30- and 60-second spots and more of everything and anything else: sponsorships, branded games, quizzes, and unusual spots—you name it. It will be less intrusive, more focused, and integrated, and will offer the viewer a lot more because it will need to attract and hold attention.

iDTV is the mainstream entertainment medium of the future; its interactive capabilities hold great promise for advertisers. Mark Iremonger of the digital advertising production firm Sleeper said, "What I can't understand is why iDTV is often sold as a direct response advertising tool. Sure, it'll be used for DR, but why focus on this when iDTV will fulfill all the advertising and marketing communication that linear TV does today?"

Sources: David Barry, "Interactive TV to Dominate European E-Commerce," *E-Commerce Times*, www.ecommercetimes.com, accessed March 27, 2000; Mark Iremonger, "iDTV Advertising: A Future to Look Forward To?," *Digitrends*, www.digitrends.com, accessed October 18, 2001; "Bcom3 Backs Future of Television through New Global Interactive Digital Venture," www.bcom3.com, accessed October 18, 2001.

36. Elizabeth Hirschman, "The Effect of Verbal and Pictorial Advertising Stimuli on Aesthetic, Utilitarian and Familiarity Perceptions," *Journal of Advertising*, 1985, 27–34.

37. B. G. Vanden Berg, S. J. Smith, and J. W. Wickes, "Internal Agency Relationships: Account Service and Creative Personnel," *Journal of Advertising*, vol. 15, no. 2 (1986), 55–60.

agencies.[38] Creativity has been found to be crucial to a positive client/advertiser relationship. Interestingly, clients see creativity as an overall agency trait, whereas agency people place the responsibility for it firmly on the shoulders of the creative department.[39] However, there is evidence that, although the client may hold the entire agency responsible for the creative output, they may still unknowingly place the creative department in a position of primary responsibility. An interview with 20 of the largest advertising clients in the United States found that failing to produce effective advertisements was the single unforgivable shortcoming an agency could have.[40]

However, many clients don't recognize their role in killing the very same effective ideas that they claim to be looking for (Exhibit 10.10). Anyone who has worked in the creative department of an advertising agency for any length of time has a full quiver of client stories—like the one about the client who wanted to produce a single 30-second spot for his ice cream novelty company. The creative team went to work and brought in a single spot that everyone agreed delivered the strategy perfectly, set up further possible spots in the same campaign, and, in the words of the copywriter, was just damn funny. It was the kind of commercial that you actually look forward to seeing on television. During the storyboard presentation, the client laughed in all the right places, and admitted the spot was on strategy. Then the client rejected the spot.

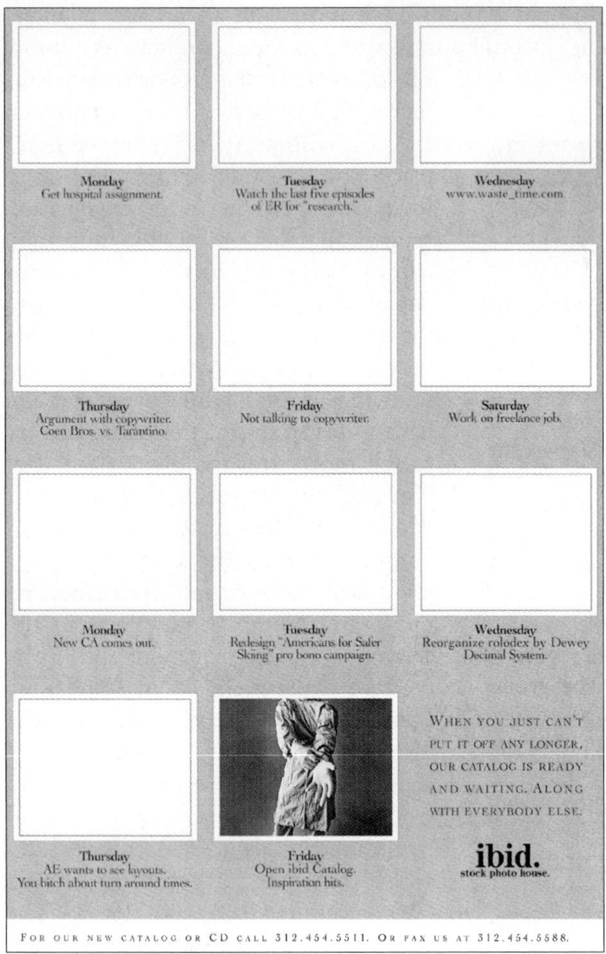

EXHIBIT 10.7

Companies like ibid (www.ibidphoto.com) cater to the creative: The ibid catalog offers images to jump-start the imagination.

The client said the agency was trying to force him into a corner where he had to approve the spot, since they didn't show him any alternatives. The agency went back to work. Thirty-seven alternatives were presented over the next six months. Thirty-seven alternatives were killed. Finally, the client approved a spot, the first spot from half a year earlier. There was much rejoicing. One week later, he canceled the production, saying he wanted to put the money behind a national couponing effort instead. Then he took the account executive out to lunch and asked why none of the creatives liked him.

Or the potato chip client that told an agency that the next campaign they came up with needed to be the best work they had ever done. The new product the client was introducing was crucial to the overall success of the company. The agency put every team in the house to work on it for 16 hours a day, two weeks straight. The result? The client loved the work, saying it was indeed the best work he had ever seen. In fact, instead of the single product-introduction ad he had asked for, the client approved four ads. There was a client/agency group hug. One week later, the client fired the agency, asking why they hadn't ever presented this kind of work before.

38. D. West, "Restricted Creativity: Advertising Agency Work Practices in the U.S., Canada and the U.K.," *Journal of Creative Behavior,* vol. 27, no. 3 (1993), 200–213.

39. P. C. Michell, "Accord and Discord in Agency-Client Perceptions of Creativity," *Journal of Advertising Research,* vol. 24, no. 5 (1984), 9–24.

40. M. Kingman, "A Profile of a Bad Advertising Agency," *Advertising Age,* November 23, 1981, 53–54.

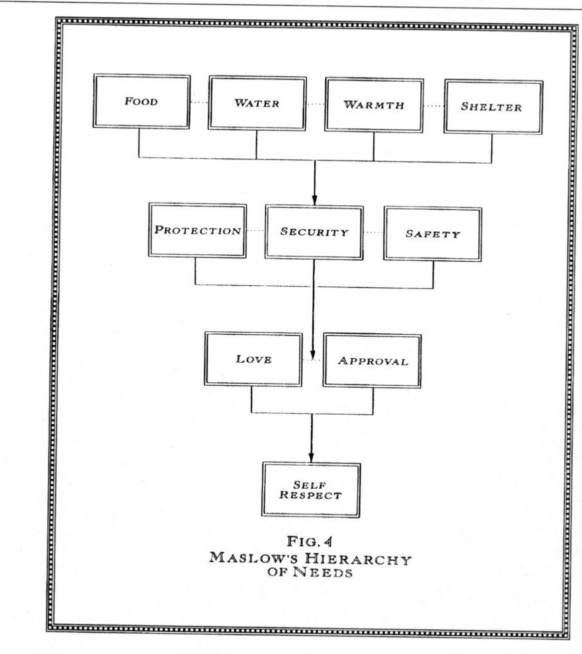

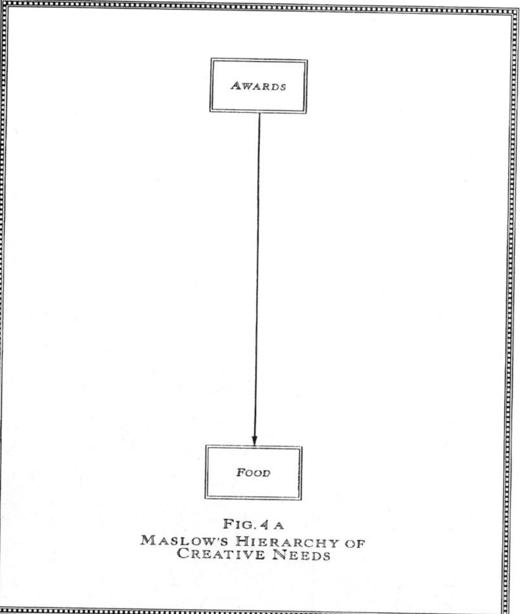

Congratulations to all the winners, and could someone please pass the green beans.

TEAM ONE ADVERTISING

EXHIBIT 10.8

Team One Advertising (www.teamoneadv.com) has an interesting spin on what motivates agency creatives; here, it parodies Maslow's hierarchy to make its point. Compare this print advertisement with the imagery, words, and ideas on display at Team One's Web site. Both are, in part, self-promotional and self-congratulatory. When an agency is both client and creator, how do the struggles for power and control of the creative product change?

$$$$$$$$$$$$

Just a reminder: winning isn't everything. Winning and getting a raise is everything.

Congratulations to the winners of the 1st annual Chicago Show. If you're interested in the real value of winning, give me a call.

NANCY RUBENSTEIN INC.

449 North Clark, Suite 300, Chicago, Illinois 60610

Phone 312-828-0560 / Fax 312-828-0561

EXHIBIT 10.9

To a creative, awards lead to better jobs and higher pay.

EXHIBIT 10.10

What clients like and what clients approve are often two very different things.

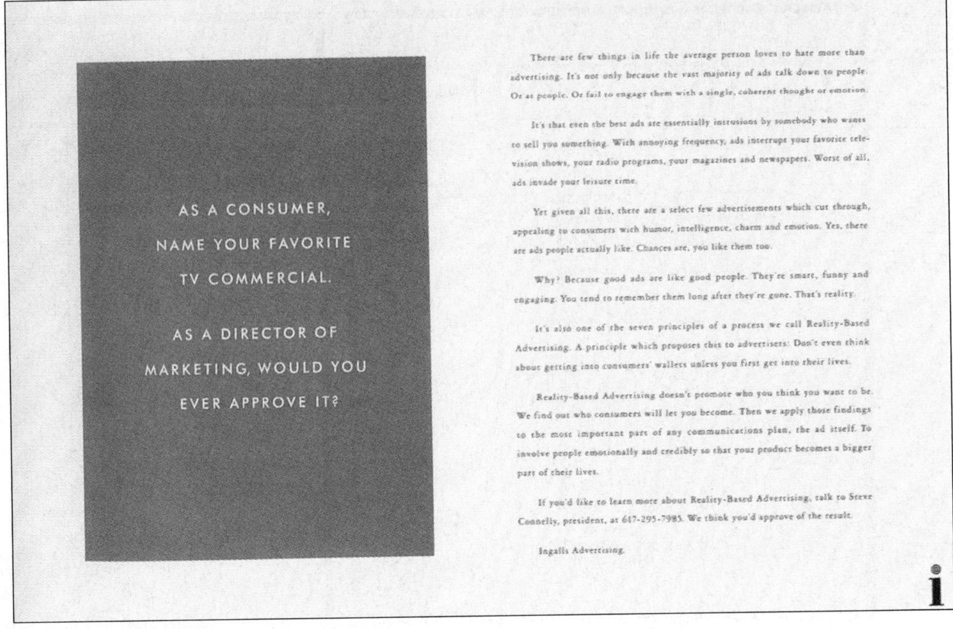

Or the newspaper client that wanted to encourage people who didn't read the newspaper to read the newspaper. Only one mandate, though. The ads had to appear in the client's newspaper since the space was free.

It's easy and sometimes fun to blame clients for all of the anxieties and frustrations of the creatives. Especially if you work in a creative department. You can criticize the clients all you want and, since they aren't in the office next to you, they can't hear you. But, despite the obvious stake that creative departments have in generating superior advertising, it should be mentioned that no creative ever put $200 million of his own money behind a campaign. Clients not only foot the bills, they also approach agencies with creative problems in the first place. Take, for instance, the challenge faced by many advertisers following the terrorist attacks of September 11, 2001, as discussed in the IBP box on page 358.

Indeed, you can't always blame the clients. Sometimes the conflicts and problems that preclude wonderful creative work occur within the walls of the advertising agency itself. To say there can be a bit of conflict between the creative department and the other departments of an advertising agency is a bit like saying there can be a bit of conflict when Jerry Springer walks into a studio. In advertising, the conflict often centers on the creative department and the account management department. It's no wonder that creatives feel as if their creative output is put under a microscope. The creative department is recognized as an essential part of an advertising agency's success. What does a potential client consider to be of primary importance when choosing an advertising agency? Creativity. What is one of the crucial factors in a positive client/agency relationship? Again, creativity.[41] So why doesn't everybody pull together and love each other within an agency?

When a client is unhappy, it fires the agency. Billings and revenue drop. Budgets are cut. And pink slips drop. It's no wonder that conflict occurs. When someone is looking out for his or her job, it's tough not to get involved in struggles over control of the creative product. Account managers function as the conduit from agency to client and back. Every day when they walk in the door, their prime

41. D. C. West, "Cross-National Creative Personalities, Processes, and Agency Philosophies," *Journal of Advertising Research*, vol. 33, no. 5 (1993), 53–62.

EXHIBIT 10.11

How to identify a good advertising executive.

For some 25 years I was an advertising agency "AE," eventually rising through the crabgrass to become a founder, president, chairman and now chairman emeritus of Borders, Perrin and Norrander, Inc.

During all those years, I pondered the eternal question: Why do some advertising agencies consistently turn out a superior creative product while others merely perpetuate mediocrity? Is the answer simply to hire great writers and art directors? Well, certainly that has a lot to do with it, but I would suggest that there is another vital component in the equation for creative success.

Outstanding creative work in an ad agency requires a ferocious commitment from all staffers, but especially from the account service person. The job title is irrelevant—account executive, account manager, account supervisor—but the job function is critical, particularly when it comes to client approvals. Yes, I am speaking of the oft-maligned AE, the "suit" who so frequently is the bane of the Creative Department.

So how in the wide world does one identify this rare species, this unusual human being who is sensitive to the creative process and defends the agency recommendations with conviction and vigor? As you might expect, it is not easy. But there are some signals, some semihypothetical tests that can be used as diagnostic tools:

To begin with, look for unflappability, a splendid trait to possess in the heat of battle. In Australia last year I heard a chap tell about arriving home to "find a bit of a problem" under his bed. An eight-foot python had slithered in and coiled around the man's small dog. Hearing its cries, he yanked the snake out from under the mattress, pried it loose from the mutt, tossed it out the door and "dispatched it with a garden hoe." Was he particularly frightened or distressed? Not at all. "I've seen bigger snakes," he said, helping himself to another Foster's Lager. Now, that's the kind of disposition which wears well in account service land.

Source: Wes Perrin, "How to Identify a Good AE," *Communication Arts Advertising Annual* 1988 (Palo Alto, Calif: Coyne and Blanchard, Inc., 1988), 210.

responsibility is to see that the client is purring and happy. Since clients hold the final power of approval over creative output, the members of the account team see an advertisement as a product they must control before the client sees it.[42] Members of the creative department resent the control. They feel as if their work is being judged by a group whose most creative input should be over what tie or scarf goes best with a pinstriped suit. Members of the account management team perceive the creatives as experts in the written word or in visual expression. However, they believe that creatives don't understand advertising strategy or business dealings.

As with most things, the truth probably lies somewhere in the murky middle. Unfortunately, except at a few fortunate agencies (Exhibit 10.11), the chances for total recognition of each department's talents are slim. As stated earlier, the backgrounds of the people in each department are just too different, the organizational structures too much of a problem.

So how does an agency successfully address this tension? The ad in Exhibit 10.12 suggests that it can be done with the right computer software. In most instances, though, the truth may be that it can't, not even with the world's largest supercomputer. Beyond the philosophy may be a simple fact: Individuals in the account service departments and creative departments of advertising agencies do not always (even usually)

42. A. J. Kover and S. M. Goldberg, "The Games Copywriters Play: Conflict, Quasi-Control, a New Proposal," *Journal of Advertising Research,* vol. 25, no. 4 (1995), 52–62.

e-SIGHTINGS

"Our shop grows because our creative side and our business side work together. That's why we use Clients& Profits."

Successful **ad agencies** and **design studios** get that way when everyone **works together**. Over 800 of today's smartest shops do it with Clients & Profits,® the best-selling **job tracking, costing, billing** and **accounting** software for the **Macintosh**. It's designed only for creative businesses, so it works just like you do. Call **800 272-4488** today for a **free guided tour** and complete information. *Or fax (619) 945-2365.*

WORKING COMPUTER
The Triangle Building
4755 Oceanside Blvd., Suite 200
Oceanside, CA 92056
(619) 945-4334

EXHIBIT 10.12

Companies like Working Computer (www.clientsandprofits.com) provide tools to help manage some of the most complex machinery imaginable: the human being. Why do you think the Clients & Profits ad highlights that the software runs on the Macintosh, given that so many of the computers in the world aren't Macs?

share the same ultimate goals for advertisements. Sorry, but that's often the way it is.

For an account manager to rise in his or her career, he or she must excel in the care and feeding of clients. It's a job of negotiation, gentle prodding, and ambassadorship. For a creative to rise, the work must challenge. It must arrest attention. It must provoke. At times, it must shock. It must do all the things a wonderful piece of art must do. Yet, as we indicated earlier, this is all the stuff that makes for nervous clients. And that is an account executive's nightmare.

This nightmare situation for the account executives produces the kind of ads that win awards for the creatives. People who win awards are recognized by the award shows in the industry. Their work gets published in *The One Show* and *Communication Arts* and appears on the Clios. These people become in demand and they are wined and dined by rival agencies (Exhibit 10.13). And they become famous and, yes, rich by advertising standards. Are they happier, better people? Some are. Some aren't. Ask one sometime. In the most honest moments, do they think about sales as much as *One Shows* and Addys? So the trick is, how do you get creatives to want to pursue cool ads that also sell? Let them win awards even though it may have nothing to do with boosting sales, or, more simply, let them keep their job?

The difficulty of assessing the effectiveness of an advertisement has also created antagonism between the creative department and the research department.[43] Vaughn states that the tumultuous social environment between creative departments and research departments represents the "historical conflict between art and science . . . these polarities have been argued philosophically as the conflict between Idealism and Materialism or Rationalism and Empiricism."[44] In the world of advertising, people in research departments are put in the unenviable position of judging the creatives (see Exhibits 10.14 and 10.15). So, again, "science" judges art. Creatives don't like this, particularly when it's usually pretty bad science, or not science at all. Of course, researchers are sometimes creative themselves, and they don't typically enjoy being an additional constraint on those in the creative department.

Why Does Advertising Need Creativity?

Who needs creativity? Clients do. Humans do. Creativity allows the consumer to see the brand in new and desired ways. It can accomplish the increasingly elusive breakthrough. Most marketing is about establishing brand relationships—creating and maintaining brand image and position. It is the creative execution that really allows this to happen. Advertising makes brands and relationships, and creative makes advertising. It puts the brand in a social context. It makes things into brands. And, as suggested by Exhibit 10.16, "bad" creatives will surely destroy a client's brand.

43. Ibid.
44. Vaughn, 1995.

EXHIBIT 10.13

Foote, Cone & Belding (www.fcb.com) is in the hunt for creatives, using a bit of sassy, pun-in-cheekiness to signal that résumés are wanted. What challenges do you think the Foote, Cone & Belding HR department faces in hiring and retaining the best and brightest (beyond borrowing some of the company's creative time to produce clever recruitment ads)?

EXHIBITS 10.14 AND 10.15

Research on an ad's effectiveness is an important, difficult, and unpopular task.

One of the advantages of being a practitioner-turned-educator is the opportunity to interact with a large number of agencies. Much like Switzerland, an academic is viewed as a neutral in current affairs and not subject to the suspicions of a potential competitor.

The result of my neutral status has been the opportunity to watch different agencies produce both great and poor work. And, as a former associate creative director, I'd like to share the trends I've seen in the development of bad creative. The revelation: Bad work is more a matter of structure than talent. Here are 12 pieces of advice if you want to institutionalize bad creative work in your agency:

1. Treat your target audience like a statistic.

Substituting numbers for getting a feel for living, breathing people is a great way to make bad work inevitable. It allows you to use your gut instinct about "women 55 to 64" rather than the instinct that evolves from really understanding a group of folks. The beauty with staying on the statistical level is that you get to claim you did your homework when the creative turns out dreadful. After all, there were 47 pages of stats on the target.

2. Make your strategy a hodgepodge.

Good ads have one dominant message, just one. Most strategies that result in lousy work have lots more than one. They are political junkyards that defy a creative wunderkind to produce anything but mediocrity. So make everybody happy with the strategy and then tell your creatives to find a way to make it all work. You'll get bad work, for sure.

3. Have no philosophy.

William Bernbach believed in a certain kind of work. His people emulated his philosophy and produced a consistent kind of advertising that built a great agency. Now, to be controversial, I'll say the exact same thing about Rosser Reeves. Both men knew what they wanted, got it, and prospered.

The agency leaders who do hard sell one day, then new wave the next, create only confusion. More important, the work does not flow from a consistent vision of advertising and a code of behavior to achieve that advertising. Instead, there is the wild embrace of the latest fashion or the currently faddish bromide making the rounds at conventions. So beware of those who have a philosophy and really are true to it. They are historically at odds with lousy work.

4. Analyze your creative as you do a research report.

The cold, analytical mind does a wonderful job destroying uncomfortable, unexpected work. Demand that every detail be present in every piece of creative and say it is a matter of thoroughness. The creative work that survives your ice storm will be timid and compromised and will make no one proud.

5. Make the creative process professional.

"Creative types collect a paycheck every two weeks. They'd better produce and do it now. This is, after all, a business." The corporate performance approach is a highly recommended way of developing drab print and TV. Treating the unashamedly artistic process of making ads as if it were an offshoot of the local oil filter assembly plant promises to destroy risk-taking and morale. Your work will become every bit as distinctive as a gray suit. More important, it will be on schedule. And both are fine qualities in business and we are a business, aren't we?

6. Say one thing and do another.

Every bad agency says all the right things about risk-taking, loving great creative, and admiring strong creative people. It is mandatory to talk a good game and then do all the things that destroy great work. This will help keep spirits low and turnover high in the creatives who are actually talented. And then you'll feel better when they leave after a few months because you really do like strong creative people—if they just weren't so damn defensive.

7. Give your client a candy store.

To prove how hard you work, insist on showing numerous half-thought-out ideas to your client. The approved campaign will have lots of problems nobody thought about and that will make the final work a mess.

Campaigns with strong ideas are rare birds, and they need a great deal of thinking to make sure they're right. So insist on numerous campaigns and guarantee yourself a series of sparrows rather than a pair of eagles.

8. Mix and match your campaigns.

Bring three campaigns to your client, and then mix them up. Take a little bit of one and stick it on another. Even better, do it internally. It's like mixing blue, red, and green. All are fine colors, but red lacks the coolness of blue. Can't we add a little? The result of the mix will be a thick muddy clump. Just like so many commercials currently on the air.

Continued

9. Fix it in production. don't agree.

Now that your procedure has created a half-baked campaign that is being mixed up with another, tell the creative to make it work by excellent production values. Then you can fire the incompetent hack when the jingle with 11 sales points is dull.

10. Blame the creative for bad creative.

After all, you told them what they should do. ("Make it totally unexpected, but use the company president and the old jingle.") The fault lies in the fact that you just can't find good talent anymore. Never mind that some creative departments have low turnover and pay smaller salaries than you do.

11. Let your people imitate.

"Chiat/Day won awards and sales for the Apple *1984* commercial, so let's do something like that for our stereo store account." This approach works wonders because your imitation appears lacking the original surprise that came from a totally expected piece of work. You can even avoid the controversy that surrounded Chiat/Day when half the industry said the ad was rotten. Your imitation can blend right in with all the other imitations and, even better, will have no strategic rationale for your bizarre execution.

12. Believe posttesting when you get a good score.

That way you can be slaughtered by your client when your sensitive, different commercial gets a score 20 points below norm. The nice things you said about posttesting when you got an excellent score with your "singing mop" commercial cannot be taken back. If you want to do good work, clients must somehow be made to use research as a tool. If you want to do bad creative, go ahead, and believe that posttesting rewards excellent work.

Naturally, a lot of bad creative results from egomania, laziness, incompetence, and client intractability—but a lot less than most believe. I have found that bad work usually comes from structures that make talented people ineffective and that demand hard work, human dedication, and tremendous financial investment to produce work that can be topped by your average high school senior.

John Sweeney, a former associate creative director at Foote, Cone & Belding, Chicago, teaches advertising at the University of North Carolina–Chapel Hill.

EXHIBIT 10.16

Assuring poor creative.

With all this talk of competition, envy, madness, constraint, and frustration, we could have written a do-it-yourself marriage counseling book. But, we had to tell you the truth. Too many books make it seem that if you just follow their good management flow chart, everything will be fine . . . peace, love, and profits. Sorry, it's not that way. Still, maybe by understanding the reasons for and the nature of the tensions, you will be able to do better. More importantly, even with all its problems, the world of advertising is as Jerry Della Femina said: "The most fun you can have with your pants on."[45] It's one of the few places left where really creative people can go to express themselves and make a living.

And remember:

What lies behind us and what lies before us are tiny matters, compared to what lies within us.

—Ralph Waldo Emerson[46]

45. Jerry Della Femina, *From Those Wonderful Folks Who Gave You Pearl Harbor, Front-Line Dispatches from the Advertising War* (New York: Simon and Schuster, 1970), 244.

46. Ralph Waldo Emerson, cited in The Quotations Archive, www.aphids.com/quotes.

IBP

Crafting the Message in the Face of Tragedy

The September 11, 2001, terrorist attacks on New York's World Trade Center and the Pentagon sent shock waves that had a profound effect on the mood of audiences in the United States and around the world. Masses stunned by the horror and magnitude of the tragedy quickly lost the appetite for entertainment-as-usual, forcing virtually every media outlet to radically change programming in order to adjust to the somber emotional and psychological climate. Radio stations around the country immediately censored rap and pop songs that depicted violence or terror, opting for more patriotic and uplifting formats, and television networks postponed fall-season premieres to revise scripts that seemed inappropriate given the nation's mournful tone. Even certain action films were postponed indefinitely from their scheduled releases.

Not only did the events of September 11 affect media programming, but advertisers were also pressured to change course and immediately respond. Agency creatives crafted new messages offering condolences to those affected by the attacks. Corporations pulled ads from current campaigns and replaced them with messages honoring the heroic rescue crews. Banner ads for the Red Cross and other nonprofit charities appeared on nearly every major Web site.

All industries were struggling to find the words to express the inexpressible, but perhaps airline advertising was buckling most under the immense pressure. Passenger volumes plummeted after the terrorist attacks, with flights booked as much as 40 percent empty as jittery travelers opted to stay home or travel by car and train. United Airlines' first TV ads after the events spoke openly with viewers about the attacks, but received mixed reviews from marketing experts. United's agency, Fallon Worldwide, ran spots for the airlines titled "Family" and "Passion," hoping to instill themes of renewal, camaraderie, a passion for flying, and confidence in the company. In the ads, airline workers talked about the thrill of flying and the "freedom" to travel anywhere, anytime in the United States. "We're not gonna let anyone take that away from us," a pilot stated. "We're Americans, and this is not going to beat us down," added an airline executive. While United's employees expressed heartfelt boldness in the face of airline tragedy, many critics rebuffed the campaign as a brilliant execution of the wrong strategy. One critic from the New England Consulting Group claimed United was "reminding people of what [United] wanted them to forget." Some reviewers, however, applauded the airline for being out there at all, recognizing the futility in hiding when the impact of the attack was so massive.

Adopting an integrated brand promotion strategy was crucial for United. With the industry facing billions in losses, marketers had to attempt to strike a balance between expressions of confidence in the airlines and subtle encouragement to fly. Jerry Dow, United's director of worldwide marketing, said, "Our customers want us out there talking to them, but they don't want the hard sell just yet." In order to stimulate business, United relied heavily on print and electronic media to offer discounts for business and leisure travelers.

For creatives, wielding advertising's powers of persuasion with such delicate precision was daunting—many advertisers just stayed home. In fact, United's two largest competitors, American Airlines and Delta, sat on the sidelines, opting to let time heal wounds before encouraging consumers to fly the friendly skies once again.

Sources: Jack Feuer, "TV Watchers More Sensitive," *AdWeek*, www.adweek.com, accessed September 25, 2001; "United Speaks on Attacks in TV Ad," *Associated Press*, www.adweek.com, accessed October 18, 2001.

SUMMARY

Describe the core characteristics of great creative minds.

A look at the shared sensibilities of great creative minds provides a constructive starting point for assessing the role of creativity in the production of great advertising. What Picasso had in common with Gandhi, Freud, Eliot, Stravinsky, Graham, and Einstein—including a strikingly exuberant self-confidence, (childlike) alertness, unconventionality, and an obsessive commitment to the work—both charms and alarms us. Self-confidence, at some point, becomes crass self-promotion; an unconstrained childlike ability to see the world as forever new devolves, somewhere along the line, into childish self-indulgence. Without creativity, there can be no advertising. How we recognize and define creativity in advertising rests on our understanding of the achievements of acknowledged creative geniuses from the worlds of art, literature, music, science, and politics.

Contrast the role of an advertising agency's creative department with that of its business managers/account executives and explain the tensions between them.

What it takes to get the right idea (a lot of hard work), and the ease with which a client or agency manager may dismiss that idea, underlies the contentiousness between an agency's creative staff and its managers and clients—between the poets and the killers. Creatives provoke. Managers control. Ads that win awards for creative excellence don't necessarily fulfill a client's business imperatives. All organizations deal with the competing agendas of one department versus another, but in advertising agencies, this competition plays out at an amplified level. The difficulty of assessing the effectiveness of an advertisement only adds to the antagonism between departments. Advertising researchers are put in the unenviable position of judging the creatives, pitting "science" against art. None of these tensions change the fact that creativity is essential to the vitality of brands. Creativity makes a brand, and it is creativity that reinvents established brands in new and desired ways.

KEY TERMS

adaptors
innovators

QUESTIONS

1. Over the years, creativity has been associated with various forms of madness and mental instability. In your opinion, what is it about creative people that prompts this kind of characterization?

2. Think about a favorite artist, musician, or writer. What is unique about the way he or she represents the world? What fascinates you about the vision he or she creates?

3. A lot of credence is given in this chapter to the idea that tension (of various sorts) fuels creative pursuits. Explain the connection between creativity and tension.

4. What role should critics play in determining what is creative and what is not?

5. Which side of this debate do you have more affinity for: Are people creative because they can produce creative results or are they creative because of the way they think? Explain.

6. Do you think everybody is creative, yet in different ways? According to the adaptation/innovation theory, what is the difference between the creativity of adaptors and that of innovators? Are both modes of creativity of equal benefit in every situation? Explain.

7. What forces inside an advertising agency can potentially compromise its creative work? Is compromise always to be avoided? Imagine that you are an agency creative. Define *compromise.* Now imagine that you are an account executive. How does your definition of compromise change?

8. Describe the conflict between the creative department and the research department. Do you think creatives are justified in their hesitancy to subject their work to advertising researchers? Why? Is science capable of judging art any more than art is capable of judging science? Explain.

9. Choose an ad from the book that represents exemplary creativity to you. Explain your choice.

10. Examine Exhibit 10.16. Using this exhibit as your guide, generate a list of ten principles to facilitate creativity in an advertising agency.

EXPERIENTIAL EXERCISES

1. Write a one-page analysis of a creative song, video, or piece of art created by an artist or musician. In your own words, describe what makes the work uniquely creative (be sure to use chapter concepts concerning creativity and creative personalities). Finally, given the contentious conflicts between creativity and management in the advertising industry, do you think this artist or musician could have succeeded in a career in advertising? Explain.

2. This chapter discussed the natural friction that occurs within the organizational structure of the advertising industry, highlighting conflicts that arise between creatives and management. Typically, creatives are experts in the written word and visual expression, but they often don't understand business strategy. Account managers, on the other hand, are trained in business strategy and client relations, but they lack an understanding of the creative process. Reread the section of this chapter concerning the tensions and challenges that occur in the industry between the creative and account management departments. Contact an employee at an advertising agency, the advertising department at your school, or any advertising professional that you know and schedule a brief phone interview concerning this issue. Ask this person for his or her professional opinion regarding organizational challenges that exist in balancing the creative and business goals of advertising, and ask for specific examples that effect the overall effectiveness of the agency.

USING THE INTERNET

10-1 Eureka!

Richard Saunders International is a think tank of strategic inventors whose mission includes inspiring breakthrough ideas in the workplace and enabling people to develop them into successful products and campaigns. Eureka! Ranch is the magical place where executives from organizations such as Nike, Walt Disney, Procter & Gamble, and other megacorporations convene for creativity training seminars focused on "capitalist creativity, the art and science of inspiring and articulating ideas that make money." Founded by famously barefooted master inventor Doug Hall, Eureka! Ranch continues to revolutionize the creative development and marketing of brands, including quantitative metrics to calculate their chances of success.

Eureka! Ranch: http://www.eurekaranch.com

1. Visit the Eureka! Ranch online and briefly describe the mission, activities, and aims of this think tank.

2. What assumptions about the nature of creativity make a resort like the Eureka! Ranch successful or even possible?

3. Describe one of the Eureka! Ranch patented services such as Merwyn or Trailblazer training, and explain how it relates to enhancing creativity.

10-2 Creativity across Domains

Thousands of sites on the Web are devoted to developing creativity in business, arts, education, and entertainment. The Innovation Network, a creative online think-space based firmly upon the motivational philosophies of Maslow and other humanistic psychologists, is dedicated to rethinking conditions around the workplace to produce more innovative creative environments for business success. Browse the following creativity site and answer the questions.

Innovation Network: http://www.thinksmart.com

1. What is the purpose of this site? Comment on the creativity displayed on this site in terms of design and artistic appeal.

2. Do you think creativity is a personality trait that resides naturally in some people but not in others, or can anyone develop creativity? Explain your answer.

3. Name and describe two or three of the site's interactive tools and functions that are designed to give your creativity a workout online. What uses might these resources have for developing creativity in advertising and promotion?

CHAPTER 11

After reading and thinking about this chapter, you will be able to do the following:

1

Identify ten objectives of message strategy.

2

Identify methods for executing each message strategy objective.

3

Discuss the strategic implications of various methods used to execute each message strategy objective.

CHAPTER 10
Creativity and Advertising

CHAPTER 11
Message Strategy

CHAPTER 12
Copywriting

CHAPTER 13
Art Direction and Production

PlayStation

There are those who say it was brilliant and inspired. Others argue it was a capricious and expensive exercise in grandstanding. In January 1984, during the third quarter of the Super Bowl, Apple Computer introduced the Macintosh with a 60-second spot. The ad, known as "1984," climaxed with a young athletic woman hurling a mallet through a huge projection screen in a monochromatic vision of a hyper-corporate and ugly future.[1] On the big screen was an Orwellian Big Brother instructing the masses. As the ad closed, with the near soulless masses obediently chanting the corporate-state mantra in the background, the following simple statement appeared on the television screens of millions of viewers: "On January 24th, Apple Computer will introduce Macintosh. And you'll see why 1984 won't be like 1984."

What made this advertisement particularly newsworthy is that it cost $400,000 to produce (very expensive for its day) and another $500,000 to broadcast, yet it was broadcast only *once*. It was a creative superevent. The three major networks covered the event on the evening news, and the ad went on to become *Advertising Age*'s Commercial of the Decade for the 1980s. But why? It wasn't just its high cost and single play. It wasn't just its very stylish, but disturbing look (directed by Ridley Scott [*Blade Runner, Alien, Gladiator, Black Hawk Down*]). It wasn't just about an ad that told us that we could be the person we wanted to be, rather than the one we had to be. It was more that the ad captured and articulated something important lying just below the surface of mid-1980s American culture. It was about us versus them, threatened individuals versus faceless corporations. It was about the defiant rejection of sterile corporate life and the celebration of individuality through, of all things, a computer. Archrival IBM was implicitly cast as the oppressive Big Blue (that is, Big Brother) and Apple as the good anticorporate corporation. The ad captured the moment and, most critically, served up a consumer product as popular ideology. Apple became the hip, the young, the cool, the democratic, the populist, the anti-establishment computer. It was the computer of the nonsellout, or at least of those who wished to think of themselves that way.

As we've said before, you can rarely go wrong by emphasizing individuality in the United States. Likewise, if you can link your product to a strong social movement, so much the better, as long as the trend lasts. If you can also serve a large and underserved market segment (for example, cyber-insecure consumers unwilling to deal with DOS, ready to use a mouse, and generally anti-button-down corporate), even better. Steve Hayden, the "1984" copywriter, described the ad this way: "We thought of it as an ideology, a value set. It was a way of letting the whole world access the power of computing and letting them talk to one another. The democratization of technology—the computer for the rest of us."[2]

With "1984," Apple and advertising agency Chiat/Day wanted to focus attention on a new product and completely distinguish Apple and the Macintosh from Big Blue, IBM. Macintosh was going to offer computing power to the people. This declaration of computing independence was made on the most-watched broadcast of the year. Forty-six percent of all U.S. households were tuned to the 1984 Super Bowl. With the Macintosh, Apple offered an alternative and very hip cyber-ethos for those who felt alienated or intimidated by the IBM world. The "1984" ad offered a clear choice, a clear instruction: Buy a Mac, keep your soul. And it worked. Macintosh and Apple grew and prospered. For quite a while, "the rest of us" was a pretty big group.

Of course, there is another lesson here: Nothing lasts forever, not even a great creative idea. Things change. Advertising has to evolve along with the situation, or the brand may suffer. As great as this ad was (and it was) and as much success as the Mac and Apple had, things didn't stay so good. Some believe that the seeds of

1. The term "ugly future" was first used in this context by Connie Johnson, University of Illinois, in the late 1970s.
2. This quote appears in Bradley Johnson, "10 Years after 1984: The Commercial and the Product That Changed Advertising," *Advertising Age,* January 10, 1994. 12.

EXHIBIT 11.1

The launch of the iMac.
www.apple.com

Apple's own near demise may have been the result of hanging on to this idea of "the rest of us" just a little too long. Apple effectively cultivated an us-versus-them ethic, which worked well to help establish a brand position and even a sense of brand community, but Apple failed to keep the Apple tent inclusive and big. The rest-of-us ethos became something of a problem.

Jump back to the present. Today, Apple's future is looking up but still is uncertain. Some believe it has forever been damaged by a failure to recognize and adapt to changes in the marketplace. Because Apple refused to license its operating system until 1995 (and then changed its mind again), Macs became a relatively expensive alternative. Coupled to a premium price, the "rest of us" came to be regarded by some as evidence of Apple's snooty and elitist attitude. The "rest of us" seemed to think they were better (more hip, cooler, more arty, more *au courant,* and so on) than us—not necessarily a desirable product attribute if a company hopes to sell a lot of computers. Once the skid hit software availability, Apple came perilously close to extinction.

With the return of co-founder Steve Jobs, Apple once again teamed up with TBWA Chiat/Day to launch the iMac (Exhibit 11.1), and it seems that things have turned around (at least some) yet again. With the return of Jobs, the company made a profit of around $309 million after a loss of $1 billion in the previous Jobs-less year. And over 278,000 people took iMacs home with them in the first six weeks on the market.[3] Is Apple back tapping into the soul of American culture? We'll have to wait and see. It is certainly doing well . . . even though its market share is still very small compared to the Windows platform. The stylish iMac has done something similar to what GM did in the 1920s, when all cars were black and were in some danger of eventually becoming undifferentiated commodities—GM began to produce them in color and introduced elements of style.

In the 1990s, computers were quickly becoming low-margin commodities—so, taking a page from GM seventy years previously, Apple introduced style and color. This was very smart marketing and required smart advertising. Still, it's unlikely that Apple will conquer the American consciousness the way it did in 1984. Back then, Apple's advertising was unquestionably superior. No one can ever take that away. It

3. David Kirkpatrick, "The Second Coming of Apple," *Fortune,* November 9, 1998, 86–92.

was truly creative, and it advanced Apple's strategy. Apple and Chiat/Day deserve a great deal of credit. Maybe they can do it again.

Message Strategy.

An advertising and promotion strategy is a summary statement of all essential and defining planning, preparation, and placement decisions. One major component of an advertising and promotion advertising strategy is the **message strategy.** The message strategy consists of objectives and methods. It defines the goals of the advertiser and how those goals will be achieved. This chapter offers ten message strategy objectives and discusses and illustrates the methods often used to satisfy them. This is not an exhaustive list, but it covers many of the most common and important message strategy objectives. Exhibit 11.2 summarizes the ten message strategy objectives presented here.

EXHIBIT 11.2

Message strategy objectives and methods.

Objective: What the Advertiser Hopes to Achieve	Method: How the Advertiser Plans to Achieve the Objective
Promote brand recall: To get consumers to recall its brand name(s) first; that is, before any of the competitors' brand names	Repetition Slogans and jingles
Link a key attribute to the brand name: To get consumers to associate a key attribute with a brand name and vice versa	Unique selling proposition (USP)
Persuade the consumer: To convince consumers to buy a product or service through high-engagement arguments	Reason-why ads Hard-sell ads Comparison ads Testimonials Demonstration Advertorials Infomercials
Instill brand preference: To get consumers to like or prefer its brand above all others	Feel-good ads Humor ads Sexual-appeal ads
Scare the consumer into action: To get consumers to buy a product or service by instilling fear	Fear-appeal ads
Change behavior by inducing anxiety: To get consumers to make a purchase decision by playing to their anxieties; often, the anxieties are social in nature	Anxiety ads Social anxiety ads
Transform consumption experiences: To create a feeling, image, or mood about a brand that is activated when the consumer uses the product or service	Transformational ads
Situate the brand socially: To give the brand meaning by placing it in a desirable social context	Slice-of-life ads Product placement/ short Internet films Light-fantasy ads
Define the brand image: To create an image for a brand by relying predominantly on visuals rather than words and argument	Image ads
Invoke a direct response: To get consumers to take immediate buying action, typically by providing a toll-free number	Call-or-click-now ads

Objective #1: Promote Brand Recall. Since the very beginning, a major goal of advertisers has been to get consumers to remember their brand's name. This is typically referred to as the brand recall objective. Of course, advertisers not only want consumers to remember their name, but also want that name to be the first brand name consumers remember. Advertisers want their brand name to be *top of mind* or at least in the *evoked set,* a small list of brand names (typically less than five) that come to mind when a product or service category (for example, airlines [United, American, Delta], soft drinks [Coke, Pepsi], or photographic film [Kodak, Fuji]) is recalled. In the case of parity products (those with few major objective differences between brands—for example, laundry soaps) and other "low-involvement" goods and services, the first brand remembered is often the most likely to be purchased. First-remembered brands are often the most popular brands. Consumers may infer popularity, desirability, and even superiority from the ease with which they recall brands. However, companies are finding that traditional branding strategies are losing their punch, as evidenced in the IBP box on this page. So, how do advertisers promote easy recall? There are several methods.

IBP

Clock Running Out on Branding Strategies

The old saying that "time waits for no one" rings ever true in the realm of advertising. In an era when product cycles are compressed into shorter and shorter increments, and the proliferation of ads creates a cluttered sea for consumers to drown in, branding may be losing ground as a vital message strategy.

For decades brands have risen to the top of their class through general branding strategies. Brands such as Coke and Pepsi benefited from big budgets and long-term commitment given to relentless, repetitive presentation of the brand name. However, there are signs that this strategy is failing as savvy consumers weed through message excesses looking for clear value and a persuasive incentive to buy. Case in point: Internet firms bilked hundreds of millions from investors to execute general communications strategies, expecting to leave a lasting positive imprint on the public. Money-drunk dot-coms tossed millions of dollars at Super Bowl commercials and megasponsorships. What is there to show for it? The demise of countless Web retailers (ignominiously called "dot-bombs") and a crippled NASDAQ.

Even successful brick-and-mortar retailers are reaching a point of diminishing returns on general branding strategies. The Gap's recent parody of "West Side Story" prodded audiences to think of khaki instead of denim and most of all to think of Gap. Downward-trending sales figures haven't vindicated the Gap's message strategy, and khaki is no more popular now than before the campaign. Underscoring the Gap's strategy was the proposition that vast sums spent on national ads would cement the chain in the collective consciousness, independent of the particular products being featured. No such luck.

In contrast, companies that emphasize integrated brand promotion seem to be hitting pay dirt. The rocketlike growth of Starbucks over the past five years occurred with nearly zero effort toward general branding techniques. Starbucks offers scores of coupons, direct-mail catalogs, and special coffee buys to provide a compelling incentive to act—and act now.

Economic activity is sure to pick up over the next few years. It remains to be seen whether marketers will redirect their budgets toward direct campaigns, point-of-purchase merchandising, and other integrated strategies to support their national creative, or continue to lasso the wind with broad, general branding strategies.

Source: Michael Klinka, "Compression Theory Bursts the Branding Bubble," *BrandEra*, www.brandera.com, accessed October 26, 2001.

2 **Method A: Repetition.** As simple as it sounds, repetition is a tried-and-true way of gaining easier retrieval from consumer's memory. This is done through buying lots of ads and/or by repeating the brand name within the ad itself. The idea is that things said more often will be remembered more easily than things said less frequently. When the consumer stands in front of the laundry detergent aisle, you can't expect deliberate and extensive consideration of product attributes: Just the recall of a brand name, a previous judgment, or (most often) habit is what does the trick and drives the purchase decision. Getting into the consumer's evoked set gets you closer to preference and, ultimately, to brand loyalty. This type of advertising tries to keep existing users as much as it tries to get new ones, usually more so.

Method B: Slogans and Jingles. Slogans are linguistic devices that link a brand name to something memorable, due to the slogan's simplicity, meter, rhyme, or some other factor. Jingles do the same thing, just set to music. Examples are numerous: "Bud-Weis-Er";

SFX: PHONE RINGING.

GUY 1: Hello . . .

CALLER: Yo! What's up?

GUY 1: Watchin' the game . . . Havin' a Bud. What's up with you?

CALLER: Nothing'. Watchin' the game. Havin' a Bud . . .

GUY 1: True, true.

(GUY 2 WEARING YELLOW JERSEY ENTERS ROOM.)

GUY 2: Whassup!

GUY 1: Whassup!

CALLER: Yo, who's that?

GUY 1: (TO GUY 2) Yo! Pick up the phone!

GUY 2: Hello!

CALLER: Whassup!

GUY 2: Whassup!

GUY 1: Whassup!

GUY 2: (TO CALLER) Yo, where's Dookie?

(CUT TO CALLER)

CALLER: (SHOUTING) Yo, Dookie!

(CUT TO DOOKIE SITTING AT HIS COMPUTER PICKING UP EXTENSION.)

DOOKIE: Yo!

GUY 2: Whassup!

GUY 1: Whassup!

CALLER: Whassup!

DOOKIE: Whassup!

SFX: INTERCOM BUZZER.

GUY 2: Yo, hold up!

(CUT TO GUY 2 PRESSING INTERCOM BUTTON.)

VISITOR VOICEOVER: Whassup!

GUY 2: Whassup!

(CUT TO OUTSIDE. WE SEE VISITOR HOLDING SIX-PACK OF BUDWEISER.)

CALLER: Whassup!

DOOKIE: Whassup!

GUY 1: Whassup!

(CUT TO GUY 2 AND DOOKIE HANGING UP PHONES. CUT BACK TO GUY 1.)

GUY 1: (TO CALLER) So what's going on, B?

CALLER: Watching the game, havin' a Bud.

GUY 1: True . . . true . . .

SUPER: Budweiser logo.

SUPER: True.

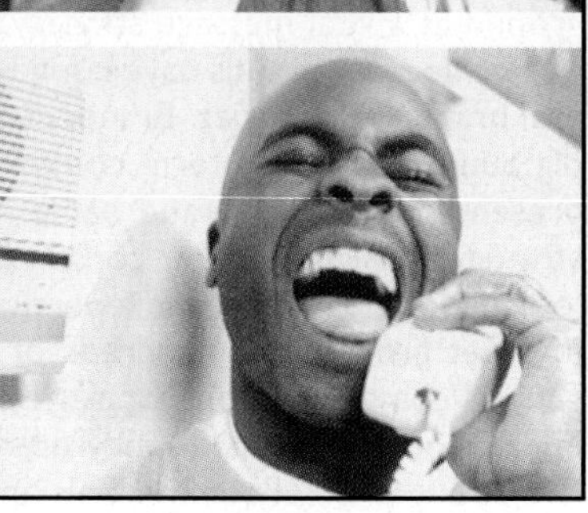

GOLD AWARD: Consumer Television Varying Lengths: Campaign
ART DIRECTORS: Chuck Taylor, Justin Reardon
WRITERS: Vinny Warren, Charles Stone III
AGENCY PRODUCER: Kent Kwiatt
PRODUCTION COMPANY: C & C–Storm Films
CLIENT: Anheuser–Busch
AGENCY: DDB/Chicago
ID 00 0096A

EXHIBIT 11.3

"Wassup" was classic repletion advertising, but it also showed that a strategy usually associated with annoyance could be fun as well. www.budweiser.com

"You Deserve a Break Today"; "Tide's In, Dirt's Out"; "The Best Part of Waking Up Is Folgers in Your Cup"; "You're in Good Hands with Allstate"; "Like a Good Neighbor, State Farm Is There"; "We Love to Fly and It Shows"; "Two, Two, Two Mints in One"; "Get Met, It Pays"; and "It Keeps on Going and Going and Going." No doubt you've heard a few of these before. Slogans and jingles allow for rehearsal and enhanced retrieval. As you know, they are hard to get out of your head (Exhibit 11.3). Success or failure of these methods is usually demonstrated by successful recall of brand name. Evaluation of repetition, slogans, and jingles is typically done through recall tests (DAR) and tracking studies.

3 Strategic Implications of Repetition, Slogans, and Jingles

 *Extremely resistant:* If you get consumers trained to remember your brand name, other advertisers' best efforts tend to fall on deaf ears.

- *Big carryover:* If it works, the residual amount of impact from the campaign is huge. If some advertisers stopped advertising today, you would remember their slogans, jingles, and names for a long, long time.
- *Long-term commitment:* For this method to work, advertisers have to sign on for the long haul. It's not easy in a cluttered media environment to build this type of easy recall. It takes lots and lots of repetition.
- *Expense:* This is an expensive method. If advertisers really want to use this method, they need to get their checkbooks out, and keep them out.
- *Competitive interference:* Even if you pay for lots of repetitions, you may, if the creative is bad, only get your brand confused with your competitor's. What a nice gesture on your part . . . paying for their advertising? Market leaders win in this situation. So be careful if you are not the category leader.
- *Creative resistance:* Creatives generally hate this type of advertising. Can you imagine why?

Objective #2: Link Key Attributes to the Brand Name. Sometimes advertisers want consumers to remember one or two attributes along with the brand name. This type of advertising is most closely identified with the "Rosser Reeves" **unique selling proposition (USP)** style. As you remember, Rosser Reeves was an important figure in 1950s advertising; he is credited with popularizing this form of advertising.

Method: USP. While one does not have to adopt a Reeves style (that is, hard sell, "tests," and an annoying style), the idea of emphasizing one and only one brand attribute is a very good idea—sometimes two if they are complementary, such as "strong, but gentle." Ads that try to link several attributes to a brand while working to establish recall often fail—they are too confusing and give too much information. Good examples of successful ads of this sort are "All-Temp-a-Cheer" and the USP offered in Exhibit 11.4. Success or failure with this method is demonstrated by successful recall of an attribute linked to a brand. Evaluation of the USP method is typically done through recall tests and tracking studies.

Strategic Implications of the USP Method

- *Resistant:* If this ad works and you can link one attribute with one brand, it is incredibly resistant to challenge. Some consumers will go to their graves remembering that Ivory is pure.
- *Big carryover:* For the reason just mentioned, the efficiency of this advertising is great once this link has been established. An investment in this kind of advertising can carry you through some lean times.
- *Long-term commitment:* If advertisers are going to do this, they have to be in it for the long haul.
- *Expense:* It will be very expensive, with lots of consumer learning to link an attribute that other brands are also trying to link.
- *Competitive interference:* For the reason just stated, you may be spending a lot of money to help the category leader.
- *Some creative resistance:* Creatives tend not to hate this as much as simple repetition, but it does seem to get old with them pretty fast. Don't expect a thank-you note.

Objective #3: Persuade the Consumer. Advertising that attempts to persuade is high-engagement advertising. Its goal is to convince the consumer, through a form of commercial discourse, that a brand is superior. The persuasion objective requires a significantly higher level of cognitive engagement with the audience. The receiver has to think about what the advertiser is saying. The receiver must engage in a form of mental argument with the commercial. For example, an ad says, "In a Mercedes, you wouldn't get

EXHIBIT 11.4

In this ad, Chevy uses a unique selling proposition: Identify a quality and sell it as unique. www.chevrolet.com/trailblazer/

stuck behind a Lexus on the road. . . . Why would you get stuck behind one at your dealer?" You might read that and say to yourself, "Hey, what's wrong with Lexus? I think Lexus is great. Forget this." Or you might say, "Yeah, if I could afford a Mercedes, I'd buy a really great car." Or maybe you would say to yourself, "Hey, that's right. . . . You know, maybe I should consider a Mercedes next time. They're probably not much more expensive than a Lexus." Or you might say, "My ex-boyfriend had a Lexus . . . what a jerk." The point is that in a persuasion ad, there is an assumed dialogue between the ad and the receiver. This style of advertising has steadily declined over the course of the last hundred years. For many reasons, it's getting pretty rare these days. This is a very wordy approach to advertising, and most ads are employing visual appeals.

Method A: Reason-Why Ads. In a reason-why ad, the advertiser reasons with the potential consumer. The ad points out to the receiver that there are good reasons why this brand will be satisfying and beneficial. Advertisers are usually relentless in their attempt to reason with consumers when using this method. They begin with some claim, like "Seven great reasons to buy Brand X," and then proceed to list all seven, finishing with the conclusion (implicit or explicit) that only a moron would, after such compelling evidence, do anything other than purchase Brand X (Exhibit 11.5). Other times, the reason or reasons why to use a product can be presented deftly. The biggest trick to this method is making sure that the reason why makes sense and that consumers care. The reason why approach is used in direct mail and other forms of promotion. (See Exhibit 11.6.)

Method B: Hard-Sell Ads. Hard-sell ads are a subcategory of reason-why ads. They are characteristically high pressure and urgent. Phrases such as "act now,"

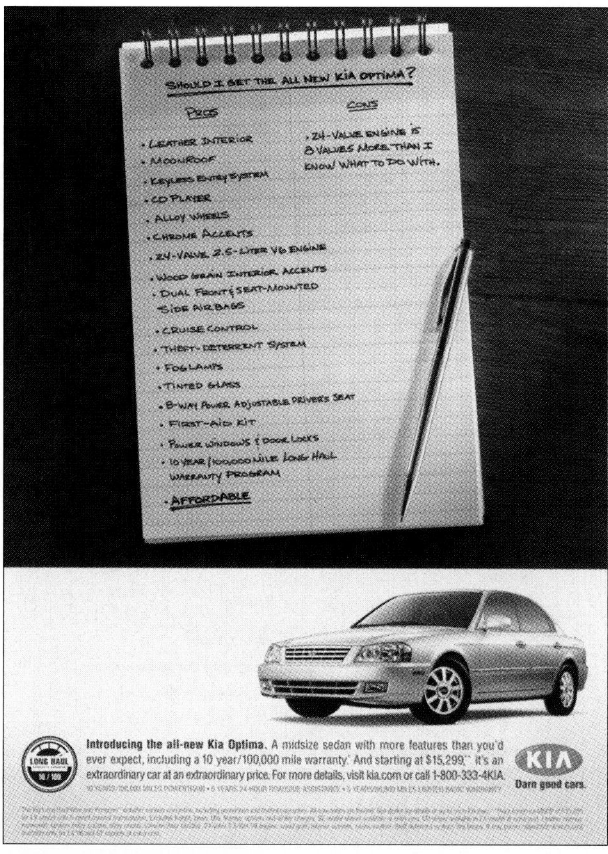

EXHIBIT 11.5

Here's why you should buy a Kia, very simple.
www.kia.com

"limited time offer," "your last chance to save," and "one-time-only sale" are representative of this method. The idea is to create a sense of urgency so consumers will act quickly. (See Exhibit 11.7.) Of course, many consumers have learned how to ignore or otherwise discount these messages. Evaluation of both hard-sell and reason-why ads is typically done through tracking studies that measure attitudes, beliefs, and preferences.

Strategic Implications of Reason-Why and Hard-Sell Approaches

- 👍 Gives consumer "permission to buy."
- 👍 Provides reasons consumers may use to defend their choice.
- 👍 If frequently rehearsed, very resistant to competitors' challenges.
- 👎 Assumes a high level of involvement; consumers really have to be paying attention for these ads to work.
- 👎 Generates considerable counterarguments.
- 👎 Requires high frequency; to break through the clutter with this style of advertising, you may have to repeat your message many times.
- 👎 For the reasons above, may lead to low efficiency.
- 👎 Legal/regulatory challenges/exposure; the makers of these ads tend to get dragged into court quite a bit. You'd better make sure that all your reasons why can stand up in court. Many haven't.

Method C: Comparison Ads. **Comparison advertisements** are another form used to persuade the consumer. Comparison ads try to demonstrate a brand's ability to satisfy consumers by comparing its features to those of competitive brands. Comparisons can be an effective and efficient means of communicating a large amount of information in a clear and interesting way, or they can be extremely confusing. Comparison as a technique has traditionally been used by marketers of convenience goods, such as pain relievers, laundry detergents, and household cleaners. Advertisers in a wide range of product categories have tried comparison advertising from time to time. For several years, AT&T and MCI had a long-running feud over whose rates were lower for household consumers. The ads seemed to have thoroughly confused everyone. Luxury car makers BMW and Lexus have targeted each other with comparative claims.[4] In one ad, BMW attacks the sluggish performance of Lexus with the message, "According to recent test results, Lexus' greatest achievement in acceleration is its price." Not to be left out, the Acura dealers of Southern California entered the luxury car advertising skirmish by stating, "We could use a lesser leather in our automobiles, but then we'd be no better than Rolls-Royce." Evaluation of comparison ads is typically done through tracking studies that measure attitudes, beliefs, and preferences; focus groups are also used.

Using comparison in an advertisement can be direct and name competitors' brands, or it can be indirect and refer only to the "leading brand" or "Brand X."

4. Jim Henry, "Comparative Ads Speed Ahead for Luxury Imports," *Advertising Age,* September 12, 1994, 10.

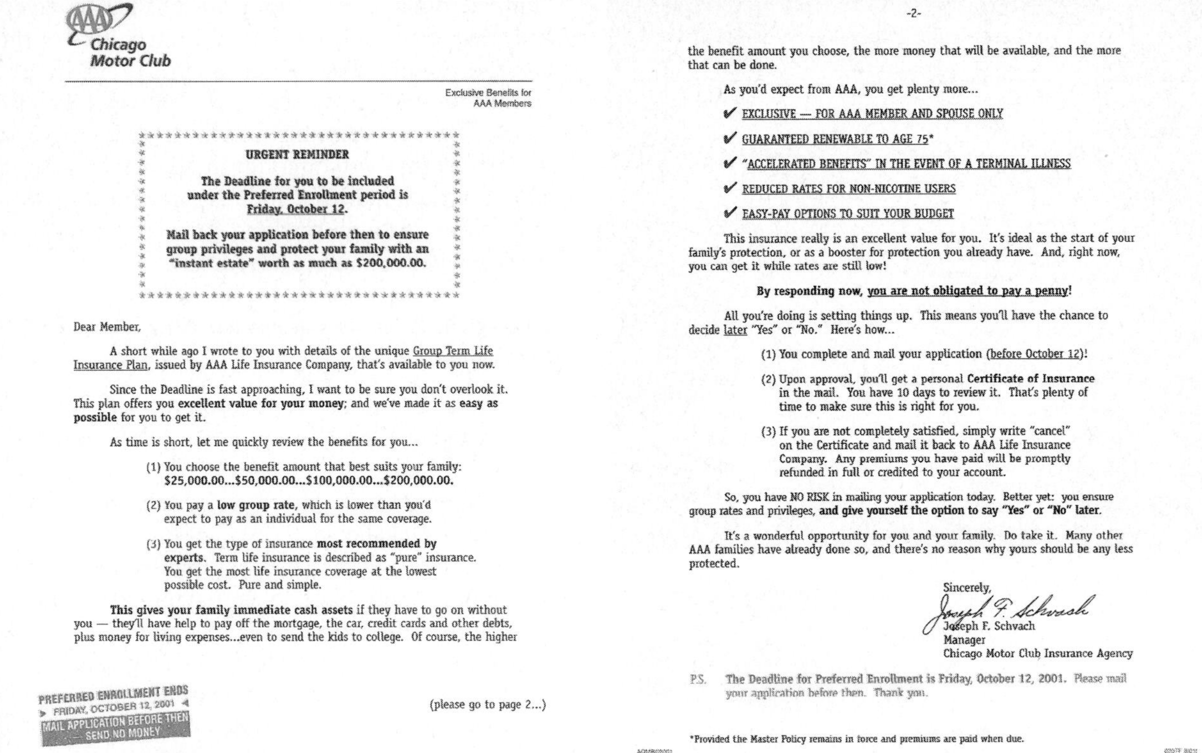

AAA Chicago Motor Club

Exclusive Benefits for AAA Members

URGENT REMINDER

The Deadline for you to be included under the Preferred Enrollment period is Friday, October 12.

Mail back your application before then to ensure group privileges and protect your family with an "instant estate" worth as much as $200,000.00.

Dear Member,

A short while ago I wrote to you with details of the unique Group Term Life Insurance Plan, issued by AAA Life Insurance Company, that's available to you now.

Since the Deadline is fast approaching, I want to be sure you don't overlook it. This plan offers you **excellent value for your money**; and we've made it as **easy as possible** for you to get it.

As time is short, let me quickly review the benefits for you...

(1) You choose the benefit amount that best suits your family: **$25,000.00...$50,000.00...$100,000.00...$200,000.00.**

(2) You pay a **low group rate**, which is lower than you'd expect to pay as an individual for the same coverage.

(3) You get the type of insurance **most recommended by experts.** Term life insurance is described as "pure" insurance. You get the most life insurance coverage at the lowest possible cost. Pure and simple.

This gives your family immediate cash assets if they have to go on without you — they'll have help to pay off the mortgage, the car, credit cards and other debts, plus money for living expenses...even to send the kids to college. Of course, the higher

PREFERRED ENROLLMENT ENDS
FRIDAY, OCTOBER 12, 2001
MAIL APPLICATION BEFORE THEN
SEND NO MONEY

(please go to page 2...)

-2-

the benefit amount you choose, the more money that will be available, and the more that can be done.

As you'd expect from AAA, you get plenty more...

✔ EXCLUSIVE — FOR AAA MEMBER AND SPOUSE ONLY

✔ GUARANTEED RENEWABLE TO AGE 75*

✔ "ACCELERATED BENEFITS" IN THE EVENT OF A TERMINAL ILLNESS

✔ REDUCED RATES FOR NON-NICOTINE USERS

✔ EASY-PAY OPTIONS TO SUIT YOUR BUDGET

This insurance really is an excellent value for you. It's ideal as the start of your family's protection, or as a booster for protection you already have. And, right now, you can get it while rates are still low!

By responding now, you are not obligated to pay a penny!

All you're doing is setting things up. This means you'll have the chance to decide later "Yes" or "No." Here's how...

(1) You complete and mail your application (before October 12)!

(2) Upon approval, you'll get a personal **Certificate of Insurance** in the mail. You have 10 days to review it. That's plenty of time to make sure this is right for you.

(3) If you are not completely satisfied, simply write "cancel" on the Certificate and mail it back to AAA Life Insurance Company. Any premiums you have paid will be promptly refunded in full or credited to your account.

So, you have NO RISK in mailing your application today. Better yet: you ensure group rates and privileges, **and give yourself the option to say "Yes" or "No" later.**

It's a wonderful opportunity for you and your family. Do take it. Many other AAA families have already done so, and there's no reason why yours should be any less protected.

Sincerely,

Joseph F. Schvach
Manager
Chicago Motor Club Insurance Agency

P.S. The Deadline for Preferred Enrollment is Friday, October 12, 2001. Please mail your application before then. Thank you.

*Provided the Master Policy remains in force and premiums are paid when due.

EXHIBIT 11.6

The Chicago Motor Club offers reasons why you should purchase its services.
www.autoclubgroup.com/chicago/

- Direct comparison by a low-share brand to a high-share brand increases the attention on the part of receivers and increases the purchase intention of the low-share brand.
- Direct comparison by a high-share brand to a low-share brand does not attract additional attention and increases awareness of the low-share brand.
- Direct comparison is more effective if members of the target audience have not demonstrated clear brand preference in their product choices.[5]

What do you think of the ads in Exhibits 11.8 and 11.9?

Strategic Implications of Comparison Ads

- 👍 Can help a very low-share brand.
- 👍 Can be very resistant to competitive advertising and promotion.
- 👎 Significant legal/regulatory exposure.
- 👎 Not done much outside the United States; in much of the world, they are either outlawed, not done by mutual agreement, or simply considered in such poor taste as to never be done.
- 👎 These ads face a fairly cynical and sophisticated audience. They are often rejected by consumers as misleading and dishonest.
- 👎 The firm sponsoring a comparative ad is sometimes perceived as less trustworthy.

5. Conclusions in this list are drawn from William R. Swinyard, "The Interaction between Comparative Advertising and Copy Claim Variation," *Journal of Marketing Research* 18 (May 1981), 175–186; Cornelia Pechmann and David Stewart, "The Effects of Comparative Advertising on Attention, Memory, and Purchase Intentions," *Journal of Consumer Research* (September 1990), 180–191; and Sanjay Petruvu and Kenneth R. Lord, "Comparative and Noncomparative Advertising: Attitudinal Effects under Cognitive and Affective Involvement Conditions," *Journal of Advertising* (June 1994), 77–90.

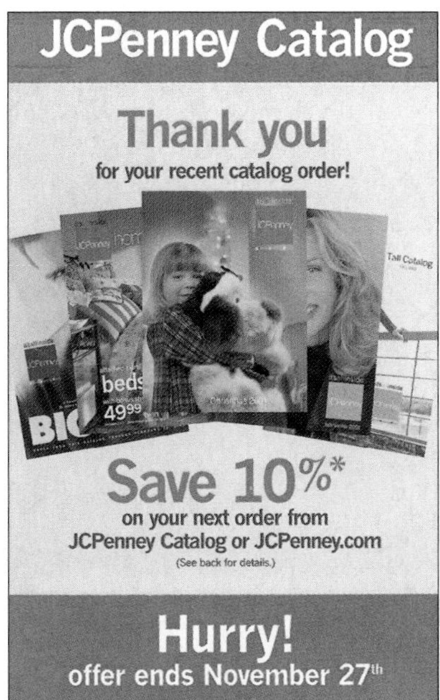

EXHIBIT 11.7

Hurry! You better act fast to get the benefits of JCPenney. This is a hard sell, and pretty typical of today's style. Hard sell used to be harder. www.jcpenney.com

EXHIBIT 11.8

A straight comparison ad. www.castrolusa.com

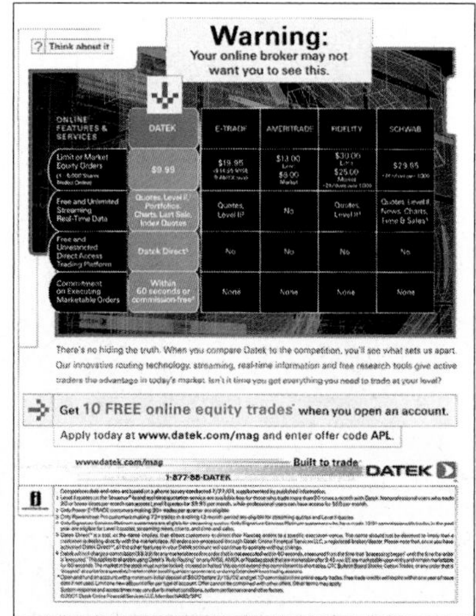

EXHIBIT 11.9

Let's see, I think Datek looks best. This is an example of straight comparison advertising. www.datek.com

- Ads are sometimes evaluated as more offensive and less interesting than non-comparative ads.
- Can tarnish your brand by association to a questionable advertising practice.

Method D: Testimonials. A frequently used message tactic is to have a spokesperson who champions the brand in an advertisement, rather than simply providing information. When an advocacy position is taken by a spokesperson in an advertisement, this is known as a **testimonial.** The value of the testimonial lies in the authoritative presentation of a brand's attributes and benefits by the spokesperson. There are three basic versions of the testimonial message tactic.

The most conspicuous version is the *celebrity testimonial.* Sports stars such as Michael Jordan (McDonald's) and Arnold Palmer (Pennzoil, Cadillac) are favorites of advertisers. Supermodels such as Cindy Crawford (Pepsi) are also widely used. The belief is that a celebrity testimonial will increase an ad's ability to attract attention and produce a desire in receivers to emulate or imitate the celebrities they admire (Exhibit 11.10).

Whether this is really true or not, the fact remains that a list of top commercials is dominated by ads that feature celebrities.[6] Of course, there is the ever-present risk that a celebrity will fall from grace, as several have in recent years, and potentially damage the reputation of the brand for which he or she was once the champion.

Expert spokespeople for a brand are viewed by the target audience as having expert product knowledge. The GM Parts Service Division created an expert in Mr. Goodwrench, who was presented as a knowledgeable source of information. A spokesperson portrayed as a doctor, lawyer, scientist, gardener, or any other expert relevant to a brand is intended to increase the credibility of the message being transmitted. There

6. Kevin Goldman, "Year's Top Commercials Propelled by Star Power," *Wall Street Journal,* March 16, 1994, B1.

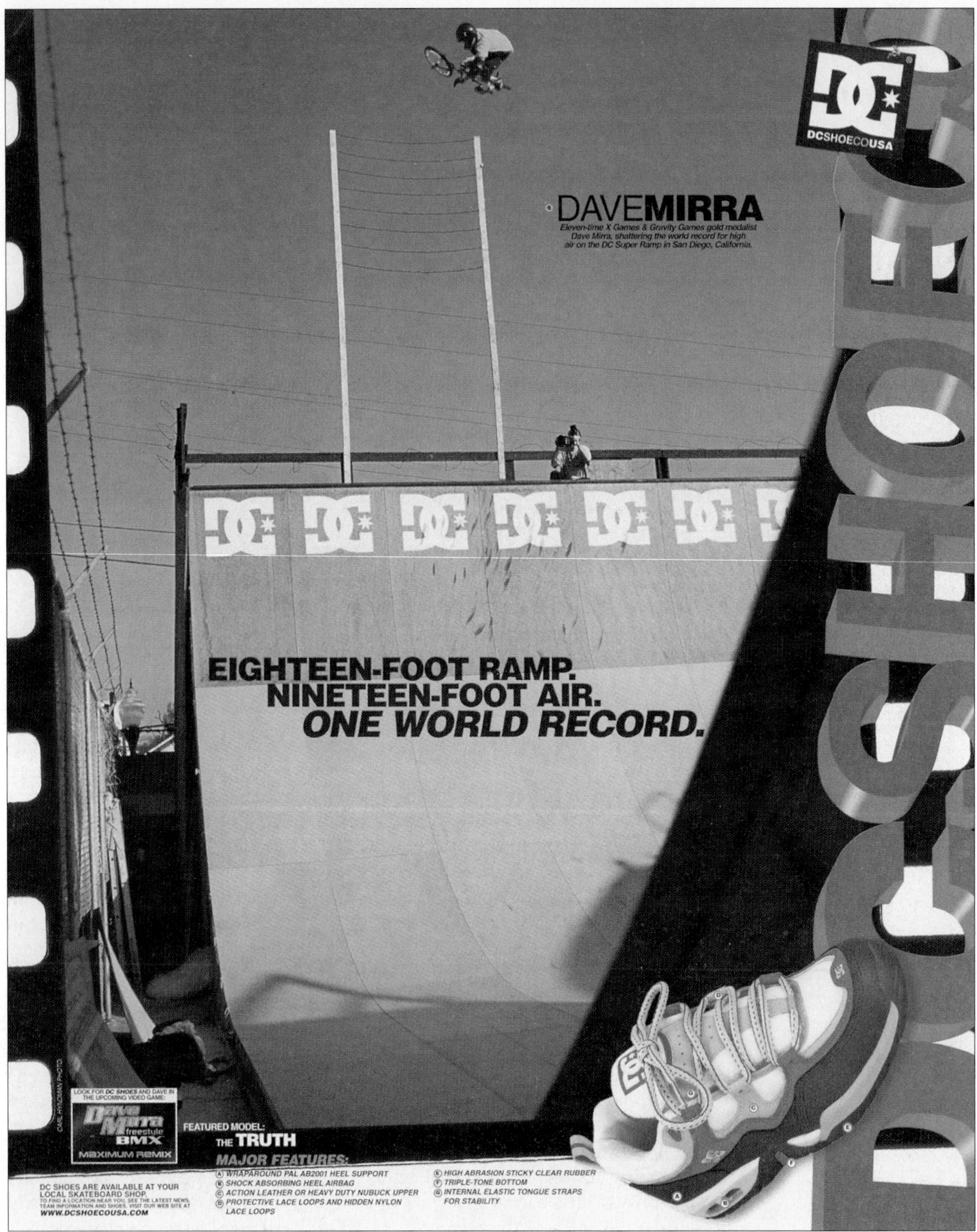

EXHIBIT 11.10

Dave Mirra is known as the Miracle Boy of freestyle BMX riding. What type of audience might find his testimonials persuasive?

EXHIBIT 11.11

This testimonial is done with facial expression, body attitude and "look." These days even testimonials don't have to have words. There is no doubt they are testifying. www.skechers.com

are also real experts. Advertising for the Club, a steering-wheel locking device that deters auto theft, uses police officers from several cities to demonstrate the effectiveness of the product. Some experts can also be celebrities. This is the case when Michael Jordan gives a testimonial for Nike basketball shoes.

There is also the *average-user testimonial.* Here, the spokesperson is not a celebrity or portrayed as an expert but rather as an average user speaking for the brand. The philosophy is that the target market can relate to this person. Solid theoretical support for this testimonial approach comes from reference group theory. An interpretation of reference group theory in this context suggests that consumers may rely on opinions or testimonials from people they consider similar to themselves, rather than on objective product information. Simply put, the consumer's logic in this situation is, "That person is similar to me and likes that brand; therefore, I will also like that brand." In theory, this sort of logic frees the receiver from having to scrutinize detailed product information by simply substituting the reference group information (Exhibit 11.11). Of course, in practice, the execution of this strategy is nowhere near that easy. Consumers are very sophisticated at detecting this attempt at persuasion. Evaluation of testimonial ads is usually done through focus groups, communication tests, and tracking studies that measure attitudes, beliefs, and preferences. Promotion efforts also use the testimonial approach, usually in a face-to-face setting after being recruited by a piece of direct mail or a phone solicitation.

Strategic Implications of Testimonial Advertising

- 👍 Very popular people can generate popularity for the brand.
- 👍 The link between star and brand gives "free" advertising to the brand every time consumers see the celebrity. Kobe slams one, some may think McDonald's.
- 👍 Can be good at breaking through clutter.
- 👎 Can seem very fake.
- 👎 Generally, poor memorability for who is promoting what.
- 👎 Can generate more popularity for the star than the brand.
- 👎 Celebrities, being human, can really screw up.

Method E: Demonstration. How close an electric razor shaves, how green a fertilizer makes a lawn, or how easy an exercise machine is to use are all product features that can be demonstrated by using a method known simply as demonstration. "Seeing is believing" is the motto of this school of advertising. When it's done well, the results are striking (Exhibit 11.12). Evaluation of demonstration ads is typically done through tracking studies that measure attitudes, beliefs, and preferences; focus groups and communication tests are also used.

Strategic Implications of Demonstration Ads

- 👍 Can create very retrievable memory.
- 👍 Can be used as social justification; helps the consumer defend his or her decision to buy.

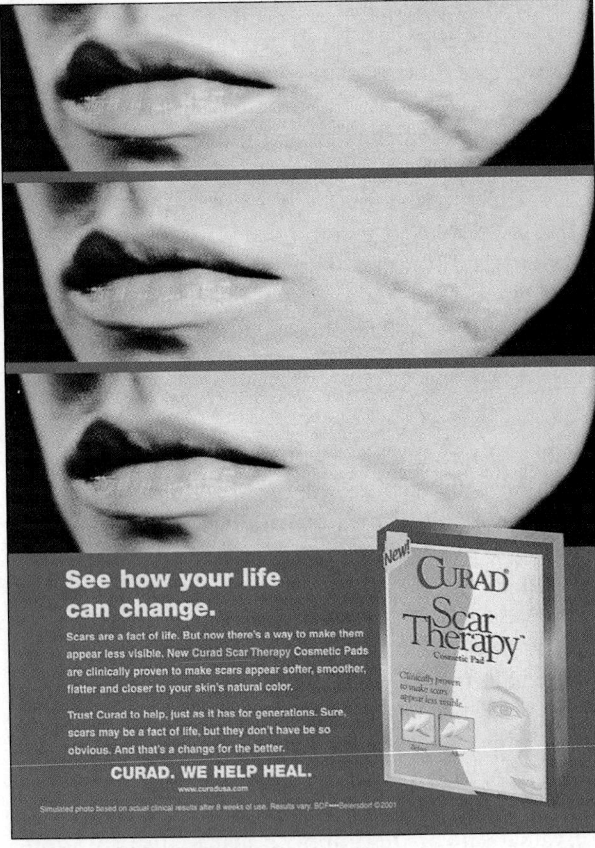

EXHIBIT 11.12

Straight demonstration of a product benefit by Curad.
www.curadusa.com

- Heavy regulatory/legal exposure.
- Faces a cynical, suspect audience.

Method F: Advertorials. An **advertorial** is a special advertising section designed to look like the print publication in which it appears. Advertorials are so named because they have the look of the editorial content of a magazine or newspaper but really represent a long and involved advertisement for a firm and its product or service. *The Wall Street Journal, Redbook, New York Magazine,* and *USA Today* have all carried advertorials. (See Exhibit 11.13.) The potential effectiveness of this technique lies with the increased credibility that comes from the look and length of the advertisement. These features have, however, raised controversy. Some critics believe that most readers aren't even aware they're reading an advertisement because of the similarity in appearance to the publication.[7] Evaluation of advertorials is typically done through communication tests, focus groups, tracking studies, and direct response measurement such as calls to 800 numbers.

Strategic Implications of Advertorials

- Can be very involving, due to their assumed identity as editorials or news.
- Less counterarguing as long as the "deception" works.
- A technique based on deception cannot be good in the long run for the brand.
- Once "busted," the advertiser is typically seen in a very negative light.

Method G: Infomercials. With the **infomercial,** an advertiser buys from 5 to 60 minutes of television time and runs a documentary/information/entertainment program that is really an extended advertisement. An infomercial is the television equivalent of an advertorial. Real estate investment programs, weight-loss and fitness products, motivational programs, and cookware have dominated the infomercial format. A 30-minute infomercial can cost from $50,000 to a few million to put on the air. The program usually has a host who provides information about a product and typically brings on guests to give testimonials about how successful they have been using the featured product. Most infomercials run on cable stations, although networks have sold early-morning and late-night time as well. Recently, big firms have used infomercials. Philips Electronics has had great success with a 30-minute adventure-like infomercial for its compact disc interactive (CD-I) player. Philips spent nearly $20 million to produce and buy primetime media for the infomercial but contends the infomercial has much more impact than the print advertising it replaced.[8] Apple Computer also ran a 30-minute infomercial as part of the advertising campaign to introduce its new lower-priced Macintosh, the Performa. The ad was targeted to families looking to buy their first computer and was a huge success. The infomercial generated four times as many telephone inquiries as Apple anticipated.[9]

7. Cynthia Crossen, "Proliferation of Advertorials Blurs Distinction between News and Ads," *Wall Street Journal,* April 21, 1988, 33.
8. Kevin Goldman, "Philips Infomercial Does Its Thing in Popular TV Watching Hours," *Wall Street Journal,* September 23, 1993, B6.
9. Kevin Goldman, "Apple Plans Infomercial Aimed at Families," *Wall Street Journal,* January 4, 1994, B3; Jacqueline M. Graves, "The Fortune 500 Opt for Infomercials," *Fortune,* March 6, 1995, 20.

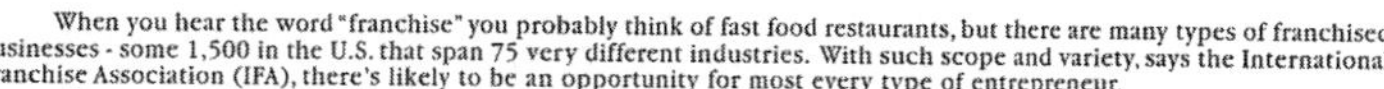
ADVERTISEMENT
THE NATION'S FRANCHISING FORUM
ADVERTISEMENT

FRANCHISING TODAY

BACK TO BASICS: WHAT IS FRANCHISING?

IFA INTERNATIONAL FRANCHISE ASSOCIATION

When you hear the word "franchise" you probably think of fast food restaurants, but there are many types of franchised businesses - some 1,500 in the U.S. that span 75 very different industries. With such scope and variety, says the International Franchise Association (IFA), there's likely to be an opportunity for most every type of entrepreneur.

For example, homes are bought and sold through franchised real estate companies. Those homes can be cleaned, painted and remodeled through franchises. We can find jobs, have our taxes prepared and even shed unwanted pounds - all through franchised businesses.

Franchising is a method of marketing a product or service. It offers individuals the freedom to operate their own small business, while relying on the expertise of the franchise system. Both the franchisor's and franchisee's obligations are spelled out in the franchise contract, which should be reviewed very carefully with an attorney.

Learn more about the basics of franchising at IFA's Web site, www.franchise.org.

Franchising Takes Us to the Cleaners

by Nancy Rathbun Scott

It was an accident. That's how we remember the event that gave birth to the dry cleaning industry. A Frenchman, Jolly Belin, made the mistake of spilling kerosene on a garment that had already been soiled. He discovered that the kerosene removed the stain. Belin continued with a series of experiments, and in the 1840's, opened the first dry cleaning establishment, in Paris.

Today it is no accident that franchisees invest in the dry cleaning industry—spills and stains still happen. Even when they don't, there's never a shortage of dirty clothes, many of them labeled "Dry Clean Only."

No one is completely sure how many dry cleaners there are in the United States. Maybe that's because, as the International Fabricare Institute (IFI) puts it, drycleaning is one of the largest industry sectors still considered a "Mom and Pop" small business.

"Although the sizes of dry cleaners vary, most commercial dry cleaners are single facility, family-owned operations, with an average of five employees working at a plant," says IFI. But are they profitable? That depends, says IFI. "Commercial drycleaning is not a high-profit business, with the median annual revenues below $250,000." But there are ways to raise the profit level. "Since one of the keys to being a successful dry cleaner is service and proximity to your customer base, dry cleaners are oftentimes integral players in their respective communities."

Statistics from BizStats.com for 2001 cite 59,250 dry cleaning proprietorships (not including dry cleaning services operating as corporations). The International Fabricare Institute (IFI) puts the figure much lower at about 30,000 establishments.

In 1997, the national sales volume for retail dry cleaners was estimated at 7 billion, according to the IFI, who says those receipts have fallen in recent years due in large part to the proliferation of launderable fabrics and more opportunities for casual dress. Still, three-fourths of the industry experiences sales between $200,000 and $300,000 per year and employs three to five workers. In total, according to the Bureau of Labor, some 217,350 people are employed as laundry and dry-cleaning workers.

Sheer dollar-value aside, dry cleaning has some recession-proof characteristics. Today's two-career families need more convenient service, and the dry cleaning industry offers them an easy answer. These families have more disposable income to spend on garment care, and they're willing to spend it because of the significant investment in their wardrobes. Natural fibers such as wools, silks, cottons, and linens in both career and recreational fashions have returned in popularity. All of these fabrics require professional dry cleaning for proper care.

Furthermore, dry cleaning is a cash and carry business that does not require investing funds in extensive inventory.

Start Ups See the Value in Pick Ups

Many investors are finding that one of the more effective ways to exploit the industry is by using a franchise concept. Ken Langone, for instance, who made his fame as a co-founder of Home Depot, has now turned his attention to franchising, raising $50 million for Micell Technologies Inc. Micell was founded in 1995 by University of North Carolina-Chapel Hill professor, Joseph M. DeSimone, and two of his students, who developed a cleaning system based on carbon dioxide technology.

The company is now rolling out a chain called Hangers Cleaners, which claims to be the "first, and only proven, environmentally responsible dry cleaning brand and franchise, cleaning clothes and other fabric items using a carbon dioxide-based technology that's safe for the consumer, gentle on fabric and non-polluting." Micell received the R&D 100 Award in 1998, being recognized as one of the 100 most technologically significant new products and processes of the year.

Other new concepts focus less on the cleaning process and more on technology to improve efficiency. PurpleTie automates the dry cleaning process by having customers use the Web (or telephone) to order home pickup of dirty clothes. The clothes are transported to a central facility, where they are cleaned and returned to the customer. Purple Tie plans to deploy delivery trucks to 25 of America's busiest cities by 2003. The company projects revenues of $10 million this year and forecasts that the San Francisco operation will be cash-flow positive early this year.

Even these projections are small next to Zoots, another upstart. Zoots hit $30 million in sales last year and expects to grow to $60 million in 2001, only its third year of operation. Like PurpleTie, Zoots builds much of its business plan around an online operation, however it has 41 stores in six states.

The convenience factor doesn't always mean building a concept around the web. 1-800-DryClean offers dry cleaning pickup and delivery service. A part of the Service Brands International network, which is best known for Molly Maids and Mr. Handyman, 1-800-DryClean is guided by a team with 13 years of working experience in the dry cleaning business. The experience has helped the network grow to 10 franchised units in its first year of operation.

If you want proof that pickup-and-deliver works over the long haul, consider Pressed4Time. The mobile dry cleaning franchisor has been in business since 1987 and franchising since 1990. In that time, they have built a system of 146 franchised units that serve 50,000 customers each week. As homebased entrepreneurs, Pressed4Time owners carry an inventory that consists of a desk, a computer with Internet access, a quality printer, a calculator, a telephone, an answering machine, and a van or mini-van.

Drop-Off Concept Still Holds On

If convenience sells, Ray Oldham knows that pairing it with service is also a business no-brainer. The former Pittsburgh Steeler Superbowl champion spent three years researching and deciding to "franchise the dry cleaning industry and bring a whole new concept to an industry that has a 150-year proven track record for stability."

But service is where Oldham's Champion Cleaners puts most of its efforts. Shirts are fitted with plastic collar butterflies to keep the collar upright and in prime condition. French cuffs are folded back and plastic clips inserted. VIP bags have a distinctive look. Customers pick up dry cleaning without ever leaving their automobiles. Champion offers drive-thru curb service and same day service.

Even though new concepts offer pick up and drive thru, the traditional dry cleaning concept still works. In 25 years, Dryclean USA has grown to be one of the largest and most recognizable names in the dry cleaning industry. Dryclean USA has more than 400 locations around the United States, the Caribbean, Central and South America.

With its years of experience, Dryclean USA has developed its own proprietary line of dry cleaning equipment that uses non-hazardous, environmentally friendly cleaning products. To keep pace with technological changes, the franchisor has developed an Internet strategy that offers customers a wide range of services beyond the scope of laundry, dry cleaning and garment care. The site also serves as a source of interactive information and solutions to clothing and textile problems.

Perhaps one of the most recognizable names in the dry cleaning industry is One Hour Martinizing. The company is the world's largest dry cleaning franchise, with 763 stores in 17 countries. In business since 1949, Martinizing was a franchising pioneer. In the early 1900's, cleaning plants were located far from the inner city because the chemicals used were flammable. Most stores operated as pick-up stations where customers dropped off their clothing and returned to claim their orders as much as a week to 10 days later. When a new nonflammable solvent was discovered in the late 1940's, Henry Martin, a New York chemist, recognized that this new development would allow for smaller, full service dry cleaning plants that could offer quick service, cost effectively. With this idea, the first Martinizing store opened in New York City in July 1949. Fifty years later, the same concept still works. Why? Customers still crave convenience. The companies who provide it last for decades. That is no accident.

EXHIBIT 11.13

Ads like this are designed to blur the line between advertising and "editorial" or news. www.franchise.org

Not all advertisers have had such good success with infomercials. After spending nearly half a million dollars to produce and air a 30-minute infomercial promoting a Broadway show, the producers pulled the ad after three weeks. The toll-free number to order tickets drew an average of only 14 calls each time the ad ran.[10] However, infomercials can have tremendous sales impact. Many leading infomercials rely on celebrity spokespeople as part of the program. Evaluation of infomercials is typically done through tracking studies that measure attitudes, beliefs, and preferences, as well as calls to 800 numbers. Infomercials are often used in an integrated communications effort with promotional efforts. The infomercial sucks you in; mail and telephone promotions follow up; and then some type of sales promotion effort, such as a "free" trip to hear more about this amazing offer, concludes the approach.

Strategic Implications of Infomercials

- 👍 Long format gives advertisers plenty of time to make their case.
- 👎 The genre of ads has a fairly negative public image, which doesn't help build credibility or trust in the advertised brand.

Objective #4: Instill Brand Preference. Advertisers want consumers to like (and better yet, prefer) their brand. Liking gets you closer to preference than does not liking. So, liking the brand is good. Liking is different from awareness or top-of-mind recall. Liking is measured in attitudes and is expressed as a feeling. There are many approaches

10. Kevin Goldman, "Broadway Hopeful Flops with Debut of Infomercial," *Wall Street Journal,* April 1992, 1.

to getting the consumer to like one's brand. Let's look at some of the general approaches; most specific executions are finer distinctions within these more general ones.

Method A: Feel-Good Ads. These ads are supposed to work through affective (feeling) association. They are supposed to link the good feeling elicited by the ad with the brand: You like the ad, you like the brand. While the actual theory and mechanics of this seemingly simple reflex are more complex than you might think (and more controversial), the basic idea is that by creating ads with positive feelings, advertisers will lead consumers to associate those positive feelings with the advertised brand, leading to a higher probability of purchase. As Steve Sweitzer of the Gal Riney and Partners advertising agency said:

> *[C]onsumers want to do business with companies they* LIKE. *If they* LIKE *us, they just may give us a try at the store. What a concept. Sometimes just being liked is a strategy.*[11]

Of course, getting from liking the ad, to liking the brand is one big jump. Still many try, typically by making a "feel good" ad and assuming that the feeling will find its way to the consumers attitude toward the brand. The evidence on how well this method works is mixed and equivocal. It may be that positive feelings are transferred to the brand, or it could be that they actually interfere with remembering the message or the brand name. Liking the ad doesn't necessarily mean liking the brand. But message strategy development is a game of probability, and liking may, more times than not, lead to a higher probability of purchase. There are certainly practitioners who continue to believe in the method's intuitive appeal.

The exact mechanisms by which this liking linkage occurs are debated or unknown. We believe that ultimately what creates a good feeling is the product of interpretation on the part of the audience member. This interpretation may be informed by fairly simple associations or by more complex and elaborated thoughts. The interpretive processes of humans are, however, very sophisticated. Humans can make sense of and otherwise "get"

CREATIVITY

Iconic Ads Better Second Time Around?

Advertisers are beginning to dust off old successful campaigns and send them back out to war. Life Cereal has resurrected the actual "Mikey" spot from decades ago, Procter & Gamble recently brought "Mr. Whipple" out of his 15-year retirement, and now Isuzu has rehashed its Joe Isuzu campaign with new spots focused around the sleazy but comical salesman. "Everybody is looking through their drawers and archives to see if they have anything that resonates with consumers," says Michael Markowitz, president of ad development firm Michael Markowitz & Associates.

While Joe is back due to popular demand from Isuzu dealers, the development signifies a new trend in this lagging economy: Rehash old successes and hope for the best. The original campaign was definitely a hit, and fans ranging from everyday consumers to academics have requested to see more Joe commercials—even *Advertising Age* recently named the original campaign on its list of Top 100 Advertising Campaigns. Recycled ad characters are a cost-effective way to connect with consumers during tough economic times. If executed effectively, vintage ad icons create in audiences a pleasant and memorable association with the product. Advertisers hope the good feelings elicited years ago will be rekindled even more powerfully a second time around. If you liked the ads years ago, you might like them even more today as they evoke nostalgic memories of happier, simpler times.

Isuzu's strategy aims to make the SUV brand fun again. However, while recycling old campaigns may be cost-effective for advertisers, it ignores the reality that what effectively reached one demographic 10 years ago will not similarly reach the same audience today. In fact, a *USA Today* Ad Track survey found that only 16 percent of respondents liked the new Joe ads a lot, well below the average 22 percent. Case in point: The Ad Track survey measured a mild response to the Joe ads that were heavily successful in the mid-eighties. The theme of the ultimate slippery salesman—a corporate strategy of self-deprecation that may have seemed fresh in the greedy eighties—is rather commonplace and ho-hum among today's more media-savvy consumers.

Even if the nostalgic rehashing of ad icons turns out to flop, one has to give some respect to Life Cereal for not even bothering to re-enact the Mikey commercials—they flat out re-aired them.

Source: Michael McCarthy, "Marketers Bring Back Vintage Ad Icons," *USA Today*, www.usatoday.com, accessed September 28, 2001.

11. The One Club e-mail discussion, July 27, 1997, as published in *One: A Magazine for Members of the One Club for Art and Copy*, vol. 1, no. 2 (Fall 1997), 18.

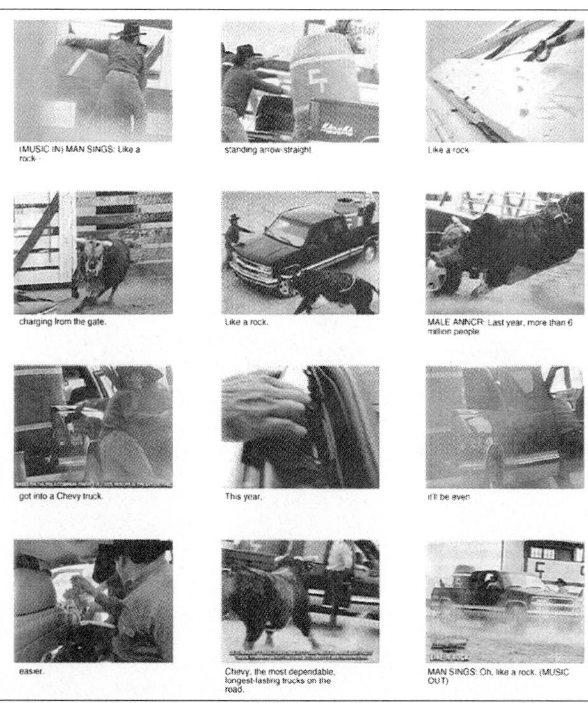

EXHIBIT 11.14

Chevy's feel-good "Like a Rock" truck ads create positive association for working-class Americans. www.chevrolet.com

complex advertising texts loaded with symbols, innuendo, jokes, and so on, in a split second. While we don't understand why some feel-good ads work and others do not, we do know that paying greater attention to the social context of likely target consumers, and the manner in which consumers "read" ads, is critical. Some positive attitudes toward the ad don't seem to result in positive attitudes toward the brand because they are not "read" for that purpose, or, it could be that consumers easily separate their feelings for the ad and their feelings for the brand. If the theory was as simple (and consumers as simple minded) as some believe, seeing *The Producers* would make you like Nazi's more. Clearly, not the intent, not the case. You may love ads for Miller Lite, but be a Budweiser drinker. You may think, "Nice ads—wish they made a good beer." Or you might love the new iMac ads, but don't ever, ever, ever want to be an Apple owner. Still, other feel-good advertising campaigns work. For example, the long-running and apparently successful Chevrolet truck television campaign "Like a Rock," shown in Exhibit 11.14, features the music of Bob Seger and scenes of hardworking, patriotic Americans and their families. It seems to work for a lot of consumers. The good feeling it produces may be the result of widely shared patriotic associations and the celebration of working-class Americans evoked by the advertising. It may map easily onto the brand because sophisticated consumers know that the brand and the advertising are symbolically consistent in theory and practice . . . and consumer experience.

Delta Air Lines could show how often its planes depart and arrive on schedule. Instead, it shows the happy reunion of family members and successful business meetings, which create a much richer message, a wider field of shared meanings. The emotions become the product attribute and are linked to the brand—or does the text simply resonate with common lived experience? Hopefully, the consumer makes the desired linkage. Consider Kodak's highly successful print and television campaign that highlighted the "Memories of Our Lives" with powerful scenes: a son coming home from the military just in time for Christmas dinner, and a father's reception dance with his newly married daughter. Here, Kodak makes it clear that it is in the memory business, and Kodak memories are good memories. Good feelings are a desirable product attribute. Back in the mid-1980s every advertiser around was scrambling to understand consumer emotions. Agencies were promising results because of their superior understanding of human emotion. Like most trends, it ran its course, and now these types of ads, while still popular, are far less common. In Exhibit 11.15, Chevy attempts to evoke warm feelings associated with the relationship between a father and son. Evaluation of feel-good ads is typically done by measuring attitude change via pre/post-exposure tests, tracking studies, theater dial-turning tests, focus groups, communication tests, and qualitative field studies.

Strategic Implications of Feel-Good Advertising

- 👍 Can be very effective short term.
- 👍 Eager creatives.
- 👎 Can have wearout problems.
- 👎 Audience reaction difficult to reliably predict for the long term.
- 👎 Only moderate success in copy-testing.

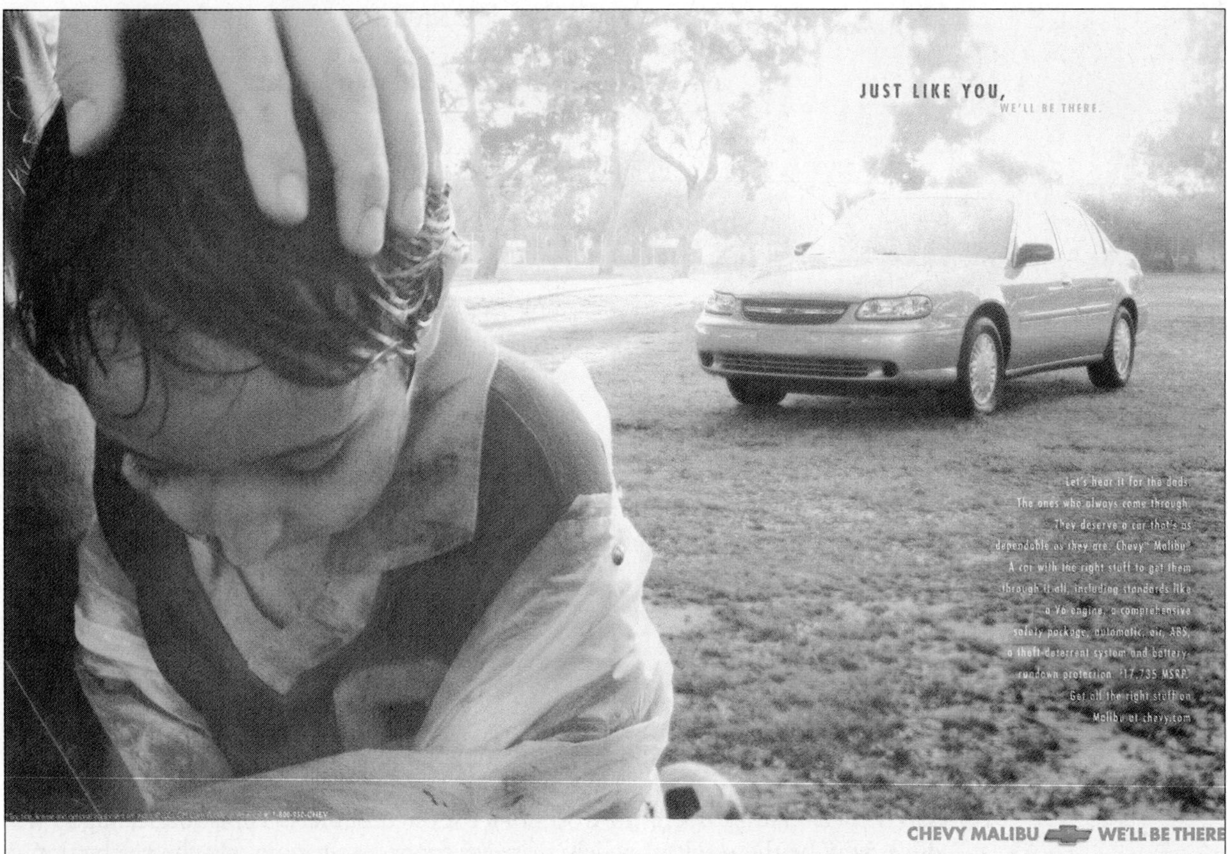

EXHIBIT 11.15

This ad is supposed to make you feel good, and feel good about Chevy Malibu.
www.chevrolet.com/malibu/

- Gets lost in high-clutter media environment.
- Affect may interfere with memory.
- Complex interpretive task.
- Evidence of effectiveness is equivocal.
- Problems with evaluation, particularly issue of test validity.
- Mechanism poorly understood.
- Must be entirely consistent with brand symbolism and real consumer experience.

Method B: Humor Ads. The goal of a humor ad is pretty much the same as that of other feel-good ads, but humor is a bit of a different animal altogether. The goal of humor in advertising is to create in the receiver a pleasant and memorable association with the product. Recent advertising campaigns as diverse as those for Miller Lite beer ("Can Your Beer Do This?"), Magnavox consumer electronics (the disappearing remote control), and Little Caesar's ("Pizza-Pizza") have all successfully used humor as the primary message theme. But research suggests that the positive impact of humor is not as strong as the intuitive appeal of the approach. Quite simply, humorous versions of advertisements often do not prove to be more persuasive than nonhumorous versions of the same ad—or research is simply inadequate to detect the difference.

How many times have you been talking to friends about your favorite ads, and you say something like, "Remember the one where the guy knocks over the drink, and then says. . . ." Everybody laughs, and then maybe someone says something like, "I can't remember who it's for, but what a great ad." Wrong; this is not a great ad. You remember the gag, but not the brand. Not good. How come with some other funny ads you can recall the brand? The difference may be that ads in which the payoff for the humor is an integral part of the message strategy better ensure the memory link between humor and brand. If the ad is merely funny and doesn't link the joke (or the punch line) to the brand name, then the advertiser may have bought some very expensive laughs. Hint: Clients rarely consider this funny.

An example of an explicitly linked payoff is the Bud Light "Give Me a Light" campaign of the early 1980s. "Miller Lite" was quickly becoming the generic term for light beer. To do something about this, Bud Light came up with the series of "Give Me a Light" ads to remind light beer drinkers that they had to be a little more specific in what they were ordering. The ads showed customers ordering "a light" and getting spotlights, landing lights, searchlights, and other types of lights. The customer would then say, "No, a Bud Light." The ads not only were funny, but also made the point perfectly: Say "Bud Light," not just "a light," when ordering a beer. In addition, the message allowed thousands of customers and would-be comedians in bars and restaurants to repeat the line in person, which amounted to a lot of free advertising. The campaign by then Needham, Harper and Steers-Chicago (now DDB Needham-Chicago) was a huge success.

Miller Brewing is an advertiser that has both reaped the benefits of humor in its recent ad campaigns and suffered from its risks. The original "Less Filling—Tastes Great" campaigns that pitted famous retired athletes against one another rose to great prominence in the late 1970s and through nearly the entire decade of the 1980s. Sports fans could hardly wait for the next installment of the campaign. But the campaign, while highly successful overall, ultimately ran into the problem of wearout. The brand began to lose market share and is still struggling to regain past glories.

Parody and self-parody are also forms of humor advertising. The 7-UP taste-test ad, the classic VW ads of the 1960s, and the unforgettable Joe Isuzu are great examples of having some fun with advertising in general. (See Exhibit 11.16.) Evaluation of humor ads is typically done through pre/post-exposure tests; dial-turning attitude tests; tracking studies that measure attitudes, beliefs, and preferences; communication tests; and focus groups.

Strategic Implications of Humor Advertising

- 👍 If the joke is integral to the copy platform, can be very effective short term.
- 👍 Very eager creatives.
- 👎 Humorous messages may adversely affect comprehension.
- 👎 Humorous messages can wear out as quickly as after three exposures, leaving no one laughing, especially the advertiser.[12]
- 👎 Humorous messages may attract attention but may not increase the effectiveness or persuasive impact of the advertisement.
- 👎 Can have wearout problems.
- 👎 Can be very expensive entertainment.

Method C: Sexual Appeal Ads. Because they are directed toward humans, ads tend to focus on sex from time to time. Not a big surprise. But does sex sell? In a literal sense, the answer is no, because nothing, not even sex, *makes* someone buy something. However, sexual appeals are attention getting and occasionally arousing, which may affect how consumers feel about a product. The advertiser is trying to get attention and link some degree of sexual arousal to the brand. Some believe in a type of classical conditioning involving sex in ads. Evidence for the effect is mixed at best. Like all other interpretation of ads by humans, context is extremely important in sexual-appeal messages. Knowing just what constitutes sex appeal is not easy. Is it showing skin? How much skin? What's the difference between the celebration of a beautiful body and its objectification? Motive? Politics? Who says?

12. This claim is made by Video Storyboards Tests, based on its extensive research of humor ads, and cited in Kevin Goldman, "Ever Hear the One about the Funny Ad?," *Wall Street Journal,* November 2, 1993, B11.

EXHIBIT 11.16

There is quite a bit of parody in this ad.
www.tgifridays.com

BOY:	Dan Patrick? At TGI Friday's? Can I have your autograph, please?
DAN:	Sure, buddy.
BOY:	Thanks, Mr. Patrick.
DAN:	Uh-huh. Don't mention it.
SUPER:	In here, it's always Friday.

MERIT AWARD: Consumer Television :20 and Under: Single
ART DIRECTOR: Manuel Moreno
WRITER: Mike Fiddleman
AGENCY PRODUCER: Harvey Lewis
PRODUCTION COMPANY: Five Union Square Productions
DIRECTOR: Tom Schiller
CLIENT: TGI Friday's
AGENCY: Publicis/Dallas
ID 00 0672A

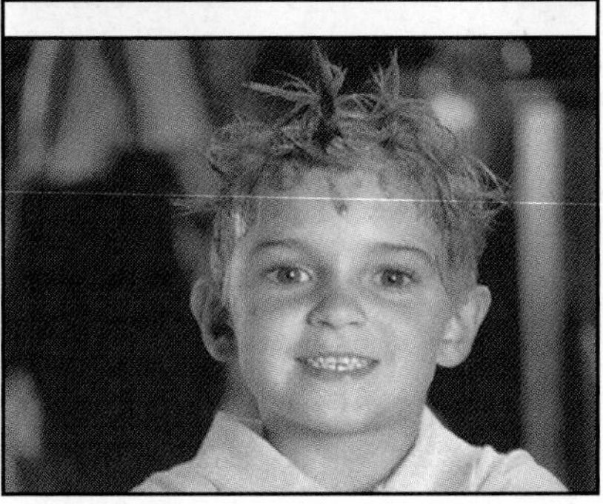

Can you use sex to help create a brand image? Sure you can. Calvin Klein and many other advertisers have used sexual imagery successfully to mold brand image. But these are for products such as clothes and perfumes, which emphasize how one looks, feels, and smells. Does the same appeal work as well for cars, telephones, computer peripherals, or file cabinets? How about breakfast cereals? In general, no. But because humans are complex and messy creatures, we cannot say that sex-appeal ads never work in such categories. Sometimes they do. In 1993, the print ads rated most successful in *Starch Tested Copy* were *ads using muted sexual appeal*[13] (see Exhibit 11.17). The ads shown in Exhibit 11.18 use a sexual-appeal message to one degree or another. How effective do you think these ads are in fulfilling the objective of instilling brand preference? Are they gratuitous? Are they on target strategically? In which of these is the sex appeal relevant, appropriate, distracting, sexist, demeaning, fun, innocent, playful, or good advertising? What do you think? Evaluation of sex-appeal ads is typically done through communication tests, focus groups, pre/post-exposure tests, and tracking studies that measure attitudes, beliefs, and preferences. Sex appeals are certainly used in all sorts of promotional efforts: remember wet T-shirt contests? But what is sexy or constitutes a sex appeal seems to vary widely according to audience members' gender, appropriateness for the product or service category, and so on. What do you think of these ads? There is more discussion of

13. Leah Richard, "Basic Approach in Ads Looks Simply Superior," *Advertising Age,* October 10, 1994, 30.

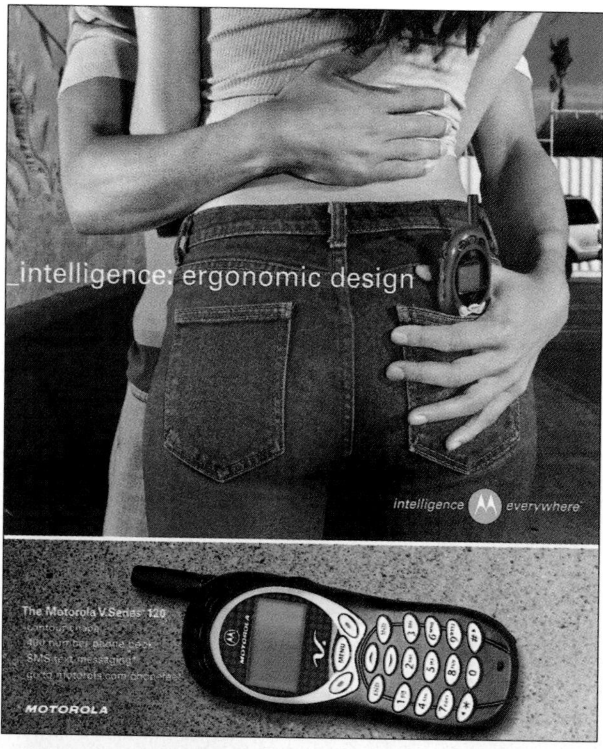

EXHIBIT 11.17

Historically, muted sex ads have scored well in recall tests. www.motorola.com/phonefeel/

sex in advertising than just about any other topic. So look at these and think about what is good, bad, effective, ineffective, OK, not OK, . . . and why. Talk about which of these ads are good advertising, gratuitous advertising, demeaning, appropriate, and so on. You will be engaging in the same debate that advertising professionals do all the time. It's good training.

> *One of the biggest problems that all agencies have is the headache of censorship. There is simply no reason to it. Censorship, any kind of censorship, is pure whim and fancy. It's one guy's idea of what is right for him. It's based on everything arbitrary. . . . There's a classic Lenny Bruce bit. He's doing a father talking to his son while they're both watching a pornographic film. Bruce says, "Son, I can't let you watch this. This is terrible and disgusting. Son, I'm going to have to cover your eyes now. That man is going to kiss that woman and they're going to make love and there's going to be pleasure and everything else and this is terrible, it's not for you until you are at least twenty-one. Instead son, I am going to take you to a nice war movie."*
>
> —Famous adman Jerry Della Femina[14]

No kidding. If you use sex in an ad, you will on occasion run into people who are sure that they know the sensibilities of the American public (and you) better than anyone else. They will take it upon themselves to tell you all the harms that can occur if you use sex. Some on the political right will tell you to avoid promoting promiscuity (and will threaten lost sales), and some on the political left will tell you they are protecting women from degrading images (and will threaten lost sales). You will run into these very morally certain and correct people at the client (occasionally), in the media (rarely), in government (too often), and in "self-regulating" review boards (like a plague). Usually the battle is about what would lose sales due to someone being offended. This is a reasonable concern on its face, but rarely (if ever) a very realistic one in practice. Just as consumers do not typically buy something (like a lawn mower) because of a poor fitting sex appeal, they will rarely refrain from buying it either.

Strategic Implications of Sexual-Appeal Advertising

- 👍 Higher attention levels.
- 👍 Higher arousal levels.
- 👎 Poor memorability due to interference from fear and anxiety at the time of exposure.
- 👎 Product-theme continuity is a necessity.
- 👎 Legal and regulatory exposure.
- 👎 Tremendous cultural differences in sexual norms makes transferability low.
- 👎 Political exposure; many political or quasi-political groups object to certain representations.

14. Jerry Della Femina, "Censorship," in *From Those Wonderful Folks Who Gave You Pearl Harbor: Front-Line Dispatches from the Advertising War,* with Charles Sopkin, ed. (New York: Simon and Schuster, 1970), 179, 190.

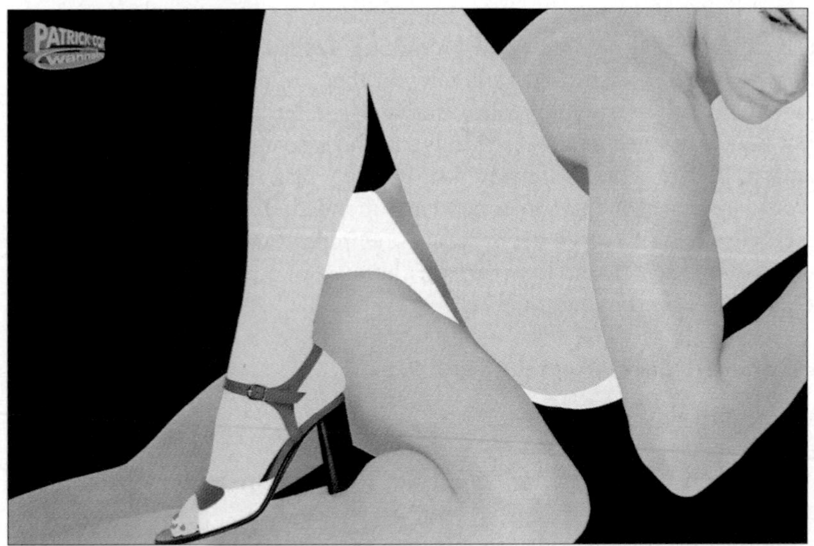

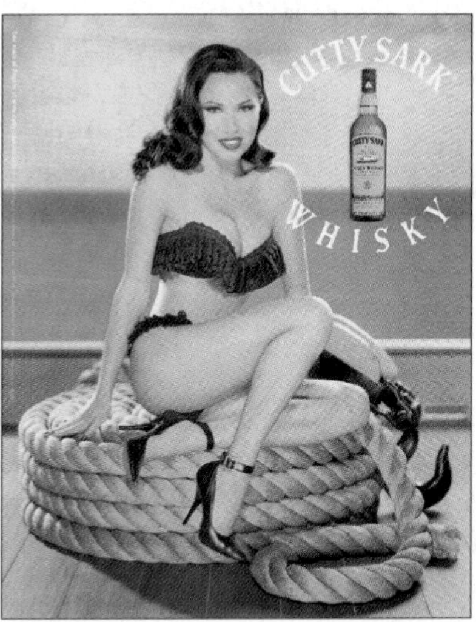

e-SIGHTINGS

EXHIBIT 11.18

Sex appeals are among the most common and the most controversial in advertising. But often the issues of "what is appropriate" and "why" get completely mixed up and confused. Here, we provide twelve current ads for your inspection and discussion. As future advertising professionals, which do you think are good, sound on-strategy advertising? Which do you think use sex inappropriately? Which are in poor taste? Which may do the brand more harm than good? What should women think and feel about these ads and the companies that sponsor them? How about men? Should there be more regulations, or not? What do you think? www.anheuser-busch.com, www.cutty-sark.co.uk, www.screenblast.com, www.michaelkors.com, *and* www.rockport.com

use me.
experience@screenblast.com
Watch me. Change me. Swap me. Use me anytime you like.
screenblast
SONY

VEGETARIAN BY DAY.
BACARDI BY NIGHT.
BACARDI
ESTD 1862

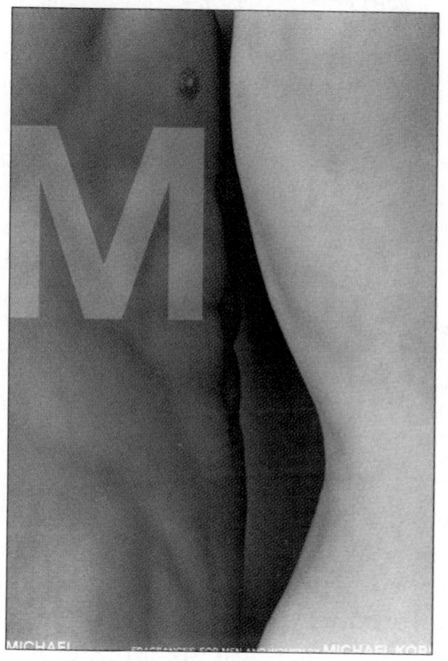
M

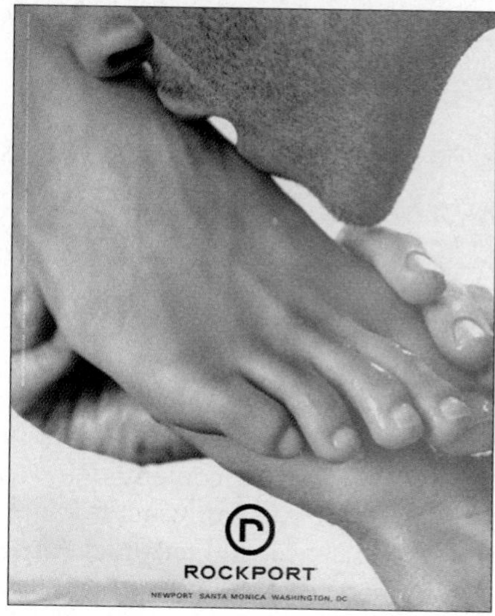
ROCKPORT
NEWPORT SANTA MONICA WASHINGTON, DC

Conker is a squirrel. Squirrels hunt for acorns.
Can you help Conker find some acorns?

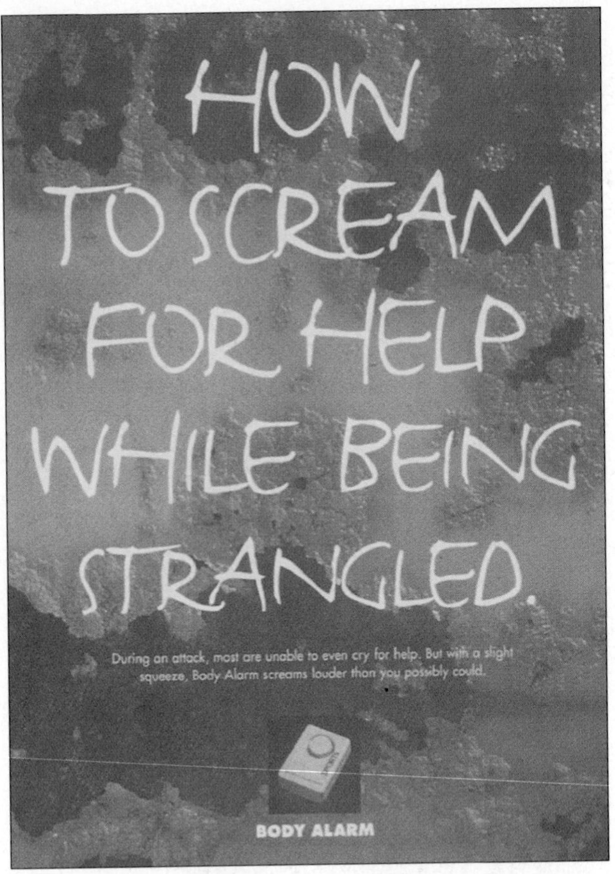

EXHIBIT 11.19

How does this ad for the Body Alarm embody the scare-the-consumer-into-action objective? Does this ad have ethical implications? How so?

Objective #5: Scare the Consumer into Action. Sometimes the idea is simply to scare the consumer. You've probably heard of fear; perhaps you've even experienced it yourself. Sometimes advertisers adopt the scare-the-consumer-into-action objective. Fear is an extraordinarily powerful emotion and may be used to get consumers to take some very important action. However, it must be used strategically and judiciously to work well, or even work at all.

Method: Fear-Appeal Ads. A fear appeal highlights the risk of harm or other negative consequences of not using the advertised brand or not taking some recommended action. The appeal is somewhere between reason-why and affect attachment. It's a little bit of thought coupled with a little bit of fear. Getting the balance right can be tricky. The intuitive belief about fear as a message tactic is that fear will motivate the receiver to buy a product that will reduce or eliminate the portrayed threat. For example, Radio Shack spent $6 million to run a series of ads showing a dimly lit unprotected house, including a peacefully sleeping child, as a way to raise concerns about the safety of the receiver's valuables, as well as his or her family. The campaign used the theme "If security is the question, we've got the answer." The ad closed with the Radio Shack logo and the National Crime Prevention Council slogan, "United against Crime."[15] Similarly, the ad in Exhibit 11.19 for Body Alarm cuts right to the chase: It capitalizes on fears of not being able to cry for help during a bodily attack.

The contemporary social environment has provided advertisers with an ideal context for using fear appeals. In an era of drive-by shootings, carjackings, gang violence, and terrorists Americans fear for their personal safety. Manufacturers of security products such as alarm and lighting security systems play on this fearful environment.[16] Other advertisers have recently tried fear as an appeal. One such advertiser, the Asthma Zero Mortality Coalition, urges people who have asthma to seek professional help and uses a fear appeal in its ad copy: "When those painful, strained breaths start coming, keep in mind that any one of them could easily be your last." The creator of the ad states, "Sometimes you have to scare people to save their lives."[17] In Exhibit 11.20, the makers of Migraleve invoke both words and a powerful image to remind migraine sufferers of the severe pain they may encounter as a result of not having Migraleve around.

Unfortunately, research does not offer such an absolute conclusion on the effectiveness of fear as a message tactic. Fear as a tactic in advertising has generated controversy. Social psychologists and marketing researchers have disagreed on the effectiveness of a fear-based appeal. Traditional research wisdom indicates that intense fear appeals actually short-circuit persuasion and result in a negative attitude toward the advertised brand.[18] It seems that receivers get so anxious about the fear-inducing

15. Jeffrey D. Zbar, "Fear!," *Advertising Age,* November 14, 1994, 18.
16. Ibid.
17. Emily DeNitto, "Healthcare Ads Employ Scare Tactics," *Advertising Age,* November 7, 1994, 12.
18. Irving L. Janis and Seymour Feshbach, "Effects of Fear Arousing Communication," *Journal of Abnormal Social Psychology* 48 (1953), 78–92.

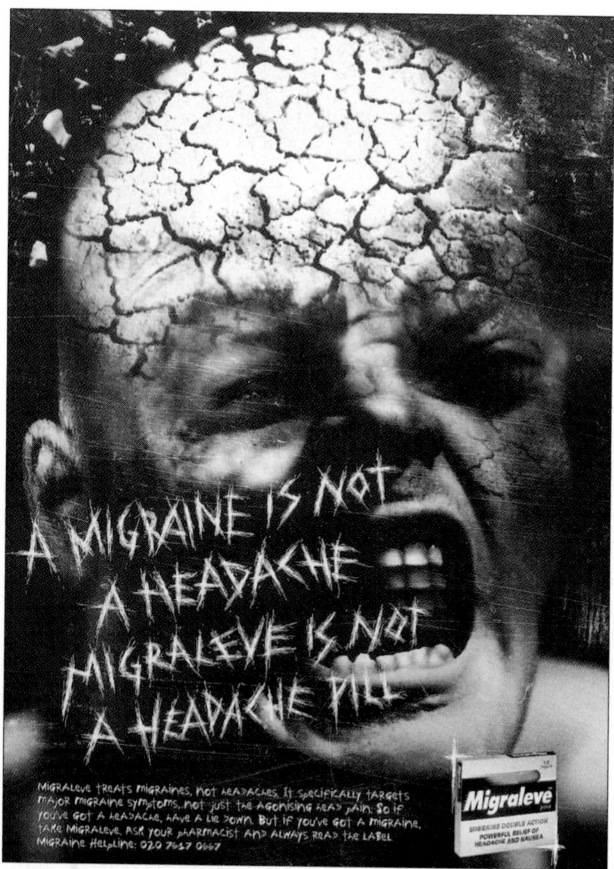

EXHIBIT 11.20

Scares us, how about you?

message that they focus on the fear and not on overcoming it. Other researchers argue that the tactic is beneficial to the advertiser.[19] More recent research on fear appeals suggests that the effectiveness of this method is difficult to evaluate. Still, it stands to reason that too much fear may occupy so much cognitive work space that the types of inferences needed to take action may never occur. It may also come down to how explicitly the suggestions for avoiding the harm are made. Using fear messages without offering a way out seems more likely to fail than does inducing moderate levels of fear coupled with suggesting an actionable behavior promised to reduce or eliminate the danger. Evaluation of fear-appeal ads is typically done through tracking studies that measure attitudes, beliefs, and preferences; pre/post-exposure tests; communication tests; and focus groups.

Strategic Implications of Fear-Appeal Advertising

- 👍 Highly compelling.
- 👍 Moderate level of fear is best (too low: insufficient arousal, motivation: result is poor memorability and attitude change. If the ad causes too much fear it becomes threatening, and the mind's processing workspace becomes overloaded with fear and anxiety. Again, the result is poor memorability of the ad and little attitude change).
- 👍 Clear, reliable solution must be offered.
- 👎 Encoding interference.
- 👎 Legal and regulatory ethical issues.
- 👎 Credibility.

Objective #6: Change Behavior by Inducing Anxiety. Like fear, anxiety is not pleasant. In fact, it's pretty awful. Most people try to avoid feeling anxious. They try to minimize, moderate, and alleviate anxiety. Often people will buy or consume things to help them in their continuing struggle with anxiety. They might watch television, smoke, exercise, eat, or take medication. They might also buy mouthwash, deodorant, condoms, a safer car, or even a retirement account, and advertisers know this. Advertisers pursue a change-behavior-by-inducing-anxiety objective by playing on consumer anxieties.

Method A: Anxiety Ads. There are many things to be anxious about. Advertisers realize this and use many settings to demonstrate why you should be anxious and what you can do to alleviate the anxiety. Social, medical, and personal-care products frequently use anxiety ads. The message conveyed in anxiety ads is that (1) there is a clear and present danger, and (2) the way to avoid this danger is to buy the advertised brand. When Head and Shoulders dandruff shampoo is advertised with the theme

19. Michael Ray and William Wilkie, "Fear: The Potential of an Appeal Neglected by Marketing," *Journal of Marketing*, vol. 34, no. 1 (January 1970), 54–62.

EXHIBIT 11.21

This ad is designed to produce anxiety. What is the target market supposed to worry about? www.ponds.com

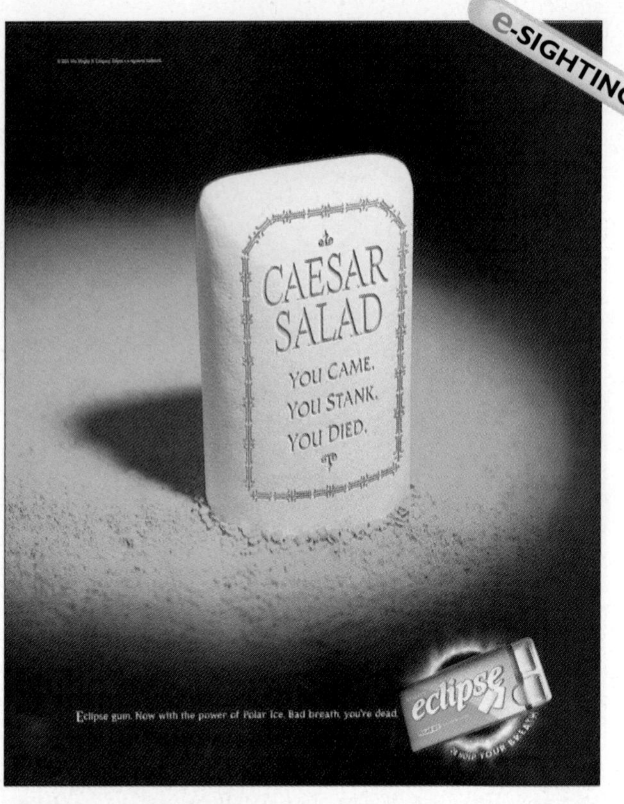

EXHIBIT 11.22

Here is another example of a social anxiety ad. Antiperspirant brands are a natural fit for advertising messages that play upon social anxiety. Do product sites for Old Spice (www.oldspice.com) *or Secret* (www.secretstrength.com) *capitalize on faux pas anxieties?*

"You never get a second chance to make a first impression," the audience realizes the power of Head & Shoulders in saving them the embarrassment of having dandruff.

Other anxiety ads tout the likelihood of being stricken by gingivitis, athlete's foot, calcium deficiency, body odor, and on and on. The idea is that these anxiety-producing conditions are out there, and they may affect you unless you take the appropriate action. What anxieties might the ad in Exhibit 11.21 arouse?

Method B: Social Anxiety Ads. This is a subcategory of anxiety ads where the danger is negative social judgment. Procter & Gamble has long relied on such presentations for its household and personal-care brands. In fact, Procter & Gamble has used this approach so consistently over the years that in some circles the anxiety tactic is referred to as the P&G approach. One of the more memorable P&G social anxiety ads is the scene where husband and wife are busily cleaning the spots off the water glasses before dinner guests arrive because they didn't use P&G's Cascade dishwashing product, which, of course, would have prevented the glasses from spotting. Most personal-care products have used this type of appeal. In Exhibit 11.22, Eclipse suggests that you might be sharing unwanted leftovers from lunch. Feel a touch of anxiety? How's your breath? Evaluation of anxiety ads is typically done by measuring attitudes and beliefs arousal and anxiety through tracking studies, focus groups, communication tests, and other qualitative methods.

EXHIBIT 11.23

Does this ad actually transform the consumption experience? That's the idea. www.budweiser.com

Strategic Implications of Anxiety Advertising

- Can generate perception of widespread threat and thus motivate action (buying and using the advertised product).
- Product-theme continuity can accomplish very good levels of product-advertising thematic consistency. The brand can become the solution to the ever present danger, and this results in long term commitment to the brand.
- Resistant to competitive advertising.
- Efficient.
- Too much anxiety, like fear, overwhelms the consumer and they may end up ignoring the ad, the threat the advertised brand becomes makes them feel too uncomfortable.
- If the anxiety producing threat is not linked tightly enough to the brand, you may increase category demand, and provide business for your competitors. The strategy typically works best for the brand leaders. If total category share goes up, you get most of it.
- Ethical issues: some believe there is enough to feel anxious about without advertisers adding more.
- Typically targeted at women.
- Makes people feel bad, contributes to anxiety of the world in general.

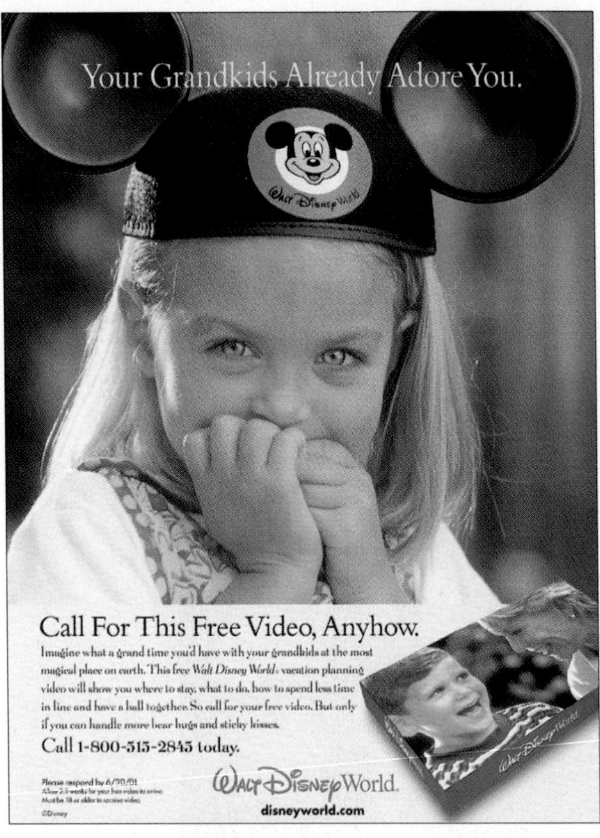

EXHIBIT 11.24

If the strategy is right, your first trip to the Magic Kingdom should be different (and better) by virtue of what you have learned (from ads like these) before getting there. www.disneyworld.com

Objective #7: Transform Consumption Experiences. You know how sometimes it's hard to explain to someone else just exactly why a certain experience was so special, why it felt so good? It wasn't just this thing, or that thing; it was that the entire experience was somehow better than the sum of the individual facets. Sometimes, that feeling is at least partly due to your expectations of what something will be like, your positive memories of previous experiences, or both. Sometimes advertisers try to provide that anticipation and/or familiarity, bundled up in a positive memory of an advertisement, to be activated during the consumption experience itself. It is thus said to have transformed the consumption experience.

Method: Transformational Ads. The idea behind transformational advertising is that it can actually make the consumption experience better. For example, after years of advertising by McDonald's, the experience of eating at McDonald's is actually transformed or made better by virtue of what you know and feel about McDonald's each time you walk in. Transformational advertising messages attempt to create a brand feeling, image, and mood that is activated when the consumer uses the product or service. Transformational ads that are acutely effective are said to connect the experience of the advertisement so closely with the brand that consumers cannot help but think of the advertisement (or in a more general sense, be informed by the memory of many ads) when they think of the brand. Exhibit 11.23 on page 389 is as much about the fun feelings connected with having a Bud with friends as it is about the taste of beer. Also check out Exhibit 11.24. Evaluation of transformational ads is typically done through field studies, tracking studies, ethnographic methods, focus groups, and communication tests.

Strategic Implications of Transformational Advertising

- 👍 Can be extremely powerful.
- 👍 Enduring.
- 👍 Resistant.
- 👎 Long-term commitment.
- 👎 Can ring absolutely false.
- 👎 Largely limited to television.
- 👎 Actual usage has to match ad-created expectations.

Objective #8: Situate the Brand Socially. Maybe you haven't given it much thought, but if you're ever going to understand advertising, you have to get this: Objects have social meanings. While it applies to all cultures, this simple truth is at the very center of consumer cultures. In consumer cultures such as ours, billions of dollars are spent in efforts to achieve specific social meanings for advertised brands. Advertisers have long known that when they place their product in the right social setting, their brand takes on some of the characteristics of its surroundings. These social settings are created in advertising. In advertising, a product is placed into a custom-created social setting perfect for the brand, a setting in which the brand excels. Hopefully, this becomes the way in which the consumer remembers the brand, as fitting into this manufactured and desirable social reality. Let us say it again: Objects have social meaning; they are not just things. As amazing as it seems, many forget this.

Method A: Slice-of-Life Ads. By placing a brand in a social context, it gains social meaning by association. Slice-of-life advertisements depict a usage situation gaining benefits and satisfaction from using the brand. Often these ads are visual and depict a social setting; the social context surrounding the brand rubs off and gives the brand social meaning (Exhibit 11.25). Other times, they do it with words. Receivers may, of course, reject or significantly alter that meaning. Think about how they work. You put the brand into a social setting and transfer meaning from that social setting to it. Look at Exhibits 11.26 and 11.27. Think about them, how they work. Evaluation of slice-of-life ads is typically done through tracking studies that measure attitudes, beliefs, and preferences; pre/post-exposure tests; communication tests; and focus groups.

Strategic Implications of Slice-of-Life Ads

- Generally, less counterargument.
- Enduring memory trace. In other words, pieces of this ad will hang around in consumer's memory for a long time.
- Legal/regulatory deniability. Advertisers attorneys like pictures more than words because determining the truth or falsity of a picture is much tougher than words.

EXHIBIT 11.25

By carefully constructing a social world within the frame of the ad into which the product is carefully placed, meaning is transferred to the product. "Background" and product meanings merge. This is the sophistication behind "slice-of-life" advertising. www.louisboston.com

EXHIBIT 11.26

Think of the meaning this carefully constructed background transfers to the Dior bag. www.dior.com

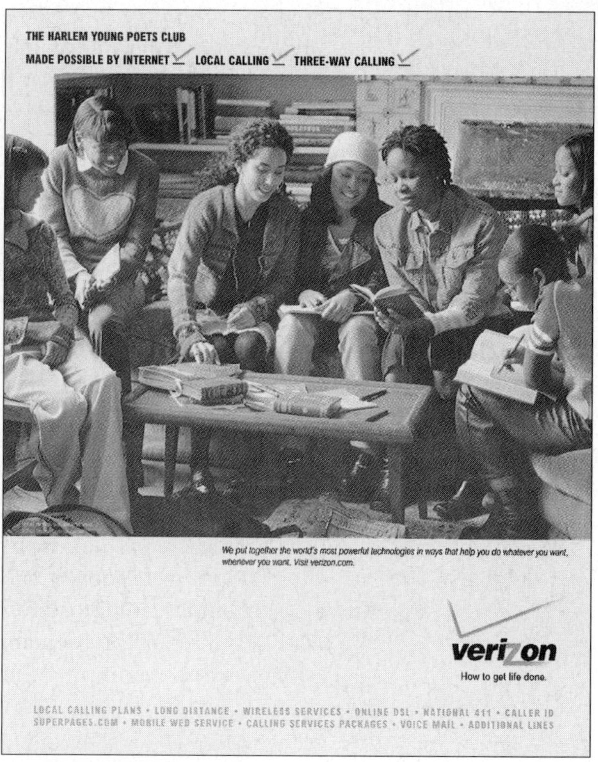

EXHIBIT 11.27

This is an excellent slice-of-life ad. It shows the phone in an idealized social context. Great ad. www.verizon.com

- 👍 Iconic potential. To make your brands another Coca-Cola is many advertisers dream. Socially set pictures of a brand give you this chance.
- 👍 Creation of ad-social-realities. You can create the desired social worlds for your brand on the page.
- 👎 Very common, can get lost in clutter.
- 👎 Rejected as clearly false.
- 👎 Don't tend to copy-test as well.
- 👎 Delayed results.

Method B: Product Placement/Short Internet Films. One way to integrate the product into a desired setting is to place the product in either a television show or film. An actor picks up a can of Coke, rather than just any soda, and hopefully the correct image association is made. Even more explicit are short films (usually less than 10 minutes) made for the Internet. Recently BMW released six such films showing its cars in dramatic contexts (www.bmwfilms.com). The most famous was a film starring Madonna and directed by her husband, British film director Guy Ritchie (*Lock, Stock and Two Smoking Barrels, Snatch*). There are no standard ways of assessing the success of these methods.

Strategic Implications of Product Placement and Internet Films

- 👍 Low counterargument, if not too obvious.
- 👍 Outside normal ad context; may reduce all sorts of defensive measures by consumers, such as source discounting.

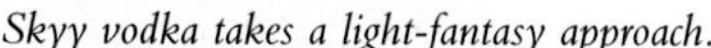
EXHIBIT 11.28

Skyy vodka takes a light-fantasy approach.

EXHIBIT 11.29

This is pure fantasy . . . and a very appropriate one for Prada.
www.prada.com

- 👍 Virtually no regulation.
- 👎 Horribly ineffective when obvious.
- 👎 No standardized rate structure.

Method C: Light Fantasy. Some ads use a form of light fantasy (Exhibit 11.28). These ads allow receivers to pretend a little and think about themselves in the position of the rich, the famous, or the accomplished. For example, the average guy wearing a particular athletic shoe can feel like an NBA all-star. Or think about the lottery, chances are you are not going to win, but it sure is fun to think about the possibilities while you wait to hear someone else's number drawn. Exhibit 11.29 presents a more dreamy type of fantasy. Which do you think works best? Evaluation of light-fantasy ads is typically done through qualitative methods such as focus groups and communication tests.

Strategic Implications of Light-Fantasy Advertising

- 👍 Evocative.
- 👍 Open text generating lots of thoughts (cognitive responses) generally don't "test" (day after recall) well.
- 👍 Consumer really gets to connect his or her thoughts and feelings.
- 👍 Eager creatives.
- 👎 Many of these thoughts may be irrelevant to your strategic goals.
- 👎 May be too dreamy and not concrete enough.
- 👎 Don't test well.

Objective #9: Define the Brand Image. Madonna has an image; Michael Jordan has an image; so do Prada and Pepsi. Even fictional characters such as the wildly popular Harry Potter have images (see the Controversy box on this page). Just like people, brands have images. Images are the most apparent and most prominently associated characteristics of a brand. They are the thing consumers most remember or associate with a brand. Advertisers are in the business of creating, adjusting, and maintaining images—in other words, they often engage in the define-the-brand-image objective.

Method: Image Ads. Image advertising means different things to different people. To some, it means the absence of hard product information. To others, it refers to advertising that is almost exclusively visual. This is an oversimplification, but it is true that most image advertising tends toward the visual. In both cases, it means an attempt to link certain attributes to the brand, rather than to engage the consumer in any kind of discourse. Sometimes these linkages are quite explicit, such as using a tiger to indicate the strength of a brand. Other times, the linkages are implicit and subtle, such as the colors and tones associated with a brand. Check out the ads in Exhibit 11.30. Evaluation of image ads is difficult. Usually qualitative methods are employed; sometimes associative tests are used, along with attribute-related tracking studies. Much advertising since the 1960s has been about figuring out what is cool, representing that cool social context in an ad, and then putting them together with the brand, transferring cool to the brand.

Strategic Implications of Image Advertising

- 👍 Enduring memory trace.
- 👍 Generally, less counterargument.
- 👍 Legal/regulatory deniability.
- 👍 Iconic potential.
- 👎 Very common, can get lost in clutter.
- 👎 Rejected as clearly false.
- 👎 Don't tend to copy-test well.
- 👎 Delayed results.

CONTROVERSY

Harry Potter: Controversial Marketing Wizard

The nonprofit Center for Science in the Public Interest (CSPI), along with more than 40 co-sponsoring organizations in a dozen countries, launched "SaveHarry.com," a campaign aimed at ending Coca-Cola's use of Harry Potter to market junk food to kids. Coca-Cola's marketing strategy uses imagery from the hit movie *Harry Potter and the Sorcerer's Stone* on packages and in advertising for some of its beverages, including Minute Maid, Coca-Cola, and Hi-C. In addition, Coca-Cola sponsors an $18 million reading and literacy program promoted through a special Web site. Coke's Potter site, called "Live the Magic," uses contests and games to entice kids to drink more soft drinks. The CSPI-sponsored Web site enables concerned consumers to send e-mail to J. K. Rowling, author of the Harry Potter books, urging her to end the deal with Coca-Cola.

Aggressive marketing campaigns aimed at children normally generate some controversy, and, although Coke likes to emphasize the Live the Magic reading program, critics are cynical. "Children and adults worldwide are outraged that their beloved Harry Potter is being used to market liquid candy to kids," said Michael F. Jacobson, executive director of CSPI. "Over-consumption of Coca-Cola and other sugar-laden soft drinks contributes to obesity and diabetes, reduced nutrient intake, and tooth decay." Nutrition-minded activists are not the only ones railing against Coke's newest campaign; advertising regulation groups are also sounding off. "Coke has transformed Harry Potter into a marketing wizard to hook our kids on its junk beverages," said Gary Ruskin, executive director of advertising watchdog Commercial Alert.

Coca-Cola's masterful sponsorship of the Live the Magic reading program portrays the company as the close ally of schoolteachers around the country. Spokeswoman Susan McDermott said Coca-Cola's association with Harry Potter is about promoting the value of reading and the magic of Harry Potter—not promoting products to children. However, while $18 million is spent on literacy, $150 million is being spent to persuade kids to have a Coke with their favorite book character. More than 850 million drink packages feature Harry Potter imagery; more than 9 million Harry Potter movie certificates will be offered to consumers; more than 29 million 20-ounce Coke products will be given away; and more than 800 customers will win trips to the Hogwarts Castle Adventure.

Children are already doing more reading because of the Harry Potter series. There can be no question that more kids will be drinking Coca-Cola products—and taking more trips to the dentist.

Sources: "Coke Marketing of Harry Potter Protested," *Associated Press*, www.cnn.com, accessed October 18, 2001; "Global Campaign Protests Coca-Cola's Use of Harry Potter to Market Junk Food," CSPI press release, www.cspinet.org, accessed October 29, 2001.

EXHIBIT 11.30

These are all image ads. Even though some people think of these ads as light and fluffy, they are anything but that. They are carefully constructed to yield the right set of connections, and images. To "get them," the reader/viewer has to give them a little thought. Think about these. Do you get it?

EXHIBIT 11.31

You'd better act now. They're going fast.
www.q4music.com

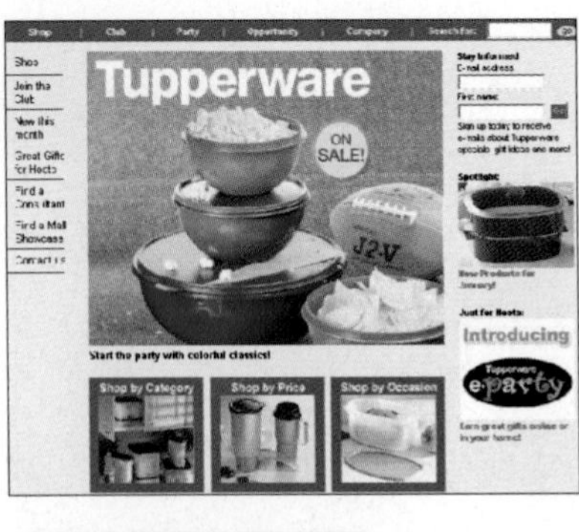

EXHIBIT 11.32

This is a great example of the direct response capabilities of the Internet.
www.tupperware.com

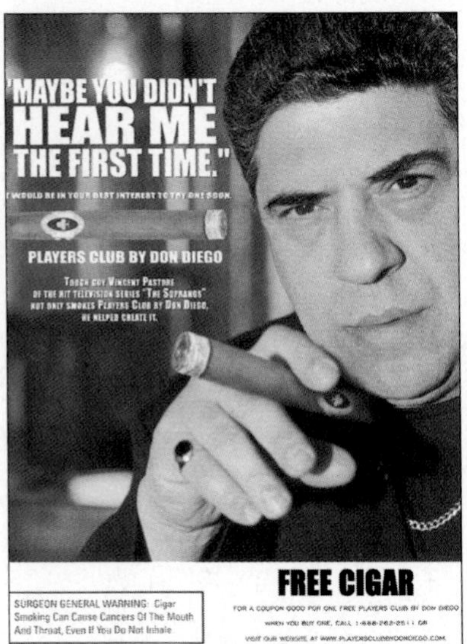

EXHIBIT 11.33

Smoke 'em if you got 'em, *particularly if you can get such a great deal.*
www.playersclubbydondiego.com

Objective #10: Invoke a Direct Response. A direct response advertising appeal implores the receiver to act immediately. It's a blend of hard selling and impulse buying. Price appeals associated with special deals (Exhibit 11.31) or the convenience of ordering from the comfort of one's home form the basis of the direct response objective. Local retailers and national direct merchants such as L. L. Bean and J. Crew are the most frequent users of this message strategy. In some cases, organizations use more feature-laden appeals in their direct response advertising. The main characteristic of such ads, however, is encouraging the audience to respond immediately by calling a toll-free number.

Method: Call-or-Click-Now Ads. Direct response ads have become more prevalent in recent years for several reasons. First, many direct response messages feature a price-oriented appeal. In today's era of value-oriented, price-conscious consumers, direct response messages provide an ideal opportunity for offering consumers a discount via a mail-in coupon or special television offer that is a price-based appeal. Second, firms have developed sophisticated databases that allow them to specifically target well-defined customer groups. Such databases can be tailored to geographic areas, demographic characteristics of audiences, or past product use as ways to target different audiences. The firm can then send a specific and different message to each target audience. Third, advertisers are demanding more evidence that the dollars they spend on advertising are having an impact. Ad agencies have found that direct response messages offer the most tangible evidence of advertising impact, and they are using the technique as a means of accountability. (See Exhibit 11.32.) Direct response is used in many promotions (Exhibit 11.33).

Strategic Implications of Direct Response Advertising and Promotion

- 👍 Easy to assess degree of success.
- 👍 Can be nicely integrated with other communication aspects and promotion.
- 👎 Creatives not all that fond of them, resistance.

- High wearout.
- Requires a lot of the consumer (even clicking takes effort).

In the End. In the end, message development is where the advertising battle is usually won or lost. It's where real creativity exists. It's where the agency has to be smart and figure out just how to turn the wishes of the client into effective advertising. It is where the creatives have to get into the minds of consumers, realizing that the advertisement will be received by different people in different ways. Great messages are developed by people who can put themselves into the minds of their audience members and anticipate their response, leading to the desired outcomes.

SUMMARY

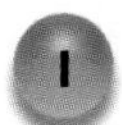

Identify ten objectives of message strategy.

Advertisers can choose from a wide array of message strategy objectives as well as methods for implementing these objectives. Three fundamental message objectives are promoting brand recall, linking key attributes to the brand name, and persuading the customer. The advertiser may also seek to link the good feelings, humor, and sex appeal of an ad with the brand itself. Such positive feelings associated with the advertised brand can lead consumers to a higher probability of purchase. The advertiser may also seek to activate negative emotional states such as fear or anxiety as the means to motivate brand purchase. Transformational advertising seeks to influence the nature of the consumption experience. A message may also feature the brand in an important social context to heighten the brand's appeal. Enhancing brand image is another common message objective and can be contrasted with designing messages to produce immediate action or to engage the consumer in cognitive discourse. Finally, many advertising messages are designed to invoke a direct response. Imploring the consumer to act immediately blends hard selling and impulse buying, and offers agencies tangible evidence of advertising impact.

Identify methods for executing each message strategy objective.

Advertisers employ any number of methods to achieve their objectives. To get consumers to recall a brand name, repetition, slogan, and jingle ads are often produced. Sometimes the objective is only to link a key attribute to a brand. For this, many turn to USP ads. If the goal is to persuade a consumer to make a purchase, reason-why ads, hard-sell ads, comparison ads, testimonials, demonstration ads, advertorials, and infomercials all do the trick. Feel-good ads, humorous ads, and sexual-appeal ads can raise a consumer's preferences for one brand over another through positive association. Fear-appeal ads, judiciously used, can motivate purchases, as can ads that play on other anxieties. Transformational ads attempt to enrich the consumption experience. With slice-of-life ads, product-placement/short Internet films, and light-fantasy ads, the goal is to situate a brand in a desirable social context. Ads that primarily use visuals work to define brand image. Finally, call- or click-now ads aim to invoke direct response.

Discuss the strategic implications of various methods used to execute each message strategy objective.

Each method used to execute a message strategy objective has pros and cons. Methods that promote brand recall or link key attributes to a brand name can be extremely successful in training consumers to remember a brand name or its specific, beneficial attributes. However, these methods require long-term commitment and repetition to work properly, and advertisers can pay high expense while generating disdain from creatives. Methods used to persuade consumers generally aim to provide rhetorical arguments and demonstrations for why consumers should prefer a brand, resulting in strong, cognitive loyalty to products. However, these methods assume a high level of involvement and are vulnerable to counterarguments that neutralize their effectiveness—more sophisticated audiences tune them out altogether, rejecting them as misleading, insipid, or dishonest. Methods used in creating affective association have short-term results and please creatives; however, the effect on audiences wears out quickly and high expense dissuades some advertisers from taking the risk. Methods designed to play on fear or anxiety are compelling, but legal and ethical issues arise, and most advertisers wish to avoid instigating consumer panic. Methods that transform consumption experiences, situate the brand socially, or define brand image have powerful enduring qualities, but often get lost in the clutter and can ring false to audiences. Finally, methods that invoke a direct response integrate well into larger campaign strategies, and can be easily measured for success. However, these methods require much of consumers and often bore creatives.

KEY TERMS

message strategy
unique selling proposition (USP)
comparison advertisements
testimonial
advertorial
infomercial

QUESTIONS

1. Review the chapter opener about the success of Apple's "1984" commercial. What was the idea at the heart of this ad that helped make the Macintosh a success? Over a decade later, Apple's big idea has failed to pan out. What went wrong?

2. Once again, reflect on the "1984" commercial. As this chapter suggested, consumers are active interpreters of ads, and one of the virtues of the "1984" ad was that it invited the audience to become involved and make an interpretation. Thinking about the "1984" ad, what sorts of interpretations could a consumer make that would benefit the brand? Conversely, what sorts of interpretations might a person make, after a single exposure to this ad, that would be detrimental to Macintosh?

3. Explain the difference between brand recall and affective association as message objectives. Which of these objectives do you think would be harder to achieve, and why?

4. Discuss the merits of unique selling proposition (USP) ads. Is it possible to have a USP that is not the "big idea" for an ad campaign?

5. Review the do's and don'ts of comparison advertising and then think about each of the brand pairs listed here. Comment on whether you think comparison ads would be a good choice for the product category in question, and if so, which brand in the pair would be in the most appropriate position to use comparisons: Ford versus Chevy trucks; Coors Light versus Bud Light beer; Nuprin versus Tylenol pain reliever; Brut versus Obsession cologne; Wendy's versus McDonald's hamburgers.

6. Procter & Gamble has had considerable success with the message strategy involving anxiety arousal. How does P&G's success with this strategy refute the general premise that the best way to appeal to American consumers is to appeal to their pursuit of personal freedom and individuality?

7. What are some of the ways advertisers can use the Internet to execute message strategy objectives?

8. Do you think product placement and short Internet films are effective in executing the message strategy of situating the brand socially? Have you ever consciously made a correlation between the products actors used during a film and your own brand preferences?

9. Think of a major purchase you have made recently. Which of the 10 message strategy objectives do you think were the most effective in influencing your purchase decision? Explain.

EXPERIENTIAL EXERCISES

1. Choose a popular radio or television slogan or jingle and evaluate its effectiveness based on what you learned in the chapter. Does the slogan or jingle immediately make you think of the brand? Does the jingle or slogan evoke a positive response? If not, does this matter? Do you think you will remember this slogan or jingle years from now? Why might creatives in the industry be averse to repetition, slogans, and jingles?

2. Beer advertisers often use ad strategy methods that are designed to achieve the objective of "affective association." Keen advertisers recognize that consumers purchase products based on their general liking of the product; such a "liking" can be prompted through good feelings evoked by advertisements. Describe a current television beer advertisement that aims to achieve affective association. Which specific method is applied in the commercial to achieve the objective? What response did you personally have to the commercial? Do you think you'd be more inclined to try this product based on the ad? What are some of the positive and negative implications of this message strategy?

USING THE INTERNET

11-1 A ChapStick for Every Pair of Lips

Whitehall-Robins has a line of lip-balm products designed to provide all-season protection against dried or cracked lips. The company has recently added a new dimension to a booming market of lip-balm products with its ChapStick LipSations. LipSations make taking care of the "old kisser" fun and flavorful all throughout the entire year.

ChapStick LipSations:
http://www.chapstick.com/lipsations

1. What key attributes does the LipSations product line add to the ChapStick brand name?

2. Explain how the concept of the unique selling proposition (USP) relates to ChapStick LipSations. What are some of the strategic implications of the USP method as they relate to this product line?

3. How does this message-strategy method help with brand name recall?

11-2 The Necessity of Healthy Hair

Pantene Pro-V is a collection of vitamin-enriched hair-care products designed to produce beautiful and healthy hair. The distinct feature of Pantene Pro-V is its focus on an individual's styling needs instead of hair type. The Pantene Pro-V collection includes a shampoo, conditioner, treatment, and styler to provide the best care for individual styling preferences. Keen advertisers have recognized that the product's focus on individuality and style integrates well with popular culture's emphasis on style and self-expression as championed by famous artists and musicians. Pantene capitalizes on these similarities by sponsoring an annual Pro-Voice music competition, a promotion established to celebrate what women have to say and to reward their songwriting talents.

Pantene Pro-Voice: http://www.pro-voice.com

Pantene Pro-V: http://www.pantene.com

1. What message-strategy objective do you think is being applied for Pantene Pro-V, and what specific methods are being used to achieve this?

2. What social meanings does Pantene hope the consumer will associate with its product? Explain. Do you think this approach will produce brand recall?

3. What are some of the pros and cons of Pantene's message strategy?

CHAPTER 12

After reading and thinking about this chapter, you will be able to do the following:

Explain the need for a creative plan in the copywriting process.

Detail the components of print copy, along with important guidelines for writing effective print copy.

Describe various formatting alternatives for radio ads and articulate guidelines for writing effective radio copy.

Describe various formatting alternatives for television ads and articulate guidelines for writing effective television copy.

CHAPTER 10
Creativity and Advertising

CHAPTER 11
Message Strategy

CHAPTER 12
Copywriting

CHAPTER 13
Art Direction and Production

WILL
WORK
FOR
FOOD
No insects left.
SBP

EXHIBIT 12.1

WARNING: The Difference Between Copywriters And Art Directors May Not Be As Great As You Think.

While copywriters are primarily responsible for writing the verbal descriptions in ads and art directors are primarily responsible for the visuals, they act as partners and often come up with great ideas outside their primary responsibility.

We live in an age when just about everything carries a warning label of some sort. Objects in rearview mirrors may be closer than they appear. Hair dryers should not be used in the shower. Using a lawn mower to trim the hedge may result in injury.

In this spirit, the authors of this book urge you to read the warning label in Exhibit 12.1. Yet, unlike the examples given earlier, the truth expressed here may not be quite so obvious, the danger not so clear. You know how some people just have to divide up the world into neat little parcels and categories. These are the same people who neatly place copywriters in one box on the organizational chart, and art directors in another. But in practice, it's not that simple. It's far too simplistic to state that copywriters are responsible for the verbal elements in an ad and art directors are responsible for the visual elements. In fact, copywriters and art directors function as partners and are referred to as the **creative team** in agencies. The creative team is responsible for coming up with the **creative concept** and for guiding its execution. The creative concept, which can be thought of as the unique creative thought behind a campaign, is then turned into individual advertisements. During this process, copywriters often suggest the idea for magnificent, arresting visuals. Likewise, art directors often come up with killer headlines.

As you can see in Exhibits 12.2 and 12.3, some ads have no headlines at all; some have no visuals. Still, in most cases, both a copywriter and an art director are equally involved in creating an ad. This doesn't mean that copywriting and art directing are one and the same. This chapter and the next will show that the talent and knowledge needed to excel in one area differ in many ways from those needed to excel in the other. Still, one must recognize that not all copywriting is done by copywriters and not all art directing is done by art directors.

Understanding copywriting is as much about the people who write copy as it is about the product studies, audience research, and other information that copywriters draw upon to create effective copy. Copywriting is, in fact, mostly about the fairly magical relationship between creator and creation, between writer and text, writer and brand. It is more about art than science. Copywriting is writing, and writing is a form of crafted magic. Magic cannot be taught. If (and it's a big if) you have a gift to begin with, then you can learn technique. But technique alone is not enough. Gifts are gifts—they come from somewhere else. Writing long paragraphs won't make you William Faulkner any more than writing self-effacing copy will make you Bill Bernbach. Likewise, trying to treat a discussion of copywriting like a step-by-step discussion of how to change the oil in your car is sadly silly and thoroughly useless. Still, there are things—some of them principles, some of them hints and tips—that can be learned from the creators of some of the greatest advertising of all time. Furthermore, even if you don't plan to be a copywriter, knowing something about the craft is essential to any working understanding of advertising. Knowing something about the craft is also essential to selling good ideas in global markets, as shown in the Global Issues box on page 408.

Lesson one:
How to avoid getting a nickname like Lefty, Stumpy or Knuckles.

CARPENTRY/CABINET MAKING CLASSES THE RICHMOND TECHNICAL CENTER
CALL 780-6237 OR ASK YOUR GUIDANCE COUNSELOR FOR DETAILS.

EXHIBIT 12.2

While most effective ads use multiple copy components—headline, subhead, body copy, visual—some ads excel by focusing on a single component. This Richmond Technical Center ad succeeds without the use of an illustration.

Let's begin with some fairly general thoughts on copywriting from some of the most influential people in the history of advertising:

If you think you have a better mousetrap, or shirt, or whatever, you've got to tell people, and I don't think that has to be done with trickery, or insults, or by talking down to people. . . . The smartest advertising is the advertising that communicates the best and respects consumers' intelligence. It's advertising that lets them bring something to the communication process, as opposed to some of the more validly criticized work in our profession which tries to grind the benefits of a soap or a cake mix into a poor housewife's head by repeating it 37 times in 30 seconds.[1]

—Lee Clow, creator of the Apple Macintosh "1984" advertisement

As I have observed it, great advertising writing either in print or television is disarmingly simple. It has the common touch without being or sounding patronizing. If you are writing about baloney, don't try to make it sound like Cornish hen, because that is the worst kind of baloney. Just make it darned good baloney.[2]

—Leo Burnett, founder of the Leo Burnett agency, Chicago

Why should anyone look at your ad? The reader doesn't buy his magazine or tune his radio and TV to see and hear what you have to say. . . . What is the use of saying all the right things in the world if nobody is going to read them? And, believe me, nobody is going to read them if they are not said with freshness, originality and imagination.[3]

—William Bernbach, cofounder of one of the most influential agencies during the 1960s, Doyle Dane Bernbach

Never write an advertisement which you wouldn't want your family to read. Good products can be sold by honest advertising. If you don't think the product is good, you have no business to be advertising it. If you tell lies, or weasel, you do your client a disservice, you increase your load of guilt, and you fan the flames of public resentment against the whole business of advertising.[4]

—David Ogilvy's ninth of eleven commandments of advertising

Finally, the following observation on the power of a good advertisement, brilliant in its simplicity, is offered by one of the modern-day geniuses of advertising:

Imagination is one of the last remaining legal means to gain an unfair advantage over your competition.[5]

—Tom McElligott, cofounder of a highly creative and successful Minneapolis advertising agency

Good copywriters must always bring spirit and imagination to advertising. Lee Clow, Leo Burnett, William Bernbach, and David Ogilvy have created some of the

1. Jennifer Pendleton, "Bringing New Clow-T to Ads, Chiat's Unlikely Creative," *Advertising Age*, February 7, 1985, 1.
2. Leo Burnett, "Keep Listening to That Wee, Small Voice," in *Communications of an Advertising Man* (Chicago: Leo Burnett, 1961), 160.
3. Cited in Martin Mayer, *Madison Avenue, U.S.A.* (New York: Pocket Books, 1954), 66.
4. David Ogilvy, *Confessions of an Advertising Man* (New York: Atheneum, 1964), 102.
5. Tom McElligott is credited with making this statement in several public speeches during the 1980s.

EXHIBIT 12.3

Some ads have no copy.

most memorable advertising in history: the "We're Number 2, We Try Harder" Avis campaign (William Bernbach); the Hathaway Shirt Man ads (David Ogilvy); the Jolly Green Giant ads (Leo Burnett); and the "1984" Apple Macintosh ad (Lee Clow). See Exhibits 12.4 and 12.5 for samples of their work. When these advertising legends speak of creating good ads that respect the consumer's intelligence and rely on imagination, they assume good copywriting.

1 Copywriting and the Creative Plan.

Writing well, rule #1: Write well.

—Luke Sullivan, copywriter and author

Copywriting is the process of expressing the value and benefits a brand has to offer, via written or verbal descriptions. Copywriting requires far more than the ability to string product descriptions together in coherent sentences. One apt description of copywriting is that it is a never-ending search for ideas combined with a never-ending search for new and different ways to express those ideas.

Imagine you're a copywriter on the MasterCard account. You've sat through meeting after meeting in which your client, account executives, and researchers have presented a myriad of benefits one gets from using a MasterCard for online purchases. You've talked to customers about their experiences. You've even gone online to try the card out for yourself. All along, your boss has been reminding you that the work you come up with must be as good as the work that focuses on the general use of the card (Exhibit 12.6). Now your job is simple. Take all the charts, numbers, and strategies and turn them into a simple, emotionally involving, intellectually challenging campaign such as the one in Exhibits 12.7 and 12.8.

Effective copywriters are well-informed, astute advertising decision makers with creative talent. Copywriters are able to comprehend and then incorporate the complexities of marketing strategies, consumer behavior, and advertising strategies into a

When you're only No.2, you try harder. Or else.

Little fish have to keep moving all of the time. The big ones never stop picking on them.

Avis knows all about the problems of little fish.

We're only No.2 in rent a cars. We'd be swallowed up if we didn't try harder.

There's no rest for us.

We're always emptying ashtrays. Making sure gas tanks are full before we rent our cars. Seeing that the batteries are full of life. Checking our windshield wipers.

And the cars we rent out can't be anything less than spanking new Plymouths.

And since we're not the big fish, you won't feel like a sardine when you come to our counter.

We're not jammed with customers.

EXHIBIT 12.4

One of the great names in advertising is William Bernbach, and the memorable and highly effective "We try harder" campaign for Avis Rent a Car was produced by his agency, Doyle Dane Berbach.
www.avis.com

Hathaway and the Duke's stud groom

IT ALL STARTED with Richard Tattersall, the Duke of Kingston's stud groom. He dressed his horses in magnificent check blankets. Then English tailors started using Mr. Tattersall's checks for gentlemen's waistcoats.

Now Hathaway takes the Tattersall one step further. With the help of an old Connecticut mill, we have scaled down this classic pattern to miniature proportions, so that you can wear it in New York. Yet its implication of landed gentry still remains.

You can get this Hathaway miniature Tattersall in red and grey (as illustrated), navy and blue, or mahogany and beige. Between board meetings you can amuse yourself counting the various hallmarks of a Hathaway shirt: 22 single-needle stitches to the inch, big buttons, square-cut cuffs. And so forth.

The price is $8.95. For the name of your nearest store, write C. F. Hathaway, Waterville, Maine. In New York, call OXford 7-5566.

EXHIBIT 12.5

David Ogilvy, to many a guru in advertising, created the Hathaway Shirt Man (complete with an eye patch) as a way to attract attention and create an image for the Hathaway brand many years ago.

brief yet powerful communication. They must do so in such a way that the copy does not interfere with but rather enhances the visual aspects of the message.

An astute advertiser will go to great lengths to provide copywriters with as much information as possible about the objectives for a particular advertising effort. The responsibility for keeping copywriters informed lies with the client's marketing managers in conjunction with account executives and creative directors in the ad agency. They must communicate the foundations and intricacies of the firm's marketing strategies to the copywriters. Without this information, copywriters are left without guidance and direction, and they must rely on intuition about what sorts of information are relevant and meaningful to a target audience. Sometimes that works; most of the time, it does not.

A **creative plan** is a guideline used during the copywriting process to specify the message elements that must be coordinated during the preparation of copy. These elements include main product claims, creative devices, media that will be used, and special creative needs a product or service might have. One of the main challenges faced by a copywriter is to make creative sense out of the maze of information that comes from the message development process. Part of the challenge is creating excitement around what can otherwise be dull product features. For example, the challenge for the copywriter responsible for the ads in Exhibits 12.9 and 12.10 was to express the expected feature of insect-killing ability in an insecticide in an unexpected fashion.

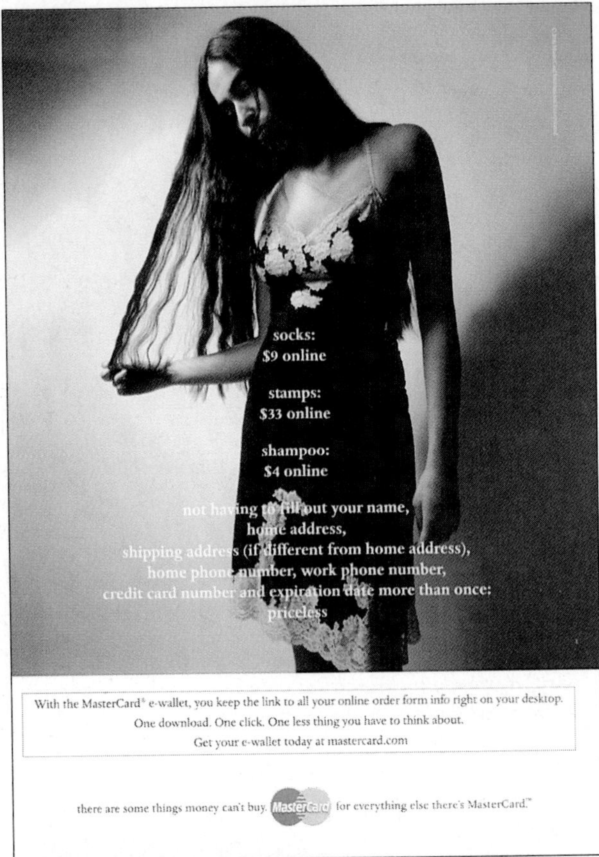

EXHIBIT 12.6

Your boss has been reminding you that the work you come up with must be as good as the work that focuses on the general use of the card.
www.mastercard.com

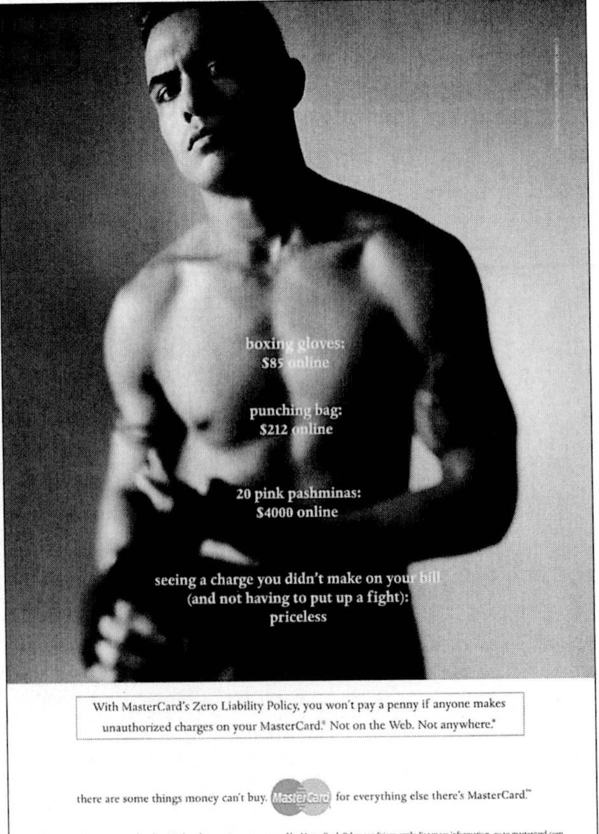

EXHIBITS 12.7 AND 12.8

Take all the charts, numbers, and strategies and turn them into a simple, emotionally involving, intellectually challenging campaign.
www.mastercard.com

EXHIBITS 12.9 AND 12.10

Expected product feature, unexpected creative delivery.

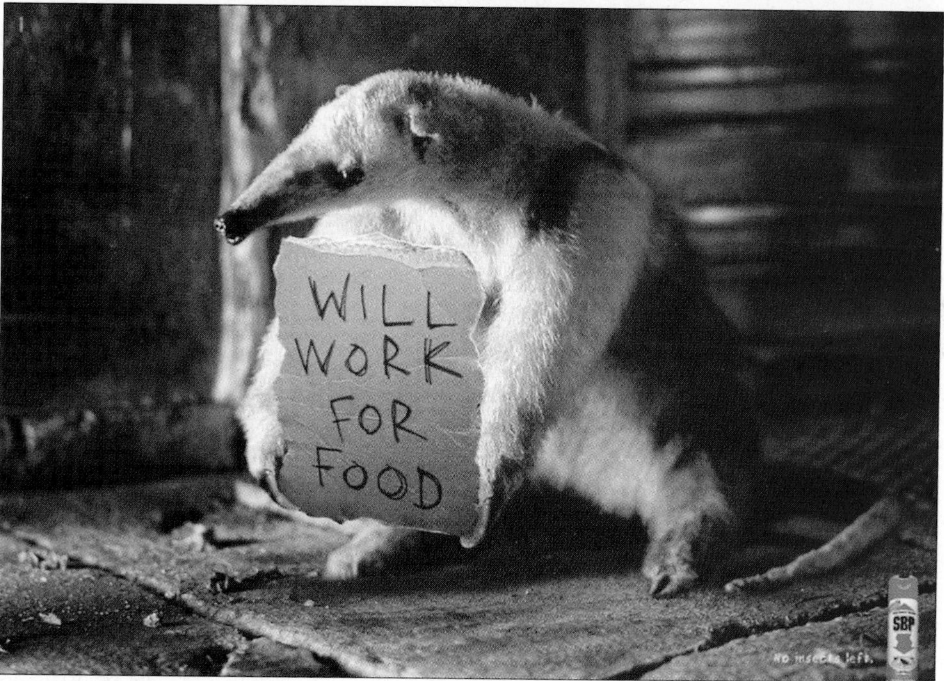

Another aspect of the challenge is bringing together various creative tools (such as illustration, color, sound, and action) and the copy. Copy must also be coordinated with the media that will be used. All of these factors are coordinated through the use of a creative plan. Some of the elements considered in devising a creative plan are the following:

- the single most important thought you want a member of the target market to take away from the advertisement
- the product features to be emphasized

- the benefits a user receives from these features
- the media chosen for transmitting the information and the length of time the advertisement will run
- the suggested mood or tone for the ad
- the ways in which mood and atmosphere will be achieved in the ad
- the production budget for the ad[6]

These considerations can be modified or disregarded entirely during the process of creating an ad. For example, sometimes a brilliant creative execution demands that television, rather than print, be the media vehicle of choice. Occasionally, a particular creative thought may suggest a completely different mood or tone than the one listed in the creative plan. A creative plan is best thought of as a starting point, not an endpoint, for the creative team. Like anything else in advertising, the plan should evolve and grow as new insights are gained. Once the creative plan is devised, the creative team can get on with the task of creating the actual advertisement.

GLOBAL ISSUES

You Know That Kissing Thing—It Works for Global Ads, Too

Years ago, some management guru said, "Keep It Simple, Stupid," giving birth to the KISS rule in American management philosophy. Well, it turns out that KISS has a place in global advertising as well.

Over the last decade, advertisers have been getting better and better at creating advertising campaigns that succeed on a global level. The International Advertising Festival at Cannes demonstrates that fact annually. More and more of the winning campaigns are global campaigns, not just domestic market campaigns. They work as well in Boston as they do in Brussels. What is also a demonstrated fact annually is that these winning campaigns are actually quite simple in terms of message theme and visual structure. Certainly, particular product categories lend themselves more readily to a global stage than do others. Lifestyle products such as soft drinks, jeans, sneakers, and candy translate well across cultures. Nike, Pepsi, and Levi's speak to the world and each has been the subject of memorable, award-winning campaigns. But what makes these brands so well suited to a global audience—even beyond the natural fit of lifestyle product categories?

The campaigns that work best on a global scale are those where the brand and its imagery are inextricably one and the same. Innovative product demonstrations or images where the pictures tell the story are the foundation of effective global advertising. Advertising that succeeds in the global arena draws on four constants: Simplicity, Clarity, Humor, and Clever demonstration. SCHC doesn't exactly spell KISS, but the reason that global ads that highlight these qualities can bridge the complexities and distinctiveness of one culture to another is simple. Granted, what is funny to a Brit may be lost on a Brazilian, but the key is to find not the culturally bound humor in a demonstration, but the culturally shared humor. When it comes to copy, simplicity and clarity rule. Aside from their inherent value, their ability to communicate across cultures is, well, clear. In short, actually *trying* to bridge cultures may be just the thing that complicates the situation. Reducing a brand and its message to the simplest and most common human values has a great chance of succeeding.

Source: Jay Schulberg, "Successful Global Ads Need Simplicity, Clarity," *Advertising Age*, June 30, 1997, 17.

2 Copywriting for Print Advertising.

In preparing copy for a print ad, the first step in the copy development process is deciding how to use (or not use) the three separate components of print copy: the headline, the subhead, and the body copy. Be aware that the full range of components applies most directly to print ads that appear in magazines, newspapers, or direct mail pieces. These guidelines also apply to other "print" media such as billboards, transit advertising, and specialty advertising, but all media are in effect different animals. More detail on these "support" media is presented in Chapter 17. The Creativity box on page 409 describes how the advertising industry itself is using print advertising to convince corporate executives of the merits of using advertising to build brands.

The Headline. The **headline** in an advertisement is the leading sentence or sentences, usually at the top or bottom of the ad, that attracts attention, communicates a key selling point, or achieves brand identification.

6. The last two points in this list were adapted from A. Jerome Jewler, *Creative Strategy in Advertising*, 3rd ed. (Belmont, Calif.: Wadsworth, 1989), 196.

CREATIVITY

Advertising Sells Itself

Ad icons like the Sunkist orange and the Energizer bunny are taking center stage in a campaign aimed to sell corporate executives on using advertising to build brands. The multiyear print advertising campaign by the American Advertising Federation (AAF) highlights the success of top brands, hoping to reinforce advertising's strategic importance in the changing business environment. A survey of top-level executives conducted by the AAF validates the need for the campaign: The survey found that while CEOs appreciated that advertising drove sales, they didn't have a complete understanding of its importance in building brands.

The new AAF campaign alters familiar ads of well-respected brands, using a persuasive mix of copy and visual to get the point across that advertising is vital to brand success. For the visual, Energizer, Sunkist, Coca-Cola, Anheuser-Busch, and Intel signed off on an unprecedented modification of their logos. The logos in the AAF ads are modified to read "Advertising" and then a specific question or statement is put forth. The copy ends with the same tagline, prompting audiences to reflect on the value of advertising.

Energizer's copy asks, "What makes one battery more powerful than another?"; Sunkist's copy states, "The average grocery store carries 16,875 brands. Why do you recognize this one?"; Coca-Cola's copy states, "The secret formula, revealed."; and Intel's copy states, "It's what makes computers more powerful." For each, the AAF tag is the same: "Advertising. The way great brands get to be great brands." The idea behind the creative was born out of the notion that advertising helped build the world's most recognized brands. "If you put your hand over the logo, you would still recognize who it was," said Randy Hughes, the creative director of the campaign.

Now seems to be an important time for advertising to sell itself, and the fact that top brands have allowed cherished logos to be altered shows the solidarity of advertisers to make their case to CEOs. Advertising currently ranks low in strategic importance among top executives, and less than half of those surveyed by the AAF believe that the importance of advertising will increase in the future. That mindset isn't likely to change soon. In fact, 27 percent of the marketers surveyed said advertising would be among the first budget items cut in a sales downturn. The AAF hopes that a little shameless self-promotion can force executives to change their minds—and, more important, their budgets.

Sources: AAF Press Release: "AAF's Next 'Great Brands' Campaign Features Intel," www.aaf.org, accessed October 31, 2001; Wendy Melillo, "AAF Debuts Print Campaign," *Advertising Week*, www.aaf.org, accessed October 31, 2001.

Many headlines fail to attract attention, and the ad itself then becomes another bit of clutter in consumers' lives. Lifeless headlines do not compel the reader to examine other parts of the ad. Simply stated, a headline can either motivate a reader to move on to the rest of an ad or lose the reader for good.

Purposes of a Headline. In preparing a headline, a copywriter begins by considering the variety of purposes a headline can have in terms of gaining attention or actually convincing the consumer. In general, a headline can be written to pursue the following purposes:

- *Give news about the brand.* A headline can proclaim a newsworthy event focused on the brand. "Champion Wins Mt. Everest Run" and "25 of 40 Major Titles Won with Titleist" are examples of headlines that communicate newsworthy events about Champion spark plugs and Titleist golf balls. The Tanqueray No. Ten ad in Exhibit 12.11 uses this approach in a powerful, straightforward manner.
- *Emphasize a brand claim.* A primary and perhaps differentiating feature of the brand is a likely candidate for the headline theme. "30% More Mileage on Firestone Tires" highlights durability. Exhibit 12.12 reminds people of the superior pickup of a Jaguar.
- *Give advice to the reader.* A headline can give the reader a recommendation that (usually) is followed by results provided in the body copy. "Increase Your Reading Skills" and "Save up to 90% on Commissions" both implore the reader to take the advice of the ad. The headline in Exhibit 12.13 advises readers to make sure that bad radio stations don't ever ruin a road trip.
- *Select prospects.* Headlines can attract the attention of the intended audience. "Good News for Arthritis Sufferers" and "Attention June Graduates" are examples of headlines designed to achieve prospect selection. The headline in the women.com ad shown in Exhibit 12.14 suggests in no uncertain terms who the intended audience is for the site.

EXHIBIT 12.11

This ad gives important news about the brand.

EXHIBIT 12.12

This headline emphasizes a straight-ahead brand feature.
www.jaguar.com

- *Stimulate the reader's curiosity.* Posing a riddle with a headline can serve to attract attention and stimulate readership. Curiosity can be stimulated with a clever play on words or a contradiction. Take, for example, the headline "With MCI, Gerber's Baby Talk Never Sounded Better." The body copy goes on to explain that Gerber Products (a maker of baby products) uses the high technology of MCI for its communication needs. Does the headline in the ad shown in Exhibit 12.15 get your attention? It was written for that purpose.
- *Set a tone or establish an emotion.* Language can be used to establish a mood that the advertiser wants associated with its product. Teva sports sandals has an ad with the headline "When you die, they put you in a nice suit and shiny shoes. As if death didn't suck enough already." Even though there is no direct reference to the product being advertised, the reader has learned quite a bit about the company doing the advertising and the types of people expected to buy the product. The headline in the ad shown in Exhibit 12.16 accomplishes the same objective.
- *Identify the brand.* This is the most straightforward of all headline purposes. The brand name or label is used as the headline, either alone or in conjunction with a word or two. The goal is to simply identify the brand and reinforce brand-name recognition. Advertising for Brut men's fragrance products often uses merely the brand name as the headline.

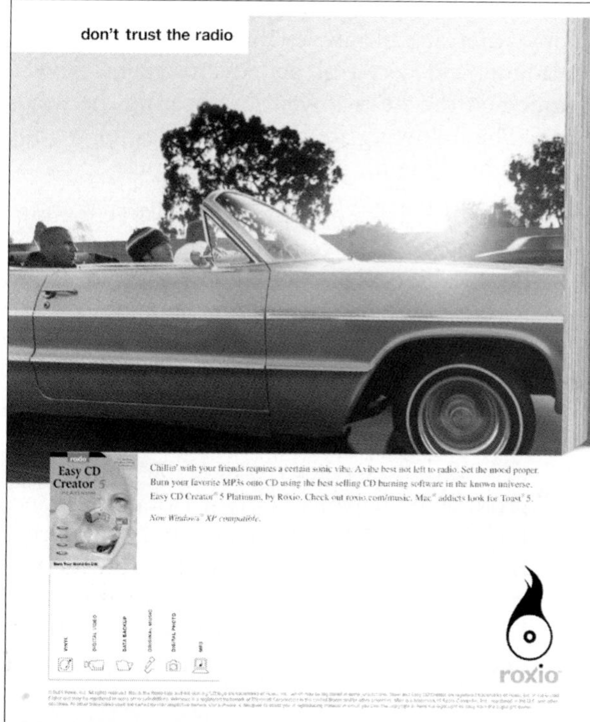

EXHIBIT 12.13

This headline offers advice. www.roxio.com

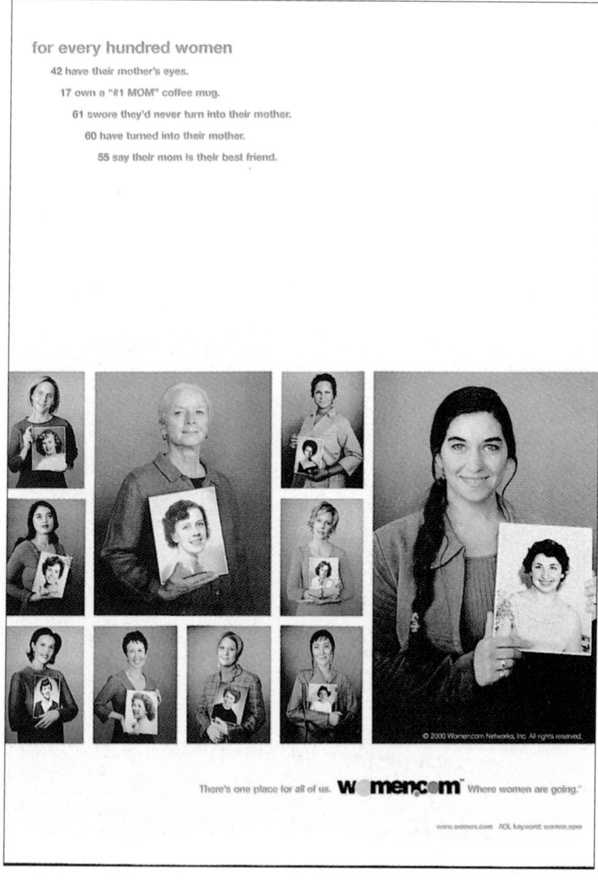

EXHIBIT 12.14

The headline in this ad suggests in no uncertain terms who the intended audience is for the site. www.women.com

EXHIBIT 12.15

A headline that creates curiosity motivates readers to continue reading, perhaps after a slight disconcerting pause. www.milk.co.uk

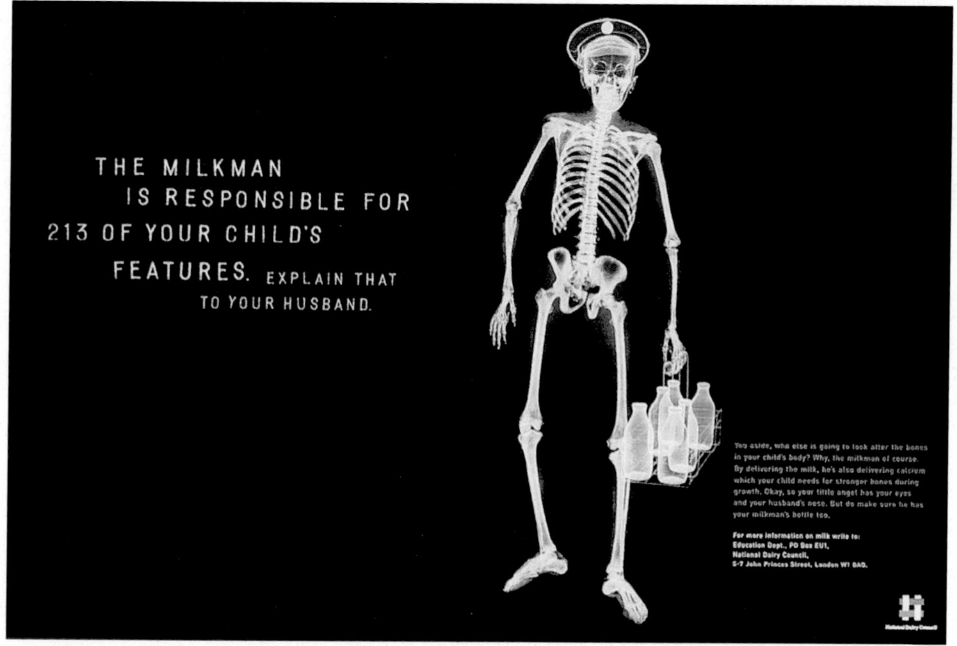

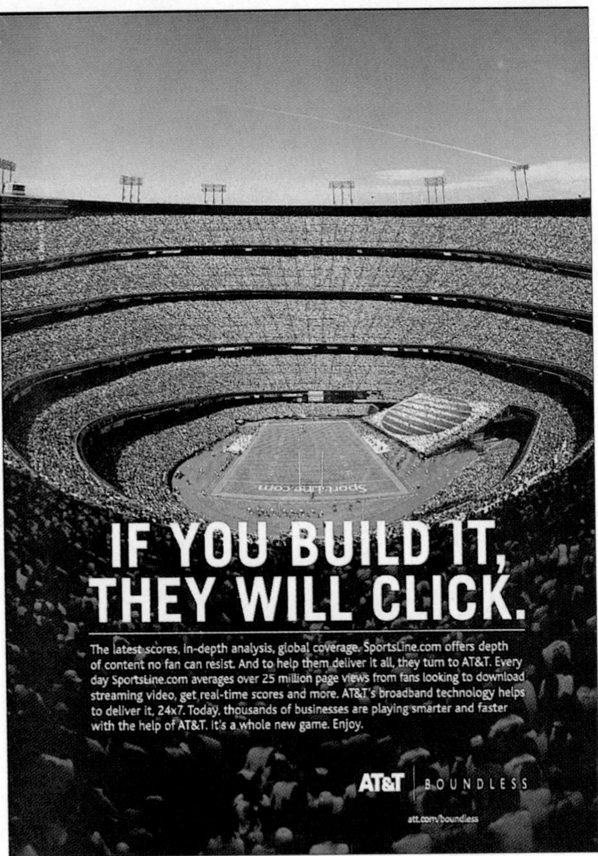

EXHIBIT 12.16

Even though there is no direct reference to the product being advertised, the reader has learned quite a bit about the company doing the advertising and the types of people expected to buy the product.
www.att.com/boundless

Guidelines for Writing Headlines. Once a copywriter has firmly established the purpose a headline will serve in an advertisement, several guidelines can be followed in preparing the headline. The following are basic guidelines for writing a good headline for print advertisements:

- Make the headline a major persuasive component of the ad. Five times as many people read the headline as the body copy of an ad. If this is your only opportunity to communicate, what should you say? The headline "New Power. New Comfort. New Technology. New Yorker" in a Chrysler ad communicates major improvements in the product quickly and clearly.
- Appeal to the reader's self-interest with a basic promise of benefits coming from the brand. For example, "The Temperature Never Drops Below Zerex" promises engine protection in freezing weather from Zerex antifreeze.
- Inject the maximum information in the headline without making it cumbersome or wordy.
- Limit headlines to about five to eight words.[7] Research indicates that recall drops off significantly for sentences longer than eight words.
- Include the brand name in the headline.
- Entice the reader to read the body copy.
- Entice the reader to examine the visual in the ad. An intriguing headline can lead the reader to carefully examine the visual components of the ad.
- Never change the typeface in a headline. Changing the form and style of the print can increase the complexity of visual impression and negatively affect the readership.
- Never use a headline whose persuasive impact depends on reading the body copy.
- Use simple, common, familiar words. Recognition and comprehension are aided by words that are easy to understand and recognize.

This set of guidelines is meant only as a starting point. A headline may violate one or even all of these basic premises and still be effective. And it is unrealistic to try to fulfill the requirements of each guideline in every headline. This list simply offers general safeguards to be considered. Test the list for yourself using the ads in Exhibits 12.17 through 12.19. Which, if any, of these ten guidelines do these ads comply with? And which ones do they torch? Which of these guidelines would you say are most important for creating effective headlines?

A truly great piece of advice:

> *Certain headlines are currently checked out. You may use them when they are returned. Lines like "Contrary to popular belief . . ." or "Something is wrong when . . ." These are dead. Elvis is dead. John Lennon is dead. Deal with it. Remember, anything that you even think you've seen, forget about it. The stuff you've never seen? You'll know when you see it, too. It raises the hair on the back of your neck.*[8]
>
> —Luke Sullivan

Originality is good.

7. Based in part on Jewler, *Creative Strategy in Advertising,* 232–233; Albert C. Book, Norman D. Cary, and Stanley I. Tannenbaum, *The Radio and Television Commercial* (Lincolnwood, Ill.: NTC Business Books, 1984), 22–26.
8. Luke Sullivan, *Hey Whipple, Squeeze This: A Guide to Creating Great Ads* (New York: Wiley), 78.

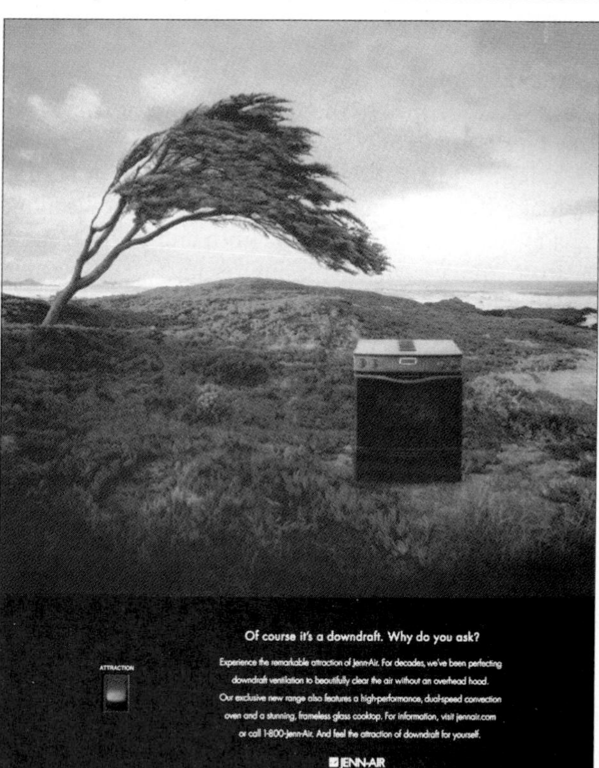

EXHIBITS 12.17 THROUGH 12.19

There are ten general guidelines for writing headlines. How do you rate the headlines in these ads relative to the guidelines? www.landrover.com, www.waterfrontbluesfest.com, *and* www.jennair.com

The Subhead. A **subhead** consists of a few words or a short sentence and usually appears above or below the headline. It includes important brand information not included in the headline. The subhead in the ad for Clorox in Exhibit 12.20 is an excellent example of how a subhead is used to convey important brand information not communicated in the headline. A subhead serves basically the same purpose as a headline—to communicate key selling points or brand information quickly. A subhead is normally in print larger than the body copy, but smaller than the headline. In many cases, the subhead is more lengthy than the headline and can be used to communicate more complex selling points. The subhead should reinforce the headline and, again, entice the reader to proceed to the body copy.

Subheads can serve another important purpose: stimulating a more complete reading of the entire ad. If the headline attracts attention, the subhead can stimulate movement through the physical space of the ad, including the visual. A good rule of thumb is the longer the body copy, the more appropriate the use of subheads. Most creative directors try to keep the use of subheads to the barest minimum, however. They feel that if an ad's visual and headline can't communicate the benefit of a product quickly and clearly, the ad isn't very good.

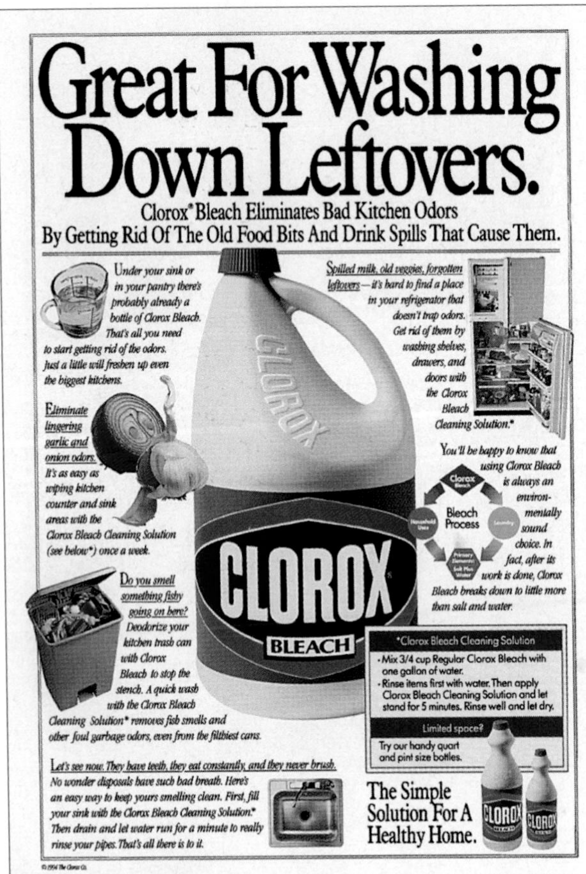

EXHIBIT 12.20

Subheads include important brand information not included in the headline. Where is the subhead in this Clorox ad? What does the subhead accomplish that the headline does not?
www.clorox.com

The Body Copy. More good advice:

I don't think people read body copy. I think we've entered a frenzied era of coffee-guzzling, fax-sending channel surfers who honk the microsecond the light turns green and have the attention span of a flashcube. If the first five words of the body copy aren't: "may we send you \$700.00," word 6 isn't read. Just my opinion, mind you.[9]

—Luke Sullivan

It's our opinion too.

Body copy is the textual component of an advertisement and tells a more complete story of a brand. Effective body copy is written in a fashion that takes advantage of and reinforces the headline and subhead, is compatible with and gains strength from the visual, and is interesting to the reader. Whether body copy is interesting is a function of how accurately the copywriter and other decision makers have assessed various components of message development, and how good the copywriter is. The most elaborate body copy will probably be ineffective if it is "off strategy." It will not matter if it's very clever, but has little to do in advancing the strategy.

There are several standard techniques for preparing body copy. The **straight-line copy** approach explains in straightforward terms why a reader will benefit from use of a brand. This technique is used many times in conjunction with a benefits message strategy. Body copy that uses **dialogue** delivers the selling points of a message to the audience through a character or characters in the ad. The Nicorette ad shown in Exhibit 12.21 is an example of the testimonial technique. A **testimonial** uses dialogue as if the spokesperson is having a one-sided conversation with the reader

9. Ibid, 85.

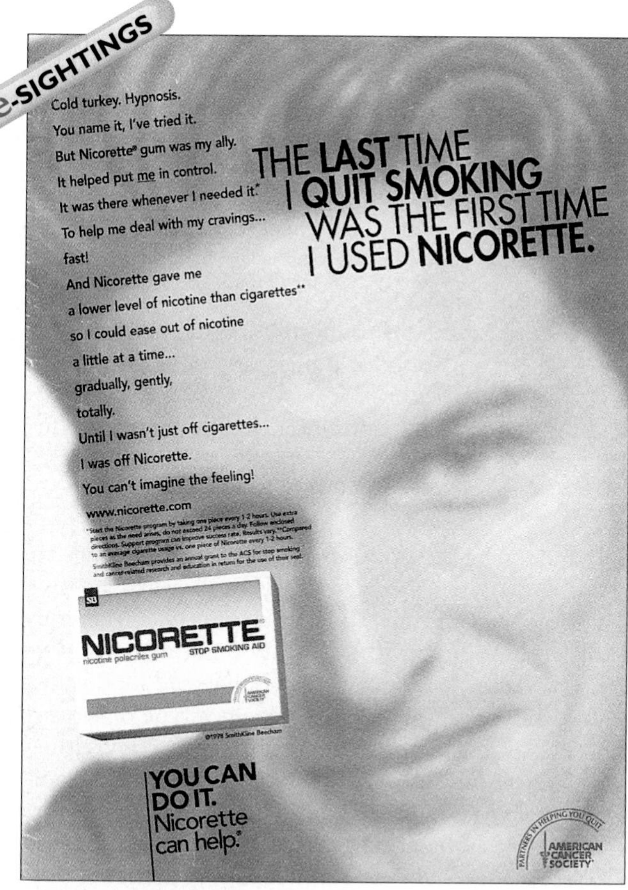

EXHIBIT 12.21

In this testimonial ad from Nicorette (www.nicorette.com), a spokesperson tells his story directly to the reader. Is this same copy technique used at the Nicorette site? What does Nicorette offer to its customers at the Committed Quitters resource site (www.committedquitters.com), and is the copy at this site more geared toward eliciting a direct response from consumers?

through the body copy. Dialogue can also depict two people in the ad having a conversation, a technique often used in slice-of-life messages.

Narrative as a method for preparing body copy simply displays a series of statements about a brand. A person may or may not be portrayed as delivering the copy. It is difficult to make this technique lively for the reader, so the threat of writing a dull ad using this technique is ever present. **Direct response copy** is, in many ways, the least complex of copy techniques. In writing direct response copy, the copywriter is trying to highlight the urgency of acting immediately. Hence, the range of possibilities for direct response copy is more limited. In addition, many direct response advertisements rely on sales promotion devices, such as coupons, contests, and rebates, as a means of stimulating action. Giving deadlines to the reader is also a common approach in direct response advertising.

These techniques for copywriting establish a general set of styles that can be used as the format for body copy. Again, be aware that any message objective can be employed within any particular copy technique. There are a vast number of compatible combinations.

Guidelines for Writing Body Copy. Regardless of the specific technique used to develop body copy, the probability of writing effective body copy can be increased if certain guidelines are followed. However, guidelines are meant to be just that—guidelines. Copywriters have created excellent ads that violate one or more of these recommendations. Generally, however, body copy for print ads has a better chance of being effective if these guidelines are followed:

- *Use the present tense whenever possible.* Casting brand claims in the past or future reduces their credibility and timeliness. Speaking to the target audience about things that have happened or will happen sounds like hollow promises.
- *Use singular nouns and verbs.* An ad is normally read by only one person at a time, and that person is evaluating only one brand. Using plural nouns and verbs simply reduces the focus on the item or brand attribute being touted and makes the ad less personal.
- *Use active verbs.* The passive form of a verb does little to stimulate excitement or interest. The use of the active verb in Pontiac's "We Build Excitement" slogan suggests that something is happening, and it's happening *now*.
- *Use familiar words and phrases.* Relying on familiar words and phrases to communicate in an interesting and unique way poses a formidable challenge for a copywriter. Familiar words can seem common and ordinary. The challenge is to creatively stylize what is familiar and comfortable to the reader so that interest and excitement result.
- *Vary the length of sentences and paragraphs.* Using sentences and paragraphs of varying lengths not only serves to increase interest but also has a visual impact that can make an ad more inviting and readable.
- *Involve the reader.* Talking at the receiver or creating a condescending mood with copy results in a short-circuited communication. Copy that impresses the reader

as having been written specifically for him or her reduces the chances of the ad being perceived as a generalized, mass communication.

- *Provide support for the unbelievable.* A brand may have features or functions that the reader finds hard to believe. Where such claims are critical to the brand's positioning in the market and value to the consumer, it is necessary to document (through test results or testimonials) that the brand actually lives up to the claims made. Without proper support of claims, the brand will lose its credibility and therefore its relevance to the consumer.
- *Avoid clichés and superlatives.* Clichés are rarely effective or attention-getting. The average consumer assumes that a brand touted through the use of clichés is old-fashioned and stale. Even though the foundation for puffery as a message method is the use of superlatives (*best, superior, unbeatable*), it is wise to avoid their use. These terms are worn out and can signal to the consumer that the brand has little new or different to offer.[10]

Copywriting for Cyberspace. While some take the position that writing is writing, we see enough evidence that the rapidly evolving medium of cyberspace has its own style, its own feel, and its own writing. Part of this is due to its history. Cybercopy evolved from a very techno-speak community, with a twentysomething, Gen-X-meets-techno-nerd kind of voice. Cybercopy's style has been influenced by this history. The medium itself, its structure and its active nature, suggests a type of writing closer to print than to television copy, but not really traditional print copy either. This is a medium where *audience* has a significantly different meaning than in traditional one-way (noninteractive) media. Audience members often come more directly to cyberads than the average print audience. In other cases, cyberads pop up as one moves from Web page to Web page. Sometimes they are downright roadblocks, but most often they are just annoyances and, thus, are pretty much like ads in other traditional media. But even in most of those cases, the cyberaudience is not as passive as television or radio audiences. All of this suggests something new. There seems to be more incentive to read cybercopy than traditional print advertising. In the beginning, there was little enough ad clutter in cyberspace, making it fairly easy to break through. (With increased Internet advertising, this has changed.) Further, much cybercopy is direct response, thus dictating copy style. At this point we believe that the basic principles of good print advertising discussed earlier in the chapter (and reconsidered in the E-Commerce box on page 418) generally apply, but a type of copy that assumes an active and engaged audience is preferred. Still, remember that odds are that they are not there for your ads, and they have mice in their hands. Consider the cyberads in Exhibits 12.22 through 12.25. What do these different forms suggest to you about cyberwriting?

Copywriting for Broadcast Advertising. Relative to the print media, radio and television present totally different challenges for a copywriter. It is obvious that the audio and audiovisual capabilities of radio and television provide different opportunities for a copywriter. The use of sound effects and voices on radio and the ability to combine copy with color and motion on television provide vast and exciting creative possibilities.

Compared to print media, however, broadcast media have inherent limitations for a copywriter. In print media, a copywriter can write longer and more involved copy to better communicate complex brand features. For consumer shopping goods such as automobiles or home satellite systems, a brand's basis for competitive differ-

10. The last three points in this list were adapted from Kenneth Roman and Jan Maas, *The New How to Advertise* (New York: St. Martin's Press, 1992), 18–19.

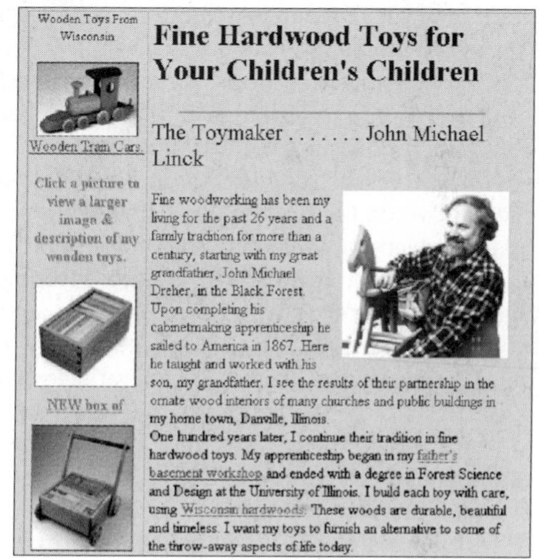

EXHIBITS 12.22 THROUGH 12.25

Cybercopy represents a new type of ad writing—closer to print than to television copy, but not really traditional print copy either. What do these four cyberads suggest to you about cyberwriting? www.garageband.com, www.johnsonville.com, www.columbia.com, *and* www.woodentoy.com.

entiation and positioning may lie with complex, unique functional features. In this case, print media provide a copywriter the time and space to communicate these details, complete with illustrations. In addition, the printed page allows a reader to dwell on the copy and process the information at a personalized, comfortable rate.

These advantages do not exist in the broadcast media. Radio and television offer a fleeting exposure. In addition, introducing sound effects and visual stimuli can distract the listener or viewer from the copy of the advertisement. Despite the additional creative opportunities that radio and television offer, the essential challenge of copywriting remains.

3 Writing Copy for Radio.

Your spot just interrupted your listener's music. It's like interrupting people having sex. If you're going to lean in the bedroom door to say something, make it good: "Hey your car's on fire."[11]

—Luke Sullivan

11. Sullivan, *Hey Whipple, Squeeze This: A Guide to Creating Great Ads,* 131.

Some writers consider radio the ultimate forum for copywriting creativity. While the radio is restricted to an audio-only presentation, a copywriter is free from some of the harsher realities of visual presentations. Yet it has been said that radio *is* visual. The copywriter must (it is almost inevitable) create images in the minds of listeners. The creative potential of radio rests in its ability to stimulate a theater of the mind, which allows a copywriter to create images and moods for an audience that transcend those created in any other medium.

Despite these creative opportunities, the drawbacks of this medium should never be underestimated. Few radio listeners ever actively listen to radio programming, much less the commercial interruptions. (Talk radio is an obvious exception.) Radio may be viewed by some as the theater of the mind, but others have labeled it audio wallpaper—wallpaper in the sense that radio is used as filler or unobtrusive accompaniment to reading, driving, household chores, or homework. If it were absent, the average person would miss it, but the average person would be hard-pressed to recall the radio ads aired during dinner last evening.

The most reasonable view of copywriting for radio is to temper both the enthusiasm of the theater-of-the-mind perspective and the pessimism of the audio-wallpaper view. (Of course, "reasonable" creative solutions often are destined to be mind-numbingly dull.) A radio copywriter should recognize the unique character of radio and exploit the opportunities it offers. First, radio adds the dimension of sound to the copywriting task, and sound (other than voices) can become a primary tool in creating copy. Second, radio can conjure images in the mind of the receiver that extend beyond the starkness of the brand "information" actually being provided. Radio copywriting should, therefore, strive to stimulate each receiver's imagination.

Writing copy for radio should begin the same way that writing copy for print begins. The copywriter must review components of the creative plan so as to take advantage of and follow through on the marketing and advertising strategies specified and integral to the brand's market potential. Beyond that fundamental task, there are particular formats for radio ads and guidelines for copy preparation the writer can rely on for direction.

Radio Advertising Formats. There are four basic formats for radio advertisements, and these formats provide the structure within which copy is prepared: the music format, the dialogue format, the announcement format, and the celebrity announcer format. Each of these formats is discussed here.

E-COMMERCE

Writing Cybercopy: Don't Abandon All the Old Rules

Writing effective copy for print and broadcast media is difficult enough, but what kind of copy does the average Net surfer find appealing? No one really knows, but we do know a few things about early users of the Internet and World Wide Web. First, users of the Internet are there first and foremost because it is an information environment. It is hard to imagine someone getting up in the morning, turning on the computer, and seeking out ads. Quite to the contrary, the beauty of the Internet in the minds of many has been its freedom from advertising.

Second, when Internet users visit a site, that visit may last only a few seconds. *HotWired* magazine says that on a good day, it can have 600,000 "hits," or visits, some lasting only a few seconds—just long enough for the visitor to quickly scan what is available and then, if not intrigued, move on to another site. The chance to communicate online thus may be even more fleeting than the opportunity offered by radio or television. Third, advertisers have to accept that cyberspace may become just as cluttered with competing ads as the traditional media.

In the end, the rules for writing effective copy in cyberspace may not be all that different from the general rules for copywriting. Once a browser is attracted to a site for the information it offers, she or he will, oh by the way, bump into ads. The new opportunity is to make these ads and their copy interactive according to an individual consumer's interest. If an IBM advertisement can lead a consumer through a series of alternative click-and-proceed paths, then customization of ads is the new copywriting opportunity offered by the interactive environment.

Sources: "Cerfin' the Net," *Sales and Marketing Management*, March 1995, 18–23; Julie Chao, "Tallies of Web-Site Browsers Often Deceive," *Wall Street Journal*, June 12, 1995, B1; Bruce Judson, "Luring Advertisers' Prospects to Web," *Advertising Age*, August 7, 1995, 16; Steven Oberbeck, "Continued Growth in Internet Ads, Users Forecast," *Salt Lake Tribune*, March 21, 1999, www.sltrib.com, accessed March 22, 1999.

Music. Since radio provides audio opportunities, music is often used in radio ads. One use of music is to write a song or jingle in an attempt to communicate in an attention-getting and memorable fashion. Songs and jingles are generally written specifically to accommodate unique brand copy. On occasion, an existing tune can be used, and the copy is fit to its meter and rhythm. This is especially true if the music is being used to capture the attention of a particular target segment. Tunes popular with certain target segments can be licensed for use by advertisers. Advertisements using popular tunes by Garbage and Barry Manilow would presumably attract two very different audiences. Singing and music can do much to attract the listener's attention and enhance recall. Singing can also create a mood and image with which the product is associated. Modern scores can create a contemporary mood, while sultry music and lyrics create a totally different mood.

But what of jingles? While some love them—and let's face it, they have survived for over a hundred years in advertising—there are some hazards in the use of singing or jingles. Few copywriters are trained lyricists or composers. The threat is ever present that a musical score or a jingle will strike receivers as amateurish and silly. To avoid this, expert songwriters are often used. Further, ensuring that the copy information dominates the musical accompaniment takes great skill. The musical impact can easily overwhelm the persuasion and selling purposes of an ad. Still, just try to get a really good jingle out of your head. You may go to your grave with it on your mind.

Another use of music in radio commercials is to open the ad with a musical score and/or have music playing in the background while the copy is being read. The role of music here is generally to attract attention. This application of music, as well as music used in a song or jingle, is subject to an ongoing debate. If a radio ad is scheduled for airing on music-format stations, should the music in the ad be the same type of music the station is noted for playing, or should it be different? One argument says that if the station format is rock, for example, then the ad should use rock music to appeal to the listener's taste. The opposite argument states that using the same type of music simply buries the ad in the regular programming and reduces its impact. There is no good evidence to suggest that music similar to or different from station programming is superior.

Dialogue. The dialogue technique, described in the section on print copywriting, is commonly used in radio. There are difficulties in making narrative copy work in the short periods of time afforded by the radio medium (typically 15 to 60 seconds). The threat is that dialogue will result in a dull drone of two or more people having a conversation. (You hear enough of that, right?) To reduce the threat of boredom, many dialogues are written with humor, like the one in Exhibit 12.26. Of course, some believe that humor is overused in radio.

Announcement. Radio copy delivered by an announcer is similar to narrative copy in print advertising. The announcer reads important product information as it has been prepared by the copywriter. Announcement is the prevalent technique for live radio spots delivered by disc jockeys or news commentators. The live setting leaves little opportunity for much else. If the ad is prerecorded, sound effects or music may be added to enhance the transmission.

Celebrity Announcer. Having a famous person deliver the copy is alleged to increase the attention paid to a radio ad. Most radio ads that use celebrities do not fall into the testimonial category. The celebrity is not expressing his or her satisfaction with the product, but merely acting as an announcer. Some celebrities (such as James Earl Jones) have distinctive voice qualities or are expert at the emphatic delivery of copy. It is argued that these qualities, as well as listener recognition of the celebrity, increase attention to the ad.

EXHIBIT 12.26

To reduce the threat of boredom, many dialogues are written with humor.
www.budweiser.com

MERIT AWARD: Consumer Radio: Single
WRITER: Steve Dildarian
AGENCY PRODUCER: Cindy Epps
CLIENT: Anheuser–Busch
AGENCY: Goodby Silverstein & Partners/San Francisco
ID 00 0555A

SFX:	SWAMP SOUNDS THROUGHOUT.
LOUIE:	Hey, Frankie.
FRANK:	What do you say, Louie?
LOUIE:	Guess who called me this morning?
FRANK:	Who?
LOUIE:	The Bud frog.
FRANK:	Oh, really. What did he say?
LOUIE:	Well, first he said, "Bud."
FRANK:	Ah hah.
LOUIE:	Then he said, "Bud," again.
FRANK:	Oh, great, okay.
LOUIE:	Yeah, I'm saying, come on, give me a little more.
FRANK:	Ah hah.
LOUIE:	But he just wanted to reminisce . . .
FRANK:	Right.
LOUIE:	. . . tell me what they are up to.
FRANK:	Well, so what are they doing?
LOUIE:	Bud is at a retirement village in Miami Beach.
FRANK:	Ooh, very nice.
LOUIE:	Yeah, he's dating a newt and he's studying tai chi.
FRANK:	Ah.
LOUIE:	And he's doing commentary for the Frog Network.
FRANK:	Well, it's good to stay active.
LOUIE:	And Er moved to New Orleans, and he's writing a book.
FRANK:	Oh yeah, what's it called?
LOUIE:	It's called, "Er. My Life As The Frog Who Said Er."
FRANK:	What a bright guy.
LOUIE:	It's just a working title.
FRANK:	Well, I hope so. Hey, how about Weis. I used to like that guy.
LOUIE:	Oooh, Weis isn't doing so well.
FRANK:	What's wrong?
LOUIE:	That nervous tic keeps getting worse.
FRANK:	Oh!
LOUIE:	He sits on his rock all day saying "Weis, weis, weis."
FRANK:	Mmm hmm.
LOUIE:	He thinks he still has the job.
FRANK:	That's a shame.
LOUIE:	That's show biz.
FRANK:	Hey, have a heart.
LOUIE:	Hey, you know what they say?
FRANK:	What?
LOUIE:	For every light on Broadway, there's a twitching frog.
FRANK:	Who says that?
LOUIE:	I was the first to say it.
FRANK:	Mmm hmm.
LOUIE:	But I'm sure there were others.
FRANK:	Oh yeah.
ANNOUNCER:	Anheuser–Busch. St. Louis, Missouri.

Guidelines for Writing Radio Copy. The unique opportunities and challenges of the radio medium warrant a set of guidelines for the copywriter to increase the probability of effective communication. The following are a few suggestions for writing effective radio copy:

- *Use common, familiar language.* The use of words and language easily understood and recognized by the receiver is even more important in radio than in print copy preparation.
- *Use short words and sentences.* The probability of communicating verbally increases if short, easily processed words and sentences are used. Long, involved, elaborate verbal descriptions make it difficult for the listener to follow the copy.
- *Stimulate the imagination.* Copy that can conjure up concrete and stimulating images in the receiver's mind can have a powerful impact on recall.
- *Repeat the name of the product.* Since the impression made by a radio ad is fleeting, it may be necessary to repeat the brand name several times before it will register. The same is true for location if the ad is being used to promote a retail organization.
- *Stress the main selling point or points.* The premise of the advertising should revolve around the information that needs to be presented. If selling points are mentioned only in passing, there is little reason to believe they'll be remembered.
- *Use sound and music with care.* By all means, a copywriter should take advantage of all the audio capabilities afforded by the radio medium, including the use of sound effects and music. While these devices can contribute greatly to attracting and holding the listener's attention, care must be taken to ensure that the devices do not overwhelm the copy and therefore the persuasive impact of the commercial.
- *Tailor the copy to the time, place, and specific audience.* Take advantage of any unique aspect of the advertising context. If the ad is specified for a particular geographic region, use colloquialisms unique to that region as a way to tailor the message. The same is true with time-of-day factors or unique aspects of the audience.[12]

The Radio Production Process. Radio commercial production highlights the role of the copywriter. There is no art director involved in the process. Further, the writer is relatively free to plan nearly any radio production he or she chooses because of the significantly reduced costs of radio execution compared to television. In radio, there are far fewer expert participants than in television. This more streamlined form of production does not mean, however, that the process is more casual. Successful fulfillment of the objectives of an advertisement still requires the careful planning and execution of the production process.

Exhibit 12.27 lists the stages and timetable of a fairly complex radio production: a fully produced commercial. Again, this is a realistic and reasonable timetable once script and budget approval have been secured. The production process for radio is quite similar to the production process for television. Once the copy strategy and methods for the commercial are approved, the process begins with soliciting bids from production houses. The producer reviews bids and submits the best bid for advertiser approval. When the best bid (not always the lowest-priced bid) is identified, the agency submits an estimate to the advertiser for approval. The bid estimate includes both the production house bid and the agency's estimates of its own costs associated with production. When the agency and the advertiser agree, then the producer can award the job to a production house.

After awarding the job to a production house, the next step is to cast the ad. A radio ad may simply have an announcer, in which case the casting job is relatively simple. If the dialogue technique is used, two or more actors and actresses may be needed. Additionally, musical scores often accompany radio ads, and either the music has to be recorded, which includes a search for musicians and possibly singers,

12. Book, Cary, and Tannenbaum, *The Radio and Television Commercial,* op. cit.

EXHIBIT 12.27

The timetable of a fully produced radio commercial, once script and budget approval have been secured.

Activity	Time
Solicit bids from production houses/other suppliers	1 week
Review bids, award job, submit production estimate to advertiser	1 week
Select a cast (announcer, singers, musicians)	1 week
Plan special elements (e.g., sound effects); make final preparations; produce tape	1 week
Edit tape	Less than 1 week
Review production (advertiser)	1 week
Mix sound	Less than 1 week
Duplicate tape; ship to stations	1 week
Total	6 to 7 weeks

or prerecorded music has to be obtained for use by permission. Securing permission for existing music, especially if it is currently popular, can be costly. Much music is in the public domain—that is, it is no longer rigidly protected by copyright laws and is available for far less cost. Closely following the casting is the planning of special elements for the ad, which can include sound effects or special effects, such as time compression or stretching, to create distinct sounds.

Final preparation and production entails scheduling a sound studio and arranging for the actors and actresses to record their pieces in the ad. If an announcer is used in addition to acting talent, the announcer may or may not record with the full cast; her or his lines can be incorporated into the tape at some later time. Music is generally recorded separately and simply added to the commercial during the sound-mixing stage.

It is during the actual production of the ad that the copywriter's efforts become a reality. As in television production, the copywriter will have drawn on the copy platform plans approved in the message development stage to write copy for the radio spot. The script used in the production of a radio advertisement serves the same purpose that the storyboard does in television production. Exhibit 12.28 is a typical radio script.

Note that the copywriter must indicate the use of sound effects (SFX) on a separate line to specify the timing of these devices. Further, each player in the advertisement is listed by role, including the announcer (ANNCR), who may or may not be needed, depending on the commercial.

One important element of writing radio copy not yet discussed is the number of words of copy to use given the length of the radio ad. As a general rule, word count relative to airtime is as follows:

10 seconds	20 to 25 words
20 seconds	40 to 45 words
30 seconds	60 to 65 words
60 seconds	120 to 125 words
90 seconds	185 to 190 words[13]

The inclusion of musical introductions, special effects, or local tag lines (specific information for local markets) reduces the amount of copy in the advertisement. Special sound effects interspersed with copy also shorten copy length. The general

13. Sandra E. Moriarty, *Creative Advertising: Theory and Practice,* 2nd ed. (Englewood Cliffs, N. J.: Prentice-Hall, 1991), 293.

MERIT AWARD: Consumer Radio: Single
WRITER: Adam Chasnow
AGENCY PRODUCER: Andy Lerner
CLIENT: Hollywood Video
AGENCY: Cliff Freeman & Partners/New York
ID 00 0542A

ANNOUNCER:	Hollywood Video presents "Sixty Second Theater," where we try, unsuccessfully, to pack all the action and suspense of a two-hour Hollywood production into 60 seconds. Today's presentation, "The Matrix."
SFX:	TECHNO/ACTION MUSIC; KNOCK KNOCK.
TRINITY:	(CARRIE-ANN MOSS SOUNDALIKE; FROM BEHIND DOOR) Hello, Neo?
NEO:	(KEANU REEVES SOUNDALIKE) Yeah.
TRINITY:	You gotta come with me to meet Morpheus and learn about the Matrix.
NEO:	But I don't know you.
TRINITY:	I'm wearing a skin-tight leather catsuit.
SFX:	DOOR OPENS.
NEO:	Oh, I'll get my coat.
SFX:	TECHNO/ACTION MUSIC TRANSITION.
TRINITY:	Morpheus, this is Neo. He's going to save the world from the machines that control the virtual reality the entire human race believes they live in.
MORPHEUS:	(LAURENCE FISHBURNE SOUNDALIKE) Hi, Neo.
NEO:	(VERY KEANU) Hey, dude.
MORPHEUS:	(TO TRINITY UNDER HIS BREATH) This guy's going to save the world?
TRINITY:	Yeah. Isn't he hot?
MORPHEUS:	We better get started. Plug the computer into his head.
SFX:	PLUG INTO HEAD.
NEO:	Ouch!
SFX:	COMPUTER SOUNDS.
MORPHEUS:	Download everything he needs to know. First, kung fu.
SFX:	COMPUTER SOUNDS.
NEO:	Hi-yah!
MORPHEUS:	Now, judo.
SFX:	KARATE SOUNDS; BODY SLAM.
NEO:	Whoa!
MORPHEUS:	And wine tasting.
SFX:	COMPUTER SOUNDS; WINE POURING FROM BOTTLE.
NEO:	Mmm. Is this a merlot or a cabernet?
MORPHEUS:	Cabernet.
SFX:	WINE GLASSES CLINKING. TECHNO/ACTION MUSIC TRANSITION.
MORPHEUS:	Now you're ready to save the world, which doesn't exist.
NEO:	Wait. This isn't actually happening?
MORPHEUS:	It is, but it isn't.
NEO:	You mean, I don't know kung fu?
MORPHEUS:	No.
NEO:	And that wasn't a cabernet?
MORPHEUS:	Sorry.
NEO:	What about her leather catsuit?
MORPHEUS:	I'm afraid not.
NEO:	Dude!
SFX:	HOLLYWOOD VIDEO THEME MUSIC.
ANNOUNCER:	If this doesn't satisfy your urge to see "The Matrix," and we can't say we blame you, then rent it today at Hollywood Video. The only place to get five-day rentals on new releases like "Prince of Egypt" and "The Mummy," available September 28th. Welcome to Hollywood. Hollywood Video. Celebrity voices impersonated.

EXHIBIT 12.28

A typical radio script. www.hollywoodvideo.com

rules for number of words relative to ad time change depending on the form and structure of the commercial.

After production, the tape goes through editing to create the best version of the production. Then, after advertiser approval, a sound mix is completed in which all music, special sound effects, and announcer copy are mixed together. The mixing process achieves proper timing between all audio elements in the ad and ensures that all sounds are at the desired levels. After mixing, the tape is duplicated and sent to radio stations for airing.

Expenses for a radio ad should be in the $30,000 to $50,000 range, although big-name talent can push that cost way up.

The most loosely structured production option essentially requires no production at all. It is called a fact sheet. A **fact sheet radio ad** is merely a listing of important selling points that a radio announcer can use to ad-lib a radio spot. This method works best with radio personalities who draw an audience because of their lively, entertaining monologues. The fact sheet provides a loose structure so the announcer can work in the ad during these informal monologues. The risk, of course, is that the ad will get lost in the chatter and the selling points will not be convincingly delivered. On the positive side, radio personalities many times go beyond the scheduled 30 or 60 seconds allotted for the ad.

Another loosely structured technique is the live script. The **live script radio ad** involves having an on-air radio personality, such as a DJ or talk-show host, read the detailed script of an advertisement. Normally there are no sound effects, since such effects would require special production. The live script ensures that all the selling points are included when the commercial is delivered by the announcer. These scripts are not rehearsed, however, and the emphasis, tone, and tempo in the delivery may not be ideal. The advantage of a live script is that it allows an advertiser to submit a relatively structured commercial for airing in a very short period of time. Most stations can work in a live script commercial in a matter of hours after it is received. Exhibit 12.29 shows that a live script is, indeed, read right over the air.

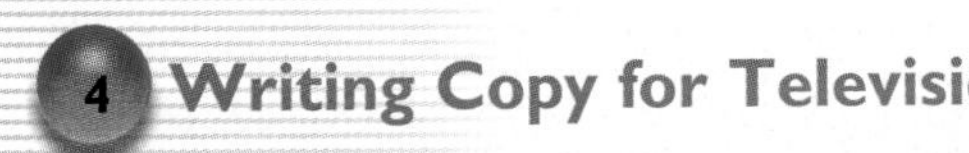

4 Writing Copy for Television.

Great print can make you famous. Great TV can make you rich.

—Anonymous[14]

Rule #1 in producing a great TV commercial. First, you must write one.

—Luke Sullivan[15]

The ability to create a mood or demonstrate a brand in use gives television wonderful capabilities; it also affords you the ability to really screw up in magnificent fashion for a very large and expensive audience (no pressure here!). Obviously, copy for television must be highly sensitive to the ad's visual aspects. It is a visual medium; you should try to not let the words get in the way.

The opportunities inherent to television as an advertising medium represent challenges for the copywriter as well. Certainly, the inherent capabilities of television can do much to bring a copywriter's words to life. But the action qualities of television can create problems. First, the copywriter must remember that words do not stand alone. Visuals, special effects, and sound techniques may ultimately convey a message far better than the cleverest turn of phrase. Second, television commercials represent a difficult timing challenge for the copywriter. It is necessary for the

14. Cited in Sullivan, *Hey Whipple, Squeeze This: A Guide to Creating Great Ads,* 103.
15. Sullivan, *Hey Whipple, Squeeze This: A Guide to Creating Great Ads,* 104.

EXHIBIT 12.29

A live script radio ad has an on-air personality read a detailed script over the air. Normally, there are no sound effects or music to accompany the ad—just the announcer's voice.

copy to be precisely coordinated with the video. If the video portion were one continuous illustration, the task would be difficult enough. Contemporary television ads, however, tend to be heavily edited (that is, lots of cuts), and the copywriting task can be a nightmare. The copywriter not only has to fulfill all the responsibilities of proper information inclusion (based on creative platform and strategy decisions), but also has to carefully fit all the information within, between, and around the visual display taking place. To make sure this coordination is precise, the copywriter, producer, and director assigned to a television advertisement work together closely to make sure the copy supports and enhances the video element. The road map for this coordination effort is known as a **storyboard.** A storyboard is a important shot-by-important-shot sketch depicting in sequence the visual scenes and copy that will be used in a television advertisement. The procedures for coordinating audio and visual elements through the use of storyboards will be presented in Chapter 13, when television production is discussed.

Television Advertising Formats. Because of the broad creative capability of the television medium, there are several alternative formats for a television ad: demonstration, problem and solution, music and song, spokesperson, dialogue, vignette, and narrative. Each is discussed here. Again, this is not an exhaustive list, but rather a sampling of popular forms.

Demonstration. Due to television's abilities to demonstrate a brand in action, demonstration is an obvious format for a television ad. Do it if you can. Brands whose benefits result from some tangible function can effectively use this format. Copy that accompanies this sort of ad embellishes the visual demonstration. The copy in a demonstration is usually straight-line copy, but drama can easily be introduced into this format, such as with the Radio Shack home security system that scares off a burglar or the Fiat braking system that saves a motorist from an accident.

Demonstration with sight and sound lets viewers appreciate the full range of features a brand has to offer. The commercial in Exhibit 12.30 was created at an agency in São Paulo, Brazil, but the clarity of the demonstration is convincing in just about any culture.

Problem and Solution. In this format, a brand is introduced as the savior in a difficult situation. This format often takes shape as a slice-of-life message, in which a consumer solves a problem with the advertised brand. Dishwashing liquids, drain openers, and numerous other household products are commonly promoted with this technique. A variation on the basic format is to promote a brand on the basis of problem prevention. A variety of auto maintenance items and even insurance products have used this approach.

Music and Song. Many television commercials use music and singing as a creative technique. The various beverage industries (soft drinks, beer, and wine) frequently use this format to create the desired mood for their brands. Additionally, the growth of image advertising has resulted in many ads that show a product in action accompanied by music and only visual overlays of the copy. This format for television advertising tends to restrict the amount of copy and presents the same difficulties for copywriting as the use of music and song in radio copywriting. Did you wonder if Burger King would ever run out of pop songs to use to peddle fast food? A logo, a few captions, a product shot, and songs ranging from "Tempted" to "So Hot" to the theme from *Welcome Back, Kotter* have been used to great success for the franchise.

Spokesperson. The delivery of a message by a spokesperson can place a heavy emphasis on the copy. The copy is given precedence over the visual and is supported by the visual, rather than vice versa. Expert, average-person, and celebrity testimonials fall into this formatting alternative. An example of the effective use of an expert spokesperson is Tiger Woods for Titleist.

Dialogue. As in a radio commercial, a television ad may feature a dialogue between two or more people. Dialogue-format ads pressure a copywriter to compose dialogue that is believable and keeps the ad moving forward. Most slice-of-life ads in which a husband and wife or friends are depicted using a brand employ a dialogue format.

Vignette. A vignette format uses a sequence of related advertisements as a device to maintain viewer interest. Vignettes also give the advertising a recognizable look, which can help achieve awareness and recognition. The Taster's Choice couple featured in a series of advertisements in the United States and Great Britain is an example of the vignette format.

Narrative. A narrative is similar to a vignette but is not part of a series of related ads. Narrative is a distinct format in that it tells a story, like a vignette, but the mood of the ad is highly personal, emotional, and involving. A narrative ad often focuses on storytelling and only indirectly touches on the benefits of the brand. Many of the "heart-sell" ads by McDonald's, Kodak, and Hallmark use the narrative technique to great effect. (See Exhibit 12.31.)

Guidelines for Writing Television Copy. Writing copy for television advertising has its own set of unique opportunities and challenges. The following are some general guidelines:

- *Use the video.* Allow the video portion of the commercial to enhance and embellish the audio portion. Given the strength and power of the visual presentation in television advertising, take advantage of its impact with copy.

EXHIBIT 12.30

Demonstration with sight and sound lets viewers appreciate the full range of features a brand has to offer; this commercial created by an ad agency in Brazil is a good example. www.honda.com

(**SFX:** MOTORCYCLE SOUNDS)	
SUPER:	Honda C-100 Dream. Up to 700 Km per liter or 30 seconds with a single drop.
SUPER:	C-100 Dream, Start It, Ride It, And Love It.
SUPER:	Honda. The World's Best Emotion.

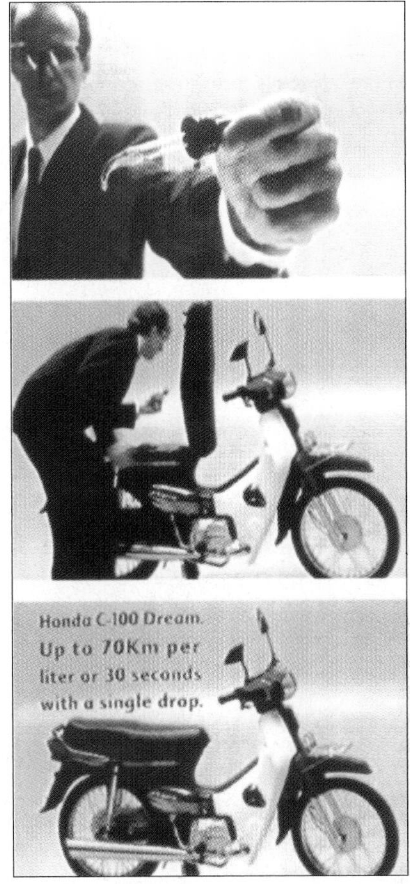

- *Support the video.* Make sure that the copy doesn't simply hitchhike on the video. If all the copy does is verbally describe what the audience is watching, an opportunity to either communicate additional information or strengthen the video communication has been lost.
- *Coordinate the audio with the video.* In addition to strategically using the video, it is essential that the audio and video do not tell entirely different stories.
- *Sell the product as well as entertain the audience.* Television ads can sometimes be more entertaining than television programming. A temptation for the copywriter and art director is to get caught up in the excitement of a good video presentation and forget that the main purpose is to deliver persuasive communication.
- *Be flexible.* Due to media-scheduling strategies, commercials are produced to run as 15-, 20-, 30-, or 60-second spots. The copywriter may need to ensure that the audio portion of an ad is complete and comprehensive within varying time lengths.
- *Use copy judiciously.* If an ad is too wordy, it can create information overload and interfere with the visual impact. Ensure that every word is a working word and contributes to the impact of the message.
- *Reflect the brand personality and image.* All aspects of an ad, copy and visuals, should be consistent with the personality and image the advertiser wants to build or maintain for the brand.
- *Build campaigns.* When copy for a particular advertisement is being written, evaluate its potential as a sustainable idea. Can the basic appeal in the advertisement be developed into multiple versions that form a campaign?[16]

16. The last three points in this list were adapted from Roman and Maas, *The New How to Advertise.*

EXHIBIT 12.31

A narrative ad often focuses on storytelling and indirectly touches on the benefits of the brand. www.jhancock.com

SUPER:	Your parents, your children, yourself.
SIGOURNEY WEAVER:	You owe it to your parents, for they brought you into this world.
SUPER:	Who do you love the least?
WEAVER:	You owe it to your children, for you did the same for them. But the day may arrive when both debts come due. When you may have no choice but to borrow from your own retirement to educate a child or care for a parent. Into whose eyes can you look and say you just can't help?
SUPER:	Insurance for the unexpected.
WEAVER:	For in both, you will surely see your own.
SUPER:	Investments for the opportunities.
SUPER:	John Hancock (Olympic rings) worldwide sponsor.

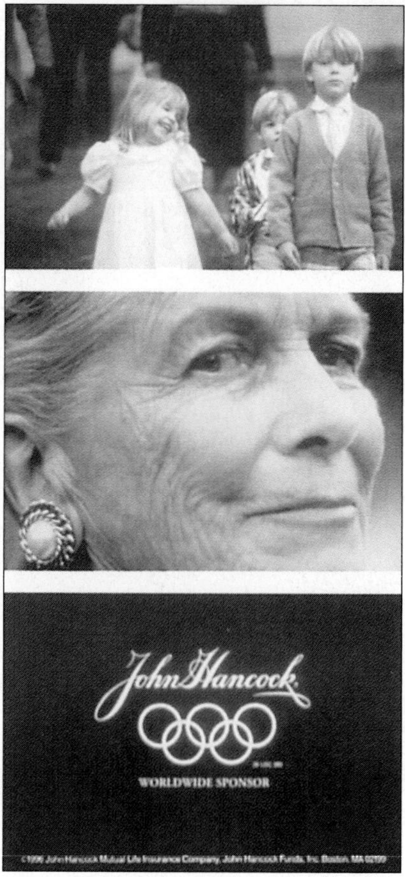

Slogans. Copywriters are often asked to come up with a good slogan or tagline for a product or service. A **slogan** is a short phrase in part used to help establish an image, identity, or position for a brand or an organization, but mostly used to increase memorability. A slogan is established by repeating the phrase in a firm's advertising and other public communication as well as through salespeople and event promotions. Slogans are often used as a headline or subhead in print advertisements, or as the tagline at the conclusion of radio and television advertisements. Slogans typically appear directly below the brand or company name, as in all Lee jeans advertising: "The Brand That Fits." Some memorable and enduring ad slogans are listed in Exhibit 12.32.

A good slogan can serve several positive purposes for a brand or a firm. First, a slogan can be an integral part of a brand's image and personality. BMW's slogan, "The Ultimate Driving Machine," does much to establish and maintain the personality and image of the brand. Second, if a slogan is carefully and consistently developed over time, it can act as a shorthand identification for the brand and provide information on important brand benefits. The long-standing slogan for Allstate Insurance, "You're in Good Hands with Allstate," communicates the benefits of dealing with a well-established insurance firm. A good slogan also provides continuity across different media and between advertising campaigns. Nike's "Just Do It" slogan has given the firm an underlying theme for a wide range of campaigns and other promotions throughout the 1990s. In this sense, a slogan is a useful tool in helping to bring about thematic integrated marketing communications for a firm. Microsoft's slogan—"Where do you want to go today?"—is all about freedom, but the company approach to integrated communications is more sophisticated than just brandishing its slogan with a vengeance.

EXHIBIT 12.32

Slogans used for brands and organizations.

Brand/Company	Slogan
Allstate Insurance	You're in Good Hands with Allstate.
American Express	Don't Leave Home Without It.
AT&T (consumer)	Reach Out and Tough Someone.
AT&T (business)	AT&T. Your True Choice.
Beef Industry Council	Real Food for Real People.
Best Buy	Turn On the Fun.
BMW	The Ultimate Driving Machine.
Budweiser	This Bud's for You.
Chevrolet trucks	Like a Rock.
Cotton Industry	The Fabric of Our Lives.
DeBeers	Diamonds are Forever.
Ford	Have You Driven a Ford Lately?
Goodyear	The Best Tires in the World Have Goodyear Written All over Them.
Harley-Davidson	The Legend Rolls On.
Lincoln	What a Luxury Car Should Be.
Maybelline	Maybe She's Born With It. Maybe It's Maybelline.
Microsoft (online)	Where Do You Want to Go Today?
Panasonic	Just Slightly Ahead of Our Time.
Prudential Insurance	Get a Piece of the Rock.
Rogaine	Stronger than Heredity.
Saturn	A Different Kind of Company. A Different Kind of Car.
Sharp	From Sharp Minds Come Sharp Products.
Toshiba	In Touch with Tomorrow.
VH1	Music First.
Visa	It's Everywhere You Want to Be.
VW	Drivers Wanted.

Common Mistakes in Copywriting. The preceding discussions have shown that print, radio, and television advertising present the copywriter with unique challenges and opportunities. Copy in each arena must be compatible with the various types of ads run in each medium and the particular capabilities and liabilities of each medium and format. Beyond the guidelines for effective copy in each area, some common mistakes made in copywriting can and should be avoided:

- *Vagueness.* Avoid generalizations and words that are imprecise in meaning. To say that a car is stylish is not nearly as meaningful as saying it has sleek, aerodynamic lines.
- *Wordiness.* Being economical with descriptions is paramount. Copy has to fit in a limited time frame (or space), and receivers bore easily. When boredom sets in, effective communication often ceases.

- *Triteness.* Using clichés and worn-out superlatives was mentioned as a threat to print copywriting. The same threat (to a lesser degree, due to audio and audiovisual capabilities) exists in radio and television advertising. Trite copy creates a boring, outdated image for a brand or firm.
- *Creativity for creativity's sake.* Some copywriters get carried away with a clever idea. It's essential that the copy in an ad remain true to its primary responsibility: communicating the selling message. However, copy that is extraordinarily funny or poses an intriguing riddle yet fails to register the main selling theme will simply produce another amusing advertising failure.

The Copy Approval Process.

"The client has some issues and concerns about your ads." This is how account executives announce the death of your labors: "issues and concerns." To understand the portent of this phrase, picture the men lying on the floor of that Chicago garage on St. Valentine's Day. Al Capone had issues and concerns with these men.

I've had account executives beat around the bush for 15 minutes before they could tell me the bad news. "Well, we had a good meeting."

Yes, you say, "but are the ads dead?"

"We learned a lot?"

"But are they dead?"

"Wellll, . . . They're really not dead. They are just in a new and better place."

—Luke Sullivan[17]

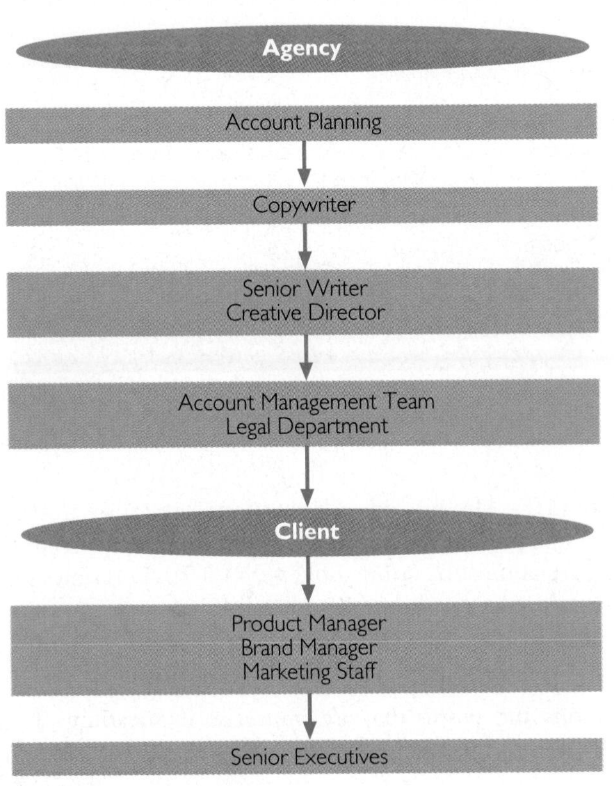

EXHIBIT 12.33

The copy approval process.

The final step in copywriting is getting the copy approved. For many copywriters, this is the most dreaded part of their existence. During the approval process, the proposed copy is likely to pass through the hands of a wide range of client and agency people, many of whom are ill-prepared to judge the quality of the copy. The challenge at this stage is to keep the creative potency of the copy intact. As David Ogilvy suggests in his commandments for advertising, "Committees can criticize advertisements, but they can't write them."[18]

The copy approval process usually begins within the creative department of an advertising agency. A copywriter submits draft copy to either the senior writer or the creative director, or both. From there, the redrafted copy is forwarded to the account management team within the agency. The main concern at this level is to evaluate the copy on legal grounds. After the account management team has made recommendations, a meeting is likely held to present the copy, along with proposed visuals, to the client's product manager, brand manager, and marketing staff. Inevitably,

17. Sullivan, *Hey Whipple, Squeeze This: A Guide to Creating Great Ads,* 182.
18. Ogilvy, *Confessions of an Advertising Man,* 101.

EXHIBIT 12.34

Advertisers should allow copywriters to exercise their creative expertise with guidance but not overbearing interference, as this Dilbert *cartoon humorously illustrates.*
www.dilbert.com

the client representatives feel compelled to make recommendations for altering the copy. In some cases, these recommendations realign the copy in accordance with important marketing strategy objectives. In other cases, the recommendations are amateurish and problematic. From the copywriter's point of view, they are rarely welcome, although the copywriter usually has to act as if they are.

Depending on the assignment, the client, and the traditions of the agency, the creative team may also rely on various forms of copy research. Typically, copy research is either developmental or evaluative. **Developmental copy research** can actually help copywriters at the early stages of copy development by providing audience interpretations and reactions to the proposed copy. **Evaluative copy research** is used to judge copy after it's been produced. Here, the audience expresses its approval or disapproval of the copy used in an ad. Copywriters are not fond of these evaluative report cards. In our view, they are completely justified in their suspicion; for many reasons, state-of-the-art evalutive copy research just isn't very good. Most of the time, it's awful, maybe even a crime. Just because someone calls it science doesn't mean a thing.

Finally, copy should always be submitted for final approval to the advertiser's senior executives. Many times, these executives have little interest in evaluating advertising plans, and they leave this responsibility to middle managers. In some firms, however, top executives get very involved in the approval process. The various levels of approval for copy are summarized in Exhibit 12.33 and parodied in Exhibit 12.34. For the advertiser, it is best to recognize that copywriters, like other creative talent in an agency, should be allowed to exercise their creative expertise with guidance but not overbearing interference. Copywriters seek to provide energy and originality to an often dry marketing strategy. To override their creative effort violates their reason for being.

SUMMARY

1 Explain the need for a creative plan in the copywriting process.

Effective ad copy must be based on a variety of individual inputs and information sources. Making sense out of these diverse inputs and building from them creatively is a copywriter's primary challenge. A creative plan is used as a device to assist the copywriter in dealing with this challenge. Key elements in the creative plan include product features and benefits that must be communicated to the audience, the mood or tone appropriate for the audience, and the intended media for the ad.

Detail the components of print copy, along with important guidelines for writing effective print copy.

The three unique components of print copy are the headline, subhead, and body copy. Headlines need to motivate additional processing of the ad. Good headlines communicate information about the brand or make a promise about the benefits the consumer can expect from the brand. If the brand name is not featured in the headline, then that headline must entice the reader to examine the body copy or visual material. Subheads can also be valuable in helping lead the reader to and through the body copy. In the body copy, the brand's complete story can be told. Effective body copy must be crafted carefully to engage the reader, furnish supportive evidence for claims made about the brand, and avoid clichés and exaggeration that the consumer will dismiss as hype.

Describe various formatting alternatives for radio ads and articulate guidelines for writing effective radio copy.

Four basic formats can be used to create radio copy. These are the music format, the dialogue format, the announcement format, and the celebrity announcer format. Guidelines for writing effective radio copy start with using simple sentence construction and language familiar to the intended audience. When the copy stimulates the listener's imagination, the advertiser can expect improved results as long as the brand name and the primary selling points don't get lost. When using music or humor to attract and hold the listener's attention, the copywriter must take care not to shortchange key selling points for the sake of simple entertainment.

Describe various formatting alternatives for television ads and articulate guidelines for writing effective television copy.

Several formats can be considered in preparing television ad copy. These are demonstration, problem and solution, music and song, spokesperson, dialogue, vignette, and narrative. To achieve effective copy in the television medium, it is essential to coordinate the copy with the visual presentation, seeking a synergistic effect between audio and video. Entertaining to attract attention should again not be emphasized to the point that the brand name or selling points of the ad get lost. Developing copy consistent with the heritage and image of the brand is also essential. Finally, copy that can be adapted to various time lengths and modified to sustain audience interest over the life of a campaign is most desirable.

KEY TERMS

creative team
creative concept
copywriting
creative plan
headline
subhead
straight-line copy
dialogue
testimonial
narrative
direct response copy
fact sheet radio ad
live script radio ad
storyboard
slogan
developmental copy research
evaluative copy research

QUESTIONS

1. Explain the applications for copy research in the copywriting process. What other forms of consumer or market research might be particularly helpful in developing effective ad copy?

2. Pull 10 print ads from your favorite magazine. Using the classifications offered in this chapter, what would you surmise was the copywriter's intended purpose for each of the headlines in your 10 print ads?

3. How does audience influence the style of writing exhibited in cyberads? How do you characterize the writing at www.peperami.com shown in Exhibit 12.23?

4. Discuss the advantages and disadvantages of music as a tool for constructing effective radio ads.

5. Listen with care to the radio ads in 30 minutes of programming on your favorite radio station. Then do the same for 30 minutes of programming on a parent's or grandparent's favorite station. Identify ads that did the best job of using terms and jargon familiar to the target audience of each station. What differences in mood or tone did you detect among ads on the two stations?

6. Compare and contrast the dialogue and narrative formats for television ads. What common requirement must

be met to construct convincing TV ads using these two formats?

7. Entertainment is both the blessing and the curse of a copywriter. Is it conceivable that ads that merely entertain could actually prove valuable in stimulating sales? If so, how so?

8. Describe the four common categories of mistakes that copywriters must avoid. From your personal experience with all types of ads, are there other common mistakes that you believe copywriters are prone to make on a regular basis?

9. Everyone has his or her own opinion on what makes advertisements effective or ineffective. How does this fundamental aspect of human nature complicate a copywriter's life when it comes to winning approval for his or her ad copy?

EXPERIENTIAL EXERCISES

1. Divide into groups. Your team assignment is to study and improve upon local car-dealer television advertising. Watch two or three television commercials by local car dealers. Discuss what you found good or bad about the ads. Seize upon the worst commercial and develop a list of suggestions to improve it. Apply your thoughts to the generation of a storyboard for a much-improved commercial.

2. Find two print ads that do not use a subhead. Craft three subheads for each ad and defend the role each plays in improving the ads.

USING THE INTERNET

12-1 Basic Components of Copy

Several major elements are used when producing advertising copy. Visit the following sites and click around individual pages in the site to read and analyze copy.

Leggs: http://www.leggs.com

Wonderbra: http://www.wonderbra.com

Pontiac: http://www.pontiac.com

1. Do these sites have headlines on the home page? What do you think makes a headline for a Web page effective?

2. Do you think that the body copy for each site supports the headline? What aspects of the body copy do you think are most effective? Least effective?

3. Does the copy support the overall creative plan of the site by integrating with various design elements such as color, illustration, sound, and interactive?

12-2 Cybercopy

Every communication medium has advantages and disadvantages in conveying a message to an audience, and good writers grasp both the opportunities and limitations inherent within each media situation. Additionally, new technology continues to affect the form and style with which we communicate as a culture. While most akin to print copy, cybercopy has certain interactive qualities that make it distinct, and many resources are available to copywriters to help them polish their craft for the Web.

Buzz Killer: http://www.buzzkiller.net

Web Grammar: http://www.webgrammar.com

1. Browse these sites and search for tips or articles pertaining to cybercopy guidelines. Based on the information you found, come up with three guidelines or rules for writing good Web copy.

2. Do these cybercopy guidelines apply equally to print copy? List similarities and differences between cybercopy and traditional print copy.

CHAPTER 13

After reading and thinking about this chapter, you will be able to do the following:

Identify the basic purposes, components, and formats of print ad illustrations.

Describe the principles and components that help ensure the effective design of print ads.

Detail the stages that art directors follow in developing the layout of a print ad.

Discuss the activities and decisions involved in the final production of print ads.

Identify the various players who must function as a team to produce television ads.

Discuss the specific stages and costs involved in producing television ads.

Describe the major formatting options for television ad production.

Remember to ski and snowboard responsibly. www.boeriusa.com
boeri®
it's your head

A hundred years ago advertisers largely relied on words to persuade consumers. They argued with consumers, attempted to reason with them, pleaded with them, and cajoled them. Then somewhere in the early 20th century, particularly noticeable after about 1910, advertisers began a move away from words and toward pictures. This trend would extend throughout the 20th century and into the 21st. Advertising has become more and more visual. There are several reasons for this. Among them are (1) improved technologies, which facilitate better and more affordable illustration; (2) the inherent advantage of pictures to quickly demonstrate goods and services; (3) the ability to build brand "images" through visuals; (4) the legalistic advantage of pictures over words in that the truth or falsity of a picture is virtually impossible to determine; (5) the widely held belief that pictures, although just as cultural as words, permit a certain type of portability that words do not; and (6) the fact that pictures allow advertisers to place brands in desired social contexts, thus transferring important social meaning to them.

Not coincidentally, the role of the art director has grown more and more important relative to the copywriter. This is a visual age, and like it or not, the primacy of the word has been challenged by pictures in contemporary advertising. Make no mistake, copywriting is still vital. This is a place where we can learn from the experience of advertising practice. So, let's show and tell.

Illustration, Design, and Layout.

We begin with a discussion of three primary visual elements of a print ad: illustration, design, and layout. We then identify aspects of each that should be specified, or at least considered, as a print ad is being prepared. An advertiser must appreciate the technical aspects of coordinating the visual elements in an ad with the mechanics of the layout and ultimately with the procedures for print production. A discussion of illustration, design, and layout brings to the fore the role of art direction in print advertising.

Initially, the art director and copywriter decide on the content of an illustration. Then the art director, often in conjunction with a graphic designer, takes this raw idea for the visual and develops it further. Art directors, with their specialized skills and training, coordinate the design and illustration components of a print ad. The creative director oversees the entire process. Most often, the copywriter is still very much in the loop.

1 Illustration.

Illustration, in the context of print advertising, is the actual drawing, painting, photography, or computer-generated art that forms the picture in an advertisement.

Illustration Purposes.

There are several specific, strategic purposes for illustration, which can greatly increase the chances of effective communication. The basic purposes of an illustration are the following:

- to attract the attention of the target audience
- to make the brand heroic
- to communicate product features or benefits
- to create a mood, feeling, or image
- to stimulate reading of the body copy
- to create the desired social context for the brand

Attract the Attention of the Target Audience. One of the primary roles of an illustration is to attract and hold attention. With all the advertising clutter out there today, this is no easy task. In some advertising situations (for example, the very early stages of a new product launch or very "low-involvement" repeat purchase items),

EXHIBITS 13.1 AND 13.2

What do you think of the impact of these ads? www.homestore.com *and* www.oddbins.com

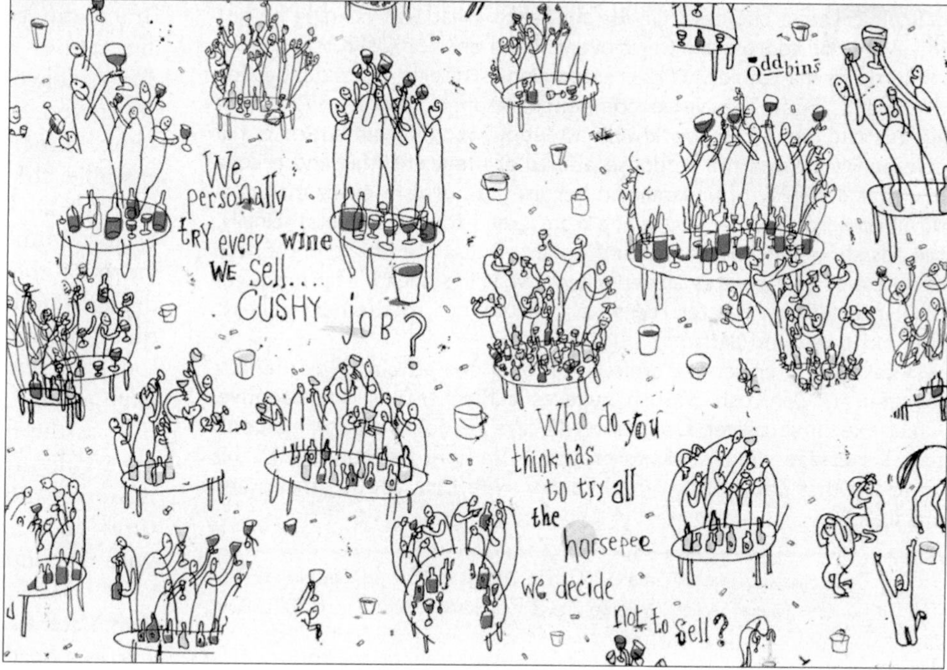

just being noticed by consumers may almost be enough. In most cases, however, just being noticed is a necessary, but not sufficient, goal. An illustration is made to communicate with a particular target audience and, generally, must support other components of the ad to achieve the intended communication impact. So, what do you think of the impact of the ads in Exhibits 13.1 and 13.2? Will they get noticed?

Make the Brand Heroic. One traditional role of art direction is to make the brand heroic. Very often this is done by the manner in which the brand is presented via illustration. Visual techniques such as backlighting, low-angle shots, and dramatic use of color can communicate heroic proportions and qualities. (See Exhibit 13.3.) David Ogilvy suggests that if you don't have a particular story to tell in the ad, then make the package the subject of the illustration.[1] The Creativity box on this page tells how OshKosh B'Gosh incorporated the tragic events of the September 11, 2001, terrorist attacks into its advertising to make its brand heroic.

CREATIVITY

We Could Be Heroes

Children's clothier OshKosh B'Gosh recently launched a national ad campaign—"What the future wears"—that produced two New York–specific ads reflecting on the terrorist events that crippled the city on September 11, 2001. Laughlin/Constable in Milwaukee produced the new ads for OshKosh B'Gosh and placed them on outdoor boards in New York City and in two magazines.

For the huge Times Square board, the agency produced a simple message in a childlike scrawl: "Every kid needs heroes. Thanks N.Y.C." The second ad depicted a young boy standing before an American flag and wearing a pair of OshKosh B'Gosh overalls, holding a crayon in his hand. Beneath him, also written in a child's hand, the tag says, "Land that I love." That ad ran in New York bus shelters, in *The New York Times* magazine, and in *People* magazine.

In the wake of terrorist attacks, advertisers have been faced with difficult creative choices: run ads similar to what was running before the events or address the tragic events head on? For OshKosh, choosing to tip its hat to New York created many strategic opportunities for the brand. First, the visual component tapped into an event that already had immediate worldwide attention. Second, the international community viewed the response efforts of the firefighting and rescue teams as a display of unparalleled heroism (a heroism every manufacturer could only dream of having transferred to its products). Finally, the ads show patriotic fervor and boldly discuss the future in the face of an event that creates anxiety about what lies ahead. The message? OshKosh B'Gosh creates rugged products worn by the next generation of heroes and patriots.

While some critics are cynical about various post-tragedy marketing efforts, OshKosh B'Gosh believes audiences will be receptive. Chief executive officer Douglas Hyde says he doesn't think his company's message will be misinterpreted: "We have a reputation as this company that comes from the Midwest. We care about families and children."

Sources: Doris Hajewski, "Attacks Spur OshKosh to Change Holiday Ad Campaign in New York," *Milwaukee Journal Sentinel*, www.jsonline.com, accessed October 24, 2001; Barry Janoff, "OshKosh Tips Hat to New York," *Media Week*, accessed October 25, 2001.

Communicate Product Features or Benefits. Perhaps the most straightforward illustration is one that simply displays brand features, benefits, or both (see Exhibit 13.4). Even though a print ad is static, the product can be shown in use through an "action" scene or even through a series of illustrations. The benefits of product use can be demonstrated with before-and-after shots or by demonstrating the result of having used the product.

Create a Mood, Feeling, or Image. Brand image is projected through illustration. The myriad of ways this is done is beyond enumeration, but the illustration, interacting with the packaging, associated brand imagery (for example, the brand logo), and evoked feelings, all contribute. The "mood" of an ad can help this along. Actually pursuing these goals with a print ad depends on the technical execution of the illustration. The lighting, color, tone, and texture of the illustration can have a huge impact. The photograph used as the illustration in the print ad for a video rental store that specializes in horror movies in Exhibit 13.5 captures an eerie, disconcerting feeling with its contrast and lighting.

Stimulate Reading of the Body Copy. Just as a headline can stimulate examination of the illustration, the illustration can stimulate reading of the body copy. Since body copy generally carries the essential selling message, any tactic that encourages reading is useful. (See Exhibit 13.6.) Illustrations can create curiosity and interest in readers. To satisfy that curiosity, readers may proceed to the body copy for clarification. (This is not easy; body copy often looks boring and tedious.) Normally, an illustration and headline need to be fully coordinated and play off each other for this level of interest to occur. One caution is to avoid making the illustration too clever a stimulus for motivating copy reading. Putting cleverness ahead of clarity in choosing an illustration can confuse

1. David Ogilvy, *Ogilvy on Advertising* (New York: Vintage Books, 1985), 77.

EXHIBIT 13.3

What makes this ad have impact? Lighting? Color? What?

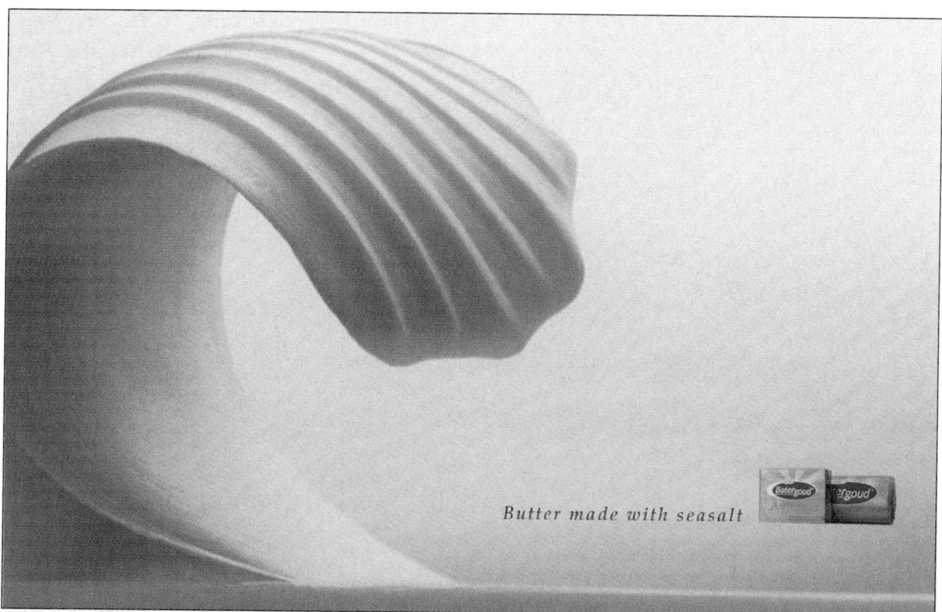

EXHIBIT 13.4

Sometimes demonstrations, even exaggerated ones, are best. This is one light bike.
www.schwinn.com

the receiver and cause the body copy to be ignored. As one expert puts it, such ads win awards but can camouflage the benefit offered by the product.[2]

Create the Desired Social Context for the Brand. As described earlier, advertisers need to associate or situate their brand within a type of social setting, thereby linking it with certain "types" of people and certain lifestyles. Establishing desired social contexts is probably the most important function of modern art direction. Look at the ad in Exhibit 13.7 and then think about what it would mean if the product were

2. Tony Antin, *Great Print Advertising* (New York: Wiley, 1993), 38.

EXHIBIT 13.5

Contrast and eerie lighting work here.

divorced from the social context. (See Exhibit 13.8.) See what we mean. Context can be (and usually is) everything.

Illustration Components. Various factors contribute to the overall visual presentation and impact of an illustration. Size, color, and medium affect viewers. Individual decisions regarding size, color, and medium are a matter of artistic discretion and creative execution. There is some evidence of the differing effects of various decisions made in each of these areas. But remember, the interpretation and meaning of any visual representation cannot be explained completely by a series of rules or prescriptive how-tos. Thankfully, it's not that simple.

Size. Does doubling the size of an illustration double the probability that the illustration will achieve its intended purpose? The answer is probably no. There is no question that greater size in an illustration may allow an ad to compete more successfully for the reader's attention, especially in a cluttered media environment. Generally speaking, illustrations with a focal point immediately recognizable by the reader are more likely to be noticed and comprehended. Conversely, illustrations that arouse curiosity or incorporate action score high in attracting attention but have been found to score low in inducing the reading of the total ad.[3]

Color. While not every execution of print advertising allows for the use of color (because of either expense or the medium being employed), color is a creative tool with important potential. Some products (such as furniture, floor coverings, or expensive clothing) may depend on color to accurately communicate a principal value. Color can also be used to emphasize a product feature or attract the reader's attention to a particular part of an ad. But remember, color has no fixed meaning, so no hard rules can be offered. Color is cultural, situational, and contextual. Saying that red always means this or blue always means that is a popular but unfounded myth. It's simply not true.

Medium. The choice of **medium** for an illustration is the decision regarding the use of drawing, photography, or computer graphics.[4] Drawing represents a wide range of creative presentations, from cartoons to pen-and-ink drawings to elaborate watercolor and oil paintings. Photos have an element of believability as representations of reality (even though they can be just as manipulated as any other form of representation.) Further, photos can often be prepared more quickly and at much less expense than other forms of art. Photographers all over the world specialize in different types of photography: landscape, seascape, portrait, food, and architecture, for example. The American Society of Magazine Photographers is a clearinghouse for nearly 5,000 photographers whose work is available as off-the-shelf images.[5] Pho-

3. Daniel Starch, *Measuring Advertising Readership and Results* (New York: McGraw-Hill, 1966), 83.
4. This section is adapted from Sandra E. Moriarity, *Creative Advertising: Theory and Practice,* 2nd ed. (Englewood Cliffs, N.J.: Prentice-Hall, 1991), 139–141.
5. G. Robert Cox and Edward J. McGee, *The Ad Game: Playing to Win* (Englewood Cliffs, N.J.: Prentice-Hall, 1990), 44.

EXHIBIT 13.6

This ad tries to get you to read the body copy. Does it work? www.becks-beer.com

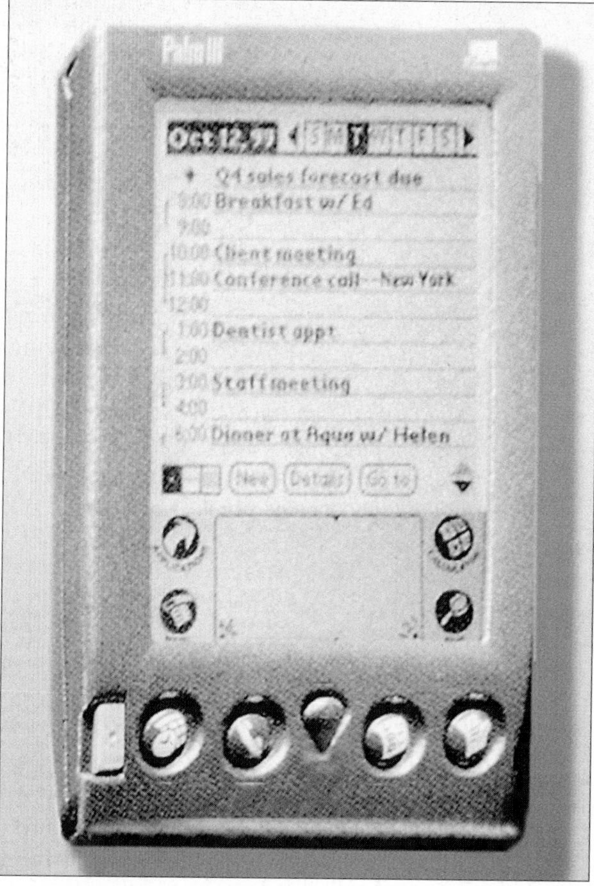

EXHIBITS 13.7 AND 13.8

3Com's Palm Computing platform with and without social context. www.3com.com

tographs can be cropped to any size or shape, retouched, color-corrected, and doctored in a number of ways to create the desired effect.

With advancing technology, artists have discovered the application of computer graphics to advertising illustrations. Computer graphics specialists can create and

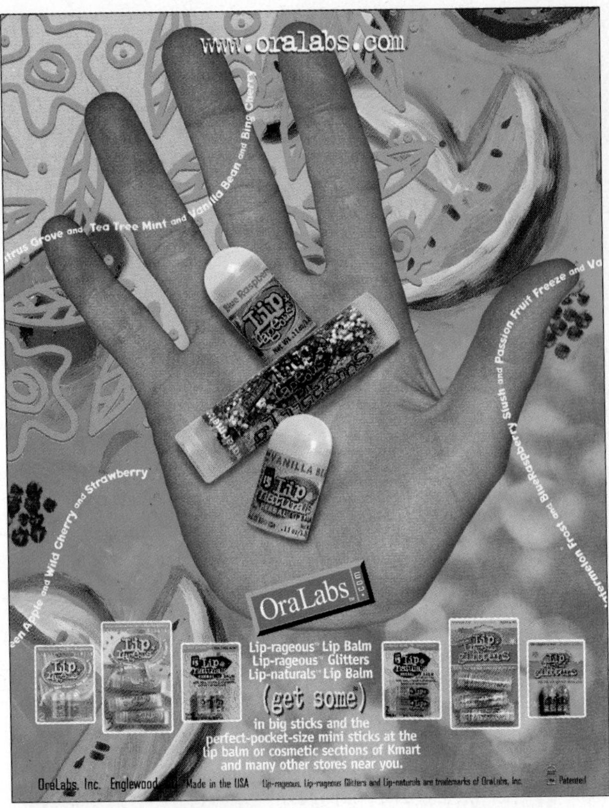

EXHIBIT 13.9

Computer graphics make this ad. www.oralabs.com

manipulate images. With respect to illustrations for print advertising, the key development has been the ability to digitize images. Digitizing is a computer process of breaking an image (illustration) into a grid of small squares. Each square is assigned a computer code for identification. With a digitized image, computer graphics specialists can break down an illustration and reassemble it or import other components into the original image. Age can be added to or taken away from a model's face, or the Eiffel Tower can magically appear on Madison Avenue. The creative possibilities are endless with computer graphics. Exhibit 13.9 is an example of an ad with multiple images imported through computer graphics. Some art directors are very fond of these software solutions.

The size, color, and media decisions regarding an illustration are difficult ones. It is likely that strategic and budgetary considerations will heavily influence choices in these areas. Once again, an advertiser should not constrain the creative process more than is absolutely necessary, and even then you should probably back off a bit.

Illustration Formats. The just-discussed components represent a series of decisions that must be made in conceiving an illustration. Another important decision is how the product or brand will appear as part of the illustration. **Illustration format** refers to the choices the advertiser has for displaying its product. There are product shots of all sorts: some emphasize the social context and meaning of the product or service; others are more abstract (see Exhibit 13.10). Obviously, the illustration format must be consistent with the copy strategy set for the ad. The creative department and the marketing planners must communicate with one another so that the illustration format selected helps pursue the specific objectives set for the total ad campaign.

The Strategic and Creative Impact of Illustration. Defining effectiveness is a matter of first considering the basic illustration purposes, components, and formats we've just discussed. Next, these factors need to be evaluated in the context of marketing strategy, consumer behavior, and campaign planning. At this point there is a lot of negotiation, discussion, and explaining. If everything works out, the ad(s) go forward.

2 Design.

Design is "the structure itself and the plan behind that structure" for the aesthetic and stylistic aspects of a print advertisement.[6] Design represents the effort on the part of creatives to physically arrange all the components of a printed advertisement in such a way that order and beauty are achieved—order in the sense that the illustration, headline, body copy, and special features of the ad are easy to read; beauty in the sense that the ad is visually pleasing to a reader.

Certainly, not every advertiser has an appreciation for the elements that constitute effective design, nor will every advertiser be fortunate enough to have highly

6. This discussion is based on Roy Paul Nelson, *The Design of Advertising,* 5th ed. (Dubuque, Iowa: Wm. C. Brown, 1985), 126.

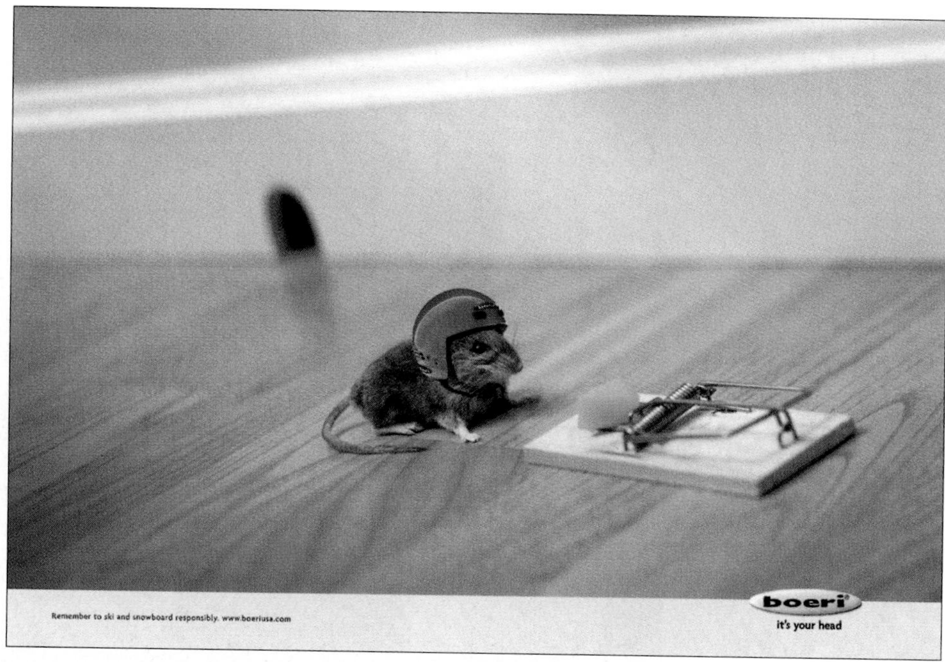

EXHIBIT 13.10

Some ads are more abstract.
www.boeriusa.com

skilled designers as part of the team creating a print ad. As you will see in the following discussions, however, there are aspects of design that directly relate to the potential for a print ad to communicate effectively based on its artistic form. As such, design factors are highly relevant to creating effective print advertising.

Principles of Design. Principles of design govern how a print advertisement should be prepared. The word *should* is carefully chosen in this context. It is used because, just as language has rules of grammar and syntax, visual presentation has rules of design. The **principles of design** relate to each element within an advertisement and to the arrangement of and relationship between elements as a whole.[7] Principles of design suggest the following:

- A design should be in balance.
- The proportion within an advertisement should be pleasing to the viewer.
- The components within an advertisement should have an ordered and directional pattern.
- There should be a unifying force within the ad.
- One element of the ad should be emphasized above all others.

We will consider each of these principles of design and how they relate to the development of an effective print advertisement. Of course, as surely as there are rules, there are occasions when the rules need to be broken. An experienced designer knows the rules and follows them, but is also prepared to break the rules to achieve a desired outcome. But first, you learn the rules.

Balance. **Balance** in an ad is an orderliness and compatibility of presentation. Balance can be either formal or informal. **Formal balance** emphasizes symmetrical presentation—components on one side of an imaginary vertical line through the ad are repeated in approximate size and shape on the other side of the imaginary line.

7. Ibid., 129–136.

EXHIBIT 13.11

This ad achieves balance.
www.greenpeace.org

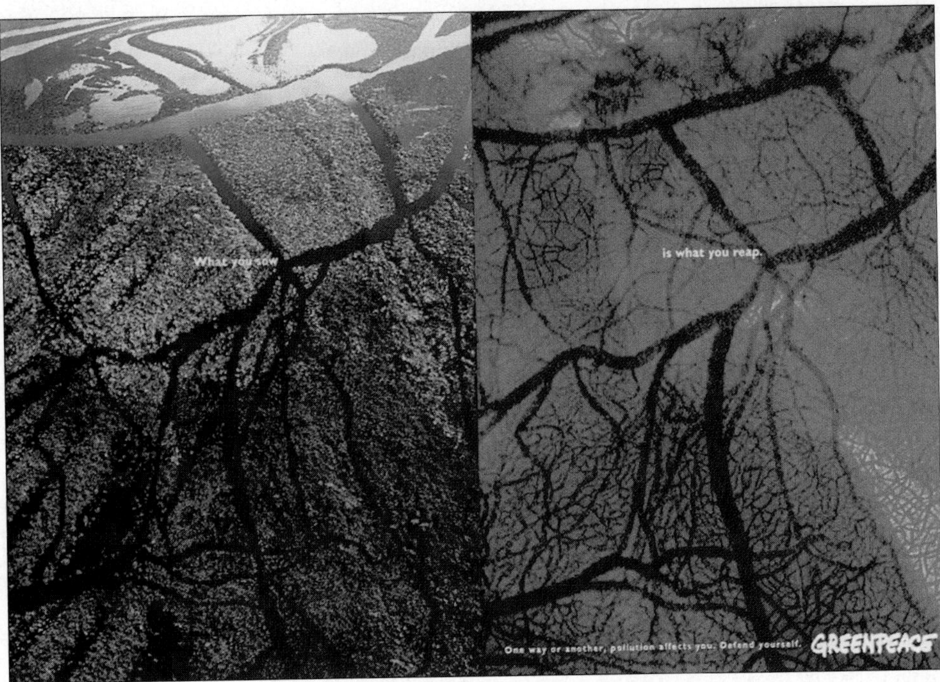

Formal balance creates a mood of seriousness and directness and offers the viewer an orderly, easy-to-follow visual presentation (see Exhibit 13.11).

Informal balance emphasizes asymmetry—the optical weighing of nonsimilar sizes and shapes. Exhibit 13.12 shows an advertisement using a range of type sizes, visuals, and colors to create a powerful visual effect that achieves informal balance. Informal balance in an ad should not be interpreted as imbalance. Rather, components of different sizes, shapes, and colors are arranged in a more complex relationship providing asymmetrical balance to an ad. Informal balance is more difficult to manage in that the placement of unusual shapes and sizes must be precisely coordinated.

Proportion. Proportion has to do with the size and tonal relationships between different elements in an advertisement. Whenever two elements are placed in proximity, proportion results. In a printed advertisement, proportional considerations include the relationship of the width of an ad to its depth; the width of each element to the depth of each element; the size of one element relative to the size of every other element; the space between two elements and the relationship of that space to a third element; and the amount of light area as opposed to the amount of dark area. Ideally, factors of proportion vary so as to avoid monotony in an ad. Further, the designer should pursue pleasing proportions, which means the viewer will not detect mathematical relationships between elements. In general, unequal dimensions and distances make for the most lively designs in advertising (Exhibit 13.13).

Order. Order in an advertisement is also referred to as sequence or, in terms of its effects on the reader, "gaze motion." The designer's goal is to establish a relationship among elements that leads the reader through the ad in some controlled fashion. A designer can create a logical path of visual components to control eye movement. The eye has a "natural" tendency to move from left to right, from up to down, from large elements to small elements, from light to dark, and from color to noncolor. Exhibit 13.14 is an example of an ad that induces the reader's eye to move from the upper right to the slogan at the lower center, based on the elements of order. Order also includes inducing the reader to jump from one space in the ad to

e-SIGHTINGS

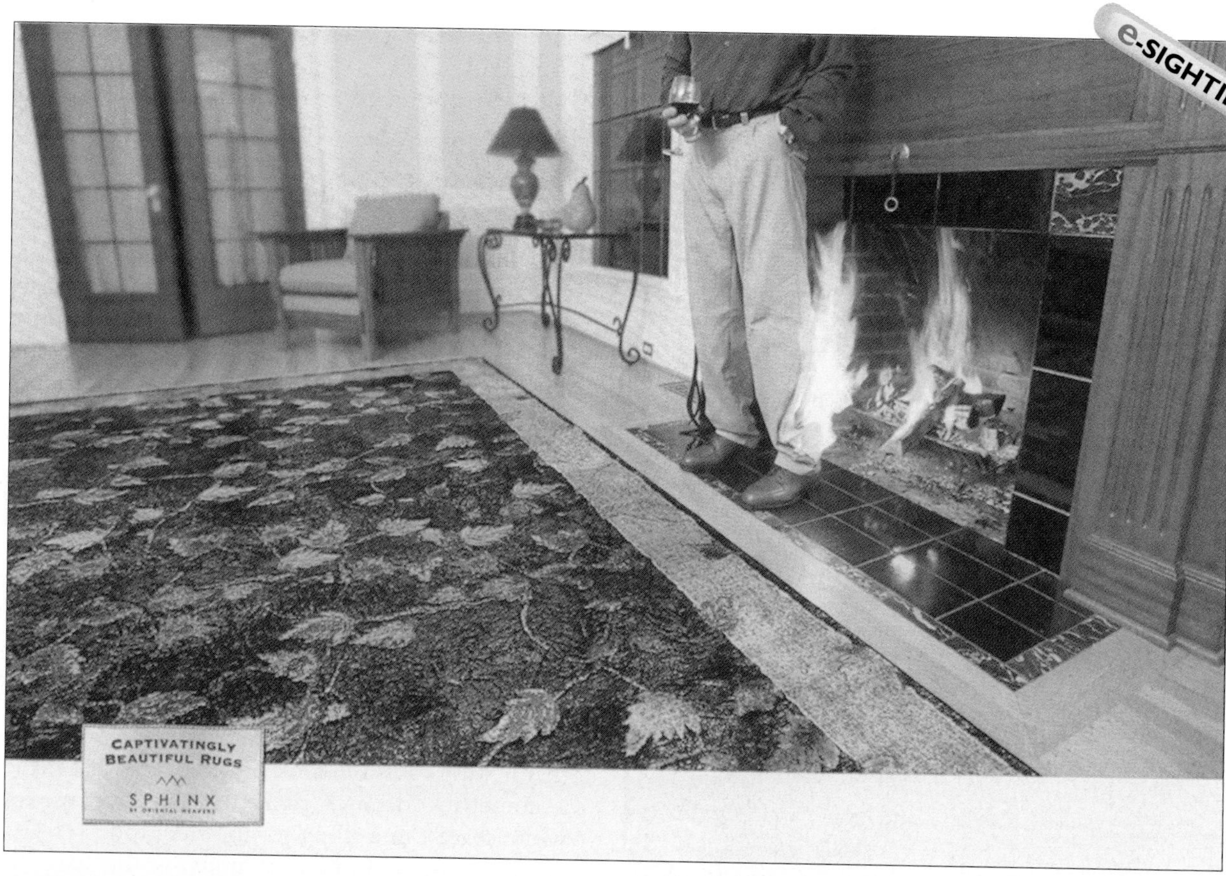
CAPTIVATINGLY
BEAUTIFUL RUGS
SPHINX

EXHIBIT 13.12

This ad uses informal balance for creative effect. Sawyer Riley Compton (www.sawyerrileycompton.com) *is a highly respected design firm. Visit the site and critique its interactive, print, and illustration portfolio samples. How well do these samples follow the basic principles of design? Are the principles of design similar across different media?* www.orientalweavers.com

EXHIBIT 13.13

Proportion, when expertly controlled, can result in an inspired display of the oversized versus the undersized.
www.parmalat.com

Parmalat
Fortified Milk.
It gives you
more energy.

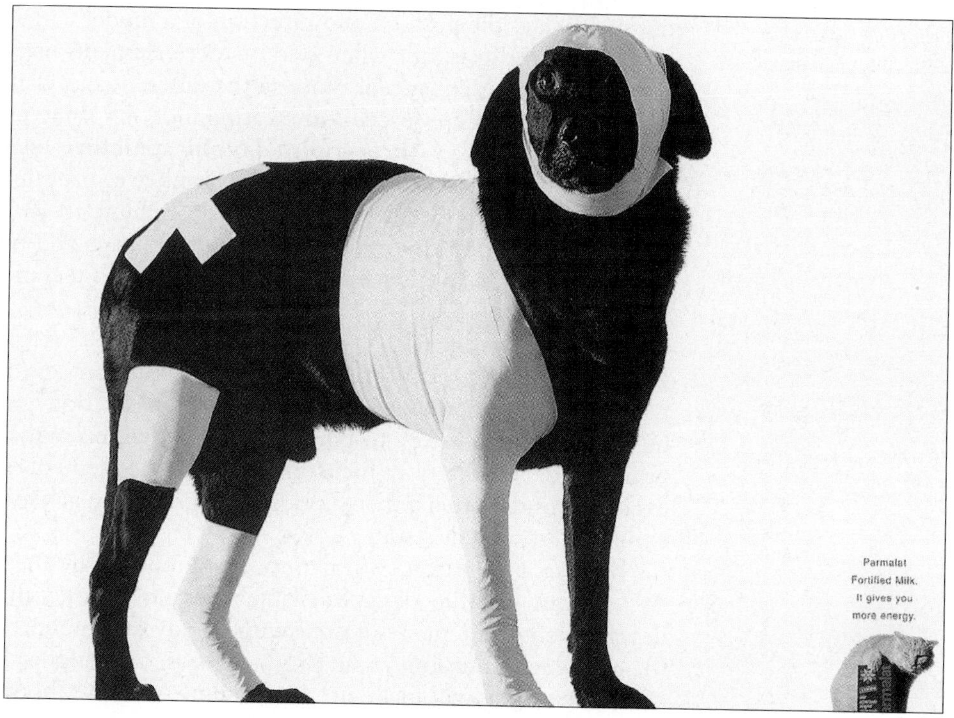

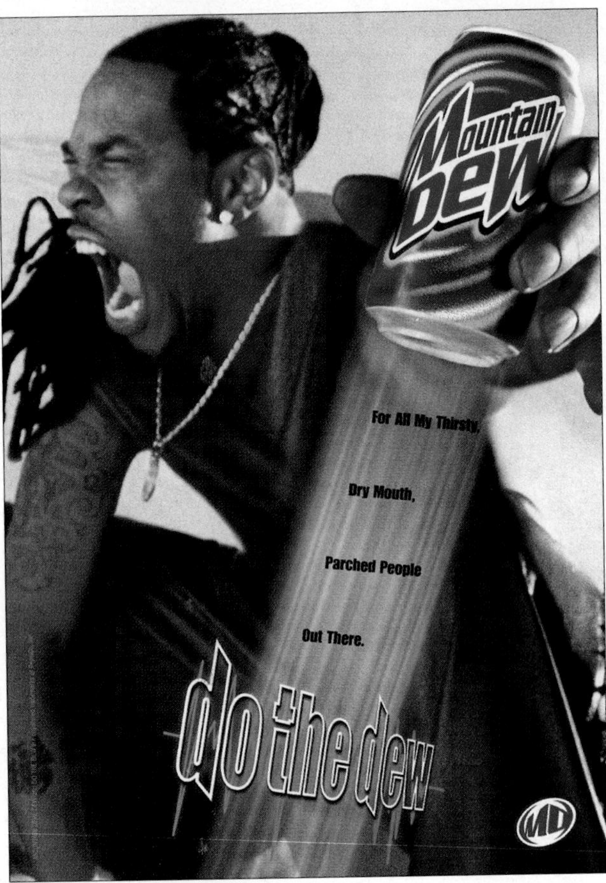

EXHIBIT 13.14

The order of elements in this ad for Mountain Dew controls the reader's eye, moving it from the upper right to the lower center.
www.mountaindew.com

another, creating a sense of action. The essential contribution of this design component is to establish a visual format that results in a focus or several focuses.

Unity. Ensuring that the elements of an advertisement are tied together and appear to be related is the purpose of unity. Considered the most important of the design principles, unity results in harmony among the diverse components of print advertising: headline, subhead, body copy, and illustration. Several design techniques contribute to unity. The **border** surrounding an ad keeps the ad elements from spilling over into other ads or into the printed matter next to the ad. **White space** at the outside edges creates an informal border effect. The indiscriminate use of white space within an ad can separate elements and give an impression of disorder. The proper use of white space can be dramatic and powerful and draw the receiver's attention to the most critical elements of an ad. Exhibit 13.15 shows a classic example of the effective use of white space. Exhibit 13.16 shows that it wasn't just the look of the Beetle that made a comeback decades later: the effective use of white space came along for the ride, too.

The final construct of unity is the axis. In every advertisement, an axis will naturally emerge. The **axis** is a line, real or imagined, that runs through an ad and from which the elements in the advertisement flare out. A single ad may have one, two, or even three axes running vertically and horizontally. An axis can be created by blocks of copy, by the placement of illustrations, or by the items within an illustration, such as the position and direction of a model's arm or leg. Elements in an ad may violate the axes, but when two or more elements use a common axis as a starting point, unity is enhanced. Note all the different axes that appear in Exhibit 13.17. A design can be more forceful in creating unity by using either a three-point layout or a parallel layout. A **three-point layout structure** establishes three elements in the ad as dominant forces. The uneven number of prominent elements is critical to creating a gaze motion in the viewer. (See Exhibit 13.18.) **Parallel layout structure** employs art on the right-hand side of the page and repeats the art on the left-hand side. This is an obvious and highly structured technique to achieve unity (see Exhibit 13.19).

Emphasis. At some point in the decision-making process, someone needs to decide which major component—the headline, subhead, body copy, or illustration—will be emphasized. The key to good design relative to emphasis is that one item is the primary but not the only focus in an ad. If one element is emphasized to the total exclusion of the others, then a poor design has been achieved, and ultimately a poor communication will result.

Balance, proportion, order, unity, and emphasis are the basic principles of design. As you can see, the designer's objectives go beyond the strategic and message-development elements associated with an advertisement. Design principles relate to the aesthetic impression an ad produces. Once a designer has been informed of the components that will make up the headline, subhead, body copy, and illustration to

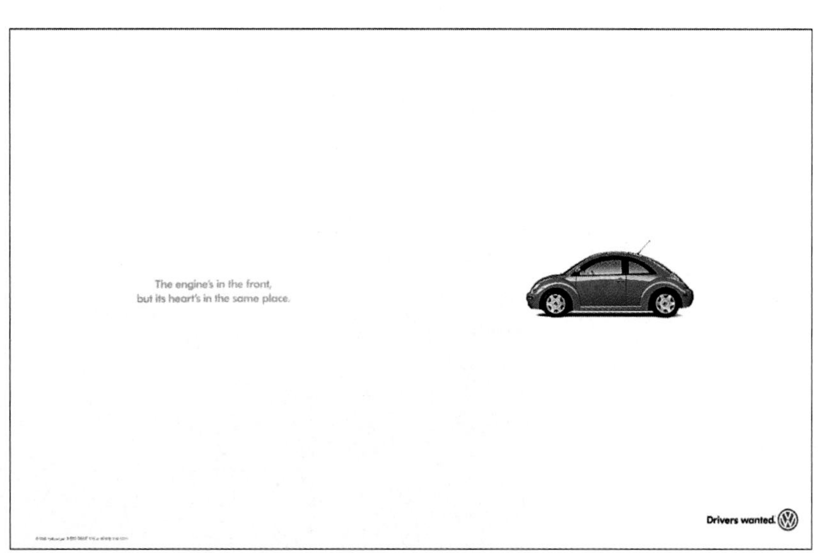

EXHIBITS 13.15 AND 13.16

The effective use of white space—past and present—to highlight the critical aspect of the ad: the product. www.vw.com

be included in the ad, then advertising and marketing decision makers *must* allow the designer to arrange those components according to the principles of creative design.

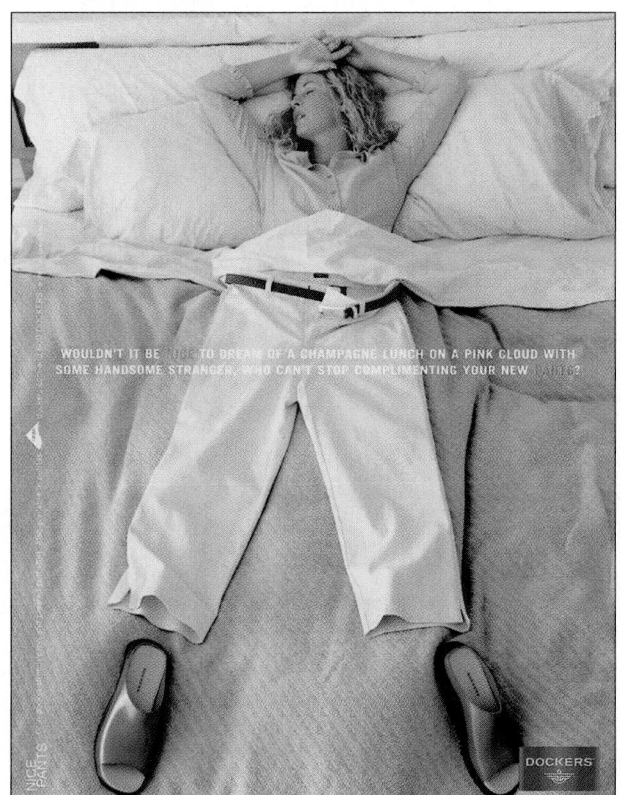

EXHIBIT 13.17

Look at all the different axes that appear in this ad. www.dockers.com

3 **Layout.** In contrast to design, which emphasizes the structural concept behind a print ad, layout is the mechanical aspect of design—the physical manifestation of design concepts. A **layout** is a drawing or digital rendering of a proposed print advertisement, showing where all the elements in the ad are positioned. An art director uses a layout to work through various alternatives for visual presentation and sequentially develop the print ad to its final stages. It is part and parcel of the design process and inextricably linked to the development of an effective design. While some art directors still work with traditional tools—layout tissue, T-square, triangle, and markers—many work in computerized layout programs, such as QuarkXPress.

An art director typically proceeds through various stages in the construction of a final design for an ad. The following are the different stages of layout development, in order of detail and completeness, that an art director typically uses.

Thumbnails. **Thumbnails** are the first drafts of an advertising layout. The art director will produce several thumbnail sketches to work out the general presentation of the ad. While the creative team refines the creative

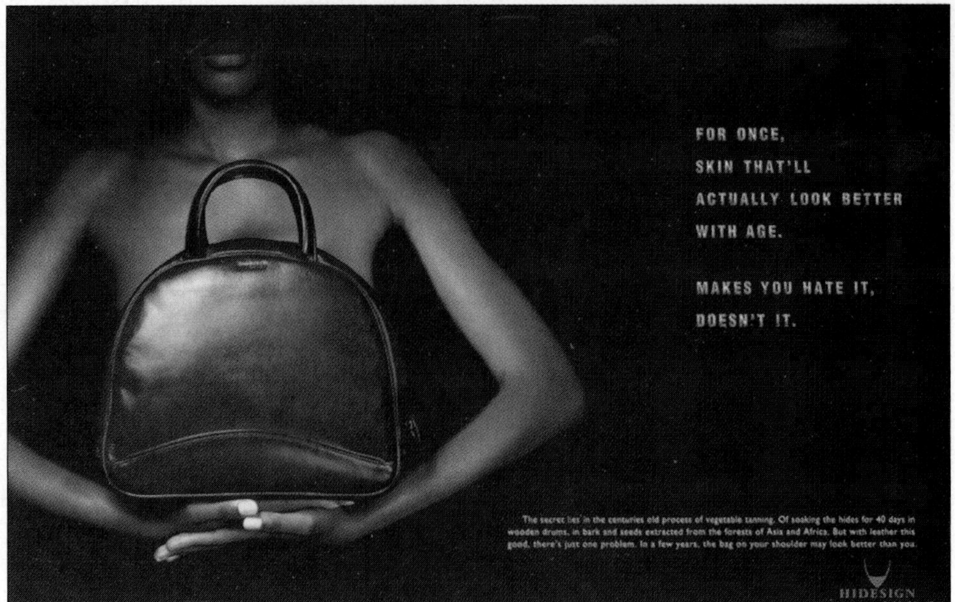

EXHIBIT 13.18

There are three prominent visual elements here.

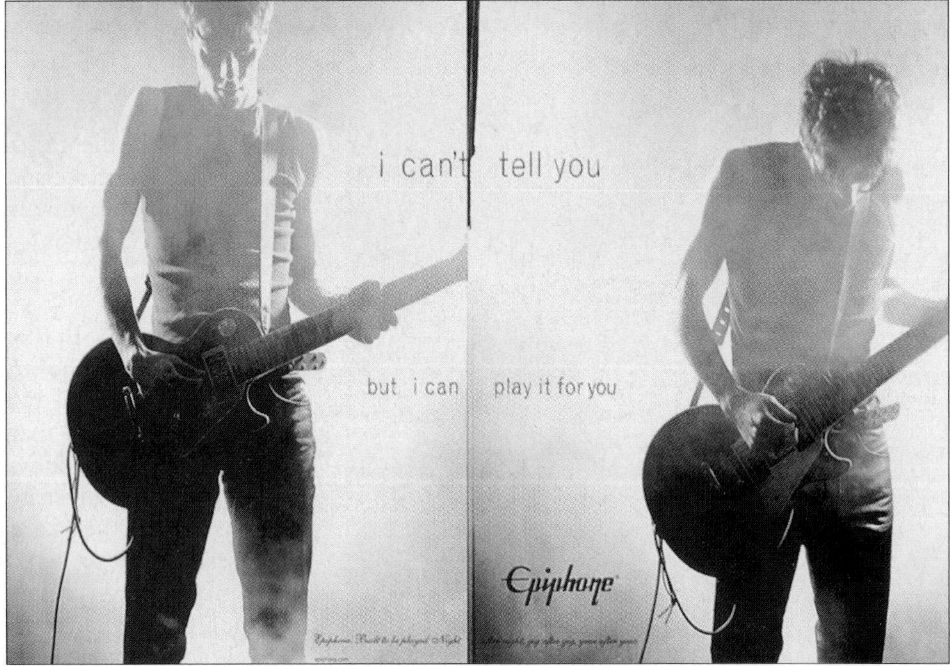

EXHIBIT 13.19

Here, the visual layout on the left is repeated on the right. www.epiphone.com

concept, thumbnails represent placement of elements—headline, images, body copy, and tagline. Headlines are often represented with zigzag lines and body copy with straight, parallel lines. An example of a thumbnail is shown in Exhibit 13.20. Typically, thumbnails are drawn at one-quarter the size of the finished ad.

Rough Layout. The next step in the layout process is the **rough layout.** Unlike a thumbnail sketch, a rough layout is done in the actual size of the proposed ad and is usually created with a computer layout program, such as QuarkXPress. This allows the art director to experiment with different headline fonts and easily manipulate the placement and size of images to be used in the ad. A rough layout is often used by the advertising agency for preliminary presentation to the client. Exhibit 13.21 features a rough layout.

Comprehensive. The comprehensive layout, or **comp,** is a polished version of an ad. Now, for the most part, computer-generated, it is a representation of what the final ad will look like. At this stage, the final headline font is used, the images to be used—photographs or illustrations—are digitized and placed in the ad, and the actual body copy is often included on the ad. Comps are generally printed in full color, if the final ad is to be in color, on a high-quality printer. Comps that are produced in this way make it very easy for the client to imagine (and approve) what the ad will look like when it is published. Exhibit 13.22 features a comp layout.

Mechanicals. After the client has approved the comprehensive layouts, the production art department creates the final version of an ad, the **mechanical,** that will be sent to the printer. Working with the art director, the production artist refines the ad by adjusting the headline spacing (kerning), making any copy changes the client has requested, and placing high-quality digitized (scanned or digitally created) versions of images (illustrations or photographs) to be used. The production artist uses a variety of computer programs such as Adobe Photoshop and Adobe Illustrator to create the ad. A layout program is used to assemble all of the elements of the ad—images and type. Although there are many programs available to perform these tasks, QuarkXPress is the standard for the advertising industry, along with the Macintosh computer platform.

The client will make one last approval of the mechanical before it is sent to the printer. Changes that a client requests, prior to the ad being sent to the printer, are still easily and quickly made. A digital file is then sent either electronically or by mail to the printer. (Prior to the use of computers to generate mechanicals, a small copy change could result in hours of work on the part of the production artists and a large bill to the client.)

The stages of layout development discussed here provide the artistic blueprint for a print advertisement (see Exhibit 13.23). At this point, the practical matters of choosing the look and style of a print ad can be considered. We now turn our attention to the matter of print production.

4 Production in Print Advertising.

The production process in print advertising represents the technical and mechanical activities that transform a creative concept and rough layout into a finished print advertisement. While the process is fundamentally technical, some aspects of print production directly relate to the strategic and design goals of the print ad. Different type styles can contribute to the design quality, readability, and mood in an advertisement. Our purpose in this section, however, is to provide a basic familiarity with production details. It is our goal to outline the sequence of activities and proper time frame related to print production and the various options available for print preparation.

The Print Production Schedule.

The advertiser is only partly in control of the timing of the print advertisement. While plans can be made to coordinate the appearance of the ad with overall marketing strategies, it must be recognized that the print media will have specifications regarding how far in advance and in what form an ad must be received to appear in print. The deadline for receipt of an ad is referred to as the **closing date.** Closing dates for newspapers can be one or two days before publication. For magazines, the closing date may be months ahead of publication. Exhibit 13.24 describes the sequence of events and the amount of time between stages for a typical magazine ad production schedule.

As you can see from this typical schedule, from the time design work begins until the ad appears in magazine publication, 13 to 21 weeks' time can be involved. For newspaper advertising, the time is typically much shorter, perhaps 1 to 2 weeks

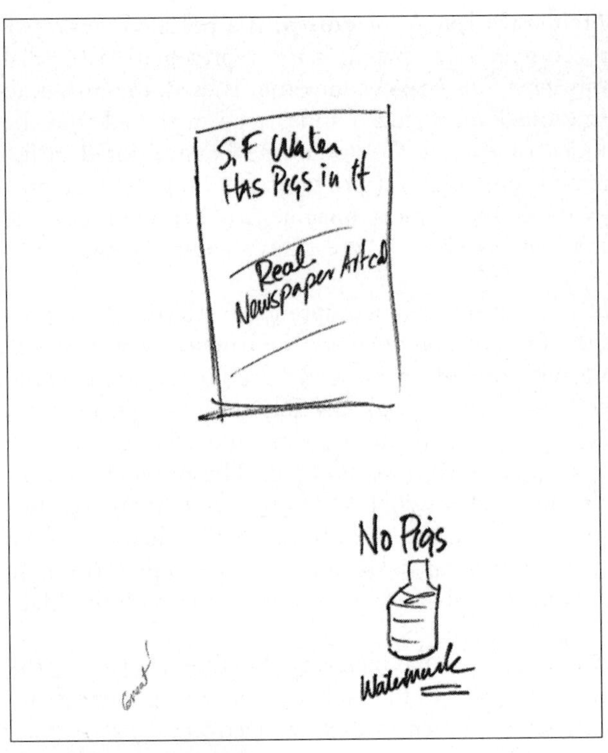

EXHIBIT 13.20

A thumbnail showing the transition from idea to advertisement.

EXHIBIT 13.21

A rough layout.

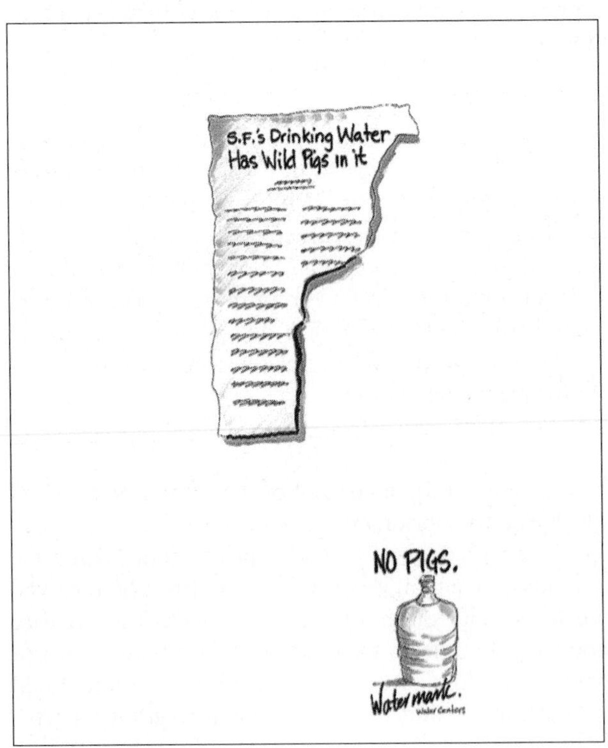

EXHIBIT 13.22

A comp layout.

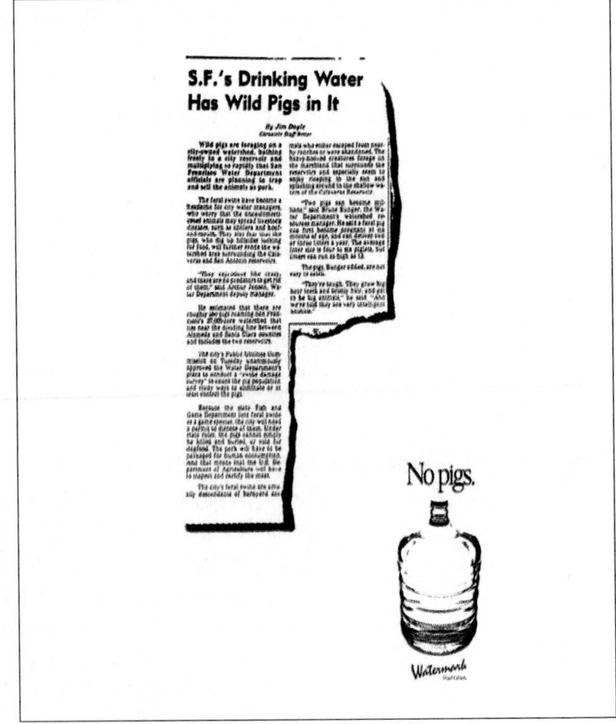

EXHIBIT 13.23

The finished ad.

EXHIBIT 13.24

Preparation and production schedule for a magazine advertisement.

Stage	Time
Creative work begins	Copy platform approved
Creative work completed and approved	2 weeks
Artwork ordered (photography or art)	1 day
Artwork completed	2 weeks
Working layout ordered	1 day
Working layout including art complete	1 week
Finished materials to printer (engraver)	5 days
First proof from printer	2 weeks
Final proof from printer	5 days
Printer (engraver) to plate preparation	5 days
Plates shipped to publication	5 days
Publication date of issue	4 to 12 weeks
Total time	13 to 21 weeks

(maybe days), but this still represents a fairly long planning and execution period. Advertisers must be aware that such advance planning is necessary to accommodate the basic nature of print production.

Print Production Processes. Seven major processes can be used in print production.[8] Depending on the medium (newspaper, magazine, direct mail, or specialty advertising), the length of the print run (quantity), the type of paper being used, and the quality desired in reproduction, one of the following processes is used: letterpress, offset lithography, gravure, flexography, electronic, laser, and inkjet printing. Advances in technology have made computer print production an ideal alternative under certain conditions.

Letterpress draws its name from the way it "presses" type onto a page. Typesetters hand-placed, or *set,* each letter for a printed page in a tray, separating lines of text with bars of lead. These trays would then be inked and "pressed" onto the paper to transfer the ink type or image, similar to how we might currently use a rubber stamp. Today, handset type is a thing of the past, and individual metal type has been replaced with metal or rubber plates that are typeset from a computer program. The most common use for the letterpress today is finishing activities, such as embossing and scoring.

Offset lithography is by far the most common printing method. This process prints from a flat, chemically treated surface—a plate—wrapped around a cylinder that attracts ink to the areas to be printed and repels ink from other areas; the basic idea is that oil and water don't mix. The inked image is then transferred to a rubber blanket on a roller and from this roller the impression is carried to paper. Depending on the length of the run (quantity of pieces needed) either a sheetfed or web (not associated with WWW) press would be used.

The **gravure** method of printing also prints from a plate. However, unlike the offset plate, the gravure plate is engraved. This method of printing is most commonly

8. This discussion is based in part on Michael H. Bruno, ed., *Pocket Pal: A Graphic Arts Production Handbook,* 13th ed. (New York: International Paper, 1983), 24–31.

used for very large runs, such as the Sunday newspaper supplements, to maintain a high quality of printing clarity.

Flexography is similar to offset lithography because it also uses a rubber blanket to transfer images. It differs from offset in that this process uses water-based ink instead of oil-based ink, and printing can be done on any surface. Because of this versatility of printing surface, flexography is most commonly used in packaging.

Electronic, laser, and inkjet printing are also known as plateless printing. The widespread use of computer technology has made printing very small runs, as few as one piece, in full color or black and white, with very sharp image quality on a variety of different papers, very easy. The advertising industry often uses software connected to a color photocopier to generate color comps for clients. The colors may not be exactly as they would be if a printer had produced the piece, but for comping purposes this method is both timely and inexpensive. Laser and inkjet printing are also plateless printing processes that are directly connected to a computer to transfer information. However, unlike the large color comping machines, laser and inkjet printers are affordable for home use. On a larger scale, both *Time* and *Fortune* use inkjet printers to address magazines to their subscribers.

Computer Print Production. Integrating the printing production process with the computer has changed the printing business considerably. First, by having digital files, printers no longer need to photograph pasted-up versions of ads. Film can be generated directly from digital files and, in turn, printing plates are made from the film. Second, the proofing process—double-checking that the colors to be printed are correct—can be performed well before the print job is on the press. Iris prints, polar proofs, and watermark prints are all extremely high-quality proofing methods. Though these proofing methods are expensive, their cost is only a small fraction of the cost to reprint a piece. Last, with the increasing use of electronic file transfer, files can be sent quickly to printers.

As stated earlier, choice of the proper printing process depends on the requirements of the advertisement with regard to the medium being used, the quantity being printed, the type of paper being printed on, and the level of quality needed. With respect to magazines, the production process is mandated by the publisher of a particular vehicle within the medium. Print production processes are independent publishing decisions.

Typography in Print Production. The issues associated with typography have to do with the typeface chosen for headlines, subheads, and body copy, as well as the various size components of the type (height, width, and running length). Designers agonize over the type to use in a print ad because decisions about type affect both the readability and the mood of the overall visual impression. For our purposes, some knowledge of the basic considerations of typography is useful for an appreciation of the choices that must be made.

Categories of Type. Typefaces have distinct personalities, and each can communicate a different mood and image. A **type font** is a basic set of typeface letters. For those of us who do word processing on computers, the choice of type font is a common decision. In choosing type for an advertisement, however, the art director has thousands of choices based on typeface alone.

There are six basic typeface groups: blackletter, roman, script, serif, sans serif, and miscellaneous. The families are divided by characteristics that reflect the personality and tone of the font. **Blackletter,** also called *gothic,* is characterized by the ornate design of the letters. This style is patterned after hand-drawn letters in monasteries where illuminated manuscripts were created. You can see blackletter fonts used today in very formal documents, such as college diplomas. **Roman** is the most common group of fonts used for body copy because of its legibility. This family is characterized by the use of thick and thin strokes in the creation of the letter forms. **Script** is easy to distinguish by the linkage of the letters in the way that cursive handwriting is connected. Script is often found on wedding invitations and documents that are intended to look elegant or of high quality. **Serif** refers to the strokes or "feet" at the ends of the letter forms. Notice the serifs that are present in these letters as you read. Their presence helps move your eye across the page, allowing you to read for a long time without losing your place or tiring your eyes. **Sans serif** fonts, as the name suggests, do not have serifs, hence the use of the French word *sans,* meaning "without." Sans serif fonts are typically used for headlines and not for body copy. **Miscellaneous** includes typefaces that do not fit easily into the other categories. Novelty display, garage, and deconstructed fonts all fall into this group. These fonts were designed specifically to draw attention to themselves and not necessarily for their legibility. The following example displays serif and sans serif type:

This line is set in serif type.
This line is set in sans serif type.

Type Measurement. There are two elements of type size. **Point** refers to the size of type in height. In the printing industry, type sizes run from 6 to 120 points. Now, with computer layout programs such as QuarkXPress, the range is much larger, between 2 and 720 points. Exhibit 13.25 shows a range of type sizes for comparison purposes. **Picas** measure the width of lines. A pica is 12 points wide, and each pica measures about one-sixth of an inch. Layout programs make it very easy for the art director to fit copy into a designated space on an ad by reducing or enlarging a font with a few strokes on the keyboard.

Readability. It is critical in choosing type to consider readability. Type should facilitate the communication process. The following are some traditional recommendations when deciding what type to use (however, remember that these are only guidelines and should not necessarily be followed in every instance):

- Use capitals and lowercase, NOT ALL CAPITALS.
- Arrange letters from left to right, not up and down.

This is 8 point type
This is 12 point type
This is 18 point type
This is 36 point type
This is 60 point type

EXHIBIT 13.25

A range of type point sizes.

- Run lines of type horizontally, not vertically.
- Use even spacing between letters and words.

Different typefaces and styles also affect the mood conveyed by an ad. Depending on the choices made, typefaces can connote grace, power, beauty, modernness, simplicity, or any number of other qualities.

Art Direction and Production in Cyberspace. Cyberspace is its own space. It is its own medium, too. It's not television or radio, but, at this point, it's closer to print than to anything else. It's an active medium rather than a passive one (people generally come to it rather than the other way around). While the basic principles of art direction (design and concept) apply, the medium is fundamentally different in the way its audience comes to it, navigates it, and responds to it. This is one of the real challenges of electronic advertising.

In most respects, cyberproduction does not differ significantly from print, radio, or television production, but it does differ from these traditional media in how aspects of production are combined with programming language, such as HTML, and with each other. Advances in streaming audio and digital video keep art direction and production in cyberspace a moving target. Still, at this point, most Internet advertising is, essentially, print advertising. Most is either produced in traditional ways and then digitized and combined with text or created entirely with computer design packages. Exhibits 13.26 through 13.29 are pretty representative of what's out there.

All media have to find their own way, their own voice. This is not just an aesthetic matter. It's figuring out what works, which has something to do with design. How the information is laid out matters. If you go back and look at the first few years of television advertising, you have to say that they really didn't fully understand the medium or the ways audiences would use this new technology. The ads went on forever and seemed to be written for radio. In fact, many of the early TV writers were radio writers. They tried to make television radio.

This same phenomenon seems to be happening with Web sites. They look more like print ads than something truly Web-ish. Yet, unlike print ads, Web sites have the ability to change almost immediately. If a client wants to change a copy point, for example, it can happen many times in one afternoon. And Web consumers demand change. Though frequent changes may seem time-consuming and expensive, they ensure return visits from audiences. Many clients, however, are slow to integrate the Web into their overall communication strategy. Thus, many sites appear to be neglected, distant relatives to their high-profile cousins, TV and print.

There is also a rapidly growing clutter problem. Web pages are often very busy, with lots of information crammed into small spaces. Advertisers, while not yet knowing what this medium can do, are convinced that they must be in it. In short, the Web is not print *or* television: It is electronic and fluid, and must be thought of in this way. In terms of design, this means trying to understand why people come to various sites, what they are looking for, what they expect to encounter, what they expect in return for their very valuable click. The design has to be an expression of this.

Art Direction and Production in Television Advertising. There have been few (if any) things that have more changed the face of advertising (or contemporary culture) than television. Like other media, television first struggled to find its best form, but soon did. In many ways, television was simply made for advertising. It is everywhere, serving as background to much of daily life. If you are in a room and a television is on, you will find yourself watching it. Want to kill a good party? Turn on a television. Did you ever try to talk to someone sitting across from you when your back is to the television? You just about have to offer money to get

EXHIBITS 13.26 THROUGH 13.29

These ads are pretty typical of contemporary cyberads. Visit the promotion site for pop group They Might Be Giants (www.tmbg.com) and its companion site (www.dialasong.com). Do these sites suggest that the future of art direction and production in cyberspace will be more like television than print, or do the interactive features make the medium unique? Do you think highly interactive Web sites add clutter, or do they make browsing a more efficient experience? Does the average Internet user have the patience to wait for interactive graphics to load and display?

EXHIBITS 13.30 AND 13.31

Two of the very best filmmakers—and storytellers—ever: John Ford and Alfred Hitchcock.

their attention. In the Oscar-winning film *Network,* a television anchorman believes that God has chosen him as a modern-day prophet. When he asks God, "Why me?" God replies, "Because you're on television, dummy." Everybody watches TV, no matter what they tell you.

Television is about moving visuals. Sometimes, it's just about leaving impressions, or setting moods, or getting you to notice; sometimes it tells stories. Many believe that the very best television ads work just as well with the sound turned off, that the best television tells its story visually. Of course, this is what film critics have said about master film directors, such as John Ford (Exhibit 13.30) and Alfred Hitchcock (Exhibit 13.31), both of whom learned their craft in silent films.

Still, it must be said that an awful lot of TV spots are very reliant on copy. In fact, entire genres of television ads rely heavily on repetitive brand mentions, or dialogue-dependent narratives. Of late, rapid cuts and sparse dialogue seem to be the way of the TV creatives, but this phase will probably change before the next full moon. Advertising is, in so many respects, fashion.

5 **Art Direction in Television Advertising.** The primary creative directive for TV is the same as for other media: effective communication. Television presents some unique challenges, however. Due to its complexity, television production involves a lot of people. These people have different but often overlapping expertise, responsibility, and authority. This makes for a myriad of complications and calls for tremendous organizational skills. At some point, individuals who actually shoot the film or the tape are brought in to execute the copywriter's and art director's concepts. At this point, the creative process becomes intensely collaborative: The film director applies his or her craft and is responsible for the actual production. The creative team (that

GLOBAL ISSUES

Ad Queen to Boost USA's Global Image

She has been called the queen of Madison Avenue and the most powerful woman in advertising. She's the only woman to have served as chairman of two top-10 worldwide advertising agencies, J. Walter Thompson and Ogilvy & Mather. She helped shape brands such as Uncle Ben's Rice and Head & Shoulders, and has graced the cover of leading magazines such as *Fortune.* Now Charlotte Beers is faced with the branding challenge of a lifetime—enhancing the USA's global image.

The Bush administration's appointment of longtime ad executive Charlotte Beers as undersecretary of state for public affairs came with the unique objective of fighting the international war on terrorism. Using an unlikely arsenal of weapons, Ms. Beers and the State Department hope to accomplish the repositioning of the quintessential global brand—the USA.

For a country with the biggest marketing industry on earth, the United States has done a surprisingly poor job of managing its own image abroad, a problem that has shifted sharply into focus in the propaganda war surrounding the September 11, 2001, terrorist attacks. "Loyal brand users" see the United States as a beacon of freedom, democracy, and tolerance. Users of the competing "brands" see the United States as a monster of self-absorption, crass commercialism, and blatant hypocrisy. The solution to this brand-identity crisis? Advertising.

The State Department has announced plans to buy television advertising on Qatar-based news channel Al Jazeera, a favored broadcast venue of well-known terrorists such as Osama bin Laden. The Arab-language station is said to have some 40 million viewers around the world. Ideas being tested for effectiveness include spotlighting famous athletes and entertainers, interviewing American Muslims about the virtues of the American system, and explaining that the United States is not a pagan paradise but a country that respects all religions. "The immediate problem is getting the message articulated and understood," said Ms. Beers.

Certainly, the stakes for directing effective television ads have never been higher. The State Department has developed an advisory council of Arab and Muslim leaders to help craft what the United States should communicate in foreign countries. In addition, Ms. Beers is working with international media-reaction teams and public affairs officers in embassies around the world to ensure that the message remains front and center.

Deeply entrenched perceptions of the United States will be hard to budge, and politicians accustomed to quick fixes could blanch under long-range branding approaches to international affairs. For Ms. Beers, this is a battle for the mind: "We are having people who are not our friends define America in negative terms. It is time for us to reignite the understanding of America."

Sources: Ira Teinowitz, "U.S. Considers Advertising on Al Jazeera TV," *Ad Age,* www.adage.com, accessed October 15, 2001; Rick Stengel, "It Is Coke vs. Pepsi," *Time,* www.time.com, accessed November 8, 2001.

is, the art director and copywriter) rarely relinquishes control of the project, even though the film director may prefer exactly that. But who really has creative authorship is typically unclear. Getting the various players to perform their particular specialty at just the right time, while avoiding conflict with other team members, is an ongoing challenge in TV ad production.

The Creative Team in Television Advertising. The vast and ever-increasing capability of the broadcast media introduces new challenges and complexities to the production process. One aspect of these complexities is that aside from the creative directors, copywriters, and art directors who assume the burden of responsibility in the production of print advertising, we now encounter a host of new and irreplaceable creative and technical participants. The proper and effective production of broadcast advertising depends on a team of highly capable creative people: agency personnel, production experts, editorial specialists, and music companies. An advertiser and its agency must consider and evaluate the role of each of these participants. Descriptions of the roles played by the participants in television advertising are provided in Exhibit 13.32. The Global Issues box on this page describes how Charlotte Beers, probably the most powerful woman in advertising, faces the challenge of assembling a creative team to enhance the USA's global image.

Creative Guidelines for Television Advertising. Just as for print advertising, there are general creative principles for television advertising.[9] These principles are not foolproof or definitive, but they certainly represent good advice. Again, truly great creative work has no doubt violated some or all of these conventions.

9. These guidelines were adapted from A. Jerome Jewler, *Creative Strategy in Advertising,* 3rd ed. (Belmont, Calif.: Wadsworth, 1989), 210–211; Nelson, *The Design of Advertising,* 296.

Agency Participants
Creative director (CD): The creative director manages the creative process in an agency for several different clients. Creative directors typically come from the art or copywriting side of the business. The main role of the CD is to oversee the creative product of an agency across all clients.
Art director (AD): The art director and the copywriter work together to develop the concept for a commercial. The AD either oversees the production of the television storyboard or actually constructs the storyboards. In addition, the AD works with the director of the commercial to develop the overall look of the spot.
Copywriter: The copywriter is responsible for the words and phrases used in an ad. In television and radio advertising, these words and phrases appear as a script from which the director, creative director, and art director work during the production process. Together with the AD, the copywriter also makes recommendations on choice of director, casting, and editing facility.
Account executive (AE): The account executive acts as a liaison between the creative team and the client. The AE has the responsibility for coordinating scheduling, budgeting, and the various approvals needed during the production process. The AE can be quite valuable in helping the advertiser understand the various aspects of the production process. Account executives rarely have direct input into either the creative or technical execution of an ad.
Executive producer: The executive producer in an agency is in charge of many line producers, who manage the production at the production site. Executive producers help manage the production bid process. They also assign the appropriate producers to particular production jobs.
Producer: The producer supervises and coordinates all the activities related to a broadcast production. Producers screen director reels, send out production bid forms, review bids, and recommend the production house to be used. The producer also participates in choosing locations, sets, and talent. Normally, the producer will be on the set throughout the production and in the editing room during postproduction, representing agency and client interests.
Production Company Participants
Director: The director is in charge of the filming or taping of a broadcast advertising production. From a creative standpoint, the director is the visionary who brings the copy strategy to life on film or tape. The director also manages the actors, actresses, musicians, and announcers used in an ad to ensure that their performances contribute to the creative strategy being pursued. Finally, the director manages and coordinates the activities of technical staff. Camera operators, sound and lighting technicians, and special effects experts get their assignments from the director.
Producer: The production company also has a producer present, who manages the production at the site. This producer is in charge of the production crew and sets up each shoot. The position of cameras and readiness of production personnel are the responsibility of this producer.
Production manager: The production manager is on the set of a shoot, providing all the ancillary services needed to ensure a successful production. These range from making sure that food service is available on the set to providing dressing rooms and fax, phone, and photocopy services. The production manager typically has a production assistant (PA) to help take care of details.
Camera department: Another critical part of the production team is the camera department. This group includes the director of photography, camera operator, and assistant camera operator. This group ensures that the lighting, angles, and movement are carried out according to the plan and the director's specification.
Art department: The art department that accompanies the production company includes the art director and other personnel responsible for creating the set. This group designs the set, builds background or stunt structures, and provides props.
Editors: Editors enter the production process at the postproduction stage. It is their job, with direction from the art director, creative director, producer, or director, to create the finished advertisement. Editors typically work for independent postproduction houses and use highly specialized equipment to cut and join frames of film or audiotape together to create the finished version of a television or radio advertisement. Editors also synchronize the audio track with visual images in television advertisements and perform the transfer and duplication processes to prepare a commercial for shipping to the media.

EXHIBIT 13.32

The creative team for television advertising production.

- *Use an attention-getting and relevant opening.* The first few seconds of a television commercial are crucial. A receiver can make a split-second assessment of the relevance and interest a message holds. An ad can either turn a receiver off or grab his or her attention for the balance of the commercial with the opening. Remember, remote controls are rarely too far away. This truism should not be ignored. Channel surfing is a very real phenomenon. It is getting so incredibly easy to avoid commercials that you, as an advertiser, must have a good hook to

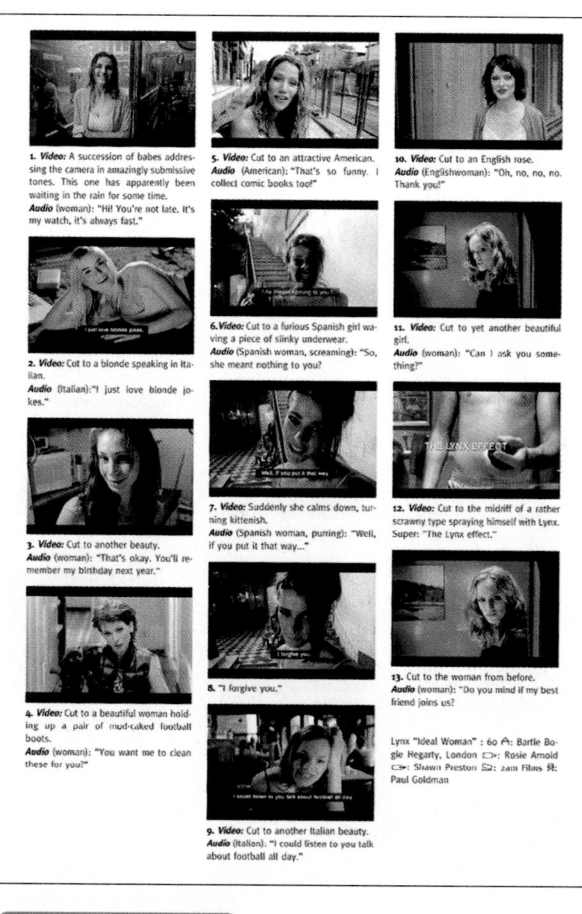

EXHIBIT 13.33

This ad wastes no time getting its message across.

suck viewers in. Ads just don't get much time to develop. Of course, there is the belief that "slower" ads (ads that take time to develop) don't wear out as quickly as the quick hit-and-run ads. So, if you have a huge (almost inexhaustible) supply of money, an ad that "builds" might be best. If you don't, go for the quick hook. In Exhibit 13.33, Lynx immediately grabbed the viewer's attention with a quite unexpected combination of words and visuals.

- *Emphasize the visual.* The video capability of television should be highlighted in every production effort. To some degree, this emphasis is dependent on the creative concept, but the visual should carry the selling message even if the audio portion is ignored by the receiver. In Exhibit 13.34, Bahlsen Cookies tells its story with a minimum of words. Exhibit 13.35 shows one of the most famous political ads of all time, an ad that helped cement Lyndon Johnson's win over Barry Goldwater in 1964 by painting Goldwater as a near madman who might get us into a nuclear war.
- *Coordinate the audio with the visual.* The images and copy of a television commercial must reinforce each other rather than pursue separate objectives. Such divergence between the audio and visual portions of an ad only serves to confuse and distract the viewer. In Exhibit 13.36, Miller High Life uses both words and visuals to create the world of a High Life man.
- *Persuade as well as entertain.* It is tempting to produce a beautifully creative television advertisement rather than a beautifully effective television advertisement. The vast potential of film lures the creative urge in all the production participants. Creating an entertaining commercial is an inherently praiseworthy goal *except* when the entertainment value of the commercial completely overwhelms its persuasive impact. In Exhibit 13.37, Hewlett-Packard sells its photo-quality printers with a humorous yet persuasive demonstration of their reproductive powers.
- *Show the product.* Unless a commercial is using intrigue and mystery surrounding the product, the product should be highlighted in the ad. Close-ups and shots of the brand in action help receivers recall the brand and its appearance.

6 **The Production Process in Television Advertising.** The television production process can best be understood by identifying the activities that take place before, during, and after the actual production of an ad. These stages are referred to as preproduction, production, and postproduction. (Hope we're not getting too technical.) By breaking the process down into this sequence, we can appreciate both the technical and the strategic aspects of each stage.

Preproduction. The **preproduction** stage is that part of the television production process in which the advertiser and the advertising agency (or in-house agency staff) carefully work out the precise details of how the creative planning behind an ad can best be brought to life with the opportunities offered by television. Exhibit 13.38 shows the sequence of six events in the preproduction stage.

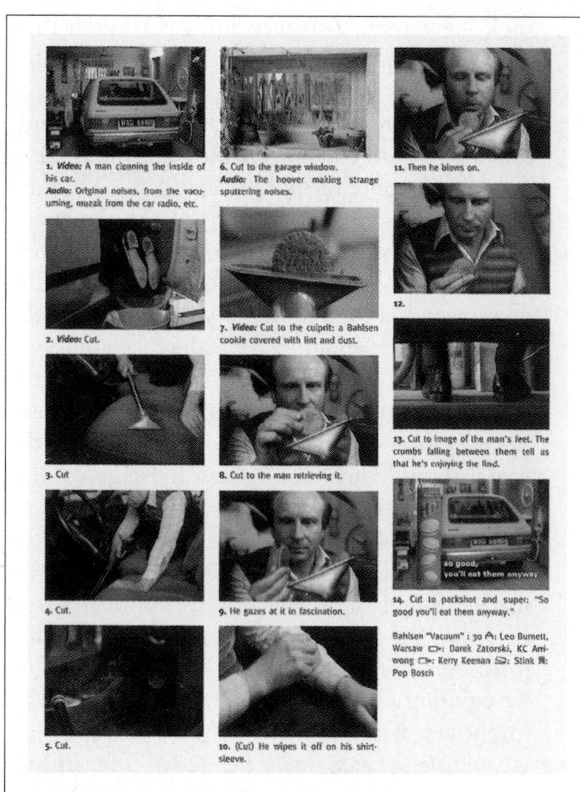

EXHIBIT 13.34

A TV ad that succeeds without words.

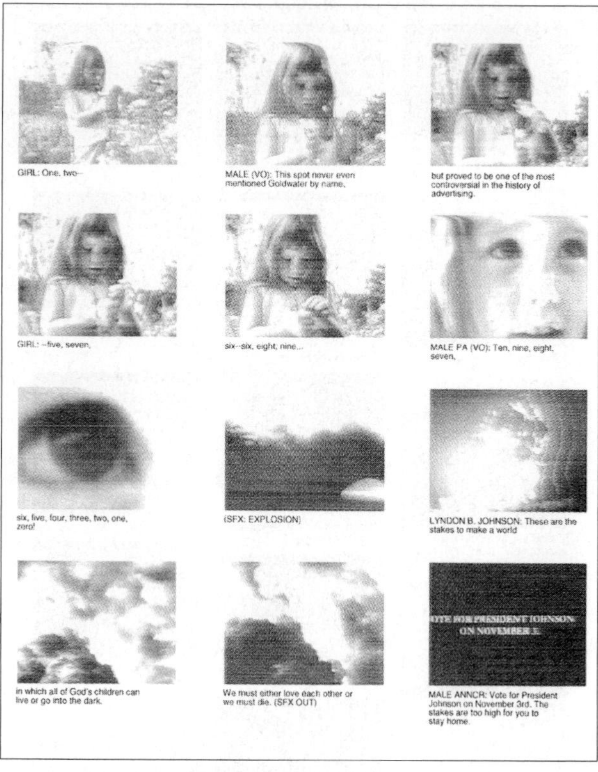

EXHIBIT 13.35

The most famous political ad of all time (Doyle Dane Bernbach).

Storyboard and Script Approval. As Exhibit 13.38 shows, the preproduction stage begins with storyboard and script approval. A **storyboard** is a shot-by-shot sketch depicting, in sequence, the visual scenes and copy that will be used in an advertisement. A **script** is the written version of an ad; it specifies the coordination of the copy elements with the video scenes. The script is used by the producer and director to set the location and content of scenes, by the casting department to choose actors and actresses, and by the producer in budgeting and scheduling the shoot. Exhibit 13.39 is part of a storyboard from the Miller Lite "Can Your Beer Do This?" campaign, and Exhibit 13.40 shows the related script. This particular spot was entitled "Ski Jump" and involved rigging a dummy to a recliner and launching the chair and the dummy from a 60-meter ski jump.

The art director and copywriter are significantly involved at this stage of production. It is important that the producer has discussed the storyboard and script with the creative team and fully understands the creative concept and objectives for the advertisement before production begins. Since it is the producer's responsibility to solicit bids for the project from production houses, the producer must be able to fully explain to bidders the requirements of the job so that cost estimates are as accurate as possible.

Budget Approval. Once there is agreement on the scope and intent of the production as depicted in the storyboard and script, the advertiser must give budget approval. The producer needs to work carefully with the creative team and the advertiser to estimate the approximate cost of the shoot, including production staging, location costs, actors, technical requirements, staffing, and a multitude of other

(single and part of series)

"Donut" :30

(OPEN ON A CLOSE-UP OF BEER, DONUTS AND A MAN'S DIRTY HANDS ON TABLE. HE PICKS UP A DONUT)

ANNCR. (VO): Sometimes a man gets too hungry to clean his hands properly.

(CUT TO CLOSE-UP OF DONUTS)

ANNCR. (VO): The powdered sugar on this donut puts a semi-protective barrier between your fingerprint and your nutrition.

(CUT TO A MAN HOLDING BEER, EATING DONUTS)

ANNCR. (VO): But even if some grease does get on that donut, that's just flavor to a High Life man.

TITLE CARD: (FADE UP) Miller Time logo.

ART DIRECTOR: Jeff Williams
WRITER: Jeff Kling
CREATIVE DIRECTOR: Susan Hoffman
PRODUCER: Jeff Selis
DIRECTOR: Errol Morris
PRODUCTION COMPANY: @radical.media
AD AGENCY: Wieden & Kennedy (Portland, OR)
CLIENT: Miller Brewing Company

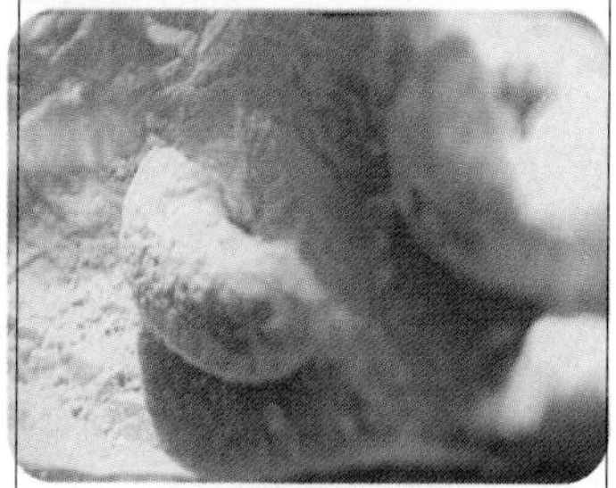

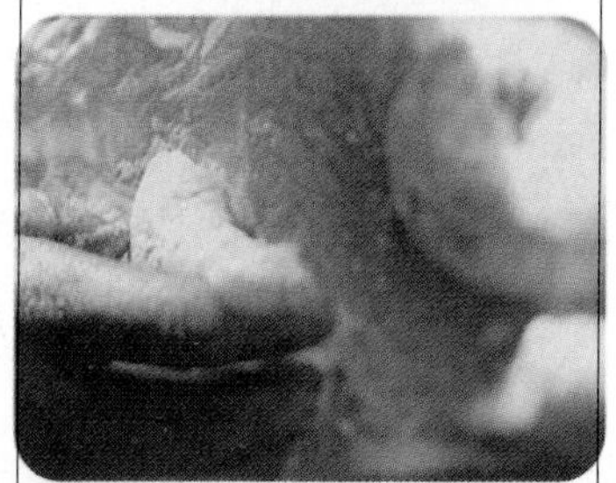

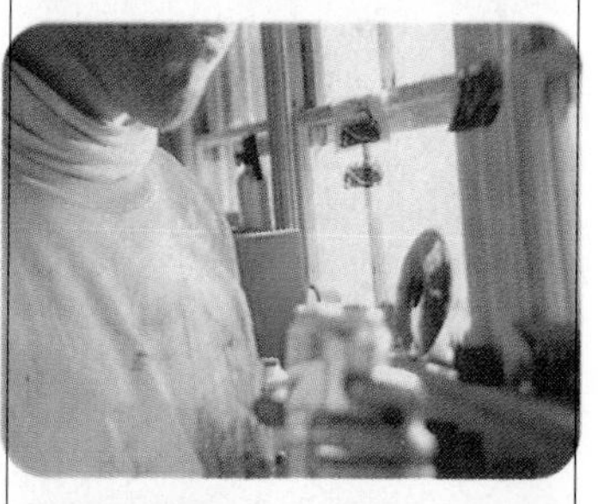

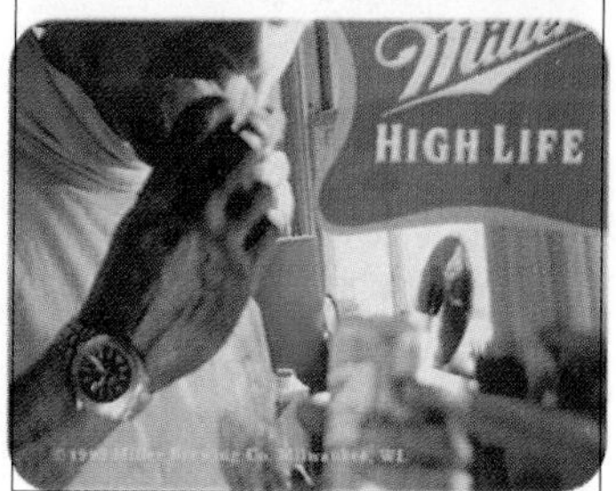

EXHIBITS 13.36

An ad that creates the world of the High Life man.
www.millerbrewing.com

EXHIBIT 13.37

Humor meets demonstration.
www.hp.com

(SFX: QUIET TICKING OF CLOCK)
(SFX: WRESTLING ON TV)
GRANDPA: Ohhhhhh!
(SFX: THUD)
BABY: Wahhhhhhhhhhh!
GRANDPA: Don't worry, honey. Mom and Dad will be right back.
GRANDPA: Pretty baby!
BABY: Wahhhhhhhhhhh!
(SFX: SUDDEN QUIET)
(SFX: CLOCK TICKING)
ANNCR: HP photo-quality printers. Good enough to fool almost anyone.
SUPER: BUILT BY ENGINEERS. USED BY NORMAL PEOPLE.

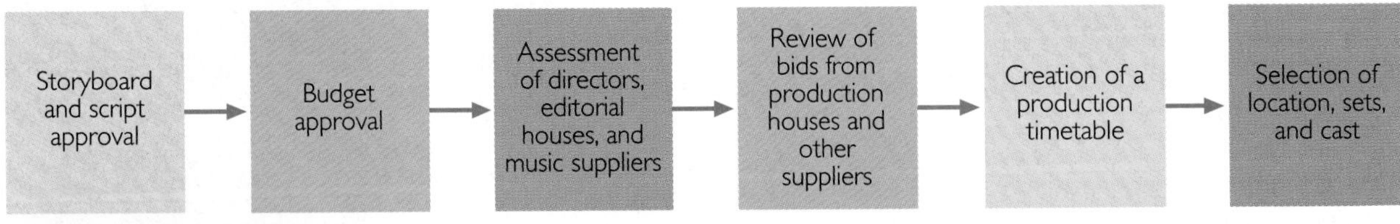

EXHIBIT 13.38

Sequence of events in the preproduction stage of television advertising.

considerations. It is essential that these discussions be as detailed and comprehensive as possible, because it is from this budget discussion that the producer will evaluate candidates for the directing role and solicit bids from production houses to handle the job.

Assessment of Directors, Editorial Houses, Music Suppliers. A producer has dozens (if not hundreds) of directors, postproduction editorial houses, and music suppliers from which to choose. An assessment of those well-suited to the task must take place early in the preproduction process. The combination of the creative talents of ad agencies and production houses can produce creative, eye-catching ads, as evidenced in the IBP box on this page. Directors of television commercials, like directors of feature films, develop specializations and reputations. Some directors are known for their work with action or special effects. Others are more highly skilled in working with children, animals, outdoor settings, or shots of beverages flowing into a glass ("pour shots").

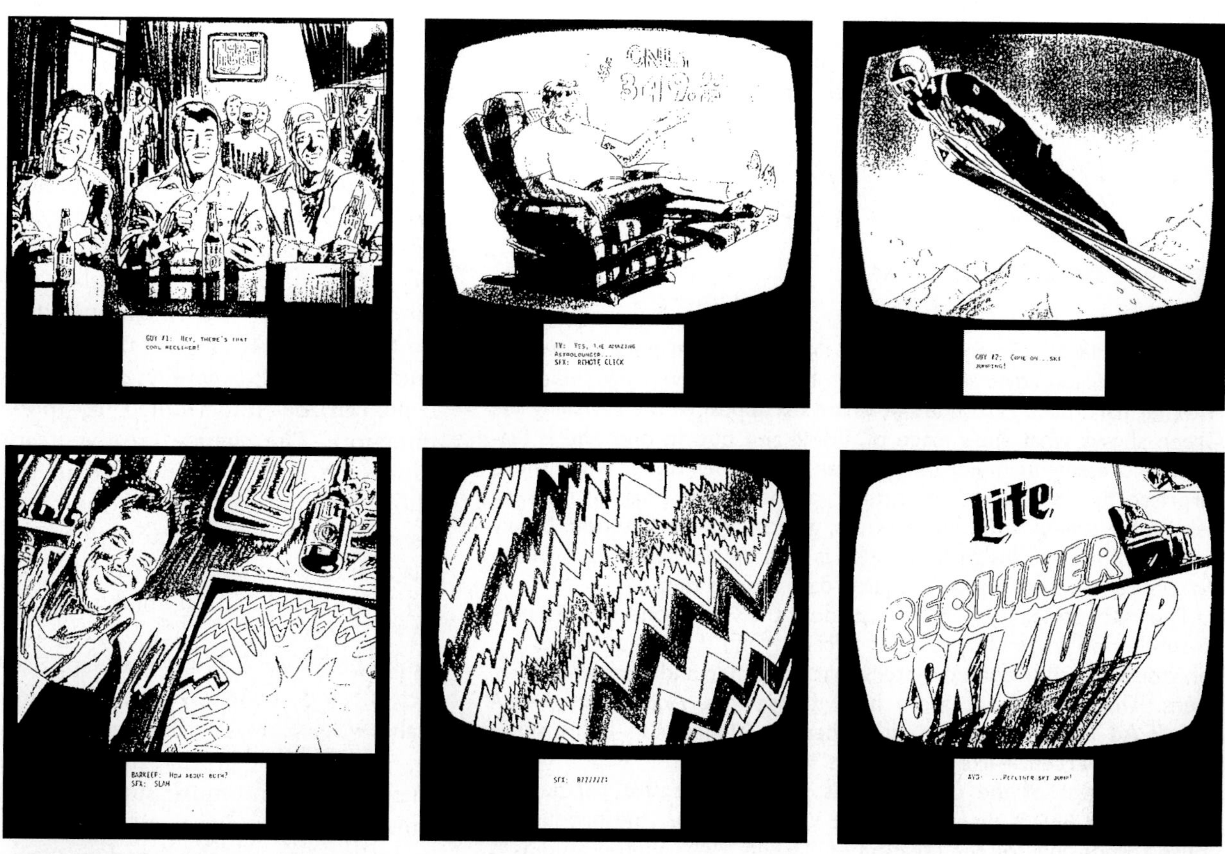

EXHIBIT 13.39

How does this storyboard for a Miller Lite Beer ad save the advertiser time and money during the television production process? www.millerlite.com

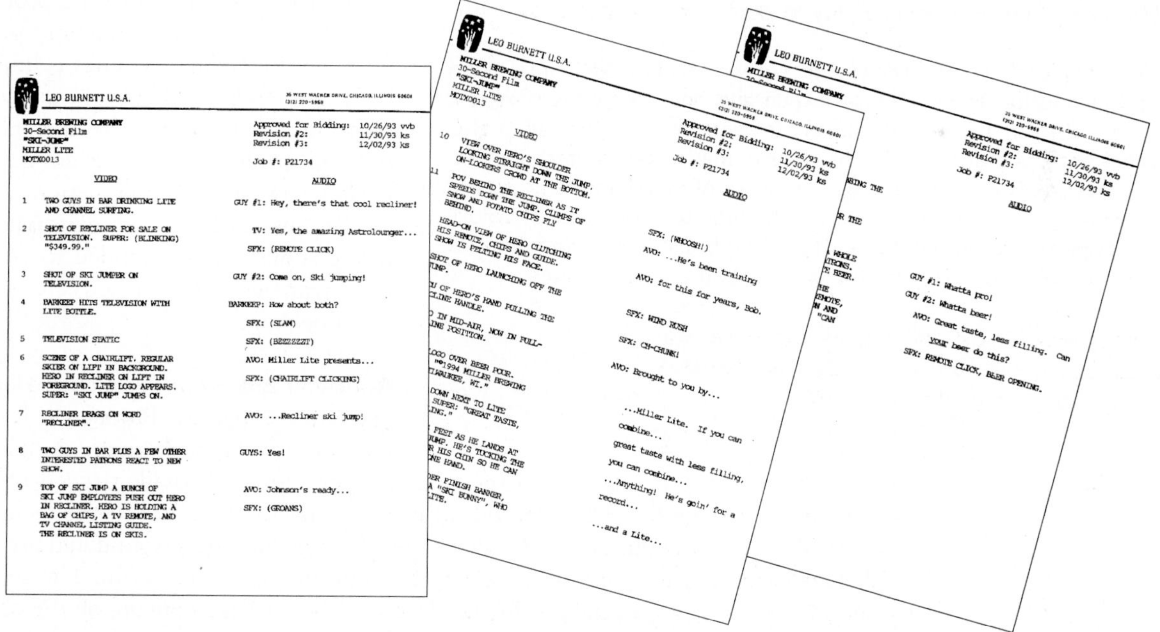

LEO BURNETT U.S.A. 35 WEST WACKER DRIVE, CHICAGO, ILLINOIS 60601 (312) 220-5959

MILLER BREWING COMPANY
30-Second Film
"SKI-JUMP"
MILLER LITE
MOTX0013

Approved for Bidding: 10/26/93 vvb
Revision #2: 11/30/93 ks
Revision #3: 12/02/93 ks

Job #: P21734

	VIDEO	AUDIO
1	TWO GUYS IN BAR DRINKING LITE AND CHANNEL SURFING.	GUY #1: Hey, there's that cool recliner!
2	SHOT OF RECLINER FOR SALE ON TELEVISION. SUPER: (BLINKING) "$349.99."	TV: Yes, the amazing Astrolounger... SFX: (REMOTE CLICK)
3	SHOT OF SKI JUMPER ON TELEVISION.	GUY #2: Come on, Ski jumping!
4	BARKEEP HITS TELEVISION WITH LITE BOTTLE.	BARKEEP: How about both? SFX: (SLAM)
5	TELEVISION STATIC	SFX: (BZZZZZZT)
6	SCENE OF A CHAIRLIFT. REGULAR SKIER ON LIFT IN BACKGROUND. HERO IN RECLINER ON LIFT IN FOREGROUND. LITE LOGO APPEARS. SUPER: "SKI JUMP" JUMPS ON.	AVO: Miller Lite presents... SFX: (CHAIRLIFT CLICKING)
7	RECLINER DRAGS ON WORD "RECLINER".	AVO: ...Recliner ski jump!
8	TWO GUYS IN BAR PLUS A FEW OTHER INTERESTED PATRONS REACT TO NEW SHOW.	GUYS: Yes!
9	TOP OF SKI JUMP A BUNCH OF SKI JUMP EMPLOYEES PUSH OUT HERO IN RECLINER. HERO IS HOLDING A BAG OF CHIPS, A TV REMOTE, AND TV CHANNEL LISTING GUIDE. THE RECLINER IS ON SKIS.	AVO: Johnson's ready... SFX: (GROANS)

EXHIBIT 13.40

This is the script for the Miller Lite "Can Your Beer Do This?" ad shown in Exhibit 13.39. The producer and director use the script to set locations and the content of scenes and for budgeting and scheduling. The script is also used to choose actors and actresses.

The director of an advertisement is responsible for interpreting the storyboard and script and managing the talent to bring the creative concept to life. A director specifies the precise nature of a scene, how it is lit and how it is filmed. In this way, the director acts as the eye of the camera. Choosing the proper director is crucial to the execution of a commercial. Aside from the fact that a good director commands a fee anywhere from $8,000 to $25,000 per day, the director can have a tremendous effect on the quality and impact of the presentation. An excellent creative concept can be undermined by poor direction. The agency creative team should be intimately involved in the choice of directors. Among the now-famous feature film directors who have made television commercials are Ridley Scott (Apple), John Frankenheimer (AT&T), Woody Allen (Campari), Spike Lee (Levi's, Nike, the Gap, Barney's), and Federico Fellini (Coop Italia). (See Exhibits 13.41 and 13.42.)

Similarly, editorial houses (and their editors) and music suppliers (and musicians) have particular expertise and reputations. The producer, the director, and the agency creative team actively review the work of the editorial suppliers and music houses that are particularly well suited to the production. In most cases, geographic proximity to the agency facilities is important; as members of the agency team try to maintain a tight schedule, editorial and music services that are nearby facilitate the timely completion of an ad. Because of this need, editorial and music suppliers have tended to cluster near agencies in Chicago, New York, and Los Angeles.

IBP

It's Not Easy Being Green

M&M/Mars has given the entertainment industry its sexiest new star—the green M&M. "Green," the sassy animated M&M personality of a recent television advertising campaign by BBDO, is winning audiences with her hard-nosed attitude and smart sex appeal. In the revealing ads Green shows what she's made of, inside and out. In one, she is featured undressing from her candy-green coat in her trailer when she is surprised by a stagehand. In another, a hot guy at a bar notices her fashionable green outfit, white boots, gloves, and pocketbook, barely paying attention to his girlfriend who is wearing the same gear. Green gloats over the situation as the jilted date storms out.

The M&M campaign—"What is it about the Green ones?"—is a not-so-subtle nod to the longstanding urban legend that green M&Ms are aphrodisiacs, candy-coated oysters that bring men and women to their knees. The colorful ads are a hit with viewers. According to *USA Today*'s Ad Track consumer poll, 40 percent of viewers—up from the average 22 percent—like them "a lot."

The success of the campaign lies with the creative partnership between the BBDO agency and Will Vinton Studios, the production house responsible for the creation of "Green." Will Vinton Studios is famous for other animated 3D wonders such as the California Raisins (of the "I Heard It through the Grapevine" campaign) and "The PJs," FOX television's funny Claymation family. The firm's award-winning work in the world of dimensional animation offers advertisers memorable ways of building brand equity through characterization and storytelling.

The ripple effect of Green's success is seen in M&M's integrated brand promotion efforts. While Green and her sexy ways remain a popular myth in the ads and in urban legends, her popularity also reaches into licensed goods, interactive media, and entertainment. M&M says she is one of the biggest movers of merchandise at its site (www.m-ms.com). Nevertheless, it's the whole assortment of colors that's popular at candy counters. The M&Ms brand in its many varieties is the number one–selling confection across the United States.

Sources: Theresa Howard, "Green Signals Go for Ad Watchers," *USA Today*, www.usatoday.com, accessed October 29, 2001; Press information on Will Vinton Studios, www.vinton.com, accessed November 2, 2001.

Review of Bids from Production Houses and Other Suppliers. Production houses and other suppliers, such as lighting specialists, represent a collection of specialized talent and also provide needed equipment for ad preparation. The expertise in production houses relates to the technical aspects of filming a commercial. Producers, production managers, sound and art specialists, camera operators, and others are part of a production house team. The agency sends a bid package to several production houses. The package contains all the details of the commercial to be produced and includes a description of the production requirements and a timetable for the production. An accurate timetable is essential because many production personnel work on an hourly or daily compensation rate.

To give you some idea of the cost of the technical personnel and equipment available from production houses, Exhibit 13.43 lists some key production house

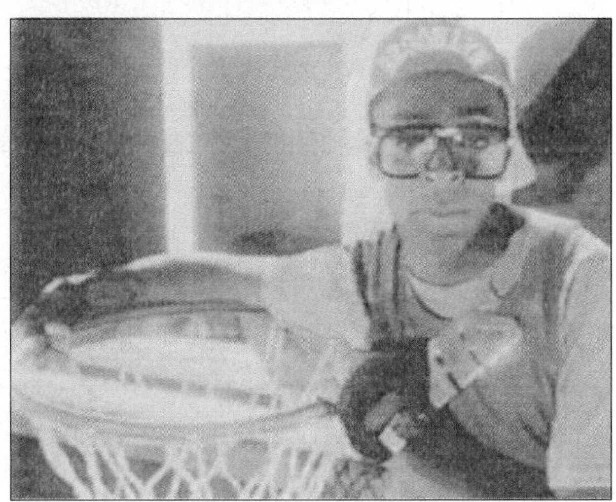

EXHIBITS 13.41 AND 13.42

Examples of famous feature film directors who have made television commercials are Ridley Scott, director of Apple's "1984" campaign and the 1982 movie Blade Runner, *and Spike Lee, who directed 1989's* Do the Right Thing *as well as the "Morris Blackman" Nike ads.* www.apple.com *and* www.nike.com

personnel who would participate in shooting a commercial, and the typical daily rates (for a 10-hour day) for such personnel and related equipment. Also listed are the rental costs of various pieces of equipment. These costs vary from market to market, but it is obvious why production expenses can run into the hundreds of thousands of dollars. The costs listed in the exhibit represent only the daily rates for production time or postproduction work. In addition to these costs are overtime costs, travel, and lodging (if an overnight stay is necessary).

Most agencies send out a bid package on a form developed by the agency. An example of such a bid form is provided in Exhibit 13.44. By using a standardized form, an agency can make direct comparisons between production house bids. A similar form can be used to solicit bids from other suppliers providing editorial or music services. The producer reviews each of the bids and revises them if necessary. From the production house bids *and* the agency's estimate of its own costs associated with production (travel, expenses, editorial services, music, on-camera talent, and agency markups), a production cost estimate is prepared for advertiser review and approval. Once the advertiser has approved the estimate, one of the production houses is awarded the job. The lowest production bid is not always the one chosen.

EXHIBIT 13.43

Sample costs for production personnel and equipment.

Personnel	Cost
Director	$8,000–25,000/day
Director of photography	3,000/day
Producer	800/day
Production assistant	200/day
Camera operator	600/day
Unit manager	450/day
Equipment	
Production van (including camera, lighting kit, microphones, monitoring equipment)	$2,500–4,000/day
Camera	750–1,000/day
Grip truck with lighting equipment and driver	400–500/day
Telescript with operator	600–700/day
Online editing with editor and assistant editor	250–400/hour

CLIENT: ____ DATE: ____
PRODUCT: ____ A. E.: ____
ACCT. SUP.: ____
WRITER: ____
A. D.: ____
C. D.: ____

NAME / LENGTH	TYPE	TALENT COUNT OC	EXT	VO
1				
2				
3.				
4.				

	ESTIMATE	ACTUAL
PRODUCTION CO.		
EDITING		
MUSIC		
TALENT		
ARTWORK/CC PACKAGES		
RECORDING STUDIO		
VIDEOTAPE TRANSFERS		
ANIMATION		
CASTING		
SUB TOTAL NET		
% A. C.		
TRAVEL		
SHIPPING		
TOTAL GROSS COST		

NOTES:

EXHIBIT 13.44

Advertising agencies use a bid form to make comparisons between production house bids and provide the client with an estimate of production costs.

Aside from cost, there are creative and technical considerations. A hot director costs more than last year's model. The agency's evaluation of the reliability of a production house also enters into the decision.

Creation of a Production Timetable. In conjunction with the stages of preproduction just discussed, the producer will be working on a **production timetable.** This timetable projects a realistic schedule for all the preproduction, production, and postproduction activities. To stay on budget and complete the production in time to ship the final advertisement to television stations for airing, an accurate and realistic timetable is essential. A timetable must allow a reasonable amount of time to complete all production tasks in a quality manner. Exhibit 13.45 is a timetable for a national 30-second spot, using location shooting.

Realize that a reasonable timetable is rarely achieved. Advertisers often request (or demand) that an agency provide a finished spot (or even several spots) in times as short as four or five weeks. Because of competitive pressures or corporate urgency for change, production timetables are compromised. Advertisers have to accept the reality that violating a reasonable timetable can dramatically increase costs and puts undue pressure on the creative process—no matter what the reason for the urgency. In fact, a creative director at one agency often told clients that they could pick any two selections from the following list for their television commercials: good, fast, and reasonably priced.[10]

10. Peter Sheldon, former creative director and current doctoral student, University of Illinois.

EXHIBIT 13.45

Example of a reasonable timetable for shooting a 30-second television advertisement.

Activity	Time
Assess directors/editorial houses/music suppliers	1 week
Solicit bids from production houses/other suppliers	1 week
Review bids, award jobs to suppliers, submit production estimate to advertiser	1 week
Begin preproduction (location, sets, casting)	1 to 2 weeks
Final preparation and shooting	1 to 2 weeks
Edit film	1 week
Agency/advertiser review of rough-cut film	1 week
Postproduction (final editing, voice mix, record music, special effects, etc.) and transfer of film to video; ship to media	2 weeks
Transfer film to videotape; ship to stations	1 week
Total	10 to 12 weeks

Selection of Location, Sets, and Cast. Once a bid has been approved and accepted, both the production house and the agency production team begin to search for appropriate, affordable locations if the commercial is to be shot outside a studio setting. Studio production warrants the design and construction of the sets to be used.

A delicate stage in preproduction is casting. While not every ad uses actors and actresses, when an ad calls for individuals to perform roles, casting is crucial. Every individual appearing in an ad is, in a very real sense, a representative of the advertiser. This is another reason why the agency creative team stays involved. Actors and actresses help set the mood and tone for an ad and affect the image of the brand. The successful execution of various message strategies depends on proper casting. For instance, a slice-of-life message requires actors and actresses with whom the target audience can readily identify. Testimonial message tactics require a search for particular types of people, either celebrities or common folks, who will attract attention and be credible to the audience. The point to remember is that successfully casting a television commercial depends on much more than simply picking people with good acting abilities. Individuals must be matched to the personality of the brand, the nature of the audience, and the scene depicted in the ad. A young male actor who makes a perfect husband in a laundry detergent ad may be totally inappropriate as a rugged outdoorsman in a chainsaw commercial.

Production. The **production stage** of the process, or the **shoot,** is where the storyboard and script come to life and are filmed. The actual production of the spot may also include some final preparations before the shoot begins. The most common final preparation activities are lighting checks and rehearsals. An entire day may be devoted to *prelight,* which involves setting up lighting or identifying times for the best natural lighting to ensure that the shooting day runs smoothly. Similarly, the director may want to work with the on-camera talent along with the camera operators to practice the positioning and movement planned for the ad. This work, known as *blocking,* can save a lot of time on a shoot day,when many more costly personnel are on the set.

Lighting, blocking, and other special factors are typically specified by the director in the script. Exhibit 13.46 is a list of common directorial specifications that show up in a script and are used by a director to manage the audio and visual components of a commercial shoot.

Script Specification	Meaning
CU	Close-up.
ECU	Extreme close-up.
MS	Medium shot.
LS	Long shot.
Zoom	Movement in or out on subject with camera fixed.
Dolly	Movement in or out on subject moving the camera (generally slower than a zoom).
Pan	Camera scanning right or left from stationary position.
Truck	Camera *moving* right or left, creating a different visual angle.
Tilt	Camera panning vertically.
Cut	Abrupt movement from one scene to another.
Dissolve	Smoother transition from one scene to another, compared to a cut.
Wipe	Horizontal or vertical removal of one image to replace it with a new image (inserted vertically or horizontally).
Split screen	Two or more independent video sources occupying the screen.
Skip frame	Replacement of one image with another through pulsating (frame insertion of) the second image into the first. Used for dramatic transitions.
Key insert, matte, chromakey	Insertion of one image onto another background. Often used to impose product over the scene taking place in the commercial.
Super title	Lettering superimposed over visual. Often used to emphasize a major selling point or to display disclaimers/product warnings.
SFX	Sound effects.
VO	Introducing a voice over the visual.
ANN	Announcer entering the commercial.
Music under	Music playing in the background.
Music down and out	Music fading out of commercial.
Music up and out	Music volume ascending and abruptly ending.

EXHIBIT 13.46

Instructions commonly appearing in television commercial scripts.

Shoot days are the culmination of an enormous amount of effort beginning all the way back at the development of the copy platform. They are the execution of all the well-laid plans by the advertiser and agency personnel. The set on a shoot day is a world all its own. For the uninformed, it can appear to be little more than high-energy chaos, or a lot of nothing going on between camera setups. For the professionals involved, however, a shoot has its own tempo and direction, including a whole lot of nothing going on.

Production activities during a shoot require the highest level of professionalism and expertise. A successful shoot depends on the effective management of a large number of diverse individuals—creative performers, highly trained technicians, and skilled laborers. Logistical and technical problems always arise, not to mention the ever-present threat of a random event (a thunderstorm or intrusive noise) that disrupts filming and tries everyone's patience. There is a degree of tension and spontaneity on the set that is a necessary part of the creative process but must be kept at a manageable level. Much of the tension stems from trying to execute the various tasks of production correctly and at the proper time.

Another dimension to this tension, however, has to do with expense. As pointed out earlier, most directors, technicians, and talent are paid on a daily rate plus overtime after 10 hours. Daily shooting expenses, including director's fees, can run $80,000 to $120,000 for just an average production, so the agency and advertiser, understandably, want the shoot to run as smoothly and quickly as possible.

There is the real problem of not rushing creativity, however, and advertisers often have to learn to accept the pace of production. For example, a well-known director made a Honda commercial in South Florida, where he shot film for only one hour per day—a half-hour in the morning and a half-hour at twilight. His explanation? "From experience you learn that cars look flat and unattractive in direct light, so you have to catch the shot when the angle [of the sun] is just right."[11] Despite the fact that the cameras were rolling only an hour a day, the $9,000-per-hour cost for the production crew was charged all day for each day of shooting. Advertisers have to accept, on occasion, that the television advertising production process is not like an assembly line production process. Sweating the details to achieve just the right look can provoke controversy—and often does.

The Cost of Television Production. Coordinating and taking advantage of the skills offered by creative talent is a big challenge for advertisers. The average 30-second television commercial prepared by a national advertiser can run up production charges from $100,000 to $500,000 and even more if special effects or celebrities are used in the spot.[12] The cost of making a television commercial increased nearly 400 percent between 1979 and 1993.[13] Now it's even more. Part of that increase is attributed to the escalating cost of creative talent, such as directors and editors. Other aspects of the cost have to do with more and better equipment being used at all stages of the production process, and longer shooting schedules to ensure advertiser satisfaction.

The average expense for a 30-second spot tends to be higher for commercials in highly competitive consumer markets, such as beer, soft drinks, autos, and banking, where image campaigns (which require high-quality production) are commonly used. Conversely, average production costs tend to be lower for advertisements in which functional features or shots of the product often dominate the spot, as with household cleansers and office equipment.

The high and rising cost of television production has created some tensions between advertisers and their ad agencies. Most agencies and production companies respond by saying that advertisers are demanding to stand out from the clutter, and to do so requires complex concepts and high-priced talent.[14] Conversely, when an advertiser is not so image-conscious, ways can be found to stand out without spending huge dollar amounts.

The important issue in the preparation of all television advertising, regardless of cost, is that the production process has direct and significant effects on the communication impact of a finished advertisement. A well-conceived copy strategy can fall flat if the execution at the point of production is poor. As one advertiser put it, "We don't want to be penny wise and pound foolish. If we're spending $10 million to buy TV time, we shouldn't threaten creative integrity just to cut production cost to $140,000 from $150,000."[15] One rule of thumb is to ask for 10 percent of the planned media buy for production. They may not give it to you, but it's nice if you can get it, unless they are planning a very small media buy.

11. Jeffrey A. Trachtenberg, "Where the Money Goes," *Forbes,* September 21, 1987, 180.
12. Joe Mandese, "Study Shows Cost of TV Spots," *Advertising Age,* August 1, 1994, 32.
13. Information for the average cost of a 30-second ad in 1979 was taken from Ronald Alsop, "Advertisers Bristle as Charges Balloon for Splashy TV Spots," *Wall Street Journal,* June 20, 1985, 29. Information for the average cost of a 30-second ad in 1993 was taken from Peter Caranicas, "4A's Survey Shows Double-Digit Hike in Spot Production Costs," *Shoot,* July 15, 1994, 1, 40–42.
14. Caranicas, "4A's Survey Shows Double-Digit Hike in Spot Product Costs," 42.
15. Alsop, "Advertisers Bristle as Charges Balloon for Splashy TV Spots," op. cit.

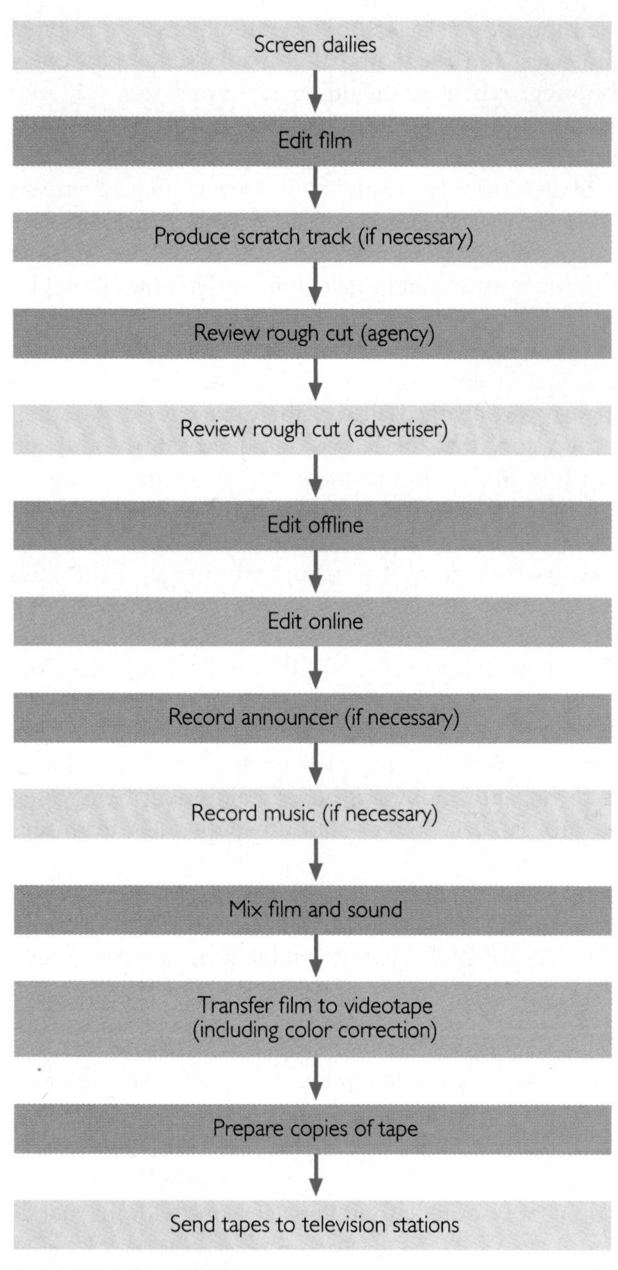

EXHIBIT 13.47

Sequence of events in television commercial postproduction.

Postproduction. Once filming is completed, several postproduction activities are required before the commercial is ready for airing. At this point, a host of additional professional talent enters the process. Film editors, audio technicians, voice-over specialists, and musicians may be contracted. Exhibit 13.47 shows the sequence of events in the postproduction phase.

The first step in postproduction is review of the **dailies**—scenes shot during the previous day's production. Such screening may result in reshooting certain segments of the ad. Once dailies are acceptable to the agency, the editing process begins. **Editing** involves piecing together various scenes or shots of scenes, called *takes,* to bring about the desired visual effect. Most editing involves making decisions about takes shot at different angles, or subtle differences in the performance of the talent. If music is to be included, it will be prepared at this point using a **scratch track,** which is a rough approximation of the musical score using only a piano and vocalists.

A rough cut of the commercial is then prepared by loading the video dailies into an *Avid computer* to digitize and timecode the tape. The **rough cut** is an assembly of the best scenes from the shoot edited together using the quick and precise access afforded by digital technology. Using the offline Avid computer on the digitized rough cut, various technical aspects of the look of a commercial can be refined—color alterations and background images, for example. The final editing of the advertisement—which includes repositioning of elements, correcting final color, and adding fades, titles, blowups, dissolves, final audio, and special effects—is done with online equipment in online rooms equipped for final editing. **Online editing** involves transferring the finalized rough cut onto one-inch videotape, which is of on-air quality suitable for media transmission.

The personnel and equipment required for postproduction tasks are costly. Film editors charge about $150 to $200 per hour, and an editing assistant is about $50 per hour. An offline computer costs about $100 per hour. When online editing begins, the cost goes up, with online rooms running about $700 per hour. The reason for the dramatic difference in cost between offline editing and online editing is that offline edits are done on a single machine to produce a rough, working version of an ad. The online room typically includes many specialized machines for all the final effects desired in the ad. Additionally, a mixing room for voice and music costs about $400 per day.

In all, it is easy to see why filmed television commercials are so costly. Scores of people with specialized skills and a large number of separate tasks are included in the process. The procedures also reflect the complexity of the process. Aside from the mechanics of production, a constant vigil must be kept over the creative concept of the advertisement. Despite the complexities, the advertising industry continues to turn out high-quality television commercials on a timely basis.

7 **Production Options in Television Advertising.** Several production options are available to an advertiser in preparing a television commercial. Eighty percent of all television commercials prepared by national advertisers use film as the medium for production. The previous discussion of production procedures, in fact, described the production process for a filmed advertisement. **Film** (typically 35-mm) is the most versatile medium and produces the highest-quality visual impression. It is, however, the most expensive medium for production and is also the most time-consuming.

A less expensive option is **videotape.** Videotape is not as popular among directors or advertisers for a variety of reasons. Tape has far fewer lines of resolution, and some say videotape results in a flatter image than film. Its visual impressions are more stark and have less depth and less color intensity. While this can sometimes add to the realism of a commercial, it can also detract from the appearance of the product and the people in the ad. The obvious advantages of videotape—its lower costs, no need to process before viewing, and its flexibility—make it very appealing. New **digital video (DV)** formats may challenge film, however. These advantages have prompted production houses (especially television station–based production facilities) to use videotape as the medium of choice in filming infomercials.[16] Infomercials can actually benefit from the starkness and realism of the videotape format.

There is always the choice of live television commercial production. **Live production** can result in realism and the capturing of spontaneous reactions and events that couldn't possibly be re-created in a rehearsed scene. It is clear, however, that the loss of control in live settings threatens the carefully worked-out objectives for a commercial. On occasion, local retailers (such as auto dealers) use live commercials to execute direct response message strategies. Such a technique can capture the urgency of an appeal.

Two techniques that do not neatly fit the production process described earlier are animation and stills. **Animation** (and the variation known as Claymation) is the use of drawn figures and scenes (such as cartoons) to produce a commercial. Keebler cookie and California Raisin commercials use characters created by animators and Claymation artists. Animated characters, such as Tony the Tiger, are frequently incorporated into filmed commercials for added emphasis. A newer form of animation uses computer-generated images. Several firms, such as TRW, have developed commercials totally through the use of computers. The graphics capabilities of giant-capacity computers make futuristic, eye-catching animation ads an attractive alternative. And the "ads" show up on time.

Still production is a technique whereby a series of photographs or slides is filmed and edited so that the resulting ad appears to have movement and action. Through the use of pans, zooms, and dissolves with the camera, still photographs can be used to produce an interesting yet low-cost finished advertisement.

The production option chosen should always be justified on both a creative and a cost basis. The dominance of filmed commercials is explainable by the level of quality of the finished ad and the versatility afforded by the technique. A local retailer or social service organization may not need or may not be able to afford the quality of film. In cases where quality is less significant or costs are primary, other production techniques are available.

16. Kevin Goldman, "CBS to Push Videotaping of Infomercials," *Wall Street Journal,* November 15, 1994, B6

SUMMARY

Identify the basic purposes, components, and formats of print ad illustrations.

With few exceptions, illustrations are critical to the effectiveness of print ads. Specifically, illustrations can serve to attract attention, make the brand heroic, communicate product features or benefits, create a mood and enhance brand image, stimulate reading of the body copy, or create the desired social context for the brand. The overall impact of an illustration is determined in part by its most basic components: size, use of color, and the medium used to create the illustration. Another critical aspect of the illustration's effectiveness has to do with the format chosen for the product in the illustration. Obviously, a print ad cannot work if the consumer doesn't easily identify the product or service being advertised.

Describe the principles and components that help ensure the effective design of print ads.

In print ad design, all the verbal and visual components of an ad are arranged for maximum impact and appeal. Several principles can be followed as a basis for a compelling design. These principles feature issues such as balance, proportion, order, unity, and emphasis. The first component of an effective design is focus—drawing the reader's attention to specific areas of the ad. The second component is movement and direction—directing the reader's eye movement through the ad. The third component is clarity and simplicity—avoiding a complex and chaotic look that will deter most consumers.

Detail the stages that art directors follow in developing the layout of a print ad.

The layout is the physical manifestation of all this design planning. An art director uses various forms of layouts to bring a print ad to life. There are several predictable stages in the evolution of a layout. The art director starts with a hand-drawn thumbnail, proceeds to the digitized rough layout, and continues with a tight comp that represents the look of the final ad. With each stage, the layout becomes more concrete and more like the final form of the advertisement. The last stage, the mechanical, is the form the ad takes as it goes to final production.

Discuss the activities and decisions involved in the final production of print ads.

Timing is critical to advertising effectiveness: Advertisers must have a keen understanding of production cycles to have an ad in the consumer's hands at just the right time. In addition, there are many possible means for actually printing an ad. These range from letterpress to screen printing to computer print production. As with many aspects of modern life, the computer has had a dramatic impact on print ad preparation and production. Before a print ad can reach its audience, a host of small but important decisions need to be made about the type styles and sizes that will best serve the campaign's purposes.

Identify the various players who must function as a team to produce television ads.

The complexity of ad production for television is unrivaled and thus demands the inputs of a variety of functional specialists. From the ad agency come familiar players such as the art director, copywriter, and account executive. Then there are a host of individuals who have special skills in various aspects of production for this medium. These include directors, producers, production managers, and camera crews. Editors will also be needed to bring all the raw material together into a finished commercial. Organizational and team-management skills are essential to make all these people and pieces work together.

Discuss the specific stages and costs involved in producing television ads.

The intricate process of TV ad production can be broken into three major stages: preproduction, production, and postproduction. In the preproduction stage, scripts and storyboards are prepared, budgets are set, production houses are engaged, and a timetable is formulated. Production includes all those activities involved in the actual filming of the ad. The shoot is a high-stress activity that usually carries a high price tag. The raw materials from the shoot are mixed and refined in the postproduction stage. Today's editors work almost exclusively with computers to create the final product—a finished television ad. If all this sounds expensive, it is!

Describe the major formatting options for television ad production.

Film is the preferred option for most TV ads because of the high-quality visual impression it provides. Videotape suffers on the quality issue, and live television is not practical in most cases. Animation is probably the second-most-popular formatting option. With continuing improvements in computer graphics, computer-generated images may one day become a preferred source of material for TV ad production. Still production can be an economical means to bring a message to television.

KEY TERMS

illustration
medium
illustration format
design
principles of design
balance
formal balance
informal balance
border
white space
axis
three-point layout structure
parallel layout structure
layout
thumbnails
rough layout
comp
mechanical
closing date
letterpress
offset lithography
gravure
flexography
electronic, laser, and inkjet printing
type font
blackletter
roman
script
serif
sans serif
miscellaneous
point
picas
preproduction
storyboard
script
production timetable
production stage, or shoot
dailies
editing
scratch track
rough cut
online editing
film
videotape
digital video (DV)
live production
animation
still production

QUESTIONS

1. Is there anyone out there who would rather watch black-and-white television than color? If not, why would any advertiser choose to run a black-and-white print ad in a medium that supports color? Can you think of a situation where a black-and-white ad might be more effective than a color ad?

2. *Effective* turns out to be a very elusive concept in any discussion of advertising's effects. In what ways might an illustration in a print ad prove to be effective from the point of view of a marketer?

3. This chapter reviewed five basic principles for print ad design: balance, proportion, order, unity, and emphasis. Give an example of how each of these principles might be employed to enhance the selling message of a print ad.

4. Creativity in advertising is often a matter of breaking with conventions. Peruse an issue of your favorite magazine or newspaper to find examples of ads that violate the five basic principles mentioned in the previous question.

5. Why is it appropriate to think of print as a static medium? Given print's static nature, explain how movement and direction can be relevant concepts to the layout of a print ad.

6. For an art director who has reached the mechanicals stage of the ad layout process, explain the appeal of computer-aided design versus the old-fashioned paste-up approach.

7. Explain the role of the production company in the evolution of a television commercial. As part of this explanation, be certain you have identified each of the unique skills and specialties that people in the production company bring to the ad development process.

8. Compare and contrast the creative guidelines for TV offered in this chapter with those offered for print ads in the previous chapter. Based on this analysis, what conclusions would you offer about the keys to effective communication in these two media?

9. Identify the six steps involved in the preproduction of a television ad and describe the issues that an art director must attend to at each step if his or her goals for the ad are to be achieved.

10. Without a doubt, a television ad shoot is one of the most exciting and pressure-packed activities that any advertising professional can take part in. List the various factors or issues that contribute to the tension and excitement that surrounds an ad shoot.

11. Review the formatting options that an art director can choose from when conceiving a television ad. Discuss the advantages of each option and describe the situation for which each is best suited.

EXPERIENTIAL EXERCISES

1. Go to the Internet and look up the following design-related sites:

http://www.lynda.com

http://www.res.com

http://www.fontsite.com

What services and benefits does each offer to art direction and production professionals? Which broad media category does each site seem most affiliated with? Identify specific agency participants that would be likely to benefit from using the site for its professional resources in art direction and production.

2. Television advertisers often list a brand's Web address at the end of commercials, prompting viewers to visit the site on their own. Evaluate a popular television advertisement that lists its Web address during the commercial. Discuss whether you think the ad follows the general creative principles for television advertising listed in this chapter and cite examples. Finally, visit the Web site and evaluate it based on the principles of design listed in this chapter. Does the particular Web site design resemble print, or does it have elements that appear more like television? List specific examples.

USING THE INTERNET

13-1 Elements of Illustration

Hillmancurtis is one of the premier design companies in the world, specializing in brand development and advertising for some of the most famous brands. The firm's regard for the power of visual design has earned it a list of clients such as Adobe, Intel, MTV, Rollingstone.com, Macromedia, and Sun Microsystems. Hillmancurtis has won prestigious honors for its work in print, broadcast, and Web media. Visit the Hillmancurtis site and browse the firm's online portfolio samples to answer the following questions.

Hillmancurtis: http://www.hillmancurtis.com

Adobe: http://www.adobe.com

1. Good illustration can make a brand more heroic. Choose a portfolio sample from the hillmancurtis.com portfolio section and explain how the firm accomplished this for its client's brand.

2. Visit Adobe's Web site and explain how Hillmancurtis designed the illustration at the site to create a mood, feeling, and image that appeal to graphic designers. How does the illustration at the site support Adobe's reputation as a leading manufacturer of publishing software and graphic design tools?

3. Browse and identify portfolio examples of Web animation at hillmancurtis.com, and describe how advancing computer technology is enabling design firms to produce endless creative possibilities for illustration.

13-2 Art Direction in Cyberspace

At this early stage in the development of the Internet, cyberspace is often compared to print and television, yet it possesses unique qualities as well. The medium is interactive, and new technology is making it possible for a variety of rich media to be used for advertising purposes. The following firm is on the pioneering edge of the Web's progression toward full-motion interactive capabilities.

eStudio: http://www.estudio.com

1. What is estudio.com, and what industries are most likely to rely heavily on its enhanced interactive design capabilities?

2. Describe how the estudio.com site combines elements of television and print into one new media experience for the user. What challenges still exist in making cyberspace a fully interactive experience for a majority of Web users?

3. Do you think traditional advertising agencies are capable of providing such advanced Internet production services to clients? Is interactive Web design influencing design elements in print or television advertising? Cite one example of a print or television ad that was influenced by the booming popularity of the Internet.

From Principles to Practice

AN INTEGRATED BRAND PROMOTION CASE

Cincinnati Bell wireless

PART 3
Cincinnati Bell Wireless: Preparing Advertising and Integrated Brand Promotion

In Parts 1 and 2 of our comprehensive IBP case, we introduced you to a client and an ad agency who together, in the spring of 1998, were preparing for the launch of a new digital phone service in the Greater Cincinnati market.

Now it is time to take an inside look at the process of actually preparing the elements of an integrated communications campaign. This stressful, stop-and-go process must be managed in such a way that the tension and stress do not stifle the creativity that is always required for breakthrough advertising. Many different types of expertise must be folded into the process to take advantage of multiple communication tools, and countless details must be attended to if the various tools are to work together to produce the synergy that is the reason for pursuing an IBP campaign in the first place. Collaboration between agency and client is key to ensure that the approval process proceeds in a timely fashion, but with all the planning and forethought there still needs to be an element of spontaneity that allows both client and agency to capitalize on the last-minute big ideas that always infiltrate the process just when you think you have everything decided.

Tension, stress, creativity, deadlines, collaboration, synergy, conflict, misunderstandings, expertise, complexity, details, details, details . . . these are all things that characterize the process of preparing to launch an IBP campaign. How is it possible for people to survive and work through the array of challenges that characterize campaign preparation? How is it possible, in the people-intensive business of advertising design and production, for order ever to emerge from the chaos?

Making Beautiful Music Together: Coordination, Collaboration, and Creativity. Metaphors help us understand, so let's use a metaphor to appreciate the challenge of executing sophisticated IBP campaigns. Executing an IBP campaign is very much like the performance of a symphony orchestra. To produce glorious music, many individuals must make their unique contributions to the performance, but it only sounds right if the maestro brings it all together at the critical moment. The next time you attend the performance of a symphony orchestra, get there early so that you can hear each individual musician warming up his or her instrument. Reflect on the many years of dedicated practice that this individual put in to master his or her instrument. Reflect on the many hours of practice that this individual put in to learn his or her specific part for tonight's performance. As you sit there listening to the warmup, notice how the random collection of sounds becomes increasingly painful to the ears. With each musician doing his or her own thing, the sound is a collection of hoots and clangs that grows louder as the performance approaches. Mercifully, the maestro finally steps to the podium to quell the cacophony. All is quiet for a moment. The musicians focus on their sheet music for reassurance, even though by now they could play their individual parts in their sleep. Finally, the maestro calls the orchestra into action. As a group, as a collective, as a team, with each person executing a specific assignment as defined by the composer, under the direction of the maestro, they make beautiful music together.

So it goes in the world of advertising. Preparing and executing breakthrough IBP campaigns is a people-intensive business. Many different kinds of expertise will be needed to pull it off, and this means many different people must be enlisted to play a variety of roles. But some order must be imposed on the collection of players. Frequently, a maestro will need to step in to give the various players a common theme or direction for their work. Beyond this need for leadership, the effort must also be guided by a strategy if this collective is to produce beautiful music together. Of course, the goal for this kind of music is a persuasive harmony that makes the cash register sing!

Without a doubt, the coordination and collaboration required for IBP execution require sophisticated teamwork. Moreover, the creative essence of the campaign can be aided and elevated by a thoughtful team approach. Teams possess a potential for synergy that allows them to rise above the talents of their individual members on many kinds of tasks.[1] (Yes, the whole can be greater than the sum of the individual parts.)

Our Cincinnati Bell Wireless example is replete with stories of successful teamwork. We will share some of those stories subsequently; however, we'd first like to make the point that successful teamwork can't be left to chance. It must be planned for and facilitated if it is to occur with regularity. In the remainder of this section we will introduce several concepts and insights about teams that are offered to encourage you to take teamwork more seriously. We will review research concerning what makes teams effective, along with basic principles for effective teamwork. Then we will turn to our Cincinnati Bell Wireless example to bring the concepts to life.

What We Know about Teams. We fully expect that every college student, by the time they read this textbook, will have taken a class where part of their grade was determined by teamwork. Get used to it. More and more instructors in all sorts of classes are incorporating teamwork as part of their courses because they know that interpersonal skills are highly valued in the real world of work. In fact, an impressive body of evidence from research on management practices indicates that teams have become essential to the effectiveness of modern organizations. In their book *The Wisdom of Teams,* management consultants Jon Katzenbach and Douglas Smith review many valuable insights about the importance of teams in today's world of work. Here we summarize several of their key conclusions.[2]

Teams Rule! There can be little doubt that teams have become the primary means for getting things done in a growing number and variety of organizations. The growing number of performance challenges faced by most businesses—as a result of factors such as more demanding customers, technological changes, government regulation, and intensifying competition—demand speed and quality in work products that are simply beyond the scope of what an individual can hope to offer. In many instances, teams are the only valid option for getting things done. This is certainly the case for executing IBP campaigns.

It's All about Performance. Research shows that teams are effective in organizations where senior management makes it perfectly clear that teams will be held

1. Arthur B. VanGundy, *Managing Group Creativity* (New York: American Management Association, 1984).
2. Jon R. Katzenbach and Douglas K. Smith, *The Wisdom of Teams: Creating the High-Performance Organization* (Boston: Harvard Business School Press, 1993).

accountable for performance. Teams are expected to produce results that satisfy the client and yield financial gains for the organization. As we will see in subsequent examples, this performance motive as the basis for teams is a perfect fit in an advertising and IBP agency such as Northlich.

Synergy through Teams. Modern organizations require many kinds of expertise to get the work done. The only reliable way to mix people with different expertise to generate solutions where the whole is greater than the sum of the parts is through team discipline. Research shows that blending expertise from diverse disciplines often produces the most innovative solutions to many different types of business problems.[3] The "blending" must be done through teams.

The Demise of Individualism? Rugged individualism is the American Way. Always look out for number one! But are we suggesting that a growing reliance on teams in the workplace must mean a devaluation of the individual and a greater emphasis on conforming to what the group thinks? Not at all. Left unchecked, of course, an "always look out for number one" mentality can destroy teams. But teams are not incompatible with individual excellence. To the contrary, effective teams find ways to let each individual bring his or her unique contributions to the forefront as the basis for their effectiveness. When an individual does not have his or her own contribution to make, then one can question that person's value to the team. Or, as Northlich's CEO Mark Serrianne is fond of saying, "If you and I both think alike, then one of us is unnecessary."

Teams Promote Personal Growth. Finally, an added benefit of teamwork is that it promotes learning for each individual team member. In a team, people learn about their own work styles and observe the work styles of others. This learning makes them more effective team players in their next assignment.

Leadership in Teams. A critical element in the equation for successful teams is leadership. Leadership in teams is a special form of leadership; it is not a matter of the most senior person in the team giving orders and expecting others to follow. Leadership in teams is not derived from the power and authority granted by one's standing in an organization. It is not a function of some mysterious accident at birth that grants some of us the ability to lead, while others must be content to follow. All of us can learn to be effective team leaders. It is a skill worth learning.

Leaders do many things for their teams to help them succeed.[4] Teams ultimately must reach a goal to justify their standing, and here is where the leader's job starts. The leader's first job is to help the team build consensus about the goals they hope to achieve and the approach they will take to reach those goals. Without a clear sense of purpose, the team is doomed. Once goals and purpose are agreed upon, then the leader plays a role in ensuring that the work of the team is consistent with the strategy or plan. This is a particularly important role in the context of creating IBP campaigns because there must always be a screen or filter applied to ensure that each element is supporting the overriding communication goal.

Leaders may also specify roles for various individuals and set and reaffirm ground rules that facilitate open communication in the team. Additionally, team leaders may serve as the point of contact for the team with others in the organization or a client outside the organization.

3. Dorothy Leonard and Susaan Straus, "Putting Your Company's Whole Brain to Work," *Harvard Business Review,* July/August 1997, 111-121.
4. Katzenbach and Smith, *The Wisdom of Teams,* Chapter 7.

Finally, team leaders must help do the real work of the team. Here the team leader must be careful to contribute ideas without dominating the team. There are also two key things that team leaders should never do: *They should not blame or allow specific individuals to fail, and they should never excuse away shortfalls in team performance.*[5] Mutual accountability must always be emphasized over individual performance.

Teams as the Engine for Coordination, Collaboration, and Creativity in the Launch of Cincinnati Bell Wireless. A multimillion-dollar product launch such as that of Cincinnati Bell Wireless will require the coordination and collaboration of hundreds of individuals. These individuals will include employees from Bell and Northlich plus a variety of outside vendors, each contributing their own particular expertise, to make the launch a success. Without skillful teamwork involving dozens of discrete teams working at various levels and on various tasks, there could be no hope of executing an integrated campaign.

That team effort has many manifestations, but it must begin with a partnership between agency and client. When Mark Serrianne of Northlich was asked what one needs to be successful in executing an IBP campaign, the first thing he said was, "You have to have a great client—a client that wants a partnership role." In the launch of Cincinnati Bell Wireless, we see client and agency working as partners to execute a successful launch. Cincinnati Bell brought to the table exactly those things that any good client must provide: technical expertise in their product category, financial resources, keen insights about competitive strategy, and a deep appreciation for the critical role of retailer support. From the agency side, Northlich brought a tireless commitment to understanding the consumer as a basis for effective communication, and a depth of expertise and experience in the design, preparation, and placement of a broad array of communication tools. Each looked to the other to do its job; in particular, we see in this example a client that trusted its agency to do the job of preparing and placing a full-scale IBP campaign. That trust is critical because it frees the agency to do its most crucial task: creating breakthrough communications that will disrupt the category and drive business results.

The Account Team. As expressed by Mark Serrianne, the Northlich philosophy on teamwork is embodied by the account team. This team of experts from the various disciplines within the agency is charged with bringing a campaign into being for its focal client. Every account team must have a leader, or account supervisor, who becomes the critical communication liaison to the client, and who seeks to facilitate and coordinate a dialogue among the disciplines represented on the team. But, consistent with our earlier discussion about team leadership, the Northlich account supervisor is definitely not identified as the highest-ranking person on the team, whose job it is to give orders, sit back, and let other people do all the work. The account supervisor is a working member of the team who also is responsible for encouraging and coordinating the efforts of other team members.

Half the battle in making teams work is getting the right people on the team in the first place. This begins with the account supervisor. The Northlich account team for the CBW launch was led by Mandy Reverman. Mandy was hired by Northlich from Campbell-Ewald, Advertising–Detroit, to direct the CBW launch. Over a seven-year period with Campbell-Ewald, Mandy had gained considerable experience in account management and team leadership through her work for Chevrolet

5. Katzenbach and Smith, *The Wisdom of Teams,* 144.

and Toyota auto dealerships. Automotive retailer groups are a demanding clientele who expect to see a direct effect on sales from the advertising they sponsor in specific metro markets. As it turns out, these were the same kinds of expectations that CBW had for its advertising in the Greater Cincinnati metro market in the spring of 1998. Mandy thus had the right background to oversee the CBW account team.

Mandy views the role of team leader as the hub of a wheel, with various spokes that reach out to diverse disciplinary expertise. The hub connects the spokes and ensures that all of them work in tandem to make the wheel roll smoothly. Using Mandy's wheel metaphor, her spokes are represented by team members from direct marketing, public relations, broadcast media, graphic design, creative, and accounting. To illustrate the multilayered nature of the team approach to IBP, each team member can also be thought of as a hub in his or her very own wheel. For example, the direct marketing member on the account team was team leader for her own set of specialists charged with preparing direct marketing materials for the CBW launch. Through this type of multilevel "hub-and-spokes" design, the coordination and collaboration essential for effective IBP campaigns can be achieved.

Teams Moderate Tension in the Copy Approval Process. In the deadline-driven and pressure-packed activity of campaign preparation, one predictable source of tension between agency and client is the copy approval process. This was certainly evident in the CBW launch, not only because of the time pressures that accompanied this launch, but also because of the unique partnership between Cincinnati Bell and AT&T that was forged in the creation of CBW. While the AT&T network was critical to the credibility of the CBW service, the partnership with AT&T also gave executives from that organization a say in the copy approval process. This turned out to be one of the most frustrating aspects of the launch for the Northlich creative team, because AT&T's executives were far removed from the actual process of ad development. According to one Northlich insider, this is the painstaking part of the process: "It is hard to keep people motivated to work the details when what appear to be insignificant changes are requested by a distant third party."

So how do you keep people motivated when these last-minute requests to shift scenes and sentences are made on work that you thought was finished? First of all, the communication that is facilitated through teamwork is essential to working through the copy approval process. Delays caused by miscommunication are certain to heighten tensions and create dysfunctional outcomes. Moreover, the mutual accountability that goes with effective teams must also come into play. The copywriters or art directors that have to respond with last-minute changes must accept their roles as team players, and move forward on the changes for the sake of the team.

Teams Liberate Decision Making. When the right combination of expertise is assembled on a team, what appears to be casual or spur-of-the-moment decision making can turn out to be more creative decision making. The value of divergent, spontaneous input as a basis for decisions is beautifully illustrated by the team-oriented approach that Northlich and CBW employed during the shoot of their television commercials. Key members of the "shoot team" included the account supervisor from Northlich, Mandy Reverman, and her steadfast partner from the client side, Mike Vanderwoude, marketing director at CBW. They joined the production manager, art director, and copywriter to create a working team that didn't just bring their storyboards to life in the shoot. Through a lively give-and-take on the site, they created engaging video that was on strategy and delivered a message that wireless customers in Cincinnati were just ready and waiting to hear.

Exhibit IBP 3.1 is an example of one of the storyboards that this working team started with at a shoot. This ad, titled "Classroom," is seeded with the core strategy

Classroom:30 (pricing/affordability)

(We open on our spokesman in classroom. He's in front of a chalkboard with a bunch of complicated formulas on it.)

Have you ever tried to figure out how much cellular service actually costs?

Hmm. Maybe you should have taken Advanced Calculus after all.

Here's a better answer:

Cincinnati Bell Wireless.

No peak calling hours. No extra charges.

(Hands of school clock spin rapidly.)

Just one low rate that's way more affordable than cellular.

(Holds up flash cards of the less than symbol., fractions)

Stop by the Store at Cincinnati Bell and see if wireless is right for you.

Unless, of course, you like homework.

EXHIBIT IBP 3.1

Cincinnati Bell Wireless Storyboard: "Classroom."

that drove much of the advertising for the launch. The message of the ad was that Cincinnati Bell Wireless is a superior solution because it is both simpler and more economical than cellular. You don't need to know advanced calculus to figure out the benefits of Cincinnati Bell Wireless. But the final ad that evolved from this board shows many departures from its rather languid script. This is because, during the shoot, the working team fed off one another's ideas to continue to develop and refine the ad's expression of "simple terms" and "it's just a better deal [than cellular]." Individual scenes were shot over and over again, testing various deliveries of new executions that the working team was creating on the spur of the moment. This liberated the team, the talent, and the director to produce a final product that delivers on the simplification message in a most compelling way.

More about Teams and Creativity. As the preceding example reflects, creativity in the preparation of an IBP campaign can be fostered by the trust and open communication that are hallmarks of effective teams. But it is also true that the creativity required for breakthrough campaigns will evolve as personal work products generated by individuals laboring on their own. Both personal and team creativity are critical in the preparation of IBP campaigns. The daunting task of facilitating both usually falls in the lap of an agency's creative director.

The position of creative director in any ad agency is very special because, much like the maestro of the symphony orchestra, the creative director must encourage personal excellence, but at the same time demand team accountability. Don Perkins, senior VP and executive creative director at Northlich, sees his job as channeling the creative energies of the dozens of individuals in his group. Don acknowledges that creativity has an intensely personal element; in his view, original creation is motivated by the desire to satisfy one's own ego or sense of self. But despite the intimate character he ascribes to creativity, Don clearly appreciates the need for team unity. Many of the principles he relies on for channeling the creativity of his group could in fact be portrayed as key tenets for team leadership. In orchestrating Northlich's creative teams, Don relies on the following principles:

- Take great care in assigning individuals to a team in the first place. Be sensitive to their existing workloads and the proper mix of expertise required to do the job for the client.
- Get to know the work style of each individual. Listen carefully. Since creativity can be an intensely personal matter, one has to know when it is best to leave people alone, versus when one needs to support them in working through the inevitable rejection.
- Make teams responsible to the client. Individuals and teams are empowered when they have sole responsibility for performance outcomes.
- Beware of adversarial relationships between individuals and between teams. They can quickly lead to mistrust that destroys camaraderie and synergy.
- In situations where the same set of individuals will work on multiple teams over time, rotate team assignments to foster fresh thinking.

To Ensure the Uniform Look, Turn to Teams. While we're probably starting to sound like a broken record on this team thing, let's take just one more example. Exhibits IBP 3.2, 3.3, and 3.4 show point-of-purchase brochures, a direct mail piece, and a billboard facing that were created by three different Northlich designers for the CBW launch. These and dozens of other elements of the launch campaign were created to have a uniform look that supported the integrated premise of the campaign. But how does one get this uniform look when in fact these dozens of different items will inevitably be the work products of dozens of different individuals? Sure. You guessed it. If you want a uniform look, you must rely on teamwork.

The materials in the three exhibits feature several common design elements, including colors, line art, fonts, background, and of course, the CBW logo. These elements were selected through an internal competition that Don Perkins and his design director orchestrated in the Northlich design department. From this competition, a design standard was chosen, and the graphic artist who created that design became the leader of an ad hoc design team. That artist thereafter coordinated the efforts of different designers as they prepared various materials for the campaign, and served the critical role that leaders often fulfill as filters to ensure collaboration, which in this specific case emerged as the "uniform look." Here we see once again that the fundamentals of effective teams—communication, trust, complementary expertise, and leadership—produce the desired performance outcome. There's simply no alternative. Teams rule!

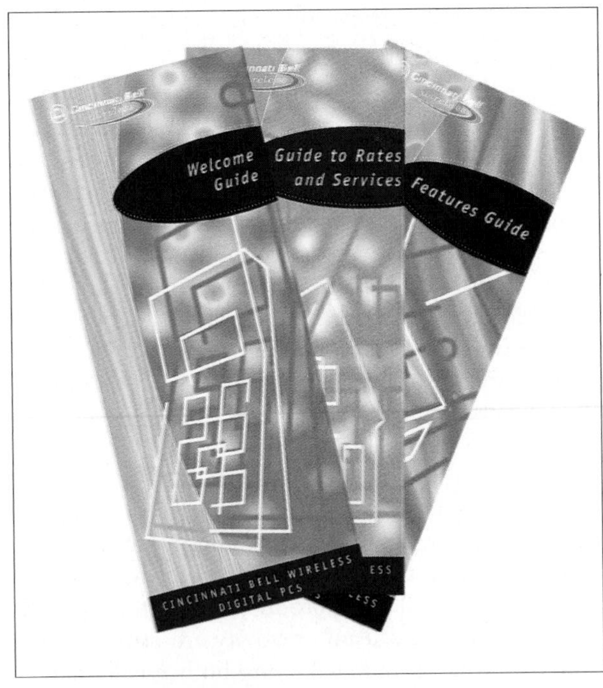

EXHIBIT IBP 3.2

CBW launch: P-O-P brochures.

EXHIBIT IBP 3.2

CBW launch: direct mail piece.

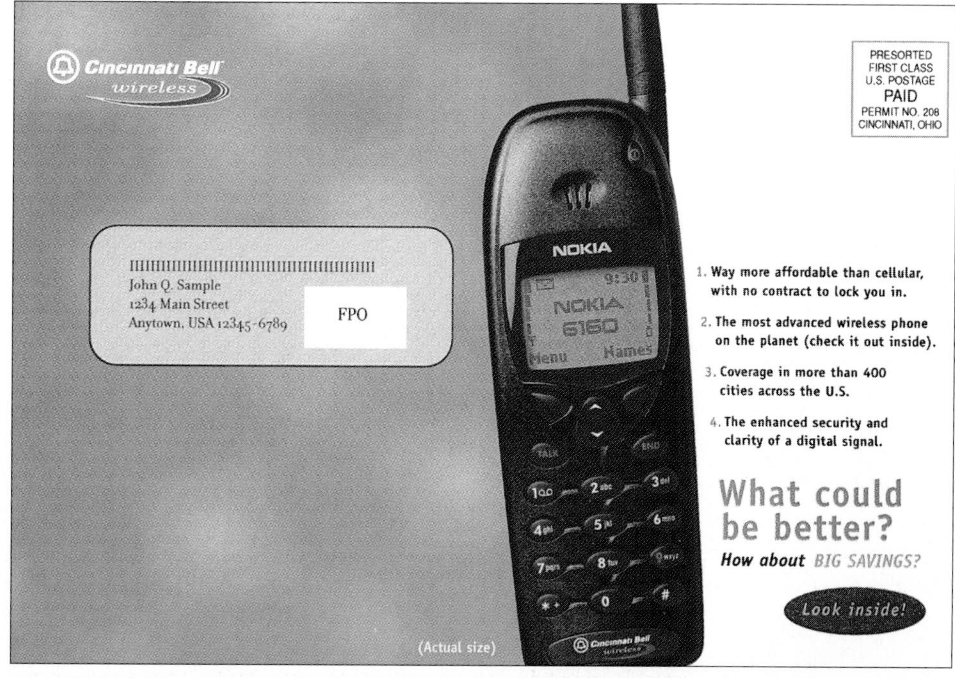

__________er than cellular

(*clear, smart, bett*)

EXHIBIT IBP 3.4

CBW launch: billboard facing.

IBP EXERCISES

1. Advertising always has been a team sport, but the advent of advertising and IBP has made effective teamwork more important than ever. It also has made it more difficult to achieve. Explain how the growing emphasis on IBP makes effective teamwork more difficult to achieve.
2. What insight(s) about teams does Mark Serrianne, CEO of Northlich, provide when he states, "If you and I both think alike, then one of us is unnecessary"?
3. In the launch of Cincinnati Bell Wireless, we see client and agency working together as a partnership to execute a product launch. What did each "bring to the table" to create the partnership? In your opinion, who plays the greater role in creating a successful partnership: the client or the agency?
4. The creative director in an advertising agency has the daunting task of channeling the creative energies of dozens of individuals, while demanding team accountability. If the expression of creativity is personal and highly individualized, how can teamwork possibly foster creativity? What might a creative director do to "allow creativity to happen" in a team environment? Explain how the saying "The whole is greater than the sum of its parts" fits into a discussion of creativity and teamwork.

PART FOUR

Placing the Message in Conventional and "New" Media

Once again we pass into a new and totally different area of advertising, "Placing the Message in Conventional and 'New' Media." We are now at the point where reaching the target audience is the key issue.

Beyond the basic and formidable challenge of effectively choosing the right media to reach a target audience, contemporary advertisers are demanding even more from the media placement decision: synergy and integration. Throughout the first three parts of the text, the issue of integrated brand communications has been raised whenever the opportunity existed to create coordinated communications. Indeed, the Cincinnati Bell sections at the end of each part are included to highlight the IBP issue. But nowhere is IBP more critical than at the media placement. Here, audiences may be exposed to an advertiser's messages through a wide range of different media each with a unique quality and tone to the communication. The advertiser is challenged to ensure that if diverse communications media options are chosen for placing the message, there is still a "one-voice" quality to the overall communication program.

14

Media Planning, Objectives, and Strategy. Maintaining integration is indeed a challenge in the contemporary media environment. Chapter 14, "Media Planning, Objectives, and Strategy for Advertising and Promoting the Brand," begins with an overview of major media options. The media-planning process is explored next, including a discussion of media objectives, strategies, choices, and scheduling issues. Next, the complexity of the current media environment is discussed. Finally, media choice is considered in the context of integrated brand communications. This chapter is enhanced with media strategy exercises and access to media data.

15

Media Planning: Print, Television, and Radio. Chapter 15, "Media Planning: Print, Television, and Radio," offers an analysis of the major media options available to advertisers. The vast majority of the creative effort—and money—is expended on print and broadcast advertising campaigns. Despite the many intriguing opportunities that new media options offer, print and broadcast media will likely form the foundation of most advertising campaigns for years to come. The chapter follows a sequence in which the advantages and disadvantages of each medium are discussed, followed by considerations of costs, buying procedures, and audience measurement techniques.

16

Media Planning: Advertising and the Internet. The newest and perhaps greatest challenge for advertisers has recently presented itself—the Internet. Chapter 16, "Media Planning: Advertising and the Internet," describes this relatively new and formidable technology available to advertisers. This chapter is key to understanding the contemporary advertising environment. Basic terminology and procedures are described. Most of the discussion in this chapter focuses on two fundamental issues: the structure of the Internet and the potential of the Internet as an advertising medium. Through these discussions, we will come to a better understanding of how to use the Internet as part of an effective advertising and integrated brand promotion effort. We will consider a short history of the Internet, an overview of cyberspace, the different types of advertising that can be used, and some of the technical aspects of the process. We also discuss where the (r)evolution stands, including triumphs, disappointments and strategic re-thinking and redeployment. A multitude of Web sites are offered for exploration.

CHAPTER 14

After reading and thinking about this chapter, you will be able to do the following:

CHAPTER 14
Media Planning, Objectives, and Strategy for Advertising and Promoting the Brand

CHAPTER 15
Media Planning: Print, Television, and Radio

CHAPTER 16
Media Planning: Advertising and the Internet

Detail the important components of the media-planning process.

Explain the applications of computer modeling in media planning.

Discuss five additional challenges that complicate the media-planning process.

FOR 4 MILLION GUYS

WE'RE BETTER THAN PORN.

Not one hot, naked female and still Sandbox.com℠ is one of the 15 most addictive sites on the Web.* We have 4 million members playing our games, and we're growing like mad. The demo: 90% male, 70% 18-34; $70K average HHI.** These guys are intelligent, loyal, highly attentive and not as elusive as you thought. Especially when we can separate your message by age, interests and other demo data. Contact Jim Keplesky at (212) 201-9801 or jkeplesky@sandbox-inc.com. For direct marketing and e-mail programs, contact Alan Laifer at (212) 201-9818 or alaifer@sandbox-inc.com.

Sandbox.com℠

It used to be a pretty simple system: Around 80 percent of all promotional dollars went to media advertising (television, radio, newspapers, magazines, and outdoor). The advertising was created, produced, and placed by full-service advertising agencies—most everything was done under one roof. The agency bought the media at a 15 percent discount, and that's how they made their money. The more advertising they could persuade a client to buy, the more money they made. It was very simple math. Those days are pretty much gone.

These days, the 15 percent commission is largely history, and in its place is a sea of individually negotiated deals that have almost nothing standard about them. The "media" now include all sorts of "new" species: the Internet, promotions, product placements, and so on. The majority of promotion dollars are not found in media advertising, but in other forms of promotion such as direct mail. The people who actually create the ads may work at an entirely different agency than the people who buy the media. Quite a bit of media planning and buying is now outsourced, or split off from the agency with the account management function, as evidenced in the IBP box on this page.

While it is absolutely true that advertising pundits never met hyperbole they didn't use, the world of advertising media has changed. Just 10 years ago, media planning was a relatively simple task. Sure, there were lots of combinations of media vehicles, which required intensive number crunching and optimization by computers. But one at least knew what was being optimized . . . what the media were. Now, all media boundaries are in flux. Promotion in all its myriad forms counts for at least as many marketing dollars as straight media advertising. Consider the use of the Internet to distribute short films by directors such as Guy Ritchie (*Lock, Stock and Two Smoking Barrels, Snatch*), Ang Lee (*Crouching Tiger, Hidden Dragon*), John Frankenheimer (*Ronin*), Wong Kar-Wai (*In the Mood for Love*), and Alejandro Gonzales Inarritu (*Amores Perros*) for BMW (see Exhibit 14.1). These are films/commercials/product placements for BMW cars. Because they are tech-

IBP

Windows XP: A Ray of Light

Microsoft unveiled a new integrated strategy with the launch of its Windows XP operating system. The optimistic campaign theme, centered on the tag "Yes you can" and the Madonna song "Ray of Light," marks a $200 million effort, with an estimated $10 million going to online initiatives.

To execute the campaign, media planners selected McCann-Erickson Worldwide to illustrate Windows XP features in print and television ads. Print ads show everyday situations such as sending digital photos of kids via e-mail against a trademark background of blue sky and green grass, the default background screen for XP. In the television ads, Madonna's "Ray of Light" pulses with upbeat optimism as energetic vignettes of people using XP are interspersed with shots of them flying against the sky background. The creative communicates frictionless, unbridled freedom. "People want to be able to do what they want when they want and how they want," said a representative from Microsoft.

For the online component of the campaign, Microsoft went with trusted interactive agency Exile on Seventh. In an unusual move, the agency negotiated the online media buy with creative that allowed sites to customize the ad units. Typically, standard ad units are deployed across multiple Web sites. Exile's president, Alan Burgis, said, "We selected ten sites and said, 'Here are the things we want to do. Who wants to play ball? What will it cost?' " Some analysts said the agency's strategy of bypassing standards for ad units risked alienating Web publishers, yet also allowed for more site-appropriate creative through customization. The strategy reflects the fact that marketers need to develop creative that can run across many Web sites, reaching a wider audience. An Ask Jeeves representative remarked, "It's about time we encouraged our clients to create units that are appropriate to the site they are advertising on."

The Windows XP campaign highlights the changes and challenges facing media planners as a broader range of communication tools and highly targeted media become integrated into media plans. The proliferation of media options has redefined the way planners go about developing and executing media plans. Increased customization and targeting also mean increased complexity: the people that actually create the ads may work at an entirely different agency than the people who execute media buys.

The increasing complexity of the media-planning environment is creating the need for a central control. While it is still unclear who will act as the hub, it is likely that media planners will emerge as more critically important to the communications process than they have ever been in the past.

Sources: Sarah J. Heim, "Microsoft Debuts Web Ads for XP," *Ad Week*, www.adweek.com, accessed October 29, 2001; "Microsoft Revs $200 Mill. XP Push," *Media Week*, www.mediaweek.com, accessed October 12, 2001.

EXHIBIT 14.1

Web films offer advertisers unique advantage. BMW spent close to an estimated $3 million per short film. According to AdAge, *"Since the site's launch in April of 2001, BMW claims the films have been downloaded 6 million times; this figure includes repeat viewings but does not count people who log off before downloading the entire film." According to Web tracker Jupiter Media Metrix, bmwfilms.com in May 2001 drew 787,000 unique visitors who spent an average of 7 minutes at the site that month, and in June 2001 drew 856,000 visitors who spent an average of 16 minutes. The Web promotion comes at a time when BMW sales are booming. "BMW's U.S. sales in June 2001 hit 20,250 vehicles, up 32% from a year ago," according to* Automotive News. *This film comes from Fallon Worldwide-Minneapolis. Visit this interesting BMW site (www.bmwfilms.com) and view the film clips. What is the link between action films and BMW automobiles? What themes do these films share in common? What subconscious message do you think BMW aims to convey to car enthusiasts through this innovative media vehicle?*

e-SIGHTINGS

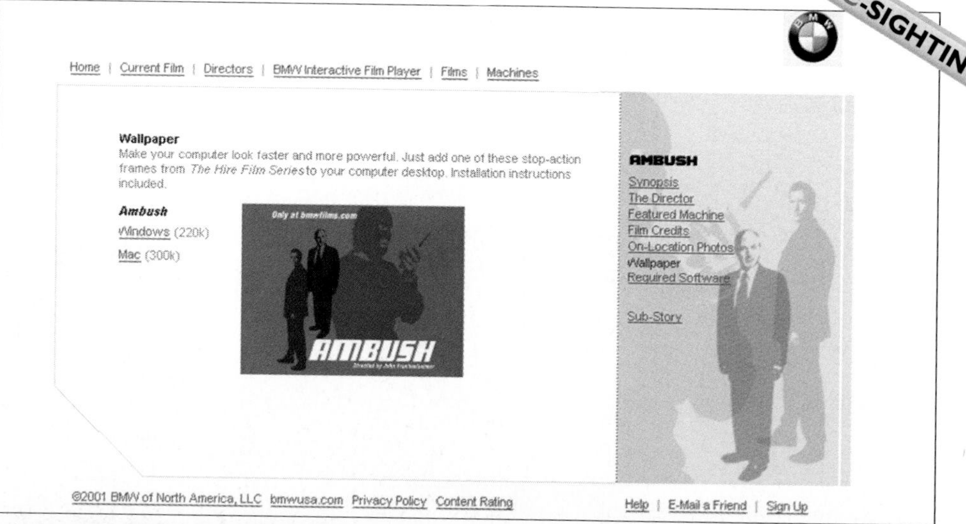

EXHIBIT 14.2

Even eggs have WWW addresses. www.goodegg.com

nically entertainment, they are beyond most regulation. Even eggs (see Exhibit 14.2) have WWW addresses stamped on them. The use of all sorts of tie-ins, cross-promotions, and other media experiments leave media planners in a brave new world. Yet despite all the change, some things remain the same: some principles, some concepts, and some methods.

First, let's set one really dumb myth aside: A few years ago a few people were saying, "Advertising is dead, long live new media." Wrong. Advertising, since that time, has done nothing but flourish, particularly traditional media advertising. In fact, traditional advertising was the big winner and not in small part due to all the advertising the now-defunct dot-coms bought in the cause of self-promotion and ratcheting their now-worthless stock prices up. Now-almost-forgotten "new economy" companies bought time on the 2000 Super Bowl to promote their now-defunct dot.com.whatever. Internet advertising rates stalled, then started falling like a rock. Well, who's still standing?

Good planning remains good planning regardless of the media employed. Some are smarter than others. While I was writing this chapter, I went downstairs to get the mail. I had an envelope from "Unique Customized Dog Food." Enclosed was a

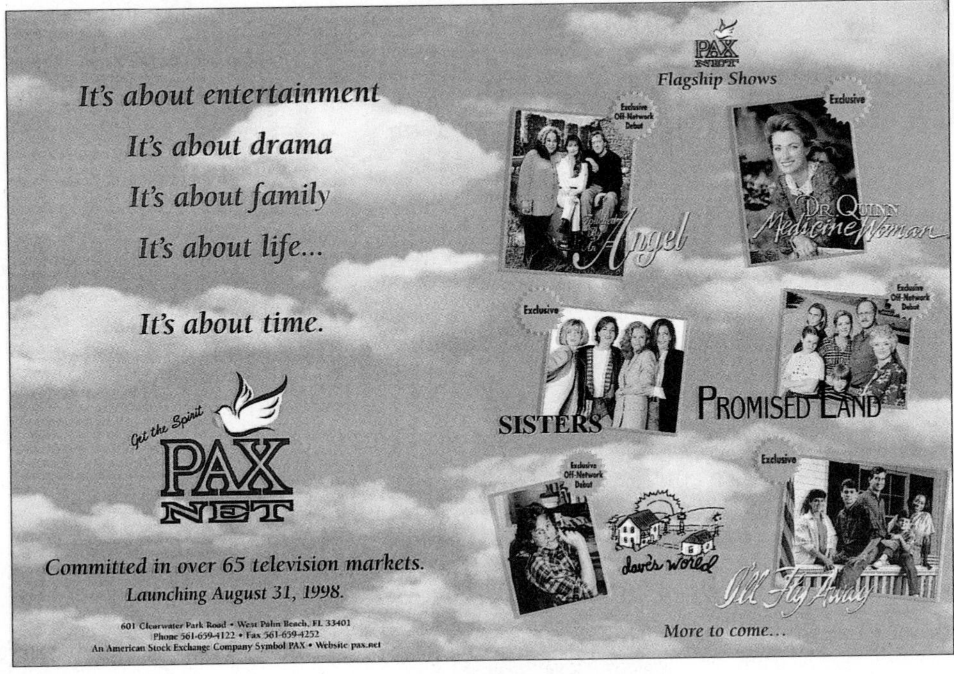

EXHIBIT 14.3

For what types of products would this medium be appropriate? www.pax.net

bright blue bag labeled "Stool Sample Collection Instructions." That's right, these guys wanted me to send them some dog feces for customized analysis, so they could make some dog food that would be "optimized for your dog's DNA (Digestive Nutrient Absorption)." I'm not making this up. This is a form of promotion. The marketer selected me to receive this offer, betting that I would be more likely than others to scoop up some of Fido's feces and send it in. Of course, there is a problem . . . I don't own a dog. I used to, but I haven't for a while. Clearly, this company relied on some bad data. Even though this effort was promotion rather than strict media advertising, planning is planning. The medium is simply the thing that carries the message to the consumer, whether it's radio, television, or in this case the mail. Now that promotion at least equals straight media advertising in the total promotional effort, we have to take a wider view of what constitutes media.

No matter how new the media are, how great a marketing plan is, and how insightful or visionary advertising strategists are, poor message placement will undermine even the best-laid plans. Advertising placed in media that do not reach the target audience—whether via new media or traditional media—will be much like the proverbial tree that falls in the forest with no one around: Does it make a sound? From an advertising standpoint, it doesn't matter. Advertising placed in media that do not reach target audiences will not achieve the communications or sales impact an advertiser desires. For example, if an ad for Victoria's Secret or for an Ultimate Fighting Championship pay-per-view event were placed on a family cable network like PaxNet (see Exhibit 14.3), it would be unlikely to affect the thoughts and actions of the audience in a positive way, at least many of them . . . we think.

To begin to appreciate the nature of media placement challenges and opportunities, let's consider the largest media organizations in the world. From the 2.9 million daily readers of the *Wall Street Journal* around the world to the estimated 250 million viewers of MTV, global reach with highly accessible media is becoming a reality. Many of these global media organizations have large audiences outside of North America. BBC Worldwide TV, based in London, has more than 7.2 million viewers throughout Asia, and NBC has 65 million viewers in Europe. Likewise, as shown in Exhibit 14.4, *Time* magazine is actively expanding all over the globe.

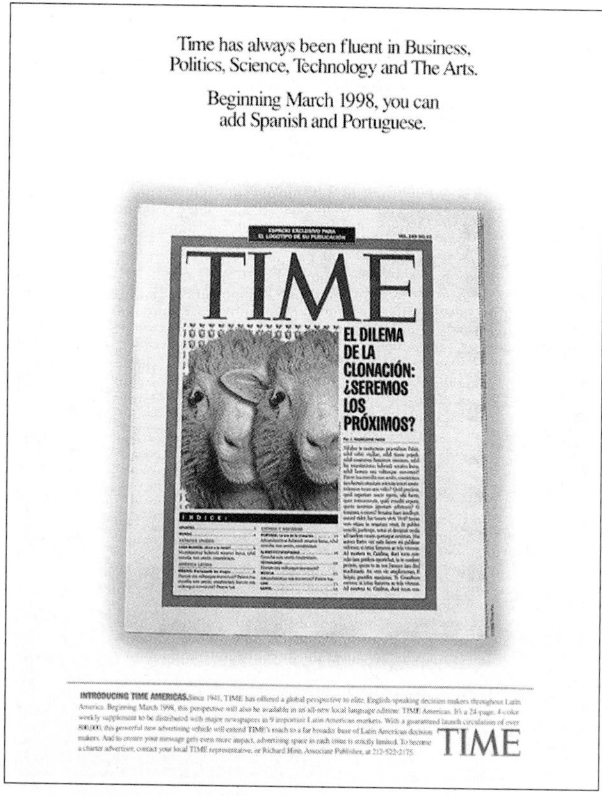

EXHIBIT 14.4

American magazines such as Time *have long pulled in news from all over the world and, increasingly, are pushing their content into the hands of non-U.S. readers, in their own languages.*
www.time.com

Another way to gain a perspective on the nature of message placement options is to examine the media environment in the United States. Exhibits 14.5 and 14.6 provide interesting information in this regard. In Exhibit 14.5, total media expenditures by media category are listed. Notice that less than half of media expenditures in the United States are made in what are referred to as measured media. The **measured media**—television, radio, newspapers, magazines, the Internet, and outdoor media—are listed in detail in Exhibit 14.5. But notice that spending on these measured media, nearly $111 billion, represents less than 46 percent of all U.S. expenditures for 2000. **Unmeasured media,** which include direct mail, promotion, co-op, couponing, catalogs, special events, and other ways to reach business, farm, and household consumers, account for the remaining 54 percent.

Exhibit 14.6 reveals a different dimension of the media placement environment in the United States. Marketers in some product categories spend more on media and rely more on certain types of media than others. Notice that this media spending list is headed by retail and then automobile marketers, who invested more than $17 and $15 billion respectively in measured media in 2000. Not surprisingly, retailers relied most on local newspapers ($6.6 billion), while the auto advertisers relied most on spot TV ($4.5 billion).

Another aspect of media placement revealed in Exhibit 14.6 is that those who are absolutely dependent on branding parity products and services such as food, medicines, and telecommunications spend the most money placing their advertisements on network television—the medium with the broadest consumer market coverage. Direct response companies, on the other hand, invest most heavily in consumer magazines, which reach the most well-defined target audiences.

1 The Media-Planning Process.

This wealth of media options demands incredible attention to detail in the media-planning process. Some basic terminology is essential to understanding this effort. A **media plan** specifies the media in which advertising messages will be placed to reach the desired target audience. A **media class** is a broad category of media, such as television, radio, or newspapers. A **media vehicle** is a particular option for placement within a media class. For example, *Newsweek* is a media vehicle within the magazine media class.

A media plan includes objectives, strategies, media choices, and a media schedule for placing a message. Exhibit 14.7 shows the specific components of a media plan. Recall from Chapter 8 that the advertising plan, developed during the planning stage of the advertising effort, is the driving force behind a media plan. Market and advertising research determines that certain media options hold the highest potential. Thus, in reality, the media-planning process takes place simultaneously with the overall development of the advertising plan.

Notice in Exhibit 14.7 that media planners set media objectives, identify strategies, make media choices, and finally set a media schedule, including the media-buying process. We will discuss each component of the media-planning process.

EXHIBIT 14.5

Advertising spending by media category in the United States, 1999–2000 (in millions of dollars).

Media	2000	1999	% Change	Media as % of total 2000	Media as % of total 1999
Magazines	$ 16,697	$ 14,672	13.8	6.9	6.6
Sunday magazines	1,110	1,006	10.3	0.5	0.5
Local newspapers	18,817	17,797	5.7	7.7	8.0
National newspapers	3,785	3,320	14.0	1.6	1.5
Outdoor	2,391	1,989	20.2	1.0	0.9
Network TV	18,417	16,354	12.6	7.6	7.4
Spot TV	17,107	15,115	13.2	7.0	6.8
Syndicated TV	2,804	2,650	5.8	1.2	1.2
Cable TV networks	9,506	8,181	16.2	3.9	3.7
Network radio	871	417	108.7	0.4	0.2
National spot radio	2,672	2,349	13.8	1.1	1.1
Internet	4,333	2,832	53.0	1.8	1.3
Yellow Pages	13,228	12,652	4.6	5.4	5.7
Total measured media	111,739	99,335	12.5	45.9	44.7
Estimated unmeasured media	131,941	122,973	7.3	54.1	55.3
Grand total	$243,680	$222,308	9.6	100.0	100.0

Source: "100 Leading National Advertisers," *Advertising Age*, September 24, 2001, S50. Reprinted with permission from the September 24, 2001, issue of *Advertising Age*. Copyright © Crain Communications Inc. 2001.

EXHIBIT 14.6

Media expenditures in the United States by selected product categories, 2000 (in millions of dollars).

Product Category	2000 Total Ad Spending	Leading Medium	1999 Medium Spending
Retail	$17,304.3	Local newspapers	$6,664.4
Automotive	15,478.3	Spot TV	4,588.4
Movies and media	6,910.1	Local newspapers	1,779.4
Financial	5,790.3	Network TV	1,356.3
Medicines and proprietary remedies	4,830.4	Network TV	1,958.6
Telecommunications	4,248.9	Local newspapers	959.1
Computer, software, Internet	4,185.5	Consumer magazine	1,362.9
Airline, ship travel, hotels, resorts	3,689.5	Local newspapers	1,201.6
Toiletries and cosmetics	3,669.6	Network TV	1,305.0
Restaurants	3,667.4	Spot TV	1,470.4

Source: "100 Leading National Advertisers," *Advertising Age*, September 24, 2001, S50. Reprinted with permission from the September 24, 2001, issue of *Advertising Age*. Copyright © Crain Communications Inc. 2001.

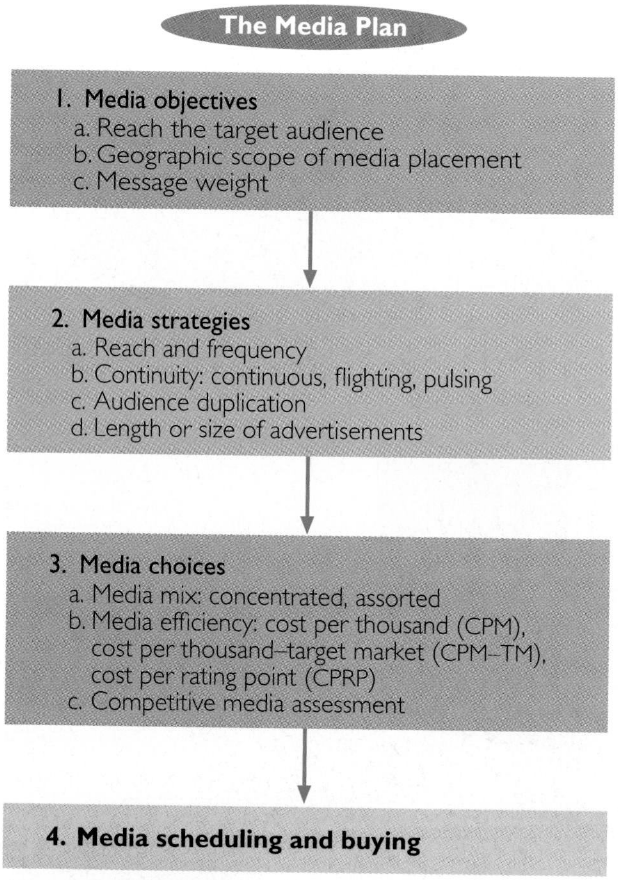

The Media Plan

1. Media objectives
a. Reach the target audience
b. Geographic scope of media placement
c. Message weight

2. Media strategies
a. Reach and frequency
b. Continuity: continuous, flighting, pulsing
c. Audience duplication
d. Length or size of advertisements

3. Media choices
a. Media mix: concentrated, assorted
b. Media efficiency: cost per thousand (CPM), cost per thousand–target market (CPM–TM), cost per rating point (CPRP)
c. Competitive media assessment

4. Media scheduling and buying

EXHIBIT 14.7

The media-planning process.

Media Objectives. **Media objectives** set specific goals for a media placement: Reach the target audience, determine the geographic scope of placement, and identify the message weight, or the total mass of advertising delivered against a target audience. In other words, what is it you are trying to do specifically with your media plan?

The first and most important media objective is that the media chosen *reach the target audience* (Exhibits 14.8 through 14.10). Recall that the definition of a target audience can be demographic, geographic, or based on lifestyle or attitude dimensions. Unfortunately, media planners are often put in the awkward and unenviable position of trying to satisfy fairly specific media objectives based on weak secondary data from media organizations. This is a common problem.

If, however, advertisers are willing to spend extra money, some media research organizations` provide detailed information on the media habits and purchase behaviors of target audiences. This information can greatly increase the precision with which media choices are made. The two most prominent providers of demographic information correlated with product usage data are Mediamark Research (MRI) and Simmons Market Research Bureau (SMRB). An example of the type of information supplied is shown in Exhibit 14.11, where market statistics for four brands of men's aftershave and cologne are compared: Eternity for Men, Jovan Musk, Lagerfeld, and Obsession for Men. The most-revealing data are contained in columns C and D. Column C shows each brand's strength relative to a demographic variable, such as age or income. Column D provides an index indicating that particular segments of the population are heavier users of a particular brand. Specifically, the number expresses each brand's share of volume as a percentage of its share of users. An index number above 100 shows particular strength for a brand. The strength of Eternity for Men as well as Obsession for Men is apparent in both the 18–24 and the 25–34 age cohorts.

Recently, even more sophisticated data have become available. Research services such as A. C. Nielsen's Home*Scan and Information Resources' BehaviorScan are referred to as **single-source tracking services,** which offer information not just on demographics but also on brands, purchase size, purchase frequency, prices paid, and media exposure. BehaviorScan is the most comprehensive, in that exposure to particular television programs, magazines, and newspapers can be measured by the service. With demographic, behavioral, and media-exposure correlates provided by research services like these, advertising and media planners can address issues such as the following:

- How many members of the target audience have tried the advertiser's brand, and how many are brand-loyal?
- What appears to affect brand sales more—increased amounts of advertising, or changes in advertising copy?
- What other products do buyers of the advertiser's brand purchase regularly?

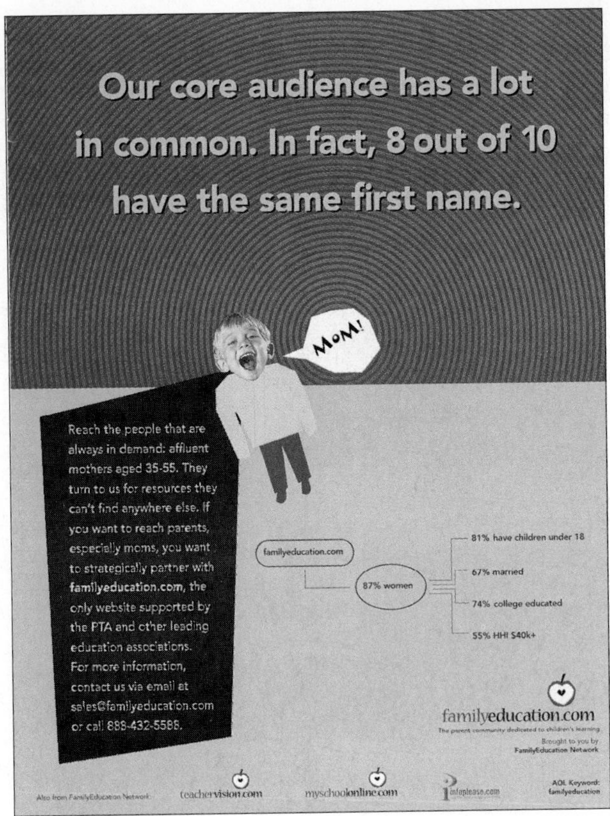

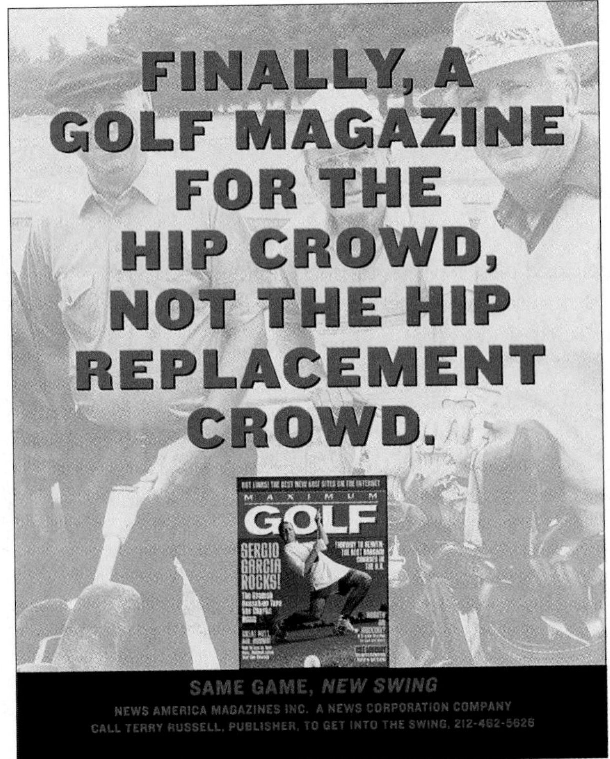

EXHIBIT 14.8 THROUGH 14.10

Here, media vehicles sell themselves to advertisers.

16 AFTERSHAVE LOTION & COLOGNE FOR MEN

		ETERNITY FOR MEN				JOVAN MUSK				LAGERFELD				OBSESSION FOR MEN			
BASE: MEN	TOTAL U.S. '000	A '000	B % DOWN	C % ACROSS	D INDEX	A '000	B % DOWN	C % ACROSS	D INDEX	A '000	B % DOWN	C % ACROSS	D INDEX	A '000	B % DOWN	C % ACROSS	D INDEX
All Men	92674	2466	100.0	2.7	100	3194	100.0	3.4	100	1269	100.0	1.4	100	3925	100.0	4.2	100
Men	92674	2466	100.0	2.7	100	3194	100.0	3.4	100	1269	100.0	1.4	100	3925	100.0	4.2	100
Women	-	-	-	-	-	-	-	-	-	-	-	-	-	-	-	-	-
Household Heads	77421	1936	78.5	2.5	94	2567	80.4	3.3	96	1172	92.4	1.5	111	2856	72.7	3.7	87
Homemakers	31541	967	39.2	3.1	115	1158	36.3	3.7	107	451	35.5	1.4	104	1443	36.8	4.6	108
Graduated College	21727	583	23.7	2.7	101	503	15.8	2.3	67	348	27.4	1.6	117	901	23.0	4.1	98
Attended College	23842	814	33.0	3.4	128	933	29.2	3.9	113	*270	21.3	1.1	83	1283	32.7	5.4	127
Graduated High School	29730	688	27.9	2.3	87	1043	32.7	3.5	102	*460	36.3	1.5	113	1266	32.2	4.3	101
Did not Graduate High School	17374	*380	15.4	2.2	82	*715	22.4	4.1	119	*191	15.0	1.1	80	*475	12.1	2.7	65
18-24	12276	754	30.6	6.1	231	*391	12.2	3.2	92	*7	0.5	0.1	4	747	19.0	6.1	144
25-34	20924	775	31.4	3.7	139	705	22.1	3.4	98	*234	18.5	1.1	82	1440	36.7	6.9	162
35-44	21237	586	23.8	2.8	104	1031	32.3	4.9	141	*311	24.5	1.5	107	838	21.3	3.9	93
45-54	14964	*202	8.2	1.4	51	*510	16.0	3.4	99	*305	24.0	2.0	149	481	12.3	3.2	76
55-64	10104	*112	4.6	1.1	42	*215	6.7	2.1	62	*214	16.9	2.1	155	*245	6.2	2.4	57
65 or over	13168	*37	1.5	0.3	10	*342	10.7	2.6	75	*198	15.6	1.5	110	*175	4.4	1.3	31
18-34	33200	1529	62.0	4.6	173	1096	34.3	3.3	96	*241	19.0	0.7	53	2187	55.7	6.6	156
18-49	62950	2228	90.4	3.5	133	2460	77.0	3.9	113	683	53.9	1.1	79	3315	84.5	5.3	124
25-54	57125	1563	63.4	2.7	103	2246	70.3	3.9	114	850	67.0	1.5	109	2758	70.3	4.8	114
Employed Full Time	62271	1955	79.3	3.1	118	2141	67.0	3.4	100	977	77.0	1.6	115	2981	76.0	4.8	113
Part-time	5250	*227	9.2	4.3	163	*141	4.4	2.7	78	*10	0.8	0.2	14	*300	7.7	5.7	135
Sole Wage Earner	21027	554	22.5	2.6	99	794	24.9	3.8	110	332	26.2	1.6	115	894	22.8	4.3	100
Not Employed	25153	*284	11.5	1.1	42	912	28.6	3.6	105	*281	22.2	1.1	82	643	16.4	2.6	60
Professional	9010	*232	9.4	2.6	97	*168	5.3	1.9	54	*143	11.3	1.6	116	504	12.8	5.6	132
Executive/Admin./Managerial	10114	*259	10.5	2.6	96	*305	9.6	3.0	88	*185	14.6	1.8	134	353	9.0	3.5	82
Clerical/Sales/Technical	13212	436	17.7	3.3	124	*420	13.2	3.2	92	*231	18.2	1.7	128	741	18.9	5.6	132
Precision/Crafts/Repair	12162	624	25.3	5.1	193	*317	9.9	2.6	76	*168	13.2	1.4	101	511	13.0	4.2	99
Other Employed	23022	631	25.6	2.7	103	1071	33.5	4.7	135	*261	20.6	1.1	83	1173	29.9	5.1	120
H/D Income $75,000 or More	17969	481	19.5	2.7	101	*320	10.0	1.8	52	413	32.5	2.3	168	912	23.2	5.1	120
$60,000 - 74,999	10346	*368	14.9	3.6	134	*309	9.7	3.0	87	*142	11.2	1.4	100	495	12.6	4.8	113
$50,000 - 59,999	9175	*250	10.2	2.7	103	*424	13.3	4.6	134	*153	12.1	1.7	122	*371	9.4	4.0	95
$40,000 - 49,999	11384	*308	12.5	2.7	102	*387	12.1	3.4	99	*134	10.6	1.2	86	580	14.8	5.1	120
$30,000 - 39,999	12981	*360	14.6	2.8	104	542	17.0	4.2	121	*126	10.0	1.0	71	*416	10.6	3.2	76
$20,000 - 29,999	13422	*266	10.8	2.0	75	*528	16.5	3.9	114	*164	12.9	1.2	89	*475	12.1	3.5	84
$10,000 - 19,999	11867	*401	16.3	3.4	127	*394	12.3	3.3	96	*67	5.3	0.6	41	*481	12.3	4.1	96
Less than $10,000	5528	*31	1.3	0.6	21	*291	9.1	5.3	153	*69	5.4	1.2	91	*194	4.9	3.5	83

Source: Mediamark Research Inc., Mediamark Research Men's, Women's Personal Care Products Report (Mediamark Research Inc., Spring 1997). 16. Reprinted with permission.

EXHIBIT 14.11

Commercial research firms can provide advertisers with an evaluation of a brand's relative strength within demographic segments. This typical data table from MediaMark Research shows how various men's aftershave and cologne brands perform in different demographic segments.

www.mediamark.com

- What television programs, magazines, and newspapers reach the largest number of the advertiser's audience?[1]

Another critical element in setting advertising objectives is determining the *geographic* scope of media placement. In some ways, this is a relatively easy objective to set. Media planners merely need to identify media that cover the same geographic area as the advertiser's distribution system. Obviously, spending money on the placement of ads in media that cover geographic areas where the advertiser's brand is not distributed is wasteful. As shown in Exhibit 14.12, the targeting of specific geographic markets has the additional benefit of allowing advertisers to cater messages directly to the people in those geographic areas.

When factors such as brand performance or competitors' activities are taken into account, media objectives for geographic scope become more complicated. For example, the strength of microbreweries in the northeastern and northwestern United States has forced major national brewers such as Miller Brewing and Anheuser-Busch not only to develop specialty beers, such as Red Wolf, but also to alter their geographic media objectives to provide different coverage based on the competitive intensity of these markets. In markets where microbreweries are particularly strong, Miller and A-B buy extra media time or run special promotions to combat the competition.

Some analysts suggest that when certain geographic markets demonstrate unusually high purchasing tendencies by product category or by brand, then geo-targeting should be the basis for the media placement decision. **Geo-targeting** is the placement of ads in geographic regions where higher purchase tendencies for a brand are evident. For example, in one geographic area the average consumer purchases of Prego spaghetti sauce were 36 percent greater than the average consumer purchases

1. Scott Donaton and Pat Sloan, "Control New Media," *Advertising Age*, March 13, 1995, 1.

EXHIBIT 14.12

Targeting local markets.
www.tvb.org

nationwide. With this kind of information, media buys can be geo-targeted to reinforce high-volume users.[2]

The final media objective is **message weight,** the total mass of advertising delivered. Message weight is the gross number of advertising messages or exposure opportunities delivered by the vehicles in a schedule. An important issue in message weight is that the measurement includes duplication of exposure; that is, an individual may be counted more than one time in a message weight calculation. Unduplicated audience measurement, known as *reach,* is discussed in the next section, dealing with media strategies. Media planners are interested in the message weight of a media plan because it provides a simple indication of the size of the advertising effort being placed against a specific market.

Message weight is typically expressed in terms of gross impressions. **Gross impressions** represent the sum of exposures to the entire media placement in a media plan. Planners often distinguish between two types of exposure. *Potential ad impressions* or *opportunities* to be exposed to ads are the most common meanings and refer to exposures by the media vehicle carrying advertisements (for example, a program or publication). *Message impressions,* on the other hand, refers to exposures to the ads themselves. Information on ad exposure probabilities can be obtained from a number of companies, including Nielsen, Simmons, Roper-Starch, Gallup & Robinson, Harvey Research, and Readex. This information can pertain to particular advertisements, campaigns, media vehicles, product categories, ad characteristics, and target groups.

For example, consider a media plan that, in a one-week period, placed ads on three television programs and in two national newspapers. The sum of the exposures to the media placement might be as follows:

		Gross Impressions	
		Media Vehicle	Advertisement
Television:	Program A audience	16,250,000	5,037,500
	Program B audience	4,500,000	1,395,000
	Program C audience	7,350,000	2,278,500
Sum of TV exposures		28,100,000	8,711,000
Newspapers:	Newspaper 1	1,900,000	376,200
	Newspaper 2	450,000	89,100
Sum of newspaper exposures		2,350,000	465,300
Total gross impressions		30,450,000	9,176,300

Of course, this does not mean that 30,450,000 separate people were exposed to the programs and newspapers or that 9,176,300 separate people were exposed to the advertisements. Some people who watched TV program A also saw program B and read newspaper 1, as well as all other possible combinations. This is called **between-**

2. This section and the example are drawn from Erwin Ephron, "The Organizing Principle of Media," *Inside Media,* November 2, 1992.

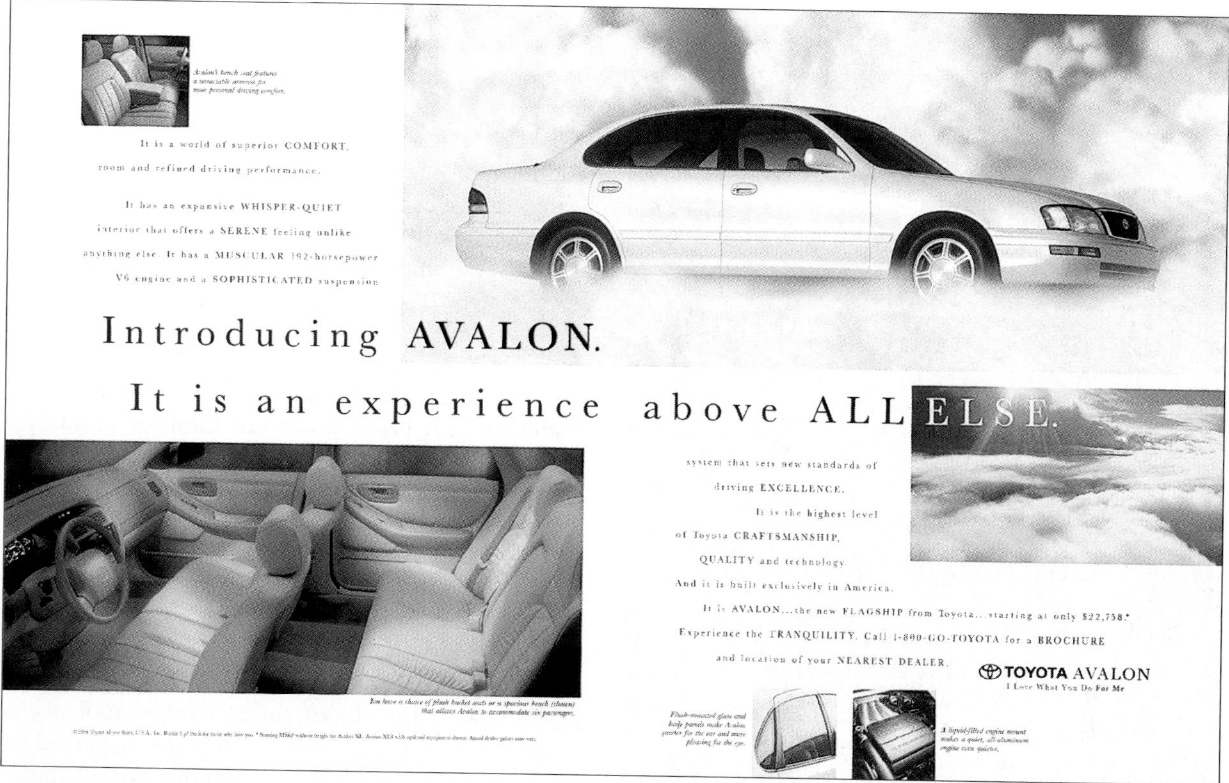

EXHIBIT 14.13

What is the importance of message weight for the introduction of a new product such as the Avalon? Is it important that the advertiser be able to distinguish between gross impressions and audience reach in this type of campaign?
www.toyota.com

vehicle duplication. It is also possible that someone who saw the ad in newspaper 1 on Monday saw it again in newspaper 1 on Tuesday. This is **within-vehicle duplication.** That's why we say that the total gross impressions number contains audience duplication. Data available from services such as SMRB report both types of duplication so that they may be removed from the gross impressions to produce the unduplicated estimate of audience, called *reach*. (You should know, however, that the math involved in such calculations is fairly complex.) The concept of reach is discussed in the next section.

The message weight objective provides only a broad perspective for a media planner. What does it mean when we say that a media plan for a week produced more than 30 million gross impressions? It means only that a fairly large number of people were potentially exposed to the advertiser's message. This does not mean that message weight is unimportant, however; it provides a general point of reference. When Toyota Motors introduced the Avalon in the U.S. market, the $40 million introductory ad campaign featured 30-second television spots, newspaper and magazine print ads (see Exhibit 14.13 for an example), and direct mail pieces. The highlight of the campaign was a nine-spot placement on a heavily watched Thursday evening TV show, costing more than $2 million. The message weight of this campaign in a single week was enormous—just the type of objective Toyota's media planners wanted for the brand introduction.[3]

Media Strategies.

Media objectives provide the foundation for media selection. The true power of a media plan, though, is in the media strategy. This strategy is expressed in decisions made with respect to a media vehicle's reach and frequency, the continuity of media placement, the audience duplication, and the length and size of advertisements.

3. Bradley Johnson, "Toyota's New Avalon Thinks Big, American," *Advertising Age,* November 14, 1994, 46.

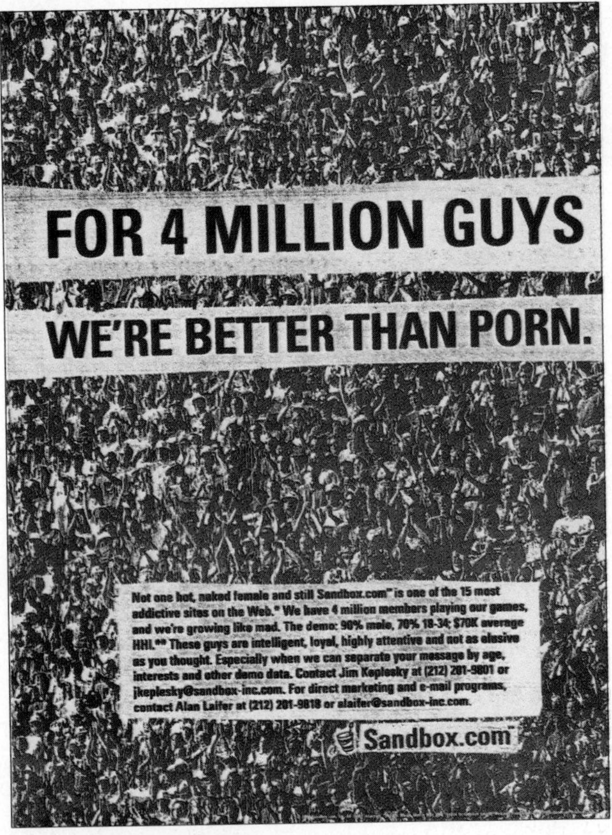

EXHIBIT 14.14

Reach is an important measure of a media vehicle's effectiveness.
www.sandbox.com

Good media strategy decisions help ensure that messages placed in chosen media have as much impact as possible.

Reach and Frequency. **Reach** refers to the number of people or households in a target audience that will be exposed to a media vehicle or schedule at least one time during a given period of time (see Exhibit 14.14). It is often expressed as a percentage. If an advertisement placed on the hit network television program *ER* is watched at least once by 30 percent of the advertiser's target audience, then the reach is said to be 30 percent. Media vehicles with broad reach are ideal for consumer convenience goods, such as toothpaste and cold remedies. These are products with fairly simple features, and they are frequently purchased by a broad cross-section of the market. Broadcast television, cable television, and national magazines have the largest and broadest reach of any of the media, due to their national and even global coverage.

Frequency is the average number of times an individual or household within a target audience is exposed to a media vehicle in a given period of time (typically a week or a month). For example, say an advertiser places an ad on a weekly television show with a 20 rating (20 percent of households) four weeks in a row. The show has an (unduplicated) reach of 43 (percent) over the four-week period. So, frequency is then equal to $(20 \times 4)/43$, or 1.9. This means that an audience member had the opportunity to see the ad an average of 1.9 times.

An important measure for media planners related to both reach and frequency is **gross rating points (GRP).** GRP is the product of reach times frequency ($GRP = r \times f$). When media planners calculate the GRP for a media plan, they multiply the rating (reach) of each vehicle in a plan times the number of times an ad will be inserted in the media vehicle and sum these figures across all vehicles in the plan. Exhibit 14.15 shows the GRP for a combined magazine and television schedule.

The GRP number is used as a relative measure of the intensity of one media plan versus another. Whether a media plan is appropriate is ultimately based on the judgment of the media planner.

Advertisers often struggle with the dilemma of increasing reach at the expense of frequency, or vice versa. At the core in this struggle are the concepts of effective frequency and effective reach. **Effective frequency** is the number of times a target audience needs to be exposed to a message before the objectives of the advertiser are met—either communications objectives or sales impact. Many factors affect the level of effective frequency. New brands and brands laden with features may demand high frequency. Simple messages for well-known products may require less-frequent exposure for consumers to be affected. While most analysts agree that one exposure will typically not be enough, there is debate about how many exposures are enough. A common industry practice is to place effective frequency at three exposures, but analysts argue that as few as two or as many as nine exposures are needed to achieve effective frequency.[4]

4. For a complete discussion of the evolution of the concepts of effective reach and effective frequency, see Jack Z. Sissors and Lincoln Bumba, *Advertising Media Planning,* 5th ed. (Lincolnwood, Ill.: NTC Business Books, 1996), 115–147.

EXHIBIT 14.15

Gross rating points (GRP) for a media plan.

Media Class/Vehicle	Rating (reach)	Number of Ad Insertions (frequency)	GRP
Television			
ER	25	4	100
Law & Order	20	4	80
Good Morning America	12	4	48
Days of Our Lives	7	2	14
Magazines			
People	22	2	44
Travel & Leisure	11	2	22
U.S. News & World Report	9	6	54
Total			**362**

Effective reach is the number or percentage of consumers in the target audience that are exposed to an ad some minimum number of times. The minimum-number estimate for effective reach is based on a determination of effective frequency. If effective reach is set at four exposures, then a media schedule must be devised that achieves at least four exposures over a specified time period within the target audience.

Continuity. The second important strategic decision in the media plan is about continuity. **Continuity** is the pattern of placement of advertisements in a media schedule. There are three strategic scheduling alternatives: continuous, flighting, and pulsing. **Continuous scheduling** is a pattern of placing ads at a steady rate over a period of time. Running one ad each day for four weeks during the soap opera *General Hospital* would be a continuous pattern. Similarly, an ad that appeared in every issue of *Redbook* magazine for a year would also be continuous. **Flighting** is another media-scheduling strategy. Flighting is achieved by scheduling heavy advertising for a period of time, usually two weeks, then stopping advertising altogether for a period, only to come back with another heavy schedule.

Flighting is often used to support special seasonal merchandising efforts or new product introductions, or as a response to competitors' activities. The financial advantages of flighting are that discounts might be gained by concentrating media buys in larger blocks. Communication effectiveness may be enhanced because a heavy schedule can achieve the repeat exposures necessary to achieve consumer awareness. For example, the ad in Exhibit 14.16 was run heavily in December issues of magazines, to take advantage of seasonal dessert consumption patterns.

Finally, **pulsing** is a media-scheduling strategy that combines elements from continuous and flighting techniques. Advertisements are scheduled continuously in media over a period of time, but with periods of much heavier scheduling (the flight). Pulsing is most appropriate for products that are sold fairly regularly all year long but have, like clothing, certain seasonal requirements.

Length or Size of Advertisements. Beyond whom to reach, how often to reach them, and in what pattern, media planners must make strategic decisions regarding the length of an ad in electronic media or the size of an ad in print media. Certainly, the advertiser, creative director, art director, and copywriter have made determinations in this regard as well. Television advertisements (excluding infomercials) can range from 10 seconds to 60 seconds, and sometimes even two minutes, in length. Is a 60-second television commercial always six times more effective than a 10-second spot? Of course, the answer is no. Is a full-page newspaper ad always more effective than a two-inch, one-column ad? Again, not necessarily. Some research shows an increase in recognition scores of print advertising with increasing image size. Some call this the **"square root law"**; that is, "the recognition of print ads increase with the square of the illustration."[5] So, a full-page ad should be twice as memorable as a quarter-page ad. Such "laws" show a general relationship, but should not be taken with such precision, nor should they be considered laws, but rather general guidelines. Too much depends on other variables. Still, advertisers use full-page newspaper ads when a product claim, brand image, or market situation warrants it (Exhibit 14.17).

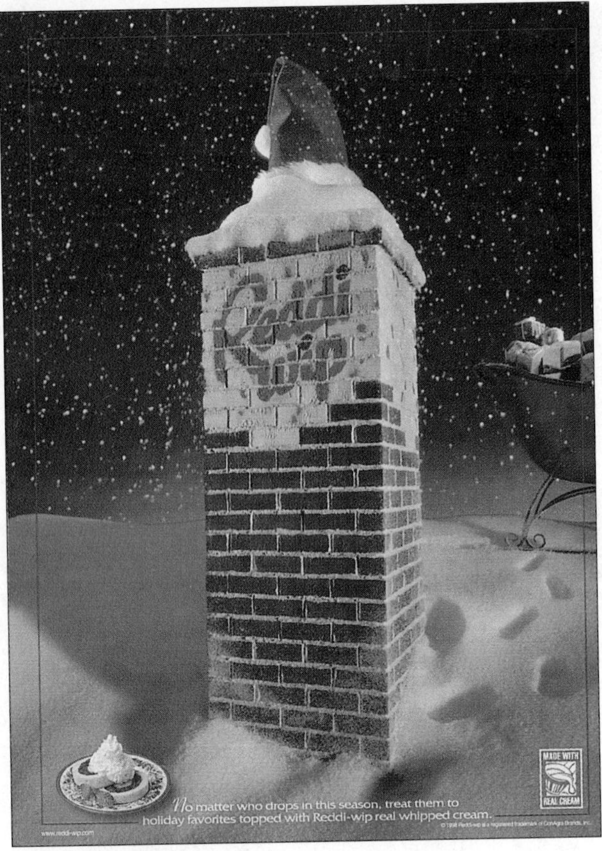

EXHIBIT 14.16

An example of a print ad that was flighted during December—a month in which whipped-cream dessert toppings figure prominently.
www.reddi-wip.com

The decision about the length or size of an advertisement depends on the creative requirements for the ad, the media budget, and the competitive environment within which the ad is running. From a creative standpoint, ads attempting to develop an image for a brand may need to be longer in broadcast media or larger in print media to offer more creative opportunities. On the other hand, a simple, straightforward message announcing a sale may be quite short or small, but it may need heavy repetition. From the standpoint of the media budget, shorter and smaller ads are, with few exceptions, much less expensive. If a media plan includes some level of repetition to accomplish its objectives, the lower-cost option may be mandatory. From a competitive perspective, matching a competitor's presence with messages of similar size or length may be essential to maintain the share of mind in a target audience. Once again, the size and length decisions are a matter of judgment between the creative team and the media planner, tempered by the availability of funds for media placement.

Media Choices. The next stage of the media-planning process focuses on media selection. Exhibit 14.18 gives general ratings for the major media. The advertiser and the agency team determine which media class is appropriate for the current effort, based on criteria similar to those listed in Exhibit 14.18. These criteria give a general orientation to major media and the inherent capabilities of each media class. The selection of magazine advertising as a medium of choice has recently declined dramatically, as illustrated in the Controversy box on page 503.

Media choice addresses three distinct issues: media mix, media efficiency, and competitive media assessment.

Media Mix. In making specific media choices for placing advertisements, media planners have to decide what sort of media mix to use. The **media mix** is the blend

5. John R. Rossiter, "Visual Imagery: Applications to Advertising," *Advances in Consumer Research* (Provo, Utah: Association for Consumer Research, 1982), 101–106.

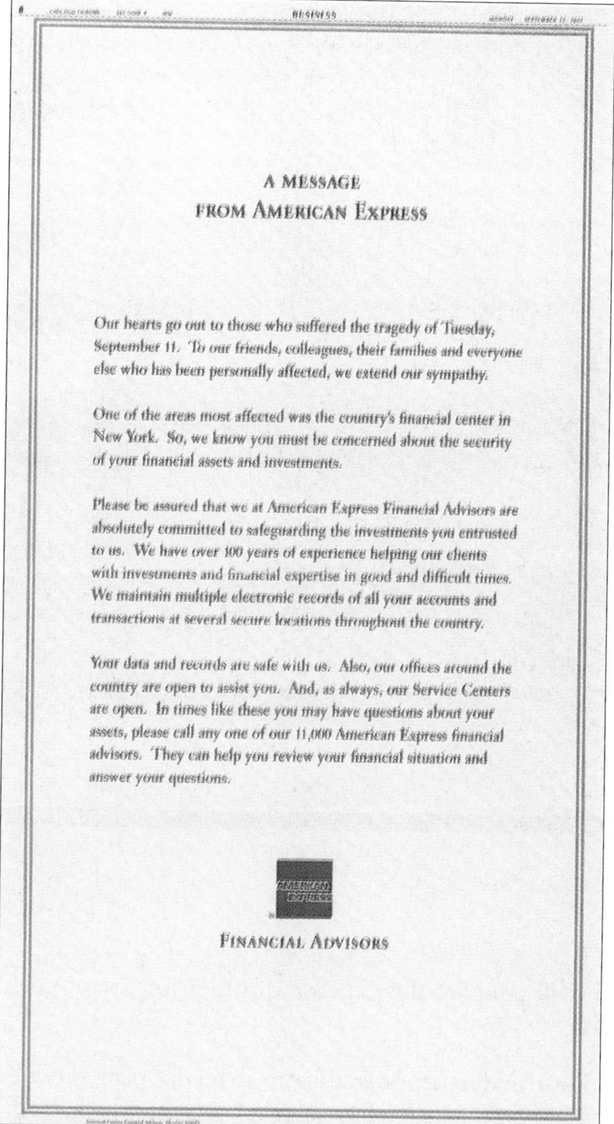

EXHIBIT 14.17

Technically, this could rightly be called sales promotion. It may also be good citizenship and compassion.

of different media that will be used to effectively reach the target audience. There are two options for a media planner with respect to the media mix: a concentrated media mix or an assorted media mix.[6] A **concentrated media mix** focuses all the media placement dollars in one medium. The rationale behind this option is that it allows an advertiser to have great impact on a specific audience segment. A highly concentrated media mix can give a brand an aura of mass acceptance, especially within an audience with restricted media exposure.[7] The range of benefits possible from a concentrated media mix are as follows:

- It may allow the advertiser to be dominant in one medium relative to the competition.
- Brand familiarity might be heightened, especially within target audiences that have a narrow range of media exposure.
- Concentrating media buys in high-visibility media, such as prime-time television or large advertising sections in premium magazines, can create enthusiasm and loyalty in a trade channel. Distributors and retailers may give a brand with heavily concentrated media exposure preferential treatment in inventory or shelf display.
- A concentration of media dollars may result in significant volume discounts from media organizations.

An **assorted media mix** employs multiple media alternatives to reach target audiences. The assorted mix can be advantageous to an advertiser because it facilitates communication with multiple market segments. By using a mix of media, an advertiser can place different messages for different target audiences in different media. In general, the advantages of an assorted media mix are as follows:

- An advertiser can reach different target audiences with messages tailored to each target's unique interests in the product category or brand.
- Different messages in different media reaching a single target may enhance the learning effect.
- Assorted media placement will increase the reach of a message, compared to concentrating placement in one medium.
- The probability of reaching audiences exposed to diverse media is greater with an assorted media mix.

One caution should be offered with the assorted media mix approach. Since different media placements require different creative and production efforts, the cost of preparing advertisements can increase dramatically. Preparing both print and broadcast versions of an ad may draw funds away from media expenditures. Using funds

6. Arnold M. Barban, Steven M. Cristol, and Frank J. Kopec, *Essentials of Media Planning: A Marketing Viewpoint,* 3rd ed. (Lincolnwood, Ill.: NTC Business Books, 1993), 76–80.

7. Leo Bogart, *Strategy in Advertising,* 2nd ed. (Lincolnwood, Ill.: NTC Business Books, 1984), 147.

Characteristics	Medium: Broadcast TV	Cable TV	Radio	News-paper	Maga-zines	Direct Mail	Outdoor	Transit	Directory
Reach									
Local	M	M	H	H	L	H	H	H	M
National	H	H	L	L	H	M	L	L	M
Frequency	H	H	H	M	L	L	M	M	L
Selectivity									
Audience	M	H	H	L	H	H	L	L	L
Geographic	L	M	H	H	M	H	H	H	H
Audience reactions									
Involvement	L	M	L	M	H	M	L	L	H
Acceptance	M	M	M	H	M	L	M	M	H
Audience data	M	L	L	M	H	H	L	L	M
Clutter	H	H	H	M	M	M	M	L	H
Creative flexibility	H	H	H	L	M	M	L	L	L
Cost factors									
Per contact	L	L	L	M	M	H	L	L	M
Absolute cost	H	H	M	M	H	H	M	M	M

H = High, M = Moderate, L = Low

EXHIBIT 14.18

Evaluation of traditional major media options.

for multiple preparations likely will come at the expense of other important goals, such as gross impressions or GRP.

Media Efficiency. Each medium under consideration in a media plan must be scrutinized for the efficiency with which it performs. In other words, which media deliver the largest target audiences at the lowest cost? A common measure of media efficiency is **cost per thousand (CPM),** which is the dollar cost of reaching 1,000 (the M in CPM comes from the roman numeral for 1,000) members of an audience using a particular medium. The CPM calculation can be used to compare the relative efficiency of two media choices within a media class (magazine versus magazine) or between media classes (magazine versus radio). The basic measure of CPM is fairly straightforward; the dollar cost for placement of an ad in a medium is divided by the total audience and multiplied by 1,000. Let's calculate the CPM for a full-page black-and-white ad in the Friday edition of *USA Today:*

$$\text{CPM} = \frac{\text{cost of media buy}}{\text{total audience}} \times 1{,}000$$

$$\text{CPM for } \textit{USA Today} = \frac{\$72{,}000}{5{,}206{,}000} \times 1{,}000 = \$13.83$$

These calculations show that *USA Today* has a CPM of $13.83 for a full-page black-and-white ad. But this calculation shows the cost of reaching the entire readership of *USA Today*. If the target audience is restricted to male college graduates in professional occupations, then the **cost per thousand–target market (CPM–TM)** calculation might be much higher for a general publication such as *USA Today* than for a more specialized publication such as *Fortune* magazine:

$$\text{CPM–TM for } \textit{USA Today} = \frac{\$72{,}000}{840{,}000} \times 1{,}000 = \$85.71$$

$$\text{CPM–TM for } \textit{Fortune} = \frac{\$54{,}800}{940{,}000} \times 1{,}000 = \$58.30$$

You can see that the relative efficiency of *Fortune* is much greater than that of *USA Today* when the target audience is specified more carefully and a CPM–TM calculation is made. An advertisement for business services appearing in *Fortune* will have a better CPM–TM than the same ad appearing in *USA Today*.

Information about ad cost, gross impressions, and target audience size is usually available from the medium itself. Detailed audience information to make a cost per thousand–target market analysis also is available from media research organizations, such as Simmons Market Research Bureau (for magazines) or A. C. Nielsen (for television). Cost information also can be obtained from Standard Rate and Data Service (SRDS) and Bacon's Media Directories, for example.

Like CPM, a **cost per rating point (CPRP)** calculation provides a relative efficiency comparison between media options. In this calculation, the cost of a media vehicle, such as a spot television program, is divided by the program's rating. (A rating point is equivalent to 1 percent of the target audience—for example, television households in the designated rating area tuned to a specific program.) Like the CPM calculation, the CPRP calculation gives a dollar figure, which can be used for comparing TV program efficiency. The calculation for CPRP is as follows, using television as an example.

$$\text{CPRP} = \frac{\text{dollar cost of ad placement on a program}}{\text{program rating}}$$

For example, an advertiser on WLTV (Univision 23) in the Miami–Ft. Lauderdale market may wish to compare household CPRP figures for 30-second announcements in various dayparts on the station. The calculations for early news and prime time programs are as follows.

$$\text{CPRP for WLTV early news} = \frac{\$2{,}205}{9} = \$245$$

CONTROVERSY

Magazine Mogul: "Business Sucks"

Amid the chaos of terrorism threats and a worsening economy, publishing executives are on edge about the fate of the magazine industry. Shortly after the fall of the World Trade Center towers, industry leaders convened at the annual American Magazine Conference to share woes and discuss the gloomy realities plaguing magazine advertising. The problem? Shell-shocked advertisers have all but abandoned magazines as a vital media vehicle, and a rebound is not expected until 2003.

The harsh economic climate has forced layoffs and the closing of well-known magazines such as *Brill's Content, Mademoiselle,* and the *Industry Standard.* Leading publishers Time Inc., Hearst, and Rodale have all made cuts, forcing top-level management to take a hard look at every aspect of the way business is done. "Publishers nationwide have to be looking in a more serious way about their operations," said Cathie Black, Hearst Magazines president.

The industry's current challenges range from flagging newsstand sales and rising postal rates to failing efforts of subscription marketing. Skittish advertisers are pulling in the reins on budget spending. "People are afraid to make commitments," said Jon Mandel, co-managing director of MediaCom Worldwide. "The September 11 attacks didn't affect the economy, but what it did affect were the brains, the heart, the psychology of advertisers." To respond, publishers are looking at cost controls and examining P&L budgets—travel, company cars, and even comp copies are being restricted.

Despite all the uncertainty, many publishers are going ahead with acquisitions and ideas for start-ups (though most are doubtful that actual launches will occur in the short term). Martha Stewart said she is considering a launch now that other publishers are on the retreat. "It's a very good time," said Stewart.

For certain, media planners will be closely examining the state of the industry before deciding how to appropriate advertising budgets. Some forecasters believe that magazines are well positioned for a solid recovery in ad spending over the next four years. In the near term, however, industry leaders will continue to circle the wagons and vent frustrations. Commenting on the recent magazine malaise, Conde Nast Publications CEO Steve Florio said it best: "Business sucks. It does indeed suck."

Source: Lisa Granatstein, "Winds of Change Ruffle Magazines," *Media Week,* www.mediaweek.com, accessed October 29, 2001.

$$\text{CPRP for WLTV prime time} = \frac{\$5{,}100}{10} = \$510$$

Clearly an early news daypart program delivers households more efficiently at $245 CPRP, less than half that of prime time, with approximately 90 percent of the typical prime-time rating.

It is important to remember that these efficiency assessments are based solely on costs and coverage. They say nothing about the quality of the advertising and thus should not be viewed as indicators of advertising effectiveness. When media efficiency measures such as CPM and CPM–TM are combined with an assessment of media objectives and media strategies, they can be quite useful. Taken alone and out of the broader campaign-planning context, such efficiency measures may lead to ineffective media buying.

Internet Media. We cover this topic in great detail in Chapter 16. We devote an entire chapter to it because Internet media has its own terms, its own unique calculation issues. Exhibits 14.19 and 14.20 give both a good glossary of Internet media terms and a sample of Internet ad rates. An absolutely excellent free resource for exploring Internet media planning and buying is *AD Resource* (adres.internet.com). Check it out. Many Internet portals will post their advertising rates. Other good resources include the Interactive Advertising Bureau (www.iab.net) and Iconocast (www.iconocast.com). The bottom line on Internet advertising, at this point, is that it has grown tremendously as a new medium, but rates have not. This is largely due to the difficulty in assessing the size of the Internet advertising audience, and what it means to say that someone was "exposed" to an ad on the Internet. It is also true that this medium is struggling to find its way in terms of what kind of ads really work. In the early days of radio and television, those media struggled to find the forms that would be best for advertising. The Internet is no different.

Competitive Media Assessment. While media planners normally do not base an overall media plan on how much competitors are spending or where competitors are placing their ads, a competitive media assessment can provide a useful perspective. A competitive media assessment is particularly important for product categories in which all the competitors are focused on a narrowly defined target audience. This condition exists in several product categories in which heavy-user segments dominate consumption—for example, snack foods, soft drinks, beer and wine, and chewing gum. Brands of luxury cars and financial services also compete for common-buyer segments.

When a target audience is narrow and attracts the attention of several major competitors, an advertiser must assess its competitors' spending and the relative share of voice its brand is getting. **Share of voice** is a calculation of any one advertiser's brand expenditures relative to the overall spending in a category:

$$\text{share of voice} = \frac{\text{one brand's advertising expenditures in a medium}}{\text{total product category advertising expenditures in a medium}}$$

This calculation can be done for all advertising by a brand in relation to all advertising in a product category, or it can be done to determine a brand's share of product category spending on a particular advertising medium, such as network television or magazines. For example, athletic-footwear marketers spend approximately $310 million per year in measured advertising media. Nike and Reebok are the two top brands, with approximately $160 million and $55 million respectively in annual expenditures in measured advertising media. The share-of-voice calculations for both brands follow.

$$\text{Share of voice, Nike} = \frac{\$160\text{ million}}{\$310\text{ million}} \times 100 = 51.6\%$$

$$\text{Share of voice, Reebok} = \frac{\$55\text{ million}}{\$310\text{ million}} \times 100 = 17.7\%$$

Ad clicks: Number of times users click on an ad banner.

Ad click rate: Sometimes referred to as "click-through," this is the percentage of ad views that resulted in an ad click.

Ad views (impressions): Number of times an ad banner is downloaded and presumably seen by visitors. If the same ad appears on multiple pages simultaneously, this statistic may understate the number of ad impressions, due to browser caching. Corresponds to net impressions in traditional media. There is currently no way of knowing if an ad was actually loaded. Most servers record an ad as served even if it was not.

B2B: B2B stands for "business-to-business," as in businesses doing business with other businesses. The term is most commonly used in connection with e-commerce and advertising, when you are targeting businesses as opposed to consumers.

Backbone: A high-speed line or series of connections that forms a large pathway within a network. The term is relative to the size of network it is serving. A backbone in a small network would probably be much smaller than many nonbackbone lines in a large network.

Bandwidth: How much information (text, images, video, sound) can be sent through a connection. Usually measured in bits per second. A full page of text is about 16,000 bits. A fast modem can move approximately 15,000 bits in one second. Full-motion full-screen video requires about 10,000,000 bits per second, depending on compression. (See also: 56K, bit, modem, T1)

Banner: An ad on a Web page that is usually "hot-linked" to the advertiser's site.

Browser caching: To speed surfing, browsers store recently used pages on a user's disk. If a site is revisited, browsers display pages from the disk instead of requesting them from the server. As a result, servers undercount the number of times a page is viewed.

Button: The term used to reflect an Internet advertisement smaller than the traditional banner. Buttons are square in shape and usually located down the left or right side of the site.

The IAB and CASIE have recognized these sizes as the most popular and most accepted on the Internet:

Standard internet ad sizes (in pixels):

468 × 60	Full banner
392 × 72	Full banner/vertical navigation bar
234 × 60	Half banner
125 × 125	Square button
120 × 90	Button #1
120 × 60	Button #2
88 × 31	Micro button
120 × 240	Vertical banner

CASIE: CASIE stands for the Coalition for Advertising Supported Information and Entertainment. It was founded in May 1994 by the Association of National Advertisers (ANA) and the American Association of Advertising Agencies (AAAA) to guide the development of interactive advertising and marketing.

CGI: Common Gateway Interface. An interface-creation scripting program that allows Web pages to be made on the fly based on information from buttons, checkboxes, text input, etc.

Click-through: The percentage of ad views that resulted in an ad click.

CPC: Cost-per-click is an Internet marketing formula used to price ad banners. Advertisers will pay Internet publishers based on the number of clicks a specific ad banner gets. Cost usually runs in the range of $0.10–$0.20 per click.

CPM: CPM is the cost per thousand for a particular site. A Web site that charges $15,000 per banner and guarantees 600,000 impressions has a CPM of $25 ($15,000 divided by 600). For more information on the average CPM rates of sites around the Web.

Cyberspace: Coined by author William Gibson in his 1984 novel *Neuromancer, cyberspace* is now used to describe all of the information available through computer networks.

Domain name: The unique name of an Internet site; for example, www.cyberatlas.com. There are six top-level domains widely used in the United States: .com (commercial) .edu (educational), .net (network operations), .gov (U.S. government), .mil (U.S. military) and .org (organization). Other two-letter domains represent countries: .uk for the United Kingdom and so on.

DTC: DTC stands for "direct-to-consumer." The term is commonly used to denote advertising that is targeted to consumers, as opposed to businesses. Television ads, print ads in consumer publications, and radio ads are all forms of DTC advertising.

Hit: Each time a Web server sends a file to a browser, it is recorded in the server log file as a "hit." Hits are generated for every element of a requested page (including graphics, text and interactive items). If a page containing two graphics is viewed by a user, three hits will be recorded—one for the page itself and one for each graphic. Webmasters use hits to measure their server's workload. Because page designs vary greatly, hits are a poor guide for traffic measurement.

Host: An Internet host used to be a single machine connected to the Internet (which meant it had a unique IP address). As a host it made available to other machines on the network certain services. However, virtual hosting now means that one physical host can now be actually many virtual hosts.

HTML: Hypertext Markup Language is a coding language used to make hypertext documents for use on the Web. HTML resembles old-fashioned typesetting code, where a block of text is surrounded by codes that indicate how it should appear. HTML allows text to be "linked" to another file on the Internet.

Hypertext: Any text that can be chosen by a reader and that causes another document to be retrieved and displayed.

IAB: IAB stands for the Interactive Advertising Bureau. The IAB is a global nonprofit association devoted exclusively to maximizing the use and effectiveness of advertising on the Internet. The IAB sponsors research and events related to the Internet advertising industry.

Continued

EXHIBIT 14.19

A handy glossary of media terms. www.internet.com/glossary

Internet: A collection of approximately 60,000 independent, interconnected networks that use the TCP/IP protocols and that evolved from ARPANet of the late '60s and early '70s.

Interstitial: Meaning "in between," refers to an advertisement that appears in a separate browser window while you wait for a Web page to load. Interstitials are more likely to contain large graphics, streaming presentations, and applets than conventional banner ads, and some studies have found that more users click on interstitials than on banner ads. Some users, however, have complained that interstitials slow access to destination pages.

IP address: Internet Protocol address. Every system connected to the Internet has a unique IP address, which consists of a number in the format A.B.C.D where each of the four sections is a number from 0 to 255. Most people use domain names instead, and the resolution between domain names and IP addresses is handled by the network and domain name servers. With virtual hosting, a single machine can act like multiple machines (with multiple domain names and IP addresses).

IRC: Internet Relay Chat is a worldwide network of people talking to each other in real time.

ISDN: Integrated Services Digital Network is a digital network that moves up to 128,000 bits per second over a regular phone line at nearly the same cost as a normal phone call.

Java: Java is a general-purpose programming language with a number of features that make the language well suited for use on the World Wide Web. Small Java applications are called Java applets and can be downloaded from a Web server and run on your computer by a Java-compatible Web browser, such as Netscape Navigator or Microsoft Internet Explorer.

Javascript: Javascript is a scripting language developed by Netscape that can interact with HTML source code, enabling Web authors to spice up their sites with dynamic content.

Jump page: A jump page, also known as a "splash page," is a special page set up for visitors who clicked on a link in an advertisement. For example, by clicking on an ad for Site X, visitors go to a page in Site X that continues the message used in the advertising creative. The jump page can be used to promote special offers or to measure the response to an advertisement.

Link: An electronic connection between two Web sites (also called "hot link").

Listserv:* The most widespread of maillists. Listervs started on BITNET and are now common on the Internet.

Log file: A file that lists actions that have occurred. For example, Web servers maintain log files listing every request made to the server. With log file analysis tools, it's possible to get a good idea of where visitors are coming from, how often they return, and how they navigate through a site. Using cookies enables Webmasters to log even more detailed information about how individual users are accessing a site.

Newsgroup: A discussion group on Usenet devoted to talking about a specific topic. Currently, there are over 15,000 newsgroups.

Opt-in e-mail: Opt-in e-mail lists are lists where Internet users have voluntarily signed up to receive commercial e-mail about topics of interest.

Page: All Web sites are a collection of electronic "pages." Each Web page is a document formatted in HTML (Hypertext Markup Language) that contains text, images or media objects such as RealAudio player files, QuickTime videos, or Java applets. The "home page" is typically a visitor's first point of entry and features a site index. Pages can be static or dynamically generated. All frames and frame parent documents are counted as pages.

Page views: Number of times a user requests a page that may contain a particular ad. Indicative of the number of times an ad was potentially seen, or "gross impressions." Page views may overstate ad impressions if users choose to turn off graphics (done to speed browsing).

RealAudio: A commercial software program that plays audio on demand, without waiting for long file transfers. For instance, you can listen to National Public Radio's entire broadcast of *All Things Considered* and *Morning Edition* on the Internet.

Rich media: *Rich media* is a term for advanced technology used in Internet ads, such as streaming video, applets that allow user interaction, and special effects.

ROI: ROI stands for "return on investment," one of the great mysteries of online advertising, and indeed, advertising in general. ROI is trying to find out what the end of result of the expenditure (in this case, an ad campaign) is. A lot depends on the goal of the campaign, building brand awareness, increasing sales, etc. Early attempts at determining ROI in Internet advertising relied heavily on the click-through of an ad.

Server: A machine that makes services available on a network to client programs. A file server makes files available. A WAIS server makes full-text information available through the WAIS protocol (although WAIS uses the term *source* interchangeably with *server*).

Splash page: See *jump page.*

Sponsorship: Sponsorships are increasing in popularity on the Internet. A sponsorship is when an advertiser pays to sponsor content, usually a section of a Web site or an e-mail newsletter. In the case of a site, the sponsorship may include banners or buttons on the site, and possibly a tagline.

Sticky: "Sticky" sites are those where the visitors stay for an extended period of time. For instance, a banking site that offers a financial calculator is stickier than one that doesn't because visitors do not have to leave to find a resource they need.

T1: A high-speed (1.54 megabits/second) network connection.

T3: An even higher-speed (45 megabits/second) Internet connection.

TCP: Transmission Control Protocol works with IP to ensure that packets travel safely on the Internet.

Unique users: The number of different individuals who visit a site within a specific time period. To identify unique users, Web sites rely on some form of user registration or identification system.

Unix: A computer operating system (the basic software running on a computer, underneath things like databases and word processors). Unix is designed to be used by many people at once ("multi-user") and has TCP/IP built-in. Unix is the most prevalent operating system for Internet servers.

Valid hits: A further refinement of hits, valid hits are hits that deliver all information to a user. Excludes hits such as redirects, error messages and computer-generated hits.

Visits: A sequence of requests made by one user at one site. If a visitor does not request any new information for a period of time, known as the "time-out" period, then the next request by the visitor is considered a new visit. To enable comparisons among sites, I/PRO, a provider of services and software for the independent measurement and analysis Web site usage, uses a 30-minute time-out.

Source: ADResources, 2001.

*Listserv is a trademark of L-Soft International, used to describe its electronic mailing list software, using it as a generic term infringes on L-Soft's trademark rights. It is however, commonly used in a generic fashion.

Nat'l Newspaper Site		E-Mail Newsletters*		Search Engine/Portal	
Impressions	**Rate**	**Impressions**	**One month**	**Run of Site**	**One month**
500,000	$40/CPM	1,000,000+	$14/CPM	1–249M	$29/CPM
860,000	$35/CPM	750–999M	$18/CPM	250–499M	$28/CPM
2,000,000	$30/CPM	500–749M	$22/CPM	500–999M	$27/CPM
4,000,000	$25/CPM	250–499M	$26/CPM	1.0–1.9 mil	$24/CPM
8,500,000	$20/CPM	249 or less	$30/CPM	2–2.9 mil	$22/CPM
				3–4.9 mil	$20/CPM
				5 mil+	$18/CPM

Ad Network		Portal–Financial Section		Technology Site	
Type of Buy	**CPM**	**Type of Buy**	**CPM**	**Monthly Impressions**	**One month**
Single site	$40+	Run of property	$20.50–31.00	100–250M	$70/CPM
Content channel	$20–$39	1–3 demo targets	$27.00–48.00	250–499M	$61/CPM
Run of network	$10–$19	3-month frequency discount	2%	500–999M	$58/CPM
		6-month frequency discount	5%	1 mil+	$56/CPM

	Average CPM by Genre	
Genre	**Q3/Q4 1999**	**Q1/Q2 2000**
Health & Fitness	$30.00	$42.50
Movies & Television	$28.84	$34.38
Yellow & White Pages	$20.00	$23.67
Kids & Family	$23.19	$26.29
Home & Garden	$40.00	$42.50
Games	$23.35	$24.13
Travel, Maps, and Local	$28.50	$38.92
General News	$37.23	$37.47
Search Engine	$25.00	$25.00
Community	$19.70	$19.70
Music & Streaming Media	$26.68	$25.05
Personal Expression	$27.50	$25.50
Portal	$29.93	$27.08
Business & Finance	$41.75	$38.30
Society, Politics, & Science	$33.75	$29.75
Sports & Recreation	$33.29	$27.53
Automotive	$39.15	$31.93
Comics & Humor	$31.44	$23.75

Source: AdRelevance
*Rates for ads across all newsletters

EXHIBIT 14.20

A sample ad rate guide.

Together, both brands dominate the product category advertising with a nearly 70 percent combined share of voice. Yet Nike's share of voice is nearly three times that of Reebok.

Research data, such as that provided by Competitive Media Reporting, can provide an assessment of share of voice in up to 10 media categories. A detailed report shows how much a brand was advertised in a particular media category versus the combined media category total for all other brands in the same product category. Knowing what competitors are spending in a medium and how dominant they might be allows an advertiser to strategically schedule within a medium. Some strategists believe that scheduling in and around a competitor's schedule can create a bigger presence for a small advertiser.[8]

Consider how Leo Burnett scheduled advertising for Miller Lite on Super Bowl Sunday in 1994. Since the Super Bowl delivers such a high proportion of the beer-drinking target audience, strategists at Burnett were faced with the prospect of a very dense competitive environment—and a very expensive one, at $1 million for a 30-second spot. Anheuser-Busch had already scheduled its "Bud Bowl" spots during the Super Bowl. So, instead of going head-to-head with Anheuser-Busch in a cluttered, million-dollar-per-spot environment, Miller bought heavily during the pregame show. In this way, the brand achieved good exposure in the target segment without extraordinary expense in a cluttered environment.

As with the media efficiency measures discussed in the previous section, a competitive media assessment is normally not the only foundation for media planning. A competitive media assessment contains valuable information; however, media objectives and media strategies should be the driving forces behind media planning.

Media Scheduling and Buying. Media scheduling and buying are activities that take place throughout the planning effort. Media scheduling focuses on several issues related to timing and impact.[9] All aspects of timing, reach, frequency, and competitive media assessment are evaluated during the scheduling phase. In addition, the total media schedule is evaluated with respect to CPM or gross impressions to gauge the impact the entire schedule delivers in each time frame. Seasonal buying tendencies in the target segment also have a major impact on scheduling. Scheduling media more heavily when consumers show buying tendencies is referred to as **heavy-up scheduling.**[10]

One of the most important aspects of the media-scheduling phase involves creating a visual representation of the media schedule. Exhibit 14.21 shows a media schedule flowchart that includes both print and electronic media placement. With this visual representation of the schedule, the advertiser has tangible documentation of the overall media plan.

Once an overall media plan and schedule are in place, the focus must turn to **media buying.** Media buying entails securing the electronic media time and print media space specified in the schedule. An important part of the media-buying process is the agency of record. The **agency of record** is the advertising agency chosen by the advertiser to purchase time and space. The agency of record coordinates media discounts and negotiates all contracts for time and space. Any other agencies involved in the advertising effort submit insertion orders for time and space within those contracts.

Rather than using an agency of record, some advertisers use a **media-buying service,** which is an independent organization that specializes in buying large blocks of media time and space and reselling it to advertisers (see Exhibit 14.22). Some

8. Andrea Rothman, "Timing Techniques Can Make Small Ad Budgets Seem Bigger," *Wall Street Journal,* February 3, 1989, B4; also see Robert J. Kent and Chris T. Allen, "Competitive Interference Effects in Consumer Memory for Advertising: The Role of Brand Familiarity," *Journal of Marketing* (July 1994), 97–105.

9. John J. Burnett, *Promotion Magazine* (Boston: Houghton Mifflin, 1993), 520–521.

10. Sissors and Bumba, *Advertising Media Planning,* 309–310.

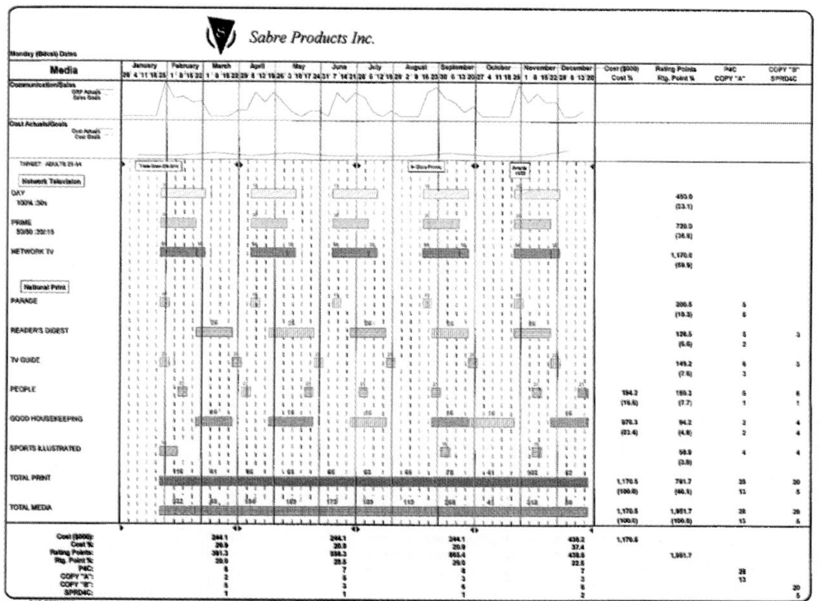

Source: Telmar Information Services Corp., FlowMaster for Windows™, New York, 1999. Reprinted with permission.

EXHIBIT 14.21

A media flowchart gives an advertiser a visual representation of the overall media plan.

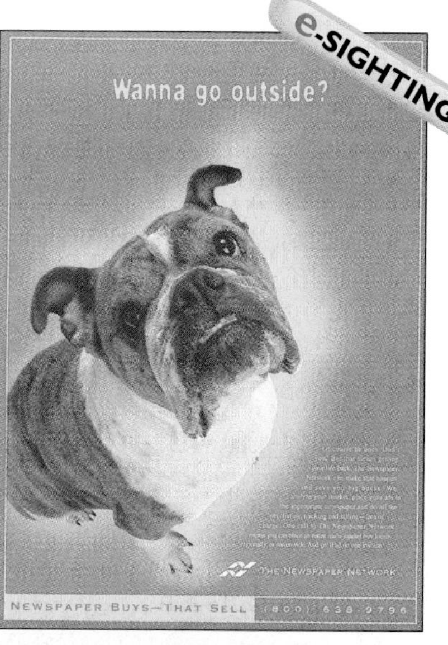

EXHIBIT 14.22

An example of a media-buying service. Internet based media-buying services enable media professionals to purchase advertising more efficiently for print, online, and broadcast media. Explore the services and capabilities of BuyMedia (www.buymedia.com) and Advertise123 (www.advertise123.com). How do these Web-based advertising-exchange services increase the efficiency of media scheduling and buying?

agencies have developed their own media-buying units to control both the planning and the buying process.[11] Regardless of the structure used to make the buys, media buyers evaluate the audience reach, CPM, and timing of each buy. The organization responsible for the buy also monitors the ads and estimates the actual audience reach delivered. If the expected audience is not delivered, then media organizations have to *make good* by repeating ad placements or offering a refund or price reduction on future ads. For example, making good to advertisers because of shortfalls in delivering 1998 Winter Olympics prime-time cost CBS an estimated 400 additional 30-second spots.[12]

2 Computer Media-Planning Models. The explosion of available data on markets and consumers has motivated media planners to rely heavily on electronic databases, computers, and software to assist with the various parts of the media-planning effort.

Nearly all of the major syndicated research services offer electronic data to their subscribers, including advertisers, agencies, and media organizations. These databases contain information helpful in identifying target markets and audiences, estimating or projecting media vehicle audiences and costs, and analyzing competitive advertising activity, among many others. Companies that offer data electronically, such as Nielsen, Arbitron, MRI, SMRB, Scarborough, and the Audit Bureau of circulations,

11. Joe Mandese, "Ayer Adjusts to Complex Media Buys," *Advertising Age,* December 12, 1994, 6.

12. "CBS Faces Olympics Make-Goods," www.adage.com, February 19, 1998.

ADplus(TM) RESULTS: SPOT TV (30S)

Walt Disney World
Off-Season Promotion
Monthly

Target: 973,900
Jacksonville DMA Adults

Message/vehicle = 32.0%

Frequency (f) Distributions

f	Vehicle % f	Vehicle % f+	Message % f	Message % f+
0	5.1	---	9.1	---
1	2.0	94.9	7.5	90.9
2	2.2	92.9	8.1	83.4
3	2.3	90.7	8.1	75.2
4	2.4	88.3	7.8	67.1
5	2.4	85.9	7.2	59.3
6	2.5	83.5	6.6	52.1
7	2.5	81.0	6.0	45.5
8	2.5	78.5	5.3	39.5
9	2.5	76.0	4.7	34.2
10+	73.5	73.5	29.5	29.5
20+	49.8	49.8	6.1	6.1

Summary Evaluation

	Vehicle	Message
Reach 1+ (%)	94.9%	90.9%
Reach 1+ (000s)	923.9	885.3
Reach 3+ (%)	90.7%	75.2%
Reach 3+ (000s)	882.9	732.8
Gross rating points (GRPs)	2,340.0	748.8
Average frequency (f)	24.7	8.2
Gross impressions (000s)	22,789.3	7,292.6
Cost-per-thousand (CPM)	6.10	19.06
Cost-per-rating point (CPP)	59	186

Vehicle List	Rating	Ad Cost	CPM-MSG	Ads	Total Cost	Mix %
WJKS-ABC-AM	6.00	234	12.51	30	7,020	5.1
WJXT-CBS-AM	6.00	234	12.51	30	7,020	5.1
WTLV-NBC-AM	6.00	234	12.51	30	7,020	5.1
WJKS-ABC-DAY	5.00	230	14.76	60	13,800	9.9
WJXT-CBS-DAY	5.00	230	14.76	60	13,800	9.9
WTLV-NBC-DAY	5.00	230	14.76	60	13,800	9.9
WJKS-ABC-PRIM	10.00	850	27.27	30	25,500	18.4
WJXT-CBS-PRIM	10.00	850	27.27	30	25,500	18.4
WTLV-NBC-PRIM	10.00	850	27.27	30	25,500	18.4
		Totals:	19.06	360	138,960	100.0

ADplus(TM) RESULTS: DAILY NEWSPAPERS (1/2 PAGE), SPOT TV (30S)

Walt Disney World
Off-Season Promotion
Monthly

Target: 973,900
Jacksonville DMA Adults

Message/vehicle = 28.1%

Frequency (f) Distributions

f	Vehicle % f	Vehicle % f+	Message % f	Message % f+
0	1.2	---	4.0	---
1	0.8	98.8	4.9	96.0
2	0.9	98.0	5.9	91.1
3	0.9	97.2	6.5	85.2
4	1.0	96.2	6.7	78.7
5	1.1	95.2	6.8	72.0
6	1.1	94.2	6.6	65.2
7	1.2	93.0	6.3	58.6
8	1.3	91.8	5.9	52.4
9	1.3	90.6	5.5	46.5
10+	89.3	89.3	41.0	41.0
20+	73.3	73.3	9.6	9.6

Summary Evaluation

	Vehicle	Message
Reach 1+ (%)	98.8%	96.0%
Reach 1+ (000s)	962.6	934.6
Reach 3+ (%)	97.2%	85.2%
Reach 3+ (000s)	946.5	829.7
Gross rating points (GRPs)	3,372.0	948.0
Average frequency (f)	34.1	9.9
Gross impressions (000s)	32,839.9	9,232.3
Cost-per-thousand (CPM)	10.96	38.99
Cost-per-rating point (CPP)	107	380

Vehicle List	Rating	Ad Cost	CPM-MSG	Ads	Total Cost	Mix %
1 DAILY NEWSPAPERS		Totals:	114.00	80	221,040	61.4
Times-Union	42.00	8,284	104.93	20	165,680	46.0
Record	4.00	866	115.18	20	17,320	4.8
News	3.20	926	153.95	20	18,520	5.1
Reporter	2.40	976	216.35	20	19,520	5.4
2 SPOT TV (30S)		Totals:	19.00	360	138,960	38.6
WJKS-ABC-AM	6.00	234	12.51	30	7,020	2.0
WJXT-CBS-AM	6.00	234	12.51	30	7,020	2.0
WTLV-NBC-AM	6.00	234	12.51	30	7,020	2.0
WJKS-ABC-DAY	5.00	230	14.76	60	13,800	3.8
WJXT-CBS-DAY	5.00	230	14.76	60	13,800	3.8
WTLV-NBC-DAY	5.00	230	14.76	60	13,800	3.8
WJKS-ABC-PRIM	10.00	850	27.27	30	25,500	7.1
WJXT-CBS-PRIM	10.00	850	27.27	30	25,500	7.1
WTLV-NBC-PRIM	10.00	850	27.27	30	25,500	7.1
		Totals:	38.99	440	360,000	100.0

Source: Kent M. Lancaster, ADplus with FlowMaster™: For Multi-Media Advertising Planning, Windows™ edition. New York, Telmar Information Services, Corp. and Media Research Institute, Inc., 1999. Reprinted with permission.

EXHIBIT 14.23

The explosion of data about markets and consumers has caused advertisers to rely more on computerized media-planning tools.

also typically provide software designed to analyze their own data. Such software often produces summary reports, tabulations, ranking, reach-frequency analysis, optimization, simulation, scheduling, buying, flowcharts, and a variety of graphical presentations.

Advertisers that use a mix of media in their advertising campaigns often subscribe to a variety of electronic data services representing the media they use or consider using. However, the various syndicated services do not provide standardized data, reports, and analyses that are necessarily comparable across media categories. Also, individual syndicated service reports and analyses may not offer the content and depth that some users prefer. Nor do they typically analyze media categories that they do not measure. Consequently, media software houses such as Interactive Market Systems (IMS) and Telmar Information Services Corp. (Telmar) offer hundreds of specialized and standardized software products that help advertisers, agencies, and media organizations worldwide develop and evaluate markets, audiences, and multimedia plans. Exhibit 14.23 shows typical screens from one such computer program. The first screen is reach and cost data for spot TV ads, and the second screen is the combined reach and cost data for spot TV and newspaper ads.

Computerization and modeling can never substitute for planning and judgment by media strategists. Computer modeling does, however, allow for the assessment of a wide range of possibilities before making costly media buys. Exhibit 14.24 shows

Industry News

***Advertising Age*:** One of the leading sources of marketing and advertising news. The online version features select articles from the print version as well as the "top" lists. Access: Free

***AdTalk*:** Home of the e-mail newsletter "The Buzz," covering trends and developments in the advertising and media worlds. Access: Free

***Adweek*:** Trade publication featuring creative, client/agency relationships and advertising strategies. Online site features select articles and classified section from print version. Access: Free

***Media Central*:** Site that combines press releases from a variety of different media and publishing industries with select articles from Cowles-related publications. Access: Free

***Media Life Magazine*:** Web-only trade publication that covers the media/advertising world on a daily basis.

***Mediaweek*:** Recently relaunched online version of trade publication. Features include several stories from print version and interactive polls on media topics. Access: Free

Research\Reference:

***American Demographics*:** Publication covering demographic trends in America from a marketer's perspective. Online version features select articles. Access: Free

A.M.I.C: Created by Telmar. A broad collection of links to media-related resources, message boards, a media book store and research tools (such as media calculators).

Audit Bureau of Circulations (ABC): Audit organization for consumer periodicals. Subscription required.

Business Publishers of America (BPA): Provider of auditing services for trade/business and consumer publications. Free access to audit statements.

Interactive Market Systems (IMS): IMS provides media planning and marketing research evaluation software, allowing users to analyze information from syndicated research databases such as MRI, Simmons, MMR, and Nielsen.

Media Plan: Describes the software planning tools available from Manas.

Mediamark Research Inc. (MRI): Provider of research data and services for the advertising industry. Site describes available research studies and tools and allows free access to some top-line data.

RedBooks: Industry's oldest resource that enables the sourcing of ad agency by client/brand and vice versa. Includes listings of senior management at corporate, brand and agency level as well as expenditures by media. Subscription required.

Simmons: A provider of syndicated and custom research for publishers and advertising agencies. Subscription required.

Standard Rate and Data Service (SRDS): Publisher of media rates and data for magazines and other media. Subscription required.

Audits & Surveys: Site describes the marketing-oriented research services available.

Telmar Media Software: Describes the advertising media-planning software and support services offered.

Verified Audit Circulation Corp: Primarily conducts audits for newspapers, including newspaper-distributed magazines.

Media Buying Sites

AdOutlet: Web site that provides an "outlet" for discounted media space in several different media.

Media Space Solutions: MSS connects advertisers with last-minute space availabilities in newspapers.

One Media Place: [Now merged with Media Passage] One Media Place facilitates electronic RFPs and lists a number of opportunistic buys.

Associations:

American Advertising Federation (AAF): Association that encompasses advertisers, agencies, and the media.

Association of Alternative Newsweeklies (AAN): The trade organization for the alternative—and mostly free—newspapers in North America.

Magazine Publishers of America (MPA): The industry association for consumer magazines; provides some valuable studies and statistics on magazine advertising impact.

American Association of Advertising Agencies (AAAA) The advertising industry's trade association gives you the "who," "why," and "what" it is they do.

Other Valuable Media & Advertising Sites:

Electronic Newsstand: Offers detailed information and low-price subscriptions for numerous magazines.

Gebbie Press: An all-in-one media directory listing TV/radio stations, newspapers, and magazines. Mostly a teaser for their subscription product, but the basics are freely accessible.

Market IQ: An organized and updated electronic library of direct marketing pieces.

Mediafinder Provides partial listings from Oxbridge's well-known directories. Fairly comprehensive listing of magazines, newspapers, catalogs, and newsletters.

MediaPassage: [CEASED OPERATION] A Web-based service that helps facilitate the buying, invoicing, and trafficing of print media.

Newspapernet (N-NET): Lists the names, addresses, and phone numbers for all U.S. newspapers.

Parrot Media: Offers user-friendly reference volumes to the entertainment industry, including direct mail and fax services.

EXHIBIT 14.24

A list of online media resources from MediaStart.

Title	Publisher	Rate Base	Circ Total	Circ Paid	Audit by	Audit Date	Rt Card Effect	Cost	Circ/ CPM
Allure	CondéNast	800,000	858,488	858,488	ABC	06/30/00	01/01/01	61,230	71.32
Cosmopolitan	Hearst	2,500,000	2,709,496	2,709,496	ABC	06/30/00	01/01/01	129,100	47.65
Details	Fairchild	400,000	400,000			08/15/00	01/01/01	34,500	86.25
Elle	Hachette	900,000	918,795	918,795	ABC	06/30/00	02/01/01	72,285	78.67
Glamour	CondéNast	2,100,000	2,207,914	2,207,914	ABC	06/30/00	01/01/01	107,470	48.67
Honey	Vanguarde	200,000	200,000			03/15/00	01/01/01	18,250	91.25
Jane	Fairchild	600,000	552,923	552,923	ABC	06/30/00	01/01/01	38,180	69.05
Lucky	CondéNast	600,000	600,000			07/01/01	07/01/01	36,000	60.00
Mode	LeWit & LeWit	600,000	602,753	602,753	ABC	06/30/00	01/01/01	34,000	56.41
more	Meredith	525,000	542,200	542,200	ABC	06/30/00	01/01/01	42,540	78.49
Nylon	Pop Media	175,000	175,000			05/01/00	01/01/01	19,260	110.06
O The Oprah	Hearst	1,300,000	1,300,000			12/01/00	01/01/01	87,100	67.00
Self	CondéNast	1,100,000	1,190,706	1,190,706	ABC	06/30/00	01/01/01	77,920	65.44
Spin	VIBE/SPIN	525,000	526,744	526,744	ABC	06/30/00	01/01/01	44,850	85.15
Sports Illustrated	Time, Inc.	400,000	400,000				01/01/01	29,500	73.75
True Story	Sterlin	500,000	258,159	258,159	ABC	06/30/00	02/01/98	16,070	62.25
YM	Gruner	2,200,000	2,202,615	2,202,615	ABC	06/30/00	02/01/01	97,400	44.22

Source: www.MediaStart.com accessed September 14, 2001.

EXHIBIT 14.25

This is a media schedule generated for free on the WWW.

a list of online media resources from Mediastart. Exhibit 14.25 shows a set of media statistics obtained from this free service. You can see that *Allure* has a circulation of about 8.6 million, a full-page, four-color ad costs $61,230 or about $71.32 per thousand (CPM). *Nylon* is comparatively more expensive at $110.06 per thousand (CPM).

3 Other Ongoing Challenges in the Media Environment.

Several additional challenges add to the complexity of media planning. To explain these additional complications, we will review five dynamic aspects of the media environment: the proliferation of media options; insufficient and inaccurate information; escalating media costs; interactive media; and the complications of media choice in the new era of integrated brand promotion.

The Proliferation of Media Options. One of the most daunting challenges for media placement is simply keeping track of the media options available. There are two areas where media proliferation is occurring. First, there has been an expansion of traditional media, both globally and in the United States. Where there were once just three broadcast television networks, there are now five or six. Cable television is also expanding rapidly, and the new smaller satellite dishes now offer consumers an even greater range of programming. New magazines are being launched at a rate of more than one per day.[13] Advertisers can reach older consumers with *Modern Maturity,*

13. Laura Loro, "Heavy Hitters Gamble on Launches," *Advertising Age,* October 19, 1992, S13–S14.

EXHIBIT 14.26

How does the proliferation of media options such as CNN's Airport Network affect strategic decisions about media scheduling and media buying? Can you think of other products or services that might benefit from an increased focus on place-based media?
www.cnn.com/airport/

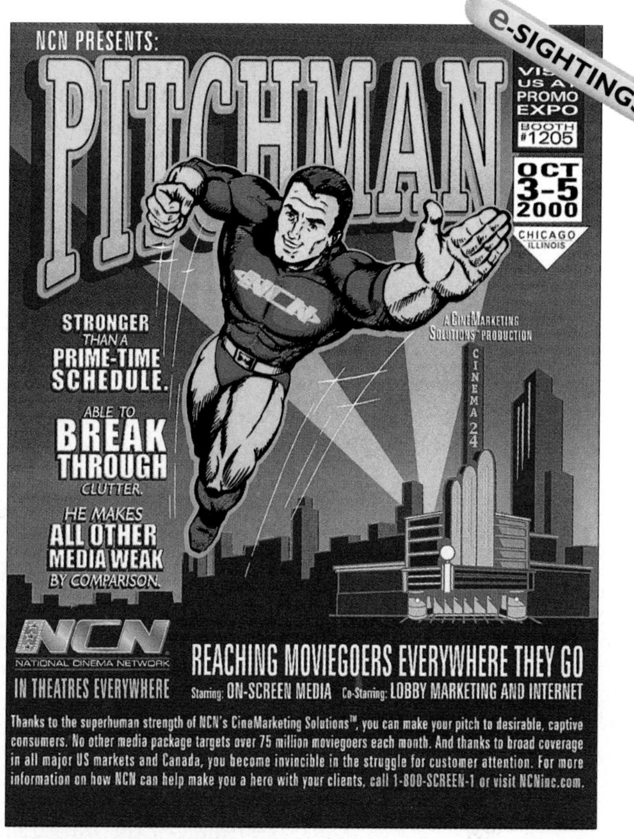

EXHIBIT 14.27

Movie-theater ads are yet another "new media" option. Other emerging media such as public Internet kiosks are creating new opportunities to effectively reach target audiences. For example, Kiosk Information Systems (www.kis-kiosk.com) is currently producing Internet kiosks for use by skateboarders and BMX freestyle riders in Vans Skateparks nationwide (www.vans.com). What advertising and marketing opportunities do public Internet kiosks offer to advertisers?

preschoolers with *Sesame Street Magazine,* and everyone in between with numerous other magazines.

Second, new media are being developed to reach consumers in more and different ways. Retailers mail videotapes to consumers in carefully designated geographic areas to entice a trip to their retail store. Interactive video kiosks in Minneapolis grocery stores dispense Minnesota Twins baseball tickets and advertise team merchandise.[14] Turner Broadcasting has developed the CNN Airport Network, one of many new place-based media that reach consumers when they're not at home. The Airport Network transmits advertising along with news and entertainment programming to airport terminal gates around the United States. Advertisers who market travel-related services, such as American Express and AT&T, find this new media vehicle an ideal option. Exhibit 14.26 illustrates this new place-based network.

Interactive video kiosks, CD-ROM ads, online information services, movie theater ads (see Exhibit 14.27)—little is left untouched by the long arm of advertising placement. Many of the players in new media are big names in traditional media as well. *Newsweek* has attracted advertisers such as Honda, Chrysler, and Fidelity Investments

14. Debra Aho, "Kiosks: The Good, the Bad & Ugly," *Advertising Age,* January 17, 1994, 13.

now that the magazine has an interactive version on the Prodigy online service. There are many new players in the new media environment as well. Overall, new-media advertising is still low-priced because the new media, at this point, lack the broad reach of traditional media. The typical CD-ROM magazine has a total audience of 150,000, versus 5 to 10 times that for a traditional magazine. Of course, the creative flexibility of interactive sound and motion available on the CD-ROM format far exceeds the capabilities of print magazines.

Finally, the evolution of what used to be called direct mail into a new form of direct marketing, which will be discussed in detail in Chapter 19, has also created new opportunities for advertisers. The evolution began with the airlines and their in-flight magazines, and now firms of all types have started to publish newsletters, news magazines, and catalogs targeted at their current customers. As a way to increase efficiency in reaching target audiences, advertisers have essentially created their own in-house media options. For example, TIAA-CREF, the largest pension fund in the world, publishes a quarterly news magazine called *The Participant.* Similarly, Physicians Mutual Insurance has a quarterly publication called *Between Friends,* which is mailed to insureds and passes along safety information, household tips, comments from customers, and a short memo from the president of the firm. These created media are efficient in that current and past customers are reached. The probability that the receiver will pay attention to the message is greater because there is some affinity for the firm sending the message.

Insufficient and Inaccurate Information. Placing ads in media that reach the intended target audience and few nontarget audience members is a tremendous challenge. The truth is that much of the information advertisers must use to make media choices is either insufficient for identifying how to reach a target audience or simply inaccurate. All the information used to identify who is using what medium at what time and in what numbers is generated as secondary data by large commercial media research organizations. Secondary data are frequently out-of-date or do not provide the category of measurement the marketer or advertiser is interested in.

Many of the problems related to media information are unique to the measurement situation; others are simply a matter of lack of availability. For example, no service provides audience measures for both AM and FM listening for *every* market in the United States. Another frustrating problem for advertisers is the accuracy of the measurement of television audience size. A nagging concern exists about the way television audiences have been measured. All television audience measurement services provide information on either individuals or homes tuned in to programs. These measures have been used as surrogates for actual exposure for many years. But, as we all know from personal experience, the fact that a household is tuned in to a program (as measured by a device attached to the television set) does not mean that exposure to the ad or attention to the ad has been achieved.

Nielsen, which holds a virtual monopoly on national television ratings in the United States, has been under pressure to improve the accuracy of its ratings.[15] Indeed, several firms, including General Electric (the parent of NBC), Disney/ABC, and CBS, have paid for a statistical analysis to examine ways of improving the ratings process. Some television stations have even dropped out of the Nielsen rating program, claiming that the measurement periods, known as sweep periods, create an artificial measurement context.[16] (See Exhibit 14.28.) Nielsen has also come under fire for the accuracy of its methods in markets outside the United States. In Japan, Nielsen has been criticized for the way it breaks down the audiences for Japanese tel-

15. See Joe Mandese, "Rivals' Ratings Don't Match Up," *Advertising Age,* February 24, 1992, 50.
16. "TV Station Drops Nielsen," *Marketing News,* March 11, 1996, 1.

Advertisers debate whether television ratings are an accurate measure of audience.

Chicago Tribune

IN THIS SECTION
Comics / 8-9
Dear Abby / 9
Bridge / 9
Crossword / 9
Magazines / 10
Horoscopes / 10

Tempo

FRIDAY, FEBRUARY 19, 1999 ■ SECTION 2

HOW TO REACH US
Tempo
435 N. Michigan Ave.
Chicago, Il. 60611
e-mail: ctc-tempo@tribune.com

A sweeping look at local news 'specials' during the all-important ratings period

Steve Johnson
ON TELEVISION

The stereotype persists about the behavior of television news operations during sweeps months: They take any excuse, from lingerie shows at local bars to unlicensed boxing matches at, well, local bars, to load up their newscasts with the kind of fare that would make Jerry Springer drool.

Sweeps are, in this view, the time of the year when "news" is most determinedly spelled with a T and an A.

The reality, at least in Chicago, is rather mundane and apparently growing more so: Sweeps-month "special reports," the kind of longer, extra-effort pieces that are heavily promoted in an attempt to boost ratings during the crucial audience-measurement periods, do tend to pander to an audience.

These linchpins in sweeps strategy are aiming, however, not at the louts who foam at the mouth over any image of a woman in her skivvies, but rather at women themselves.

Witness, already this sweeps month, the two-night takeouts on moisturizing lotions (WMAQ-Ch. 5); on disposable diapers (WLS-Ch. 7); on children's software (WLS); on heart attacks, especially as they relate to women (WMAQ); and on dads more willing to stay at home with the kids (WLS).

The demographically dominant sex tends to be the primary audience for local TV news and also the maker of the news-viewing decision, which explains why local newscasts during the quarterly sweeps periods look not

SEE SWEEPS, PAGE 3

Rating the reports

'SMACK'
Eddie Arruza, **WGN-Ch. 9**
Heroin use is up among high school students.
Strength: Telling interviews with real addicts.
Flaw: Thin on Chicagoland-specific info.
Special moment: Seductive black-and-white images of heroin preparation.

'SKIN DEEP' (2 parts)
Robin Meade, **WMAQ-Ch. 5**
A lab and real people test skin moisturizers.
Strength: Products rated by name.
Flaw: Ratings confusing, mealy-mouthed.
Special moment: Moisturizer by Walgreen's, a WMAQ news sponsor, does well in both tests.

'A SHELTER GAME'
Chuck Goudie, **WLS-Ch. 7**
Many registered sex offenders officially listed as homeless shelter residents aren't.
Strength: Highlights flaws in sex-perp tracking system.
Flaw: Thin on context, relevance of such lists.
Special moment: Goudie at man's door: "Sir, I need to speak to you about your sex registration."

'MURDER: FOR HIRE'
Larry Yellen, **WFLD-Ch. 32**
More plain folks seem to be employing hit men.
Strength: Thorough reporting on topic often in news.
Flaw: More exploration than, as billed, "investigation."
Special moment: Jailed perp philosophizes: "In the '90s... you pay to have everything done."

'THE GREAT DIAPER DEBATE' (2 parts)
Janet Davies, **WLS-Ch. 7**
Disposable diapers explained, then tested by moms.
Strength: Interesting history of product.
Flaw: No discernible "debate."
Special moment: Pampers wins mom ratings, but WLS anchor, weatherman say they like Huggies best.

'EAT, DRINK AND STILL BE WARY'
Pam Zekman, **WBBM-Ch. 2**
Follow-ups to November's attention-getting hidden-camera look at restaurant sloth.
Strength: Secret video of chef licking fingers shown again.
Flaw: Includes pol praising Zekman by name.
Special moment: Pizzeria owner forced to clean up act looks ready to clock Zekman.

CARMEN ELECTRA INTERVIEW
Allison Payne, **WGN-Ch. 9**
Publicity-tour chat with star of WGN show.
Strength: Well-packaged, for a puff piece.
Flaw: No new info on Rodman marriage.
Special moment: Failure to mention series, "Hyperion Bay," was put on hiatus that day.

'UNDER LOCK AND KEY' (2 parts)
Lisa Parker, **WMAQ-Ch. 5**
Locks that come with luggage are not secure.
Strength: Included people scoffing at story concept.
Flaw: Belaboring obvious hits new extreme.
Special moment: Head of luggage trade association tells reporter she has a "non-story."

'RICKY'S STORY' (2 parts)
Dave Savini, **WMAQ-Ch. 5**
Boy's death suggests problems when transit-system buses sub for school buses.
Strength: Demonstrates need for added safety features.
Flaw: Ignores past reports on yellow bus flaws.
Special moment: Footage of tearful, surviving twin brother used both nights.

evision broadcast programs.[17] Problems with media-audience measurement are among the reasons why so much pretesting of messages is done. Pretesting provides a "controlled" (albeit artificial) measure of effectiveness.

Finally, media organizations often provide information to advertisers in ways that are only marginally useful. While it is possible to get detailed information on the age, gender, and geographic location of target audiences, these characteristics may not be relevant to audience identification. Not all brands show clear tendencies among consumer groups based on Simmons or MRI data. Rather, consumer behavior is much more often influenced by peer groups, lifestyles, attitudes, and beliefs—which don't show up on commercial research reports. If we base our target marketing on these behavioral and experiential factors, then we would logically want to choose our media in the same way. But such information is often not available from media organizations, nor is it likely to be forthcoming (due to the cost of gathering these data). In fairness, some media kits from magazines targeted to upper-income consumers (such as *Smithsonian Magazine*) provide fairly detailed information on past purchase behaviors and some leisure activities. This information is the exception rather than the rule, however, and even then a lot is being assumed.

Escalating Media Costs. While advertisers have always complained about media costs, the situation may be reaching a critical point. The cost of newspaper and magazine ads can reach into the hundreds of thousands of dollars for a single page. In 1998, the average cost for a 30-second spot during the Super Bowl was $1.3 million and in 1999 it escalated to $1.6 million. Spots during prime-time network television programs cost $80,000 to $500,000 for 30 seconds.

These sorts of price increases, as well as the high absolute dollar amount for media placement, have made advertisers scrutinize their media costs. Some advertisers are questioning the wisdom of massive expenditures on media with broad reach, such as network television. For the time being, big advertisers are still investing more

17. Jennifer Cody, "Broadcasters Pan Nielsen Japan's Ratings," *Wall Street Journal*, November 9, 1994, B8.

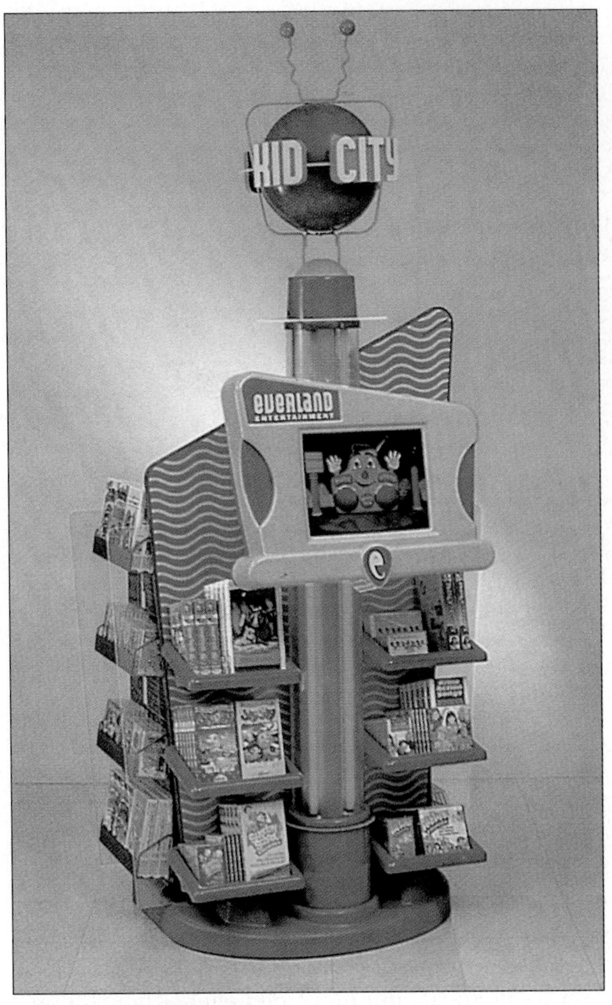

EXHIBIT 14.29

This example of point-of-purchase advertising won an award from the Point-of-Purchase Advertising Institute. www.everlandentertainment.com

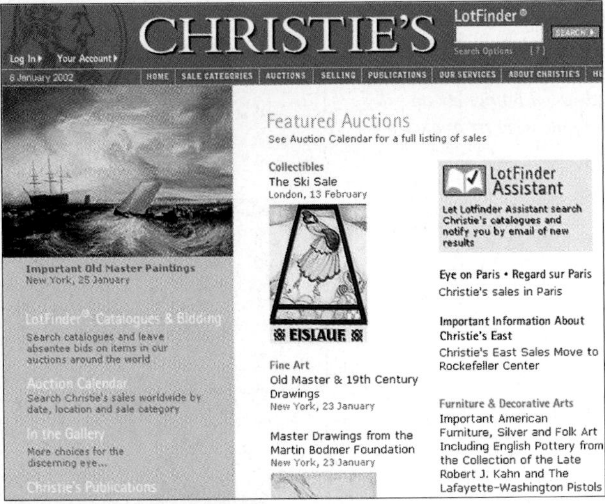

EXHIBIT 14.30

Online and interactive media have become popular even among upscale, traditional organizations. www.christies.com

in all forms of traditional mass media, but that might be changing with the growth of interactive media and the greater attention being paid to integrated brand promotion.[18]

Interactive Media. Aside from the escalating cost of traditional mass media options, the media environment has gotten considerably more challenging as interactive media have been refined. **Interactive media** reach beyond television and include kiosks (Exhibit 14.29 shows an award-winning interactive kiosk) in shopping malls or student unions. Also included are interactive telephones, interactive CDs, online services, the Internet, and online versions of magazines. Absolut Vodka has developed a successful interactive Internet campaign, as discussed in the E-Commerce box on page 517. Even such traditional, upscale outlets as Christie's auction house have started using home pages on the World Wide Web to publicize upcoming events (see Exhibit 14.30). The confounding factor for media placement decisions is that if consumers

18. Robert J. Coen, "Look for Bid Up of Desirable Media," *Advertising Age*, November 7, 1994, S20–S22.

E-COMMERCE

Absolut Value

While most marketers aim to capitalize on the Internet's targeted ad-serving, e-commerce, and cybermarketing capabilities, Absolut is conquering cyberspace by exploiting an edgy brand-building technique: interactive entertainment. Absolut Vodka has an interactive and innovative site where surfers can create music mixes, play games, and watch film shorts. This top international brand has shown visionary zeal and a knack for creating relationships with consumers that blur the lines between online and offline marketing. By turning brand images into electronic entertainment and leveraging the interactive nature of the Net to build customer loyalty, Absolut is reinforcing its brand well beyond the confines of classic marketing channels.

Early on, the company made a conscious decision to avoid banner ads, site sponsorships, e-coupons, and other digital marketing gadgets. Instead, Absolut followed market research that confirmed suspicions that its customers were Web-savvy netizens, artistic types, film buffs, and literati. To build a rapport with this audience, the company developed a myriad of online art experiences where the brand is wrapped within an entertaining interactive experience. The site's visually stunning interactive images weave in and out of the most recognized silhouette in advertising history—the Absolut bottle.

Critics of this approach to new media branding say "show me the clicks." Absolut's marketers dismiss that hyper-quantitative, bottom-line thinking. Measuring click-throughs is just the tip of the iceberg. For a brand like Absolut, there has always been a strong balance between the qualitative and the quantitative. Absolut's campaigns keep viewers engaged in a way that many others have failed to achieve. Considering that the company generated roughly $1 billion in U.S. sales last year, or about 60 percent of the vodka market, it's clear that Absolut has found a formula that translates its edgy, artsy campaigns into effective marketing vehicles online.

Source: Scott Hays, "Cool, Edgy, Artistic Absolut," Mediapost, www.mediapost.com, accessed on November 5, 2001.

truly do begin to spend time with interactive media, they will have less time to spend with traditional media such as television and newspapers. This will force advertisers to choose whether to participate in (or develop their own) interactive media. (Chapter 16 deals exclusively with the Internet, media buying on the Internet, and audience measurement problems.)

In the beginning, a few shopping networks, such as QVC, and a few retailers, such as Macy's and Nordstrom, found interactive technology well suited to serving their customers with greater ease and convenience. But interactive media are growing beyond a few retail-shopping experiments. Although no one knows for sure whether consumers will use interactive television for home shopping, education, games, movie rental, or other entertainment programming, the chairman and CEO of U.S. West, Richard D. McCormick, says firmly, "We want consumers to have access to any piece of information in the multimedia sense, anytime they want it."[19] Big players such as Time Warner, Bell Atlantic, Tele-Communications, and Cablevision Systems see similar potential in interactive media, because they are all developing their own interactive options for advertisers.

Media Choice and Integrated Brand Promotions.

A final complicating factor in the media environment is that more firms are adopting an integrated brand promotion (IBP) perspective, which relies on a broader mix of communication tools. IBP is the use of various promotional tools, including advertising, in a coordinated manner to build and maintain brand awareness, identity, and preference. Promotional options such as event sponsorship, direct marketing, sales promotion (Exhibit 14.31), and public relations are drawing many firms away from traditional mass media advertising. But even these new approaches, like the one shown in Exhibit 14.32, will still require coordination with the advertising that remains. Some of the more significant implications for media planning to achieve IBP are as follows:

- The reliance on mass media will be reduced as more highly targeted media are integrated into media plans. Database marketing programs and more sophisticated single-source data research will produce more tightly focused efforts through direct marketing and interactive media options.

19. Leslie Cauley, "U.S. West Prepares to Make a Big Splash in Multimedia," *Wall Street Journal,* January 10, 1994, B4.

EXHIBIT 14.31

This is sales promotion. Sunglass Hut and American Pie 2 *cross-promote.*

EXHIBIT 14.32

What it has come to.

- More precise media impact data, not just media exposure data, will be needed to compare media alternatives. Advertisers will be looking for proof that consumers exposed to a particular medium are buyers, not just prospects.
- Media planners will need to know much more about a broader range of communication tools: event sponsorship, interactive media, direct marketing, and public relations. They will need to know more about the impact and capabilities of these other forms of promotion to fully integrate communications.
- Central control will be necessary for synergistic, seamless communication. At this point, it is unclear who will provide this central control—the advertiser, the advertising agency, the copywriter, or the media planner. There is some reason to believe that, because of the need for integration and coordination, media planners will emerge as more critically important to the communications process than they have ever been in the past.[20]

20. Adapted from Sissors and Bumba, *Advertising Media Planning,* 6–7, 51–60.

SUMMARY

Detail the important components of the media-planning process.

A media plan specifies the media vehicles that will be used to deliver the advertiser's message. Developing a media plan entails setting objectives such as effective reach and frequency and determining strategies to achieve those objectives. Media planners use several quantitative indicators, such as CPM and CPRP, to help them judge the efficiency of prospective media choices. The media-planning process culminates in the scheduling and purchase of a mix of media vehicles expected to deliver the advertiser's message to specific target audiences at precisely the right time to affect their consumption decisions.

Explain the applications of computer modeling in media planning.

As is true in so many aspects of modern life, the computer has become an essential tool for the media planner. The detailed information available and the myriad of choices that must be made in working up a media schedule lend themselves to computer modeling. Modeling allows a planner to economically gauge the potential impact of alternative plans before making a media buy. Computer models can also be used to rate media vehicles in terms of their efficiency in reaching a target segment. These models are important decision-support tools in media planning.

Discuss five additional challenges that complicate the media-planning process.

Several additional factors complicate media planning. Simply keeping track of all the options is a challenge, given that new options are constantly being invented. Inadequate information and rising media costs are additional hurdles. The emergence of interactive media presents advertisers with new, untested vehicles. This incredible array of choices creates many dilemmas for the media planner who seeks to achieve integrated marketing communications.

KEY TERMS

measured media
unmeasured media
media plan
media class
media vehicle
media objectives
single-source tracking services
geo-targeting
message weight
gross impressions
between-vehicle duplication
within-vehicle duplication
reach
frequency
gross rating points (GRP)
effective frequency
effective reach
continuity
continuous scheduling
flighting
pulsing
"square root law"
media mix
concentrated media mix
assorted media mix
cost per thousand (CPM)
cost per thousand–target market (CPM–TM)
cost per rating point (CPRP)
share of voice
heavy-up scheduling
media buying
agency of record
media-buying service
interactive media

QUESTIONS

1. The opening section of this chapter describes radical changes that have taken place in the world of media planning. Compare and contrast the way things used to be and the way things are now. What factors contributed to this shift? Do you think the job of media planning has become more or less complicated? Explain.

2. The claim has been made that traditional media advertising is dead. In rebuttal, many advertisers point out that traditional advertising flourished during the massive dot-com media buys of the late 1990s. Now that the dot-com craze has dramatically collapsed, do you believe that traditional advertising can continue to hold its own? Justify your answer.

3. Media plans should of course take a proactive stance with respect to customers. Explain how geo-targeting and heavy-up scheduling can be used in making a media plan more proactive with respect to customers.

4. Carefully watch one hour of television and record the time length of each advertisement. Using your perceptions about the most and least persuasive ads during this hour of television, develop a hypothesis about the value of long versus short advertising messages. When should an advertiser use long instead of short ads, to accomplish what goals?

5. Review the mathematics of the CPM and CPRP calculations, and explain how these two indicators can be used to assess the efficiency and effectiveness of a media schedule.

6. Assume that you are advising a regional snack-food manufacturer whose brands have a low share of voice. Which pattern of continuity would you recommend for such an advertiser? Would you place your ads in television programming that is also sponsored by Pringles and Doritos? Why or why not?

7. Media strategy models allow planners to compare the impact of different media plans, using criteria such as reach, frequency, and gross impressions. What other kinds of criteria should a planner take into account before deciding on a final plan?

8. Discuss the issues raised in this chapter that represent challenges for those who champion integrated brand promotions. Why would central control be required for achieving IBP? If media planners wish to play the role of central controller, what must they do to qualify for the role?

EXPERIENTIAL EXERCISES

1. Choose two of your favorite magazines or newspapers and visit their Web sites to find information pertaining to ad rates. To do this, search for links on the home pages that say "advertising" or "media kit" (you may have to browse various magazine and newspaper sites until you find this information). Once you locate the advertising information at the site, describe the type of data that is available to potential advertisers and media buyers. List two or three specific examples of data and explain how this information helps media buyers make effective decisions during the media-planning process.

2. Go to the Internet and make a list of the banner ads you see at the following sites. Make a note of which ads appear on each site, and state whether or not you think the placement of these ads is likely to accomplish the objectives of the advertisers. Give your reasoning.

http://www.ivillage.com

http://www.vibe.com

http://www.ellegirl.com

http://www.thirdage.com

http://www.theonion.com

USING THE INTERNET

14-1 Strategies for Promoting Hip Brands

Hi Frequency is a national youth-marketing company that implements custom-built campaigns through a nationwide organization of teams that operate at street level to make a connection to today's media-savvy youth market. The firm's army of hip, young reps appear at music stores, skateboarding parks, and shopping malls with a mission to create a buzz over a pop star's latest CD or a designer's new clothing line. By sparking interest in new concepts through guerrilla marketing methods, Hi Frequency has been instrumental in the success of alternative bands such as Radiohead and Limp Bizkit, and continues to be a favorite promotion firm for the entertainment industry.

Hi Frequency Marketing: http://www.hifrequency.com

1. Describe Hi Frequency's clients, and explain why the firm's campaigns provide some of the most targeted message placement available for these clients.

2. Read about the firm's services at the site. Name three unique methods the company employs to reach influential trendsetters and consumers of youth culture. Would Hi Frequency's methods for message placement be best categorized as measured media or unmeasured media?

3. Briefly define the concept of media efficiency, and explain why there are difficulties in determining the efficiency of the advertising and promotion techniques that are employed by Hi Frequency.

14-2 Computerized Media Planning

Standard Rate and Data Service (SRDS) has been a leading provider of media rates and information to the advertising industry for over 80 years. The company's data sources offer comprehensive coverage of traditional and alternative media.

Standard Rate and Data Service: http://www.srds.com

1. List and describe two or three specific products or services SRDS offers to its subscribers.

2. Who is likely to subscribe to SRDS and what are some of the ways the site can be used as a tool to meet customers' media planning and buying needs?

3. A media plan includes objectives, strategies, media choices, and a media schedule for placing a message. For each of these four important components, identify a service, tool, or resource at the SRDS site that can help guide media planners through the media-planning process.

4. What are some of the pitfalls media strategists face in utilizing electronic data and computerized modeling for media planning?

CHAPTER 15

After reading and thinking about this chapter, you will be able to do the following:

Detail the pros and cons of newspapers as a media class, identify newspaper types, and describe buying and audience measurement for newspapers.

Detail the pros and cons of magazines as a media class, identify magazine types, and describe buying and audience measurement for magazines.

Detail the pros and cons of television as a media class, identify television types, and describe buying and audience measurement for television.

Detail the pros and cons of radio as a media class, identify radio types, and describe buying and audience measurement for radio.

CHAPTER 14
Media Planning, Objectives, and Strategy for Advertising and Promoting the Brand

CHAPTER 15
Media Planning: Print, Television, and Radio

CHAPTER 16
Media Planning: Advertising and the Internet

The acquisition of Time Warner by America Online, Inc. is easily the biggest media event of the early 21st century. With Federal Communications Commission approval, the $103 billion deal united the biggest provider of Internet service (with nearly 30 million subscribers) with the largest media company in the United States, whose holdings include two major movie studios, 20 cable TV channels, 20 million cable subscribers, seven record labels, and 36 magazines.[1] When the approval came from the FCC, America Online Chairman Steve Case described the merger as a "historic moment . . . when we transform the landscape of media and communications."[2]

Indeed, the AOL Time Warner megamedia conglomerate just might transform media and communications. The combined "properties" of the two entities include such important television media options as TBS, TNT, the WB network, and HBO; magazine media options including *Time, People, Sports Illustrated, Fortune,* and *Entertainment Weekly*; film properties including the Warner Bros. and New Line film studios; and, of course, Internet access provided by America Online, which includes AOL, Compuserve, and Netscape, among other Internet entities. All totaled, the revenues from these various media sum to nearly $40 billion annually.

But sheer size and revenue are not the basis for the importance and power of this new media giant. Rather, the ability of the new AOL to provide advertisers with effective and efficient media reach is the real power in the complexity and size of this media organization. The value for advertisers (and the real revenue-generating opportunity for AOL) lies in the opportunity for cross-media advertising buys (see Exhibits 15.1 and 15.2). The combined media available from AOL allow an advertiser to reach vast but carefully defined target audiences. For example, General Motors might run print ads promoting the Chevy Blazer SUV to 25-to-34-year-old men in *Sports Illustrated*—nothing remarkable there. But GM can then also simultaneously advertise the vehicle on AOL's sports and finance cable channels and place banner ads through AOL's Internet division. This array of advertising messages in multiple media does much to create an integrated brand promotion for a brand. In addition, GM would have a one-stop-shopping contact for a wide range of media placement needs. To validate the "cross-selling" option, AOL has announced deals with Compaq Computer, Cendant, Nortel Networks, and Purchase Pro, each buying a package of ad space in online, print, and television properties.[3]

Which Media: Strategic Planning Considerations.

Media decisions made by advertisers ultimately determine which media companies, or media conglomerates such as AOL, earn the billions of dollars of revenue for print, television/cable, and radio advertising slots. This chapter focuses on the challenge advertisers face in evaluating these major media options as key ways to reach their audiences. As the discussion of media planning in the previous chapter emphasized, even great advertising can't achieve communications and sales objectives if the media placement misses the target audience.

Our discussion of print, television, and radio media will concentrate on several key aspects of using these major media. With respect to the print media—newspapers and magazines—we will first consider the advantages and disadvantages of the media themselves. Both newspapers and magazines have inherent capabilities and limitations that advertisers must take into consideration in building a media plan. Next, we will look at the types of newspapers and magazines from which advertisers can choose. Finally, we will identify buying procedures and audience measurement techniques.

1. Jill Carroll, "AOL-Time Warner Merger Clears FCC," *Wall Street Journal,* January 12, 2001, A3.
2. Jennifer Gilbert, "AOL's Dilemma," *Business 2.0,* May 29, 2001, 41.
3. Jon Fine, "Crunchtime," *Advertising Age,* May 7, 2001, 1, 16–19.

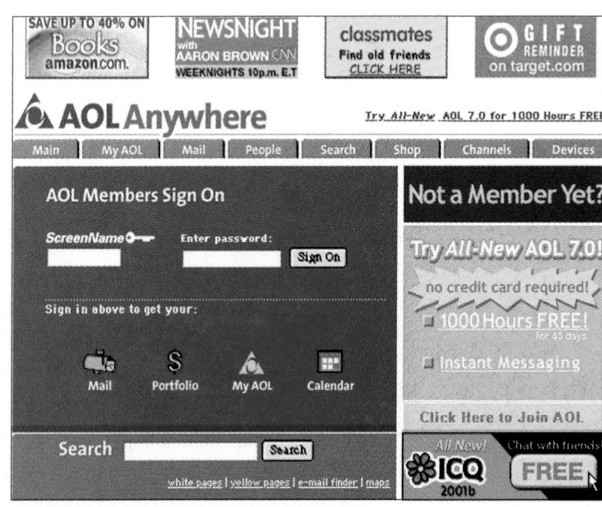

EXHIBITS 15.1 AND 15.2

The acquisition of Time Warner by America Online, Inc. provides advertisers such diverse media placement choices as Time *magazine and AOL. The merger of two giant media companies offers advertisers the opportunity for "cross buying" media in order to reach a wide range of target markets.* www.aoltimewarner.com

Discussion of television and radio media follows. First, the types of television and radio options are described. Next, the advantages and disadvantages of television and radio are examined. The buying procedures and audience measurement techniques are identified. Finally, the future of television and radio in the context of new Internet, satellite, and broadband technology is considered.

Print, television, and radio media represent major alternatives available to advertisers for reaching audiences. While much has been said—and more will be said in the following chapters—about increased spending on new media, about 50 percent of all advertising dollars in the United States still go to traditional print, radio, and television media.[4] In addition, the vast majority of the creative effort—and money—is expended on print and broadcast advertising campaigns. Despite the many intriguing opportunities that new media options offer, print and broadcast media will likely form the foundation of most advertising campaigns for years to come. The discussions in this chapter will demonstrate why these media represent such rich communication alternatives for advertisers.

Print Media.

You might think that the print media are lifeless and lack impact compared to the broadcast media options. Think again. Consider the problems that faced Absolut vodka. In 1980, Absolut was on the verge of extinction. The Swedish brand was selling only

4. R. Craig Endicott, "100 Leading National Advertisers," *Advertising Age,* September 24, 2001, S12.

12,000 cases a year in the United States—not enough to even register a single percentage point of market share. The name Absolut was seen as gimmicky; bartenders thought the bottle was ugly and hard to pour from; and to top things off, consumers gave no credibility at all to a vodka produced in Sweden, which they knew as the land of boxy-looking cars and hot tubs.

The TBWA advertising agency in New York set about the task of overcoming these liabilities of the brand and decided to rely on print advertising *alone*—primarily because spirits ads were banned from broadcast at the time. The agency took on the challenge of developing magazine and newspaper ads that would build awareness, communicate quality, achieve credibility, and avoid Swedish clichés etched in the minds of American consumers. The firm came up with one of the most famous and successful print campaigns of all time. The concept was to feature the strange-shaped Absolut bottle as the hero of each ad, in which the only copy was a two-word tag line always beginning with *Absolut* and ending with a "quality" word such as *perfection* or *clarity*. The two-word description evolved from the original quality concept to a variety of clever combinations. "Absolut Centerfold" appeared in *Playboy* and featured an Absolut bottle with all the printing removed, and "Absolut Wonderland" was a Christmas-season ad with the bottle in a snow globe like the ones that feature snowy Christmas scenes.

In the end, the Absolut campaign was not only a creative masterpiece, but also a resounding market success. Absolut has become one of the leading imported vodkas in the United States. The vodka with no credibility and the ugly bottle has become sophisticated and fashionable with a well-conceived and well-placed print campaign.[5] To this day, the same campaign is being used for the Absolut brand with continued success. The reason print media alone have been able to accomplish this task relates to some of the inherent capabilities and qualities of print as an advertising media option.

1 **Newspapers.** Newspaper is the medium that is most accessible to the widest range of advertisers. Advertisers big and small—even you and I when we want to sell that old bike or snowboard—can use newspaper advertising. In fact, investment in newspaper advertising reached $50.4 billion in 2001—second only to television in attracting advertising dollars.[6] Exhibits 15.3 and 15.4 show the top 10 advertisers in national and local newspapers. Notice three features of the spending data in these exhibits. First, the list of national newspaper advertisers includes many business products and services. Several national newspapers reach primarily business audiences. Second, notice that the list of local newspaper advertisers is dominated by retailers. Newspapers are, of course, ideally suited to reaching a narrow geographic area—precisely the type of audience retailers want to reach. Finally, look at how much more money is spent by the top 10 local advertisers than by the national advertisers. This is because the national advertisers use newspaper advertising as part of a multimedia plan, while local advertisers, even though they are often national companies, tend to rely on newspapers as the primary medium for reaching their well-defined geographic target audiences.

There are some sad truths, however, about the current status of newspapers as a medium. Since the early 1980s, newspapers across the United States have been suffering circulation declines, and the trend has continued into the 21st century.[7] What may be worse is that the percentage of adults reading daily newspapers is also declining. About 60 percent of adults in the United States read a daily newspaper, com-

5. Information about the Absolut vodka campaign was adapted from information in Nicholas Ind, "Absolut Vodka in the U.S.," in *Great Advertising Campaigns* (Lincolnwood, Ill.: NTC Business Books, 1993), 15–32.
6. Mercedes M. Cardona, "The Party's Over," *Advertising Age,* January 1, 2001, 11.
7. Jon Fine, "Bad News for Newspapers: ABC's Figures Show Circ. Falls," *Advertising Age,* November 6, 2000, 36.

EXHIBIT 15.3

Top 10 national newspaper advertisers (U.S. dollars in millions).

		National Newspaper Ad Spending		
Rank	Advertiser	2000	1999	% Change
1	AOL Time Warner	$75.0	$63.8	17.5
2	IBM Corp.	63.1	48.7	29.6
3	General Motors Corp.	62.5	62.8	–0.05
4	Ford Motor Co.	48.8	39.9	22.1
5	FMR Corp.	45.4	48.7	–6.7
6	Verizon Communications	44.8	35.3	26.7
7	Walt Disney Co.	44.3	51.1	–13.3
8	Sony Corp.	41.6	33.9	22.6
9	Federated Dept. Stores	41.1	37.0	10.9
10	Viacom	36.6	32.5	12.6

Source: *Advertising Age*, September 24, 2001, S16. Reprinted with permission from the September 24, 2001, issue of *Advertising Age*. Copyright © Crain Communications Inc. 2001.

EXHIBIT 15.4

Top 10 local newspaper advertisers (U.S. dollars in millions).

		National Newspaper Ad Spending		
Rank	Advertiser	2000	1999	% Change
1	Federated Dept. Stores	$537.4	$496.2	8.3
2	May Dept. Stores	457.0	420.7	8.6
3	News Corp.	361.3	382.4	–5.5
4	Verizon Communications	303.3	140.6	115.7
5	General Motors Corp.	297.2	541.1	–45.1
6	AOL Time Warner	261.3	251.8	3.7
7	Target Corp.	211.9	214.1	–1.0
8	SBC Communications	211.5	138.8	52.4
9	Dillard's	208.4	193.3	7.8
10	Circuit City Stores	208.2	300.9	–30.8

Source: *Advertising Age*, September 24, 2001, S16. Reprinted with permission from the September 24, 2001, issue of *Advertising Age*. Copyright © Crain Communications Inc. 2001.

pared with about 78 percent in 1970.[8] Much of the decline in both circulation and readership comes from the fact that both morning and evening newspapers have been losing patronage to television news programs. While shows such as *Good Morning America* cannot provide the breadth of coverage that newspapers can, they still offer news, and they offer it in a lively multisensory format.

Advantages of Newspapers. Newspapers may have lost some of their luster over the past two decades, but they do reach more than 50 percent of U.S. households, representing more than 150 million adults. And, as mentioned earlier, the newspaper is still an excellent medium for retailers targeting local geographic markets.

8. *Facts about Newspapers 1995* (Reston, Va.: Newspaper Association of America, 1995), 4.

But broad reach isn't the only attractive feature of newspapers as a medium. Newspapers offer other advantages to advertisers:

- *Geographic selectivity.* Daily newspapers in cities and towns across the United States offer advertisers the opportunity to reach a well-defined geographic target audience. Some newspapers are beginning to run zoned editions, which target even more narrow geographic areas within a metropolitan market. Zoned editions are typically used by merchants doing business in the local area; national marketers such as Kellogg and Colgate can use the paper carrier to deliver free samples to these zoned areas.
- *Timeliness.* The newspaper is one of the most timely of the major media. Because of the short time needed for producing a typical newspaper ad and the regularity of daily publication, the newspaper allows advertisers to reach audiences in a timely way. This doesn't mean on just a daily basis. Newspaper ads can take advantage of special events or a unique occurrence in a community.
- *Creative opportunities.* While the newspaper page does not offer the breadth of creative options available in the broadcast media, there are things advertisers can do in a newspaper that represent important creative opportunities. Since the newspaper page offers a large and relatively inexpensive format, advertisers can provide a lot of information to the target audience at relatively low cost. This is important for products or services with extensive or complex features that may need lengthy and detailed copy. The Tire America ad in Exhibit 15.5 needs just such a large format to provide detail about tire sizes and prices.
- *Credibility.* Newspapers still benefit from the perception that "if it's in the paper it must be the truth." This credibility element played a role in Microsoft's decision to use the *Wall Street Journal* and *New York Times* for its "Five Nines" campaign, which touted that Windows 2000 servers stay up and running 99.999% of the time.[9]
- *Audience interest.* Newspaper readers are truly interested in the information they are reading. While overall readership may be down in the United States, those readers that remain are loyal and interested. Many readers buy the newspaper specifically to see what's on sale at stores in the local area, making this an ideal environment for local merchants. And newspapers are the primary medium for local classified advertising despite an early concern that the Internet would cut deeply into classified revenue, as the E-Commerce box on page 530 suggests.
- *Cost.* In terms of both production and space, newspapers offer a low-cost alternative to advertisers. The cost per contact may be higher than with television and radio options, but the absolute cost for placing a black-and-white ad is still within reach of even a small advertising budget.

Disadvantages of Newspapers. Newspapers offer advertisers many good opportunities. Like every other media option, however, newspapers have some significant disadvantages.

- *Limited segmentation.* While newspapers can achieve good geographic selectivity, the ability to target a specific audience ends there. Newspaper circulation simply cuts across too broad an economic, social, and demographic audience to allow the isolation of specific targets. The placement of ads within certain sections can achieve minimal targeting by gender, but even this effort is somewhat fruitless. Some newspapers are developing special sections to enhance their segmentation capabilities such as the kids' section shown in Exhibit 15.6. Many papers are developing sections on e-business and film reviews to target specific audiences.[10] In addition, more and more newspapers are being published to serve specific ethnic groups, which is another form of segmentation.

9. Tobi Elkin, "Microsoft Blitz Pushes Server," *Advertising Age,* January 1, 2000, 29.
10. Jon Fine, "Tribute Seeks National Ads with 3 New Special Sections," *Advertising Age,* October 9, 2000, 42.

EXHIBIT 15.5

The newspaper medium offers a large format for advertisers. This is important when an advertiser needs space to provide the target audience with extensive information, as Tire America has done with this ad featuring tire sizes and prices.

Courtesy of the Peoria Journal Star

EXHIBIT 15.6

Many newspapers are trying to increase their target selectivity by developing special sections for advertisers, as in this kids' section.

- *Creative constraints.* The opportunities for creative executions in newspapers are certainly outweighed by the creative constraints. First, newspapers have poor reproduction quality. Led by *USA Today,* most newspapers now print some of their pages in color. But even the color reproduction does not enhance the look of most products. For advertisers whose product images depend on accurate, high-quality reproduction (color or not), newspapers simply have severe limitations compared to other media options. Second, newspapers are a unidimensional medium—no sound, no action. For products that demand a broad creative execution, this medium is not the best choice.
- *Cluttered environment.* The average newspaper is filled with headlines, subheads, photos, and announcements—not to mention news stories. This presents a terribly cluttered environment for an advertisement. To make things worse, most advertisers in a product category try to use the same sections to target audiences. For example, all the home equity loan and financial services ads are in the business section, and all the women's clothing ads are in the local section.
- *Short life.* In most U.S. households, newspapers are read quickly and then discarded (or, hopefully, stacked in the recycling pile). The only way advertisers can

overcome this limitation is to buy several insertions in each daily issue, buy space several times during the week, or both. In this way, even if a reader doesn't spend much time with the newspaper, at least multiple exposures are a possibility.

The newspaper has creative limitations, but what the average newspaper does, it does well. If an advertiser wants to reach a local audience with a simple black-and-white ad in a timely manner, then the newspaper is the superior choice.

Types of Newspapers. All newspapers enjoy the same advantages and suffer from the same limitations to one degree or another. But there are different types of newspapers from which advertisers can choose. Newspapers are categorized by target audience, geographic coverage, and frequency of publication.

- *Target audience.* Newspapers can be classified by the target audience they reach. The five primary types of newspapers serving different target audiences are general-population newspapers, business newspapers, ethnic newspapers, gay and lesbian newspapers, and the alternative press. **General-population newspapers** serve local communities and report news of interest to the local population. Newspapers such as the *Kansas City Star,* the *Dayton Daily News,* and the *Columbus Dispatch* are examples. **Business newspapers** such as the *Wall Street Journal, Investor's Business Daily* (United States), and the *Financial Times* (United Kingdom) serve a specialized business audience. **Ethnic newspapers** that target specific ethnic groups are growing in popularity. Most of these newspapers are published weekly. The *New York Amsterdam News* and the *Michigan Chronicle* are two of the more than 200 newspapers in the United States that serve African-American communities. The Hispanic community in the United States has more than 300 newspapers. One of the most prominent is *El Diario de las Americas* in Miami. **Gay and lesbian newspapers** exist in most major (and many smaller) markets. Readership typically extends considerably beyond gay and lesbian readers. So-called **alternative press newspapers,** such as the *L.A. Weekly* (www.laweekly.com), the *Austin Chronicle* (www.auschron.com/current/), and the *Octopus* of Champaign-Urbana, Illinois

E-COMMERCE

Myth: The Web Will Dominate Classified Advertising. Reality: Newspapers Don't Have to Worry.

Classified advertising is the lifeblood of local newspapers. It often represents 30 to 40 percent of a newspaper's total revenues. In addition, classified ads are the fastest-growing area of newspaper advertising, adding about $1 billion in additional revenue a year to newspaper coffers. Currently, classifieds bring in about $18.7 billion a year, according to the Newspaper Association of America.

It is no wonder that when big portals like Yahoo!, Microsoft, and America Online began creating local sites to compete with newspapers, there was serious concern that Web-based classifieds would seriously cut into newspaper revenues. After all, wasn't the Web a better and more accessible venue for classified ads? A consumer-seller could submit a photo of the house or the bike or the dog that was for sale. This is a much enhanced presentation over the itty-bitty box with the three terse lines of description. Similarly, the consumer-buyer could come to the classified advertising environment anytime—no need to trek out onto the lawn to grab the paper that never quite seems to make it to front porch. It seemed like such a much better idea than newspaper-based classifieds that dot-com companies such as Monster.com (help wanted/employees available) and autobytel.com (automobile classifieds) were attracting outside investors and establishing a foothold online by offering classified free of charge supported by banner ads. How could newspapers ever compete with a better presentation format *and* free advertising space?

Well, the prospect of the Web swallowing up all the classified advertising dollars never turned into a reality. While the Net classifieds have had some success at the expense of newspapers, the best estimate is that the Web-based classifieds have merely slowed traditional classified advertising growth to about 2 percent per year as opposed to the 6 to 8 percent historical rate. Local newspapers have combatted the Web attack by providing their own localized version of ads on the Internet. But in the end, interactive media analysts suggest that neither the big Internet companies such as Yahoo! or the more specialized competitors such as Monster.com will ever displace newspapers in their home markets. As one analyst put it, "In the long term, these guys don't have the roots in the local community. Newspapers do."

Source: Dan Mitchell, "Hello, Webmaster—Get Me Rewrite," *Business 2.0,* March 6, 2001, 42.

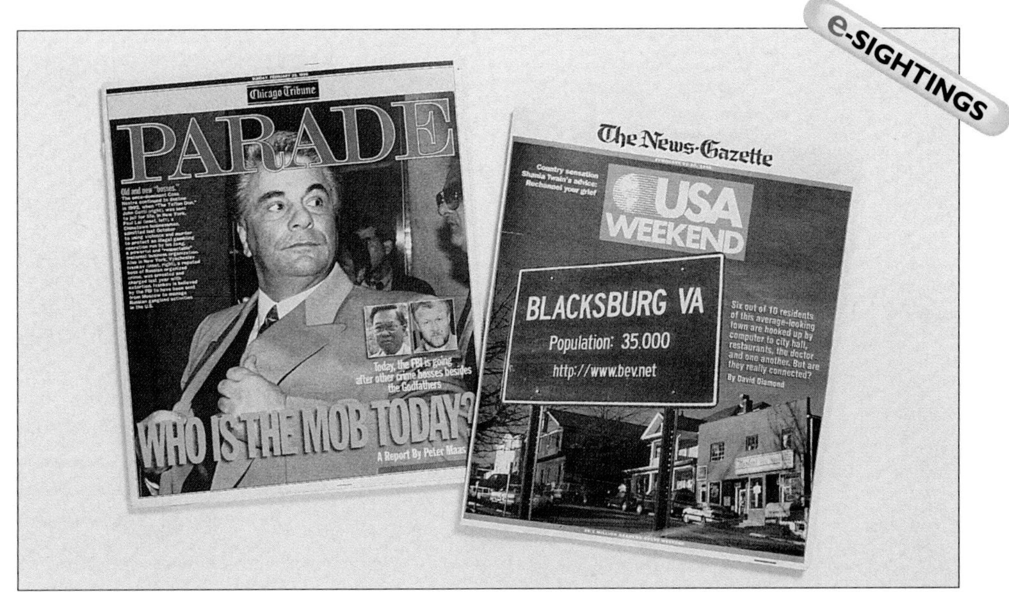

EXHIBIT 15.7

Sunday supplements such as Parade *magazine* (www.parade.com) *and* USA Weekend (www.usaweekend.com) *offer advertisers another alternative for placing newspaper ads. How do these differ from alternative press weeklies such as the* Village Voice (www.villagevoice.com)*? Does* USA Weekend*'s Web site offer any features that attract repeat visits from readers, thus increasing the life of the weekly publication?*

(www.cuoctopus.com), are very viable vehicles for reaching typically young and entertainment-oriented audiences.

- *Geographic coverage.* As noted earlier, the vast majority of newspapers are distributed in a relatively small geographic area—either a large metropolitan area or a state. Newspapers such as the *Tulsa World* and the *Atlanta Journal,* with circulations of 170,000 and 140,000, respectively, serve a local geographic area. The other type of newspaper in the United States is a national newspaper. *USA Today* and the *Wall Street Journal* were, from their inception, designed to be distributed nationally, and each currently has a circulation of about 1.8 million. The *New York Times* and the *Los Angeles Times,* each with a circulation of about 1.1 million, have evolved into national newspapers.[11]
- *Frequency of publication.* The majority of newspapers in the United States are called *dailies* because they are published each day of the week, including Sunday. There are a smaller number of *weeklies,* and these tend to serve smaller towns or rural communities. Finally, another alternative for advertisers is the Sunday supplement, which is published only on Sunday and is usually delivered along with the Sunday edition of a local newspaper. The most widely distributed Sunday supplements—*Parade* magazine and *USA Weekend*—are illustrated in Exhibit 15.7.

Categories of Newspaper Advertising. Just as there are categories of newspapers, there are categories of newspaper advertising: display advertising, inserts, and classified advertising.

- *Display advertising.* Advertisers of goods and services rely most on display advertising. **Display advertising** in newspapers includes the standard components of a print ad—headline, body copy, and often an illustration—to set it off from the news content of the paper. An important form of display advertising is co-op advertising sponsored by manufacturers. In **co-op advertising,** a manufacturer pays part of the media bill when a local merchant features the manufacturer's brand in advertising. Co-op advertising can be done on a national scale as well. (See Exhibit 15.8.) Intel invests heavily in co-op advertising with PC manufacturers who feature the "Intel Inside" logo in their ads.

11. Jon Fine, "Daily papers see circ. decline," *Advertising Age,* May 21, 2001, S37.

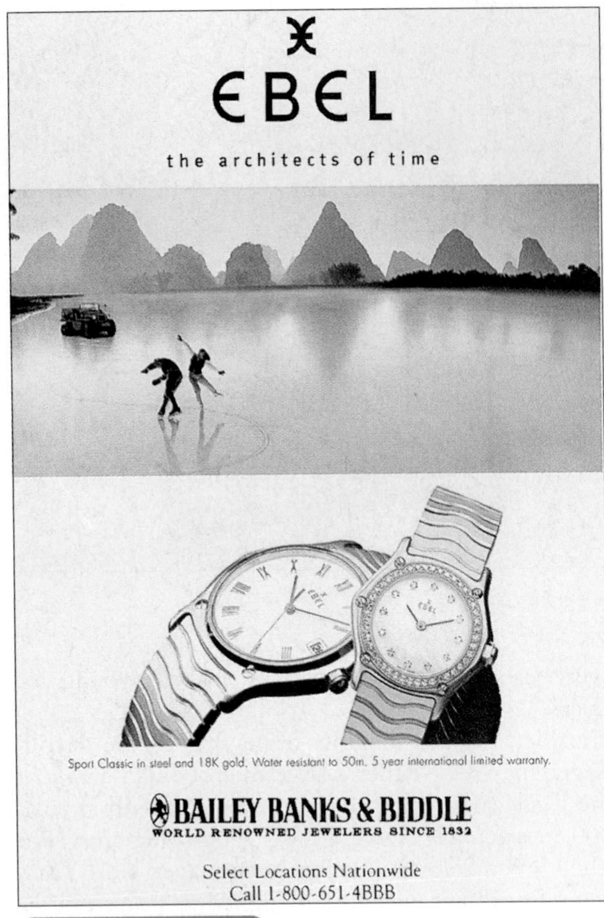

EXHIBIT 15.8

Retailers who feature a particular brand can receive co-op advertising money for media placement. www.ebel.com

EXHIBIT 15.9

This example of a free-standing insert (FSI) from Pizza Hut shows how an ad can be delivered via a newspaper distribution system without having to become part of the paper itself. What are the production and attention-getting advantages that this insert provides? www.pizzahut.com

- *Inserts.* There are two types of insert advertisements. Inserts do not appear on the printed newspaper page but rather are folded into the newspaper before distribution. An advertiser can use a **preprinted insert,** which is an advertisement delivered to the newspaper fully printed and ready for insertion into the newspaper. The second type of insert ad is a **free-standing insert (FSI),** which contains cents-off coupons for a variety of products and is typically delivered with Sunday newspapers. The Pizza Hut ad in Exhibit 15.9 is part of a free-standing insert.
- *Classified advertising.* **Classified advertising** is newspaper advertising that appears as all-copy messages under categories such as sporting goods, employment, and automobiles. Many classified ads are taken out by individuals, but real estate firms, automobile dealers, and construction firms also buy classified advertising.

Costs and Buying Procedures for Newspaper Advertising. When an advertiser wishes to place advertising in a newspaper, the first step is to obtain a rate card from the newspaper. A **rate card** contains information on costs, closing times (when ads have to be submitted), specifications for submitting an ad, and special pages or features available in the newspaper. The rate card also summarizes the circulation for the designated market area and any circulation outside the designated area.

The cost of a newspaper ad depends on how large the advertisement is, whether it is black-and-white or color, how large the total audience is, and whether the newspaper has local or national coverage. Advertising space is sold in newspapers by the **column inch,** which is a unit of space one inch deep by one column wide. Each column is 2$\frac{1}{16}$ inches wide. Most newspapers have adopted the **standard advertising unit (SAU)** system for selling ad space, which defines unit sizes for advertisements. There are 57 defined SAU sizes for advertisements in the system, so that advertisers can prepare ads to fit one of the sizes. Many newspapers offer a volume discount to advertisers who buy more than one ad in an issue or buy multiple ads over some time period.

When an advertiser buys space on a **run-of-paper (ROP)** basis, which is also referred to as a *run-of-press basis,* the ad may appear anywhere, on any page in the paper. A higher rate is charged for **preferred position,** in which the ad is placed in a specific section of the paper. **Full position** places an ad near the top of a page or in the middle of editorial material.

Measuring Newspaper Audiences. There are several different dimensions to measuring newspaper audiences. The reach of a newspaper is reported as the newspaper's circulation. **Circulation** is the number of newspapers distributed each day (for daily newspapers) or each week (for weekly publications). **Paid circulation** reports the number of copies sold through subscriptions and newsstand distribution. **Controlled circulation** refers to the number of copies of the newspaper that are given away free. The Audit Bureau of Circulations (ABC) is an independent organization that verifies the actual circulation of newspapers.

Rates for newspaper advertising are not based solely on circulation numbers, however. The Newspaper Association of America estimates that 2.28 people read each copy of a daily newspaper distributed in the United States. **Readership** of a newspaper is a measure of the circulation multiplied by the number of readers of a copy. This number, of course, is much higher than the circulation number and provides a total audience figure on which advertisers base advertising rates. To give you some idea of costs, a full-page four-color ad in *USA Today* costs about $100,000, and a full-page black-and-white ad in the *Wall Street Journal* costs about $175,000. A full-page ad in your local newspaper is, of course, considerably less—probably around $10,000 to $15,000 for a good-sized city and much less for small-town newspapers. Remember, though, that few advertisers, national or local, purchase an entire page.

The Future of Newspapers. At the outset of this chapter, we talked about the fact that newspaper circulation has been in a long, sustained downward trend, and that readership is following the same pattern. To survive as a viable advertising medium, newspapers will have to evolve with the demands of both audiences and advertisers, who provide them with the majority of their revenue. To compete in the future as a viable advertising medium, newspapers will have to do the following:

- Continue to provide in-depth coverage of issues that focus on the local community.
- Increase coverage of national and international news.
- Provide follow-up reports of news stories.
- Maintain and expand their role as the best local source for consumers to find specific information on advertised product features, availability, and prices.
- Provide the option of shopping through an online newspaper computer service.
- Become more mainstream in integrated brand promotions particularly relating to new media (see Exhibit 15.10).

2 **Magazines.** The marketing director for Schwinn Cycling & Fitness wanted to resurrect the company's bicycle division. Schwinn had been pummeled by worthy competitors such as Trek and Specialized, and he felt certain that one of the underlying problems was that the image of the Schwinn brand was outdated. To begin solving this image problem, the marketing director first instructed the firm's advertising agency to

EXHIBIT 15.10

The future of newspapers will be greatly enhanced if the medium adapts to the demands of a new media environment and particularly if newspapers can become part of the integrated brand promotion process that includes new media. This ad touts just such a role for newspapers in IBP.
www.nnn-naa.com

develop a $10 million magazine campaign. One of Schwinn's ads from this campaign is shown in Exhibit 15.11. The ads were placed in specialty biking magazines and were aimed at mountain-biking and race-biking enthusiasts. Schwinn created an integrated brand promotion supporting the magazine campaign with event sponsorships and interactive mall kiosks. While Schwinn is still a distant third in the U.S. bike market, sales climbed 18.4 percent during the restructured IBP period.

Schwinn's emphasis on magazine advertising was part of an effort to upgrade the brand image and turned out to be an excellent strategic decision. Magazines, more than any other media option, provide advertisers with a choice of highly selective alternatives that offer a wide variety of formats and contexts. Magazines are a highly valued media choice with advertisers spending over $3 billion for advertising space in magazines annually.[12] The top 10 magazines in the United States, based on circulation, are listed in Exhibit 15.12. This list suggests the diversity of magazines as a media class. Exhibit 15.13 shows the top 10 advertisers in magazines.

Like newspapers, magazines have advantages and disadvantages, come in different types, offer various ad costs and buying procedures, and measure their audiences in specific ways. We will consider these issues now.

Advantages of Magazines. Magazines have many advantages relative to newspapers. These advantages make them more than just an ideal print medium—many analysts conclude that magazines are, in many ways, superior to even broadcast media alternatives.

- *Audience selectivity.* The overwhelming advantage of magazines relative to other media—print or broadcast—is the ability of magazines to attract, and therefore target, a highly selective audience. This selectivity can be based on demographics (*Woman's Day*), lifestyle (*Muscle & Fitness*), or special interests (*Business 2.0*), as shown in Exhibit 15.14. The audience segment can be narrowly defined, as is the one that reads *Modern Bride,* or it may cut across a variety of interests, as does the one for *Newsweek.* Magazines also offer geographic selectivity on a regional basis, as does *Southern Living* or city magazines, such as *Atlanta,* which highlight happenings in major metropolitan areas. Also, large national publications have multiple editions for advertisers to choose from. *Better Homes & Gardens* has 85 different specific market editions, and *Time* offers advertisers a different edition for each of the 50 states. Recently, publishers of leading women's magazines, such as *Elle* and *Cosmopolitan,* have discovered that global expansion to places such as Russia and Asia is facilitated by the ability of magazines to be tightly targeted.[13]
- *Audience interest.* Perhaps more than any other medium, magazines attract an audience because of content. While television programming can attract audiences through interest as well, magazines have the additional advantage of voluntary exposure to the advertising. Golfers are interested in golf equipment like

12. R. Craig Endicott, "Magazine 300," *Advertising Age,* June 18, 2001, S1.
13. Claire Wilson and Rebecca A. Fannin, "Magazine Marathon," *Ad Age International,* May 1997, 116.

EXHIBIT 15.11

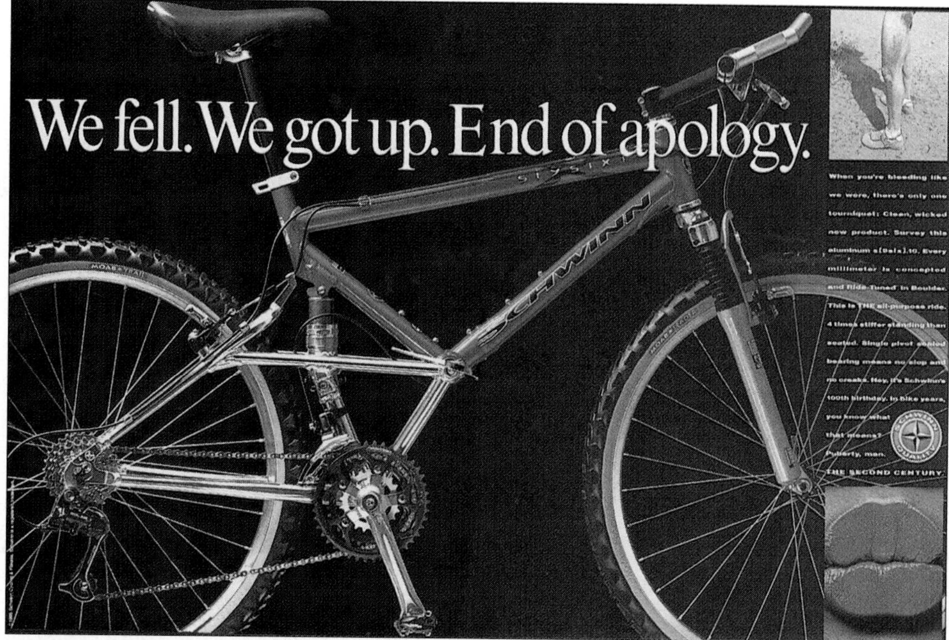

Schwinn Cycling & Fitness relied on magazine ads like this one to upgrade its brand image and regain lost market share from Trek and Specialized.
www.schwinn.com

EXHIBIT 15.12

Top 10 magazines by circulation for 2000.

Rank	Publication	Circulation	% Change
1	*Modern Maturity*	20,963,870	2.4
2	*Reader's Digest*	12,566,047	0.1
3	*TV Guide*	9,948,792	−10.5
4	*National Geographic*	7,828,642	−8.1
5	*Better Homes & Gardens*	7,617,985	0.1
6	*Family Circle*	5,002,042	0.0
7	*Good Housekeeping*	4,558,524	0.2
8	*Woman's Day*	4,244,383	−0.9
9	*Ladies' Home Journal*	4,101,550	−9.4
10	*Time*	4,056,150	−1.6

Source: *Ad Age Data Place*, www.Adage.com. Accessed April 15, 2001.

that shown in Exhibit 15.15 and advertised in *Golf Digest,* while auto enthusiasts find the auto accessory equipment advertised in *Car and Driver* appealing.

- *Creative opportunities.* Magazines offer a wide range of creative opportunities. Because of the ability to vary the size of an ad, use color, use white space, and play off the special interests of the audience, magazines represent a favorable creative environment. Also, because the paper quality of most magazines is quite high, color reproduction can be outstanding—another creative opportunity. In an attempt to expand the creative environment even further, some advertisers have tried various other creative techniques: pop-up ads, scratch-and-sniff ads, ads with perfume scent strips, and even ads with small computer chips that have flashing lights and play music. The Clarins ad in Exhibit 15.16 shows how an advertiser can take advantage of the creative opportunities offered by magazines.
- *Long life.* Many magazines are saved issue-to-issue by their subscribers. This means that, unlike newspapers, a magazine can be reexamined over a week or a month. Some magazines are saved for long periods for future reference, such as

EXHIBIT 15.13

Top 10 magazine advertisers (U.S. dollars in millions).

		Magazine Ad Spending		
Rank	**Advertiser**	**2000**	**1999**	**% Change**
1	Philip Morris Cos.	$592.8	$479.2	23.7
2	General Motors Corp.	485.6	502.5	–3.4
3	Procter & Gamble Co.	448.6	462.9	–3.1
4	AOL Time Warner	351.3	293.4	19.7
5	DaimlerChrysler	300.1	328.6	–8.6
6	Ford Motor Co.	250.0	334.4	–25.2
7	Toyota Motor Corp.	194.8	183.2	6.4
8	L'Oreal	188.8	136.9	37.7
9	Pfizer	181.9	171.9	28.8
10	Johnson & Johnson	171.6	153.4	11.9

Source: *Advertising Age*, September 24, 2001, S16. Reprinted with permission from the September 24, 2001, issue of *Advertising Age*. Copyright © Crain Communications Inc. 2001.

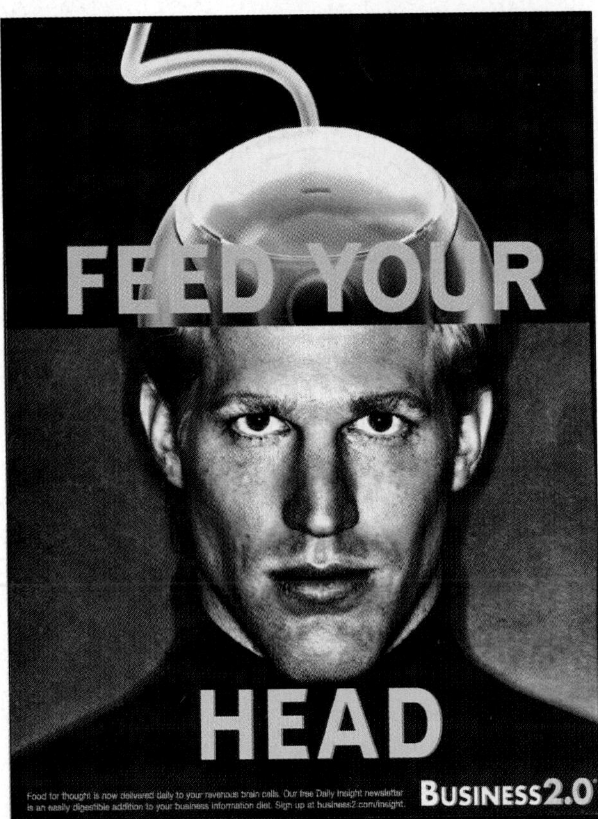

EXHIBIT 15.14

One distinct advantage of magazines over most other media options is the ability to attract and target a highly selective audience. Magazines such as Business 2.0 *attract an audience based on special interests and activities—in this case, readers interested in high-tech and Internet business issues.*

e-SIGHTINGS

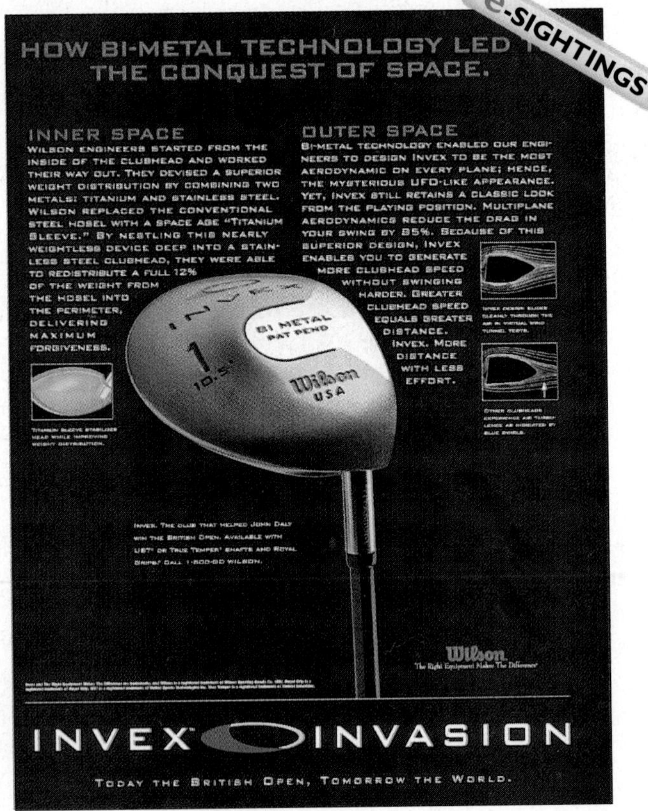

EXHIBIT 15.15

Magazines can attract readers with specialized content, and in so doing, they attract advertisers. This ad by Wilson (www.wilsonsports.com) appeared in Golf Digest. *Does* Golf Digest*'s site (www.golfdigest.com) follow the same monthly publication cycle as the magazine? Do advertisers benefit from the digital versions of popular magazines? What useful interactive features does* Golf Digest *offer to golf enthusiasts? What does the magazine hope to accomplish with such interactive site features?*

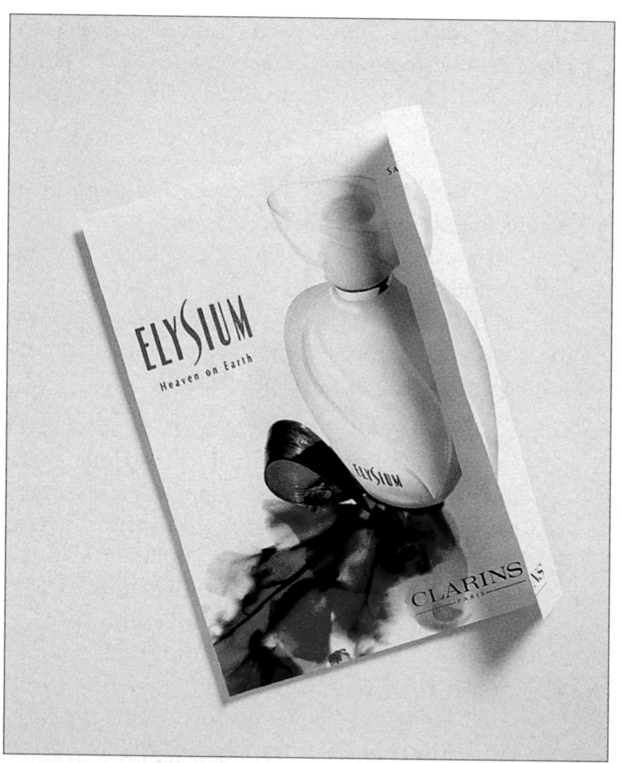

EXHIBIT 15.16

Magazines offer unique creative opportunities to advertisers. Perfume marketers such as Clarins include scent strips in the magazine ads for consumers to sample.

Architectural Digest, National Geographic, and *Travel & Leisure.* In addition to multiple subscriber exposure, this long life increases the chance of pass-along readership as people visit the subscriber's home (or professional offices) and look at magazines.

Many magazines are experiencing some difficulty in growing both circulation and revenue. General-interest publications such as *Time* and *Good Housekeeping* are experiencing little growth. Specialty magazines with narrow target audiences, such as *Maxim* and *InStyle,* are showing solid gains, however.[14] It would appear that the main advantage of magazines to appeal to a selective audience is translating into market success.

Disadvantages of Magazines. The disadvantages of magazines as a media choice have to do with their being too selective in their reach and with the recent proliferation of magazines.

- *Limited reach and frequency.* The tremendous advantage of selectivity discussed in the previous section actually creates a limitation for magazines. The more narrowly defined the interest group, the less overall reach a magazine will have.

Since most magazines are published monthly or perhaps every two weeks, there is little chance for an advertiser to achieve frequent exposure using a single magazine. To overcome this limitation, advertisers often use several magazines targeted at the same audience. For example, many readers of *Better Homes & Gardens* may also be readers of *Architectural Digest.* By placing ads in both publications, an advertiser can increase both reach and frequency within a targeted audience.

- *Clutter.* Magazines are not quite as cluttered as newspapers, but they still represent a fairly difficult context for message delivery. The average magazine is about half editorial and entertainment content and half advertising material, but some highly specialized magazines can contain as much as 80 percent advertising. And this advertising, given the narrowly defined audiences, tends to be for brands in direct competition with each other. In addition to this clutter, there is another sort of clutter that has recently begun to plague magazines. As soon as a new market segment is recognized, there is a flood of "me-too" magazines. This may be good in terms of coverage, but it may devalue individual ads and the vehicles in which they appear.
- *Long lead times.* Advertisers are required to submit their ads as much as 90 days in advance of the date of publication. If the submission date is missed, there can be as much as a full month's delay in placing the next ad. And once an ad is submitted, it cannot be changed during that 90-day period, even if some significant event alters the communications environment.
- *Cost.* While the cost per contact in magazines is not nearly as high as in some media (direct mail in particular), it is more expensive than most newspaper space, and many times the cost per contact in the broadcast media. The absolute cost for a single insertion can be prohibitive. For magazines with large circulation,

14. Jon Fine, "New ABC Report on Six-Month Circ. Shows Mixed Bag," *Advertising Age,* August 21, 2000, 33.

such as *Modern Maturity* (20 million) and *Good Housekeeping* (5 million), the cost for a one-time four-color ad runs from $100,000 to about $250,000.

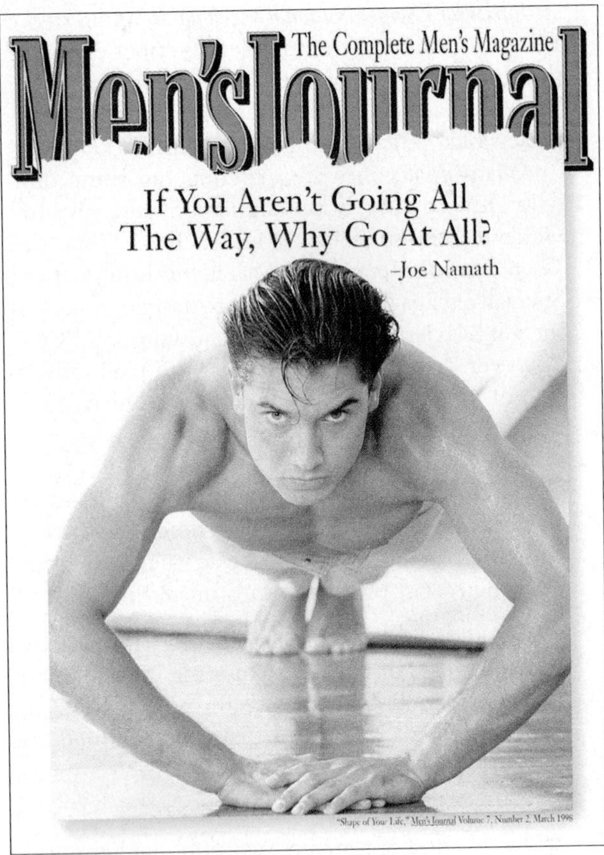

EXHIBIT 15.17

In the consumer magazine category, publishers try to appeal to target audiences' special interests. Men's Journal *deals with contemporary issues facing men in health, fitness, and career challenges.*
www.mensjournal.com

Types of Magazines. The magazine medium is highly fragmented, with more than 12,000 magazine titles published annually in the United States and literally hundreds of titles introduced every year. A useful classification scheme for magazines is to categorize them by major target audience: consumer, business, and farm publications.

- *Consumer publications.* Magazines that appeal to consumer interests run the gamut from international news to sports, education, age-group information, and hobbies. These include magazines written specifically for men (*Men's Journal*—see Exhibit 15.17), women (*Woman's Day*), and ethnic groups (*Ebony*). Many new consumer magazines appeal to the lifestyle changes of the 1980s and 1990s: *New Woman, Men's Health.* Advertisers invested more than $13 billion in advertising in consumer magazines in 2001.[15] The top five magazines in this category are listed in Exhibit 15.18.
- *Business publications.* Business magazines come in many different forms. Each major industry has a trade publication, such as *InfoWorld* in the computer industry, that highlights events and issues in that industry. Professional publications are written for doctors, lawyers, accountants, and other professional groups. *American Family Physician* publishes articles for family practitioners and carries advertising from many pharmaceutical manufacturers. General-interest business magazines such as *Fortune* and *Forbes* cut across all trades, industries, and professions. The leading business magazine categories are listed in Exhibit 15.19.
- *Farm publications.* The three major farm publications in the United States and their approximate paid circulations are *Farm Journal* (197,000), *Successful Farming* (476,000), and *Progressive Farmer* (286,000). These magazines provide technical information about farming techniques as well as business management articles to improve farmers' profitability. In addition to national publications, regional farm magazines and publications focus on specific aspects of the industry.

In this new media environment, it is important to recognize that many consumer and business publications are now available in digital format over the Internet. Magazines that are available electronically have been dubbed "digizines." Over 250 magazines now offer their titles in a digital version. There are several advantages of the digizine format for both the publisher and the subscriber. First, a publisher is often able to tap a different segment—the Internet-savvy user—with an electronic format. Second, the publisher also may realize lower costs in publishing a digizine in that there are no paper costs and distribution costs are greatly reduced. Finally, some advertisers may find the digital version a better environment for advertising than the more cluttered printed version.

15. Cardona, "The Party's Over," 11.

Magazine Category	Total Revenue	Ad Revenue	Ad Revenue 1999–2000 % Change	Top Magazine in Classification
Newsweeklies	$5,490.3	$3,455.4	0.1	*People*
Women's	4,489.9	2,969.6	12.2	*Good Housekeeping*
General editorial	3,308.6	1,977.9	10.3	*Reader's Digest*
Business and finance	2,682.8	2,215.1	27.4	*Business Week*
Home service and home	2,435.0	1,686.7	10.5	*Better Homes & Gardens*

Source: *Advertising Age*, June 18, 2001, S18. Reprinted with permission from the June 18, 2001, issue of *Advertising Age*. Copyright © Crain Communications Inc. 2001.

EXHIBIT 15.18

Top five consumer magazine categories, ranked by revenue, 2000 (U.S. dollars in millions).

Magazine Category	Total Revenue	Ad Revenue	Ad Revenue 1999–2000 % Change	Top Magazine in Classification
Computers/Internet	$2,764.9	$2,455.4	12.0	*PC Magazine*
Business	323.7	285.5	88.6	*Fast Company*
Electronic engineering	318.9	318.6	21.2	*EE Times*
Travel, retail	239.2	237.9	9.0	*Travel Agent*
Medical and surgical	145.5	112.3	1.2	*New England Journal of Medicine*

Source: *Advertising Age*, June 18, 2001, S18. Reprinted with permission from the June 18, 2001, issue of *Advertising Age*. Copyright © Crain Communications Inc. 2001.

EXHIBIT 15.19

Top five business magazine categories, ranked by revenue, 2000 (U.S. dollars in millions).

From the subscriber's standpoint, the digizine is easily accessible through the subscriber's PC, movement through the magazine is facilitated by standard keyword search conventions, and, for the environmentally conscious, no recycling is needed. Finally, for subscribers to magazines that deal with computer or Internet content, the digizine is the ideal and preferred format. Ziff-Davis Publishing discovered that consumers with acute interest in the Internet were far more likely to subscribe to a digital version of the company's *Yahoo! Internet Life* than the traditional print version, with 75 to 80 percent of new subscribers coming from Internet-based subscriptions.[16]

Costs and Buying Procedures for Magazine Advertising. The cost for magazine space varies dramatically. As with newspapers, the size of an ad, its position in a publication, its creative execution (black-and-white or color or any special techniques), and its placement in a regular or special edition of the magazine all affect costs. The main cost, of course, is based on the magazine's circulation. A full-page four-color ad in *Reader's Digest* costs about $150,000; a full-page four-color ad in *People* costs about $106,000; a full-page ad in *Skiing* costs about $25,000; and a full-page ad in *Surreal,* a Gen-X magazine with a paid circulation of 3,000, is only $500.

Each magazine has a rate card that shows the cost for full-page, half-page, two-column, one-column, and half-column ads. A rate card also shows the cost for black-and-white, two-color, and four-color ads. Rate cards for magazines, as with

16. Ann Marie Kerwin, "Internet Life Taps Yahoo! Site for Subscribers," *Advertising Age,* June 15, 1998, 60.

EXHIBIT 15.20

Gatefold ads display extra-wide advertisements, like this one for Lenox dishes. www.lenox.com

newspapers, have been the standard pricing method for many years. In recent years, however, more and more publishers have been willing to negotiate rates and give deep discounts for volume purchases—discounts as large as 30 to 40 percent off the published card rate.[17]

In addition to standard rates, there is an extra charge for a **bleed page.** On a bleed page, the background color of an ad runs to the edge of the page, replacing the standard white border. **Gatefold ads**, or ads that fold out of a magazine to display an extra-wide advertisement, also carry an extra charge. Gatefolds are often used by advertisers on the inside cover of upscale magazines. An example is the ad for dishes and flatware in Exhibit 15.20.

When buying space in a magazine, advertisers must decide among several placement options. A run-of-paper advertisement, as mentioned earlier, can appear anywhere in the magazine, at the discretion of the publisher. The advertiser may pay for several preferred positions, however. **First cover page** is the front cover of a magazine; **second cover page** is the inside front cover; **third cover page** is the inside back cover; and **fourth cover page** is the back cover. When advertisers prepare **double-page spreads**—advertisements that bridge two facing pages—it is important that no headlines or body copy run through the *gutter,* which is the fold between the magazine pages.

Buying procedures for magazine advertising demand that an advertiser follow several guidelines and honor several key dates. A **space contract** establishes a rate for all advertising placed in a publication by an advertiser over a specified period. A **space order,** also referred to as an *insertion order,* is a commitment by an advertiser to advertising space in a particular issue. It is accompanied by production specifications for the ad or ads that will appear in the issue. The dates that an advertiser must be aware of are as follows:

- **Closing date:** The date when production-ready advertising materials must be delivered to a publisher for an ad to make an issue.
- **On-sale date:** The date on which a magazine is issued to subscribers and for newsstand distribution. Most magazines put issues on sale far in advance of the cover date.
- **Cover date:** The date of publication appearing on a magazine.

17. Joe Mandese, "Magazines Cut Deeper into Rates, Despite Ad Gains," *Advertising Age,* October 16, 2000, 1, 22.

Measuring Magazine Audiences. Most magazines base their published advertising rates on **guaranteed circulation,** which is a stated minimum number of copies of a particular issue that will be delivered to readers. This number guarantees for advertisers that they are achieving a certain minimum reach with an ad placement. In addition, publishers estimate **pass-along readership,** which is an additional number of people, other than the original readers, who may see a publication. Advertisers can verify circulation through the Audit Bureau of Circulations, which reports total and state-by-state circulation for magazines, as well as subscriber versus newsstand circulation. When an advertiser wants to go beyond basic circulation numbers, the syndicated magazine research services such as Simmons Market Research Bureau and Mediamark Research can provide additional information. Through personal interviews and respondent-kept diaries, these services provide advertisers with information on reader demographics, media use, and product usage.

The Future of Magazines. Magazines have had a roller-coaster history over the past 10 to 15 years. Currently, revenues and ad pages are up, and advertisers are finding the advantages of magazines well suited to their current needs. Two factors are likely to be major influences on magazines as an advertising medium in the future. First, magazines will, like other media options, have to determine how to adapt to new media options. More than 250 magazines now offer online versions with computer services such as America Online, CompuServe, and Prodigy. As discussed earlier, these electronic versions have several advantages to both the publisher and the subscriber, but it remains to be seen whether advertisers believe there are advantages. To date, these digizines have attracted minimal ad spending. Some analysts feel that for online advertising to be successful, it must be unintrusive. Such ads will have to be interactive, educational, or entertaining and seem as though they are part of the digizine itself. Until online magazine publication proves viable from the standpoint of reach, advertisers are likely to stay with traditional formats.

The second factor affecting the future of magazines is a robust environment for mergers and acquisitions. Recent years have seen dozens of merger and acquisition deals each year in the magazine industry. Buyers are looking for two benefits in acquiring publications: economies of scale in traditional print publication and new media outlets. In the last few years, the pursuit of these advantages has resulted in over $2 billion a year in mergers and acquisitions. The U.S. unit of German publisher Bartelsmann alone invested $600 million in acquiring new titles during 2000.[18]

Television and Radio: Strategic Planning Considerations.

When you say the word *advertising,* the average person thinks of television and radio advertising. It's easy to understand why. Television advertising can be advertising at its very best. With the benefit of sight and sound, color and music, action and special effects, television advertising can be the most powerful advertising of all. It has some other advantages as well. In many parts of the world, particularly in the United States, television is the medium most widely used by consumers for entertainment and information. Radio advertising also has key advantages. The ability to reach consumers in multiple locations and the creative power of radio rank as important communications opportunities. Advertisers readily appreciate the power of television and radio advertising and invest billions of dollars a year in these media.

3 **Television.** To many, television is the medium that defines what advertising is. With its multisensory stimulation, television offers the chance for advertising to be all that it can be. Television presents two extraordinary opportunities to advertisers. First, the diversity

18. Tom Lowry, "How Many Magazines Did We Buy Today?" *Business Week,* January 22, 2001, 98–99.

of communication possibilities allows for outstanding creative expression of a brand's value. Dramatic color, sweeping action, and spectacular sound effects can cast a brand in an exciting and unique light. Second, once this expressive presentation of a brand is prepared, it can be disseminated to millions of consumers, often at a fraction of a penny per contact.

These opportunities have not been lost on advertisers. In the United States in 2001, advertisers invested more than $55 billion in television advertising for media time alone—this does not include the many billions of dollars spent on production costs.[19] To fully appreciate all that television means to advertisers, we need to understand much more about this complex medium.

Television Categories. Without careful evaluation, the natural tendency is to classify television as a single type of broadcast medium. When we turn on the television, we simply decide what program we find interesting and then settle in for some entertainment. The reality is that over the past 15 to 20 years, several distinct versions of television have evolved, from which consumers can choose for entertainment and advertisers can choose for reaching those consumers. There are four different alternatives: network, cable, syndicated, and local television. Exhibit 15.21 shows the spending in these television categories for 2000 and 2001. Notice that while all the options showed solid growth in advertising receipts, the fastest growth by far was in cable television.

Let's examine the nature of each of the four options for television advertising and the growing satellite/closed-circuit option as well.

- *Network television.* **Network television** broadcasts programming over airwaves to affiliate stations across the United States under a contract agreement. Advertisers can buy time within these programs to reach audiences in hundreds of markets. There are currently six major broadcast television networks in the United States. The original big three networks were American Broadcasting Company (ABC, now owned by Disney), the Columbia Broadcasting System (CBS), and the National Broadcasting Company (NBC). The next broadcast company to be added was Fox network. Two additional competitors in network television have recently begun to broadcast. WB, a new network financed by Time Warner (now part of AOL), estimates it will reach about 80 percent of U.S. households. The other new network is United Paramount Network (UPN), which began broadcasting in January 1995. Exhibit 15.22 shows the top 10 advertisers on network television.

  Despite speculation over the last decade that alternative television options (discussed next) would ultimately undermine broadcast television, the broadcast networks still continue to flourish—mostly due to innovative programming. For example, the final episode of *Survivor 2001* on CBS drew an audience of 35.8 million viewers.[20] No other television option gives advertisers that sort of breadth of reach.
- *Cable television.* From its modest beginnings as community antenna television (CATV) in the 1940s, cable television has grown into a worldwide communications force. **Cable television** transmits a wide range of programming to subscribers through wires rather than over airwaves. In the United States, more than 70 million households (nearly 68 percent of all U.S. households) are wired for cable reception and receive on average more than 30 channels of sports, entertainment, news, music video, and home-shopping programming.[21] Cable's power as an advertising option has grown enormously over the past decade as cable's share of the prime time viewing audience has grown.

19. Wayne Friedman, "The Party's Over," *Advertising Age,* January 1, 2001, 10.
20. Associated Press News Release, WSJ.com, accessed May 5, 2001.
21. National Cable & Telecommunications Association, data available at www.ncta.com, accessed May 18, 2001

EXHIBIT 15.21

Spending by advertisers in the four television categories (U.S. dollars in billions).

	Total Measured Advertising Spending		
	2001	2000	% Change
Spot TV	$12.0	$11.9	−1.0
Network TV	15.9	15.7	1.0
Cable TV	10.1	9.0	12.5
Syndicated TV	3.3	3.1	6.0

Source: Wayne Friedman, "The Party's Over," *Advertising Age*, January 1, 2001, 10. Reprinted with permission from the January 1, 2001, issue of *Advertising Age*. Copyright © Crain Communications Inc. 2001.

EXHIBIT 15.22

Top 10 network TV advertisers (U.S. dollars in millions).

		Network TV Ad Spending		
Rank	Advertiser	2000	1999	% Change
1	General Motors	$965.7	$887.4	8.8
2	Philip Morris Corp.	511.5	486.0	5.2
3	Procter & Gamble Co.	495.8	640.4	–22.6
4	Johnson & Johnson	436.4	475.2	–8.2
5	Pfizer	364.8	364.7	0.0
6	Pepsi Co.	338.1	295.6	14.4
7	Walt Disney Co.	317.1	243.1	30.4
8	Unilever	313.5	299.3	4.7
9	AOL Time Warner	307.8	209.2	47.1
10	GlaxoSmithKline	303.9	265.4	14.5

Source: *Advertising Age*, September 24, 2001, S16. Reprinted with permission from the September 24, 2001, issue of *Advertising Age*. Copyright © Crain Communications Inc. 2001.

Aside from more programming on cable, which distinguishes this category of television from the networks, another aspect is the willingness of cable networks to invest in original programming. With the success of programs such as USA network's *La Femme Nikita* and *JAG*, cable networks are investing record dollar amounts in new programs to continue to attract well-defined audiences (see Exhibit 15.23).[22]

- *Syndicated television.* Television syndication is either original programming or programming that first appeared on network television. It is then rebroadcast on either network or cable stations. Syndicated programs provide advertisers with proven programming that typically attracts a well-defined, if not enormous, audience. There are several types of television syndication. **Off-network syndication** refers to programs that were previously run in network prime time. Some of the most popular off-network syndicated shows are *Home Improvement* and *Seinfeld*. **First-run syndication** refers to programs developed specifically for sale to individual stations. The most famous first-run syndication show is *Star Trek: The Next Generation*. **Barter syndication** takes both off-network and first-run syndication shows and offers them free or at a reduced rate to local television stations, with some national advertising presold within the programs. Local stations can then sell the remainder of the time to generate revenues. This option allows

22. Andrew Bowser, "Networks Increase Original Programming," *Advertising Age*, June 8,1998, A4.

David Young-Wolff/Photo Edit

EXHIBIT 15.23

The power and success of cable comes from offering very specific programming that targets and attracts well-defined audiences such as the teens watching this Carson Daly program on MTV (www.mtv.com). *Cable's power as an advertising option has grown enormously over the past decade as cable's share of the prime-time viewing audience has grown. Another example is the Food Network, which offers programming on health and nutrition. What is ESPN Radio* (www.espnradio.com), *and how does the cable network benefit from adding an online Web radio component to its list of media? Does ESPN Radio offer any ad space to advertisers?*

national advertisers to participate in the national syndication market conveniently. Some of the most widely recognized barter syndication shows are *Jeopardy* and *Wheel of Fortune.*

- *Local television.* **Local television** is the programming other than the network broadcast that independent stations and network affiliates offer local audiences. Completely independent stations broadcast old movies, sitcoms, or children's programming. Network affiliates get about 90 hours of programming a week from the major networks, but they are free to broadcast other programming beyond that provided by the network. News, movies, syndicated programs, and community-interest programs typically round out the local television fare.
- *Satellite/Closed-Circuit.* New technology offers another version of television available to advertisers. Programming can now be transmitted to highly segmented audiences via **satellite and closed-circuit** transmission. The best known of these systems is the *CNN Airport Network,* which transmits news and weather programming directly to airport terminals around the world. A growing segment in this area is programming being delivered via satellite to college campuses. CTN (College Television Network) reaches 7 million college students each week through closed-circuit programming delivered by satellite to thousands of TV monitors on 150 college and university campuses.[23]

As you can see, while all television may look the same to the average consumer, advertisers actually have five distinct options to consider. Regardless of which type of television transmission advertisers choose, television offers distinct advantages to advertisers as a way to communicate with target audiences.

Advantages of Television. Throughout the book, we have referred to the unique capability of television as an advertising medium. There must be some very good reasons why advertisers such as AT&T, General Motors, and Procter & Gamble invest hundreds of millions of dollars annually in television advertising. The specific advantages of this medium are as follows:

- *Creative opportunities.* The overriding advantage of television compared to other media is, of course, the ability to send a message using both sight and sound. With recent advances in transmission and reception equipment, households now have brilliantly clear visuals and stereo-enhanced audio to further increase the impact of television advertising. In addition, special effects perfected for films such as *The Matrix* are now making their way into advertising prepared for television.
- *Coverage, reach, and repetition.* Television, in one form or another, reaches more than 98 percent of all households in the United States—an estimated 270 million people. These households represent every demographic, economic, and ethnic

23. Kate Fitzgerald, "Nets Pull Out Stops to Win Campus Crowd," *Advertising Age,* April 16, 2001, S26.

segment in the United States, which allows advertisers to achieve broad coverage. We have also seen that the cable television option provides reach to hundreds of millions of households throughout the world. Further, no other medium allows an advertiser to repeat a message as frequently as television.

- *Cost per contact.* For advertisers that sell to broadly defined mass markets, television offers a cost-effective way to reach millions of members of a target audience. The average prime-time television program reaches 11 million households, and top-rated shows can reach more than 20 million households. This brings an advertiser's cost-per-contact figure down to an amount unmatched by any other media option—literally fractions of a penny per contact.
- *Audience selectivity.* Television programmers are doing a better job of developing shows that attract well-defined target audiences. **Narrowcasting** is the development and delivery of specialized programming to well-defined audiences. Cable television is far and away the most selective television option. Cable provides not only well-defined programming, but also entire networks—such as MTV and ESPN—built around the concept of attracting selective audiences. The ability to narrowcast is enhanced ever further when cable is combined with other media, as the IBP box highlights.

IBP

Using Cable (and the Web) to Reach Tight Markets

The discussion of cable broadcast in the chapter highlights that one of the key advantages of cable is the ability to reach narrowly defined target segments. There are several other advantages of cable with respect to such narrowcasting, including combining cable with Web placement to achieve an integrated brand promotion effect. Overall, the key advantages of cable, including the advantage of combining cable with the Web, include the following:

- *The expanded reach of cable.* Cable's growing appeal is growing among key demographic groups such as teens who spend more time watching cable than broadcast television. Overall, cable now reaches nearly 85 percent of all U.S. households.
- *The growing appeal of cable.* Consumers are highly favorable toward cable as a medium. In a recent survey of consumer perceptions of quality across major media (TV, radio, magazines, and newspapers), cable ranked first in 15 of 25 ratings while broadcast television only ranked first in two categories.
- *Minimal waste.* Cable is much more efficient in reaching target markets than broadcast television. Viewers have more choices and those more precisely defined choices attract a more well defined demographic, psychographic, and geographic audience than broadcast television.
- *Integrated brand promotion.* For advertisers who want to add new media options to the media mix, cable offers an interesting combination with the Internet. Cable offers many branded Web sites. In fact, cable branded Web sites attract more than 60 percent of the audience that is attracted to media-affiliated Web sites.

Source: Joe Ostrow, "Cable Exec. Cites Value in Tight Market," *Advertising Age*, April 16, 2001, S26.

Disadvantages of Television.

Television has great capabilities as an advertising medium, but it is not without limitations. Some of these limitations are serious enough to significantly detract from the power of television advertising.

- *Fleeting message.* One problem with the sight and sound of a television advertisement is that it is gone in an instant. The fleeting nature of a television message, as opposed to a print ad (which a receiver can contemplate), makes message impact difficult. Some advertisers invest huge amounts of money in the production of television ads to overcome this disadvantage.
- *High absolute cost.* While the cost per contact of television advertising is the best of all media, the absolute cost may be the worst. The average cost of airtime for a single 30-second television spot during prime time is just over $200,000, with the most popular shows such as *ER* and *Friends* commanding up to $640,000 for a 30-second spot.[24] In addition, the average cost of producing a quality 30-second

24. Joe Mandese, "ER tops price charts, Regis wears the crown," *Advertising Age,* October 2, 2000, A1, A24.

television spot is around $200,000 to $300,000. These costs make television advertising prohibitively expensive for many advertisers. Of course, large, national consumer products companies—for which television advertising is best suited anyway—find the absolute cost acceptable for the coverage, reach, and repetition advantages discussed earlier.

- *Poor geographic selectivity.* While programming can be developed to attract specific audiences, program transmission cannot target geographic areas nearly as well. For a national advertiser that wants to target a city market, the reach of a television broadcast is too broad. Similarly, for a local retailer that wants to use television for reaching local segments, the television transmission is likely to reach a several-hundred-mile radius—which will increase the advertiser's cost with little likelihood of drawing patrons.
- *Poor audience attitude and attentiveness.* Since the inception of television advertising, consumers have bemoaned the intrusive nature of the commercials. Just when a movie is reaching its thrilling conclusion—on come the ads. The involuntary and frequent intrusion of advertisements on television has made television advertising the most distrusted form of advertising among consumers.

  Along with—and perhaps as a result of—this generally bad attitude toward television advertising, consumers have developed ways of avoiding exposure. Making a trip to the refrigerator or conversing with fellow viewers are the preferred low-tech ways to avoid exposure. On the high-tech side, **channel grazing,** or using a remote control to monitor programming on other channels while an advertisement is being broadcast, is the favorite way to avoid commercials. When programs have been videotaped for later viewing, zapping and zipping are common avoidance techniques. **Zapping** is the process of eliminating ads altogether from videotaped programs. **Zipping** is the process of fast-forwarding through advertisements contained in videotaped programs.

  New technology has created yet another potential method for avoiding advertising—and this development has advertisers greatly concerned. The problems centers on the so-called "V-chip." The **V-chip** is a device that can block television programming based on the newly developed program rating system. It was developed as a way for parents to block programming that they do not want their children to see. While that was the original and intended use for the V-chip, the technology can be easily adapted to block advertisements as well. Two manufacturers, RCA and Panasonic, say they want to build television sets with this sort of technology. Advertisers and broadcasters, of course, are challenging the rights of these manufacturers to build such sets. The consequences of sets with V-chips that block ads could be devastating to advertising revenues.
- *Clutter.* All the advantages of television as an advertising medium have created one significant disadvantage: clutter. The major television networks run about 13 minutes of advertising during each hour of prime-time programming, and cable broadcasts carry about 17 minutes of advertising per hour. A communications environment cluttered with advertising can cause viewers to invoke various information overload defenses, as we discussed in Chapter 5.

Buying Procedures for Television Advertising. Discussions in Chapter 13 as well as in this chapter have identified the costs associated with television advertising from both a production and a space standpoint. Here we will concentrate on the issue of buying time on television. Advertisers buy time for television advertising through sponsorship, participation, and spot advertising.

- *Sponsorship.* In a **sponsorship** arrangement, an advertiser agrees to pay for the production of a television program and for most (and often all) of the advertising that appears in the program. Sponsorship is not nearly as popular today as it

EXHIBIT 15.24

Television broadcast dayparts (in Eastern time zone segments).

Morning	7:00 A.M. to 9:00 A.M., Monday through Friday
Daytime	9:00 A.M. to 4:30 P.M., Monday through Friday
Early fringe	4:30 P.M. to 7:30 P.M., Monday through Friday
Prime-time access	7:30 P.M. to 8:00 P.M., Sunday through Saturday
Prime time	8:00 P.M. to 11:00 P.M., Monday through Saturday 7:00 P.M. to 11:00 P.M., Sunday
Late news	11:00 P.M. to 11:30 P.M., Monday through Friday
Late fringe	11:30 P.M. to 1:00 A.M., Monday through Friday

was in the early days of network television. Contemporary sponsorship agreements have attracted big-name companies such as AT&T and IBM, who often sponsor sporting events, and Hallmark, known for its sponsorship of dramatic series.

- *Participation.* The vast majority of advertising time is purchased on a participation basis. **Participation** means that several different advertisers buy commercial time during a specific television program. No single advertiser has a responsibility for the production of the program or a commitment to the program beyond the time contracted for.
- *Spot advertising.* **Spot advertising** refers to all television advertising time purchased from and aired through local television stations. Spot advertising provides national advertisers the opportunity to either adjust advertising messages for different markets or intensify their media schedules in particularly competitive markets. Spot advertising is the primary manner in which local advertisers, such as car dealers, furniture stores, and restaurants, reach their target audiences with television.

A final issue with respect to buying television advertising has to do with the time periods and programs during which the advertising will run. Once an advertiser has determined that sponsorship, participation, or spot advertising (or, more likely, some combination of the last two) meets its needs, the time periods and specific programs must be chosen. Exhibit 15.24 shows the way in which television programming times are broken into **dayparts,** which represent segments of time during a television broadcast day.

The dayparts are important to advertisers because the size and type of audience varies by daypart. Morning audiences tend to be predominantly made up of women and children. The daytime daypart is dominated by women. Prime time has the largest and most diverse audiences. Once dayparts have been evaluated, specific programs within dayparts are chosen. As we have discussed, programs are developed and targeted to specific audiences, and advertisers match their ad buying to the program audience profiles. Let's turn our attention to these television audience issues.

Measuring Television Audiences. Television audience measurements identify the size and composition of audiences for different television programming. Advertisers choose where to buy time in television broadcasts based on these factors. These measures also set the cost for television time. The larger the audience or the more attractive the composition, the more costly the time will be.

The only source for *both* network and local audience information is A. C. Nielsen. Arbitron is another source for network measurement, but it abandoned local measurement in 1993.

The following are brief summaries of the information used to measure television audiences.

- *Television households.* **Television households** is an estimate of the number of households that are in a market and own a television. Since more than 98 percent of all households in the United States own a television, the number of total households and the number of television households are virtually the same, about 101 million. Markets around the world do not have the same level of television penetration.
- *Households using television.* **Households using television (HUT),** also referred to as *sets in use,* is a measure of the number of households tuned to a television program during a particular time period.
- *Program rating.* A **program rating** is the percentage of television households that are in a market and are tuned to a specific program during a specific time period. Expressed as a formula, program rating is

$$\text{program rating} = \frac{\text{TV households tuned to a program}}{\text{total TV households in the market}}$$

  A **ratings point** indicates that 1 percent of all the television households in an area were tuned to the program measured. If an episode of *The X-Files* is watched by 19.5 million households, then the program rating would be calculated as follows:

$$\textit{X-Files}\text{ rating} = \frac{19{,}500{,}000}{95{,}900{,}000} = 20 \text{ rating}$$

  The program rating is the best-known measure of television audience, and it is the basis for the rates television stations charge for advertising on different programs. Recall that it is also the way advertisers develop their media plans from the standpoint of calculating reach and frequency estimates, such as gross rating points.

- *Share of audience.* **Share of audience** provides a measure of the proportion of households that are using televisions during a specific time period and are tuned to a particular program. If 65 million households are using their televisions during the *X-Files* time slot, the share of audience measure is:

$$\textit{X-Files}\text{ share} = \frac{\text{TV households tuned to a program}}{\text{total TV households using TV}} = \frac{19{,}500{,}000}{65{,}000{,}000} = 30 \text{ share}$$

The Future of Television. The future of television is exciting for several reasons. First, the emerging interactive era will undoubtedly affect television as an advertising medium. Prospects include viewer participation in mystery programs and game shows in which household viewers play right along with studio contestants. Equally important, though, is that technology is creating the ability to transmit advertising to a wide range of new devices from cell phones to personal digital assistants to pagers. Estimates are that by 2005, global interactive advertising will represent an $83 billion industry.[25] And, recall the discussion from Chapter 3 regarding the growth of broadband access. By 2004, it is estimated that 15 percent of U.S. households (about 16 million households and 40 million people) will have broadband connections.[26]

Advertisers will have to seriously consider the implications of this mode of communication and how well it will serve as a way to send persuasive communications. Most specifically, broadband connections will increase the prospect that television advertising will be transmitted via the Internet to either PCs or handheld devices (see Exhibit 15.25).

25. Russ Banham, "Advertising's Future," *Critical Mass,* Fall 2000, 51–56.
26. Anna Bernasek, "How Broadband Adds Up," *Fortune,* October 9, 2000, 28–29.

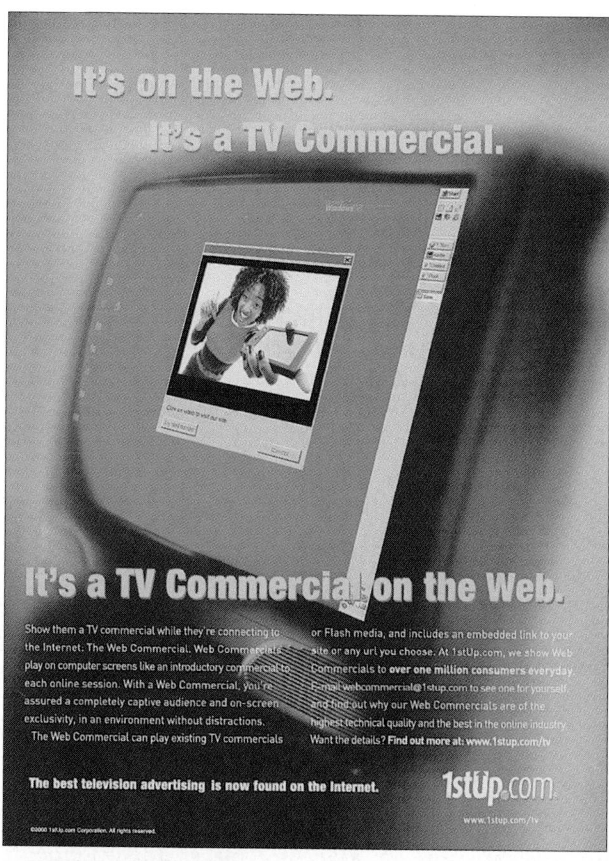

EXHIBIT 15.25

The future of television advertising will be greatly affected by new technology. Specifically, broadband technology will allow delivery of television advertising via the Internet to PCs and handheld devices.

Another major change that will affect the future of television is emerging transmission technology. **Direct broadcast by satellite (DBS)** is a program delivery system whereby television (and radio) programs are sent directly from a satellite to homes equipped with small receiving dishes. This transmission offers the prospect of hundreds of different channels. While advertisers will still be able to insert advertising in programs, the role of networks and cable stations in the advertising process will change dramatically. Recently, DBS technology has added a new capability. Rather than transmitting directly to homes, a Japanese company has developed a system to deliver programming to automobiles.

Finally, **high-definition television (HDTV)** promises to offer consumers picture and audio clarity that is a vast improvement over current technology. While HDTV equipment will certainly have the capability to reproduce images and sound with extraordinary quality, the uncertainties of visual and audio transmission may compromise the ability of the new HDTV sets to do so.

While it is hard to predict what the future will hold, one thing seems sure—television will continue to grow as an entertainment and information medium for households. The convenience, low cost, and diversity of programming make television an ideal medium for consumers. Additionally, television's expansion around the world will generate access to huge new markets. Television, despite its limitations, will continue to be an important part of the integrated communications mix of many advertisers.

4 **Radio.** Radio may seem the least glamorous and most inconspicuous of the major media. This perception does not jibe with reality. Radio plays an integral role in the media plans of some of the most astute advertisers. Because of the unique features of radio, advertisers invested $20.8 billion in the medium in 2001.[27] There are good reasons why advertisers of all sorts invest in radio as a means to reach target audiences. Let's turn our attention to the different radio options available to advertisers.

Radio Categories. Radio offers an advertiser several options for reaching target audiences. The basic split of national and local radio broadcasts presents an obvious, geographic choice. More specifically, though, advertisers can choose among the following categories, each with specific characteristics: networks, syndication, and AM versus FM.

- *Networks.* **Radio networks** operate much like television networks in that they deliver programming via satellite to affiliate stations across the United States. Network radio programming concentrates on news, sports, business reports, and

27. Cardona, "The Party's Over," 10.

short features. Some of the more successful radio networks that draw large audiences are ABC, CNN, and AP News Network.

- *Syndication.* **Radio syndication** provides complete programs to stations on a contract basis. Large syndicators offer stations complete 24-hour-a-day programming packages that totally relieve a station of any programming effort. Aside from full-day programming, they also supply individual programs, such as talk shows. Large syndication organizations such as Westwood One and Satellite Music Network place advertising within programming, making syndication a good outlet for advertisers.
- *AM versus FM.* AM radio stations send signals that use amplitude modulation (AM) and operate on the AM radio dial at signal designations 540 to 1600. AM was the foundation of radio until the 1970s. Today, AM radio broadcasts, even the new stereo AM transmissions, cannot match the sound quality of FM. Thus, most AM stations focus on local community broadcasting or news and talk formats that do not require high-quality audio. Talk radio has, in many ways, been the salvation of AM radio. Radio is, of course, now available via the Web. (For example, check out the very cool *Roe and Garry Show* on www.wlsam.com, 3 to 7 P.M. Central Time, Monday through Friday.) Since 1990, the number of stations that have devoted the bulk of their programming to the talk format has nearly tripled from 405 stations to 1,130.[28] FM radio stations transmit using frequency modulation (FM). FM radio transmission is of a much higher quality. Because of this, FM radio has attracted the wide range of music formats that most listeners prefer.

Types of Radio Advertising. Advertisers have three basic choices in radio advertising: local spot radio advertising, network radio advertising, or national spot radio advertising. Spot radio advertising attracts 80 percent of all radio advertising dollars in a year. In **local spot radio advertising,** an advertiser places advertisements directly with individual stations rather than with a network or syndicate. Spot radio dominates the three classes of radio advertising because there are more than 9,000 individual radio stations in the United States, giving advertisers a wide range of choices. And spot radio reaches well-defined geographic audiences, making it the ideal choice for local retailers.

Network radio advertising is advertising placed within national network programs. Since there are few network radio programs being broadcast, only about $600 million a year is invested by advertisers in this format.

The last option, **national spot radio advertising,** offers an advertiser the opportunity to place advertising in nationally syndicated radio programming. The leading national spot radio advertisers are listed in Exhibit 15.26. An advertiser can reach millions of listeners by contracting with Westwood One for *Casey Kasem's Top 40 Countdown,* which is carried by thousands of stations across the United States.

Advantages of Radio. While radio may not be the most glamorous or sophisticated of the major media options, it has some distinct advantages over newspapers, magazines, and television.

- *Cost.* From both a cost-per-contact and absolute-cost basis, radio is often the most cost-effective medium available to an advertiser. A full minute of network radio time can cost between $5,000 and $10,000—an amazing bargain compared to the other media we've discussed. In addition, production costs for preparing radio ads are quite low; an ad often costs nothing to prepare if the spot is read live during a local broadcast.
- *Reach and frequency.* Radio has the widest exposure of any medium. It reaches consumers in their homes, cars, offices, and backyards, and even while they exer-

28. Kelly Shermach, "Talk Radio Attracts Ads as Well as Listeners," *Marketing News,* January 30, 1995, 8.

EXHIBIT 15.26

Top 10 national spot radio advertisers (U.S. dollars in millions).

		National Spot Radio Ad Spending		
Rank	Advertiser	2000	1999	% Change
1	Verizon Communications	$72.1	$54.0	33.5
2	SBC Communications	58.0	43.6	33.2
3	AT&T Corp.	46.1	12.6	265.5
4	AOL Time Warner	44.7	38.3	16.9
5	Viacom	43.2	32.9	31.2
6	General Motors Corp.	34.8	28.4	22.5
7	General Electric Corp.	31.0	20.6	50.3
8	News Corp.	28.5	30.1	–5.1
9	Diageo	27.1	34.4	–21.4
10	U.S. Government	25.3	22.0	15.0

Source: *Advertising Age*, September 24, 2001, S12. Reprinted with permission from the September 24, 2001, issue of *Advertising Age*. Copyright © Crain Communications Inc. 2001.

EXHIBIT 15.27

Radio dayparts.

Morning drive time	6:00 A.M. to 10:00 A.M.
Daytime	10:00 A.M. to 3:00 P.M.
Afternoon/evening drive time	3:00 P.M. to 7:00 P.M.
Nighttime	7:00 P.M. to 12:00 A.M.
Late night	12:00 A.M. to 6:00 A.M.

cise. The wireless and portable features of radio provide an opportunity to reach consumers that exceeds all other media. The low cost of radio time gives advertisers the opportunity to frequently repeat messages at low absolute cost and cost per contact.

- *Target audience selectivity.* Radio can selectively target audiences on a geographic, demographic, and psychographic basis. The narrow transmission of local radio stations gives advertisers the best opportunity to reach narrowly defined geographic audiences. For a local merchant with one store, this is an ideal opportunity. Radio programming formats and different dayparts also allow target audience selectivity. CBS Radio made the decision several years ago to convert 4 of 13 stations to a rock-and-roll oldies format to target 35-to-49-year-olds—in other words, the baby boomers.[29] Hard rock, new age, easy listening, country, classical, and talk radio formats all attract different audiences. Radio dayparts, shown in Exhibit 15.27, also attract different audiences. Morning and afternoon/evening drive times attract a male audience. Daytime attracts predominantly women; nighttime, teens.
- *Flexibility and timeliness.* Radio is the most flexible medium because of very short closing periods for submitting an ad. This means an advertiser can wait until close to an air date before submitting an ad. With this flexibility, advertisers can take advantage of special events or unique competitive opportunities in a timely fashion.
- *Creative opportunities.* While radio may be unidimensional in sensory stimulation, it can still have powerful creative impact. Recall that radio has been described as

29. Kevin Goldman, "CBS Radio Retunes to Music of the '70s," *Wall Street Journal,* December 30, 1993, B5.

the theater of the mind. Ads such as those containing the folksy tales of Tom Bodett for Motel 6 or the eccentric humor of Stan Freberg are memorable and can have tremendous impact on the attitude toward a brand. In addition, the musical formats that attract audiences to radio stations can also attract attention to radio ads. Audiences that favor certain music may be more prone to an ad that uses recognizable, popular songs.[30]

Disadvantages of Radio. As good as radio can be, it also suffers from some severe limitations as an advertising medium. Advertising strategists must recognize these disadvantages when deciding what role radio can play in an integrated marketing communications program.

- *Poor audience attentiveness.* Just because radio reaches audiences almost everywhere doesn't mean that anyone is paying attention. Remember that radio has also been described as audio wallpaper. It provides a comfortable background distraction while a consumer does something else—hardly an ideal level of attentiveness for advertising communication. When a consumer is listening and traveling in a car, he or she often switches stations when an ad comes on and divides his or her attention between the radio and the road. This lack of attentiveness, indeed an aversion to advertising on the radio, represents a threat to the very existence of radio, as the Controversy box on page 553 discusses.
- *Creative limitations.* While the theater of the mind may be a wonderful creative opportunity, taking advantage of that opportunity can be difficult, indeed. The audio-only nature of radio communication is a tremendous creative compromise. An advertiser whose product depends on demonstration or visual impact is at a loss when it comes to radio. And like its television counterpart, a radio message creates a fleeting impression that is often gone in an instant.
- *Fragmented audiences.* The large number of stations that try to attract the same audience in a market has created tremendous fragmentation. Think about your own local radio market. There are probably four or five different stations that play the kind of music you like. Or, consider that in the past few years, more than 1,000 radio stations in the United States have adopted the talk radio format. This fragmentation means that the percentage of listeners tuned to any one station is likely very small.
- *Chaotic buying procedures.* For an advertiser who wants to include radio as part of a national advertising program, the buying process can be sheer chaos. Since national networks and syndicated broadcasts do not reach every geographic market, an advertiser has to buy time in individual markets on a station-by-station basis. This could involve dozens of different negotiations and individual contracts.

Buying Procedures for Radio Advertising. While buying procedures to achieve national coverage may be chaotic, this does not mean they are completely without structure. Although the actual buying may be time-consuming and expensive if many stations are involved, the structure is actually quite straightforward. Advertising time can be purchased from networks, syndications, or local radio stations. Recall that among these options, advertisers invest most heavily in local placement. About 80 percent of annual radio advertising is placed locally. About 15 percent is allocated to national spot placement, and only 5 percent is invested in network broadcasts.

The other factor in buying radio time relates to the time period of purchase. Refer again to Exhibit 15.27, which shows the five basic daypart segments from which an advertiser can choose. The time period decision is based primarily on a demographic description of the advertiser's target audience. Recall that drive-time

30. Kevin Goldman, "Hot Songs Are Wooing Younger Ears," *Wall Street Journal,* January 2, 1993, B1.

dayparts attract a mostly male audience, while daytime is primarily female, and nighttime is mostly teen. This information, combined with programming formats, guides an advertiser in a buying decision.

As with magazine buying, radio advertising time is purchased from rate cards issued by individual stations. Run-of-station ads—ads that the station chooses when to run—cost less than ads scheduled during a specific daypart. The price can also increase if an advertiser wants the ad read live on the air by a popular local radio personality hosting a show during a daypart.

The actual process of buying radio time is relatively simple. A media planner identifies the stations and the dayparts that will reach the target audience. Then the rates and daypart availabilities are checked to be sure they match the media-planning objectives. At this point, agreements are made regarding the number of spots to run in specified time frames.

CONTROVERSY

The Death of Radio?

In early 2001, Sirius Radio launched its third satellite into space from the Soviet Union's once-secret Baikonur Cosmodrome in Kazakhstan. This is the same site where the first earth satellite was launched in 1957 and where the first human in orbit blasted off in 1961. Will this site also be known as the place where the slow death of radio began?

Sirius plans to broadcast 100 channels—from gospel music to heavy metal to science news and from CNBC to NPR—to cars anywhere in the United States. The broadcast will boast CD-quality sound and there will be little if any advertising. Radio listeners will, for the first time ever, be asked to pay a $9.95 per month subscription fee for this new radio option. If the advantages of subscription radio are appealing to consumers, it could rattle the very foundations of the $17-billion-a-year radio industry.

There are some very high-profile believers. Corporations like General Motors, DaimlerChrysler, and Clear Channel, as well as financiers like Prime 66 Partners, Apollo, and Blackstone, have sunk almost $3 billion into Sirius and its main competitor XM. The auto dealers have struck a deal to install satellite radio as original equipment in their cars as soon as the broadcast is perfected. One industry analyst believes that satellite radio is "the next major consumer phenomenon" and predicts that by 2007 it will be generating up to $10 billion a year in revenue.

While all that sounds very convincing, the reality is that no satellite radio company has earned a penny in revenues yet. Critics point out that the technology really is rocket science and there is some question as to whether providers can deliver on the promise of stellar sound anywhere, anytime. And the crucial question is, will people actually pay to listen to the radio—something they have never had to do?

So what would you rather do? Pay about $120 year for on-demand, crystal-clear radio in your car, or put up with advertising and the channel surfing required to avoid it? Is the death of radio greatly exaggerated?

Source: Bethany McLean, "Satellite Killed the Radio Star," *Fortune*, January 22, 2001, 95.

Measuring Radio Audiences. There are two primary sources of information on radio audiences. Arbitron ratings cover 260 local radio markets. The ratings are developed through the use of diaries maintained by listeners who record when they listened to the radio and to what station they were tuned. The *Arbitron Ratings/Radio* book gives audience estimates by time period and selected demographic characteristics. Several specific measures are compiled from the Arbitron diaries:

- **Average quarter-hour persons:** The average number of listeners tuned to a station during a specified 15-minute segment of a daypart.
- **Average quarter-hour share:** The percentage of the total radio audience that was listening to a radio station during a specified quarter-hour daypart.
- **Average quarter-hour rating:** The audience during a quarter-hour daypart expressed as a percentage of the population of the measurement area. This provides an estimate of the popularity of each station in an area.
- **Cume:** The cumulative audience, which is the total number of different people who listen to a station for at least five minutes in a quarter-hour period within a specified daypart. Cume is the best estimate of the reach of a station.
- RADAR (Radio's All Dimension Audience Research) is the other major measure of radio audiences. Sponsored by the major radio networks, RADAR collects audience data twice a year based on interviews with radio listeners. Designated listeners are called daily for a one-week period and asked about their listening

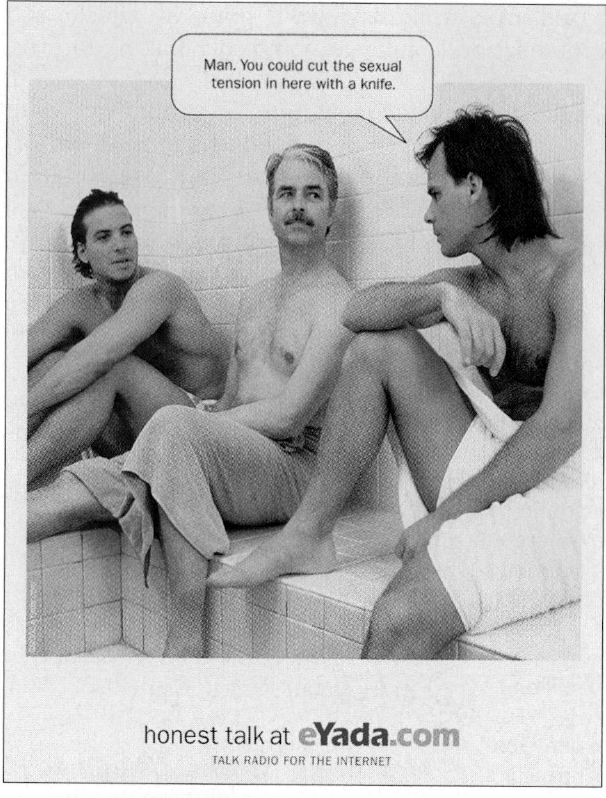

EXHIBIT 15.28

Much like television advertising, new technologies will affect the prospect of delivering radio (programming and) advertising via the Internet.

behavior. Estimates include measures of the overall audience for different network stations and audience estimates by market area. The results of the studies are reported in an annual publication, *Radio Usage and Network Radio Audiences*. Media planners can refer to published measures such as Arbitron and RADAR to identify which stations will reach target audiences at what times across various markets.

The Future of Radio. Two factors must be considered with respect to the future of radio. First, the prospects for successful subscription radio should not be underestimated. Subscription radio does away with radio advertising clutter and offers listeners multiple, detailed choices to match their listening preferences.[31] The only issue, of course, is whether radio listeners will be willing to pay for an entertainment medium that has been free from its inception.

Second, radio will be affected by emerging technologies much in the same way that television will be affected. The potential for transmitting radio programming—and advertising—via the Internet is very real (see Exhibit 15.28). As broadband technology grows, so will the attractiveness of Internet transmission of radio programming and advertising.

31. Bethany McLean, "Satellite Killed the Radio Star," *Fortune*, January 22, 2001, 95.

SUMMARY

1 Detail the pros and cons of newspapers as a media class, identify newspaper types, and describe buying and audience measurement for newspapers.

Newspaper types cluster into three categories: target audience, geographic coverage, and frequency of publication. As a media class, newspapers provide an excellent means for reaching local audiences with informative advertising messages. Precise timing of message delivery can be achieved at modest expenditure levels. But for products that demand creative and colorful executions, this medium simply cannot deliver. Newspaper costs are typically transmitted via rate cards and are primarily a function of a paper's readership levels.

2 Detail the pros and cons of magazines as a media class, identify magazine types, and describe buying and audience measurement for magazines.

Three important magazine types are consumer, business, and farm publications. Because of their specific editorial content, magazines can be effective in attracting distinctive groups of readers with common interests. Thus, magazines can be superb tools for reaching specific market segments. Also, magazines facilitate a wide range of creative executions. Of course, the selectivity advantage turns into a disadvantage for advertisers trying to achieve high reach levels. Costs of magazine ad space can vary dramatically because of the wide array of circulation levels achieved by different types of magazines.

Detail the pros and cons of television as a media class, identify television types, and describe buying and audience measurement for television.

The four basic forms of television are network, cable, syndicated, and local television. Television's principal advantage is obvious: Because it allows for almost limitless possibilities in creative execution, it can be an extraordinary tool for affecting consumers' perceptions of a brand. Also, it can be an efficient device for reaching huge audiences; however, the absolute costs for reaching these audiences can be staggering. Lack of audience interest and involvement certainly limit the effectiveness of commercials in this medium. The three ways that advertisers can buy time are through sponsorship, participation, and spot advertising. As with any medium, advertising rates will vary as a function of the size and composition of the audience that is watching.

Detail the pros and cons of radio as a media class, identify radio types, and describe buying and audience measurement for radio.

Advertisers can choose from three basic types of radio advertising: local spot, network radio, or national spot advertising. Radio can be a cost-effective medium, and because of the wide diversity in radio programming, it can be an excellent tool for reaching well-defined audiences. Poor listener attentiveness is problematic with radio, and the audio-only format places obvious constraints on creative execution. Radio ad rates are driven by considerations such as the average number of listeners tuned to a station at specific times throughout the day.

KEY TERMS

general-population newspapers
business newspapers
ethnic newspapers
gay and lesbian newspapers
alternative press newspapers
display advertising
co-op advertising
preprinted insert
free-standing insert (FSI)
classified advertising
rate card
column inch
standard advertising unit (SAU)
run-of-paper (ROP)
preferred position
full position
circulation
paid circulation
controlled circulation
readership
bleed page
gatefold ads
first cover page
second cover page
third cover page
fourth cover page
double-page spreads
space contract
space order
closing date
on-sale date
cover date
guaranteed circulation
pass-along readership
network television
cable television
off-network syndication
first-run syndication
barter syndication
local television
satellite and closed-circuit
narrowcasting
channel grazing
zapping
zipping
V-chip
sponsorship
participation
spot advertising
dayparts
television households
households using television (HUT)
program rating
ratings point
share of audience
direct broadcast by satellite (DBS)
high-definition television (HDTV)
radio networks
radio syndication
local spot radio advertising
network radio advertising
national spot radio advertising
average quarter-hour persons
average quarter-hour share
average quarter-hour rating
cume

QUESTIONS

1. Magazines certainly proved to be the right media class for selling Absolut vodka. Why are magazines a natural choice for vodka advertisements? What has Absolut done with its advertising to take full advantage of this medium?

2. What advantages do publishers perceive of "digizines" versus a traditional, printed version of a magazine?

3. Reach and frequency can be perceived as conflicting goals in media planning. Evaluate each of the four major media classes discussed in this chapter in terms of how well they would serve reach-versus-frequency objectives.

4. Peruse several recent editions of your town's newspaper and select three examples of co-op advertising. What objectives do you believe the manufacturers and retailers are attempting to achieve in each of the three ads you've selected?

5. Place your local newspaper and an issue of your favorite magazine side by side and carefully review the content of each. From the standpoint of a prospective advertiser, which of the two publications has a more dramatic problem with clutter? Identify tactics being used by advertisers in each publication to break through the clutter and get their brands noticed.

6. The costs involved in preparing and placing ads in television programming such as the Super Bowl broadcast can be simply incredible. How is it that advertisers such as Pepsi or Nissan can justify the incredible costs that come with this media vehicle?

7. Think about the television viewing behavior you've observed in your household. Of the four means for avoiding TV ad exposure discussed in this chapter, which have you observed in your household? What other avoidance tactics do your friends and family use?

8. The choice between print and broadcast media is often portrayed as a choice between high- and low-involvement media. What makes one medium inherently more involving than another? How will the characteristics of an ad's message affect the decision to employ an involving versus an uninvolving medium?

9. For an advertiser that seeks to achieve nationwide reach, can radio be a good buy? What frustrations are likely to be encountered in using radio for this purpose?

10. How will new technologies affect television and radio advertising?

EXPERIENTIAL EXERCISES

1. Look up the following four sites on the Internet and evaluate which medium (radio, television, magazines, or newspaper) you think is best suited for advertising the brands. Justify your choices based on an evaluation of these brands, and based on the pros and cons of each medium discussed in the chapter.

K2 Snowboards: http://www.k2snowboards.com

Cover Girl: http://www.covergirl.com

Metro Goldwyn Mayer: http://www.mgm.com

Southgate House: http://www.southgatehouse.com

2. This chapter discusses the cost and buying procedures of four different types of media. Select one of your favorite magazines or newspapers, or choose a local television or radio station, and look over its costs and buying procedures. (You can normally view rate cards on the company's Internet site. If the information is not listed there, contact someone in the sales department.)

3. Using the cost-and-buying information in the text as your guide, gather specific rate information from the publication or station you selected. List how the rates and specifications compare to what is listed in the text. If the rates or buying procedures for your selected medium seem different from the ones listed in the text, explain why you think they varied. Do you think the costs are justified for advertisers seeking to place ads in the media company you selected?

USING THE INTERNET

15-1 Alternative Press

While newspapers across the United States have been suffering a decline in circulation and readership, alternative press weeklies, such as the *Village Voice* and *L.A. Weekly,* have been growing. In the past, national advertisers often avoided these smaller papers due to their relatively small circulation. In recent years, however, hundreds of alternative press papers formed a network to give advertisers opportunities to transact national advertising buys across the country. This network provides them with an affordable, national reach.

Alternative Weekly Network: http://www.awn.org

1. Do alternative press papers provide advertisers with useful segmentation? What kinds of advertisers are likely to be interested in reaching the audience that alternative weeklies provide? Explain.

2. Search around the Alternative Weekly Network site for its demographics information, and read over some of the facts and figures. How is the average alternative-weekly reader depicted? Name an advertiser you think might not wish to target an alternative press audience, and give your reason.

3. Explain the benefits the Alternative Weekly Network provides to national advertisers. How does the service work?

15-2 Making Media Decisions

All media have inherent capabilities and limitations that advertisers must take into account when building a media plan. Even the most creative ad can't achieve sales and communications objectives if placement misses the target audience. These sites represent four major media, each having its unique pros and cons. Visit the sites and rank the usefulness of the media companies to advertisers based on the criteria listed in the questions below.

Fox: http://www.fox.com

The Chicago Tribune: http://www.chicagotribune.com

97X: http://www.woxy.com

Spin: http://www.spin.com

1. Which medium is normally considered the best in terms of audience selectivity? What attributes give it this advantage over other media?

2. Which medium is normally considered the most accessible to the widest range of advertisers? What attributes give it this advantage over other media?

3. Which medium is normally considered the best at providing creative opportunities for an advertiser to express a brand's value? What attributes give it this advantage over other media?

4. Which medium is normally considered to have the greatest frequency and reach? What attributes give it this advantage over other media?

CHAPTER 16

After reading and thinking about this chapter, you will be able to do the following:

Identify the basic components of the Internet.

Identify the Internet media available for communicating over the World Wide Web.

Describe the different types of search engines used to surf the Web.

Describe the different advertising options on the Web.

Discuss the issues involved in establishing a site on the World Wide Web.

CHAPTER 14
Media Planning, Objectives, and Strategy for Advertising and Promoting the Brand

CHAPTER 15
Media Planning: Print, Television, and Radio

CHAPTER 16
Media Planning: Advertising and the Internet

DOES YOUR CONTENT ?
Or does it hide quietly in places it won't be seen?
Distribute your news, features and photos to niche and special interest web sites, generating an easy revenue stream and extending your brand to audiences you wouldn't reach otherwise. Call or visit our web site.
OUR SUBSCRIBERS:
America Online, drkoop.com, Microsoft, MotherNature.com, ProgressiveFarmer.com, and hundreds more.
OUR CONTENT PROVIDERS:
New York Times Syndicate, Red Herring, Knight Ridder/Tribune, USATODAY.com, Christian Science Monitor, Salon.com, New York Post, and over 500 others.
SCREAMING MEDIA
www.screamingmedia.com
Contact m.howatson@screamingmedia.com
or call toll-free 877.720.7400

EXHIBIT 16.1

Pepsi has found that developing individual Web sites with engaging content can help the firm communicate effectively with its 25-and-under market.
www.pepsiworld.com

So would you buy a can of Pepsi online? Seems like kind of a dumb question, doesn't it? There is obviously no reason to go to the Web to order a Pepsi or any other soda. Hardly any product is more widely available than a can of Pepsi—grocery stores, convenience stores, vending machines, street vendors, and so on. That soda is widely distributed is almost an inalienable consumer right. Then why would Pepsi be developing a wider and wider presence on the Web?

Obviously, not to sell the product over the Web. Pepsi is developing a range of programs accessible through the Web, from music sites to games to banner ads to sweepstakes. While only about 3 percent of Pepsi's $400 million brand advertising budget is devoted to virtual air, that percentage does not reveal the company's commitment to cyberspace. John Vail is the director of digital media and marketing for Pepsi-Cola and describes the firm's investment in the Internet this way: "This medium is here to stay and we buy that."[1]

There are several reasons Vail is sold on the Internet as a way to advertise Pepsi products and promote the brand name. First, the Internet is a good medium for reaching the 25-and-under target market. This segment of the population has the heaviest Internet use. Second, and the most important reason for Vail, is that while there are difficulties in measuring online advertising effects, Pepsi has launched campaigns that have paid off big-time. For example, in a barter deal with Yahoo!, Pepsi plastered the Yahoo! logo on 1.5 *billion* cans of Pepsi. In exchange, Yahoo! took the company's well-established loyalty program—PepsiStuff—to another level of success. At a Web site co-developed between Yahoo! and Pepsi, the loyalty points were redeemable for highly prized items such as electronics and concert tickets. The results were impressive. Three million consumers registered at the PepsiStuff Web site, giving the company detailed consumer data virtually for free that would normally have to be paid for through marketing research. And information that once took months to gather took only a matter of days. Vail contends that Pepsi sales volume rose 5 percent during the online promotion and the cost was about one-fifth of a direct mail campaign.

Given the early success with the PepsiStuff site, Pepsi is pushing forward aggressively with its Internet program. Banner ads will be included in the program, but the real power will be in creating a variety of engaging Pepsi sites (see Exhibit 16.1). These sites will feature Pepsi celebrities from NASCAR racing (Jeff Gordon) or Pepsi television advertising (Britney Spears). While Pepsi might not be able to sell you a can of Pepsi over the Internet, it just might be able to communicate with you in a new and much more interesting way.

The Role of the Internet in the Advertising Process.

So just what is the role of the Internet in the advertising process? Certainly Pepsi has found a way to successfully integrate the Internet into its integrated brand promotion strategy. But what about the Internet overall as a medium? In the late 1990s, everyone thought the Internet was going to all but eliminate all other forms of advertising! Now, Internet advertising spending has plummeted from earlier estimates, and there

1. Ellen Neuborne, "Pepsi's Aim Is True," *Business Week e.biz,* January 22, 2001, 2.

is a growing list of high-profile Internet sites that went from dot-darlings to dot-nots—eToys, Garden.com, and Pets.com, to name a few.[2] To appreciate the magnitude of the change, consider that at its peak, eToys had a market capitalization of $10.1 billion. In early 2000, Johnson & Johnson (the consumer drug and household items conglomerate) was the leading organization in buying up eToys' assets and inventory for a paltry $20 million.[3] In the understatement of the Internet era, one analyst with a prominent Wall Street hedge fund said "Obviously, the original thought of what the eToys brand was worth has changed."[4] Duh.

But what can and what will likely be the role of the Internet in the advertising effort? That may be the question of the decade. A few "truths" have made themselves evident to this point. No, the Internet will obviously *not* be replacing all other forms of advertising. Nor is it likely that advertisers will use the Internet as even the main method of communicating with a target audience. But, as we saw in the Pepsi example, advertisers will be discovering ways to use the Internet as a key component of integrated brand promotions. While Pepsi was featured here, firms such as Virgin Group Ltd., Arthur Andersen, and RCA Records have incorporated the Internet as a key feature in brand advertising and promotion.[5]

We will spend most of our time in this chapter focusing on two fundamental issues: the structure of the Internet and the potential of the Internet as an advertising medium. Through these analyses, we will come to a better understanding of how to use the Internet as part of an effective overall advertising and integrated brand promotion effort. First, we will consider a short history of the evolution of the Internet. Then, we'll have an overview of cyberspace and some of the basics of the way the Internet works. Next, we will consider the different types of advertising that can be used and some of the technical aspects of the process. Finally, we will look at the issues involved in establishing a Web site and developing a brand in the "e-community."

The (R)evolution of the Internet.

Technology changes everything—or at least it has the power and potential to change everything. When it's communications technology, such as the Internet, it can change something very fundamental about human existence. The Internet-connected consumer is connected to other consumers in real time, and with connection comes community, empowerment, even liberation.

Is the proliferation of the Internet an evolution in communication or a revolution? While revolutions are more common than they used to be, the Internet certainly is going through some growing pains. Still, what can be truly revolutionary about the Internet is its ability to alter the basic nature of communication within a commercial channel. And, despite the recent and ongoing shakeout of Internet sites, if you want a revolutionary perspective on the Internet and advertising, consider the short history of communication in this channel.[6] In 1994, advertisers began working with Prodigy and CompuServe, who were the first Internet service providers (ISPs). These advertisers had the idea that they would send standard television commercials online. Well, the technology was not in place back then for that to work. That technological fact sent the advertisers and the ISPs back to the drawing board. With the emergence of more commercial ISPs such as America Online, the new Web browsers were worth exploring as a way to send commercial messages. The first Web browser was Mosaic, the precursor to Netscape 1.0, and the first ads began appearing in *HotWired* magazine (the online version of *Wired* magazine) in October

2. "World Web Advertising," *Business 2.0,* February 20, 2001, 64.
3. Lara Christianson, "E-Assets for Sale—Dirt Cheap," *Business Week e.biz,* May 14, 2001, 20–22.
4. Ibid., 20.
5. See, for example, Erin White, "Chatting a Singer up the Pop Charts," *Wall Street Journal,* December 5, 1999, B1, B4; and Kerry Capell, "Virgin Takes E-Wing," *Business Week e.biz,* January 22, 2001, 30–34.
6. Gene Koprowski, "A Brief History of Web Advertising," *Critical Mass,* Fall 1999, 8–14.

1994. The magazine boasted 12 advertisers including MCI, AT&T, Sprint, Volvo, and ClubMed. Each marketer paid $30,000 for a 12-week run of online banner ads with no guarantee of the number or profile of the viewers.

Now, the Internet is being accessed worldwide by about 400 million users.[7] Advertising revenues on the Internet were estimated at about $8.2 billion in 2000 and could grow to over $30 billion by 2004.[8] The medium is used by all forms of companies, large and small, bricks and mortar, virtual, e-commerce, you name it. Further, the medium is home to thousands of personal Web sites, and the value of the Internet to individual consumers is growing daily. Let's turn our attention to the technical aspects of the Internet at this point and then we will explore the Internet as a strategic advertising and IBP option for advertisers.

An Overview of Cyberspace.

We refer to the Internet casually because it has become so prominent in the technological landscape. But, just what is this thing called the Internet? The **Internet** is a global collection of computer networks linking both public and private computer systems. It was originally designed by the U.S. military to be a decentralized, highly redundant, and thus reliable communications system in the event of a national emergency. Even if some of the military's computers crashed, the Internet would continue to perform. Today the Internet comprises a combination of computers from government, educational, military, and commercial sources. In the beginning, the number of computers connected to the Internet would nearly double every year, from 2 million in 1994 to 5 million in 1995 to about 10 million in 1996. But beginning in 1998 the top blew off Internet use, with around 90 million people connected to the Internet in the United States and Canada and 155 million people worldwide. Exhibit 16.2 shows that Internet access around the world has continued its accelerated rate of increase with over 407 million current users worldwide. As you can see, the United States, Japan, and Western Europe account for most of the world's Web traffic. Internet users are, at present, disproportionately affluent white American males. The United Kingdom, Western Europe, parts of Southeast Asia, and Latin America are growing in both absolute and relative terms.[9]

Do not overlook the potential that still remains for Internet communications. The 407 million current Internet users represent only about 7 percent of the world's population. Further, countries with large populations, such as Russia and China, are only now connecting to the Internet. Like many communication technologies, the Internet started rather upscale, but is now broadening to middle- and lower-income consumers with the advent of more affordable PCs and Web TV. Wireless technology will spread the application even further and faster to poor countries that cannot afford the infrastructure needed for wired connections.

1 The Basic Parts.

While many of you are no doubt frequent and savvy Web users, you may never have had the chance to explore the foundations of the Internet. Let's take some time to look at the basic parts of the Internet that allow all of us to surf and that give advertisers the opportunity to use the Web as another tool in the promotional mix. There are four main components of the Internet: electronic mail, IRC, Usenet, and the World Wide Web. **Electronic mail (e-mail)** allows people to send messages to one another. In 2000, more than 1.5 trillion e-mails were sent from within the United States, which may explain the proliferation of services, technologies, and devices that support electronic messaging and the advertising associated with them—

7. NUA Internet Surveys, www.nua.net/surveys/, accessed May 26, 2001.
8. Internet Advertising Bureau, "Total Ad Spend for 2000 Reached USD8.2 bn," April 22, 2001, www.iab.com, accessed May 25, 2001.
9. Jeffery D. Zbar, "Web Hot: Net Marketing Surges in Latin America," *Advertising Age,* February 14, 2000, 28.

EXHIBIT 16.2

Estimates of Internet users worldwide as of 2001.

Country	Number Online	Percent of Total Population
Europe		
Austria	30.0 million	36.9%
Belgium	2.7 million	36.4
Czech Republic	350,000	3.4
Denmark	2.6 million	48.4
France	9.0 million	44.0
Germany	20.1 million	24.3
Hungary	650,000	6.4
Italy	13.4 million	23.3
Netherlands	7.3 million	45.9
Norway	2.4 million	52.6
Spain	5.5 million	13.4
Brazil	9.9 million	5.7
Mexico	2.5 million	2.5
China	16.9 million	1.4
Japan	38.6 million	30.6
Russia	9.2 million	6.3
United Kingdom	20.0 million	34.0
United States	153.9 million	55.9
World Total	**407.1 million**	**6.7%**

Source: N U A Internet Surveys, www.nua.com, accessed May 26, 2001.

an example of which is seen in Exhibit 16.3. **Internet Relay Chat (IRC)** makes it possible for people to "talk" electronically in real time with each other, despite their geographical separation. For people with common interests, **Usenet** provides a forum for sharing knowledge in a public "cyberspace" that is separate from their e-mail program. Finally, with the **World Wide Web (WWW),** people can access an immense "web" of information in a graphical environment through the use of programs called Web browsers (such as Netscape and Internet Explorer). Many Web sites are still listed with the prefix http://, which stands for *hypertext transfer protocol,* or rules of interaction between the Web browser and the Web server that are used to deal with hypertext. Currently, many Web browsers assume that the file will be in hypertext, so they don't require users to type out the prefix.

To use the Internet, the user's personal computer must be connected to the network in some way. The most common way to access the Internet is by using a modem to call a *host computer,* which then provides the *client computer* access to the Internet. The four most common access options are through a commercial online service, such as America Online or Juno; a corporate gateway, such as AT&T's WorldNet Service; a local Internet service provider; or an educational institution. In addition to using one of these networks, a personal computer needs software to communicate and move around while online, such as a Web browser and/or e-mail application. For example, if one is interested in the graphic-oriented World Wide

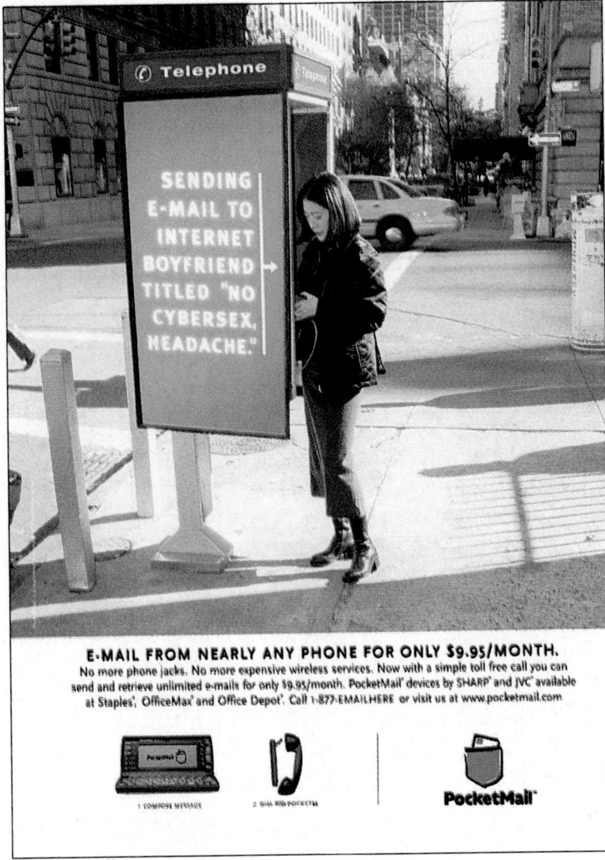

EXHIBIT 16.3

The 24/7, come-as-you-are convenience of Internet access is being fostered by new technology and new devices. www.pocketmail.com

Web, then software such as Netscape Navigator or Microsoft Internet Explorer is needed. If one is interested only in e-mail, then a program such as Eudora will suffice. A new option for novice users and those not in need of computing capability is Web TV. With a simple keyboard and Internet connection, the user's television provides access to the World Wide Web. The user can then surf Web sites and send and receive e-mail. It's not exactly computing, but it is a connection to the Web.

While much of the vocabulary of the Web is common knowledge or intuitive, some of the language of the Web is, well, a mystery. The short glossary in Exhibit 16.4 defines some of the terms you have heard dozens of times, but may have had no idea what they really meant.

2 Internet Media.

Internet media for advertising consist of e-mail (including electronic mailing lists), Usenet, and the World Wide Web.

E-Mail. E-mail is frequently used by advertisers to reach potential and existing customers. A variety of companies collect e-mail addresses and profiles that allow advertisers to direct e-mail to a specific group. The DM Group (www.dm1.com) maintains a list of e-mail groups and has reportedly collected hundreds of thousands of e-mail addresses. Widespread, targeted e-mail advertising is just now materializing through organizations like Advertising.com (www.advertising.com) due to significant consumer resistance to advertisers' direct mailing to personal e-mail addresses (see Exhibit 16.5). Advertising.com will target, prepare, and deliver e-mails to highly specific audiences for advertisers. As techniques and guidelines are better established for direct e-mail advertising, it may become more accepted in the future. Many believe it's only a matter of time, because, historically, advertisers have rarely worried about being too intrusive.

People who wish to discuss specific topics through the Internet often join **electronic mailing lists.** Thousands of mailing lists are available on an incredible variety of topics. Currently there are nearly 200,000 lists with a total of 123 million members (remember that one person can be on several lists).[10] A message sent to the list's e-mail address is then re-sent to everybody on the mailing list. Organizations such as L-Soft International (www.lsoft.com) offer software for managing electronic mailing lists; this software can be downloaded for a few thousand dollars (see Exhibit 16.6). It is currently considered in very bad taste to openly sell products via topical electronic mailing lists, particularly when there is no apparent connection between the mailing list's topic and the advertised product. Product information shared through these mailing lists is similar to traditional word-of-mouth communications and is, at the moment, still in the hands of users.

10. Data obtained from L-Soft, www.lsoft.com, accessed May 27, 2001.

applet	A Java program that can be inserted into an HTML page (see definition for HTML below).
banner ad	An advertisement, typically rectangular in shape, used to catch a consumer's eye on a Web page. Banner ads serve as a gateway to send a consumer to an expanded Web page where more extensive information is provided for a firm or a product. Many include an electronic commerce capability whereby a product or service can be ordered through the banner itself.
bandwidth	The capacity for transmitting information through an Internet connection. Internet connections are available through phone lines, cable, or various wireless options.
baud	A measure of data transmission speed, typically referring to a modem.
click-through	The process of a Web site visitor clicking on a banner ad and being sent to a marketer's home page for further information. Ad banner click-through rates average about 1 percent.
cookie	A piece of information sent by a Web server to a Web browser that tracks Web page activity. Because they identify users and their browsing habits, cookies are at the center of Web privacy issues.
CPM	Cost per thousand impressions, the long-standing measure of advertising rates used in traditional media and now carried over as a standard for the Internet.
domain name	The unique name of a Web site chosen by a marketer. There are twelve designations for domain names after the unique name chosen by the marketer: .com and .net refer to business and commercial sites; .org refers to an institution or nonprofit organization; .gov identifies government Web sites; .edu refers to academic institutions; .aero for the air transport industry; .biz for businesses; .coop for cooperatives; .info, unrestricted by organizational type; .museum for museums; .name for individuals; .pro for accountants, lawyers, and other professionals.
e-mail	Text messages exchanged via computer, Web TV, and various wireless devices such as Palm Pilots and cell phones.
HTML	An acronym that stands for *hypertext markup language*, which is used to display and link documents to the Web.
interstitial	Pop-up ads that appear when a Web user clicks on a designated (or not designated) area of a Web page.
intranet	An online network *internal* to a company that can be used by employees. Intranets are even showing up in some households.
spam	"Junk" e-mail sent to consumers who haven't requested the information. Not an acronym, the Internet term is said to have derived from a Monty Python skit about a restaurant where everything comes with Spam—the Hormel lunch meat, that is.

EXHIBIT 16.4

A glossary of basic Internet terminology.

Usenet. As we saw earlier, Usenet is a collection of discussion groups in cyberspace. People can read messages pertaining to a given topic, post new messages, and answer messages. For advertisers, this is an important source of consumers who care about certain topics. For example, the Usenet group alt.beer is an excellent place for a new microbrewery to promote its product. Advertisers can also use Usenet as a source of unobtrusive research, getting the latest opinions on their products and services. Television shows such as *The X-Files* often monitor Usenet groups, such as alt.tv.x-files, to find out what people think about the show. Usenet is also used as a publicity vehicle for goods and services. Usenet represents a relatively self-segmented word-of-mouth channel.

Uninvited commercial messages sent to electronic mailing lists, Usenet groups, or some other compilation of e-mail addresses is a notorious practice known as **spam.** In one instance, more than 6 million people were spammed at a cost of only $425. In retaliation, such organizations as the Coalition Against Unsolicited Commercial

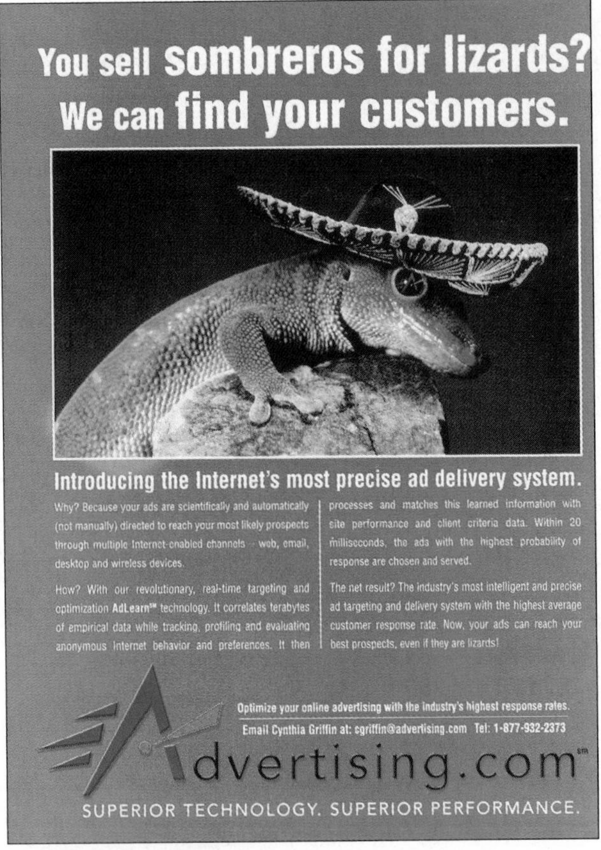

EXHIBIT 16.5

Several new service firms have emerged to help marketers place highly targeted e-mail messages on the Internet that serve as customized one-by-one advertising. www.advertising.com

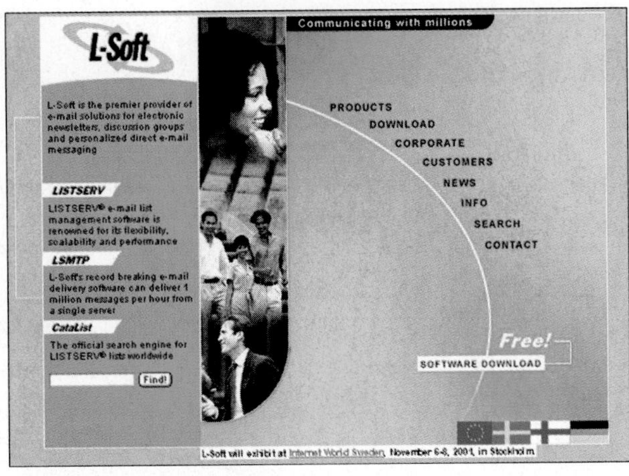

EXHIBIT 16.6

Similar to e-mail messaging, firms can buy complete listservs, lists of e-mail groups, from companies L-Soft for a few thousand dollars.

E-mail (www.cauce.org) have compiled resources for fighting spam as well as a blacklist of advertisers who have used spam. For an ambitious and gutsy marketer, such a tactic could prove an enormously cost-effective advertising buy, or it could provoke a great deal of hate mail, resentment, or even more dire consequences, including a loss of business reputation. Loss of reputation is a distinct possibility because surveys of consumers find that they trust the government more than they trust e-mail advertisers to regulate the use of e-mail as a communications medium.[11] Again, the point is for advertisers to make sure they are wanted guests, and not despised intruders into what often amount to valuable virtual communities.[12]

The World Wide Web. Finally, the World Wide Web (WWW) is a "web" of information available to most Internet users, and its graphical environment makes navigation simple and exciting. Of all the options available for Internet advertisers, the WWW holds the greatest potential. It allows for detailed and full-color graphics, audio transmission, delivery of in-depth messages, 24-hour availability, and two-way information exchanges between the marketer and customer. For some people, spending time on the Web is replacing time spent viewing other media, such as

11. "No Taste for Spam," *PROMO Magazine,* May 2000, 57–58.

12. For a discussion of spamming versus targeted e-mail pitches, see Dana Garber, "Spam Has Choicer Cuts," *CNN Interactive,* August 10, 1998, cnn.com/TECH/computing/9808/10/tastyspam.idg/, accessed March 28, 1999.

IBP

Chatting a Star up the Charts

When executives at RCA records started plotting the advertising strategy for Christina Aguilera's debut album, they knew the Internet would play a crucial role in the introductory campaign. Most important, they understood that the teen target audience was skeptical and not receptive to traditional marketing tactics. Or, in the words of one Internet marketing strategist, "they have their B.S detectors on 11." With that knowledge, RCA put into motion an Internet-based advertising/word-of-mouth strategy to create an Internet buzz around Ms. Aguilera and her new album. The strategy was executed in four stages by Electric Artists, an Internet marketing firm that specializes in music marketing.

- Stage 1: To monitor what teens already knew about Aguilera and what they were saying, Electric Artists began monitoring popular teen sites such as www.alloy.com and www.gurl.com as well as sites created for other teen stars such as the Backstreet Boys and Britney Spears. The firm compiled some important information about fans' reactions to Aguilera's single "Genie in a Bottle" and also learned that there was a budding rivalry between Aguilera fans and Spears fans.
- Stage 2: Electric sent a team of cybersurfers to popular sites to start chatting up Aguilera, her single, her past, and the rumor of her new album. The surfers posted messages on sites or e-mailed individual fans with comments like "Does anyone remember Christina Aguilera—she sang the song from *Mulan* called 'Reflection'? I heard she has a new song out called 'Genie in a Bottle' and a new album is supposed to be out this summer." Electric strategists point out, "It's kids marketing to each other."
- Stage 3: The promotional strategy ascended to a new level as Electric shifted the emphasis of its Internet communication from Aguilera's single to the album itself. One challenge included motivating fans to go from a $1.98 purchase to a $16.00 purchase. Another hurdle was to convince big music retailers such as Amazon.com and CDNow that Aguilera deserved prominent visibility on their Web sites. To complement these strategies, Electric ensured that the album cover and album name were highly memorable to parents who were shopping for their teenagers. This included lots of major magazine and entertainment television media coverage that parents, particularly mothers, would come in contact with.
- Stage 4: To retain the momentum gained from the initial Internet effort, Electric continued to strengthen and broaden Aguilera's fan base using a variety of additional Internet strategies. The continually updated Web site offers teen audiences access to concert and TV appearances, chats, fan club information, merchandise, and e-mail. Electric also continues to monitor teen interest in competitors such as Mariah Carey and Whitney Houston to stay connected to the broader teen music scene.

The result of this Internet-based campaign was a number one album and eventually the Best New Artist award at the 2000 Grammy Awards. The story of Christina Aguilera shows that the power of Internet advertising lies in its ability to specifically target and communicate in very specific language to an audience. That is the distinguishing feature of the Internet as an advertising media alternative. And the Aguilera story demonstrates that Internet advertising is much more than just banner ads.

Sources: Erin White, "Chatting a Singer up the Pop Charts," *Wall Street Journal*, December 5, 1999, B1, B4; Christopher John Farley and David E. Thigpen, "Christina Aguilera: Building a 21st Century Star," *Time*, March 6, 2000, 70–71.

print, radio, and television. There is one great difference between the Web and other cyberadvertising vehicles: The consumer actively searches for the marketer's home page. Of course, Web advertisers are attempting to make their pages much easier to find and, in reality, harder to avoid.

To learn how a firm can make highly effective use of all the Internet media, see the IBP box on this page which describes how RCA records put together a Web-based strategy to create a buzz around Christina Aguilera's debut album.

3 Surfing the World Wide Web. Using software such as Netscape, consumers can simply input the addresses of Web sites they wish to visit and directly access the information available there. However, the Web is a library with no card catalog. There is no central authority that lists all possible sites accessible via the Internet. This condition leads to **surfing**—gliding from page to page. Users can seek and find different sites in a variety of ways: through search engines, through direct links with other sites, and by word of mouth.

A **search engine** allows an Internet user to type in a few keywords, and the search engine then finds all sites that contain the keywords. Search engines all have the same basic user interface but differ in how they perform the search and in the amount of the WWW accessed. There are four distinct styles of search engines: hierarchical, collection, concept, and robot. There are also the special cases of portals, Web community sites, and mega–search engines.

Hierarchical Search Engines. Most of you are familiar with Yahoo!, which is an example of a search engine with a hierarchical, subject-oriented system (see Exhibit 16.7). In a **hierarchical search engine,** all sites fit into categories. For example, Nike is indexed as Business and Economy/Shopping and Services/Apparel/Footwear/Athletic

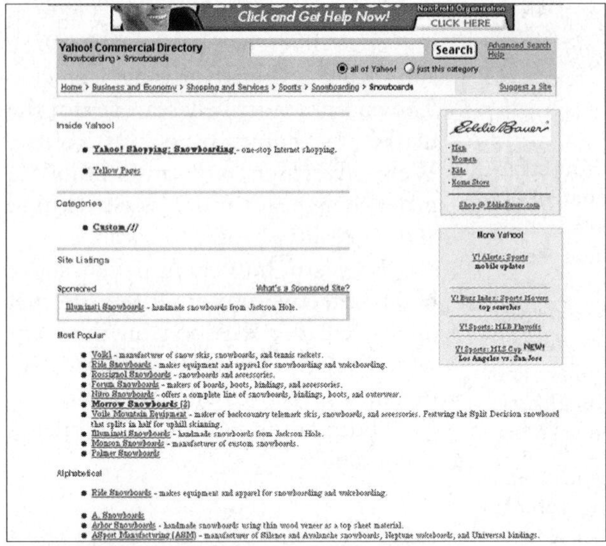

EXHIBIT 16.7

Big Internet sites like Yahoo! offer Internet users a hierarchical search engine to seek out information on the Internet. Notice also that sites like Yahoo!, Lycos, and Excite provide all sorts of links for travel, games, chat, e-mail, and news and sports information.
www.yahoo.com

Shoes/Brand Names. Users are thus able to find and select a category as well as all the relevant Yahoo! sites. Going to Business and Economy/Shopping and Services/Sports/Snowboarding/Snowboards, for instance, gives a list of nearly 60 companies that sell snowboards on the Web. By checking these sites, a person could find a snowboard company and buy a snowboard over the Web. Although hierarchical sites like Yahoo! are great for doing general searches, they do have some significant limitations. For example, Yahoo!'s database of Web sites contains only submissions. That is, Yahoo! does not actually perform a search of the Web for sites, but contains only sites that users tell it about. Because of this, Yahoo! omits a significant portion of the vast information available on the Web.

Collection Search Engines. A second type of search engine is exemplified by AltaVista. **Collection search engines** use a **spider,** which is an automated program that crawls around the Web and collects information. As of mid-2000, the collection of Web pages indexed by AltaVista stood at over 3 million. With AltaVista, a person can perform a text search on all of these sites, resulting in access to literally tens of billions of words. For example, the search for the phrase "alpine skiing" returned 22,493 pages that contain this exact phrase. By comparison, the same phrase entered in a Yahoo! search turned up 128 category matches.

Because of the sheer quantity of Web pages, AltaVista ranks the best matches first. The relatively large amount of information available on AltaVista mandates that users know what they are really interested in; otherwise, they will be flooded with useless information.

Concept Search Engines. Excite is a concept search engine. With a **concept search engine,** a concept rather than a word or phrase is the basis for the search. Using the alpine skiing example, the top sites with the concept "alpine skiing" are listed in an Excite search. This is a very efficient way of searching, producing relatively focused results compared to AltaVista and with the added ability of using the results of a search to further modify the search. The downside is that concept search engines such as Excite lack the comprehensiveness of collection search engines. Ask Jeeves, another concept search engine, allows users to conduct searches using natural-language questions such as, "Who was the fourteenth president of the United States?" (Answer: Franklin Pierce, 1853–1857.)

Robot Search Engines. The newest technique, **robot search engines,** employs **robots** ("bots") to do the work for the consumer by roaming the Internet in search of information fitting certain user-specified criteria. For example, shopping robots specialize in finding the best deals for your music needs (see Exhibit 16.8), insurance needs (www.insuremarket.com), or traveling needs (www.travelocity.com). Web retailers concerned that such robots will result in an electronic marketplace governed entirely by price rather than brand loyalty have designed their sites to either refuse the robot admission to the site or confuse the robot.[13] Still, some analysts believe that future e-commerce will be governed by "shopbots" and that loyalty will shift to the

13. *Wall Street Journal,* September 3, 1998, B1, B8.

EXHIBIT 16.8

The newest way to search the Internet is with "shopbots" or "bots." These automated Internet search engines take directions on what to search for and then deliver it automatically back to the user. www.mysimon.com

EXHIBIT 16.9

Community portals like Latina.com offer the opportunity to visit a site that matches surfers' interests for information on a variety of topics from politics to culture to entertainment. What is Teen.com (www.teen.com) *doing to make sure it wins the community portal war? Are the search functions and navigational features of Teen.com designed to direct surfers to particular sites? Does it offer search access to the World Wide Web?*

shopbot sites rather than retail brand names. We will explore this issue in great detail in Chapter 10 on direct marketing and e-commerce.

Portals. *Portal* has assumed the position as the most overused, misused, abused, and confused term in Internet vocabulary. A **portal** is a starting point for Web access and search. Portals can be vertical (serving a specialized market or industries, such as Chemdex [www.chemdex.org] for the chemical industry), horizontal (providing access and links across industries, such as Verticalnet [www.verticalnet.com] with its 53 different business trade communities), or ethnic (www.latina.com; see Exhibit 16.9) or community-based.[14] Several of the large search engines, such as Yahoo! and Lycos, are focusing their attention on becoming portals for Internet exploring. In addition to providing its own content, AOL serves as a convenient and well-organized entrance to the Web. From AOL a Web surfer can jump to many locations highlighted by AOL, particularly commercial sites who are partnering with AOL and have paid a fee for preferred placement on the site.[15] Portals are more interested in channeling surfers to particular sites, especially commercial ones.

14. Mougayar Walid, "The New Portal Math," *Business 2.0,* January 2000, 245.
15. Chip Bayers, "Capitalist Econstruction," *Wired,* March 2000, 211–218.

The portal wars are already hot, with each portal trying to provide access and incentive for using their service as a gateway to the Internet or commerce. Each is trying to top the other in monthly traffic and advertising revenue. This battle is going to only get hotter in the near term as portals vie for superiority and dominance in the wireless Web. In 1999, 3.6 million households had wireless Web browsing capability. By 2003, this number is expected to grow to over 40 million households, with wireless-directed ad revenue reaching as high as 17 billion.[16]

Other Ways to Find Sites. Many people have created their own Web pages that list their favorite sites. This is a fabulous way of finding new and interesting sites—as well as feeding a person's narcissism. For example, the Web address for this book, http://oguinn.swcollege.com, is a resource for information about advertising, including links to a wide range of industry resources. Since this page is maintained, updated, and checked regularly, it is a good resource for someone interested in advertising. Although most people find Web pages via Internet resources (over 80 percent of respondents in one survey found Web pages through search engines or other Web pages), sites can also be discovered through traditional word-of-mouth communications. Internet enthusiasts tend to share their experiences on the Web through discussions in coffeehouses, by reading and writing articles, and via other non-Web venues. There are also Web community sites such as www.theglobe.com and mega–search engines that combine several search engines at once (www.dogpile.com).

4 Advertising on the Internet.

In 1995, $54.7 million was spent advertising on the Internet. Spending in 1996 was around $300 million. In 1997 it jumped to just around $1 billion, in 1998 it was somewhere around $2 billion, and the year 2000 logged in at just over $8.2 billion. As we saw earlier, advertising revenues on the Internet are expected to grow to $30 billion by 2004—an astronomical growth rate.[17] At the same time, the cost of advertising on the Internet is falling; it dropped about 6 percent in 1998 alone and has continued to fall. So as demand for cyberadvertising goes up, apparently so does supply. But don't let the big numbers impress you too much. Internet advertising still represents only about 1.5 percent of all U.S. advertising; when one counts all promotion dollars it's less than half of 1 percent. And as we have seen, beginning in 2001, ad spending on the Internet plummeted. Advertising spending at Web portal Yahoo! plunged 22 percent, prompting massive layoffs.[18]

A wide range of issues are associated with using the Internet for advertising purposes. This section begins by exploring the advantages of Internet advertising. Then we'll look at who is advertising on the internet, the costs associated with Internet advertising, and the different types of Internet advertising.

The Advantages of Internet Advertising.

Internet advertising has emerged as a legitimate advertising option for advertisers—and it is not just because the Web represents a new and different technological option. Several unique characteristics of Internet advertising offer advantages over traditional forms.

Target Market Selectivity. The Web offers advertisers a new and precise way to target market segments. Not only are the segments precisely defined (you can place an ad on the numismatist [coin collecting] society page, for example), but the

16. Patricia Riedman, "Portals Find More Wars to Wage on Wireless Web," *Advertising Age,* March 6, 2000, S34; Pui-Wing Tam, "Show of Hands," *Wall Street Journal,* April 23, 2001.
17. Internet Advertising Bureau, "Total Ad Spend for 2000 Reached USD8.2 bn," op. cit.
18. Beth Snyder Bulik, "Not by Ads Alone," *Business 2.0,* February 20, 2001, 70–72.

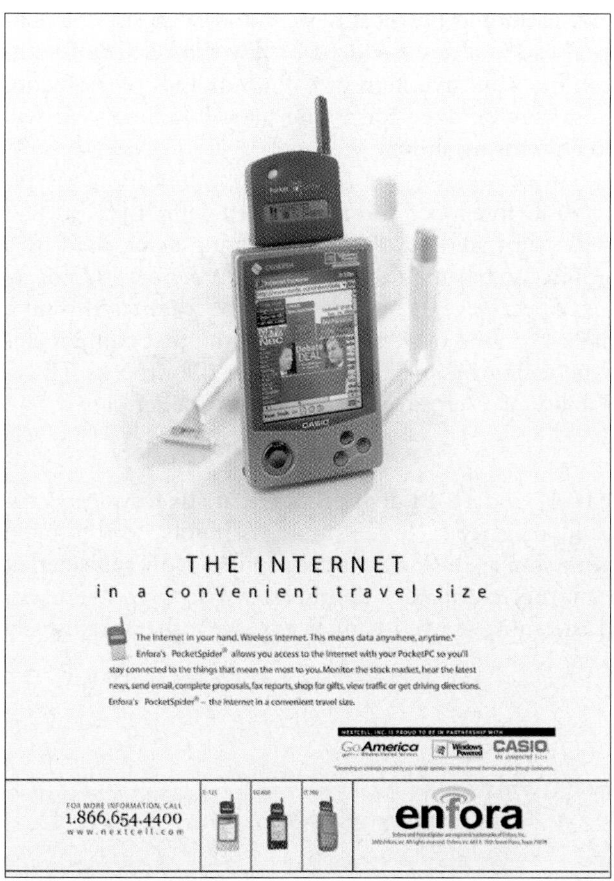

EXHIBIT 16.10

Wireless delivery of Internet information is expected to explode over the next few years. www.enfora.com

Internet allows forms of targeting that truly enhance traditional segmentation schemes such as demographics, geographics, and psychographics. Advertisers can focus on specific interest areas, but they can also target based on geographic regions (including global), time of day, computer platform, or browser.

Tracking. The Internet allows advertisers to track how users interact with their brands and learn what interests current and potential customers. Banner ads and Web sites also provide the opportunity to measure the response to an ad (number of hits), which is a measure that is unattainable in traditional media.

Deliverability and Flexibility. Online advertising and Web site content is delivered 24 hours a day, 7 days a week, at the convenience of the receiver. Whenever receivers are logged on and active, advertising is there and ready to greet them. Just as important, a campaign can be tracked on a daily basis and updated, changed, or replaced almost immediately. This is a dramatic difference from traditional media, where changing a campaign might be delayed for weeks, given media schedules and the time needed for production of ads in traditional media. GMbuy.com (www.globalbuypower.com) is a perfect example of this kind of deliverability and flexibility. The site allows consumers considering a GM car or truck to visit the site at any time to dig for information about GM vehicles. And, as mentioned earlier, as Web delivery goes wireless, there will be even more flexibility and deliverability for Web communications (see Exhibit 16.10).

Interactivity. A lofty and often unattainable goal for a marketer is to engage a prospective customer with the brand and the firm. This can be done with Internet advertising in a way that just cannot be accomplished in traditional media. A consumer can go to a company Web site or click through from a banner ad and take a tour of the brand's features and values. A **click-through** is a measure of the number of page elements (hyperlinks) that have actually been requested (that is, "clicked through" from the banner ad to the link). Software is a perfect example of this sort of advantage of the Web. Let's say you are looking for software to do your taxes. You can log on to taxes.yahoo.com, where (through H&R Block tax consulting) you will find all the software, tax forms, and online information you need to prepare your taxes. Then you can actually file your taxes with both the IRS and your state tax agency! And this sort of interactivity is not reserved for big national companies. Try this as an exercise. Find a sign company in your local phone directory. It is likely that one will have a Web site where you can design your own sign, order it, and ask for it to be delivered. You have complete interaction with the firm and its product without ever leaving your computer.

Cost. While the cost-per-thousand numbers on reaching audiences through the Web are still relatively high (see the next section) compared to radio or television, they compare very favorably with magazines, newspapers, and direct marketing. And the cost for producing a Web ad, including both banner ads and Web sites, is relatively low. Banner ads are very cheap at a few hundred or few thousand dollars to produce and place. Web sites can be expensive, tens or even hundreds of thousands of dollars to develop, but the cost may be fixed for a long period of time. We will cover more on the cost of Web advertising shortly.

Integration. Web advertising is easily integrated and coordinated with other forms of promotion. In the most basic sense, all traditional media advertising being used by a marketer can carry the Web site URL. Web banner ads can highlight themes and images from television or print campaigns. Special events or contests can be featured in banner ads and on Web sites. Overall, the integration of Web activities with other components of the marketing mix is one of the easiest integration tasks in the IBP process. This is due to the flexibility and deliverability of Web advertising discussed earlier.

Who Advertises on the Internet?

Exhibits 16.11 and 16.12 demonstrate that advertising on the Web, compared to television and magazines, for example, is highly concentrated among a very few advertisers with similar business model profiles. You can see that the big users of the Web are Internet companies themselves. The top advertisers, based on both impressions and the most-viewed banner ads, are either exclusively

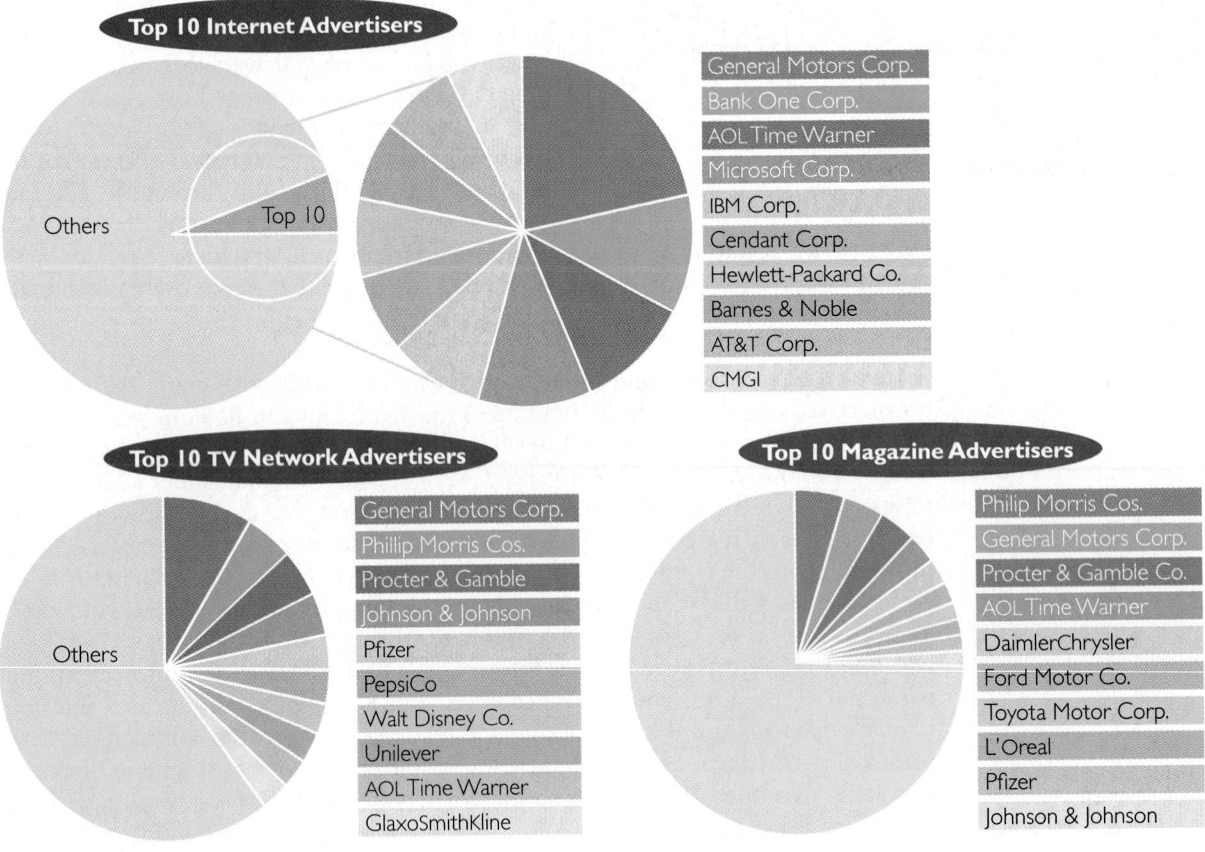

EXHIBIT 16.11

Top advertisers on the Web, ranked by impressions.

Rank	Advertiser	Unique Audience	Reach %
1	Bonzi.com Software	10,030,000	13.3
2	ClassMates.com	9,969,000	13.2
3	JP Morgan Chase	5,714,000	7.6
4	Providian Financial Corp.	5,525,000	7.3
5	American Airlines	5,383,000	7.1
6	JP Morgan Chase	5,375,000	7.1
7	Colonize.com	5,356,300	7.1
8	Consumer Cnslg. of America	4,488,000	6.0
9	Ebates	4,215,000	5.6
10	Consumer Cnslg. of America	4,073,000	6.0
11	Ebates	4,002,000	5.4
12	GetSmart.com	3,984,000	5.3
13	Ameritrade	3,973,000	5.3
14	Ebates	3,933,000	5.2
15	Amazon.com	3,800,000	5.0

Source: *Advertising Age*, April 21, 2001, 32

EXHIBIT 16.12

Top banner advertisers, ranked by unique audience and reach.

EXHIBIT 16.13

The cost per thousand (CPM) for banner ads has been falling steadily over the last several years. However, compared to television or radio broadcasts, banner ad CPM is still relatively high. Notice, however, that the absolute cost in dollars of placing banner ads and other Internet-based communications can be much lower than traditional media.

	Absolute Cost	Cost per Thousand (CPM)
Traditional Media		
Local TV (30-second spot)	$4,000 to $45,000	$12 to $15
National TV (30-second spot)	80,000 to 600,000	10 to 20
Cable TV (30-second spot)	5,000 to 10,000	3 to 8
Radio (30-second spot)	200 to 1,000	1 to 5
Newspaper (top-10 markets)	40,000 to 80,000	80 to 120
Magazines (regional coverage)	40,000 to 100,000	50 to 120
Direct mail (inserts)	10,000 to 20,000	15 to 40
Billboards	5,000 to 25,000	—
Internet Media		
Banner ads	$1,000 to $5,000	$5 to $50
Rich media	1,000 to 10,000	40 to 50
E-mail newsletters	1,000 to 5,000	25 to 200
Sponsorship	Variable based on duration	30 to 75

Sources: Forrester Research, www.forrester.com; Jennifer Rewick, "Choices, Choices," *Wall Street Journal*, April 23, 2001, R12.

Web organizations or those with significant Web presence. This will have to change if the WWW is to really challenge traditional media.

The Cost of Internet Advertising. On a cost-per-thousand (CPM) basis, the cost of Web ads for the most part compares favorably with ads placed in traditional media. Exhibit 16.13 shows the comparison of absolute cost and cost per thousand (CPM) for ads placed in traditional media and Web-based ads. The real attraction of the Internet is not found in raw numbers and CPMs, but rather in terms of highly desirable, highly segmentable, and highly motivated audiences (Exhibit 16.14). The Internet is ideally suited for niche marketing—that is, for reaching only those consumers most likely to buy what the marketer is selling. This aspect of the Internet as an advertising option has always been its great attraction: the ability to identify segments and deliver almost-customized (or in the case of e-mail, actually customized) messages directly to them—one by one.

The current Internet audience is relatively affluent, so the Internet audience does have the means to buy. In cases where there is an active search for product or service information on the Internet, there is also a predisposed and motivated audience. This makes the Internet fairly special among advertising-supported vehicles. On the other hand, there are enormous audience measurement problems; we don't really know who sees or notices Internet advertising with much certainty. So advertisers don't know exactly what they are buying. This bothers them. Further, there is some evidence that audience tolerance for Web advertising is actually declining. Recent studies find that Web surfers are even less tolerant of advertising than are average consumers. The number of Web users who say they actively avoid the ads is up, and the number who say they notice ads is down.[19] This is consistent with the experience of advertising history in general: As advertising becomes more common, fewer

19. *The Economist*, "Advertising That Clicks," October 9, 1999, 71–72.

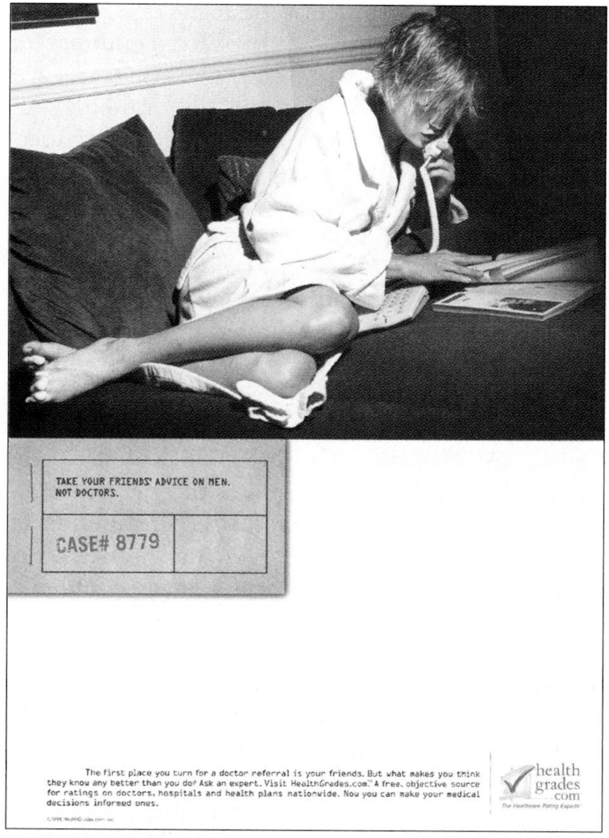

EXHIBIT 16.14

One of the key advantages of the Internet is that Web sites can be targeted to the very specific information needs of narrowly defined segments. www.healthgrades.com

ads are noticed, fewer are accepted, and fewer make any impact at all. Each ad thus becomes less powerful as ads become more common, familiar, and annoying. Advertising has always had a way of being a victim of its own success. What's more, Internet advertising comes into an already crowded and highly cluttered media and information environment.

Regardless of the lack of effective measurement and evaluation of reach, the narrow audience composition, and the unknown impact of Web advertising, companies seem to be afraid of being left behind. Apparently, there is some prestige attached to advertising on the WWW, or at least a feeling of inadequacy to not be there. In addition, most advertisers want to have a well-established Web image in the future, so getting involved now makes sense, even if the best strategy for doing so is unclear. Keeping on eye on the future seems like a good idea, too. By 2005, it is expected that there will be 77 million Internet users under age 18. This means that a new generation of Net surfers and users will be emerging and will be searching the Web with ease.[20]

Types of Internet Advertising. There are several ways for advertisers to place advertising messages on the Web. The most widely known of these options is the banner ad, which includes several variations. But more complex and elaborate variations on Internet advertising include pop-up ads, e-mail communication, streaming video and audio, corporate Web sites, and virtual malls. We will consider the features and advantages of each of these types of Internet advertising options.

Banner Ads. Banner ads, which account for about 50 percent of all online advertising revenue,[21] are paid placements of advertising on other sites that contain editorial material. A variation on the banner that you may encounter is the **skyscraper,** a tall, skinny banner ad that is a variation on the traditional top-of-the-screen rectangle. A feature of banner ads is that consumers not only see the ad but also can make a quick trip to the marketer's home page by clicking on the ad (this the "click-through" defined earlier). Thus, the challenge of creating and placing banner ads is not only to catch people's attention but also to entice them to visit the marketer's home page and stay for a while. Many high-traffic Web sites that provide information content have started to rely on advertisers to support their services. General consumer sites such as Yahoo! and HotWired have banner advertisements as part of their revenue-generation scheme.

A more targeted option is to place banner ads on sites that attract specific market niches. For example, a banner ad for running shoes would be placed on a site that offers information related to running. This option is emerging as a way for advertisers to focus more tightly on their target audiences. Currently, advertisers

20. Bernadette Burke, "Meeting Generation Y," NUA Internet Surveys, July 19, 1999 at www.nua.net/surveys/, accessed March 22, 2000.

21. Heather Green and Ben Elgin, "Do E-Ads Have a Future?," *Business Week e.biz,* January 22, 2001, 46–49.

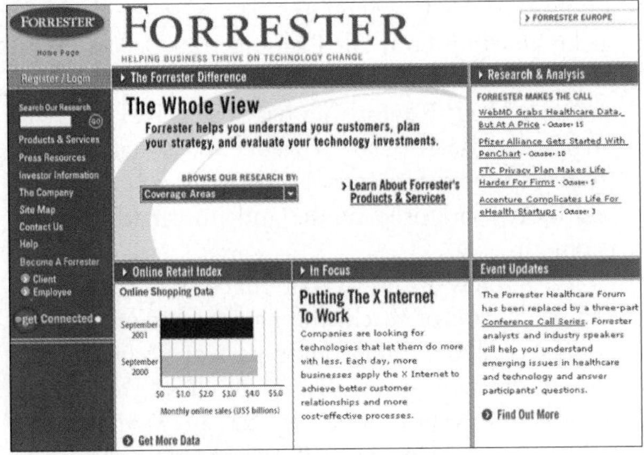

EXHIBIT 16.15

New services can track advertising cost and audience delivered for various Web sites. www.forrester.com

consider WWW users to be a focused segment of their own. However, as the Web continues to blossom, advertisers will begin to realize that, even across the entire Web, there are sites that draw specific subgroups of Web users. These niche users have particular interests that may represent important opportunities for the right marketer.

A pricing evaluation service for banner ads is offered by Interactive Traffic. The I-Traffic Index computes a site's advertising value based on traffic, placement and size of ads, ad rates, and evaluations of the site's quality.[22] Firms such as Forrester Research (see Exhibit 16.15) assess the costs of banner ads on a variety of sites and provide an estimate to advertisers of the audience delivered. Complicating the matter now is the fact that consumer resistance to banner ads is increasing. First, most online consumers do not click on Web banner ads. For example, one survey found that only 1 percent of surfers click on banner ads.[23] Second, many consumers resent banner ads, which they see as intrusive and annoying; banner ads increase Web page load times due to their complex graphics and animation. (Thus, banner advertisements should be designed with downloading time in mind.) Supporting this trend are fixes called *ad blockers,* which allow consumers to screen out banner ads. For example, one ad blocker program called AdWipe allows a surfer to load pages sans banner ads.[24]

There is currently wide debate about the value and even the future of banner ads. Banner ads represent over half of all advertising on the Internet, but they are also the most reviled of all elements of online marketing.[25] One Web site, Mediconsult.com, announced that it was abandoning banner ads altogether after completing extensive focus groups with its users. The 3.5 million annual visitors to the site now surf banner-free.[26] On the plus side, banner ads are accounting for the majority of all online spending by companies trying to use the Web as part of their integrated brand promotion strategy. This, of course, accounts for most of the revenue of the pure online promotion organizations. In addition, a study of recall for banner ads shows that recall for a single ad banner exposure is about 12 percent, which compares favorably with the 10 percent recall for a single exposure to a television ad.

On the negative side of the argument, eMarketer estimates that 99.9 percent of all banner ads don't get clicked. In addition, eMarketer's data suggests that 49 percent of Web surfers don't even look at a banner ad while they surf, and in order to develop any brand recognition a consumer would have to be exposed to a banner ad 27 times—not a good combination of statistics. The current thinking is that most users of banner advertising will shift their Web spending from banners to strategic partnerships and sponsorships.[27]

Pop-Up Ads. The only thing surfers hate more than banner ads is pop-up Internet ads. The idea is borrowed from TV. A **pop-up ad** is an Internet advertisement that appears as a Web site page is loading or after a page has loaded. A surfer wants to go to a certain site but has to wade through an ad page first, just as a television

22. K. Cleland, "SRDS, I Join Interactive Frenzy," *Advertising Age,* October 16, 1995, 22.
23. *The Economist,* September 26, 1998.
24. *San Francisco Chronicle,* August 26, 1998.
25. Kim Cross, "Whither the Banner," *Business 2.0,* December 1999, 137.
26. Ibid.
27. "Consumer Attitudes toward Web Marketing," eMarketing Report published July 7, 1999, www.emarketing.com, accessed March 22, 2000.

EXHIBIT 16.16

E-mail as an advertising alternative can meet with some heavy resistance from Web users. One way to avoid the resistance is to use a permission marketing firm. These firms have lists of consumers who "opt in," or agree to have e-mail sent to them by commercial sources. www.edirect.com

viewer must watch a commercial before seeing a favorite show. It is often not merely a word from a sponsor, but invitations to link to another related site. A pop-up ad opens a separate window. The more times people click on these ads, the more money can be charged for the privilege of advertising. If the future of banner ads is uncertain, then the future of pop-ups must be doomed—a recent study found that 62 percent of surfers said that pop-ups interfered with their use of a Web page.[28] A new version of the pop-up called the bulky box was recently introduced by CNet on its Web site.[29] The **bulky box** is simply a very large pop-up that can cover about 25 percent of the Web page—that ought to convert the other 38 percent of the surfers who didn't already hate pop-ups! But as long as marketers are willing to give pop-up ads a try, then we'll all have our pleasant surfing interrupted with unwanted commercial messages.

E-Mail Communication. As mentioned earlier, e-mail communication may be the Internet's most advantageous application. Through e-mail, the Internet is the only mass medium capable of customizing a message for thousands or even millions of receivers. The message is delivered in a unique way, one at a time, which no other medium is capable of doing. E-mail advertising is expected to grow from about $164 million in advertising in 1999 to about $7 billion in 2005, with over 260 billion e-mail promotional messages being sent.[30] The attitude toward e-mail advertising varies, of course, depending on whether people are "spammed" with unwanted e-mail or have signed up and given permission for e-mail to be delivered. When Web users agree to receive e-mails from organizations, this is called **permission marketing.** Some Web firms, such as edirect.com (see Exhibit 16.16), specialize in developing what are called "opt-in" lists of Web users who have agreed to accept commercial e-mails.

The data on permission-based e-mailing versus spamming are compelling. Sixty-six percent of Web users who give their permission to have e-mail sent to them indicate that they are either eager or curious to read the e-mail. This compares to only 15 percent of Web users who receive e-mail through spamming.[31] And e-mail advertisers are turning to some traditional message strategies such as humor to make the e-mail messages more palatable and interesting. BitMagic, an Amsterdam-based Web advertising specialty firm, has Web users download software containing a joke, cartoon, or game along with the e-mail message.[32]

Through e-mail and electronic mailing lists, advertisers can encourage viral marketing. **Viral marketing** is the process of consumers marketing to consumers over the Internet through word of mouth transmitted through e-mails and electronic mailing lists. Hotmail (www.hotmail.com) is the king of viral marketing. Every e-mail by every Hotmail subscriber used to conclude with the tagline "Get your private, free e-mail at http://www.hotmail.com." That viral marketing program helped

28. NUA Internet Surveys, May 3, 2001, www.nua.i.e, accessed May 28, 2001.
29. Mylene Magalindan, "CNet to Roll Out New Internet Ad Styles," *Wall Street Journal,* January 24, 2001, B10.
30. Cara Beardi, "This Party Is Just Started," *Advertising Age,* February 5, 2001, 14.
31. Ibid.
32. Kathryn Kranhold, "Internet Advertisers Use Humor in Effort to Entice Web Surfers," *Wall Street Journal,* August 17, 1999, B9.

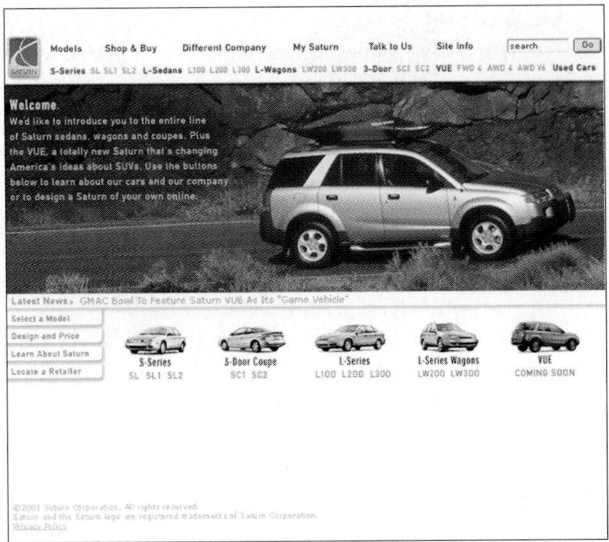

EXHIBIT 16.17

Some corporate Web sites are developed to be purely information sites. The Saturn site provides extensive product information for the full line of Saturn vehicles.
www.saturnbp.com

sign up 12 million subscribers, with 150,000 being added every day.[33]

Streaming Video and Audio. **Streaming video and audio** is merely the process of inserting TV- and radio-like ads into music and video clips that marketers send to Web users as they visit content networks. Firms such as RealNetworks, NetRadio, and MusicVision insert ads for advertisers. The future of such ads will depend on the ability to deliver bandwidth to accommodate the transmission and consumer access to high-speed Internet connections. The advantage, aside from being more interesting than a banner or a pop-up, is that streaming audio and video can realize click-through rates of 3.5 percent—or hundreds of times greater than banner click-throughs.[34]

Corporate Home Pages. A **corporate home page** is a Web site where a marketer provides current and potential customers information about the firm in great detail. The best corporate home pages not only provide corporate and product information but also offer other content of interest to site visitors. The Saturn site (www.saturnbp.com) in Exhibit 16.17 allows people to find out about the line of Saturn cars, pricing, specifications, and the closest dealers. This product-oriented site also allows consumers to request brochures, communicate their comments and questions to the Saturn corporation, and find a dealer when they are ready to make a purchase. A corporate site that falls toward the lifestyle end of the spectrum is the Crayola site (www.crayola.com) displayed in Exhibit 16.18. Rather than focusing on its rather famous product, the company decided to focus on the needs of the parents and children that use Crayola crayons. Visitors can do such things as read bedtime stories, search for local child-care providers, discover hints on getting kids to help with housework, and browse movie reviews for family-oriented flicks. And, of course, there is a link to areas where kids can create art with computerized Crayolas (the crayons on the right side of the page).

Virtual Malls. A variation on the corporate Web site is a Web site placed inside a virtual mall. A **virtual mall** is a gateway to a group of Internet storefronts that provide access to mall sites by simply clicking on a category of store, as shown on the Mall Internet site (www.mall-internet.com) in Exhibit 16.19. Notice that many of the resident stores at this Web site have their own corporate Web sites and home pages, but have chosen to also set up a site in the virtual mall. Mall visitors can be led directly to the corporate site. Having this additional presence just gives stores such as the Gap and J. Crew more exposure.

The nature of virtual malls varies widely from mall to mall. MetroWest's Virtual Mall (www.virtmall.com) features local orientation from west Boston. The advantage of malls for a marketer is the opportunity to attract browsers to its site, much as window shopping works in the physical world. Check out CyberShop at www.cybershop.com: This online mall allows virtual shoppers to browse by department or brand. Offerings range from gourmet foodstuffs to housewares to women's accessories, and include constantly updated sale items.

33. Steve Jurvetson, "Turning Customers into a Sales Force," *Business 2.0,* March 2000, 231.
34. Green and Elgin, "Do E-Ads Have a Future," 48.
35. Beth Snyder Bulik, "Procter & Gamble's Great Web Experiment," *Business 2.0,* November 28, 2000, 48–50.

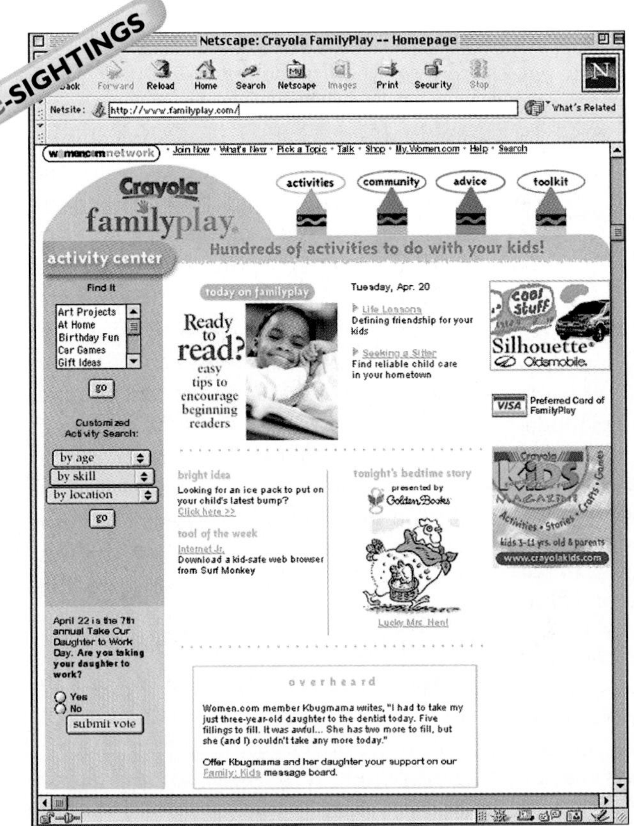

EXHIBIT 16.18

In contrast to purely information sites, other Web sites are more "lifestyle" sites. The Crayola site (www.crayola.com) offers parents, educators, and kids all sorts of interesting, entertaining, and educational options. Compare the Crayola site to the Good Humor–Breyer's Popsicle site (www.popsicle.com), and evaluate which one does a better job of focusing on the needs of parents and children. Lycos also hosts a kid-friendly site (www.lycoszone.com). Why is this "kids' zone" an important option for a search engine to provide? What does Lycos hope to achieve with this special corporate home page?

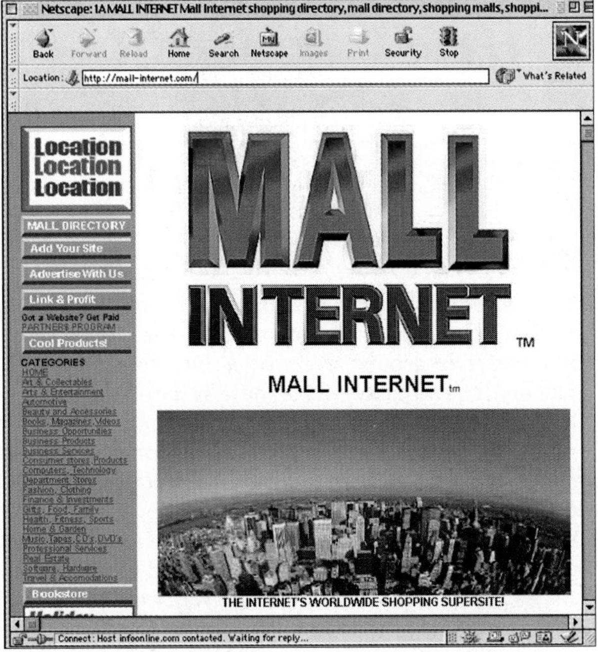

EXHIBIT 16.19

Virtual malls provide advertisers another way to reach surfers. Malls like this one provide links to corporate Web sites that consumers might not go to directly. www.mall-internet.com

5 Establishing a Site on the World Wide Web.

While setting up a Web site can be done fairly easily, setting up a commercially viable one is a lot harder and a lot more expensive. The top commercial sites today cost $1 million to develop, about $4.9 million for the initial launch and about $500,000 to over a million dollars a year to maintain.[35] Setting up an attractive site costs so much because of the need for specialized designers to create the site and, most important, to constantly update the site. The basic hardware for a site can be a personal computer, and the software to run the site ranges from free to several thousand dollars, depending on the number of extras needed. A site anticipating considerable traffic will need to plan for higher-capacity connections—and hence, a bigger phone bill.

But what if you're not a big IPO Internet firm with several million to spend for the first year of operating of a Web site? Not to fear. There are actually some very inexpensive ways of setting up a site and finding hosts to maintain it if you are a small or medium-size business and want an Internet presence. Some of the big players are actually coming to the rescue of the little guys. Yahoo!, AT&T, Intel, MindSpring,

35. Beth Snyder Bulik, "Procter & Gamble's Great Web Experiment," *Business 2.0,* November 28, 2000, 48–50.

and others have begun to offer low-cost hosting and browser-based development tools that allow small businesses to get started on the Internet for about $300 a month.[36] But there is even better news. A new class of Web builders is emerging with an even better deal. One startup based in Emeryville, California, FreeMerchant.com (www.freemerchant.com), will set up a Web page and e-commerce site for free. The company makes its revenue by partnering with vendors who want to reach a small business audience. By the end of 1999, nearly 37 percent of small businesses had developed Web sites.[37] We also need to keep in mind that using the Web as a key component of a brand-building strategy is not reserved just for consumer brands. Business products advertisers are discovering the power of the Web for brand building as well. Plus, from a corporate perspective, the Web is an ideal global medium, as Arthur Andersen, the global consulting firm, discovered when it set out to revamp its brand image.[38] The Global Issues box on this page tells the whole story.

In order for a Web site to attract visitors and build consumer loyalty and confidence, advertisers must conceive a Web strategy that addresses the issues in the next section.

GLOBAL ISSUES

Using the Net to Take a Brand Global

Arthur Andersen is a $7.3 billion professional services and consulting firm that helps clients navigate through the complexities of new economic realities around the world. But the company itself recently woke up to new reality—its brand was mired in an old business model with a market perception that was fading into a conservative and staid image. This definitely did not match the company's current objective, which was to be viewed as a global expert on the "new economy." What made things worse is that Arthur Andersen regional operations around the world were pursuing their own individual strategies. In the words of Matthew Gonring, global managing partner of communications and integrated marketing, "The way we went to market was confusing and diluting the brand. We had to go to one Arthur Andersen master brand around the world."

To reverse the slide and rejuvenate the brand image, Arthur Andersen devised a new promotional program that relied heavily on the Web and attacked the image problem in a way that would provide not only a contemporary look, but also a global presence as well. The first step was to redesign the Arthur Anderson Web site. Ogilvy Interactive was the agency called on to revamp and redesign the site. They immediately cut more than half the content and added new updated material on the firm's services (www.arthurandersen.com). The site also highlighted a new brand logo and bold language—"maverick and inventive"—to describe the company's services. Then 13,000 direct mail pieces, containing miniature CD-ROMs that guided both existing clients and potential customers to the new Web site, were sent to executives worldwide.

Remember that all this reinventing and redesigning was undertaken for arguably the most recognized and respected brand in corporate consulting. But in Gonring's words, "While we recognized that the Arthur Andersen brand is one of the strongest, the brand research was saying that if we wanted to capture the new business . . . tweaking the status quo wasn't going to get us there."

Source: Amanda Beeler, "Arthur Andersen Takes Wraps off Global Image," *Advertising Age*, February 14, 2000, 24.

Getting Surfers to Come Back. Once a site is set up, getting those who spend considerable time on the Internet (**netizens,** as they are commonly called) to spend time at the site and to come back often is a primary concern. When a site is able to attract visitors over and over again and keep them for a long time, it is said to be a **sticky site** or have features that are "sticky." A site with pages and pages showing the product and its specifications may have no appeal beyond attracting a single visit. Even a quick tour of various home pages reveals countless, boring corporate Web pages. According to recent research, most Web sites merely include rich product descriptions that simply mimic printed brochures.[39] Although such Web sites might satisfy the needs of netizens searching for specific product information, they are unlikely to attract and capture the interest of surfers enough to get them to come back. The whole idea is to satisfy visitors and get them to come back.

36. G. Beato, "Web-O-Matic," *Business 2.0,* October 1999, 190.
37. "Small Biz Web Sites on the Rise," Prodigy Communications Corporation, www.prodigy.com, accessed March 17, 2000.
38. Amanda Beeler, "Arthur Andersen Takes Wraps off Global Image," *Advertising Age,* February 14, 2000, 24.
39. Ann E. Schlosser and Alaina Kanfer, "Current Advertising on the Internet," in D. Schumann and E. Thurson, eds., *Advertising and the World Wide Web* (Mahwak, NJ: Lawrence Erlbaum Associates, 1999) 41–60.

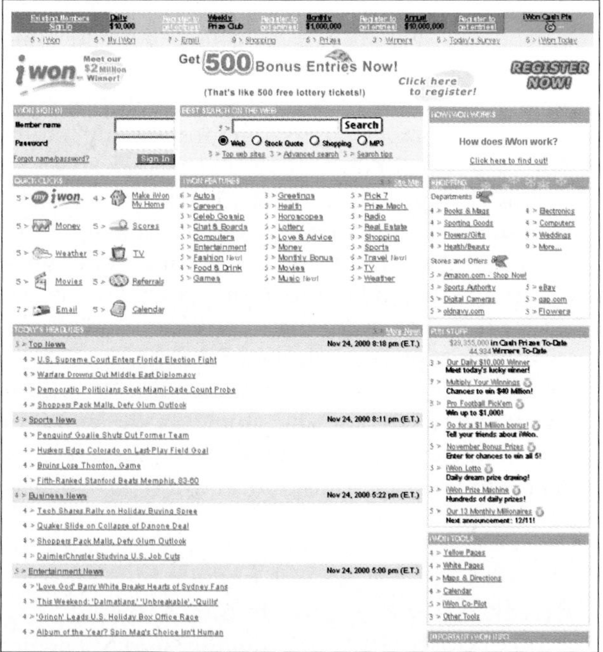

EXHIBIT 16.20

One of the biggest challenges facing Web marketers is making a site "sticky." A sticky site gets consumers to stay long and come back often. Notice that at the iwon.com site, you not only have a chance to win big money on a daily basis and bigger money on a monthly basis, but you also have access to all sorts of options such as checking sports scores, sending greeting cards, or visiting a chat room.
www.iwon.com

To make a site sticky, a marketer should incorporate engaging, interactive features into the site. For the major hosting sites and portals, recurring information such as the weather, late-breaking news, sports scores, and stock quotes are key to attracting visitors daily or even several times a day. In an effort to break into the world of portals, iwon.com (www.iwon.com) offers all sorts of links to current information—as well as the chance to win $10,000 a day or $1 million each month for using the site—pretty much an all-out assault on trying get surfers to come back (see Exhibit 16.20). For home pages or Web sites, entertaining features such as online games or videos can also get surfers to stay at a site and get them to come back.[40] One area in the Cartoon Network site (www.cartoon-network.com) allows kids to help direct the action in a special made-for-the-Web interactive cartoon called *Robot Frenzy*. Thus, it is important for advertisers to be sure to learn about their customers before setting up a site. Good consumer and communications research can be useful in this context.

A well-developed site can keep customers coming back for more. A good example is the New Jersey Devils Web page (www.newjerseydevils.com). Visitors can do more than just read about how their favorite NHL team did the night before. They can read in-depth interviews with players, coaches, and even team trainers. Visitors compete for fan-of-the-month awards, while younger fans get a chance to be sportswriters. Tickets, schedules, and team merchandise are readily available. And, of course, no visit to the New Jersey Devils site is complete without a rousing game of Zamboni Master, where players race around the Devils' arena in a Zamboni machine, repairing damage inflicted by invasions of opposing teams. These features give people multiple reasons to continue to visit the site. Such an approach to Web-presence design has been referred to as **rational branding** and stresses the need for a brand's Web site to provide some unique informational resource to justify visiting it. These features give people multiple reasons to continue to visit the site. Some firms provide advertisers with all the tools they need to develop a sticky site. One such firm is ScreamingMedia (www.screamingmedia.com), which provides design and features for Web sites to attract visitors and keep them coming back (see Exhibit 16.21).

One crucial Web site feature (regardless of whether consumers are searching for specific information or browsing the Web) is the presence of multiple navigational tools; the more navigational tools available, the more the visitor will like the site.[41] Navigational tools help guide the visitor around the site; examples include home and section icons, a search engine that is specific to the site, and a site index. Just as consumers need a cable guide to help them enjoy their cable services, so too do consumers need resources to help them realize and enjoy all the possibilities of the site. Remodeling a site is a costly investment: According to Forrester Research, adding search and other personalization features to a site can cost $300,000 to $425,000. Many argue that such an investment is worthwhile, since the consequences of a poorly designed site include lost revenues and the erosion of brand image.

40. Anne E. Schlosser and Alaina Kanfer, "Culture Clash in Internet Marketing," in M. J. Shaw, R. Blanning, T. Strader, and A. Whinston, eds., *Handbook on Electronic Commerce* (New York: Springer-Verlag, 1999).

41. Schlosser and Kanfer, "Current Advertising on the Internet," 41–60.

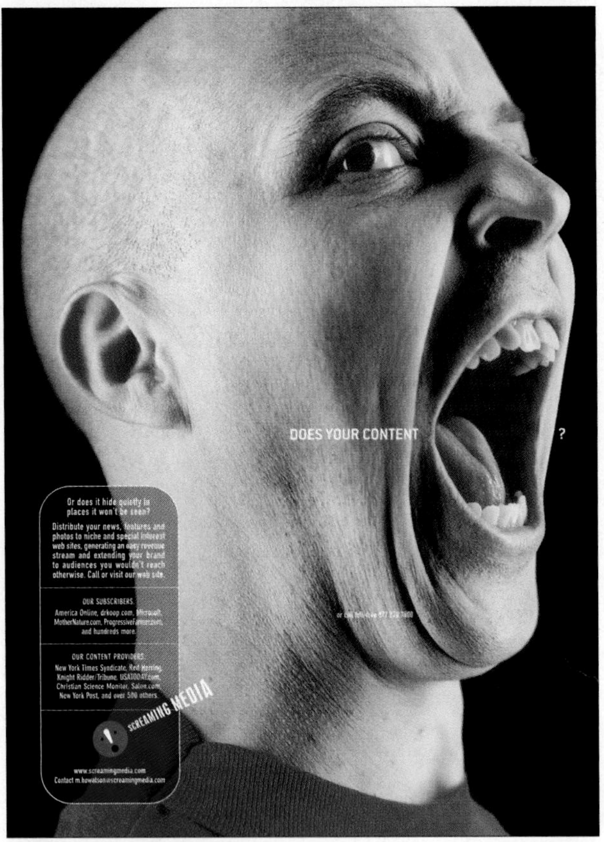

EXHIBIT 16.21

Marketers can turn to firms like ScreamingMedia (www.screamingmedia.com) to help them develop sites that attract Web surfers and keep them coming back.

Thus, the objective of having repeat customers depends on substance, ease of use, and entertainment value. Netizens are discriminating in that while nice pictures are interesting, sites that have considerable repeat users offer something more. This can be product information and ongoing technical support, or it can be general news about a product, original writing, or the latest or most comprehensive information about just about anything. At the same time, the company should ensure that the advertising information and graphics can be easily downloaded by their consumers. Above all, it has to satisfy the consumer's goal for visiting the site—pure and simple. In the words of one Web development consultant, "To stay on a Web site, customers need incentive, convenience, and competitive prices."[42]

Purchasing Keywords and Developing a Domain Name. Online search engines such as Yahoo! sell keywords. A marketer can purchase a keyword such that its banner appears whenever users select that word for a search. For example, when a user searches for a keyword such as "inn" on the search engine Lycos, he or she will see an ad from a directory for bed-and-breakfast inns. Keyword sponsorship on Lycos, for example, costs around five cents per impression ($50 CPM), but has been dropping recently due competitive pressures. These search engines let advertisers pay a flat monthly fee or a per-impression fee (based on how many people see the ad). Thus, getting a popular word may result in a considerable number of impressions and a higher bill. The other factor is effectiveness. The Infoseek search engine claims buy rates from 2 to 36 percent, while other engines claim that keyword ads do not significantly differ from the banner ads in effectiveness. However, keyword ads are a great way to get a product in front of someone interested in that general category.

Purchasing keywords helps consumers find your site while they search for information. But before purchasing a keyword, a marketer must decide on a domain name first, which establishes the basis for a keyword. A **domain name** is the unique URL through which a Web location is established. If you are The Gap or Sony, your domain name is your corporate name and consumers know how to search for your location. But for thousands of Web startups that provide specialized Web products and services, the domain name issue is a dilemma. You want the name to be descriptive but unique, and intuitive but distinctive. That was the strategy used by Dennis Scheyer, a consultant, when he recommended that GoToTix.com, a ticketing and entertainment site, stick with its original name. The name was intuitive and easy to remember. But the firm insisted on running a consumer contest to rename the company. Scheyer said of the names that made the final cut, "One sounded like a breakfast cereal you wouldn't eat. One sounded like a cough medicine. And one sounded like a prophylactic." In the end, the firm chose Acteva.com (we suspect this is Scheyer's cough medicine entry) because "Act conveys activity. E signifies E-commerce and 'va'

42. Anu Shukla, "Sticking to the Basics," *Business 2.0,* March 2000, 129.

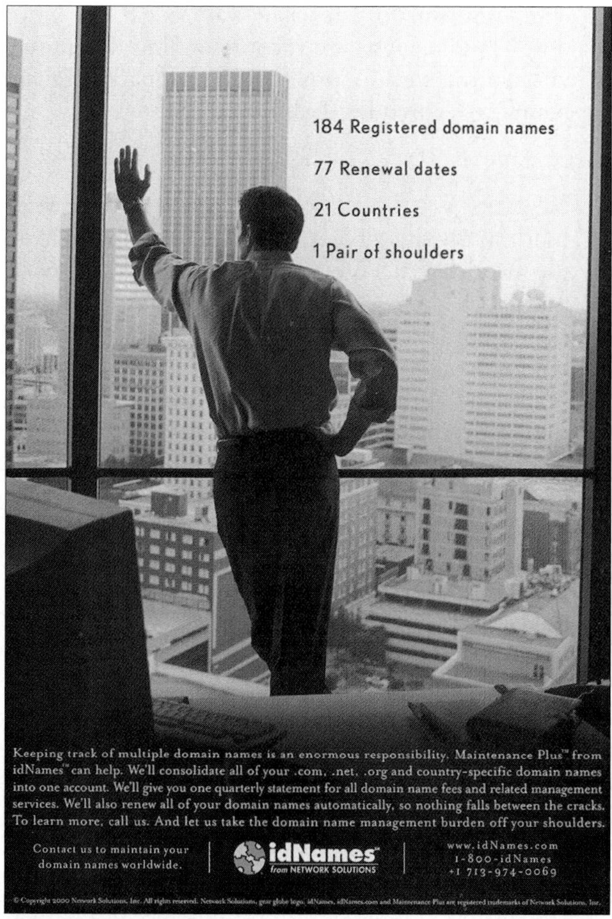

EXHIBIT 16.22

Firms like idNames, now part of Verisign, are in the business of registering names so surfers have direct access to company Web sites—a process made considerably more complicated by the introduction of TLDs (top-level domains) such as .biz and .name.
www.idnames.com

has that international flavor."[43] Fortunately, companies such as idNames (www.idnames.com) now part of Verisign, help companies identify, register, and manage Internet names and keywords in both domestic and global markets (see Exhibit 16.22).

The newest issue in domain names is the issuance of seven new top-level domains. The **top-level domain (TLD)** is the suffix that follows the Web site name. Until late 2000, there were only five TLDs—.com, .edu, .org, .gov, and .net. In November 2000, the Internet Corporation for Assigned Names and Numbers (ICANN)—a nonprofit formed in 1998 to coordinate technical management of the domain name system—approved seven new TLDs: [44]

- .aero for the air transport industry
- .biz for businesses
- .coop for cooperatives
- .info, unrestricted by organizational type
- .museum for museums
- .name for individuals
- .pro for accountants, lawyers, and other professionals

The whole idea behind releasing new TLDs, of course, is to relieve the pressure on the original five top-level domains. But there is the prospect of a degree of confusion among consumers as similar or identical prefixes are paired with the new suffixes.

Promoting Web Sites. Building a Web site is only the first step; the next is promoting it. Throughout the text, you have seen advertising by companies promoting their Web sites. Several agencies, including BBDO, Wieden & Kennedy, and Ogilvy One, specialize in promoting Web sites. The quickest and lowest-cost way to promote a Web site is to notify Usenet groups. The other key method is to register the site with search engines such as Yahoo! and AltaVista. With Yahoo!, because it is a hierarchical search engine, it is important to pick keywords that are commonly chosen, yet describe and differentiate that site. Other places to register are with the growing Yellow Pages on the Internet (for example, www.bigyellow.com) and with appropriate electronic mailing lists. It is also important to send out press releases to Internet news sites. E-mail as a form of direct mail is another method to promote the site.

In the past, dot-com companies found the allure of traditional mass media irresistible. Offline ad spending by online companies topped $1 billion in 1999. About half of the $1 billion was spent on television advertising and the bulk of the remainder on magazine ads. Some firms, such as E-Stamp and NetRadio.com, were so lavish in their spending that they actually spent $4 to $6 on marketing for every $1 of *revenue*—not a sustainable cash "burn" rate. By 2001, many dot-coms had "burned" most of their cash reserves, and spending on traditional media plummeted. Most dot-coms returned to the friendly confines of the Internet environment or relied on

43. Laurie Freeman, "Domain-Name Dilemma Worsens," *Advertising Age,* November 8, 1999, 100.
44. Karen D. Schwartz, "Here Come Da Names," *Business 2.0,* December 26, 2000, 34–41.

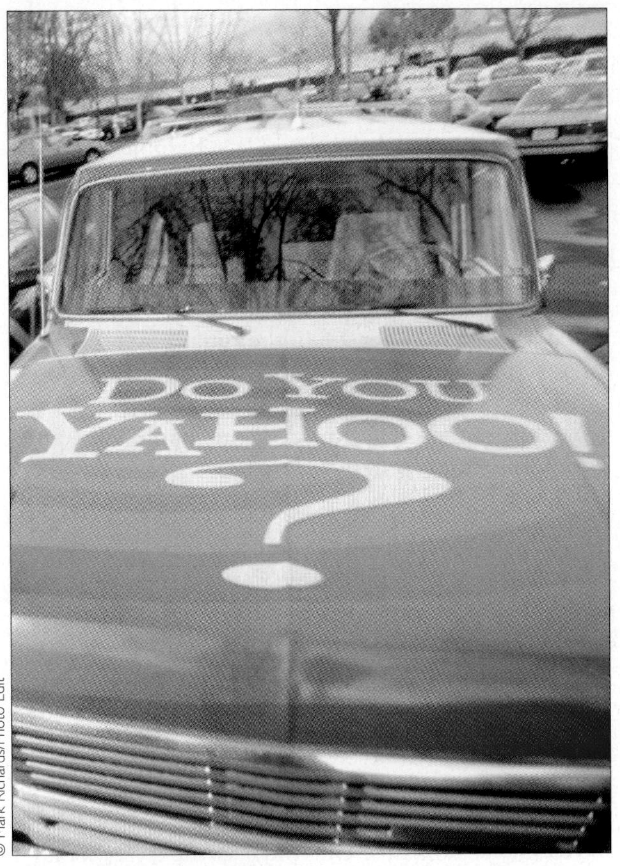

© Mark Richards/Photo Edit

EXHIBIT 16.23

Dedicated Yahoo employee cars with the familiar Yahoo! company logo illustrates one way that virtual firms can promote their companies through more traditional methods. www.yahoo.com

co-sponsorship of sites as a way to get the word out.[45] And analysts are recommending that purely virtual firms turn to more traditional marketing and branding techniques (Exhibit 16.23).[46]

Security and Privacy Issues. Any Web user can download text, images, and graphics from the World Wide Web. Although advertisers place trademark and copyright disclaimers on their online displays, advertisers on the Web have to be willing to accept the consequence that their trademarks and logos can be copied without authorization. Currently, there is no viable policing of this practice by users. Thus far, advertisers have taken legal action only against users who have taken proprietary materials and blatantly used them in a fashion that is detrimental to the brand or infringes on the exclusivity of the marketer's own site. This may change.

In Chapter 4 we discussed privacy as an ethical and regulatory issue. At this point, we can consider privacy from a strategic management standpoint. Also, as we saw in Chapter 4, privacy is a very complex and sensitive topic. Discussions at the highest levels focus on the extent to which regulations should be mandated for gathering and disseminating information about Web use. The concern among advertisers is not just the regulatory aspects of the issue. In addition, consumers are expressing concerns about using the Internet for fear of invasion of privacy—clearly a strategic management issue. A recent survey found that a whopping 78 percent of consumers surveyed were either very or somewhat concerned that a company would use their personal information to send them unwanted information. This is up from 65 percent two years earlier.[47]

At the center of this debate is the Web research and profiling firm DoubleClick (www.doubleclick.com). DoubleClick is in the business of helping Web companies identify and understand customer groups to better develop and target marketing efforts. Using DoubleClick's Hyperion division, a company such as 3Com can keep track of the buying habits and traffic patterns of the 30 million people who visit the 3Com Web site each week. But as we learned in Chapter 4, this sort of profiling has come under intense scrutiny. In response, profiling research firms such as DoubleClick and Avenue A have issued privacy statements and even appointed Chief Privacy Officers as a way to assure consumers (and regulators) that consumer profile information is used strictly to improve customer service and not to dig into (or sell) information about consumers' private affairs.[48] This would seem to be the right approach because consumers claim that with some assurance of privacy, their concerns about surfing or shopping the Web are greatly diminished.[49] With respect to consumer privacy, the Coalition for Advertising Supported Information

45. Jennifer Gilbert, "Running on Empty," *Advertising Age,* November 6, 2000, S2–S5.
46. Patricia Riedman, "After the Crash: Where from Here?," *Advertising Age,* August 7, 2000, S2–S4.
47. Heather Green et al., "It's Time for Rules in Wonderland," *Business Week,* March 20, 2000, 82–96.
48. "DoubleClick Appoints Chief Privacy Officer and Privacy Advisory Board Chairman," company press release, March 8, 2000, http://biz.yahoo.com, accessed March 17, 2000.
49. Green et al., "It's Time for Rules in Wonderland," 84.

EXHIBIT 16.24

CASIE—the Coalition for Advertising Supported Information and Entertainment—has issued a set of goals for advertisers on the Internet.

1. We believe it is important to educate consumers about how they can use interactive technology to save time and customize product and service information to meet their individual needs. By choosing to share pertinent data about themselves, consumers can be provided the product information most relevant to them and can help marketers service them more economically and effectively.
2. We believe any interactive electronic communication from a marketer ought to disclose the marketer's identity.
3. We believe that marketers need to respect privacy in the use of "personal information" about individual consumers collected via interactive technology. "Personal information" is data not otherwise available via public sources. In our view, personal information ought to be used by a marketer to determine how it can effectively respond to a consumer's needs.
4. We believe that if the marketer seeks personal information via interactive electronic communication, it ought to inform the consumer whether the information will be shared with others. We also believe that before a marketer shares such personal information with others, the consumer ought to be offered an option to request that personal information not be shared. Upon receiving such a request, the marketer ought to keep such personal information confidential and not share it.
5. We believe consumers ought to have the ability to obtain a summary of what personal information about them is on record with a marketer that has solicited them via interactive electronic communication. In addition, a consumer ought to be offered the opportunity to correct personal information, request that such information be removed from the marketer's database (unless the marketer needs to retain it for generally accepted and customary accounting and business purposes), or request that the marketer no longer solicit the customer.

Source: Coalition for Advertising Supported Information and Entertainment, www.casie.com/guide1/priv.html, accessed March 28, 1999.

and Entertainment (CASIE) has suggested five goals for advertisers, which we've reproduced in Exhibit 16.24. Striving for these goals will certainly contribute to the loyalty and confidence that consumers possess for a brand. Privacy is a legitimate concern for Internet users, and will likely continue to be one for civil libertarians and regulators as well. But one analyst assessed the privacy issue as a situation where, with the exception of DoubleClick, there have been almost no instances where a company has suffered financial loss from a privacy controversy. "A lot of companies take a PR hit, but it is uncertain if that seriously damages their reputation or their customers' good will," said the founder of a consumer advocacy firm.[50]

Measuring the Effectiveness of Internet Advertising.

The information a Web site typically gets when a user connects with a site is the IP address of the Internet site that is requesting the page, what page is requested, and the time of the request. This is the minimum amount of information available to a Web site. If a site is an opt-in site and requires registration, then additional information (for example, e-mail address, zip code, gender, age, or household income) is typically requested directly from the user. Attempts at registration (and easy audience assessment) have been largely rejected by consumers because of the privacy concern, but plenty of service providers, such Nielsen//NetRatings (www.nielsen-netratings.com), are available to guide marketers through Web measurement options (Exhibit 16.25).

Several terms, such as *hits, click-throughs, pages, visits, users,* and *reach,* are used in Web audience measurement. We will consider the most meaningful of these

50. Ann Harrison, "Privacy? Who Cares," *Business 2.0,* June 12, 2001, 48–49.

EXHIBIT 16.25

Because of the technology of the Web, tracking the behavior of Web site visitors is relatively easy. Firms like Nielsen//NetRatings help marketers measure the behavior of Web visitors. www.nielsen-netratings.com

measurement factors. **Hits** represent the number of elements requested from a given page and consequently provide almost no indication of actual Web traffic. For instance, when a user requests a page with four graphical images, it counts as five hits. Thus by inflating the number of images, a site can quickly pull up its hit count. Consider what might happen at the *Seventeen* magazine site (www.seventeen.com). The *Seventeen* site may get three million hits a day, placing it among the top Web sites. However, this total of three million hits translates into perhaps only 80,000 people daily. Thus, hits do not translate into the number of people visiting a site. Another measure of site effectiveness is the extent to which a site will motivate visitors to click through, as we have discussed before. Most analysts feel that the click-through number (and percentage) is the best measure of the effectiveness of banner advertising. If an ad is good enough to motivate a visitor to click on it and follow the link to more information, then that is verification that the ad was viewed and was motivating (more on this later).

Pages (or page views) are defined as the pages (actually the number of HTML files) sent to the requesting site. However, if a downloaded page occupies several screens, there is no indication that the requester examined the entire page. Also, it "doesn't tell you much about how many visitors it has: 100,000 page views in a week could be 10 people reading 10,000 pages, or 100,000 people reading one page, or any variation in between."[51] **Visits** are the number of occasions in which a user *X* interacted with site *Y* after time *Z* has elapsed. Usually *Z* is set to some standard time such as 30 minutes. If the user has not interacted with the site until after 30 minutes has passed, this would be counted as a new visit. **Users** (also known as unique visitors) are the number of different "people" visiting a site (a new user is determined from the user's registration with the site) during a specified period of time. Besides the address, page, and time, a Web site can find out the referring link address. This allows a Web site to discover what links people are taking to the site. Thus, a site can analyze which links do in fact bring people to the site. This can be helpful in Internet advertising planning. The problem is that what is really counted are similar unique IP numbers. Many Internet service providers use a dynamic IP number, which is different every time a given user logs in through the service, so "you might show up as 30 different unique visitors to a site you visited daily for a month."[52] *Advertising Age* provides a weekly overview of the visits to both Web sites and hits on banner ads, as we saw displayed in Exhibit 16.12.

Log analysis software is measurement software that not only provides information on hits, pages, visits, and users, but also lets a site track audience traffic within the site. A site could determine which pages are popular and expand on them. It is

51. "Let's Get This Straight: Reach for the Hits," www.salonmagazine.com/21st/rose/laag/02/05straight2.html, is an article that focuses exclusively on measurement issues. Also see Alan L. Baldinger, "Integrated Communication and Measurement: The Case for Multiple Measures," in Esther Thorson and Jeri Moore, eds., *Integrated Communications* (Mahwah, N.J.: Lawrence Erlbaum Associates, 1996), 271–283.

52. Ibid.

also possible to track the behavior of people as they go through the site, thus providing inferential information on what people find appealing and unappealing. An example of this software is MaxInfo's WebC, which allows marketers to track what information is viewed, when it is viewed, how often it is viewed, and where users go within a site.[53] An advertiser can then modify the content and structure accordingly. It can also help marketers understand how buyers make purchase decisions in general. It still isn't possible, however, to know what people actually do with Web site information.

Plenty of companies, such as I/PRO, NetCount, and Interse, offer measurement services for interactive media. Yet there is no industry standard for measuring the effectiveness of one interactive ad placement over another. There also is no standard for comparing Internet with traditional media placements. Moreover, demographic information on who is using the WWW is severely limited to consumers who have signed up for opt-in programs and, for example, allow targeted e-mails to be sent to them. Until these limitations are overcome, many marketers will remain hesitant about spending substantial dollars for advertising on the World Wide Web.

The new deal in town is the Media Metrix reach index (see Exhibit 16.26). Media Metrix and its competitors (for example, NetRatings, owned by Nielsen) are invoking older technology to address the problem: sampling through a "Nielsen family" model. Sampling is used to draw a representative set of families. Tracking software is installed on the users' computers, and then data are collected and transmitted back to the companies. These data are projected to the universe of Internet users. The figure that has become the standard is the reach figure; here it represents the percentage of users who visit a site in any one-month period. Of course, there are systematic biases built in, such as undercounting of workplace surfing. Some critics simply have a problem with applying the reach concept to this new medium at all.

As a measure of Web use, reach is weighted toward the superficial: It favors sprawling sites with vast collections of largely unrelated pages (like, for instance, GeoCities, now owned by Yahoo!) over well-focused sites that collect specific groups of users with shared interests. Say one site has 200,000 loyal users who visit regularly; another has little regular traffic, but its wide variety of pages turn up in enough disparate search engine results to attract brief visits during the course of a month from, say, five million visitors. The two sites may have identical page view counts. The former site may actually have a more valuable franchise to sell to marketers or to hand over to e-commerce partners—but the latter site wins the reach contest by a landslide.

Technical Aspects of the Internet Measurement Problem. When a computer is connected to the Internet, it has a unique IP address, such as 204.17.123.5. When a link to a Web site such as www.yahoo.com is clicked on, a computer converts this textual representation into a number that is the unique IP address for Yahoo!. This computer then requests from Yahoo! its home page, and in return it gives Yahoo! its unique IP address so Yahoo! knows the address of the requester. Thus the only information a computer at a site such as Yahoo! receives is an IP address, along with the material the user is actually requesting. Note that a textual IP address is not the same thing as an e-mail address. E-mail addresses are similar but follow a different protocol on the Internet.

A Web site log file contains the IP addresses of the computers requesting information. However, an IP address does not usually correspond to just one person. Many systems dynamically assign IP addresses to computers connected to the Internet.

53. Ibid.

EXHIBIT 16.26

Firms like Media Metrix have developed programs to track the use of the Internet by signing up households who have agreed to have their surfing and clicking activities monitored.
www.mediametrix.com

Therefore a person visiting a site in two different sessions may have a different IP address each time. For a marketer, this means it is unclear exactly how many different people visited the site. Even if a requesting computer has a permanent static address, thus allowing a site to keep track of a specific computer, the site still doesn't know who is actually using the computer. The computer could be used by one graduate student in his or her apartment, or it could be in a computer lab where hundreds of different people have access to the same computer.

A Web site can track how many machines accessed the site, but this does not correspond to how many people actually visited the Web site. One estimate is that the number of visitors exceeds IP addresses by about 15 percent.[54] Thus it is currently difficult to know exactly who is visiting a site, and whether the visitors are revisiting. The only obvious enhancement would be implementing unique IDs in Web browsers. This would identify a specific computer visiting the site. However, this has not been seen as feasible due to current privacy concerns. It also leaves the possibility of many different people using the same computer, such as would occur in a computer lab.

The Caching Complication in Internet Measurement. To conserve resources on the Web, there is a system known as caching. **Caching** is a memory function in Web and computer technology. Once a page is downloaded, the cache on the computer saves that page so it can be immediately accessed. Commercial online services such

54. J. Udell, "Damn Lies," *Byte,* February 1996, 137.

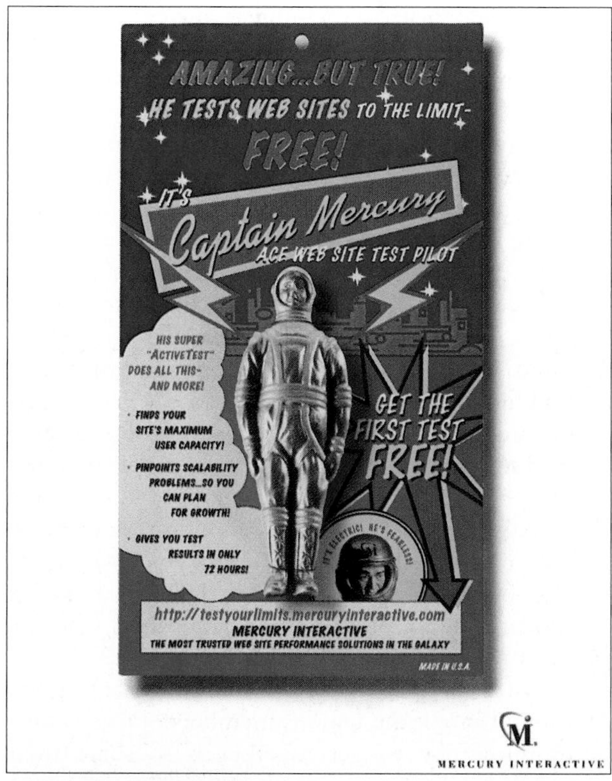

EXHIBIT 16.27

Aside from merely measuring the audience, Web site "performance" is also being measured so that firms can know the capacity and expandability of their sites.
www.merc-int.com

as America Online cache heavily trafficked sites on their computers so users get quicker response times when they request that page. Suppose a person first goes to a Web site's home page. After clicking on a link to go somewhere else, the user decides to go back to the home page. Instead of asking the Web site again for that home page, the cache will have stored it in anticipation of the user wanting it again. This conserves Internet resources, commonly called **bandwidth,** because the user is not needlessly requesting the same material twice. However, this complicates matters in measuring activity at the site because once a person has cached a page, the Web site has no idea whether the user spent considerable time at the page in one visit, returned to the page several times, or immediately moved on.

Technological solutions can reduce the amount of caching, thus allowing sites better data on how often a page is viewed, but it comes with the cost of additional bandwidth for the site and a slower response time for the person viewing the site. Caching may result in fewer page requests to a Web site than have actually occurred. Moreover, if a person hits the reload button, a Web site will register more traffic than there actually is. While cache-busting technology (technology that allows sites to look inside users' computer caches to determine the true number of pages) does exist, its widespread use seems unlikely in the near future. What is possible is for firms to measure the performance of their sites in terms of capacity and expandability (see Exhibit 16.27).

Internet Measurement and Payment. Internet marketers pay for ads in several ways but they all, in one way or another, depend on the measurement of activity related to Web site visits where banner ads appear. Many pay in terms of impressions. It's supposed to mean the number of times a page with your ad on it is viewed; in reality these are roughly equivalent to hits, or opportunities to view. Often these are priced as flat fees—so many dollars for so many impressions. Others price with pay-per-click, which is in all reality the same as impressions. Others pay in click-throughs. "The overall average for click-throughs for all Web advertising, as we have seen, is an astoundingly low 0.1 percent."[55] That's one person out of a thousand who bothers to click on a banner ad to seek more information! These rates, down from about 2 percent, are driving prices down on banner ad placement costs—as you might expect. Others will buy on cost per lead (documented business leads) or cost per actual sale (very rare). A net rate refers to the 15 percent discounted rate given to advertising agencies, although direct deals with portals and browsers are very common.

Managing the Brand in an E-Community.

A final strategic issue to be considered is the concept of creating a brand community, or e-community, for a brand by using the Internet. The Internet, in addition to providing a new means for advertisers

55. Gary Khermouch and Tom Lowry, "The Future of Advertising," *Business Week,* March 26, 2001.

e-SIGHTINGS

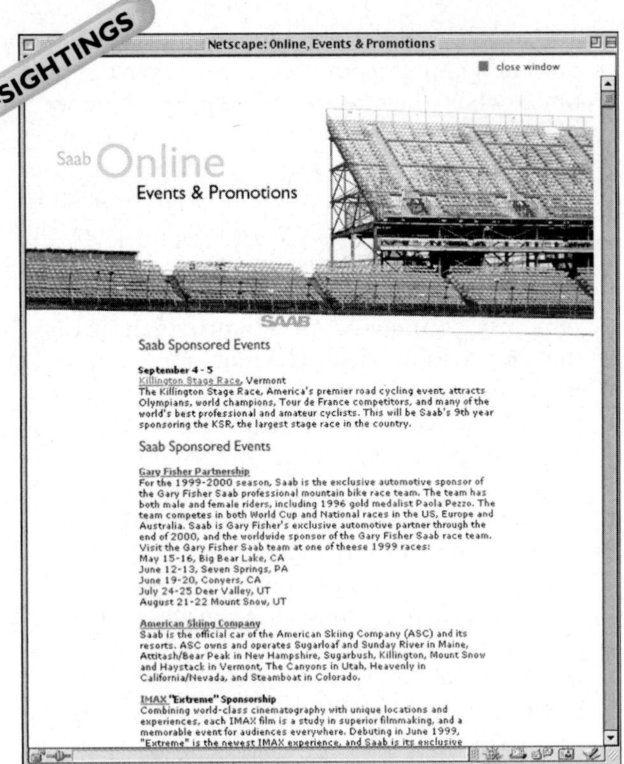

EXHIBIT 16.28

Building an e-community with great loyalty to a site is a tall task. Firms like Saab (www.saabusa.com) will devote at least a portion of their sites to promoting community among brand users. Visit the special BMW site www.bmwfilms.com and compare it with the Saab site. What is the link between action films and BMW automobiles? What does the "e-mail a friend" and "sign up" functionality offer to loyal users? What features could BMWFilms add to help foster more of a sense of community? Do BMW drivers prefer urbane discreteness to the bustle of crowds, or does the home site (www.bmwusa.com) offer better community features that satisfy users?

to communicate to consumers, also provides consumers a new and efficient way to communicate with one another. In fact, the social aspect of the Internet is one of the most important reasons for its success. Via Usenet newsgroups, e-mail, IRC, and even Web pages, consumers have a new way to interact and form communities. Sometimes communities are formed online among users of a particular brand. These online brand communities behave much like a community in the traditional sense, such as a small town or ethnic neighborhood. They have their own cultures, rituals, and traditions. Members create detailed Web pages devoted to the brand. Members even feel a sense of duty or moral responsibility to other members of the community. For example, among many Volkswagen drivers, it is a common courtesy to pull over to help another VW broken down on the side of the road. Harley-Davidson riders feel a similar sense of obligation to help others who use the same brand when they are in trouble.

In most respects, such communities are a good thing. One of the reasons members of these communities like to get together is to share their experiences in using the brand. They can share what they like about the brand and what it means to them, or suggest places to go to buy replacement parts or have the product serviced. However, advertisers need to be careful not to alienate members or turn them off to the brand. These consumers can also share their dislikes about recent changes in the brand and its advertising, rejecting them if severe enough. Since the Internet makes it easier for members of these communities to interact, brand communities are likely to proliferate in coming years. Consequently, dealing effectively with these communities will be one of the challenges facing advertisers. Several firms, such as MyEvents.com (www.myevents.com), have emerged to facilitate the community interaction process by providing shared access to a site that promotes communication between members. The Saab site featured in Exhibit 16.28 tries to accomplish just that sort of e-community interaction. Another technique is to create a community around the brand in a portal-like manner—that is, drawing consumers to a brand site with content and features that include lifestyle and entertainment information much like what the big portals provide. One firm that is trying such a strategy is teen apparel manufacturer Candie's (www.candies.com). See the Creativity box on page 592 for details on how Candie's goes about creating an e-community.

Of course, these sorts of e-community strategies create new management issues as well. One of the most intriguing ideas for advertisers has been how to access and use consumer word-of-mouth. The Internet has made the collection and management of these data much easier. Advertisers can monitor Usenet discussions, develop proprietary search engines that scour the Web to find who is saying what about new products, and so on—just as Electric Artists did when building a buzz around Christina Aguilera. Another firm that relied exclusively on the Web to build awareness of its brand was the Israeli company ICQ (formally known as Mirabilis). This company never spent a dime on traditional promotional tools. Rather, it used only "word of mouse" to spread the word about its chat and instant messaging technology. Two years after launching a chat-room- and Usenet-only campaign, the company had 30 million users worldwide and America Online bought the firm for $400 million.[56]

The Future of Advertising and the Internet.

When it comes to the Internet, talking about the future is usually futile. The future seems to come with every new issue of *Business Week, Fortune, Wired,* or *Business 2.0.* But the future of the Internet and the advertising that gets placed there seems unavoidably linked to two types of technology: wireless communication and video. The AOL/Time Warner merger in 2001 signals the future direction for the Web and Web advertising. As we saw in Chapter 15, Time Warner brought to this merger all of its movie studio properties as well as an emerging Internet movie business and digital delivery of Warner Bros. movies on demand. Time Warner also has Time Warner cable television. What AOL brought to the merger, of course, was AOL's online services, including Netscape, CompuServe, MovieFone, and Instant Messenger. Oh, did I forget to mention AOL's nearly 30 million subscribers? Together, AOL and Time Warner can offer speedier and more diverse Internet and interactive TV services using Time Warner's cable lines.[57]

Mergers and partnerships of broadcast and Internet firms is one side of the story. On the other side, advertisers and advertising agencies are preparing for new opportunities with "broadcast Web." For example, Sears, Roebuck and *Forbes* are testing a new technology that can instantly connect TV sets to specific Internet sites. With this technology, TV watchers can click on an icon during a television program and be connected to Web sites pertaining to the nature of the programming—sports, entertainment, news, and so forth.[58] Not only does this technology merge the Net with television programming, but it can also provide advertisers with general demographic and preference data to its registered users without resorting to names or e-mail addresses—the crux of the privacy concerns we have discussed. In the words of one agency executive, "This will revolutionize advertising on the Web because it establishes accountability and connection. I know that every one of our clients that has been shown this technology has been blown away."[59] And there may be some good reasons to get excited. In an Arbitron Internet Information Services/Edison Media research study, "streamies" (the nickname for Webcast viewers and online radio listeners) were twice as likely as general online users to click on banner ads or buy from a Web site, with 40 percent reporting that they had made a purchase online.[60]

Does this mean that in the near future every television ad is really a Web ad? Well, maybe it won't be that extreme, but the technology is available to provide direct links to Web sites for information and purchasing through television ads—a huge opportunity and potential for advertisers. The possibilities are attracting all the big players—Microsoft, ABC, CBS, and Warner Brothers Online, to name just a few. They all see video streaming as another piece of this Web broadcast puzzle.[61] Of course, this next step in the evolution of the Internet and its potential as an advertising alternative depends on the consumer's willingness to allow the communication to occur. Some things never change.

56. Tania Hershman, "Word of Mouth," *Business 2.0,* December 1999, 371.
57. Maryanne Murray Buechner et al., "Happily Ever After?," *Time,* January 24, 2000, 39–44.
58. Diane Mermigas, "Net Technology Connects Data with Marketers," *Advertising Age,* January 17, 2000, 2.
59. Ibid.
60. Amanda Beeler, "Marketers Find Lucrative Audience in 'Streamies,' " *Advertising Age,* February 21, 2000, 48.
61. Dana Blankenhorn, "Where TV, Net Link," *Advertising Age,* January 17, 2000, s20.

CREATIVITY

Skipping Sales in Favor of Community

Most consumers put firms that target teenage consumers in a category with Attila the Hun and the Wicked Witch of the West. But one firm is using its Web site primarily as a community-building portal rather than as a sales-generating site. Read on to see why this teen-focused firm came to such a seemingly contradictory strategic conclusion.

Candie's, a teen-focused, hip shoe and apparel maker, knew that the world was going online and it felt that it needed to keep up. But the New York–based company faced a problem. As a wholesaler, Candie's was hesitant to bypass retailers and go direct to consumers with online sales. First, such a strategy could damage relationships in the supply chain. Second, the firm was ill-equipped to even handle a direct-to-consumer selling effort.

Instead of establishing a sales site, the firm decided to establish a brand community portal. Candies.com was designed to be a site for teenage girls with a host of e-community features—free e-mail, online chat, Web page hosting, entertainment news, and the like. But it wanted to go further than traditional e-community options. To do so, Candie's also became a publisher of sorts. In a deal with *Rolling Stone* magazine, the site also publishes music news and CD reviews. The original agreement with Rolling Stone has now been extended to include television and film entertainment reviews.

Of course, the whole idea behind the content-based, rather than sales-based, focus of the site is to keep girls coming back. David Conn, vice president of marketing for Candie's, explains, "We felt if we could build a site that became a prime gather point for our customer, that gave them a platform and entertained them, we could data-mine and learn a lot about our market, which is really important when marketing to fickle teenage girls."

Aside from being primarily community oriented, another interesting feature of the Candie's Web strategy is that it flies in the face of the lessons learned by the ill-fated Levi's online strategy. Levi's began its online effort with what was described at the time as an attempt to create "a platform for kids to see what other kids are doing." But, after a short time, Levi's abandoned the "no sales" strategy in favor of a more e-commerce-oriented site. It would seem that Candie's is heading down the same path. But the Candie's site is more broad-based and elaborate and includes partnership content that Levi's did not. So it remains to be seen whether the Candie's strategy will survive. So far, so good, but go to www.candies.com and see if the strategy is still working!

Sources: Joe Ashbrook Nickell, "501 Blues," *Business 2.0,* January 2000, 53; Joe Ashbrook Nickell, "Teen Scene Maker," *Business 2.0,* March 2000, 108–110.

The final issue regarding the future of the Web is the sort of revenue model that must evolve for the mere survival of most Web firms. Clearly, the advertising revenue model is not working. When the biggest and the best—Yahoo! and Amazon—are struggling, then clearly something has to change. The best bet is that more sites will demand payment.[62] This seems like heresy for a medium that has been free (except for connection charges). But there has to be revenue from somewhere, and the various forms of advertising revenue have not been sufficient.

Some sites are highly successful as pay sites. Consumer Reports is the most successful of the pay sites. At $24.95 per month, it has a long and successful history as a pay site. TheStreet.com has struggled, but it has survived as a site that offers professional and often highly technical analysis of the stock market and individual securities. Yahoo! appears to most of us to be free, but there are actually sections of the portal that cost money or soon will, given the struggle Yahoo! has had to maintain a sufficient revenue stream. The future of the Internet is certainly at a crossroads, and the next five years will be telling with respect to the future of advertising and this medium.

62. Timothy J. Mullaney, "Sites Worth Paying For?" *Business Week e.Biz,* May 14, 2001, 10–12.

SUMMARY

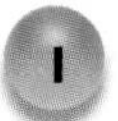

Identify the basic components of the Internet.

There are four main components of the Internet: electronic mail, IRC, Usenet, and the World Wide Web. Electronic mail (e-mail) allows people to send messages to one another using the Internet. Internet Relay Chat (IRC) makes it possible for people to "talk" electronically in real time with each other, despite their geographical separation. For people with common interests, Usenet provides a forum for people with common interests to share knowledge in a public "cyberspace" that is separate from their e-mail program. The World Wide Web (WWW) allows people to access an immense "web" of information in a graphical environment through the use of programs called Web browsers (such as Netscape and Internet Explorer).

Identify the Internet media available for communicating over the World Wide Web.

E-mail allows users to communicate much as they do using standard mail. People who wish to discuss specific topics through the Internet often join electronic mailing lists. Thousands of mailing lists are available on an incredible variety of topics. A message sent to the list's e-mail address is then re-sent to everybody on the mailing list. Usenet is a collection of discussion groups in cyberspace. People can read messages pertaining to a given topic, post new messages, and answer messages. The World Wide Web (WWW) is the "web" of information available to most Internet users, and its graphical environment makes navigation simple and exciting. Of all the options available for Internet marketers, the WWW holds the greatest potential as an advertising medium.

Describe the different types of search engines used to surf the Web.

In a hierarchical search engine, such as Yahoo!, all sites fit into categories. Collection search engines, such as AltaVista, use a spider, which is an automated program that crawls around the Web and collects information. With a concept search engine, a concept rather than a word or phrase is the basis for the search. The top sites that match the concept are listed in order after a search. The newest technique, robot search engines, employs robots ("bots") to do the "legwork" for the consumer by roaming the Internet in search of information fitting certain user-specified criteria. A portal is a starting point for Web access and search.

Describe the different advertising options on the Web.

Banner ads are paid placements of advertising on other sites that contain editorial material. A pop-up ad is an Internet advertisement that appears as a Web site page is loading or after a page has loaded. E-mail can be used to customize a message for thousands or even millions of receivers. A corporate home page is a Web site where a marketer provides current and potential customers information about the firm in great detail. A variation on the corporate Web site is the virtual mall, which is a gateway to a group of Internet storefronts that provide access to mall sites by simply clicking on a category of store.

Discuss the issues involved in establishing a site on the World Wide Web.

There are three key issues to successfully establishing and maintaining a site on the World Wide Web: getting surfers to come back by creating a "sticky" site; purchasing keywords and developing a domain name; and promoting the Web site.

KEY TERMS

Internet
electronic mail (e-mail)
Internet Relay Chat (IRC)
Usenet
World Wide Web (WWW)
electronic mailing lists
spam
surfing
search engine
hierarchical search engine
collection search engine
spider
concept search engine
robot search engine
robots
portal
click-through
banner ads
skyscraper
pop-up ad
bulky box
permission marketing
viral marketing
streaming video and audio
corporate home page
virtual mall
netizens
sticky site
rational branding
domain name
top-level domain (TLD)
hits
pages
visits
users
log analysis software
caching
bandwidth

QUESTIONS

1. In the face of considerable uncertainty about audience size, audience composition, and cost-effectiveness, marketers have nonetheless been flocking to the World Wide Web. What is it about the Web that advertisers have found so irresistible?

2. How can an understanding of search engines and how they operate benefit an organization initiating an ad campaign on the WWW?

3. Explain the two basic strategies for developing corporate home pages, exemplified in this chapter by Saturn and Crayola.

4. Niche marketing will certainly be facilitated by the WWW. What is it about the WWW that makes it such a powerful tool for niche marketing?

5. Visit some of the corporate home pages described in this chapter, or think about corporate home pages you have visited previously. Of those you have encountered, which would you single out as being most effective in giving the visitor a reason to come back? What conclusions would you draw regarding the best ways to motivate repeat visits to a Web site?

6. Why is an agreement between AOL and Time Warner such big news for marketers with an interest in the WWW? Regarding the agreement between the two, what new opportunities do you see for marketers to use advertising on the Internet?

7. The Internet was obviously not conceived or designed to be an advertising medium. Thus, some of its characteristics have proven perplexing to advertisers. If advertising professionals had the chance to redesign the Internet, what single change would you expect they would want to make to enhance its value from an advertising perspective?

EXPERIENTIAL EXERCISES

1. While the much-ballyhooed Y2K threat came and went without incident, the turn of the millennium was indeed apocalyptic for many Internet companies. Enterprising dot-com businesses (such as pets.com and gov-works.com) went broke and were later dubbed "dot-bombs" by international press and financial wizards. Conduct research online or at the library and write a short report on the rise and fall of one of these dot-bomb Internet sites. Explain the history and e-business model that procured early success for the company, then list the reasons why it ultimately failed and went bust. What lessons can surviving Internet businesses learn from the sudden downturn of the dot-com technology sector?

2. Visit some of your favorite digizines, portal sites, or other Web pages that have banner advertising. Click on numerous banner ads that appeal to you and describe what happens. Did you simply get transferred to another Web site? Were you taken to an online promotion such as a sweepstakes? What purpose did the company have in prompting your click-throughs, and what incentives were you given to oblige the advertiser with your time and effort? Finally, describe the different experiences you had clicking through different banner ads and rate their effectiveness from a consumer perspective.

USING THE INTERNET

16-1 Establishing a Site on the World Wide Web

When CBS needed to establish a Web site to help build the brand of its wildly popular *Survivor* series, it turned to Xceed, a strategic consulting and digital solutions firm known for its expertise with highly interactive e-business solutions. CBS aimed to capitalize on all the suspense and interest associated with the program and capture it in an interactive format that would keep fans coming back to the site.

Survivor: http://www.cbs.com

Xceed: http://www.xceed.com

1. Visit the CBS site and search for the *Survivor* Web page. What makes this site "sticky," and how does it capitalize on the program's interesting features?

2. What is "rational branding"? Does the *Survivor* site make full use of this concept? Have you ever visited the *Survivor* site before? If so, how did you use it?

3. Visit Xceed's site and research its list of clients. Visit one of the Web sites it has produced for another client, and compare and contrast that site's features with those of the *Survivor* site. Do you think this site is as effective as the *Survivor* site? Why?

16-2 E-Mail Innovations

Advertising and marketing through e-mail is one of the most promising and useful Internet developments in recent years. The popularity of electronic messaging has led to the proliferation of e-mail-based tools that help advertisers reach extremely targeted audiences around the globe at a very low cost. XactMail is one of many Internet firms leading the way in harnessing the power of messaging-based advertising.

XactMail—Permission E-Mail:
http://www.xactmail.com

Coalition Against Unsolicited Commercial E-Mail:
http://www.cauce.org

1. What services does XactMail offer, and what is "opt-in" e-mail?

2. How does the text define *spam,* and how does spam relate to XactMail? Does XactMail run the risk of being blacklisted by the Coalition Against Unsolicited Commercial e-mail? Why?

3. What are the benefits of e-mail-based advertising to advertisers? How do most businesses allow consumers to avoid getting electronic junk mail?

4. Do you ever receive electronic ads or promotions in your mailbox? How do you respond to them?

PART 4
Cincinnati Bell Wireless: The Launch Campaign

As noted in Part 2 of this case history, one of the most laudable aspects of the launch campaign designed and executed by Northlich was the skillful mix of persuasion tools deployed on behalf of Cincinnati Bell Wireless in the spring of 1998. As you will see, it is reasonable to conclude that these tools worked in harmony from both the standpoint of communicating a multifaceted value proposition and creating awareness, credibility, and excitement for the CBW brand, which culminated in a desire to purchase this service.

From Part 2 you should also recall the launch strategy that guided the preparation of the campaign: MOPEs (managers, owners, professionals, entrepreneurs) using other wireless services were targeted for conversion to PCS digital from Cincinnati Bell. The value proposition communicated through a diversified IBP campaign advanced this package of benefits:

- *Simple pricing, better value.* Subscribers sign no contracts; they choose a simple pricing plan, such as 500 minutes for $49.95/month or 1,600 minutes for $99.95/month.
- *The coolest phone on the planet.* CBW launched its service with the feature-laden Nokia 6160 phone.
- *Member of the AT&T wireless network.* As a member of AT&T's network, CBW offered customers wireless access in over 400 cities at one "hometown rate."
- *Worry-free security.* Digital PCS allows secure business transactions that may be compromised over analog cellular.

As you will see in the sample communication materials that follow, the critical points advanced throughout the launch campaign were superiority over cellular, simplification, and hey, it's a cool phone! Various ads played different parts to yield precisely the kind of beautiful music that Jack Cassidy and others at CBW were waiting to hear: These ads made the cash register sing!

An Overview of the CBW Launch Campaign. Here we will describe and provide examples of many of the different persuasion tools deployed in this multimillion-dollar launch. You will see that this was a multilayered campaign with different elements called on to contribute the best of what each has to offer, as represented in Chapters 14 through 20. We will discuss TV, print, radio, and outdoor ads, special events and promotions, direct mail, and point-of-purchase advertising. Each built on the other to advance the CBW brand. But we begin at the beginning, with public relations.

Public Relations. As you will learn in Chapter 20, there can be at least six different objectives for public relations activities. Two of these six were very clearly being pursued by public relations staff on behalf of CBW: the use of press releases and staged events to develop

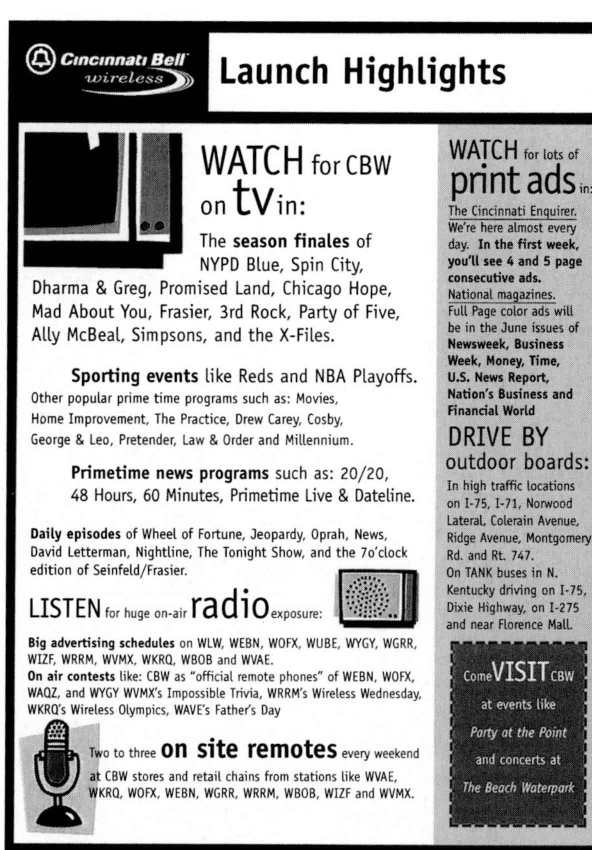

EXHIBIT IBP 4.1

CBW internal newsletter: launch preview.

awareness for CBW, and active development and direct dissemination of information to employees of Cincinnati Bell to turn them into knowledgeable spokespeople for the company's newest offering. Public relations efforts often are initiated in advance of more conventional advertising. In this case, press releases were created and circulated as early as February 1998 to announce newsworthy developments such as the signing of the partnership agreement between Cincinnati Bell and AT&T, which established the infrastructure to support CBW. One could think of this activity as preparatory awareness building.

Another excellent example of the PR function at work is illustrated through Exhibit IBP 4.1. This "Launch Highlights" document was part of a corporate newsletter distributed to Cincinnati Bell employees to advise them of the forthcoming launch. It provides a wonderful synopsis of the complete launch campaign in an effort to create interest and enthusiasm for the new service from within the company. Other internal corporate communications included a special invitation to attend an employees-only sneak preview for CBW on May 5, 1998. Hundreds of Cincinnati Bell employees turned out to watch the official countdown and blastoff for the new service. But guess who else got a special invitation to this "employees-only" event? That's right, the press! All the Cincinnati media were in attendance to make sure the whole scene was reported that evening on the local news and in the next day's newspapers. So here again, we see the two PR objectives of awareness building and internal selling working for CBW.

Television. May 11, 1998, was the official start of the advertising support for CBW. Three television advertisements were at the center of the advertising barrage. One of these, "Classroom," was described briefly in Part 3 (see Exhibit IBP 3.1). The other two were titled "The Big Easy" (see the storyboard in Exhibit IBP 4.2) and "X-Ray: Cool Phone." These two ads advanced different aspects of the CBW value proposition. Many of the programs where these ads were initially aired are listed in Exhibit IBP 4.1.

Throughout this text we have emphasized that good advertising must be based on an understanding of the customer's wants and needs. Northlich lives by this principle, and we see it brought to life very vividly in the two spots "Classroom" and "The Big Easy." Northlich's consumer research repeatedly identified that consumers were frustrated by the complexity of the wireless category. Their complaints were that the deals were confusing; they got locked in by a contract; and it was hard, even after the fact, to understand the pricing plan that applied to them. CBW's service tackled these concerns with its simple pricing plan and no-contracts offer. "The Big Easy" presents CBW as a breakthrough service that eliminates all the hassles people associate with cellular. What's more, this is a service from "people you know you can rely on." "The Big Easy" set the stage for all that would follow.

Print, Radio, and Outdoor. Television is the ultimate medium for achieving broad reach for an appeal almost instantly. However, when repetition of the basic message is called for, the high absolute cost of this medium makes it an expensive option to rely on exclusively. It is

EXHIBIT IBP 4.2

Bell Wireless storyboard: "The Big Easy."

common to use other, more economical media as a complement to television to achieve frequency or repetition of the basic message(s). For the CBW launch, Northlich made heavy use of both print and radio ads to complement the messages being advanced in the television campaign. Actual spending levels for TV, radio, print, and outdoor are detailed in Exhibit IBP 4.3.

As reflected in Exhibit IBP 4.3, there was a consistent commitment to print ads as a means to keep the CBW offer on the table on almost a daily basis. Print ads like the one in Exhibit IBP 4.4 hammered away at the point that CBW is simply a better deal than cellular and that the world's most advanced digital phone is part of the package. Additionally, the actor shown in Exhibit IBP 4.4 is the same one featured in all CBW TV ads, which again reinforces the integrated look of the campaign. Per Exhibit IBP 4.1, print ads ran in both local newspapers and regional editions of several major magazines.

As you learned in Chapter 15, radio is a very cost-effective medium for executing high levels of message repetition in a targeted geography. Northlich deployed radio ads to achieve frequency of exposure of the campaign's basic themes. Using several different executions, the radio ads reinforced the claims that with CBW you get the best coverage, a great phone, no contracts, and much better prices than cellular. One sample of the radio ad copy is featured in Exhibit IBP 4.5. This particular ad emphasizes the point that, with CBW, you can roam far and wide and still stay in touch. The main actor in the radio ad is the same actor who appeared in the TV and print ads. Are you starting to get the picture that the folks at Northlich took this "one look," "one voice" integration thing pretty seriously?

From the spending levels in Exhibit IBP 4.3, it should be clear that outdoor advertising was not a major emphasis but instead served its traditional role as a support

Description	January	February	March	April	May	June	July
TV					$142,982	$ 95,887	$ 0
Radio					49,904	22,844	27,536
Print					153,977	65,265	63,374
Outdoor					8,339	8,339	6,589
Production Totals	$19,179	$50,053	$281,165	$344,835	246,118	202,306	169,507
Media Totals	0	0	0	0	355,202	192,335	97,499
Total Spending	**$19,179**	**$50,053**	**$281,165**	**$344,835**	**$601,320**	**$394,641**	**$267,006**

EXHIBIT IBP 4.3

CBW launch: media billing summary for the first half of 1998.

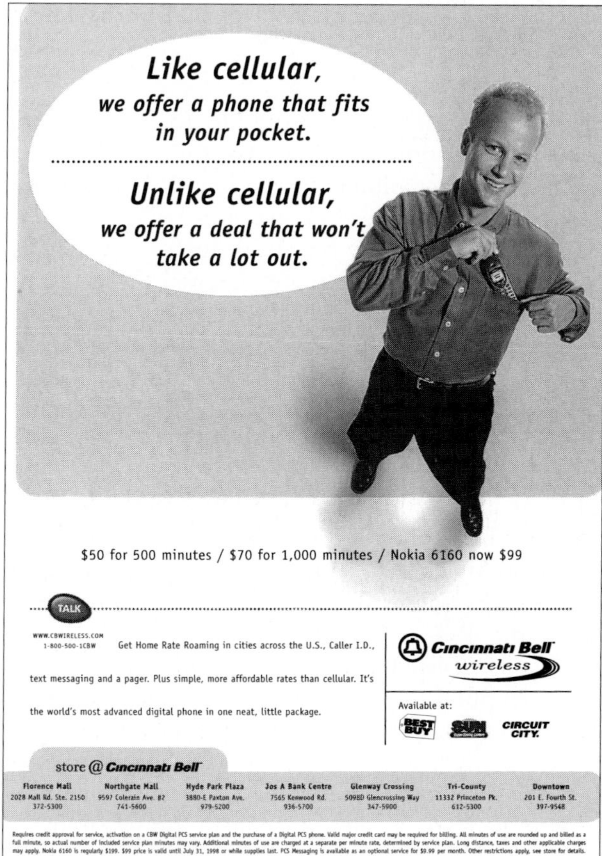

EXHIBIT IBP 4.4

Sample print ad from the CBW launch.

(Sound effects: outdoor, nature sounds.)

Scott: This truly is a modern way to travel, Roy.

Roy: Yeah, the largest mobile home ever made. Theater-style seating. Sleeps 52. So big, it beeps when I back up . . . and when I'm going forward.

Scott: Wow! Now where have you been, what have you seen?

Roy: The world's largest talking cow in Georgia. A bicycle-eating tree in Washington. And pretty much everything in between.

Scott: Oh, that's great . . . now, you know, if you had a Cincinnati Bell Wireless phone, you could talk to virtually anyone, anywhere you went.

Roy: Oh yeah, is that right, even at the sand sculpture of the last supper?

Scott: Oh, the sand sculpture of the last supper . . .

Roy: All right, how about the lickable house of salt?

Scott: Oh . . . yeah, wherever that is. You know . . . plus home-rate roaming in AT&T cities across the U.S.

Roy: Well, what are we waiting for?!

(Sound effects: engine starts, then the familiar beeping sound a truck makes when it's backing up, continues under Scott.)

Scott: Get the nationwide coverage and simple more affordable rates than cellular: 100 minutes for 25 bucks or 500 minutes for $50. Stop by the Store@Cincinnati Bell or call 565-1CBW for details.

NOTE: This ad was voted *Best of Show* by the 1998–99 Addy Awards, Cincinnati Advertising Club.

EXHIBIT IBP 4.5

Radio copy: Roadside America (:60).

medium. Billboard and transit ads bolstered the basic proposition that CBW is clearer, smarter, and better than cellular. As we pointed out in Part 3 of this case, the billboards definitely contributed to the uniform look of the campaign.

Promotions and Events. Northlich and CBW also made adept use of promotions and special events for a variety of purposes. The schedule of launch events and promotions for May and June 1998 is listed in Exhibit IBP 4.6. Several points are evident here. First, there was participation in citywide spring outdoor events, such as Taste of Cincinnati, Day in Eden (Park), and Kid Fest, that provided exposure and lead generation for CBW at virtually no cost. Note as well that with an event like Kid Fest, CBW was also probing customers who were not part of the primary launch target. This gave CBW an opportunity to gauge the appeal of their service with a broader base of potential users, without diluting the focus of their primary advertising campaign.

Second, from Exhibit IBP 4.6 we see that CBW offered price promotions around traditional gift-giving occasions such as Mother's Day, Father's Day, and graduation. These promotions were supported by special radio and print ads and direct mail. One advantage CBW has over any local competitor is that its parent company, Cincinnati Bell Telephone, makes regular mailings to nearly every household in the city in the form of monthly phone bills. For CBW, the bill insert is a very cost-effective way to announce promotions.

Finally, Exhibit IBP 4.6 also notes CBW's participation as a sponsor of professional baseball and the women's professional golf tour. Through their "businessmen's special" promotions at Cincinnati Reds' games, CBW was afforded an awareness-building opportunity with its primary target segment—MOPEs. An affiliation with the Ladies' Professional Golf Association facilitated outreach to the primary target segment and beyond.

Direct Marketing. The set of communication tools previously described—from PR, to various forms of mass-media advertising, to event participation—set the stage for the success of CBW by building awareness, excitement, and credibility for the brand. At this point, a MOPE may have been convinced to walk into a Store@Cincinnati Bell to purchase a cool phone and activate this new service; however, Northlich was clearly leaving no stone unturned. To build on the broad base of awareness created by the communication tools described thus far, direct marketing specialists on the account team prepared a coordinated and extensive direct mail campaign.

The goal for this campaign was to prompt action in one of several ways. Recipients of the direct mail brochure were invited to either sign up immediately for wireless service by calling an 800 number or get more details at the CBW Web site. Or, as the brochure explained, they could sign up by visiting any Store@Cincinnati Bell or another CBW-authorized dealer. As part of this mailing, MOPEs also received a letter from Mike Vanderwoude, CBW's marketing director, detailing the benefits of CBW for the sophisticated business user. Attached to Mike's letter was a $10 coupon redeemable on any CBW purchase. Again, the goal of this direct marketing effort was to sway hesitant MOPEs to close the deal.

With the help of a list broker that specialized in geodemographic segmentation (remember Chapter 6?), Northlich identified nearly 100,000 households in greater Cincinnati that contained a MOPE. Simultaneously, they were planning a campaign that included a built-in experiment. As you will see in Chapter 19, the mindset of the direct marketing specialist always includes experimentation to benefit future programs. For the CBW launch, four groups were created to facilitate this research:

1. 46,000 MOPE households were designated to receive the complete mailing package plus outbound telemarketing follow-up *and* an extra offer of a free leather case for their Nokia 6160 phone.
2. 46,000 MOPE households were designated to receive the complete mailing package plus outbound telemarketing follow-up, but no offer for the free leather case.

EXHIBIT IBP 4.6

CBW launch: promotion and events schedule.

May	June
Taste of Cincinnati Target: Adults 25–54 Objective: Introduce CBW and build awareness; generate leads (database) Vehicles: Event only Promo: Booth at event; free trial (phone calls); contest entry **Mother's Day** Target: Users and nonusers Objective: Drive response; store traffic Message: Safety; multiple phones per household Vehicles: Radio and print; bill inserts Promo: Special price package; radio contest (best mother; mother in most need of wireless) **Graduate Program (high school and college)** Target: Nonusers (soon-to-be young professionals); users (families) Objectives: Drive response Message: Safety and productivity benefits Vehicles: Radio and print; bill inserts Promo: Special price package **Baseball** Target: Businessmen (Businessmen's Special) Objective: Build awareness; drive response Message: Productivity benefits Vehicles: Event only Promo: Coupon on back of ticket for discount; raffle free phone/service	**Day in Eden** Target: Adults 25–54 Objective: Introduce CBW and build awareness; generate leads (database) Vehicles: Event only Promo: Booth at event; free trial (phone calls); contest entry **Kid Fest** Target: Users and nonusers Objective: Build awareness; drive response Message: Safety Vehicles: Event only Promo: Booth at event giving away safety-related item (windshield distress sign; emergency flag) logo'd CBW; special offer to sign up for service and receive family pass to local amusements **Father's Day** Target: Users and nonusers Objective: Drive response; traffic in stores Message: Productivity benefits Vehicles: Radio and print; bill inserts Promo: Special price package; radio contest (best father; father in most need of wireless) **LPGA** Target: Nonusers and users Objective: Drive response Message: Safety and convenience Vehicles: Event only Promo: Coupon on back of ticket for discount; raffle free phone/service

3. 5,000 MOPE households were designated to receive the complete mailing package with follow-up by a second direct mail contact in place of telemarketing.
4. 1,500 MOPE households were designated to receive outbound telemarketing only.

It should be apparent that Northlich's direct marketing department expected direct mail followed by outbound telemarketing to be the best combination to drive response. The overwhelming majority of the targeted MOPEs received this combination. Groups 3 and 4 were used to assess the relative effectiveness of other combinations for future campaigns. In addition, the comparison of responses from group

1 versus group 2 showed Northlich the value of the leather case offer, again for future reference. As it turned out, the incremental responses generated by the leather case offer were not enough to justify the extra costs associated with that offer. Looking to the future, there would be no more leather freebies, and direct mail followed by outbound telemarketing was established as the most effective tactical combination.

P-O-P Advertising, Collateral, and Sales Support. The final layer that must be addressed as part of any multilayered IBP campaign is point-of-purchase. At P-O-P, everything the customer hears, sees, touches, tastes, and smells must support the promises that were made by other communication tools. While there isn't much tasting or smelling to worry about in activating a new mobile phone, there are plenty of other details.

At P-O-P, and particularly in the Stores@Cincinnati Bell, the prospective customer was reminded of the larger IBP campaign in many ways. As you saw in Part 3 of this case history (see especially Exhibit IBP 3.3), the numerous informational brochures developed by Northlich shared many design features with other materials from the campaign, as did the interior design of the Stores@Cincinnati Bell. Northlich also used the same design features for the package sleeve that slid over the protective packaging of the Nokia 6160 phone.

In-store salespeople were also well versed in the messages and details of the larger IBP campaign. As already mentioned, the details of the campaign were communicated to all employees throughout the CBW system by newsletter announcements (see Exhibit IBP 4.1). Additionally, the multiple benefits of CBW's value proposition were recast as a list of the top 10 reasons why one should become a CBW subscriber (for example, reason number one was "No contracts to sign!"). This top 10 list was featured on in-store placards and window posters to reinforce the benefit promises that customers may have heard in other campaign executions.

An IBP plan should also anticipate brand contacts. Brand contacts are all the ways in which prospective customers come in contact with the organization—through packaging, employees, in-store displays, and sales literature, as well as media or event exposure. Each contact must be evaluated for consistency with the overall IBP program. We see this drive for consistency at every level of the CBW launch campaign.

Gauging the Impact of the CBW Launch Campaign. Hopefully, this overview has given you an appreciation for the breadth of the IBP campaign that Northlich orchestrated on behalf of its client and partner, Cincinnati Bell Wireless. But were the campaign's objectives achieved? Did the client consider the campaign a success? Looking back now, we are able to accurately assess the outcomes from this launch campaign, and this assessment must start with the issue of objectives. You may recall from Part 2 that the client's primary objective targeted new subscribers. Success for CBW begins with service activations. The campaign's goal was 16,868 subscribers by the end of the calendar year, a conservative and attainable goal that both the client and agency hoped to surpass. But no one really anticipated how much was possible.

It didn't take long for all parties to realize that they needed to think bigger. After just one week into the launch campaign, they had 10,500 activations. While this pace could not continue, the new-subscriber goal for the campaign was easily surpassed in the first 90 days. By the end of 1998, CBW had over 60,000 subscribers, over three and a half times the original goal. And the profile of these subscribers was truly remarkable. About half of these activations came from MOPEs who were converting to CBW from another mobile phone service. As you know by now, these MOPEs were the primary target segment. The other 30,000 activations came from young professionals who hadn't previously subscribed to a mobile phone service. To explain the outcome, Jack Cassidy, president of CBW, surmised that the launch campaign had been exceptionally effective in communicating the *no hassles, great pricing,* and *cool phone* elements of the CBW value proposition. Users and nonusers alike were persuaded that CBW was different and better than anything available previously. Users switched carriers, and nonusers signed on in about equal numbers. As you might expect, Jack Cassidy was very pleased with this outcome.

There are other concrete indicators of the campaign's success. One has to do with CBW's realized churn rate. *Churn rates* are expressed as a percentage and indicate the percent of current customers that a company is losing each month. Average monthly churn in the wireless business is about 4 percent. If a company is losing 4 percent of its customers every month, then after just a year, it will have lost nearly half its customers. Obviously, high churn rates are an indication of customer dissatisfaction. In 1998, CBW's churn rate was less than 1.5 percent per month, indicating that CBW customers were considerably more satisfied than the industry average. It also indicates that there was a good balance between the benefits promised in CBW advertising and the actual benefits realized in the use of the service. Striking this balance is one mark of great advertising.

You probably also will recall that the primary reason MOPEs were targeted had to do with their usage potential. The thinking was that MOPEs (that is, business users) make heavier use of their mobile phones each month than do household users. Thus, if Northlich targeted their advertising efforts properly, they would attract heavy (more profitable) users. Here again, Northlich delivered the goods. Industry averages provide the critical point of reference: Average revenue per customer per month for analog cellular companies is $29, and for other PCS digital companies it is $45. In 1998, CBW's average revenue per customer per month was just over $60, which means that Northlich's communication tools were delivering the high-value mobile phone customers to Jack Cassidy's door, again making him very happy.

Finally, in the spring of 1998, CBW had intended to spend about $3 million on its launch campaign. But astute marketers monitor their own successes carefully and make budget adjustments to support programs that clearly are working. Strong programs get budget increases and weak programs get budget cuts. Given that this campaign clearly was working, which became obvious to all just one week into the campaign, what do you suppose Jack Cassidy did with his advertising and IBP budget? Well, he effectively doubled it. By the end of 1998, CBW had spent $6 million to support its aggressive launch. This spending is yet another indicator of the campaign's unprecedented success. As 1998 came to a close, investment analysts, AT&T executives, business journalists, and Jack Cassidy were all drawing the same conclusion about the CBW campaign: By any measure, this was the most successful PCS digital launch in North America.

IBP EXERCISES

1. Compare this CBW launch campaign with the iMac campaign described at the beginning of Chapter 8. How are they similar? How are they different? What aspects of the iMac campaign would have made it a more complex undertaking than the CBW launch?
2. In this CBW example we see that direct marketing people are most prone to learning through trial and error. Why is this type of learning so important to direct marketers? What is it about direct marketing that makes learning in this way more feasible? What did the direct marketers on Northlich's account team learn in the CBW launch?
3. Make a list of at least five different communication tools that were used as part of the IBP campaign for CBW. Now critique each tool with respect to how well it supported or reinforced key aspects of the CBW value proposition.
4. Visit the CBW Web site at www.cbwireless.com. Obviously, the launch campaign described was just the beginning for CBW. From the Web site, can you infer any changes in marketing strategy? Has the value proposition changed? What about the primary target segment? Given the effectiveness of their launch campaign, how could CBW justify any changes in their marketing strategy, on the Web or elsewhere?

PART FIVE

Integrated Brand Promotion

Part Five of the text brings us to the end of our journey in the study of advertising. This part of the text highlights the full range of communications tools a firm can use in creating an integrated brand promotion campaign. Throughout the text, we have been emphasizing that IBP is a key to effective overall brand development in the market. You will find that the variety and breadth of communications options discussed here truly represent a tremendous opportunity for a marketer to support the main advertising effort. Each of the tools discussed in this section has unique capability in affecting the audience's perception of and desire to own a brand.

Support Media, P-O-P Advertising, and Event Sponsorship Chapter 17, "Support Media, P-O-P Advertising, and Event Sponsorship," reflects the extraordinary range of options available to today's advertiser, from billboards and transit advertising to event sponsorship or point-of-purchase (P-O-P) advertising. The chapter focuses on P-O-P advertising and event sponsorship because of the dramatic growth and impact of these activities. The examples in this chapter highlight how creative marketers and their IBP agencies must be in finding compelling ways to reach target markets. 17

Sales Promotion Chapter 18, "Sales Promotion," describes the ways that contests, sweepstakes, and price incentives attract the attention of customers. The impact of many sales promotion techniques is much easier to measure than the impact of advertising, thus prompting many marketers to shift spending from advertising to sales promotion in their integrated brand promotion campaigns. Highlighted in this chapter are the fundamental differences between the purpose of advertising and the purpose of sales promotion. This chapter also features discussions of both consumer market sales promotion techniques *and* sales promotion for use with trade and business market buyers. Finally, the risks of relying on sales promotional tools are revealed in this chapter. 18

Direct Marketing Consumers' desire for greater convenience and marketers' never-ending search for competitive advantage has spawned growth in direct marketing. Chapter 19, "Direct Marketing," considers this area, which is a combination of both marketing and promotion. With direct marketing, advertisers communicate to a target audience, but they also seek an immediate response. The ultimate "immediate response" that a direct marketer seeks is an order to buy. 19

Public Relations and Corporate Advertising Chapter 20, "Public Relations and Corporate Advertising," concludes the discussion of integrated brand promotion. Public relations offers the opportunity for positive communication but also provides damage control when negative events affect an organization. Corporate advertising is image-, cause-, or advocacy-focused and can serve a useful role in supporting an advertiser's broader brand advertising programs. These two separate and important areas can be key aspects of an organization's overall integrated brand promotion effort—particularly in the context of negative publicity. Each has the potential to make a distinct and important contribution to the single and unified message and image of an organization, which is the ultimate goal of IBP. 20

CHAPTER 17

After reading and thinking about this chapter, you will be able to do the following:

1

Describe the role of support media in a comprehensive media plan.

2

Explain the appeal of P-O-P advertising as an element of integrated brand promotion.

3

Justify the growing popularity of event sponsorship as another supporting component of a media plan.

4

Discuss the challenges presented by the ever-increasing variety of media for achieving integrated brand promotion.

CHAPTER 17
Support Media, P-O-P Advertising, and Event Sponsorship

CHAPTER 18
Sales Promotion

CHAPTER 19
Direct Marketing

CHAPTER 20
Public Relations and Corporate Advertising

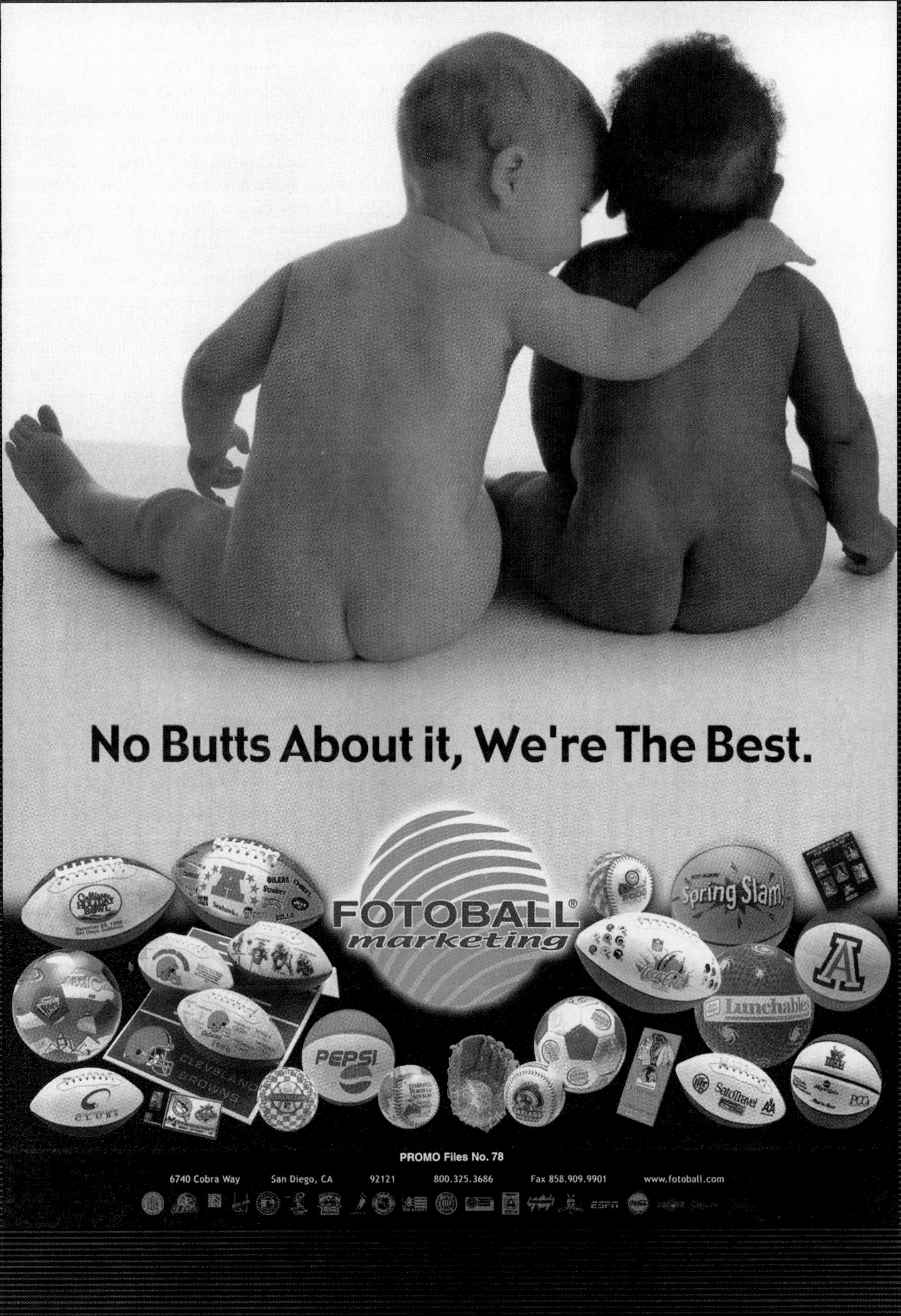

No Butts About it, We're The Best.

PROMO Files No. 78

6740 Cobra Way San Diego, CA 92121 800.325.3686 Fax 858.909.9901 www.fotoball.com

David Dorfman, co-owner of Insite Advertising, sells media space. But not just any media space. David and his partner Marc Miller sell access to the ad space in 250 restrooms of trendy bars, restaurants, and nightclubs throughout New York City. Marketers such as RJR Nabisco, the Joe Boxer Corporation, and Procter & Gamble have bought into Mr. Dorfman's program. He comments: "What we sell to advertisers is a captive audience with a prime demographic of 21 to 35 years old. And it's gender specific! So you can get either men or women and eliminate the waste."[1]

Marketers of the Noxzema brand decided that women's restrooms throughout Manhattan was a place they wanted to be. The thinking was that Noxzema had been around forever, and it was time for a facelift. Noxzema needed something fresh, edgy, unexpected, and new. It needed to be part of a medium that would help it move up the hip scale and that would challenge women to think, "Whoa, what brand has the nerve to do and say that?" It needed to be in the restroom.

So working with the company's ad agency, Leo Burnett, Noxzema brand managers created a series of small advertising signs like those shown in Exhibit 17.1, featuring in-your-face humor such as "It's not the lighting" and "Did someone miss her beauty sleep?," with the common tagline "Next time Noxzema." Oh yeah, one more detail. These signs were hung in frames on the walls across from the mirrors in about 115 trendy restaurants and clubs in chic Manhattan neighborhoods. The

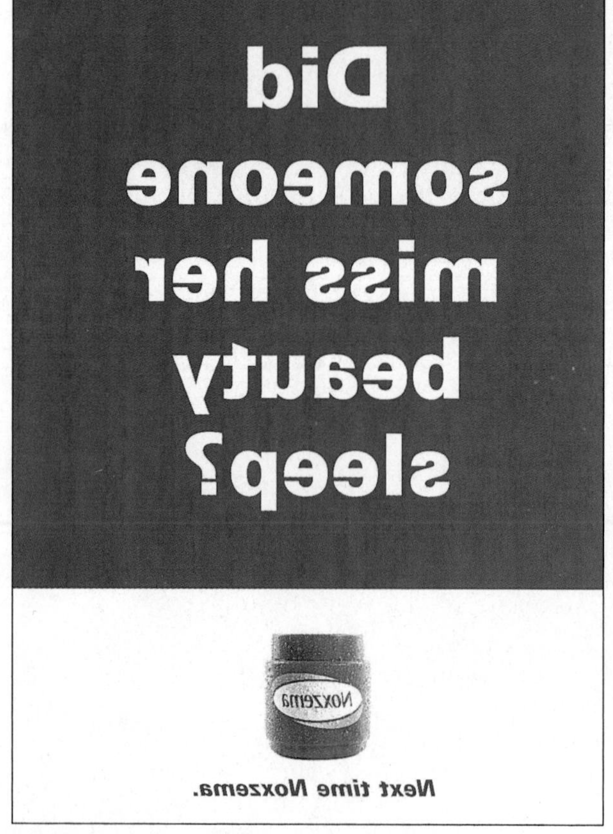

EXHIBIT 17.1

These are two of the ad posters created for Noxzema's assault on women's restrooms in Manhattan. All the posters were meant to be read in the mirror. Hold this exhibit up to a mirror, and you too may see the light. www.pg.com

1. Stuart Elliott, "P&G Takes a Most Unusual Tack with Its New, In-Your-Face Ads," *New York Times*, June 3, 1998.

signs were meant to be read in the mirror exactly at that point in time when a woman might be thinking about her face and appearance before returning to the crowded dance floor. Perhaps, then, this is an example of being at the right place at the right time to deliver an in-your-face, "Hey, look at me" message, for a brand that had become a little too familiar and a little too boring. In addition, quirky campaigns like this one often attract the attention of business writers in conventional media and lead to valuable, free exposure for the brand. Indeed, many of the details of this example are drawn from an article about it that appeared in a business column from the *New York Times*. Not bad coverage for bathroom advertising!

As you no doubt have already recognized, perhaps in a restroom near you, advertisers are always on the lookout for new venues to advance their messages. And this can lead them to unconventional places. The Noxzema example reflects the growing interest among marketers in finding unusual media vehicles meant to reach niche markets, particularly in urban locations, where new market trends often originate. Other such niche media include trucks that drive endlessly through city streets as mobile billboards; ads beamed onto the sides of office buildings; racks of postcard ads, which are again placed in trendy restaurants and nightspots; ads printed on coffee cups with coordinated signage attached to coffee carts; and even small signs attached to the backs of messenger bikes that patrol the canyons of downtown corporate America.

The Noxzema restroom affair is also a nice prelude to this chapter because it illustrates several of the chapter's basic themes. It makes the point that advertisers are constantly on the lookout for new, cost-effective ways to break through the clutter of competitors' advertisements to register their appeals with carefully targeted consumers. Of course, as soon as a new method begins to deliver results, many will make it part of their media plans, and the clutter problem returns. Edgy, inexpensive promotional initiatives executed in major urban markets have become so popular with mainstream marketers that they now have their own name—**guerrilla marketing.** Additional examples of guerrilla marketing activities are listed in Exhibit 17.2. How long before such tactics lose their novelty and thus their effectiveness? Three to five years seems a reasonable estimate.[2]

Although print and broadcast media continue to draw the lion's share of advertising expenditures, many other options exist for communicating with consumers. This chapter will examine a set of options commonly referred to as support media. Traditional support media such as signs and billboards have been around for many years, but are enjoying renewed interest from advertisers. Additionally, alternatives such as point-of-purchase advertising and event sponsorship continue to produce impressive results and thus are receiving more and more funding from many marketers. Many of the communication options discussed in this chapter present low-cost means for trying something different—and unleashing the creative forces that can generate breakthrough results.

1 Traditional Support Media.

This section will feature traditional support media: outdoor signage and billboard advertising, transit and aerial advertising, specialty advertising, and directory advertising. **Support media** are used to reinforce or extend a message being delivered via some other media vehicle; hence the name *support media.* They can be especially productive when used to deliver a message near the time or place where consumers are actually contemplating product selections. Since these media can be tailored for local markets, they can have value to any organization that wants to reach consumers in a particular venue, neighborhood, or metropolitan area.

2. Michael Mechanic, "Taking It to the Streets," *Industry Standard,* February 26, 2001, 62–63.

Client	Product	Agency	Street Strategy
Best Buy	Best Buy	Momentum Marketing	Stage a Sting concert in Central Park. Uniformed teams hit streets of the Big Apple with branded CD samplers containing $10 store coupons; 30,000 recipients also to win Sting tix.
Bloomberg News	New radio coverage of politics, entertainment	Margeotis Fertitta & Partners	Dispatch fake news hawkers—"Extra! Extra!"—to tollbooths, cinemas, and New York's City Hall. Dole out hundreds of thousands of radios that get only one station: Bloomberg's.
Brown & Williamson	Lucky Strike cigarettes	Big Fat	Approach workers on cigarette breaks in six metropolitan areas. In winter, smokers get cups of coffee; in summer, chairs to sit on. Smokers are told: "Lucky loves you!"
Haagen-Dazs	Gelato	Aronow & Pollock	Three Italian chefs compete in an ice cream scoop-off at New York's Columbus Circle. The winner gets a $25,000 charity donation in his name. Onlookers gorge on gelato samples.
Hasbro	Shoezies—tiny shoes for kids' fingertips	Alliance, a spinoff of Grey Advertising	Send a brand-wrapped van to malls and teen hangouts in major cities; 20 girls in Shoezies gear pop out, perform a choreographed dance and hand out samples of the tiny collectibles.
Levi Strauss & Co.	Levi's Jeans	TBWA Chiat/Day	Buy old UPS trucks, repaint in Levi's colors and build mock college dorm rooms inside. Drive to raves, clubs and other youth hangouts, and sell jeans right off the truck.

Source: Companies listed.

EXHIBIT 17.2

Guerrilla marketers take to the streets.

Outdoor Signage and Billboard Advertising. Billboards, posters, and outdoor signs are perhaps the oldest advertising form.[3] Posters first appeared in North America when they were used during the Revolutionary War to keep the civilian population informed about the war's status. In the 1800s they became a promotional tool, with circuses and politicians being among the first to adopt this new medium. Exhibit 17.3 shows a classic ad execution for "The Greatest Show on Earth." With the onset of World War I, the U.S. government turned to posters and billboards to call for recruits, encourage the purchase of war bonds, and cultivate patriotism. By the 1920s outdoor advertising also enjoyed widespread commercial applications and, until the invention of television, was the medium of choice when an advertiser wanted to communicate with visual imagery.

While the rise of television stifled the growth of outdoor advertising, the federal highway system that was laid across the nation in the sixties pumped new life into billboards. The 40-foot-high burgers and pop bottles were inevitable, but throughout the seventies and eighties billboards became an outlet for creative expression in advertising. One exceptional example of using the medium to its fullest was a Nike campaign run in the mid-eighties featuring high-profile athletes, such as Olympian Carl Lewis, performing their special artistry.[4] Today, the creative challenge posed by outdoor advertising is as it has always been—to grab attention and communicate with minimal verbiage and striking imagery, as do the billboards in Exhibits 17.4 and 17.5.

In excess of $4.8 billion was spent to deliver advertisers' messages on the 400,000 billboards across the United States in 1999.[5] Outdoor advertising offers several dis-

3. Ann Cooper, "All Aboards," *Adweek,* May 9, 1994, 3–10.
4. Ibid.
5. Ellen Neubourne, "Road Show: The New Face of Billboards," *Business Week,* May 8, 2000, 75.

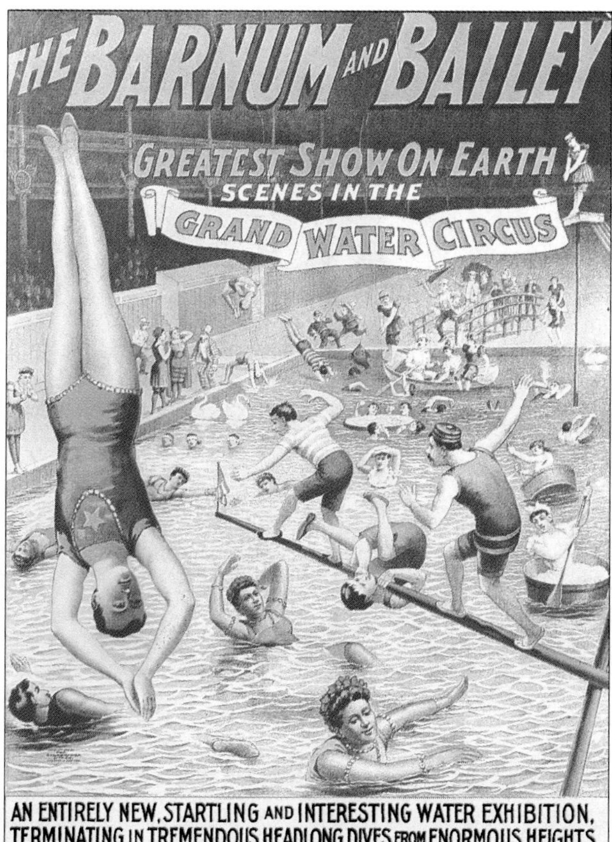

EXHIBIT 17.3

Advertising in the United States began with posters and billboards. Circuses were the early pioneers in this medium.
www.ringling.com

tinct advantages.[6] This medium provides an excellent means to achieve wide exposure of a message in specific local markets. Size is, of course, a powerful attraction of this medium, and when combined with special lighting and moving features, billboards can be captivating. Billboards created for Dayton Hudson in Minneapolis have even wafted a mint scent throughout the city as part of a candy promotion for Valentine's Day.[7] Billboards also offer around-the-clock exposure for an advertiser's message and are well suited to showing off a brand's distinctive packaging or logo.

Billboards are especially effective when they reach viewers with a message that speaks to a need or desire that is immediately relevant. For instance, they are commonly deployed by fast-food restaurants along major freeways to help hungry travelers know where to exit to enjoy a Whopper or Big Mac. A clever example of putting one's outdoor signage in the right place at the right time to enhance its appeal is illustrated by Exhibit 17.6.

Billboards have obvious drawbacks. Long and complex messages simply make no sense on billboards; some experts suggest that billboard copy should be limited to no more than six words.[8] Also, the impact of billboards can vary dramatically depending on their location, and assessing locations is tedious and time-consuming. To assess locations, companies may have to send individuals to the site to see if the location is desirable.[9] This activity, known in the industry as **riding the boards,** can be a major investment of time and money. Moreover, the Institute of Outdoor Advertising rates billboards as expensive in comparison to several other media alternatives.[10] Considering that billboards are constrained to short messages, are often in the background, and are certainly not the primary focus of anyone's attention, their costs may be prohibitive for many advertisers.

Despite the costs, and the criticism by environmentalists that billboards represent a form of visual pollution, spending on outdoor advertising has been increasing, and because of important technological advances, the future looks secure for billboards.[11] The first of these advances combines the videotaping of billboard sites and their surroundings with software from International Outdoor Systems of London.[12] This tool reduces the amount of time and money that executives must spend riding the boards, and it helps them design boards to fit in with the surroundings at a particular location. The software package not only allows advertisers to view billboard sites via videotape, but also allows them to insert mock-ups of different billboard executions into the specific location pictured on their computer screen. This design tool and time-saving system should make outdoor advertising a more attractive option for many advertisers.

6. Jack Z. Sissors and Lincoln Bumba, *Advertising Media Planning* (Lincolnwood, Ill.: NTC Business Books, 1993).
7. Ronald Grover, "Billboards Aren't Boring Anymore," *Business Week,* September 21, 1998, 88–89.
8. *Yellow Pages and the Media Mix* (Troy, Mich.: Yellow Pages Publishers Association, 1990).
9. Kevin Goldman, "Spending on Billboards Is Rising; Video Tool Makes Buying Easier," *Wall Street Journal,* June 27, 1994, B6.
10. Sissors and Bumba, *Advertising Media Planning.*
11. Grover, "Billboards Aren't Boring Anymore," op. cit.
12. Goldman, "Spending on Billboards Is Rising," op. cit.

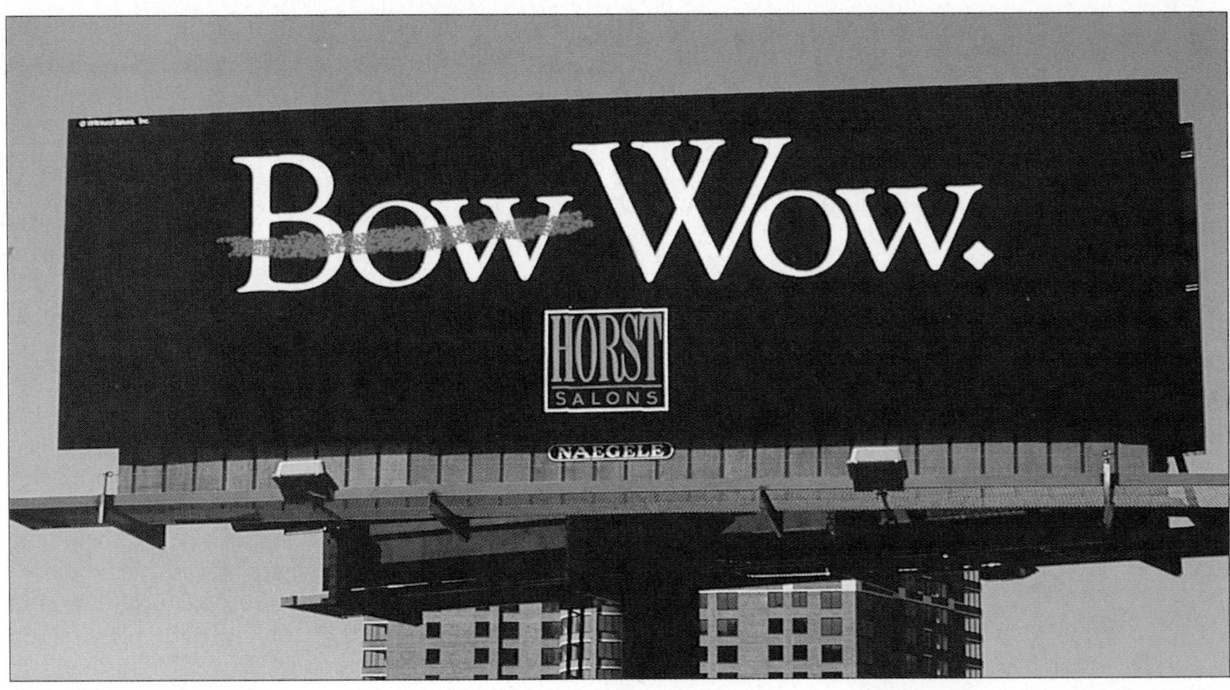

EXHIBIT 17.4

Minimal verbiage is one key to success with billboard advertising. This example easily satisfies the minimal-verbiage rule. www.horst-salons.com

EXHIBIT 17.5

As with all media, creativity is a must in making effective use of billboards. Soaring above the clutter to grab the attention of passing motorists is the goal of this execution.

EXHIBIT 17.6

This sign uses the perfect slogan for a sports venue. Has there ever been a referee who didn't need glasses?

Perhaps even more important to the future of billboard advertising is the development of computer-aided production technology for board facings.[13] Until a few years ago, billboard creation and painting was a labor-intensive process that could take a crew of workers several days to complete, and quality control from board to board was always problematic. Now, thanks to computer graphics, the biggest players are designing their boards digitally. One consequence of computer-aided design is that the time needed to get a campaign up and running on multiple boards has been reduced from months to days. Additionally, board facings can be produced in unlimited quantities with total quality control. The advent of computer-directed painting brings magazine-quality reproduction to billboards in any market. And digital design has set the stage for a major infusion of creativity in billboard advertising. If the designer can think it, he or she now can execute it on a billboard. The rapid deployment, quality control, and creative expression that now are possible in executing billboards and outdoor signage have attracted a whole new group of big-name advertisers—such as Disney, Sony, Microsoft, America Online, and Amazon.com—to the great outdoors.[14]

Transit and Aerial Advertising. **Transit advertising** is a close cousin to billboard advertising, and in many instances it is used in tandem with billboards. The phrase **out-of-home media** is commonly used to refer to the combination of transit and billboard advertising; this is a popular advertising form around the world with global revenues approaching $20 billion in 2000.[15] As illustrated in Exhibits 17.7, 17.8, and 17.9, out-of-home ads appear in many venues, including on backs of buildings, in subway tunnels, and throughout sports stadiums. Transit ads may also appear as signage on terminal and station platforms, or actually envelop mass transit vehicles, as exemplified in Exhibit 17.10. One of the latest innovations in out-of-home media is taxi-top

13. Cyndee Miller, "Outdoor Gets a Makeover," *Marketing News,* April 10, 1995, 26.
14. Grover, "Billboards Aren't Boring Anymore," op. cit.
15. Alastair Ray, "A Market on the Move," *adageglobal,* April 2001, 36.

EXHIBIT 17.7

This wonderful old building has a big, flat backside, facing a major interstate freeway. No wonder then that the Gap wants to keep it in jeans. Does the Gap site (www.gap.com) show signs of integrated brand promotion? Have you noticed any relationship between the location and placement of local transit ads with demographic trends? Can you cite an example where a transit ad or billboard seemed entirely out of place?

EXHIBIT 17.8

Happy Berliners enjoy their Cokes at 3 degrees Celsius while waiting on the U-bahn (subway).

electronic billboards that deliver customized messages by neighborhood using wireless Internet technology.[16] We've come a long way from the circus poster . . .

Transit advertising can be valuable when an advertiser wishes to target adults who live and work in major metropolitan areas.[17] The medium reaches people as they travel to and from work, and because it taps into daily routines repeated week after week, transit advertising offers an excellent means for repetitive message exposure. In large metro areas such as New York—with its 200 miles of subways and

16. Evantheia Schibsted, "Zip-Coding: Taxi-Top Advertising Targets the 'Hood," *Business 2.0,* April 17, 2001, 56.
17. Sissors and Bumba, *Advertising Media Planning.*

e-SIGHTINGS

EXHIBIT 17.9

As this Fenway Park scoreboard shows, signage and advertiser slogans are standard fare at the ballpark. None of these scoreboard ads sport Web addresses, although Crackerjack (www.crackerjack.com) and these advertised brands all have homes on the Web. Does it matter? Which of the advertised brands might you need more information on? Is selection of a cream- versus jam-filled doughnut predicated on nutritional research, or is Dunkin' Donuts (www.dunkindonuts.com) just hoping you'll pick up a dozen on the way home from the park? Why do you think each advertiser chose to pick this particular place to advertise?

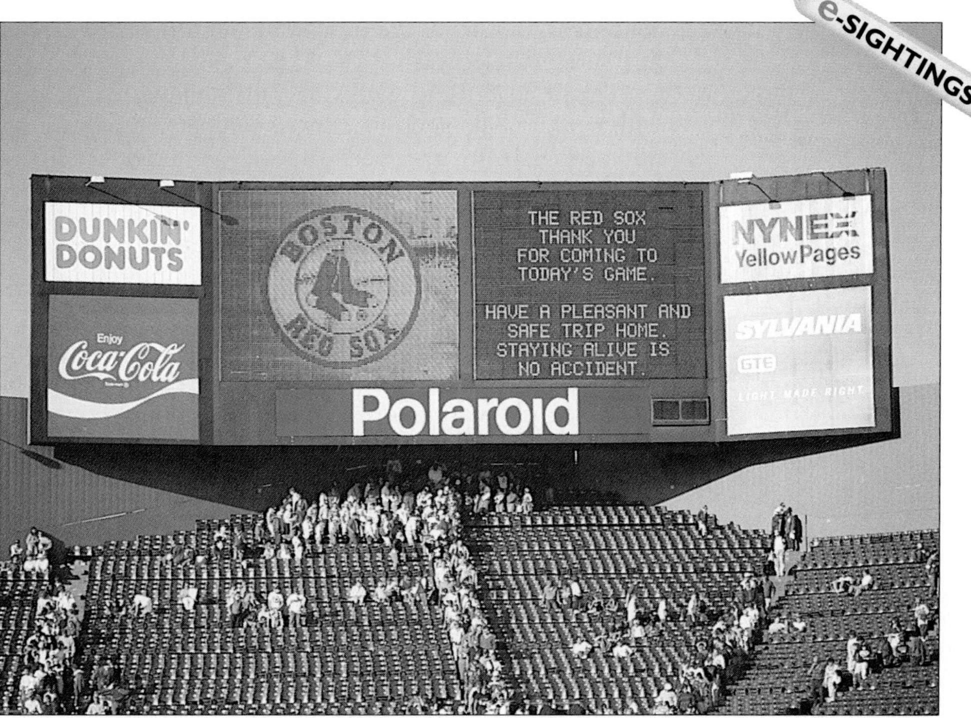

EXHIBIT 17.10

The story is the same all over the world. Mass transit has become an advertising vehicle too. Can you identify this European city?
www.converse.com

3 million subway riders—transit ads can reach large numbers of individuals in a cost-efficient manner.

When working with this medium, an advertiser may find it most appropriate to buy space on just those trains or bus lines that consistently haul people from the demographic segment being targeted. This type of demographic matching of vehicle with target is always preferred as a means of deriving more value from limited ad budgets. Transit advertising can be appealing to local merchants because their messages may reach a passenger as he or she is traveling to a store to shop. For some consumers, transit ads are the last medium they are exposed to before making their final product selection.

Transit advertising works best for building or maintaining brand awareness; as with outdoor billboards, lengthy or complex messages simply cannot be worked into this medium. Also, transit ads can easily go unnoticed in the hustle and bustle of daily life. People traveling to and from work via a mass transit system are certainly one of the hardest audiences to engage with an advertising message. They can be bored, exhausted, absorbed by their thoughts about the day, or occupied by some other medium. Given the static nature of a transit poster, breaking through to a harried commuter can be a tremendous challenge.

When an advertiser can't break through on the ground or under the ground, it may have to look skyward. **Aerial advertising** can involve airplanes pulling signs or banners, skywriting, or those majestic blimps. For several decades, Goodyear had blimps all to itself; however, in the nineties, new blimp vendors came to the market with smaller, less-expensive blimps that made this medium surge in popularity with other advertisers.[18] Virgin Lightships created a fleet of small blimps that measure 70,000 cubic feet in size and can be rented for advertising purposes for around $200,000 per month. Not to be outdone, Airship International flies full-size blimps, about 235,000 cubic feet in size, promising 200 percent more usable ad space than the competition's mini-blimps.

Sanyo, Fuji Photo, MetLife, and Anheuser-Busch have clearly bought into the appeal of an airborne brand presence. The Family Channel has also been a frequent user of Virgin Lightships' mini-blimps at sporting events such as the Daytona 500 NASCAR race. A recall study done after one such event showed that 70 percent of target consumers remembered the Family Channel as a result of the blimp flyovers.[19] Blimps carrying television cameras at sporting events also provide unique video that can result in the blimp's sponsor getting several on-air mentions. This brand-name exposure comes at a small fraction of the cost of similar exposure through television advertising.

When a medium proves itself, more and more marketers will want it in their media plans. Of course, the irony is that as a medium becomes more attractive and hence cluttered, its original appeal begins to be diluted. We see this occurring with aerial advertising. With more and more blimps showing up at sporting events, networks can be choosy about which one gets the coveted on-air mention. Besides carrying an overhead camera for them, networks now demand that blimp sponsors purchase advertising time during the event if they want an on-air mention. Additionally, the sportscasters' casual banter about the beautiful overhead shots from so-and-so's wonderful blimp have now been replaced by scripted commentary that is written out in advance as part of the advertising contract.[20] As we've noted before, this cycle of uniqueness and effectiveness, followed by clutter and dilution of effectiveness, repeats itself over and over again. Are there any clutter-free places left for building a brand? Well, as described in the Creativity box on page 617, Radio Shack has its sights set on the moon. That's right, the *moon*.

Specialty Advertising. No one can say for sure, but it is believed that modern-day specialty advertising came into being around 1840. An insurance salesperson in Auburn, New York, wanted local businesses to post information about his insurance offerings. When the owners declined to help, he bought calendars, attached the information

18. Fara Warner, "More Companies Turn to Skies as Medium to Promote Products," *Wall Street Journal,* January 5, 1995, B6.
19. Ibid.
20. Bill Richards, "Bright Idea Has Business Looking Up for Ad Blimps," *Wall Street Journal,* October 14, 1997, B1.

he had wanted to post, and presented the wall calendars as gifts. The local business owners were pleased with the gift, hung the calendars in their stores, and the rest, as they say, is history. Lest you think that items such as calendars and kitchen magnets are too trivial to be worth serious consideration, *PROMO Magazine*'s estimate of expenditures on such items for 2000 was $16.3 billion, up more than 10 percent from the previous year.[21]

The insurance salesperson's wall calendar illustrates the essence of all modern specialty advertising. **Specialty-advertising items** have three defining elements: (1) they contain the sponsor's logo and perhaps a related promotional message; (2) this logo and message appear on a useful or decorative item; and (3) the item is given freely, as a gift from the sponsor. This third element distinguishes specialty-advertising items from those referred to as premiums.[22] **Premiums** are items that carry the logo of a sponsor and are offered "free" or at a reduced charge to motivate the purchase of a related product or service. For example, the next time you receive a "free" souvenir movie cup with the purchase of a super-size Coke at McDonald's, you're taking home a premium.

Literally thousands of different items have been used for specialty-advertising purposes, but the majority of these fall into five broad categories: wearables, writing instruments, desk or office accessories, calendars, and glassware or ceramics.[23] T-shirts, bumper stickers, coffee mugs, matchbooks, ashtrays, cups and glasses, buttons, decals, clocks, pens and pencils, mouse pads, balloons, litter bags, coin holders, notepads, rulers, and yardsticks are all examples of specialty-advertising items. As illustrated in Exhibit 17.11, customized Post-it Notes can have hypnotic appeal, but if sports balls are your thing, you're probably going to want to check out www.fotoball.com. See their ad in Exhibit 17.12.

Using specialty-advertising items to carry a brand name has several appealing aspects.[24] First, they can be made available on a selective basis. Whether they are sent

CREATIVITY

Brand Building by Way of the Moon

On an earth cluttered with advertising messages at every turn, how does the creative marketer stand out from the crowd? Well, Radio Shack Corporation, the Texas-based retail giant, has decided it must go where no advertiser has gone before. Working as the lead corporate sponsor with its partner LunaCorp, Radio Shack is designing a most unusual marketing event. Radio Shack has made a multimillion-dollar commitment to support a mission to explore the moon with an advanced robotic vehicle that will carry the Radio Shack logo boldly into space. This novel moon expedition is scheduled tentatively for 2003.

Beyond its logo on the moon rover, several other kinds of visibility are expected to accrue to Radio Shack as a result of this unique sponsorship. The logo will be transmitted from moon to earth via well-placed cameras, and it will also appear prominently on the Web site that LunaCorp is developing to monitor every aspect of the event. Additionally, the Radio Shack presence will be significant in the simulators that LunaCorp is planning for science centers across America, where the public will have a chance to experience a rover ride on the moon. The purported scientific purpose of the mission is to search for water and ice and to collect other data through high-definition television cameras. Call us cynical if you must, but the real science we see at work here is the science of brand building.

Radio Shack makes no bones about it. For them, this sponsorship is all about enhancing the image of Radio Shack as a company that knows technology and makes it accessible to the mass market. As described by Jim McDonald, a senior vice president who championed this unique alliance, the LunaCorp moon mission is a good fit (for Radio Shack) because it is all about "trying to democratize space and demystify space as well." If Radio Shack can succeed as a space pioneer, its credibility as a merchant of wireless phones, satellite dishes, and other high-tech gadgetry is likely to soar to new heights as well.

Source: Jeff Cole, "Advertisers Find One of the Last Clutter-Free Places," *Wall Street Journal*, June 15, 2000, B1.

21. "Proceed with Caution: *PROMO*'s Exclusive Annual Report of the U.S. Promotion Industry," *PROMO Magazine*, May 2001, S13.
22. Dan S. Bagley, *Understanding Specialty Advertising* (Irving, Tex.: Specialty Advertising Association International, 1990).
23. Ibid.
24. Rebecca Piirto Heath, "An Engraved Invitation," *Marketing Tools*, November/December 1997, 36–42.

EXHIBIT 17.11

As we see here, the handy Post-it Note can be adapted as a specialty-advertising item with many appealing aspects. It carries information that will be at a customer's fingertips, note after note, day after day. Check out the possibilities at www.3m.com/promote.

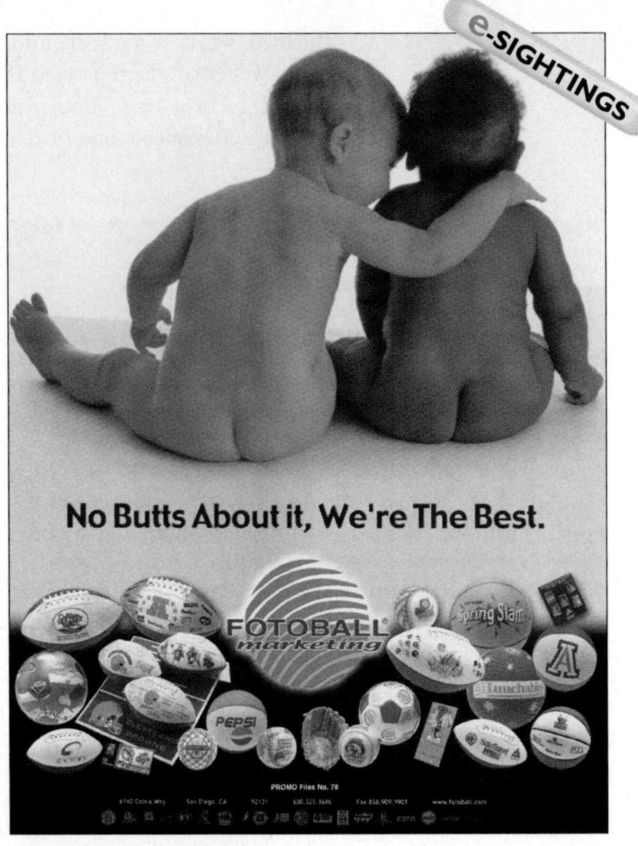

EXHIBIT 17.12

*Specialty-advertising items come in all shapes and sizes. Fotoball Marketing of San Diego, California, wants to be your one-stop shopping headquarters for the ever-popular sports ball. Visit the site (*www.fotoball.com*) and read about the company and types of collectibles and products it creates as marketing souvenirs. How do advertisers use Fotoball products to reach targeted audiences? Compare the longevity of these items compared to other items such as Promo Partner (*www.promopartner.com*). What are some inherent limitations of specialty advertising?*

by mail, distributed only in a local trading area, or passed out by salespeople to target customers, the dispensing of these items can be carefully monitored. This ensures cost-effectiveness and literally puts a message into the hands of prospective customers. Second, unlike other media options, specialty-advertising items can hang around for long periods of time. For example, a Friskies wall calendar will reinforce the virtues of Friskies cat food day in and day out for at least a year. Third, specialty advertising can help build goodwill. Young or old, people like to receive gifts. When executed with good taste, specialty-advertising programs can generate the goodwill that is an important asset for any brand.

Specialty advertising shares the space limitation problems of many other support media. Coffee mugs, coin holders, and the like provide little space for detailing the virtues of a brand; relative to the vast array of information that people are exposed to on a daily basis, what can be said on the back of a matchbook is easily overlooked. In addition, the mind-boggling variety of items to choose from for specialty advertising makes selection complex and time-consuming. (See for yourself at www.promomart.com.) This decision must be made carefully, because asso-

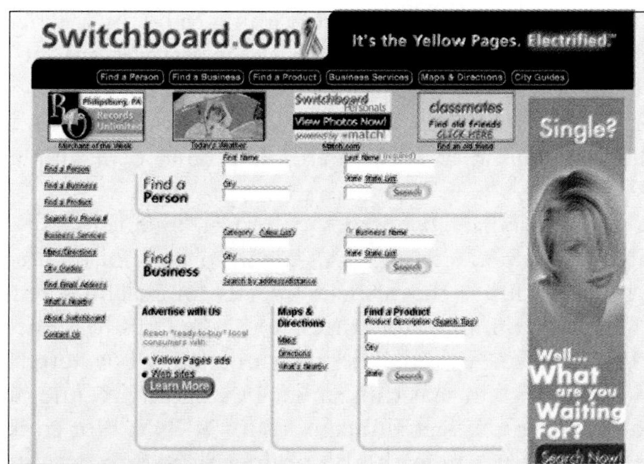

EXHIBIT 17.13

When you need a phone number in a hurry, do you pull out the Yellow Pages or pull up a site like Switchboard.com (www.switchboard.com) to get your answer?

ciating a brand name with items that some might see as junk or trinkets always has the potential of backfiring by cheapening the brand's image.

Directory Advertising. The last time you reached for a phone directory to appraise the local options for Chinese or Mexican food, you probably didn't think about it as a traditional support medium. However, Yellow Pages advertising plays an important role in the media mix for many types of organizations, as is evidenced by the $12.7 billion that was spent in this medium in 1999.[25] A wealth of current facts and figures about this media option are available at www.yppa.org.

A phone directory can play a unique and important role in consumers' decision-making processes. While most support media keep a brand name or key product information in front of a consumer, Yellow Pages advertising helps people follow through on their decision to buy. By providing the information that consumers need to actually find a particular product or service, the Yellow Pages can serve as the final link in a buying decision. Because of their availability and consumers' familiarity with this advertising tool, Yellow Pages directories provide an excellent means to supplement awareness-building and interest-generating campaigns that an advertiser might be pursuing through other media.

On the downside, the proliferation and fragmentation of phone directories can make this a difficult medium to work in.[26] Many metropolitan areas are covered by multiple directories, some of which are specialty directories designed to serve specific neighborhoods, ethnic groups, or interest groups. Selecting the right set of directories to get full coverage of large sections of the country can be a daunting task. Additionally, working in this medium requires long lead times; over the course of a year, information in a Yellow Pages ad can easily become dated. There is also limited flexibility for creative execution in the traditional paper format.

Growth of the Internet was once viewed as a major threat to providers of old-style phone directories.[27] Many Web sites such as www.switchboard.com and www.superpages.com provide online access to Yellow Pages–style databases that allow individualized searches at one's desktop. Exhibit 17.13 features the home page for Switchboard.com. Other high-profile Web players such as Yahoo! and MSN have also developed online directories as components of their service offerings for Web surfers. But as it turns out, consumers still want their old-style Yellow Pages; market research has established that people who spend the most time on the Internet searching for addresses and phone numbers are also the same people who make heavy use of paper directories.[28] When people are in an information-gathering mode, they commonly use multiple media. So, thus far the Internet has been more of an opportunity than a threat for Yellow Pages publishers, and old-fashioned Yellow Pages directories continue to produce something that has been hard to find on the Web—profitability!

25. Yellow Pages Publishers Association, www.yppa.org, accessed May 25, 2001.
26. *Yellow Pages and the Media Mix.*
27. *Yellow Pages: Facts & Media Guide 1998* (Troy, Mich.: Yellow Pages Publishers Association, 1998), 4, 5.
28. Rachel E. Silverman, "Print Yellow Pages Are Still Profitable," *Wall Street Journal,* May 22, 2000, B16.

When Support Media Are More Than Support Media. There are going to be times when the capabilities and economies of support media lead them to be featured in one's media plan. Obviously, in such instances, it would be a misnomer to label them as merely supportive. Out-of-home media used creatively and targeted in major metropolitan markets are especially compelling in this regard. A couple of examples should make this point clear.

There will be times when the particular advantages of transit advertising fit a marketer's communication objectives so perfectly that this medium will not be used merely as a support medium, but instead, as the primary means for reaching customers. Donna Karan's DKNY line of clothing, accessories, and cosmetics has relied heavily on transit advertising to reach its target audience in Manhattan.[29] For starters, the firm bought out the ten-car subway train that runs under Lexington Avenue on Manhattan's East Side and filled it with sophisticated image ads for DKNY. Not coincidentally, this particular subway train runs under the Bloomingdale's store on 59th Street, where DKNY had a supershop featuring all the products in its extensive line. DKNY ads have also appeared on the shuttles from Times Square to Grand Central Terminal, and at subway stations in the city. For DKNY, extensive advertising on and under the streets of New York City reflects its general strategy of using unconventional locations to create awareness and distinctive imagery for the DKNY product line.

Altoids, "the curiously strong mints" made in England since 1780, used a similar strategy to invigorate its brand in 12 major U.S. cities. Turns out that Altoids' target segment of young, socially active adults living in urban neighborhoods are very hard to reach with conventional broadcast or print advertising. Perhaps they are just too busy being socially active. Whatever, using geodemographic segmentation systems like those described in Chapter 6, it is not hard to identify their neighborhoods. So Altoids and its ad agency, Leo Burnett, set out to plaster those neighborhoods with quirky advertising signage on telephone kiosks, bus shelters, and the backs of buses. Once again, quirky rules! In each of the 12 targeted metro areas, sales of Altoids increased by more than 50 percent.[30] Now that's invigorating.

2 Point-of-Purchase (P-O-P) Advertising. From 1981 to 2000, marketers' annual expenditures on point-of-purchase (P-O-P) advertising rose from $5.1 to $17 billion per year.[31] Why this dramatic growth? First, consider that P-O-P is the only medium that places advertising, products, and a consumer together in the same place at the same time. Then, think about these results. Research conducted by the Point-of-Purchase Advertising Institute (www.popai.com) indicates that 70 percent of all product selections involve some final deliberation by consumers at the point of purchase. (Data cited in *POPAI U.S. Consumer Buying Habits Study,* 1995, pp. 17–18. Conducted by POPAI in conjunction with Meyers Research Center.) Additionally, a joint study sponsored by Kmart and Procter & Gamble found that P-O-P advertising boosted the sales of coffee, paper towels, and toothpaste by 567 percent, 773 percent, and 119 percent, respectively.[32] With results like these, it is plain to see why P-O-P advertising is one of the fastest-growing categories in today's marketplace.

P-O-P advertising refers to materials used in the retail setting to attract shoppers' attention to one's product, convey primary product benefits, or highlight pricing information. As will be discussed in Chapter 18, P-O-P displays may also feature price-off deals or other consumer sales promotions. A corrugated cardboard dump

29. Fara Warner, "DKNY Takes Upscale Ads Underground," *Wall Street Journal,* October 6, 1994, B5.
30. Brad Emondson, "The Drive/Buy Equation," *Marketing Tools,* May 1998, 28–31.
31. Data cited in Lisa Z. Eccles, "P-O-P Scores with Marketers," *Advertising Age,* September 26, 1994, P1–P4; Leah Haran, "Point of Purchase: Marketers Getting with the Program," *Advertising Age,* October 23, 1995, 33; "Proceed with Caution: PROMO's Exclusive Annual Report of the U.S. Promotion Industry," *PROMO Magazine,* May 2001, S10–S12.
32. Eccles, "P-O-P Scores with Marketers," P1–P4; Haran, "Point of Purchase: Marketers Getting with the Program," 33.

bin and an attached header card featuring the brand logo or related product information can be produced for pennies per unit. When filled with a product and placed as a freestanding display at retail, sales gains usually follow.

A dump bin with tower display was designed for Nabisco's Barnum's Animals crackers. This colorful 76-inch-tall cardboard tower spent 14 weeks in design before being mass-produced and rolled out across the country. The gorilla towers, along with their tiger and elephant predecessors, hold small boxes of animal crackers, and are the cornerstone of the advertising strategy for Barnum's.[33] While other Nabisco brands such as Oreo's, Chips Ahoy, and Nilla Wafers are supported by more comprehensive advertising programs, they too benefit from P-O-P displays.

Effective deployment of P-O-P advertising requires careful coordination with the marketer's sales force. Gillette found this out in 1996 when it realized it was wasting money on lots of P-O-P materials and displays that retailers simply ignored.[34] Gillette sales reps visit about 20,000 stores per month, and are in a position to know what retailers will and will not use. Gillette's marketing executives finally woke up to this fact when their sales reps told them, for example, that 50 percent of the shelf signs being shipped to retailers from three separate suppliers were going directly to retailers' garbage bins. Reps helped redesign new display cards that mega-retailers such as Wal-Mart approved for their stores and immediately put into use. Now any time Gillette launches a new P-O-P program, it tracks its success through the eyes and ears of 20 of its sales reps who have been designated as monitors for the new program. Having a sales force that can work with retailers to develop and deliver effective P-O-P programs is a critical element for achieving integrated brand promotion.

A myriad of displays and presentations are available to marketers. P-O-P materials generally fall into two categories: **short-term promotional displays,** which are used for six months or less, and **permanent long-term displays,** which are intended to provide point-of-purchase presentation for more than six months. Within these two categories, marketers have a wide range of choices:[35]

- *Window and door signage:* Any sign that identifies and/or advertises a company or brand or gives directions to the consumer.
- *Counter/shelf unit:* A smaller display designed to fit on counters or shelves.
- *Floor stand:* Any P-O-P unit that stands independently on the floor.
- *Shelf talker:* A printed card or sign designed to mount on or under a shelf.
- *Mobile/banner:* An advertising sign suspended from the ceiling of a store or hung across a large wall area.
- *Cash register:* P-O-P signage or small display mounted near a cash register designed to sell impulse items such as gum, lip balm, or candy, as in Exhibit 17.14.
- *Full line merchandiser:* A unit that provides the only selling area for a manufacturer's line. Often located as an end-of-aisle display.
- *End aisle display/gondola:* Usually a large display of products placed at the end of an aisle, as in Exhibit 17.15.
- *Dump bin:* A large bin with graphics or other signage attached.
- *Illuminated sign:* Lighted signage used outside or in-store to promote a brand or the store.
- *Motion display:* Any P-O-P unit that has moving elements to attract attention.
- *Interactive unit:* A computer-based kiosk where shoppers get information such as tips on recipes or how to use the brand. Can also be a unit that flashes and dispenses coupons.

33. Yumiko Ono, "'Wobblers' and 'Sidekicks' Clutter Stores, Irk Retailers," *Wall Street Journal,* September 8, 1998, B1.

34. Nicole Crawford, "Keeping P-O-P Sharp," *PROMO Magazine,* January 1998, 52, 53.

35. *The Point-of-Purchase Advertising Institute's Retailer Guide to Maximizing In-Store Advertising Effectiveness* (Washington, D.C.: Point-of-Purchase Advertising Institute, 1999), 5–7.

EXHIBIT 17.14

Displays in a cash register checkout lane are designed to sell impulse items such as candy, or easily forgotten items such as batteries.

EXHIBIT 17.15

End of aisle displays provide space to draw attention to a large display of product.

EXHIBIT 17.16

A shopping cart ad carries an immediate message to shoppers.

- *Overhead merchandiser:* A display rack that stocks product and is placed above the cash register. The cashier can reach the product for the consumer. The front of an overhead merchandiser usually carries signage.
- *Cart advertising:* Any advertising message adhered to a shopping cart, as in Exhibit 17.16.
- *Aisle directory:* Used to delineate contents of a store aisle; also provides space for an advertising message.

This array of in-store options gives marketers the opportunity to attract shoppers' attention, induce purchase, and provide reinforcement for key messages that are being conveyed through other components of the advertising plan. Retailers are increasingly looking to P-O-P displays as ways to differentiate and provide ambience for their individual stores, which means that the kind of displays valued by Wal-Mart versus Walgreens versus Albertson's versus Target (to name just a few) will often vary considerably. Once again, it is the marketer's field sales force that will be critical in developing the right P-O-P alternative for each retailer stocking that marketer's products.[36] Without the retailers' cooperation, P-O-P advertising has virtually no chance to work its magic.

Event Sponsorship.

Marketers large and small have realized that the effectiveness of traditional broadcast media continues to erode as media become more fragmented and consumers become more distracted. No one knows this better than one of the world's biggest advertisers—General Motors. GM spends more than $2 billion annually in traditional media such as TV, radio, and magazines.[37] But throughout the nineties, GM saw growing expenditures in these media producing no real gains in market share. One GM executive concluded, "You have to find other ways to touch customers than hammering them with network television."[38]

GM has experimented with a number of ways to "get closer" to its prospective customers. Most entail sponsoring events that get consumers in direct contact with its vehicles, or sponsoring events that associate the GM name with causes or activities that are of interest to its target customers. For example, GM has sponsored a traveling slave-ship exhibition, a scholarship program for the Future Farmers of America, and Seventh Avenue's week of fashion shows in New York City. GM has also launched a movie theater on wheels that travels to state fairs, fishing contests, and auto races to show its 15-minute "movie" about the Silverado pickup truck. Like many marketers large and small, GM is shifting more of its advertising budget into event sponsorship.[39]

Event sponsorship has some similarities with the other advertising and promotional options discussed thus far in this chapter. Event sponsorship often is used to support or supplement other ongoing advertising efforts. Thus, while it is not quite accurate to think of event sponsorship as a support *medium,* there will be times when it plays a supportive role in the media plan akin to that of out-of-home or specialty advertising. Additionally, event sponsorship can provide a base for wonderful synergies with other tactical options such as sales promotions and public relations. Some of these synergies will be made apparent in this chapter, and are then elaborated on in Chapters 18 and 20. As always, the challenge is to get multiple tactical alternatives working together to break through the clutter of the marketplace and register the message with the target customer.

3 Who Else Uses Event Sponsorship?

Event sponsorship is a special and increasingly popular way to reach consumers. **Event sponsorship** involves a marketer providing financial support to help fund an event, such as a rock concert or golf tournament. In return, that marketer acquires the rights to display a brand name, logo, or advertising message on-site at the event. If the event is covered on TV, the marketer's brand and logo may also receive exposure with the television audience. In 2000, marketers in North America spent $8.7 billion for sponsorship rights, with about two-thirds of this total going for sports sponsorships.[40]

Event sponsorship can take many forms. The events can be international in scope, like the Olympics, or they may have a local flavor, like a chili cook-off in Amarillo, Texas. The events may have existed on their own, with marketers offering funding after the fact, or marketers may create an event they can sponsor, in hopes of engaging a segment of their customers. Events provide a captive audience, may receive live coverage by radio and television, and often are reported in the print

36. Matthew Kinsman, "The Last Stand," *PROMO Magazine,* January 2001, 29–34.
37. Fara Warner, "Under Pressure, GM Takes Its Sales Show on the Road," *Wall Street Journal,* November 4, 1998, B1.
38. Ibid.
39. Ibid.
40. "Proceed with Caution: PROMO's Exclusive Annual Report of the U.S. Promotion Industry," *PROMO Magazine,* May 2001, S17.

media. Hence, event sponsorship can both yield face-to-face contact with real consumers and receive simultaneous and follow-up publicity in the mass media.

The list of companies participating in event sponsorships seems to grow with each passing year. Best Buy, Sprint, Atlantic Records, Pepsi, Citibank, and a host of other companies have sponsored tours and special appearances for recording artists such as Brandy, Jewel, Sting, Britney Spears, Elton John, and the Rolling Stones. Sprint reportedly paid $6 million to the Stones to fund their Bridges to Babylon tour and, as suggested by the ad in Exhibit 17.17, were grateful for the opportunity to be associated with "the World's Greatest Rock 'n' Roll Band." The growing popularity of women's soccer led Hyundai Motor America to be among the first national sponsors of the new Women's United Soccer Association.[41] If you have ever hit the beaches for spring break, you already know that companies such as Coca-Cola, MCI, and Sega will be there to greet you. Research conducted by Intercollegiate Communications, Inc., has even established that 65 percent of college students on break not only accept corporate events on the beach, they expect and look forward to them.[42] With the growing interest in stock-car racing and an expanded NASCAR circuit that includes races all over the United States, major brands such as Canon, Tide, Gillette, Winston, McDonald's, and Kodak have scrambled for the privilege to spend $4 million a year to sponsor their very own race car.[43] Andersen Consulting has dabbled in golf and auto racing funding, and was also a proud sponsor of the "Van Gogh Masterpieces" art exhibit at the National Gallery of Art in Washington, D.C.[44] There can be no doubt that more marketers of all types will pursue event sponsorship in the future, and as indicated by the Global Issues box on page 625, this is by no means a development unique to North America.

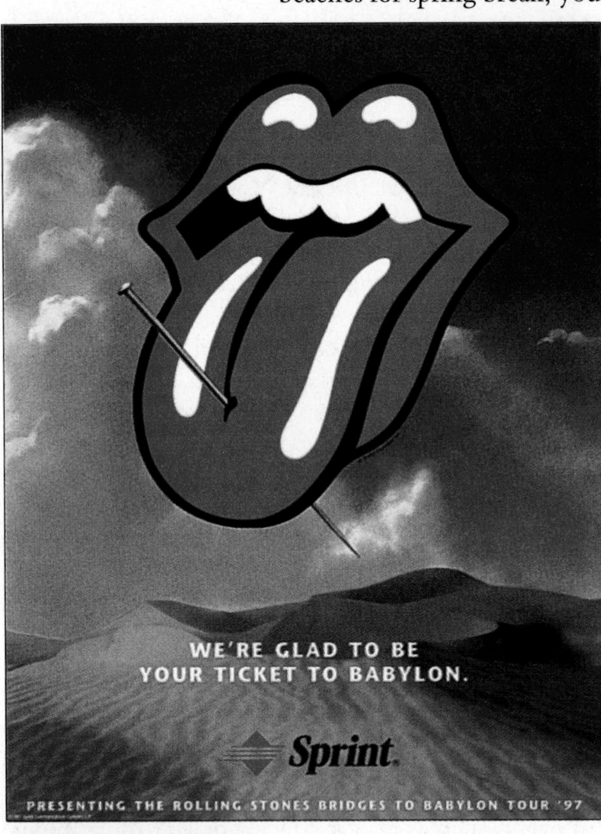

EXHIBIT 17.17

Over the years, one-time bad boys of rock and roll have been courted by all manner of corporate sponsors. Cries of "Sellout!" were directed at the Stones for the $6 million deal they signed with Sprint (www.sprint.com). But the Rolling Stones (est. 1962) could legitimately argue that they (not Sprint) are the bigger brand name, and that only the truly naive believe that people who actually make the music are less deserving of the rewards than the big corporations.
www.stones.com

The Appeal of Event Sponsorship. In the early days of event sponsorship, it often wasn't clear what an organization was receiving in return for its sponsor's fee. Even today, many critics contend that sponsorship, especially of sporting events, can be ego-driven and thus a waste of money.[45] Company presidents are human, and they like to associate with sports stars and celebrities. This is fine, but when sponsorship of a golf tournament, for example, is motivated mainly by a CEO's desire to play in the same foursome as Jack Nicklaus or Tiger Woods, the company is really just throwing away advertising dollars.

41. Patrick M. Reilly, "Rich Marketing Alliances Keep Music Stars Glowing," *Wall Street Journal,* January 22, 1998, B1; Ken Liebeskind, "Women's Soccer Takes Shot at Pro's," *Advertising Age,* April 16, 2001, S8.
42. Dan Hanover, "School's Out!" *PROMO Magazine,* February 1998, 42–46.
43. Chris Roush, "Red Necks, White Socks, and Blue-Chip Sponsors," *Business Week,* August 15, 1994, 74; Alex Taylor III, "Can NASCAR Run in Bigger Circles?" *Fortune,* February 5, 1996, 38.
44. "Andersen Revamps Logo, Readies $100 Million," *Brandweek,* June 22, 1998, 1.
45. William M. Bulkeley, "Sponsoring Sports Gains in Popularity; John Hancock Learns How to Play to Win," *Wall Street Journal,* June 24, 1994, B1.

One of the things fueling the growing interest in event sponsorship is that many companies are now finding ways to make a case for the effectiveness of their sponsorship dollars. Boston-based John Hancock Mutual Life Insurance has been a pioneer in developing detailed estimates of the advertising equivalencies of its sponsorships.[46] John Hancock began sponsoring a college football bowl game in 1986 and soon after had a means to judge the value of its sponsor's fee. Hancock employees scoured magazine and newspaper articles about their bowl game to determine name exposure in print media. Next they'd factor in the exact number of times that the John Hancock name was mentioned during television broadcast of the game, along with the name exposure in pregame promos. In 1991, Hancock executives estimated that they received the equivalent of $5.1 million in advertising exposure for their $1.6 million sponsorship fee. One John Hancock executive called this result "an extraordinarily efficient media buy."[47] However, as the television audience for the John Hancock bowl dwindled in subsequent years, Hancock's estimates of the bowl's value also plunged. Subsequently, Hancock moved its sports sponsorship dollars into other events, such as the Olympics and the U.S. Gymnastics Championships.

GLOBAL ISSUES

Event Sponsorship Hits China

Marketers around the world want to be associated with culturally appropriate events. These events provide exposure and networking opportunities that foster global expansion. And with China being one of the largest developing economies in the world, it is a hot spot for event sponsorship. Thus, when the decision was made to perform Puccini's classic opera *Turandot* in the Forbidden City, international marketers were ready with their checkbooks to help underwrite the lavish $15 million production.

Of course, the location is perfect: Giacomo Puccini set his opera in Beijing's Forbidden City. The opera was conducted by Zubin Mehta, directed by Zhang Yimou, and performed outdoors by a cast of 1,000. The extravagant production was expected to draw 20,000 spectators, even with the equally extravagant ticket prices ranging from $150 to $1,500. Sponsors covet the association with affluent, cosmopolitan people that an event like this attracts. Banks and accounting firms were at the head of the line for sponsorship rights, and were joined by companies such as Time Inc., Ericsson Telecommunications, and Tricon Global Restaurants. To be a sponsor, any international firm needed to first establish a joint-venture relationship with a Chinese company, as required by the Chinese government.

So what is there to eat at the opera? Fortunately, Tricon's Pizza Hut and KFC were part of the event, selling their fast food on site. Chicken wings, Puccini, and the Forbidden City: It just doesn't get any better than that . . .

Source: Kate Fitzgerald, "China's International Culture Club," *Advertising Age,* August 3, 1998, 22, 23.

Other research is also providing hard evidence for the value of sponsorship. Studies conducted with various types of sports fans by Performance Research of Newport, Rhode Island, indicate that fan loyalty can be converted to sales. Among stock-car racing fans, 70 percent say they frequently buy the products they see promoted at the racetrack. For baseball, tennis, and golf, these commitment levels run at 58 percent, 52 percent, and 47 percent, respectively.[48] These findings suggest that racing fans in particular have specific product preferences that advertisers can identify and appeal to, and explain why marketers are flocking to the racetrack to get their brand names on the hood of a stock car or on the cap of a stock-car driver.

So how is it conceivable that a company such as Procter & Gamble could justify sponsorship of the Tide Car, shown in Exhibit 17.18? Well, first of all, lots of women are NASCAR fans and lots of women buy Tide. Additionally, P&G's own research jibes with that mentioned in the previous paragraph: NASCAR fans really

46. Michael J. McCarthy, "Keeping Careful Score on Sports Tie-Ins," *Wall Street Journal,* April 24, 1991, B1.
47. Ibid.
48. Roush, "Red Necks, White Socks, and Blue-Chip Sponsors," 74.

EXHIBIT 17.18

Automobile racing attracts big crowds with lots of purchasing power. Is it any surprise that advertisers want to be part of the action? www.pg.com

are loyal to the brands that sponsor cars and have absolutely no problem with marketers plastering their logos all over their cars and their drivers. This translates into incredible visibility and exposure for the Tide brand during a race and in subsequent race coverage. Indeed, when it comes to TV exposure, NASCAR's average per-event TV ratings are second only to NFL football,[49] and without a doubt, brands are truly the stars of the show during any NASCAR event. P&G and the Kroger Company recently expanded their racing participation by signing a sponsorship agreement with Sarah Fisher, billed as the fastest woman driver in the world. Ms. Fisher's race car carries P&G logos for Bounty, Crest, Folgers, Gain, IAMS, Olay, Pantene, and Always, along with a great big KROGER.[50]

Adding to their appeal, event sponsorships can furnish a unique opportunity to foster brand loyalty. When marketers connect their brand with the potent emotional experiences often found at rock concerts, in sport stadiums, or on Fort Lauderdale beaches in late March, positive feelings may be attached to that brand that linger well beyond the duration of the event. As part of its spring break promotion, Coca-Cola sponsors dance contests on the beach, where it hands out thousands of cups of Coke and hundreds of Coca-Cola T-shirts each day. The goal is to build brand loyalty with those 18-to-24-year-old students who've come to the beach for fun and sun. As assessed by one of Coke's senior brand managers, "This is one of the best tools in our portfolio."[51]

Since various types of events attract well-defined target audiences, marketers can and should choose to sponsor just those events that help them reach their desired target. Such is the case for the sponsors featured in Exhibit 17.19. Notice that JBL Electronics is teaming up with TREK to sponsor nationwide mountain biking events. These so-called "gravity" sports are particularly attractive to cynical teens who reject

49. Sam Walker, "NASCAR Gets Coup as Anheuser Is Set to Raise Sponsorship Role," *Wall Street Journal,* November 13, 1998, B6.

50. Kate Fitzgerald, "On Track with Fisher," *Advertising Age,* March 26, 2001, 35.

51. Bruce Horovitz, "Students Get Commercial Crash Course," *USA Today,* March 22, 1995, B1–B2.

e-SIGHTINGS

EXHIBIT 17.19

One of the best uses of events is in reaching well-defined audiences that may be hard to reach through other channels. JBL and TREK have teamed up to support events that reach a target segment that interests them both. Visit the TREK site (www.trekbikes.com) *and look for examples of tie-ins to events such as the Tour de France. How many examples of sponsorship can you find at the TREK site? While the relationship between TREK and biking events is obvious, why does JBL* (www.jbl.com) *think racing fans will respond to its sponsorship of such events? Are there certain benefits to event sponsorship that are fundamentally different than anything traditional media can provide?*

traditional media advertising and are even starting to reject other forms of promotion. Their support of these sports at least puts JBL and TREK on the radar screen of this demanding target audience.[52] A more comprehensive set of guidelines for selecting those events that will most benefit any brand is outlined in Exhibit 17.20.

Seeking a Synergy around Event Sponsorship. As we have seen, one way to justify event sponsorship is to calculate the number of viewers who will be exposed to a brand either at the event or through media coverage of the event, and then assess whether the sponsorship provides a cost-effective way of reaching the target segment. This approach assesses sponsorship benefits in direct comparison with traditional advertising media. Some experts now maintain, however, that the benefits of sponsorship can be fundamentally different from anything that traditional media might provide. These additional benefits can take many forms.

Events can be leveraged as ways to entertain important clients, recruit new customers, motivate the firm's salespeople, and generally enhance employee morale. Events provide unique opportunities for face-to-face contact with key customers. Marketers commonly use this point of contact to distribute specialty-advertising items so that attendees will have a branded memento to remind them of the rock concert or soccer match. Marketers may also use this opportunity to sell premiums such as T-shirts and hats, administer consumer surveys as part of their marketing research efforts, or distribute product samples. As you will see in Chapter 20, a firm's event participation may also be the basis for public relations activities that then generate additional media coverage.

John Hancock Mutual Life has shown remarkable creativity in maximizing the benefits it derived from the $24 million it spent for its five-year sponsorship of the Olympic Games.[53] Of course, association with a high-profile event such as the Summer Games in Atlanta yields broad exposure for the John Hancock name, but Hancock has also been skillful in taking advantage of its sponsor status with local programs. For instance, in conjunction with the Winter Games, Hancock sponsored hockey clinics featuring Olympians from the 1980 gold medal–winning team. Children and their parents turned out in droves. While the clinics were designed for children, the parents who brought them became immediate prospects for Hancock sales representatives. It is this sort of synergy between sponsorship and local selling efforts that organizations often fail to strive for in maximizing the benefits of their sponsorship expenditures. The IBP box on page 629 provides more insights regarding crucial questions to ask in gauging the benefits of event sponsorship.

52. Laura Petrecca, "Defying Gravity: NBC, Peterson Connect with Cynical Teens via Sports Fest," *Advertising Age,* October 11, 1999, 36.
53. Bulkeley, "Sponsoring Sports Gains in Popularity."

EXHIBIT 17.20

Guidelines for event sponsorship.

Guidelines for Event Sponsorship

1. Match the brand to the event. Be sure that the event matches the brand personality. Stihl stages competitions at Mountain Man events featuring its lumbering equipment. Would the Stihl brand fare as well sponsoring a boat race or a triathalon? Probably not.

2. Tightly define the target audience. Closely related to point number one is the fact that the best event in the world won't create impact for a brand if it's the wrong target audience. Too often the only barometer of success is the number of bodies in attendance. Far more important is the fact that the brand is getting exposure to the right audience. This is what JBL and TREK accomplished with the mountain bike tour sponsorship.

3. Stick to a few key messages. Most events try to accomplish too much. People are there to experience the event and can only accommodate a limited amount of persuasion. Don't overwhelm them. Stick to a few key messages and repeat them often.

4. Develop a plot line. An event is most effective when it is like great theater or a great novel. Try to develop a beginning, a middle, and an exciting ending. Sporting events are naturals in this regard, which explains much of their popularity. In non-sporting events, the plot line needs to be developed and delivered in small increments so the attendees can digest both the event and the brand information.

5. Deliver exclusivity. If you staging a special event, make it by invitation only. Or, if you are a featured sponsor, invite only the most important customers, clients, or suppliers. The target audience wants to know that this event is special. The exclusivity provides a positive aura for the brand.

6. Deliver relevance. Events should build reputation, awareness, and relationships. Trying to judge the success of an event in terms of sales is misleading and short-sighted. Don't make the event product-centric; make it a brand-building experience for the attendees.

7. Use the Internet. The Internet is a great way to promote the event, maintain continuous communication with the target audience, and follow up with the audience after an event. Plus, it's a good way to reach all the people who can't attend the event in person. pga.com gets viewers involved with each event on the tour and gives sponsors another chance to reach the target audience.

8. Plan for the before and after. Moving prospects from brand awareness to trial to brand loyalty doesn't happen overnight. The audience needs to see the event as part of a broad exposure to the brand. This is the synergy that needs to be part of the event-planning process. The event must be integrated with advertising, sales promotions, and advertising specialty items.

Source: Laura Shuler, "Make Sure to Deliver When Staging Events," *Marketing News*, September 13, 1999, 12.

4 The Coordination Challenge. When we add various support media to the many options that exist in print and broadcast media, we have an incredible assortment of choices for delivering messages to a target audience. And it doesn't stop there. As you have seen, marketers and advertisers are constantly searching for new, cost-effective ways to break through the clutter and reach consumers. Important developments in information technologies will only accelerate this search for new options as the traditional mass media undergo profound changes.

In concluding this chapter, a critical point about the media explosion needs to be reinforced. Advertisers have a vast and ever-expanding array of options for delivering messages to their potential customers. From cable TV to national newspapers, from virtual billboards to home pages on the World Wide Web, the variety of options is staggering. The keys to success for any advertising campaign are choosing the right set of options to engage a target segment and then coordinating the placement of messages to ensure coherent and timely communication.

Many factors work against coordination. As advertising has become more complex, organizations often become reliant on functional specialists. For example, an organization might have separate managers for advertising, event sponsorship, and direct marketing. Specialists, by definition, focus on their specialty and can lose sight of what others in the organization are doing.[54] Specialists also want their own budgets and typically argue for more funding for their particular area. Internal competition for budget dollars often yields rivalries and animosities that work against coordination.

Coordination is also complicated by the fact that few ad agencies have all the internal skills necessary to fulfill clients' complete communication needs.[55] The interactive media discussed in Chapter 16 have been a special challenge for traditional ad agencies in recent years. This point was also made way back at the beginning of Chapter 2 with the Lipton Brisk example. You may recall that Lipton felt the need to bring in an interactive specialist to assist with Web site design.[56] But with each additional external organization employed to help deliver messages to customers, coordination problems become more complicated.[57] The complications Lipton encountered led them to abandon their interactive specialist in less than a year.

Remember also that the objective underlying the need for coordination is to achieve a synergistic effect. Individual media can work in isolation, but advertisers get more from their advertising dollars if various media and promotional tools build on one another and work together. Even marketing giants such as Gillette are challenged by the need for coordination. In fact,

IBP

Stop, Look, and Listen

Sponsorships yield their greatest benefit when they foster a relationship or deep connection between the target consumer and the sponsoring company or brand. This connection is created when the consumer's passion for the event in question (say, World Cup soccer) becomes associated with a sponsoring brand (such as Adidas, Fujifilm, or MasterCard). There is no guarantee that all brands will realize an emotional connection to the events they sponsor. Indeed, most won't. And while traditional evaluation tools like telephone interviewing or media analysis are important in assessing the value of sponsorships, they cannot reveal deep connections. Careful listening is key to uncovering these connections.

When we know the right questions to ask, listening to the consumer can prove very rewarding. Three areas of questioning can provide important insights for evaluating the relationship-building benefits of event sponsorship. This qualitative research process should begin by exploring eventgoers' subjective experience of an event. Do they have strong feelings about the events they attend? What is it that ignites their passion for an event? Next, it is critical to explore whether fans really understand the role of the sponsor. Most fans know little about the benefits that sponsors provide; research has shown that the more they know, the more the sponsor benefits. Auto-racing fans have the greatest understanding of the role of the sponsor, which helps explain the eagerness of companies to get involved as sponsors of this sport. Finally, one needs to probe the issue of connection: what specific brands do people connect with specific events and how have their opinions of those brands been affected, if at all?

Tapping emotional connections will require sophisticated listening. Listen for fans' descriptions of their emotional experiences, their understanding of the role of the sponsor, and the connections they take away regarding what brands stood out as contributors to what events. Keen listening in these areas will help reveal whether sponsorships are deepening a brand's relevance and meaning in the lives of eventgoers.

Source: Julie Zdziarski, "Evaluating Sponsorships," *PROMO Magazine*, March 2001, 92, 93.

54. Don E. Schultz, Stanley I. Tanenbaum, and Robert F. Lauterborn, *Integrated Marketing Communications* (Lincolnwood, Ill.: NTC Business Books, 1993).

55. Kate Fitzgerald, "Beyond Advertising," *Advertising Age*, August 3, 1998, 1, 14; Laura Q. Hughes and Kate MacArthur, "Soft Boiled: Clients Want Integrated Marketing at Their Disposal, but Agencies Are (Still) Struggling to Put the Structure Together," *Advertising Age*, May 28, 2001, 3, 54.

56. Joan E. Rigdon, "Hip Advertisers Bypass Madison Avenue When They Need Cutting-Edge Web Sites," *Wall Street Journal*, February 28, 1996, B1. For an in-depth description of the Lipton Brisk example, see Kathryn Kranhold, "Ice-Tea Bottler Finds Silicon Alley Ad Firm Too Cool for Its Taste," *Wall Street Journal*, July 21, 2000, A1, A4.

57. Don E. Schultz, "New Media, Old Problem: Keeping Marcom Integrated," *Marketing News*, March 29, 1999, 11, 12.

large size and global scale probably just make things harder. As we saw back in Chapter 6, Gillette is determined to dominate the wet-shaving business for men and women around the world. This will involve the launch of new products such as its Venus triple-blade razor for women with multimillion-dollar advertising campaigns and loyalty-building promotional activities on Florida's beaches,[58] and perhaps even a bumper sticker on Gillette's NASCAR entry. But it also requires effective deployment of Gillette's sales force to negotiate and schedule P-O-P displays for Venus so that the brand stands out from the crowd in the retail setting, inviting shoppers to act on the interest that was created for the brand by mass media advertising. Making all these components work together and speak to the targeted consumer with a "single voice" is the essence of advertising and integrated brand promotion. But easier said than done.

The coordination challenge does not end here. Chapters that follow will add more levels of complexity to this challenge. Topics to come include sales promotion, direct marketing, and public relations. These activities entail additional contacts with a target audience that should reinforce the messages being delivered through broadcast, print, and support media. Integrating these efforts to speak with one voice represents a marketer's best and maybe only hope for breaking through the clutter of competitive advertising to engage with a target segment in today's crowded marketplace.

58. Betsy Spethmann, "Venus Rising," *PROMO Magazine,* April 2001, 52–61.

SUMMARY

Describe the role of support media in a comprehensive media plan.

The traditional support media include out-of-home media along with specialty and directory advertising. Billboards and transit advertising are excellent means for carrying simple messages into specific metropolitan markets. Aerial advertising can be a great way to break through the clutter. Specialty-advertising items and premiums are useful for getting and keeping a brand name in front of a customer. Finally, directory advertising can be a sound investment because it helps a committed customer locate an advertiser's product.

Explain the appeal of P-O-P advertising as an element of integrated brand promotion.

Expenditures on P-O-P advertising continue to grow at a rapid pace. The reason is simple: P-O-P can be an excellent sales generator when integrated with an overall advertising campaign. P-O-P displays may call attention to one's brand, remind consumers of key benefits provided by one's brand, or offer price-off deals as a final incentive to purchase. Retailers' cooperation is key in making P-O-P programs work; getting their cooperation requires diligent efforts from the marketer's sales force in the field.

Justify the growing popularity of event sponsorship as another supporting component of a media plan.

The list of companies sponsoring events grows with each passing year, and the events include a wide variety of activities. Of these various activities, sports attract the most sponsorship dollars. Sponsorship can help in building brand familiarity; it can promote brand loyalty by connecting a brand with powerful emotional experiences; and in most instances it allows a marketer to reach a well-defined target audience. Events can also facilitate face-to-face contacts with key customers and present opportunities to distribute product samples, sell premiums, and conduct consumer surveys.

Discuss the challenges presented by the ever-increasing variety of media for achieving integrated brand promotion.

The tremendous variety of media options we have seen thus far represents a monumental challenge for an advertiser who wishes to speak to a customer with a single voice. Achieving this single voice is critical for breaking through the clutter of the modern advertising environment. However, the functional specialists required for working in the various media have their own biases and subgoals that can get in the way of integration. We will return to this issue in subsequent chapters as we explore other options available to marketers in their quest to persuade customers.

KEY TERMS

guerrilla marketing
support media
riding the boards
transit advertising
out-of-home media
aerial advertising
specialty-advertising items
premiums
P-O-P advertising
short-term promotional displays
permanent long-term displays
event sponsorship

QUESTIONS

1. Explain the important advancements in technology that are likely to contribute to the appeal of billboards as an advertising medium.

2. Critique the out-of-home media as tools for achieving reach-versus-frequency objectives in a media plan.

3. Explain the unique role for directory advertising in a media plan. Given what you see happening on the Internet, what kind of future do you predict for traditional Yellow Pages advertising?

4. When would it be appropriate to conclude that tools such as transit or P-O-P advertising are serving more than just a supportive role in one's media plan? Give an example of each of these tools being used as the principal element in the advertising plan, either from your own experience or from examples that were offered in this chapter.

5. During your next visit to the grocery store, identify three examples of P-O-P advertising. How well were each of these displays integrated with other aspects of a more comprehensive advertising campaign? What would you surmise are the key factors in creating effective P-O-P displays?

6. Present statistics to document the claim that the television viewing audience is becoming fragmented. What are the causes of this fragmentation? Develop an argument that links this fragmentation to the growing popularity of event sponsorship.

7. Event sponsorship can be valuable for building brand loyalty. Search through your closets, drawers, or cupboards and find a premium or memento that you acquired at a sponsored event. Does this memento bring back fond memories? Would you consider yourself loyal to the brand that sponsored this event? If not, why not?

8. Explain why interactive media contribute to the need for functional specialists in ad preparation. What problems do these and other functional specialists create for the achievement of integrated brand promotion?

EXPERIENTIAL EXERCISES

1. This chapter gives two general categories of P-O-P displays and identifies over a dozen examples of in-store options such as floorstands, shelf talkers, and the dump bin. Take that list and go to any retail store or grocer. Make a list of how many examples you can find to match the displays discussed in the text, and identify the advertisers that used each display you found. Briefly describe each and evaluate its usefulness based on what you learned in the chapter.

2. Event sponsorship is becoming more important to advertisers, as the effectiveness of traditional broadcast media continues to erode with increasing fragmentation. Event sponsorship can be international, like the Olympics, or have local color, such as a chili cook-off. Find an example of event sponsorship and describe the relationship between the advertiser and the event. What role does the advertiser perform during the event? Why do companies think sponsoring this event is an effective means of reaching target audiences? As a consumer, do you think event sponsorships have influenced your decision to use a product?

USING THE INTERNET

17-1 P-O-P Advertising

In 1981, entrepreneur Phil Johnson started selling 100-pound sacks of whole-bean arabicas to gourmet shops. While shopping at his local supermarket, he had an idea that changed the way consumers think of coffee. Johnson designed a retail distribution and placement model that would later put the Millstone Coffee Company front-and-center in supermarkets everywhere. By placing clear bean bin displays in stores, consumers would have a strong visual incentive to bypass competing brands and purchase the numerous gourmet coffees that have made Millstone famous.

Millstone Coffee: http://www.millstone.com

1. Using the text, define P-O-P advertising. In the case of Millstone Coffee, describe how the actual beans become part of the P-O-P display. Have you ever purchased Millstone coffee because of the attraction of the clear bins full of rich coffee beans?

2. What research conclusions have to led the dramatic rise of annual expenditures on P-O-P advertising by large companies? Why do you think P-O-P advertising is so effective in persuading customers to buy Millstone coffee?

3. Explain the important role of the sales force in the successful deployment of P-O-P materials and displays. What can happen if sales reps aren't coordinating the deployment of P-O-P displays with retail managers?

17-2 Billboards

Billboards, posters, and outdoor signs are considered by some to be the oldest forms of advertising. From the time of the Revolutionary War, when posters were used for propaganda, outdoor signage has been used to promote events such as circuses, political campaigns, and military recruiting. Although the advent of television put the future of outdoor signage in question, the establishment of a federal highway system in the 1960s brought new promise, and billboards and other creative outdoor displays were revitalized by new opportunity.

Beach 'N Billboard: http://www.beachnbillboard.com

1. What types of markets are best suited for outdoor signage?

2. Describe how Beach 'N Billboard has seized upon a unique market opportunity, as outdoor signage such as posters and billboards did in advertising's history.

3. Explain how Beach 'N Billboard represents an environmentalist response to the notion that billboards represent a form of visual pollution.

CHAPTER 18

After reading and thinking about this chapter, you will be able to do the following:

Explain the importance and growth of different types of sales promotion.

Describe the main sales promotion techniques used in the consumer market.

Describe the main sales promotion techniques used in the trade and business markets.

Identify the risks to the brand of using sales promotion.

Explain the coordination issues for integrated brand promotion associated with using sales promotion.

CHAPTER 17
Support Media, P-O-P Advertising, and Event Sponsorship

CHAPTER 18
Sales Promotion

CHAPTER 19
Direct Marketing

CHAPTER 20
Public Relations and Corporate Advertising

VERY CHERRY.

VERY CHERRY.

ENTER THE "VERY CHERRY SWEEPSTAKES" AND WIN A NEW BEETLE.

America's Favorite Jelly Bean gives you a chance to win America's favorite new car! It's easy. Just tell us what name appears on every Jelly Belly® bean and the name of your favorite Jelly Belly retailer. To enter, visit your nearest participating retailer and ask for your official "Very Cherry Sweepstakes" entry form, or enter online at www.jellybelly.com. One lucky winner will receive the Grand Prize, a 1999 New Beetle,® and 40 second-prize winners will receive a Jelly Belly Bean Machine. Enter to win, and a hot New Beetle could be yours! Sweepstakes runs from 1/1/99 thru 5/31/99. For your nearest retailer, call **1-800-JB-BEANS**.

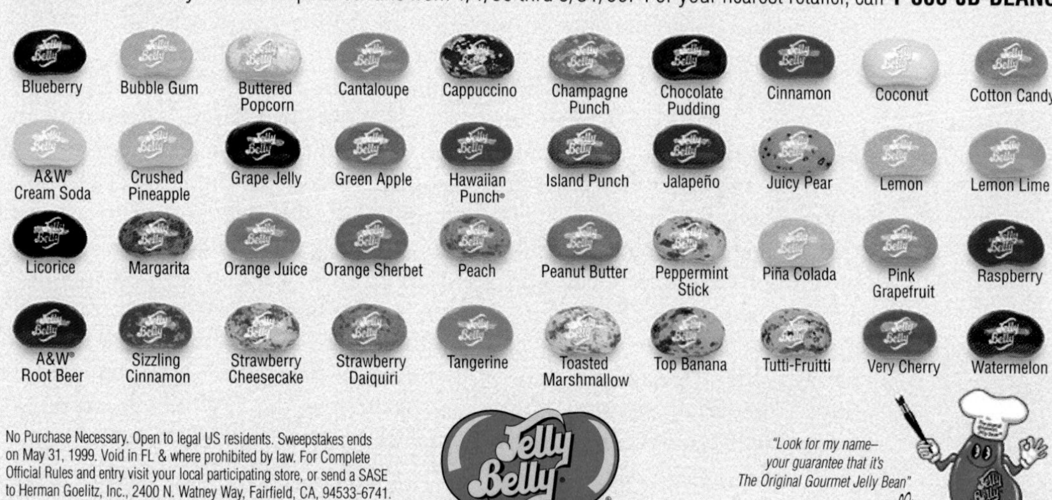

No Purchase Necessary. Open to legal US residents. Sweepstakes ends on May 31, 1999. Void in FL & where prohibited by law. For Complete Official Rules and entry visit your local participating store, or send a SASE to Herman Goelitz, Inc., 2400 N. Watney Way, Fairfield, CA, 94533-6741. Residents of VT & WA omit return postage.

Jelly Belly
The original gourmet jelly bean.®

"Look for my name– your guarantee that it's The Original Gourmet Jelly Bean"

Mr Jelly Belly

It's America's Favorite Jelly Bean.

How important is sales promotion in the household products market? Well, no matter how important it was before, it's even more important now. Big brand marketers such as Procter & Gamble, Johnson & Johnson, and Clorox are realizing that unless they support their household product brands, such as Tide and Glad, with a heavy sales promotion effort, the low-priced private-label brands are going to step in and take away market share.

When the big brand names—Tide, Pledge, Pampers—lack sales promotions such as couponing, contests, or trade channel incentives, the private-label or "house" brands can make inroads on the big names. This is exactly what has happened over the past few years. The long-sluggish house brand market shares are soaring in household product and personal care categories for the first time since 1992. Some of the categories experiencing the greatest growth are air fresheners (40.8%), batteries (32.2%), food storage containers (65.3%), and toilet tissue (25.4%). Overall, the private labels have increased market share by 6 to 7 percent across 35 product categories.[1]

So what is the explanation behind this surge in sales? Is the "brand" still king in consumers' minds? Aren't house brands just cheap substitutes? Well, the answer to those questions is no if consumers lose the perception that big national brands have more value to offer than the house brands. And the answer to those questions is also no if the retailers and wholesalers are convinced (by being given better profit margins and higher volume) that it is in their best interest to feature the big brand names over the private-label house brands. When a marketer offers coupons or runs a sweepstake for a big brand, then consumers feel as if they are getting a little extra for paying a premium price. Even though they typically believe that the big-name brand is better quality than the private-label house brand, consumers still want to feel that they are getting the best value. A little extra goes a long way in increasing the perceived value of the brand.

Recently, though, national brand marketers have innovated less, charged more, and, frankly, brought down the perceived value of their brands. A good example of this is in the disposable diaper category, where private-label house brand share has increased over 26 percent. As a result, retailers such as Wal-Mart have held the line on price increases, and their private (and well-trusted) house brand sold under the White Cloud name is now priced about 7 percent below Luvs and Pampers. Conversely, strong promotional efforts by national-brand marketers and new products have contained private-label growth in some categories such as toothpaste and shampoo, where no ground has been gained on the big-name brands.

One part of the solution to combating the market share erosion is for the big-brand marketers to begin re-investing in sales promotion. This strategy is being used by Clorox—finally.[2] When Clorox acquired the Glad brand (plastic bags and wraps) from First Brands in 1998, it applied its standard turnaround strategy to the brand—cut trade and consumer price promotion and revive the brand through media advertising. Well, the brand has been on a downhill slide ever since the acquisition, and Clorox strategists have had to re-think the process. Without trade and consumer promotions support, Glad sales were down overall about 15 percent the first year after the acquisition. So, to help sagging market share, Clorox is increasing trade promotion dollars to be used for in-store display and merchandising assistance. Simultaneously, the marketer will issue more coupons. Sales promotion, coupled with continued media advertising, is expected to revive the brand. Check out the Glad display next time you're in the supermarket and see how Clorox is doing.

1. Jack Neff, "Black Eye in Store for Big Brands," *Advertising Age,* April 30, 2001, 1, 34.
2. Jack Neff, "Clorox Gives In on Glad, Hikes Trade Promotion," *Advertising Age,* November 27, 2000, 22.

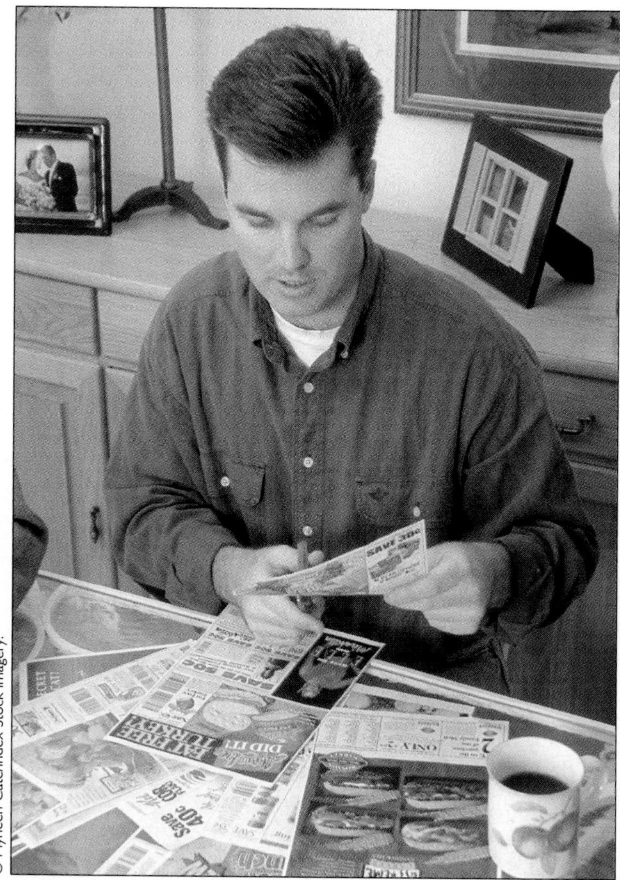

EXHIBIT 18.1

Sales promotions, like these coupons, attract attention and drive short-term sales.

Sales Promotion Defined.

Sales promotion can be a key alternative for advertisers within a integrated brand promotion campaign. As the Glad example highlights, sales promotions, dealer incentives, and coupons can attract attention and give new energy to the advertising and integrated brand promotion effort. While mass media advertising is designed to build a brand image over time, sales promotion is conspicuous and designed to make things happen in a hurry. Used properly, sales promotion is capable of the almost instant demand stimulation that some contests and sweepstakes can create. The message in a sales promotion features price reduction (or free samples), a prize, or some other incentive for consumers or business buyers to try a brand or for a retailer to feature the brand in the store. Sales promotion has proven to be a popular complement to mass media advertising because it accomplishes things advertising cannot (Exhibit 18.1).

Formally defined, **sales promotion** is the use of incentive techniques that create a perception of greater brand value among consumers, the trade, and business buyers. The intent is to create a short-term increase in sales by motivating trial use or encouraging larger purchases or repeat purchases. **Consumer-market sales promotion** includes coupons, price-off deals, premiums, contests and sweepstakes, sampling and trial offers, brand (product) placements, rebates, loyalty/frequency programs, phone and gift cards, and event sponsorship. All are ways of inducing household consumers to purchase a firm's brand rather than a competitor's brand. Notice that some incentives reduce price, offer a reward, or encourage a trip to the retailer. **Trade-market sales promotion** uses point-of-purchase displays, incentives, allowances, or cooperative advertising as ways of motivating distributors, wholesalers, and retailers to stock and feature a firm's brand in their merchandising programs. **Business buyer sales promotion** is designed to cultivate buyers in large corporations who are making purchase decisions about a wide range of products including computers, office supplies, and consulting services. Techniques used for business buyers are similar to the trade market techniques and include trade shows, premiums, incentives, and loyalty/frequency programs.

1 The Importance and Growth of Sales Promotion.

Sales promotion is designed to affect demand differently than advertising. As we have learned throughout the text, most advertising is designed to have awareness-, image-, and preference-building effects for a brand over the long run. The role of sales promotion, on the other hand, is primarily to elicit an immediate purchase from a customer. Coupons, samples, rebates, contests and sweepstakes, and similar techniques offer a consumer an immediate incentive to choose one brand over another, as exemplified in Exhibit 18.2. Notice that Oreck is offering a free product (referred to as a premium offer) just for trying the Oreck vacuum cleaner.

Other sales promotions, such as brand placements (getting the company's brand placed in a movie or on a TV show) and frequency programs (for example, frequent-flyer programs), provide an affiliation value with a brand, which increases a consumer's

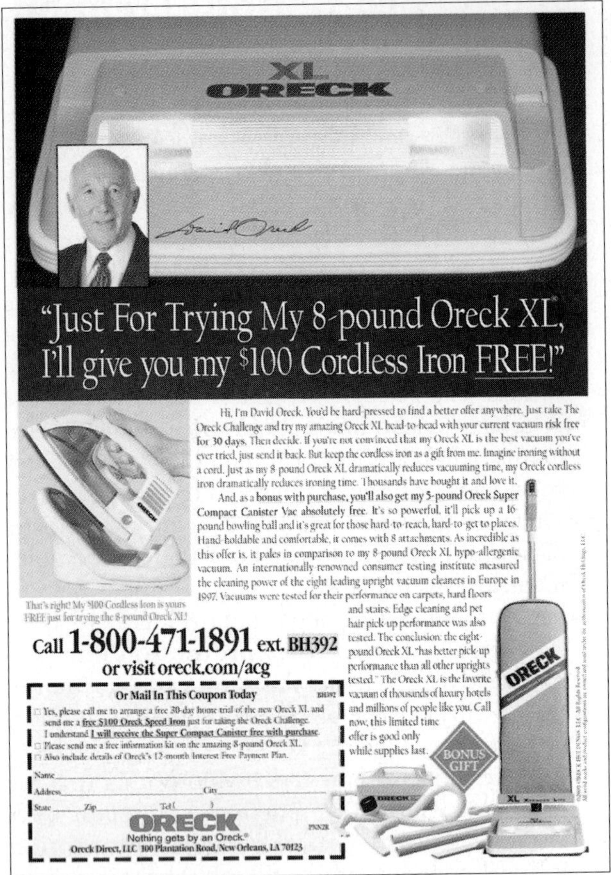

EXHIBIT 18.2

Marketers use a wide range of incentives to attract attention to a brand. Here, David Oreck is offering new buyers a free iron for trying the Oreck lightweight vacuum. www.oreck.com

ability and desire to identify with a particular brand. Sales promotions featuring price reductions, such as coupons, are effective in the convenience goods category, where frequent purchases, brand switching, and a perceived homogeneity among brands characterize consumer behavior.

Sales promotions are used across all consumer goods categories and in the trade market as well. When a firm determines that a more immediate response is called for—whether the target customer is a household, business buyer, distributor, or retailer—sales promotions are designed to provide the incentive. The goals for sales promotion versus advertising are compared in Exhibit 18.3. Notice the key differences in the goals for these different forms of promotion. Sales promotion encourages more immediate and short-term responses, while the purpose of advertising is to cultivate loyalty and repeat purchases over the long term.

The Importance of Sales Promotion.

The importance of sales promotion in the United States should not be underestimated. Sales promotion may not seem as stylish and sophisticated as mass media advertising, but expenditures on this tool are impressive. In recent years, sales promotion expenditures have grown at an annual rate of about 9 to 12 percent, compared to a 6 to 8 percent rate for advertising. By 2000, investment by advertisers in sales promotions reached over $100 billion.[3] Add to that figure consumer savings by redeeming coupons and rebates and the figure exceeds $150 billion.[4] Exhibit 18.4 shows the spending, percent increase, and proportion of total sales promotion spending for the most frequently used sales promotion techniques.

It is important to realize that full-service advertising agencies specializing in advertising planning, creative preparation, and media placement typically do not prepare sales promotion materials for clients. These activities are normally assigned to sales promotion agencies that specialize in couponing, event management, premiums, or other forms of sales promotion that require specific skills and creative preparation.

The development and management of an effective sales promotion program require a major commitment by a firm. During any given year, as much as 30 percent of brand management time is typically spent on designing, implementing, and overseeing sales promotions. The rise in the use of sales promotion and the enormous amount of money being spent on various programs make it one of the most prominent forms of marketing activity. But again, it must be undertaken only under certain conditions and then carefully executed for specific reasons.

Growth in the Use of Sales Promotion. Marketers have shifted the emphasis of their promotional spending over the past decade. Most of the shift has been away from mass media advertising and toward consumer and trade sales promotions. Currently, the

3. 2001 Annual Report of the Promotion Industry, "Introduction: Proceed with Caution," May 2001, compiled by *PROMO Magazine,* www.industryclick.com, accessed June 5, 2001.
4. Betsy Spethmann, "So Much for Targeting," *PROMO Magazine,* April 2000, 69.

EXHIBIT 18.3

Sales promotion and advertising serve very different purposes in the promotional mix. What would you describe as the key difference between the two, based on the features listed here?

Purpose of Sales Promotion	Purpose of Advertising
Stimulate short-term demand	Cultivate long-term demand
Encourage brand switching	Encourage brand loyalty
Induce trial use	Encourage repeat purchases
Promote price orientation	Promote image/feature orientation
Obtain immediate, often measurable results	Obtain long-term effects, often difficult to measure

EXHIBIT 18.4

Marketers rely on several different sales promotion techniques to complement and support the advertising effort. This list shows spending on those techniques as well as the amount spent on promotion agency services and research.

Segments	1999	2000	% Change	% of total
Premiums	$26,300	$26,900	2.3%	26.6
P-O-P	14,400	17,000	18.1	16.8
Ad Spec	14,800	16,300	10.1	16.1
Sponsorships	7,600	8,700	14.5	8.6
Coupons	6,980	6,920	–0.9	6.9
Printing	6,200	6,100	–1.6	6.0
Licensing	5,500	5,775	5.0	5.7
Fulfillment	3,297	3,800	15.3	3.8
Agency	2,178	2,614	20.0	2.6
Interactive	1,471	1,800	22.4	1.8
Games, Contests, Sweeps	1,380	1,504	9.0	1.5
Research	1,340	1,460	9.0	1.4
Sampling	1,120	1,200	7.1	1.2
In-store	870	904	3.9	0.9
Total	**$93,436**	**$100,977**	**8.1%**	**100.0%**

Source: Copyright *PROMO Magazine*, Stamford, CT. May 1, 2001.

budget allocation stands at about 53 percent for advertising, 18 percent for trade promotions, and 23 percent for consumer promotions.[5] There are several reasons why many marketers have been shifting funds from mass media advertising to sales promotions:

Demand for Greater Accountability. In an era of cost cutting and downsizing, companies are demanding greater accountability across all functions, including marketing, advertising, and promotions. When activities are evaluated for their contribution to sales and profits, it is often difficult to draw specific conclusions regarding the effects of advertising. Conversely, the immediate effects of sales promotions are typically easier to document. Another plus for the accountability of sales promotion is that ACNielsen and IPSOs-ASI research firms have developed Market Drivers, a new research program that evaluates the effects of sales promotions.[6] The program

5. 2001 Annual Report of the Promotion Industry, "Introduction: Proceed with Caution," op. cit.
6. James B. Arndorfer, "ACNielsen Market Drivers Will Gauge Promos' Punch," *Advertising Age,* February 23, 1998, 8.

combines Nielsen's store sales data with the IPSOs-ASI copy-testing measures to identify the effects of sales promotions versus ads in communicating to target segments. But this measurement is not cheap. The companies estimate that using the Market Drivers program runs about $100,000 per project.

Short-Term Orientation. Several factors have created a short-term orientation among managers. Pressures from stockholders to produce better quarter-by-quarter revenue and profit per share are one factor. A bottom-line mentality is another factor. Many organizations are developing marketing plans—with rewards and punishments for performance—based on short-term revenue generation. This being the case, tactics that can have short-term effects are sought. Nabisco found that a contest directed at kids had just the sort of short-term effect the firm was looking for. In its "Don't Eat the Winning Oreo" promotion, which featured a Volkswagen Beetle filled with Oreos, sales jumped 29 percent during the time the promotion was running.[7]

Consumer Response to Promotions. The precision shopper in the contemporary market place is demanding greater value across all purchase situations, and the trend is battering overpriced brands.[8] These precision shoppers search for extra value in every product purchase. Coupons, premiums, price-off deals, and other sales promotions increase the value of a brand in these shoppers' minds. The positive response to sales promotion goes beyond value-oriented consumers, though. For consumers who are not well informed about the average price in a product category, a brand featuring a coupon or price-off promotion is sensed to be a good deal and will likely be chosen over competitive brands—this is a basic tenet of consumer behavior analysis.[9] Overall, consumers report that coupons, price, and good value for their money influence 75 to 85 percent of their brand choice decisions.[10] (Be careful here—coupons, price, and value, in particular, do not necessarily mean consumers are choosing the *lowest* price item. The analysis suggests that these sales promotion techniques act as an incentive to purchase the brand using a promotion.)

Proliferation of Brands. Each year, thousands of new brands are introduced into the consumer market. The drive by marketers to design products for specific market segments to satisfy ever more narrowly defined needs has caused a proliferation of brands that creates a mind-dulling maze for consumers. At any point in time, consumers are typically able to choose from about 60 spaghetti sauces, 100 snack chips, 50 laundry detergents, 90 cold remedies, and 60 disposable diaper varieties. As you can see in Exhibit 18.5, gaining attention in this blizzard of brands is no easy task. Often marketers turn to sales promotions—brand placements, contests, coupons, and premiums—to gain some recognition in a consumer's mind and stimulate a trial purchase.

Increased Power of Retailers. Retailers such as Home Depot, The Gap, Toys "R" Us, and the most powerful of all, Wal-Mart, now dominate retailing in the United States. These powerful retailers have responded quickly and accurately to the new environment for retailing, where consumers are demanding more and better products and services at lower prices. Because of the lower-price component of the retailing environment, these retailers are demanding more deals from manufacturers. Many of the deals are delivered in terms of trade-oriented sales promotions: point-of-purchase displays, slotting fees (payment for shelf space), case allowances, and cooperative advertising allowances. In the end, manufacturers use more and more

7. Stephanie Thompson, "Nabisco Stuffs More into Oreo Promotion," *Advertising Age,* January 10, 2000, 8.
8. Neff, "Black Eye in Store for Big Brands," op. cit.
9. Leigh McAlister, "A Model of Consumer Behavior," *Marketing Communications,* April 1987, 26–28.
10. Cox Direct 20th Annual Survey of Promotional Practices, Chart 22, 1998, 37.

EXHIBIT 18.5

As you can see by this shelf of spaghetti sauces, getting the consumer to pay attention to any one brand is quite the challenge. This proliferation of brands in the marketplace has made marketers search for ways to attract attention to their brands, and sales promotion techniques often provide an answer. Notice the point-of-purchase promotion attached to the shelves.

sales promotion devices to gain and maintain good relations with the new, powerful retailers—a critical link to the consumer. And retailers use the tools of sales promotion as competitive strategies against each other. The Creativity box on page 642 describes how Toys "R" Us relied on a contest and other promotional tools to combat competitive challenges from Wal-Mart and Kmart.

Media Clutter. A nagging and traditional problem in the advertising process is clutter. Many advertisers target the same customers because their research has led them to the same conclusion about whom to target. The result is that advertising media are cluttered with ads all seeking the attention of a common target. One way to break through the clutter is to feature a sales promotion. In print ads, the featured deal is often a coupon. In broadcast advertising, sweepstakes and premium offers can attract listeners' and viewers' attention. The combination of advertising and creative sales promotions has proven to be a good way to break through the clutter.

2 Sales Promotion Directed at Consumers.

It is clear that U.S. consumer-product firms have made a tremendous commitment to sales promotion in their overall marketing plans. During the 1970s, consumer goods marketers allocated only about 30 percent of their budgets to sales promotion, with about 70 percent allocated to mass media advertising. Estimates show that for many consumer goods firms, the percentages are just the opposite, with nearly 75 percent being spent on sales promotions—considerably higher than the across industries allocation we saw earlier.[11] With this sort of investment in sales promotion as part of the integrated brand promotion process, let's examine in detail the objectives for sales promotion in the consumer market and the wide range of techniques that can be used.

11. Cox Direct 20th Annual Survey of Promotional Practices, Chart 24, 1998, 39.

CREATIVITY

This Is Fun?

Video games, skateboards, doll houses—all fun and games. Not quite. In the $23-billion-a-year toy industry, the stakes are too high for competitors to have much fun at all. And the challenges are particularly tough for the industry leader, Toys "R" Us. Everyone is out to get an industry leader, and Warren Kornblum, senior VP and chief marketing officer, is using all forms of promotion to protect the company's leadership position.

The need to rely on broad-based promotions can be traced back to the early 1990s. At that time, Toys "R" Us watched its market share get sniped by formidable foes. Wal-Mart expanded its toy department and made toys a key draw for shoppers at the Wal-Mart SuperCenters that were being put in place. Kmart reconfigured its stores and gave more shelf space to toys. And upstart KB Toys used an arsenal of tiny shops to divert billions of dollars of toy spending into its coffers.

Toys "R" Us was shell-shocked. The toy giant's first competitive reaction was to tweak the merchandise and fiddle with the store layouts. But that wasn't good enough. Between 1990 and 1997, market share fell from 25 percent to 18 percent. To add insult to injury, in 1998, Wal-Mart officially became the largest toy retailer in the United States—ouch! The loss of industry leadership motivated Kornblum to look for a more aggressive response to competition. That response was a new marketing plan that was anchored primarily in new and innovative promotions.

The first step was to rein in the scattered marketing effort and plan fewer but more robust promotional campaigns. As an example, Toys "R" Us teamed with Buzz Lightyear and was a key partner in the launch of *Toy Story 2*. The main strategy in this promotion was an innovative "scan and win" promotion that lured shoppers to Toys "R" Us stores and got them interacting with the *Toy Story* characters. This is how it worked. Toys "R" Us distributed 250 million unique UPC (universal product code) game pieces through newspaper inserts. Buzz Lightyear and Woody encouraged consumers to stop by Toys "R" Us stores and scan in. When they arrived armed with their UPC game pieces, players held the UPC up to scanners placed throughout the store to see if they had won. Prizes included a $1 million grand prize, trips to Disney World, Chevy Astro Vans, and $1,000 Toys "R" Us shopping sprees. The results were powerful. One million consumers scanned in to see if they had won a prize, and store traffic increased dramatically.

But in-store promotions was only the first in a series of sales promotion techniques used by Toys "R" Us to help bolster sagging market share. Other techniques included sponsorship of Major League Baseball's Diamond Skills campaign, aimed at developing youth baseball skills. Stores featured promotions with prizes such as the chance to throw out the ceremonial first ball at the All-Star Game. Another sales promotion was sponsorship of the Fox Kids World Tour, a traveling interactive theme park that showcased the Fox Kids Network shows. Promotions like these are helping Toys "R" Us reclaim its leadership in the toy industry.

Source: Dan Hanover, "The Real Toy Story," *PROMO Magazine*, April 2000, 84–88.

Objectives for Consumer-Market Sales Promotion.

To help ensure the proper application of sales promotion, specific strategic objectives should be set. The following basic objectives can be pursued with sales promotion in the consumer market:

- *Stimulate trial purchase.* When a firm wants to attract new users, sales promotion tools can reduce the consumer's risk of trying something new. A reduced price or offer of a rebate may stimulate trial purchase. When Keebler wanted to attract trial use in eight key Hispanic markets, it created the Keebler Kids Club, which featured giveaways and the *Keebler Kids Quiz Show,* which gave Spanish-speaking youngsters the chance to win college scholarships.[12] Exhibit 18.6 is a demonstration of attempting to stimulate trial use.
- *Stimulate repeat purchases.* In-package coupons good for the next purchase, or the accumulation of points with repeated purchases, can keep consumers loyal to a particular brand. The most prominent frequency programs are found in the airline industry, where competitors such as Delta, American, and United try to retain their most lucrative customers by enrolling them in frequency programs. Frequent flyers can earn free travel, hotel stays, gifts, and numerous other perks through the programs. Recently, fast-food chains such as McDonald's have started frequency programs (the McExtra card) to keep customers coming back in the brand switching–prone fast-food industry.[13]
- *Stimulate larger purchases.* Price reductions or two-for-one sales can motivate consumers to stock up on a brand, thus allowing firms to reduce inventory or increase

12. "Best in the World," *PROMO Magazine,* November 1995, 39.
13. Louise Kramer, "McD's Eyes Rollout of Loyalty Card," *Advertising Age,* April 27, 1998, 3.

e-SIGHTINGS

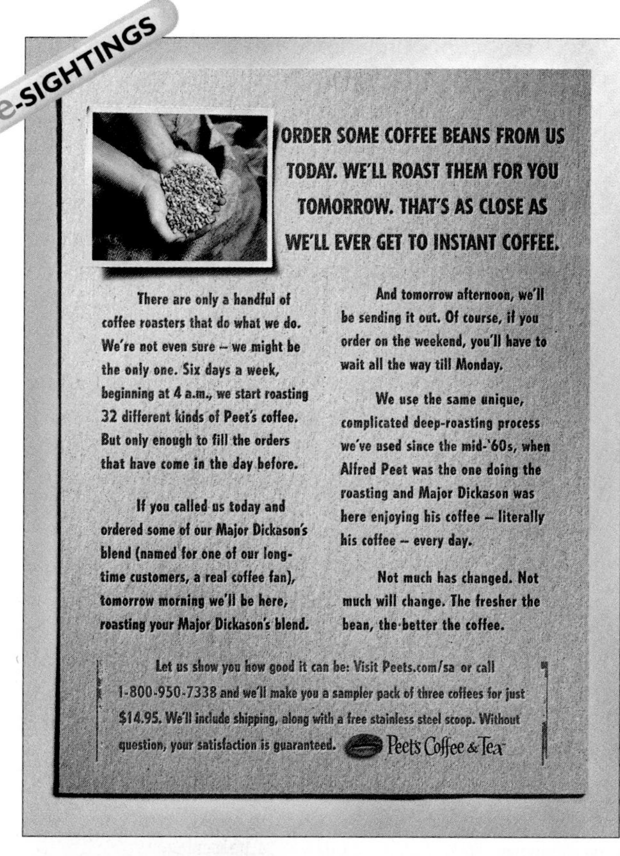

EXHIBIT 18.6

One objective for sales promotion in the consumer market is to stimulate trial use. Here, Peet's Coffee and Tea (www.peets.com) is offering consumers a sample pack that they can request either online or by calling a toll-free number. What current sales promotion techniques are being used at the Peet's Web site? (Search the main page and the online store.) What is the primary objective for the promotion? Does Peet's offer consumers any incentives that might encourage repeat purchases or the trial of a new brand?

EXHIBIT 18.7

Sales promotions are often used to encourage larger purchases. This coupon for SpaghettiOs offers consumers the chance to stock up on three cans. www.spaghettios.com

cash flow. Shampoo is often double-packaged to offer a value to consumers. Exhibit 18.7 is a sales promotion aimed at stimulating a larger purchase.

- *Introduce a new brand.* Because sales promotion can attract attention and motivate trial purchase, it is commonly used for new brand introduction. When the makers of Curad bandages wanted to introduce their new kid-size bandage, 7.5 million sample packs were distributed in McDonald's Happy Meal sacks. The promotion was a huge success, with initial sales exceeding estimates by 30 percent.[14]
- *Combat or disrupt competitors' strategies.* Because sales promotions often motivate consumers to buy in larger quantities or try new brands, they can be used to disrupt competitors' marketing strategies. If a firm knows that one of its competitors is launching a new brand or initiating a new advertising campaign, a well-timed sales promotion offering deep discounts or extra quantity can disrupt the competitors' strategy. Add to the original discount an in-package coupon for future purchases, and a marketer can severely compromise competitors' efforts. *TV Guide* magazine used a sweepstakes promotion to combat competition. In an effort to address increasing competition from newspaper TV supplements and

14. Glen Heitsmith, "Still Bullish on Promotion," *PROMO Magazine,* July 1994, 40.

cable-guide magazines, *TV Guide* ran a shopping spree sweepstakes in several regional markets. Winners won $200 shopping sprees in grocery stores—precisely where 65 percent of *TV Guide* sales are realized.[15]

- *Contribute to integrated marketing communications.* In conjunction with advertising, direct marketing, public relations, and other programs being carried out by a firm, sales promotion can add yet another type of communication to the mix. Sales promotions suggest an additional value, with price reductions, premiums, or the chance to win a prize. This is an additional and different message within the overall communications effort.

Consumer-Market Sales Promotion Techniques. Several techniques are used to stimulate demand and attract attention in the consumer market. Some of these are coupons, price-off deals, premiums and advertising specialties, contests and sweepstakes, samples and trial offers, phone and gift cards, brand placement, rebates, frequency programs, and event sponsorship.

Coupons. A **coupon** entitles a buyer to a designated reduction in price for a product or service. Coupons are the oldest and most widely used form of sales promotion. The first use of a coupon is traced to around 1895, when the C.W. Post Company used a penny-off coupon as a way to get people to try its Grape-Nuts cereal. Annually, about 350 billion coupons are distributed to American consumers, with redemption rates ranging from 2 percent for gum purchases to nearly 45 percent for disposable diaper purchases. Exhibit 18.8 shows coupon redemption rates for several product categories. In 2000, marketers invested $6.92 billion in coupons as a sales promotion technique, and about 4.4 billion of those coupons were redeemed by consumers for over $3.6 billion in savings.[16]

There are five advantages to the coupon as a sales promotion tool:

- The use of a coupon makes it possible to give a discount to a price-sensitive consumer while still selling the product at full price to other consumers. A price-

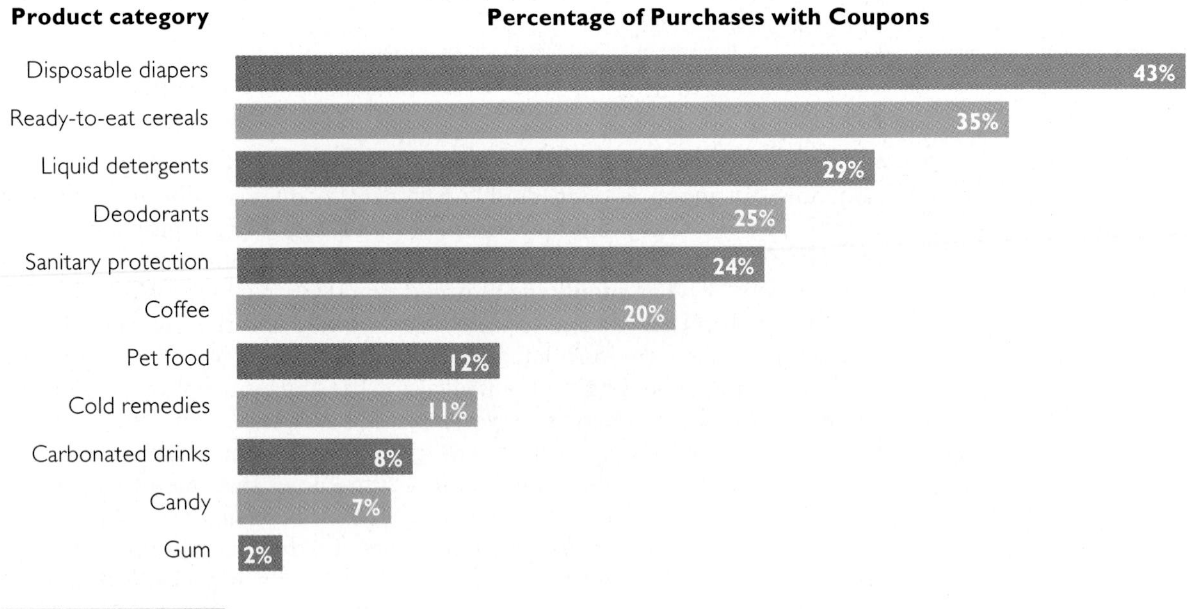

EXHIBIT 18.8

Percentage of purchases made with coupons in various product categories.

15. "*TV Guide* Tunes In Sweepstakes," *PROMO Magazine,* November 1995, 1, 50.
16. 2001 Annual Report of the Promotion Industry, "Coupons: Nowhere to Go But Up," May 2001, compiled by *PROMO Magazine,* www.industryclick.com, accessed June 5, 2001.

sensitive customer takes the time to clip the coupon and carry it to the store; a regular consumer merely buys the product at full price.

- The coupon-redeeming customer is often a competitive-brand user, so the coupon can induce brand switching.
- A manufacturer can control the timing and distribution of coupons. This way a retailer is not implementing price discounts inappropriately.
- A coupon is an excellent method of stimulating repeat purchases. Once a consumer has been attracted to a brand, with or without a coupon, an in-package coupon can induce repeat purchase. The long-standing belief is that in-package coupons stimulate greater brand loyalty than media-distributed coupons. While an in-package coupon is designed to encourage repeat purchase and brand loyalty, retailers believe that coupons attached to the store shelf and distributed at the point of purchase are the most effective.[17]
- Coupons can get regular users to trade up within a brand array. For example, users of low-price disposable diapers may be willing to try a premium variety with a coupon.

The use of coupons is not without its problems. There are administrative burdens and risks with coupon use:

- While coupon price incentives and the timing of distribution can be controlled by a marketer, the timing of redemption cannot. Some consumers redeem coupons immediately; others hold them for months. Expiration dates printed on coupons help focus the redemption time but may compromise the impact of coupons.
- Coupons do attract competitors' users and some nonusers, but there is no way to prevent current users from redeeming coupons with their regular purchases. Heavy redemption by regular buyers merely reduces a firm's profitability. This has led some firms to seriously consider eliminating coupons from their arsenal of marketing tools.
- Couponing entails careful administration. Coupon programs include much more than the cost of the face value of the coupon. There are costs for production and distribution and for retailer and manufacturer handling. In fact, the cost for handling, processing, and distribution of coupons is equal to about two-thirds of the face value of the coupon.[18] Historically, Procter & Gamble has distributed as many as 700 million coupons for its Folgers coffee brand, with administrative costs totaling more than $14 million.[19] Marketers need to track these costs against the amount of product sold with and without coupon redemption.
- Fraud is a chronic and serious problem in the couponing process. The problem relates directly to misredemption practices. There are three types of misredemption that cost firms money: redemption of coupons by consumers who do not purchase the couponed brand; redemption of coupons by salesclerks and store managers without consumer purchases; and illegal collection or copying of coupons by individuals who sell them to unethical store merchants, who in turn redeem the coupons without the accompanying consumer purchases. Unfortunately, this sort of fraud has spread to the online, Internet-based distribution of coupons as well.[20]

Price-Off Deals. The price-off deal is another straightforward technique. A **price-off deal** offers a consumer cents or even dollars off merchandise at the point of purchase through specially marked packages. The typical price-off deal is a 10 to

17. Data displayed in *Advertising Age,* May 10, 1993, S5.
18. "1998 Annual Report of the Promotion Industry," compiled by *PROMO Magazine,* May, 1998, S37.
19. "Coffee's On," *PROMO Magazine,* February 1996, 48–49.
20. Michael Scroggie, "Online Coupon Debate," *PROMO Magazine,* April 2000, 53.

25 percent price reduction. The reduction is taken from the manufacturer's profit margin rather than the retailer's. Manufacturers like the price-off technique because it is controllable. Plus, the price off, judged at the point of purchase, can effect a positive price comparison against competitors. Consumers like a price-off deal because it is straightforward and automatically increases the value of a known brand. Regular users tend to stock up on an item during a price-off deal. Retailers are less enthusiastic about this technique. Price-off promotions can create inventory and pricing problems for retailers. Also, most price-off deals are snapped up by regular customers, so the retailer doesn't benefit from new business.

Premiums and Advertising Specialties. **Premiums** are items offered free, or at a reduced price, with the purchase of another item. Many firms offer a related product free, such as a free granola bar packed inside a box of granola cereal. Service firms, such as a car wash or dry cleaner, may use a two-for-one offer to persuade consumers to try the service. Premiums represent the single largest category of investment by firms in a sales promotion technique, with over $26.9 billion spent on premiums during 2000.[21]

Two options are available for the use of premiums. A **free premium** provides consumers with an item at no cost; the item is either included in the package of a purchased item or mailed to the consumer after proof of purchase is verified. The most frequently used free premium is an additional package of the original item or a free related item placed in the package. Some firms do offer unrelated free premiums, such as balls, toys, and trading cards. These types of premiums are particularly popular with cereal manufacturers.

A **self-liquidating premium** requires a consumer to pay most of the cost of the item received as a premium, as shown in Exhibit 18.9. Self-liquidating premiums are particularly effective with loyal customers. However, these types of premiums must be used cautiously. Unless the premium is related to a value-building strategy for a brand, it can, like other sales promotions, serve to focus consumer attention on the premium rather than on the benefits of the brand. Focusing on the premium rather than the brand erodes brand equity.

Advertising specialties have three key elements: a message, placed on a useful item, given to consumers with no obligation. Popular advertising specialties are baseball caps, T-shirts, coffee mugs, computer mouse pads, pens, and calendars. Industry sources estimate that firms spend $14 billion a year on advertising specialties, which is one of the fastest growing areas of sales promotion.[22] The Promotional Products Association International (www.ppa.org) puts promotional products into 17 different categories ranging from buttons/badges/bumper stickers to jewelry and watches.[23]

Contests and Sweepstakes. Contests and sweepstakes can draw attention to a brand like no other sales promotion technique. Technically, there are important differences between contests and sweepstakes. A **contest** has consumers compete for prizes based on skill or ability. Winners in a contest are determined by a panel of judges or based on which contestant comes closest to a predetermined criterion for winning, such as picking the total points scored in the Super Bowl. Contests tend to be somewhat expensive to administer because each entry must be judged against winning criteria.

A **sweepstakes** is a promotion in which winners are determined purely by chance. Consumers need only to enter their names in the sweepstakes as a criterion for winning. Sweepstakes often use official entry forms as a way for consumers to enter the sweepstakes. Other popular types of sweepstakes use scratch-off cards.

21. 2001 Annual Report of the Promotion Industry, "Coupons: Nowhere to Go But Up."

22. 2001 Annual Report of the Promotion Industry, "Introduction: Proceed with Caution."

23. Dan S. Bagley III, *Understanding and Using Promotional Products* (Irving, Tex.: Promotional Products Association International, 1999), 6.

EXHIBIT 18.9

One form of premium is the "self-liquidating" premium. What makes this offer by Jell-O self-liquidating? www.jello.com

EXHIBIT 18.10

Instant-winner sweepstakes are popular with consumers, attract attention, and generate excitement at the point of purchase. Webstakes.com (www.webstakes.com) *is an online sweepstakes service that claims to have daily instant winners. Is the online version of instant winning the same as its traditional offline counterpart? Popular culture e-zines such as alloy.com* (www.alloy.com) *and ellegirl.com* (www.ellegirl.com) *often feature sweepstakes, but visitors need to check back often to see if they won. What benefit is this to the Web site? Search any one of these links to learn more about an online sweepstakes or contest. Are the regulations and restrictions of the contest distracting? Does the intended message of the IBP effort get lost in the context of the game aspect of the promotion?* www.gillette.com

Instant-winner scratch-off cards tend to attract customers. Exhibit 18.10 shows an instant-winner sweepstakes run by Gillette. Gasoline retailers, grocery stores, and fast-food chains commonly use scratch-off card sweepstakes as a way of building and maintaining store traffic. Sweepstakes can also be designed so that repeated trips to the retail outlet are necessary to gather a complete set of winning cards. In order for contests and sweepstakes to be effective, advertisers must design them in such a way that consumers perceive value in the prizes and find playing the games intrinsically interesting.

Contests and sweepstakes can span the globe. British Airways ran a contest with the theme "The World's Greatest Offer," in which it gave away thousands of free airline tickets to London and other European destinations. While the contest increased awareness of the airline, there was definitely another benefit. Contests like these create a database of interested customers and potential customers. All the people who didn't win can be mailed information on future programs and other premium offers.

Contests and sweepstakes often create excitement and generate interest for a brand, but the problems of administering these promotions are substantial. Primary among the problems are the regulations and restrictions on such promotions. Advertisers must be sure that the design and administration of a contest or sweepstakes comply with both federal and state laws. Each state may have slightly different regulations. The legal problems are complex enough that most firms hire agencies that specialize in contests and sweepstakes to administer the programs.

Another problem is that the game itself may become the consumer's primary focus, while the brand becomes secondary. The technique thus fails to build long-term consumer affinity for a brand. This problem is inherent to most forms of sales promotion, not just contests and sweepstakes.

The final problem with contests and sweepstakes relates to the IBP effort a firm may be attempting. It is hard to get any meaningful message across in the context of a game. The consumer's interest is focused on the game, rather than on any feature or value message included in the contest or sweepstakes communication. A related problem is that if a firm is trying to develop a quality or prestige image for a brand, contests and sweepstakes may contradict this goal.

Samples and Trial Offers. Getting consumers to simply try a brand can have a powerful effect on future decision making. **Sampling** is a sales promotion technique designed to provide a consumer with an opportunity to use a brand on a trial basis with little or no risk. Saying that sampling is a popular technique is an understatement. Most consumer-product companies use sampling in some manner, and invest approximately $1.2 billion a year in the technique.[24] A recent survey shows that consumers are very favorable toward sampling, with 43 percent indicating that they would consider switching brands if they liked a free sample that was being offered.[25] Sampling is particularly useful for new products, but should not be reserved for new products alone. It can be used successfully for established brands with weak market share in specific geographic areas. Ben & Jerry's "Stop & Taste the Ice Cream" tour gave away more than a million scoops of ice cream in high-traffic urban areas in an attempt to re-establish a presence for the brand in weak markets.[26] Six techniques are used in sampling:

- **In-store sampling** is popular for food products and cosmetics. This is a preferred technique for many marketers because the consumer is at the point of purchase and may be swayed by a direct encounter with the brand. Increasingly, in-store demonstrators are handing out coupons as well as samples.
- **Door-to-door sampling** is extremely expensive because of labor costs, but it can be effective if the marketer has information that locates the target segment in a well-defined geographic area. Some firms enlist the services of newspaper delivery people, who pack the sample with daily or Sunday newspapers as a way of reducing distribution costs.
- **Mail sampling** allows samples to be delivered through the postal service. Again, the value here is that certain zip-code markets can be targeted. A drawback is that the sample must be small to be economically feasible. Specialty-sampling firms, such as Alternative Postal Delivery, provide targeted geodemographic door-to-door distribution as an alternative to the postal service. Cox Target Media has developed a multisample mailer that samples industry-specific products—such as car care products—that can reach highly targeted market segments.[27]

24. 2001 Annual Report of the Promotion Industry, "Sampling: Brand Handing," May 2001, compiled by *PROMO Magazine*, www.industryclick.com, accessed June 5, 2001.
25. Cox Direct 20th Annual Survey of Promotional Practices, 1998, 28.
26. Betsy Spethmann, "Branded Moments," *PROMO Magazine*, September 2000, 84.
27. Cara Beardi, "Cox's Introz Mailer Bundles Samples in Industry," *Advertising Age*, November 2000, 88.

- **Newspaper sampling** has become very popular in recent years, and 42 percent of consumers report having received samples of health and beauty products in this manner.[28] Much like mail sampling, newspaper samples allow very specific geographic and geodemographic targeting. Big drug companies such as Eli Lilly and Bristol-Myers Squibb are using newspaper distribution of coupons to target new users for antidepressant and diabetes drugs.[29]
- **On-package sampling,** a technique in which the sample item is attached to another product package, is useful for brands targeted to current customers. Attaching a small bottle of Ivory conditioner with a regular-sized container of Ivory shampoo is a logical sampling strategy.
- **Mobile sampling** is carried out by logo-emblazoned vehicles that dispense samples, coupons, and premiums to consumers at malls, shopping centers, fairgrounds, and recreational areas. Strategists at Iomega, makers of the popular computer Zip drive, used a mobile display to introduce its new product, the HipZip portable digital audio player, to target consumers on college campuses. Personal contact with the new product was used to increase awareness.[30]

Of course, sampling has its critics. Unless the product has a clear value and benefit over the competition, simple trial of the product is unlikely to persuade a consumer to switch brands. This is especially true for convenience goods, because consumers perceive a high degree of similarity among brands, even after trying them. The perception of benefit and superiority may have to be developed through advertising in combination with sampling. In addition, sampling is expensive. This is especially true in cases where a sufficient quantity of a product, such as shampoo or laundry detergent, must be given away for a consumer to truly appreciate a brand's values. In-store sampling techniques are being devised that can reduce the cost of traditional sampling methods.[31] Finally, sampling can be a very imprecise process. Despite the emergence of special agencies to handle sampling programs, a firm can never completely ensure that the product is reaching the targeted audience.

Trial offers have the same goal as sampling—to induce consumer trial use of a brand—but they are used for more expensive items. Exercise equipment, appliances, watches, hand tools, and consumer electronics are typical of items offered on a trial basis. Trial offers can be free for low-priced products, as we saw in Exhibit 18.6, or trials can be offered for as little as a day to as long as 90 days for more expensive items such as vacuum cleaners and computer software. The expense to the firm, of course, can be formidable. Segments chosen for this sales promotion technique must have high sales potential.

Phone and Gift Cards. Phone and gift cards represent a new and increasingly popular form of sales promotion. This technique could be classified as a premium offer, but it has enough unique features to warrant separate classification as a sales promotion technique. The use of phone and gift cards is fairly straightforward. Manufacturers or retailers offer either for free or for purchase debit cards that provide the holder with either minutes of phone time or some preset spending limit in the case of a gift card. The cards are designed to be colorful and memorable. A wide range of marketers, including luxury car manufacturers such as Lexus and retailers such as The Gap, have made effective use of phone and gift cards.[32] In Exhibit 18.11, Oldsmobile is trying to lure shoppers to dealerships with a $50 gift card to Blockbuster Video.

28. Cox Direct 20th Annual Survey of Promotional Practices, 1998, 27.
29. Susan Warner, "Drug Makers Print Coupons to Boost Sales," Knight Ridder Newspapers, June 4, 2001.
30. Kate Fitzgerald, "Iomega Makes Music," *Advertising Age,* October 30, 2000, 42.
31. Debbie Usery, "What's In-Store," *PROMO Magazine,* May 2000, 54.
32. Carolyn Shea, "Calling All Cards: Pre-Paid Phone Cards Are Racking Up Sales," *PROMO Magazine,* March 1995, 42.

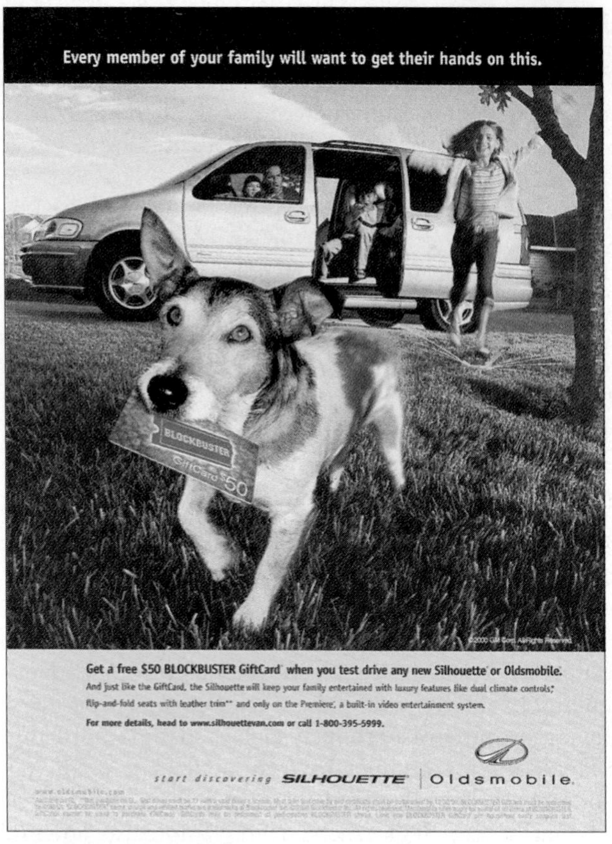

EXHIBIT 18.11

Phone and gift cards have emerged as a popular new sales promotion device among a wide range of marketers. www.oldsmobile.com

Brand Placement. **Brand placement** (previously referred to as product placement) is the sales promotion technique of getting a marketer's brand featured in movies and television shows. The use of a brand by actors and actresses or the mere association of a brand with a popular film or television show can create a positive image or, occasionally, a demonstrated sales impact for a brand. Advertisers used to think brand placements affected only consumers' perceptions of a brand, much like advertising. But recent brand placements have shown that the technique can have a sales impact like that of a traditional sales promotion. For example, consider these results:

- When British agent 007, James Bond, switched from his traditional Aston-Martin sports car to the new BMW Z3, a brand placement in the Bond film *Goldeneye,* along with a tightly coordinated dealer promotion program, resulted in 6,000 predelivery orders for the Z3.
- Sales of Nike sneakers and apparel jumped after the release of the hit movie *Forrest Gump.* The film featured the star Tom Hanks getting a pair of Nike running shoes as a gift, which his character, Gump, believes is "the best gift anyone could get in the whole wide world." Later in the film, Gump wears a Nike T-shirt during a cross-country run.
- When Jennifer Grey danced in retro oxford sneakers in the film *Dirty Dancing,* the shoe's manufacturer, Keds, saw a huge increase in sales.
- One of the biggest beneficiaries of a brand placement was Bausch and Lomb. Tom Cruise wore distinctive Bausch and Lomb Ray-Ban sunglasses in the film Risky Business, and the glasses were featured on the movie poster as well. Ray-Ban sales rocketed to all-time highs after the film's release.[33] More recently, Cruise sparked a wave of interest in Oakley's X-Metal Romeo glasses after wearing them in the beginning of the film *Mission Impossible 2.* Obviously, Tom is the king of sunglasses brand placement.
- In an episode of *Friends,* Phoebe and Rachel spent most of the show discussing the merits of Pottery Barn, a retailer of home accessory items. While there is no estimate of the sales effect on the retailer, "Pottery Barn" was uttered by the two stars at least 50 times.

The newfound power of brand placement has been surprising, but the process is relatively simple. Once a movie studio or television production team approves a script and schedules production, placement specialists, either in-house or working for specialty agencies, go to work. They send the script to targeted companies in an effort to sell the placement opportunities. If a company agrees, then little more is involved than having the brand sent to the studio for inclusion in the film or program. Marketers such as BMW and Coke play a more formative role, but they are exceptions.

Brand placement, like any other communications effort, shows varying results. If the brand name is spoken aloud, such as Gene Hackman telling Tom Cruise to help

33. Blair R. Fischer, "Making Your Product the Star Attraction," *PROMO Magazine,* July 1996, 58.

himself to a Red Stripe beer during the film *The Firm,* the impact can be dramatic. Similarly, prominent use by a celebrity of a featured brand, such as Mel Gibson clearly drinking a Dr Pepper or Dennis Quaid eating at McDonald's, can achieve 40 to 50 percent recognition within an audience. Less obvious placements, such as when Bond smashes a car into a Heineken beer truck—referred to as background placements—are considered by some analysts to be a waste of money.

e-SIGHTINGS

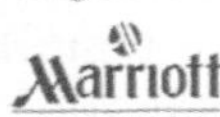

EXHIBIT 18.12

Frequency (continuity) programs build customer loyalty and offer opportunities for building a large, targeted database for other promotions. Online services such as points.com (www.points.com) *and marketing firms such as Netcentives* (www.netcentives.com) *specialize in building brand loyalty through frequency programs. What role does each of these companies have in developing and executing frequency programs? Which sales promotion objectives guide the development of frequency programs? How do these rewards help counter the effects of the proliferation of brands in the marketplace?* www.marriott.com

Rebates. Rebates started in the mid-1970s when auto dealers feared price freezes would be imposed by the government as a means to curb inflation. Auto dealers discovered that a rebate on the purchase price of a car was a way around the impending freeze. The price freeze never materialized, but the rebate survived as a sales promotion technique. A **rebate** is a money-back offer requiring a buyer to mail in a form requesting the money back from the *manufacturer* rather than the retailer (as in couponing). The rebate technique has been refined over the years and is now used by a wide variety of marketers. Rebates are particularly well suited to increasing the quantity purchased by consumers, so rebates are commonly tied to multiple purchases. For example, if you buy a ten-pack of Kodak film, you can mail in a rebate coupon worth $2.00.

Another reason for the popularity of rebates is that few consumers take advantage of the rebate offer after buying a brand.[34] The best estimate of consumer redemption of rebate offers by the research firm Market Growth Resources is that only 5 to 10 percent of buyers ever bother to fill out and then mail in the rebate request. This may signal a waning popularity of the rebate with consumers. Extensive rebate efforts in the SUV market have recently been unable to reenergize flagging sales.[35]

Frequency (Continuity) Programs. In recent years, one of the most popular sales promotion techniques among consumers has been frequency programs. **Frequency programs,** also referred to as *continuity programs,* offer consumers discounts or free product rewards for repeat purchase or patronage of the same brand or company. These programs were pioneered by airline companies. Frequent-flyer programs such as Delta Air Lines' SkyMiles, frequent-stay programs such as Marriott's Honored Guest Award program, and frequent-renter programs such as Hertz's #1 Club are examples of such loyalty-building activities. But frequency programs are not reserved for big national airline and auto-rental chains. Chart House Enterprises, a chain of 65 upscale restaurants, successfully launched a frequency program for diners, who earned points for every dollar spent. Frequent diners were issued "passports," which were stamped with each visit. Within two years, the program had more than 300,000 members.[36] Exhibit 18.12 features Marriott's frequency program.

34. William H. Buckeley, "Rebates' Secret Appeal to Manufacturers: Few Consumers Actually Redeem Them," *Wall Street Journal,* February 10, 1998, B1.
35. David Kiley, "Car Sales Slow Despite Deals," *USA Today,* June 1, 2001, 3B.
36. Kerry J. Smith, "Building a Winning Frequency Program—The Hard Way," *PROMO Magazine,* December 1995, 36.

Event Sponsorship. When a firm sponsors or co-sponsors an event, such as an auto race, charity marathon, or rock concert, the brand featured in the event immediately gains a credibility with the event audience. The audience attending (or participating) in an event already has a positive attitude and affinity for the context—they chose to attend or participate voluntarily. When this audience encounters a brand in this very favorable reception environment, the brand benefits from the already favorable audience attitude.

Advocates of events as a promotional tool point to the fact that entertainment tie-ins provided for a brand touch consumers in a way that advertising cannot. When Nissan launched its Xterra SUV, the firm decided that the best way to demonstrate the powers of the vehicle to a demand audience was to assume the title sponsorship of a series of off-road, extreme competitions. The fit was good and the audience was a perfect target.[37] Sponsorship has grown to be the fourth most popular form of promotion used by U.S. firms, with about $8.7 billion invested annually and a growth rate exceeding 8.6 percent per year.[38]

The most preferred venue for sponsorship is, not surprisingly, sporting events, which attract about $5 billion in sponsorship dollars. The next most popular activities for attracting sponsors are entertainment tours at about $893 million, festivals and fairs at $777 million, cause fundraisers with $769 million, and art events saw about $599 million in sponsorship spending.[39] And with sporting events comes the chance to promote a brand globally. There is no better global venue than the Olympics. The Global Issues box on page 653 shows that firms have found sales promotion well suited to gaining international attention for a brand.

3 Sales Promotion Directed at the Trade and Business Buyers.

Sales promotions can also be directed at members of the trade—wholesalers, distributors, and retailers—and business buyers. For example, Compaq Computer designs sales promotion programs for its retailers, such as Circuit City, in order to ensure that the Compaq line gets proper attention and display. But Compaq will also have sales promotion campaigns aimed at business buyers like Accenture (formerly Andersen Consulting) or IHC HealthCare. The purpose of sales promotion as a tool does not change in the trade market or business buyer markets. It is still intended to stimulate demand in the short term and help push the product through the distribution channel or cause business buyers to act more immediately and positively toward the marketer's brand.

Effective trade and business market promotions can generate enthusiasm for a product and contribute positively to the loyalty distributors show for a brand. In the business market, sales promotions can mean the difference between landing a very large order and missing out entirely on a revenue opportunity. With the massive proliferation of new brands and brand extensions, manufacturers need to stimulate enthusiasm and loyalty among members of the trade and also need a way to get the attention of business buyers suffering from information overload.

Objectives for Promotions in the Trade Market. As in the consumer market, trade-market sales promotions should be undertaken with specific objectives in mind. Generally speaking, when marketers devise incentives for the trade market, they are executing a **push strategy**; that is, sales promotions directed at the trade help push

37. Kate Fitzgerald, "Events Offer New Level of Brand Immersion," *Advertising Age,* April 17, 2000, 22.
38. 2001 Annual Report of the Promotion Industry, "Sponsorship: Getting In On the Action," May 2001, compiled by *PROMO Magazine,* www.industryclick.com, accessed June 5, 2001.
39. Ibid.

a product into the distribution channel until it ultimately reaches the consumer. Four primary objectives can be identified for these promotions:

- *Obtain initial distribution.* Because of the proliferation of brands in the consumer market, there is fierce competition for shelf space. Sales promotion incentives can help a firm gain initial distribution and shelf placement. Like consumers, members of the trade need a reason to choose one brand over another when it comes to allocating shelf space. A well-conceived promotion incentive may sway them.

  Bob's Candies, a small family-owned business in Albany, Georgia, is the largest candy cane manufacturer in the United States. But Bob's old-fashioned candy was having trouble keeping distributors. To reverse the trend, Bob's designed a new name, logo, and packaging for the candy canes. Then, each scheduled attendee at the All-Candy Expo trade show in Chicago was mailed three strategically timed postcards with the teaser question "Wanna Be Striped?" The mailing got a 25 percent response rate, and booth visitations at the trade show were a huge success.[40]
- *Increase order size.* One of the struggles in the channel of distribution is over the location of inventory. Manufacturers prefer that members of the trade maintain large inventories so the manufacturer can reduce inventory-carrying costs. Conversely, members of the trade would rather make frequent, small orders and carry little inventory. Sales promotion techniques can encourage wholesalers and retailers to order in larger quantities, thus shifting the inventory burden to the channel.
- *Encourage cooperation with consumer-market sales promotions.* It does a manufacturer little good to initiate a sales promotion in the consumer market if there is little cooperation in the channel. Wholesalers may need to maintain larger inventories, and retailers may need to provide special displays or handling during consumer-market

GLOBAL ISSUES

Bring On the World

You've finally reached that pinnacle of performance that so many dream about but so few actually achieve. The endless hours of work and dedication, away from the family on weekends, no time to yourself, finally pay off in your chance to show the world that you are the best in the world at what you do. This is the Olympic Games. And you are an Olympic sponsor. Is there any event bigger than the Olympic Games? When it comes to sponsorships and promotions for marketers, the answer is no—not even close.

The Olympic Games is a key sponsorship opportunity for many global firms such as Kodak, General Motors, and Home Depot. But for Visa International, the Olympics always hold special promise. Each year the Olympics are staged is a chance for Visa to tout, once again, that Visa's sponsorship means that it is the only card accepted at the Games—a promotional message the firm relishes in its competition with MasterCard and American Express.

Visa used a multifaceted promotional campaign in the months leading to the 2000 Summer Games in Sydney, Australia. To drive the point home that Visa was a sponsor and the exclusive card at the games, banks issued Olympic-themed credit cards beginning in January 2000. Within the country, the company developed several promotions around the campaign theme "Dream with No Boundaries." The centerpiece of the promotion was the "Dream Trips Sweepstakes," in which cardholders were entered to win one of five Games travel packages every time they made a purchase. The sweepstakes was touted on Visa's Web site, via billing statement inserts, and through P-O-P signage in retail shops. Yet another sweepstakes called "Your Dream, Your Team" offered 10 winners $5,000, with Visa donating a matching amount to the U.S. Olympic team of the winner's choice.

At the games themselves, Visa used tie-ins with local merchants at the point of purchase. Michael Lynch, VP for event and sponsorship marketing for Visa, explained that the firm worked with local merchants as a way to "customize programs specific to their marketplace needs to build their profitability." This might include Visa promotional tie-ins or even appearances by athletes.

While promotions are important to many firms across a wide variety of applications, the Olympics offer a special opportunity. Few firms have taken advantage of an opportunity as well as Visa International takes advantage of its Olympic opportunities.

Source: Bob Woods, "They Got Games," *PROMO Magazine*, April 2000, 79–82.

40. Lee Duffey, "Sweet Talk: Promotions Position Candy Company," *Marketing News*, March 30, 1998, 11.

sales promotions. To achieve synergy, marketers often run trade promotions simultaneously with consumer promotions. As it turned out, when Toys "R" Us ran its "scan and win" promotion, the company actually ran out of several very popular toy items during the critical holiday buying season because distributors (and Toys "R" Us) were unprepared for the magnitude of the response to the promotion.

- *Increase store traffic.* Retailers can increase store traffic through special promotions or events. Door-prize drawings, parking-lot sales, or live radio broadcasts from the store are common sales promotion traffic builders. Burger King has become a leader in building traffic at its 6,500 outlets with special promotions tied to Disney movie debuts. Beginning in 1991 with a *Beauty and the Beast* tie-in promotion, Burger King has set records for generating store traffic with premium giveaways. The *Pocahontas* campaign distributed 55 million toys and glasses. Most recently, a promotion tie-in with Disney's huge success *Toy Story* resulted in 50 million toys, based on the film's characters, being given away in $1.99 Kid Meals.[41]

Manufacturers can also design sales promotions that increase store traffic for retailers. A promotion that generates a lot of interest within a target audience can drive consumers to retail outlets. A good example of this is shown in Exhibit 18.13. Jelly Belly jelly beans ran this giveaway of a New Beetle as a way to attract attention to the brand. But notice the copy in the ad: "To enter, visit your nearest participating retailer and ask for your Very Cherry Sweepstakes entry form. . . ." Supporting retailer traffic in this way creates strong and lasting relationships between marketers and their trade channel partners.

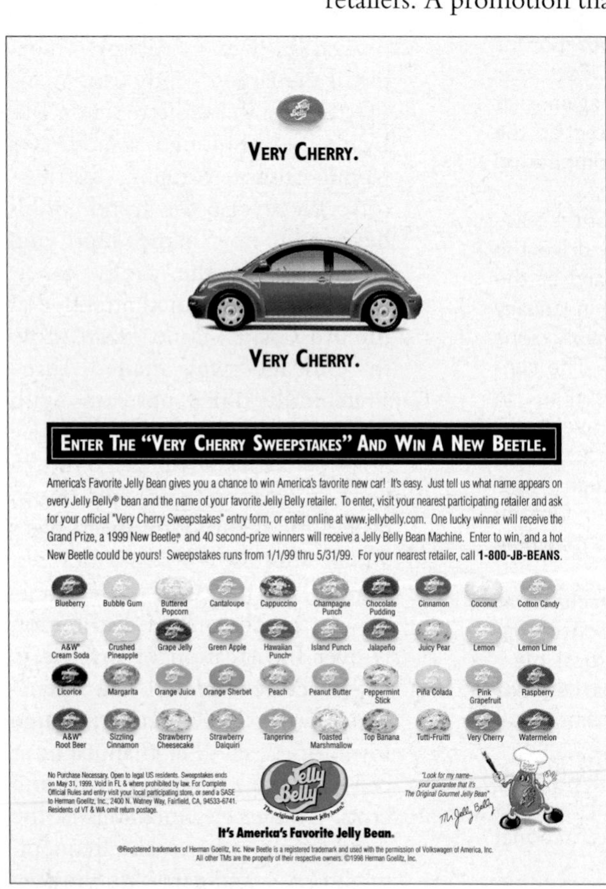

EXHIBIT 18.13

One of the objectives for sales promotion at the trade market level is to build store traffic. While retailers often use sales promotion techniques to do so, occasionally a manufacturer will try to stimulate store traffic for a retailer, as the Very Cherry Sweepstakes attempts to do.
www.jellybelly.com

Trade-Market Sales Promotion Techniques. The sales promotion techniques used with the trade are point-of-purchase displays, incentives, allowances, trade shows, sales training programs, and cooperative advertising.

Point-of-Purchase Displays. Product displays and information sheets are useful in reaching the consumer at the point of purchase and often encourage retailers to support one's brand. P-O-P promotions can help win precious shelf space and exposure in a retail setting. From a retailer's perspective, a P-O-P display should be designed to draw attention to a brand, increase turnover, and possibly distribute coupons or sweepstakes entry forms. Exhibit 18.14 shows a typical P-O-P display. Advertisers invested $17.0 billion on P-O-P materials in 2000—an 18.1 percent increase over the prior year. This is more than was spent on either magazine or radio advertising.[42]

In an attempt to combat the threat of losing business to online shopping, retailers are trying to enliven the retail environment, and point-of-purchase displays are part of the strategy. Both brand advertisers and retailers are trying to create a better and

41. Editors' Special Report, "Having It Their Way," *PROMO Magazine,* December 1995, 79–80.
42. 2001 Annual Report of the Promotion Industry, "P-O-P Displays: On Solid Ground," May 2001, compiled by *PROMO Magazine,* www.industryclick.com, accessed June 5, 2001.

EXHIBIT 18.14

Point of purchase is an important competitive battleground for attracting attention to a brand. Here we see an excellent illustration of one advertiser's effort to take control of that battleground.
www.gillette.com

more satisfying shopping experience. The president of a large display company says, "We're trying to bring more of an entertainment factor to our P-O-P programs."[43]

Incentives. Incentives to members of the trade include a variety of tactics not unlike those used in the consumer market. Awards in the form of travel, gifts, or cash bonuses for reaching targeted sales levels can induce retailers and wholesalers to give a firm's brand added attention. The incentive does not have to be large or expensive to be effective. Weiser Lock offered its dealers a Swiss Army knife with every dozen cases of locks ordered. The program was a huge success. A follow-up promotion featuring a Swiss Army watch was an even bigger hit.

Another form of trade incentive is referred to as push money. In **push money** programs, retail salespeople are offered a monetary reward for featuring a marketer's brand with shoppers. The program is quite simple. If a salesperson sells a particular brand of refrigerator for a manufacturer as opposed to a competitor's brand, the salesperson will be paid an extra $50 or $75 "bonus" as part of the push money program.

One risk with incentive programs for the trade is that salespeople can be so motivated to win an award or extra push money that they may try to sell the brand to every customer, whether it fits that customer's needs or not. Also, a firm must carefully manage such programs to minimize ethical dilemmas. An incentive technique can look like a bribe unless it is carried out in a highly structured and open fashion.

Allowances. Various forms of allowances are offered to retailers and wholesalers with the purpose of increasing the attention given to a firm's brands. Allowances are typically made available to wholesalers and retailers about every four weeks during a quarter. **Merchandise allowances,** in the form of free products packed with regular shipments, are payments to the trade for setting up and maintaining displays. The payments are typically far less than manufacturers would have to spend to maintain the displays themselves.

43. Ibid.

In recent years, shelf space has become so highly demanded, especially in supermarkets, that manufacturers are making direct cash payments, known as **slotting fees,** to induce food chains to stock an item. The proliferation of new products has made shelf space such a precious commodity that these fees now run in the hundreds of thousands of dollars per product. Another form of allowance is called a bill-back allowance. **Bill-back allowances** provide retailers a monetary incentive for featuring a marketer's brand in either advertising or in-store displays. If a retailer chooses to participate in either an advertising or display bill-back program, the marketer requires the retailer to verify the services performed and provide a bill for the services. A similar program is the **off-invoice allowance,** where advertisers allow wholesalers and retailers to deduct a set amount from the invoice they receive for merchandise. This program is really just a price reduction offered to the trade on a particular marketer's brand. The incentive for the trade with this program is that the price reduction increases the margin (and profits) a wholesaler or retailer realizes on the off-invoiced brand.

Sales Training Programs. An increasingly popular trade promotion is to provide training for retail store personnel. This method is used for consumer durables and specialty goods, such as personal computers, home theater systems, heating and cooling systems, security systems, and exercise equipment. The increased complexity of these products has made it important for manufacturers to ensure that the proper factual information and persuasive themes are reaching consumers at the point of purchase. For personnel at large retail stores, manufacturers can hold special classes that feature product information, demonstrations, and training about sales techniques.

Another popular method for getting sales training information to retailers is the use of videotapes and brochures. Manufacturers can also send sales trainers into retail stores to work side by side with store personnel. This is a costly method, but it can be very effective because of the one-on-one attention it provides.

Cooperative (Co-Op) Advertising. **Cooperative advertising** as a trade promotion technique is referred to as vertical cooperative advertising. (Such efforts are also called *vendor co-op programs*.) Manufacturers try to control the content of this co-op advertising in two ways. They may set strict specifications for the size and content of the ad and then ask for verification that such specifications have been met. Alternatively, manufacturers may send the template for an ad, into which retailers merely insert the names and locations of their stores. Such an ad is featured in Exhibit 18.15. Notice that the James Bond and Omega watch components are national, with the co-op sponsorship of the Hawaiian retailer highlighted in the lower right.

Business Market Sales Promotion Techniques.

Often the discussion of sales promotion focuses only on consumer and trade techniques. It is a major oversight to leave the business buyer market out of the discussion. The Promotional Product Association estimates that several billion dollars a year in sales promotion is targeted to the business buyer.[44]

Trade Shows. **Trade shows** are events where several related products from many manufacturers are displayed and demonstrated to members of the trade. Literally every industry has trade shows, from gourmet products to the granddaddy of them all, COMDEX. COMDEX is the annual computer and electronics industry trade show held in Las Vegas that attracts over a quarter of a million business buyers.

44. Bagley, *Understanding and Using Promotional Products,* 5.

EXHIBIT 18.15

Here is a classic example of co-op advertising between manufacturer and retailer. Omega is being featured by this Hawaiian retailer in a magazine ad. Is another form of sales promotion going on here as well?
www.omega.ch

At a typical trade show, company representatives are on hand staffing a booth that displays a company's products or service programs. The representatives are there to explain the products and services and perhaps make an important contact for the sales force. The use of trade shows must be carefully coordinated and can be an important part of the business market promotional program. Trade shows can be critically important to a small firm that cannot afford advertising and has a sales staff too small to reach all its potential customers. Through the trade-show route, salespeople can make far more contacts than would be possible with direct sales calls.

Trade shows are also an important route for reaching potential wholesalers and distributors for a company's brand. But the proliferation of trade shows has been so extensive in recent years that the technique is really more oriented to business buyers these days.

Business Gifts. Estimates are that nearly half of corporate America gives business gifts.[45] These gifts are given as part of building and maintaining a close working relationship with suppliers. Business gifts that are part of a promotional program may include small items such as logo golf balls, jackets, or jewelry. Extravagant gifts or expensive trips that might be construed as "buying business" are not included in this category of business market sales promotion.

Premiums and Advertising Specialties. As mentioned earlier, a key chain, ball cap, T-shirt, mouse pad, or calendar that reminds a buyer of a brand name and slogan can be an inexpensive but useful form of sales promotion. A significant portion of the $14 billion premium and advertising specialty market is directed to business buyers. While business buyers are professionals, they are not immune to the value perceptions that an advertising specialty can create. In other words, getting something for nothing appeals to business buyers as much as it does to household consumers. Will a business buyer choose one consulting firm over another to get a sleeve of golf balls? Probably not. But advertising specialties can add to the satisfaction of a transaction nonetheless.

Trial Offers. Trial offers are particularly well suited to the business market. First, since many business products and services are high cost and often result in a significant time commitment to a brand (that is, many business products and services have long life), trial offers provide a way for buyers to lower the risk of making a commitment to one brand over another. Second, a trial offer is a good way to attract new customers who need a good reason to try something new. The GoldMine software offer in Exhibit 18.16 is a perfect demonstration of these points. Software installation and use require both a time and money commitment on the part of a business buyer. And using software for sales force team communications and planning may

45. Ibid.

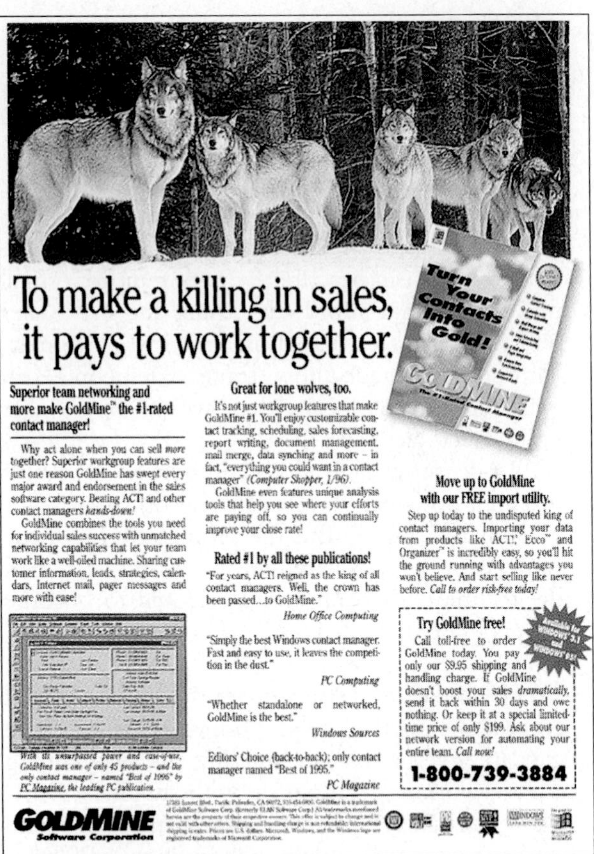

EXHIBIT 18.16

Business products often require a large time and money commitment. A risk-free trial offer, such as this one for GoldMine software, allows business buyers the chance to try something new at a very low risk.
www.goldminesw.com

be new to many organizations. The chance to try a new product for 30 days with no financial risk can be a compelling offer.

Frequency Programs. The high degree of travel associated with many business professions makes frequency programs an ideal form of sales promotion for the business market. Airline, hotel, and restaurant frequency programs are dominated by the business market traveler. But frequency programs for the business market are not restricted to travel-related purchases. Retailers of business products, such as Staples, Office Max, and Costco, have programs designed to reward the loyalty of the business buyer. Costco has teamed with American Express to offer business buyers an exclusive Costco/American Express credit card. Among the many advantages of the card is a rebate at the end of the year based on the level of buying—the greater the dollar amount of purchases, the greater the percentage rebate. The IBP box on page 660 gives an example of how frequency programs can be used in the professional business market.

Sales Promotion, the Internet, and New Media.

Sales promotion has entered the era of new media as well. Marketers are expanding their use of sales promotion techniques in the consumer, trade, and business markets by using the Internet and other new media options. In a recent survey, 49 percent of advertisers said they used Internet-based promotions.[46] There are two parts to the issue of sales promotion in new media applications. First, there is the *use by* Internet and new media companies of sales promotion techniques. Second, there is the *use of* the Internet and new media to implement various sales promotion techniques.

The Use of Sales Promotion by Internet and New Media Organizations. The new titans of technology—AOL, Yahoo!, Network Associates—have discovered a new way to generate revenue fast: They give their products away. More specifically, they have discovered the power of sales promotion in the form of distributing free samples. These fast-growing, highly successful companies have discovered an alternative to advertising—sales promotion.

Of course, giving away free samples, as we have seen, is not a new sales promotion technique. But giving away intellectual property, such as software, is new and America Online is the Godzilla of giveaways (see Exhibit 18.17). With each new release, AOL blankets the United States with diskettes and CD-ROMs offering consumers a free one-month trial of its Internet services. No distribution channel is left untapped in trying to reach consumers with the free diskettes. They have been stashed in boxes of Rice Chex cereal, in United Airlines in-flight meals, and in packages of Omaha Steaks—not to mention inside the plastic sack along with your local Sunday paper that the neighborhood kid delivers.

46. 2001 Annual Report of the Promotion Industry, "Introduction: Proceed with Caution."

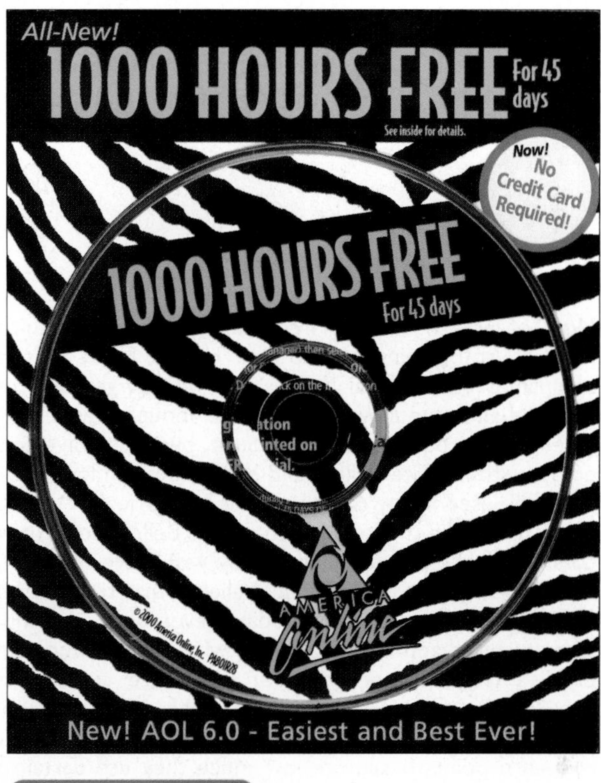

EXHIBIT 18.17

Internet and new media firms such as AOL have discovered the power of sales promotion. www.aol.com

What makes sampling so attractive for AOL is that it helps take all the risk away from consumer trial. Consumers with computers, of course, can give AOL or Yahoo! a try without investing a penny or making a long-term commitment to a piece of software. If they like what they see, they can sign up for a longer period of time. The technology companies have embraced the concept and accepted the main liabilities of sampling—cost and time.[47]

But sampling is not the only sales promotion tool discovered by the dot-coms. In their desire to create "sticky" Web sites, Internet firms have relied heavily on incentives as a way to attract and retain Web surfers. Many of them are offering loyalty programs, and others have devised offers to make members out of visitors. In an attempt to make the incentive programs more interesting, many of the Web companies allow participants to review their standings in contests and then take a virtual tour of prizes—including exotic travel destinations that typically constitute a grand prize.[48]

These technology companies have discovered that sales promotion can be a valuable component of the overall promotional program—and that the potential impact of sales promotion is quite different from advertising. Internet and new media companies have invested heavily in advertising as a way to develop brand recognition. Now they have discovered sales promotion as a way to help drive revenues.

47. Patricia Nakache, "Secrets of the New Brand Builders," *Fortune,* June 22, 1998, 167–170.

48. "Motivating Matters," Promotion Trends 2000, Annual Report of the Promotion Industry, May 2000, compiled by *PROMO Magazine,* A13.

The Use of the Internet and New Media to Implement Sales Promotions.

It is interesting to see Internet and new media companies rely on traditional sales promotions. But it is also interesting to see how companies of all types are learning to use the Internet and new media to implement sales promotion techniques. In a survey of firms using various promotional techniques, more than half responded that the Internet and new media were having a large impact on their promotional planning. Estimates are that marketers invested about $926 million in Web-based promotions in 1999, including online sweepstakes, couponing, and loyalty and sampling programs.[49]

There are a variety of ways in which the Internet is being used to implement sales promotions. First, companies like Halo.com (www.halo.com) are emerging that increase the efficiency of the sales promotion process. Halo.com operates online promotional "stores" for corporate customers. Other online companies help firms determine how to use the Internet to implement sales promotion programs such as sweepstakes (see Exhibit 18.18).[50] Second, the Internet is being used as a distribution system for couponing. In the packaged-goods area, Internet-"triggered" coupons (either printed from a Web page or requested online for mail delivery) have become so popular that a coupon-based Web site, coolsavings.com, now boasts over 11 million members.[51] As an example, PetsMart launched a Petsmart.com Store Savings Center. Site visitors enter their zip code, then print out coupons to redeem at their neighborhood PetsMart Store.[52] Rebates are also being distributed through the Internet, as shown in Exhibit 18.19. Finally, sweepstakes are highly popular on the Web, as we have seen before. A General Motors game for the new Chevy Tracker drew 1.3 million Web-based entries.

While the Internet attracts most of the attention for sales promotion implementation, new media applications are also taking hold. The CD-ROMs distributed by Netscape represent one form of new media application. In-store coupon dispensers is another. Finally, interactive kiosks in retail locations that provide both information and incentives are being developed.

IBP

IBP in B to B

Most of us are used to frequency programs in which a company rewards us for being loyal to their brands. From multinational airline companies to the local bagel shop, we can get our frequency card punched and reap rewards. But what about a frequency program targeted to the business market? Sure, business travelers will rack up points with favorite airlines and hotels, but can loyalty/frequency programs be used in any other product categories?

As far as the marketing manager at Bell Atlantic (now Verizon) is concerned, the answer is absolutely yes! Steve McVeigh, senior marketing manager at Bell Atlantic, believes that to most business users, telephone service is a commodity—everybody is going to offer the same services and options. That's why Bell Atlantic started Business Link—a frequency program for corporate customers. Companies enrolled in the program can save roughly 15 percent on their direct-dial calls when their monthly usage exceeds a set amount. They can also earn points based on how much they use certain specified Bell Atlantic services.

Kodak has a similar program called ProRewards. This is a points-based program for professional photographers. With their accumulated points, photographers can get discounts on a wide array of items—except film. As a Kodak spokesperson so succinctly put it: "What we want to do is get them to *buy* the film."

A real payoff for both firms is that once they have business users enrolled in the frequency programs, a database is developed of these loyal customers. With the database, specialized product promotions can be developed and mailed to these frequent buyers and loyal customers.

To get the most from a loyalty/frequency program in the business market, the following guidelines are offered:

- Give rewards or discounts only to those who spend enough to make the discounts profitable.
- Track buying habits and customer information to create targeted marketing programs and to develop special offers.
- Offer your best customers special rewards—an exclusive customer service phone number, e-mail bulletins, or early release of products—that show you recognize their value to your company.

Source: Chad Kaydo, "How to Build a B-to-B Frequency Program," *Sales and Marketing Management*, April 1999, 79.

49. "Internet Invasion," Promotion Trends 2000, Annual Report of the Promotion Industry, May 2000, compiled by *PROMO Magazine*, A30.
50. Peter Breen, "Straight from the Source," *Premiums*, April 2000, S4–S9.
51. Roger O. Crockett, "Penny Pinchers' Paradise," *Business Week E-Biz*, January 22, 2000, 12.
52. Ibid.

EXHIBIT 18.18

New Internet companies like ePrize are emerging to help firms plan and execute sales promotions using the Web. www.eprize.net

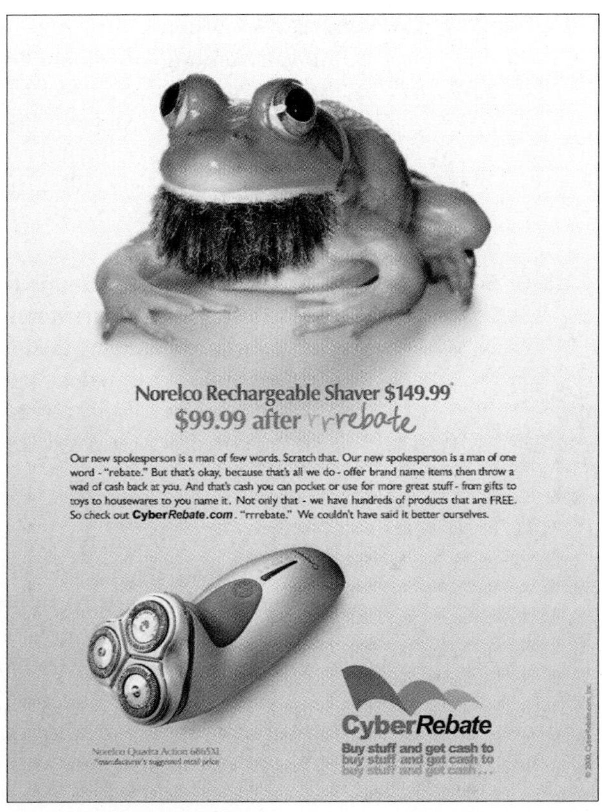

EXHIBIT 18.19

Rebates can effectively be distributed through the Internet, as this Norelco rebate program demonstrates. www.norelco.com

The Risks of Sales Promotion.

Sales promotion can be used to pursue important sales objectives. As we have seen, there are a wide range of sales promotion options for both the consumer and trade markets. But there are also significant risks associated with sales promotion, and these risks must be carefully considered.

Creating a Price Orientation.

Since most sales promotions rely on some sort of price incentive or giveaway, a firm runs the risk of having its brand perceived as cheap, with no real value or benefits beyond low price. Creating this perception in the market contradicts the concept of integrated brand promotion. If advertising messages highlight the value and benefit of a brand only to be contradicted by a price emphasis in sales promotions, then a confusing signal is being sent to the market.

Borrowing from Future Sales.

Management must admit that sales promotions are typically short-term tactics designed to reduce inventories, increase cash flow, or show periodic boosts in market share. The downside is that a firm may simply be borrowing from future sales. Consumers or trade buyers who would have purchased the brand anyway may be motivated to stock up at the lower price. This results in reduced sales during the next few time periods of measurement. This can play havoc with the measurement and evaluation of the effect of advertising campaigns or other image-building communications. If consumers are responding to sales promotions, it may be impossible to tease out the effects of advertising.

Alienating Customers. When a firm relies heavily on sweepstakes or frequency programs to build loyalty among customers, particularly their best customers, there is the risk of alienating these customers with any change in the program. Airlines suffered just such a fate when they tried to adjust the mileage levels needed for awards in their frequent-flyer programs. Ultimately, many of the airlines had to give concessions to their most frequent flyers as a conciliatory gesture.

Time and Expense. Sales promotions are both costly and time-consuming. The process is time-consuming for the marketer and the retailer in terms of handling promotional materials and protecting against fraud and waste in the process. As we have seen in recent years, funds allocated to sales promotions are taking dollars away from advertising. Advertising is a long-term, franchise-building process that should not be compromised for short-term gains.

Legal Considerations. With the increasing popularity of sales promotions, particularly contests and premiums, there has been an increase in legal scrutiny at both the federal and state levels. Legal experts recommend that before initiating promotions that use coupons, games, sweepstakes, and contests, a firm should check into lottery laws, copyright laws, state and federal trademark laws, prize notification laws, right of privacy laws, tax laws, and FTC and FCC regulations.[53] The best advice for staying out of legal trouble with sales promotions is to carefully and clearly state the rules and conditions related to the program so that consumers are fully informed.

5 The Coordination Challenge—Sales Promotion and IBP.

There is an allure to sales promotion that must be put into perspective. Sales promotions can make things happen—quickly. While managers often find the immediacy of sales promotion valuable, particularly in meeting quarterly sales goals, sales promotions are rarely a viable means of long-term success. But when used properly, sales promotions can be an important element in a well-conceived IBP campaign. Key to their proper use is coordinating the message emphasis in advertising with the placement and emphasis of sales promotions. When advertising and sales promotion are well coordinated, the impact of each is enhanced—a classic case of synergy. When advertisers were surveyed about their perspective on sales promotion, 57 percent said that they employed a mix of brand building and sales incentives in the promotional process. Similarly, the majority of respondents indicated that sales promotion was an ancillary part of their IBP campaigns rather than a core component or the key component.[54]

Message Coordination. The typical sales promotion should either attract attention to a brand or offer the target market greater value: reduced price, more product, or the chance to win a prize or an award. In turn, this focused attention and extra value acts as an incentive for the target market to choose the promoted brand over other brands. One of the coordination problems this presents is that advertising messages designed to build long-term loyalty may not seem totally consistent with the extra-value signal of the sales promotion.

This is the classic problem that marketers face in coordinating sales promotion with an advertising campaign. First, advertising messages tout brand features or emo-

53. Maxine S. Lans, "Legal Hurdles Big Part of Promotions Game," *Marketing News,* October 24, 1994, 15.
54. 2001 Annual Report of the Promotion Industry, "Introduction: Proceed with Caution," May 2001, compiled by *PROMO Magazine,* www.industryclick.com, accessed June 5, 2001.

tional attractions. Then, the next contact a consumer may have with the brand is an insert in the Sunday paper offering a cents-off coupon. These mixed signals can be damaging for a brand.

Increasing the coordination between advertising and various sales promotion efforts requires only the most basic planning. First, when different agencies are involved in preparing sales promotion materials and advertising materials, those agencies need to be kept informed by the advertiser regarding the maintenance of a desired theme. Second, simple techniques can be used to carry a coordinated theme between promotional tools. The use of logos, slogans, visual imagery, or spokespersons can create a consistent presentation. As illustrated in Exhibit 18.3, even if advertising and sales promotion pursue different purposes, the look and feel of both efforts may be coordinated. The more the theme of a promotion can be tied directly to the advertising campaign, the more impact these messages will generally have on the consumer.

Media Coordination. Another key in coordination involves timing. Remember that the success of a sales promotion depends on the consumer believing that the chance to save money or receive more of a product represents enhanced value. If the consumer is not aware of a brand and its features and benefits, and does not perceive the brand as a worthy item, then there will be no basis for perceiving value—discounted or not. This means that appropriate advertising should precede price-oriented sales promotions for them to be effective. The right advertising can create an image for a brand that is appropriate for a promotional offer. Then, when consumers are presented with a sales promotion, the offer will impress the consumer as an opportunity to acquire superior value. This is precisely why Internet firms began investing so heavily in advertising before turning to sales promotions as a way of attracting visitors. In coordinating online with offline media, the chief marketing officer of a high-tech promotions shop observes, "Online promotions used to be ugly stepchildren. But brands are now starting to use the Web smartly. They're combining the media and no longer treating online and offline separately."[55]

Conclusions from Research. The synergy theme prominent in the preceding discussion is not just a matter of speculation. Research using single-source data generated by ACNielsen reaffirms many of the primary points of this chapter.[56] The major conclusions of this research are the following:

- The short-term productivity of promotions working alone is much more dramatic than that of advertising. Promotions that involve price incentives on average yield a 1.8 percent increase in sales for each 1 percent price reduction. A 1 percent increase in advertising yields just a 0.2 percent sales increase on average.
- The average cost of a 1 percent reduction in price is always far greater than the cost of a 1 percent increase in advertising. Thus, more often than not, sales promotions featuring price incentives are actually unprofitable in the short term.
- It is rare that a sales promotion generates a long-term effect. Hence, there are no long-term revenues to offset the high cost of promotions in the short run. Successful advertising is much more likely to yield a profitable return over the long run, even though its impact on short-run sales may be modest.
- While both advertising and sales promotions may be expected to affect sales in the short run, the evidence suggests that the most powerful effects come from a combination of the two. The impact of advertising and promotions working together is dramatically greater than the sum of each sales stimulus working by itself.

55. "Internet Invasion," op. cit.
56. John Philip Jones, *When Ads Work* (New York: Lexington Books, 1995).

According to the researchers, "The strong synergy that can be generated between advertising and promotions working together points very clearly to the need to integrate the planning and execution of both types of activity: the strategy of Integrated Marketing Communications."[57]

57. Ibid., 56.

SUMMARY

Explain the importance and growth of different types of sales promotion.

Sales promotions use diverse incentives to motivate action on the part of consumers, members of the trade channel, and business buyers. They serve different purposes than does mass media advertising, and for some companies, receive substantially more funding. The growing reliance on these promotions can be attributed to the heavy pressures placed on marketing managers to account for their spending and meet sales objectives in short time frames. Deal-prone shoppers, brand proliferation, the increasing power of large retailers, and media clutter have also contributed to the rising popularity of sales promotion.

Describe the main sales promotion techniques used in the consumer market.

Sales promotions directed at consumers can serve various goals. For example, they can be employed as means to stimulate trial, repeat, or large-quantity purchases. They are especially important tools for introducing new brands or for reacting to a competitor's advances. Coupons, price-off deals, phone and gift cards, and premiums provide obvious incentives for purchase. Contests, sweepstakes, and brand placements can be excellent devices for stimulating brand interest. A variety of sampling techniques are available to get a product into the hands of the target audience. Rebates and frequency programs provide rewards for repeat purchase.

Describe the main sales promotion techniques used in the trade and business markets.

Sales promotions directed at the trade can also serve multiple objectives. They are a necessity in obtaining initial distribution of a new brand. For established brands, they can be a means to increase distributors' order quantities or obtain retailers' cooperation in implementing a consumer-directed promotion. P-O-P displays can be an excellent tool for gaining preferred display space in a retail setting. Incentives and allowances can be offered to distributors to motivate support for a brand. Sales training programs and cooperative advertising programs are additional devices for effecting retailer support.

In the business market, professional buyers are attracted by various sales promotion techniques. Frequency (continuity) programs are very valuable in the travel industry and have spread to business product advertisers. Trade shows are an efficient way to reach a large number of highly targeted business buyers. Gifts to business buyers are a unique form of sales promotion for this market. Finally, premiums, advertising specialties, and trial offers have proven successful in the business market.

Identify the risks to the brand of using sales promotion.

There are important risks associated with heavy reliance on sales promotion. Offering constant deals for a brand is a good way to erode brand equity, and it may simply be borrowing sales from a future time period. Constant deals can also create a customer mindset that leads consumers to abandon a brand as soon as a deal is retracted. Sales promotions are expensive to administer and fraught with legal complications. Sales promotions yield their most positive results when carefully integrated with the overall advertising plan.

Explain the coordination issues for integrated brand promotion associated with using sales promotion.

One of the coordination problems is message coordination. Advertising messages designed to build long-term loyalty may not seem to consumers to be totally consistent with the extra-value message of the sales promotion. This is the classic problem that marketers face in coordinating sales promotion with an advertising campaign. First, advertising messages promote brand features or emotional attractions. Then, the next contact a consumer may have with the brand is an insert in the Sunday paper that touts a price reduction or contest.

Another key in coordination involves media coordination. The success of a sales promotion depends on the consumer believing that the chance to save money or receive extra quantity of a product represents enhanced value. If the consumer is not aware of a brand and its features and benefits, and does not perceive the brand as a worthy item, then there will be no basis for perceiving value—discounted or not. This means that appropriate advertising should precede price-oriented sales promotions for them to be effective.

KEY TERMS

sales promotion
consumer-market sales promotion
trade-market sales promotion
business buyer sales promotion
coupon
price-off deal
premiums
free premium
self-liquidating premium
advertising specialties
contest
sweepstakes
sampling
in-store sampling
door-to-door sampling
mail sampling
newspaper sampling
on-package sampling
mobile sampling
trial offers
brand placement
rebate
frequency programs
push strategy
push money
merchandise allowances
slotting fees
bill-back allowances
off-invoice allowance
cooperative advertising
trade shows

QUESTIONS

1. Compare and contrast sales promotion and mass media advertising as promotional tools. In what ways do the strengths of one make up for the limitations of the other? What specific characteristics of sales promotions account for the high levels of expenditures that have been allocated to them in recent years?

2. What is brand proliferation and why is it occurring? Why do consumer sales promotions become more commonplace in the face of rampant brand proliferation? Why do trade sales promotions become more frequent when there is excessive brand proliferation?

3. Pull all the preprinted and free-standing inserts from the most recent edition of your Sunday newspaper. From them find an example of each of these consumer-market sales promotions: coupon, free premium, self-liquidating premium, contest, sweepstakes, and trial offer.

4. In developing an advertising plan, synergy may be achieved through careful coordination of individual elements. Give an example of how mass media advertising might be used with on-package sampling to effect a positive synergy. Give an example of how event sponsorship might be used with mobile sampling to achieve a positive synergy.

5. Consumers often rationalize their purchase of a new product with a statement such as, "I bought it because I had a 50-cent coupon and our grocery was doubling all manufacturers' coupons this week." What are the prospects that such a consumer will emerge as a loyal user of the product? What must happen if he or she is to become loyal?

6. Early in the chapter, it was suggested that large retailers such as Wal-Mart are assuming greater power in today's marketplace. What factors contribute to retailers' increasing power? Explain the connection between merchandise allowances and slotting fees and the growth in retailer power.

7. In your opinion, are ethical dilemmas more likely to arise with sales promotions directed at the consumer or at the business market? What specific forms of consumer or business promotions seem most likely to involve or create ethical dilemmas?

8. Many marketers argue that consumer sales promotions do not work unless a great deal of time and money are first invested in advertising. What logic might you offer to support this contention? Why would advertising be required to make a sales promotion work?

EXPERIENTIAL EXERCISES

1. This chapter lists over a dozen consumer-market sales promotion techniques. List five promotion techniques that you have participated in during the past year. For each, explain what prompted you to participate in the promotion, and explain what real benefits you gained as a result. Based on the objectives for consumer-market sales promotion listed in the chapter, explain what specific objective you believe the advertiser was trying to achieve with the specific promotions you listed. Do you think these promotions had short-term or long-term benefits to the advertiser?

2. Browse the following links and identify the different kinds of sales promotion techniques. Describe how they function online and explain how they compare to their offline counterparts. Do you think all products and brands can benefit from Internet-based sales promotions? Why? Are most of these sites targeted to trade and business buyers, or consumers? Try to find one example of an online sales promotion directed at trade and business buyers and explain what it offers.

http://www.sweepstakes.com

http://www.ebates.com

http://www.callingcards.com

http://www.myfree.com

http://www.coolsavings.com

USING THE INTERNET

18-1 The Wonderful World of Disney

Integrated brand promotion involves a strategic coordination of multiple communication tools to promote products and services. Instead of viewing advertising, public relations, sales promotions, and other marketing functions as separate, the IBP approach aims to streamline them together to execute campaigns with a clear, consistent, and persuasive tone. Megacorporations such as Disney use the IBP approach for the promotion of their brands on a global level.

Disney.com: http://www.disney.com

Disney Store Affiliates:
http://www.disneystoreaffiliates.com

Disney Store: http://www.disneystore.com

1. From the disney.com home page, list features of the site that suggest that integrated brand promotion is an important concept in Disney's advertising and marketing efforts.

2. List a consumer-market sales promotion technique that you see on the disney.com home page. Explain the strengths of that promotion technique and describe how visitors participate in the promotion via the Internet.

3. What is the purpose of the Disney Store Affiliates program, and how does it work? What is a push strategy, and how does it relate to the Disney Store Affiliates program?

18-2 Sales Promotion Agencies

Marketing services companies such as Marketing Drive Worldwide develop marketing programs that attempt to establish emotional bonds between consumers and world-famous brands. The firm's creative and promotional-mix services drive product differentiation and educate consumers about the value of a brand. Marketing Drive's campaigns cross borders and cultures to reinforce a successful brand promotion on all levels.

Marketing Drive Worldwide:
http://www.marketingdrive.com

Marketing Drive Worldwide Services Group:
http://www.marketingdrive.com/servicesgroup

1. List some of Marketing Drive Worldwide's clients.

2. What is the Marketing Drive Worldwide Services Group, and what specific sales promotion services are offered? What are some risks to the brand that are associated with using sales promotion?

3. Click around the Services Group section to find examples of case studies that explain how these promotions helped clients develop their brands. Why is message and media coordination essential in an IBP campaign?

CHAPTER 17
Support Media, P-O-P Advertising, and Event Sponsorship

CHAPTER 18
Sales Promotion

CHAPTER 19
Direct Marketing

CHAPTER 20
Public Relations and Corporate Advertising

CHAPTER 19

After reading and thinking about this chapter, you will be able to do the following:

Identify the three primary purposes served by direct marketing and explain its growing popularity.

Distinguish a mailing list from a marketing database and review the many applications of each.

Describe the prominent media used by direct marketers in delivering their messages to the customer.

Articulate the added challenge created by direct marketing for achieving integrated brand promotion.

UNSOLICITED EMAIL SUCKS

MONEY FROM YOUR BOTTOM LINE.

Try YesMail™ instead—where the future of direct marketing is reaching people who have already said "Yes."

Permission email is a marketing concept so powerful it will forever change the way you think of direct response marketing. And yesmail.com™ has developed the most advanced permission email marketing capabilities in the industry... providing you with a total online direct marketing solution from customer acquisition to retention and ongoing relationship management. How?

yesmail.com offers you access to a growing network of over 12 million consumers and business professionals, who have said "yes" to receiving promotional email in their areas of interest. By applying proprietary technology, yesmail.com's experienced direct marketing professionals help you reach those who have said "yes." The result is response rates that are substantially higher than traditional direct mail or banner advertising. To learn more about how you can maximize your marketing dollars, call or visit our Web site at **www.yesmail.com** today!

1-877-YESMAIL
www.yesmail.com

a cmgi company

Check your wallet and see if you agree with John Hashman, CEO of NextCard Inc. According to Mr. Hashman, "Very few people . . . need another credit card."[1] Indeed, with about three billion credit card solicitations being stuffed into people's mailboxes every year ("You've Been Pre-Approved!"), how could anyone need another credit card?

As a veteran of the credit card business, John Hashman was well aware of the facts. But in 1997 he helped launch NextCard Inc. as an Internet-only credit card issuer. And after the dot-com meltdown of the late 1990s, Mr. Hashman's e-business was one of the few left standing. How has NextCard survived in the saturated business of extending credit? The answer: direct marketing, with an Internet twist. By making a simple comparison between NextCard and the usual suspects in the credit industry, we can get an immediate appreciation for the old and the new methods of direct marketing.

Traditional credit card issuers such as Capital One and Providian Financial Corporation have built massive businesses using a primary tool of the direct marketer–direct mail. Their business model is based upon wave after wave of direct mail offers. In each wave, different tactical elements are manipulated to encourage consumers to open the envelope and submit an application. Type size, colors, logo placement, and wording are some of the factors that are tinkered with over time in an effort to find those features that will improve response. But there are limits to creativity in a direct mail piece, and for that matter, everything doable has been tried over and over again. No surprise that direct mail response rates across the industry have been on the decline.[2]

In a lot of ways, NextCard's business model parallels that of its old-style competition, but the Web enables many more possibilities. NextCard has about 100 different banner ads at work on the Web at any moment, drawing from its repertoire of more than 2,000 designs. In any given month its ads appear roughly three billion different times across about 200 different Web sites. In a single year it will conduct on the order of 200,000 tests where it can gauge, in as little as two weeks, what combinations of design elements and Web positionings are most likely to provoke a "click-through," and ultimately an online credit card application. NextCard's Web-enabled direct marketing approach also allows precise assessment of how much business is generated per advertising dollar spent. As expressed by one industry analyst, NextCard has taken direct marketing to a level that makes even the best direct mail campaigns "look like the Flintstones chiseling an offer out of stone tablets."[3] But whether low-tech or high-tech, direct marketing methods are all about generating positive and quantifiable results. This results-oriented mindset drives business success, and so it naturally follows that marketers in all types of organizations are allocating larger chunks of their budgets to direct marketing activities.

1 **The Evolution of Direct Marketing.** In this chapter we will examine the growing field of direct marketing and explain how it may be used to both complement and supplant other forms of advertising. Carefully coordinated advertising campaigns and direct marketing programs produce the synergy that spells the difference between success and failure in the marketplace. Before we examine the evolution of direct marketing and look at the many reasons for its growing popularity, we need a better appreciation for what people mean when they use the term *direct marketing*. The "official" definition of *direct marketing* from the Direct Marketing Association (DMA) provides a starting point:

1. Paul Beckett, "Dot-Com Rarity: NextCard Finds Online Ads Work," *Wall Street Journal*, January 29, 2001, B1, B4.
2. Ibid.
3. Ibid.

Direct marketing *is an interactive system of marketing which uses one or more advertising media to effect a measurable response and/or transaction at any location.*[4]

When examined piece by piece, this definition furnishes an excellent basis for understanding the scope of direct marketing.[5]

Direct marketing is interactive in that the marketer is attempting to develop an ongoing dialogue with the customer. Direct marketing programs are commonly planned with the notion that one contact will lead to another and then another, so that the marketer's message can become more focused and refined with each interaction. The DMA's definition also notes that multiple media can be used in direct marketing programs. This is an important point for two reasons. First, we do not want to equate direct mail and direct marketing. Any media can be used in executing direct marketing programs, not just the mail. Second, as we have noted before, a combination of media is likely to be more effective than any one medium used by itself.

Another key aspect of direct marketing programs is that they almost always are designed to produce some form of immediate, measurable response.[6] In the NextCard example, that immediate response would come in the form of an online credit card application. Direct marketing programs may also be designed to produce an immediate sale. The customer might be asked to return an order form with check or money order for $189 to get a stylish Klaus Kobec Couture Sports Watch, or to call an 800 number with credit card handy to get 22 timeless hits on a CD called *The Very Best of Tony Bennett.* Because of this emphasis on immediate response, direct marketers are always in a position to judge the effectiveness of a particular program. As we shall see, this ability to gauge the immediate impact of a program has great appeal to marketers.

The final phrase of the DMA's definition notes that a direct marketing transaction can take place anywhere. The key idea here is that customers do not have to make a trip to a retail store for a direct marketing program to work. Follow-ups can be made by mail, over the telephone, or on the Internet. At one point in time the thinking was that Web-based direct marketers such as Amazon.com, pets.com, and eToys.com could ultimately provide so much convenience for shoppers that traditional retail stores might fall by the wayside.[7] Not! It now seems clear that consumers like the option of contacting companies in many ways. So smart retailers like Best Buy (Exhibit 19.1) and Coldwater Creek (Exhibit 19.2) make themselves available in both the physical and virtual worlds.[8] Customers are then free to choose where and how they want to shop.

Direct Marketing—A Look Back. From Johannes Gutenberg and Benjamin Franklin to Richard Sears, Alvah Roebuck, and Lillian Vernon, the evolution of direct marketing has involved some of the great pioneers in business. As Exhibit 19.3 shows, the practice of direct marketing today is shaped by the successes of many notable mail-order companies and catalog merchandisers.[9] Among these, none is more exemplary than L. L. Bean. Bean founded his company in 1912 on his integrity and $400. His first product was a unique hunting shoe made from a leather top and rubber bottom sewn together. Other outdoor clothing and equipment soon followed in the Bean catalog.

4. Bob Stone, *Successful Direct Marketing Methods* (Lincolnwood, Ill.: NTC Business Books, 1994), 5.
5. The discussion to follow builds on that of Stone, *Successful Direct Marketing Methods,* op. cit.
6. Don E. Schultz and Paul Wang, "Real World Results," *Marketing Tools,* April/May 1994, 40–47.
7. Patrick M. Reilly, "In the Age of the Web, a Book Chain Flounders," *Wall Street Journal,* February 22, 1999, B1, B4.
8. Allanna Sullivan, "From a Call to a Click," *Wall Street Journal,* July 17, 2000, R30.
9. See Edward Nash, "The Roots of Direct Marketing," *Direct Marketing Magazine,* February 1995, 38–40; Cara Beardi, "Lillian Vernon Sets Sights on Second Half-Century," *Advertising Age,* March 19, 2001, 22.

EXHIBIT 19.1

Among other things, pure-play Internet retailers came to realize that when shoppers are dissatisfied with their purchases, many want a physical store where they can return the merchandise for a refund or a trade. In this ad BestBuy.com has some fun with this issue in the context of online CD shopping. At Best Buy, if Folksongs from Rumania *is not what you thought it would be, you can always return it to one of their retail stores.* www.bestbuy.com

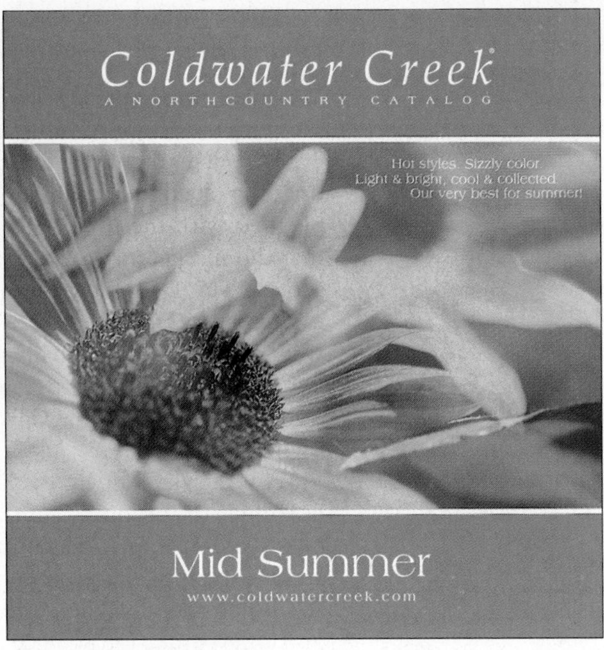

EXHIBIT 19.2

Sophisticated retailers like Coldwater Creek let customers decide when and how they want to shop, whether it be by catalog, online at www.coldwatercreek.com/, *or in one of their conventional retail stores.*

A look at the L. L. Bean catalog of 1917 (black and white, just 12 pages) reveals the fundamental strategy underlying Bean's success. It featured the Maine Hunting Shoe and other outdoor clothing with descriptive copy that was informative, factual, and low-key. On the front page was Bean's commitment to quality. It read: "Maine Hunting Shoe—guarantee. We guarantee this pair of shoes to give perfect satisfaction in every way. If the rubber breaks or the tops grow hard, return them together with this guarantee tag and we will replace them, free of charge. Signed, L. L. Bean."[10] Bean realized that long-term relationships with customers must be based on trust, and his guarantee policy was aimed at developing and sustaining that trust.

As an astute direct marketer, Bean also showed a keen appreciation for the importance of building a good mailing list. For many years he used his profits to promote his free catalog via advertisements in hunting and fishing magazines. Those replying to the ads received a rapid response and typically became Bean customers. Bean's obsession with building mailing lists is nicely captured by this quote from his friend, Maine native John Gould: "If you drop in just to shake his hand, you get home to find his catalog in your mailbox."[11]

10. Allison Cosmedy, *A History of Direct Marketing* (New York: Direct Marketing Association, 1992), 6.
11. Ibid.

EXHIBIT 19.3

Direct-marketing milestones.

c. 1450	Johannes Gutenberg invents movable type.
1667	The first gardening catalog is published by William Lucas, an English gardener.
1744	Benjamin Franklin publishes a catalog of books on science and industry and formulates the basic mail-order concept of customer satisfaction guaranteed.
1830s	A few mail-order companies began operating in New England, selling camping and fishing supplies.
1863	The introduction of penny postage facilitates direct mail.
1867	The invention of the typewriter gives a modern appearance to direct-mail materials.
1872	Montgomery Ward publishes his first "catalog," selling 163 items on a single sheet of paper. By 1884 his catalog grows to 240 pages, with thousands of items and a money-back guarantee.
1886	Richard Sears enters the mail-order business by selling gold watches and makes $5,000 in his first six months. He partners with Alvah Roebuck in 1887, and by 1893 they are marketing a wide range of merchandise in a 196-page catalog.
1912	L. L. Bean founds one of today's most admired mail-order companies on the strength of his Maine Hunting Shoe and a guarantee of total satisfaction for the life of the shoe.
1917	The Direct Mail Advertising Association is founded. In 1973 it becomes the Direct Mail/Direct Marketing Association.
1928	Third-class bulk mail becomes a reality, offering economies for the direct-mail industry.
1950	Credit cards first appear, led by the Diners' Club travel and entertainment card. American Express enters in 1958.
1951	Lillian Vernon places an ad for a monogrammed purse and belt and generates $16,000 in immediate business. She reinvests the money in what becomes the Lillian Vernon enterprise. Vernon recognizes early on that catalog shopping has great appeal to time-pressed consumers.
1953	Publishers Clearing House is founded and soon becomes a dominant force in magazine subscriptions.
1955	Columbia Record Club is established, and eventually becomes Columbia House—the music-marketing giant.
1967	The term *telemarketing* first appears in print, and AT&T introduces the first toll-free 800 service.
1983	The Direct Mail/Direct Marketing Association drops Direct Mail from its name to become the DMA, as a reflection of the multiple media being used by direct marketers.
1984	Apple introduces the Macintosh personal computer.
1992	The number of people who shop at home surpasses 100 million in the United States.
1998	The Direct Marketing Association, www.the-dma.org, eager to adapt its members' bulk mailing techniques for the Internet, announces it will merge with the Association for Interactive Media, www.interactivehq.org.

Sources: Adapted from the DMA's "Grassroots Advocacy Guide for Direct Marketers" (1993). Reprinted with permission of the Direct Marketing Association, Inc.; Rebecca Quick, "Direct Marketing Association to Merge with Association of Interactive Media," *Wall Street Journal,* October 12, 1998, B6.

By 1967 Bean sales approached $5 million, and by 1990 they had exploded to $600 million, as the product line was expanded to include more apparel and recreation equipment. Today, L. L. Bean is still a family-operated business that emphasizes the basic philosophies of its founder, which are carefully summarized at the company's Web site at www.llbean.com. Quality products, understated advertising, and sophisticated customer-contact and distribution systems still drive the business. Additionally, L. L.'s 100-percent-satisfaction guarantee can still be found in every Bean catalog, and it remains at the heart of the relationship between Bean and its customers.

Direct Marketing Today. Direct marketing today is rooted in the legacy of mail-order giants and catalog merchandisers such as L. L. Bean, Lillian Vernon, Publishers Clearing House, and JCPenney. Today, however, direct marketing has broken free from its mail-order heritage to become a tool used by all types of organizations throughout the world. Although many types of businesses and not-for-profit organizations are using direct marketing, it is common to find that such direct-marketing programs are not carefully integrated with an organization's other advertising efforts. Integration should be the goal for advertising and direct marketing; impressive evidence supports the thesis that integrated programs are more effective than the sum of their parts.[12]

Because many different types of activities are now encompassed by the label *direct marketing,* it is important to remember the defining characteristics spelled out in the DMA definition given earlier. Direct marketing involves an attempt to interact or create a dialogue with the customer; multiple media are often employed in the process, and direct marketing is characterized by the fact that a measurable response is immediately available for assessing a program's impact. With these defining features in mind, we can see that direct marketing programs are commonly used for three primary purposes.

As you might imagine, the most common use of direct marketing is as a tool to close a sale with a customer. This can be done as a stand-alone program, or it can be carefully coordinated with a firm's other advertising. Telecommunications companies such as AT&T, MCI WorldCom, Sprint, and Verizon make extensive use of the advertising/direct marketing combination. High-profile mass media ad campaigns build awareness for their latest offer, followed by systematic direct marketing follow-ups to close the sale.

A second purpose for direct marketing programs is to identify prospects for future contacts and, at the same time, provide in-depth information to selected customers. Any time you respond to an offer for more information or for a free sample, you've identified yourself as a prospect and can expect follow-up sales pitches from a direct marketer. The StairMaster ad in Exhibit 19.4 is a marketer's attempt to initiate a dialogue with prospective customers. Ordering the free catalog and video, whether through the 800 number or at the Web site, begins the process of interactive marketing designed to ultimately produce the sale of another FreeClimber 4600.

Direct marketing programs are also initiated as a means to engage customers, seek their advice, furnish helpful information about using a product, reward customers for using a brand, and in general foster brand loyalty. For instance, the manufacturer of Valvoline motor oil seeks to build loyalty for its brand by encouraging young car owners to join the Valvoline Performance Team.[13] To join the team, young drivers just fill out a questionnaire that enters them into the Valvoline database. Team members receive posters, special offers on racing-team apparel, news about racing events that Valvoline has sponsored, and promotional reminders at regular intervals that reinforce the virtues of Valvoline for the driver's next oil change.

12. Ernan Roman, *Integrated Direct Marketing* (Lincolnwood, Ill.: NTC Business Books, 1995).
13. Nash, "The Roots of Direct Marketing," op. cit.

EXHIBIT 19.4

Most people are not going to buy a major piece of exercise equipment based on this or any other magazine ad. That's not the intent of this ad. The purchase process could start here, however, with the simple act of ordering that free video either through the 800 number or at www.stairmaster.com.

What's Driving the Growing Popularity of Direct Marketing? The growth in popularity of direct marketing is due to a number of factors. Some of these have to do with changes in consumer lifestyles and technological developments that in effect create a climate more conducive to the practice of direct marketing. In addition, direct marketing programs offer unique advantages vis-à-vis conventional mass media advertising, leading many organizations to shift more of their marketing budgets to direct marketing activities.

From the consumer's standpoint, direct marketing's growing popularity might be summarized in a single word—*convenience*. Dramatic growth in the number of dual-income and single-person households has reduced the time people have to visit retail stores. Direct marketers provide consumers access to a growing range of products and services in their homes, thus saving many households' most precious resource—time.

More liberal attitudes about the use of credit and the accumulation of debt have also contributed to the growth of direct marketing. Credit cards are the primary means of payment in most direct marketing transactions. The widespread availability of credit cards makes it ever more convenient to shop from the comfort of one's home.

Developments in telecommunications have also facilitated the direct marketing transaction. After getting off to a slow start in the late sixties, toll-free 800 numbers have exploded in popularity to the point where one can hardly find a product or a catalog that does not include an 800 number for interacting with the manufacturer. Whether one is requesting that StairMaster video, ordering a twill polo shirt from Eddie Bauer, or inquiring about the free bottle of Nasonex per Exhibit 19.5, the preferred mode of access for most consumers has been the 800 number.

Another technological development having a huge impact on the growth of direct marketing is the computer. Did you know that your parents' new Buick has more computer power than the Apollo spacecraft that took astronauts to the moon? The incredible diffusion of computer technology sweeping through all modern societies has been a tremendous boon to direct marketers. The computer now allows firms to track, keep records on, and interact with something like five million customers for what it cost to track a single customer in 1950.[14] As we will see in an upcoming discussion, the computer power now available for modest dollar amounts is fueling the growth of direct marketing's most potent tool—the marketing database.

And just as the computer has provided marketers with the tool they need to handle massive databases of customer information (see also the E-Commerce box on page 677), it too has provided convenience-oriented consumers with the tool they need to comparison shop with the point and click of a mouse. What could be more convenient than logging on to the Internet and pulling up a shopping agent like www.pricescan.com or www.mysimon.com to check prices on everything from toaster ovens to snowboards? If you haven't yet taken the plunge, check out a few

14. Don Peppers and Martha Rogers, "The End of Mass Marketing," *Marketing Tools*, March/April 1995, 42–51.

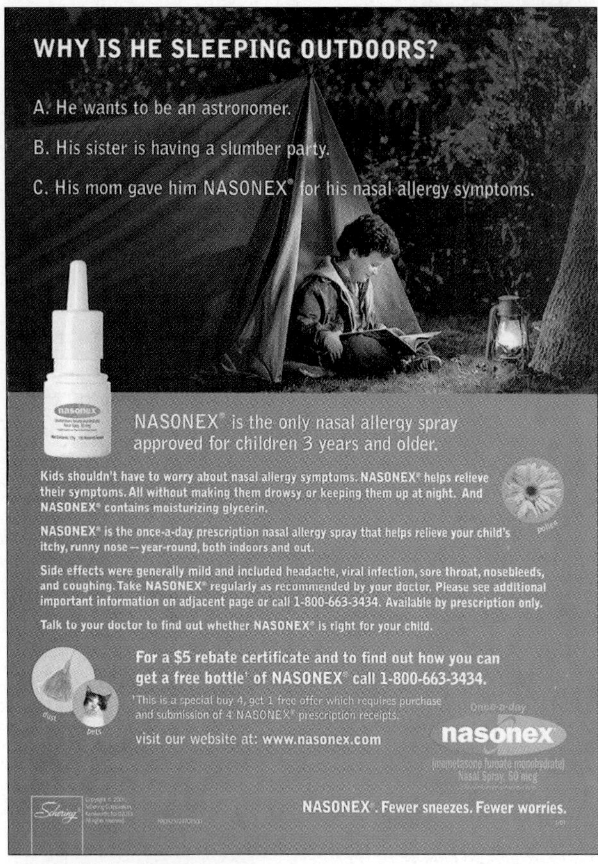

EXHIBIT 19.5

Another way interactive marketing can begin is with a request for more information about a special offer. In this case a $5 rebate offer is the enticement to initiate a dialogue with Nasonex. www.nasonex.com

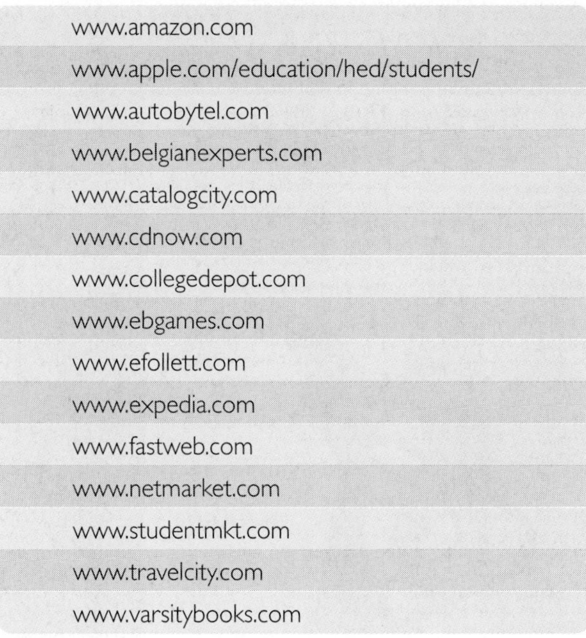

www.amazon.com
www.apple.com/education/hed/students/
www.autobytel.com
www.belgianexperts.com
www.catalogcity.com
www.cdnow.com
www.collegedepot.com
www.ebgames.com
www.efollett.com
www.expedia.com
www.fastweb.com
www.netmarket.com
www.studentmkt.com
www.travelcity.com
www.varsitybooks.com

EXHIBIT 19.6

Fifteen diverse shopping destinations on the Internet.

of the sites listed in Exhibit 19.6, and draw your own conclusions about the future of online shopping.

Direct marketing programs also offer some unique advantages that make them appealing compared with what might be described as conventional mass marketing. A general manager of marketing communications with AT&T's consumer services unit put it this way: "We want to segment our market more; we want to learn more about individual customers; we want to really serve our customers by giving them very specific products and services. Direct marketing is probably the most effective way in which we can reach customers and establish a relationship with them."[15] As you might expect, AT&T is one of those organizations that has shifted more and more of its marketing dollars into direct-marketing programs.

The appeal of direct marketing is enhanced further by the persistent emphasis on producing measurable effects. For instance, in direct marketing, it is common to find calculations such as **cost per inquiry (CPI)** or **cost per order (CPO)** being featured in program evaluation.[16] These calculations simply divide the number of responses to a program by that program's cost. When calculated for every program an organization conducts over time, CPI and CPO data quickly help an organization appreciate what works and what doesn't work in its competitive arena.

15. Gary Levin, "AT&T Exec: Customer Access Goal of Integration," *Advertising Age,* October 10, 1994, S1.
16. Stone, *Successful Direct Marketing Methods,* 620.

This emphasis on producing and monitoring measurable effects is realized most completely through an approach called *database marketing*. Working with a database, direct marketers can target specific customers, track their actual purchase behavior over time, and experiment with different programs for affecting the purchasing patterns of these customers.[17] Obviously, those programs that produce the best outcomes become the candidates for increased funding in the future. Let's look into database marketing.

2 Database Marketing.

If any ambiguity remains about what makes direct marketing different from marketing in general, that ambiguity can be erased by the database. The one characteristic of direct marketing that distinguishes it from marketing more generally is its emphasis on database development.[18] Knowing who the best customers are along with what and how often they buy is a direct marketer's secret weapon. This knowledge accumulates in the form of a marketing database.

Databases used as the centerpieces in direct marketing campaigns take many forms and can contain many different layers of information about customers. At one extreme is the simple mailing list that contains nothing more than the names and addresses of possible customers; at the other extreme is the customized marketing database that augments names and addresses with various additional information about customers' characteristics, past purchases, and product preferences. Understanding this distinction between mailing lists and marketing databases is important in appreciating the scope of database marketing.

Mailing Lists.

A **mailing list** is simply a file of names and addresses that an organization might use for contacting prospective or prior customers. Mailing lists are plentiful, easy to access, and inexpensive.[19] For example, CD-ROM phone directories available for less than $200 provide a cheap and easy way to generate mailing lists.[20] More-targeted mailing lists are available from a variety of suppliers. These suppliers offer lists such as the 107,521 active members of the Association of Catholic Senior Citizens; the 174,600 Kuppenheimer

E-COMMERCE

It Takes a Warehouse . . .

Data warehousing refers to the use of huge databases filled with information about consumers and their shopping habits as a means to create marketing promotions and programs. How huge is huge, you ask. Well, Wal-Mart has a whopper. Wal-Mart uses NCR equipment to house the 100 terabytes of data that it has collected on shoppers thus far. That's 100 trillion bytes, which translates into about 16,000 bytes of data for every one of the world's six billion people. However, because Wal-Mart does most of its business in North America, most of these bytes are about shoppers in North America. The insights Wal-Mart executives glean from this massive data file help them decide what products to stock and where and how to shelve them. Store signage and the Wal-Mart in-store radio network are also programmed to take advantage of what is learned from the data warehouse. Since on the order of 100 million customers visit a Wal-Mart every week, and Wal-Mart knows a ton about these customers, it makes perfect sense for Wal-Mart to use its stores as its primary advertising medium.

By comparison, Fingerhut, a mail-order unit of Federated Department Stores, keeps a data warehouse of a mere six terabytes. But that's enough bytes to keep 30 analysts employed full-time just trying to ascertain key insights about shoppers from these data. Fingerhut mails on average 100 catalogs per year to each name in its customer file of six million people, so judging when and to whom to mail is something they have turned into a data-based science. What's next on Fingerhut's list of database applications? The direct marketer's new favorite tool: targeted e-mail.

So does it follow that he or she with the most data wins? Judging from Wal-Mart's success, maybe so . . .

Source: Dana Blankenhorn, "Marketers Hone Targeting," *Advertising Age*, June 18, 2001, T16.

17. Schultz and Wang, "Real World Results," op. cit.
18. Stone, *Successful Direct Marketing Methods*, Chapter 2.
19. John Kremer, *The Complete Direct Marketing Sourcebook* (New York: John Wiley & Sons, 1992).
20. Ira Teinowitz, "Let Your Keyboard Do the Walking," *Advertising Age*, February 20, 1995, 22.

male-fashion buyers; the 825,000 subscribers to *Home* magazine; and the 189,000 buyers of products from the Smith & Hawken gardening catalog.[21]

Each time you subscribe to a magazine, order from a catalog, register your automobile, fill out a warranty card, redeem a rebate offer, apply for credit, join a professional society, or log in at a Web site, the information you provided about yourself goes on another mailing list. These lists are freely bought and sold through many means, including over the Internet. Sites such as www.worldata.com and www.edirect.com allow one to buy names and addresses, or e-mail address lists, for as little as 25 cents per record.

Two broad categories of lists should be recognized: the internal, or house list, versus the external, or outside list. **Internal lists** are simply an organization's records of its customers, subscribers, donors, and inquirers. **External lists** are purchased from a list compiler or rented from a list broker. At the most basic level, internal and external lists facilitate the two fundamental activities of the direct marketer: Internal lists are the starting point for developing better relationships with current customers, whereas external lists help an organization cultivate new business.

List Enhancement. Name-and-address files, no matter what their source, are merely the starting point for database marketing. The next step in the evolution of a database is mailing-list enhancement. Typically this involves augmenting an internal list by combining it with other, externally supplied lists or databases. External lists can be appended or integrated with a house list.

One of the most straightforward list enhancements entails simply adding or appending more names and addresses to an internal list. Proprietary name-and-address files may be purchased from other companies that operate in noncompetitive businesses.[22] With today's computer capabilities, adding these additional households to an existing mailing list is simple. Many well-known companies such as Sharper Image, American Express, Bloomingdale's, and Hertz sell or rent their customer lists for this purpose.

A second type of list enhancement involves incorporating information from external databases into a house list. Here the number of names and addresses remains the same, but an organization ends up with a more complete description of who its customers are. Typically, this kind of enhancement includes any of four categories of information:

- *Demographic data*—the basic descriptors of individuals and households available from the Census Bureau.
- *Geodemographic data*—information that reveals the characteristics of the neighborhood in which a person resides.
- *Psychographic data*—data that allow for a more qualitative assessment of a customer's general lifestyle, interests, and opinions.
- *Behavioral data*—information about other products and services a customer has purchased; prior purchases can help reveal a customer's preferences.[23]

List enhancements that entail merging existing records with new information rely on software that allows the database manager to match records based on some piece of information the two lists share. For example, matches might be achieved by sorting on zip codes and street addresses.

Many suppliers gather and maintain databases for the sole purpose of list enhancement. Infobase Premier is an enhancement file offered by Infobase Services and is particularly notable for its size and array of available information. Infobase Pre-

21. Kremer, *The Complete Direct Marketing Sourcebook.*
22. Terry G. Vavra, "The Database Marketing Imperative," *Marketing Management,* vol. 2, no. 1 (1993), 47–57.
23. Ibid.

mier contains 170 different pieces of information about 200 million American consumers. Because of its massive size, this database has a high match rate (60 to 80 percent) when it is merged with clients' internal lists.[24] A more common match rate between internal and external lists is 45 to 60 percent. As with most things, list enhancement services are now available on the Web at sites such as www.imarket-inc.com. For its product named MarketPlace Pro, iMarket Inc. promises match rates of 50 to 75 percent.

The Marketing Database. Mailing lists come in all shapes and sizes, and by enhancing internal lists they obviously can become rich sources of information about customers. But for a mailing list to qualify as a marketing database, one important additional type of information is required. Although a marketing database can be viewed as a natural extension of an internal mailing list, a **marketing database** also includes information collected directly from individual customers.[25] Developing a marketing database involves pursuing dialogues with customers and learning about their individual preferences and behavioral patterns. This can be potent information for hatching marketing programs that will hit the mark with consumers (Exhibit 19.7).

Aided by the dramatic escalation in processing power that comes from every new generation of computer chip, marketers see the chance to gather and manage more information about every individual who buys, or could buy, from them. Their goal might be portrayed as an attempt to cultivate a kind of cybernetic intimacy with the customer. A marketing database represents an organization's collective memory, which allows the organization to make the kind of personalized offer that once was characteristic of the corner grocer in small-town America. For example, working in conjunction with the American Occupational Therapy Association (AOTA), L. L. Bean created a backpack promotion it labeled *Gear Up Safely,* including a direct mail piece that was used as part of the promotion. This piece was mailed to health care professionals with school-age children whose L. L. Bean Visa card entitled them to free shipping on all L. L. Bean merchandise. Now that's cybernetic intimacy! Is *your* backpack loaded properly?

While you might find this concept of cybernetic intimacy a bit far-fetched, it certainly is the case that a marketing database can have many valuable applications. Before we look at some of these applications, let's review the terminology introduced thus far. We now have seen that direct marketers use mailing lists, enhanced mailing lists, and/or marketing databases as the starting points for developing many of their programs. The crucial distinction between a mailing list and a marketing database is that the latter includes direct input from customers. Building a marketing database entails pursuing an ongoing dialogue with customers and continuous updating of records with new information. While mailing lists can be rich sources of information for program development, a marketing database has a dynamic quality that

EXHIBIT 19.7

The ability to tailor a specific program or campaign based on how a target market behaves is a distinct advantage of a marketing database. In this exhibit, how do you think Sony and American Express select card members as good targets for this ad?

24. Ibid.
25. Herman Holtz, *Database Marketing* (New York: John Wiley & Sons, 1992).

sets it apart. A marketing database can be an organization's living memory of who its customers are and what they want from the organization.

Marketing Database Applications. Many different types of customer-communication programs are driven by marketing databases. One of the greatest benefits of a database is that it allows an organization to quantify how much business the organization is actually doing with its current best customers. A good way to isolate the best customers is with a recency, frequency, and monetary (RFM) analysis.[26] An **RFM analysis** asks how recently and how often a specific customer is buying from a company, and how much money he or she is spending per order and over time. With this transaction data, it is a simple matter to calculate the value of every customer to the organization and identify customers that have given the organization the most business in the past. Past behavior is an excellent predictor of future behavior, so yesterday's best customers are likely to be any organization's primary source of future business.

RFM analysis allows an organization to spend marketing dollars to achieve maximum return on those dollars. Promotions targeted at best customers will typically pay off with handsome returns. For example, Claridge Hotel & Casino uses its frequent-gambler card—CompCard Gold—to monitor the gambling activities of its 350,000 active members.[27] Promotions such as free slot-machine tokens, monogrammed bathrobes, and door-to-door limo services are targeted to best customers. Such expenditures pay for themselves many times over because they are carefully targeted to people who spend freely when they choose to vacation at Claridge's resort hotels.

A marketing database can also be a powerful tool for organizations that seek to create a genuine relationship with their customers. The makers of Ben & Jerry's ice cream use their database for two things: to find out how customers react to potential new flavors and product ideas, and to involve their customers in social causes.[28] In one program, their goal was to find 100,000 people in their marketing database who would volunteer to work with Ben & Jerry's to support the Children's Defense Fund. Jerry Greenfield, cofounder of Ben & Jerry's, justifies the program as follows: "We are not some nameless conglomerate that only looks at how much money we make every year. I think the opportunity to use our business and particularly the power of our business as a force for progressive social change is exciting."[29] Of course, when customers feel genuine involvement with a brand like Ben & Jerry's, they also turn out to be very loyal customers.

Reinforcing and recognizing preferred customers can be another valuable application of the marketing database. This application may be nothing more than a simple follow-up letter that thanks customers for their business or reminds them of the positive features of the brand to reassure them that they made the right choice. As illustrated in Exhibit 19.8, BMW uses its "branded" magazine as a way to inform owners about all the latest and greatest developments for "The Ultimate Driving Machine."

To recognize and reinforce the behaviors of preferred customers, marketers in many fields are experimenting with frequency-marketing programs that provide concrete rewards to frequent customers. **Frequency-marketing programs** have three basic elements: a *database,* which is the collective memory for the program; *a benefit structure,* which is designed to attract and retain customers; and *a communication strategy,* which emphasizes a regular dialogue with the organization's best customers.[30] As suggested by the Global Issues box on page 682, these loyalty-building programs can be found in all corners of the world.

26. Rob Jackson and Paul Wang, *Strategic Database Marketing* (Lincolnwood, Ill.: NTC Business Books, 1994).
27. Jonathan Berry, "Database Marketing," *Business Week,* September 5, 1994, 56–62.
28. Murray Raphel, "What's the Scoop on Ben & Jerry?" *Direct Marketing Magazine,* August 1994, 23–24.
29. Ibid.
30. Richard Barlow, "Starting a Frequency Marketing Program," *Direct Marketing Magazine,* July 1994, 34.

EXHIBIT 19.8

Building relationships with existing customers is a key application of the marketing database. No company builds a stronger bond with its customers than BMW. www.bmwusa.com

Spectrum Foods, a San Francisco–based company with 15 upscale restaurants in California, has had considerable success with its frequency-marketing program known by diners as Table One.[31] Table One members earn points each time they dine. They can earn $25 award certificates, $250 shopping sprees at Nordstrom, or, for really frequent diners, trips to Italy and Mexico. Spectrum's program also includes free benefits such as valet parking, preferred reservations, and exclusive invitations to wine tastings and special dinners. Spectrum Foods has received a positive response to this program. Table One members dine at Spectrum's restaurants more often, spend more money each time they dine, and recommend the program to their friends—which has helped Spectrum increase its business at twice the industry average.

Another common application for the marketing database is **cross-selling**.[32] Since most organizations today have many different products or services they hope to sell, one of the best ways to build business is to identify customers who already purchase some of a firm's products and create marketing programs aimed at these customers but featuring other products. If they like our ice cream, perhaps we should also encourage them to try our frozen yogurt. If they have a checking account with us, can we interest them in a credit card? If customers dine in our restaurants on Fridays and Saturdays, with the proper incentives perhaps we can get them to dine with us midweek, when we really need the extra business. A marketing database can provide a myriad of opportunities for cross-selling.

A final application for the marketing database is a natural extension of cross-selling. Once an organization gets to know who its current customers are and what they like about various products, it is in a much stronger position to go out and seek new customers. Knowledge about current customers is especially valuable when an organization is considering purchasing external mailing lists to append to its marketing database. If a firm knows the demographic characteristics of current customers—knows what they like about products, knows where they live, and has insights about their lifestyles and general interests—then the selection of external lists will be much more efficient. The basic premise here is simply to try to find prospects who share many of the same characteristics and interests with current customers. And what's the best vehicle for coming to know the current, best customers? Marketing-database development is that vehicle.

The Privacy Concern. One very large dark cloud looms on the horizon for database marketers: consumers' concerns about invasion of privacy. It is easy for marketers to gather a wide variety of information about consumers, and this is making the general public nervous. Many consumers are uneasy about the way their personal information is being gathered and exchanged by businesses and the government without their knowledge, participation, or consent. Of course, the Internet only amplifies these concerns

31. Greg Gattuso, "Restaurants Discover Frequency Marketing," *Direct Marketing Magazine,* February 1995, 35–36.
32. Jackson and Wang, *Strategic Database Marketing.*

because the Web makes it easier for all kinds of people and organizations to get access to personal information.

In response to public opinion, state and federal lawmakers have proposed and sometimes passed legislation to limit businesses' access to personal information. But thus far such legislation has had little impact on the practices of direct marketers.[33] Direct marketers have been effective in blocking or minimizing the effect of regulation by convincing lawmakers that they can police themselves. For example, the Direct Marketing Association has an online service (www.the-dma.org/consumers/offmailinglist.html) that allows individuals to remove their names from mailing lists. However, it is not widely used by consumers, and some question its effectiveness. While people can do something about taking ownership over their personal information in today's world of database and Internet marketing, most don't take the time.

If you're interested, a good place to go to learn more about how to protect the privacy of personal information is www.ftc.gov/privacy/protect.htm. Or if you'd like to really get serious and buy some protection for when you go online, check out the company featured in Exhibit 19.9. Zeroknowledge uses a pretty dramatic emotional trigger in this ad, don't you think?

Companies can address their customers' concerns about privacy if they remember two fundamental premises of database marketing. First, a primary goal for developing a marketing database is to get to know customers in such a way that an organization can offer them products and services that better meet their needs. The whole point of a marketing database is to keep junk mail to a minimum by targeting only exciting and relevant programs to customers. If customers are offered something of value, they will welcome being in the database.

Second, developing a marketing database is about creating meaningful, long-term relationships with customers. If you want someone's trust and loyalty, would you collect personal information from them and then sell it to a third party behind their back? We hope not! When collecting information from customers, an organization must help them understand why it wants the information and how it will use it. If the organization is planning on selling this information to a third party, it must get customers' permission. If the organization pledges that the information will remain confidential, it must honor that pledge. Integrity is fundamental to all meaningful relationships, including those involving direct marketers and their customers. Recall that it was his integrity as much as anything else that enabled L. L. Bean to launch his successful career as a direct marketer. It will work for you too.

GLOBAL ISSUES

Loyalty Programs Know No Boundaries

Loyalty programs such as frequent-flyer plans or credit card points are familiar by now to consumers around the world. But when an economy goes into recession, local marketers must fight even harder to retain their customers. So what does your local video rental store offer as a reward for your repeat business? Discounts? Coupons? Store merchandise? Free popcorn or soda? How about a blood test?

To win the loyalty of its customers, KPS Video of Hong Kong launched its new Elite Card with the usual discounts on future rentals and store merchandise. But in a unique offer made in conjunction with Asian Medical Diagnostic Centers, the card also allowed renters to accumulate points that could be redeemed for blood counts, AIDS tests, cholesterol screenings, and other medical procedures. Was this an act of desperation by a local merchant in tough economic times, or savvy marketing based on keen insight about local market conditions? That's a hard call to make, but we should add that the program was launched in the same year that Hong Kong residents experienced widespread concern and near panic about the so-called bird flu epidemic. Turns out this was a banner year for blood testing in Hong Kong. Olivia Kan, marketing director for KPS Retail Stores, put it this way: "We found that because of the disease epidemic earlier this year in Hong Kong, people are more conscious about this kind of thing."

But will the free blood test have global appeal as an incentive for movie rentals? Well, while we would always defer to the judgment of local marketers such as Olivia Kan, our best advice on this one is, isn't free popcorn a whole lot more fun?

Source: Sarah Tilton, "Asia's Loyalty Card Promotions Multiply in Crisis, and Get Stranger," *Wall Street Journal*, September 1, 1998, B2.

33. Jerry Markon, "Don't-Call Laws Raise False Hopes for Peace, Quiet," *Wall Street Journal*, December 22, 2000, B1, B4.

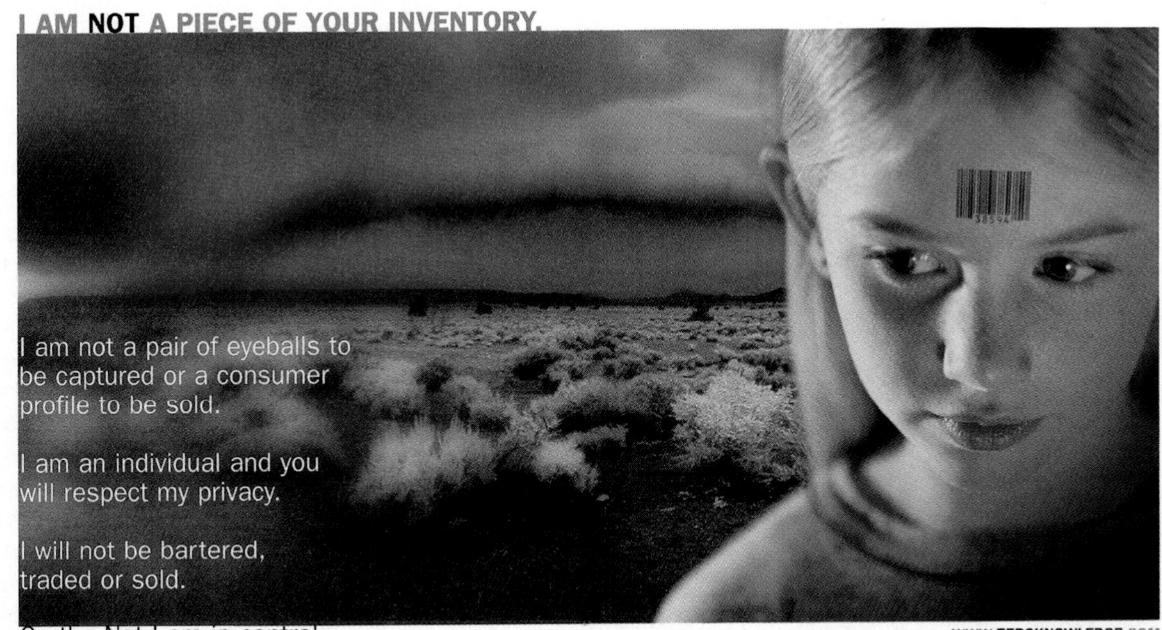

EXHIBIT 19.9

This Orwellian ad paints a dark picture of our future if database marketers go unchecked. There is definitely something about the Internet that has heightened people's concerns about who is in control of their personal information. Who controls your personal information? Does it matter to you? How might the Online Privacy Alliance (www.privacyalliance.org) keep database marketers from going too far with personal information? Are there any reasons to think this organization might not be able to regulate database marketing abuses? www.zeroknowledge.com

3 Media Applications in Direct Marketing.

While mailing lists and marketing databases are the focal point for originating most direct marketing programs, information and arguments need to be communicated to customers in implementing these programs. As we saw in the definition of direct marketing offered earlier in this chapter, multiple media can be deployed in program implementation, and some form of immediate, measurable response is typically an overriding goal. The immediate response desired may be an actual order for services or merchandise, a request for more information, or the acceptance of a free trial offer. Because advertising conducted in direct marketing campaigns is typified by this emphasis on immediate response, it is commonly referred to as **direct response advertising.**

As you probably suspect, **direct mail** and **telemarketing** are the direct marketer's prime media. However, all conventional media, such as magazines, radio, and television, can be used to deliver direct response advertising; nowadays, a wide array of companies are also deploying e-mail as a most economical means of interacting with customers. In addition, a dramatic transformation of the television commercial—the infomercial—has become especially popular in direct marketing. Let's begin our examination of these media options by considering the advantages and disadvantages of the dominant devices—direct mail and telemarketing.

Direct Mail.

Direct mail has some notable faults as an advertising medium, not the least of which is cost. It can cost 15 to 20 times more to reach a person with a direct mail piece than it

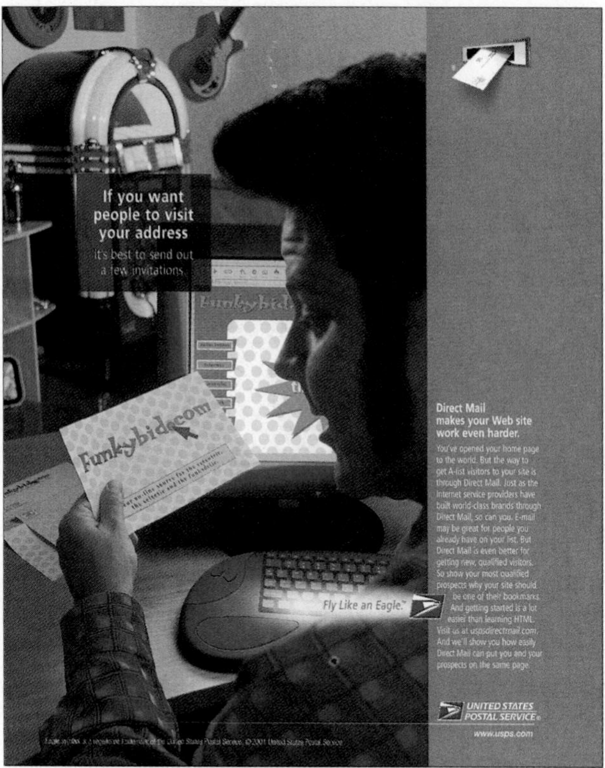

EXHIBIT 19.10

The U.S. postal service is saying, use our services to drive consumers to your Web site. They make a great point: With millions of Web sites out there in cyberspace, you really must find economical ways to help people notice yours. For more help reaching qualified visitors, they suggest you visit www.uspsdirectmail.com. *Imagine that . . .*

would to reach that person with a television commercial or newspaper advertisement.[34] Additionally, in a society where people are constantly on the move, mailing lists are commonly plagued by bad addresses. Each bad address represents advertising dollars wasted. And direct mail delivery dates, especially for bulk, third-class mailings, can be unpredictable. When the timing of an advertising message is critical to its success, direct mail can be the wrong choice.

But as suggested by the ad from the U.S. Postal Service in Exhibit 19.10, there will be times when direct mail is the right choice. Direct mail's advantages stem from the selectivity of the medium. When an advertiser begins with a database of prospects, direct mail can be the perfect vehicle for reaching those prospects with little waste. Also, direct mail is a flexible medium that allows message adaptations on literally a household-by-household basis.[35] For example, through surveys conducted with its 15 million U.S. subscribers, *Reader's Digest* amassed a huge marketing database detailing the health problems of specific subscribers.[36] In the database are 771,000 people with arthritis, 679,000 people with high blood pressure, 206,000 people with osteoporosis, 460,000 smokers, and so on. Using this information, *Reader's Digest* sends its subscribers disease-specific booklets containing advice on coping with their afflictions, wherein it sells advertising space to drug companies that have a tailored message that they want to communicate to those with a particular problem. This kind of precise targeting of tailored messages is the hallmark of direct marketing.

Direct mail as a medium also lends itself to testing and experimentation. For example, with direct mail it is common to test two or more different appeal letters using a modest budget and a small sample of households.[37] The goal is to establish which version effects the largest response. When a winner is decided, that form of the letter is backed by big-budget dollars in launching the organization's primary campaign.

In addition, with direct mail, the array of formats an organization can send to customers is substantial. It can mail large, expensive brochures; videotapes; computer disks; or CDs. It can use pop-ups, foldouts, scratch-and-sniff strips, or just simple postcards. If a product can be described in a limited space with minimal graphics, there really is no need to get fancy with the direct mail piece. The double postcard (DPC) format has an established track record of outperforming more expensive and elaborate direct mail packages.[38] Moreover, if an organization follows U.S. postal service guidelines carefully in mailing DPCs, the pieces can go out as first-class mail for reasonable rates. Since the Postal Service supplies address corrections on all first-class mail, using DPCs usually turns out to be a winner on either CPI or CPO measures, and DPCs can be an effective tool for cleaning up the bad addresses in a mailing list!

34. Stone, *Successful Direct Marketing Methods,* 362.
35. Jack Z. Sissors and Lincoln Bumba, *Advertising Media Planning* (Lincolnwood, Ill.: NTC Business Books, 1994).
36. Sally Beatty, "Drug Companies Are Minding Your Business," *Wall Street Journal,* April 17, 1998, B1, B3.
37. Pamela Sebastian, "Charity Tries Two Letters to Melt Cold Hearts," *Wall Street Journal,* November 22, 1994, B1.
38. Michael Edmondson, "Postcards from the Edge," *Marketing Tools,* May 1995, 14.

Telemarketing. Telemarketing is probably the direct marketer's most invasive tool. As with direct mail, contacts can be selectively targeted, the impact of programs is easy to track, and experimentation with different scripts and delivery formats is simple and practical. Because telemarketing involves real, live, person-to-person dialogue, no medium produces better response rates.[39] Telemarketing shares many of direct mail's limitations. Telemarketing is very expensive on a cost-per-contact basis, and just as names and addresses go bad as people move, so do phone numbers. It is typical in telemarketing programs to find that 15 percent of the numbers called are inaccurate.[40] Further, telemarketing does not share direct mail's flexibility in terms of delivery options. When you reach people in their home or workplace, you have a limited amount of time to convey information and request some form of response.

If you have a telephone, you already know the biggest concern with telemarketing. It is a powerful yet highly intrusive medium that must be used with discretion. High-pressure telephone calls at inconvenient times can alienate customers. Telemarketing gives its best results over the long run if it is used to maintain constructive dialogues with existing customers and qualified prospects.[41]

E-Mail. Perhaps the most controversial tool deployed of late by direct marketers has been unsolicited or "bulk" e-mail. Commonly referred to as spam, this junk e-mail can get you in big trouble with consumers. In a worst-case scenario, careless use of the e-mail tool can earn one's company the label of a "spammer" across the Internet, and because of the community-oriented character of Internet communications, can then be a continuing source of negative publicity. But is this discouraging direct marketers from deploying this tool? Hardly. According to eMarketer, a New York-based market research firm, by 2003, three-quarters of all the e-mail you receive will be unsolicited contacts from direct marketers.[42] As shown in the IBP box on page 686, even marketing giants such as Nike have experimented with targeted e-mail messaging as part of their integrated brand promotion programs.

It is easy to understand why marketers have fallen in love with e-mail. First, it's cheap. A $20,000 "snail-mail" execution will run you about $1,000 using e-mail. In addition, response rates have been superior for e-mail. A good snail-mail campaign may be expected to generate a response of around 2 percent, whereas e-mail marketers have been touting response in the 10 percent range. But look for this difference in response to fall off dramatically as more and more organizations deploy this tactic. Like anything else in marketing and advertising, the more organizations that use the tactic, the less effective it becomes. Donna Hoffman, co-director of the eLab at Vanderbilt University, predicts that "e-mail marketing is going to go the way of banner ads," which of course now are pulling a response rate of less than 0.5 percent.[43]

39. Sissors and Bumba, *Advertising Media Planning.*
40. Ibid.
41. Stone, *Successful Direct Marketing Methods,* Chapter 14.
42. Jodi Mardesich, "Too Much of a Good Thing," *Industry Standard,* March 19, 2001, 84.
43. Ibid.

IBP

Nike Marketers Decide to Do E-Mail

When it comes to using the tools of direct marketing, it would be fair to say that just about everybody has gotten into the game. Take, for example, Nike Inc. Renowned for its high-profile TV ad campaigns featuring the royalty of professional sports, Nike decided to take a more integrated approach in launching Engineered for Women Athletes, a new line of women's-only products. The initial launch included 11 new shoes such as the Air Propensity, a walking shoe, as well as a bevy of basketball shoes endorsed by WNBA stars such as Lisa Leslie and Sheryl Swoopes. Six months later Nike would add 11 more products to its women's-only repertoire, all of which had undergone specific design and engineering to make them anatomically correct for a woman's foot. With so much to explain and so many different products to talk about, Nike marketers decided to rely more heavily on the tools of direct marketing in an integrated launch campaign. As with any IBP campaign, the goal was to get the right message to just the right consumer.

Like any good direct marketer, Nike built its launch campaign around its customer database. Through its established relationships with numerous leagues and sports associations nationwide, its Internet site, and its in-box mail-in program that generates 180,000 response cards monthly, Nike has amassed a customer database of more than 6 million Nike users. About 2.4 million of these are women. Obviously, these 2.4 million previous Nike customers became a focal point in the launch of the Engineered for Women Athletes line. Of course, once you know who your customer are, where they live physically and electronically, and what they've purchased from you in the past, broadcast media such as television are not your best choice for delivering a targeted appeal about a specific new product. Targeted messages in this launch were delivered via postcards, product brochure mailings, and e-mail—more proof that direct marketing tools and tactics may have been conceived initially by the likes of L. L. Bean and Lillian Vernon, but now have been embraced by marketers in most companies large and small.

Source: Theresa Howard, "Nike Set to Run with Two New Product Lines: Postcards, E-Mail Will Help Shoemaker Target Women," *DM News*, July 20, 1998, 1, 58.

There definitely is a school of thought that says some consumers are not averse to receiving targeted e-mail advertisements, and that as the Internet continues to evolve as an increasingly commercial medium, those companies that observe proper etiquette on the Net (dare we say "Netiquette"?) will be rewarded through customer loyalty.[44] The key premise of netiquette is to get the consumer's permission to send information about specific products or services, or using the current buzzword, they must "opt in." This opt-in premise has spawned a number of e-marketing service providers who claim to have constructed e-mail lists of consumers who have "opted in" for all manner of products and services. Exhibits 19.11 and 19.12 show ads from two of the many firms that have quickly emerged to fill this niche. As noted in the ad for YesMail.com, the future of direct marketing may be in reaching those people who have already said "Yes."

Our advice is to stay away from the low-cost temptations of bulk e-mail. The quickest way to get flamed and damage your brand name is to start sending out bulk e-mails to people who do not want to hear from you. Instead, through database development, ask your customers for permission to contact them via e-mail. Honor their requests. Don't abuse the privilege by selling their e-mail addresses to other companies, and when you do contact them, have something important to say. Seth Godin, whose 1999 book *Permission Marketing* really launched the "opt-in" mindset, puts it this way: "The best way to make your (customer) list worthless is to sell it.

44. Kenneth Leung, "Marketing with Electronic Mail without Spam," *Marketing News*, January 19, 1998, 11; Cara Beardi, "Opt-In Taken to Great Heights," *Advertising Age*, November 6, 2000, S54.

EXHIBIT 19.11

Purveyors of permission e-mail have sprung up like mushrooms in the forest after a rain. It is hard to argue with the premise that Unsolicited Email Sucks. Wouldn't you agree? www.yesmail.com

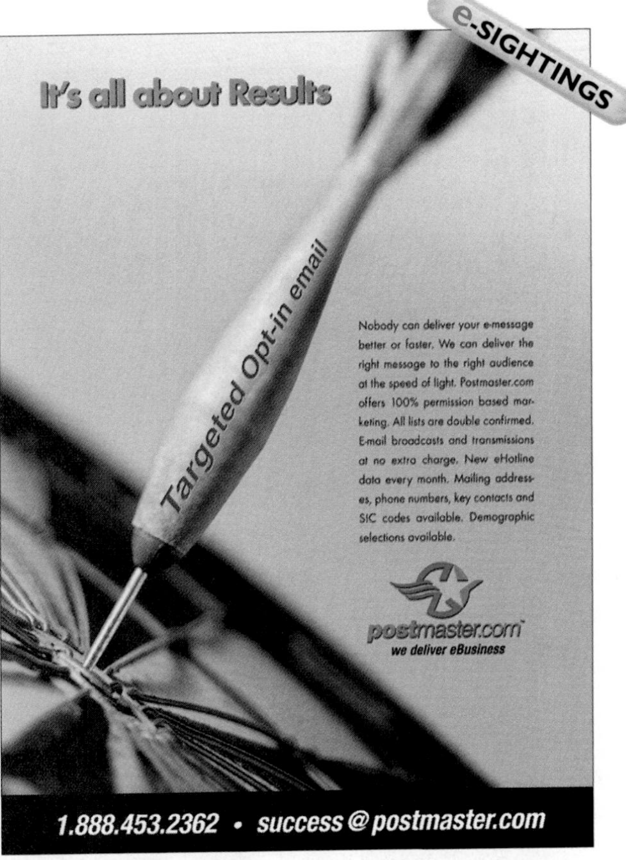

EXHIBIT 19.12

In direct marketing, it is always all about results. Targeted opt-in e-mail is currently all the rage. We'll see how long it lasts. YesMail.com (www.yesmail.com) is the leader in e-mail marketing. Does the site go out of its way to distinguish its services from "spamming"? How do you feel about receiving unsolicited e-mail messages from organizations? Do your feelings differ based on the product or idea being marketed?

The future is, this list is mine and it's a secret."[45] Isn't it funny. . . . You can imagine L. L. Bean feeling exactly the same way about his customer list 90 years ago.

Direct Response Advertising in Other Media. Direct marketers have experimented with many other methods in trying to convey their appeals for a customer response. In magazines, a popular device for executing a direct marketer's agenda is the bind-in insert card.[46] Thumb through a copy of any magazine and you will see how effective these light-cardboard inserts are in stopping the reader and calling attention to themselves. Insert cards not only promote their products but also offer the reader an easy way to order things such as Murray's All-Natural Chicken Dinner Kit from www.epicurious.com, request a free sample of Skoal smokeless tobacco, or select those 12 CDs for the price of one that will make the reader a member of the BMG Music Club.

45. Mardesich, "Too Much of a Good Thing," 85.
46. Stone, *Successful Direct Marketing Methods,* 250–252.

EXHIBIT 19.13

Nothing fancy here. Just good, sound direct marketing. www.oreck.com

When AT&T introduced the first 800 service in 1967, it simply could not have known how important this service would become to direct marketing. Newspaper ads from the *Wall Street Journal* provide toll-free numbers for requesting everything from really cheap online trading services (1-800-619-SAVE) to high-speed color copiers (1-800-OK-CANON). If you watch late-night TV, you may know the 800 number to call to order the Grammy-winning CD by Walter Ostanek and his polka band. IDS Financial Services, a division of American Express, featured its 800 number in radio ads as part of a two-step offer designed to generate prospects for its financial planning business. IDS operators took the caller's name, address, phone number, and age to input into a marketing database, and they offered to book the caller for a consultation. IDS found this radio-based campaign more than twice as profitable as the direct mail campaigns it had used previously.[47] Finally, per Exhibit 19.13, magazine ads like this one out of *Bon Appetit* are commonly used to provide an 800 number to initiate contact with customers. As these diverse examples indicate, toll-free numbers make it possible to use nearly any medium for direct response purposes.

Infomercials. The infomercial is a novel form of direct response advertising that merits special mention. An **infomercial** is fundamentally just a long television advertisement made possible by the lower cost of ad space on many cable and satellite channels. They range in length from 3 to 60 minutes, but the common length is 30 minutes. Although producing an infomercial is more like producing a television program than it is like producing a 30-second commercial, infomercials are all about selling. There appear to be several keys to successful use of this unique vehicle.

A critical factor is testimonials from satisfied users. Celebrity testimonials can help catch a viewer as he or she is channel surfing past the program, but celebrities aren't necessary, and, of course, they add to the production costs. Whether testimonials are from celebrities or from folks just like us, one expert summarizes matters this way: "Testimonials are so important that without them your chances of producing a profitable infomercial diminish hugely."[48]

Another key point to remember about infomercials is that viewers are not likely to stay tuned for the full 30 minutes. An infomercial is a

47. Nancy Coltun Webster, "Radio Tuning In to Direct Response," *Advertising Age,* October 10, 1994, S14–S15.
48. Herschell Gordon Lewis, "Information on Infomercials," *Direct Marketing Magazine,* March 1995, 30–32.

30-minute direct response sales pitch, not a classic episode of *Seinfeld* or *The Simpsons*. The implication here is that the call to action should come not just at the end of the infomercial; most of the audience could be long gone by minute 28 into the show. A good rule of thumb in a 30-minute infomercial is to divide the program into 10-minute increments and close three times.[49] Each closing should feature the 800 number or Web address that allows the viewer to order the product or request more information. And an organization should not offer information to the customer unless it can deliver speedy follow-up; same-day response should be the goal in pursuing leads generated by an infomercial.

Many different types of products and services have been marketed using infomercials, and now via Internet extensions such as www.iqvc.com. CD players, self-help videos, home exercise equipment, kitchen appliances, and Annette Funicello Collectible Bears have all had success with the infomercial. While it is easy to associate the infomercial with things such as the Ronco Showtime Rotisserie & BBQ (yours for just four easy payments of $39.95!), many familiar brands have experimented with this medium. Brand marketers such as Quaker State, America Online, Primestar, Lexus, Monster.com, Hoover, Kal Kan, and yes, Mercedes-Benz, have all used infomercials to help inform consumers about their offerings.[50]

While the infomercial has become a versatile tool, one final point needs to be made about making profitable use of this tool. If the primary goal in running infomercials is order solicitation, it is difficult to generate a profit for any item priced below $40 or $50.[51] The costs to produce and air an infomercial make it almost impossible to generate adequate cash flow from an item that can support a price of, say, only $19.95. If a firm is working with moderately priced items, the solution may be to bundle them together. If the product can justify a price of only $19.95, sell it in sets of three for $49.99, or, better yet, offer two for $49.99 with a third item free for those who call the 800 line immediately. Then, the firm must be prepared: 80 percent of all calls generated by infomercials occur within five minutes of the focal call to action.[52] If callers get a busy signal or are put on hold, many will have second thoughts, and will put their credit cards back in their wallets.

4 The Coordination Challenge Revisited. As you have seen throughout this book, the wide variety of media available to an advertiser poses a tremendous challenge with respect to coordination and integration. Organizations are looking to achieve the synergy that can come when various media options reach the consumer with a common and compelling message. However, to work in various media, functional specialists both inside and outside an organization need to be employed. It then becomes a very real problem to get the advertising manager, special events manager, sales promotion manager, and new-media manager to work in harmony.[53] And now we must add to the list of functional specialists the direct marketing manager.

The evolution and growing popularity of direct marketing raise the challenge of achieving integrated communication to new heights. In particular, the development of a marketing database commonly leads to interdepartmental rivalries and can create major conflicts between a company and its advertising agency. The marketing database is a powerful source of information about the customer; those who do not have direct access to this information will be envious of those who do. Additionally, the growing use of direct marketing campaigns must mean that someone else's

49. Ibid.

50. Kathy Haley, "Infomercials Score for Brand-Name Advertisers," *Advertising Age,* September 8, 1997, A1, A2; Evantheia Schibsted, "Ab Rockers, Ginsu Knives, E320s," *Business 2.0,* May 29, 2001, 46–49.

51. Lewis, "Information on Infomercials," op. cit.

52. Paul Kerstetter, "When Consumers Actually Respond to Infomercial Airings," *Adweek Infomercial Sourcebook,* 1994, 12–15.

53. Laura Q. Hughes and Kate MacArthur, "Soft Boiled," *Advertising Age,* May 28, 2001, 3, 54.

budget is being cut. Typically, direct marketing programs come at the expense of conventional advertising campaigns that might have been run on television, in magazines, or in other mass media.[54] Since direct marketing takes dollars from activities that have been the staples of the traditional ad agency business, it is easy to see why a pure advertising guru like Saatchi's Kevin Roberts views direct marketing with some disdain.[55]

There are no simple solutions for achieving integrated communication, but one recommended approach is the establishment of a marketing communications manager, or marcom manager for short.[56] A **marcom manager** plans an organization's overall communications program and oversees the various functional specialists inside and outside the organization to ensure that they are working together to deliver the desired brand-building message to the customer.

One company that has experimented with this marcom manager system is AT&T. As already mentioned, AT&T, like its telecommunications rivals, makes heavy use of both direct marketing programs and mass media advertising to reach out and touch its customers. George Burnett, the marcom manager for AT&T, explains the value of integrating direct mail and advertising this way: "Honestly, I think it is simplicity and clarity. . . . That is one of the goals of integrated communications, because in this complicated world, adding complication on top of the competitiveness is really not in our customers' interest."[57]

Burnett adds emphasis to a theme we have developed throughout this book. Perhaps the major challenge in the world of advertising today is to find ways to break through the clutter of competitors' ads—and really all advertising in general—to get customers' attention and make a point with them. If the various media and programs an organization employs are sending different messages or mixed signals, the organization is only hurting itself. To achieve the synergy that will allow it to overcome the clutter of today's marketplace, an organization has no choice but to pursue advertising and integrated brand promotion.

54. Kate Fitzgerald, "Beyond Advertising," *Advertising Age,* August 3, 1998, 1, 14.

55. Alessandra Galloni, "Is Saatchi Helping Publicis Bottom Line?" *Wall Street Journal,* June 22, 2001, B6.

56. Don E. Schultz, Stanley I. Tannenbaum, and Robert F. Lauterborn, *Integrated Marketing Communications* (Lincolnwood, Ill.: NTC Business Books, 1993).

57. Levin, "AT&T Exec," op. cit.

SUMMARY

Identify the three primary purposes served by direct marketing and explain its growing popularity.

Many types of organizations are increasing their expenditures on direct marketing. These expenditures serve three primary purposes: direct marketing offers potent tools for closing sales with customers, for identifying prospects for future contacts, and for offering information and incentives that help foster brand loyalty. The growing popularity of direct marketing can be attributed to several factors. Direct marketers make consumption convenient: Credit cards, 800 numbers, and the Internet take the hassle out of shopping. Additionally, today's computing power, which allows marketers to build and mine large customer information files, has enhanced direct marketing's impact. The emphasis on producing and tracking measurable outcomes is also well received by marketers in an era when everyone is trying to do more with less.

Distinguish a mailing list from a marketing database and review the many applications of each.

A mailing list is a file of names and addresses of current or potential customers, such as lists that might be generated by a credit card company or a catalog retailer. Internal lists are valuable for creating relationships with current customers, and external lists are useful in generating new customers. A marketing database is a natural extension of the internal list, but includes information about individual customers and their specific preferences and purchasing patterns. A marketing database allows organizations to identify and focus their efforts on their best customers. Recognizing and reinforcing preferred customers can be a potent strategy for building loyalty. Cross-selling opportunities also emerge once a database is in place. In addition, as one gains keener information about the motivations of current best customers, insights usually emerge about how to attract new customers.

Describe the prominent media used by direct marketers in delivering their messages to the customer.

Direct marketing programs emanate from mailing lists and databases, but there is still a need to deliver a message to the customer. Direct mail and telemarketing are the most common means used in executing direct marketing programs. E-mail has recently emerged as a low-cost alternative. Because the advertising done as part of direct marketing programs typically requests an immediate response from the customer, it is known as direct response advertising. Conventional media such as television, newspapers, magazines, and radio can also be used to request a direct response by offering an 800 number or a Web address to facilitate customer contact.

Articulate the added challenge created by direct marketing for achieving integrated brand promotion.

Developing a marketing database, selecting a direct mail format, or producing an infomercial are some of the tasks attributable to direct marketing. These and other related tasks require more functional specialists, who further complicate the challenge of presenting a coordinated face to the customer. Some organizations employ marcom managers, who are assigned the task of coordinating the efforts of various functional specialists working on different aspects of a marketing communications program. To achieve an integrated presence that will break through in a cluttered marketplace, this coordination is essential.

KEY TERMS

direct marketing
cost per inquiry (CPI)
cost per order (CPO)
mailing list
internal lists
external lists
marketing database
RFM analysis
frequency-marketing programs
cross-selling
direct response advertising
direct mail
telemarketing
infomercial
marcom manager

QUESTIONS

1. Direct marketing is defined as an interactive system of marketing. Explain the meaning of the term *interactive system*. Give an example of a noninteractive system. How would an interactive system be helpful in the cultivation of brand loyalty?

2. Start a collection of the direct mail pieces you receive at your home or apartment. After you have accumulated at least 10 pieces, review the three main purposes for direct marketing discussed in this chapter. For each piece in your collection, what would you surmise is the direct marketer's purpose?

3. Review the major forces that have promoted the growth in popularity of direct marketing. Can you come up with any reasons why its popularity might be peaking? What are the threats to its continuing popularity as a marketing approach?

4. Describe the various categories of information that a credit card company might use to enhance its internal mailing list. For each category, comment on the possible value of the information for improving the company's market segmentation strategy.

5. What is RFM analysis, and what is it generally used for? How would RFM analysis allow an organization to get more impact from a limited marketing budget? (Keep in mind that every organization views its marketing budget as too small to accomplish all that needs to be done.)

6. Compare and contrast frequency-marketing programs with the tools described in Chapter 18 under the heading "Sales Promotion Directed at Consumers." What common motivators do these two types of activities rely on? How are their purposes similar or different? What goal is a frequency-marketing program trying to achieve that would not be a prime concern with a sales promotion?

7. There's a paradox here, right? On the one hand, it is common to talk about building relationships and loyalty with the tools of direct marketing. On the other hand, direct-marketing tools such as junk e-mail and telephone interruptions at home during dinner are constant irritants. How does one build relationships by using irritants? In your opinion, when is it realistic to think that the tools of direct marketing could be used to build long-term relationships with customers?

8. What is it about direct marketing that makes its growing popularity a threat to the traditional advertising agency?

EXPERIENTIAL EXERCISES

1. This chapter discusses serious privacy concerns raised by database marketing. Today's marketers are gathering enormous amounts of information about individuals, and much of the database development occurs without the consent or awareness of consumers. Visit the following sites and explain the contribution of each to the issue of online privacy.

http://www.bbbonline.org

http://www.truste.com

2. Identify some of the recent direct mail and e-mail marketing items you have received. Did they target your relevant hobbies, interests, or work-related needs? If so, how did the marketer know of your specific interests? What previous consumer relationship have you had with these marketers, and do you react favorably to their direct marketing efforts? What convenience do consumers gain from today's direct marketing initiatives, and do you feel more loyalty to specific brands as a result of these efforts?

USING THE INTERNET

19-1 Database Marketing

MyPoints.com is a leading provider of Internet direct marketing services. The company's service features a true "opt-in" database of more than 16 million members, and provides advertisers with an integrated suite of rewards-based media products that target, acquire, and retain customers. Web users can earn free rewards from name-brand merchants such as Blockbuster Video, Barnes & Noble Booksellers, and BMG by regularly visiting Web sites, responding to targeted e-mail promotions, filling out surveys, shopping, or taking advantage of trial offers. The ultimate purpose of these rewards programs is to help marketers develop databases that track the shopping and surfing habits of Web consumers, resulting in more effective future marketing and advertising efforts.

MyPoints.com: http://www.mypoints.com

MyPoints.com Corporate Site:
http://www.corp.mypoints.com

1. Based on the definition in the text, is MyPoints.com an example of a frequency-marketing program? What are the three basic elements that constitute a frequency-marketing program?

2. Read over the company information on MyPoints.com and explain how members accumulate and redeem loyalty points. How can one spend and earn points?

3. Visit the MyPoints.com corporate site and read about its advertising solutions. Who are some clients that partner with MyPoints.com, and what benefits do they receive? What are some of the ultimate benefits of database marketing?

19-2 The Challenges of Integrated Communication

Marketers have evolved basic models for setting up and managing an e-commerce branch of their businesses. Keen marketers recognize that when customers encounter a positive online shopping experience, they are likely to become loyal users—however, complications or inconveniences quickly drive them away. Marketers of successful e-commerce businesses are masters of managing various "behind-the-scenes" facilitators and enabler companies that work together to create a seamless, positive shopping experience for the end user.

PETsMART.com: http://www.petsmart.com

1. What are some of the challenges created by direct marketing on the Web as it relates to achieving integrated communication? What factors are driving the growing popularity of direct marketing?

2. Browse around PETsMART.com and cite examples of direct marketing. Do you think PETsMART executes its direct marketing campaigns "in-house"?

3. Based on what you learned in this chapter concerning the history and evolution of direct marketing, what impact do you think the digital revolution will have on traditional forms of direct marketing? What impact might the digital revolution have on the future of direct marketing?

CHAPTER 20

After reading and thinking about this chapter, you will be able to the following:

1

Explain the role of public relations as part of an organization's overall integrated brand promotion strategy.

2

Detail the objectives and tools of public relations.

3

Describe how firms are using the Internet to assist their public relations activities.

4

Describe two basic strategies motivating an organization's public relations activities.

5

Discuss the applications and objectives of corporate advertising.

CHAPTER 17
Support Media, P-O-P Advertising, and Event Sponsorship

CHAPTER 18
Sales Promotion

CHAPTER 19
Direct Marketing

CHAPTER 20
Public Relations and Corporate Advertising

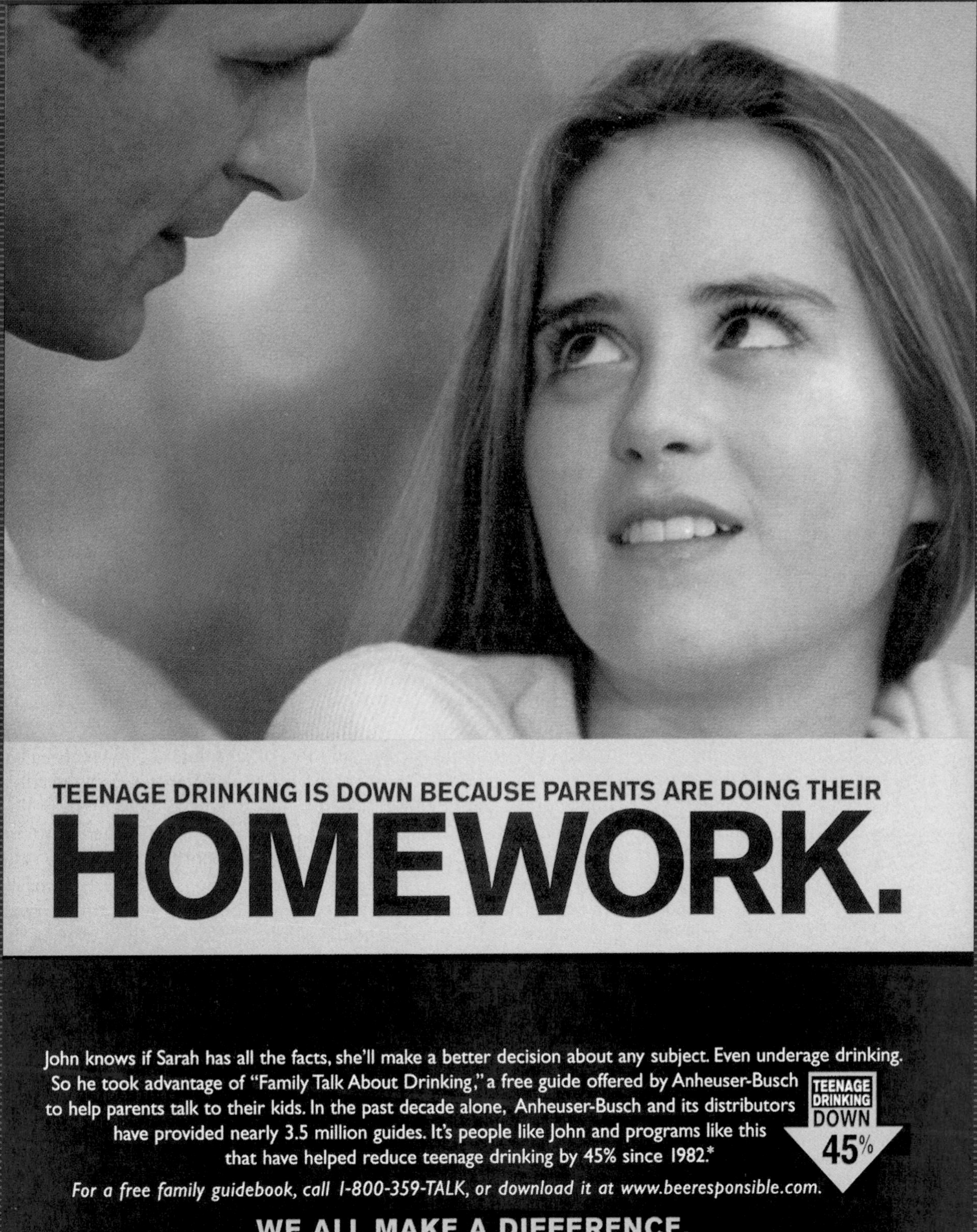

TEENAGE DRINKING IS DOWN BECAUSE PARENTS ARE DOING THEIR

HOMEWORK.

John knows if Sarah has all the facts, she'll make a better decision about any subject. Even underage drinking. So he took advantage of "Family Talk About Drinking," a free guide offered by Anheuser-Busch to help parents talk to their kids. In the past decade alone, Anheuser-Busch and its distributors have provided nearly 3.5 million guides. It's people like John and programs like this that have helped reduce teenage drinking by 45% since 1982.*

TEENAGE DRINKING DOWN 45%

For a free family guidebook, call 1-800-359-TALK, or download it at www.beeresponsible.com.

WE ALL MAKE A DIFFERENCE.

www.beeresponsible.com

*Department of Health & Human Services, 1999.

Firestone and Ford: two major corporations and one gigantic public relations challenge. In August 2000, public awareness began to rise that Ford Explorer SUVs outfitted with Firestone Wilderness AT tires had been involved in a large number of fatal and serious-injury accidents. Many of the fatalities were the result of Firestone tire failure causing rollovers. Ford was the first to act and urged a rapid recall of 6.5 million tires.[1] Bridgestone/Firestone, a unit of Japan's Bridgestone and makers of the suspect tires, didn't share Ford's sense of urgency. Despite daily newspaper and television publicity and Internet chat room buzz that was deafening, Firestone's response was that there were no unique problems with the Firestone Wilderness AT tires produced at its Decatur, Illinois, plant. As time passed, Firestone joined in the recall and began a careful evaluation of the tires. The firms began to blame each other for the "failure" of the tires. Ford claimed the tires were defective. Firestone executives claimed that the Wilderness AT was failing at a much higher rate on Ford Explorers than on any other vehicle fitted with the tire. In the end, both firms suffered serious loss of consumer confidence—although the big loser was clearly Firestone, with the firm's Corporate Reputation Index score (a 0–100 scale) falling from the high 60s to about 20 in one year.[2]

This was and will remain a classic and unique public relations event in the history of corporate America. On the one hand, both Ford and Firestone needed to be concerned about the negative publicity surrounding their individual brands. But given the fact that both brands were involved in the same tragic incidents, the situation created adversaries out of century-old corporate partners that up to this point had had a long and profitable history together.[3] As one analyst put it, "You have two brands pitted against each other trying to emerge from this debacle—the buddyship has ended."[4]

The challenge in the situation facing Ford and Firestone was enormous—a situation calling for swift and effective public relations to minimize the damage to the brands. The biggest loser, it appears, was Firestone. Despite challenges to the design of the Ford Explorer (Firestone tires were failing on the Explorer at a much higher rate than on other SUVs, including other Ford SUVs), the Firestone brand was taking the brunt of the public relations damage and loss of consumer confidence.[5] The initial denial and then delay in accepting responsibility hurt Firestone's image badly. When the firm finally did respond with direct communications to consumers, in the form of print and television advertising and Web content devoted to the issue (see Exhibits 20.1 and 20.2), analysts believed the company's response was a classic case of "too little, too late" and the brand had already suffered serious damage.[6] To make things worse, during the time Firestone was apparently deciding what to do, rival tire makers were filling the void by running ads with headlines like "Not everybody had to think about their tires this week."[7] Ouch!

The problem with all this negative publicity, of course, is that it damages the brand image, which in turn damages the market potential for the brand. Dealing with negative publicity is the province of public relations, primarily, with the support of corporate advertising. This chapter will consider in detail the role of these two separate and important areas that can be key aspects of an organization's overall integrated brand promotion effort—particularly in the context of negative publicity. Each has the potential to make a distinct and important contribution to the single and unified message and image of an organization, which is the ultimate goal of IBP.

1. William J. Holstein, "Guarding the Brand Is Job 1," *U.S. News & World Report,* September 11, 2000, 64–66.
2. Jean Halliday, "Ford, Firestone Suffer Damage in Tire Blowout," *Advertising Age,* May 28, 2001, 57.
3. Joann Muller and Nicole St. Pierre, "Ford vs. Firestone: A Corporate Whodunit," *Business Week,* June 11, 2001, 46–47.
4. Holstein, "Guarding the Brand Is Job 1," op. cit.
5. David Grainger, "Who Can Save 'Dead Brand Driving,' " *Fortune,* January 22, 2001.
6. Bob Garfield, "Firestone's Bid to Rebuild Trust Comes Too Late for the Wary," *Advertising Age,* April 30, 2001, 35.
7. David Welch, "Firestone: Is This Brand Beyond Repair?" *Business Week,* June 11, 2001, 48.

Making It Right.

You have our word on that.

When you buy tires, you're not just buying rubber and steel... you want the confidence that your tires will get you to your destination—safely. Your safety is our primary concern. We want you to have confidence in the way Firestone tires are made and the way they perform. We'll do whatever it takes, however long it takes to gain your trust.

We call this our "*Making It Right*" plan. With your satisfaction as our goal, Firestone is expanding warranties and making important enhancements in manufacturing and quality control. In the role of watchdogs, a new team of top technical and quality control managers has been assembled to continuously analyze tire and safety data. They'll act to uncover issues ***before*** they become problems. We believe in our tires. We want to prove to you that you can believe in them as well. ***We'll make it right. It's that simple.***

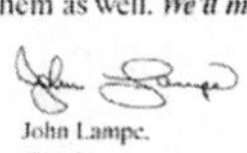

John Lampe,
CEO, Firestone

For a free copy of this safety brochure with information that's important for you and your family, visit our web site or your nearest Firestone retailer.

www.firestonetire.com

EXHIBIT 20.1

As part of a public relations campaign, Firestone used print advertisements as a way to communicate with consumers about the company's commitment to high quality and customer satisfaction. (Image courtesy of Bridgestone/Firestone Americas Holding Inc.)
www.firestone.com

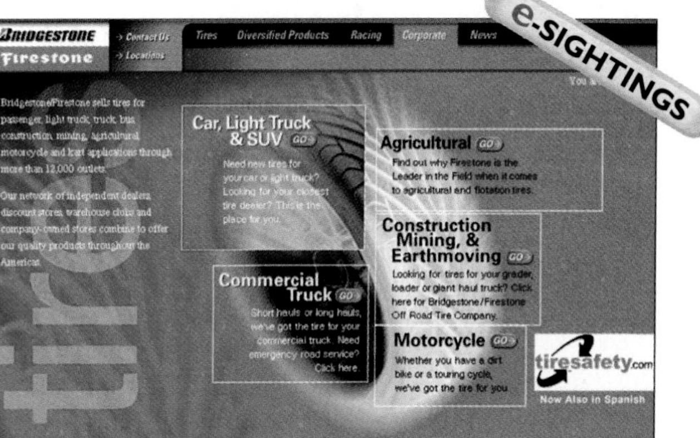

EXHIBIT 20.2

The Internet provided an ideal medium for updating consumers on Firestone's tire replacement program and offering them information that they may not have been seeing in the public media. Also, Firestone's corporate homepage (www.firestone.com) provided a direct link to TireSafety.com (www.tiresafety.com) where consumers could learn about proper tire care and maintenance. (Image courtesy of Bridgestone/Firestone Americas Holding Inc.)

Each also has the potential for effective and supportive communication, but they achieve this in different ways. Public relations is often a "behind the scenes" process. We will discuss the many tools and objectives of public relations throughout this chapter. Corporate advertising uses major media to communicate a unique, broad-based message that is distinct from the typical brand advertising a firm might do. Corporate advertising contributes to the development of an overall image for the firm without touting an individual brand or the brand's unique features. While public relations and corporate advertising are rarely the foundation of an IBP program, they do represent key communications tools under certain conditions. We will explore the nature of these two specialized promotional tools and the conditions under which they are ideally suited for the IBP effort.

Public Relations.

Public relations is a marketing and management communications function that deals with the public issues encountered by firms across a wide range of situations. An important component of public relations is **publicity**—news media coverage of events related to a firm's products or activities. Publicity presents both challenges (as Firestone and Ford have learned) and opportunities. News reports about problems, such as those Firestone had to deal with, represent challenges. Large investment projects in facilities or new product discoveries represent opportunities for positive publicity.

Public relations problems can arise from either a firm's own activities or from external forces completely outside a firm's control. Aside from the very recent situation facing Firestone and Ford, let's consider two classic public relations incidents that occurred at highly visible companies—Intel and Pepsi—and the problems they faced. In one case, the firm caused its own public relations and publicity problems; in the other, an external, uncontrollable force created problems for the firm.

Intel is one of the great success stories of American industry. Intel has risen from relative techno-obscurity as an innovative computer technology company to number 41 on the Fortune 500 list. Sales have grown from $1.3 billion to more than $33 billion in just 20 years.[8] But all this success did not prepare Intel for the one serious public relations challenge that the firm encountered. In early 1994, Intel introduced its new-generation chip, the Pentium, as the successor to the widely used line of X86 chips. The Pentium processor was another leap forward in computing speed and power. But in November 1994, Pentium users were discovering a flaw in the chip. During certain floating-point operations, some Pentium chips were actually producing erroneous calculations—albeit the error showed up in only the fifth or sixth decimal place. While this might not affect the average consumer who's trying to balance a checkbook, power users in scientific laboratories require absolute precision and accuracy in their calculations.

Having a defect in a high-performance technology product such as the Pentium chip was one thing; how Intel handled the problem was another. Intel's initial "official" response was that the flaw in the chip was so insignificant that it would produce an error in calculations only once in 27,000 years. But then IBM, which had shipped thousands of PCs with Pentium chips, challenged the assertion that the flaw was insignificant, claiming that processing errors could occur as often as every 24 days. IBM announced that it would stop shipment of all Pentium-based PCs immediately.[9]

From this point on, the Pentium situation became a runaway public relations disaster. Every major newspaper, network newscast, and magazine carried the story of the flawed Pentium chip. Even the cartoon series *Dilbert* got in on the act, running a whole series of cartoon strips that spoofed the Intel controversy. One of these *Dilbert* cartoons can be seen in Exhibit 20.3. One observer characterized it this way: "From a public relations standpoint, the train has left the station and is barreling out of Intel's control."[10] For weeks Intel publicly argued that the flaw would not affect the vast majority of users, and the firm did nothing.

Ultimately, public pressure and user demands forced Intel to change its position. Consumers were outraged at Intel's initial policy of refusing to replace Pentium chips unless Intel thought the user needed one. Finally, in early 1995, Intel decided to provide a free replacement chip to any user who believed he or she was at risk. Andy Grove, Intel's highly accomplished CEO, in announcing the $475 million program to replace customers' chips, admitted publicly that "the Pentium processor divide problem has been a learning experience for Intel."[11]

8. "The Fortune 500," *Fortune,* April 16, 2001, F1.
9. Barbara Grady, "Chastened Intel Steps Carefully with Introduction of New Chip," *Computerlink,* February 14, 1995, 11.
10. James G. Kimball, "Can Intel Repair the Pentium PR?" *Advertising Age,* December 19, 1994, 35.
11. Grady, "Chastened Intel Steps Carefully with Introduction of New Chip," op. cit.

Source: Dilbert reprinted by permission of United Features Syndicate, Inc.

EXHIBIT 20.3

When Intel did not respond quickly and positively to problems with its Pentium chip, the press unloaded a barrage of negative publicity on the firm. Even Dilbert *got into the act with this parody of Intel decision making.* www.dilbert.com

Intel's public relations and publicity problems were mostly of its own doing. But in many cases, firms are faced with public relations crises that are totally beyond their control. One of these cases, which goes down in history as a classic, happened to Pepsi. In 1993, Pepsi had a public relations nightmare on its hands. Complaints were coming in from all over the United States that cans of Pepsi, Diet Pepsi, and Caffeine Free Diet Pepsi had syringes inside them. Other callers claimed their cans of Pepsi contained such things as a screw, a crack vial, a sewing needle, and brown goo in the bottom. Unlike Intel, Pepsi assembled a management team that was mobilized to handle the crisis. The team immediately considered a national recall of all Pepsi products—no matter what the cost. The Food and Drug Administration (FDA) told Pepsi there was no need for such action, since no one had been injured and there was no health risk. The Pepsi team was sure that this was not a case of tampering in the production facility. A can of Pepsi is filled with cola and then sealed in nine-tenths of a second—making it virtually impossible for anyone to get anything into a can during production.

The president of Pepsi went on national television to explain the situation and defend his firm and its products. Pepsi enlisted the aid of a powerful and influential constituent at this point—the Food and Drug Administration. The commissioner of the FDA, David Kessler, said publicly that many of the tampering claims could not be substantiated or verified. A video camera in Aurora, Colorado, caught a woman trying to insert a syringe into a Pepsi can. Pepsi was exonerated in the press, but the huge public relations problem had significantly challenged the firm to retain the stature and credibility of a truly global brand.

What happened to Intel and Pepsi highlights why public relations is such a difficult form of communication to manage. In many cases, a firm's public relations program is called into action for damage control, as the Pepsi ad in Exhibit 20.4 illustrates. Intel and Pepsi had to be totally reactive to the situation rather than strategically controlling it, as with the other tools in the integrated communications process. But while many episodes of public relations must be reactive, a firm can be prepared with public relations materials to conduct an orderly and positive goodwill and image-building campaign among its many constituents. To fully appreciate the role and potential of public relations in the broad communications efforts of a firm, we will consider the objectives of public relations, the tools of public relations, and basic public relations strategies.

2 **Objectives of Public Relations.** The public relations function in a firm, usually handled by an outside agency, is prepared to engage in positive public relations efforts and to deal with any negative events related to a firm's activities. Within the broad guidelines of

Pepsi is pleased to announce...

...nothing.

As America now knows, those stories about Diet Pepsi were a hoax. Plain and simple, not true. Hundreds of investigators have found no evidence to support a single claim.

As for the many, many thousands of people who work at Pepsi-Cola, we feel great that it's over. And we're ready to get on with making and bringing you what we believe is the best-tasting diet cola in America.

There's not much more we can say. Except that most importantly, we won't let this hoax change our exciting plans for this summer.

We've set up special offers so you can enjoy our great quality products at prices that will save you money all summer long. It all starts on July 4th weekend and we hope you'll stock up with a little extra, just to make up for what you might have missed last week.

That's it. Just one last word of thanks to the millions of you who have stood with us.

Drink All The Diet Pepsi You Want.
Uh Huh®.

DIET PEPSI and UH HUH are registered trademarks of PepsiCo Inc.

EXHIBIT 20.4

When the truth about the tampering with Pepsi cans was finally resolved, the firm took the opportunity for some positive public relations by running this ad.
www.pepsi.com

image building and establishing relationships with constituents, it is possible to identify six primary objectives of public relations:

- *Promoting goodwill.* This is an image-building function of public relations. Industry events or community activities that reflect favorably on a firm are highlighted. When Pepsi launched a program to support school music programs—programs hard hit by funding decreases—the firm garnered widespread public relations goodwill. The Creativity box on page 702 tells the whole story of this program.
- *Promoting a product or service.* Press releases or events that increase public awareness of a firm's brands can be pursued through public relations. Large pharmaceutical firms such as Merck and Glaxo Wellcome issue press releases when new drugs are discovered or FDA approval is achieved.
- *Preparing internal communications.* Disseminating information and correcting misinformation within a firm can reduce the impact of rumors and increase employee support. For events such as reductions in the labor force or mergers of firms, internal communications can do much to dispel rumors circulating among employees and in the local community.
- *Counteracting negative publicity.* This is the damage control function of public relations. The attempt here is not to cover up negative events, but rather to prevent the negative publicity from damaging the image of a firm and its brands. When a lawsuit was filed against NEC alleging that one of its cellular phones had caused cancer, McCaw Cellular Communications used public relations activities to inform the public and especially cellular phone users of scientific knowledge that argued against the claims in the lawsuit.[12] And one industry's public relations problems are another industry's golden opportunity, as the ad in Exhibit 20.5 shows.
- *Lobbying.* The public relations function can assist a firm in dealing with government officials and pending legislation. Recall that Microsoft reportedly spent $4.6 billion on such lobbying efforts. Industries maintain active and aggressive lobbying efforts at both the state and federal levels. As an example, the beer and wine industry has lobbyists monitoring legislation that could restrict beer and wine advertising.
- *Giving advice and counsel.* Assisting management in determining what (if any) position to take on public issues, preparing employees for public appearances, and helping management anticipate public reactions are all part of the advice and counsel function of public relations.

Tools of Public Relations. There are several vehicles through which a firm can make positive use of public relations and pursue the objectives just cited. The goal is to gain as much control over the process as possible. By using the methods discussed in the follow-

12. John J. Keller, "McCaw to Study Cellular Phones as Safety Questions Affect Sales," *Wall Street Journal,* January 29, 1993, B3.

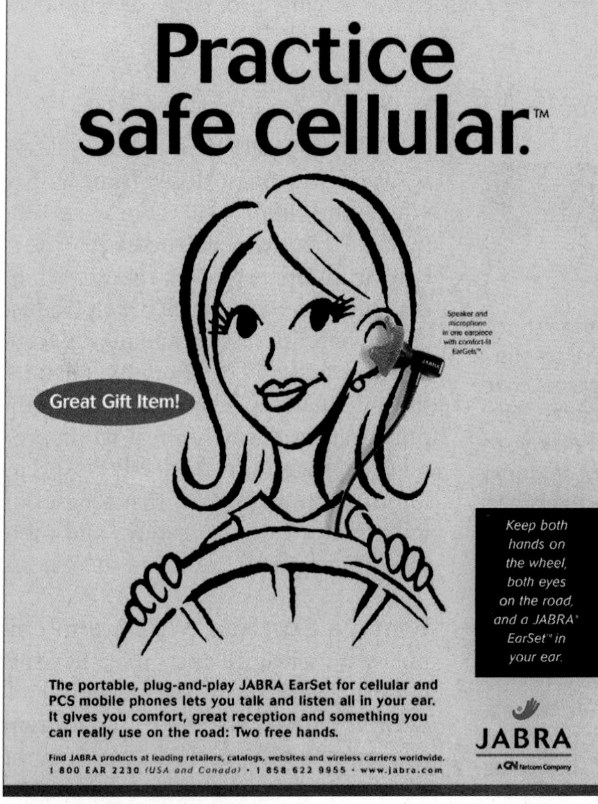

EXHIBIT 20.5

Public relations problems in one industry create opportunities in another. When medical research suggested that extensive cellular phone use could be linked to brain tumors, firms developed cell phone accessories to address the issue. Here, Jabra is alluding to the negative publicity and the medical research as the basis for its brand appeal. www.jabra.com

Tuesday, June 5, 6:30 A.M. Eastern Time

Press Release

SOURCE: Myriad Genetics, Inc.

Myriad Genetics Discovers High Cholesterol Gene

CHD2 Enzyme is in Novel Pathway, May Lead to New Class of Cholesterol Lowering Drugs

Salt Lake City, June 5/PRNewswire/—Myriad Genetics, Inc. (NASDAQ: MYGN-news), has discovered a human gene responsible for high total cholesterol and low HDL (also known as "good cholesterol"), in individuals with early age myocardial infarction. The research shows that the gene's protein product is produced in abnormal amounts in these individuals and has enzymatic activity and other characteristics that suggest it will be readily amenable as a drug target. The CHD2 (Coronary Heart Disease 2) protein acts in a novel, previously unknown pathway, distinct from the cholesterol synthesis pathway that is acted upon by the statin class of drugs and other classes of drugs.

The CHD2 gene, and its function, was discovered by a combination of genetic analyses of families whose members had heart attacks at an early age and an analysis of biological pathways. In total, more than 5,000 individuals from 145 families were analyzed to identify the gene. The discovery in this population, made by Myriad in collaboration with scientists from the Cardiovascular Genetics Research Clinic at the University of Utah, means that abnormal levels of the CHD2 protein are critical to the development of disease. Because disorders of the CHD2 gene lead to high LDL cholesterol, low HDL cholesterol, and early-onset heart disease, inhibition of the gene with a small molecule drug is expected to lower cholesterol and reduce the risk of heart disease across the general population of individuals with high cholesterol. Current therapies, including the statins, are inadequate in lowering the total cholesterol to recommended levels in many patients. Heart disease remains the most common cause of death in the United States. Studies estimate that half of all men and one-third of women will develop heart disease during their lives.

"The discovery of this novel drug target for the treatment of heart disease points to the strengths of Myriad's integrated approach to drug development incorporating the best technologies of genomics and proteomics in a high-throughput, industrialized fashion," said Peter Meldrum, President and Chief Executive Officer of Myriad Genetics, Inc. "Myriad now has a full pipeline of earlier stage preclinical compounds to back up our lead prostate cancer drug, which has completed a Phase IIa human clinical trial, and we intend to aggressively advance these compounds toward commercialization."

EXHIBIT 20.6

A press release is good way to communicate positive information about a firm to a wide variety of constituents and stakeholders. Here, Myriad Genetics has issued a press release regarding a new drug designed to lower cholesterol. www.myriad.com

ing sections, a firm can integrate its public relations effort with other marketing communications.

Press Releases. Having a file of information that makes for good news stories puts the firm in a position to take advantage of free press coverage. Press releases allow a firm to pursue positive publicity from the news media. Exhibit 20.6 is a press release announcing the discovery by Myriad Genetics of a gene related to high cholesterol. Items that make for good public relations include the following:

- new products
- new scientific discoveries
- new personnel
- new corporate facilities

- innovative corporate practices, such as energy-saving programs or employee benefit programs
- annual shareholder meetings
- charitable and community service activities

CREATIVITY

Pepsi's School Effort Makes Sweet Music

The cola wars have taken to the schoolyard—well, at least the school music rooms. Pepsi has launched a school fund-raising effort to support school music education programs. These are the programs that have been particularly hard hit by government funding cutbacks. The program is called "Share the Joy with Music" and will run every year around the Thanksgiving, Christmas, and Chanukah holiday seasons. Pepsi offers schools free musical equipment and supplies in exchange for collecting Pepsi "Notes." The notes are printed on hundreds of millions of larger-sized packages of Pepsi, Diet Pepsi, Pepsi One, and Mountain Dew. The notes can also be found on packages of Frito-Lay potato chips, Frito's, and Rold Gold Pretzels.

To help schools participate, Pepsi sends a mailer to over 100,000 school principals and music educators in public and private schools for grades K–12. The materials include enrollment forms and directions on how schools can send in their Pepsi Notes as well as instructions on communicating with the firm through the program Web site at www.pepsinotes.com. The site has links to online music retailer Music123.com and offers more than 100,000 items that schools can choose from, including music-writing software for 300 notes, a violin for 2,115 notes, and a tuba for 22,500 notes.

Aside from the involvement of Pepsi at the corporate level, the firm hopes that local retailers will see the benefit in participating in a positive contribution to the schools at the local level. Retailers are being encouraged to "adopt" local schools and facilitate the Pepsi Note acquisition and redemption process. To ensure access to the program by all schools, Pepsi supports the program with national radio advertising and print ads targeted to music educators by being placed in education journals.

Pepsi is by no means the first advertiser to be involved with school promotional programs. Campbell Soup began its "Labels for Education" program 27 years ago. General Mills' "Boxtops for Education" program is in its fifth year. This program offers the chance to exchange boxtops for 10 cents each in cash. So far, General Mills has donated over $32 million to schools serving kindergartners through eighth-graders.

In the end, firms that get involved with promotional programs like this sincerely hope that their efforts benefit participating schools. But they are also keenly aware of the good public relations such programs can generate. They are also, as you might suspect, carefully monitoring such programs to see if there is any appreciable effect on sales. Such programs are also being scrutinized by watchdog groups who are concerned about the "commercialization" of the educational environment.

Source: Stephanie Thompson, "Pepsi Hits High Note with Schools," *Advertising Age*, October 9, 2000, 30.

The only drawback to press releases is that a firm often doesn't know if or when the item will appear in the media. Also, the news media are free to edit or interpret a news release, which may alter its meaning. To help reduce these liabilities, consultants recommend carefully developing relationships with editors from publications the organization deems critical to its press release program.[13] And editors prefer information from firms that focuses on technical or how-to features and more case studies about company successes.[14]

Feature Stories. While a firm cannot write a feature story for a newspaper or televise a story over the local television networks, it can invite journalists to do an exclusive story on the firm when there is a particularly noteworthy event. A feature story is different from a press release in that it is more controllable. A feature story, as opposed to a news release, offers a single journalist the opportunity to do a fairly lengthy piece with exclusive rights to the information. Jupiter Communications, a leading research organization that tracks Internet usage and generates statistics about the Internet, has a simple philosophy when it comes to using feature stories as a public relations tool. The CEO says that "It is our goal to get every research project we do covered somewhere. We know this is the cheapest, and maybe most effective, way to market ourselves."[15]

Company Newsletters. In-house publications such as newsletters can disseminate positive information about a firm through its employees. As members of the community, employees are proud of achievements by their firm. Newsletters can also be distributed to important constituents in the

13. Adriana Cento, "7 Habits for Highly Effective Public Relations," *Marketing News*, March 16, 1998, 8.
14. Chad Kaydo, "How to Boost Your Press Coverage," *Sales and Marketing Management*, July 1998, 76.
15. Andy Cohen, "The Jupiter Mission," *Sales and Marketing Management*, April 2000, 56.

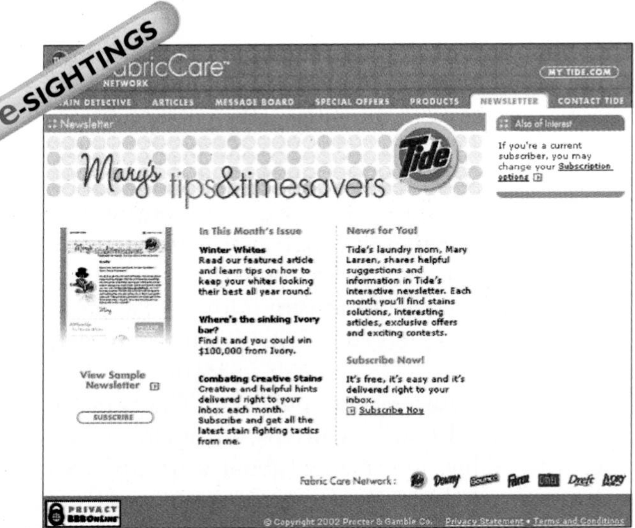

EXHIBIT 20.7

Companies have discovered that electronic distribution of newsletters is an effective and efficient way to offer consumers information in a low-key way. Here, Procter & Gamble has created an electronic newsletter that not only gets information out about the Tide brand of laundry detergent, but also helps create a community around Tide. How does Cheer (www.cheer.com) use its electronic newsletter to reinforce the notion that hip, young people use the product? Is competing brand Purex (www.purex.com) finding a way to build positive, ongoing relations with its consumers through its product site? What real effect do you think these public relations initiatives have?

community, such as government officials, the chamber of commerce, or the tourism bureau. Suppliers often enjoy reading about an important customer, so newsletters can be mailed to this group as well.[16] Firms are also discovering that the Internet is an excellent way to distribute information that traditionally has been the focus of newsletters.[17] Procter & Gamble has done just that at www.tide.com/newsletter (see Exhibit 20.7).

Interviews and Press Conferences. As in the Pepsi tampering crisis, interviews and press conferences can be a highly effective public relations tool. Often, interviews and press conferences are warranted in a crisis management situation. But firms have also successfully called press conferences to announce important scientific breakthroughs or explain the details of a corporate expansion. The press conference has an air of importance and credibility because it uses a news format to present important corporate information. New technology is fostering the use of press conferences as a means of getting the word out (see Exhibit 20.8).

Sponsored Events. Sponsored events were discussed as a form of support media in Chapter 17. Sponsoring events can also serve as an important public relations tool. Sponsorships run the gamut from supporting local community events to sponsoring global events such as the World Cup soccer competitions. At the local level, prominent display of the corporate name and logo offers local residents the chance to see that an organization is dedicated to the community.

Another form of sponsorship is fund-raisers. Fund-raisers of all sorts for nonprofit organizations give positive visibility to corporations. For many years, Chevrolet has sponsored college scholarships through the NCAA by choosing the offensive and defensive player of a game. The scholarships are announced weekly at the conclusion of televised games. This sort of notoriety for Chevrolet creates a favorable image for viewers.

One of the most difficult aspects of investing in sponsorships is determining the positive payoff the organization can expect from such an investment. Typically, corporations will try to assess the effect of sponsorships by (a) establishing an evaluation procedure that tracks awareness generated from sponsorships, (b) establishing an event-tracking model that can identify target audience attitudes and purchase behavior, and (c) identifying the components of the sponsorship that were most effective in achieving awareness and attitude goals. While these are general criteria for assessing the effects of sponsorship, there is an important image effect of the sponsorship. This is where the public relations role for sponsored events is manifested. Current research shows that there is a positive transfer of image from the event to the brand—precisely the effect being sought by a public relations tool.[18]

16. Joanne Cleaver, "Newsletters Prove to Be Both Effective and Cost-Effective," *Marketing News,* January 4, 1999, 6.
17. Jeffery D. Zbar, "Marketers Buoy Brands with E-Mail Newsletters," *Advertising Age,* October 25, 1999, 74.
18. Kevin P. Gwinner and John Eaton, "Building Brand Image through Event Sponsorship: The Role of Image Transfer," *Journal of Advertising,* vol. 28, No. 4 (Winter 1999), 47–57.

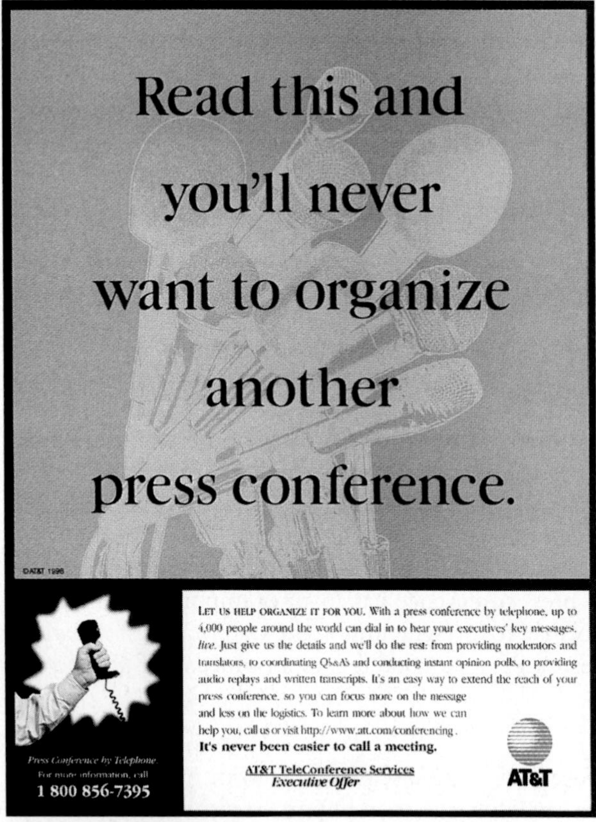

EXHIBIT 20.8

New technology is allowing firms to use press conferences more effectively.
www.att.com

Publicity. **Publicity** is unpaid-for media exposure about a firm's activities or its products and services. Publicity is dealt with by the public relations function but cannot, with the exception of press releases, be strategically controlled like other public relations efforts. This lack of control was demonstrated earlier in the chapter with respect to the situations faced by Firestone, Intel, and Pepsi. In addition, publicity can turn into a global problem for a firm. Benetton, the Italian sportswear maker, is another classic case of a firm that regularly has to deal with negative publicity. The firm has learned several times (or maybe not at all) the lesson that public information about a brand is not always controllable. Benetton has created much of this uncontrollable publicity with its controversial advertising. In one instance the firm ran an ad depicting a white child wearing angel's wings alongside a black child wearing devil's horns. In another campaign, the firm featured death row inmates to promote its clothing line, although company officials argued they were merely trying to raise public consciousness of the death penalty.[19] The reaction to such advertising was severe enough that at one point German retailers refused to carry the company's products.

Public relations professionals can react swiftly to publicity, as the team from Pepsi did, but they cannot control the flow of information. Despite the lack of control, publicity can build an image and heighten consumer awareness of brands and organizations. An organization needs to be prepared to take advantage of events that make for good publicity and to counter events that are potentially damaging to a firm's reputation.

One major advantage of publicity—when the information is positive—is that it tends to carry heightened credibility. Publicity that appears in news stories on television and radio and in newspapers and magazines assumes an air of believability because of the credibility of the media context. Not-for-profit organizations often use publicity in the form of news stories and public interest stories as ways to gain widespread visibility at little or no cost.

And publicity is not always completely out of the companies' control. During the 2001 Academy Awards, a bracelet worn by Academy Award–winning actress Julia Roberts caused quite a publicity stir. After Ms. Roberts won the award for best actress, she stood smiling (which we all know she does so well) and waving to the cameras and suddenly the whole world wanted to know about the snowflake-design Van Cleef & Arpels bracelet that adorned her right (waving) wrist. What a lucky break! Not. The whole episode was carefully planned by Van Cleef's PR agency, Ted, Inc. The agency lobbied hard to convince Ms. Roberts that the bracelet and matching earrings were stunning with her dress and knew that if she won the Oscar, she would be highly photographed wearing (and waving) the bracelet.[20]

19. John Rossant, "The Faded Colors of Benetton," *Business Week,* April 10, 1995, 87, 90.
20. Beth Snyder Bulik, "Well-Healed Heed the Need for PR," *Advertising Age,* June 11, 2001, s2.

3 Public Relations and New Media. The fact that firms large and small are using the Internet to distribute newsletters reveals only one application of new media for public relations purposes. Firms are using the Internet for a variety of public relations activities. Procter & Gamble, cited earlier for its use in distributing newsletters, has also created a special section at its Web site (www.pg.com/rumor) to battle nagging rumors that the firm has some sort of connection to satanic cults. The site offers facts about P&G's moon-and-stars logo (the 13 stars represent the 13 original colonies, not a satanic symbol). The site also carries testimonials posted from the Billy Graham Evangelistic Association. The rumors were being spread through the Web, so P&G is fighting fire with fire by using the Web for a public relations counterattack.[21]

New Web companies are finding that their needs for public relations are just as great as, if not greater than, established, non-Web-based firms. One Internet startup, Digital Island, attributes most of its early success to the effects of proactive public relations strategies. One public relations expert believes that "Every positive article is worth $1 million in valuation" to an Internet startup. Further, analysts believe that without third-party endorsement (the press and industry analysts), it is doubtful that a startup can be successful.[22]

The issue was raised earlier that new media can create a "buzz" through word-of-mouth that is more effective with certain target segments than any other tactic. In a noisy and crowded competitive environment, mainstream promotional tools such as advertising, sales promotion, and sponsorships may get lost in the clutter. Public relations using new media, particularly Web sites, chat room posts, and Web press releases, can reach targeted audiences in a different way that carries more credibility than "in your face" company self-promotion.[23]

Finally, there is a major drawback to new media when it comes to public relations. Because of the speed with which information is disseminated, staying ahead of negative publicity is indeed challenging. While word-of-mouth can be used to create a positive buzz, it can also spread bad news or, even worse, misinformation just as fast. When a crisis hits the Internet, one PR expert says that "act quickly becomes act *even more* quickly."[24] Acting quickly and responding with the right facts is the topic of the next section. And new Web sites, in an effort to get recognized (and these days even survive), are less likely to scrutinize public relations press releases as carefully as perhaps they should (see the IBP box on page 707 for a detailed discussion).

4 Basic Public Relations Strategies. Given the breadth of possibilities for using public relations as part of a firm's overall integrated brand promotion effort, we need to identify basic public relations strategies. Public relations strategies can be categorized as either proactive or reactive. **Proactive public relations strategy** is guided by marketing objectives, seeks to publicize a company and its brands, and takes an offensive rather than defensive posture in the public relations process. **Reactive public relations strategy** is dictated by influences outside the control of a company, focuses on problems to be solved rather than opportunities, and requires a company to take defensive measures.[25] These two strategies involve different orientations to public relations.

Proactive Public Relations Strategy. In developing a proactive public relations strategy, a firm acknowledges opportunities to use public relations efforts to accomplish something positive. Companies often rely heavily on their public relations firms

21. Nicholas Kulish, "Still Bedeviled by Satan Rumors, P&G Battles Back on the Web," *Wall Street Journal,* September 21, 1999, B1.
22. "The Future of Public Relations Is the Internet," *The Strategist,* Spring 1999, 6–10.
23. Dana James, "Dot-Coms Demand New Kind of Publicity," *Marketing News,* November 22, 1999, 6, 11.
24. Kathryn Kranhold, "Handling the Aftermath of Cybersabotage," *Wall Street Journal,* February 10, 2000, B22.
25. These definitions were developed from discussions offered by Jordan Goldman, *Public Relations in the Marketing Mix* (Lincolnwood, Ill.: NTC Business Books, 1992), xi–xii.

EXHIBIT 20.9

The biotechnology industry is taking a proactive approach to the controversies surrounding the industry and its processes. www.whybiotech.com

to help them put together a proactive strategy. The biotechnology industry is subject to much controversy in the press regarding genetically altered food and seed products. The advertisement in Exhibit 20.9 from the biotechnology industry attempts to take a proactive approach to dealing with the controversies by presenting a positive image and information.

In many firms, the positive aspects of employee achievements, corporate contributions to the community, and the organization's social and environmental programs go unnoticed by important constituents. To implement a proactive public relations strategy, a firm needs to develop a comprehensive public relations program. The key components of such a program are as follows:

1. *A public relations audit.* A **public relations audit** identifies the characteristics of a firm or the aspects of the firm's activities that are positive and newsworthy. Information is gathered in much the same way as information related to advertising strategy is gathered. Corporate personnel and customers are questioned to provide information. The type of information gathered in an audit includes descriptions of company products and services, market performance of brands, profitability, goals for products, market trends, new product introductions, important suppliers, important customers, employee programs and facilities, community programs, and charitable activities.
2. *A public relations plan.* Once the firm is armed with information from a public relations audit, the next step is a structured public relations plan. A **public relations plan** identifies the objectives and activities related to the public relations communications issued by a firm. The components of a public relations plan include the following:
   - *Current situation analysis.* This section of the public relations plan summarizes the information obtained from the public relations audit. Information contained here is often broken down by category, such as product performance or community activity.
   - *Program objectives.* Objectives for a proactive public relations program stem from the current situation. Objectives should be set for both short-term and long-term opportunities. Public relations objectives can be as diverse and complex as advertising objectives. As with advertising, the focal point is not sales or profits. Rather, factors such as the credibility of product performance (that is, placing products in verified, independent tests) or the stature of the firm's research and development efforts (highlighted in a prestigious trade publication article) are legitimate statements of objective.
   - *Program rationale.* In this section, it is critical to identify the role the public relations program will play relative to all the other communication efforts—particularly advertising—being undertaken by a firm. This is the area where an integrated brand promotion perspective is clearly articulated for the public relations effort.

- *Communications vehicles.* This section of the plan specifies precisely what means will be used to implement the public relations plan. The public relations tools discussed earlier in the chapter—press releases, interviews, newsletters—constitute the communications vehicles through which program objectives can be implemented. There will likely be discussion of precisely how press releases, interviews, and company newsletters can be used.[26]
- *Message content.* Analysts suggest that public relations messages should be researched and developed in much the same way that advertising messages are researched and developed. Focus groups and in-depth interviews are being used to fine-tune PR communications. For example, a pharmaceutical firm learned that calling obesity a "disease" rather than a "condition" increased the overweight population's receptivity to the firm's press release messages regarding a new anti-obesity drug.[27]

A proactive public relations strategy has the potential for making an important supportive contribution to a firm's IBP effort. Carefully placing positive information targeted to important and potentially influential constituents—such as members of the community or stockholders—supports the overall goal of enhancing the image, reputation, and perception of a firm and its brands.

IBP

Where Is the Spin Control?

Throughout the text, we have seen that the Internet is a great place to create a buzz and spread the "word" at lightning speed. But the way "content" can be splashed across the Web, it is getting difficult to know what is real content and news versus what is corporate PR.

Here is the crux of the problem. The trend toward "dressing" public relations as "news" is being driven by economics. A standard press release on the Internet costs only a few hundred dollars to compose and distribute electronically, which makes the Web a bargain for information dissemination—but we knew that. Entering the scene, however, are content-hungry publishers. In an effort to provide their outlets with fresh text fast and cheap, they simply forward corporate news releases. Content consulting firm ScreamingMedia (www.screamingmedia.com) estimates that a company that wants to create significant online presence with advertising would need to spend about $500,000 monthly on various advertising and content development and placement. But the price to news sites for most of the PR content is zero.

This issue is particularly relevant when you consider that of the dot-com failures in 2000, 30 percent of those shutdowns were content providers. Despite the shakeout, the need for content continues to grow. If you're a firm seeking a PR presence on the Internet, this is certainly good news, partly because the remaining number of sites featuring "news" areas (such as portals or special-interest sites) is nearly inestimable. But almost 42 million users currently visit the top 10 general news sites. The pressure within content providers to attract those eyeballs is huge. One analyst notes, "Online news outlets are not only competing against one another but against traditional media. The pressure to be the first or to scoop the others is immense. Rushed stories can mean less time for fact-checking and less time to interview subjects."

As a test, visit some of these sites and see whether it's "news" or a company PR press release:

abcnews.com: Go to the MoneyScope section, http://money.go.com.

America Online: Go to the Channels and click "news." Locate the stories by selecting the "News Search" button at the top of the menu.

CNET: Click "CNET Investor" or go directly to http://investor.cnet.com and check out the company press releases.

Newsalert.com: Press releases are mixed in with news stories on the site from all the major wire organizations—CBS, Reuters, Business Wire, and UPI.

Source: Joanne R. Helperin, "Spinning Out of Control?," *Business 2.0,* May 1, 2001, 54–56.

Reactive Public Relations Strategy. A reactive public relations strategy seems a contradiction in terms. As stated earlier, firms must implement a reactive public relations strategy when events outside the control of the firm create negative publicity. Coca-Cola was able to rein in the publicity and negative public reaction by acting swiftly after an unfortunate incident

26. Ibid., 4–14.
27. Geri Mazur, "Good PR Starts with Good Research," *Marketing News,* September 15, 1997, 16.

occurred in Europe. Seven days after a bottling glitch at a European plant caused teens in Belgium and France to become sick after drinking Coke, the firm acted quickly and pulled all Coca-Cola products from European shelves, and the CEO issued an apology.[28] But Coca-Cola's actions did not prevent negative consequences. Because of the incident, Coca-Cola went from being one of the most admired and trusted names in Europe to a company that ultimately had to start giving the product away to regain people's trust. The event was so catastrophic that Coke sales dropped 21 percent, and earnings were pummeled as well. But Coke's President of the Greater Europe Group said, "We re-evaluated and re-tailored our marketing programs to meet the needs of consumers on a country-by-country basis and continue to reach out with marketing programs specifically designed to reconnect the brands with consumers."[29] The programs relied heavily on integrated brand promotion strategies including free samples; dealer incentive programs; and beach parties featuring sound and light shows, live music DJs, and cocktail bars with free Cokes to win back the critical teen segment.[30] By early 2000, Coca-Cola was well on its way to recapturing the lost sales and market share.

It is much more difficult to organize for and provide structure around reactive public relations. Since the events that trigger a reactive public relations effort are unpredictable as well as uncontrollable, a firm must simply be prepared to act quickly and effectively. Two steps help firms implement a reactive public relations strategy:

- *The public relations audit.* The public relations audit that was prepared for the proactive strategy helps a firm also prepare its reactive strategy. The information provided by the audit gives a firm what it needs to issue public statements based on current and accurate data. In the Pepsi situation, a current list of distributors, suppliers, and manufacturing sites allowed the firms to quickly determine that the problems were not related to the production process.
- *The identification of vulnerabilities.* In addition to preparing current information, the other key step in a reactive public relations strategy is to recognize areas where the firm has weaknesses in its operations or products that can negatively affect its relationships with important constituents. These weaknesses are called *vulnerabilities* from a public relations standpoint. If aspects of a firm's operations are vulnerable to criticism, such as environmental issues related to manufacturing processes, then the public relations function should be prepared to discuss the issues in a broad range of forums with many different constituents. Leaders at Pepsi, Quaker Oats, and Philip Morris were taken somewhat by surprise when shareholders challenged the firms on their practices with respect to genetically modified foods. While the concern was among a minority of shareholders, there were enough concerned constituents to warrant a proxy vote on the genetically modified foods issue.[31]

Public relations is an prime example of how a firm can identify and then manage aspects of communication in an integrated and synergistic manner to diverse audiences. Without recognizing public relations activities as a component of the firm's overall communication effort, misinformation or disinformation could compromise more mainstream communications such as advertising. The coordination of public relations into an integrated program is a matter of recognizing and identifying the process as an information source in the overall IBP effort.

5 Corporate Advertising.

As we learned in Chapter 1, corporate advertising is not designed to promote a specific brand but rather is intended to establish a favorable attitude toward a company as a whole. A variety of highly regarded and highly suc-

28. Kathleen V. Schmidt, "Coke's Crisis," *Marketing News,* September 27, 1999, 1, 11.
29. Amie Smith, "Coke's European Resurgence," *PROMO Magazine,* December 1999, 91.
30. Ibid.
31. James Cox, "Shareholders Get to Put Bio-Engineered Foods to Vote," *USA Today,* June 6, 2000, 1B.

cessful firms use corporate advertising to enhance the image of the firm and affect consumers' attitudes. This perspective on corporate advertising is gaining favor worldwide, as the Global Issues box on this page describes. Firms with the stature of Toyota, Hewlett-Packard, Rockwell, and Coopers & Lybrand have invested in corporate advertising campaigns. The Coopers & Lybrand corporate campaign was conceived to show how the firm helps manage change in a dynamic, global environment. The goal was to establish the image of Coopers & Lybrand as a contemporary and visionary organization.[32] One of the ads from the Coopers & Lybrand campaign before its merger with Pricewaterhouse Coopers is shown in Exhibit 20.10.

GLOBAL ISSUES

Good Humor Is a Good Cause

Every year Unilever's Bestfoods division unveils a slew of ice cream novelties to catch kids' attention during the critical summer selling season. But now the firm is trying to build some excitement among parents as well, who aren't always thrilled about their kids diving into fattening, cavity-causing ice cream treats. Unilever managers have invested in something more altruistic than in the past by linking the company's Popsicle brand with a program involving the conservation group World Wildlife Fund (WWF).

The centerpiece (no pun intended) of the program is a panda-shaped Wildlife Ice Cream Bar. The ice cream bar was featured in newspaper inserts that featured three endangered species appealing to kids with the headline "We need you." The same line was repeated on point-of-purchase displays. Packaging for the special promotional campaigned featured the panda-shaped logo of the WWF. Facts about each of the featured animals were contained on the packages, and kids could send to the company for animal-themed items including trading cards and watches.

The firm believes it has received extensive and positive coverage for the program. Managers with Unilever explain that "the efforts in support of wildlife programs across the world have been a huge selling point in presentations to retailers." One U.S. retailer explained the product's quick acceptance by saying simply, "We support any manufacturer donating proceeds to a nonprofit."

While this program by Unilever was one of its first efforts in cause-related advertising and integrated brand promotion, it will unlikely be its last. In an executive study by Cone Cause Branding Practice, 69 percent of respondents said they planned to increase their commitment to social causes. This bodes well for firms like Unilever who are contemplating using cause-related efforts. And it certainly bodes well for all the nonprofit organizations who so desperately need the financial support of corporations.

Source: Stephanie Thompson, "Good Humor's Good Deeds," *Advertising Age*, January 8, 2001, 6.

The Scope and Objectives of Corporate Advertising.

Corporate advertising is a significant force in the overall advertising carried out by organizations in the United States. Billions of dollars are invested annually in media for corporate advertising campaigns. Interestingly, most corporate campaigns run by consumer goods manufacturers are undertaken by firms in the shopping goods category, such as appliance and auto marketers. Studies have also found that larger firms (in terms of gross sales) are much more prevalent users of corporate advertising than are smaller firms. Presumably, these firms have broader communications programs and more money to invest in advertising, which allows the use of corporate campaigns. An example of a company using just such a campaign is Apple Computer in its "Think Different" campaign featuring historic events (Exhibit 20.11).

In terms of media use, firms have found both magazine and television media to be well suited to corporate advertising efforts.[33] Corporate advertising appearing in magazines has the advantage of being able to target particular constituent groups with image- or issue-related messages. Hewlett-Packard chose to use both television and magazine ads in its corporate campaign (see Exhibit 20.12).[34] The campaign was designed to unify the image of the firm after its new CEO, Carly Fiorina, determined that the firm's image had become fragmented in the market. Magazines also provide the space for lengthy copy, which is often needed to achieve

32. Kevin Goldman, "Coopers & Lybrand TV Ads Paint Inspirational Image for Accounting," *Wall Street Journal*, January 3, 1994, 12.
33. David W. Schumann, Jan M. Hathcote, and Susan West, "Corporates Advertising in America: A Review of Published Studies on Use, Measurement and Effectiveness," *Journal of Advertising*, vol. 20, no. 3 (September 1991), 40.
34. Greg Farrell, "And Then There Was One H-P," *USA Today*, June 1, 2000, 5B.

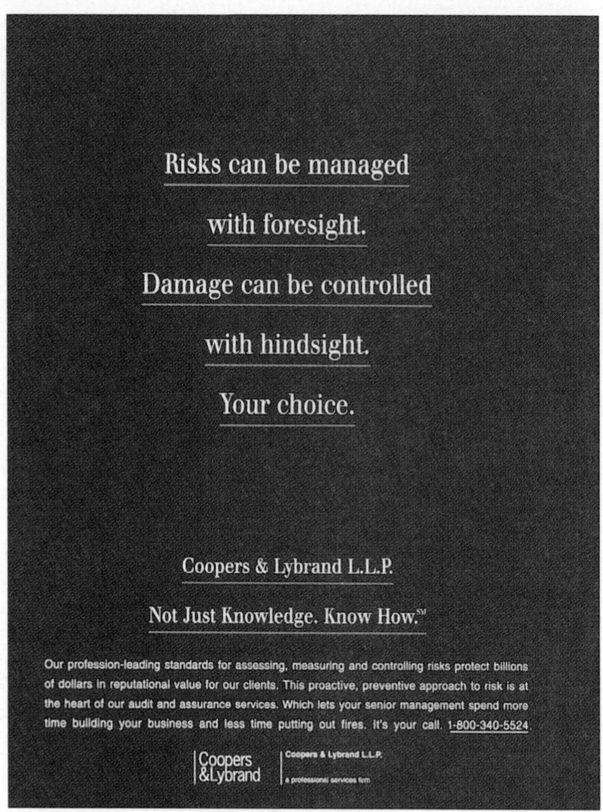

EXHIBIT 20.10

Coopers & Lybrand created this ad for their corporate image campaign a few years ago. Although the ad is for an accounting firm, does the headline remind you of public relations?

© Michael Newman/Photo Edit

EXHIBIT 20.11

Corporate image advertising is meant to build a broad image for the company as a whole rather than tout the features of a brand. Does this ad qualify as a corporate image ad? www.applecomputer.com

corporate advertising objectives. Television is a popular choice for corporate campaigns, especially image-oriented campaigns, because the creative opportunities provided by television can deliver a powerful, emotional message.

The objectives for corporate advertising are well focused. In fact, corporate advertising shares similar purposes with proactive public relations when it comes to what firms hope to accomplish with the effort. While corporate managers can be somewhat vague about the purposes for corporate ads, the following objectives are generally agreed upon:

- to build the image of the firm among customers, shareholders, the financial community, and the general public
- to boost employee morale or attract new employees
- to communicate an organization's views on social, political, or environmental issues
- to better position the firm's products against competition, particularly foreign competition, which is often perceived to be of higher quality
- to play a role in the overall integrated brand promotion of an organization as support for main product or service advertising

Notice that corporate advertising is not always targeted strictly at consumers. A broad range of constituents can be targeted with a corporate advertising effort. For example, when Glaxo Wellcome and SmithKline Beecham merged to form a $73 billion pharmaceutical behemoth, the newly created firm, known as GlaxoSmithKline,

EXHIBIT 20.12

Hewlett-Packard felt the company's image had become fragmented. This is one of the ads in a new corporate image campaign designed to unify the image of the firm. www.hp.com

launched an international print campaign aimed at investors who had doubts about the viability of the new corporate structure. The campaign was broadly image oriented and led with the theme "Disease does not wait. Neither will we."[35]

Types of Corporate Advertising.

Three basic types of corporate advertising dominate the campaigns run by organizations: image advertising, advocacy advertising, and cause-related advertising. Each is discussed in the following sections.

Corporate Image Advertising. The majority of corporate advertising efforts focus on enhancing the overall image of a firm among important constituents—typically customers, employees, and the general public. When IBM promotes itself as the firm providing "Solutions for a small planet" or when Toyota uses the slogan "Investing in the things we all care about" to promote its five U.S. manufacturing plants, the goal is to enhance the broad image of the firm. Bolstering a firm's image may not result in immediate effects on sales, but as we saw in Chapter 5, attitude can play an important directive force in consumer decision making. When a firm can enhance its overall image, it may well affect consumer predisposition in brand choice.[36] Exhibit 20.13 is an example of an image-oriented corporate ad. Here, Bristol-Myers Squibb is touting the life-saving impact of its high technology line of pharmaceuticals.

A distinguishing feature of corporate image advertising is that it is not designed to directly or immediately influence consumer brand choice. Bayer Corporation's corporate advertising campaign launched in 1995 had two specific goals: first, to announce its name change from Miles Laboratories Inc. to Bayer Corporation; second, to change the perception of the company from that of an aspirin-product firm to that of a diverse, research-based international company with businesses in health care, chemicals, and imaging technologies. The ads show a wide range of non-aspirin and often non-consumer products to demonstrate how Bayer regularly touches people's lives in meaningful ways. The target audience is business decision makers and opinion leaders. The media schedule reflects this non-consumer target: the *Wall Street Journal* and *Business Week* in print and *Face the Nation* and *Meet the Press* in television.

While most image advertising intends to communicate a general, favorable image, several corporate image advertising campaigns have been quite specific. When PPG Industries undertook a corporate image campaign to promote its public identity, the firm found that over a five-year period the number of consumers who claimed to have heard of PPG increased from 39.1 percent to 79.5 percent. The perception of the firm's product quality, leadership in new products, and attention to environmental problems were all greatly enhanced over the same period.[37] Another organization that has decided that image advertising is worthwhile is the national

35. David Goetzl, "GlaxoSmithKline launches print ads," *Advertising Age*, January 8, 2001, 30.

36. For an exhaustive assessment of the benefits of corporate advertising, see David M. Bender, Peter H. Farquhar, and Sanford C. Schulert, "Growing from the Top," *Marketing Management*, vol. 4, no. 4 (Winter/Spring 1996), 10–19, 24.

37. Schumann, Hathcote, and West, "Corporate Advertising in America," 43, 49.

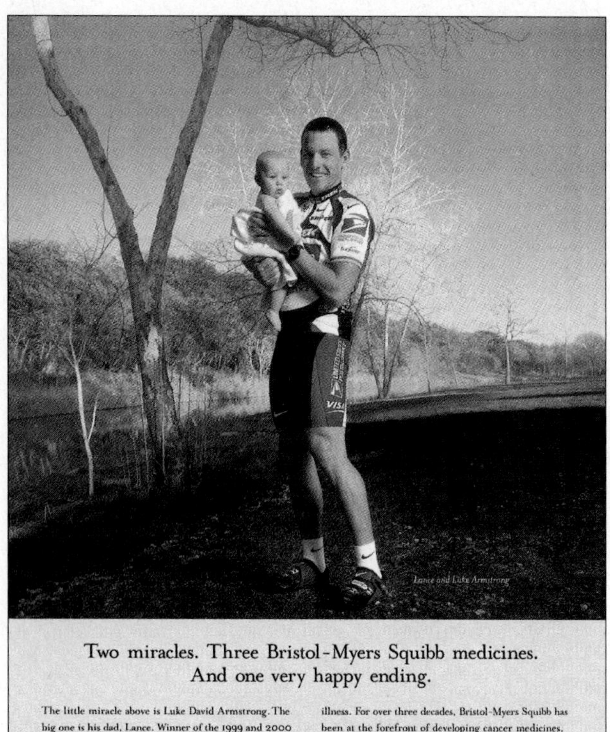

EXHIBIT 20.13

This corporate image ad for Bristol-Myers Squibb is touting the beneficial, life-enhancing effects of its high-technology pharmaceuticals. www.bms.com

newspaper *USA Today*.[38] The newspaper has spent $1 million on print and outdoor ads that highlight the four color-coded sections of the newspaper: National, Money, Sports, and Life.

Advocacy Advertising. **Advocacy advertising** attempts to establish an organization's position on important social, political, or environmental issues. Advocacy advertising is advertising that attempts to influence public opinion on issues of concern to a firm and the nature of its brands. For example, in a corporate advertising program begun in the early 1990s, Phillips Petroleum links its commitment to protect and restore bird populations and habitats to its efforts to reduce sulfur in gasoline. Some of the ads from this campaign can be viewed at www.phillips66.com/about/Flyway/Tradition-Advertising.htm. Typically, the issue in advocacy advertising is directly relevant to the business operations of the organization.

Cause-Related Advertising. **Cause-related advertising** features a firm's affiliation with an important social cause—reducing poverty, increasing literacy, and curbing drug abuse are examples—and takes place as part of the cause-related marketing efforts undertaken by a firm. The idea behind cause-related marketing and advertising is that a firm donates money to a non-profit organization in exchange for using the company name in connection with a promotional campaign. The purpose of cause-related advertising is that a firm's association with a worthy cause enhances the image of the firm in the minds of consumers. The ad in Exhibit 20.14 fits this definition perfectly. Anheuser-Busch is promoting the control of teenage drinking. This campaign helps establish the firm as a responsible marketer of alcoholic beverages, its primary business, while the firm is also helping society deal with a widespread social problem.

Cause-related advertising is thus advertising that identifies corporate sponsorship of philanthropic activities. Each year, *PROMO Magazine* provides an extensive list of charitable, philanthropic, and environmental organizations that have formal programs in which corporations may participate. Most of the programs suggest a minimum donation for corporate sponsorship and specify how the organization's resources will be mobilized in conjunction with the sponsor's other resources.

Some very high-profile cause-related marketing programs have made extensive use of cause-related advertising. The Dixie Chicks promoted the World Wildlife Fund during a summer tour and donated album sales to the organization. Kraft Foods Balance Bar is used as a sponsoring brand for the American Forest's ReLeaf program.[39]

Firms are also finding that new media outlets such as the World Wide Web offer opportunities to publicize their cause-related activities. This is especially true for

38. Keith J. Kelly, "*USA Today* Unveils Image Ads," *Advertising Age,* February 6, 1996, 8.
39. Stephanie Thompson, "Good Humor's Good Deeds," *Advertising Age,* January 8, 2001, 6.

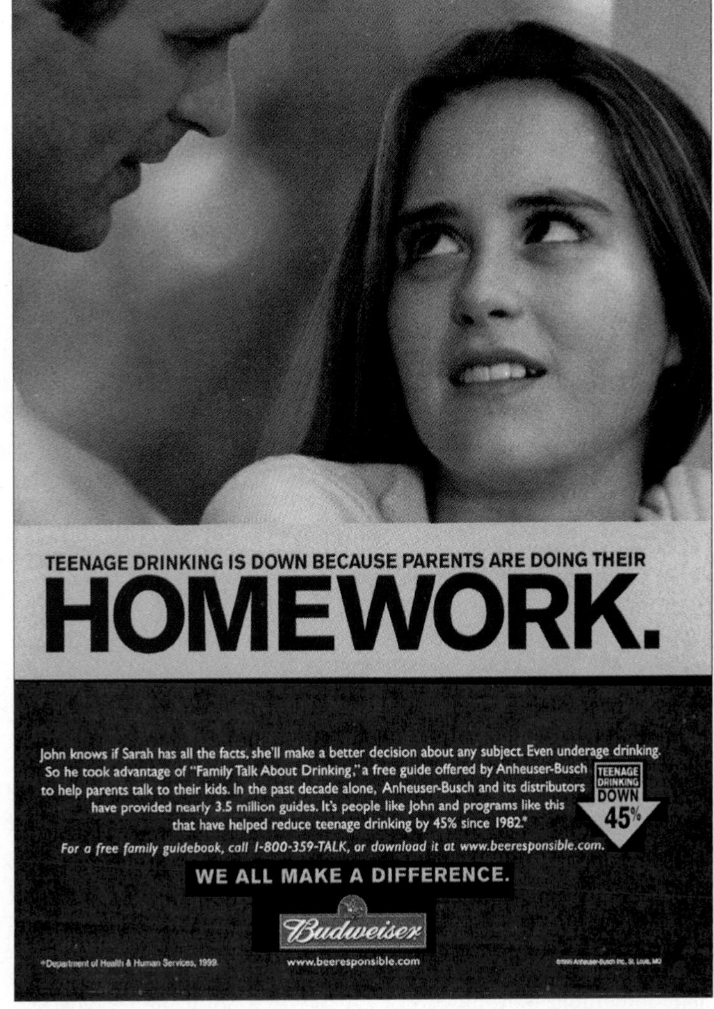

EXHIBIT 20.15

In this cause-related corporate campaign, Anheuser-Busch is promoting the control of teenage drinking. This campaign helps establish the firm as a responsible marketer of alcoholic beverages.
www.beeresponsible.com

environmental activities that firms are engaged in. The higher-education, upscale profile of many Web users matches the profile of consumers who are concerned about the natural environment. When firms engage in sound environmental practices, the Web is a good place for these firms to establish a "green" presence. "Green site" operators (www.greenmarketplace.com and www.envirolink.org are examples) give firms a forum to describe their environmental activities.[40]

While much good can come from cause-related marketing, there is some question as to whether consumers see this in a positive light. In a study by Roper Starch Worldwide, 58 percent of consumers surveyed believed that the only reason a firm was supporting a cause was to enhance the company's image.[41] The image of a firm as self-serving was much greater than the image of a firm as a philanthropic partner.

The belief among consumers that firms are involved with causes only for revenue benefits is truly unfortunate. Firms involved in causes do, indeed, give or raise millions of dollars for worthy causes. And the participation by U.S. firms in supporting worthy causes is broad based. About 92 percent of all U.S. companies contribute to a cause and spend over $770 million annually supporting causes.[42] While

40. Jacquellyn Ottman, *Marketing News,* February 26, 1996, 7.
41. Geoffrey Smith and Ron Stodghill, "Are Good Causes Good Marketing?," *Business Week,* March 21, 1994, 64–65.
42. John Palmer, "We Are the Children," *PROMO Magazine,* February 2001, 55–57.

there is some suspicion among adult consumers, there is growing evidence that cause marketing and advertising may be much more effective with teenagers. Researchers have found that 67 percent of teens shop for clothing and other items with a "cause" in mind, and more than half said they would switch to brands or retailers that were associated with a good cause.[43] In the words of one teen, "I bought a lot of my clothes at the Gap because they support the environment."[44] Some firms believe that cause-related advertising and integrated brand promotions are effective in a global marketing effort as well. The Global Issues box on page 709 described one such firm and its global cause-related effort.

Corporate advertising will never replace brand-specific advertising as the main thrust of corporate communications. But it can serve an important supportive role for brand advertising, and it can offer more depth and breadth to an integrated brand promotion program. One fundamental criticism corporate managers have of corporate advertising is the difficulty of measuring its specific effects on sales. If the sales effects of brand-specific advertising are difficult to measure, those for corporate advertising campaigns may be close to impossible to gauge.

43. Melinda Ligos, "Mall Rats with a Social Conscience," *Sales and Marketing Management,* November 1999, 115.
44. Ibid.

SUMMARY

Explain the role of public relations as part of a firm's overall integrated brand promotion strategy.

Public relations represents another aspect of an organization's IBP programming that can play a key role in determining how the organization's many constituents view the organization and its products. Public relations is a marketing and management communications function that deals with the public issues encountered by firms across a wide range of constituents. An important component of public relations is publicity—news media coverage of events related to a firm's products or activities.

Detail the objectives and tools of public relations.

An active public relations effort can serve many objectives, such as building goodwill and counteracting negative publicity. Public relations activities may also be orchestrated to support the launch of new products or communicate with employees on matters of interest to them. The public relations function may also be instrumental to the firm's lobbying efforts and in preparing executives to meet with the press. The primary tools of public relations experts are press releases, feature stories, corporate newsletters, interviews, press conferences, and participation in the firm's event sponsorship decisions and programs.

Describe how firms are using the Internet to assist their public relations activities.

Firms are using the Internet for a variety of public relations activities. In Chapter 16, we saw that new media can create a "buzz" through word-of-mouth that is more effective with certain target segments than any other tactic. In a noisy and crowded competitive environment, mainstream promotional tools such as advertising, sales promotion, and sponsorships may get lost in the clutter. Public relations using new media, particularly Web sites, chat room posts, and Web press releases, can reach targeted audiences in a different way that carries more credibility than "in your face" company self-promotion.

New Web companies themselves are finding that their needs for public relations are just as great as, if not greater than, established, non-Web-based firms. Analysts believe that without the third-party endorsement that public relations provides from the press and industry analysts, it is doubtful that a startup can be successful.

Finally, there is a major drawback to new media when it comes to public relations. Because of the speed with which information is disseminated, staying ahead of negative publicity is indeed challenging. While word-of-mouth can be used to create a positive buzz, it can also spread bad news or, even worse, misinformation just as fast.

 Describe two basic strategies motivating an organization's public relations activities.

When companies perceive public relations as a source of opportunity for shaping public opinion, they are likely to pursue a proactive public relations strategy. With a proactive strategy, a firm strives to build goodwill with key constituents via aggressive programs. The foundation for these proactive programs is a rigorous public relations audit and a comprehensive public relations plan. The plan should include an explicit statement of objectives to guide the overall effort. In many instances, however, public relations activities take the form of damage control, and in these instances the firm is obviously in a reactive public relations strategy mode. While a reactive strategy may seem a contradiction in terms, it certainly is the case that organizations can be prepared to react to bad news. Organizations that understand their inherent vulnerabilities in the eyes of important constituents will be able to react quickly and effectively in the face of hostile publicity.

 Discuss the applications and objectives of corporate advertising.

Corporate advertising is not undertaken to support an organization's specific brands, but rather to build the general reputation of the organization in the eyes of key constituents. This form of advertising uses various media—but primarily magazine and television ads—and serves goals such as image enhancement and building fundamental credibility for a firm's line of products. Corporate advertising may also serve diverse objectives, such as improving employee morale, building shareholder confidence, or denouncing competitors. Corporate ad campaigns generally fall into one of three categories: image advertising, advocacy advertising, or cause-related advertising. Corporate advertising may also be orchestrated in such a way to be very newsworthy, and thus it needs to be carefully coordinated with the organization's ongoing public relations programs.

KEY TERMS

public relations
publicity
proactive public relations strategy
reactive public relations strategy
public relations audit
public relations plan
advocacy advertising
cause-related advertising

QUESTIONS

1. Describe the two basic strategies a firm can select in determining its approach to the public relations function. Which of these two strategies do you believe Firestone operated under in dealing with the public relations challenges of the Justice Department case against the firm?

2. Review the criteria presented in this chapter and in Chapter 12 regarding the selection of events to sponsor. Obviously, some events will have more potential for generating favorable publicity than others. What particular criteria should be emphasized in event selection when a firm has the goal of gaining publicity that will build goodwill via event sponsorship?

3. Would it be appropriate to conclude that the entire point of public relations activity is to generate favorable publicity and stifle unfavorable publicity? What is it about publicity that makes it such an opportunity *and* threat?

4. There is an old saying to the effect that "there is no such thing as bad publicity." Can you think of a situation in which bad publicity would actually be good publicity?

5. Most organizations have vulnerabilities they should be aware of to help them anticipate and prepare for unfavorable publicity. What vulnerabilities would you associate with each of the following companies:

   R. J. Reynolds—makers of Camel cigarettes

   Procter & Gamble—makers of Pampers disposable diapers

   Kellogg's—makers of Kellogg's Frosted Flakes

   Exxon—worldwide oil and gasoline company

   McDonald's—worldwide restauranteur

6. Review the three basic types of corporate advertising and discuss how useful each would be as a device for generating brand image. Is corporate image advertising necessarily the best image builder?

EXPERIENTIAL EXERCISES

1. Visit the following link to about.com and research any one of the current public relations articles listed on the page. Summarize the article, answering some of the following questions: What is the main focus of the article? What specific information does it try to convey to people in the industry? Who is likely to benefit from this information? Name one main topic discussed in this chapter that relates to the article and explain the connection.

About.com: http://www.publicrelations.about.com

2. This chapter discusses the many ways new media contributes to the activities of public relations. Read the section of this chapter on Public Relations and New Media. Visit the following sites and explain how each contributes to the online public relations industry.

Arista Army: http://www.aristaarmy.com

Atomic PR: http://www.atomicpr.com

Internet PR Guide: http://www.internetprguide.com

eReleases: http://www.ereleases.com

USING THE INTERNET

20-1 Objectives for Public Relations

The goal of the public relations function is to manage positive public relations efforts as well as to soften the impact of negative events that threaten the relationship between businesses and consumers. Agencies must set very specific objectives for promoting healthy public relations, and must use the right tools to maintain the good reputation of their clients. McSpotlight is a consumer-protection organization that directs its efforts to raise awareness among fast-food customers.

McSpotlight: http://www.mcspotlight.org

1. What is the purpose of the McSpotlight organization?

2. Of the six primary objectives for public relations listed in the chapter, which is most likely to direct the McDonald's public relations effort in response to McSpotlight?

3. What public relations tools is McSpotlight using to achieve its goals? What public relations tools do you suppose McDonald's uses most often to counteract negative publicity?

20-2 Public Relations Agencies

Carter Ryley Thomas ranks among the largest independent agencies in the nation. CRT boasts a values-based philosophy that guides the firm's employee-owners in their everyday decisions. The agency was recently recognized as the Best PR Agency to Work for in America, and was named One of Five Best Mid-Sized PR Firms in the Country.

Carter Ryley Thomas Public Relations: http://www.crtpr.com

1. Browse the site and describe one of the recent public relations campaigns CRT has conducted for its clients.

2. What objectives and tools guided the campaign?

3. Was the effort characteristic of a proactive public relations strategy or a reactive one?

4. What direct benefits do you believe the client received as a result of this public relations strategy?

PART 5

Cincinnati Bell Wireless: Sustaining and Growing the Brand after Launch

There's a predictable aspect to advertising and marketing: Last year's results are last year's results. After a few bottles of champagne are popped to celebrate a good year, it's time to do it all again. And the new year will most certainly present opportunities and challenges that will need to be addressed in one's advertising and IBP planning, if a brand like Cincinnati Bell Wireless is to continue to thrive and grow. As we saw at the end of Part 4 of this case, 1998 was a very good year for Cincinnati Bell Wireless. Could CBW and its partner Northlich hope for a repeat performance in 1999? What were the prospects for continued growth of their wireless business? Jack Cassidy was proud of what CBW had been able to accomplish in its launch year, but by the fourth quarter of 1998, planning was already under way to make 1999 even better.

There were good reasons to be optimistic about CBW's prospects, heading into 1999. Consumers responded immediately to the superior features of digital PCS technology versus analog cellular, and CBW had emerged as the market leader for digital PCS in Cincinnati and surrounding communities. More generally, wireless phone service was evolving from a specialized technology adopted by a few to a mass-market product. The 30 percent annual growth rates in adoption of wireless phone services were projected to continue into 1999, making Cincinnati a marketplace with substantial, unfulfilled market potential.

Another thing that is predictable in advertising and marketing: If you have spotted a great opportunity for growing your business, rest assured that many of your competitors will have spotted it too. This would be CBW's biggest challenge headed into 1999. At least five wireless competitors envious of CBW's success in 1998 were preparing to do everything in their power to rob CBW of some of that success in 1999. These included Nextel, AirTouch Cellular, GTE Wireless, Ameritech, and Sprint PCS. Sprint represented an especially formidable foe because they offered the same state-of-the-art technology as CBW, and as a nationwide player were prepared to spend heavily behind their own brand-building campaign in 1999. No one expected that the Cincinnati market could support six wireless service providers. Only the strong would survive, and 1999 would prove to be a critical year in separating the weak from the strong.

Refining the CBW Advertising and IBP Plan for 1999. The launch plan implemented by Northlich on behalf of Cincinnati Bell Wireless had produced outstanding results. But before moving forward to create new executions for 1999, Northlich reassessed the plan by re-evaluating the key strategic issues from Thorson and Moore's strategic planning triangle (see Part 2 of this case if you need a refresher). Before selecting the mix of persuasion tools to be deployed in 1999, Northlich reassessed both appropriate target segment(s) and focal value proposition(s) for the brand. Direct feedback from the marketplace was essential in this re-evaluation.

Target Segment Identification. You may recall that CBW and Northlich had initially targeted MOPES (managers, owners, professionals, and entrepreneurs) in the launch campaign. While the campaign was effective in reaching these high-value business users, it was also clear that a market existed beyond those who would use the phone for business purposes. Almost overnight, wireless phone service had moved from novelty to necessity in the lifestyles of affluent, time-starved consumers. So Northlich entered 1999 with two target segments clearly specified. One was young (25+), college-educated, working professionals who (much like the MOPES) represented a high-value segment that used their phones to enhance on-the-job productivity. The second was an older (45 to 54) group of well-educated professionals who appeared to be adopting wireless phone service as a convenient alternative to the wired phone for everyday communication. These two segments were labeled Charter 500 Customers and Charter 100 Customers, respectively, indicating the pool of monthly minutes (that is, 500 versus 100) that was expected to be most attractive to each.

Consolidating the Value Proposition for the CBW Brand. Northlich and Cincinnati Bell launched the wireless brand with a value proposition featuring the functional benefits of this new service. To assess whether this proposed value was in fact being recognized by its customers, Northlich conducted a series of focus groups in January 1999 to hear directly from CBW customers what they liked most about this new service. In their customers' own words, CBW stood for *flexible, best choice, simple and affordable, no surprises, no contracts, reliable,* and *putting me in control.* Based on this qualitative research, the CBW value proposition for 1999 became a more focused version of what it had been in 1998. The goal for all advertising was to convince target audiences that CBW represented the "Simple Choice" for wireless communication. Additionally, to be in sync with Nokia's increasingly fashionable phones, CBW also aspired to be perceived as current and cool. The smart choice, cool enough to set current trends, was the brand equity that CBW set out to own in 1999.

Building the Brand and Growing the Business.

Here we will describe several of the various persuasion tools that were deployed to build the CBW brand in 1999. Much as it had done in the launch campaign, Northlich again called on its multidisciplinary teams to generate a sophisticated, multilayered advertising and IBP campaign, to sustain and grow the CBW brand. The campaign in 1999 integrated nearly all the tools that you have learned about in the previous 20 chapters, but in the following discussion we will emphasize the IBP tools that were featured in Chapters 17 through 20.

Equity Building. As the foundation for continuing success, Northlich used several tools to cultivate CBW brand equity. Brand equity is what consumers know about you; CBW aspired to be known as the smart choice, cool enough to set current trends. Several television spots were developed with the goal of reinforcing this brand equity. Like the "Classroom" and "Big Easy" spots described in Part 4, the emphasis of the new ads for 1999 was to position CBW as the simple, smart choice in wireless, and to portray signing contracts and complicated pricing schemes as an old-fashioned way of doing business. One particularly creative execution in 1999 was an ad that spoofed *Antiques Road Show,* PBS's most popular prime-time program at the time. In this ad a clunky analog cellular phone was written off as a worthless artifact of some bygone era, with of course a CBW phone being represented as the only appropriate choice for modern living. If imitation is the sincerest form of flattery, the creatives at Northlich must have been very flattered when Sprint PCS basically copied this ad execution as part of its national television campaign in 2001.[1]

1. Suzanne Vranica, "Madison Avenue Plays on Antiques' Lure," *Wall Street Journal,* May 16, 2001, B7.

In 1999 the creatives at Northlich also generated several out-of-the-box outdoor ad executions to contribute to the equity-building effort. A sample is provided in Exhibit IBP 5.1. This "Carol & Ted" ad was designed for one of the city's most prominent billboards; this billboard is equipped with a special feature where it can support three rotating panels, which can be programmed to rotate on any sequence that a client wants. So panels A, B, and C in the Exhibit below were designed to be rotated in a methodical sequence, delivering the punch line that if contracts scare you, then CBW is definitely the right choice.

Carol, will you marry me?
— Ted

Ted, NO.
— Carol

Trouble with commitment?
NO CONTRACTS. Cincinnati Bell wireless

EXHIBIT IBP 5.1

The "Carol & Ted" three-panel billboard.

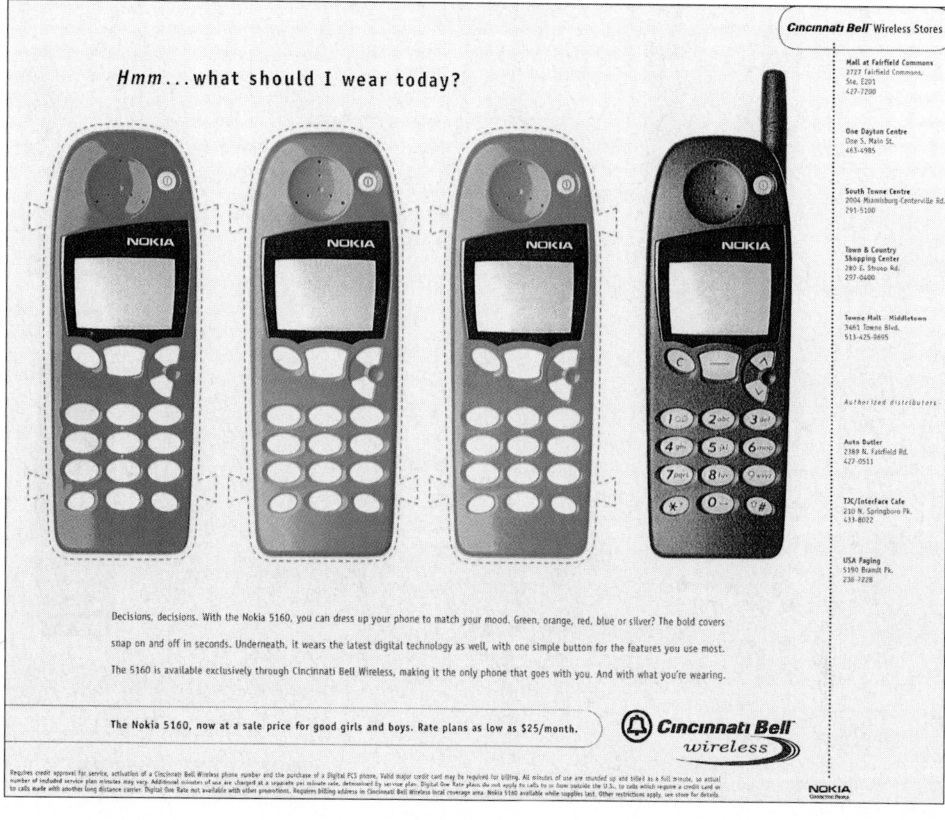

EXHIBIT IBP 5.2

Brand building around a cool Nokia phone.

The special genius associated with this outdoor ad came in how it was deployed to create a public relations coup for Cincinnati Bell. Rather than rotate through all the panels initially, only panel A from Exhibit IBP 5.1 was displayed for the first week. This drove all the local TV news departments wild with curiosity, and became a regular topic during the evening news. Why make your marriage proposal on the city's most visible billboard? Who was Ted? Carol? Did they live and work in Cincinnati? On and on it went. In week two, panel B was revealed. Carol said no! Poor Ted. He must be heartbroken. Would we ever hear from Ted again? By the time the third week came, when CBW was ready to reveal panel C, the local media had drummed up so much attention around this billboard that nearly everyone in the city would ultimately learn that the punch line was CBW's swipe against wireless service providers that make you sign contracts. This is a wonderful example of how a little creativity can pay big dividends in getting low-cost, mass exposure for a brand-building message.

Another sample of Northlich's brand-building work is the print ad in Exhibit IBP 5.2. Remember, CBW aspired to be the smart choice, cool enough to set current trends, like taking a pretty candy-colored phone to work to demonstrate your savoir faire. Much as Swatch did for the inexpensive wristwatch, and iMac did for the personal computer, Nokia in 1999 was hard at work in North America converting the cell phone from a plain utilitarian device into a fashion badge. CBW was quick to catch on to Nokia's agenda, and Northlich developed the ads to champion CBW as the brand that was cool enough to set current trends, at least for people age 25 to 54. (People under age 25 would get their own brand: more on that at the end.)

Closing the Sale. As noted in Chapter 18, many diverse sales promotion tactics are employed by marketers to supplement their advertising for the purpose of closing the sale. The kind of tactics used and the frequency of use depends on one's industry and competitive

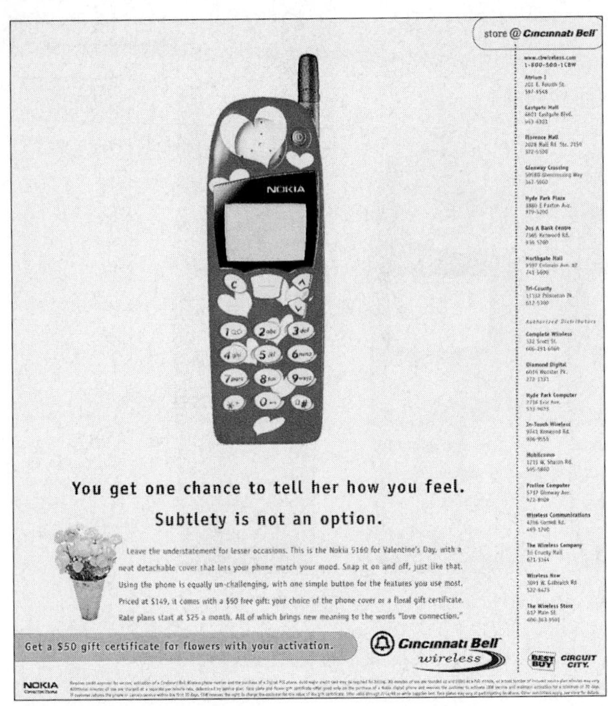

EXHIBIT IBP 5.3

There's nothing like a $50 gift certificate for flowers to get people's attention in mid-February.

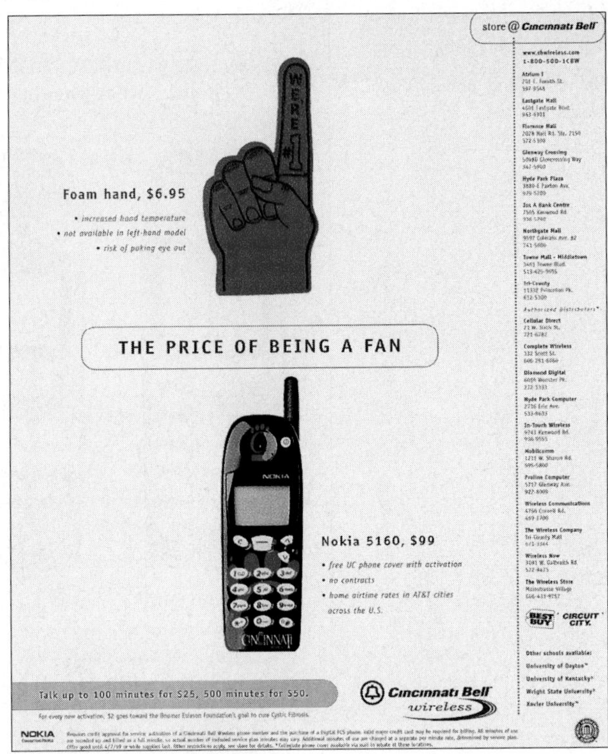

EXHIBIT IBP 5.4

March Madness is the perfect time to help sports fans show their true colors.

field. Turns out that the telecommunications business is intensely competitive, and 1999 would be a year of wireless warfare in Cincinnati.[2] So, beyond the general brand-building ads, Northlich and CBW also worked fervently to create and advertise a series of sales promotions designed to persuade new customers to take that plunge and activate their wireless phone service with Cincinnati Bell.

The competitive intensity of the wireless phone business means that, ideally, one should have a fresh sales promotion ready to go each and every month. Northlich pretty much delivered on this demanding schedule. Sample print ads from the Valentine's Day promotion of February 1999 and the March Madness promotion of March 1999 appear in Exhibits IBP 5.3 and 5.4. Other sales promotions included a Mother's Day event, a Summer Splash, Fall Football Faceplates, and a host of offers during the holiday season in late fall, where 40 percent of annual activations are typically generated. All of these events included a price deal on a Nokia phone, and/or a freebie such as a $50 floral gift certificate, to help close the sale.

Another tool for delivering news about an exciting sales promotion to carefully targeted households is direct mail. Northlich and CBW deployed this tool skillfully in 1999. An example of their collaboration from the Summer Splash promo is shown in Exhibit IBP 5.5. Examine this direct mail piece carefully and you'll find all the right elements for closing a sale. The piece features a great offer: a nice price on a spiffy Nokia phone plus four free tickets to the then newly opened Newport Aquarium—everyone's #1 destination in the summer of 1999. Note as well the clear call to action: "Hurry, this incredible offer ends August 14!" How can I sign up? With

2. Mike Boyer, "Wireless Wars," *Cincinnati Enquirer,* November 15, 1998, E1, E4.

CBW it's always easy. Take your pick: the toll-free number; www.cbwireless.com; or any Cincinnati Bell Wireless retail outlet, including Best Buy, Circuit City, Office Depot, and Staples. This is great local sales execution, making the smart choice an obvious choice.

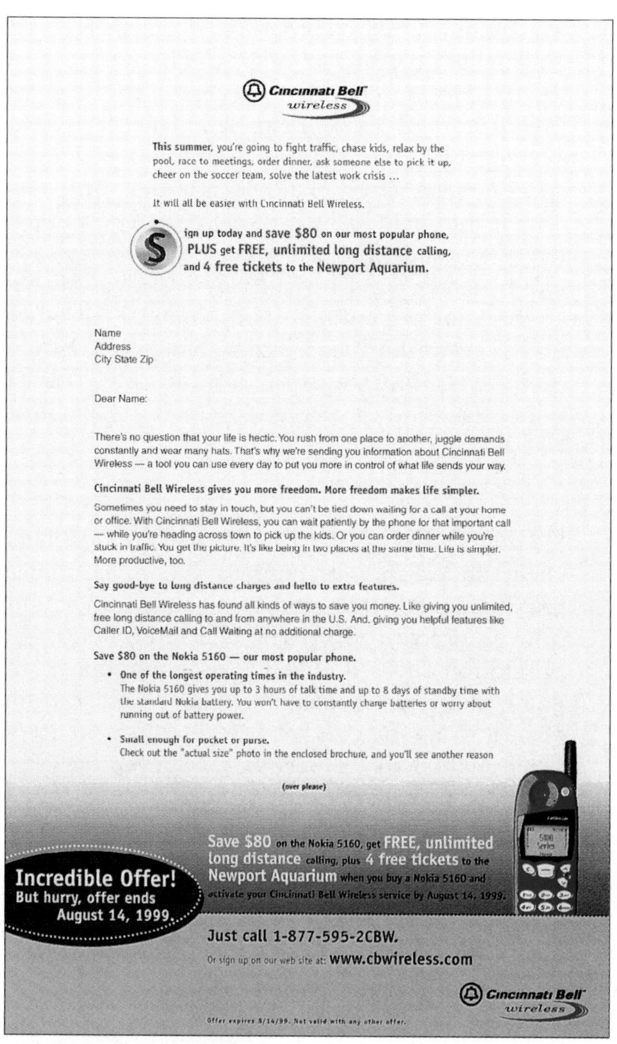

Cincinnati Bell wireless

This summer, you're going to fight traffic, chase kids, relax by the pool, race to meetings, order dinner, ask someone else to pick it up, cheer on the soccer team, solve the latest work crisis ...

It will all be easier with Cincinnati Bell Wireless.

Sign up today and save $80 on our most popular phone, PLUS get FREE, unlimited long distance calling, and 4 free tickets to the Newport Aquarium.

Name
Address
City State Zip

Dear Name:

There's no question that your life is hectic. You rush from one place to another, juggle demands constantly and wear many hats. That's why we're sending you information about Cincinnati Bell Wireless — a tool you can use every day to put you more in control of what life sends your way.

Cincinnati Bell Wireless gives you more freedom. More freedom makes life simpler.

Sometimes you need to stay in touch, but you can't be tied down waiting for a call at your home or office. With Cincinnati Bell Wireless, you can wait patiently by the phone for that important call — while you're heading across town to pick up the kids. Or you can order dinner while you're stuck in traffic. You get the picture. It's like being in two places at the same time. Life is simpler. More productive, too.

Say good-bye to long distance charges and hello to extra features.

Cincinnati Bell Wireless has found all kinds of ways to save you money. Like giving you unlimited, free long distance calling to and from anywhere in the U.S. And, giving you helpful features like Caller ID, VoiceMail and Call Waiting at no additional charge.

Save $80 on the Nokia 5160 — our most popular phone.

- **One of the longest operating times in the industry.** The Nokia 5160 gives you up to 3 hours of talk time and up to 8 days of standby time with the standard Nokia battery. You won't have to constantly charge batteries or worry about running out of battery power.
- **Small enough for pocket or purse.** Check out the "actual size" photo in the enclosed brochure, and you'll see another reason

(over please)

Incredible Offer! But hurry, offer ends August 14, 1999.

Save $80 on the Nokia 5160, get FREE, unlimited long distance calling, plus 4 free tickets to the Newport Aquarium when you buy a Nokia 5160 and activate your Cincinnati Bell Wireless service by August 14, 1999.

Just call 1-877-595-2CBW.

Or sign up on our web site at: www.cbwireless.com

Cincinnati Bell wireless

Offer expires 8/14/99. Not valid with any other offer.

EXHIBIT IBP 5.5

This direct mail piece carried all the incredible news about Summer Splash.

Nurturing Relationships with Customers. Cincinnati Bell is an experienced database marketer. Working with Northlich, the company created a number of innovative programs in 1999 designed to reward, engage, and build a bond with existing CBW customers. Too often marketers make the mistake of spending all their advertising dollars trying to win new customers, and they take existing customers for granted. Then they wonder why their churn rates exceed industry averages. As we saw in Part 4 of this case, in its first year CBW had churn rates well below industry averages. No slippage would be acceptable in 1999.

Database marketing at its best is about building enduring relationships with customers, and CBW used its customer database in an attempt to do just that in 1999. Relationships depend on communication, and to foster that communication CBW launched its own branded newsletter—*The Talk.* The cover page of the summer 1999 issue is shown in Exhibit IBP 5.6. The communication goals for *The Talk* involved things such as keeping customers aware of changes taking place in the wireless industry, tips for making your phone more convenient to use and program, and details about special promotions designed exclusively for CBW customers. *The Talk* also encouraged customer comments and complaints by phone (877-CBW-8877) or e-mail (thetalk@cinbell.com).

Well, a newsletter like *The Talk* can be a great thing when you have something special to talk about. So, as part of its Summer Splash extravaganza, CBW decided to throw a party to celebrate the first anniversary of its launch. But what kind of party makes sense if your brand stands for *smart, current, and cool*? And whom should we invite? How about a rock-and-roll concert for 10,000 of our closest friends—only CBW customers allowed. Perfect. Using *The Talk* to deliver its exclusive invitations, CBW was able to attract about 10,000 of its customers to a free concert featuring Hootie & the Blowfish. In addition, Nokia got so caught up in the activity that they ended up footing most of the bill for the evening's entertainment, turning it into a huge win for CBW and CBW customers.

An event like this Hootie concert works in several ways to stir passion for a brand. First, the band puts on a great show, leaving everyone with memories of a pleasant evening that are now connected to the CBW brand. Additionally, the local news media would of course create a big fuss over this event, making anyone who attended feel that, as a CBW customer, they really did get to be part of something special. Pity those poor souls who haven't gotten the message about which wireless brand in Cincinnati is *smart, current, and cool.*

It also turns out that every time someone activates a CBW phone, Cincinnati Bell sets aside two dollars for Boomer Esiason's foundation for the cure of cystic fibrosis.

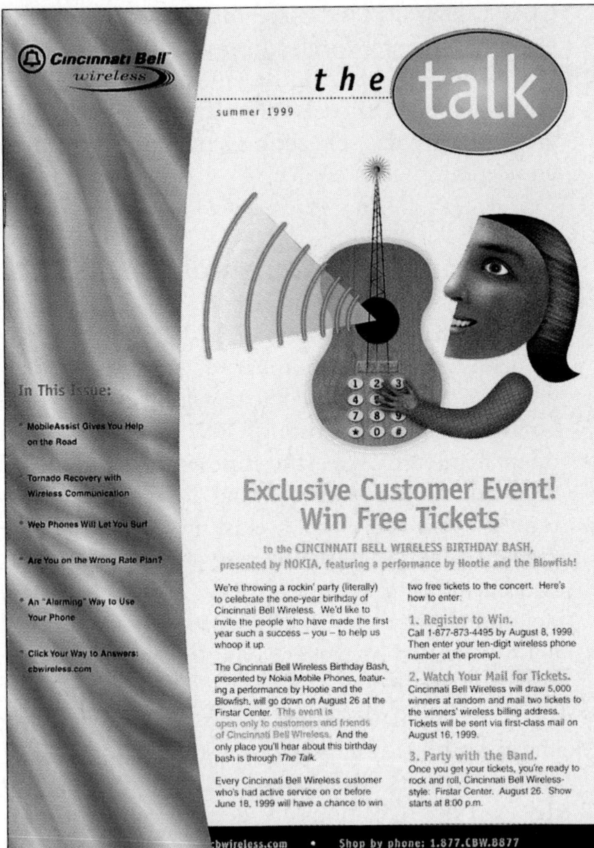

EXHIBIT IBP 5.6

Newsletters are an increasingly common tool for would-be relationship builders.

Mr. Esiason, a retired professional athlete, is one of Cincinnati's mega-celebrities, and he was on hand for the Hootie concert to accept a check to his foundation for more than $200,000. It was an evening filled with passion and emotion. Passion and emotion drive brand loyalty and turn customers into brand advocates who then go out and tell two friends who tell two friends who tell two more friends, and all of a sudden you've touched a whole lot of customers and potential customers with a powerful brand-building message. You're probably starting to get the hint that 1999 turned out to be another very good year for Cincinnati Bell Wireless.

Measuring Up in 1999. When a client understands its business and its customers like Cincinnati Bell, and an agency understands how to execute advertising and integrated brand promotion like NORTHLICH, good things are going to happen in the marketplace. This certainly proved to be the case for CBW's launch in 1998, when 60,000 activations were achieved by year's end. But things turned out just as well or maybe even a little better for CBW in 1999. By December 1999 Cincinnati Bell had activated over 150,000 customers for its wireless business; CBW's market share had more than doubled versus one year earlier, with much of this gain coming from consumers who were abandoning the rapidly fading analog cellular format. With creative advertising, aggressive promotions like March Madness and Summer Splash, adept direct marketing, and a flair for public relations, CBW established itself as a feisty local brand ready to defend its home turf against telecommunication heavyweights such as Sprint and AT&T. Smart, current, and cool is right where they wanted to be.

When Opportunity Comes Knockin'. To close this saga about the wireless business, it only seems appropriate that we provide a glimpse of the next big thing for Cincinnati Bell. Put yourself in the shoes of Jack Cassidy at Cincinnati Bell. What would you do if information like the following was brought to your attention in the fall of 1999?

- The U.S. prepaid wireless phone business is expected to grow to 28 percent of the overall market by 2003, up from 3.5 percent in 1998.
- About 35 percent of Cincinnati's residents are under age 25.
- Wireless market penetration in the 16-to-24 age group was about 7 percent in the United States in 1998, versus more than 30 percent in Western Europe.
- British Telecom doubled the size of its business in the U.K. by launching a brand called "U phone" to people in the 16-to-24 age group.

With all the good business sense you've developed at this point, we hope you can see that Jack Cassidy had an obvious call to make in the fall of 1999. He needed a prepaid wireless brand for the market of young consumers in Cincinnati that was currently being poorly served. So why not just go after them with a prepaid version

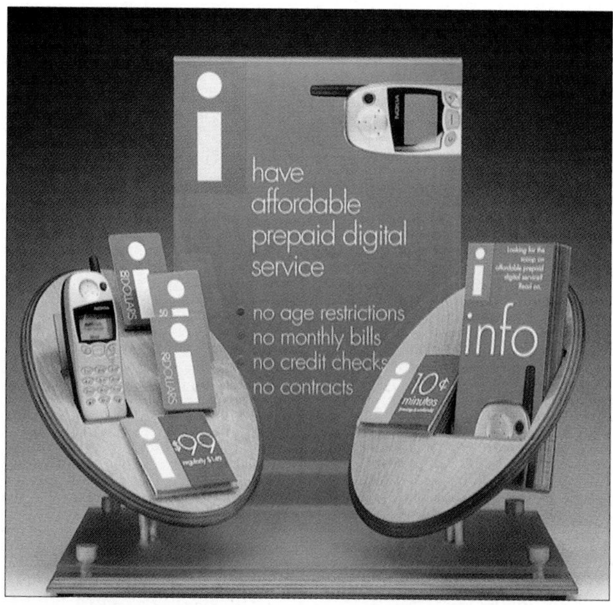

EXHIBIT IBP 5.7

Every aspect of the i-wireless brand was conceived to differentiate it from CBW, including point-of-purchase displays. (Photo provided by JHPhotography.*)*

of Cincinnati Bell Wireless? Think about that one. Making a brand smart, current, and cool for people 25 to 54 years old, and then having it also connect with people in the 16-to-24 age range, is a tall order. Jack Cassidy was way too savvy a brand builder to fall into that trap. It thus was time to launch another brand.

In the fall of 1999 Cincinnati Bell launched i-wireless, the first service in the United States marrying a wireless phone with a Web portal and targeted to the 16-to-24 age group.[3] This would not be your parents' phone service. The launch campaign featured some naughty advertising, a new Web site (www.i-ontheweb.com), and a heavy emphasis on guerrilla marketing tactics. For example, the launch glorified the I-crew, 25 high school and college students in customized VW Beetles traveling around the city to promote i-wireless at bars and school events. Of course, the Beetles were emblazoned with the i-wireless logo and slogan, *i live by my terms*. Key components of the i-wireless value proposition are apparent in the point-of-purchase display shown in Exhibit IBP 5.7: no age restrictions, no monthly bills, no credit checks, and of course, no contracts! It didn't take long for this new service to find an enthusiastic audience, but would it become another success story on the magnitude of the CBW launch? We'll save that one for next time. Happy trails.

3. Mike Boyer, "Prepaid Appeals to Parents," *Cincinnati Enquirer,* December 14, 1999, B10.

IBP EXERCISES

1. Review Thorson and Moore's strategic planning triangle from Part 2 of this case study. What were the key strategic issues that Northlich had to reconsider as part of the planning process for 1999? What changes (if any) did this reconsideration lead to in the advertising and IBP campaign that Northlich would execute for CBW in 1999?
2. Using this CBW example, explain how equity-building advertising, sales promotions, and direct marketing programs can be used in combination to produce the kind of outcome that all clients are looking for. What makes the combination of these tools more potent than any one of the tools by itself?
3. Local brands need to be creative in capitalizing on their local roots if they are to stave off the attacks of powerful national brands. The folks at Northlich and CBW seem keenly aware of this point. Provide three examples from the 1999 campaign that illustrate CBW's willingness to connect to issues or events that are meaningful in its local community.
4. Compare the Web sites for Cincinnati Bell Wireless (www.cbwireless.com) and i-wireless (www.i-ontheweb.com). What features or aspects of the two Web sites serve to effectively differentiate these two brands? Based on what you find at these Web sites, how would you describe the similarities and differences in the value propositions for these two brands?

GLOSSARY

A

account planner A relatively recent addition to many advertising agencies; it is this person's job to synthesize all relevant consumer research and use it to design a coherent advertising strategy.

account planning A system by which, in contrast to traditional advertising research methods, an agency assigns a co-equal account planner to work alongside the account executive and analyze research data. This method requires the account planner to stay with the same projects on a continuous basis.

account services A team of managers that identify the benefits a brand offers, its target audiences, and the best competitive positioning, and then develops a complete promotion plan.

Action for Children's Television (ACT) A group formed during the 1970s to lobby the government to limit the amount and content of advertising directed at children.

adaptors In reference to the *adaptation/innovation theory* generated by a study of creativity in employees, adaptors are the ones who, when faced with creative tasks, tend to work within the existing paradigm.

advertisement A specific message that an organization has placed to persuade an audience.

advertising A paid, mass-mediated attempt to persuade.

advertising agency An organization of professionals who provide creative and business services to clients related to planning, preparing, and placing advertisements.

advertising campaign A series of coordinated advertisements and other promotional efforts that communicate a single theme or idea.

advertising clutter An obstacle to advertising resulting from the large volume of similar ads for most products and services.

advertising plan A plan that specifies the thinking and tasks needed to conceive and implement an effective advertising effort.

advertising response function A mathematical relationship based on marginal analysis that associates dollars spent on advertising and sales generated; sometimes used to help establish an advertising budget.

advertising specialties A sales promotion having three key elements: a message, placed on a useful item, given to consumers with no obligation.

advertising substantiation program An FTC program initiated in 1971 to ensure that advertisers make available to consumers supporting evidence for claims made in ads.

advertorial A special advertising section designed to look like the print publication in which it appears.

advocacy advertising Advertising that attempts to influence public opinion on important social, political, or environmental issues of concern to the sponsoring organization.

aerial advertising Advertising that involves airplanes (pulling signs or banners), skywriting, or blimps.

affirmative disclosure An FTC action requiring that important material determined to be absent from prior ads must be included in subsequent advertisements.

agency of record The advertising agency chosen by the advertiser to purchase media time and space.

alternative press newspapers Newspapers geared toward a young, entertainment-oriented audience.

animation The use of drawn figures and scenes (like cartoons) to produce a television commercial.

appropriation The use of pictures or images owned by someone else without permission.

aspirational groups Groups made up of people an individual admires or uses as role models but is unlikely to ever interact with in any meaningful way.

association tests A type of projective technique that asks consumers to express their feelings or thoughts after hearing a brand name or seeing a logo.

assorted media mix A media mix option that employs multiple media alternatives to reach target audiences.

attitude An overall evaluation of any object, person, or issue that varies along a continuum, such as favorable to unfavorable or positive to negative.

attitude-change study A type of advertising research that uses a before-and-after ad exposure design.

audience A group of individuals who may receive and interpret messages sent from advertisers through mass media.

average quarter-hour persons The average number of listeners tuned to a radio station during a specified 15-minute segment of a daypart.

average quarter-hour rating The radio audience during a quarter-hour daypart expressed as a percentage of the population of the measurement area.

average quarter-hour share The percentage of the total radio audience that was listening to a radio station during a specified quarter-hour daypart.

axis A line, real or imagined, that runs through an advertisement and from which the elements in the ad flare out.

B

balance An orderliness and compatibility of presentation in an advertisement.

bandwidth A measure of the computer resources used by a Web site on the Internet.

banner ads Advertisements placed on World Wide Web sites that contain editorial material.

barter syndication A form of television syndication that takes both off-network and first-run syndication shows and offers them free or at a reduced rate to local television stations, with some national advertising presold within the programs.

beliefs The knowledge and feelings a person has accumulated about an object or issue.

benefit positioning A positioning option that features a distinctive customer benefit.

benefit segmentation A type of market segmenting in which target segments are delineated by the various benefit packages that different consumers want from the same product category.

between-vehicle duplication Exposure to the same advertisement in different media.

bill-back allowances A monetary incentive provided to retailers for featuring a marketer's brand in either advertising or in-store displays.

blackletter A style patterned after monastic hand-drawn letters characterized by the ornate design of the letters. Also called gothic.

bleed page A magazine page on which the background color of an ad runs to the edge of the page, replacing the standard white border.

border The space surrounding an advertisement; it keeps the ad elements from spilling over into other ads or into the printed matter next to the ad.

brand A name, term, sign, symbol, or any other feature that identifies one seller's good or service as distinct from those of other sellers.

brand attitudes Summary evaluations that reflect preferences for various products and brands.

brand communities Groups of consumers who feel a commonality and a shared purpose grounded or attached to a consumer good or service.

brand equity Developed by a firm that creates and maintains positive associations with the brand in the mind of consumers.

brand extension An adaptation of an existing brand to a new product area.

branding The strategy of developing brand names so that manufacturers can focus consumer attention on a clearly identified item.

brand-loyal users A market segment made up of consumers who repeatedly buy the same brand of a product.

brand loyalty A decision-making mode in which consumers repeatedly buy the same brand of a product as their choice to fulfill a specific need.

brand placement The sales promotion technique of getting a marketer's brand featured in movies and television shows.

brand switching An advertising objective in which a campaign is designed to encourage customers to switch from their established brand.

broadband A high-speed network providing the capability of transmitting video as well as voice transmission over the Internet.

build-up analysis A method of building up the expenditure levels of various tasks to help establish an advertising budget.

bulky box A very large pop-up that can cover about 25 percent of the Web page.

business buyer sales promotion Incentive techniques designed to cultivate buyers in large corporations who are making purchase decisions about a wide range of products.

business markets The institutional buyers who purchase items to be used in other products and services or to be resold to other businesses or households.

business newspapers Newspapers like the *Financial Times,* which serve a specialized business audience.

C

cable television A type of television that transmits a wide range of programming to subscribers through wires rather than over airwaves.

caching The use of a kind of active memory to conserve computer system resources.

cause-related advertising Advertising that identifies corporate sponsorship of philanthropic activities.

cease-and-desist order An FTC action requiring an advertiser to stop running an ad within 30 days so a hearing can be held to determine whether the advertising in question is deceptive or unfair.

celebrity A unique sociological category that matters a great deal to advertisers.

celebrity endorsements Advertisements that use an expert or celebrity as a spokesperson to endorse the use of a product or service.

channel grazing Using a television remote control to monitor programming on other channels while an advertisement is being broadcast.

circulation The number of newspapers distributed each day (for daily newspapers) or each week (for weekly publications).

classified advertising Newspaper advertising that appears as all-copy messages under categories such as sporting goods, employment, and automobiles.

click-throughs When Web users click on advertisements that take them to the homepages of those advertisers.

client The company or organization that pays for advertising. Also called the *sponsor.*

closing date The date when production-ready advertising materials must be delivered to a publisher for an ad to make a newspaper or magazine issue.

cognitive consistency The maintenance of a system of beliefs and attitudes over time; consumers' desire for cognitive consistency is an obstacle to advertising.

cognitive dissonance The anxiety or regret that lingers after a difficult decision.

cognitive responses The thoughts that occur to individuals at that exact moment in time when their beliefs and attitudes are being challenged by some form of persuasive communication.

collection search engine An automated program that crawls (a Spider) around the Web and collects information.

column inch A unit of advertising space in a newspaper, equal to one inch deep by one column wide.

commission system A method of agency compensation based on the amount of money the advertiser spends on the media.

communication tests A type of pretest message research that simply seeks to see if a message is communicating something close to what is desired.

community A group of people loosely joined by some common characteristic or interest.

comp A polished version of an ad.

comparison advertisements Advertisements in which an advertiser makes a comparison between the firm's brand and competitors' brands.

competitive field The companies that compete for a segment's business.

competitive positioning A positioning option that uses an explicit reference to an existing competitor to help define precisely what the advertised brand can do.

competitor analysis In an advertising plan, the section that discusses who the competitors are, outlining their strengths, weaknesses, tendencies, and any threats they pose.

concentrated media mix A media mix option that focuses all the media placement dollars in one medium.

concept search engine A concept rather than a word or phrase is the basis for the search.

concept test A type of developmental research that seeks feedback designed to screen the quality of a new idea, using consumers as the final judge and jury.

consent order An FTC action asking an advertiser accused of running deceptive or unfair advertising to stop running the advertisement in question, without admitting guilt.

consideration set The subset of brands from a particular product category that becomes the focal point of a consumer's evaluation.

consultants Individuals that specialize in areas related to the promotional process.

consumer behavior Those activities directly involved in obtaining, consuming, and disposing of products and services, including the decision processes that precede and follow these actions.

consumer culture A way of life centered around consumption.

consumerism The actions of individual consumers to exert power over the marketplace activities of organizations.

consumer markets The markets for products and services purchased by individuals or households to satisfy their specific needs.

consumer-market sales promotion A type of sales promotion designed to induce household consumers to purchase a firm's brand rather than a competitor's brand.

contest A sales promotion that has consumers compete for prizes based on skill or ability.

continuity The pattern of placement of advertisements in a media schedule.

continuous scheduling A pattern of placing ads at a steady rate over a period of time.

controlled circulation The number of copies of a newspaper that are given away free.

coolhunts Researchers actually go to the site where they believe cool resides, stalk it, and bring it back to be used in the product and its advertising.

co-op advertising *See* **cooperative advertising.**

cooperative advertising The sharing of advertising expenses between national advertisers and local merchants. Also called *co-op advertising.*

copywriting The process of expressing the value and benefits a brand has to offer, via written or verbal descriptions.

corporate advertising Advertising intended to establish a favorable attitude toward a company as a whole, not just toward a specific brand.

corporate home page A site on the World Wide Web that focuses on a corporation and its products.

corrective advertising An FTC action requiring an advertiser to run additional advertisements to dispel false beliefs created by deceptive advertising.

cost per inquiry (CPI) The number of inquiries generated by a direct-marketing program divided by that program's cost.

cost per order (CPO) The number of orders generated by a direct-marketing program divided by that program's cost.

cost per rating point (CPRP) The cost of a spot on television divided by the program's rating; the resulting dollar figure can be used to compare the efficiency of advertising on various programs.

cost per thousand (CPM) The dollar cost of reaching 1,000 members of an audience using a particular medium.

cost per thousand–target market (CPM–TM) The cost per thousand for a particular segment of an audience.

coupon A type of sales promotion that entitles a buyer to a designated reduction in price for a product or service.

cover date The date of publication appearing on a magazine.

creative boutique An advertising agency that emphasizes copywriting and artistic services to its clients.

creative concept The unique creative thought behind an advertising campaign.

creative plan A guideline used during the copywriting process to specify the message elements that must be coordinated during the preparation of copy.

creative revolution A revolution in the advertising industry during the 1960s, characterized by the "creatives" (art directors and copywriters) having a bigger say in the management of their agencies.

creative services A group that develops the message that will be delivered through advertising, sales promotion, direct marketing, event sponsorship, or public relations.

creative team The copywriters and art directors responsible for coming up with the creative concept for an advertising campaign.

cross-selling Marketing programs aimed at customers that already purchase other products.

culture What a people do—the way they eat, groom themselves, celebrate, mark their space and social position, and so forth.

cume The cumulative radio audience, which is the total number of different people who listen to a station for at least five minutes in a quarter-hour period within a specified daypart.

customer satisfaction Good feelings that come from a favorable postpurchase experience.

D

dailies Newspapers published every weekday; also, in television ad production, the scenes shot during the previous day's production.

database agency Agency that helps customers construct databases of target customers, merge databases, develop promotional materials, and then execute the campaign.

dayparts Segments of time during a television broadcast day.

deception Making false or misleading statements in an advertisement.

defamation When a communication occurs that damages the reputation of an individual because the information was untrue.

delayed response advertising Advertising that relies on imagery and message themes to emphasize the benefits and satisfying characteristics of a brand.

demographic segmentation Market segmenting based on basic descriptors like age, gender, race, marital status, income, education, and occupation.

design The structure (and the plan behind the structure) for the aesthetic and stylistic aspects of a print advertisement.

designers Specialists intimately involved with the execution of creative ideas and efforts.

developmental copy research A type of copy research that helps copywriters at the early stages of copy development by providing audience interpretations and reactions to the proposed copy.

dialogue Advertising copy that delivers the selling points of a message to the audience through a character or characters in the ad.

dialogue balloons A type of projective technique that offers consumers the chance to fill in the dialogue of cartoonlike stories, as a way of indirectly gathering brand information.

differentiation The process of creating a perceived difference, in the mind of the consumer, between an organization's brand and the competition's.

digital video (DV) A less expensive and less time-consuming alternative to film, it produces a better quality image than standard videotape.

direct broadcast by satellite (DBS) A program delivery system whereby television (and radio) programs are sent directly from a satellite to homes equipped with small receiving dishes.

direct mail A direct-marketing medium that involves using the postal service to deliver marketing materials.

direct marketing According to the Direct Marketing Association, "An interactive system of marketing which uses one or more advertising media to affect a measurable response and/or transaction at any location."

direct-marketing agency Agency that maintains large databases of mailing lists; some of these firms can also design direct-marketing campaigns either through the mail or by telemarketing.

direct response advertising Advertising that asks the receiver of the message to act immediately.

direct response agency Also called direct marketing agency.

direct response copy Advertising copy that highlights the urgency of acting immediately.

display advertising A newspaper ad that includes the standard components of a print ad—headline, body copy, and often an illustration—to set it off from the news content of the paper.

domain name The unique URL through which a Web location is established.

door-to-door sampling A type of sampling in which samples are brought directly to the homes of a target segment in a well-defined geographic area.

double-page spreads Advertisements that bridge two facing pages.

E

e-commerce agency Agency that handles a variety of planning and execution activities related to promotions using electronic commerce.

economies of scale The ability of a firm to lower the cost of each item produced because of high-volume production.

editing In television ad production, piecing together various scenes or shots of scenes to bring about the desired visual effect.

effective frequency The number of times a target audience needs to be exposed to a message before the objectives of the advertiser are met.

effective reach The number or percentage of consumers in the target audience that are exposed to an ad some minimum number of times.

elaboration likelihood model (ELM) A model that pertains to any situation where a persuasive communication is being sent and received.

electronic, laser, and inkjet printing A printing process that uses computers, electronics, electrostatics, and special toners and inks to produce images.

electronic mail (e-mail) An Internet function that allows users to communicate much as they do using standard mail.

electronic mailing list A collection of e-mail addresses.

emergent consumers A market segment made up of the gradual but constant influx of first-time buyers.

emotional benefits Those benefits not typically found in some tangible feature or objective characteristic of a product or service.

ethics Moral standards and principles against which behavior is judged.

ethnic newspapers Newspapers that target a specific ethnic group.

ethnocentrism The tendency to view and value things from the perspective of one's own culture.

evaluative copy research A type of copy research used to judge an advertisement after the fact—the audience expresses its approval or disapproval of the copy used in the ad.

evaluative criteria The product attributes or performance characteristics on which consumers base their product evaluations.

event-planning agencies Experts in finding locations, securing dates, and putting together a "team" of people to pull off a promotional event.

event sponsorship Providing financial support to help fund an event, in return for the right to display a brand name, logo, or advertising message on-site at the event.

extended problem solving A decision-making mode in which consumers are inexperienced in a particular consumption setting but find the setting highly involving.

external facilitator An organization or individual that provides specialized services to advertisers and agencies.

external lists Mailing lists purchased from a list compiler or rented from a list broker and used to help an organization cultivate new business.

external position The competitive niche a brand pursues.

external search A search for product information that involves visiting retail stores to examine alternatives, seeking input from friends and relatives about their experiences with the products in question, or perusing professional product evaluations.

eye-tracking systems A type of physiological measure that monitors eye movements across print ads.

F

fact sheet radio ad A listing of important selling points that a radio announcer can use to ad-lib a radio spot.

Federal Trade Commission (FTC) The government regulatory agency that has the most power and is most directly involved in overseeing the advertising industry.

fee system A method of agency compensation whereby the advertiser and the agency agree on an hourly rate for different services provided.

field work Research conducted outside the agency, usually in the home or site of consumption.

film The most versatile and highest quality medium for television ad production.

first cover page The front cover of a magazine.

first-run syndication Television programs developed specifically for sale to individual stations.

flexography A printing technique similar to offset printing but that uses water-based ink, allowing printing to be done on any surface.

flighting A media-scheduling pattern of heavy advertising for a period of time, usually two weeks, followed by no advertising for a period, followed by another period of heavy advertising.

focus group A brainstorming session with a small group of target consumers and a professional moderator, used to gain new insights about consumer response to a brand.

formal balance A symmetrical presentation in an ad—every component on one side of an imaginary vertical line is repeated in approximate size and shape on the other side of the imaginary line.

fourth cover page The back cover of a magazine.

free premium A sales promotion that provides consumers with an item at no cost; the item is either included in the package of a purchased item or mailed to the consumer after proof of purchase is verified.

free-standing insert (FSI) A newspaper insert ad that contains cents-off coupons for a variety of products and is typically delivered with Sunday newspapers.

frequency The average number of times an individual or household within a target audience is exposed to a media vehicle in a given period of time.

frequency-marketing programs Direct-marketing programs that provide concrete rewards to frequent customers.

frequency programs A type of sales promotion that offers consumers discounts or free product rewards for repeat purchase or patronage of the same brand or company.

fulfillment center Centers that ensure customers receive the product ordered through direct mail.

full position A basis of buying newspaper ad space, in which the ad is placed near the top of a page or in the middle of editorial material.

full-service agency An advertising agency that typically includes an array of advertising professionals to meet all the promotional needs of clients.

functional benefits Those benefits that come from the objective performance characteristics of a product or service.

G

gatefold ads Advertisements that fold out of a magazine to display an extra-wide ad.

gay and lesbian newspapers Newspapers targeting a gay and lesbian readership.

gender The social expression of sexual biology or choice.

general-population newspapers Newspapers that serve local communities and report news of interest to the local population.

geodemographic segmentation A form of market segmentation that identifies neighborhoods around the country that share common demographic characteristics.

geo-targeting The placement of ads in geographic regions where higher purchase tendencies for a brand are evident.

global advertising Developing and placing advertisements with a common theme and presentation in all markets around the world where the firm's brands are sold.

global agencies Advertising agencies with a worldwide presence.

globalized campaigns Advertising campaigns that use the same message and creative execution across all (or most) international markets.

government officials and employees One of the five types of audiences for advertising; includes employees of government organizations, such as schools and road maintenance operations, at the federal, state, and local levels.

gravure A print production method that uses a plate or mat; it is excellent for reproducing pictures.

gross domestic product (GDP) A measure of the total value of goods and services produced within an economic system.

gross impressions The sum of exposures to all the media placement in a media plan.

gross rating points (GRP) The product of reach times frequency.

guaranteed circulation A stated minimum number of copies of a particular issue of a magazine that will be delivered to readers.

guerrilla marketing Edgy, inexpensive promotional initiatives executed in major urban markets.

H

habit A decision-making mode in which consumers buy a single brand repeatedly as a solution to a simple consumption problem.

headline The leading sentence or sentences, usually at the top or bottom of an ad, that attract attention, communicate a key selling point, or achieve brand identification.

heavy-up scheduling Placing advertising in media more heavily when consumers show buying tendencies.

heavy users Consumers who purchase a product or service much more frequently than others.

hierarchical search engine A database engine divided into categories for searching.

high-definition television (HDTV) Television that displays picture and produces sound from a satellite that sends a digital signal.

highly industrialized countries Countries with both a high GNP and a high standard of living.

hits The number of pages and graphical images requested from a Web site.

household consumers The most conspicuous of the five types of audiences for advertising; most mass media advertising is directed at them.

households using television (HUT) A measure of the number of households tuned to a television program during a particular time period.

I

illustration In the context of advertising, the drawing, painting, photography, or computer-generated art that forms the picture in an advertisement.

illustration format The way the product is displayed in a print advertisement.

impressions One way an advertiser can pay for space on a Web site page. In this case, a flat fee is charged for each time the advertisement is viewed.

Industrial Revolution A major change in Western society beginning in the mid-eighteenth century and marked by a rapid change from an agricultural to an industrial economy.

industry analysis In an advertising plan, the section that focuses on developments and trends within an industry and on any other factors that may make a difference in how an advertiser proceeds with an advertising plan.

inelasticity of demand Strong loyalty to a product, resulting in consumers being less sensitive to price increases.

infomercial A long advertisement that looks like a talk show or a half-hour product demonstration.

informal balance An asymmetrical presentation in an ad—nonsimilar sizes and shapes are optically weighed.

information intermediator An organization that collects customer purchase transaction histories, aggregates them across many firms that have sold merchandise to these customers, and then sells the customer names and addresses back to the firms that originally sold to these customers.

in-house agency The advertising department of a firm.

innovators In reference to the *adaptation/innovation theory* generated by a study of creativity in employees, innovators are the ones who, when faced with creative tasks, treat the existing paradigm as an obstacle.

inquiry/direct response measures A type of posttest message tracking in which a print or broadcast advertisement offers the audience the opportunity to place an inquiry or respond directly through a reply card or toll-free number.

in-store sampling A type of sampling that occurs at the point of purchase and is popular for food products and cosmetics.

integrated brand promotion (IBP) The use of various promotional tools, including advertising, in a coordinated manner to build and maintain brand awareness, identity, and preference.

integrated marketing communications (IMC) The process of using promotional tools in a unified way so that a synergistic communications effect is created.

interactive agencies Advertising agencies that help advertisers prepare communications for new media like the Internet, interactive kiosks, CD-ROMs, and interactive television.

interactive media Media that allow consumers to call up games, entertainment, shopping opportunities, and educational programs on a subscription or pay-per-view basis.

intergenerational effect When people choose products based on what was used in their childhood household.

internal lists An organization's records of its customers, subscribers, donors, and inquirers, used to develop better relationships with current customers.

internal position The niche a brand achieves with regard to the other similar brands a firm markets.

internal search A search for product information that draws on personal experience and prior knowledge.

international advertising The preparation and placement of advertising in different national and cultural markets.

international affiliates Foreign-market advertising agencies with which a local agency has established a relationship to handle clients' international advertising needs.

Internet A vast global network of scientific, military, and research computers that allows people inexpensive access to the largest storehouse of information in the world.

Internet Relay Chat (IRC) A component of the Internet that makes it possible for users to "talk" electronically with each other, despite their geographical separation.

involvement The degree of perceived relevance and personal importance accompanying the choice of a certain product or service within a particular context.

J, K, L

layout A drawing of a proposed print advertisement, showing where all the elements in the ad are positioned.

less-developed countries Countries whose economies lack almost all the resources necessary for development: capital, infrastructure, political stability, and trained workers.

letterpress The oldest and most versatile method of printing, in which text and images are printed from a plate or mat.

libel Defamation that occurs in print and would relate to magazine, newspaper, direct mail, or Internet reports.

lifestyle segmentation A form of market segmenting that focuses on consumers' activities, interests, and opinions.

limited problem solving A decision-making mode in which consumers' experience and involvement are both low.

live production The process of creating a live television commercial, which can result in realism and the capturing of spontaneous reactions and events but comes with a loss of control that can threaten the objectives of the commercial.

live script radio ad A detailed script read by an on-air radio personality.

local advertising Advertising directed at an audience in a single trading area, either a city or state.

local agency An advertising agency in a foreign market hired because of its knowledge of the culture and local market conditions.

localized campaigns Advertising campaigns that involve preparing different messages and creative executions for each foreign market a firm has entered.

local spot radio advertising Radio advertising placed directly with individual stations rather than with a network or syndicate.

local television Television programming other than the network broadcast that independent stations and network affiliates offer local audiences.

log analysis software Measurement software that allows a Web site to track hits, pages, visits, and users as well as audience traffic within the site.

logo A graphic mark that identifies a company and other visual representations that promote an identity for a firm.

M

mailing list A file of names and addresses that an organization might use for contacting prospective or prior customers.

mail sampling A type of sampling in which samples are delivered through the postal service.

marcom manager A marketing-communications manager who plans an organization's overall communications program and oversees the various functional specialists inside and outside the organization to ensure that they are working together to deliver the desired message to the customer.

market analysis In an advertising plan, the section that examines the factors that drive and determine the market for a firm's product or service.

marketing The process of conceiving, pricing, promoting, and distributing ideas, goods, and services to create exchanges that benefit consumers and organizations.

marketing database A mailing list that also includes information collected directly from individual customers.

marketing mix The blend of the four responsibilities of marketing—conception, pricing, promotion, and distribution—used for a particular idea, product, or service.

market niche A relatively small group of consumers who have a unique set of needs and who typically are willing to pay a premium price to a firm that specializes in meeting those needs.

market segmentation The breaking down of a large, heterogeneous market into submarkets or segments that are more homogeneous.

markup charge A method of agency compensation based on adding a percentage charge to a variety of services the agency purchases from outside suppliers.

measured media Media that are closely measured to determine advertising costs and effectiveness: television, radio, newspapers, magazines, and outdoor media.

mechanical A carefully prepared pasteup of the exact components of an advertisement, prepared specifically for the printer.

media buying Securing the electronic media time and print media space specified in a given account's schedule.

media-buying service An independent organization that specializes in buying media time and space, particularly on radio and television, as a service to advertising agencies and advertisers.

media class A broad category of media, such as television, radio, or newspapers.

media mix The blend of different media that will be used to effectively reach the target audience.

media objectives The specific goals for a media placement: Reach the target audience, determine the geographic scope of placement, and identify the message weight, which determines the overall audience size.

media plan A plan specifying the media in which advertising messages will be placed to reach the desired target audience.

media vehicle A particular option for placement within a media class (e.g., *Newsweek* is a media vehicle within the magazine media class).

medium The means by which an illustration in a print advertisement is rendered: either drawing, photography, or computer graphics.

membership groups Groups an individual interacts with in person on some regular basis.

members of business organizations One of the five types of audiences for advertising; the focus of advertising for firms that produce business and industrial goods and services.

members of a trade channel One of the five types of audiences for advertising; the retailers, wholesalers, and distributors targeted by producers of both household and business goods and services.

merchandise allowances A type of trade-market sales promotion in which free products are packed with regular shipments as payment to the trade for setting up and maintaining displays.

message strategy A component of an advertising strategy, it defines the goals of the advertiser and how those goals will be achieved.

message weight A sum of the total audience size of all the media specified in a media plan.

miscellaneous In regard to font styles, a category that includes display fonts which are used not for their legibility, but for their ability to attract attention. Fonts like garage and novelty display belong in this category.

mobile sampling A type of sampling carried out by logo-emblazoned vehicles that dispense samples, coupons, and premiums to consumers at malls, shopping centers, fairgrounds, and recreational areas.

monopoly power The ability of a firm to make it impossible for rival firms to compete with it, either through advertising or in some other way.

multi-attribute attitude models (MAAMs) A framework and set of procedures for collecting information from consumers to assess their salient beliefs and attitudes about competitive brands.

N

narrative Advertising copy that simply displays a series of statements about a brand.

narrowcasting The development and delivery of specialized television programming to well-defined audiences.

national advertising Advertising that reaches all geographic areas of one nation.

National Advertising Review Board A body formed by the advertising industry to oversee its practice.

national spot radio advertising Radio advertising placed in nationally syndicated radio programming.

need state A psychological state arising when one's desired state of affairs differs from one's actual state of affairs.

netizens A person who spends considerable time on the Internet.

network radio advertising Radio advertising placed within national network programs.

network television A type of television that broadcasts programming over airwaves to affiliate stations across the United States under a contract agreement.

newly industrialized countries Countries where traditional ways of life that have endured for centuries change into modern consumer cultures in a few short years.

newspaper sampling Samples distributed in newspapers to allow very specific geographic and geodemographic targeting.

nonusers A market segment made up of consumers who do not use a particular product or service.

normative test scores Scores that are determined by testing an ad and then comparing the scores to those of previously tested, average commercials of its type.

O

objective-and-task approach A method of advertising budgeting that focuses on the relationship between spending and advertising objectives by identifying the specific tasks necessary to achieve different aspects of the advertising objectives.

off-invoice allowance A program allowing wholesalers and retailers to deduct a set amount from the invoice they receive for merchandise.

off-network syndication Television programs that were previously run in network prime time.

offset lithography A printing process in which a flat, chemically treated surface attracts ink to the areas to be printed and repels ink from other areas; the inked image is then transferred to a rubber blanket on a roller, and from the roller the impression is carried to paper.

online editing The transferring of the finalized rough cut of a television ad onto one-inch videotape, which is of on-air quality suitable for media transmission.

on-package sampling A type of sampling in which a sample item is attached to another product package.

on-sale date The date on which a magazine is issued to subscribers and for newsstand distribution.

out-of-home media The combination of transit and billboard advertising.

P

pages The particular pages sent from a Web site to a requesting site.

paid circulation The number of copies of a newspaper sold through subscriptions and newsstand distribution.

parallel layout structure A print ad design that employs art on the right-hand side of the page and repeats the art on the left-hand side.

participation A way of buying television advertising time in which several different advertisers buy commercial time during a specific television program.

pass-along readership An additional number of people, other than the original readers, who may see a magazine.

pay-for-results A compensation plan that results when a client and its agency agree to a set of results criteria on which the agency's fee will be based.

percentage-of-sales approach An advertising budgeting approach that calculates the advertising budget based on a percentage of the prior year's sales or the projected year's sales.

peripheral cues The features of an ad other than the actual arguments about the brand's performance.

permanent long-term displays P-O-P materials intended for presentation for more than six months.

permission-based e-mail An advertiser-originated e-mail to consumers who have granted permission for e-mail to be sent to them.

permission marketing Web users agree to receive e-mails from organizations.

physiological measures A type of pretest message research that uses physiological measurement devices to detect how consumers react to messages, based on physical responses.

pica A measure of the width or depth of lines of type.

picturing Creating representations of things.

pilot testing A form of message evaluation consisting of experimentation in the marketplace.

point A measure of the size of type in height.

P-O-P advertising Advertising that appears at the point of purchase.

pop-up ad An Internet advertisement that appears as a Web site page is loading or after a page has loaded.

portal A starting point for Web access and search.

positioning The process of designing a product or service so that it can occupy a distinct and valued place in the target consumer's mind, and then communicating this distinctiveness through advertising.

positioning strategy The key themes or concepts an organization features for communicating the distinctiveness of its product or service to the target segment.

posttest message tracking Advertising research that assesses the performance of advertisements during or after the launch of an advertising campaign.

preferred position A basis of buying newspaper ad space, in which the ad is placed in a specific section of the paper.

premiums Items that feature the logo of a sponsor and that are offered free, or at a reduced price, with the purchase of another item.

preprinted insert An advertisement delivered to a newspaper fully printed and ready for insertion into the newspaper.

preproduction The stage in the television production process in which the advertiser and advertising agency (or in-house agency staff) carefully work out the precise details of how the creative planning behind an ad can best be brought to life with the opportunities offered by television.

price-off deal A type of sales promotion that offers a consumer cents or even dollars off merchandise at the point of purchase through specially marked packages.

primary demand The demand for an entire product category.

primary demand stimulation Using advertising to create demand for a product category in general.

principle of limited liability An economic principle that allows an investor to risk only his or her shares of a corporation, rather than personal wealth, in business ventures.

principles of design General rules governing the elements within a print advertisement and the arrangement of and relationship between these elements.

proactive public relations strategy A public relations strategy that is dictated by marketing objectives, seeks to publicize a company and its brands, and is offensive in spirit rather than defensive.

production facilitator An organization that offers essential services both during and after the production process.

production services A team that takes creative ideas and turns them into advertisements, direct mail pieces, or events materials.

production stage The point at which the storyboard and script for a television ad come to life and are filmed. Also called the *shoot*.

production timetable A realistic schedule for all the preproduction, production, and postproduction activities involved with making a television commercial.

professionals One of the five types of audiences for advertising, defined as doctors, lawyers, accountants, teachers, or any other professionals who require special training or certification.

program rating The percentage of television households that are in a market and are tuned to a specific program during a specific time period.

projective techniques A type of developmental research designed to allow consumers to project thoughts and feelings (conscious or unconscious) in an indirect and unobtrusive way onto a theoretically neutral stimulus.

promotion agencies Specialized agencies that handle promotional efforts.

psychogalvanometer A type of physiological measure that detects galvanic skin response—minute changes in perspiration that suggest arousal related to some stimulus (such as an advertisement).

psychographics A form of market research that emphasizes the understanding of consumers' activities, interests, and opinions.

publicity Unpaid-for media exposure about a firm's activities or its products and services.

public relations A marketing and management function that focuses on communications that foster goodwill between a firm and its many constituent groups.

public relations audit An internal study that identifies the characteristics of a firm or the aspects of the firm's activities that are positive and newsworthy.

public relations firms Firms that handle the needs of organizations regarding relationships with the local community, competitors, industry associations, and government organizations.

public relations plan A plan that identifies the objectives and activities related to the public relations communications issued by a firm.

puffery The use of absolute superlatives like "Number One" and "Best in the World" in advertisements.

pulsing A media-scheduling strategy that combines elements from continuous and flighting techniques; advertisements are scheduled continuously in media over a period of time, but with periods of much heavier scheduling.

purchase intent A measure of whether or not a consumer intends to buy a product or service in the near future.

Pure Food and Drug Act A 1906 act of Congress requiring manufacturers to list the active ingredients of their products on their labels.

push money A form of trade incentive in which retail salespeople are offered monetary reward for featuring a marketer's brand with shoppers.

push strategy A sales promotion strategy in which marketers devise incentives to encourage purchases by members of the trade to help push a product into the distribution channel.

Q, R

radio networks A type of radio that delivers programming via satellite to affiliate stations across the United States.

radio syndication A type of radio that provides complete programs to stations on a contract basis.

rate card A form given to advertisers by a newspaper and containing information on costs, closing times, specifications for submitting an ad, and special pages or features available in the newspaper.

ratings point A measure indicating that 1 percent of all the television households in an area were tuned to the program measured.

rational branding A Web-presence design that gives people multiple reasons to continue to visit the site.

reach The number of people or households in a target audience that will be exposed to a media vehicle or schedule at least one time during a given period of time. It is often expressed as a percentage.

reactive public relations strategy A public relations strategy that is dictated by influences outside the control of a company, focuses on problems to be solved rather than opportunities, and requires defensive rather than offensive measures.

readership A measure of a newspaper's circulation multiplied by the number of readers of a copy.

rebate A money-back offer requiring a buyer to mail in a form requesting the money back from the manufacturer.

reference group Any configuration of other persons that a particular individual uses as a point of reference in making his or her own consumption decisions.

regional advertising Advertising carried out by producers, wholesalers, distributors, and retailers that concentrate their efforts in a particular geographic region.

repeat purchase A second purchase of a new product after trying it for the first time.

repositioning Returning to the process of segmenting, targeting, and positioning a product or service to arrive at a revised positioning strategy.

resonance test A type of message assessment in which the goal is to determine to what extent the message resonates or rings true with target audience members.

RFM analysis An analysis of how recently and how frequently a customer is buying from an organization, and of how much that customer is spending per order and over time.

riding the boards Assessing possible locations for billboard advertising.

rituals Repeated behaviors that affirm, express, and maintain cultural values.

robots A software that roams the Internet through a user-specified criteria.

robot search engine Employs the use of "bots" to roam the Internet in search of information fitting certain user-specified criteria.

roman The most popular category of type because of its legibility.

rough cut An assembly of the best scenes from a television ad shoot edited together using digital technology.

rough layout The second stage of the ad layout process, in which the headline is lettered in and the elements of the ad are further refined

run-of-paper or **run-of-press (ROP)** A basis of buying newspaper or magazine ad space, in which an ad may appear anywhere, on any page in the paper or magazine.

S

sales promotion The use of incentive techniques that create a perception of greater brand value among consumers or distributors.

salient beliefs A small number of beliefs that are the critical determinants of an attitude.

sampling A sales promotion technique designed to provide a consumer with a trial opportunity.

sans serif A category of type that includes typefaces with no small lines crossing the ends of the main strokes.

satellite and closed-circuit A method of transmitting programming to highly segmented audiences.

scratch track A rough approximation of the musical score of a television ad, using only a piano and vocalists.

script The written version of an ad; it specifies the coordination of the copy elements with the video scenes.

search engine A software tool used to find Web sites on the Internet by searching for keywords typed in by the user.

secondary data Information obtained from existing sources.

second cover page The inside front cover of a magazine.

selective attention The processing of only a few advertisements among the many encountered.

selective demand stimulation Using advertising to stimulate demand for a specific brand within a product category.

self-expressive benefits What consumers gain by using products that they perceive will send a set of signals identifying them with their desired reference group.

self-liquidating premium A sales promotion that requires a consumer to pay most of the cost of the item received as a premium.

self-reference criterion (SRC) The unconscious reference to one's own cultural values, experiences, and knowledge as a basis for decisions.

self-regulation The advertising industry's attempt to police itself.

sentence and picture completion A type of projective technique in which a researcher presents consumers with part of a picture or a sentence with words deleted and then asks that the stimulus be completed; the picture or sentence relates to one or several brands.

serif The small lines that cross the ends of the main strokes in type; also the name for the category of type that has this characteristic.

share of audience A measure of the proportion of households that are using television during a specific time period and are tuned to a particular program.

share of voice A calculation of any advertiser's brand expenditures relative to the overall spending in a category.

shoot *See* **production stage.**

short-term promotional displays P-O-P materials that are used for six months or less.

single-source tracking measures A type of posttest message tracking that provides information about brand purchases, coupon use, and television advertising exposure by combining grocery store scanner data and devices that monitor household television-viewing behavior.

single-source tracking services Research services that offer information not just on demographics but also on brands, purchase size, prices paid, and media exposure.

situation analysis In an advertising plan, the section in which the advertiser lays out the most important factors that define the situation, and then explains the importance of each factor.

skyscraper A tall, skinny banner ad that is a variation on the traditional top-of-the-screen rectangle.

slander Oral defamation that in the context of promotion would occur during television or radio broadcast of an event involving a company and its employees.

slogan A short phrase used in part to help establish an image, identity, or position for a brand or an organization, but mostly used to increase memorability.

slotting fees A type of trade-market sales promotion in which manufacturers make direct cash payments to retailers to ensure shelf space.

social class A person's standing in the hierarchy resulting from the systematic inequalities in the social system.

social meaning What a product or service means in a societal context.

society A group of people living in a particular area who share a common culture and consider themselves a distinct and unified entity.

space contract A contract that establishes a rate for all advertising placed in a magazine by an advertiser over a specified period.

space order A commitment by an advertiser to advertising space in a particular issue of a magazine. Also called an *insertion order.*

spam To post messages to many unrelated newsgroups on Usenet.

specialty-advertising items Items used for advertising purposes and that have three defining elements: (1) they contain the sponsor's logo and perhaps a related promotional message; (2) this logo and message appear on a useful or decorative item; and (3) the item is given freely, as a gift from the sponsor.

spider An automated program used in collection search engines.

split-cable transmission A type of pilot testing in which two different versions of an advertisement are transmitted to two separate samples of similar households within a single, well-defined market area; the ads are then compared on measures of exposure, recall, and persuasion.

split-list experiment A type of pilot testing in which multiple versions of a direct mail piece are prepared and sent to various segments of a mailing list; the version that pulls the best is deemed superior.

split-run distribution A type of pilot testing in which two different versions of an advertisement are placed in every other issue of a magazine; the ads are then compared on the basis of direct response.

sponsor *See* **client.**

sponsorship A way of buying television advertising time in which an advertiser agrees to pay for the production of a television program and for most (and often all) of the advertising that appears in the program.

spot advertising A way of buying television advertising time in which airtime is purchased through local television stations.

"square root law" The recognition of print ads increases with the square of the illustration.

standard advertising unit (SAU) One of 57 defined sizes of newspaper advertisements.

sticky site A site that is able to attract visitors over and over again and keep them for a long time.

still production A technique of television ad production whereby a series of photographs or slides is filmed and edited so that the resulting ad appears to have movement and action.

storyboard A frame-by-frame sketch or photo sequence depicting, in sequence, the visual scenes and copy that will be used in an advertisement.

story construction A type of projective technique that asks consumers to tell a story about people depicted in a scene or picture, as a way of gathering information about a brand.

STP marketing (**S**egmenting, **T**argeting, **P**ositioning) A marketing strategy employed when advertisers focus their efforts on one subgroup of a product's total market.

straight-line copy Advertising copy that explains in straightforward terms why a reader will benefit from use of a product or service.

streaming video and audio The process of inserting TV and radio-like ads into music and video clips.

subhead In an advertisement, a few words or a short sentence that usually appears above or below the headline and includes important brand information not included in the headline.

subliminal advertising Advertising alleged to work on a subconscious level.

support media Media used to reinforce a message being delivered via some other media vehicle.

surfing Gliding from Web site to Web site using a search engine, direct links, or word of mouth.

sweepstakes A sales promotion in which winners are determined purely by chance.

switchers A market segment made up of consumers who often buy what is on sale or choose brands that offer discount coupons or other price incentives. Also called *variety seekers.*

symbolic value What a product or service means to consumers in a nonliteral way.

T

target audience A particular group of consumers singled out for an advertisement or advertising campaign.

target segment The subgroup (of the larger market) chosen as the focal point for the marketing program and advertising campaign.

taste A generalized set or orientation to consumer preferences.

telemarketing A direct-marketing medium that involves using the telephone to deliver a spoken appeal.

television households An estimate of the number of households that are in a market and own a television.

testimonial An advertisement in which an advocacy position is taken by a spokesperson.

third cover page The inside back cover of a magazine.

thought listing A type of pretest message research that tries to identify specific thoughts that may be generated by an advertisement.

three-point layout structure A print ad design that establishes three elements in an ad as dominant forces.

thumbnails, or **thumbnail sketches** The rough first drafts of an ad layout, about one-quarter the size of the finished ad.

top-level domain (TLD) The suffix that follows the Web site name.

top-of-the-mind awareness Keen consumer awareness of a certain brand, indicated by listing that brand first when asked to name a number of brands.

trade-market sales promotion A type of sales promotion designed to motivate distributors, wholesalers, and retailers to stock and feature a firm's brand in their merchandising programs.

trade reseller Organizations in the marketing channel of distribution that buy products to resell to customers.

trade shows Events where several related products from many manufacturers are displayed and demonstrated to members of the trade.

transit advertising Advertising that appears as both interior and exterior displays on mass transit vehicles and at terminal and station platforms.

trial offers A type of sales promotion in which expensive items are offered on a trial basis to induce consumer trial of a brand.

trial usage An advertising objective to get consumers to use a product new to them on a trial basis.

type font A basic set of typeface letters.

U

unfair advertising Defined by Congress as "acts or practices that cause or are likely to cause substantial injury to consumers, which is not reasonably avoidable by consumers themselves and not outweighed by the countervailing benefits to consumers or competition."

unique selling proposition (USP) A promise contained in an advertisement in which the advertised brand offers a specific, unique, and relevant benefit to the consumer.

unit-of-sales approach An approach to advertising budgeting that allocates a specified dollar amount of advertising for each unit of a brand sold (or expected to be sold).

unmeasured media Media less-formally measured for advertising costs and effectiveness (as compared to the measured media): direct mail, catalogs, special events, and other ways to reach business and household consumers.

Usenet A collection of more than 13,000 discussion groups on the Internet.

user positioning A positioning option that focuses on a specific profile of the target user.

users The number of different people visiting X Web site during Y time.

V

value A perception by consumers that a product or service provides satisfaction beyond the cost incurred to acquire the product or service.

value proposition A statement of the functional, emotional, and self-expressive benefits delivered by the brand, which provide value to customers in the target segment.

values The defining expressions of culture, demonstrating in words and deeds what is important to a culture.

variety seekers *See* **switchers.**

variety seeking A decision-making mode in which consumers switch their selection among various brands in a given category in a random pattern.

V-chip A device that can block television programming based on the recently developed program rating system.

vertical cooperative advertising An advertising technique whereby a manufacturer and dealer (either a wholesaler or retailer) share the expense of advertising.

videotape An option for television ad production that is less expensive than film but also of lower quality.

viral marketing The process of consumers marketing to consumers over the Internet through word of mouth transmitted through e-mails and electronic mailing lists.

virtual mall A gateway to a group of Internet storefronts that provides access to mall sites by simply clicking on a storefront.

visits The number of occasions on which a user X looked up Y Web site during Z time.

W

white space In a print advertisement, space not filled with a headline, subhead, body copy, or illustration. White space is not just empty space: it is typically used to mark qualities that include luxury, elegance and simplicity.

within-vehicle duplication Exposure to the same advertisement in the same media at different times.

World Wide Web (WWW) A universal database of information available to Internet users; its graphical environment makes navigation simple and exciting.

X, Y, Z

Zaltman Metaphor Elicitation Technique (ZMET) A research technique to draw out people's buried thoughts and feelings about products and brands by encouraging participants to think in terms of metaphors.

zapping The process of eliminating advertisements altogether from videotaped programs.

zipping The process of fast-forwarding through advertisements contained in videotaped programs.

NAME/BRAND/COMPANY INDEX

Page references in **bold** print indicate ads or photos. Page references in *italics* indicate tables, charts, or graphs. Page references followed by "n" indicate footnotes.

A

A. C. Nielsen, *252,* 310, 493, 496, 503, 509, 514, 585, 639, 663
Aaker, David, 234n, 235n, 259n
Aaker, Jennifer L., 313n
Abacus Direct, 141
ABC, 550
Abion, Mark S., 30n
Absolut Vodka, 56, 108, 517, 525–526
Accenture, **224,** 652
Acteva.com, 582–583
Action for Children's Television (ACT), 140
Acura, 371
Acxiom, 116
Adbusters, 140
Adidas, **194**
AD Resource, 504
Ad Track, 378
Advertising Age, 586
Advertising.com, 564, **566**
AdWipe, 576
Aetna Life & Casualty, 124
Agency.com Ltd, 44–45
Agres, Stuart J., 255n
Aguilera, Christina, 567, 590
Aho, Debra, 513n
AIDS prevention campaign, 124
Airbus, **312**
Airship International, 616
AirTouch Cellular, 330, 718
Ajzen, Icek, 175n
Alastair, Ray, 613n
Albertson's, 52
Albion, Mark S., 129n
Alizé, **198**
AllAdvantage.com, 65
All detergent, **32**
Allen, Chris T., 181n, 508n
Allen, Woody, 464
Alliance, *610*
Allstate Insurance, 428, *429*
Alpo, 96, **96**
Alsop, Ronald, 469n
AltaVista, 568, 583
Alternative Postal Delivery, 648
Altoids, 56, **259,** 620
Amazon.com, 567, *573,* 592, 613
American Advertising Federation, *137,* 198–199, 409
American Airlines, 57, 358, 367, *573,* 642
American Association of Advertising Agencies, 98, *132, 137,* 138–139
American Broadcasting Company, 542
American Business Press, *137*
American Community Survey, 248
American Express, 21, *23,* 65, **198, 278, 279,** *429,* **501,** 513, 653, *673,* 678
American Family Physician, 538
American Forest's ReLeaf program, 712
American Lock & Supply, 52
American Occupational Therapy Association (AOTA), 679
American Pie 2, **518**
American Wine Association, *137*
America Online, 524, **525,** 530, 541, 561, 563, 569, 589, 591, 613, 658–659, **659,** 689
Ameritech, 718
Ameritech Cellular, 330
Ameritrade, *573*
Amnesty International, **101**
Anacin, 94
Andersen Consulting, 624
Anderson, Benedict, 199n
Anheuser-Busch, 118, **118,** 119, 409, 495, 508, 616, 712, **713**
Animal Planet, *314*
Antin, Tony, 439n
AOL Time Warner, *49,* 67, 349, *527, 536, 543, 551, 572,* 591
AP News Network, 550
Apollo, 553
Apple Computers, 34, 272–276, **273–276,** 343, 364–366, **365,** 376, **465**
Aqueous 9H20, **232**
Arbitron, 509
Arbitron Internet Information Services/Edison Media, 591
Arbitron Ratings/Radio, 553
Architectural Digest, 537
Arm & Hammer Dental Care, 214
Arndorfer, James B, 639n
Arnould, Eric J., 185n
Aronow & Pollock, *610*
Arthur Andersen, 561, 580
Artzt, 109
Artzt, Edwin L., 98
Asian Medical Diagnostic Centers, 682
Asian Pacific AIDS Intervention Team, Pacific Asian Language Services of Special Service for Groups and Healthier Solutions Inc., **118**
Ask Jeeves, 568
Assael, Henry, 320n
Association for Interactive Media, *673*
Association of American Soap and Glycerin Products, **86**
Association of National Advertisers, *137*
Asthma Zero Mortality Coalition, 386

Atlanta, 534
Atlanta Journal, 531
Atlantic Records, 624
Atlas Tires, **91**
AT&T Corporation, *23, 49,* 65, 304, 322, 371, **412,** *429,* 480, 513, 544, 547, *551,* 562, 563, *572,* 579, *673,* 674, 676, 688, 690, **704**
Audit Bureau of Circulations, 509, 533, 541
Austin Chronicle, 530
Australian Direct Marketing Association (ADMA), 139
Avis, **405**
Avon, 151, 231
Ayer, Francis W., 80

B

Bacardi, **385**
Bacon's Media Directories, 503
Bad Girl Clothing Co., **189**
Bagley, Dan S., 617n, 646n, 656n, 657n
Bahlsen cookies, **460**
Bailey Banks & Biddle, **532**
Baldinger, Alan L., 586n, 587n
Banham, Russ, 47n, 548n
Bank Marketing Association, *137*
Bank One Corporation, *572*
Barack, Lauren, 47n
Barban, Arnold M., 501n
Barich, Howard, 223n
Barlow, Richard, 680n
Barnes, Beth E., 37n, 66n
Barnes & Noble, *572*
Barnum, P. T., 81
Barnum and Bailey, **611**
Barnum's Animals, **622**
Barry, David, 349n
Bartelsmann, 541
Barton, Bruce, 84–85, 85n
Bath & Body Works, 173
Batra, Rajeev, 259n
Baudot, Barbara Sundberg, 310n
Bausch and Lomb, 650
Bayer Corporation, *35,* 711
Bayers, Chip, 569n
BBC Worldwide, *314,* 490
BBDO, 85, *303,* 464, 583
Bcom3 Group, 46, *55,* 349
Beardi, Cara, 577n, 648n
Beato, G., 141n, 580n
Beatty, Sally, 89n, 217n, 218n, 341n, 684n
Beaty, Sally Goll, 19n
Beckett, Paul, 670n
Beck's, **441**
Beef Industry Council, *429*
Beeler, Amanda, 580n, 591n
Beers, Charlotte, 457
Bell Atlantic, 517, 660
Bender, David M., 711n
Benetton, 704
Ben & Jerry's, 27, **28,** 648, 680
Bennett, Peter D., 21n
Bernasek, Anna, 47n, 102n, 548n
Bernbach, William, 90, 348, 403, 404, **405**
Berry, Jonathan, 107n, 680n
Best Buy, 18, *429, 610,* 624, **672**
Bestfoods, 231, 709
Better Business Bureau, 136–138
National Advertising Division of, 131
Better Homes & Gardens, 534, 537, *539*
Between Friends, 514
Bierley, Calvin, 181n
Big Fat, *610*
Binkley, Christina, 236n
Bird, Laura, 128n
Birkenstock, 343
BitMagic, 577
Black, Cathie, 503
Black Flag, 124
Blackstone, 553
Blackwell, Roger D., 170n
Blankenhorn, Dana, 59n, 591n, 677n
Blockbuster, 280, 649
Bloomberg News, *610*
Bloomingdale's, 678
Bloomstrom, John, *154*
Blue Martini Software, **5,** 16, **16**
Bluestreak, **43, 56**
BMW, 27, 371, 392, 428, *429,* **489,** 650, 680, **681**
BMX Bikes, 315
Bobbi Brown Essentials, 213
Bob's Candies, 653
Bodett, Tom, 552
Body Alarm, **386**
Body Shop, The, 122, **123**
Boeri, **435, 443**
Bogart, Leo, 501n
Bon Appetit, 688
Bonzi.com Software, *573*
Book, Albert C., 412n, 421n
Borden, Neil H., 33n
Borden's Evaporated Milk, **84**
Boston News Letter, 79
Botergoud, **439**
Bounty, 626
Bourdieu, Pierre, 188n
Bowser, Andrew, 543n
Boyer, Mike, 330n, 722n
Brandwise.com, 99
Brandy, 624
Braniff, **93**
Breen, Peter, 38n, 660n
Brienes, Wini, 87n
Brill's Content, 503
Bristol-Myers Squibb, *35,* 649, 711, **712**
British Airways, 647
Britt, Stewart Henderson, 285n
Brooks, Janet Rae, 129n
Brown & Williamson, *610*
Bruno, Michael H., 451n
Bruzzone, 259
BSKyB, 349
Buckeley, William H., 651n
Bud Light, 119, 381
Budweiser, 78, 119, 284, **368, 389,** *420, 429,* **695, 713**
Buechner, Maryanne Murray, 591n
Buhl, Claus, 37n, 203n, 256n
Bulik, Beth Snyder, 99n, 294n, 570n, 578n, 579n, 704n
Bulkeley, William, 89n, 624n, 627n
Bumba, Lincoln, 498n, 508n, 519n, 611n, 614n, 684n, 685n
Burger King, 654
Burgis, Alan, 488
Burke, Bernadette, 575n
Burke International, 64
Burnett, George, 690
Burnett, John J., 508n
Burnett, Leo, 403, 404
Burrell, Thomas, 94–95, **95**
Burrell Advertising, 94–95, **95**
Burrows, Peter, 276n
Business 2.0, **523,** 534, **536**
Business/Professional Advertising Association, *137*
Business Week, 314, 539
Buystream, **116**
Buzzsaw, 52

C

Cablevision Systems, 517
Cacioppo, John T., 179n, 181n
Cadillac, *175*
Calfee, John E., 130n
Calgon, 24
Calhoon, Don, 6
Calkins, Earnest Elmo, 80
Calvin Klein, 382
Campbell Soup Company, *35,* 94, 167, **167,** 174, 215, 702
Candie's, **183, 194,** 592
Canon, 624
Capell, Kerry, 561n
Capital One, 670
Car and Driver, 167, 535
Caranicas, Peter, 469n
Cardona, Mercedes M., 9n, 19n, 24n, 48n, 313n, 526n, 538n, 549n
Carey, James W., 78n
Carlton, Jim, 272n
Carreyrou, John, 283n
Carroll, Jill, 524n
Carter, Jimmy, 94
Cartoon Network, *314,* 581
Cary, Norman D., 412n, 421n
Case, Steve, 524
Casey Kasem's Top 40 Countdown, 550
Casio, **170,** 199
Cassidy, Jack, 333, 718
Castrol Syntec, **373**
Cauley, Leslie, 517n
Caves, Richard, 120n
CBS, 509, 514, 551
CDNow, 567
Cendant, 524, *572*
Census Bureau, 248
Centers for Disease Control (CDC), 124
Cento, Adriana, 702n
Chanel, 48
Chao, Julie, 418n
Charmin, 78
Charter Club, 33
Chart House Enterprises, 651
Cheer, **28**
Chevrolet, 27, **370,** 379, **379, 380,** *429,* 703
Chiat, Jay, 60, 264
Chiat/Day, 60, 61, 364
Chicago Motor Club, **372**
Children's Advertising Review Unit, *137*
Chivas, **190**
Christianson, Lara, 561n
Christie's, **516**
Chrysler, **223,** 513
Chura, Hillary, 37n, 46n, 55n
Church & Dwight Company, 214
Cincinnati Bell Wireless, 38, 148, 152–157, **156,** 326–335, **329,** 479–483, **481–484,** 596–603, **597, 599,** 718–725, **720–724**
Circuit City, *35, 527,* 652
Cisco, *23,* 57
Citibank, *23,* 198, 624
Claridge Hotel & Casino, 680
Clarins, 188, **537**
Claritas, 249
ClassMates.com, *573*
Clear Channel, 553
Cleaver, Joanne, 703n
Cleland, K., 576n
Clinique, 213, **214**
Clinton, Bill, 126
Clorox, **414,** 636
Clow, Lee, 403, 404
ClubMed, 562
CMGI, *572*
CNBC, *314*
CNN, 95, *314,* 315, **513,** 550
CNN Airport Network, 544
Coca-Cola Company, **6,** 6–7, 15, **15,** 21, *23,* 78, 88, **88,** 124, 140, 173, 174, **241,** 246, **254,** 300, *304,* 318, 343, 367, 392, 394, 409, **614, 615,** 624, 626, 707–708
Cody, Jennifer, 515n
Coen, Robert J., 516n
Cohen, Andy, 702n
Coldwater Creek, **672**
Cole, Jeff, 617n
Colgate, 29
Colgate-Palmolive, 214, 286

Collier, James Lincoln, 85n, 86n, 96n
Colonize.com, *573*
Columbia Broadcasting System (CBS), 542
Columbia Record Club, *673*
Columbus Dispatch, 530
COMDEX, 656
Comedy Central, **494**
Commerce One, **282**
Communication Arts, 354
Compaq Computer, 524, 652
CompCard Gold, 680
Competitive Media Reporting, 508
CompuServe, 524, 541, 561
Computerworld, 314
ConAgra, 21, *35*
CondéNast, *512*
Conde Nast Publications, 503
Conn, David, 592
Consumer Consolidating of America, *573*
Consumer Federation of America (CFA), 140
Consumer Mail Panel, *252*
Consumer Reports, 140, 167, 592
Consumers Union, 140
Converse, **254, 615**
Cook, Clive, 308n
Cooper, Ann, 610n
Coopers & Lybrand, 709, **710**
Coors Brewing, 231
Cordiant Communications Group, *55*
Cosmedy, Allison, 672n
Cosmopolitan, 534
Costco, 658
Cotton Industry, *429*
Coty, 24
Council for Biotechnology Information, **706**
County Seat, 32
Cox, G. Robert, 440n
Cox, James, 708n
Cox Target Media, 648
Cramer-Krasselt, 55
Crawford, Cindy, 373
Crawford, Nicole, 621n
Crayola, 578
Creating Minds (Gardner), 344
Crest, 78, **95, 245,** 626
Crispy Corn, **182**
Cristol, Steven M., 501n
Crockett, Roger O., 660n
Cross, Kim, 576n
Crossen, Cynthia, 376n
Crumley, Bruce, 316n
CSPI, 394
CTN, 544
Cuneo, Alice Z., 33n, 63n
Curad, **376,** 643
Current Population Survey, 248
Cutty Sark, **384**
C.W. Post Company, 644
CyberRebate, **661**
CyberShop, 578
Cyrk-Simon Worldwide, 151

D

DaimlerChrysler, *49, 536,* 553, *572*
Danskin, **291**
Darwin Digital, 294
Datek, **373**
Dates, Jannette L., 196n
Daugherty, Will, 102n
Davis, Howard, 61
Davis, Wendy, 46n, 53n
Days of Our Lives, 499
Dayton Daily News, 530
Dayton Hudson, 611
DC Shore Co. USA, 374
DDB Worldwide, *303*
DeBeers, **172,** *429*
Deesse, **115, 118**
Dell, 34, *35*
Delta Air Lines, 358, 367, 379, 642, 651
Del Valle, Christina, 219n
DeNitto, Emily, 386n
Denny's, **197**
Dentsu, 46, *55, 303*
Destiny's Child, **194**
Detroit, Michigan, **180**
Deveny, Kathleen, 128n, 214n
Diageo, *551*
Diamond Information Center, **172**
Dichter, Ernest, 89
DieselStyleLab, **395**
Digital Island, 705
Dilbert, 431
Dillard's, 52, *527*
Diner's Club, *673*
Dior, **392**
Direct Debit, **396**
Direct Mail Advertising Association, *673*
Direct Mail Marketing Association, *137*
Direct Marketing Association (DMA), 139, 670–671, *673,* 682
Direct Media, 57
Direct Selling Association, *137*
Discovery Communications, *314*
Disney, *23,* **24,** *49,* 50, 67, 173, **186,** 244, *314,* **390,** 514, *527, 543, 572,* 613
Distilled Spirits Association, *137*
Ditcher, Ernest, 37n
Dixie Chicks, 712
DKNY, 620
DM Group, 564
Dockers, **447**
Doc Martens, 35, 199
Dolce & Gabbana, **161, 189**
Domino's, 305
Donaton, Scott, 495n
Dorfman, David, 608
Doritos, 284
DoubleClick, **47,** 57, 141, 584, 585
Dove, **123**
Dow, Jerry, 358
Dow Jones & Co, *314*
Doyle Dan Bernbach, 7, **7,** 90, **405**
Dr. Pepper, 651
Dr. West's, **86**
Drucker, Peter F., 27n
Dubitsky, Tony M., 255n
Duffey, Lee, 653n
Duffy's, **20**
Dun & Bradstreet Market Identifiers, *252*
Duncan, Tom, 46n
Dunkin' Donuts, **615**
Dunn, Mike, 340n
DuPont, 247, **404,** 709, **710**
Dutta, Lara, 188
DVC Group, 46

E

Eaton, John, 703n
Ebates, *573*
Ebel, **532**
Ebony, 538
Eccles, Lisa Z., 620n
Eclipse, **388**
Economist, 314
Economist Group, *314*
Edell, Julie A., 255n
eDirect.com, **577,** 678
Edmondson, Michael, 684n
Edwards, Rob, 139
EE Times, 539
Einstein, Albert, 344, 345
eLab, 686
El Diario de las Americas, 530
Electolux, 300
Electric Artists, 567, 590
Elgin, Ben, 575n, 578n
Eli Lilly, 649
Eliot, Richard, 203n
Eliot, T. S., 344, 345
Elkin, Tobi, 19n, 528n
Elle Deco, 314
Elliot, Stuart, 98n
Elliott, Stuart, 123n, 608n
Elmquist, Marion L., 33n
eMarketer, 576, 685
Emerson, Ralph Waldo, 357
Emondson, Brad, 620n
Endicott, R. Craig, 48n, 49n, 52n, 126n, 525n, 534n
Energizer, 409
Enfora, **103, 571**
Engel, James F., 170n
Entertainment Weekly, 524
Ephron, Erwin, 496n
Epiphone, **448**
ePrize, **661**
ER, 499, 545
Ericsson, 19, 625
ESPN, 95, *314,* 545
Esrey, William T., 98
E-Stamp, 583
Estée Lauder, *35,* 120, 213
Estrey, 109
Eternity, 493, *495*
eToys, 561
E*Trade, 284
Eudora, 564
Euro RSCG Worldwide, *303*
Evaliant Media Resources, 256
Evans, Walker, **85**
Everland Entertainment, **516**
Evian, **395**
Excedrin, 231
Excite search, 568
Exile on Seventh, 488
Experian, 219
eYada.com, **554**

F

Fairchild, *512*
Fallon McElligott, 61
Fallon Worldwide, 358
Family Channel, 616
Familyeducation.com, **494**
Fannin, Rebecca A., 534n
Farley, Christopher John, 567n
Farm Journal, 538
Farquhar, Peter H., 711n
Farrell, Greg, 709n
Farris, Paul W., 30n, 129n
Fast Company, 539
Featherly, Kevin, 345n
Federated Department Stores, 32–33, *527*
FedEx, 173, **224,** 225
FeedRoom, 67
Fellini, Federico, 464
Fels-Naptha, **82**
Femina, Jerry Della, 357n, 383
Fender Stratocaster, 199, **200**
Fendi, 25, **27**
Feshbach, Seymour, 386n
Feuer, Jack, 358n
Fiat, 425
Fidelity Investments, 513
Financial Times, 314, 530
Fine, Jon, 524n, 526n, 528n, 531n, 537n
Fingerhut, 677
Fiorina, Carly, 709
Firestone, 696–697, **697**
First Brand, 636
1stUp.com, **549**
Fischer, Blair R., 650n
Fish, Stanley, 202n
Fishbein, Martin, 175n
Fisher, Christy, 131n
Fisher, Sarah, 626
Fitzgerald, Kate, 21n, 148n, 150n, 152n, 544n, 625n, 626n, 629n, 649n, 652n, 690n
FJCandN, **61**
Fleischmann's Yeast, 87
Florida Department of Citrus, 29, **30**

Florio, Steve, 503
FMR Corp, *527*
Folgers, 626, 645
Food Network, **544**
Foote, Cone & Belding, **355**
Forbes, *314*
Forbes, 314, 538, 591
Ford, *23, 35, 49,* **91,** 151, 174, **261,** *304,* 321, *429, 527, 536, 572,* 696–697
Ford, Gary T., 130n
Ford, John, **456**
Forrester Research, **576,** 581
Fortune, 314, 524, 538
40 Acres and a Mule Production Company, 290
Fotoball Marketing, **607, 618**
Four Seasons Hotel, 37
Fox, Stephen, 79n, 80n, 87n, 90n, 122n
Frank, Robert, 148n
Frank, Thomas, 94n, 242n
Frankena, Mark, 128n
Frankenheimer, John, 464, 488
Freberg, Stan, 552
Freedman, Alix M., 140n
Freeman, Laurie, 583n
FreeMerchant.com, 580
Freud, Sigmund, 344, 345, 345n
Friedman, Wayne, 542n
Friends, 545
Frost, Geoffrey, 61
Fuji, 281, 367, 616
Fulton, Sue, 155n

G

Gain, 626
Galbraith, John Kenneth, 33n
Galloni, Alessandra, 690n
Gallup & Robinson, 496
Gal Riney and Partners, 378
Gandhi, Mahatma, 344, 345
Gannett Co., *314*
Gap, 48, 367, 578, **614,** 640, 649
Garbagebandrecords, **417**
Garber, Dana, 566n
Gardner, Howard, 344n, 345n, 346n
Garfield, Bob, 6n, 696n
Gateway, 34
Gator, 345
Gattuso, Greg, 681n
GE, *23*
General Electric, *49,* 514, *551*
General Foods, 50, **83**
General Mills, 53, 140, 702
General Motors, 19, *35,* 48–49, *49,* 63, **228,** 228–229, **261,** *304, 527, 536, 543,* 544, *551,* 553, 571, *572,* 623, 653, 660
GeoCities, 587
Geo Metro, 165, **166**
Gerber, 173
Gershman, Michael, 233n
GetSmart.com, *573*
Gibney, Frank Jr., 67n
Gilbert, Jennifer, 63n, 66n, 141n, 524n, 584n
Gillette, *23, 35,* 210–212, **211,** 225, **292, 293,** 320, 621, 624, 629–630, **647, 655**
Glad, 636
Gladwell, Malcolm, 251n
GlaxoSmithKline, *543, 572,* 710–711
Glaxo Wellcome, 89, 700, 710
Gobe, Marc, 342n
Godin, Seth, 149n, 178n, 686–687
Goetzl, David, 711n
Goldberg, S. M., 353n, 354n
Goldman, Jordan, 705n, 707n
Goldman, Kevin, 124n, 373n, 376n, 377n, 381n, 471n, 551n, 552n, 611n, 709n
Gold Medal Flour, **84**
GoldMine software, 657, 658, **658**
Goldsmith, R. E., 346n, 347n
Goldstein, Jeffrey, 128n
Golf Digest, 535
Gonring, Matthew, 580
Goodby, Silverstein & Partners, 264, 294
Goodegg.com, **489**
Good Housekeeping, 537, 538, *539*
Goodman, Kevin, 98n
Good Morning America, 499
Goody, Silverstein and Partners, 60
Goodyear, **93,** *429,* 616
Gordon, DeeDee, 250
Gordon, Jeff, 560
Gore, Al (political campaign), **11**
GoToTix.com, 582
Gould, John, 672
Gouldner, Alvin W., 187n
Grady, Barbara, 698n
Graham, Jeffrey, 345n
Graham, Martha, 344, 345
Grainger, David, 696n
Granatstein, Lisa, 503n
Graves, Jacqueline M., 376n
Green, Heather, 226n, 575n, 578n, 584n
Greenfield, Jerry, 680
Green Giant, **280**
Greenpeace, **444**
Gregg, B. G., 126n
Grey, Jennifer, 650
Grey Global Group, *55*
Grove, Andy, 698
Gruner, *512*
GTE Wireless, 330, 718
Gucci, **36,** 37, **209, 231**
Guess?jeans, 35
Guinness, **100,** 343
Guinot, **121**
Gulf Refining Company, **82**
Gwinner, Kevin P., 703n

H

Haagen-Dazs, *610*
Hachette, *512*
Hachette Filipacchi, *314*
Hackman, Gene, 650
Hajewski, Doris, 438n
Haley, Kathy, 689n
Halliday, Jean, 63n, 290n, 696n
Hallmark, 174, 426, 547
Halo.com, 660
Han, S., 308n
Hanover, Dan, 624n, 642n
Happy Kreme, **455**
Haran, Leah, 620n
Hard Candy, **214**
Hardee's, 6, 34
Harley-Davidson, 173, **185, 204,** *429,* 590
Harrah's Entertainment, 236
Harrison, Ann, 585n
Hartman, Michael, 44
Harvard Business Review, 314
Harvey Research, 496
Hasbro, *610*
Hashman, John, 670
Hathaway Shirt Man, **405**
Hathcote, Jan M., 709n, 711n
Hau, Louis, 321n
Havas Advertising, *55*
Hayden, Steve, 364
Hays, Scott, 517n
HBO, 524
Head and Shoulders, 387–388
Health Education Authority (United Kingdom), **10**
Healthgrades.com, **575**
Healthy Choice, 21
Hearst, 503
Heckman, James, 143n
Heim, Sarah J., 488n
Heineken, **104,** 173, **307,** 651
Heitsmith, Glen, 643n
Helperin, Joanne R., 707n
Henke, Lucy L., 128n
Henkel, *304*
Henry, Jim, 371n
Hershman, Tania, 591n
Hertz, 651, 678
Hewlett-Packard, *23,* **462,** *572,* 709, **711**
Hi-C, 394
Hidden Persuaders, The (Packard), 87
Hidesign, **448**
Himelstein, Linda, 38n
HipZip, 649
Hirschman, Elizabeth, 349n
Hitchcock, Alfred, **456**
Hoffman, Donna, 686
Holstein, William J., 696n
Holtz, Herman, 679n
Home Depot, 150, 640, 653
Home*Scan, 493
Homestore, **437**
Honda, **26,** 34, *35,* 55, **223, 427,** 513
Hooley, Graham J., 287n
Hootie & the Blowfish, 723
Hoover, 689
Hopkins, Claude, 80
Hormel, **184**
Horovitz, Bruce, 626n
Horst Salons, **612**
Hotmail, 577
HotWired, 561, 575
Howard, Theresa, 686n
Hughes, Laura Q., 293n, 629n, 689n
Hughes, Laura W., 46n, 53n
Hughes, Randy, 409
Hughes Network Systems, **103**
Hurley, John, 80n
Hyde, Douglas, 438
Hyperion, 66, **67,** 584, **584**
Hyundai Motor, 624

I

IAMS, 170–171, **171,** 626
ibid, **350**
IBM Corporation, 17, *23,* 32, *35,* 52, **91,** 198, **284,** 308, **309,** 364, *527,* 547, *572,* 698, 711
Iconocast, 504
Idaho Department of Commerce, **54**
IDG, *314*
idNames, 583, **583**
IDS Financial Services, 688
IHC HealthCare, 652
iMac, 272–276, **273–276,** 364–366, 365, **365,** 376
iMarket Inc., 679
Inarritu, Alejandro Gonzales, 488
INC, 33
Industry Standard, 503
Infiniti, **529**
Infinium, 66
Infobase Premier, 678
Infobase Services, 678
Information Resources, *252,* 493
Infoseek, 582
InfoWorld, 538
Ingrassia, Paul, 228n
Insite Advertising, 608
Instinet, 69, **69**
InStyle, 537
Intel, *23, 35,* 78, 409, 531, 579, 698–700
Interactive Advertising Bureau, 504
Interactive Internet Advertising, 345
Interactive Market Systems (IMS), 510
Interactive Traffic, 576
Interbrand, 21
Intercollegiate Communications, Inc., 624
International Herald Tribune, 314
International Outdoor Systems, 611
International Social Survey Programme, 248

Interpretation of Dreams (Freud), 345
Interpublic Group, 46, *55*
Interse, 587
Investor's Business Daily, 530
Invisalign, **230**
Iomega, **230,** 649
I/PRO, 587
IPSOs-ASI research, 639
Iremonger, Mark, 349n
Isuzu, **169,** 378
Ivory, 22, 78
iwon.com, 581, **581**

J

J. Crew, 396, 578
J. Walter Thompson, 44–45, **45,** 61, 83–84, 152, 457
Jabra, **701**
Jack Daniel's, **319**
Jackson, Rob, 680n, 681n
Jacobson, Michael F., 394
JAG, 543
Jaguar, **265,** 290, **410**
James, Dana, 705n
Janis, Irving L., 386n
Janoff, Barry, 438n
JBL Electronics, 626–627, **627**
JCPenney, *35,* 38, **373**
Jeep, 164
Jell-O, 185, **186, 647**
Jelly Belly, **635, 654**
Jenn-air, **413**
Jewel, 624
Jewler, A. Jerome, 408n, 412n, 457n
Jobs, Steve, 272, 273, 276, 277, 293, 365
Joe Boxer, **204,** 608
Johansson, Johny, 308n
John, Elton, 624
John Hancock Mutual Life, **428,** 625, 627
Johnnie Walker, **309**
Johnson, Bradley, 19n, 56n, 116n, 272n, 276n, 364n, 497n
Johnson, Connie, 364n
Johnson, Greg, 341n
Johnson & Johnson, *35, 49,* **121, 165,** *536, 543,* 561, *572,* 636
Johnston & Murphy, 201, **202**
Jones, John Philip, 261n, 284n, 663n, 664n
Jones, Larry, 59
Jones, Susan, *154*
Jordan, Michael, 135, 373, 394
Jovan, 493, *495*
Joy, 162, **163**
JP Morgan Chase, *573*
Judson, Bruce, 418n
Jung, Carl G., 344
Juno, 563
Jupiter Media Metrix, 244
Jurvetson, Steve, 578n

K

Kal Kan, 689
Kan, Olivia, 682
Kanfer, Alaina, 580n, 581n
Kansas City Star, 530
Kao Corporation, 162
Karan, Donna, 620
KarWai, Wong, 488
Katona, George, 122n
Katz, Marian, 310n
Katzenbach, Joe R., 477n, 478n, 479n
Kaydo, Chad, 660n, 702n
Kazaa, 244
KB Toys, 642
Keds, 650
Keebler, 642
Keller, John J., 700n
Keller, Kevin, 24n, 149n, 203n, 247n
Kellogg, *35,* **92**
Kelly, Keith J., 712n
Kemper Insurance, 55
Kennedy, John E., 80
Kent, Robert J., 508n
Kerstetter, Paul, 689n
Kerwin, Ann Marie, 539n
Kessler, David, 699
KFC, 625
Kia, **371**
Kiley, David, 651n
Killarney's, **384**
Killbourne, Jean, 87
Kimball, James G., 698n
Kimberly-Clark, 140
Kingman, M., 350n
Kinsman, Matthew, 623n
Kirby, Robert, 300n
Kirkpatrick, David, 365n
Kirton, M., 346n, 347n
Klinka, Michael, 367n
Kluegal, James R., 187n
Kmart, 620, 641
Kodak, **84,** 281, 367, 379, 426, 624, 651, 653, 660
Kohler, **455**
Kopec, Frank J., 501n
Koprowski, Gene, 561n
Koss-Feder, Laura, 197n, 198n
Kotler, Philip, 212n, 223n, 225n, 229n
Kover, A. J., 353n, 354n
Kover, Amy, 106n
KPMG Consulting, 69
KPS Video, 682
Kraft, **186, 254, 637,** 712
Kramer, Louise, 642n
Kranhold, Kathryn, 44n, 46n, 63n, 577n, 629n, 705n
Krauss, Michael, 66n, 141n
Kremer, John, 677n, 678n
Kroger Company, 626
Kulish, Nicholas, 705n
Kuperman, Bob, 342

L

L90, 66
L. L. Bean, 396, 671–674, **679**
L.A. Weekly, 530
Lactia, 246
Lady Protector, **311**
Lady Speed Stick, **230**
La Femme Nikita, 543
Lagerfeld, 493, *495*
Lake Capital, 46
Lambesis, 250
Lancaster, Kent M., *510*
Landers, Peter, 308n
Land Rover, **413**
lang, k. d., 213
Lans, Maxine S., 662n
Lasker, Albert, 80
Latina.com, **569**
Laughlin/Constable, 438
Lauterborn, Robert F., 629n, 690n
Law & Order, 499
Leading Web Advertisers, 256
Lee, **12,** 13, 428
Lee, Louise, 310n
Lee, Spike, 290, 464, **465**
Lefton, Terry, 285n
Lennon, John, 90n
Lenox, **540**
Leo Burnett, 46, 90, **92,** *303,* 508, 608, 620
Leonard, Dorothy, 478n
Leslie, Lisa, 686
Leung, Kenneth, 686n
Levin, Gary, 676n, 690n
Levi Strauss, 17, **36,** 37, 38, 56, 78, **101,** 173, 408, 592, *610*
Lewis, Byron, 95
Lewis, Carl, 610
Lewis, Herschell Gordon, 688n, 689n
LeWit & LeWit, *512*
Lexus, 37, 371, 649, 689
LG Electronics, 310
Lieber, Ronald B., 247n
Liebeskind, Ken, 256n
Lifebuoy, **82,** 83, 87
Life Cereal, 378
Ligos, Melinda, 714n
Limited, The, 52
Lincoln, **261,** *429*
Linnett, Richard, 56n, 127n
Lipton Brisk, 44–45, **45,** 629
Listerine, 82, 94
Little Caesar's, 380
Locander, William B., 191n, 247n
Lois, George, 348
Lord, Kenneth R., 372n
Lord and Thomas, 80
L'Oréal, 34, *35,* 188, *304, 536, 572*
Loro, Laura, 512n
Los Angeles Times, 531
LouisBoston, **391**
Lowe Lintas & Partners, *303*
Lowry, Tom, 541n, 589n
L-Soft International, 564, **566**
LuckySurf.com, **142**
Luik, J. C., 30n
Lull, James, 266n
Luvs, 636
Lux laundry soap, 76, **76,** 87
Lycos, 569, 582
Lycra Stretch, **404**
Lynch, James E., 287n
Lynch, Michael, 653
Lyndon B. Johnson ad, **460**
Lynx, **459**

M

Maas, Jan, 416n, 427n
M.A.C., 213
MacArthur, Kate, 6n, 7n, 37n, 55n, 629n, 689n
Machleit, Karen A., 181n
Macintosh computers, 343, 364–366, 376
MacManus group, 46
Macy's, 517
Madden, Thomas J., 181n
Mademoiselle, 503
Madonna, 392, 394, 488
Magalindan, Mylene, 577n
Magma Group, 141
Magnavox, 380
Majorica, **255**
Mall Internet, 578, **579**
Mandel, Jon, 503
Mandese, Joe, 109n, 469n, 509n, 514m, 540n, 545n
Man Nobody Knows, The (Barton), 85
Marathon Oil, 170
Marchand, Roland, 197n
Mardesich, Jodi, 685n, 686n, 687n
Maremont, Mark, 210n, 211n, 320n
Margeotis, Fertitta & Partners, *610*
Marie Callender, 21
Market Drivers, 639–640
Market Growth Resources, 651
MarketPlace Pro, 679
Markon, Jerry, 682n
Markowitz, Michael, 378
Marlboro, *23,* 151
Marriott, **651**
Mars, 22, **260,** *304,* 320
Marshall, Gordon, 183n, 185n, 199n
Maslow, A. H., 120n
Massingill, Teena, 116n
MasterCard, 21, **97, 193, 406,** 653
Matherly, T. A., 346n, 347n
Matrix, The, 544
Maxim, 537
Maximum Golf, **494**
MaxInfo, 587
Maxwell House, 78

Maybelline, *429*
May Department Stores, *527*
Mayer, Martin, 403n
Mazur, Geri, 707n
McAlister, Leigh, 640n
McCann-Erickson Worldwide, 17, 19, 55, 488
McCarroll, Thomas, 315n
McCarthy, Michael, 378n, 625n
McCartney, Paul, 90n
McCartney, Scott, 227n
McCaw Cellular Communications, 700
McCormick, Richard D., 517
McCracken, Grant, 201, *202*
McDermott, Susan, 394
McDonald, Jim, 617
McDonald's, 6, *23, 49,* 52, 135, 174, 235–236, 283, 305, 373, 390, 426, 624, 642, 643, 651
McElligott, Tom, 403, 404
McGee, Edward J., 440n
McGraw-Hill Co., *314*
MCI, 50, 371, 410, 562, 624, 674
McLean, Bethany, 554n
McSweeney, Frances K., 181n
McVeigh, Steve, 660
MeccaUSA, **195**
Mechanic, Michael, 609n
MediaCom Worldwide, 503
Mediamark Research, 493, *495,* 541
Media Metrix, 106, 587, **588**
MediaStart, 511, 512
Mediconsult.com, 576
Mehta, Zubin, 625
Meiji Milk Products, 246
Melcher, Rischar A., 320n
Men's Health, 538
Men's Journal, **538**
Mercedes, *23*
Mercedes Benz, 165, **166,** 689
Merck, 700
Mercury Interactive, **589**
Meredith, *512*
Mermigas, Diane, 591n
Merrell Performance Footwear, **232**
Merrill Lynch, *23,* 51
MessageMedia, 57, 59
MetLife, 616
Metro, Zoe, 48
Metromail, 116
Metro West's Virtual Mall, 578
Meyers, John G., 259n
Mic, David Glenn, 37n
Michael Kor, **385**
Michael Markowitz & Associates, 378
Michell, P. C., 350n
Michigan Chronicle, 530
Mick, David Glenn, 203n, 256n
Microsoft, *23, 35,* 66, *429,* 488, 528, 530, 564, *572,* 613
Migraleve, **387**
Miles Laboratories Inc., 711
Milillo, Wendy, 409n
Milk council, **411**
Miller, Joe, 19n
Miller, Marc, 608
Miller, Rick, *154*
Miller Brewing, 47, **254,** 381, **461,** 495
Miller Cyndee, 613n
Miller Lite, 78, **190,** 340–341, 380, 381, **463,** 508
Millman, Joel, 305n
MindShare, 56
MindSpring, 579
Miniard, Paul W., 170n
Minute Maid, 394
Mirage Resorts, 127–128
Mirra, Dave, **394**
Misunas, Kathy, 106
Mitchell, Dan, 530n
Mitchell, Susan, 219n
Mizerski, Richard, 128n
M&M, **184,** 464
Mobil Oil Corporation, 217, 224, **226,** 227
Modern Bride, 534
Modern Maturity, 512, 538
Momentum Marketing, *610*
Monahan, 125n
Monster.com, 530, 689
Moore, Jeri, 149n, 326n
Moore, Timothy E., 125n
Moriarity, Sandra E., 46n, 422n, 440n
Morpheus, 244
Morton, Bruce Simon, 128n
Mosaic, 561
Motion Picture Association of America, *137*
Motorola, 17, 19, 61, **383**
Mountain Dew, 199, 343, **446**
Movie Addict, **440**
MRI, 509
MSN, 619
MTV, 97, **101,** *314,* 315, 320, 490, 545
Mullaney, Timothy J., 592n
Muller, Joann, 696n
Muniz, Albert Jr., 199n, 231n
Munk, Nina, 120n, 213n
Murphy, 125n
Muscle & Fitness, 534
Museum of Flight, **612**
MusicVision, 578
MyEvents.com, 590
Myriad Genetics, 701, **701**
MySimon.com, **569**

N

N. W. Ayer, 80
Nabisco, 234, **622,** 640
Nakache, Patricia, 659
Nancy Rubenstein Inc., **339, 351**
Napster, 244
NASCAR, 625
Nash, Edward, 671n, 674n
Nasonex, **676**
National Advertising Division/ National Advertising Review Board, *137*
National Archives and Records Administration, 248
National Association of Broadcasters, *137,* 139
National Broadcasting Company (NBC), 542
National Cinema Network, **513**
National Fluid Milk Processor Promotion Board, 29, **30**
National Geographic, 314, 537
National Guard, 53
National Purchase Diary Panel, *252*
National Swimming Pool Institute, *137*
Nature Conservancy, 53
NEC, 56, 700
Needham, Harper and Steers, 381
Neff, Jack, 24n, 131n, 321n, 636n, 640n
Nelson, Roy Paul, 442n, 443n, 457n
Nestlé, *35,* 48, *304*
Netcentives, 57, **58**
NetCount, 587
NetRadio, 578, 583
NetRatings, 585, **586**
Netscape, 524, 561, 564, 660
Network, 456
Network Associates, 658
Neubourne, Ellen, 560n, 610n
New Corporation, *527*
New England Journal of Medicine, 539
New Jersey Devils, 581
New Line film studio, 524
News America Magazines Inc., **494**
News Corporation, *551*
Newspaper Association of America, 530
Newspaper National Network, **534**
Newspaper Network, **509**
Newsweek, 314, 513, 534
New Woman, 538
New York Amsterdam News, 530
New York Magazine, 376
New York Times, 314, 528, 531
NextCard Inc, 670
Nextel, 718
Nickell, Joe Ashbrook, 592n
Nickelodeon, 67, 95
Nicorette, **415**
Nike, 48, 56, **104,** 126, 235–236, 300–301, **301,** 343, 408, 428, **465,** 504, 508, 610, 650, 686
Nikon, **320**
1984 (Orwell), 116
Nissan, 340, **340,** 652
Nixon, Richard, 94
Nokia, 19, *23,* **307**
Nordstrom, 32, 517
Norelco, **661**
Norris, Vincent P., 78n
Nortel Networks, 524
Northlich, 38, 148, 152–157, **153,** 326–335, **329,** 479–483, **481–484,** 596–603, **597, 599,** 718–725, **720–724**
Northwest Airlines, **168**
Novell, 66
Noxzema, **608,** 608–609
Nynex, 124
Nynex Yellow Pages, **615**

O

Oakley, 650
Oberbeck, Steven, 418n
Obsession, 218, **219,** 493, *495*
O'Connell, Vanessa, 234n, 282n
Octopus, 530
Oddbins, **437**
Office Max, 658
Ogilvy, David, 90, 403, 404, **405,** 430, 438n
Ogilvy & Mather, 90, **92,** *303,* 457, 580, 583
O'Guinn, Thomas, 199n, 231n, 266n
Olay, **187,** 626
Old Dutch Cleanser, **84**
Old Navy, 57
Oldsmobile, 234, **243, 261,** 649
Old Spice, 218, **219**
Oliver, Richard W., 109n
Olsen, G. Douglas, 266n
O'Malley, Chris, 328n, 330n
Omega, **657**
Omnicom Group, *55,* 317
One Show, The, 354
Ono, Yumiko, 621n
Oolong Socha, 246
Oracle, 66
OraLabs, **442**
Oreck, 637, **638, 688**
Oregon Food Bank, **413**
Orenstein, Susan, 280n
Oreos, **622,** 640
Oriental Weavers, USA Inc., **445**
OshKosh B'Gosh, 438
Osterman, Jim, 150n
Ostrow, Joe, 545n
Ottman, Jacquellyn, 713n
Outdoor Advertising Association of America, *137*

P

Pace, Stella, 48
Packard, Vance, 87n, 121n
Palm, 343
Palmer, Arnold, 373
Palmer, John, 218n, 713n
Palm III, **441**
Pampers, **197,** 636

Panasonic, 29, *429,* 546
Pantene, 626
Parade, **531**
Paris Garters, **75, 86**
Park, C. Whan, 190n
Parker Pen, 300
Parmalat, **445**
Participant, The, 514
Partnership for a Drug-Free America, 9, 126, **127**
Pastore, Michael, 244n
Patrick Cox Wannabe, **384**
Paxnet, **490**
PC Magazine, 539
PC World, 314
Pearson PLC, *314*
Pechmann, Cornelia, 372n
Peckham, James O., 286n
Pedigree, 320
Peet's Coffee and Tea, **643**
Pendleton, Jennifer, 403n
Penn Railroad, **88**
Pennsylvania Gazette, 79
Pentium chip, 698
People, 499, 524, 539, *539*
Peppers, Don, 675n
PepsiCo, 37, 44, *49,* **93, 98,** 151, 284, 300, 315, 343, 367, 373, 394, 408, *543,* **560,** *572,* 624, 699, **700,** 702, 708
Performance Research, 625
Perkins, Don, *154,* 481–482
Perrin, West, 353n
Pet Milk, **83**
Petrecca, Laura, 46n, 62n, 63n, 148n, 627n
Petruvu, Sanjay, 372n
Pets.com, 99, **102**
Petsmart.com, 660
Petty, Richard, 179n, 181n
Pfizer, *49, 536, 543, 572*
Pharmaceutical Manufacturers Association, *137*
Philip Morris, *49,* 78, 151, **254,** *304, 536, 543, 572,* 708
Philips Electronics, 376
Phillips Petroleum, 32, 712, **713**
Physicians Mutual Insurance, 514
Picasso, Pablo, 344, **344,** 345
Piirto, Rebecca, 215n, 220n, 221n, 617n
Pillsbury, 220, **221**
Pirelli, 17
Pizza Hut, 305, **532,** 625
Placid Planet, 250
Plastics Manufacturers Council, **34**
Players Club by Don Diego, **396**
Play Station, **363, 395**
Pleats Please, **395**
Pledge, 636
PocketMall, **564**
Polaroid, 94, **95, 615**
Pollio, Howard, 191n, 247n
Pond's, **388**
Pontiac, **228,** 228–229, **261,** 415
Pope, Daniel, 79n
Pop Media, *512*
Post-it Note, **618**
postmaster.com, **687**
Pottery Barn, 650
Power Beads, 48
PowerQuest, 8, **8**
Powers, John E, 80
PPG Industries, 711
Pracejus, John W., 266n
Prada, 343, **393,** 394
Presbrey, Frank, 79n, 80n
Preston, Ivan, 130n, 131n
Preston, James E., 231
Prevacid, 16, **17**
PricewaterhouseCoopers, 52
Priester, Joseph R., 179n, 181n
Prime 66 Partners, 553
Primestar, 689
Pringles, **255**
Privada, **142**
Prizm, 248–249
PR Newswire, 58
Procter & Gamble, 24, 27, **28,** *35,* 48, *49,* 50, 63, 78, 98, 99, **102,** 106, **107,** 109, 140, 162, **163,** 214, *304,* 310, 321, 378, 388, *536, 543,* 544, *572,* 608, 620, 625, 626, 636, 645, **703,** 705
Prodigy, 541, 561
Progressive Farmer, 538
Project Research, Inc., **355**
PROMO Magazine, 712
Promotional Products Association International, 646
Proprietary Association, *137*
Providian Financial Corporation, *573,* 670
Prudential Insurance, *429*
Pruzan, Todd, 315n
PSA Peugeot Citroen, *304*
Publicis SA, 318
Publishers Clearing House, 142, *673*
Pulblicis Group, *55*
Purchase Pro, 524
Pussyfoot, **105**

Q

Quaid, Dennis, 651
Quaker Oats, 708
Quaker State, 689
Quart, Alissa, 116n, 141n
Quasar, 29
Quick, Rebecca, 673n
Quixi, **271, 282**
QVC, 517

R

R. L. Polk, 116
Radio Shack, 386, 425, 617
Radio Usage and Network Radio Audiences, 554
Raffi, **384**
Ralph Lauren, 38
Raphel, Murray, 680n
Rasmusson, Erika, 116n
Ray, Michael, 387n
Ray-Ban, **36,** 650
RCA, 29, 546, 561, 567
Reader's Digest, 89, *314,* 315–316, 539, *539,* 684
Reagan, Ronald, 96, **97**
RealNetworks, 578
Rebello, Kathy, 107n
Redbook, 376
Reddi-wip, **500**
Red Sky Interactive, 56
Red Stripe, 651
Red Wolf, 495
Reebok, 250–251, 504, 508
Reeves, Rosser, 89, 369
Reilly, Patrick M., 624n, 671n
Renault, *304*
Resor, Helen, 83–84
Resor, Stanley, 83
Retsky, Maxine Lans, 131n
Reverman, Mandy, 479, 480
Revlon, 188
Richard, Leah, 382n
Richards, Bill, 616n
Richmond Technical Center, **403**
Rickard, Leah, 310n
Ricks, David, 312n
Riedman, Patricia, 99n, 570n, 584n
Ries, Al, 229n
Rigdon, Joan E., 629n
Ritchie, Guy, 392, 488
Ritson, Mark, 203n
RJR Nabisco, 608
Roberts, Julia, 704
Roberts, Kevin, 342, 690
Robertson, Thomas S., 223n
Rockport, **385**
Rockwell, 709
Rodale, 503
Roe and Garry Show, 550
Rogaine, *429*
Rogers, Martha, 675n
Rogers, Stuart, 88n
Rolex, 17, **18**
Rolling Stone, 592
Rolling Stones, 624
Rolls-Royce, **92**
Roman, Ernan, 674n
Roman, Kenneth, 416n, 427n
Roper Starch, *252,* 310, 496, 713
Ross, Chuck, 67n
Ross, David, **347**
Rossant, John, 704n
Rossiter, John R., 500n
Rothman, Andrea, 508n
Roush, Chris, 624n, 625n
Rowling, J. K., 394
Roxio, **411**
Royal Peacock Hotel, **100**
Rubel, Chad, 226n, 227n
RuPaul, 213
Rust, Roland, 109n
Rykä, **232**

S

Saab, 34, 199, 590, **590**
Saatchi & Saatchi, *303,* 342, 690
Salomon Smith Barney, **279**
Sandbox.com, **487, 498**
Sanyo, 616
Saporito, Bill, 320n
SAS, 66
Satellite Music Network, 550
Saturn, 199, **200,** 203, *429,* **578**
SBC Communications, *527, 551*
SBP, **401, 407**
Scammon, Debra L., 135n
Scarborough, 509
Scheyer, Dennis, 582
Schibsted, Evantheia, 108n, 216n, 614n, 689n
Schiff, 24, **25**
Schiller, Zachary, 320n
Schlosser, Anne E., 580n, 581n
Schmalensee, Richard, 129n
Schmidt, Kathleen V., 708n
Schmitt, Bernd H., 346n
Schulberg, Jay, 408n
Schulert, Sanford C., 711n
Schultz, Don E., 37n, 66n, 139n, 149n, 629n, 671n, 677n, 687n, 690n
Schumann, David W., 709n, 711n
Schwartz, Karen D., 583n
Schwinn Cycling & Fitness, **439,** 533–534, **535**
Scientific American, 314
Scott, Linda, 203n, 257n
Scott, Ridley, 364, 464, **465**
ScreamingMedia, **559,** 581, **582,** 707
Screenblast, **385**
Scroggie, Michael, 645n
Sears, 38, 49, *49,* 52, **176,** 231, 591
Sebastian, Pamela, 684n
Sega, 315, 624
Sellers, Patricia, 62n, 226n
Semenik, Richard J., 135n
Serrianne, Mark, *154,* 155, 478, 479
Serta, **91**
Sesame Street Magazine, 513
Sesame Street Snacks, **194**
7up, **455**
SFX Entertainment, 38, 50, 53
Shapiro, **20**
Sharp, *429*
Sharper Image, 678
Shavitt, S., 308n
Shea, Carolyn, 649n
Sheldon, Peter, 466n
Shephard Associates, 64
Sheridan, Patrick J., 127n
Shermach, Gary, 589n
Shermach, Kelly, 550n

Shirouzu, Norihiko, 246n
Shroer, James C, 286n
Shukla, Anu, 582n
Shuler, Laura, 628n
Silverman, Rachel E., 619n
Simmons Market Research Bureau, 64, 493, 496, 503, 541
Simon, Julian, 77n
Singapore Airlines, 17
Singapore's Tourism Board, **180**
Sirius Radio, 553
Sissors, Jack Z., 498n, 508n, 519n, 611n, 613n, 684n, 685n
Skechers, 343, **375**
Ski-Doo, 55
Skiing, 539
Skippy, 218
SkyDigital TV, 349
SkyPort, **316**
Skyy Vodka, **393**
Sloan, Pat, 62n, 286n, 495n
Smith, Amie, 708n
Smith, Douglas K., 477n, 478n, 479n
Smith, Eliot R., 187n
Smith, Geoffrey, 231n, 713n
Smith, Karen H., 128n
Smith, Kerry E., 46n
Smith, Kerry J., 651n
Smith, S. J., 349n
SmithKline Beecham, 710–711
Smithsonian Magazine, 515
SMRB, 509
SnackWell, 234
Snickers, 22
Snyder, Wally, 198–199
Sobe Beverage Company Inc., **455**
Socrates, 344
Solomon, Michael R., 192n
Sony, 17, *23,* 50, 173, **177,** *304, 527,* 613
Sookdeo, Richard, 308n
Sorell, Martin, 55n
Southern Living, 534
Southwest Airlines, 227
SpaghettiOs, **643**
Spain, William, 99n
Spears, Britney, 560, **560,** 624
Special K, **92**
Spectrum Foods, 681
Spethmann, Betsy, 47n, 53n, 63n, 148n, 150n, 151n, 152n, 211n, 292n, 630n, 638n, 648n
Spirit, 96, **96**
Sports Illustrated, 524
Spring Communications, 349
Sprint, *49,* 98, 109, 126, 330, 562, 624, **624,** 674, 718
SRI International, 64, 220–221, **222**
St. Pierre, Nicole, 696n
StairMaster, 674, **675**
Standard Rate and Data Service (SRDS), 503
Standard Sanitary, **84**
Staples, 658
Starband, **69**
Starbucks, 173, 367
Starch, 259, **260**
Starch, Daniel, 440n
Starch INRA Hooper, 64
Star-Kist, 231
STAR TV, 315
State Farm Insurance, 227, **228**
Statistical Yearbook, 305
Steel, Jon, 60, 60n, 264n
Stengel, Rick, 457n
Stepanek, Marcia, 66n, 141n
Sterlin, *512*
Stevens, Gillian, 248n
Stewart, David, 216n, 372n
Stewart, Martha, 503
Stigler, George J., 117n, 118n
Sting, 624
Stodghill, Ron, 713n
Stone, Bob, 671n, 676n, 677n, 684n, 685n
Strathman, Alan J., 179n, 181n
Straus, Susaan, 478n
Stravinsky, Igor, 344, 345
Strout, Erin, 10n
Stutz, Mary Ann, 128n
Subway, 305
Successful Farming, 538
Suissa Miller, 55
Sullivan, Allanna, 217n, 671n
Sullivan, Luke, 348, 404–408, 412, 414, 417, 424, 430
Sunbeam, 311–312
Sunglass Hut, **518**
Sunkist, 409
Surreal, 539
Survivor 2001, 542
Svetlana, **226**
Swartz, Jon, 276n
Swatch, 300–301, **301,** 315
Sweeney, John, 357n
Sweitzer, Steve, 378
Swimming Suits (Ross), **347**
Swinyard, William R., 372n
Swiss Army knife, 655
Switchboard.com, 619, **619**
Swoopes, Sheryl, 686
Sylvania, **615**

T

Taco Bell, 340–341, **342**
Tag Heuer, 199
Takada Junji, 162, 163
Tam, Pui-Wing, 276n, 570n
Tampax, **124**
Tannenbaum, Stanley I., 412n, 421n, 629n, 690n
Tanqueray No. Ten, **410**
Target, **343,** *527*
Taster's Choice, 426
TBS, 95, 524
TBWA, 108, *303,* 526
TBWA Chiat/Day, 276, 340–341, 342, **342,** 365, **365,** *610*
Teachout, Terry, 321n
Team One Advertising, **351**
Ted, Inc., 704
Ted Bated agency, 89
Teinowitz, Ira, 10n, 66n, 141n, 142n, 457n, 677n
Tele-Communications, 517
Television Bureau of Advertising, **496**
Telmar Information Services Corp, 510
Teradyne, **103**
Teva, 410
TGI Friday's, **382**
Thailand tourism, **312**
TheStreet.com, 592
Thigpen, David E., 567n
Thomas, Bob, 340
Thomas, Dave, 6, **6, 173**
Thompson, Craig J., 191n, 247n
Thompson, Stephanie, 21n, 22n, 231n, 640n, 702n, 709n, 712n
Thorson, Esther, 149n, 326n
3Com, 584
3M, 57
TIAA-CREF, 514
Tide, 624, 625–626, **626,** 636, **703**
Tilles, Daniel, 318n
Tilton, Sarah, 682n
Time, 314, 490, **491,** 524, **525,** 534, 537
Time Inc., 503, *512*
Time Warner, *314,* 517, 524, **525,** 542, 591
Timex, 25, 199
Tire America, **529**
Titleist, 426
T.J.Maxx, **195**
TNT, *314,* 524
Tommy Hilfiger, 38, 343
Toshiba, **31,** *429*
Toy Manufacturers Association, *137*
Toyota Motor Company, *23, 49,* 165, **166,** *304,* 497, **497,** *536, 572,* 709, 711
Toys "R" Us, 640, 642, 654
Toy Story 2, 642
Trachtenberg, Jeffrey A., 469n
Trackstar Motorsports Inc., **105**
Tracy-Locke, 61
Travel Agent, 539
Travel & Leisure, 499, 537
Treasure Island, 127
TREK, 626–627, **627**
Tricon Global Restaurant, 625
Trojan, **10**
Tropicana, 30, **31, 306**
Trout, Jack, 229n
True North Communications, *55*
Tsui, Bonnie, 216n, 284n
Tulley, Shawn, 321n
Tulsa World, 531
TUMI, 19
Tupperware, **396**
Turner Broadcasting, 513
TV Guide, 643–644
TV Land, 67
Twain, Mark, 109
Twinkies, 218, **219**
Tylenol, 231–232, **233, 622**

U

Udell, J., 588n
Umo, 310
Uncle Ben's Rice, 22
Unilever, 17–18, *49,* 56, 62, *304,* 310, *543, 572,* 709
United, 642
United Airlines, **36,** 198, 358, 367
United Paramount Network (UPN), 542
United States Brewers Association, *137*
United Way, 53
Uniworld, 95
Urbanski, Al, 57n
U.S. Armed Forces, **214,** 216
U.S. Government, *49, 551*
U.S. News & World Report, 499
U.S. Postal service, **684**
U.S. West, 517
USA Today, 376, 529, 531, 533, 712
USA Today International, 314
USA Weekend, **531**
Usery, Debbie, 649n
Utumporn, Pichayaporr, 123n

V

Vagnoni, Anthony, 340n, 342n
Vail, John, 560
Valvoline, 674
Van Cleef & Arpels, **299, 311,** 704
Vanden Berg, B. G., 349n
Vanderwoude, Mike, 480
Vanguarde, *512*
VanGundy, Arthur B., 477n
Vaughn, 354n
Vavra, Terry G, 168n
Vavra, Terry G., 678n, 679n
Vazquez, Ignacio, 305n
Velveeta, 78
Venus, **292, 293**
Verisign, 583
Verizon, *49,* **392,** *527, 551,* 660, 674
Versace Couture, **123**
VerticalNet, 52, **53**
VH1, 67, *429*
ViaCom, *49*
Viacom, 67, *314,* 315, *527, 551*
Vicary, James, 88
Vinton, Marcus, 349

Virgin Group Ltd, 561
Virgin Lightships, 616
Visa, 21, **312,** *429*
Volkswagen, 7, **7,** *35,* **93,** 284, *304, 429,* **447,** 590
Volney Palmer, 79
Volvo, 562
Vranica, Suzanne, 148n, 152n, 719n
Vuitton, Louis, 48

W

Walid, Mougayar, 569n
Walker, Sam, 626n
Wallendorf, Melanie, 185n
Wall Street Journal, 376, 490, 528, 530, 531, 533
Wal-Mart, 32, 34, *35,* 53, 150, 170, **184,** 621, 636, 640, 641, 642, 677
Wanamaker, John, 292
Wang, Paul, 671n, 677n, 680n, 681n, 687n
Warhol, Andy, 125, **125**
Warn, Colston E., 33n
Warner, Fara, 164n, 616n, 620n, 623n
Warner, Susan, 649n
Warner Bros., 524
Warner-Lambert, 94
Washington Post Co., *314*
Wassong, Kevin, 44
Waterford, **36**
Waterson, M. S., 30n
Waterson, Michael J., 129n
WB, 542
WB network, 524
Webster, Nancy Coltun, 688n
Wehling, Bob, 321
Weinberg, Steve, 144n
Weiser Lock, 655
Welch, David, 696n
Wells, Mary, 90, **93**
Wells Fargo Bank, 217, **217**
Wells Rich and Green, 90
Wendy's, **6,** 34, **173**
Wentz, Laurel, 108n
Wessel, David, 317n
West, D., 350n
West, D. C., 352n
West, Susan, 709n, 711n
Westwood One, 550
Whirlpool, 106
White, Erin, 561n, 567n
White, Joe, 234n
White Cloud, 636
Whitestrips, **245**
Wickes, J. W., 349n
Wieden & Kennedy, 583
Wightman, Baysie, 250–251
Wild Turkey, **395**
Wilkie, William, 387n
Wilkins, Ronnie, 80n
Will Vinton Studios, 464
Wilson, **536**
Wilson, Christopher P., 78n
Wilson, Claire, 534n
Windex, 244, **245**
Wine Institute, *137*
Wingert, Pat, 129n
Winmx, 244
Winneker, Allen, 64n
Winston, 624
Wisk, **257**
Woman's Day, 534, 538
Women.com, **411**
Wonderbra, **26**
Wood, James P., 79n
Woods, Bob, 653n
Woods, Tiger, 426
Working Computer, **354**
Worldata.com, 678
WorldNet Service, 563
World Wildlife Fund, 57
World Wildlife Fund (WWF), 709, 712
Worthy, Ford S., 308n
WPP Group, *55,* 317
Wunderman Cato Johnson, 151
Wynter, Leon E., 319n

Xerox, 32
X-Files, 565
X-Metal Romeo, 650
Xootr, **233**

Y

Yahn, Steve, 98n
Yahoo!, 107, 530, **568,** 569, 575, 579, 582, 583, 587, 592, 619, 658
Yellow Pages, 583, 619, **619**
Yerlagsgruppe Hoitzbrinck, *314*
yesmail.com, **669, 687**
Yimou, Zhang, 625
Yokohama, **322**
Young, James Webb, 83–84
Young & Rubicam, 55, 152, *303*

Z

Zajonc, 125n
Zantac, 89
Zbar, Jeffery D., 562n, 703n
Zbar, Jeffrey D, 386n
Zdziarski, Julie, 629n
Zenith Electronics, 55
Zentropy Partners, 294
Zeroknowledge, 682, **683**
Ziff-Davis Publishing, 539
Ziploc, **131**

SUBJECT INDEX

Page references in **bold** print indicate ads or photos. Page references in *italics* indicate tables, charts, or graphs. Page references followed by "n" indicate footnotes.

A

Accommodation in communication process, 14, *14*
Account executive, for television advertising production, *458*
Account planning, 60
  advertising planning and strategy, 290
  advertising research, 264–265
  defined, 242
Account services, 59
  tension between creative department and account services, 349
Action for Children's Television (ACT), 94, 132
Activities, interest and opinions (AIOs), 220, 245–246
Adaptation/innovation theory, 346–347
Adaptors, 346–347
Ad blockers, 576
Administrative services, 62
Advertisers, 49–54
  federal, state and local government as, 52–53
  manufacturers as, 50–52
  service firms as, 50–52
  social organizations, 53–54
  trade resellers as, 52
Advertising. *See also* Evolution of advertising
  annual expenditures on, 48–49, *49, 50*
  as art, 125
  in brand development and management, 21–24
  as business process, 19–37
  challenges/opportunities for, 488–491
    proliferation of media options, 512–513
  as communication process, 13–15
  defined, 8–11
  economic effects of, 33–37
  fundamental rules of, 294
  global nature of, 301–303
  informative nature of, 117–118
  marketing role of advertising, 19–24
  mass media and effect of, 126
  nature of, 4–5
  offensive nature of, 123–124
  political, 9–11
  psychological processes of, 174–181
  vs. publicity, 8–9
  public's attitude toward, 7–8
  vs. sales promotion, 637–638, *639*
  sensitivity shown by, 122
  social aspects of, 117–126
  as social text, 201–204
  society's social priorities and, 122
  spending on, 34, *35*
  strengths of traditional, 488
  superficiality of, 118–119
  truth in, 126–127
  types of
    corporate, 32–33
    delayed response, 31–32
    direct response, 30–31
    primary demand stimulation, 29–30
    selective demand stimulation, 30
Advertising agencies, *51,* 54–58
  agencies winning the most creative awards, *303*
  compensation plans
    commission, 62
    fee system, 63
    markup charges, 62–63
    pay-for-results, 63–64
  creative process in, 348–354
  defined, 54
  global agencies, 317
  income of, 54, *55*
  international affiliates, 317–318
  local agencies, 318–319
  professionals of, 54
  role of, in advertising plan, 293–294
  self-regulation of, 138–139
  services of, 59–62
    account services, 59
    administrative services, 62
    creative and production services, 60–61
    marketing research services, 59–60
    media planning and buying services, 61
  types of
    creative boutique, 55
    full-service agencies, 55
    in-house agency, 56
    interactive agencies, 55–56
    media buying and planning services, 56
    promotion agencies, 56–58
Advertising campaign, 11–13
Advertising industry
  annual expenditures on, 48–49, *49, 50*
  scope of, 48–49
  structure of
    advertisers, 49–54
    advertising agencies, *51,* 54–58
    external facilitators, 50, *51,* 64–66
    media organizations, 50, *51,* 66–69
    target audiences, 50, *51*
  transition of, 46–48
  trends of, 46–47
    budget fragmentation, 46
    communication/distribution channels, 47
    consolidation and globalization, 46
    interactivity, 46–47
    media clutter, 47
    media evolution, 47

Advertising plan
  for Apple Computer, 272–276
  components of
    budgeting, 285–290
    evaluation, 292–293
    execution, 290–292
    introduction, 277
    objectives, 281–285
    situation analysis, 278–281
    strategy, 290
    summary, *277*
  defined, 277
  role of advertising agencies in, 293–294
Advertising research
  vs. account planning, 264–265
  by advertising agencies as service of, 59–60
  brief history of, 243
  British, 182
  copy research, 249–265
    attitude-change study, 260–262
    communication tests, 256
    direct response, 263
    evaluative criteria, 253–256
    frame-by-frame test, 264
    motives and expectations, 249, 252–253
    physiological tests, 262
    pilot testing, 262–263
    recall tests, 257–259
    recognition tests, 259–260
    resonance test, 256–257
    single-source data, 263–264
    thought listing, 257
    tracking studies, 263
  copywriting
    developmental copy research, 431
    evaluative copy research, 431
  cross-cultural audience research, 305
  developmental, 243–248
    audience definition, 245
    audience profiling, 245–246
    concept testing, 244
    field work, 247–248
    focus group, 246
    idea generation, 244
    projective techniques, 246–247
  Internet sites for, *511*
  meaningfulness of, 243
  need for naturalistic methods of, 265–266
  reliability of, 242
  secondary data sources
    commercial data sources, 248–249, *252*
    government sources, 248
    internal company sources, 248–249
    professional publications, 249
  share of voice, 504, 508
  single-source tracking services, 493, 495
  trustworthiness of, 242
  uses for, 242
  validity of, 242
Advertising research firms, 64
Advertising response function, 287
Advertising specialties
  as business buyer sales promotion, 657
  as consumer-market sales promotion, 646
Advertising substantiation program, 135
Advertorials, 376
Advocacy advertising, 712
Aerial advertising, 616
Affirmative disclosure, 135
African Americans, 198, 290
  in advertising, 94–95
  online shopping, 216
  projected U.S. population of, *196*
Agency of record, 508
Aided recall, 258
AIO (activities, interests and opinions), 220, 245–246
Airline industry, media expenditures by, *492*
Alcohol, Tobacco and Firearms, Bureau of
  areas of advertising regulation by, *134*
Alcoholic beverage advertising
  advertising to decrease abuse of, 119
  ethics of, 128–129
Allowances, as trade-market sales promotion, 655–656
Alternate evaluation, 168
Alternative press newspapers, 530–531
American Advertising Federation, advertising selling itself to business, 409
American Association of Advertising Agencies, 98
  Creative code of, 138–139
  guidelines for comparison advertising, *132*
American Dreams segment, 219
American Indians, projected U.S. population of, *196*
AM radio stations, 550
Animation, for television advertising, 471
Announcements, in radio advertising, 419
Anxiety ads, 387–388
  social anxiety, 388–389
  strategic implications of, 389
Applet, *565*
Appropriations, 144
Argentina, Internet use in, 315
Art, advertising as, 125
Art department, for television advertising production, *458*
Art director
  growing importance of role, 436
  Internet, 454
  print media, typography, 452–454
  television advertising, 454–459, 460
  working with copywriters, 402, 436
Asian Americans, 198
  online shopping, 216
  projected U.S. population of, *196*
Aspirational groups, 192
Association tests, 247
Assorted media mix, 501–502
Attitude-change studies, 260–262
Attitudes
  attitude-change studies, 260–262
  brand attitude, 175
  changing
    as advertising objectives, 281–282
    assessing advertising effectiveness and, 255
  defined, 174
  formation
    elaboration likelihood model, 179–181
    by peripheral cues, 181
  multi-attribute attitude models, 175–177
  relationship to values, 184, *185*
Audience, 67, 69
  audience definition, 245
  audience profiling, 245–246
  better assessment of, 149
  business organizations member as, 16
  cross-cultural audience research, 305
  defined, 15
  geography of, 17–19
  government officials/employees as, 16–17
  household consumers, 15–16
  Internet advertising, difficulty in assessing size of, 504
  magazine
    audience interest, 534–535
    measuring, 541
    selectivity of, 534
  newspaper
    audience interests, 528
    measuring, 533
  professionals as, 16
  radio
    fragmented, 552
    poor audience attentiveness, 552
    target audience selectivity, 551
  television, 546
    measuring, 548
    problems with measuring size of, 514–515
    selectivity, 545
  trade channel members as, 16
Australia, self-regulation of direct marketing, 139
Austria
  advertising regulations in, 316
  Internet users in, *563*
Automobile industry
  advertising-to-sale ratio, *35*
  media expenditures by, *492*
Average quarter-hour person, 553
Average quarter-hour rating, 553
Average quarter-hour share, 553
Average-user testimonials, 375
Axis, 446, **447**

B

Baby boomers, 89, 278
Balance, as design principle, 443–444, **444, 445**
Bandwidth, *565,* 589
Banner ads, 575–576
  ad blockers, 576
  consumer's resentment of, 576
  cost of, 572
  defined, *565*
  pricing evaluation service for, 576
  recall for, 576
  skyscrapers, 575–576
  top banner advertisers, *573*
Barter syndication, 543
Belgium, Internet users in, *563*
Beliefs, 175
  in MAAMs, 176
  objectives of advertising plan and, 281
Benefit positioning, 229–231
Benefit segmentation, 221–222
Between-vehicle duplication, 496–497

Bill-back allowances, 656
Billboard advertising, 610–613
riding the boards, 611
Bind-in insert cards, 687
Blackletter typeface, 452
Bleed page, 540
Blimp advertising, 616
Blocking, 467
Body copy
defined, 414
dialogue, 414
direct response copy, 415
guidelines for writing, 415
illustrations to stimulate reading of, 438–439
narrative, 415
straight-line copy, 414
testimonial, 414–415
Bomb shelters, 87, **90**
Border, 446
Bots, 568–569
Boycotts as regulation, 140
Brand
creativity and, 343
defined, 21
link key attributes to brand name, 369
most valuable brands in world, 21, *23*
proliferation of, and sales promotion, 640
social meaning, 36–37
symbolic value, 35
value and, 34–37
Brand attitude, 175
Brand awareness, as objectives of advertising plan, 281, 282
Brand communities, 199
Brand development and management. *See also* Integrated brand promotion (IBP)
brand extension introduction, 22–23
creating image and meaning for brand, 24
defining brand image as message strategy, 394–395
differentiation, 25
in evolution of advertising, 78, 80
headlines and, 409–410
house brand market, 636
illustrations to make brand heroic, 437–438
information and persuasion, 21
Internet advertising, 589–590
manufacturers' power in branding and evolution of advertising, 78
positioning, 26–27
role of advertising in, 21–24
share of voice, 504, 508
situate brand socially
light fantasy, 393
product placement/short Internet films, 392–393
slice-of-life, 391–392
Brand equity, 24
Brand extension, 22
Brand loyalty
building and maintaining
among consumers, 23–24
among trade, 24
consumer decision-making and, 173–174
defined, 23
Digital Story Telling (DST), 174
emotional benefit, 173
event sponsorship, 625–626
functional benefit, 173
vs. habits, 173
India, 310
Brand-loyal users, 216
Brand placement, 637, 650–651
Brand preference
instilling as message strategy objective, 377–386
feel-good ads, 378–380
humor ads, 380–381
sexual appeal ads, 381–385
Brand recall
evoked set, 367
repetition method, 367
slogans/jingles method, 367–369
Brand switching, 645
as objectives of advertising plan, 283
Brazil, 310
expenditures on advertising in, *302*
Internet users in, 315, *563*
British research, 182
Broadband, 548
defined, 47
speculation on future trends in, 106–107
tobacco settlement and, 102
Broadcast advertising. *See* Radio advertising; Television advertising
Broadcast media, 67, *68*
Broadcast Web, 591
Budgeting
of advertising plan, 285–290
objective-and-task, 287–290
percentage-of-sales approach, 286
response models, 287
share of market/share of voice, 286–287
unit-of-sales approach, 286
fragmentation trend in, 46
television advertising production approval, 460, 462
Build-up analysis, 288–289
Bulky box, 577
Business-buyers sales promotion, 637
goals of, 652
techniques for, 656–658
advertising specialties, 657
business gifts, 657
frequency programs, 658
premiums, 657
trade shows, 656–657
trial offers, 657
Business cycle, advertising's effect on, 33
Business gifts, as business buyer sales promotion, 657
Business magazines, 538
Business markets, 222–224
Business newspapers, 530
Business organization members, 16
Business process, advertising as, 19–37
economic effects of, 33–37
marketing role of advertising, 19–24
types of advertising, 29–32

C

Cable television, 95, 542–543
combined with Web, 545
Caching, complication of Internet measurement, 588–589
Call-or-click-now ads, 396
Camera department, for television advertising production, *458*
Canada, 321
expenditures on advertising in, *302*
Capitalism, 77
Cast selection, 467
Cause-related advertising, 712–714
CD-ROM, 513, 660
Cease-and-desist order, 135
Celebrities
celebrity announcer in radio advertising, 419
rules for endorsements by, 135
as social category, 193
testimonials, 373
as direct marketing, 688–689
Channel grazing, 546
Channel of distribution. *See* Distribution channel
Children's advertising
alcoholic beverage advertising, 128–129
cigarette advertising, 128–129
ethics of, 127–128
marketing junk food to, 394
guidelines for, 132
obesity and, 129
regulation of, 94, 132–133
Children's Online Privacy Protection Act (COPPA), 218
China
event sponsorship, 625
Internet users in, *563*
Cigarette, advertising ethics of, 128–129
Cincinnati Bell Wireless case study, 148, 152–157
assessing prior to launch
historical context, 327–328
industry analysis, 328, 330
local competition, 330
market analysis, 330–331
background of participants, 148, 152–155
building brand and growing business
closing sale, 721–723
equity building, 719–721
nurturing relationships with customers, 723–724
future of, 724–725
gauging impact of, 602–603
launch strategy
mix of persuasion tools, 334–335
objectives and budget, 333–334
measuring up in 1999, 724
model for, 326–335
overview of launch, 596–602
direct marketing, 600–602
P-O-P advertising, collateral and sales support, 602
print, radio, and outdoor, 597–600
promotion and events, 600
public relations, 596–597
television, 597
planning for, 326

refining advertising and IBP plan for 1999, 718–719
consolidating value proposition for CBW brand, 719
target segment identification, 719
target segmenting for, 331–333
teamwork in launch
account team, 479–480
copy approval process, 480
decision making, 480–481
value proposition, 333
Cinco de Mayo, 305
Civil Aeronautics Board, 133
Classified advertising, 532
Claymation, 471
Clichés, 416, 430
Click-through, *565,* 571, 575, 586
Client, 8
role in killing effective ideas, 350
Clios, 302
top winning agencies of, *303*
Closing date, 449, 540
Clutter, 47, 178
advertising, 178
increase in, 150
magazine advertising, 537
newspaper advertising, 529
sales promotion and, 641
support media, 609, 616
television advertising, 546
Coalition for Advertising Supported Information and Entertainment (CASIE), 584–585
goals for advertisers on Internet, *585*
Cognitive consistency, 178
Cognitive dissonance, 169
Cognitive response, 179
elaboration likelihood model, 179–181
Collection search engines, 568
Collectivism, 308
College student, 216–217
Color, as illustration component, 440
Column inch, 533
Commercial data sources, 248–249, *252*
Commission, 62
Commitment level, 215–217
Communication process in advertising
accommodation and negotiation process in, 14, *14*
communications vs. sales objectives, 283–284
as mass-mediated communication, 9, 13–15
new communication channels, 47
production process in, 14, *14*
reception process in, 14, *14*
Communication tests, 256
Community, 199
Company newsletters, 702–703
Comparison advertisements, 131–132, 371–373
guidelines for, *132*
Compensation plans for advertising agencies
commission, 62
fee system, 63
markup charges, 62–63
pay-for-results, 63–64
Competition
advertising's effect on, 33
comparison advertisements, 131–132
competitive media assessment, 504, 508
monopoly power, 132
regulation of, 131–132
sales promotion to combat, 643–644
vertical cooperative advertising, 131
Competitive field, 225
Competitive positioning, 231
Competitor analysis, 281
Comprehensive layout, 449, **450**
Computer graphics, 441–442
Computer industry
advertising-to-sale ratio, *35*
economies of scale, 34
media expenditures by, *492*
Computer models, for media-planning process, 509–512
Computer print production, 452
Concentrated media mix, 501
Concept search engines, 568
Concept testing, 244
Consent order, 135
Consideration set, 168, 176
Consultants, 64
Consumer magazines, 538
Consumer markets, 222
Consumer-market sales promotion, 57–58, 637, 641–652
objectives for, 642–644
techniques for, 644–652
brand placement, 650–651
contests, 646–648
coupons, 644–645
event sponsorship, 652
frequency programs, 651
phone and gift cards, 649
premiums and advertising specialties, 646
price-off deals, 645–646
rebates, 651
samples, 648–649
sweepstakes, 646–648
trial offers, 649
Consumer organizations, as regulatory agent on advertising, 140
Consumers. *See also* Consumers, as decision makers; Consumers, as social beings
building brand loyalty among, 23–25
controlling information flow, 66
defined, 163
education provided by advertising, 117–118
establishment of consumer culture, 80
household consumer, 15–16
increased sophistication and power of, 149–150
persuading
advertorials, 376
comparison ads, 371–373
demonstrations, 375–376
hard-sell ads, 370–371
infomercials, 376–377
reason-why ads, 370, 371
testimonials, 373–375
as regulatory agents, 139–140, 140
scare into action as message strategy objective, 386–387
transform consumption experiences of, 390
Consumers, as decision makers, 164–181
decision-making modes
brand loyalty, 173–174
extended problem solving, 171
habit or variety seeking, 172–173
limited problem solving, 171–172
source of involvement, 170–171
decision-making process
information search and alternative evaluation, 165–168
need recognition, 164–165
post purchase use and evaluation, 168–169
purchase, 168
psychological processes
elaboration likelihood model (ELM), 179–181
information processing and perceptual defense, 177–179
multi-attribute attitude model, 175–177
Consumers, as social beings, 181–204
advertising as social text, 201–204
community, 199
cool, 193
culture, 183–184
family, 190–191
gender, 197–199
object meaning and, 199–201
race and ethnicity, 196–197
reference groups, 191–193
ritual, 185–187
social class, 187–190
values, 184–185
Contests
as consumer-market sales promotion, 646–648
direct mail, regulatory issues of, 142–143
regulation on, 143
Continuity, 499
Continuity programs, 651
Continuous scheduling, 499
Controlled circulation, 533
Cookie
defined, *565*
privacy issues, 141
Cool
coolhunts, 248, 250–251
defined, 193
Cooperative advertising, 19, 531
as trade-market sales promotion, 656
Copy research, 249–265
attitude-change study, 260–262
communication tests, 256
direct response, 263
evaluative criteria, 253–256
attitude change, 255
behavior, 256
feelings and emotions, 255
getting it, 253
knowledge, 253
physiological change, 256
frame-by-frame test, 264
motives and expectations, 249, 252–253
physiological tests, 262

Copy research (*continued*)
pilot testing, 262–263
recall tests, 257–259
recognition tests, 259–260
resonance test, 256–257
single-source data, 263–264
thought listing, 257
tracking studies, 263
Copyright infringement, 144
Copywriters/copywriting
characteristics of, 404–405
common mistakes in, 429–430
copy approval process, 430–431
creative plan and, 404–408
defined, 404
for Internet, 416, 418
for print media
body copy, 414–416
headlines, 408–413
subheads, 414
for radio, 417–424
challenge of, 416–418
formats for, 418–419
guidelines for, 421
production process, 421–424
research
developmental, 431
evaluative, 431
slogans, 428, *429*
strategy for, in advertising plan, 291
television advertising, 424–427, *458,* 460
challenge of, 416–417, 424–425
guidelines for, 426–427
working with art director, 402, 436
Corporate advertising, 32–33, 708–714
institutional advertising, 32
objectives of, 710
scope of, 709
types of
advocacy advertising, 712
cause-related advertising, 712–714
corporate image advertising, 711–712
Corporate home pages, 578
Corporate image advertising, 711–712
Corrective advertising, 135
Cost per inquiry (CPI), 676
Cost per order (CPO), 676
Cost per rating point (CPRP), 503–504
Cost per thousand (CPM), 502
Cost per thousand-target market (CPM-TM), 502–503
Costs
direct mail, *574,* 683
escalating media costs, 515–516
Internet advertising, 571–572, *574,* 574–575
magazine advertising, 537–540, *574*
media efficiency, 502–504
newspaper advertising, 528, 532–533, *574*
outdoor advertising, *574*
radio advertising, 550, *574*
television advertising, 545–546, *574*
Coupons, 644–645
advantages to, 644–645
burden and risks of, 645
fraud, 645
on Internet, 660
product categories with highest percentage use, *644*
Cover date, 540
CPM, *565*
Creative boutique, 55
Creative concept, 402
Creative director, for television advertising production, *458*
Creative plan, 405–408
challenge of, 405
copywriters and, 405–408
defined, 405
elements of, 407–408
Creative revolution, 90–94
Creative services, 60–61
Creative team
defined, 402
television advertising, 457, *458*
Creativity
across domains
becoming creative question, 346
in business world, 346
as gift, 344
traits of famous creative minds, 344–346
adaptation/innovation theory, 346–347
creating brands through, 343
creative process in advertising agencies, 348–354
client's role in killing effective ideas, 350
creative department and account management tension, 352–354
creativity as overall agency trait, 350
tension between creative and research departments, 354
tension between creative department and account services, 349
tips for bad creative work in, 356–357
importance of, 343, 354, 357
international advertising and creative challenge of, 311–313
poets vs. killers analogy of, 340–343
Cross-cultural audience research, 305
customs, 309–310
demographic characteristics, 307–308
economic conditions, 305–307
product use and preferences, 310–311
rituals, 309–310
secondary data for, 305
values, 308
Cross-selling, 681
Cultural capital, 188
Culture, 183–184
barriers of, in international advertising, 303–311
cultural capital, 188
nature of, 183
picturing, 312–313
rituals and, 185
Cume, 553
Customer satisfaction, 169
Customs, cross-cultural research, 309–310
Cyberagencies, 56
Czech Republic, Internet users in, *563*

D

Dailies, 79
for television advertising postproduction, 470
Database agencies, 57
Database consultant, 64
Database marketing, 116, 677–682
list enhancement, 678–679
mailing lists, 677–678
marketing database, 679–681
merging offline and online information, 141
pharmaceutical marketers, 89
privacy issues, 116–117, 141
technology improvements in and IBP, 150
Data warehousing, 677
Day-after recall (DAR) scores, 253, 258
Dayparts
radio, *551*
television advertising, 547
Deception
affirmative disclosure, 135
consent order, 135
deceptive acts of commerce, 87
defined, 126
ethics of, 126–127
FTC's definition of, 130
regulation of, 130–131
Decision-making process. *See* Consumers, as decision makers
Defamation, 144
Delayed response advertising, 31–32, 167
Demand
Industrial Revolution and, 77
manufacturers' pursuit of power in channel of distribution, 78
primary, 129
shuffling of existing total demand by advertising, 119–120
Demographics/demographic segmentation, 217–218
cross-cultural research, 307–308
product usage data, 493, *495*
single-source tracking services, 493, 495
transit advertising and, 615
universal trends in, 321
usage patterns and, 217
Demonstration ads, 375–376
in television advertising, 425–426
Denmark, Internet users in, *563*
Depression era advertising, 85–87
Design, 442–447
defined, 442
principles of
balance, 443–444, **444, 445**
emphasis, 446–447
order, 444–446, **446**
proportion, 444, **445**
unity, 446, **447**
Designers, 58
Design firms, 58
Developmental advertising research, 243–248
audience definition, 245
audience profiling, 245–246
concept testing, 244
field work, 247–248
focus group, 246

idea generation, 244
methods in, 246–248
projective techniques, 246–247
Developmental copy research, 431
Dialogue
as body copy, 414
in radio advertising, 419
in television advertising, 426
Dialogue balloons, 247
Differentiation, 25
Digital Story Telling (DST), 174
Digital video (DV), for television advertising, 471
Digizines, 538–539
Direct broadcast by satellite (DBS), 315, 549
Direct mail advertising, 683–684
advantages of, 684
contests and sweepstakes, regulatory issues of, 142–143
cost, *574,* 683
disadvantages of, 684
double postcard, 684
evolution of, 514
general rating for, *502*
self-regulation, 139
split-list experiment, 263
Direct marketing, 514, 670–690
advantages of, 675–676
applications of
e-mail, 685–687
infomercials, 688–689
insert cards, 687
telemarketing, 685
toll free numbers, 688
characteristics of
interactive nature of, 671
measurable response of, 671
Code Administration Authority in Australia, 139
coordination challenge of, 689–690
database marketing, 677–682
defined, 671
direct mail, 683–684
evolution of, 670–677
brief history of, 671–674
current state of, 674–677
milestones in, *673*
growing popularity of, 675–677
Internet, 670, 675–676
marcom manager, 690
purpose of, 674
Direct marketing agencies, 57
Director
for television advertising production, *458*
in television advertising production, 462, 464
Directory advertising, 618–619
general rating for, *502*
online, 619
Direct response advertising, 30–31, 263, 396–397, 683
Direct response agencies, 57
Direct response copy, as body copy, 415
Display advertising, 531
Distribution channel
Industrial Revolution and, 77
manufacturers' pursuit of power in, 78
sales promotion and retailers power in, 640–641
trends in, 47
Distribution/distributors
as advertisers, 52
in marketing mix, 20, *22*
Domain name, 582–583
defined, *565*
top-level domain (TLD), 583
Door-to-door sampling, 648
Dot-com companies, 63, 99, 561
Double-page spread, 540
Double postcard (DPC), 684
Drugs. *See* Pharmaceutical advertising

E

E-commerce. *See* Internet; Internet advertising
E-commerce agencies, 57
Economic conditions
in cross-cultural research, 305–307
Economies of scale, 29
standard of living and, 119
Editing, for television advertising postproduction, 470
Editorial houses, in television advertising production, 462, 464
Editors, for television advertising production, *458*
Education, social class and, 187
Effective frequency, 498
Effective reach, 499
Elaboration likelihood model (ELM), 179–181
Electronic mailing lists, as media for Internet advertising, 564
Electronic printing, 452
E-mail, 562, *565*
E-mail advertising, 564
as direct marketing, 685–687
cost and, 686
opt-in, 685, *686*
spam, 685
opt-in lists, 577
peer-to-peer marketing, 141
permission-based, 108, 577
potential growth of, 577
as promotional option, 59
spam, 108
viral marketing, 577–578
Emergent consumers, 216
Emotional benefit, 165, **165**
brand loyalty, 173
positioning strategy, 229, 231
value proposition, 235–236
Emotions
anxiety ads, 387–388
change in, and assessing advertising effectiveness, 255
fear-appeal ads, 386–387
feel-good ads, 378–380
illustrations to create, 438
Emphasis, as design principle, 446–447
Ethics, 126–129
advertising controversial products, 128–129
advertising to children, 127–128
marketing junk food to, 394
alcoholic beverage advertising, 128–129
cigarette advertising, 128–129
deception, 126–127
defined, 126
peer-to-peer music networks, 244
targeting pathological gamblers, 236
truth in advertising, 126–127
Ethnicity, 196–197
Ethnic newspapers, 530
Ethnocentrism, 304
Evaluation of advertising plan, 292–293
Evaluative copy research, 431
Evaluative criteria, 168, 176
Evaluative research. *See* Copy research
Event-planning agencies, 58
Event sponsorship, 623–628
appeal of, 624–627
brand loyalty and, 625–626
as consumer-market sales promotion, 652
defined, 623
evaluating benefit from, 625, 627, 629
guidelines for, *628*
Olympic sponsor, 652, 653
as public relations tool, 627, 703
seeking synergy around, 627
users of, 623–624
Evoked set, 367
Evolution of advertising
fundamental influences on, 76–79
Industrial revolution, 77
manufacturers' pursuit of power in channel of distribution, 78
rise of capitalism, 77
rise of modern mass media, 78–79
periods in
pre-1800, 79
1800–1875, 79–80
1875–1918, 80–81
1918–1929, 81–85
1929–1941, 85–87
1941–1960, 87–90
1960–1972, 90–94
1973–1980, 94–96
1980–1992, 96–98
1993–2000, 98–99
2001–present, 99–108
speculation on future trends in, 106–108
value of evolutionary perspective, 109
Execution of advertising plan, 290–292
Executive producer, for television advertising production, *458*
Executive summary, 277
Expert spokespeople, 373, 375
Extended problem solving, 171
External facilitators, 50, *51,* 64–66
consultants, 64
defined, 64
information intermediators, 65–66
marketing and advertising research firms, 64
production facilitators, 64–65
software firms, 66
External mailing lists, 678
External position, 26–27
External search, 167–168
Eye-tracking systems, 262

F

Fact sheet radio ad, 424
Fair Credit Reporting Act, 133
Fair Packaging and Labeling Act, 133
Family
  consumer behavior of, 190–191
  intergenerational effect, 191
  by type and selected characteristics, *192*
Fantasy, ads, 393
Farm magazines, 538
Fear-appeal ads, 386–387
Feature stories, 702
Federal Communications Commission (FCC), 128
  areas of advertising regulation by, *134*
Federal Trade Commission (FTC), 87, 94
  areas of advertising regulation by, *134*
  children's advertising, 132
  historical perspective on legislative mandates of, 133–134
  policy on deception, 130
  regulatory programs and remedies by
    advertising substantiation program, 135
    affirmative disclosure, 135
    cease-and-desist order, 135
    celebrity endorsement, 135
    consent order, 135
    corrective advertising, 135
  unfair advertising, 131
Feel-good ads
  to instill brand preference, 378–380
  recycled ad characters, 378–380
  strategic implications of, 379–380
Fee system, 63
Field work, 247–248
  coolhunts, 248, 250–251
Film, for television advertising, 471
Financial industry, media expenditures by, *492*
First cover page, 540
First-run syndication, 543
Flexography, 452
Flighting, 499
FM radio stations, 550
Focus groups, 246
Food and Drug Administration, areas of advertising regulation by, *134*
Food industry, advertising-to-sale ratio, *35*
Formal balance, 443–444, **444**
Fourth cover page, 540
Frame-by-frame tests, 263–264
France, 283, 310
  expenditures on advertising in, *302*
  Internet users in, *563*
Fraud, coupons, 645
Free premium, 646
Free-standing insert, 532
Frequency
  defined, 498
  effective, 498
  gross rating points, 498, *499*
  magazine advertising, 537
  of newspapers, 531
  radio advertising, 550–551
Frequency-marketing programs, 637, 642, 680–681
  as business buyer sales promotion, 658, 660
  as consumer-market sales promotion, 651
  in Hong Kong, 682
Fulfillment centers, 57
Full position, 533
Full-service agencies, 55
Functional benefit, 165, **166**
  brand loyalty, 173
  positioning strategy, 229
  value proposition, 235–236
Fur Products Labeling Act, 133

G

Galvanic skin response (GSR), 262
Gambling
  ethics of advertising for, 129, 236
Gatefold ad, 540
Gay newspapers, 530
Gays, 198
Gaze motion, 444
Gender, 197–199
General Agreement on Tariffs and Trade (GATT), 303
General-population newspapers, 530
Generation X, 97, 216
Generation Y, 216
Geodemographic segmentation, 219
Geographic segmentation, 218–219
  newspaper advertising, 526, 528
  television, 546
Geo-targeting, 495–496
Germany
  advertising regulations in, 316
  Discount Law, 317
  expenditures on advertising in, *302*
  Free Gift Act, 317
  Internet users in, *563*
  media availability in, 313
  price sensitivity in, 310
Gift cards, 649
Global advertising. *See also* International advertising
  defined, 17
  global vs. localized campaign, 319–322
Global agencies, 317
Global brands, 300–301
Globalization
  of advertising industry, 46
  of media organizations, 490
Goodwill, 700
Government
  as advertisers, 52–53
  as audience, 16–17
Government data sources, 248
Gravure, 451–452
Great Britain, 321
Greece, advertising regulations in, 316
Gross domestic product (GDP)
  advertising's effect on, 33
Gross impressions, 496
Gross rating points, 498, *499*
Guaranteed circulation, 541
Guerrilla marketing, 609, *610*
Gutter, 540

H

Habit, 172
  vs. brand loyalty, 173
Hard-sell ads, 370–371
Headlines, 408–413
  defined, 408
  guidelines for, 412
  purposes of, 409–410
  as slogan, 428
Heavy-up scheduling, 508
Heavy users, 215
Hierarchical search engines, 567–568
High-definition television (HDTV), 549
Highly industrialized countries, 306–307
Hispanics
  online shopping, 216
  projected U.S. population of, *196*
Historical context, 279
Historical perspective of advertising. *See* Evolution of advertising
Hits, 586
Hong Kong, frequency programs, 682
House brand market, 636
Household consumers, 15–16
  number of, 15
  by type and selected characteristics, *192*
Households using television (HUT), 548
HTML, *565*
Humor ads
  to instill brand preference, 380–381
  strategic implications of, 381
Hungary, Internet users in, *563*
Hypertext transfer protocol, 563

I

Idea generation, 244
iDTV, 256
Illustrations, 436–442
  components of color, 440
    medium, 440–441
    size, 440
  defined, 436
  formats, 442
  purposes of, 436–440
    attracting attention of target audience, 436–437
    communicating product features and benefits, 438
    creating desired social context for brand, 439–440
    creating mood, feeling and image, 438
    making brand heroic, 437–438
    stimulate reading of body copy, 438–439
  square root law, 500
  strategic and creative impact of, 442
Image ads, 394–395
Importance weights, in MAAMs, 176
Improvement Act, 133
Incentives, as trade-market sales promotion, 655
Income, social class and, 187
India
  brand loyalty in, 310
  value shift in, 188

Individualism, 185, 308, 364
teamwork and, 478
Industrial Revolution, 77
advertising during, 79–80
Industry analysis, 280
Inelasticity of demand, 29
Infomercials, 97–98, 376–377
defined, 57
as direct marketing, 688–689
Informal balance, 444, **445**
Information
in brand development, 21
New Class and, 187
Information intermediators, 65–66
Information processing, 177–179
elaboration likelihood model, 179–181
Information search, 165–168
In-house agency, 56
Inkjet printing, 452
Innovators, 347
Inquiry/direct response measures, 263
Insert cards, 687
Insertion order, 540
Inserts, 532
Institutional advertising, 32
In-store sampling, 648
Integrated brand promotion (IBP)
challenges of, 150–152
Cincinnati Bell Wireless case study, 148, 152–157, 326–335, 479–484, 596–603, 718–725
coordination and collaboration of, 476–477, 628–630
defined, 13
examples of
Jaguar, 290
Levi Strauss, 38
M&M/Mars, 464
Nike, 686
Saturn, 203
United, 358
hierarchy of, 150–151
importance of, 13
vs. integrated marketing communication (IMC), 37, 149
Internet
PepsiStuff, 560
RCA records, 567
luxury brand marketers, 48
media choice and media-planning process, 517, 519
model for, 326–335
need for
accountability, 150
better audience assessment, 149
channel power, 150
consumer empowerment, 149–150
database technology, 150
fragmentation of media, 149
increased advertising clutter, 150
sales promotion
conclusions from research, 663–664
media coordination, 663
message coordination, 662–663
strategic planning triangle, 326–327
strategy for, in advertising plan, 291–292
teamwork in, 477–479
Integrated marketing communication (IMC)
defined, 37
vs. integrated brand promotion, 37, 149
Interactive advertising, 99
speculation on future trends in, 106–107
Interactive agencies, 55–56
Interactive digital television (iDTV), possible changes in advertising from, 349
Interactive kiosks, 513, 516, *516,* 660
Interactive media, *68,* 99, 516–517
Interactivity, 46–47
of Internet advertising, 571
Intergenerational effect, 191
Internal company sources, 248
Internal mailing lists, 678
Internal position, 26–27
Internal search, 165, 167–168
International advertising, 17–18
advertising agencies in
global agencies, 317
international affiliates, 317–318
local agencies, 318–319
advertising spending by top ten countries in world, 301–302, *302*
creative challenge
language, 311–312
picturing, 312–313
cultural barriers to, 303–311
cross-cultural audience research, 305
custom and ritual, 309–310
demographic characteristics, 307–308
economic conditions, 305–307
ethnocentrism, 304
product use and preference, 310–311
self-reference criterion, 304–305
values, 308
defined, 17, 300
globalized vs. localized campaigns, 319–322
Americanization of consumption values, 321
global communications, 320
global teenagers, 320–321
universal demographic and lifestyle trends, 321
global nature of advertising, 301–303
Internet and, 315
media challenge of
media availability and coverage, 313–315
media cost and pricing, 315–316
newspaper advertising, 313
regulatory challenge, 316
revenues of, 562
Simplicity, Clarity, Humor and Clever (SCHC), 408
television advertising, 313
International affiliates, 317–318
International Trade Administration (ITA), 305
Internet
art direction, 454
basic parts of
e-mail, 562, 564
glossary of terms for, *565*r
Internet Relay Chat (IRC), 563
usenet, 563
World Wide Web (WWW), 563, 566–567
brand building and, 174
broadband, 47, 102
cable TV combined with, 545
cause-related advertising, 712–713
Children's Online Privacy Protection Act (COPPA), 218
company newsletters, 703
copywriting for, 416, 418
Digital Story Telling (DST), 174
direct marketing, 675–676, 685–687
e-commerce agencies, 57
e-mail, 108
as promotional option, 59
ethics
peer-to-peer music networks, 244
glossary of media terms for, *505–506*
information intermediators for, 65–66
interactive agencies, 55–56
as international advertising, 315
magazine, digizines, 538–539
news vs. public relations press release on, 707
privacy issues
cookies, 66
peer-to-peer marketing, 141
public relations, 705
research firms for, 256
sales promotion, 658–660
sticky Web sites, 659
short Internet films, 392–393
size of, 27
surfing web, 567–570
collection search engines, 568
concept search engines, 568
hierarchical search engines, 567–568
portals, 569–570
robot search engines, 568–569
target segments and, 215, 216
users of worldwide, 315, *563*
Web site
development and management consultants, 64
wireless technology, 562
Internet advertising
ad rate for sample page, *507*
advantages of
cost, 571–572
deliverability and flexibility, 571
integration, 572
interactivity, 571
target market selectivity, 570–571
tracking, 571
audience, difficulty in assessing size of, 504
beginning of, 561–562
branding by, 589–590
cost, *574,* 574–575
databases, merging offline and online information, 141
defined, 562
direct marketing, 685–687
directory advertising, 619
disadvantages of, 574–575
e-communities strategies, 589–590

Internet advertising (*continued*)
emergence of, as threat to traditional advertising, 98
examples of
Absolut Vodka, 517
PepsiStuff, 560
RCA records, 567
Whirlpool, 106
expenditures on, *492*
future of, 591–592
broadcast Web, 591
speculation on trends in, 106–108
wireless technology, 591
growth of online advertising, 99
lack of creativity, 345
magazine advertising, 541
measuring effectiveness, 585–589
caching complications, 588–589
hits, 586
log analysis software, 586–587
measurement and payment, 589
pages, 586
reach, 587
technical aspect of, 587–588
users, 586
visits, 586
media for
e-mail, 564
usenet, 565–566
World Wide Web, 566–567
media planning, 504
newspaper, classified ads, 529
online media resources
associations, *511*
industry news, *511*
media buying sites, *511*
research/references, *511*
popularity of, around world, 302
revenues from, 570
role in advertising process, 560–561
top advertisers on, *572, 573*
types of
banner ads, 575–576
corporate home pages, 578
e-mail communications, 577–578
pop-up ads, 576–577
streaming video and audio, 578
virtual malls, 578
Web site, establishing
getting surfers to come back, 580–582
keywords and domain names, 582–583
promoting site, 583–584
rational branding, 581
security and privacy issues, 584–585
Internet Corporation for Assigned Names and Numbers (ICANN), 583
Internet Relay Chat (IRC), 563
Interstitial, *565*
Interviews, as public relations, 703
Intranet, *565*
Introduction of advertising plan, 277
Involvement
brand loyalty, 173–174
defined, 170
elaboration likelihood model, 179–181
extended problem solving, 171
habit, 172
limited problem solving, 171–172
sources of, 170–171
variety seeking, 172–173
Italy
advertising regulations in, 316
expenditures on advertising in, *302*
Internet users in, *563*

J

Japan, 321
collectivism, 308
dishwashing soap and, 162–163
expenditures on advertising in, *302*
Internet users in, *563*
price sensitivity in, 310
teenage girls predicting product success, 246
Jingles
brand recall and, 367–369
in radio advertising, 419
Junkbusters, 116

K

Keywords, purchasing, 582
KISS rule, 408
Knockoffs, 48

L

Laser printing, 452
Latinos. *See* Hispanics
Layout, 447–449
comprehensive, 449, **450**
defined, 447
mechanical, 449, **450**
parallel layout structure, 446, **448**
rough, 448, **450**
three-point layout structure, 446, **448**
thumbnails, 447–448, **450**
Leadership, teamwork and, 478–479
Legal issues. *See also* Regulation
sales promotion, 662
Lesbian newspaper, 530
Lesbians, 198
Less-developed countries, 306
Letterpress, 451
Libel, 144
Library of Congress, 133
Lifestyle research, 245–246
universal trends in, 321
Lifestyle segmentation, 220–221
Light fantasy ads, 393
Limited liability, principle of, 77
Limited problem solving, 171–172
List enhancement, 678–679
Live production, for television advertising, 471
Live script radio ad, 424
Lobbying, as objective of public relations, 700
Local advertising, 18
Local agencies, 317–318
Localized campaign, vs. globalized campaign, 319–322
Local newspapers, 531
Local spot radio advertising, 550
Local television, 544
Location selection, 467
Log analysis software, 586–587
Logo, 58
Lotteries, 129
Love and belonging needs, 120
Luxury brand marketers, 48

M

Mad cow disease, 283
Magazine
digizines, 538–539
rise of, and evolution of advertising, 78
top ranking
advertisers in, *536, 572*
business magazines, *539*
consumer magazines, *539*
magazines by circulation, *535*
types of
business, 538
consumer, 538
farm, 538
Magazine advertising
advantages of
audience interest, 534–535
audience selectivity, 534
creative opportunities, 535
long life, 535, 537
audience measurement
circulation, 541
readership, 541
buying procedures for, 539–540
CD-ROM for, 514
costs, 515, 537–540, *574*
decline in use of, 503
disadvantages of
clutter, 537
cost, 537–538
frequency, 537
long lead time, 537
reach, 537
escalating cost of, 515
expenditures on, *492*
future of, 541
general rating for, *502*
Internet, 541
production schedule, 449, 450, *450*
recall tests for, 258–259
self-regulation, 139
Mailing lists, 677–678
external lists, 678
internal lists, 678
list enhancement, 678–679
Mail sampling, 648
Make good, 509
Malaysia, 306
Manufacturers
as advertisers, 50–52
pursuit of power in channel of distribution by, 78
Marcom manager, 690
Marginal analysis, 287, *288*
Market analysis, 280
Marketing. *See also* STP marketing
brand development and management, 21–24
defined, 20
differentiation, 25
guerrilla, 609, *610*
market segmentation, 25

positioning, 26–27
revenue and profit generation, 27–29
Marketing database, 679–681
applications for, 680–681
cross-selling, 681
frequency-marketing programs, 680–681
RFM analysis, 680
defined, 679
privacy concerns, 681–682
Marketing mix
defined, 20
distribution in, 20, *22*
price in, 20, *22*
product in, 20, *22*
promotion in, 20, *22*
role of advertising in, 20–21
Marketing research firms, 64
Marketing research services
by advertising agencies, 59–60
Market niche, 225–226
Market segmentation
advertising's role in, 25–27
benefit segmentation, 221–222
business-to-businsess markets, 222–223
competitive field, 225
defined, 25, 215
demographic segmentation, 217
geographic segmentation, 218–219
Internet and, 216, 570–571
lifestyle segmentation, 220–221
market niche, 225–226
newspaper advertising and limited, 528
prioritizing, 224–226
psychographics and, 220
usage patterns and commitment levels, 215–217
Market segments. *See* STP marketing
Markup charges, 62–63
Mass media
affordability of, 126
diversity of, 126
effects of advertising on, 126
financial support of, by advertising, 78–79, 126
fragmentation of, 149
rise of, and evolution of advertising, 78–79
Mass-mediated communication, 9, 13–15
Mass production, 77
Materialism, 121–122
Meaning
object, 199–201
symbolic, 170, 193
textual, 203
transmission of sociocultural meaning, 201–204
Measured media, 491
expenditures on, *492*
Mechanical, 449, **450**
Media
competitive media assessment, 504, 508
cross-media advertising buying, 524
evolution in, and advertising, 47
expenditures by media category, 491, *492*
fragmentation of, 47
interactive, 516–517
international availability, coverage, cost and pricing, 313–316
measured, 491
proliferation of media options, 488–489, 512–513
unmeasured, 491
Media buying, 61, 508
Media-buying services, 56, 508–509
Media class, 491
Media clutter. *See* Clutter
Media conglomerates, 67, *68*
Media mix, 500–502
assorted media mix, 501–502
concentrated media mix, 501
defined, 500–501
Media objectives, 493–497
geographic scope of media placement, 495–496
message weight, 496–497
reach target audience, 493–495
Media organizations, 50, *51,* 66–68, *68*
self-regulation, 139
Media planner, 61
Media-planning process, 61, 491–512
challenges of
escalating media costs, 515–516
insufficient and inaccurate information, 514–515
interactive media, 516–517
media choice and integrated brand promotion, 517, 519
proliferation of media options, 488–489, 512–513
computer models for, 509–512
defined, 491
geographic scope, 495–496
media choices
competitive media assessment, 504, 508
Internet advertising, 504
media efficiency, 502–504
media mix, 500–502
media objectives, 493–497
geographic scope of media placement, 495–496
message weight, 496–497
reach target audience, 493–495
media scheduling and buying, 508–509
media strategies
continuity, 499
length or size of advertisement, 499–500
reach and frequency, 498–499
overview of, *493*
strategic planning considerations
in advertising plan, 291
Internet advertising, 570–592
magazines, 533–541
newspaper, 526–533
radio, 549–554
television, 541–549
Media researcher, 61
Media scheduling, 508–509
Media strategies, 497–500
Media vehicle, 491
Medium, as illustration component, 440
Membership groups, 192
Merchandise allowances, 655
Message evaluation
evaluative criteria, 253–256
attitude change, 255
behavior, 256
feelings and emotions, 255
getting it, 253
knowledge, 253
physiological change, 256
Message impressions, 496
Message strategy
defined, 366
objectives for
change behavior by inducing anxiety, 387–389
define brand image, 394–395
instill brand preference, 377–385
invoke direct response, 396–397
link key attribute to brand name, 369
persuade consumer, 369–377
promote brand recall, 367–369
scare consumer into action, 386–387
situate brand socially, 390–393
transform consumption experience, 390
Message weight
defined, 496
identifying, as media objective, 496–497
Mexico, 321
fast food in, 305
Internet users in, 315, *563*
movie advertising in, 108
newspaper advertising in, 313
Middle class, 79
Mind control, 87
Miscellaneous typeface, 453
Mobile sampling, 649
Modernity themes, in advertising, 81–83
Monopoly power, 132
Morning in America ad, 97, **97**
Movie theater ads, 513
Multi-attribute attitude models (MAAMs), 175–177
Music
peer-to-peer music networks, 244
in radio advertising, 419
for television advertising, 426
in television advertising production, 462, 464

N

Narrative
as body copy, 415
for television advertising, 426
Narrowcasting, 545
National advertising, 18
National Advertising Division of Better Business Bureau, 131
flow diagram of regulatory process, *138*
National Advertising Review Board, 94, 136
flow diagram of regulatory process, *138*
National spot radio advertising, 550
Needs
created by advertising, 120
hierarchy of, 120
need recognition, 164–165
need state, 164
Negotiation in communication process, 14, *14*

Netherlands
  advertising regulations in, 316
  Internet users in, *563*
  media availability in, 313
  newspaper advertising in, 313
Netizens, 580
Network radio advertising, 550
Network television, 542
Newly industrialized countries, 306
Newsletters, company, 702–703
Newspaper
  circulation of, 533
  readership, 526
  types of
    frequency of publication, 531
    geographic coverage, 531
    target audience, 530
Newspaper advertising
  advantages of, 527–528
    audience interest, 528
    cost, 528
    creative opportunities, 528
    credibility, 528
    geographic selectivity, 528
    timeliness of, 528
  audience measurement
    circulation, 533
    readership, 533
  buying procedures for, 532–533
  categories of
    classified advertising, 532
    display advertising, 531
    inserts, 532
  circulation, 526–527
  classified ads vs. Internet classified ads, 529
  cost of, 515, 528, 532–533, *574*
  dailies, 79
  disadvantages of
    cluttered environment, 529
    creative constraints, 529
    limited segmentation, 528
    short life of, 529–530
  escalating cost of, 515
  expenditures on, *492*
  first, 79
  future of, 533
  general rating for, *502*
  international availability and, 313
  length of, 500
  popularity of, around world, 302
  self-regulation, 139
  square root law, 500
  top advertisers, *527*
Newspaper sampling, 649
Nonusers, 216
Normative test scores, 252
North American Free Trade Agreement (NAFTA), 303
Norway, Internet users in, *563*
Nutrition Labeling and Education Act (NLEA), 133–134

O

Objective-and-task budgeting, 287–290
  build-up analysis, 288–289
  compare costs against industry and corporate benchmarks, 289
  defined, 288
  determine time frame for payout, 289
  reconcile and modify budget, 289
Objectives of advertising plan, 281–285
  beliefs, 281
  brand awareness, 281, 282
  brand switching, 283
  changing attitudes as, 281–282
  characteristics of workable, 284–285
  communications vs. sales objectives, 283–284
  purchase intent, 282
  repeat purchase, 283
  trial usage, 283
Object meaning, 199–201
Occupation
  social class and, 187
Off-invoice allowances, 656
Off-network syndication, 543
Offset lithography, 451
Olympic sponsor, 652, 653
Online editing, for television advertising postproduction, 470
Online information services, 513
On-package sampling, 649
On-sale date, 540
Opt-in lists, 577
Order, as design principle, 444, 446, **446**
Outdoor signage and billboard advertising, 610–613
  cost, *574*
  general rating for, *502*
Out-of-home media, 613

P

Pages, 586
Paid circulation, 533
Parallel layout structure, 446, **448**
Participation, for television advertising, 547
Pass-along readership, 541
Patent medicines, **80,** 80–81
Patent Office, 133
Pay-for-results, 63–64
Peer-to-peer marketing, 141
Peer-to-peer music networks, 244
Peoplemeters, 264
Percentage-of-sales budgeting, 286
Perceptual defense, 177–179
Perceptual space, 26
Peripheral cues, 181
Permanent long-term displays, 621
Permission marketing, 117
  e-mail advertising, 108, 577
Personal care products, 310
  advertising-to-sale ratio, *35*
  anxiety ads, 387–389
  media expenditures by, *492*
Personal video recorders (PVRs), 46–47
Persuasion, in brand development, 21
Persuasive ads
  advertorials, 376
  comparison ads, 371–373
  demonstrations, 375–376
  hard-sell ads, 370–371
  infomercials, 376–377
  reason-why ads, 370, 371
  testimonials, 373–375
Pharmaceutical advertising
  advertising-to-sale ratio, *35*
  database marketing, 89
  media expenditures by, *492*
  patent medicines, **80,** 80–81
Phone cards, 649
Photos, 440–441
Physiological changes, assessing advertising effectiveness by, 256
Physiological measures, 262
Physiological needs, 120
Physiological tests, 262
Picas, 453
Picturing, 312–313
Pilot testing, 262–263
Point, typeface, 453
Point-of-purchase (P-O-P) advertising, *516,* 620–623
  permanent long-term displays, 621
  range of choices for, 621–622
  short-term promotional displays, 621
  trade-market sales promotion, 654–655
Political advertisement, 9–11
Pop art, 125
Pop-up ads, 576–577
  bulky box, 577
  consumer resentment of, 577
Portals, 569–570
Portugal, advertising regulations in, 316
Positioning. *See also* STP marketing
  defined, 26, 212
  external position, 26–27
  internal position, 26–27
  perceptual space, 26
Positioning strategy
  benefit positioning, 229–231
  competitive positioning, 231
  consistency, 227
  defined, 212, 226–234
  distinctiveness, 228–229
  emotional benefit, 229, 231
  essentials for effective, 227–229
  functional benefits, 229
  fundamental themes, 229–232
  self-expressive benefits, 231
  simplicity, 228
  substantive value, 227
  user positioning, 231
Postal Service, U.S., **684**
  areas of advertising regulation by, *134*
Posters, 610
Postpurchase reinforcement programs, 169
Posttest message tracking, 263
Potential ad impressions, 496
Preferred position, 533
Prelight, 467
Premiums, 617
  as business buyer sales promotion, 657
  as consumer-market sales promotion, 646
  regulations of, 143
Pre-post design, 260–262
Preprinted insert, 532

Press conferences, as public relations, 703
Press releases, 701–702
Price
advertising's effect on, 33–34
economies of scale, 34
inelasticity of demand, 29
in marketing mix, 20, *22*
Price-off deals, 645–646
Price sensitivity
Germany, 310
Japan, 310
Primary demand, 129
Primary demand stimulation, 29–30
Principles of design, 443–447
Printing methods
computer print production, 452
electronic, 452
flexography, 452
gravure, 451–452
inkjet, 452
laser, 452
letterpress, 451
offset lithography, 451
Print media, *68*
art direction
design, 442–447
illustration, 436–442
layout, 447–449
typography, 452–454
copywriting for
body copy, 414–416
headlines, 408–413
subheads, 414
production in
processes for, 451–452
schedule, 449–451
typography in, 452–454
square root law, 500
Privacy issues
cookies, 66, 141
establishing Web sites and, 584–585
marketing databases, 116–117, 141, 681–682
peer-to-peer marketing, 141
permission marketing, 117
public relations and, 144
Privacy Rights Clearing House, 117
PRIZM (potential rating index by ZIP marketing), 219
Proactive public relations strategy, 705–707
Problem and solution ad
for television advertising, 426
Problem solving
extended, 171
limited, 171–172
Producer, for television advertising production, *458*
Product, in marketing mix, 20, *22*
Product differentiation, strategy for, 214
Production facilitators, 64–65
Production houses, in television advertising production, 464
Production in communication process, 14, *14*
Production manager, for television advertising production, *458*
Production services, 61
Production stage, 467–469
Product placement, 392–393
Product use and preferences
cross-cultural research, 310–311
illustration to communicate product features/benefits, 438
Professional publications, 249
Professionals, as audience, 16
Program rating, 548
Projective techniques, 246–247
association tests, 247
dialogue balloons, 247
sentence and picture completion, 247
story construction, 247
Zaltman Metaphor Elicitation Technique, 247
Promotion
in marketing mix, 20, *22*
Promotion agencies, 56–58
defined, 56–57
types of
design firms, 58
direct marketing agencies, 57
direct response agencies, 57
e-commerce agencies, 57
event-planning agencies, 58
public relations firms, 58
sales promotion agencies, 57–58
Proportion, as design principle, 444, **445**
Psychogalvanometer, 262
Psychographics, 220
Psychological processes
attitude, 174
elaboration likelihood model (ELM), 179–181
information processing and perceptual defense, 177–179
multi-attribute attitude model, 175–177
P.T. Barnum era, 80–81
Publicity
advantages of, 704
vs. advertising, 8–9
defined, 698
negative, 696–698, 704
Public relations, 696–708
event sponsorship, 627
examples of
Firestone and Ford, 696–697
Intel, 698–699
Pepsi, 699
Internet, 705
news vs. public relations press release on, 707
objectives of, 699–700
counteracting negative publicity, 700
giving advice and council, 700
lobbying, 700
preparing internal communications, 700
promoting goodwill, 700
promoting product, 700
public relations audit, 706
public relations plan, 706–707
regulation issues in, 143–144
appropriations, 144
copyright infringement, 144
defamation, 144
strategies for
proactive, 705–707
reactive public relations strategy, 707–708
tools of, 700–704
company newsletter, 702–703
feature stories, 702
interviews and press conferences, 703
press release, 700–702
publicity, 704
sponsored events, 703
Public relations audit, 706
Public relations firms, 58
Public relations plan, 706–707
Public service announcements, 9
Puffery, 127, 130
Pulsing, 499
Purchase intent, 282
Pure Food and Drug Act, 81
Push money, 655
Push strategy, 652–653

Q

QuarkXPress, 447, 448, 449

R

Race, 196–197
projected U.S. population by race, *196*
RADAR (Radio's All Dimension Audience Research), 553–554
Radio
advantages of
creative opportunities, 551–552
flexibility and timeliness, 551
target audience selectivity, 551
categories of
AM vs. FM, 550
networks, 549–550
syndication, 550
dayparts, *551*
Radio advertising
advantages of
cost, 550
reach and frequency, 550–551
audience measurement, 553–554
buying procedures for, 552–553
copywriting for, 417–424
challenge of, 416–418
formats for, 418–419
guidelines for, 421
cost of, 550, *574*
disadvantages
chaotic buying procedures, 552
creative limitations, 552
fragmented audience, 552
poor audience attentiveness, 552
emergence of, 86
expenditures on, *492,* 549
fact sheet radio ad, 424
format for
announcement, 419
celebrity announcer, 419
dialogue, 419
music, 419
future of, 554
general rating for, *502*
live script radio ad, 424

Radio advertising (*continued*)
production process, 421–424
elements of, 421–422
script for, 420, 423
timetable for, *422*
word count relative to airtime, 422
top ten national spot advertisers, *551*
types of
local spot radio advertising, 550
national spot radio advertising, 550
network radio advertising, 550
Radio networks, 549–550
Radio syndication, 550
Rate card
for magazine advertising, 539–540
for newspaper advertising, 532
Rational branding, 581
Reach, 496, 497
defined, 498
effective, 499
gross rating points, 498, *499*
Internet advertising, 587
magazine advertising, 537
radio advertising, 550–551
television advertising, 544–545
Time Warner and AOL merge and, 524
Reactive public relations strategy, 707–708
Readership
circulation, 541
magazine, 541
newspapers, 533
Reason-why ads, 370, 371
Rebates, 651
Recall test, 257–259
Reception in communication process, 14, *14*
Recognition tests, 259–260
Reference groups, 191–193
Regional advertising, 18
Regulation, 129–144
advertising aimed at children, 94, 132–133, 218
areas of
advertising to children, 132–133
competitive issues, 131–132
deception and unfairness, 130–131
current concerns in
direct marketing, 141–142
Internet privacy, 141–142
public relations, 143–144
sales promotion, 143
international advertising and, 316
Internet, 141–142
children privacy protection, 218
legislation
during depression, 87
Pure Food and Drug Act, 81
during 1970s, 94
during P.T. Barnum era, 81
Pure Food and Drug Act, 81
regulatory agents, 133–140
consumers as, 139–140
government, 133–136
industry self-regulation, 136–139
tobacco settlement and, 102
Repeat purchase, 283, 642, 645
Repetition, as brand recall, 367
Repositioning, 233–234
Research. *See* Advertising research
Resellers, as advertisers, 52
Resonance tests, 256–257
Response models of budgeting, 287
Restaurants, media expenditures by, *492*
Retailers
as advertisers, 52
advertising-to-sale ratio, *35*
increase in channel power by big retailers, 150
interactive media, 517
media expenditures by, *492*
newspaper advertising, 526
sales promotion, and power in channel of distribution, 640–641
RFM analysis, 680
Riding the boards, 611
Rituals, 185–187
of beauty pageants, 188
cross-cultural research, 309–310
Roaring Twenties, 81–85
Robinson-Patman Act, 133, 143
Robots, 568–569
Robot search engines, 568–569
Roman typeface, 452–453
Rosie the Riveter ads, 87, **88**
Rough cut, for television advertising postproduction, 470
Rough layout, 448, **450**
Run-of-paper (ROP), 533
Rural Industria segment, 219
Russia, 310
Internet users in, *563*

S

Safety needs, 120
Sales objectives, vs. communication objectives, 283–284
Sales promotion, vs. advertising, 637–638, *639*
business buyer, techniques for, 656–658
consumer-market sales promotion, 641–652
objectives for, 642–644
techniques for, 644–652
defined, 637
expenditures on, 638, *639*
forms of, 637
goals of, 628, *629,* 637
growth in
consumer response to promotions, 640
demand for greater accountability, 639–640
increased power of retailers, 640–641
media clutter, 641
proliferation of brands, 640
short-term orientation, 640
house brand vs. big brand names, 636
IBP coordination challenge
conclusions from research, 663–664
media coordination, 663
message coordination, 662–663
importance of, 637–638
Internet, 658–660
regulatory issues in, 143
risks of
alienating customers, 662
borrowing from future sales, 661
creating price orientation, 661
legal considerations, 662
time and expense of, 662
trade-market sales promotion
objectives for, 652–654
techniques for, 654–656
Sales promotion agencies, 57–58, 638
Sales training programs, 656
Salient beliefs, 175
Samples
as consumer-market sales promotion, 648–649
Sans serif, 453
Satellite/closed-circuit television, 544
Scheduling
continuous scheduling, 499
flighting, 499
heavy-up scheduling, 508
pulsing, 499
Science, 89
in evolution of advertising, 82–83
worship of, 243
Scratch track, for television advertising postproduction, 470
Scripts, for television advertising, 460, *468*
Script typeface, 453
Search, robot, 568–569
Search engines
collection, 568
concept, 568
defined, 567
hierarchical search engines, 567–568
Secondary data
for cross-cultural research, 305
out-of-date, 514
single-source tracking services, 493, 495
sources
commercial data sources, 248–249, *252*
government sources, 248
internal company sources, 248–249
professional publications, 249
weak information from, 493
Second cover page, 540
Securities and Exchange Commission
areas of advertising regulation by, *134*
Selective attention, 178
Selective demand stimulation, 30
Self-actualization needs, 120
Self-expressive benefit, 193
positioning strategy, 231
value proposition, 235–236
Self-liquidating premium, 646
Self-reference criterion (SRC), 304
Self-regulation
advertising agencies and associations, 138–139
Better Business Bureaus, 136–138
list of organizations supporting, 137
media organizations, 139
National Advertising Review Board, 136
Sentence and picture completion, 247
Serif, 453
Service firms, as advertisers, 50–52
Set selection, 467
Sex appeal ads
to instill brand preference, 381–385
strategic implications of, 383
Share of audience, 548

Share of market budgeting, 286–287
Share of voice, 504, 508
Share of voice budgeting, 286–287
Shoot, 467–468
Short-term promotional displays, 621
Simplicity, Clarity, Humor and Clever (SCHC), 408
Singapore, 306
Single-source data, 263–264
Single-source tracking measures, 263–264
Single-source tracking services, 493, 495
Situation analysis, 278–281
  competitor analysis, 281
  defined, 278
  historical context, 279
  industry analysis, 280
  market analysis, 280
Skyscraper, 575
Slander, 144
Slice-of-life ads, 391–392
Slogans
  brand recall and, 367–369
  copywriting, 428, *429*
  elements of good, 428
Slotting fees, 656
Social anxiety ads, 388–389
Social aspects of advertising, 117–126
  affects on happiness and general well-being, 120–122
  demeaning and deceitful vs. liberating and artful, 122–125
  educates consumers, 117–119
  effect on mass media, 126
  standard of living improvements, 119–120
Social class, 187–190
  consumption and, 188–190
  cultural capital, 188
  defined, 187
  education, 187
  income, 187
  occupation, 187
  taste and, 188
Social context
  illustration to create, 439–440
  importance of, in Roaring Twenties, 82–83
Social meaning, 36–37
  defined, 36
  situate brand socially, 390–393
Social organizations, as advertisers, 53–54
Software firms, 66
South Korea, 306, 308
  expenditures on advertising in, *302*
Space contract, 540
Space order, 540
Spain
  expenditures on advertising in, *302*
  Internet users in, *563*
Spam, 108, 565–566, 685
Specialty advertising, 616–618
Spiders, 568
Split-cable transmission, 262
Split-list experiment, 263
Split-run distribution, 262–263
Spokesperson, for television advertising, 426
Sponsor, 8
Sponsorship, for television advertising, 546–547
Spot advertising, 547
Square root law, 500
Standard advertising unit (SAL), 533
Standard Industrial Classification (SIC), 223
Standard of living
  improvements of, by advertising, 119–120
Stereotypes, perpetuating by advertising, 122
Sticky Web sites, 580–581
  sales promotion and, 659
Still production, for television advertising, 471
Storyboard, 425
  in television advertising production, 460
Story construction, 247
STP marketing
  continuous nature of, 213–215
  evolution of marketing strategies, 212–215
  positioning strategy, 226–234
    essentials for effective, 227–229
    fundamental themes, 229–232
    repositioning, 233–234
  target segments
    benefit segmentation, 221–222
    business-to-businsess markets, 222–223
    demographic segmentation, 217
    geographic segmentation, 218–219
    lifestyle segmentation, 220–221
    prioritizing, 224–226
    psychographics and, 220
    usage patterns and commitment levels, 215–217
Straight-line copy, 414
Strategic planning triangle, 326–327
Streaming video and audio
  Internet advertising, 578
Subheads
  purpose of, 414
  as slogan, 428
Subliminal advertising, 87–88, 125
Super Bowl commercials, 284, 364–365, **365**, 508, 515
Superlatives, 416
Support media, *68*
  coordination challenge of, 628–630
  event sponsorship, 623–628
  point-of-purchase (P-O-P) advertising, 620–623
  role of, 609, 620
  traditional, 609–620
    aerial advertising, 616
    directory advertising, 618–619
    outdoor signage and billboard advertising, 610–613
    specialty advertising, 616–618
    transit advertising, 613–616
Surfing, 567
Sweden, 321
Sweepstakes
  as consumer-market sales promotion, 646–648
  direct mail regulatory issues of, 142–143
  on Internet, 660
  regulation on, 143
Switchers, 216
Switzerland, advertising regulations in, 316
Symbolic meaning, 170, 193
  picturing, 312
Symbolic value, 35
Syndicated television, 543–544

T

Taiwan, 306
Target audience, 50, *51*
  defined, 15
  illustration to attract attention of, 436–437
  newspapers, 526, 528
  product usage data, 493, *495*
  radio, 551
  reaching as objective in media-planning process, 493
  single-source tracking services, 493, 495
Target market, 212
Target segment. *See* STP marketing
Taste, 188
Teamwork
  facts about, 477–478
  individualism and, 478
  leadership and, 478–479
  principles for, 482
  uniform look, 482
Technology, 89
  broadband, 102
  broadcast Web, 591
  in evolution of advertising, 82–83
  growth in communication technology in 1970s, 95
  interactive, 99
  New Class and, 187
  wireless, 102, 591
Teenagers, global teenagers, 320–321
Telecommunications industry
  media expenditures by, *492*
Telemarketing, 683, 685
  regulation on practices of, 143
Telephone Consumer Fraud and Abuse Prevention Act, 143
Television
  cable, 95
  categories of
    cable, 542–543
    local, 544
    network television, 542
    satellite/closed-circuit, 544
    syndicated, 543–544
  future of, 548–549
  interactive digital television (iDTV)
    possible changes in advertising from, 349
Television advertising
  advantages of
    audience selectivity, 545
    cost per contact, 545
    coverage, reach and repetition, 544–545
    creative opportunities, 544
  art director, 454–459
  audience measurement
    households using television, 548
    program rating, 548
    share of audience, 548
    television households, 548

Television advertising (*continued*)
buying procedures for
participation, 547
sponsorship, 546–547
spot advertising, 547
copywriting
challenge of, 416–417, 424–425
guidelines for, 426–427
cost of, 515, 545–546, *574*
creative guidelines for, 457–459
creative team in, 457, *458*
disadvantages of
clutter, 546
fleeting message, 545
high absolute cost, 545–546
poor audience attitude and attentiveness, 546
poor geographic selectivity, 546
effect on programming, 126
emergence of, 89
escalating cost of, 515
expenditures on, *492,* 542, *543*
formats for
demonstration, 425–426
dialogue, 426
music and song, 426
narrative, 426
problem and solution, 426
spokesperson, 426
vignette, 426
general rating for, *502*
infomercial, 97–98
interactive media as threat to, 98
international availability and, 313
length of, 500
pilot testing, 262–263
popularity of, around world, 302
postproduction, 470
preproduction
budget approval, 460, 462
directors, editorial houses, music suppliers, 462, 464
production timetable, 466, *467*
review bids, 464–466
selecting location, set, cast, 467
storyboard and script approval, 459, 460
production, 467–469
cost of, 466, 469
creative team for, *458*
options for, 471
timetable for, 466, *467*
rating system, accuracy of measurement of audience size, 514–515
recall tests for, 258
self-regulation, 139
storyboard, 425
top advertisers, *543, 572*
Television households, 548
Television networks, 67, *68*
Testimonials
average-user, 375
as body copy, 414–415
celebrity, 373
as direct marketing, 688–689
expert spokespeople, 373, 375
in infomercials, 376
Textile Fiber Products Identification Act, 133
Textual meaning, 203
Third cover page, 540
Thought listings, 257
Three-point layout structure, 446, **448**
Thumbnails, 447–448, **450**
Tobacco advertising, 102
Toll free numbers, as direct marketing, 687
Top-level domain (TLD), 583
Top-of-mind, 281, 367
Tracking studies, 260–262, 263
Trade allowances, regulation on, 143
Trade channel
building and maintaining brand loyalty within, 24
institutional advertising, 32
members as audience, 16
vertical trade communities, 52
Trade-market sales promotion, 58, 637
goals of, 652
objectives for, 652–654
push strategy, 652–653
techniques for
allowances, 655–656
cooperative advertising, 656
incentives, 655
point-of-purchase displays, 654–655
sales training programs, 656
Trade resellers, as advertisers, 52
Trade shows, 656–657
Transformational ads, 390
Transit advertising, 613–616
general rating for, *502*
Trial offer
as business buyer sales promotion, 657–658
as consumer-market sales promotion, 649
Trial purchase, 642
Trial usage, 283
Truth in Lending Act, 133
Turkey, newspaper advertising in, 313
Twinkie tax, 129
Type font, 452
Typography, 452–454
categories of, 452–453
readability of, 453–454
type measurement, 453

U

Unaided recall, 258
Unfair advertising, defined, 131
Unique selling proposition (USP), 369
United Kingdom
advertising regulations in, 316
expenditures on advertising in, *302*
Internet users in, *563*
media availability in, 313
United States
boosting global image of, 457
expenditures on advertising in, *302*
Internet users in, 315, *563*
Unit-of-sales budgeting, 286
Unity as design principle, 446, **447**
axis, 446, **447**
border, 446
parallel layout structure, 446, **448**
three-point layout structure, 446, **448**
white space, 446, **447**
Unmeasured media, 491
expenditures on, *492*
Usage patterns, 215–217
demographic segmentation, 217
Usenet
defined, 563
as media for Internet advertising, 565–566
User positioning, 231
Users, 586

V

VALS (values and lifestyles, 220–221, *222*
Value proposition, 234–236
defined, 234
emotional benefit, 235–236
functional benefit, 235–236
self-expressive benefit, 235–236
Values, 184–185
advertising's effect on, 34–37
cross-cultural research, 308
defined, 34
relationship to attitudes, 184, *185*
social meaning, 36–37
symbolic, 35
Variety seeking, 172–173, 216
V-chip, 546
VCRs, 29
Vertical cooperative advertising, 131
Vertical trade communities, 52
Videotape, for television advertising, 471
Vignette, for television advertising, 426
Viral marketing, 577–578
Virtual malls, 578
Visits, 586
Voice response analysis, 262

W

Web sites. *See also* Internet; Internet advertising
corporate home pages, 578
cost of, 572
development and management consultants, 64
establishing, 579–585
getting surfers to come back, 580–582
keywords and domain names, 582–583
promoting site, 583–584
rational branding, 581
security and privacy issues, 584–585
payment for use of, 592
for small businesses, 580
sticky sites, 580–581
sales promotion and, 659
Web TV, 564
Weeklies, 531
Wheeler-Lea Amendment, 87, 133
White space, 446, **447**
Wholesalers, as advertisers, 52
Wireless technology, 562
future growth potential, 102
Internet advertising, 591
Within-vehicle duplication, 497

Women
  feminist movement, 94
  as primary target of advertising, 82
  in workforce, during WWII, 87
Wool Products Labeling Act, 133
Woopies, 218
World War I, 81
World War II
  advertising during and right after, 87–90
World Wide Web (WWW), 563, 566–567.
  See also Internet; Web sites

Y

Yellow Pages advertising, 619
  expenditures on, *492*

Z

Zaltman Metaphor Elicitation Technique
  (ZMET), 247
Zapping, 546
Zipping, 546

CREDITS

For permission to reproduce the images on the pages indicated, acknowledgment is made to the following:

Chapter 1

5 © 2001, Blue Martini Software, Inc.
6 Courtesy Wendy's International, Inc.
7 Courtesy of Volkswagen (left). Courtesy of Volkswagen and Arnold Communications, Inc. (middle). © 1995 The Coca-Cola Company. Reprinted by permission (right).
8 Advertising Agency: Tanhouse Creative. Client: PowerQuest Corporation.
10 Reprinted with permission from Medpointe, Inc. All rights reserved (top). Courtesy of the Health Education Authority (bottom).
11 Gore/Lieberman campaign 2000.
12 All photos © Geof Kern.
15 Courtesy of The Coca-Cola Company.
16 © 2001, Blue Martini Software, Inc.
17 Courtesy of TAP Pharmaceuticals.
18 Courtesy of Rolex Watch U.S.A., Inc. (top left and right).
20 Courtesy of Daffy's (top). Courtesy of Shapiro Luggage, Gifts, Leather (bottom).
24 Copyright 2000 Disney.
25 Weider Nutrition International © 1995.
26 Courtesy Taramask S.A. Switzerland (top). Courtesy of Honda Motor Co., Inc. (bottom left). Courtesy of Wonderbra (right).
28 Courtesy of Ben & Jerry's® (left). Procter & Gamble Company. Reprinted by permission (right).
30 Courtesy of Panasonic (left). © 1996 National Fluid Milk Processor Promotion Board. Reprinted by permission of Bozell Worldwide, Inc. (middle). Courtesy of State of Florida, Department of Citrus, 1994/95 (right).
31 Reprinted with permission of FCB (left). Courtesy of Toshiba America Consumer Products, Inc. (right).
32 Permission granted by The Franklin Mint and Sheffield Enterprises (left). © 1995 Lever Brothers Company "All" Laundry Detergent. Courtesy of Lever Brothers Company (right).
34 © 1993 American Plastics Council. Reprinted by permission.
36 Photo courtesy of Levi Strauss & Co. (top left). Ray-Ban sunglasses by Bausch & Lomb. © 1995 Bausch & Lomb Incorporated (top right). Courtesy of United Airlines (bottom left). © 1994 Waterford Wedgwood USA, Inc. Reprinted by permission (bottom middle). Courtesy of Gucci (bottom right).

Chapter 2

43 Bluestreak.
45 Courtesy Pepsi Company.
47 Courtesy of DoubleClick.
53 VerticalNet Solutions.
54 Idaho Department of Commerce.
56 Bluestreak.
58 Photography: Copyright © 2000 by Aaron Rapoport. Creative: Copyright © 2000 by Welch, Nehlen, Groome Advertising, Inc.
61 Courtesy Richter 7, formerly FJC&N.
65 Courtesy Alladvantage.com.
67 Courtesy of Hyperion.
69 Reprinted by permission of StarBand Communications, Inc. and Tony Stone Images/New York Inc. (left). Instinet Corporation; Ad Agency: Brouillard; Art Director: George Noszagh, Writer: Ted Speck (right).

Chapter 3

76 Courtesy of Lever Brothers Company.
82 Courtesy of Lever Brothers Company (left).
85 Reproduced from the Collections of the Library of Congress.
88 Courtesy of the Coca-Cola Company (left).
90 © Archive Photos, Inc. (left). Courtesy of H. Armstrong Roberts, Inc. (right).
91 Courtesy of IBM Corporation (top right). Courtesy of Serta, Inc., Des Plaines, Illinois (bottom left).
92 ® Kellogg Company, © 1968 Kellogg Company; used with permission (left).
93 Courtesy of Volkswagen (top left). Courtesy of Braniff (top right). Courtesy of Goodyear Tire & Rubber Company (bottom left). Reproduced with the permission of PepsiCo, Inc., 1995 Purchase, New York (bottom right).
95 Photo courtesy of Polaroid Corporation; "Polaroid" and "One Step"® (left). © The Procter & Gamble Company. Used by permission (right).
96 Courtesy of Nestle, U.S.A, Inc. (left). Courtesy of Chrysler Corporation (right).
97 Courtesy of the Republican National Committee (left). Courtesy of MasterCard (right).
98 Reproduced with the permission of PepsiCo, Inc., 1995, Purchase, New York.
100 Courtesy of Mocha Blend (top left). Courtesy of The Royal Peacock (top right). Title: Cue Ball; Copywriter: Andy Greenaway; Art Director: Craig Smith Photographer: Julian Watt; Retouching: Procolor (bottom).
101 Courtesy of Levis SilverTab (top). Goodby, Silverstein & Berlin (bottom left). © 1998 MTV Networks. All rights reserved. MTV, MUSIC TELEVISION and all related titles, characters and logos are trademarks owned by MTV Networds, a division a Viacom International Inc. (bottom right).
102 Courtesy of Pets.com (left). Courtesy of Procter & Gamble (right).
103 Advertisement Courtesy of Hughes Network Systems, Germantown, Maryland (top right). Holland Mark Boston for Teradyne, Inc. (bottom left). Artwork by loudthöt, Inc.; Copy written by Angelia Pinaga of Enfora, Inc. (bottom right).
104 Courtesy of Nike (top). © Heineken Brouwerijen (bottom).
105 Courtesy of Pussyfoot (top). Trackstar Motorsports.com (bottom).
107 Courtesy of Procter & Gamble.

Chapter 4

115 Courtesy of Deesse.
116 Courtesy of Buystream.
118 © 1990 Anheuser-Busch, Inc., St. Louis, MO. Reprinted by permission (left). The Facing HIV and AIDS campaign is a collaborative effort by the Asian Pacific AIDS Intervention Team and Pacific Asian Language Services of Special Service for Groups and Healthier Solutions, Inc., under a CARE grant from the County of Los Angeles Department of Health Services, AIDS Programs office (middle). Courtesy of Deesse (right).
121 Courtesy of Johnson & Johnson (left). Courtesy of Lachman Imports (right).
123 Richard Avedon for Gianni Versace (left). Courtesy, © Unilever United States, Inc. (middle). Courtesy of The Body Shop (right).
124 Courtesy of Procter & Gamble.
125 © Darlene Hammond/Archive Photos.
127 Courtesy of Partnership for a Drug-Free America.
131 Courtesy S.C. Johnson & Son, Inc.
142 Courtesy of Privada (left). Courtesy of Luckysurf.com (right).

Chapter 5

161 Dolce & Gabbana.
163 © The Procter & Gamble Company. Used by permission.
165 Courtesy Johnson & Johnson.
166 © General Motors Corp. (top). David Le Bon (bottom right). Courtesy of Toyota (bottom left).
167 Courtesy of Campbell Soup Company.

168 Courtesy of Northwest Airlines.
169 Courtesy of American Isuzu Motors Inc.
170 Courtesy of Casio, Inc.
171 Courtesy of IAMS Food Company.
172 Courtesy of DeBeers Consolidated Mines, Ltd., and J. Walter Thompson.
173 Courtesy Wendy's International.
176 Courtesy of Sears, Roebuck and Co.
177 Courtesy of Sony Electronics, Inc. Client: Sony Electronics, Inc.; Agency: Bagby and Company, Chicago; Creative Directors: Steve Bagby, Lary Larsen; Writers: Erin McCarty, Ted Wahlberg; Photographer: Steve Nozicka, Chicago.
180 Courtesy of Detroit (left). Singapore Tourism Board (right).
182 Photo by Thomas C. O'Guinn.
183 Photo by Thomas C. O'Guinn.
184 CURE 81 and HORMEL are registered trademarks of Hormel foods, LLC, and are used with permission by Hormel Foods (left). TM/® "M&M's," "M" and the "M&M's" Characters are registered trademarks of Mars, Incorporated and its affiliates. All are used with permission. Mars Incorporated is not associated with the Advertising and Integrated Brand Promotion or O'Guinn, Allen & Semenik the authors (middle). Courtesy of Wal-Mart Inc. (right).
185 Paul Wakefield/B & A.
186 Courtesy of Kraft Foods, Inc. (left). © Disney Enterprises, Inc. (right).
187 © Charles Purvis, Saatchi & Saatchi for the Procter & Gamble Company. Used by permisson.
189 Courtesy of Bad Girl Clothing Co. (top). Courtesy of Dolce & Gabbana (bottom).
190 Chivas Regal and the Chivas Regal Logo are trademarks of Chivas Brothers Limited (left). Courtesy of Miller Brewing Company Archives (right).
191 © Gonalco Productions, Inc./CBS.
193 Courtesy MasterCard International, Incorporated.
194 Hard Top—Adidas America, Burrell Communications (Agency) featuring Antawn Jamison. Illustration by Eddie Guy (top). © Sesame Workshop. Sesame Street, Tickles and their logos are trademarks and or servicemarks of Sesame Workshop. All rights reserved (bottom left). Cramer-Krasselt/Phoenix (center). Candie's, Inc. (bottom right).
195 Copyright © 2002 T.J. Maxx (top). Reproduced by permission of Mecca USA (bottom).
197 Used with permission of DFO, Inc. (left). Courtesy of Pampers (right).
198 ©1997 American Express Financial Corporation. Reprinted with permission (left). Ad Concept by Mad Dogs & Englishmen. Illustration by Stuart Patterson (right).
200 Courtesy of Saturn Corporation (top). Courtesy of Fender Museum (bottom).
202 Courtesy Johnston & Murphy, Nashville, TN.
204 Creative Directors: Michael Wilde/Jeff Odiorne/Nicolas Graham; Art Director: Erich Pfeifer; Copywriter: Jim Lansbury (top). © Shawn Michienzi, RipSaw, Inc. (bottom).

Chapter 6

209 Courtesy of Gucci.
211 Courtesy of Gillette (both).
214 Neither the United States Marine Corps nor any other component of the Department of Defense has approved, endorsed, or authorized this product. USMC advertising creative by J. Walter Thompson (left). Courtesy of Clinique (middle). Courtesy of Hard Candy (right).
217 Courtesy of Wells Fargo.
219 Reprinted with permission of Simmons Market Research Bureau, Inc. (both).
221 Courtesy of Pillsbury Company; created by Foote, Cone & Belding (left). Courtesy of Pillsbury Company; created by Leo Burnett (Chicago) (right).
223 American Honda Motor Co., Inc. (top). Courtesy of Chrysler (bottom).
224 Courtesy of Accenture (left). ©2001 Federal Express Corporation. All Rights Reserved (right).
226 Reprinted by permission of Svetlana Electron Devices. Created in house by Svetlana Eletron Devices. Creative Director: Terri Bates; Photographer: Jared Cassidy.
228 Courtesy of State Farm Insurance Companies (left). Courtesy of Pontiac Division of General Motors Corporation (right).
230 Agency: DSW Partners. Photographer: Michael O'Brien (top). Courtesy of Mennen (bottom left). Courtesy of Invisalign (bottom right).
231 Courtesy of Gucci.
232 Courtesy of Rykä and Mullen Advertising (left). Courtesy of Merrell Footwear (right).
233 Courtesy of Saatchi & Saatchi (left). Courtesy of Nova Cruz Products and Lunar Design (right).

Chapter 7

241 Courtesy of The Coca-Cola Company.
243 Courtesy of Oldsmobile Division of General Motors Corporation.

245 Courtesy of SC Johnson & Son, Inc. (left). Courtesy of Procter & Gamble (right).
254 Phillip Morris Companies, Inc. (top left). Courtesy The Coca-Cola Company (top right). Client: Converse; Agency: Pyro, Dallas; Art Directors: Andy Mahr, Shannon; Copywriter: Todd Tillford, Gail Barlow, Josh Cannon Photographer: Cheryl Dunn. (bottom).
255 Courtesy of Procter & Gamble (left). Client: Majorica; Agency: Vinizius/Y&R, Barcelona; Art Directors: Victor Arrianzu, Luíz Moreno; Copywriters: Christian Martinell, Txema Escolano; Photographer: David Levin (right).
257 Reproduced courtesy of Lever Bros. Co.
258 Photo by Lloyd DeGrane.
259 Courtesy of Leo Burnett and Altoids, a product of Collard & Bowser.
260 Client: Mars. Agency: D'Arcy, London. Art Director: Susan Byrne, Michelle Power. Copywriter: Michelle Power, Susan Byrne. Photographer: Julie Fisher (top). Courtesy of Starch (inset).
261 Reprinted with permission of General Motors Corporation (left). Courtesy of Ford Motor Company (top right). Reprinted with permission of General Motors Corporation (bottom right).
263 Courtesy of Walt Disney World.
265 Screengrabs courtesy of Jaguar Cars North America 2001.
266 *Agency* Magazine.

Chapter 8

271 Courtesy of Quixi Inc. & Cliff Freeman.
273 Courtesy of Apple Computer, Inc.
274 Courtesy of Apple Computer, Inc.
275 Courtesy of Apple Computer, Inc.
276 Courtesy of Apple Computer, Inc. Portions ©Netscape Communications Corporation, 1999.
278 © 1996 American Express Travel Related Services Company, Inc. Reprinted with permission.
279 Courtesy American Express Corporation (left). Courtesy of Solomon Smith Barney (right).
280 Courtesy of the Pillsbury Company.
282 Courtesy of Commerce One (left). Courtesy of Quixi (right).
284 Photographer: Chris Buck; Agency: Ogilvy & Mather; CD/CW: Josh Tavlin, Kristen Steele; CD/AD: John McNeil, Mark Graham
291 Danskin, Inc.
292 The Gillette Company.
293 The Gillette Company.

Chapter 9

299 Courtesy of Boucheron, Paris.
301 Courtesy of Nike (left). Courtesy of Swatch (right).
306 Courtesy of Tropicana Dole Beverages North America.
307 © Heineken Brouwerijen (left). Courtesy of Nokia (right).
309 Courtesy of Schieffelin & Somerset Co., 2 Park Avenue, New York, NY 10016 (left). Courtesy of International Business Machines Corporation (right).
311 Courtesy of Warner-Lambert Company. Lady Protector de Wilkinson is available in the French Market; it is a trademark of Wilkinson Sword GmbH (left). Courtesy of Boucheron, Paris (right).
312 Courtesy of FashionMall.com (left). Courtesy of Tourism Authority of Thailand (middle). Courtesy of Alan Powdrill, photographer, and Euro RSCG Wnek Gosper. Art director: Oliver Caporn (right).
316 Courtesy SkyPort TV, CS Service Center Corporation, Yokohama, Japan.
319 Courtesy of Jack Daniel Distillery (both).
320 Courtesy of Nikon GMBH.
322 Courtesy of Yokohama Rubber Company, Tokyo, Japan; advertising agency IDUE.
334 Agency: The Richards Group; Client: Nokia Mobile Phones.

Chapter 10

339 Courtesy of Nancy Rubenstein Inc.
340 Courtesy of Nissan Motor Co. Ltd.
341 Courtesy of Taco Bell.
343 Courtesy of Target.
344 © Philadelphia Museum of Art.
347 Doing Business: The Art of David Ross, p. 10/Andrews and McMeel, A Universal Press Syndicate Company, 4520 Main Street, Kansas City, MO 64111, ©1996,Library of Congress # 96-83993,TCRN: 0-8362-2178-8
350 Courtesy of ibid Stock Photo House.
351 Courtesy of Nancy Rubenstein Inc. (bottom).
354 Courtesy of Working Computer.
355 Courtesy of Foote, Cone & Belding (top). Courtesy of Project Research, Inc. (bottom left and right).

Chapter 11

363 Courtesy of Sony Computer Entertainment, Foster City, CA.
365 Courtesy of Apple Computer, Inc.
368 Courtesy of Anheuser-Busch, St. Louis, MO.

370 Courtesy of GM Corp., Detroit, MI.
371 Courtesy of Kia Corporation.
372 Courtesy Chicago Motor Club, Chicago, IL.
373 Courtesy of JC Penny, Inc., Dallas, TX (left). Courtesy of Castrol North America, Inc. (middle). Courtesy of Datek Online Financial Services LLC (right).
374 Courtesy of DC Shoes, Inc., Vista, CA.
375 Courtesy of Sketchers USA, Inc.
376 Courtesy of Beiersdorf Inc.
377 Courtesy of International Franchise Association.
379 Courtesy of GM Corp., Detroit, MI
380 Courtesy of GM Corp., Detroit, MI.
382 Courtesy of Carlson Restaurants, Dallas TX.
383 Courtesy of Motorola.
384 Courtesy of Raffi, Inc. (top left). Courtesy of Anheuser-Busch, St. Louis, MO (top right). Courtesy of Patrick Cox, International, London, England (bottom left). Courtesy of Cutty Sark Scots Whiskey (bottom right).
385 Courtesy of Sony Computer Entertainment, Foster City, CA (top left). Courtesy of Bacardi U.S.A., Inc., Miami, FL (top right). Courtesy of Michael Kors Fragrances for Men and Women, New York (center left). Courtesy of Rockport (center right). Courtesy of Rare Rareware and Nintendo (bottom).
386 Courtesy of Omega Research & Development, Douglasville, GA.
387 Courtesy of Pfizer, Inc., New York.
388 Courtesy of Chesebrough-Pond's USA Co. (left). Courtesy of Wm. Wrigley Jr. Company (right).
389 Courtesy Anheuser-Busch, St. Louis, MO.
390 © Disney Enterprises, Inc.
391 Courtesy of Danny Lyon and Magnum Photos, New York.
392 Courtesy of Christian Dior (left). Courtesy of Verizon (right).
393 Courtesy of Skyy Spirits. LLC, San Francisco, CA (top). Courtesy of Prada (bottom).
395 Courtesy of Evian Natural Spring Water (top left). Courtesy of Wild Turkey, Lawrenceburg, KY (top right). Courtesy of Sony Computer Entertainment, Foster City, CA (center left). Courtesy of DieselSytleLab, New York. (center right). Courtesy of Issey Miyake, New York (bottom).
396 Courtesy of Q Magazine and Ben Holland, Leicestershire, UK (left). Courtesy of Tupperware Corporation, Orlando, FL (middle). Courtesy of Altadis USA, Tampa, FL (right).

Chapter 12

401 Manolo Moran.
403 Reprinted by permission of Richmond Technical Center. Art Director: Rich Wakefield, Writer: Peter Sheldon, Agency: Hawley Martin Partners, Richmond.
405 Courtesy of Avis Rent A Car System, Inc. (left). Courtesy of C. F. Hathaway (right).
406 Courtesy of MasterCard International, Incorporated (all).
407 Manolo Moran (both).
410 Courtesy of Tanqueray (left). Photo courtesy of Jaguar Cars North America (right).
411 Courtesy of Roxio, Inc. (top right). The women.com screen shot made available courtesy of iVillage Inc. © 2001 iVillage Inc. All rights reserved. "iVillage" and the iVillage logo are trademarks of iVillage Inc. (top left). Courtesy of the Dairy Council (bottom).
412 Reprinted with permission of AT&T.
413 Permission to reprint granted by Land Rover North America, Inc. (top left). Courtesy of Oregon Food Bank (middle). Courtesy of Jenn-Air (bottom).
414 Courtesy of the Clorox Company.
415 Courtesy of the American Cancer Society.
417 Courtesy of Garageband Records (top left). Layout and Design by Bryon D. Zimmerman/Sherry L. Smies at ZDO-Sheboygan, WI. Creative Direction by Anthony R. Rammer/Johnsonville Sausage, LLC-Johnsonville, WI (top right). Copyright © Columbia Sportswear 2001. All rights reserved (bottom left). John Michael Linck- Toymaker - www.woodentoy.com (bottom right).
420 Anhaeuser–Busch.
423 Hollywood Video.
425 Stephen Frisch/Stock Boston SUF3230R.
427 Courtesy of Honda.
428 Courtesy of John Hancock.
431 Dilbert © United Feature Syndicate, Inc. Reprinted by Permission.

Chapter 13

435 Art Director: Mary Rich; Copy: Stephen Meitelski; Photo: Craig Orsini.
437 Reprinted by permission of Homestore.com, Inc. (top). Illustrator: Andy Smith; Copy writer: Nigel Roberts; Art Director, Paul Bedford; Ad created for Oddbins Ltd. by TBWA London (bottom).

439 Courtesy of Botergoud (top). Schwinn, A division of Pacific Cycle, Madison, WI (bottom).
440 Kai Zastrow, Amsterdam.
441 Courtesy of Beck's (top). Courtesy of Palm III (bottom left and right).
442 Katharine Kieppe Nelson is a graphic designer from Grand Haven, Michigan and now lives in Denver, Colorado.
443 Art Director: Mary Rich; Copy: Stephen Meitelski; Photo: Craig Orsini.
444 Courtesy of Greenpeace.
445 Sawyer Riley Compton, Atlanta, GA: Creative Director, Bart Cleveland; Writer, Al Jackson; Art Director, Kevin Thoem (top). Courtesy of Parmalat.
446 Courtesy of Pepsi-Cola Company.
447 Courtesy of Volkswagen and Arnold Fortuna Lawner & Cabot Inc., Advertising (top left). Courtesy of Volkswagen (top right). Client: Dockers® / Levi Strauss & Co.; Agency: Foote, Cone & Belding SF; Photographer: Tim Walker (bottom).
448 Reprinted with permission from Hidesign (top). Client: The Epiphone Company, a division of Gibson Guitar Corp.; Agency: CORE, St. Louis; Creative Director: Eric Tilford; Art Director: Eric Tilford; Copy Writer: Wade Paschall; Strategy: Jeff Graham; Photographer: James Schwartz (bottom).
450 Courtesy Arnold, Finnegan & Martin (all).
455 All rights reserved. SoBe Beverage Company, Inc. (top left). Courtesy of Kohler (top right). Reprinted by permission of Krispy Kreme Doughnut Corporation (center). 7 UP and SEVEN UP are registered trademarks of © Dr Pepper/Seven Up, Inc. 2000. (bottom)
456 © Kobal Collection (left). © Paramount (Courtesy Kobal Collection) (right).
459 Client: Lynx; Agency: Bartle Bogle Hegarty, London; Artist: Rosie Arnold; Copywriter: Shawn Preston; Production Company: 2am Films; Photographer: Paul Goldman.
460 Client: Balsen; Agency: Leo Burnett, Warsaw; Artists: Darek Zalorski, KC Ariwong; Copywriter: Kerry Keenan; Production Company: Stink; Photographer: Pep Bosch (left). Courtesy of Doyle Dane Bernbach (right).
461 Courtesy of Miller Brewing Company. "Donut" television commercial. Jeff Williams: art director; Jeff Kling: writer; Susan Hoffman: creative director; Jeff Selis: producer; Errol Morris: director; @radical.media: production company; Wieden & Kennedy (Portland, OR): ad agency.
462 Courtesy of Hewlett-Packard (top).
463 Courtesy of Miller Brewing Company (both).
465 © Apple Computer, Inc. Used with permission. All rights reserved. Apple® and the Apple logo are registered trademarks of Apple Computer, Inc. (top left). © Ladd Co. (Courtesy Kobal Collection) (top right). © Universal (Courtesy Kobal Collection) (bottom left). With permission of Nike, Inc., and 40 Acres and a Mule Filmworks (bottom right).

Chapter 14

487 Courtesy of Sandbox.com.
489 Courtesy of BMW (top). Courtesy of Good Egg.com (bottom).
490 Courtesy of Paxson Communications Corporation.
491 Courtesy of *Time* Magazine.
494 Courtesy of Comedy Central, New York (top left). Courtesy of Family Education Network, Boston, MA. (top right). Courtesy of News America Magazines Inc., A News Corporation Company (bottom).
495 Courtesy of Mediamark Research, Inc.
496 Courtesy of Television Bureau of Advertising.
497 Courtesy of Toyota and Saatchi & Saatchi DFS; photos by Michael Raushe, David Lebon, and John Early.
498 Courtesy of Sandbox.com.
500 Courtesy of Reddi-Wip.
501 Courtesy of American Express.
505 Copyright, 2001 INT Media Group, Inc. All rights reserved. Reprinted with permission from http://www.internet.com.
509 Courtesy of the Newspaper Network (right).
511 Courtesy of MediaStart.com.
512 Courtesy of MediaStart, New York.
513 © 1998 Turner Private Networks, Inc. All rights reserved. Used by permission of TPNI (left). Courtesy of National Cinema Network (right).
515 © copyrighted 1999 Chicago Tribune Company. All rights reserved. Used with permission.
516 Courtesy of Everland Entertainment, Nashville, TN (left). Courtesy of Christie's Inc. (right).
518 Courtesy of Sunglass Hut, Cincinnati, Ohio (top). Reprinted with permission from Felipe Galindo (Feggo) (bottom).

Chapter 15

523 Courtesy of Business2.0.
525 From *Time,* October 2, 2000. Copyright © 2000 Time Inc. Reprinted by permission (left). Courtesy of America Online (right).

529 Copyright, Nissan 1994. Reproduced by permission. Infiniti and the Infiniti logo are registered trademarks of Nissan (left): Courtesy of Tire America (right).
531 Photography by Joe Higgins.
532 Ebel USA, Inc. (left). Photo courtesy of Pizza Hut (right).
534 Reprinted by permission of Newspaper National Network.
535 Courtesy of Schwinn Corporation.
536 Courtesy of Business2.0 (bottom left). Courtesy of Ogilvy & Mather, Chicago (bottom right).
537 Courtesy of Clarins Corporation.
538 Courtesy of Men's Journal Co., L. P. Photograph by James McLoughlin.
540 Company: Lenox Brands 1998. Agency: Grey Advertising, N.Y.
544 Courtesy of the Food Network.
549 Courtesy of 1stUp.com.
554 Courtesy of eYada.com.

Chapter 16

559 Courtesy of Screaming Media. Art Director: Nick Cohen; Copywriter: Mikel Reich; Designer: Agatha Sohn; Photographer: Joseph Cuttice.
560 Courtesy of PepsiCo, Inc.
564 Reprinted by permission of PocketMail.
566 Reprinted by permission of advertising.com. (left). Courtesy of L-Soft (right).
568 Courtesy of Yahoo.
569 MySimon, Inc. Courtesy CNET.com (left). Courtesy of Latina Online (right).
571 Artwork by loudthöt, Inc. Copy written by Angelia Pinaga of Enfora, Inc.
575 Used by permission from Healthgrades.com, Inc. © Healthgrades, photo by Grant Leighton.
576 Courtesy of Forrester.
577 Ad campaign and slogan created and reprinted by permission of Scott Hirsch, Founder and CEO of eDirect.com.
578 Courtesy of Saturn Corporation.
579 Courtesy women.com Networks. Portions © Netscape Communications Corporation, 1999. Netscape, Netscape Navigator and the Netscape N Logo, are registered trademarks of Netscape in the United States and other countries (left). Courtesy Naomi Evan Info Edge Internet Services. Portions © Netscape Communications Corporation, 1999 (right).
581 Courtesy of iwon.com.
582 Courtesy of Screaming Media. Art Director: Nick Cohen; Copywriter: Mikel Reich; Designer: Agatha Sohn; Photographer: Joseph Cuttice.
583 Courtesy of idNames from Network Solutions.
584 Courtesy of Hyperion.
586 Courtesy NetRatings, Inc., Nielsen Media Research.
588 Courtesy Jupiter Media Metrix.
589 Courtesy of Mercury Interactive.
590 Courtesy Saab Cars USA, Inc. Portions © Netscape Communications Corporation, 1999.

Chapter 17

607 Reprinted by permission of Fotoball.
608 Courtesy of Procter & Gamble.
611 Courtesy of The Bettmann Archive.
612 Courtesy of Horst Salons. Carol Henderson, art director; Like Sullivan, writer: Fallon McElligot, Minneapolics, agency (top). Courtesy of the Museum of Flight, Seattle, Washington (bottom).
613 Courtesy of David Auerback Optitians.
614 © Chris T. Allen, photographer.
615 © Bob Kramer/Stock Boston (top). © Chris T. Allen, photographer (bottom).
618 Courtesy of 3M Company (left). Reprinted by permission of Fotoball (right).
619 Courtesy of Switchboard.com.
622 Courtesy of Nabisco a division of Kraft Foods, Inc. (left and middle). Courtesy of McNeil Consumer & Specialty Pharmaceuticals, a Division of McNeil- PPC, Inc. (right).
624 Courtesy of Sprint.
626 © The Procter & Gamble Company. Used by permission.
627 Courtesy of Trek Bikes.

Chapter 18

635 Courtesy of Jelly Belly Candy Company, Inc.
637 Courtesy of Kraft Foods, Inc.
638 Courtesy of Oreck Corporation, New Orleans, Louisiana.
641 Photography of Jeff Greenberg.
643 © Vitro Robertson. Ad: "Instant Coffee"; Client: Peet's Coffee & Tea; Agency: VITROROBERTSON; Creative Directors: John Roberston, John Vitro; Art Director: Dave Huerta; Copywriter: John Robertson; Inset Image: Chuck Eaton; Letterpress; Ken West; Account Executive: DelBracht (left). Courtesy of Campbell Soup Company (right).

647 JELL-O and JIGGLERS are registered trademarks of Kraft Foods, Inc.; used with permission (left). Courtesy of the Gillette Company (right).
650 Courtesy of Oldsmobile Division of General Motors Corporation.
651 Reprinted by permission of Marriot International, Inc.
654 Courtesy of Jelly Belly Candy Company, Inc.
655 Photography of Jeff Greenberg.
657 Courtesy Omega—Swiss made since 1848.
658 Courtesy of Goldmine Software Corporation.
659 Courtesy of America Online.
661 Copyright 2002 – ePrize, LLC. All Rights Reserved. Reprinted by permission (left). Courtesy of CyberRebate.com, Inc. (right).

Chapter 19

669 Courtesy of YesMail, Chicago, IL.
672 Courtesy of Best Buy Co., Inc., Minneapolis, MN (left). Courtesy of Coldwater Creek, Inc. Sandpoint, Idaho (right).
675 Courtesy of StairMaster, Inc., Kirkland, WA.
676 Courtesy of Schering Corporation, Kenilworth, NJ.
679 Courtesy of LLBean, Freeport, ME.
681 Courtesy of BMW of North America, LLC, Woodcliff Lake, NJ.
683 Courtesy of Zero-Knowledge System, Inc., Montreal, Quebec, Canada.
684 Courtesy of United States Postal Service, Washington, DC.
687 Courtesy of YesMail, Chicago, IL (left). Courtesy of eDirect, Boca Raton, FL (right).
688 Courtesy of Oreck Corporation, New Orleans, Louisiana.

Chapter 20

695 Courtesy of Anheuser-Busch Inc.
697 Courtesy of Firestone (both).
699 DILBERT reprinted by permission of United Feature Syndicate, Inc.
700 Reprinted with permission of PepsiCo. Inc. Diet Pepsi, Pepsi, Pepsi-Cola, and the Pepsi Globe design are registered trademarks.
701 Courtesy © 2000 JABRA Corporation. Reprinted by permission.
703 Courtesy of Procter & Gamble.
704 Reproduced with permission of AT&T.
706 Courtesy of Council for Biotechnology Information.
710 Courtesy of Coopers & Lybrand LLP (left). Courtesy of DuPont, Inc. (right).
711 Courtesy of Hewlett-Packard Company.
712 Courtesy of Bristol-Myers Squibb Company.
713 Courtesy of Phillips Petroleum Company (left). Courtesy of Anheuser-Busch Inc. (right).
725 Photo provided by JH Photography.